# The Routledge Handbook of Language and Intercultural Communication

*The Routledge Handbook of Language and Intercultural Communication* constitutes a comprehensive introduction to the multidisciplinary field of intercultural communication, drawing on the expertise of leading scholars from diverse backgrounds. The *Handbook* is structured in five sections and covers historical perspectives, core issues and topics, and new debates in the field, with a particular focus on the language dimension. Among the key themes addressed are: the contested nature of culture; the language and culture nexus; the complex relationship between language, culture, identity, agency, power and context; conceptions of intercultural (communicative) competence; English as the principal medium for intercultural communication; and developments in intercultural communication research and praxis, among others. The *Handbook* includes an introduction and overview by the editor, which provides readers with an indication of the focus of each section and chapter.

*The Routledge Handbook of Language and Intercultural Communication* is an essential resource for advanced undergraduates and postgraduate students of applied linguistics as well as those in related degrees such as applied English language and TESOL/TEFL. It will also be useful for researchers and students in other fields such as speech communication, cross-cultural communication, psychology and sociology, and anyone interested in language and intercultural communication.

**Jane Jackson** is Professor of Applied Linguistics at the Chinese University of Hong Kong.

# The Routledge Handbook of Language and Intercultural Communication

*Edited by*
*Jane Jackson*

Routledge
Taylor & Francis Group

LONDON AND NEW YORK

First published in paperback 2014
First published 2012
by Routledge
2 Park Square, Milton Park, Abingdon, Oxon OX14 4RN

Simultaneously published in the USA and Canada
by Routledge
711 Third Avenue, New York, NY 10017

*Routledge is an imprint of the Taylor & Francis Group, an informa business*

*British Library Cataloguing in Publication Data*
A catalogue record for this book is available from the British Library

*Library of Congress Cataloging in Publication Data*
The Routledge handbook of language and intercultural communication / edited by Jane
Jackson.
p. cm. – (Routledge handbook of applied linguistics)
Includes bibliographical references and index.
1. Intercultural communication–Handbooks, manuals, etc. 2. Language and culture–
Handbooks, manuals, etc. I. Jackson, Jane, 1954-
P94.6.R68 2012
400–dc22
2011007373

ISBN: 978-0-415-57254-5 (hbk)
ISBN: 978-0-415-70982-8 (pbk)
ISBN: 978-0-203-80564-0 (ebk)

Typeset in Bembo
by Taylor & Francis Books

Printed and bound in the United States of America by Publishers Graphics,
LLC on sustainably sourced paper.

# Contents

Contents

**Adrian Holliday** is Professor of Applied Linguistics at Canterbury Christ Church University, UK, where he supervises doctoral research in the critical sociology of language education and intercultural issues. The first half of his career was spent in Iran, Syria and Egypt as a curriculum developer.

**Prue Holmes** is Senior Lecturer in International and Intercultural Education at Durham University, UK. Before coming to Durham, she taught intercultural communication for 10 years at the Waikato Management School, University of Waikato, New Zealand. Recent research includes intercultural competence and intercultural dialogue.

**Juliane House** is Professor Emerita of Applied Linguistics at Hamburg University, Germany, and a senior member of the German Science Foundation's Research Center on Multilingualism. She has published widely in the areas of translation theory, contrastive pragmatics, politeness, intercultural communication and English as a lingua franca.

**Hyi-sung Hwang** is a research scientist at Humintell, LLC, USA. Her research interests include emotion, nonverbal behaviour and culture.

**Gavin Jack** is Professor of Management at the Graduate School of Management, La Trobe University, Australia. He researches in the area of critical management studies, and his books include (with Alison Phipps, 2005) *Tourism and Intercultural Exchange: Why Tourism Matters*.

**Jane Jackson** is Professor in the English Department at the Chinese University of Hong Kong in the Hong Kong SAR. Her research interests include intercultural communication/pragmatics, identity (re)construction and education abroad. Recent monographs include *Language, Identity, and Study Abroad: Sociocultural Perspectives* (Equinox, 2008) and *Intercultural Journeys: From Study to Residence Abroad* (Palgrave Macmillan, 2010). She is a fellow of the International Academy for Intercultural Research and a member scholar of the International Institute for Qualitative Methodology.

**Liz Jones** (PhD, Queensland) is an Associate Professor in Organizational Psychology at Griffith University, Australia. Her research interests include intergroup communication in health and organizational contexts. She is also interested in organizational change and health care service improvements.

**Istvan Kecskes** is Professor of Linguistics and Communication at the State University of New York, Albany, USA. He is the founding editor of the linguistics journal *Intercultural Pragmatics* and the *Mouton Series in Pragmatics* published by Mouton de Gruyter, Berlin/New York.

**Michael Kelly** is Professor of French at the University of Southampton, UK. He publishes on French cultural history and language education policy. He led a study of language teacher education in Europe for the European Commission (2002–4) and is editor of the *European Journal for Language Policy*.

**Young Yun Kim** is Professor of Communication at the University of Oklahoma, USA. She has researched and published extensively in intercultural/interethnic communication and cross-cultural adaptation. She is a fellow of the International Communication Association and the International Academy for Intercultural Research.

**Claire Kramsch** is Professor of German at the University of California, Berkeley, USA, where she teaches graduate and undergraduate courses in applied linguistics. She has written extensively on language, discourse and culture in the teaching and learning of foreign languages.

**Juliet Langman** is Associate Professor of Applied Linguistics in the Department of Bicultural–Bilingual Studies at the University of Texas, San Antonio, USA. Her research interests focus on minority youth populations in multilingual settings, exploring the intersection between language use, language learning and identity.

**Peih-ying 'Peggy' Lu** (PhD, University of Glasgow) is Associate Professor in the Center for General Education, Kaohsiung Medical University, Taiwan. She has published articles on intercultural language education in Taiwan and the use of art, literature and problem-based learning in medical education. Her research involves the integration of intercultural language education and the medical humanities with preclinical and clinical medical training.

**Malcolm N. MacDonald** (PhD) is Associate Professor in the Centre of Applied Linguistics at the University of Warwick, UK. His main areas of research are intercultural communication, critical theory and pedagogic discourse. He is editor of *Language and Intercultural Communication* (Taylor and Francis). He has taught ESP (the Seychelles), EAP (Kuwait), business (Singapore), human sciences (Scotland), applied linguistics and language education (the Universities of Stirling, St Andrews and Exeter) and postgraduate TESOL courses (Malaysia).

**Jennifer Mahon** (PhD) is an Assistant Professor of Sociocultural Education at the University of Nevada, Reno, USA. Growing out of the critical tradition, her work focuses on the development of intercultural awareness among educators, especially how notions of conflict affect understanding.

**Judith N. Martin** is Professor of Intercultural Communication at Arizona State University, USA. She has authored and co-authored many research publications on the topics of cultural adaptation and sojourner communication, ethnic identity and interracial communication, intercultural relationships and new media and intercultural communication.

**David Matsumoto** is Professor of Psychology at San Francisco State University and Director of Humintell, LLC, USA. His research interests centre on emotion, facial expression, nonverbal behaviour and culture.

**Thomas K. Nakayama**, Professor and Chair of Communication Studies at Northeastern University, USA, has authored and contributed to publications on racial, national and sexual identities and critical intercultural communication. He is the first editor of the *Journal of International and Intercultural Communication*.

**Kimberly A. Noels** is Professor in the Department of Psychology at the University of Alberta, Canada. Her research focuses on the social contexts of language learning and the implications of intercultural communication for ethnic identity, psychological well-being and intergroup relations.

**Robert O'Dowd** teaches at the University of León, Spain, and is the University's Secretary for International Training. He has written a book, *Telecollaboration and the Development of Intercultural Communicative Competence* (2006), and edited the volume *Online Intercultural Exchange: An Introduction for Foreign Language Teachers* (2007). He has coordinated national and international projects on telecollaboration and two Eurocall Regional Workshops on the topic. Homepage: http://www3.unileon.es/personal/wwdfmrod/

**John P. O'Regan** is a Lecturer in Languages in Education at the Institute of Education, University of London, UK, where he leads the MA in World Englishes. He is also co-editor of the international journal *Language and Intercultural Communication*.

**Alison Phipps** is Professor of Languages and Intercultural Studies and Co-Convener of the Glasgow Refugee, Asylum and Immigration Research Network (GRAMNET) at the University of Glasgow, UK, where she teaches languages, comparative literature, anthropology and intercultural education. She has published numerous books and articles on critical and intercultural theory, identity, intercultural communication, critical/modern language pedagogy and tourism. Her first collection of poetry, *Through Wood*, is with Wild Goose Publications (2009).

**Ben Rampton** is Professor of Applied and Sociolinguistics and Director of the Centre for Language Discourse and Communication at King's College London, UK. He does interactional sociolinguistics, and his interests cover urban multilingualism, ethnicity, class, youth and education. He has written *Crossing: Language and Ethnicity among Adolescents* (Longman, 1995/St Jerome, 2005) and *Language in Late Modernity: Interaction in an Urban School* (CUP, 2006), co-authored *Researching Language: Issues of Power and Method* (Routledge, 1992) and co-edited *The Language, Ethnicity and Race Reader* (Routledge, 2003).

**Karen Risager** is Professor in Cultural Encounters, Roskilde University, Denmark. Her main research areas are the structure of the relationship between language and culture in a global and transnational perspective, including the concept of linguaculture, especially as it relates to language and intercultural learning, and to language hierarchies and policies at the international university.

**Phyllis Ryan** is Associate Professor (retired) in the Centro de Ensenanza de Lenguas Extranjeras, Universidad Nacional Autonoma de Mexico, Mexico. She has taught in the graduate programme of applied linguistics and advised PhD student research. Her main interests include multilingualism and intercultural communication.

**Farzad Sharifian** is Associate Professor and Director of the Language and Society Centre within the School of Languages, Cultures and Linguistics, Monash University, Melbourne, Australia. He has published widely in international journals in various areas of applied linguistics such as intercultural communication, World Englishes, English as an international language and pragmatics.

**Xingsong Shi** is Associate Professor in the School of International Studies at the University of International Business and Economics, Beijing, China. Her main research areas include intercultural communication, language socialization, business communication and second language acquisition.

**Kathryn Sorrells** is Professor in the Department of Communication Studies at California State University, Northridge, USA, where she teaches courses in intercultural communication, cultural studies and feminist theory. Dr Sorrells is author of a forthcoming book entitled *Globalizing Intercultural Communication*; she has published a variety of articles related to intercultural communication.

**Rebecca B. Speer** is a doctoral student in communication at the University of California, Santa Barbara, USA. Her research interests centre on intergroup dynamics within family, organizational and intercultural contexts. She has published work on stepfamilies and anti-/pro-social communication.

**Stella Ting-Toomey** is Professor of Human Communication Studies at California State University, Fullerton, USA. She is the author and editor of 17 books. She has also published more than 90 journal articles and chapters in various communication journals and monographs.

**Michiko Uryu** completed her PhD dissertation at the University of California, Berkeley, USA. With Claire Kramsch, she has co-authored 'Ecological perspectives on intercultural communication' in the *Intercultural Communication Review* (2010) 8: 15–34.

**Martin Warren** is Professor of Applied English Language Studies in the Department of English at the Hong Kong Polytechnic University, the Hong Kong SAR. He currently teaches and conducts research in the areas of corpus linguistics, discourse analysis, intercultural communication and pragmatics.

**Bernadette Watson** (PhD, Queensland) is a Senior Lecturer in Psychology at the University of Queensland, Australia. A health psychologist who studies communication, her research focuses on effective communication between health professionals and patients. She researches the influence of identity and intergroup processes on both patient–health professional communication and on communication in multidisciplinary health teams.

**Jane Wilkinson** is Lecturer in German at the University of Leeds, UK. She was chair of the International Association for Languages and Intercultural Communication (IALIC) between 2008 and 2010. Her research focuses on borders and border crossings in contemporary German-speaking culture, and she is author of *Performing the Local and the Global: The Theatre Festivals of Lake Constance* (Peter Lang, 2007) and several articles on cross-border cultural events at the German–Polish border.

**Tomoko Yashima** is Professor of Applied Linguistics and Intercultural Communication at Kansai University, Japan. Her research interests include intercultural contact and affective variables in L2 acquisition. Her studies have been published in the *Modern Language Journal, Language Learning, Psychological Reports* and the *International Journal of Intercultural Relations*.

**Rui Zhang** is currently a doctoral student in social and cultural psychology at the University of Alberta, Canada. His research centres on the psychological dynamics of intercultural contact in the contexts of immigration and societal change.

# Abbreviations

| | |
|---|---|
| AACTE | American Association of Colleges of Teacher Education |
| ACTFL | American Council on the Teaching of Foreign Languages |
| AERA | American Educational Research Association |
| AIC | Assessment of Intercultural Competence |
| ALD | Assessment of Language Development |
| ASLPR | Australian Second Language Proficiency Ratings |
| ATE | Association for Teacher Educators |
| BASIC | Behavioural Assessment Scale for Intercultural Communication |
| BEVI | Beliefs, Events and Values Inventory |
| BICS | Basic Interpersonal Communication Skills |
| C1 | First/native culture |
| C2 | Second culture |
| CA | Conversational analysis |
| CAFIC | China Association for Intercultural Communication |
| CAL | Critical Applied Linguistics |
| CALL | Computer-Assisted Language Learning |
| CALP | Cognitive Academic Language Proficiency |
| CAT | Communication accommodation theory |
| Cb | Backward-looking centre |
| CBTE | Community-based tourism enterprise |
| CC | Cultural competence |
| CCA | Cross-cultural assessor |
| CCAI | Cross-Cultural Adaptability Inventory |
| CCC | Culturally competent communication |
| CCR | Critical contrastive rhetoric |
| CCSARP | Cross-Cultural Speech Act Realization Project |
| CDA | Critical discourse analysis |
| CEFR | Common European Framework of Reference for Languages |
| Cf | Forward-looking centre |
| CLA | Critical language awareness |
| CLIL | Content and Language Integrated Learning |
| CLL | Community Language Learning |
| COI | Cultural Orientations Indicator® |
| Cp | Preferred centre |
| CPD | Continuing professional development |

| | |
|---|---|
| CQ | Cultural intelligence |
| CR | Contrastive rhetoric |
| D | Distance |
| DCT | Discourse completion test |
| DMIS | Developmental Model of Intercultural Sensitivity |
| DRAI | Display Rule Assessment Inventory |
| DST | Discourse segment topic |
| EAIE | European Association for International Education |
| EC | Ethnographies of Communication |
| ECFA | Economic Cooperation Framework Agreement |
| EFL | English as a foreign language |
| EID | Emotional intelligence and diversity |
| EIEGL | *Échanges interculturels exolingues en groupe en ligne* |
| EIL | English as an international language |
| ELF | English as a lingua franca |
| ELL | English language learner |
| ELP | European Language Portfolio |
| ELT | English language teaching |
| ERASMUS | European Region Action Scheme for the Mobility of University Students |
| ESL | English as a second language |
| ESP | English for specific purposes |
| EU | European Union |
| FL | Foreign language |
| FSI | Foreign Service Institute (US) |
| FSL | French as a second language |
| FT | Foreigner talk |
| FTA | Face threatening acts |
| GEPT | General English Proficiency Test |
| GMS | Global Mindedness Scale |
| GSP | Grand Strategy of Politeness |
| H | Hearer |
| IAIR | International Academy for Intercultural Research |
| IALIC | International Association for Language and Intercultural Communication |
| IAM | Interactive acculturation model |
| IAWE | International Association for World Englishes |
| IC | Intercultural contact |
| IC1 | *Inter*cultural contact |
| IC2 | *Intra*cultural contact |
| ICC | Intercultural communicative competence |
| ICOPROMO | Intercultural Competence for Professional Mobility |
| ICT | Information and communications technology |
| ICW | Intercultural Communication Workshop |
| IDI | Intercultural Development Inventory |
| IECC | Intercultural E-mail Classroom Connections |
| INTASC | Interstate New Teachers Assessment and Support Consortium |
| IP1 | *Inter*personal contact |
| IP2 | *Intra*personal contact |
| IR | Intercultural rhetoric |

| | |
|---|---|
| IRA | International Reading Association |
| ISLPR | International Second Language Proficiency Ratings |
| ITALS | Italiano come Lingua Straniera |
| JCIC | Japan Center for Intercultural Communications |
| LACE | Languages and Cultures in Europe |
| LANQUA | Language Network for Quality Assurance |
| L1 | First/native language |
| L2 | Second language |
| LC1 | First languaculture |
| LC2 | Second languaculture |
| MAXSA | Maximizing Study Abroad |
| MFL | Modern foreign language |
| MLA | Modern Language Association |
| MoE | Ministry of Education (People's Republic of China) |
| NBLT | Network-based language teaching |
| NCATE | National Council for Accreditation of Teacher Education |
| NCLB | No Child Left Behind |
| NCTE | National Council on the Teaching of English |
| NGO | Non-governmental organization |
| NIC | Nordic Network for Intercultural Communication |
| NVB | Nonverbal behaviours |
| OECD | Organization for Economic Cooperation and Development |
| P | Power |
| PCAT | Peterson Cultural Awareness Test |
| PCE | Panamanian Creole English |
| PCSI | Peterson Cultural Style Indicator |
| PISA | Programme for International Student Assessment |
| R | Rating of imposition |
| S | Speaker |
| SAGE | Study Abroad for Global Engagement |
| SIETAR | Society for International Education, Training, and Research |
| SCA | Sociocognitive approach |
| SLA | Second language acquisition |
| Standards | National Standards in Foreign Language Education: Preparing for the 21st Century (USA) |
| SVS | Schwartz Value Survey |
| TESOL | Teachers of English to Speakers of Other Languages |
| TNC | Transnational corporation |
| TT | Tourist talk |
| TPR | Total physical response |
| UNESCO | United Nations Educational, Scientific, and Cultural Organization |
| URL | Uniform Resource Locator |
| WE | World Englishes |
| YOGA | Your Objectives, Guidelines and Assessment |

# Acknowledgements

I owe a debt of gratitude to the Editorial Advisory Board, whose methodical and insightful reviews helped shape the contents of the individual chapters. They are (in alphabetical order):

Michael Byram, Professor Emeritus, Durham University, UK
Winnie Cheng, Hong Kong Polytechnic University, Hong Kong SAR
Alvino E. Fantini, Professor Emeritus, World Learning's SIT Graduate Institute, USA
Adrian Holliday, Canterbury Christ Church University, UK
Karen Risager, Roskilde University, Denmark

I would like to acknowledge the support and hard work of all the contributors, as well as the editorial assistance and encouragement provided by the Routledge team, especially Nadia Seemungul, Sophie Jacques, Louisa Semlyen, Megan Graieg and the copy editor. I also wish to thank Ron Carter and the anonymous reviewers who provided helpful feedback on the proposal for this *Handbook*.

The editor and publisher appreciate the permission granted to reproduce the copyright material in this book:

Figure 2.1 adapted from A. Holliday, *Intercultural Communication and Ideology*, 2011. With kind permission from Sage Publications.

In Chapter 8: Figures 8.1 and 8.4, photos taken by David Matsumoto; Figure 8.2, photos © Bob Willingham; Figure 8.3, a graph from D. Matsumoto, S.H. Yoo, J. Fontaine, A.M. Anguas-Wong, M. Arriola, B. Ataca *et al.* (2008) 'Mapping expressive differences around the world: the relationship between emotional display rules and individualism v. collectivism', *Journal of Cross-Cultural Psychology*, 39(1): 55–74 (a Sage publication).

John Benjamins Publishing Company for Table 9.2, from Culpeper (1996), cited in D. Bousfield, *Impoliteness in Interaction*, 2008.

Figures 14.1 and 14.2 taken from Y.Y. Kim, *Becoming Intercultural: An Integrative Theory of Communication and Cross-cultural Adaptation*, © Sage, 2001.

John Berry for Figure 15.1 taken from J.W. Berry (1980) 'Acculturation as varieties of adaptation', in A. Padilla (ed.) *Acculturation: Theory, Models, and Some New Findings*, Boulder, CO: Westview, pp. 9–25, Sage; Figure 15.2 from H. Giles and J. Giles in A. Kuyulo (ed.) *Inter/cultural Communication: Representation and Construction of Culture in Everyday Interaction* (in press); Sage for Figure 15.3 taken from J. Harwood (2010) 'The contact space: a novel framework for intergroup contact research', *Journal of Language and Social Psychology*, 29: 147–77.

Table 21.2, a chart taken from R. O'Dowd and P. Ware (2009) 'Critical issues in - telecollaborative task design', *Computer Assisted Language Learning*, 22(2): 173–88. Figure 21.1, a chart from R. O'Dowd and M. Ritter (2006) 'Understanding and working with "failed communication" in telecollaborative exchanges', *CALICO Journal*, 23: 623–42.

For Figure 24.2, the 'gemstone model' from A. Fantini (2000–2001) 'Designing quality intercultural programs: a model and a process', *Interspectives: A Journal on Transcultural Education*, 18: 100–105.

Michael Byram for Figure 26.1, the intercultural communicative competence model.

Elsevier Limited for Table 34.1 from C.M. Echtner and P. Prasad, 'The context of Third World tourism marketing', *Annals of Tourism Research*, 30(3): 660–82.

Every effort has been made to contact copyright holders. If any have been inadvertently overlooked, the publishers will be pleased to make the necessary arrangements at the first opportunity.

# Introduction and overview

*Jane Jackson*

## 1. Language and intercultural communication

Across the globe, migration, travel, business and international education are facilitating face-to-face intercultural contact. Advances in technology (e.g. the internet, social networking sites) are also making it easier to link people virtually in different parts of the world. As we become increasingly interconnected, the demand for individuals who can communicate effectively and appropriately with people who have a different cultural/linguistic background becomes ever more pressing.

In the last few decades, the challenges and promise of intercultural interaction have been capturing the attention of scholars from many disciplines (e.g. anthropology, applied linguistics, communication studies, education, language, psychology, sociology). Not surprisingly, the field of intercultural communication has become more and more diverse, multidisciplinary and international.

In past years, there was limited interaction between researchers and educators from different disciplines who had a particular interest in intercultural communication. Disciplinary networks rarely intersected and, consequently, many scholars were unaware of developments in intercultural communication research and practice outside their own area of specialization. For example, applied linguists were unfamiliar with the intercultural communication research of communication scholars and did not pay sufficient attention to the (inter)cultural dimension in second language (L2) communication/education. Conversely, speech communication specialists and cross-cultural psychologists often ignored the language dimension in intercultural communication and were not familiar with publications by applied linguists that focused on the (inter)cultural dimension. While lack of awareness of work in different disciplines remains an issue, the situation is changing.

With the advent of accelerating globalization and increasing intercultural contact, both in person and online, whether at home or abroad, it is imperative that scholars reach outside their own disciplinary sphere to better understand the nature and impact of intercultural communication. Of course, this may bring tension as a result of differing definitions and conceptions of the field (e.g. understandings of culture, cultural difference) and different methodological traditions. Nonetheless, this interaction is vital if we are to gain deeper insight into the cultural, social, linguistic, cognitive, psychological and communicative dimensions of intercultural interaction, especially when it involves a second language. To propel ourselves and others towards intercultural communicative competence (ICC) and global, intercultural citizenship, we need to develop more awareness of the elements and processes involved.

The *Handbook* raises readers' awareness of the contested nature of culture, largely rejecting reductive and hegemonic interpretations. Throughout, the authors reflect on the complex connection between language, culture, identity, agency, power and context, citing examples of intercultural contact and competence in diverse settings. The chapters draw from a wide range of disciplines and practices (e.g. anthropology, bilingualism and multilingualism, business education, cognition, cultural theory, discourse analysis, ecology of language, education, ethnography of communication, language and gender, language and social psychology, literacy, pragmatics, psycholinguistics, rhetoric, sociolinguistics, translation, to name a few). The contributions explicate and demonstrate the breadth of this area of study and offer insight into the depth of knowledge required of an interculturalist in today's complex, globalizing world where languages and cultures frequently intermingle.

This volume outlines the central themes and challenges for current research in the field of intercultural communication, paying particular attention to the language dimension. Many of the authors discuss the impact of the rise and expanding influence of English as a lingua franca on present and future intercultural communication/education. The status of English as a global, pluricentric language, and the principal medium for international and intranational communication, are developments that we cannot ignore.

The *Handbook* provides compelling evidence of growing maturity in the field of intercultural communication. As this volume is included in the *Routledge Handbooks in Applied Linguistics* series, it also sends a clear signal of the importance of intercultural communication research and practice in the wider field of applied linguistics.

## 2. Aim, contents and organization

This *Handbook* aims to provide an accessible introduction and guide to the field of language and intercultural communication, with chapters written by leading scholars, both established and up-and-coming. The intended audience is advanced undergraduates, graduates and research students, as well as established researchers and scholars in applied linguistics, TESOL and language education courses. It will also be very useful for students and researchers in other fields such as anthropology, general education, management studies, speech communication, cross-cultural communication, psychology and sociology, as well as anyone interested in intercultural communication.

Reflecting the distinctive multidisciplinary character of this field of study, the authors have diverse backgrounds and span a number of disciplines (e.g. anthropology, applied linguistics, business/management education, cross-cultural psychology, international education, law, L2/ general education, medicine, speech communication, interpretation/translation, management training, teacher education, among others). They also come from different parts of the globe: Australia, Canada, China, Cyprus, Denmark, Finland, Germany, the Hong Kong SAR, Japan, Mexico, Portugal, Spain, Taiwan, the UK and the USA, so the collection is also international. Twelve of the chapters have two or more collaborating authors; in some cases, co-authors are from different disciplinary backgrounds and traditions. Their collaboration demonstrates the potential for the blurring of disciplinary boundaries.

The *Handbook* underscores the multidisciplinary nature of the discipline in terms of theories, research and practice. It provides a comprehensive and historical survey of the study of language and intercultural communication, addressing the following questions: What is the state of the art? What are the key debates and issues that pertain to this field of study? Who are the leading experts in each area of concern? What are the primary approaches to language and intercultural communication research and practice? Where is the discipline going? The *Handbook* contains a critical assessment of past and present theory, research methods, tools and practices, and also looks towards the future. In accord with the multifaceted, multidisciplinary character of intercultural communication enquiry, it emphasizes theoretical diversity within the field and explores ways to integrate and build on these perspectives through a range of methodologies and approaches. Recognizing the changing landscape of the field in the face of rapid globalization and increasing interconnectedness, the *Handbook* is international in scope and encourages dialogue, discussion and interdisciplinary collaboration/experimentation. The chapters are replete with examples of intercultural communication interaction, research and practice in a variety of languages and international settings.

The organization of the *Handbook* moves from the general to the specific, and from the past to the present and future. In general, each chapter comprises an overview of a particular area of intercultural communication, covering its historical development, research methods, current issues/tensions and potential future developments. Contributors explain why the issue is important and critically discuss the leading views. There is cross-referencing to related chapters; each chapter (except for Chapter 35) includes a list of other topics in the volume to which readers may find it useful to refer. To facilitate more exploration of key issues and topics, each chapter also contains a section on further reading; a brief description is provided with each work that is cited. The last chapter (Chapter 35) provides a list of relevant peer-refereed academic journals and professional organizations. Endnotes (if any are used) and bibliographical references are placed at the end of each chapter; a detailed index is placed at the end of the volume.

Following this introduction, the thirty-five chapters are organized into five major sections:

- Section I: Foundations of language and intercultural communication
- Section II: Core themes and issues
- Section III: Theory into practice: towards intercultural (communicative) competence and citizenship
- Section IV: Language and intercultural communication in context
- Section V: New debates and future directions

## Section I: Foundations of language and intercultural communication

Section I comprises five chapters. They locate the multidisciplinary study of language and intercultural communication, offering insight into the history, theory-building, modes of research and pedagogical approaches that have been driven by differing perceptions of culture. The contested nature of culture, race and ethnicity is explored as well as the impact of (de)colonization and globalizing forces on language and intercultural communication research and practice, including the rise of English as the primary language of international/intercultural communication.

In Chapter 1, 'The history and development of the study of intercultural communication and applied linguistics', Judith Martin, Thomas Nakayama and Donal Carbaugh draw on their training in different research paradigms (functionalist/postpositivist, interpretive, critical) to present a survey of the major strands of research that have influenced the historical foundations of contemporary intercultural communication and applied linguistics. They observe that these areas of study developed 'in different ways at different times in various world regions, with scholars in each region following particular research trajectories'. Their review is necessarily selective as it is impossible to cover all developments in a single chapter. The first part focuses on the foundation of the study of intercultural communication in the United States and Japan. The authors then describe the research trajectory in Europe, which centred on language and followed an interpretive research paradigm. The third part centres on the convergence of paradigms and the growing influence of critical theory. They conclude by posing provocative questions about the future of the multidisciplinary study of language and intercultural communication.

In Chapter 2, 'Culture, communication, context and power', Adrian Holliday reviews two sociological paradigms that profoundly influence current understandings of intercultural communication: 'neo-essentialism' and the 'critical cosmopolitan' paradigm. Derived from structural–functionalism and essentialist models of culture, the former maintains that behaviour and values are defined by national social structures. Although claiming distance from essentialism, Holliday argues that much of today's work in intercultural communication retains a positivist adherence to a priori cultural descriptions; hence, behaviour that differs from national stereotypes is often viewed as 'exceptions to the essentialist rule rather than as a reality in its own right'. In contrast, in a 'critical cosmopolitan' approach, the individual has the potential of dialogue with national social structures and is not contained by them. Holliday urges researchers and educators in intercultural communication to recognize and understand the ideology underpinning the ways in which they present culture. His discussion involves considerations of core issues related to third space, hybridity, globalization, multiculturalism and the role of language.

In Chapter 3, 'Language, identity and intercultural communication', Kimberly A. Noels, Tomoko Yashima and Rui Zhang critically examine how scholars in social psychology, communication and applied linguistics have defined identity and described its function in intercultural communication. They explain how 'the languages we learn and use open up possibilities for new identities, while at the same time our identities can have implications for engagement in language learning and use'. Their review highlights the complex relation between language and identity in intercultural communication, drawing attention to 'the role of sociostructural status and power, the relational and discursive nature of identity, and use of language as a tool of identity negotiation'. The authors explain how theory and research on these dimensions can guide practice in intercultural communication training and L2 learning and teaching. They call for more interdisciplinary research on language, identity and intercultural communication.

In Chapter 4, 'Interculturality and intercultural pragmatics', Istvan Kecskes contrasts intercultural pragmatics with cross-cultural pragmatics, explaining that the former is concerned with 'how the language system is put to use in social encounters between human beings who have different first languages, communicate in a common language, and, usually, represent different cultures'. He stresses that this relatively new field of enquiry offers a new perspective on communicative processes from a sociocognitive angle. Kecskes draws our attention to four foci of research in intercultural pragmatics: (1) interaction between native speakers and non-native speakers of a language; (2) lingua franca communication when none of the interlocutors has the same first language; (3) multilingual discourse; and (4) the language use and development of individuals who speak more than one language. This chapter is enriched by numerous examples of intercultural dialogue in various contexts.

The final chapter (Chapter 5) in Section I is 'Conceptualizing intercultural (communicative) competence and intercultural citizenship' by Michael Byram. The author considers what it means to be and act interculturally in today's increasingly interconnected, globalizing world. Delving into such notions as interculturality, bilingualism/biculturalism, intercultural (communicative) competence' (ICC) and 'intercultural citizenship', Byram draws connections between relevant theory and practice. In his discussion, he points to interesting examples of citizenship education programmes in Europe. He argues that the aims and purposes of citizenship education should be combined with those of foreign language education to help young people develop both ICC and intercultural citizenship. Byram urges foreign language teacher educators to pay attention to the dimensions of intercultural citizenship and promote the design/development of theory-driven materials that can enhance the teaching and assessment of intercultural citizenship competences.

## Section II: Core themes and issues

The fourteen chapters in Section II are divided into four subsections, namely: 'Verbal/nonverbal communication and culture', 'Language, identity and intercultural communication', 'Understanding intercultural transitions: from adjustment to acculturation' and 'Intercultural communicative competence: multiple conceptual approaches'. In each chapter, core themes and issues in the study of language and intercultural communication are examined, providing state-of-the-art coverage of a wide array of topics, including linguaculture, intercultural rhetoric, nonverbal communication, facework, identity and acculturation, among others. Section II also explores differing conceptualizations of intercultural (communicative) competence and intercultural citizenship, drawing attention to major positions and approaches.

## Culture and verbal/nonverbal communication

This subsection comprises four chapters, which provide discussions of the impact of culture on verbal and nonverbal dimensions of intercultural communication. In the first, Chapter 6, 'Linguaculture and transnationality: the cultural dimensions of language', Karen Risager presents historical perspectives on the multifarious relationship between language and culture. Citing the most influential sources, she traces the development of diverse conceptualizations of linguaculture (or languaculture) and their implications for language teaching and learning. She observes that studies of linguaculture and discourse are being incorporated into the larger field of intercultural communication, and this is raising awareness of language complexity as a product of transnational practices and processes. Risager calls for more studies of the language–culture nexus, including qualitative research that examines 'subjects' complex personal language histories over time' (e.g. Kramsch 2009).

Chapter 7, 'Intercultural rhetoric and intercultural communication' (Dwight Atkinson), reviews the historical development and current state of intercultural/contrastive rhetoric, with a focus on the 'vexed notion of culture'. Atkinson's account is rich in detail, offering insight into the challenges that scholars/researchers in this speciality have faced since its inception as contrastive rhetoric in 1966. He suggests possible future directions for research in intercultural rhetoric and calls for more critical attention to such notions as 'culture', 'intercultural' and 'rhetoric' within the context of 'global cultural flows'. He argues that this is essential if intercultural rhetoric is to 'produce a better understanding of culture–writing connections' and inspire more effective ways to teach L2 writing.

In Chapter 8, 'Nonverbal communication: the messages of emotion, action, space, and silence', David Matsumoto and Hyi-sung Hwang review the primary findings of research that has examined the influence of culture on various nonverbal behaviours (NVB) (e.g. facial expressions, gestures, gaze, voice, interpersonal space, touch, posture, gait). The authors delve into the relationship between verbal and nonverbal communication and explore its impact on intercultural relations. Drawing on recent studies, they provide numerous examples to illustrate how cultural differences in NVB make intercultural interactions more complex than intra-cultural communication, and lead to greater potential difficulties in relationships. The authors discuss the implications for intercultural understanding and communication.

In Chapter 9, 'Speech acts, facework and politeness: relationship-building across cultures', Winnie Cheng examines notions of face, facework, politeness and impoliteness from historical perspectives. Drawing on empirical cross-cultural and intercultural communication research, she provides examples of cultural variability in speech act performance (e.g. apology, complaint, compliment response, correction, greeting, promise, refusal, request) and its impact on facework and politeness in intercultural interactions in a variety of settings. Cheng maintains that research on speech acts, facework and politeness has the potential to enhance intercultural education and professional communication, and concludes by offering recommendations for future studies.

## Language, identity and intercultural communication

In this subsection, there are four chapters, all of which explore the connections between language, identity and intercultural interaction from various perspectives. In Chapter 10, 'Gender, language, identity and intercultural communication', Xingsong Shi and Juliet Langman discuss the major topics and theoretical approaches that have shaped language, gender and identity studies since the 1970s, with a particular focus on the intercultural difference model of the 1980s. They argue that research that draws on feminist poststructural theory and social constructivist theory allows for a re-examination of the assumed and essentialized duality that sees 'women' and 'men' as different but undifferentiated groups. Further, with border crossers in mind, they contend that a deeper 'understanding of L2 learners' discursive negotiation of gendered identities and language practices in intercultural contexts and institutions' can help mitigate 'the sociocultural barriers that complicate the newcomers' development in the host communities'.

Chapter 11, 'Cultural identity, representation and Othering' (Fred Dervin), draws our attention to challenges facing researchers who work on questions of identity, biases and other-ization in this age of rapid globalization. In his discussion, Dervin draws on six studies from various fields that have examined how cultural identity is constructed, represented and contested in diverse intercultural contexts. Stressing the importance of intersubjectivity in the construction of identities, he argues that intercultural researchers should embrace 'reflexivity, criticality and the idea of "diverse diversities"' in future explorations of representations, stereotypes and biases.

In Chapter 12, 'Other language learning, identity and intercultural communication in contexts of conflict', Constadina Charalambous and Ben Rampton explore the interface of language, identity and culture in environments affected by intergroup/interethnic animosity. They begin by offering a detailed example of other language learning in Cyprus and then draw on evidence from language education programmes in Israel and Macedonia, as well as bilingual programmes in Canada. In their discussion, they identify challenges to established theories of language and culture teaching presented by contexts of conflict. Charalambous and Rampton argue that sensitive, well-designed language and peace education programmes may help overcome hostile 'ideological representations of "us" and "them"'; however, more research is needed to better understand the 'practical, ideological and emotional difficulties' that can impact on the teaching and learning of languages associated with the 'Other'.

In Chapter 13, 'Intercultural contact, hybridity, and third space', Claire Kramsch and Michiko Uryu employ a discourse approach to intercultural communication to explore the 'traffic in meaning' (Pratt 2002) that occurs when people from different cultures enter into contact with one another. In their discussion, they draw on work in anthropology, cultural theory and applied linguistics. Problematizing traditional notions of identity, they argue that '[b]y conceptualizing one's identity only as attributable to one's linguistic, cultural, ethnic, national or social background, one runs the risk of essentializing such characteristics and making them into stable, nonnegotiable features of the Self'. Citing examples of intercultural contact in diverse contexts, they draw attention to the opportunities and dangers of hybridity and 'third spaces', including those that have recently opened up online. Advocating 'truly ecological or poststructuralist methods of inquiry', they argue that the study of intercultural contact should address issues of power and ideology, historicity and subjectivity, within a poststructuralist framework.

## Understanding intercultural transitions: from adjustment to acculturation

This subsection contains two chapters. In Chapter 14, 'Beyond cultural categories: communication, adaptation and transformation', Young Yun Kim addresses the phenomenon of cross-cultural adaptation, with a special emphasis on the potential for identity transformation. After briefly reviewing major developments in micro-level studies of long-term and short-term cross-cultural adaptation, Kim discusses the integrative communication theory of cross-cultural adaptation, which has implications for L2 sojourners. Emerging issues in this important area of research are discussed within the broader context of globalization and the increasing impact of mass media and computer-mediated means of intercultural communication. Kim concludes by offering suggestions for individuals who seek to facilitate their own cross-cultural adaptation, while cultivating a more open, intercultural identity.

In Chapter 15, 'Acculturating intergroup vitalities, accommodation and contact', Howard Giles, Douglas Bonilla and Rebecca Speer review past conceptualizations of acculturation phenomena. They provide a comprehensive and critical review of theoretical and empirical research that centres on mobility, intercultural contact and accommodation. Building on Berry's (1980) acculturative framework and Bourhis et al.'s (1997) interactive acculturation model (IAM), they offer a new perspective on acculturation that blends and integrates notions of social identity, group vitality, intergroup contact and communication accommodation theories.

## Intercultural communicative competence: multiple conceptual approaches

The last group of chapters in Section II contains four chapters. In Chapter 16: 'Language: an essential component of intercultural communicative competence', Alvino E. Fantini puts forward a new paradigm for language and intercultural educators – one that integrates language (linguistic, paralinguistic, extralinguistic and sociolinguistic dimensions) with small 'c' culture aspects (behavioural and interactive dimensions). Providing multiple examples, he discusses the implications and applications of this expanded model for intercultural communication. Fantini argues that '[w]hen speaking about abilities needed for effective and appropriate cross-cultural interactions, the languages of both parties must form part of the equation'. For him, the process of learning an additional language must be 'direct, experiential (as well as "intellectual"), reflective and introspective, and focus on learning to be and to do in alternative ways'. He argues that L2/intercultural educational experience has the potential to change 'our approach to the world' and 'enrich us for the rest of our lives'.

Chapter 17, 'Understanding intercultural conflict competence: multiple theoretical insights', is authored by Stella Ting-Toomey. She discusses three theoretical approaches that may help us to better understand the complex layers of intercultural conflict issues that can arise, especially in situations where an L2 is used: social ecological theory, integrated threat theory and face negotiation theory. She draws our attention to critical issues related to the criteria and components of intercultural conflict competence, stressing the critical role of mindfulness and the 'mindful transformation process'. Ting-Toomey advocates the incorporation of specific identity threat management and facework management strategies into intercultural conflict competence.

In Chapter 18, 'The intercultural speaker and the acquisition of intercultural/global competence', Jane Wilkinson reviews the literature on the 'intercultural speaker', drawing heavily on the work of Michael Byram (e.g. Byram *et al.* 2001). She then focuses on the acquisition of intercultural or global competence through foreign language education, and the progression towards intercultural speaker status through formal education at home or education abroad. Wilkinson problematizes current conceptualizations of the intercultural speaker and intercultural/global competence, observing that: 'While born of a desire to replace the idealism of the native speaker concept, the intercultural speaker has itself become a somewhat idealistic and overly theorized concept which does not apply to all language learners and to all contexts'. To better understand the 'space of the intercultural speaker', she recommends 'further exploitation of the synergies between theories of intercultural communication and border theories' that have emerged in such disciplines as geography, sociology and anthropology.

Chapter 19, 'World Englishes, intercultural communication and requisite competences' (Farzad Sharifian), discusses the status of English as a global, pluricentric language and the principal medium for international and intranational communication. Although intercultural communication now frequently occurs between individuals who speak different varieties of English, Sharifian observes that the critical link between studies of World Englishes (WEs) and intercultural communication/competence has largely been ignored. He critiques the Kachruvian paradigm of WEs and then discusses more recent approaches to the study of WEs (e.g. cognitive sociolinguistics, cognitive linguistics) and their relevance to intercultural communication and intercultural citizenship. Examples from a variety of WEs are provided (e.g. Australia, Cameroon, Iran). Sharifian concludes that '[s]uccess in international/intercultural communication is now tied to competences such as multidialectal competence, intercultural competence, and meta-cultural competence'. He calls for more systematic investigations of new varieties of WEs and their associated cultural conceptualizations, arguing that '[t]he relevance of World Englishes to more practical areas such as intercultural communication and English language teaching cannot be overestimated'.

## Section III: Theory into practice: towards intercultural (communicative) competence and citizenship

The five chapters in this section examine the practical applications of intercultural communication theories to the promotion of intercultural (communicative) competence and citizenship. In their discussion, the authors draw our attention to current developments in intercultural communication pedagogy and training (e.g. critical perspectives, experiential learning, innovative online programmes that facilitate interaction between L2 learners from different parts of the globe). In the process, the authors build on the theoretical notions and issues that were explained in Sections I and II.

In Chapter 20, 'An intercultural approach to second language education and citizenship', Peih-ying Lu and John Corbett discuss common ground between citizenship education and intercultural language learning. In their discussion, they make reference to influential documents issued as guidelines to language teachers in America, Australasia and Europe. They delve into the complex relationship between politics, language, identity and 'bounded' citizenship, drawing on Taiwan as a case study. Lu and Corbett raise awareness of how broad curriculum guidelines can impact on L2 teaching, especially the intercultural dimension and citizenship education. Their writing is richly illustrated with examples of L2 classroom practice and resources (e.g. intercultural language activities, citizenship education materials) from many parts of the world. The authors stress the need for education for both global citizenship and intercultural communicative competence.

Chapter 21, 'Intercultural communicative competence through telecollaboration', is authored by Robert O'Dowd. After defining key terms, he traces the development and use of online intercultural exchanges in foreign language education and then describes several current models (e.g. ethnographic interviewing, *Cultura*). His chapter explains how online communication tools may enhance the participants' foreign language skills and intercultural competence. O'Dowd argues that '[i]f telecollaboration is to become a long-term, integral part of foreign language education, it needs to be seen as a fundamental part of classroom activity and language programmes rather than an extra or supplementary activity'. For this to happen, a range of challenges must be overcome (e.g. 'a lack of stability in project partners, the limited support and understanding of practitioners' institutions and the practical difficulties in integrating online exchanges in course syllabi and course evaluation schemes').

In Chapter 22, 'Critical language and intercultural communication pedagogy', Manuela Guilherme explores the potential contribution of critical pedagogy in language and intercultural communication education that aims to foster 'critical cosmopolitan citizenship' through the promotion of 'intercultural responsibility' and global ethics. She argues that the possibilities, challenges and pressing needs for intercultural dialogue and civic commitment must be made explicit in language and intercultural communication education. Drawing on a current inter-cultural project in Europe (ICOPROMO), she shows how this theory-in-practice approach entails the cultivation of critical awareness, reflection, transformation and action 'to overcome avoidance, suspicion, prejudice and misunderstanding'. Guilherme concludes that critical pedagogy can promote interculturality and help build a 'bridge between the achievement of intercultural competence and intercultural responsibility'.

Chapter 23, 'Intercultural training in the global context' (Kathryn Sorrells), provides an his-torical overview of intercultural training and addresses the ways theoretical shifts manifest in terms of practice. Within the contemporary context of globalization, Sorrells explores four critical trends in intercultural training: the impact of differing notions of 'culture'; the emerging emphasis in the intercultural communication field on broader historical contexts and geopoli-tical relationships of power; the increasing importance of technology and the focus on various forms of 'intelligences'; and the turn towards social justice and global engagement in inter-cultural praxis. In her discussion, she provides numerous examples of intercultural training/ education programmes, including those centred on study abroad and re-entry.

In Chapter 24, 'Multiple strategies for assessing intercultural communicative competence', Alvino E. Fantini stresses that lack of clarity about the nature of intercultural communicative competence (ICC) and its components makes its assessment particularly challenging. After dis-cussing definitions of this construct, he reviews basic assessment principles, paying particular attention to the assessment of L2 proficiency and ICC. Fantini warns that 'the purposes of training and education and the outcomes assessed must be inextricably linked' and '[g]iven the complex nature of intercultural competence, traditional assessment approaches are clearly insufficient'. Therefore, he argues that 'multiple assessment modes and strategies' are required. To assist L2 education/intercultural practitioners, various assessment instruments are reviewed, with details provided about their purpose and source.

## Section IV: Language and intercultural communication in context

The ten chapters in this section focus on the application of language and intercultural communication theories and research in a variety of contexts, namely: second language teacher education; the English as a foreign or international language classroom; the multicultural classroom; education abroad; business and management education; professional and workplace settings; translation and interpreting; health care settings; legal contexts; and tourism. Reflecting the importance of the intercultural dimension in education and professional development, the first five chapters in this section continue an exploration of the issues that dominate Section III.

Many of the chapters in Section IV discuss how culture, language, power relations and positioning affect intercultural contact and discourse in various settings. Some authors address differing conceptualizations of culture and culture difference and the implications for the enhancement of intercultural communicative competence and intercultural citizenship in a particular environment. Examples centre on diverse situations and sites of engagement (e.g. teacher–student and student–student interaction in the multicultural or foreign language classroom, host–sojourner relations, doctor–patient discourse, lawyer–client interaction, tourist–host interaction). Although many local and international contexts are explored, this section is necessarily incomplete as intercultural communication occurs in all contexts imaginable.

Chapters 25–29 address intercultural communication issues in educational contexts. Chapter 25, 'Second language teacher education' (Michael Kelly), examines the intercultural dimension in the pre-service education and continuing professional development of second or foreign language teachers, primarily in European contexts. Kelly begins by providing an historical review of models of L2 teacher education in Europe, noting that traditionally only a few countries dealt with intercultural or sociocultural pedagogy. When the *Common European Framework* was introduced in 1996, the intercultural nature of language learning was made more explicit. Since then, a number of initiatives (e.g. the *European Profile for Language Teacher Education*) have aimed to develop the intercultural awareness of L2 teachers. Kelly identifies challenges that teacher educators must address if they are to help teachers acquire the knowledge, skills and strategies needed to incorporate a stronger intercultural dimension into their language teaching and meet the growing social demand for intercultural communicative competence.

In Chapter 26, 'The English as a foreign or international language classroom', Phyllis Ryan examines the relationship between language and culture within the context of the learning and teaching of English as an additional language in non-English-speaking countries. Drawing heavily on the work of Risager (2007), she looks at the debate between the teaching of English as a national language and the more recent transnational paradigm, which is described in detail in Chapter 6. Discussion then centres on teacher thinking about culture and intercultural communicative competence (ICC) and its implications for the teaching of English as a foreign or international language. Ryan compares models of ICC and discusses their practical implications for the teaching of English as a foreign or global language. She concludes her chapter by proposing several lines of enquiry that might further enhance the intercultural learning of foreign language learners.

In Chapter 27, 'The multicultural classroom', Jennifer Mahon and Ken Cushner address the ways in which culture influences communication in the context of teaching and learning in the general education classroom. Discussion centres on challenges facing US American teachers who must manage the academic and psychosocial needs of a large group of culturally and linguistically diverse students. Mahon and Cushner stress that concepts related to intercultural communicative competence should be central to the preparation and development of teachers for multicultural and multilingual environments. As 'all classrooms are multicultural', the authors argue that 'teachers must be interculturally skilled mediators who enable learning to occur for everyone'. Their chapter provides concrete examples and recommendations for the establishment of effective learning communities in the multicultural classroom.

In Chapter 28, 'Education abroad', Jane Jackson identifies critical issues and topics that have emerged in the literature on education abroad learning and highlights variations in the theoretical underpinnings and methodologies that have guided research on the language and intercultural learning of L2 sojourners. She then discusses the practical implications of the findings for the enhancement of education abroad programming and, more specifically, the language, identity, (inter)cultural development and 'whole person' learning of L2 students. Jackson calls for more interdisciplinary research that makes use of a range of methodologies, arguing that we need to 'deepen our understanding of the multifaceted education abroad experience' if we are to 'propel more L2 sojourners towards intercultural communicative competence and intercultural, global citizenship'.

In Chapter 29, 'Business and management education', Prue Holmes draws our attention to the intercultural communication knowledge and skills that are needed in today's increasingly complex, ambiguous and pluricultural workplace. Within the context of business and management education, she describes critical responses to essentialist notions of culture and intercultural communication, including recent approaches that promote experiential language and culture learning, and critical/reflective intercultural action. Central to her discussion is the notion of the 'intercultural speaker' as negotiator/mediator. Throughout, Holmes stresses the importance of educating business/management students to be critical, culturally aware, socially connected citizens who are well prepared for the realities of the multicultural workplace.

Chapter 30, 'Professional and workplace settings' (Martin Warren), explores the situated nature and challenges of intercultural communication in 'white collar' occupations and other work environments. He draws on the work of Sarangi (2002), who stresses the importance of understanding 'professional practice and knowledge representations from their insiders' perspective'. In his discussion, Warren reviews multiple studies that sought to explain the complexities of intercultural workplace communication. Reflecting on future directions in research, he advocates an interdisciplinary approach, which 'embraces situated, thick, data-driven descriptions of workplace intercultural communication, and intercultural communication between professionals'.

In Chapter 31, 'Translation, interpreting and intercultural communication' Juliane House provides a window into the challenging work of translators and interpreters. After discussing the relationship between language and culture, she presents a functional–pragmatic theory of translation/interpreting as re-contextualization in intercultural communication. Empirical evidence is provided in the form of contrastive pragmatic and discourse analyses conducted with a particular language pair. Multiple German–English examples of 'cultural filtering in translations' in a variety of situations vividly illustrate patterns of cross-cultural difference. In her chapter, House also raises awareness of the increasing dominance of English in intercultural communication and the resulting 'trend towards cultural universalism and neutralism in many languages and cultures'.

Chapter 32, 'Culture and health care: intergroup communication and its consequences', is written by a multidisciplinary team of authors who span a number of disciplines: health/intercultural communication, medicine and psychology. Bernadette Watson, Cindy Gallois, David G. Hewett and Liz Jones review the literature on culture and health communication, with a particular emphasis on language/intercultural issues as they apply to the hospital setting. The authors draw our attention to cultural, linguistic and ethnic differences that may lead to intergroup conflict and miscommunication in health care. They conclude that '[u]nderstanding the history of the relations between speakers and the power structure that exists and is embedded in the health and particularly the hospital system is paramount to effecting good communication'.

Chapter 33, 'Legal contexts' (Christoph A. Hafner), reviews studies of legal discourse and intercultural communication in three principal cultural contexts of interaction: professional and lay culture; dominant culture and minority groups; and multilingual and multicultural contexts. Throughout, Hafner provides examples of intercultural communication in legal situations in a range of international settings. He maintains that 'as an increasingly global and culturally diverse population comes into contact with the local legal system, culture is likely to grow in importance as a factor in communication in legal contexts'. Consequently, he calls for more studies that focus on the intercultural dimension in legal education and explore ways to accommodate cultural differences in legal contexts.

In Chapter 34, 'Tourism', Gavin Jack and Alison Phipps describe, illustrate and critically evaluate three principal approaches to the study of tourism, language and intercultural communication: the tourism impacts approach; the language of tourism approach; and the intercultural encounters approach. Noting the limited research on intercultural communication in tourism contexts, they call for more multidisciplinary investigations, including ethnographic studies that can provide 'the lived and rich contextual insights that are currently missing from much of the tourism impacts and language of tourism approaches'.

## Section V: New debates and future directions

The concluding chapter (Chapter 35), 'A global agenda for intercultural communication research and practice', highlights key issues and views in the *Handbook*, and discusses the future of the study of intercultural communication within the context of globalization and transnational mobility. Malcolm N. MacDonald and John P. O'Regan draw attention to such emergent themes as diverse conceptualizations of culture (Holliday 2011) and intercultural/global citizenship; localism and globalism; the complex relationship between language, culture and identity; 'asymmetries of power' and the impact of ideology on intercultural relations; multiculturalism and the vital need for intercultural dialogue/conflict resolution; the 'political and ethical dimensions of intercultural pedagogy and intercultural competence' and 'the dominance of hegemonic global languages', among others. The authors reflect on 'the move towards more interpretive and critical approaches to intercultural communication research' and offer suggestions for further development in research and praxis to create new possibilities for interculturality in both private and public spheres. To facilitate this, MacDonald and O'Regan provide a comprehensive list of peer-refereed academic journals and professional bodies in the field of intercultural communication.

## 3. Conclusion

This collection of specially commissioned chapters demonstrates the importance of language and intercultural communication in today's increasingly diverse and interconnected world. The *Handbook* raises awareness of the critical role that language plays in intercultural relations, whether in the local environment or abroad. As expressed by many of the contributors, we cannot overlook the dominance of English, as it has emerged as the primary language of international and intercultural communication. This status is impacting on language choice/use, intercultural relations and intercultural interaction/education in all corners of the globe. With the development of multiple world Englishes (Kirkpatrick 2010) and the 'decentring of the native speaker' in L2/intercultural/citizenship education (Byram 2008; Pennycook 1994), we are recognizing the need for more profound understandings of the dimensions of intercultural communicative competence and intercultural/global citizenship.

Theories and research in a variety of disciplines have influenced our current views about the challenges and benefits of intercultural discourse and interaction, and what it means to be intercultural. The findings have impacted on developments in intercultural communication praxis, L2/intercultural teacher education, L2 pedagogy and citizenship education. Much more work is needed, however, to fully comprehend the complex dimensions of intercultural communication, determine the most effective and appropriate ways to empower 'intercultural speakers/mediators' (Byram *et al.* 2001) and nurture intercultural communicative competence and intercultural/global citizenship in various contexts and spaces.

This *Handbook* opens a window on different ways of conceptualizing, researching and facilitating intercultural interaction, especially when a second language is involved. Many of the chapters illustrate the benefits of cooperation between scholars from different fields/nations/backgrounds who share an interest in intercultural communication and dialogue. I hope this volume inspires more border crossings, collaboration and systematic explorations that will further enrich this exciting, multidisciplinary field.

## References

Berry, J.W. (1980) 'Acculturation as varieties of adaptation', in A. Padilla (ed.) *Acculturation: Theory, Models, and Some New Findings*, Boulder, CO: Westview, pp. 9–25.

Bourhis, R., Moise, L.C., Perreault, S. and Senecal, S. (1997) 'Towards an interactive acculturation model: a social psychological approach', *International Journal of Psychology*, 32: 369–86.

Byram, M. (2008) *From Foreign Language Education to Education for Intercultural Citizenship: Essays and Reflections*, Clevedon: Multilingual Matters.

Byram, M., Nichols, A. and Stevens, D. (2001) 'Introduction', in M. Byram, A. Nichols and D. Stevens (eds) *Developing Intercultural Competence in Practice*, Clevedon: Multilingual Matters, pp. 1–8.

Holliday, A. (2011) *Intercultural Communication and Ideology*, London: Sage.

Kirkpatrick, A. (2010) *Routledge Handbook of World Englishes*, London/New York: Routledge.

Kramsch, C. (2009) *The Multilingual Subject*, Oxford: Oxford University Press.

Pennycook, A. (1994) *The Cultural Politics of English as an International Language*, London: Longman.

Pratt, M.L. (2002) 'The traffic in meaning: translation, contagion, infiltration', *Profession*, 2002, 12: 25–36.

Risager, K. (2007) *Language and Culture Pedagogy: From a National to a Transnational Paradigm*, Clevedon: Multilingual Matters.

Sarangi, S. (2002) 'Discourse practitioners as a community of interprofessional practice: some insights from health communication research', in C. Candlin (ed.) *Research and Practice in Professional Discourse*, Hong Kong: City University of Hong Kong Press, pp. 95–133.

# Section I
# Foundations of language and intercultural communication

# The history and development of the study of intercultural communication[1] and applied linguistics

*Judith N. Martin, Thomas K. Nakayama and Donal Carbaugh*

## 1. Introduction

Communication scholar Wendy Leeds-Hurwitz describes how contemporary intercultural communication scholars can benefit from knowing the historical foundations of current scholarship:

> Multiple strands of research have influenced what we study today and how we study it … Modern scholars can benefit from studying the past because it will help to reveal why we study what we do, and why we use the methods that we do … Knowing our own history permits decisions about whether some of our assumptions should perhaps be revised, or whether they still serve researchers well. If modern-day researchers continue to do in the present what our predecessors did in the past, it should at least be the result of a deliberate choice.
>
> *Leeds-Hurwitz (2011: 30)*

We approach the writing of this chapter with some trepidation, knowing that any attempt to describe the "multiple strands of research" in our discipline's history is a daunting task and in the end is also necessarily incomplete, constructed through our particular lens of experience, and invariably contested. As sociologist Immanuel Wallerstein (1999) reminds us in "Writing History", there is 'no rapid consensus today or tomorrow' among persons who call themselves historians' and in a sense all inquiry is historical as "any sense of knowing that reality at any given point in time is the consequence of what happened at previous points in time, including of course all the radical disjunctures that have occurred" (p. 7).

Even a cursory review of the literature reveals that the study of intercultural communication and applied linguistics developed in different ways at different times in various world regions, with scholars in each region following particular research trajectories, including accepted practices as well as disjunctures. As authors, we are aware that a description of this history could be configured in various ways: chronologically, with emphasis on dates and important intellectual events; geographically, with emphasis on scholarly development in particular world regions; or topically, highlighting the development of particular research paradigms. In the end, we decided on a combination of geography and paradigms. As scholars trained in three distinct research paradigms (functionalist/postpositivist, interpretive, critical), our goal is to provide here a review of *some* of these strands of research that form *some* of the historical foundations of contemporary intercultural communication research and applied linguistics.

The first part of the chapter describes key interdisciplinary ideas and events that formed the foundation for the study of intercultural communication in the United States and Japan. Using the broadest of Kuhn's (1970) meanings for paradigm—strongly held worldviews and beliefs that undergird scholarship—we show how the initial scholarship was interdisciplinary and aparadigmatic, and later became dominated by functionalist/postpositive research traditions. We then describe the very different research trajectory in Europe, which centered on language and followed an interpretive research paradigm. The third section describes the convergence of paradigms, as many US communication scholars embraced interpretivism, and then—like scholars in many places—were influenced by critical theory. We conclude the chapter by summarizing current paradigmatic research and posing several questions concerning the future of the multidisciplinary study of language and intercultural communication.

## 2. Intercultural communication in the United States and Japan: from aparadigmatic to functionalism

The academic study of intercultural communication and applied linguistics is built on many disciplinary foundations including the work of key intellectuals in the nineteenth and early eighteenth century. For example, Charles Darwin's evolutionary theory and his 1872 book, *The Expressions of the Emotions in Man and Animals*, helped found ethology (the study of animal behavior), which informed later investigations into cross-cultural comparisons of nonverbal communication. Sigmund Freud's (1954) concept of the unconscious influenced assumptions that nonverbal cultural behavior lies outside of the awareness of individuals (Rogers and Hart 2002). Karl Marx's notions about base and superstructure influenced critical approaches to intercultural communication by emphasizing larger social and structural relationships, as well as ideology (Jameson 1971; Kellner 1989). Rogers *et al.* (2002) note that sociologist Georg Simmel's (1908/1921) concept of the stranger influenced decades of investigations into cultural transitions and adaptation (cf. Carbaugh and Berry 2001; Cooks 2001). Sociologist William Graham Sumner's (1906/1940) concept of ethnocentrism was integrated as a key element in intercultural communication studies.

In the mid-1930s and 1940s, the work of a core group of US American anthropologists, including Margaret Mead, Ruth Benedict, Gregory Bateson, and Clyde Kluckhohn, led to important assumptions that set the stage for the formation of the intercultural communication discipline in the United States (Leeds-Hurwitz 2011). Three core assumptions—known as national character, culture and personality, and "culture at a distance"—together led to a view of peoples within national boundaries as essentially homogeneous, possessing certain core characteristics, and a belief that one did not have to travel to foreign cultures to "study" them. About the same time, Benjamin Whorf, a student and colleague of Edward Sapir, advanced the notion of linguistic relativity through the Sapir–Whorf hypothesis—the notion that differences in the way *languages* encode cultural and cognitive categories significantly affect the way people perceive the world around them. This assumption became another important foundational concept in the study of language and intercultural communication (Rogers and Hart 2002).

According to Leeds-Hurwitz (1990) and others, it was in the mid-twentieth century that a formal (sub)discipline of intercultural communication developed as a result of the collaboration of linguists and anthropologists (influenced by the traditions of US scholars Mead, Benedict, etc., described above) who were hired by the US government at the Foreign Service Institute (FSI) to help train government and business personnel involved in the overseas postwar rebuilding efforts (Kitao 1989; Rogers and Hart 2002; Rogers *et al.* 2002). The FSI staff included a number of notable scholars—including linguists George Trager and Ray Birdwhistell and anthropologist Edward T. Hall—recognized by many as the "founding father" of the formal study of intercultural communication (Leeds-Hurwitz 1990).

First and foremost, it was an interdisciplinary effort, as these scholars recognized that no one discipline could explore, explain, predict, and train people to interact effectively in intercultural contexts. Anthropologists generally focused on *macro*-level structures—investigating the economic, government, kinship, and religious practices of a single cultural group. The linguists of the day focused on analyzing *micro*-elements of language and were quite successful at teaching language at the FSI; however, both the FSI staff and trainees recognized that they needed more than language training in order to communicate effectively with individuals from cultures different from their own.

According to Rogers *et al.* (2002), E.T. Hall began to meet every weekday afternoon with linguist George Trager to discuss how to reconceptualize the anthropology curriculum at FSI. Influenced by psychoanalytic theory, Hall was most interested in the unconscious aspects of cultural behavior—particularly nonverbal cues (which he termed "microculture"). It was a novel idea that nonverbal communication, just like language, varies across cultures and, in E.T. Hall's opinion, played a large role in intercultural encounters (Hall 1955; Leeds-Hurwitz 1990; Rogers *et al.* 2002). His first book, *The Silent Language* (1959), introduced the concept of proxemics, the study of how people use personal space to communicate. In a subsequent book, *Hidden Dimension* (1966), he elaborated on the concept of proxemics and identified systematic variation of personal space in many countries and regions (Europe, the Middle East, Asia, North, Latin, and South America). He noted that each cultural group has its own set of rules for personal space and that respecting these cultural differences is critical to smooth communication.

Following the theoretical taxonomies already established in linguistics through the work of Kenneth Pike (e.g., phonemes, phonetics), Hall and colleagues developed similar taxonomies in various nonverbal meaning systems (kinesics with kinemorphs), chronemics (polychronic and monochronic time), and proxemics (personal space). Another tenet was nonjudgmental ethnorelativism, and a final one was a strong relationship between culture and communication. The influence of Hall's work (emphasis on nonverbal variations and broad-based cultural differences in international contexts) can be seen even today in intercultural communication scholarship and textbooks, particularly in the US and Asia (Leeds-Hurwitz 1990).

However, unlike Dell Hymes's proposed "ethnography of speaking" in 1962 (Gumperz and Hymes 1972; see below), Hall was not interested in establishing a new academic specialty. He continued to see himself as an anthropologist for his entire life even as he became quite famous, writing for the popular press and leaving it to other scholars to carry on his theoretical and applied scholarship (E.T. Hall 1992; Rogers *et al.* 2002). As noted earlier, in Kuhn's (1970) terms, the fledgling field of intercultural communication was aparadigmatic in its early years—the 1960s and 1970s. There were no agreed upon theories or methods, just an "invisible college of scholars" mostly in the communication discipline, working to better understand nonverbal and verbal aspects of intercultural communication (Rogers and Hart 2002: 4). The first published scholarly works reflect the multidisciplinarity of this young field. For example, Alfred Smith's

(1966) edited volume, *Communication and Culture*, was organized within a linguistic framework (theory, syntactics, semantics, and pragmatics) and included contributions from linguists Noam Chomsky, Kenneth Pike, Ray Birdwhistell, and Jurgen Ruesch as well as other prominent scholars such as Erving Goffman, Robert Bales, Joshua Fishman, Elihu Katz, Gregory Bateson, Basil Bernstein, Charles Osgood, and, of course, E.T. Hall.

By the 1970s, the subdiscipline was becoming formalized within the academy in the United States, mostly in communication departments. The first university courses were taught at the University of Pittsburgh and Michigan State University, and the first textbooks were *Intercultural Communication: A Reader* (Samovar and Porter 1972), *Intercultural Communication* (Harms 1973), and *An Introduction to Intercultural Communication* (Condon and Yousef 1975). The International Communication Association established a division of Intercultural Communication in 1970, The Speech Communication Association (now the National Communication Association) established a similar division in 1975, and the Society for International Education, Training, and Research (SIETAR) was established in 1974. In 1977, the first issue of the *International Journal of Intercultural Relations* was published, edited by Dan Landis, and this became an important outlet for intercultural communication scholarship (Landis and Wasilewski 1999). By the 1980s, about sixty US universities offered graduate-level courses, and more than 200 offered undergraduate-level courses in intercultural communication (Kitao 1989).

There were similar efforts in Japan. As early as 1953, the Japan Center for Intercultural Communications (JCIC) was established by private-sector volunteers to increase mutual international understanding in the wake of a devastating world war (http://home.jcic.or.jp/en/enkaku_02.html) (accessed August 6, 2010). In subsequent decades, as Japan and the US became economic powers, there was a great deal of collaboration and exchange between Japanese and US scholars, e.g., John (Jack) Condon and Dean Barnlund both taught at Japanese universities for many years (Kitao and Kitao 1989). Mitsuko Saito, a prominent scholar at the International Christian University, and John Condon organized two conferences in Japan, bringing together an international and interdisciplinary group of scholars, which resulted in two publications (Condon and Saito 1974, 1976). Another Japanese scholar who greatly influenced intercultural communication was Masao Kunihiro, who, along with Professor Saito, translated Hall's *The Silent Language* (*Chinmoku No Kotoba*) into Japanese. These two Japanese scholars were trained in linguistics and English, and identified Japanese concepts that have no equivalence in English and vice versa (Kunihiro 1973). Like their counterparts in the US, they realized that to be effective in intercultural communication required more than mastery of foreign languages. Further, they highlighted the importance of contrasting cultural values and nonverbal patterns of communication (Kitao and Kitao 1989). As Rogers *et al.* (2002) describe it, in the 1970s and 1980s, Japanese scholars explored many aspects of nonverbal communication—silence, facial expressions, hand gestures, bowing, eye contact, touching, and personal space (Ishii 1973)—and this led to a long tradition of culture-specific and comparative work by Japanese scholars (Ito 2000; Kitao and Kitao 1989; Miike and Ishii 1997, 1998).

Much of the early scholarly work focused on concepts directly connected to East–West cultural differences, comparing Asian collectivism with Western individualism and the concomitant communication behaviors, which continues to this day. More recent studies extend the earlier research, identifying specific individualistic/collectivistic influences on various communication behaviors, including face negotiation, conflict resolution styles, and also Eastern and Western contrasts of Hall's (1976) notions of high- and low-context communication (Gudykunst *et al.* 2005; Hofstede 1980; Kincaid 1987). There have been more studies of Japanese/US American communication than of intercultural communication between any two other cultural groups (Ito 2000; Shuter 1998).

By the mid-1980s, intercultural communication scholarship in the US (and Japan) moved from being aparadigmatic to paradigmatic. That is, research became increasingly influenced by the behavioral social psychological approaches (within the functionalist/postpositive paradigm) that were becoming increasingly influential in the broader communication discipline (Bormann 1980). In fact, the results of a survey of intercultural communication researchers in the mid-1990s show how their disciplinary influences shifted away from anthropology and linguistics (an exception was work by Alvino Fantini 1997) to social psychology (and the functionalist paradigm) in the 1980s and early 1990s (see Harman and Briggs 1991; Hart 1999). This movement from aparadigmatic to an acceptance of functionalism as a dominant paradigm is described by Moon (1996) as a "disjuncture", an abrupt shift when a fairly rigid paradigm became established; she speculates that it was partially motivated by a desire on the part of intercultural communication scholars to gain credibility and acceptance from their communication colleagues. Leeds-Hurwitz (1990) concurs, confirming that US researchers in the fledgling (sub)discipline of intercultural communication felt pressured to conduct research in the increasingly dominant paradigm of the communication discipline.

Functionalist research has its philosophical foundations in the work of social theorists such as Auguste Comte and Emile Durkheim, and assumes that the social world is composed of knowable empirical facts that exist separately from the researcher. Researchers who work in this paradigm attempt to apply models and methods of the natural sciences to the study of human behavior (Burrell and Morgan 1988; Gudykunst and Nishida 1989; Mumby 1997). Scholars investigating culture and communication phenomena in this tradition generally view culture as a stable variable defined by group members (usually on a national level); these researchers attempt to establish causal relationships between culture and communication behaviors (Moon 1996). Intercultural communication research in the 1980s and early 1990s emphasized extending interpersonal communication theories to intercultural contexts or discovering theoretically based cross-cultural differences in interpersonal communication, from an "etic" perspective (Headland et al. 1990). For example, Gudykunst and colleagues extended uncertainty reduction theory (labeled anxiety uncertainty management) to intercultural contexts (Gudykunst et al. 2005), whereas Giles and colleagues combined ethnolinguistic theory and speech accommodation theory into the communication accommodation theory (CAT) (Gallois et al. 2005) (see also Chapter 15, this volume).

Although no longer dominant, the functionalist research paradigm (more commonly referred to as postpositivist) remains quite viable and is followed by a number of contemporary US communication and culture researchers (e.g., Barnett and Lee 2002; Gudykunst et al. 2005). For example, individualism/collectivism and other value frameworks continue to be used to predict various communication behaviors including conflict styles (Ting-Toomey and Oetzel 2002), face concerns (Ting-Toomey 2005), conversational constraints (M.-S. Kim 2005), and anxiety/uncertainty management strategies (Gudykunst et al. 2005), and other strong examples of continuing intercultural communication research focus on intercultural communication competence (Wiseman and Koester 1993), communication and sojourner adaptation (Y.Y. Kim 2001, 2005, this volume), and Bennett's (1993) development of a scale measuring attitudes toward cultural differences.

In 1997, there was a move to facilitate primarily functionalist/positivist research across disciplinary lines. To this end, a group of researchers led by Dr. Dan Landis, editor of the *International Journal of Intercultural Relations*, formed the International Academy for Intercultural Research (IAIR). The primary mission continues to be the promotion and encouragement of interdisciplinary research, theory, and practice in the field of intercultural relations.

## 3. Intercultural communication and applied linguistics in Europe: the interpretive paradigm

The study of intercultural communication in Europe differed from the US and Japanese trajectory in at least four important ways: (1) motivation to establish the study of intercultural communication; (2) focus; (3) disciplinary foundations; and (4) preferred research paradigm.

First, according to Kramsch (2001)—a prominent scholar in culture-based language education—the study of intercultural communication in Europe grew out of the social and political challenges resulting from the huge influx of immigration into industrialized European countries. This was especially evident early in the 1990s in Finland as programs and courses in intercultural communication were being established at universities in Jyväskylä, Tampere, and the Turku School of Business.

Second, in contrast to US and Asian scholarship where nonverbal behavior was a common research focus, the study of intercultural communication in Europe was firmly oriented toward language issues—the role of language in intercultural encounters and the role of intercultural communication in language education (Corbett 2003, 2009; Dahl 1995; Kramsch 2001). There may be several reasons for the focus on language, perhaps because of the immigrant situation and the influx of non-native speakers needing language training. Also, there was a concern about European unity through mutual understanding, reflected in the development of the Common European Framework of Reference for Languages: Learning, Teaching, Assessment (CEFR) (Council of Europe 2001; Byram and Zarate 1997; Byram et al. 2002). CEFR, the result of extensive theoretical and applied research, provided guidelines for language teaching, learning, and assessment. From its inception, the framework was firmly based in a sociocultural approach to language learning/teaching that recognized the importance of cultural dimensions of language and emphasized intercultural competence as an important goal for language learners (Byram 1997, 2003; Lofman et al. 1993; Zarate 2003a).

In addition to intercultural communication competence, applied linguists continue to investigate other aspects of intercultural contact of interest to their US and Asian colleagues, including attitudes toward cultural others and inter/bicultural identities (Bredella 2003; Petkova and Lehtonen 2005; Zarate 2003b), cultural variations in communication style (FitzGerald 2003), and culture learning, both theoretically and in applied contexts (Delanoy 2006).

In contrast to the US, where the field became established in the communication discipline, intercultural communication scholars in Europe emerged from language-oriented disciplines including applied linguistics, linguistics, and language education (Berry and Carbaugh 2004; Kramsch 1998). For example, the Nordic Network for Intercultural Communication (NIC), which was established in the early 1990s, included many members in language centers with interests in applied linguistics and intercultural communication. In the early 1990s, in the Department of Communication at the University of Jyväskylä in Finland, a program in intercultural communication was established under the leadership of Rector Aino Sallinen and Liisa Salo-Lee; study in this area was also becoming prominent at the Turku School of Economics and Business Administration through Michael Berry's works and at the University of Tampere through Nancy Aalto in the Language Center. Similar work was conducted at the University of Stavanger in Norway through Orvind Dahl and at the University of Göteborg in Sweden through the works of Jens Allwood.

A fourth and final contrast concerns the dominant paradigm of the emerging field in Europe. Although some intercultural communication scholarship in European disciplines such as psychology and sociology or applied fields such as business and management followed a functionalist/

postpositive paradigm (e.g., Geert Hofstede 1980, 1991), some applied linguists adopted an interpretive research paradigm, often utilizing ethnographic methods in culture learning and teaching (Byram and Feng 2004).

Scholars who work from the interpretive paradigm are concerned with understanding the world as enacted through meaningful social activity, as well as describing the subjective, creative communication of individuals, usually using qualitative research methods (B. Hall 1992). This work is partly based on the philosophical foundations of contemporary phenomenology (Merleau-Ponty 1962), hermeneutics (Gadamer 1976, 1989; Schleiermacher 1977), the pragmatics of John Dewey, and symbolic interaction (Mead 1934). Interpretivist research emphasizes, according to one scholar, the "knowing mind as an active contributor to the constitution of knowledge" (Mumby 1997: 6), but more importantly, explores the meanings that symbolic practices presumably have to the people who produce them (Geertz 1973). Culture, in an interpretive paradigm, is generally understood to be a socially constructed and emergent practice, rather than a reified entity that is defined *a priori* (Carbaugh 1990a). The relationship between culture and communication is seen as more reciprocal than causal, where culture may influence communication but is also constructed and enacted through communication. From this view, communication can be viewed as the primary social process in which practices are culturally coded, with the coding process serving as bases not only for integrating persons but also for transformative or creative functions (Carbaugh 1988a, 1988b, 1990b, 1990c; Philipsen 1997; Philipsen *et al.* 2005).

In the European works cited above, scholarship often focuses on language and meaning-centered approaches, as is evident in the Nordic Network for Intercultural Communication (NIC) and its concerns with a variety of linguistic contexts including business and politics in addition to education (see, for example, the early compendium by Dahl 1995). The northern European network is also complemented by recent important work in Great Britain in linguistic ethnography, a tradition evident today in the journal *Language and Intercultural Communication*. It is noteworthy that these works have drawn principally upon the ethnographic study of language-in-use as a site of culture and meaning-making.

As noted, the works of European scholars have focused at times on the role of language in intercultural communication and language education (Byram and Feng 2004). Several programs in the study of intercultural communication, in addition to those mentioned above, have been developing in Russian universities since the late 1990s (e.g., at the University at Rostov-on-Don under the direction of Professor Irina Rozina, at Moscow State University through the earlier works of Professor Anna Pavlovskaya, and at Tver State University under the early direction of Dean Mikhail Makarov). There is also the new *Russian Journal of Communication* edited by Igor Klyukanov, which includes studies of intercultural communication among its entries. Increasingly, as in the Italian school at the University of Modena, works are focusing on culture-based studies of language, human relationships, identities, and intercultural communication (e.g., Baraldi *et al.* 2010). There is also the *Journal of Intercultural Communication* at the Immigrant Institute established in Sweden in 1999.

Similarly, the establishment of the International Association for Language and Intercultural Communication (IALIC) in 1999 in the UK focused on:

> an abiding concern with the tension between competences as a set of abstractions, a sleek instrument for assessment, audit and course management, and the inevitably messy lived experiences of increasingly skilled language practitioners.
>
> *Corbett (2009: 215)*

## 4. Convergence: interpretive and critical approaches

By the 1990s, there was a move in the US toward more interpretive and critical approaches to studying intercultural communication. These paradigms were closely aligned with European scholarship in language education, international business contacts, political encounters, and other issues that have been subjected to careful linguistic, cultural, or ethnographic study (Isaksson and Røkaas 2000; Kelly and Tomic 2001). Similarly, there is parallel research in Asia, notably in China and Japan. There is also a considerable body of work in a number of courses in China, where the leader is Jia Yuxin at the Harbin Institute of Technology and the China Association for Intercultural Studies. Similarly, at Wuhan University as well as several universities in Beijing, there is considerable momentum building in the study of intercultural communication.

This section first outlines the various themes in interpretive research conducted by various language and communication scholars—most notably the ethnography of communication. Then, we discuss critical and cultural features in this work, describing how these features have been integrated into research agendas that examine language and intercultural communication.

A strong exemplar of interpretive research is discourse-based approaches. For example, Ron Scollon and Suzanne Wong Scollon (1995/2001) built their studies on the analytic frameworks of sociolinguist John J. Gumperz (1982a, 1982b), who links discourse and social identity, and Dell Hymes's (1962, 1972) work on the ethnography of communication. Compared with the more cross-cultural (comparative) postpositive work described earlier, these scholars focus on face-to-face interactions in conversation (how people *do things* with language) within specific contexts (social conversations, political events, professional meetings, native and non-native dynamics, interviews), based on data gathered using qualitative, ethnographic research methods. They conceptualize intercultural (interdiscourse) communication as systems of discourse and examine interactional dimensions such as politeness, face, identity, action, emotion, and dwelling-in-places within it.

Another major interpretive research program is based on the communication theory of identity (Hecht 1993; Hecht et al. 2005). Examples include: Witteborn's (2004) study of Arab women's expressions of cultural identity before and after 9/11, Ribeau et al.'s (2003) study of African-American identity, and Collier's (2005) interpretive theory of identity. Perhaps the best developed exemplar of intercultural interpretive research continues to be the ethnography of communication (e.g., studies conducted by Donal Carbaugh and colleagues). This body of work has explored how intercultural interactions can be sites of deeply held identities and actions that are intricately emergent through cultural discourses (Carbaugh 1990c, 2007; Witteborn 2007); how these involve communication codes that are diverse and, thus, vary from scene to scene and culture to culture (Berry 2009; Boromisza-Habashi 2007; Wilkins and Isotalus 2009); and how intercultural interactions can lead to misunderstandings, disadvantage, injustice, and other outcomes in intercultural interactions (Carbaugh 2005). Some of these studies have focused on communication contrasts between Russian and US American, Blackfeet Indian and White US Americans, as well as comparisons of Finnish and US American patterns of conversational speech and silence (Wilkins and Isotalus 2009).

Ethnographic studies of communication have developed a distinctive approach to intercultural communication (Carbaugh 1990b, 1990c, 2005, 2007), and in the process have issued challenges for future works. Early work in this tradition was designed to respond to several dynamics described above and below. One impetus was the lack of a coherent approach to intercultural communication, which stood at the nexus of language use, discourse, and cultural study (Hymes 1962, 1972). The development of ethnographic studies provided one such coherent, integrative approach. Following the works of Dell Hymes, ethnography of communication scholars designed a program of research that examined cultural practices of communication in contexts, including moments of intercultural contact, as is illustrated in an early reader by Carbaugh (1990b), which assembled studies of cultural communication, intercultural encounters, and cross-cultural studies of communication.

A second impetus was the paucity of research which examined, in detail, actual instances of intercultural interactions as the primary data for analysis. As noted by several scholars within the field (Blommaert 1998; Gudykunst and Ting-Toomey 1988; Leeds-Hurwitz 1990), empirical studies of actual instances of intercultural contact were not common or apparent within the field of intercultural communication, and thus an approach was needed that made intercultural interactions themselves primary data for analysis and, thus, a focal concern. Ethnographic work was needed that explored, empirically, the intricate dynamics of actual moments of intercultural communication.

A third impetus for such study was the lack of a critical dimension in research on intercultural communication. Earlier studies within the tradition of the ethnography of communication had explored in depth how interactional dynamics between races and ethnic members created inequities, injustice, and disadvantages. This is perhaps most evident in John Gumperz's studies (1982b) concerning inequities in interracial and interethnic contacts, but also in many others. A review was published of the "critical voice in ethnography of communication research" in such studies, drawing attention to the critical move within this tradition, identifying its various dimensions and types (Carbaugh 1990c). The point in the review was to respond to popular misconceptions of that time that this approach lacked a critical dimension, and to identify ways in which prior and subsequent works within this approach could advance cultural and critical studies (as below).

EC (ethnographies of communication) studies of intercultural communication therefore provided a coherent and complex philosophy, theory, and methodology for such study. This approach has produced a body of research by scholars around the world that focuses on actual practices of intercultural interactions in contexts and, as a result, provides empirical analyses that are useful bases for critical inquiry. The theory has been explicated and reviewed, as have case studies using the approach (Carbaugh 1990b, 2007). Important to emphasize here is that the approach is an interpretive one, but it is more than that. It includes five distinctive modes of inquiry, the interpretive being one, and the others being theoretical, descriptive, comparative, and critical (Carbaugh 1990c, 1996, 2007). Each mode has its own concepts and procedures; each is designed for making its own claims. It is useful to describe each mode because attention to each builds robust research, as it also builds a useful bridge between the interpretive studies mentioned above and the critical studies reviewed below. Taken together, this system of inquiry helps set the stage for producing the necessary ingredients in intercultural communication research today and provides challenges for our future works (as mentioned below).

## Theoretical inquiry

Ideas have been developed that *conceptualize intercultural interaction as communication and cultural practice*. This development is helping to create new concepts, ways of understanding issues such as identity, power, gender, nation, adaptation, anxiety, and the like as an interactional and largely linguistic process. This relocates the site of theoretical concern from individuals' or aggregate minds or abstract structures into social practices. Conceptualizing these concerns as communication practices contributes to developing an understanding of these as processes steeped in cultural traditions, economic circumstances, and histories (e.g., Bailey 2000). Some developments along these lines include a cyclical research design with a focus on communication theory development (Carbaugh and Hastings 1992), the communication of identity in intercultural contexts (Carbaugh 2005; Wieder and Pratt 1990), and a focus on interactional asynchrony as an historically based source of racial discrimination (Bailey 2000; Chick 1990).

## Descriptive inquiry

As mentioned above, a descriptive mode of inquiry painstakingly documents in as exacting a way as is possible the *actual details of intercultural interactions*. This is evident in ethnographic studies that include detailed transcriptions, such as Gumperz (1982b), Chick (1990), and Bailey (2000) cited above. This allows readers and analysts to see (feel, hear) actual interactional moments in which, for example, racial discrimination and ethnically based disrespect, respectively, are active. Assessments of such intercultural matters are then based upon specific empirical knowledge, with exacting analyses of how each works in social and cultural contexts.

## Interpretive inquiry

Ethnographic studies of intercultural communication seek to *make claims about the meaning of interactional practices to the people who produce them*. Interpretive procedures of data analysis build these claims of interpretation and bring to the fore different meaning systems, or codes, as these are active in the empirical data of concern (Philipsen 1997). By watching and listening to what people are doing, including ourselves, through descriptive analyses, and then interpreting the meaning of those actions to participants through interpretive analyses, we situate our inquiries with an attentive eye to actual interactions and their socially occasioned meaningfulness. A conceptual vocabulary and set of procedures is available and used systematically in such work (Carbaugh 1990b, 2007).

## Comparative inquiry

Intercultural communication involves, by definition, at least two *expressive systems in interaction that are placed in cross-cultural perspective*. Comparative analyses help bring to the fore a sustained cross-cultural study of what is relevant in intercultural interaction (its empirical grounds) and what is meaningful within it (through interpretive analyses). Earlier ethnographic studies have examined the interactional management of face, identity, and meanings (Chick 1990), whereas recent studies have revealed contrastive forms of narrative within particular social contexts (Scollon and Wong Scollon 2007). By juxtaposing differences in communication practices through systematic comparative study, we better understand both what is culturally distinct in the intercultural communication and what is common across expressive systems in these interactions.

## Critical inquiry

As mentioned above, ethnographic studies of intercultural communication have long been keenly attentive to problems of power, injustice, and inequities (e.g., Blommaert 2009; Gumperz 1982b) and have included a "critical voice" within them (Carbaugh 1990c). Several studies of Native American and "Anglo" communication in classrooms show how these intercultural dynamics have disadvantaged Native American students because of Anglo assumptions about proper interaction and what constitutes knowledge in classrooms (Braithwaite 1997; Carbaugh 2005; Philips 1993; Scollon and Wong Scollon 2007). Studies such as these are self-consciously based in an ethnographic ethic; they examine various dimensions of the critical voice and employ it in diverse ways. It is this type of critical inquiry, based upon prior theoretical, descriptive, interpretive, and comparative work, that is attentive to the diversity of practices of concern in intercultural communication. This form of inquiry provides adequate bases for "critical assessment, but only after demonstrating a deep understanding of their situated nature and use" (Berry 2009).

## 5. Critical intercultural communication

The critical paradigm arose from critiques by many scholars—including Europeans, US Americans, and Asians—of the theoretical and methodological shortcomings of the traditional functionalist/postpositive paradigm and some interpretive research. That is, some versions of these paradigms overlooked questions about the relationship between and among culture, communication, and politics, in terms of situated power interests, historical contextualization, global shifts and economic conditions, different politicized identities in terms of race, ethnicity, gender, sexuality, region, socioeconomic class, generation, and diasporic positions. Not only did the critical perspective see the traditional approach as reinforcing stereotypes and homogenizing cultures, the critical perspective asked scholars to think about the political impact of intercultural contact, as well as intercultural communication scholarship (Corbett 2003; Kramsch 2001). This critical stance is congruent with European scholars such as Phillipson's (1992) and Pennycook's (1994) work on linguistic imperialism; Claire Kramsch (2001: 205) places the critical response to the more traditional cross-cultural research much later in language-based intercultural approaches:

> At the beginning of the twenty-first century, the essentialization of national traits and cultural characteristics—i.e., the comparison of differences between one native and one foreign culture seen as stable spaces on the map and permanent in time—seems too reductionistic.

Similarly, in the language-teaching research context, Holliday (1999) advocates distinguishing between the "large culture" paradigm, referring to national and ethnic groups, which tend to promote essentialist thinking and postpositivist research orientations, and the "small culture" paradigm, referring to smaller social groups, which promote non-essentialist thinking and more interpretive research orientations. In more recent work, he continues to reject the center's "old" notions of culture in the context of English language instruction and calls for a more decentered view, whereby speakers of Englishes who are on the periphery define their cultural and language realities in their own terms.

Halualani et al.'s (2009) discussion of the junctures and moves that paved the way for the critical approach in the US are consonant with similar calls by European language scholars (Byram and Feng 2004; Holliday 2009). First, they discuss the importance of scholars' calls for closer attention to historical specificity and contextual grounding in intercultural studies (see Asante 1980; Gonzalez and Peterson 1993; Lee et al. 1995; Mendoza 2005; Moon 1996; Smith 1979; as well as the ethnography of communication scholars' calls detailed above). Second were critiques of the predominant theoretical construct of culture as nation (e.g., Altman and Nakayama 1992; Asante 1980; Gonzalez and Peterson 1993; Holliday 1999, 2009; Moon 1996; Ono 1998; Smith 1981).

A third juncture was the rise of works arguing for the re-theorizing of culture as "sites of struggle" based on power relations and ideologies (Collier et al. 2001; Cooks 2001; Martin and Nakayama 1999; Moon 1996; Starosta and Chen 2003). These arguments are also made by

European language education scholars, as described in a recent literature review by Byram and Feng (2004: 164) who acknowledge that "language teaching has always been susceptible to political and social influences"; they describe how critical approaches have "resulted in reassessment and redefinition of many common sense assumptions, with respect to notions such as native speakers, standard language, national identities, homogenous target cultures" (Byram and Feng 2004: 158). These junctures gradually opened up and stretched the boundaries of intercultural communication inquiry and research and ignited new, complex questions about culture and communication for language and intercultural communication scholars everywhere. Their call to situate intercultural communication in larger contexts has given rise to more awareness of cultural hybridity, cultural conflicts, and transnational movements that create multiple identities (Zarate 2003b). These larger contexts include historical relations, economic relations, as well as political engagements.

These critiques led to the perspective known as "critical intercultural communication studies", a power-based research lens (Halualani *et al.* 2009). What followed from these critiques were: the identification of gaps in knowledge; calls to fill voids in research; and the urging of scholars to approach intercultural communication in a different way. As noted above, some EC scholars responded to these critiques by incorporating notions of power inequities into their investigations of the intersections of culture and communication.

The critical paradigm shares many of the same metatheoretical assumptions with the interpretive—an ontological assumption that reality is socially constructed and an emphasis on the voluntaristic characteristic of human behavior (Martin and Nakayama 1999; Mumby 1997). However, critical scholars emphasize that human behavior is always constrained by societal ideological superstructures and material conditions that privilege some and disadvantage others. Culture is not a benignly socially constructed variable, but a site of struggle where various communication meanings are contested within social hierarchies—the ultimate goal is to examine systems of oppression and ultimately work for system change. Critical scholars vary in their emphasis, focusing on either the "consciousness" as the basis for a radical critique of society or structural relationships within a realist social world (Burrell and Morgan 1988: 34). It is becoming increasingly common for scholars, e.g., EC scholars identified earlier, to incorporate both interpretive and critical impulses in their research.

The field of cultural studies is one of the strongest critical influences on the field of language and intercultural communication (Byram 1986; Byram and Feng 2004). Cultural studies was formalized by the establishment of the Centre for Contemporary Cultural Studies at the University of Birmingham in the UK in 1964. The Centre, which was interdisciplinary and multimethodological, drew from a wide range of theories and traditions in order to study and understand culture. One of the most influential scholars was Stuart Hall (1996), whose work on race and gender added to the already established scholarship on social class and national identity. In the 1980s, cultural studies also flourished in the US, largely as a result of the work of Lawrence Grossberg (1993).

Ultimately, at the same time that cultural studies and critical theory began to influence the study of intercultural communication, cultural studies began to circulate globally and unevenly. On the one hand, cultural studies spread around the world and national (and regional) traditions began to develop. For example, the development of cultural studies in South Africa is reflected in the journal *Critical Arts*, founded in 1980. Similarly, *Topia: A Journal of Canadian Cultural Studies* aims to develop Canadian cultural studies, as well as to remain engaged with international concerns. Cultural studies has also taken off in Australia and New Zealand. The Cultural Studies Association of Australia was established in 1992, and became the Cultural Studies Association of Australasia in 2002 (Magee 2002). They host their own journal, *Continuum*. And in Asia, particularly Taiwan, led largely by the work of Kuan-hsing Chen, cultural studies began to be undertaken to discuss Asian issues. One important forum for this discussion is the journal *Inter-Asia Cultural Studies*. Needless to say, the reach and impact of cultural studies around the globe makes it impossible to list all the journals, scholars, and sites where it has taken root.

Recent writings by Asian scholars critiquing Eurocentric biases in Western intercultural communication theory are consonant with a critical perspective. More than 20 years ago, Ishii (1984) noted the limitations of Western theorizing in intercultural communication and called for more indigenous perspectives. Gordon (1998/99) also critiqued the ethnocentric Western bias in communication theorizing, cautioning that the communication theory developed in the US should not become the communication theory for the world, and called for multicultural communication perspectives to be generated and shared internationally. Many scholars have heeded these exhortations, resulting in a "multicultural turn in communication theory" (Miike 2007: 272). For example, Min Sun Kim (2002) has critiqued Western bias in the positivistic communication research on self-related variables (e.g., communication styles, self-disclosure, conflict styles) and called for a shift from an Anglo-centered field to one that questions the pervasive European–American belief in the autonomous individual: "we need to recognize one major stumbling block in knowledge production in Western contexts: a cultural view that the individual, *a priori*, is separate and self-contained, and must resist the collective" (Kim 2007: 283).

Miike (2003, 2004, 2006) has written extensively on how Asiacentric epistemological, ontological, and methodological traditions might transform Eurocentric communication research into culturally reflexive and sensitive theories and practice. It remains to be seen whether these calls will result in new paradigms or whether the Asiacentric scholarship will be incorporated into current communication conceptualization and research endeavors.

In 2008, the International Communication Association launched *Communication, Culture, and Critique*, a journal devoted to "critical, interpretive and qualitative" approaches to the study of cultural criticism and communication. Also in 2008, the National Communication Association launched the *Journal of International and Intercultural Communication*. This journal's mission was cast more broadly, as it invites manuscripts from any theoretical or methodological approach. The critical perspective in a way is a bridge across the various research traditions in Europe, North America, Asia, and other regions of the world. As noted earlier, in Europe, critical views on language/culture and language education are seen in the establishment of associations and journals such as the International Association for Language and Intercultural Communication (IALIC) in 1999 and its associated journal *Language and Intercultural Communication*. Outgoing editor John Corbett (2009: 215) noted "political engagement remains a hallmark of the journal" and "critical perspectives are firmly in place". These new venues for intercultural communication scholarship in journals around the world reflect the importance of critical work and are healthy signs for the place of critical work in intercultural communication and for the study of intercultural communication more broadly.

## 6. Future directions

In summary, this cursory review of the history of language and intercultural communication studies reveals, first and foremost, that the study is alive and well. There continue to be increasing numbers of academic programs, professional associations, journals and other publications in many geographic regions—so many that it is not possible to provide a comprehensive worldwide history of this area of scholarship.

Second, scholars in various world regions have examined a variety of verbal and nonverbal dimensions of intercultural encounters, with various disciplinary foundations, paradigmatic traditions, and contexts. Intercultural communication scholars need to continue to conceptualize their field with a very wide lens. This means that they recognize that it developed and continues to be built upon a number of disciplinary foundations. The history of intercultural communication highlights this multidisciplinarity, but it also raises a number of questions and issues.

First, should intercultural communication be explicitly interdisciplinary? If so, does it risk losing an academic identity? How does it manage this interdisciplinary approach to building scholarship?

Second, how does intercultural communication maintain the productive tension between the local and the global? In other words, how do intercultural communication scholars research local identities and cultures in the context of their relationships with other cultures and identities in a hybrid, global world? How do intercultural communication scholars maintain this tension without oversimplifying or sacrificing one or the other?

Third, how would intercultural communication scholarship maintain its multiparadigmatic approaches when scholars are often trained in one methodological paradigm? What would multiparadigmatic research look like? Would it have to be done by multidisciplinary research teams?

And finally, given the variety of relevant research that is not conducted by "communication" scholars in Europe, Asia, and other regions, should intercultural communication be housed in departments of communication? Or the field of communication? Or is it transforming itself into something else that is not anthropology, not sociology, not language acquisition and pedagogy, and so on?

The history of intercultural communication raises more questions than answers, but it is important for intercultural communication scholars to begin the process of thinking through the many questions and issues that confront this area of study in the twenty-first century.

## Related topics

Communication, context, and power; critical intercultural communication; culture; essentialism; language, identity, and intercultural communication

## Further reading

Hall, B. (1992) 'Theories of culture and communication', *Communication Theory*, 2: 50–70 (Review of three paradigms of intercultural communication research).
Kramsch, C. (2001) 'Intercultural communication', in R. Carter and D. Nunan (eds) *The Cambridge Guide to Teaching English to Speakers of Other Languages*, New York: Cambridge University Press, pp. 201–6 (History of intercultural communication studies in Europe).
Leeds-Hurwitz, W. (1990) 'Notes on the history of intercultural communication: the Foreign Service Institute and the mandate for intercultural training', *The Quarterly Journal of Speech*, 76: 262–81 (History of intercultural communication studies in the US).
Rogers, E.M., Hart, W.B. and Miike, Y. (2002) 'Edward T. Hall and the history of intercultural communication: The United States and Japan', *Keio Communication Review* 24: 3–26 (An analysis of the development of intercultural communication in the US and Japan).

## Note

1 We should note that we use the term "intercultural" rather than "cross-cultural", although they are sometimes used interchangeably. Cross-cultural communication generally refers to the comparison of

communication behaviors across cultures; intercultural communication involves communication between people from different cultures. Cultural communication often refers to communication among people belonging to the same cultural group (Gudykunst 2002).

## References

Altman, K. and Nakayama, T. 'The fallacy of the assumption of a unitary culture', paper presented at the annual meeting of the Speech Communication Association, Chicago, November 1992.

Asante, M.K. (1980) 'Intercultural communication: an inquiry into research direction', *Communication Yearbook*, 4: 401–10.

Bailey, B. (2000) 'Communicative behavior and conflict between African-American customers and Korean immigrant retailers in Los Angeles', *Discourse and Society*, 11: 86–108.

Baraldi, C., Borsari, A. and Carli, A. (eds) (2010) *Culture and the Human Sciences*, Aurora, CO: The John Davies Group.

Barnett, G.A. and Lee, M. (2002) 'Issues in intercultural communication research', in W.B. Gudykunst and B. Mody (eds) *Handbook of International and Intercultural Communication*, 2nd edn, Thousand Oaks, CA: Sage, pp. 275–90.

Bennett, M.J. (1993) 'Towards ethnorelativism: a developmental model of intercultural sensitivity', in R.M. Paige (ed.) *Education for the Intercultural Experience*, Yarmouth, ME: Intercultural Press, pp. 21–71.

Berry, M. (2009) 'The social and cultural realization of diversity: an interview with Donal Carbaugh', *Language and Intercultural Communication*, 9: 230–41.

Berry, M. and Carbaugh, D. (2004) 'Communicating Finnish quietude: a pedagogical process for discovering implicit cultural meanings in languages', *Language and Intercultural Communication*, 4: 261–80.

Blommaert, J. 'Different approaches to intercultural communication: a critical survey', plenary lecture, Lernen und Arbeiten in einer international vernetzten und multikulturellen Gesellschaft, Expertentagung Universität Bremen, Institut für Projektmanagement und Witschaftsinformatik (IPMI), 27–28 February 1998.

——(2009) 'Ethnography and democracy: Hymes' political theory of language', *Text and Talk*, 29: 257–76.

Bormann, E.G. (1980) *Communication Theory*, New York: Holt, Rinehart and Winston.

Boromisza-Habashi, D. (2007) 'Freedom of expression, hate speech, and models of personhood in Hungarian political discourse', *Communication Law Review*, 7: 54–74.

Braithwaite, C. (1997) 'Sa'ah naaghai bik'eh hozhoon: an ethnography of Navajo educational communication practices', *Communication Education*, 46: 219–33.

Bredella, L. (2003) 'For a flexible model of intercultural understanding', in G. Alred, M. Byram and M. Fleming (eds) *Intercultural Experience and Education*, Clevedon: Multilingual Matters, pp. 14–30.

Burrell, G., and Morgan, G. (1988) *Sociological Paradigms and Organizational Analysis*, Portsmouth, NH: Heinemann.

Byram, M. (1986) 'Cultural studies in foreign language teaching', *Language Teaching*, 19: 322–36.

——(1997) *Teaching and Assessing Intercultural Communicative Competence*, Clevedon: Multilingual Matters.

——(ed.) (2003) *Intercultural Competence*, Strasbourg, France: Council of Europe.

Byram, M. and Feng, A. (2004) 'Culture and language learning: teaching, research and scholarship', *Language Teaching*, 37: 149–68.

Byram, M. and Zarate, G. (1997) 'Definitions, objectives, and assessment of sociocultural competence', in M. Byram, G. Zarate and G. Neuner (eds) *Sociocultural Competence of Language Learning and Teaching*, Strasbourg, France: Council of Europe, pp. 7–43.

Byram, M., Gribkova, B. and Starkey, H. (2002) *Developing the Intercultural Dimension in Language Teaching*, Strasbourg, France: Council of Europe.

Carbaugh, D. (1988a) 'Comments on "culture" in communication inquiry', *Communication Reports*, 1: 38–41.

——(1988b) *Talking American*, Norwood, NJ: Ablex.

——(1990a) 'Toward a perspective on cultural communication and intercultural contact', *Semiotica*, 80: 15–35.

——(ed.) (1990b) *Cultural Communication and Intercultural Contact*, Hillsdale, NJ: Erlbaum.

——(1990c) 'The critical voice in ethnography of communication research', *Research on Language and Social Interaction*, 23: 261–82.

——(1996) *Situating Selves: The Communication of Social Identities in American Scenes*, Albany, NY: State University of New York.

——(2005) *Cultures in Conversations*, New York: Routledge.

——(2007) 'Cultural discourse analysis: communication practices and intercultural encounters', *Journal of Intercultural Communication Research*, 36(3): 167–82.

Carbaugh, D. and Berry, M. (2001) 'Communicating history, Finnish and American discourses: an ethnographic contribution to intercultural communication inquiry', *Communication Theory*, 11(3): 352–66.

Carbaugh, D. and Hastings, S. (1992) 'A role for communication theory in ethnography and cultural analysis', *Communication Theory*, 2: 156–65.

Chick, J.K. (1990) 'The interactional accomplishment of discrimination in South Africa', in D. Carbaugh (ed.) *Cultural Communication and Intercultural Contact*, Hillsdale, NJ: Lawrence Erlbaum, pp. 225–52.

Collier, M.J. (2005) 'Theorizing cultural identification: critical updates and continuing evolution', in W.B. Gudykunst (ed.) *Theorizing about Intercultural Communication*, Thousand Oaks, CA: Sage, pp. 235–56.

Collier, M.J., Hegde, R.S., Lee, W.S., Nakayama, T.K., and Yep, G.A. (2001) 'Dialogue on the edges: ferment in communication and culture', in M.J. Collier (ed.) *Transforming Communication about Culture: Critical New Directions, International and Intercultural Communication Annual*, Volume 24, Thousand Oaks, CA: Sage, pp. 219–80.

Condon, J.C. and Saito, M. (eds) (1974) *Intercultural Encounters with Japan: Communication: Contact and Conflict*, Tokyo: Simul Press.

——(eds) (1976) 'Communication across Cultures for What?', a symposium on Humane Responsibility in Intercultural Communication, Tokyo: Simul Press.

Condon, J.C. and Yousef, F. (1975) *An Introduction to Intercultural Communication*, Indianapolis, IN: Bobbs-Merrill.

Cooks, L. (2001) 'From distance and uncertainty to research and pedagogy in the borderlands: implications for the future of intercultural communication', *Communication Theory*, 11: 339–51.

Corbett, J. (2003) *An Intercultural Approach to English Language Teaching*, Clevedon: Multilingual Matters.

——(2009) 'Editorial', *Language and Intercultural Communication*, 9(4): 215–16.

Council of Europe (2001) *Common European Framework of Reference for Languages: Learning, Teaching, Assessment (CEFR)*. Cambridge: Cambridge University Press.

Dahl, O. (ed.) (1995) *Intercultural Communication and Contact*, Stavanger, Norway: Misjohnshogskolens Forlag.

Delanoy, W. (2006) 'Transculturality and (inter-)cultural learning in the EFL Classroom' in W. Delanoy and L. Volkmann (eds) *Cultural Studies in the EFL Classroom*, Heidelberg, Germany: Winter, pp. 233–48.

Fantini, A.E. (1997) *New Ways in Teaching Culture*, Alexandria, VA: TESOL Inc.

FitzGerald, H. (2003) *How Different are We?*, Clevedon: Multilingual Matters.

Freud, S. (1954) *Aus den Aufäugen der Psychoanalyse (Psychoanalyses)*, New York: Basic Books.

Gadamer, H.G. (1976) *Philosophical Hermeneutics*, ed. and trans. D.E. Linge, Berkeley, CA: University of California Press.

——(1989) *Truth and Method*, New York: Crossroad Publishing.

Gallois, C., Ogay, T. and Giles, H. (2005) 'Communication accommodation theory', in W.B. Gudykunst (ed.) *Theorizing about Intercultural Communication*, Thousand Oaks, CA: Sage, pp. 121–48.

Geertz, C. (1973) *The Interpretation of Culture*, New York: Basic Books.

Gonzalez, A., and Peterson, T.R. (1993) 'Enlarging conceptual boundaries: a critique of research in intercultural communication', in S. P. Bowen (ed.) *Transforming Visions: Feminist Critiques in Communication Studies*, New York: Hampton Press, pp. 249–78.

Gordon, R. (1998/99) 'A spectrum of scholars: multicultural diversity and human communication theory', *Human Communication: Journal of the Asian and Pacific Communication Association*, 2(1): 1–7.

Grossberg, L. (1993) 'Cultural studies and/in new worlds', *Critical Studies in Mass Communication*, 10: 1–22.

——(ed.) (2005) *Theorizing about Intercultural Communication*, Thousand Oaks, CA: Sage.

Gudykunst, W.B. (2002) 'Issues in cross-cultural communication research', in W.B. Gudykunst and B. Mody (eds) *Handbook of International and Intercultural Communication*, 2nd edn, Thousand Oaks, CA: Sage, pp. 165–77.

Gudykunst, W.B. and Nishida, T. (1989) 'Theoretical perspectives for studying intercultural communication', in M.F. Asante and W.B. Gudykunst (eds) *Handbook of International and Intercultural Communication*, Newbury Park, CA: Sage, pp. 17–46.

Gudykunst, W.B. and Ting-Toomey, S. (1988) *Culture and Interpersonal Communication*, Newbury Park, CA: Sage.

Gudykunst, W.B., Lee, C.M., Nishida, T. and Ogawa, N. (2005) 'Theorizing about intercultural communication', in W.B. Gudykunst (ed.) *Theorizing about Intercultural Communication*, Thousand Oaks, CA: Sage, pp. 3–32.

Gumperz, J.J. (1982a) *Discourse Strategies*, New York: Cambridge University Press.

——(ed.) (1982b) *Language and Social Identity*, Cambridge: Cambridge University Press.

Gumperz, J.J. and Hymes, D.H. (eds) (1972) *Directions in Sociolinguistics*, New York: Holt, Rinehart, and Winston.

Hall, B. (1992) 'Theories of culture and communication', *Communication Theory*, 1: 50–70.

Hall, E.T. (1955) 'The Anthropology of Manners', *Scientific American*, 192: 85–89.

——(1959) *The Silent Language*, New York: Doubleday.

——(1966) *The Hidden Dimension*, New York: Doubleday.

——(1976) *Beyond Culture*, New York: Doubleday.

——(1992) *An Anthropology of Everyday Life*, New York: Doubleday/Anchor.

Hall, S. (1996) 'Cultural studies and its theoretical legacies', in D. Morley and K.H. Chen (eds) *Stuart Hall: Critical Dialogues in Cultural Studies*, London: Routledge, pp. 262–75.

Halualani, R.T., Mendoza, S.L. and Drzewiecka, J.A. (2009) 'Critical junctures in intercultural communication studies: a review', *The Review of Communication*, 9(1): 17–35.

Harman, R.C. and Briggs, N.E. (1991) 'SIETAR survey: perceived contributions to the social sciences to intercultural communication', *International Journal of Intercultural Relations*, 15(1): 19–28.

Harms, L.S. (1973) *Intercultural Communication*, New York: Harper and Row.

Hart, W.B. (1999) 'Interdisciplinary Influences in the study of intercultural relations: a citation analysis of the International Journal of Intercultural Relations', *International Journal of Intercultural Relations*, 23: 575–90.

Headland, T.N., Pike, K.L. and Harris, M. (1990) *Emics and Etics: The Insider/Outsider Debate*, Newbury Park, CA: Sage.

Hecht, M.L. (1993) 'A research odyssey: towards the development of a communication theory of identity', *Communication Monographs*, 60: 76–82.

Hecht, M.L., Warren, J.R., Jung, E. and Krieger, J.L. (2005) 'A communication theory of identity: development, theoretical perspective and future directions', in W.B. Gudykunst (ed.) *Theorizing about Intercultural Communication*, Thousand Oaks, CA: Sage, pp. 257–78.

Hofstede, G.H. (1980) *Culture's Consequences: International Differences in Work-Related Values*, Beverly Hills, CA: Sage.

——(1991) *Cultures and Organizations: Software of the Mind*, London: McGraw-Hill.

Holliday, A. (1999) 'Small cultures', *Applied Linguistics*, 20: 237–64.

——(2009) 'The role of culture in English language education: key challenges', *Language and Intercultural Communication*, 9: 144–55.

Hymes, D.H. (1962) 'The ethnography of speaking', in W.T. Sturtevant (ed.) *Anthropology and Human Behavior*, Washington, DC: Anthropological Society of Washington, pp. 13–53.

——(1972) 'Models of the interaction of language and social life', in J.J. Gumperz and D.H. Hymes (eds) *Directions in Sociolinguistics*, New York: Holt, Rinehart, and Winston, pp. 35–71.

Isaksson, M and Røkaas, F.A. (eds) (2000) *Conflicting Values: An Intercultural Challenge*, selected papers from the 1999 NIC Symposium in Oslo, Oslo: Nordic Network for Intercultural Communication (NIC).

Ishii, S. (1973) 'Characteristics of Japanese nonverbal communicative behavior', *Communication* (Journal of the Communication Association of the Pacific), 2(3): 43–60.

——(1984) '*Enryo-Sasshi* communication: a key to understanding Japanese interpersonal relations', *Cross Currents*, 11(1): 49–58.

Ito, Y. (2000) 'What causes the similarities and differences among the social sciences in different cultures? focusing on Japan and the West', *Asian Journal of Communication*, 10(2): 93–123.

Jameson, F. (1971) *Marxism and Form*, Princeton, NJ: Princeton University Press.

Kellner, D. (1989). *Critical Theory, Marxism and Modernity*, Baltimore, MD: Johns Hopkins University Press.

Kelly, M. and Tomic, A. (2001). 'Editorial', *Language and Intercultural Communication*, 1(1): 1–5.

Kim, M.-S. (2002) *Non-Western Perspectives on Human Communication*, Thousand Oaks, CA: Sage.

——(2005) 'Culture-based conversational constraints theory: individual- and culture-level analyses', in W. Gudykunst (ed.) *Theorizing about Intercultural Communication*, Thousand Oaks, CA: Sage, pp. 93–118.

——(2007) 'The four cultures of cultural research', *Communication Monographs*, 74(2): 279–85.

Kim, Y.Y. (2001) *Becoming Intercultural: An Integrative Theory of Communication and Cross-Cultural Adaptation*, Thousand Oaks, CA: Sage.

——(2005) 'Adapting to a new culture: an integrative communication theory', in W. Gudykunst (ed.) *Theorizing about Intercultural Communication*, Thousand Oaks, CA: Sage, pp. 375–400.

Kincaid, D.L. (ed.) (1987) *Communication Theory: Eastern and Western Perspectives*, New York: Academic Press.

Kitao, K. (1989) 'The state of intercultural communication in the United States: a brief history to the early 1980s', in K. Kitao and S.K. Kitao (eds) *Intercultural Communication: Between Japan and the United States*, Tokyo: Eichosha Shinsha, pp. 3–26.

Kitao, K. and Kitao, S.K. (eds) (1989) *Intercultural Communication: Between Japan and the United States*, Tokyo: Eichosha Shinsha.

Kramsch, C.J. (1998) *Language and Culture*, Oxford: Oxford University Press.

——(2001) 'Intercultural Communication', in R. Carter and D. Nunan (eds) *The Cambridge Guide to Teaching English to Speakers of Other Languages*, New York: Cambridge University Press, pp. 201–6.

Kuhn, T.S. (1970) *The Structure of Scientific Revolutions*, Chicago: University of Chicago Press.

Kunihiro, M. (1973) 'Indigenous Barriers to Communication', *The Japanese Interpreter*, 10(3/4): 270–83.

Landis, D. and Wasilewski, J.H. (1999) 'Reflections on 22 years of the *International Journal of Intercultural Relations* and 23 years in other areas of intercultural practice', *International Journal of Intercultural Relations*, 23: 535–74.

Lee, W.S., Chung, J., Wang., J. and Hertel, E. (1995) 'A sociohistorical approach to intercultural communication', *Howard Journal of Communications*, 6: 262–91.

Leeds-Hurwitz, W. (1990) 'Notes on the history of intercultural communication: the Foreign Service Institute and the mandate for intercultural training', *The Quarterly Journal of Speech*, 76: 262–81.

——(2011) 'Writing the intellectual history of intercultural communication', in T.K. Nakayama and R.T. Halualani (eds) *Handbook of Critical Intercultural Communication*, Malden, MA: Blackwell, pp. 21–33.

Lofman, L., Kurki-Suonio, L., Pellinen, S. and Lehtonen, J. (eds) (1993) *The Competent Intercultural Communicator: AFinLA Yearbook*, Publications de l'association Finlandaise de Linguistique Appliqué (Publications of Finland's Association in Applied Linguistics), 51: 117–29.

Magee, P. (2002) 'President's welcome', Cultural Studies Association of Australasia website. Online. Available www.csaa.asn.au/about/welcome.php (accessed 5 November 2010).

Martin, J.N. and Nakayama, T.K. (1999) 'Thinking about culture dialectically', *Communication Theory*, 9: 1–25.

Mead, G.H. (1934) *Mind, Self, and Society*, Chicago, IL: University of Chicago Press.

Mendoza, S.L. (2005) 'Tears in the archive: creating memory to survive and contest empire', in R. Lustig and J. Koester (eds) *Among US: Essays on Identity, Belonging and Intercultural Competence*, Boston, MA: Pearson, pp. 233–45.

Merleau-Ponty, M. (1962) *Phenomenology of Perception*, trans. C. Smith, London: Routledge and Kegan Paul.

Miike, Y. (2003) 'Toward an alternative metatheory of human communication: an Asiacentric vision', *Intercultural Communication Studies*, 12(4): 39–63.

——(2004) 'Rethinking humanity, culture, and communication: Asiacentric critiques and contributions', *Human Communication*, 7(1): 67–82.

——(2006) 'Non-Western theory in western research? an Asiacentric agenda for Asian communication studies', *Review of Communication*, 6 (1/2): 4–31.

——(2007) 'An Asiacentric reflection on Eurocentric bias in communication theory', *Communication Monographs*, 74(2): 272–78.

Miike, Y. and Ishii, S. (1997) 'An analysis of English–Language literature on Japanese nonverbal communication (1966–97): Part I' (in Japanese), *Intercultural Communication Studies*, 11: 119–35.

——(1998) 'An analysis of English-language literature on Japanese nonverbal communication (1966–97): Part II' (in Japanese), *Intercultural Communication Studies*, 11: 137–50.

Moon, D.G. (1996) 'Concepts of culture: implications for intercultural communication research', *Communication Quarterly*, 44: 70–84.

Mumby, D.K. (1997) 'Modernism, postmodernism, and communication studies: a rereading of an ongoing debate', *Communication Theory*, 7: 1–28.

Ono, K.A. (1998) 'Problematizing "nation" in intercultural communication research', in D. Tanno and A. Gonzalez (eds) *Communication and Identity across Cultures*, Thousand Oaks, CA: Sage, pp. 34–55.

Pennycook, A. (1994) *The Cultural Politics of English as an International Language*, London: Longman.

Petkova, D. and Lehtonen, J. (eds) (2005) *Cultural Identity in an Intercultural Context*, Publications of the Department of Communication, No. 27. University of Jyväskylä, Finland.

Philips, S.U. (1993) *The Invisible Culture: Communication in Classroom and Community on the Warm Springs Indian Reservation*, Prospect Heights, IL: Waveland.

Philipsen, G. (1997) 'A theory of speech codes', in G. Philipsen and T. Albrecht (eds) *Developing Communication Theories*, Albany, NY: State University of New York Press, pp. 119–56.

Philipsen, G., Coutu, L.M. and Covarrubias, P. (2005) 'Speech codes theory: restatement, revisions, and response to criticisms', in W.B. Gudykunst (ed.) *Theorizing about Intercultural Communication*, Thousand Oaks, CA: Sage, pp. 55–68.

Phillipson, R. (1992) *Linguistic Imperialism*, Oxford: Oxford University Press.

Ribeau, S.A., Hecht, M.L. and Jackson, R.L. (2003) *African American Communication: Exploring Identities and Culture*, New York: Routledge.

Rogers, E.M. and Hart, W.B. (2002) 'The histories of intercultural, international, and development communication', in W.B. Gudykunst and B. Mody (eds) *Handbook of International and Intercultural Communication*, 2nd edn, Thousand Oaks, CA: Sage, pp. 1–18.

Rogers, E.M., Hart, W.B. and Miike, Y. (2002) 'Edward T. Hall and the history of intercultural communication: the United States and Japan', *Keio Communication Review*, 24: 3–26.

Samovar, L.A. and Porter, R.E. (eds) (1972) *Intercultural Communication: A Reader*, Belmont, CA: Wadsworth.

Schleiermacher, F.D.E. (1977) *Hermeneutics: The Handwritten Manuscripts*, trans. J. Duke and J. Forstman, Missoula, MT: Scholars Press for the American Academy of Religion.

Scollon, R. and Wong Scollon, S. (1995; 2nd edn 2001) *Intercultural Communication: A Discourse Approach*, Malden, MA: Blackwell.

——(2007) Nexus analysis: refocusing ethnography on action, *Journal of Sociolinguistics*, 11: 608–25.

Shuter, R. (1998) 'Revisiting the Centrality of Culture', in J.N. Martin, T.K. Nakayama and L.A. Flores (eds) *Readings in Cultural Contexts*, Mountain View, CA: Mayfield, pp. 38–48.

Simmel, G. (1908/1921) *Soziologie: Untersuchungen über die Formen der Vergesellschaftung (Sociology: Studies of the Forms of Societization)*, Leipzig, Germany: Duncker and Humblot.

Smith, A.G. (ed.) (1966) *Communication and Culture: Readings in the Codes of Human Interaction*, Austin, TX: Holt, Rinehart, and Winston.

——(1981) 'Content decisions in intercultural communication', *Southern Speech Communication Journal*, 47: 252–62.

Smith, A.L. (1979) *Rhetoric of Black Power*, Westport, CT: Greenwood.

Starosta, W.J. and Chen, G.M. (eds) (2003) 'Ferment in the intercultural field: axiology/value/praxis', *International and Intercultural Communication Annual* 26, Thousand Oaks, CA: Sage.

Sumner, W.G. (1906; 2nd edn 1940) *Folkways: A Study of The Sociological Importance of Usages, Manners, Customs, Mores, and Morals*, Boston, MA: Ginn and Co.

Ting-Toomey, S. (2005) 'Identity negotiation theory: crossing cultural boundaries', in W.B. Gudykunst (ed.) *Theorizing about Intercultural* Communication, Thousand Oaks, CA: Sage, pp. 211–33.

Ting-Toomey, S. and Oetzel, J.G. (2002) 'Cross-cultural face concerns and conflict styles: current status and future directions', in W.B. Gudykunst and B. Mody (eds) *Handbook of International and Intercultural Communication*, 2nd edn, Thousand Oaks, CA: Sage, pp. 153–64.

Wallerstein, I. (1999) 'Writing history', paper presented at the 'Colloquium on History and Legitimisation: [Re]constructing the past', Brussels, 24–27 February 1999. Online. Available: http://fbc.binghamton.edu/iwchv-hi.htm (accessed 5 December 2010).

Wieder, L. and Pratt, S. (1990) 'On being a recognizable Indian among Indians', in D. Carbaugh (ed.) *Cultural Communication and Intercultural Contact*, Hillsdale, NJ: Lawrence Erlbaum Associates, Inc., pp. 45–64.

Wilkins, R. and Isotalus, P. (eds) (2009) *Speech Culture in Finland*, Lanham, MD: University Press of America.

Wiseman, R.L. and Koester, J. (eds) (1993) *Intercultural Communication Competence*, Newbury Park, CA: Sage.

Witteborn, S. (2004) 'On being an Arab woman before and after September 11: the enactment of communal identities in talk', *Howard Journal of Communications*, 15: 83–98.

——(2007) 'The expression of Palestinian identity in narratives about personal experience: implications for the study of narrative, identity, and social interaction', *Research on Language and Social Interaction*, 40: 145–70.

Zarate, G. (2003a) 'Identities and plurilingualism: preconditions for recognition of intercultural competences', in M. Byram (ed.) *Intercultural Competence*, Strasbourg, France: Council of Europe, pp. 85–118.

——(2003b) 'The recognition of intercultural competence: from individual experience to certification', in G. Alred, M. Byram and M. Fleming (eds) *Intercultural Experience and Education*, Clevedon: Multilingual Matters, pp. 213–24.

# 2

# Culture, communication, context and power

*Adrian Holliday*

## 1. Introduction/definitions

This chapter reviews two sociological paradigms that govern the way we think about intercultural communication. I use the term 'neo-essentialism' to refer to the dominant approach both within the academy and in everyday attitudes, which follows the essentialist and highly influential work of theorists such as Hofstede, while claiming a more liberal, non-essentialist vision. Much current work in intercultural communication studies rejects essentialism and cultural overgeneralization and acknowledges cultural diversity. However, this work remains neo-essentialism because important essentialist elements are still maintained. Although it does seek to go beyond national categories and deals with the smaller cultures or discourses of business or educational organizations, the same items of literature are invariably pulled back towards the traditional, essentialist use of national cultures as the basic unit, either employing Hofstedian categories of difference or others like them. Behaviour that goes against national stereotypes tends therefore to be framed as exceptions to the essentialist rule rather than as a reality in its own right.

This contrasts with a 'critical cosmopolitan' paradigm, which comes from a critical sociology literature, in which the notion of 'culture' is considered to be a social construction that is manipulated by politics and ideology. It is generally accepted that 'cultures' or constructions of 'culture' operate at local and global levels, from small communities, work groups, households and so on to whole nations and even larger entities. However, because of current concerns with world travel, migration and globalization, it is the global that occupies much current literature and research, and is the major concern here.

## 2. Historical perspectives

To place these paradigms within a historical context, it is necessary to go back to some of the basics of sociological theory.

### Structural–functionalism

Neo-essentialism can be located within the sociological tradition of structural–functionalism, which can be traced back to Emile Durkheim (e.g. 1964), who presented society as an organic system that achieves equilibrium through the functioning of its parts. Derived from biological science, this gave the impression of a society as a solid object, and enabled the development of social theory based on detailed descriptions of how the parts of society, such as the institutions of education, the military, the family and politics, contribute to the whole. Talcott Parsons' *The Social System* (1951) developed this notion, providing a detailed description of all the interconnected parts of society; this contributed greatly to our understanding of the way in which society works.

However, problems arise when these descriptions are used to explain and indeed predict cultural behaviour and values as though they are contained within the system, giving the impression that individual behaviour is determined rather than autonomous. Therefore, if a culture is deemed collectivist, 'any' behaviour within it can be explained as contributing to (or as an exception to) its collectivism. Each countable culture is also considered as a differentiated unit between which precise comparisons can be made. This approach underpins the influential work of Hofstede within intercultural communication studies, who draws on Talcott Parsons to gain support for the notion of a culture as a 'complete' social system that is 'characterized by the highest level of self-sufficiency in relation to its environments' (Hofstede 2001: 10). There is also a strong normative sense to this thinking, which enables the evaluation of behaviour and values depending on whether they are functional or dysfunctional (or deviant) to the equilibrium of the whole.

## Social action theory

Critical cosmopolitanism is supported by social action theory, which presents a very different model by asserting the potential independence of social action. Here, culture is a negotiated 'process' that is far more difficult to pin down. Social action theory can be traced back to the work of Max Weber (1964), who maintained that the precise nature of human behaviour could never be determined. Part of his strategy against pinning things down was remembering that coherent ideas about societies should be regarded as 'ideal types' – imagined models or heuristic devices (i.e. for the purpose of investigation) – which might be used to imagine what society 'might' be like but should never be taken as descriptions of how things actually are (Stråth 2008: 33–34; Weber 1968: 23). Although Weber did much to describe the social structures of Protestantism and Confucianism, it was made very clear that the social action of individuals could be expressed in dialogue with them (Bendix 1966: 261; Dobbin 1994: 118). Whereas political and other circumstances may severely reduce the degree to which individual social action can be acted out, this does not mean that the potential is not there. The example of critical thinking, which has become a common focus in intercultural communication studies, can be used to clarify the difference in the two approaches:

- The structural–functionalist view: If a society is structured in such a way that students are not allowed to express critical views in the classroom, they will lack critical thinking everywhere.
- The social action view: Not being allowed to express critical views in classrooms in one particular social system does not mean that students do not think critically in private or that they cannot express critical views when moving to other social systems.

Rather than being subjected to an organism of cultural containment, social action theory considers at least the possibility of individuals being able to change existing orders, for example by means of charisma (Bendix 1966: 265). Unlike the neat layering depicted by structural–functionalism, social action theory indicates a messy, shifting, uncertain complexity of cultural reality which is ideology dependent on the perspectives of the people concerned.

One must, however, avoid projecting too neat a case for Weber's social action theory and its relationship with critical cosmopolitanism. It has been argued that he was still preoccupied with nation to the degree that he failed completely 'to treat it as problematic social and historical construction' (Schudson 1994: 21).

## 3. Critical issues and topics

Critical cosmopolitan provides the basis for a powerful critique of what I have termed neo-essentialism and existing thought and practice within intercultural communication.

### The centrality of ideology

The key to this critique is the positioning of ideology. Whereas the structural–functionalist position places ideology as a feature of the structure of the culture being investigated, critical cosmopolitanism places ideology within the domain of the investigator and therefore maintains that the descriptions of culture are themselves ideological, and that the structural–functionalists' claim to scientific neutrality and objectivity comprise a naïve denial of ideology.

Ideology can be defined as a system of ideas that are 'systematically distorted' or 'bent out of shape' (Wallace 2003: 23, citing Eagleton and Habermas) to promote the interests of a particular group of people (Spears 1999: 19). Gellner (2005: 2) characterizes the drawing power of ideology by suggesting that it has 'powerful sex appeal'. Within the current historical climate, this ideology is placed very much within a global politics where the power of 'the West' takes centre position in defining the Periphery 'non-West'. The terms 'Centre' and 'Periphery', 'West' and 'non-West' need to be used with caution. For me, they only make sense as psychological concepts, although West and non-West clearly also have a geographical aspect. Hannerz (1991) defines the relationship between Centre and Periphery as one of imposing and taking meaning within an unequal global order. This can apply strategically or emotionally to different groups of people, events or attitudes at different times.

### Methodological nationalism

National culture as a concept is thus considered to be ideologically driven – projected in different ways at different times to suit political agendas (e.g. Hall 1991a: 20); and its longstanding influence in the explanation of cultural behaviour has been attributed to the politics of nineteenth-century European nationalism. This 'methodological nationalism' is accused of having dominated science ever since with simplistic explanations that do not recognize the true complexity of culture in which boundaries are blurred and diversity is the norm (Ahmad and Donnan 1994; Beck and Sznaider 2006: 2; Crane 1994; Delanty 2006; Grande 2006; Rajagopalan 1999; Schudson 1994; Tomlinson 1991: 69).

It is further argued that the preoccupation with structural–functionalist theories of culture has served a need within the academy for accountability, especially during the Reagan and Thatcher era of the 1980s (Moon 2008: 15). Shuter (2008: 38) argues that this need for accountable theories thrives on and encourages tightly specialist concepts such as 'uncertainty reduction', 'initial interaction', 'intercultural communication competence', 'communication apprehension', 'intercultural adaptation' and 'relationship development'. Kumaravadivelu

(2007: 68) makes a similar point about the proliferation of technical terms such as 'accommodation, acculturation, adaptation, adoption, assimilation, enculturation, integration'.

Critical cosmopolitanism thus connects with Kuhn's (1970) *The Structure of Scientific Revolutions*, which blew apart the modernist illusion that science was neutral and argued that the development of paradigms in science is influenced by the career-serving academic politics and the ideologies of schools of thought.

## The individualist Self vs. the collectivist Other

A particularly influential description to which the critical cosmopolitan critique can be applied is that of collectivist and individualist cultures, most commonly associated with Triandis (1995). In summary, 'people from individualist cultures' are presented as 'North Americans of European backgrounds, North and West Europeans, Australians, New Zealanders', and are associated with autonomy, personal goals, improvement, achievement, assertiveness, self-reliance, consistency, openness to change, fun, equality and choice. In contrast, 'people from collectivist cultures' are presented as 'Latin Americans, Southern Europeans, East and South Asians, Africans', and are associated with group and family membership and loyalty, interdependence, circular thinking, stability, conservatism, silence and few choices (Triandis 2004: x–xi).

Although it might be argued that these descriptions are ideal types in the Weberian sense, or 'prototypes' of national culture which exist to varying degrees in all countries (Triandis 2004: ix), they have taken on a powerful geographical reality in intercultural studies, where they are assumed to be neutral descriptions. The critical cosmopolitanism critique is that they are ideological constructions in that they represent a veiled demonization of a non-Western Other by an idealized Western Self, and that the collectivist attributes thus represent cultural deficiency (Kim 2005: 108; Kumaravadivelu 2007: 15; Moon 2008: 16). The outcome is therefore essentialist Othering – the defining of a particular group of people or a person by means of negative characteristics – so that the behaviour of someone from a so-called 'collectivist culture' is explained entirely according to imagined and negative collectivist characteristics. That the collectivism description relates more to a generalized notion of low achievement, rather than to specific national cultural groups, is evidenced by the use of the same descriptions for low-achieving mainstream American schoolchildren (Kubota 2001). Triandis himself (2006: 29) gives away his own association between collectivism and deficiency when he connects it with 'poverty', societies with '*only* one normative system' (my emphasis), which are 'not cosmopolitan', and with the 'lower social classes of any society' or among people who 'have not travelled', not 'been socially mobile' or who 'have not been exposed to the modern mass media'.

## The struggle for Periphery cultural recognition

One of the arguments in support of the collectivism–individualism distinction is that it preserves the integrity of non-Western cultures against conforming with Western values. The critical cosmopolitan response is that the distinction itself is constructed by Western academia – that definitions of the Other that are produced by the West are so powerful that they obliterate any recognition of non-Western realities.

Here, it is important to note the difference between critical cosmopolitanism and a centre-led picture of a cosmopolitan world that has been variously termed 'global cosmopolitanism', 'globalism' and 'global mass culture' (Bhabha 1994: xiv; Canagarajah 1999: 207–9; Fairclough 2006: 40; Hall 1991a: 20). This less critical picture suggests an attractive liberalization and integration of markets which serves progress, democracy and prosperity, global villages and silicon valleys, all of which serve Western economies – the 'nice world' that ignores inequality and needs to be protected by the 'war on terror'.

The critical cosmopolitan viewpoint counters this picture of harmony with an uncomfortable picture of global inequality (e.g. Hannerz 1991). It presents a hidden, alternative, 'vernacular', local cosmopolitanism that needs to struggle for recognition (Bhabha 1994: xv–xvi), but 'has always been there in non-Western communities' with villagers dealing easily across small linguistic boundaries; this has largely been destroyed by colonial powers that have 'divided these communities arbitrarily into nation-states for their convenience' (Canagarajah 1999: 207–9). Various theorists are relatively optimistic about a revolutionary reclaiming of cultural space from the margins – a globalization from below (Fairclough 2006: 121; Hall 1991a: 34).

## Liberal multiculturalism as neo-racism

This picture of a defining Western order that has hidden the expression of peripheral cultural realities adds to the criticism of the way in which culture is perceived in society generally in what has been referred to as liberal multiculturalism – a recognized response to the 'foreign' within Western societies over the past 40 years. I locate liberal multiculturalism within neo-essentialism because, although there is a liberal desire to move away from essentialism, the result is otherwise.

The liberal multiculturalist interest in the celebration and sharing of artefacts, festivals, ceremonies, dress, food, and customs has been widely criticized as hiding a deeper racism. It is asserted that its 'bland', 'indulgent' superficiality has resulted in a commodified packaging that has been far from faithful to the complexity of lived cultural experience, and has instead focused on 'the exotica of difference', which demean and alienate personal identities as though they are a 'spectacle' (e.g. Ahmad and Donnan 1994: 5; Hall 1991b: 55; Kubota 2004: 35; Kumaravadivelu 2007: 104–6; Sarangi 1995; Wallace 2003: 55). The annoyance at the superficiality of this approach is well expressed as follows:

> Ritualized celebration of difference has become an end in itself … aestheticized and packaged as an exciting consumable collage: brown hands holding yellow hands holding white hands holding male hands holding female hands holding black hands … 'boutique multiculturalism'.
>
> *Kumaravadivelu (2007: 109), citing Radhakrishnan, and Stanley and Fish*

Hence, what appears to be an inclusive, celebratory recognition of cultural diversity turns into an Othering of non-Western groups by a Western definition of who they are. An example of this is that whatever any 'Asian' says or does is 'interpreted with stunning regularity as a consequence of their "Asianness", their "ethnic identity", or the "culture" of their "community"' (Baumann 1996: 1).

An outcome is neo-racism, where race is rationalized, hidden and denied under the 'nice' heading of culture (Delanty *et al.* 2008: 1; Spears 1999). At a macro level, the self-perception of a democratic West as 'de facto anti-racist' leads to a 'depoliticization', which 'masks the embeddedness of the idea of "race"' (Lentin 2008: 102–3). At a micro level, there are everyday 'disclaimer' statements of denial – '"I have nothing against [ … ], but", "my best friends are [ …], but", "we are tolerant, but", "we would like to help, but"'(Wodak 2008: 65). There is also an implicit ethos of a deeply patronizing 'tolerant' 'helping' of the non-Western Other (Delanty *et al.* 2008: 9), which can be connected with a modernistic desire to tie down identities and to hide aggression beneath education, progress and civilization (Latour 2006). Rather than building bridges, a naïve multiculturalism has thus failed to escape from a deeper Centre–Western psychosis, which we see in the expanding world of tourism, where ethnic imagery is reconstructed, generalized, mythologized and fixed for the best effect in satisfying the high-status activity of what amounts to 'shopping for difference' and 'authenticity' (Jordan and Weedon 1995: 150; MacCannell 1992: 158–70; Urry 2002: 2, 5, 10).

## The indelible intercultural line

Like Weber's ideal types, the concepts of critical cosmopolitanism and neo-essentialism are of course themselves both fictions that help us to focus on particular issues. One such issue is raised by the now fairly established concepts of the third space, in which it is possible for intercultural travellers to negotiate their position with regard to the new culture, and hybridity, where someone at the same time maintains the attributes of their own culture while taking on in a limited way those of another. Although these concepts are used to struggle with the problems of essentialism, especially in the search for postcolonial spaces (e.g. Bhabha 1994: 5; Canagarajah 1999: 208; Delanty 2006: 33; Guilherme 2002: 167; Kramsch 1993; Young 2006: 159; Zhu 2008), they also seem to imply a neo-essentialist preoccupation with an indelible line between two cultures. As with liberal multiculturalism, on the surface, this line may appear to represent respect for difference and potential for intercultural creativity (e.g. Fay 1996: 55ff). However, the intercultural line may also indicate a division of values that reflects a division in what people are prepared to do or are capable of doing. Although there is a concept of a line between 'our culture' and 'their culture', it cannot remain at a level of mutual respectfulness. The notions of a third space or hybridity also have at least the potential of denying the possibility of complexly diverse cultural ownership. Kumaravadivelu puts this well:

> Proponents of cultural hybridity would expect me to create a – third culture, or a – third space, without allowing either my inherited Indian culture or my learned American culture to fully determine my values and beliefs ... a state of ambivalence ... in-betweenness that is supposed to result when individuals ... displace themselves from one national/cultural context ... into another. I do not believe I am dangling in cultural limbo. Instead I believe I live in several cultural domains at the same time – jumping in and out of them, sometimes with ease and sometimes with unease. ... In fact one does not even have to cross one's national borders to experience cultural complexity.
>
> *Kumaravadivelu (2007: 5)*

Kumaravadivelu goes on to suggest that the concept of hybridity 'wrongly places the margin at the centre and, in doing so, it conflates the distinction between the oppressed and the oppressor' (ibid: 112).

## 4. Current contributions and research

Taking Kumaravadivelu's critique further, if the notion of not being restricted by the cultural line is put together with the critical cosmopolitan notion of Periphery cultural realities that are hidden by powerful Centre discourses of culture (described above), there is the possibility that there are unrecognized potentials for individuals to negotiate national cultural boundaries and claim a broader world. This suggests that individuals can transcend national cultural boundaries as they travel from place to place. In the following subsection, I cite some research in support of this view.

## The ability to move and cross

The possibility of transcending cultural lines is supported by work that focuses at the level of discourses or small cultures. Small cultures could be a wide range of social groupings from neighbourhoods or communities to work, friendship or leisure groups (e.g. Beales *et al.* 1967: 8; Holliday 1999). They are built from the micro basics of how individuals manage image within the group (e.g. Goffman 1972) to how groups are formed and routinized (e.g. Wenger 2000). They represent the 'intermediate level of social structuring' in which there are identifiable discourses (Fairclough 1995: 37); and it is at the level of discoursal strategies that we see the individual's ability to acquire the social competence to move through a multiplicity of cultural experiences within the complexity of society (e.g. Lankshear *et al.* 1997; The New London Group 1996). It is at this level that we can see the detail of the building of 'normal' thinking through social construction, normalization and reification (Berger and Luckmann 1979; Gergen 2001) – in the formation of 'imaginary representations of how the world will be or should be within strategies for change which, if they achieve hegemony, can be operationalised to transform these imaginaries into realities' (Fairclough 2006: 26). These are the bases for the social action that is in dialogue with and not confined by social structure within the social action picture of society.

This picture of society can be seen in Angouri and Harwood's (2008) discussion of how people co-construct multiple writing genres in response to different communities of practice, and in Baumann's (1996) ethnographic study of how people in the multicultural London borough of Southall construct different discourses of culture in different ways at different times depending on who and what they are relating to, and also in schoolchildren playing creatively with culture in urban classrooms (Rampton *et al.* 2008). Angouri and Glynos (2009) show us how, in a complex world of culture play, 'culture' as 'a floating signifier' is a label that is invoked for a variety of purposes to make sense of interactions in organizations.

Of course, this type of discussion is as full of interpretation as it claims for the nature of 'culture'. An interesting point of focus here is Eva Hoffman's (1998) seminal description of being a Polish immigrant in North America. Whereas this is often cited as an example of the problems with crossing cultural lines, my own reading of Hoffman did not begin from a preoccupation with an indelible intercultural line and therefore inspired me with accounts of someone struggling to write herself into and take ownership of a new and strange cultural universe.

Political positioning, as discussed by the critical cosmopolitans above, can make the difference here. Where cultural struggle is underpinned by the intense desire to throw off the stereotypes imposed by a Western order, the emphasis on the ability to cross cultural lines and take ownership of the foreign becomes all important. Implicit in this struggle is the dissatisfaction with the Western monopoly on key concepts of cultural proficiency such as modernity and self-determination. An interesting text on this subject is Honarbin-Holliday's (2009) ethnography of Iranian women claiming the modern world as their own cultural heritage and tracing it back to the deep indigenous modernity implicit in the generation of their grandmothers.

Implicit in this assertion that people are not what they appear to be is a stand against the Orientalist trope that the non-West is characterized as cultural deficient (Said 1978), as associated with the image of collectivist cultures described above. There is therefore a similar stand against unjust stereotyping in research into chauvinistic depictions of 'non-native speakers' in English language education, which argues that the assumption that they lack the ability to participate, plan and organize is a professional misrepresentation (Holliday 2005b; Holliday and Aboshiha 2009; Kubota and Lin 2006; Kumaravadivelu 2006; Nayar 2002; Pennycook 1998).

There is similarly a growing body of research arguing against the negative 'collectivist' stereotyping of Chinese students in British universities and elsewhere as culturally unable to take part in educational activities (e.g. Clark and Gieve 2006; Grimshaw 2007; Quach *et al.* 2009). See also Montgomery and McDowell's (2009) discussion of how university students from a range of cultural backgrounds form their own international community of practice.

## Cultural realism

The discussion so far maintains that the common image of cultures as national structures that define and confine us is an illusion forged by Western ideology both in the academy and in society more generally. Kumaravadivelu (2007: 143) usefully rationalizes this point of view by taking the cultural realism implicit in the social action theory of Weber, as described above – acknowledging the substantial reality of national structures, but in a contextual rather than a confining role – and coupling it with a social constructivist acknowledgement that culture is socially constructed (see also Fairclough 2006: 18).

My own attempt to resolve this relationship between reality and illusion is expressed in Figure 2.1, which is consciously complex, with full realization that there are no easy answers. The figure represents the dialogue between underlying universal cultural processes, in the right centre, and the particularities of national or other structures.

Although the particularities of what might be called large cultural structures ([i] in Figure 2.1) have undeniable influence, both cultural resources and global positioning are drawn upon in different ways at different times depending on the needs and orientation of the individual. Whether or not these are positive or negative influences and the degree of power that they exercise depends on the particular personal cultural trajectories through life of each individual [ii], which are a major link between the universal and the particular. Strong examples of such trajectories are recorded in interviews with thirty-eight informants from across the world who, despite their different cultural backgrounds, spoke very similarly about how family, ancestry, peers and profession influenced them (Holliday 2010; 2011: 42).

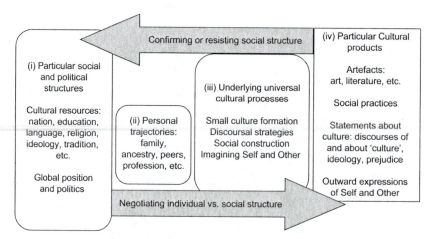

*Figure 2.1* Aspects of cultural reality
*Source*: Adapted from Holliday (2011: 131). Reproduced with permission.

It is underlying universal cultural processes [iii] that are employed to make sense of and realize this mediation. These comprise the small culture and discoursal strategies described above, and provide the basic cultural competence that allow individuals to transcend cultural lines. The outcome of this dialogue between universal processes and particular structures is the particular cultural products [iv]. Artefacts are the physical, visible aspects of society (as indicated by the box), which relate to many people's popular view of culture, and have been the superficial focus of liberal multiculturalism, as discussed above. The artefacts listed in Figure 2.1 just scratch the surface of what they might include – so many aspects of the appearance of a society and what people do in it, from how buses and streets look to how animals are killed and where screws are sold. They will also be empty references until they are set against the ideologically driven statements about culture [iv], and may confirm or resist the social and political structures.

The core of the issue of reality vs. illusion resides in the imagining of Self and Other. In one respect, this is part of the universal process through which any social group establishes an image of strength and superiority in the face of other groups. Businesses, professional groups, families, football teams and so on may emphasize efficiency, specialism, ideology or morality. The cult of the 'mission statement' is part of this. Equivalent negative attributes to competing groups will also be projected. The degree to which these projections are based on reality or really are imagined may be hard to establish. However, placing this core of cultural chauvinism within the universality of what we all do ([iii] in Figure 2.1) also indicates that responsibility has to be taken for it by everybody at every level. It underlies everything that takes on the presence of neutrality in cultural difference and attempts to solve this difference. It is at the core of what is denied within neo-essentialism.

In another respect, the imagining of Self and Other results in the substantive cultural product in the form of statements about culture [iv]. These are what people say or otherwise project consciously about their 'culture'. These are not descriptions of what their cultural group is actually like – except that there are people who wish to project themselves in this manner. Thus, although such statements are cultural acts, they are also artefacts of the culture. At another level, they indicate cultural agendas. Thus, when people state that their culture is individualist and is marked by self-determination, it does not necessarily mean that self-determination is a defining characteristic of their group, but that this is the ideal with which they wish to be associated. They are thus the products of discourses of and about 'culture', and are ideologically driven by the global and political positioning on the left of Figure 2.1. The statement 'British people like football' does not mean that all British people like football. One would need to look at the conditions within which the statement is made to begin to understand its deeper meanings.

The major significance of the universality of underlying universal cultural processes is that they have the potential to be transported across national cultural boundaries. This possibility leads to a very different way of looking at cultural behaviour. What has become a classic example, of East Asian students being quiet in British classrooms, can be used to illustrate this point. There are two very different ways of looking at this:

- The dominant neo-essentialist view: This behaviour derives from collectivist national cultures in which loyalty to the group inhibits individual expression, which in turn reflects a lack of self-determination. This therefore reflects different values that have to be appreciated and understood. We (from individualist cultures) need to be sensitive and to adjust our expectations.
- The critical cosmopolitan view: This may well be influenced by national traditions and educational practices, but the students do not have to be confined by them. The behaviour reflects the employment of universal discoursal strategies to deal with unfamiliar cultural

practice (different structures of power and authority). Silence may be a form of resistance which involves strategic withdrawal. With appropriate cultural learning and opportunity, other strategies may be employed to develop 'successful' behaviour, which may well enrich and improve the cultural practice of the British classroom.

The second reading is partly informed by doctoral and master's dissertations in which Japanese language students who are noisy in Japan go quiet in front of British teachers who demand controlled talk (Hayagoshi 1996); Taiwanese language students who are quiet because they do not understand task instructions and then get what they need outside the classroom (Cheng 2000); and Hong Kong Chinese high school students who demonstrate highly 'communicative' behaviour in resistance to their teachers (Tong 2002) – all discussed in Holliday (2005b). There is also the important factor that, when people are newcomers in a particular cultural domain, they must not be seen negatively as deficient in the foreign practices they find, but as people with enhanced cultural skills 'because' they have travelled, building positively on their cultural experience as they go – hence the very real possibility that 'international' students who have the opportunity to rationalize more than one educational institutional experience are in a better position to contribute creatively than 'home' students who have not travelled (Holliday 2011: 174ff). Strategic withdrawal by marginal groups as resistance to powerful symbolic violence is also well known in other domains (Flam and Bauzamy 2008; Sawyer and Jones 2008: 245). The first reading, although pretending sensitivity and understanding, in effect represents the patronizing Othering implicit in liberal multiculturalism described above by positioning the foreign in another place from which it is not able to contribute.

## 5. Main research methods

The critical cosmopolitan approach suggests an interpretivist methodology that seeks to allow meanings to emerge from the non-aligned, de-centred piecing together of what is found, rather than imposing the *a priori* narratives implicit in a neo-essentialist approach. If Periphery cultural realities are to be revealed, the aim must therefore be (1) to put aside established descriptions, (2) to seek a broader picture and (3) to look for the hidden and the unexpressed. This is a difficult aim to achieve within the ideological and politicized domain that critical cosmopolitanism attributes to culture. This is particularly problematic because interpretivism itself has different shades of criticality. Much interpretive attention is already given to cultural difference in the neo-essentialist paradigm; but it is not sufficient to undo the power of the essentialist roots in models such as Hofstede's or to undo the denial of ideology. The first reading, above, employs interpretation, which does not go sufficiently far or dig sufficiently deep to arrive at the more critical second reading. It is certainly the case that Far Eastern students will tell researchers things that comply with the first reading. These are statements about culture, as described in Figure 2.1 [iv]. However, all statements require deeper investigation. To take such statements at face value and not to dig deeper is to ignore social complexity. There has already been much work done on the use of ethnographic narrative and autobiography in developing young people's intercultural awarenesses, which go into developed detail concerning the role and demeanour of the language learner as an integrative social researcher (Byram 2008: 115ff). This is an important start, but there needs to be careful consideration of the deep cultural prejudices that researchers inevitably carry with them.

### Postmodern qualitative research

The postmodernism implicit in critical cosmopolitanism does lend itself to the postmodern end of qualitative research, which recognizes the inevitability of the influence of researcher subjectivity and ideology within the research setting and seeks to address it (e.g. Denzin and Lincoln 2005; Gubrium and Holstein 1997: vi, 38; Hammersley and Atkinson 1995: 11; Holliday 2007: 19). There are similar developments in more critical versions of ethnography (Blackman 2007; Clifford and Marcus 1986). Disciplines that help the researcher to 'make the familiar strange' are crucial. One such is bracketing, which, often associated with phenomenology, can be described as locating prejudices that will colour the viewpoint of the researcher and consciously putting them aside, to 'temporarily suspend all commonsense assumptions' in order to set aside judgements about the expected 'nature', 'essence' and 'reality' of things (Schutz 1970: 316), and to 'make visible the practices through which taken-for-granted realities are accomplished' (Gubrium and Holstein 1997: 40). It employs the methodology of the stranger (Schutz 1964) approaching a new set of social practices and having to work out from first principles how the culture works in terms of its basic structures, and seeing through the discourses and ideologies of culture that have become reified to insiders.

In my own study of Hong Kong Chinese students (Holliday 2005b: 88ff), I knew that the stereotype of Chinese culture was so deeply embedded in my thinking that I had to bracket it. If I was to avoid the 'easy answer' that Chinese students are 'collectivist' and 'passive', I had to work hard to think of them first as students, not as Chinese. In Holliday (2004, 2007: 107ff.), I explore a number of ways in which qualitative researchers try to dig down to deeper realities and counter cultures, including reconstructed and fictionalized narratives; and I attempt to use these methods in Holliday (2011: x). The researcher's deconstruction of their own professional prejudices can help them to see similar prejudices in their research subjects. I and Aboshiha thus use personal narratives of our own professional history to help us see the cultural chauvinism among so-called 'native speaker' English language teachers (Holliday 2005a; Holliday and Aboshiha 2009).

## Critical reading

Critical discourse analysis has an obvious role in investigating hidden ideologies. Wallace employs this in her teaching of critical cultural awareness through what she terms 'critical reading' (2003: 25–26, citing Fairclough, Kress and Halliday). This involves students from different cultural backgrounds working together to investigate ideology and power relations, which inevitably underpin texts that depict cultural life (Wallace 2003: 102). It is through the students sharing their readings that critical reading significantly transcends the preoccupation with the line between 'our culture' and 'their culture'. It is necessary not just to compare what people in different societies do, but to invite everyone to look at profound texts of interaction from every side. The texts should not be a depiction of 'the other, foreign culture', which would encourage a vision of how 'they' are different from or the same as 'us'. They should represent cultural interface. The students thus look at texts with both familiar and unfamiliar content in each other's company. Wallace provides the example of a 'cross-cultural dialogue' within a classroom setting in a university in London 'where students, both from mainstream, dominant cultural groups and marginalized ones may make strange their own cultural practices', 'negotiate a range of different cultural understandings' and 'gain some distance from their readings of familiar texts'. Hence, 'in a multicultural classroom a diversity of readings provides a cultural and critical resource for the whole class' (2003: 75). As with Schutz's notion of the stranger, above, outsiders can see ideology which insiders cannot, especially if they come from more politically challenging countries. 'Traditional ways of life, relations between men and women, ways of doing things, are necessarily open to challenge and can no longer be taken for granted in *any* society' (Wallace 2003: 57–58, her emphasis).

## 6. Future directions

A predominant theme running through the discussion in this chapter has been that of a global inequality which underpins the manner in which culture and cultural difference have been projected both in the academy and in everyday life. The result is a sustained and profound cultural disbelief with regard to an imagined non-Western Other. Adding to this issue is what I have argued to be the fact that this inequality is largely denied in the dominant approach to intercultural communication studies, where it is believed that cultural descriptions such as those of so-called collectivist and individualist societies, although possibly overgeneralized, are technically neutral.

Future directions therefore need to be in two areas. Research into cultural difference and education towards cultural awareness both need to focus on cultural 'belief' rather than disbelief. This very subtle change in gear suggests that we focus on what the cultural Other 'can' do and contribute – that that line between cultures can be crossed, with positive contribution and even cultural improvement. An important aspect of this focus is the domain of underlying universal cultural processes, which provide the potential for cultural competence regardless of where people come from. These underlying processes need to be observed and understood as the basis for what brings us together and enables us to read critically both what is going on between us and what fuels the ideology that keeps us apart. Recognizing and understanding the ideology beneath the ways in which we present culture is the second area.

## Related topics

Cosmopolitanism; culture, essentialism; hybridity, multiculturalism; Othering; race; research methodology, stereotyping; third space

## Further reading

Delanty, G, Wodak, R. and Jones, P. (eds) (2008) *Identity, Belonging and Migration*, Liverpool: Liverpool University Press (Although focusing mainly on migration within Europe, this edited collection represents the major discussions within a critical cosmopolitan theme. The often unrecognized prejudices of centre–Western ideology are explored, with reference to Othering, discourses of discrimination, neo-racism, multiculturalism, symbolic violence and resistence).

Fairclough, N. (2006) *Language and Globalization*, London: Routledge (Within the context of Romania's developing relations with Western European institutions, this book provides a detailed analysis of the role of discourse within globalization. It provides perceptive descriptions of the manner in which cultural realities develop and change in everyday life).

Holliday, A.R. (2011) *Intercultural Communication and Ideology*, London: Sage (This book provides an alternative, critical cosmopolitan view of culture and suggests that common, established theories of cultural difference are ideological within unequal global politics. It is the denial of such ideology that prevents the West from appreciating the cultural realities of the Periphery).

King, A.D. (ed.) (1991) *Culture, Globalization and the World-System*, New York: Palgrave (This classic edited text provides discussions from key theorists who, between them, present the basic sociological arguments for how notions of culture are constructed by a global politics. The concepts of globalization, Centre and Periphery, postcolonial identity, nation and class are explored).

Kumaravadivelu, B. (2007) *Cultural Globalization and Language Education*, Yale: Yale University Press (Although the backdrop is English language education, this book provides a powerful discussion of established views of culture. It critiques the notions of hybridity, multiculturalism and cultural assimilation. There is also excellent coverage of intercultural communication literature).

## References

Ahmad, A.S. and Donnan, H. (1994) 'Islam in the age of postmodernity', in A.S. Ahmad and H. Donnan (eds) *Islam, Globalization and Postmodernity*, London: Routledge, pp. 1–20.

Angouri, J. and Glynos, J. (2009) 'Managing cultural difference and struggle in the context of the multi-national corporate workplace: solution or symptom?', *Working Paper in Ideology in Discourse Analysis*, 26: 1–20.

Angouri, J. and Harwood, N. (2008) 'This is too formal for us … : a case study of variation in the written products of a multinational consortium', *Journal of Business and Technical Communication*, 22(1): 38–64.

Baumann, G. (1996) *Contesting Culture*, Cambridge: Cambridge University Press.

Beales, A.R., Spindler, G. and Spindler, L. (1967) *Culture in Process*, New York: Holt, Rinehart.

Beck, U. and Sznaider, N. (2006) 'Unpacking cosmopolitanism for the social sciences: a research agenda', *British Journal of Sociology*, 57(1): 1–23.

Bendix, R. (1966) *Max Weber: An intellectual portrait*, London: Methuen.

Berger, P. and Luckmann, T. (1979) *The Social Construction of Reality*, Harmondsworth: Penguin.

Bhabha, H.K. (1994) *The Location of Culture*, London: Routledge.

Blackman, S.J. (2007) '"Hidden ethnography": crossing emotional borders in qualitative accounts of young people's lives', *Sociology*, 41(4): 699–716.

Byram, M. (2008) *From Foreign Language Education to Education for Intercultural Citizenship: Essays and Reflections*, Clevedon: Multilingual Matters.

Canagarajah, A.S. (1999) 'On EFL teachers, awareness and agency', *ELT Journal*, 53(3): 207–14.

Cheng, X. (2000) 'Asian students' reticence revisited', *System*, 28(3): 435–46.

Clark, R. and Gieve, S.N. (2006) 'On the discursive construction of "the Chinese learner"', *Language, Culture and Curriculum*, 19(1): 54–73.

Clifford, J. and Marcus, G.E. (eds) (1986) *Writing Culture: The Poetica Of Politics of Ethnography*, Berkeley, CA: University of California Press.

Crane, D. (1994) 'Introduction: the challenge of the sociology of culture to sociology as discipline', in D. Crane (ed.) *The Sociology of Culture*, Oxford: Blackwell, pp. 1–19.

Delanty, G. (2006) 'The cosmopolitan imagination: critical cosmopolitanism and social theory', *British Journal of Sociology*, 57(1): 25–47.

Delanty, G., Wodak, R. and Jones, P. (2008) 'Introduction: migration, discrimination and belonging in Europe', in G. Delanty, R. Wodak and P. Jones (eds) *Identity, Belonging and Migration*, Liverpool: Liverpool University Press, pp. 1–20.

Denzin, N.K. and Lincoln, Y.S. (2005) 'The discipline and practice of qualitative research', in N.K. Denzin and Y.S. Lincoln (eds) *Handbook of Qualitative Research*, 3rd edn, Thousand Oaks, CA: Sage, pp. 1–30.

Dobbin, F.R. (1994) 'Cultural models of organization: the social construction of rational organizing principles', in D. Crane (ed.) *The Sociology of Culture*, Oxford: Blackwell, pp. 117–41.

Durkheim, E. (1964) *The Division of Labour in Society*, trans. G. Simpson, New York: Free Press.

Fairclough, N. (1995) *Critical Discourse Analysis: The Critical Study of Language*, London: Addison Wesley Longman.

——(2006) *Language and Globalization*, London: Routledge.

Fay, B. (1996) *Contemporary Philosophy of Social Science: A Multicultural Approach*, Oxford: Blackwell.

Flam, H. and Bauzamy, B. (2008) 'Symbolic violence', in G. Delanty, R. Wodak and P. Jones (eds) *Identity, Belonging and Migration*, Liverpool: Liverpool University Press, pp. 221–40.

Gellner, E. (2005) *Words and Things*, Oxford: Routledge.

Gergen, K.J. (2001) *Social Construction in Context*, London: Sage.

Goffman, E. (1972) *Relations in Public*, Harmondsworth: Penguin.

Grande, E. (2006) 'Cosmopolitan political science', *British Journal of Sociology*, 57(1): 87–111.

Grimshaw, T. (2007) 'Problematizing the construct of 'the Chinese learner': insights from ethnographic research', *Educational Studies*, 33: 299–311.

Gubrium, J.F. and Holstein, J.A. (1997) *The New Language of Qualitative Research*, New York: Oxford University Press.

Guilherme, M. (2002) *Critical Citizens for an Intercultural World: Foreign Language Education as Cultural Politics*, Clevedon: Multilingual Matters.

Hall, S. (1991a) 'The local and the global: globalization and ethnicity', in A.D. King (ed.) *Culture, Globalization and the World-System*, New York: Palgrave, pp. 19–39.

——(1991b) 'Old and new identities, old and new ethnicities', in A.D. King (ed.) *Culture, Globalization and the World-System*, New York: Palgrave, pp. 40–68.

Hammersley, M. and Atkinson, P. (1995) *Ethnography, Principles and Practice*, 2nd edn, London: Routledge.

Hannerz, U. (1991) 'Scenarios of peripheral cultures', in A.D. King (ed.) *Culture, Globalization and the World-system*, New York: Palgrave, pp. 107–28.

Hayagoshi, H. (1996) 'British teachers' perceptions of Japanese students in contrast with Japanese students' perceptions of their own needs and wants', unpublished master's dissertation, Department of English and Language Studies, Canterbury Christ Church University, Canterbury, UK.

Hoffman, E. (1998) *Lost in Translation*, London: Vintage.

Hofstede, G.H. (2001) *Culture's Consequences: Comparing Values, Behaviours, Institutions and Organizations Across Cultures*, London: Sage.

Holliday, A.R. (1999) 'Small cultures', *Applied Linguistics*, 20(2): 237–64.

——(2004) 'The value of reconstruction in revealing hidden or counter cultures', *Journal of Applied Linguistics*, 1(3): 275–94.

——(2005a) 'How is it possible to write?', *Journal of Language, Identity and Education*, 4(4): 304–9.

——(2005b) *The Struggle to Teach English as an International Language*, Oxford: Oxford University Press.

——(2007) *Doing and Writing Qualitative Research*, 2nd edn, London: Sage.

——(2010) 'Complexity in cultural identity', *Language and Intercultural Communication*, 10(2): 165–77.

——(2011) *Intercultural Communication and Ideology*, London: Sage.

Holliday, A.R. and Aboshiha, P.A. (2009) 'The denial of ideology in perceptions of "nonnative speaker" teachers', *TESOL Quarterly*, 43(4): 669–89.

Honarbin-Holliday, M. (2009) *Becoming Visible In Iran: Women in Contemporary Iranian Society*, London: I.B. Tauris.

Jordan, G. and Weedon, C. (1995) 'The celebration of difference and the cultural politics of racism', in B. Adam and S. Allan (eds) *Theorizing Culture: An Interdisciplinary Critique After Postmodernism*, London: UCL Press, pp. 149–64.

Kim, M.-S. (2005) 'Culture-based conversational constraints theory', in W.B. Gudykunst (ed.) *Theorizing About Intercultural Communication*, Thousand Oaks, CA: Sage, pp. 93–117.

Kramsch, C. (1993) *Context and Culture in Language Teaching*, Oxford: Oxford University Press.

Kubota, R. (2001) 'Discursive construction of the images of us classrooms', *TESOL Quarterly*, 35(1): 9–37.

——(2004) 'Critical multiculturalism and second language education', in B. Norton and K. Toohey (eds) *Critical Pedagogies and Language Learning*, Cambridge: Cambridge University Press, pp. 30–52.

Kubota, R. and Lin, A.M.Y. (2006) 'Race and TESOL: introduction to concepts and theories', *TESOL Quarterly*, 40(3): 471–93.

Kuhn, T.S. (1970) *The Structure of Scientific Revolutions*, Chicago, IL: University of Chicago Press.

Kumaravadivelu, B. (2006) 'Dangerous liaison: globalization, empire and TESOL', in J. Edge (ed.) *(Re)Locating TESOL in an Age of Empire: Language and Globalization*, London: Palgrave, pp. 1–26.

——(2007) *Cultural Globalization and Language Education*, Yale, CT: Yale University Press.

Lankshear, C., Gee, J. P., Knobel, M. and Searle, C. (1997) *Changing Literacies*, Buckingham: Open University Press.

Latour, B. (2006) War of the worlds – What about peace? *Matrix, Bridge The Gap*. Online. Available: www.btgjapan.org/catalysts/bruno.html (accessed 19 August 2006).

Lentin, A. (2008) 'Racism, anti-racism and the western state', in G. Delanty, R. Wodak and P. Jones (eds) *Identity, Belonging and Migration*, Liverpool: Liverpool University Press, pp.101–9.

MacCannell, D. (1992) *Empty Meeting Grounds*, London: Routledge.

Montgomery, C. and McDowell, L. (2009) 'Social networks and the international student experience: an international community of practice?' *Journal of Studies in International Education*, 13(4): 455–66.

Moon, D.G. (2008) 'Concepts of "culture": implications for intercultural communication research', in M.K. Asante, Y. Miike and J. Yin (eds) *The Global Intercultural Communication Reader*, New York: Routledge, pp. 11–26.

Nayar, B. (2002) 'Ideological binarism in the identities of native and non-native English speakers', in A. Duszac (ed.) *Us and Others: Social Identities across Languages, Discourse and Cultures*, Amsterdam: John Benjamin, pp. 463–80.

The New London Group (1996) 'A pedagogy of multiliteracies: designing social futures', *Harvard Educational Review*, 66(1): 60–93.

Parsons, T. (1951) *The Social System*, London: Routledge and Kegan Paul.

Pennycook, A. (1998) *English and the Discourses of Colonialism*, London: Routledge.

Quach, L.H., Jo, J.-Y.O. and Urrieta, L. (2009) 'Understanding the racialized identities of Asian students in predominantly white schools', in R. Kubota and A.M.Y. Lin (eds) *Race, Culture, and Identities in Second Language Education*, New York: Routledge, pp. 118–37.

Rajagopalan, K. (1999) 'Of EFL teachers, conscience and cowardice', *ELT Journal*, 53(3): 200–206.

Rampton, B., Harris, R., Georgakopoulou, A., Leung, C., Small, L. and Dover, C. (2008) 'Urban classroom culture and interaction: end-of-project report', unpublished Working Papers in Urban Language and Literacies, King's College, London University, London.

Said, E. (1978) *Orientalism*, London: Routledge and Kegan Paul.

Sarangi, S. (1995) 'Culture', in J. Vershueren, J. Östman and J. Blomaert (eds) *Handbook of Pragmatics*, Amsterdam: John Benjamins, pp. 1–30.

Sawyer, L. and Jones, P. (2008) 'Voices of migrants: solidarity and resistance', in G. Delanty, R. Wodak and P. Jones (eds) *Identity, Belonging and Migration*, Liverpool: Liverpool University Press, pp. 241–60.

Schudson, M. (1994) 'Culture and the integration of national societies', in D. Crane (ed.) *The Sociology of Culture*, Oxford: Blackwell, pp. 21–43.

Schutz, A. (1964) *Collected Papers*, Vol. 2, The Hague: Martinus Nijhoff.

——(1970) *On Phenomenology and Social Relations*, Chicago, IL: University of Chicago Press.

Shuter, R. (2008) 'The centrality of culture', in M.K. Asante, Y. Miike and J. Yin (eds) *The Global Intercultural Communication Reader*, New York: Routledge, pp. 37–43.

Spears, A.K. (1999) 'Race and ideology: an introduction', in A.K. Spears (ed.) *Race and Ideology; Language, Symbolism, and Popular Culture*, Detroit, IL: Wayne State University Press, pp. 11–58.

Stråth, B. (2008) 'Belonging and European identity', in G. Delanty, R. Wodak and P. Jones (eds) *Identity, Belonging and Migration*, Liverpool: Liverpool University Press, pp. 21–37.

Tomlinson, J. (1991) *Cultural Imperialism*, London: Pinter Publications.

Tong, W. M. (2002) '"Filial piety": a barrier or a resource? A qualitative case study of English classroom culture in Hong Kong secondary schools', unpublished PhD thesis, Department of English and Language Studies, Canterbury Christ Church University, Canterbury, UK.

Triandis, H.C. (1995) *Individualism and Collectivism*, Boulder, CO: Westview Press.

——(2004) 'Forward', in D. Landis, J.M. Bennett and M.J. Bennett (eds) *Handbook of Intercultural Training*, 3rd edn, Thousand Oaks, CA: Sage: pp. ix–xii.

——(2006) 'Culture and conflict', in L.A. Samovar and R.E. Porter (eds) *Intercultural Communication: A Reader*, Belmont, CA: Wadsworth, pp. 22–31.

Urry, J. (2002) *The Tourist Gaze*, 2nd edn, London: Sage.

Wallace, C. (2003) *Critical Reading in Language Education*, Basingstoke: Palgrave Macmillan.

Weber, M. (1964) *The Theory of Social and Economic Organization*, New York: The Free Press.

——(1968) 'Ideal types and theory construction', in M. Brodbeck (ed.) *Readings in the Philosophy of the Social Sciences*, London: Macmillan, pp. 496–507.

Wenger, E. (2000) 'Communities of practice and social learning systems', *Organization*, 7(2): 225–46.

Wodak, R. (2008) '"Us and them": inclusion and exclusion', in G. Delanty, R. Wodak and P. Jones (eds) *Identity, Belonging and Migration*, Liverpool: Liverpool University Press, pp. 54–77.

Young, R. (2006) 'The cultural politics of hybridity', in B. Ashcroft, G. Griffiths and H. Tifflin (eds) *The Post-Colonial Studies Reader*, London: Routledge, pp. 158–62.

Zhu, H. (2008) 'Duelling languages, duelling values: codeswitching in bilingual intergenerational conflict talk in diasporic families', *Journal of Pragmatics*, 40(10): 1799–816.

# Language, identity and intercultural communication

*Kimberly A. Noels, Tomoko Yashima and Rui Zhang*

## 1. Introduction

It is commonly noted that, owing to technological advances in transportation and communication, the redistribution of production and labour, and other reasons, the potential for intercultural contact is currently greater than it has ever been in human history. Moreover, with an estimated 6,900 languages across the approximately 200 countries of the world (Lewis 2009), it is very likely that intercultural contact will involve encounters between people who speak different languages. Sometimes, these encounters take place between members of groups with a long history of inter-action and thus they are rather routine, such that personal and normative expectations regarding language use effectively guide the communication process to predictable, if not mutually satis-fying, outcomes. At other times, we are less well acquainted with our interlocutors' practices, and so part of the process of communication involves grappling with the acquisition of new verbal and nonverbal communication systems. Regardless of the level of familiarity, a variety of sociopsychological and sociocultural processes operate within every intercultural interaction.

In this chapter, we focus on how the languages we speak are linked to feelings of identity in intercultural encounters. This relation is a reciprocal one: the languages we learn and use open up possibilities for new identities, while at the same time our identities can have implications for engagement in language learning and use. We begin with a review of how scholars in social psychology, communication studies and applied linguistics have defined identity and described its function in intercultural communication. We discuss some prominent themes that reverbe-rate (or not) across disciplines, particularly as they relate to notions of identity, language and culture, and we consider what the various conceptualizations of these constructs imply for research methodology. In so doing, we highlight areas where we believe that theory and research can be informed through interdisciplinary rapprochement.

## 2. Disciplinary perspectives on identity, language and intercultural communication

### Social psychology

The view on language, identity and intercultural communication taken by many social psy-chologists might be described as an 'intergroup' perspective, in that it focuses on the social context in terms of the relations between two or more groups that differ in their relative sociostructural status (cf. Brabant *et al.* 2007). In this section, we describe two lines of research, both of which were conceived in sociohistorical contexts involving considerable sociopolitical tension between ethnolinguistic groups. The first line of research, originating in Montreal, Canada, highlights the implications of interethnic contact for patterns of bilingualism and ethnic identity, and the second, initially formulated in Bristol, UK, centres on how interlocutors adjust their communication behaviour in line with their group memberships. These are not unrelated bodies of theory and research; indeed, during the formative years there was considerable cross-Atlantic interaction between the two research groups (H. Giles, personal communication, 2007).

## Sociostructural status, bilingualism and identity

One of the earliest psychologists to examine the relation between language and identity was Wallace Lambert (1956, 1978), who observed that the acquisition of a new language and cultural identity did not necessarily entail the loss of the original language and identity. Rather, he argued that the relative status of the language groups in contact was an important predictor of patterns of bilingualism. He suggested that people belonging to a relatively subordinate, minority group were likely to lose their original language and identity as a result of learning the language of the majority group, a process known as subtractive bilingualism. In contrast, people belonging to a dominant, majority group could acquire a new language and culture without compromising their original language and culture, a process known as additive bilingualism. In contrast to the prevailing opinion at the time, Lambert's work emphasized that being bilingual could be associated with advantages not experienced by monolinguals, and that sociopolitical disparities often lay at the heart of social psychological differences between ethnolinguistic groups.

Lambert's work has inspired many researchers interested in cognitive and social psychological aspects of bilingualism and interethnic relations (for overviews, see Dil 1972; Reynolds 1991). Working initially with Lambert, Gardner proposed that people's motivation to learn a second language (L2) was supported to the extent that they hold positive attitudes towards that language community and want to learn the language in order to more readily interact with that community, a motivational orientation termed the 'integrative orientation' (Gardner and Lambert 1959, 1972). Over 50 years of research has underlined the importance of this concept of 'integrativeness', which encompasses the notion of identity in the sense that one has a willingness to be like valued members of the language community, even to the point of identifying with that community (Masgoret and Gardner 2003). This prominent formulation has been critiqued, however, for a variety of reasons (for an overview, see Dörnyei and Ushioda 2011). Notably, the experience of many learners of English suggests that the claim that integrativeness is necessary for motivated learning is tenuous because these learners do not necessarily identify with a specific English community. Instead, it is perhaps more appropriate to frame identification with reference to a global community (Lamb 2004), or in terms of adopting an 'international posture' (Yashima 2002). Dörnyei and Ushioda (2011) maintain that 'integrativeness' should be reconceptualized as that part of the self-concept representing the L2 and culture, such that it is an idealized vision of what one would like to become as a language speaker within an imagined community (see also Kramsch 2010; Norton 2001). Thus, in recent years, there has been a shift from examining whether learners categorize themselves as members of particular language groups to understanding whether and how learners envisage themselves as speakers of other languages, invest in that vision, and internalize that vision into their sense of self, sometimes to the point of identifying with a new language community.

## Social identity and communication accommodation

Communication accommodation theory (CAT) (see Chapter 15, this volume) and related theories such as ethnolinguistic identity theory (e.g. Giles *et al.* 1977; Giles and Johnson 1981) and the intergroup theory of L2 learning (Giles and Byrne 1982) articulate some of the identity dynamics implicated in language behaviour and the societal consequences arising therefrom. From this perspective, social identity derives from knowing in which social category one belongs and assuming the characteristics of that social group. Identity becomes salient through comparisons with other groups, and this process of social comparison is influenced by a motivational desire to see one's own group, and thus oneself, in a positive light. Social identity is linked to language when language serves as a marker of group distinctiveness. In such cases, people adjust their verbal and nonverbal styles in order to create and maintain positive identities and to create a desired level of social distance between themselves and their interlocutors (among other goals). Similarity and affiliation can be demonstrated through convergence on linguistic, paralinguistic and nonverbal features in such a way as to become more similar to their interlocutor's behaviour, and difference can be demonstrated through divergence in communication style that accentuates differences between the speaker and the interlocutor. Actual convergence or divergence may be otherwise intended by the speaker or interpreted by the interlocutor, and thus perceptions and attributions for these communicative strategies determine the effectiveness of language strategies and have implications for future encounters.

The social psychological processes outlined by CAT have consequences for larger scale relations between groups and long-term language shift and/or maintenance. Depending on one's strength of ethnolinguistic identity and perceptions regarding the relations between the two language groups (e.g. the perceived legitimacy of status differentials between groups and the penetrability of group boundaries), identity can be managed through language choices that maintain the status quo or contribute to social change in the relative status and relations between ethnolinguistic groups.

With its emphasis on how perceptions of intergroup boundaries and relative status relate to identity and language variations, the theoretical work of Giles and his colleagues complements Lambert's foundational work linking sociostructural variables at the macro level of the society with psychological variables at the micro level of the individual (for recent research with other models in this tradition, see Clément *et al.* 2003; Gilbert *et al.* 2005). Moreover, Lambert's notion of additive and subtractive bilingualism underlines the multiplicity of possible relations between language and identity, whereas CAT and its satellite theories highlight the fact that identities are managed through language use.

## *Applied linguistics*

Discussions in applied linguistics of the role of identity in language learning and intercultural communication have been informed by social psychological theories of intergroup dynamics and, more recently, by social science theorizing relating to what can be termed a 'sociocultural' perspective (Zuengler and Miller 2006). One major contribution of the sociocultural perspective to the study of language, identity and intercultural communication is that it theorizes language as a tool for achieving social and psychological ends, and hence as a resource for managing everyday activities, including the negotiation of identities. A second contribution is its detailed analysis of the power dynamics at play in situated interactions where one or both parties must use a language they have not yet mastered.

## Vygotskyan/social–historical perspective

The Vygotskyan/social–historical perspective emphasizes the relations between individuals and the society as well as culturally created artefacts in understanding individual and collective human development. Human development is a socially and culturally mediated process of learning or gaining self-regulation as an autonomous individual. The identity of individuals are forged as they gain a fuller control of their environment and of themselves. As Holland and Lachicotte (2007: 108) write regarding semiotic mediation in the formation of the self, 'The self comes to use the signs, once directed to others or received from others, in relation to the self'. Through conversations, a child learns to see himself or herself as the object of meaning. Further, symbolic artefacts such as inner speech mediate self-regulation and thoughts, whereas narratives mediate making sense of the self and of life events. According to Lantolf and Thorne (2006), learning and using an L2 amounts to acquiring a new way of mediation and can thus lead to a renewed or additional identity for an individual.

## Community of practice perspective

In Lave and Wenger's (1991) situated learning theory, learners acquire knowledge and skills as they move towards fuller participation in the practices of a language community, a process that results in changes in their relationships with old timers and in the learners' identities. Participating in the practices of the host-national community means, in a sense, acculturating through acquiring normative behaviours or symbolic competences in that community. Thus, expanded behavioural repertoires in multiple languages and cultures can result in a wider range of identity options to choose from, and can affect how effectively an individual can manage identities in intercultural communication.

Community of practice perspectives are used to connect how learners' imagined identities can guide learning trajectories (Lamb 2009; Yashima and Zenuk-Nishide 2008). McMahill's (1997) study demonstrates that, as Japanese women participated in a local community of learners of English with feminism as its content, these women imagined a link to the international community of feminists. Communities of practice have also been used to understand how newcomers in a community participate peripherally but legitimately or, conversely, how their entries are rejected, which affects their L2 learning and their L2-mediated identities. Morita's (2004) study of Japanese graduate students in Canadian universities showed that non-participation in classroom discussions was socially constructed and that, in the struggle to participate more fully in the community, these learners faced their identity as Asian women with less knowledge and less than the desired level of English competence. Unless one speaks like other members of the speech community, one may not be an accepted member of that community, whereas the acquisition of symbolic competence increases audibility and intelligibility.

Language identity issues have also been taken up in recent research on study-abroad experiences (Jackson 2008; Kinginger 2008). Moving from studies mostly analysing language acquisition using pre- and post-test designs, recent research often uses narratives to describe individual learners' unique experiences as they try to participate in communities of practice available in the host countries, or it focuses on the contexts influencing language acquisition outcomes. Research demonstrates that, in study-abroad contexts, identity struggles are part of learners' daily interactions. Some learners face not only their ethnic identities but also L2 user' identities (Pellegrino 2005) and gendered identities (Mori 1997; Siegal 1996) as they try to communicate with host nationals. For instance, American female students studying in Russia or France often encounter sexual harassment, which hampers their participation in the host community (Brecht and Davidson 1995; Kline 1993). Many opt for resistance or non-participation in the community.

## Poststructuralist/critical perspective

The recent surge of interest in identity among applied linguists was instigated by researchers taking poststructuralist critical perspectives, including Block (2007), Norton (2000) and Pavlenko and Blackledge (2004), among others. Their theorizing is influenced by Bourdieu's (1977) conceptualization of cultural and symbolic capital, which underlines symbolic imbalances among interactants as well as the notion of the right to speak and be heard. For poststructuralists, language is not a neutral medium of communication, and the value of speech cannot be separated from who uses it. Instead, speech is used and understood with reference to the social positioning of the interactants. Language use is a site of struggle where individuals negotiate identities. Identity, then, is not a product of an individual's mind but is discursively co-constructed through interactions in the social sphere.

Much poststructuralist research has centred on migrant situations, with a focus on how learners struggle to negotiate identities in order to adapt to the more influential host community (Block 2006; Norton 2000; Toohey and Norton 2003). This inequity in power relations is inherent in the learning context as the hosts do not necessarily need to hear the voices of the newcomers, but the newcomers do need to be heard and accepted to be members of the society. In this sense, interactional patterns reflect the macro-sociopolitical situations surrounding those who participate. A number of studies have featured learners' 'identity work' through oral and written narratives (Block 2006, 2007; see also Norton 2000; Pavlenko and Lantolf 2000). Often, desired identities are not endorsed by host nationals, and the learners must resist imposed identities, often by appropriating languages 'to legitimize, challenge, and negotiate identities and open new identity options for oppressed and subjected groups and individuals' (Pavlenko and Blackledge 2004: 13). These identities negotiated through discourses are complex and multiple, as is demonstrated by Norton's (2000) study of how immigrant women's ethnic, gendered and class identities intertwine with language learner identities in complex ways.

## Communication

Although the study of intercultural communication within the discipline of communication is increasingly informed by research in other geographical locations, many of the current identity-based theories were developed in the US (Leeds-Hurwitz 1990; Chapter 1, this volume). Despite the fact that these theories reflect varied metatheoretical paradigms (Martin and Nakayama 1999), we seek to briefly review the shared interests among major theories of identity validation and negotiation during intercultural interactions, while highlighting their key differences.

There are a number of theories that give considerable weight to the construct of identity, especially identity management in relation to others during intercultural interactions. What drives these theories is the assumption that the identity one wishes to avow or negate may be at odds with what is granted or affirmed by one's intercultural partner; thus, identity is not only flexible but mutually negotiable (cf. Y.Y. Kim 2007). For example, both identity management theory (IMT; Imahori and Cupach 2005) and identity negotiation theory (INT; Ting-Toomey 2005) underline such mutuality of intercultural communication, whereby desired identities need to be mutually recognized and validated; the lack of mutuality or negotiation competence can lead to feelings of not being understood, respected or affirmatively valued. Both conceptualize identity as the interpretive framework for understanding one's self and the surrounding world and focus on cultural and relational identities. INT extends IMT in also viewing intercultural communication as balancing the identity dialectics of security/vulnerability, inclusion/differentiation, predictability/unpredictability, connection/autonomy and consistency/change. Meeting those identity challenges by expanding one's cognitive, affective and behavioural repertoire could potentially transform one into a 'dynamic biculturalist' who is attuned to both self-identity and other-identity negotiation issues.

A similar conceptualization of identity as negotiable and hence inherently communicative is reflected in Hecht *et al.*'s (2005) communication theory of identity. Its central argument is that identity is formed, expressed and modified through social interaction. To capture this, it proposes four interpenetrating layers of identity (personal, enacted, relational and communal). Identity negotiation is recast in terms of the way individuals negotiate the four different layers in communicating who they are, managing the dialectical tensions between and among one's layers of identity while avoiding or resolving 'identity gaps' (Hecht *et al.* 2005).

Perhaps an even more dynamic account of identity is provided by Y.Y. Kim's (1988, 2005; Chapter 14, this volume) theory of cross-cultural adaptation that seeks to capture the evolving nature and growth-oriented aspects of adaptation as a result of one's extensive and accumulative experiences with a new cultural environment. It builds upon the open-systems principle about one's natural tendency to restore the internal disequilibrium created by the challenges associated with acculturation. Specifically, Kim proposes a stress–adaptation–growth dynamic that explains how psychological transformation gradually evolves out of the stress–adaptation dialectic. The product of this steady self-transformation is the emergence of an intercultural identity, a mindset that is both increasingly individualized and universalized. Not only does the theory envisage the intercultural identity as possibly transcending ascribed group boundaries, it also provides a developmental framework that has the advantage of explaining the emergent and reciprocal nature of identity and communication.

Finally, the poststructuralist/critical paradigm is gaining prominence in intercultural communication (e.g. cultural identifications theory, Collier 2005), partly due to the influence of applied linguistics in European scholarship (Chapter 1, this volume). Such an interpretive framework is often articulated through ethnographic work involving a 'thick description' of a particular community and gleaning insights into its distinctive communicative practices (Carbaugh 2005; Philipsen *et al.* 2005). This paradigm highlights power inequities, the production of privileging ideologies and politicalization of identity, all of which are undertheorized in interpersonal approaches to identity in intercultural communication. Its engagement with the sociostructural context thus makes it compatible with the intergroup approach in social psychology reviewed above.

## 3. Issues in the study of identity, language and culture

Although they are informed by different disciplinary traditions and, to some extent, different metatheoretical traditions, social psychological, communication and applied linguistics scholars have wrestled with some common issues in their discussion of identity, language and culture. We turn to a consideration of these themes, with the goals of making connections between relevant work across the disciplines and indicating some areas for future scholarly enquiry.

### Identity

The first theme relates to the notion that identities are multiple; most theorists eschew simplistic conceptualizations of identity in which people are categorically ascribed to externally defined social groups, a practice that was not uncommon in the early decades of research (Leets *et al.* 1996). From an intergroup perspective, this multiplicity is asserted in the premise that certain identities are more salient in some situations than in others, such that ethnolinguistic identity is only one of a number of social identities that a person can entertain, and multiple identities may be relevant in any given encounter (Clément and Noels 1992). Moreover, intercultural encounters can be either or both intergroup or interpersonal in nature, such that, in the former, the relative status and power of the groups in contact play an important role in how the encounter unfolds and, in the latter, personal characteristics and interpersonal histories play a more prominent role (cf. Deaux and Martin 2003). In other, more relational perspectives, identity is also assumed to be multiple, in that each interaction involves the (co-)construction of identities anew, often through ongoing boundary marking and remarking as well as crossing boundaries to create new identities.

Identities can also be multiple in the sense that one might claim multiple ethnolinguistic identities. Particularly in contexts where there is continued intercultural contact (arguably including global English), it might be argued that few people come together with no knowledge of the target culture and no notion of how to communicate with its members. Thus, the researcher must consider the extent to which a person has been exposed to the target language and culture, interacted with native speakers, taken on that culture's values, norms and/or practices and identifies with that group, all of which could make the person more or less an ethnolinguistic hybrid. Moreover, there are likely to be a myriad of ways in which people can integrate ethnolinguistic identities, such that hybridity itself could be construed in different ways, depending upon the context (Dallaire and Denis 2001).

The notion that people negotiate multiple identities is closely tied to the idea that identity is contingent upon context. Defining context, however, has proven challenging. One approach is to describe macro-social factors, such as the dimensions of demographic representation, institutional support and prestige subsumed in the notion of ethnolinguistic vitality (Giles *et al.* 1977), through impersonal indicators, such as census data. The 'objective' context's influence on identity and language, however, is assumed to be mediated by social and psychological processes, such that it is the subjective perceptions of the intergroup context that predict cognitive, affective and behavioural responses to members of other groups. In a reciprocal manner, these attitudes and actions are the basis for solidifying or changing the macro-level, societal dynamics. In contrast with this conceptualization, sociocultural theorists argue against a dualist model of the individual and social context, in which context is construed as a layer that surrounds the individual, or as an independent factor influencing individuals' thoughts and actions. Rather, context is inseparable from the individuals' lived experiences; in every interaction, interlocutors constitute context and are constituted by context.

A third theme is that identity in intercultural communication is problematic in at least three respects. The first aspect concerns the competence of interactants. By definition, language learners lack the competence or the confidence to interpret host culture perspectives and/or the communication skills, including language skills, necessary to achieve effective communication outcomes, including identity negotiation. These difficulties can contribute to poorer intercultural adjustment (cf. Gudykunst 2005). To be an effective communicator, then, one must become more knowledgeable and skilled in the ways of the target culture and adopt a positive affective orientation towards that culture, two challenges that can be difficult to meet.

A second aspect concerns the power relations between interlocutors. From an intergroup perspective, a power imbalance between social groups contributes to feelings of threat, which in turn can lead to intergroup conflict. Likewise, much sociocultural research has focused on how power dynamics play into how people claim, contest and resist identities (cf. Pavlenko and

Blackledge 2004), emphasizing that, despite one's skills and knowledge, power dynamics can restrict access to resources, including those necessary for improving communicative competence and enabling identity negotiation.

A third problem arises from the premise that that identity is negotiable, and hence variable. This emphasis on the dynamism of identity stands in contrast to identity models associated with the psychodynamic tradition of Erik Erikson and his followers (Erikson 1968; Marcia 1966), which highlight the importance of the self as a unifying process, and the idea that self-consistency and coherence are essential to psychological well-being. Although this perspective has received extensive critique (e.g. Rattansi and Phoenix 2005), this dialectic between identity stability and dynamism merits greater consideration in intercultural communication research. We need to address questions such as: 'How do people maintain a sense of consistency in the face of inevitable change?'; 'What purpose do these feelings of coherence serve?'; 'In what contexts does (the need for) a sense of self-consistency arise?'; 'How are sameness and continuity (and conversely difference and change) constructed through dialogue in intercultural interactions?' (cf. Spreckels and Kotthoff 2007).

## Language

Social psychological research on language use has generally been directed at understanding how these choices affect impression formation and other psychological and behavioural reactions, rather than on particular linguistic and nonverbal characteristics (Brabant et al. 2007). From this perspective, language tends to be broadly defined, for instance in terms of accent, dialect, language, or in terms of more or less accommodative or non-accommodative styles. In order to demonstrate that social psychological processes are associated with variations in communicative competence, social psychologists have used more concrete measures of language competence. These include course grades, standardized test scores, cloze tests and tests designed specifically for a particular study, as well as self-assessments of competence, usually in terms of reading, writing, speaking and understanding (although these self-evaluations might be better interpreted as indices of self-confidence in using the target language rather than indices of competence; see MacIntyre et al. 1994). More recently, emphasis has been placed on predicting interactional tendencies, such as a willingness to communicate with others, rather than linguistic or communicative competence (Clément et al. 2003). An inadvertent consequence of this correlational approach, however, is that it tends to frame language as a cognitive process relatively independent of social processes.

In communication research, language seems at best tangential unless it is assumed that language constitutes part of the process of message encoding and decoding that occurs during intercultural interaction. There is a continued interest in how nonverbal and verbal behaviour differs across cultures, concerning mainly what transpires in the immediate context of meaning or message transaction (e.g. M.-S. Kim 2005; Ting-Toomey 1988). Little explicit attention, however, has been paid to how language and identity are conceptualized in relation to each other and the extent to which language can be said to constitute an important part of identity (but see Croucher 2009; Matsunaga et al. 2010). This conspicuous omission is perhaps due in part to the fact that many intercultural communication theories were generated to explain intercultural communication within the US, where the use of one single, dominant language is assumed, and in part to the emphasis on the non-linguistic aspects of culture and communication during its formative years (Chapter 1, this volume).

Not surprisingly, in applied linguistics, language is at the core of inquiries into identity. In Vygotskyan cultural–historical theory concerning mediated mental development, language is viewed in terms of intra- or interpersonal speech and conceptual meaning of words that mediates thinking, rather than as linguistic forms or referential meaning (Lantolf and Thorne 2006). Conceptual metaphors that are culturally influenced also carry importance in this framework. Critical poststructuralists, on the other hand, have devised ethnographic studies using interviews and observation and/or looked closely at conversations to analyse how identity tied to language use is constructed and negotiated discursively in interactions using L1 (first language) or L2 (Block 2006; Goldstein 1997; Kanno 2000). They often hope to disclose power relations that may be stated or unstated but assumed in the discourse. Thus, this perspective places greater emphasis on the social rather than the cognitive aspect of language.

## Culture

Any examination of the relation between language and identity in intercultural interactions requires a definition of culture to clarify what it is (if anything) that sets such interactions apart from intracultural interactions. The notion of culture, however, has received varied elaboration across the three disciplines. Driven by an intergroup approach that frames intercultural relations in terms of groups' relative social status and power differentials, the social psychological perspective has had rather little to say about culture. This is perhaps because the historically established patterns of beliefs, norms and social practices more or less shared by members within an ethnolinguistic group are not assumed to systematically influence the process of intergroup communication; the intergroup dynamics of categorization, identification and comparison are considered to be sufficient to explain patterns of language learning and use. Although it is conceivable that cultural patterns might moderate intergroup processes (e.g. collectivistically oriented groups might enforce stricter boundaries between in-groups and out-groups than individualistically oriented groups; cf. Brewer and Yuki 2007), to date, little research has addressed this kind of intersection between culture and communication within the context of intercultural communication.

The notion of culture has been more extensively articulated by communication scholars, often with reference to definitions forwarded by researchers interested in cross-cultural comparisons. Such research tends to characterize cultural groups, typically nations, on a limited set of dimensions pertaining to values, self-construals and so on, such as individualism/collectivism (Hofstede 2001) or independence/interdependence (Markus and Kitayama 1991). Scholars from this tradition emphasize that these are not essential, categorical differences between cultural groups, but rather chronic 'mental habits' that predispose people to think along particular lines (Oyserman and Lee 2008). Because they are tendencies, this frame of reference varies among members of a cultural group and may shift within any individual depending upon the context. Despite such admonitions, this approach lends itself to the conceptualization of 'culture-typed identities' (Kim and Hubbard 2007: 231), which tends to pit 'individualistic' Western against 'collectivistic' East Asian nations, raising concerns pertaining to the questionable assumption that cultures are internally cohesive and externally distinctive (see Chapter 2, this volume). Moreover, such a perspective does not adequately take into account cultural complexity in the era of globalization (e.g. Dervin and Ljalikova 2008; Hannerz 1992). These concerns suggest that we reframe thinking of cultures in isolation and move from looking at mean tendencies that distinguish one culture from another to tackling the contact zone of living with and committing to multiple cultures.

Sociocultural applied linguists regard culture as the shared activity or practice of a community. From a Vygotskyan cultural–historical perspective, social relationships and culturally created artefacts are central to human development. Cultural contexts are, therefore, seen as vital in determining the nature of that development because different cultures create different artefacts, both physical and symbolic, which individuals use to mediate learning. To understand a different culture, therefore, includes understanding culturally influenced metaphors and conceptual meanings that are related to the culture's worldviews and thought patterns. In a move further away from essentialized notions of culture, some poststructuralist critical researchers focus on linguistic and discursive construction of cultural categories and how power is implicated in this process.

## 4. Research methodology

Like most areas of the social sciences, scholars studying language and identity in intercultural interactions have had to grapple with the different, possibly incommensurate, perspectives on ontology and epistemology that characterize positivism and constructivism. These decades-old discussions have highlighted problems with older, established points of view and offered new avenues for theory and research. At the same time, critical reflection (and self-reflection) on newer perspectives have revealed limitations in their formulations (cf. Cromby and Nightingale 1999; Kim 2007), emphasizing that it is probably counterproductive to 'throw the baby out with the bathwater' (MacIntyre et al. 2009). In response to these debates, some have argued that we need a third way that can resolve the discrepancies between paradigms (e.g. Dörnyei and Ushioda's (2011) discussion of dynamic systems theory), and others have argued that the tensions between paradigms serve a useful dialectic for creating new perspectives (Noels and Giles 2009; Varghese et al. 2005).

Discussions of the nature of reality and how we can understand it inevitably lead to discussions of appropriate methodology. Although there has been a marked increase in qualitative research, across the disciplines, intercultural communication research has tended to rely on quantitative data, collected primarily through survey methods and, less often, experimental methods. These include questionnaires designed to tap psychological constructs and self-reports of behaviour in intercultural encounters, responses to hypothetical scenarios and reactions to written or recorded speech samples. It is perhaps a curious fact, given that language and communication are action-oriented processes, that much of the research involves self-reports acquired through survey methods (cf. Brabant et al. 2007). Although self-reports of the type gathered in questionnaires and interviews provide insight into people's reflections on their intercultural communication experiences, a drawback of this method is that self-reports often do not reliably correspond with people's actual behaviour (Nisbett and Wilson 1977). It is thus incumbent upon researchers to supplement self-reports with observations of intercultural encounters as they happen, whether in the laboratory or in the field.

Regardless of whether one chooses to gather and analyse quantitative or qualitative information, research design needs to better address some common assumptions about language, identity and intercultural communication. First, although few scholars across the three disciplines construe identity, communication or cultural processes as static and unchangeable, much research to date gives just such an impression because it is carried out at only one point in time. Moreover, developments in structural equation modelling (usually using quantitative, self-report data) have led researchers to emphasize unidirectional, causal relations between variables rather than dynamic, reciprocal interactions between them. Increasingly, researchers are emphasizing the need to employ longitudinal research designs that can better model the contextual and temporal dynamics of identity and intercultural communication, and better capture the reciprocal relations within and between systems. Recent advances in developmental science include quantitative analytical techniques, such as multilevel modelling and latent growth curve analysis, which offer greater power to examine identity and language as dynamic, contextualized and interrelated systems.

Second, in order to explain the role of the social context in language, identity and intercultural communication, we should not shy away from research that adopts a comparative perspective. To date, much intercultural communication research has been comparative primarily in the sense that it contrasts the characteristics and practices of two cultures to see where there is the potential for miscommunication. This kind of comparison runs the risk of ethnocentric interpretations of cultural differences that favour privileged positions (cf. Moon 1996). Moreover, it does not provide the kind of insight that helps us to understand differences between contexts of intercultural communication (Clément et al. 2007). For instance, interactions between members of groups that have a long history of interaction (e.g. Anglophones and Francophones in Canada) are likely to involve different dynamics than intercultural interactions between members of groups with shorter histories (English Canadian sojourners in France). Likewise, the acquisition of a new language is likely to involve different dynamics for learners who have little opportunity for face-to-face contact with the language community outside the classroom than for those who regularly interact with speakers of the target language. This kind of comparative analysis offers more than an extensive cataloguing of intercultural interactions. As pointed out by MacIntyre et al. (2010), the contexts in which we carry out our research frame our theory-building, such that certain themes are brought to light and others disappear from relevance. By systematically comparing the particularities of the contexts within which we conduct our studies, we can better understand the limits and possibilities of our findings to inform theory development, research and teaching.

## 6. Conclusion

In this review, we have brought together representative theoretical approaches to examine the relation between language and identity across three disciplines that share a common interest in understanding how this relation is relevant for intercultural communication. Limitations of space preclude us from delving into each theory more deeply or from considering other important frameworks, but we hope that we have adequately described some major traditions and paradigms within social psychology, applied linguistics and communication studies. Their different foci highlight different aspects of the relation between language and identity in intercultural communication, including the role of sociostructural status and power, the relational and discursive nature of identity and the use of language as a tool in identity negotiation. As well, each brings into relief various understandings and debates about the constructs of identity, language and culture. The reader has no doubt anticipated that we would conclude that the understanding of language, identity and intercultural communication would benefit from more discussion between scholars in each of these disciplines, and we hope that this review will be a step towards facilitating that conversation.

## Related topics

Biculturalism; bilingualism; communication accommodation; community of practice; culture; education abroad; identity; intercultural adjustment; intergroup conflict; language and identity; motivation; poststructuralism; social psychology; sociocultural theory

## Further reading

Brabant, M., Watson, B. and Gallois, C. (2007) 'Psychological perspectives: social psychology, language, and intercultural communication', in H. Kotthoff and H. Spencer-Oatey (eds) *Handbook of Intercultural*

Communication, Berlin: Mouton de Gruyter, pp. 55–75 (focuses on language and intercultural communication from a social psychological perspective).

Noels, K.A. and Giles, H. (2009) 'Social identity and language learning', in W.C. Ritchie and T.K. Bhatia (eds) *The New Handbook of Second Language Acquisition*, Bingley, UK: Emerald, pp. 647–70 (further discussion of various theoretical perspectives on the role of identity in language learning).

Pavlenko, A. and Blackledge, A. (eds) (2004) *Negotiation of Identities in Multilingual Contexts*, Clevedon: Multilingual Matters (provides a good introduction to the poststructural perspective on language and identity).

Spreckels, J. and Kotthoff, H. (2007) 'Communicating identity in intercultural communication', in H. Kotthoff and H. Spencer-Oatey (eds) *Handbook of Intercultural Communication*, Berlin: Mouton de Gruyter, pp. 467–90 (focuses on identity research in communication studies).

# References

Block, D. (2006) *Multilingual Identities in a Global City: London Stories*, London: Palgrave.

——(2007) *Second Language Identities*, London: Continuum.

Bourdieu, P. (1977) *Outline of a Theory of Practice*, New York: Cambridge University Press.

Brabant, M., Watson, B. and Gallois, C. (2007) 'Psychological perspectives: social psychology, language, and intercultural communication', in H. Kotthoff and H. Spencer-Oatey (eds) *Handbook of Intercultural Communication*, Berlin: Mouton de Gruyter, pp. 55–75.

Brecht, R. and Davidson, D. (1995) 'Predictors of foreign language gain during study abroad', in B. Freed (ed.) *Second Language Acquisition in a Study Abroad Context*, Amsterdam: John Benjamins, pp. 37–66.

Brewer, M.B. and Yuki, M. (2007) 'Culture and social identity', in S. Kitayama and D. Cohen (eds) *Handbook of Cultural Psychology*, New York: Guilford Press, pp. 307–22.

Carbaugh, D. (2005). *Cultures in Conversation*, Mahwah, NJ: Lawrence Erlbaum.

Clément, R. and Noels, K.A. (1992) 'Towards a situated approach to ethnolinguistic identity: the effects of status on individuals and groups', *Journal of Language and Social Psychology*, 11: 203–32.

Clément, R., Baker, S.C. and MacIntyre, P.D. (2003) 'Willingness to communicate in a second language: the effects of context, norms and vitality', *Journal of Language and Social Psychology*, 22: 190–209.

Clément, R., Noels, K.A. and MacIntyre, P.D. (2007) 'Three variations on the social psychology of biliguality: context effects in motivation, usage and identity', in A. Weatherall, B. Watson, and C. Gallois (eds) *Language, Discourse and Social Psychology*, Melbourne: Palgrave Macmillan, pp. 51–77.

Collier, M.J. (2005) 'Theorizing about cultural identifications: critical updates and continuing evolution', in W.B. Gudykunst (ed.) *Theorizing about Intercultural Communication*, Thousand Oaks, CA: Sage, pp. 235–56.

Cromby, J. and Nightingale, D.J. (1999) 'What's wrong with social constructionism?', in D.J. Nightingale and J. Cromby (eds) *Social Constructionist Psychology: A Critical Analysis of Theory and Practice*, Buckingham, UK/Philadelphia, PA: Open University Press, pp. 1–19.

Croucher, S.M. (2009) 'How limiting linguistic freedoms influences the cultural adaptation process: an analysis of the French Muslim population', *Communication Quarterly*, 57: 302–18.

Dallaire, C. and Denis, C. (2001) 'Asymmetrical hybridities: youths at Francophone games in Canada', *Canadian Journal of Sociology*, 30: 143–68.

Deaux, K. and Martin, D. (2003) 'Interpersonal networks and social categories: specifying levels of context in identity processes', *Social Psychology Quarterly*, 66: 101–17.

Dervin, F. and Ljalikova, A. (2008) *Regards sur les Mondes Hypermobile: Mythes et Réalités*, Paris: L'Harmattan.

Dil, A.S. (1972) *Language, Psychology and Culture: Essays by Wallace E. Lambert*, Stanford, CA: Stanford University Press.

Dörnyei, Z. and Ushioda, E. (2011) *Teaching and Researching Motivation*, Harlow, UK: Pearson Education.

Erikson, E. (1968) *Identity: Youth and Crisis*, New York: W.W. Norton.

Gardner, R.C. and Lambert, W.E. (1959) 'Motivational variables in second language acquisition', *Canadian Journal of Psychology*, 13: 266–72.

——(1972) *Attitudes and Motivation in Second Language Learning*, Rowley, MA: Newbury House.

Gilbert, A., Langlois, A., Landry, R. and Aunger, E. (2005) 'L'environnement et la vitalité communautaire des minories francophones: vers un modèle conceptuel', *Francophones d'Amérique*, 20: 51–62.

Giles, H. and Byrne, J.L. (1982) 'An intergroup approach to second language acquisition', *Journal of Multicultural Multilingual Development*, 3: 17–39.

Giles, H. and Johnson, P. (1981) 'The role of language in ethnic group relations', in J.C. Turner and H. Giles (eds) *Intergroup Behaviour*, Chicago, IL: University of Chicago Press, pp. 199–243.

Giles, H., Bourhis, R.Y. and Taylor, D.M. (1977) 'Towards a theory of language in ethnic group relations', in H. Giles (ed.) *Language, Ethnicity and Intergroup Relations*, London: Academic Press, pp. 307–48.

Goldstein, T. (1997) *Two Languages at Work: Bilingual Life on the Production Floor*, New York/Berlin: Mouton de Gruyter.

Gudykunst, W.B. (2005) 'An anxiety/uncertainty management (AUM) theory of strangers' intercultural adjustment', in W.B. Gudykunst (ed.) *Theorizing about Intercultural Communication*, Thousand Oaks, CA: Sage, pp. 419–57.

Hannerz, U. (1992) *Cultural Complexity: Studies in the Social Organisation of Meaning*, New York: Columbia University Press.

Hecht, M.L., Warren, J.R., Jung, E. and Krieger, J.L. (2005) 'A communication theory of identity: development, theoretical perspective, and future directions', in W.B. Gudykunst (ed.) *Theorizing about Intercultural Communication*, Thousand Oaks, CA: Sage, pp. 257–78.

Hofstede, G.H. (2001) *Culture's Consequences: Comparing Values, Behaviours, Institutions and Organizations across Nations*, 2nd edn, London: Sage.

Holland, D. and Lachicotte, W. (2007) 'Vygotsky, Mead, and the new sociocultural studies of identity', in H. Daniels, M. Cole and J.V. Wertsch (eds) *The Cambridge Companion to Vygotsky*, New York: Cambridge University Press, pp. 101–35.

Imahori, T. and Cupach, W. (2005) 'Identity management theory: facework in intercultural relationships', in W.B. Gudykunst (ed.) *Theorizing about Intercultural Communication*, Thousand Oaks, CA: Sage, pp. 195–210.

Jackson, J. (2008) *Language, Identity and Study Abroad: Sociocultural Perspectives*, London: Equinox.

Kanno, Y. (2000) 'Bilingualism and identity: the stories of Japanese returnees', *International Journal of Bilingual Education and Bilingualism*, 3: 1–18.

Kim, M.-S. (2005) 'Culture-based conversational constraints theory: individual- and culture-level analyses', in W.B. Gudykunst (ed.) *Theorizing about Intercultural Communication*, Thousand Oaks, CA: Sage, pp. 148–69.

Kim, M.-S. and Hubbard, A.S.E. (2007) 'Intercultural communication in the global village: how to understand "the other"', *Journal of Intercultural Communication Research*, 36: 223–35.

Kim, Y.Y. (1988) *Communication and Cross-Cultural Adaptation: An Integrative Theory*, Clevedon: Multilingual Matters.

——(2005) 'Adapting to a new culture: an integrative communication theory', in W.B. Gudykunst (ed.) *Theorizing about Intercultural Communication*, Thousand Oaks, CA: Sage, pp. 375–400.

——(2007) 'Ideology, identity and intercultural communication: an analysis of differing academic conceptualizations of cultural identity', *Journal of Intercultural Communication Research*, 36: 237–53.

Kinginger, C. (2008) 'Language learning in study abroad: case studies of Americans in France', *The Modern Language Journal Monograph Series*, Volume 1.

Kline, R. (1993) 'The social practice of literacy in a program of study abroad', unpublished PhD dissertation, Pennsylvania State University, Philadelphia, PA.

Kramsch, C. (2010) *The Multilingual Subject*, Oxford: Oxford University Press.

Lamb, M. (2004) 'Integrative motivation in a globalizing world', *System*, 32: 3–19.

——(2009) 'Situating the L2 self: two Indonesian school learners of English', in Z. Dörnyei and E. Ushioda (eds) *Motivation, Language Identity and the L2 Self*, Clevedon: Multilingual Matters, pp. 229–47.

Lambert, W.E. (1956) 'Developmental aspects of second-language acquisition: III. A description of developmental changes', *Journal of Social Psychology*, 43: 99–104.

——(1978) 'Cognitive and socio-cultural consequences of bilingualism', *Canadian Modern Language Review*, 34: 537–47.

Lantolf, J.P. and Thorne, S.L. (2006) *Sociocultural Theory and the Genesis of Second Language Development*, Oxford: Oxford University Press.

Lave, J. and Wenger, E. (1991) *Situated Learning: Legitimate Peripheral Participation*, Cambridge: Cambridge University Press.

Leeds-Hurwitz, W. (1990) 'Notes in the history of intercultural communication: the Foreign Service Institute and the mandate for intercultural training', *Quarterly Journal of Speech*, 76: 262–81.

Leets, L., Giles, H. and Clément, R. (1996) 'Explicating ethnicity in communication theory and research', *Multilingua*, 15: 115–47.

Lewis, M.P. (ed.) (2009) *Ethnologue: Languages of the World*, Dallas, TX: SIL International. Online. Available: http://www.ethnologue.com (accessed 5 August 2010).

MacIntyre, P.D., Noels, K.A. and Clément, R. (1994) 'Biases in self-ratings of second language proficiency: the role of anxiety', *Language Learning*, 47: 265–87.

MacIntyre, P.D., MacKinnon, S. and Clément, R. (2009) 'The baby, the bathwater, and the future of language learning motivation research', in Z. Dörnyei and E. Ushioda (eds) *Motivation, Language Identity and the L2 Self*, Bristol: Multilingual Matters, pp. 43–65.

MacIntyre, P.D., Noels, K.A. and Moore, B. (2010) 'Perspectives on motivation in second language acquisition: lessons from the Ryoanji garden', in M.T. Prior, Y. Watanabe and S.-K. Lee (eds) *Selected Proceedings of the 2008 Second Language Research Forum*, Somerville, MA: Cascadilla Proceedings Project.

McMahill, C. (1997) 'Communities of resistance: a case study of two feminist English classes in Japan', *TESOL Quarterly*, 31: 612–21.

Marcia, J. (1966) 'Development and validation of ego identity status', *Journal of Personality and Social Psychology*, 3: 551–58.

Markus, H. and Kitayama, S. (1991) 'Culture and the self: implications for cognition, emotion, and motivation', *Psychological Review*, 98: 224–52.

Martin, J. and Nakayama, T. (1999) 'Thinking dialectically about culture and communication', *Communication Theory*, 1: 1–25.

Masgoret, A. and Gardner, R.C. (2003) 'Attitudes, motivation, and second language learning: a meta-analysis of studies conducted by Gardner and associates', *Language Learning*, 53: 123–63.

Matsunaga, M., Hecht, M.L., Elek, E. and Ndiaye, K. (2010) 'Ethnic identity development and acculturation: a longitudinal analysis of Mexican-heritage youth in the southwest United States', *Journal of Cross-Cultural Psychology*, 41: 410–27.

Moon, D.G. (1996) 'Concepts of culture: implications for intercultural communication research', *Communication Quarterly*, 44: 70–84.

Mori, K. (1997) *Polite Lies: On Being a Woman Caught between Cultures*, New York: Henry Holt and Company.

Morita, N. (2004) 'Negotiating participation and identity in second language academic communities', *TESOL Quarterly*, 38: 573–601.

Nisbett, R.E. and Wilson, T.D. (1977) 'Telling more than we can know: verbal reports on mental processes', *Psychological Review*, 84: 231–59.

Noels, K.A. and Giles, H. (2009) 'Social identity and language learning', in W.C. Ritchie and T.K. Bhatia (eds) *The New Handbook of Second Language Acquisition*, Bingley, UK: Emerald, pp. 647–70.

Norton, B. (2000) *Identity and Language Learning: Gender, Ethnicity, and Educational Change*, London: Longman.

——(2001) 'Non-participation, imagined communities and the language classroom', in M.P. Breen (ed.) *Learner Contributions to Language Learning: New Directions in Research*, Harlow, UK: Pearson Education Limited, pp. 159–71.

Oyserman, D. and Lee, S. (2008) 'Does culture influence what and how we think? Effects of priming individualism and collectivism', *Psychological Bulletin*, 134: 311–42.

Pavlenko, A. and Blackledge, A. (eds) (2004) *Negotiation of Identities in Multilingual Contexts*, Clevedon: Multilingual Matters.

Pavlenko, A. and Lantolf, J.P. (2000) 'Second language learning as participation and the (re)construction of selves', in J.P. Lantolf (ed.) *Sociocultural Theory and Second Language Learning*, Oxford: Oxford University Press, pp. 155–77.

Pellegrino, V.A. (2005) *Study Abroad and Second Language Use: Constructing the Self*, Cambridge: Cambridge University Press.

Philipsen, G., Coutu, L.M. and Covarrubias, P. (2005) 'Speech codes theory: restatement, revisions, and a response to criticisms', in W.B. Gudykunst (ed.) *Theorizing about Intercultural Communication*, Thousand Oaks, CA: Sage, pp. 55–68.

Rattansi, A. and Phoenix, A. (2005) 'Rethinking youth identities: modernist and postmodernist frameworks', *Identity: An International Journal of Theory and Research*, 5: 97–123.

Reynolds, A.G. (ed.) (1991) *Bilingualism, Multiculturalism, and Second Language Learning: The McGill Conference in Honour of Wallace E. Lambert*, Mahwah, NJ: Lawrence Erlbaum Associates.

Siegal, M. (1996) 'The role of learner subjectivity in second language sociolinguistic competency: Western women learning Japanese', *Applied Linguistics*, 17: 356–82.

Spreckels, J. and Kotthoff, H. (2007) 'Communicating identity in intercultural communication', in H. Kotthoff and H. Spencer-Oatey (eds) *Handbook of Intercultural Communication*, Berlin: Mouton de Gruyter, pp. 467–90.

Ting-Toomey, S. (1988) 'Intercultural conflicts: a face-negotiation theory', in Y.Y. Kim and W.B. Gudykunst (eds) *Theories in Intercultural Communication*, Newbury Park, CA: Sage, pp. 213–35.

——(2005) 'Identity management theory: facework in intercultural relationships', in W.B. Gudykunst (ed.) *Theorizing about Intercultural Communication*, Thousand Oaks, CA: Sage, pp. 195–210.

Toohey, K. and Norton, B. (2003) 'Autonomy as learner agency in sociocultural settings', in D. Palfreyman and R. Smith (eds) *Learner Autonomy across Cultures*, London: Palgrave Macmillan, pp. 58–72.

Varghese, M., Morgan, B., Johnston, B. and Johnson, K.A. (2005) 'Theorizing language teacher identity: three perspectives and beyond', *Journal of Language, Identity, and Education*, 4: 21–44.

Yashima, T. (2002) 'Willingness to communicate in a second language: the Japanese EFL context', *Modern Language Journal*, 86: 54–66.

Yashima, T. and Zenuk-Nishide, L. (2008) 'The impact of learning contexts on proficiency, attitudes, and L2 communication: creating an imagined international community', *System*, 36: 566–85.

Zuengler, J. and Miller, E. (2006) 'Cognitive and sociocultural perspectives: two parallel SLA worlds?', *TESOL Quarterly*, 40: 35–58.

# 4

# Interculturality and intercultural pragmatics

*Istvan Kecskes*

## 1. Introduction

### What is intercultural pragmatics?

Intercultural pragmatics is a relatively new field of inquiry that is concerned with how the language system is put to use in social encounters between human beings who have different first languages, communicate in a common language, and, usually, represent different cultures (Kecskes 2004, 2011). The communicative process in these encounters is synergistic in the sense that it is a merger in which the pragmatic norms of each participant are represented to some extent. Intercultural pragmatics represents a sociocognitive perspective in which individual prior experience and actual situational experience are equally important in meaning construction and comprehension. Research in intercultural pragmatics has four main foci: (1) interaction between native speakers and non-native speakers of a language; (2) lingua franca communication in which none of the interlocutors has the same first language (L1); (3) multilingual discourse; and (4) language use and development of individuals who speak more than one language.

### Interlanguage pragmatics and cross-cultural pragmatics

Difference should be made between "interlanguage pragmatics", "cross-cultural pragmatics", and "intercultural pragmatics". Although these terms are often used interchangeably, they do not refer to the same inquiry. "Interlanguage pragmatics" focuses on the acquisition and use of pragmatic norms in a second language (L2): how L2 learners produce and comprehend speech acts, and how their pragmatic competence develops over time (e.g., Kasper 1998; Kasper and Blum-Kulka 1993). Boxer (2002) argued that interlanguage pragmatics focuses on the language learner's appropriation and/or acquisition of pragmatic norms represented in the host language community. To date, many cross-sectional, longitudinal, and theoretical studies have been conducted that have mainly focused on L2 classroom interaction; this has resulted in a special tie between interlanguage pragmatics and second language acquisition (SLA) research.

In a way, interlanguage pragmatics incorporates cross-cultural pragmatics, although there is some difference between the two. Cross-cultural pragmatics "takes the view that individuals from two societies or communities carry out their interactions (whether spoken or written) according to their own rules or norms, often resulting in a clash of expectations and, ultimately, misperceptions about the other group" (Boxer 2002: 151). Cross-cultural studies focus mainly on speech act realizations in different cultures, cultural breakdowns, and pragmatic failures, such as the way some linguistic behaviors considered polite in one language may not be polite in another language. A significant number of these studies use a comparative approach to different cultural norms reflected in language use (e.g., House 2000; Spencer-Oatey 2000; Thomas 1983).

Interlanguage pragmatics and cross-cultural pragmatics are based primarily on three theoretical constructs: Gricean pragmatics, Brown and Levinson's politeness theory, and the so-called "interlanguage hypothesis" (Selinker 1972). Recently, attempts have been made to integrate relevance theory (e.g., Escandell-Vidal 1996; Jary 1998) and conversation analysis (e.g., Kasper 2004; Markee 2000) into interlanguage pragmatics, although the main foci of research have remained pragmatic competence, speech acts, politeness, and pragmatic transfer. The ability to comprehend and produce a communicative act is referred to as pragmatic competence (Kasper 1996; Paradis 1995). This concept usually includes awareness of social distance, speakers' social status, cultural knowledge such as politeness, and linguistic knowledge, of both the explicit and implicit kind. Kecskes (2005) argued that the problem with interlanguage pragmatics is that it represents a monolingual and cross-cultural rather than a multilingual and intercultural view, inasmuch as all of its theoretical resources (Gricean theory, politeness theory, and the interlanguage hypothesis) advocate the relative independence, rather than the interdependence, of language systems and cultures, and proclaim the universality of principles such as those of cooperation and politeness. Wierzbicka (1985), Goddard and Wierzbicka (1997), and Meier (1997), among others, have questioned the claims made for the universality of Grice's cooperative principle (Grice 1961) and Brown and Levinson's theory of politeness (Brown and Levinson 1987). For instance, they have made a case for the cultural relativity of definitions of sincerity and relevance in a given speech community, or the ranking of imposition when a request is made.

The concerns of intercultural pragmatics differ significantly from those of both interlanguage pragmatics and cross-cultural pragmatics. Differences are based on two factors: the understanding of interculturality and the sociocognitive approach (e.g., Kecskes and Zhang 2009; Kecskes 2010a).

## 2. Interculturality and intraculturality

### Definition

In order for us to understand the perspective of intercultural pragmatics, we should first define interculturality in communication and separate it from intraculturality. There have been several attempts (e.g., Gudykunst and Mody 2002; Nishizaka 1995; Samovar and Porter 2001; Ting-Toomey 1999) to explain the difference between the two terms. According to Samovar and Porter (2001), "intracultural communication" is "the type of communication that takes place between members of the same dominant culture, but with slightly different values", as opposed to "intercultural communication", which is the communication between two or more distinct cultures. This approach has led to a common mistake that several researchers have committed. They have considered interculturality as the main reason for miscommunication (e.g., Hinnenkamp 1995; Thomas 1983; Ting-Toomey 1999). In fact, some researchers' findings show the opposite (e.g., House 2003; Kecskes 2008, 2007). The use of semantically transparent language by non-native speakers results in fewer misunderstandings and communication breakdowns than expected. The insecurity experienced by lingua franca speakers makes them establish a unique set of rules for interaction, which may be referred to as an "interculture", according to Koole and ten Thije (1994: 69) a "culture constructed in cultural contact".

Blum-Kulka *et al.* (2008: 164) defined interculturality as "a contingent interactional accomplishment" from a discoursive–constructivist perspective. They argued that a growing literature explores interculturality as a participant concern (e.g., Higgins 2007; Markee and Kasper 2004; Mori 2003). Nishizaka (1995) pointed out that interculturality is a situationally emergent rather than a normatively fixed phenomenon. The sociocognitive approach (Kecskes 2008, 2010a; Kecskes and Zhang 2009), which is explained in the next section, goes one step further and defines interculturality as a phenomenon that is not only interactionally and socially constructed in the course of communication but also relies on relatively definable cultural models and norms that represent the speech communities to which the interlocutors belong. Consequently, interculturality has both relatively normative and emergent components. In order for us to understand the dynamism and ever-changing nature of intercultural encounters, we need to approach interculturality dialectically. Cultural constructs and models change diachronically, whereas cultural representation and speech production by individuals changes synchronically. "Interculturality is a situationally emergent and co-constructed phenomenon that relies both on relatively definable cultural norms and models as well as situationally evolving features" (Kecskes 2011). Intercultures are ad hoc creations. They are created in a communicative process in which cultural norms and models brought into the interaction from prior experience of interlocutors blend with features created ad hoc in the interaction in a synergetic way. The result is intercultural discourse in which there is mutual transformation of knowledge and communicative behavior rather than transmission. The emphasis is on transformation rather than on transmission.

## Interculturality as an emergent, co-constructed phenomenon

Interculturality has both an *a priori* side and an emergent side that occur and act simultaneously in the communicative process. Consequently, intercultures are not fixed phenomena, but they are created in the course of communication in which participants belong to different L1 speech communities, speak a common language, and represent different cultural norms and models that are defined by their respective L1 speech community. The following conversation between a Brazilian girl (B) and a Polish woman (P) illustrates this point well.

(1)
B: And what do you do?
P: I work at the university as a cleaner.
B: As a janitor?
P: No, not yet. Janitor is after the cleaner.
B: You want to be a janitor?
P: Of course.

*Albany English Lingua Franca Dataset collected by PhD students*

In this conversation, interlocutors represent two different languages and cultures (Brazilian and Polish), and use English as a lingua franca. This is the prior knowledge that participants bring to the interaction. They create an interculture, which belongs to none of them but emerges in the course of conversation. Within this interculture, the two speakers have a smooth conversation about the Polish woman's job. Although neither of them is sure what the right term is for the job, there are no misunderstandings in the interaction because each participant is careful to use semantically transparent language in order to be as clear as possible. The Polish woman sets up a "hierarchy" that is non-existent in the target language culture ("cleaner → janitor") but is an emergent element of the interculture that the interlocutors have been constructing.

Intercultures come and go; they are neither stable nor permanent. They just occur. They are both synergetic and blended. Interculturality is constituted on the spot by speakers who participate in the conversation. But is this not a phenomenon that also occurs in intracultural communication? Why and how should we distinguish intercultural communication from intracultural communication? Basically, the currently dominant approach to this issue is that there is no "principled" difference between intracultural and intercultural communication (e.g., Winch 1997; Wittgenstein 2001). This is true as far as the mechanism of the communicative process is concerned. However, there is a qualitative difference in the nature and content of an intracultural interaction and an intercultural interaction. Speakers in intracultural communication rely on prior knowledge and culture of a relatively definable speech community, which is privatized by individuals belonging to that speech community. No language boundaries are crossed; however, subcultures are relied upon and representations are individualized. What is created on the spot enriches the given culture, contributes to it, and remains within the fuzzy but still recognizable confines of that language and culture. In the case of intercultural communication, however, prior knowledge that is brought into and privatized in the communicative process belongs to different cultures and languages, and what participants create on the spot will disappear and not become an enrichment and/or addition to any particular culture or language. Intercultures are ad hoc creations that may enhance the individual and the globalization process but can hardly be said to contribute to any particular culture. This is exactly what we see in example (1). The speakers created a hierarchy between "cleaner" and "janitor" just to establish common ground and assure their own mutual private understanding of a given situation. However, this interculture disappears when they stop talking.

## Regularity and variability

In understanding the dialectical relationship of regularity and variability characterizing intercultural and intracultural communication, one must rely on Leibniz (1976 [1679]): " … si nihil per se concipitur, nihil omnino concipietur" (" … if nothing can be understood by itself nothing at all can ever be understood"). The reason we can speak about a language or a culture is that, although these entities have fuzzy boundaries, they are still definable. They can be defined because there are qualitative differences between them. Chinese, Russian, English, Arabic, etc. are different languages. Meanings of words or expressions in different languages can be determined because words and expressions pull together information about the history of their use in actual situational contexts and sociocultural encounters in a particular speech community (see an opposite view in Evans 2009). Of course, these meanings are privatized by individual prior experience. The following example in which an American student and a Korean are conversing demonstrates individual privatization (see Kecskes 2008):

(2)
CONTEXT:   Korean and American students talking. Both study linguistics and are required to write an essay.
KOREAN:   Jill, do you want me to help you with your essay?

AMERICAN: *Don't patronize me, please.*
KOREAN: You say, you don't want support?
AMERICAN: Please just don't … . Okay?

Although both speakers work with lexical units from the same language, their private meaning construction system may give different interpretations to the same items. Differences can be significant depending on the speakers' prior experience (frequency, familiarity, motivation, etc.) with the same words, expressions, and utterances. This is especially so in intercultural communication; because of cultural differences, not only may the speakers' private contexts differ significantly, but also the public contexts tied to the same lexical item.

In the above scenario, there is a difference in how the American student uses the word "patronize" and how the South Korean student understands it. The main sense of "patronize" can be described as follows: to act as a patron to someone or something. This is the sense both interlocutors are supposed to have because in conversation it is usually the core sense of a lexical unit that constitutes the minimum set of features that we can assume to be shared by interlocutors. However, especially in intercultural communication, when interlocutors represent different languages and cultures, the same word may have different culture-specific conceptual property for the native speaker and the non-native speaker. This is what may have happened in example (2). In American culture, the word "patronize" usually has quite a negative culture-specific conceptual property if the direct object of the verb is animate and referring to a person or persons ("patronize someone"). In South Korean culture, the closest equivalent of the English word "patronize" is *huwonhada*, which has a positive culture-specific conceptual property. For Koreans, if they are patronized, it means that they receive a favor. This positive cultural load may be transferred to the English word when used by a Korean speaker. This may be the reason why the South Korean student does not seem to have understood the negative attitude of the American speaker.

Words from a particular language can create context because they encapsulate prior situational contexts in which a speaker has used them (e.g., Kecskes 2008; Violi 2000). When "get out of here" or "license and registration, please" are uttered without any actual situational context, these expressions will create a situational context in the mind of hearers because of their prior experience with the lexical units. This relative regularity attached to lexical units of a language changes diachronically, whereas variety changes synchronically. They are two sides of the same phenomenon. From this perspective, it sounds redundant to suggest replacing the notion of language groups with that of "communities of practice" (e.g., Chaiklin and Lave 1993; Hall *et al.* 2006; Wenger 2000).

## Crossing language boundaries

An example of intracultural communication would be if a dentist in the dominant culture, say, in the United States, spoke about dental issues with a plumber belonging to the same US culture. Their negotiation may not be that smooth because the plumber might not be very knowledgeable about dental terms. If, however, the dentist speaks with another dentist about dental issues, they would certainly understand each other's language use quite well, although there still might be individual differences. This is what prompts the argument that a US dentist would understand an English-speaking French dentist better that she would understand an English native-speaker plumber. However, we must be very careful with judgments like this. Intercultural situations may differ from intracultural situations to a great extent.

I have argued elsewhere (Kecskes 2010b) that it is important to make a distinction between a "quantitative" change and a "qualitative" change, and between changes occurring within a culture or across cultures. If a person moves from Albany, New York, to New Orleans, Louisiana, and makes adjustments to the new Louisiana subculture, he may start to say things such as "I could do this". This scenario, however, cannot be compared "qualitatively" with the case of a person who moves from Albany, New York, to Lille, France. In the first case, we can speak about peripheral rather than core changes in the language use of the person. Louisiana culture and upstate New York culture can be considered subcultures of American culture, and the Louisiana dialect and the upstate New York dialect are dialects of American English. The change is different, however, when an American moves from Albany, New York, to Lille, France. Comparing the upstate New York dialect with the Picard dialect of Lille is not the same as comparing it with the Louisiana dialect. In the latter, we are speaking about dialects of different languages (English and French), whereas the first case involves dialects of the same language (English). There is a qualitative difference between crossing language boundaries and crossing dialects (but staying within the confines of the core of one particular language).

The same is true for cultures. The relationship between American and French cultures differs qualitatively from the relationship between Louisiana subculture and upstate New York sub-culture. English–French bilingualism may create qualitatively different changes in the mind and behavior of a person than Louisiana–upstate New York bidialectalism (Kecskes 2010b). I would like to emphasize that this view does not represent a homogeneous approach to language and culture. Languages and cultures are never homogeneous. What is temporarily and relatively homogeneous-like is the linguistic faculty (language system) that changes diachronically, whereas language changes both synchronically and diachronically.

There is one more major difference between intracultural and intercultural communication. Intracultural communication is dominated by preferred ways of saying things (Wray 2002) and preferred ways of organizing thoughts within a particular speech community (Kecskes 2008). This is not the case in intercultural communication because the development of "preferred ways" requires time and conventionalization within a speech community. Human languages are very flexible. They can lexicalize whatever their speakers find important to lexicalize. There are preferred ways of lexicalizing certain actions, phenomena, and things. Americans "shoot a film", "dust the furniture", "make love", "do the dishes", etc. One language has a word for a phenomenon that is important in that culture, and the other does not. In Russian, they have the word *spargal'ki* to denote tools for cheating. In Hungarian, the same phenomenon is denoted by the word *puska*. We have no word for this in English. Knowing what expressions to select, what is appropriate or inappropriate in different situations may be an important sign of "group-inclusiveness" and, God forbid, "native-likeness". In intercultural communication, this group-inclusiveness is created on the spot by speakers with different linguistic and cultural backgrounds who can hardly rely on the advantageous use of formulaic and figurative elements of a common language. In an empirical study, Kecskes (2007) demonstrated that, in lingua franca communication, the use of formulaic language by the participants was less than 10%. Lingua franca speakers relied on semantically transparent language to make sure that their interlocutor could follow what they said.

In sum, it is erroneous to think that intercultural communication differs from intracultural communication because the former is more complicated than the latter, and the former leads to more miscommunication than the other. As we saw above, the dissimilarity is qualitative rather than quantitative, because there is a qualitative difference between crossing language boundaries and crossing dialects.

## 3. Theoretical foundation of intercultural pragmatics

The study of intercultural pragmatics supports a less idealized, more down-to-earth approach to communication than current pragmatic theories usually do. Although not denying the decisive role of cooperation, context, and politeness in communication, intercultural pragmatics also gives equal importance to egocentrism, chaos, aggression, trial-and-error, and salience in the analysis of language production. Intercultural pragmatics adopts a sociocognitive approach (SCA) to pragmatics that takes into account both societal and individual factors including cooperation and egocentrism that, as claimed here, are not antagonistic phenomena in interaction (Kecskes 2008, 2010a). SCA is considered an alternative to current theories of pragmatics that may not give an adequate account of what really happens in the communicative process.

Sociocognitive theorists consider communication an idealistic, cooperation-based, context-dependent process in which speakers are supposed to carefully construct their utterances for the hearer, taking into account all contextual factors, while hearers do their best to figure out the intentions of the speakers. This approach relies mainly on the positive features of communication including cooperation, context, rapport, and politeness, but almost completely ignores the untidy, trial-and-error nature of the process and the importance of prior and emerging contexts captured in the individual use of linguistic expressions. The overemphasis on cooperative, societal, politeness, and contextual factors has led to the neglect of individual factors such as egocentrism and salience that are as important contributors to the communicative process as cooperation, context, and rapport. The sociocognitive approach is presented as a theoretical framework for intercultural pragmatics to incorporate and reconcile two seemingly antagonistic sides of the communicative process and explain the dynamic interplay of prior and actual situational contexts.

### The dialectical relationship of social and cognitive factors

Before describing the main tenets of SCA, we have to make a clear distinction between my approach and van Dijk's understanding of the sociocognitive view in language use. Van Dijk (2008: X) said that in his theory it is not the social situation that influences (or is influenced by) discourse, but the way the participants define the situation. He goes further and claims that "contexts are not some kind of objective conditions or direct cause, but rather (inter)subjective constructs designed and ongoingly updated in interaction by participants as members of groups and communities" (van Dijk 2008: X). SCA adopts a more dialectical perspective by considering communication to be a dynamic process in which individuals are not only constrained by societal conditions, but also shape them at the same time. Speakers and hearers are equal participants in the communicative process. They both produce and comprehend speech relying on their most accessible and salient knowledge expressed in their private contexts in production and comprehension. Consequently, only a holistic interpretation of utterance and discourse from the perspective of both the speaker and the hearer can give us an adequate account of language communication. As I said earlier, when referring to Leibniz, it is very important that we realize that there are social conditions and constraints (contexts) that have some objectivity from the perspective of individuals. Of course, there can always be slight differences in how individuals process those relatively objective societal factors based on their prior experience. But it would be a mistake to deny the presence of any objectivity in social contexts.

When language is used, its unique property is activated in two ways. When people speak or write, they craft what they need to express to fit the situation or context in which they are communicating. But, at the same time, the way people speak or write the words, expressions, and utterances they use creates that very situation, context, sociocultural frame in which the given communication occurs. Consequently, two things seem to happen simultaneously: people attempt to fit their language to a situation or context that their language, in turn, helped to create in the first place (e.g., Gee 1999). This dynamic behavior of human speech and reciprocal process between language and context basically eliminates the need to ask the ever-returning question: Which comes first? The situation the speakers are in (e.g., faculty meeting, car renting, dinner ordering, etc.) or the particular language that is used in the given situation (expressions and utterances representing ways of talking and interacting)? Is this a "car rental" because participants are acting and speaking that way, or are they acting and speaking that way because this is a "car rental"? Acting and speaking in a particular way constitutes social situations, sociocultural frames, and these frames require the use of a particular language. "Which comes first?" does not seem to be a relevant question synchronically. Social and cultural routines result in recurring activities and institutions. However, these institutions and routinized activities have to be rebuilt continuously in the here and now. The question is whether these cultural models, institutions, and frames exist outside language or not. The social constructivists insist that models and frames have to be rebuilt again and again, so it is just our impression that they exist outside language (see van Dijk 2008). However, the sociocognitive approach argues that these cultural mental models have some kind of psychological reality in the individual mind and, when a concrete situation occurs, the appropriate model is recalled, which supports the appropriate verbalization of triggered thoughts and activities. Of course, building and rebuilding our world occurs not merely through language but through the interaction of language with other real-life phenomena such as non-linguistic symbol systems, objects, tools, technologies, etc.

## Sociocognitive approach to pragmatics

The sociocognitive approach to communication and pragmatics (Kecskes 2008, 2010a; Kecskes and Zhang 2009) emphasizes not only the role of co-construction but also the importance of prior knowledge in the interaction. SCA points out the complex role of cultural models and private mental models, how these are applied categorically and/or reflectively by individuals in response to sociocultural environmental feedback mechanisms, and how this leads to and explains different meaning outcomes and knowledge transfer. In meaning construction and comprehension, individuals rely both on pre-existing encyclopedic knowledge based on their prior experience and current knowledge created in the process of interaction.

In the sociocognitive paradigm, communication is driven by the interplay of "cooperation" required by societal conditions and "egocentrism" rooted in the prior experience of the individual. Consequently, egocentrism and cooperation are not mutually exclusive phenomena. They are both present in all stages of communication to a different extent because they represent the individual and societal traits of the dynamic process of communication (Kecskes and Zhang 2009). On the one hand, speakers and hearers are constrained by societal conditions but, as individuals, they all have their own goals, intention, desire, etc. that are freely expressed, and recognized in the flow of interaction.

This is not the denial of the pragmatic theories that have grown out of the cooperation-centered Gricean approach. Recognizing the important egocentrism of speaker–hearers, the sociocognitive approach is more like "a synthesis of the cooperation-centered view of communication and the egocentrism-based cognitive psychological approach".

Several researchers (e.g., Barr and Keysar 2005; Giora 2003; Keysar and Bly 1995) have indicated that speakers and hearers are egocentric to a surprising degree, and individual, egocentric endeavors of interlocutors play a much more decisive role in the initial stages of

*Table 4.1* The dynamic model of meaning

| Individual trait | Social trait |
| --- | --- |
| attention | intention |
| private experience | actual situational experience |
| egocentrism | cooperation |
| salience | relevance |

production and comprehension than current pragmatic theories envision. Their egocentric behavior is rooted in the interlocutors' greater (suggestion) reliance on their own knowledge instead of mutual knowledge. Recent research (e.g., House 2003; Kecskes 2007) in intercultural communication also affiliates with cognitive dynamism. Kecskes (2007) argued that, especially in the first phase of the communicative process, instead of looking for common ground, which is absent to a great extent, lingua franca speakers articulate their own thoughts with linguistic means that they could easily use.

In the sociocognitive approach framed by the dynamic model of meaning (Kecskes 2008; Kecskes and Zhang 2009), communication is characterized by the interplay of two traits that are inseparable, mutually supportive, and interactive (see Table 4.1).

Communication is the result of the interplay of intention and attention motivated by socio-cultural background that is privatized individually by interlocutors. The sociocultural background is composed of encyclopedic knowledge of interlocutors deriving from their "prior experience" tied to the linguistic expressions they use and "current experience" in which those expressions create and convey meaning.

The sociocognitive approach integrates the pragmatic view of cooperation and the cognitive view of egocentrism, and emphasizes that both cooperation and egocentrism are manifested in all phases of communication to a varying extent. Whereas cooperation is an intention-directed practice and measured by relevance, egocentrism is an attention-oriented trait and measured by salience. Intention and attention are identified as two measurable forces that affect communication in a systematic way. The measurement of intention and attention by means of relevance and salience is distinct from earlier explanations (e.g., Giora 2003; Sperber and Wilson 1986/1995; Wilson and Sperber 2004).

## 4. Application of SCA in intercultural pragmatics

The application of SCA as a theoretical framework results in two main distinctive features of intercultural pragmatics.

### Intercultural pragmatics is discourse segment centered rather than utterance centered

The focus of pragmatic theories is on communicative actions (speech acts, pragmatic action, utterance), whereas intercultural pragmatics focuses on interaction. Pragmatic theories are utterance centered, which means that in these theories the most significant difference between a sentence and an utterance is that sentences are judged according to how well they make sense "grammatically", whereas utterances are judged according to their "communicative validity" (Habermas 1979: 31). Austin's work (1976) is widely associated with the concept of the speech act and the idea that speech is itself a form of action. In his opinion, language is not just a passive practice of describing a given reality, but a particular practice to invent and affect those realities.

What can we do/achieve with words and utterances? This question has been one of the main driving forces of contemporary pragmatics research. So the main focus of pragmaticians since Austin has been meaning conveyed by an utterance in its actual situational context in intracultural communication. However, utterance analysis in intercultural pragmatics may be problematic for two reasons. On the one hand, utterances in intercultural communication are often not quite properly formed because of language proficiency issues. On the other hand, in an experimental study, Kecskes (2007) demonstrated that the creativity of lingua franca speakers is detectable at the discourse level rather than utterance level. A similar claim was made by Prodromou (2008). Consequently, in intercultural communication, it makes more sense to analyze discourse segments rather than utterances. And indeed, the criticism of intercultural interaction as characterized by miscommunication, lack of systematic coherence, and a low level of creativity is seen to be invalid when we analyze the phenomenon on a discourse segment rather than an utterance level and in the sociocognitive paradigm in which we treat creativity and coherence as discourse in progress.

Instead of considering coherence as a formal text- and product-oriented concept, we should perceive it as an interactively negotiated process that is dependent on the context and interlocutors. Coates (1995) argued that much real language data are coherent without the application of any cohesive devices. Thus, coherence is closely connected to interpretability, acceptability in context, and involves both intra- and extratextual factors. It is not the text that coheres but people who cohere when ascribing meaning to utterances. Understanding takes place when the speaker's and hearer's contributions cohere. All human communication underlies a "default principle of coherence" (Bublitz and Lenk 1999): a basic assumption that our interlocutors produce coherent discourse.

Recently, serious efforts have been made to introduce conversational analysis (CA) in SLA and interlanguage pragmatics research. Although CA application received quite a critical response from SLA researchers, it has become fully acceptable in interlanguage pragmatics. CA has been used mainly to analyze classroom talk (e.g., Markee and Kasper 2004; Mori 2003) and institutional talk (e.g., Bardovi-Harlig and Hartford 2005; Félix-Brasdefer 2008). CA can also be used efficiently in intercultural pragmatics because it requires description and analysis of the sequencing of action and organization of turns at the micro level of verbal and nonverbal acts. CA is empirically based, and it has clearly defined methodological procedures for developing participant-relevant analyses of talk-in-interaction, and is concerned with the possibility of replication.

Another analytical methodology that can be used successfully in intercultural pragmatics derives from the "centering theory" developed first by Grosz and Sidner (1986) to stress the role of purpose and processing in discourse. This theory is compatible with the sociocognitive approach because it focuses on the interplay and change in intention and attention within discourse segments and underlines both *a priori* and emergent features in the discursive process. The theory attempts to relate focus of attention, choice of referring expression, and perceived coherence of utterances within a discourse segment. It provides a model of discourse structure and meaning well suited to intercultural interaction, where an understanding of the ways in which the focus of attention affects both the production and the understanding of various linguistic expressions in discourse is crucial.

In the centering theory of discourse, we distinguish among three components of discourse structure: linguistic structure, intentional structure, and attentional state. Linguistic structure groups utterances into discourse segments. Intentional structure consists of discourse segment purposes and the relations between them. The attentional state is an abstraction of the focus of attention of the participants as the discourse unfolds. The attentional state, being dynamic, records the objects, properties, and relations that are salient at each point of the discourse.

In the theory, there are two levels of attentional state. The global level is concerned with the relations between discourse segments and the ways in which attention shifts between them; it depends on the intentional structure. The local level is concerned with changes in attention within discourse segments. "Centering" (Grosz *et al.* 1995), an element of the local level, pertains to the interaction between the form of linguistic expression and local discourse coherence. In particular, it relates local coherence to choice of referring expression (pronouns in contrast to definite description or proper name), and argues that differences in coherence correspond in part to the different demands for inference made by different types of referring expressions, given a particular attentional state.

The centering theory claims that discourses contain constituent segments, and each segment is represented as part of a discourse model. Centers are semantic entities that are part of the discourse model for each utterance in a discourse segment.

- Cf: forward-looking center
- Cb: backward-looking center
- Cp: preferred center

Centering theory predicts four transition states:

- CONTINUE: If the current Cb is not only the same as the previous one, but also the same as the current Cp.
- RETAIN: If the current Cb is the same as the previous one, but different from the current Cp.
- SMOOTH-SHIFT: If the current Cb is different from the previous one, but the same as the current Cp.
- ROUGH-SHIFT: If the current Cb is neither the same as the previous one nor the same as the current Cp.

The following simple example demonstrates how centering theory can be applied to explain an earlier example (1):

(3)
U1   Brazilian (B): – And what do you do?
        Cf: you
U2   Pole (P): – I work at the university as a cleaner.
        Cf-cb: you (I) Cf: cleaner               CONTINUE
U3   B: – As a janitor?
        Cf-cb: you; janitor (cleaner)            CONTINUE
U4   P: – No, not yet. Janitor is after the cleaner.
        Cf-cb: cleaner (janitor)                 RETAIN
U5   B: – You want to be a janitor?
        Cf-cb: janitor                           CONTINUE
U6   P: – Of course.

Several researchers (e.g., Hu and Pan 2001; Walker 1998) argued that the restriction of centering to operating within a discourse segment should be abandoned in order to integrate centering within a model of global discourse structure. According to Walker (1998), the within-segment restriction causes three problems. The first problem is that centers are often continued over discourse segment boundaries with pronominal referring expressions whose form is identical to those that occur within a discourse segment. The second problem is that recent work has shown that listeners perceive segment boundaries at various levels of granularity. It is almost impossible that each listener will have the same segment boundaries within discourse process. The third issue is that, even for utterances within a discourse segment, there are strong contrasts between utterances whose adjacent utterance within a segment is hierarchically recent and those whose adjacent utterance within a segment is linearly recent. Hu and Pan (2001) argued that the centering theory makes wrong predictions in center computation because the theory does not distinguish a backward-looking center (Cb) from the discourse segment topic (DST). Although Cb and DST share many properties, they are conceptually different, and should thus be differentiated from each other. Cb is used to process the local coherence of discourse between utterances, whereas DST is used to process the more global coherence of discourse between discourse segments. In our example, the DST is "cleaner". The DST changes in U3 to "janitor". However, this is only a semantic change; the dialog continues to be about the same thing (cleaner; janitor).

We have no space here to go into a detailed explanation of how to use the centering theory to analyze intercultural interaction data. However, there is no doubt that, beside CA, this type of analysis looks most promising in intercultural pragmatics.

## Priority of salience in both production and comprehension

In neo-Gricean pragmatics, cooperation occurs as the main driving force of the communicative process. In the relevance theory, this role is played by relevance. In contrast, intercultural pragmatics emphasizes the priority of "salience" in both production and comprehension. Although cooperation is an intention-directed practice measured by relevance, egocentrism is an attention-oriented trait measured by salience (Kecskes 2008; Kecskes and Zhang 2009). The simplest definition of salience is that it is the most probable out of all possible (Kecskes 2007).

The two main debates in current pragmatics theory focus on the controversies surrounding the conscious vs. the automatic processing of available contextual information and the distinction between literal and nonliteral meaning. In fact, these issues are two sides of the same question: the literal/nonliteral distinction is closely bound with the distinction between the automatic and conscious retrieval of information. Giora (2003: 33) wrote:

> Though literal meanings tend to be highly salient, their literality is not a component of salience. The criterion or threshold a meaning has to reach to be considered salient is related only to its accessibility in memory due to such factors as frequency of use or experiential familiarity.

Intercultural communication clearly demonstrates the priority of salience over contextual factors in both production and comprehension. What is most salient for the speaker–hearer based on his/her prior experience counts as the decisive factor. Gibbs (1999: 33) argued that "context becomes operative only at a post-access stage, guiding the selection of the contextually relevant meaning of the ambiguous words". The critical variable in language processing is saliency and not the literalness of lexical units (e.g., Giora 2003; Katz 2005; Kecskes 2004). Both speakers and hearers rely on their most accessible and salient knowledge expressed in their private contexts in production and comprehension. The main claim of Giora's graded salience hypothesis is that salient meanings are processed automatically (although not necessarily solely), irrespective of contextual information and strength of bias in the first phase of comprehension when lexical processing and contextual processing run parallel (Giora 2003: 24). Other cognitive psychologists also emphasized that the individual, egocentric endeavors of speakers and hearers play a much more decisive role in communication than current pragmatic theories envision (Keysar and Barr 2002). Language processing is anchored in the assumption that what is salient or accessible to oneself will also be accessible to one's interlocutors (Barr and Keysar 2005; Colston 2005; Kecskes 2007). This is what is called the "egocentrism" of speaker–hearer. However, egocentrism is not a negative phenomenon. It is something interlocutors cannot help, cannot subdue. What is salient, based on their prior experience, is always on their mind subconsciously and automatically. This is why it is not enough to emphasize only the co-constructed, emergent part of the communicative process. Together with societal factors, emphasis must also be put on individual cognitive factors (prior experience). Giora's graded salience hypothesis (1997, 2003) does this, and claims that, instead of postulating the priority of literal meaning, the priority of salient (e.g., conventional, familiar, frequent, predictable) meaning should be assumed.

Salience is a crucial factor in intercultural pragmatics. Interlocutors participating in intercultural encounters have their main prior experience rooted in different cultures and languages. They share more limited common ground than interlocutors in intracultural communication. This common ground is usually restricted to universal knowledge, so participants in intercultural communication must create most of the common ground in the course of interaction. This unique situation raises the importance of a linguistic code tied to prior experience as opposed to actual situational context in meaning production and comprehension in intercultural encounters. Language as a system encapsulates basic core meaning (usually called "literal meaning") for each user of that code system. Some studies in English lingua franca (ELF) use (e.g., House 2003; Kecskes 2007; Philip 2005) found that ELF speakers rely on semantically more transparent language rather than formulaic and/or figurative language that may carry more native-likeness. Based on the results of an empirical study, Kecskes (2007) claimed that ELF users usually avoided the use of formulaic expressions, not necessarily because they did not know those phrases but because they were worried that their interlocutors would not understand them properly. They were reluctant to use language that they knew or perceived to be, figurative or semantically, less transparent (see also Philip 2005). ELF speakers tried to come as close to the compositional meaning of expressions as possible because they thought that, if there was no figurative and/or metaphorical meaning involved, their interlocutors would process the English words and expressions the way they meant them. As lingua franca speakers come from different sociocultural backgrounds and represent different cultures, the mutual knowledge they may share is the knowledge of the primary meaning of words and expressions. Consequently, semantic analyzability plays a decisive role in ELF speech production. This assumption was supported in Kecskes's study (2007) by the fact that the most frequently used formulaic expressions were the fixed semantic units (as a matter of fact; on the other hand), phrasal verbs (put up with; come across), and speech formulas (you know; right; not bad) in which there is semantic transparency to a much greater extent than in idioms (spill the beans) or situation-bound utterances (welcome aboard; I'll talk to you later). The following conversation between a Chinese and a Turkish student illustrates this point.

(4)

CHINESE:  I think Peter drank a bit too much at the party yesterday.

TURKISH:  Eh, *tell me about it*. He always drinks too much.

CHINESE:  When we arrived he drank beer. Then Mary gave him some vodka. Later he drank some wine. Oh, too much.

TURKISH:  Why are you telling me this? I was there.

CHINESE:  Yes, but you told me to tell about it.

*Albany English Lingua Franca database collected by PhD students*

In this example, the use of the expression "tell me about it" by the Turkish student in a figurative sense leads to misunderstanding because the Chinese student processed it literally.

In both intracultural and intercultural communication, salience overrides literalness because, given the fact that lexical units encapsulate the history of their prior use, the usages that will get priority in the meaning hierarchy are those that represent the most familiar and frequent encounters. However, although the most salient meaning in intracultural communication can be either literal or figurative or both, in intercultural communication, the most salient meaning for interlocutors is usually the literal meaning.

Although Giora (1997, 2003) argued that cognitively prominent salient meanings, rather than literal meanings, play the most important role in both production and comprehension of language, most attention in pragmatics research has been paid to comprehension rather than production. The sociocognitive approach (Kecskes 2008) claims that salience plays as important a role in language production as in comprehension. The role of salience in language production involves a relation between the prominence of entities in a ranking and preference of a choice among alternatives.

When the speaker is faced with having to choose a word or an expression, a ranking of the available choices is obtained on the basis of the degree of salience of entities in the context of generation. The word or phrase is then selected for utterance on the basis of maximum salience. Once a speaker has either an *a priori* or an emergent, co-constructed intention to communicate, s/he should find an appropriate linguistic representation to transfer this message to the hearer. In intercultural communication, the problem is that interlocutors lack or have very little collective salience that is the basis for common ground. Consequently, they can rely on individual salience and situational salience. The following example demonstrates how salience works in production:

(5) A Pakistani, a Chinese, and a Colombian student are talking.

PAK:  You said you live with your son. So your wife is not here.

CH:  Yes, I am alone. I am with my son.

COL:  Will your wife come to visit?

CH:  Yes, she came yesterday.

PAK:  Did she come from China?

CH:  Yes, she arrived from Nanjing.

The Pakistani wants the Chinese to confirm that he lives with his son. He concludes that the Chinese student's wife was not there. The Chinese reacts to this first, saying that he is alone but then with another utterance he confirms that his son is with him. The two statements seem to contradict each other. However, if we consider that the Chinese student responded to two separate utterances, the contradicting utterances make sense. Salience is a psychological phenomenon that often results in an automatic response to the latest piece of information.

## 5. Summary and future directions

Intercultural pragmatics is a relatively new subfield of pragmatics. With its support of a less idealized, more down-to-earth approach to communication than current pragmatic theories, intercultural pragmatics may help us better understand the real nature of human communication. Interculturality was defined as a situationally emergent and co-constructed phenomenon that relies on both relatively definable cultural norms and models as well as situationally evolving features. Intercultures are created as a result of blending cultural norms and models brought into the interaction from prior experience of interlocutors with features created ad hoc in the interaction.

Intercultural interactional data pose a special challenge for analysts for two reasons. First, the relatively short existence of the notion of "interculturality" makes it difficult to decide what to analyze, what to pay attention to, and what methods to use for analysis. Second, intercultural interaction necessitates the study of discourse segments rather than utterance analysis because coherence and creativity are clearly detectable at the discourse level. It is not through the individual utterance that language users demonstrate they are cooperative, but rather it is how they behave over the course of the conversation. I have discussed two analytical methods (conversational analysis and centering theory) that can be used to give us more insight into what exactly happens in intercultural encounters.

Further research should rely on these tools to investigate: how meaning is constructed and comprehended; what may cause misunderstandings; how prior context and actual situational context relate to each other in interaction; how the three types of salience (individual, collective, and situational) affect production and comprehension; how common ground is sought and created; and what role formulaic language plays in intercultural communication, to mention just a few out of many open questions that are expected to be answered in the paradigm of intercultural pragmatics.

## Related topics

Cognition; intercultural communication; interculturality; lingua franca; politeness; speech acts

## Further reading

Grundy, P. (2000) *Doing Pragmatics*, London: Arnold (book on basic concepts of pragmatics).

Kecskes, I. (2004) 'Lexical merging, conceptual blending, cultural crossing', *Intercultural Pragmatics*, 1(1): 1–26 (editorial in the first issue of the journal with key definitions).

Kiesling, F.S. and Bratt Paulston, C. (eds) (2004) *Intercultural Discourse and Communication: The Essential Readings*, London: Wiley-Blackwell (collection of core readings).

Moeschler, J. (2004) 'Intercultural pragmatics: a cognitive approach', *Intercultural Pragmatics*, 1(1): 49–70 (an introduction to the cognitive approach in intercultural pragmatics).

Wierzbicka, A. (1991) *Cross-Cultural Pragmatics: The Semantics of Human Interaction*, Berlin/New York: Mouton de Gruyter (seminal work on cross-cultural pragmatics).

## References

Austin, J.L. (1976) *How to Do Things with Words*, Oxford: Oxford University Press.

Bardovi-Harlig, K. and Hartford, B. (eds) (2005) *Interlanguage Pragmatics: Exploring Institutional Talk*, Mahwah, NJ: Erlbaum.

Barr, D.J. and Keysar, B. (2005) 'Making sense of how we make sense: the paradox of egocentrism in language use', in H.L. Colston and A.N. Kayz (eds) *Figurative Language Comprehension*, Mahwah, NJ: Lawrence Erlbaum, pp. 21–43.

Blum-Kulka, S., Blondheim, M., House, J., Kasper, G. and Wagner, J. (2008) 'Intercultural pragmatics, language and society', in P. van Sterkenburg (ed.) *Unity and Diversity of Languages*, Amsterdam/Philadelphia, PA: Benjamins, pp. 155–73.

Boxer, D. (2002) 'Discourse issues in cross-cultural pragmatics', *Annual Review of Applied Linguistics*, 22: 150–67.

Brown, P. and Levinson, S.C. (1987) *Politeness: Some Universals in Language Usage*, Cambridge: Cambridge University Press.

Bublitz, W. and Lenk, U. (1999) 'Disturbed coherence: "fill me in"', in W. Bublitz, U. Lenk and E. Ventola (eds) *Coherence in Spoken and Written Discourse*, Amsterdam/Philadelphia, PA: Benjamins, pp. 153–75.

Chaiklin, S. and Lave, J. (eds) (1993) *Understanding Practice: Perspectives on Activity and Context*, Cambridge: Cambridge University Press.

Coates, J. (1995) 'The negotiation of coherence in face-to-face interaction: some examples from the extreme bounds', in M.-A. Gernsbacher and T. Givon (eds) *Coherence in Spontaneous Text*, Amsterdam: John Benjamins, pp. 41–58.

Colston, H.L. (2005) 'On sociocultural and nonliteral: a synopsis and a prophesy', in H.L. Colston and A.N. Katz (eds) *Figurative Language Comprehension: Social and Cultural Influences*, Hillsdale, NJ: Lawrence Erlbaum, pp. 1–20.

Escandell-Vidal, V. (1996) 'Towards a cognitive approach to politeness', *Language Science*, 18: 629–50.

Evans, V. (2009) *How Words Mean: Lexical Concepts, Cognitive Models, and Meaning Construction*, Oxford: Oxford University Press.

Félix-Brasdefer, J.C. (2008) 'Sociopragmatic variation: six preferred responses in Mexican and Dominican Spanish', *Journal of Politeness Research*, 4(1): 81–110.

Gee, J.P. (1999). *An Introduction to Discourse Analysis*, London: Routledge.

Gibbs, R.W., Jr. (1999) *Intentions in the Experience of Meaning*, Cambridge: Cambridge University Press.

Giora, R. (1997) 'Understanding figurative and literal language: the graded salience hypothesis', *Cognitive Linguistics*, 8(3): 183–206.

——(2003) *On our Mind: Salience, Context and Figurative Language*, Oxford: Oxford University Press.

Goddard, C. and Wierzbicka, A. (1997) 'Discourse and culture', in T.A. van Dijk (ed.) *Discourse as Social Interaction*, London: Sage, pp. 231–57.

Grice, H.P. (1961) 'The causal theory of perception', *Proceedings of the Aristotelian Society*, Supplementary Volume 35: 121–52.

Grosz, B.J. and Sidner, C.L. (1986) 'Attention, intentions, and the structure of discourse', *Computational Linguistics*, 12(3): 175–204.

Grosz, B.J., Joshi, A.K. and Weinstein, S. (1995) 'Centering: a framework for modelling the local coherence of discourse', *Computational Linguistics*, 21(2): 203–25.

Gudykunst, W.B. and Mody, B. (2002) *Handbook of International and Intercultural Communication*, Thousand Oaks, CA: Sage, pp. 259–75.

Habermas, J. (1979) *Communication and the Evolution of Society*, Toronto: Beacon Press.

Hall, J.K., Cheng, A. and Carlson, M. (2006) 'Reconceptualizing multicompetence as a theory of language knowledge', *Applied Linguistics*, 27(2): 220–40.

Higgins, C. (ed.) (2007) 'A closer look at cultural differences, "interculturality" in talk-in interaction', *Pragmatics*, Special issue 17(1).

Hinnenkamp, V. (1995) 'Intercultural communication', in J. Verschueren, J.-O. Östman and J. Blommaert (eds) *Handbook of Pragmatics*, Amsterdam/Philadelphia, PA: John Benjamins.

House, J. (2000) 'Understanding misunderstanding: a pragmatic-discourse approach to analysing misman-aged rapport in talk across cultures', in H. Spencer-Oatey (ed.) *Culturally Speaking: Managing Rapport Through Talk Across Cultures*, London: Continuum, pp. 146–64.

——(2003) 'Misunderstanding in intercultural university encounters', in J. House, G. Kasper and S. Ross (eds) *Misunderstanding in Social Life: Discourse Approaches to Problematic Talk*, London: Longman, pp. 22–56.

Hu, J. and Pan, H. (2001) 'Processing local coherence of discourse in centering theory', proceedings of the 15th Pacific Asia Conference on Language, Information and Computation, Hong Kong: City University of Hong Kong.

Jary, M. (1998) 'Relevance theory and the communication of politeness', *Journal of Pragmatics*, 30: 1–19.

Kasper, G. (1996) 'The development of pragmatic competence', in E. Kellerman, B. Weltens and T. Bongaerts (eds) *EUROSLA 6: A Selection of Papers*, 55(2): 103–20.

——(1998) 'Interlanguage pragmatics', in H. Byrnes (ed.) *Learning Foreign and Second Languages: Perspectives in Research and Scholarship*, New York: The Modern Language Association of America, pp. 183–208.

——(2004) 'Speech acts in (inter)action: repeated question', *Intercultural Pragmatics*, 1(1): 125–35.

Kasper, G. and Blum-Kulka, S. (1993) 'Interlanguage pragmatics: an introduction', in G. Kasper and S. Blum-Kulka (eds) *Interlanguage Pragmatics*, Oxford: Oxford University Press, pp. 3–17.

Katz, A. (2005) 'Discourse and social–cultural factors in understanding nonliteral language', in H. Colston and A. Katz (eds) *Figurative Language Comprehension: Social and Cultural Influences*, Mahwah, NJ: Erlbaum and Associates, pp. 183–207.

Kecskes, I. (2004) 'Lexical merging, conceptual blending, cultural crossing', *Intercultural Pragmatics*, 1(1): 1–26.

——(2005) 'Pragmatics aspects of multilingualism', in K. Brown (ed.) *Encyclopedia of Language and Linguistics*, 2nd edn, Oxford: Elsevier Science.

——(2007) 'Formulaic language in English lingua franca', in I. Kecskes and L. Horn (eds) *Explorations in Pragmatics: Linguistic, Cognitive and Intercultural Aspects*, Berlin/New York: Mouton de Gruyter, pp. 191–219.

——(2008) 'Dueling context: a dynamic model of meaning', *Journal of Pragmatics*, 40(3): 385–406.

——(2010a) 'The paradox of communication: a socio-cognitive approach', *Pragmatics and Society*, 1(1): 50–73.

——(2010b) 'Dual and multilanguage systems', *International Journal of Multilingualism*, 7(2): 1–19.

——(2011) 'Intercultural pragmatics', in D. Archer and P. Grundy (eds) *Pragmatics Reader*, London: Routledge, pp. 371–87.

Kecskes, I. and Zhang, F. (2009) 'Activating, seeking and creating common ground: a socio-cognitive approach', *Pragmatics and Cognition*, 17(2): 331–55.

Keysar, B., and Barr, D.J. (2002) 'Self anchoring in conversation: why language users do not do what they "should"', in T. Gilovich, D.W. Griffin and D. Kahneman (eds) *Heuristics and Biases: The Psychology of Intuitive Judgment*, Cambridge: Cambridge University Press, pp. 150–66.

Keysar, B. and Bly, B. (1995) 'Intuitions of the transparency of idioms: can one keep a secret by spilling the beans?', *Journal of Memory and Language*, 34: 89–109.

Koole, T. and Thije, J.D. ten (1994) *The Construction of Intercultural Discourse: Team Discussions of Educational Advisers*, Amsterdam/Atlanta: RODOPI.

Leibniz, G.W. (1679; 2nd edn 1976) *Philosophical Papers and Letters*, Selection translated and edited with an introduction by L.E. Loemker, 2nd edn, Dordrecht, Holland/Boston, MA: D. Reidel.

Markee, N. (2000) *Conversation Analysis*, Mahwah, NJ: Lawrence Erlbaum.

Markee, N. and Kasper, G. (2004) 'Classroom talks: an introduction', *Modern Language Journal*, 88(4): 491–500.

Meier, A.J. (1997) 'Teaching the universals of politeness', *ELT Journal*, 51(1): 21–28.

Mori, J. (2003) 'The construction of interculturality: a study of initial encounters between American and Japanese students', *Research on Language and Social Interaction*, 36(2): 143–84.

Nishizaka, A. (1995) 'The interactive constitution of interculturality: how to be a Japanese with word?', *Human Studies*, 18: 301–26.

Paradis, M. (1995) *Aspects of Bilingual Aphasia*, London: Pergamon.

Philip, G. (2005) 'Figurative language and the advanced learner', *Research News: The Newsletter of the IATEFL Research SIG*, 16: 16–20.

Prodromou, L. (2008) *English as a Lingua Franca: A Corpus-Based Analysis*, London: Continuum.

Samovar, L.A. and Porter, R.E. (2001) *Intercultural Communication Reader*, New York: Thomas Learning Publications.

Selinker, L. (1972) 'Interlanguage', *International Review of Applied Linguistics in Language Teaching*, 10: 209–31.

Spencer-Oatey, H. (2000) 'Rapport management: a framework for analysis', in H. Spencer-Oatey (ed.) *Culturally Speaking: Managing Rapport Through Talk across Cultures*, London: Continuum, pp. 11–46.

Sperber, D. and Wilson, D. (1986; 2nd edn 1995) *Relevance: Communication and Cognition*, Oxford: Blackwell.

Thomas, J. (1983) 'Cross-cultural pragmatic failure', *Applied Linguistics*, 4(2), 91–112.

Ting-Toomey, S. (1999) *Communicating Across Cultures*, New York/London: The Guilford Press.

van Dijk, T.A. (2008) *Discourse and Context: A Sociocognitive Approach*, Cambridge: Cambridge University Press.

Violi, P. (2000) 'Prototypicality, typicality and context', in L. Albertazzi (ed.) *Meaning and Cognition*, Amsterdam: John Benjamins, pp. 103–23.

Walker, M.A. (1998) 'Centering, anaphora resolution, and discourse structure', in M.A. Walker, A.K. Joshi and E.F. Prince (eds) *Centering in Discourse*, Oxford: Oxford University Press, pp. 401–35.

Wenger, E. (2000) *Communities of Practice*, New York: Cambridge University Press.

Wierzbicka, A. (1985) 'Different cultures, different languages, different speech acts', *Journal of Pragmatics*, 9: 145–78.

Wilson, D. and Sperber, D. (2004) 'Relevance theory', in L.R. Horn and G. Ward (eds) *The Handbook of Pragmatics*, Oxford: Blackwell, pp. 607–32.

Winch, P. (1997) 'Can we understand ourselves?', *Philosophical Investigations*, 20(3): 193–204.

Wittgenstein, L. (2001) *Philosophical Investigations*, 3rd edn, Oxford/Malden, MA: Blackwell Publishers Ltd.

Wray, A. (2002) *Formulaic Language and the Lexicon*, Cambridge: Cambridge University Press.

# 5

# Conceptualizing intercultural (communicative) competence and intercultural citizenship

*Michael Byram*

## 1. Defining terms

As any literature and web search will show, terms such as 'interculturality', 'cross-cultural', 'transcultural' or 'intercultural' competence abound and are used in confusing ways. The phrase 'intercultural citizenship' is less widespread, but being used increasingly. Definitions are best seen in the light of usage, and this chapter does not attempt to present definitive dictionary-like definitions but to consider the questions that arise in the relationship between 'intercultural (communicative) competence' and 'intercultural citizenship' in theory and practice. The first stage examines the notion of 'interculturality' before moving to matters of 'competence' as a means of analysing the state of being intercultural and of being a citizen.

## 2. Being and acting interculturally

A useful starting point is to consider linguistic competence and, in particular, bilingualism, not least because research on and analysis of bilingualism has a much longer history and also because linguistic competence and cultural competence are often assumed to be related.

Definitions of being bilingual range from minimum ability to say something in two or more languages[1] to the ability to be accepted, or 'pass', as a native speaker in two or more languages. Passing as a native speaker linguistically implies, however, also being seen or identified as someone who 'fits in' to a group of native speakers in terms of behaviour, of appearance, of opinions and beliefs, in short, of culture. Being a bilingual therefore implies being bicultural, either in a minimal sense corresponding to minimal bilingualism, or in the maximal sense of being accepted as a 'native' of two language groups who speak two different languages, and of identifying with them. There is, however, remarkably little research literature on being bicultural in this sense.

Bilingual people may simply switch from one language to the other according to the circumstances and the group in which they find themselves, thus keeping their languages and identifications with two groups separate. On the other hand, they may also act as interpreters and translators between the groups whose languages they speak. They can do this even if they only have minimal bilingual ability and, in some circumstances, minimal ability is crucial; many people who think they do not speak a language discover this when there are no other options except to use the little they know to interpret. At this point, bilingual people find themselves 'between' languages, and between the cultures of the people for whom they are interpreting or translating. If they do this on an occasional basis and in an amateur way, they often assume that what one person says and the behaviours and beliefs they express can be transferred whole and in a simple one-to-one relationship to the language and behaviour and belief systems of the other. On the other hand, professional interpreters and translators are aware that this is not the case and that sometimes they cannot transfer the whole or that they have to give some further explanation if they are to do so. Interpreters under pressure of time often have to settle for transferring less than the whole, whereas translators, with the luxury of the written language and the time to consult works of reference and other sources, may add footnotes to their text or use other devices such as paraphrase.

The ability to act between languages and cultures in this way is a competence to which we shall return. The consequences of this activity – let us call it the state of 'being intercultural' – for the individual concerned are also important. For it may be the case that being positioned between two individuals or groups gives a perspective on the languages and cultures of each that is different from identifying with one or switching between two without taking note of the relationships between them. Being intercultural and the state of 'interculturality' may follow from acting interculturally, and is different from being bilingual/bicultural. If we think taking a third perspective in this way is worthwhile, perhaps because it allows deeper understanding, then we might wish to encourage people who are bilingual and bicultural, even to only a minimal degree, to become intercultural. We might then include this as one of the purposes of the teaching of languages as an educational endeavour, in whatever location or institution people are taught. In short, we might then embrace the notion of 'interculturalism', i.e. a belief in the value of being and acting as an intercultural person.

Like other '-isms', interculturalism is an ideology or belief system. It has recently, in the European context at least, been contrasted with 'multiculturalism', which is seen, in a negative light, as a belief in encouraging different social groups with different languages and cultures to live side by side in a spirit of mutual acceptance, each remaining within their own language and culture and essentially monolingual. The ideology of multiculturalism is thought to have led to problems because groups living side by side cannot simply ignore each other and, particularly when resources such as housing and jobs are scarce, they compete with each other in often aggressive ways. Interculturalism, on the other hand, encourages 'dialogue' among groups, and this became the basis for the promotion from 2008, in the European Year of Intercultural Dialogue, of an interpretation of interculturality that specifically builds on dialogue. The Council of Europe's White Paper on Intercultural Dialogue argues that:

> [I]ntercultural dialogue ( … ) allows us to prevent ethnic, religious, linguistic and cultural divides. It enables us to move forward together, to deal with our different identities constructively and democratically on the basis of shared universal values.
>
> *Council of Europe (2008: 2)*

However, dialogue presupposes bilingualism and biculturalism, to some degree, in at least some members of each group, and preferably in all, and this is not fully recognized in the White Paper. Dialogue also implies that bilingual and bicultural people act in intercultural ways as interpreters or translators – or even as 'mediators' – and thereby become intercultural people. The notion of 'mediator' becomes relevant particularly when there is a potential conflict among groups, but it is also a more accurate term in most 'in-between' situations because there are often linguistic and cultural differences or conflicting perspectives that the intercultural person has to explain to each group from his/her third place perspective.

Ultimately, however, the intercultural person depends on those for whom they are mediating to resolve the 'conflict' themselves, whether this is a matter of 'mere' misunderstanding of meanings or an actual physical conflict. The intercultural person's action is limited to the act of mediating as a neutral agent, unless they take a different but related role of intercultural citizen, as we shall see below.

## 3. Intercultural 'communicative' competence

As Fleming (2009) says, the term 'competence' has had a chequered history but can usefully be adopted to refer to observable behaviours as well as to the implicit understandings within them. His examples demonstrate the flexibility of the concept:

> For example, a dental nurse who has been declared competent in being 'able to sterilise equipment' must know the technical procedures but he must also know that if he drops the implement in the dirt after sterilisation he must begin the process all over again. This implies understanding of process and purpose which is not necessarily made explicit in the performance statement itself ( ... ). Similarly, it is fairly clear that to judge that a trainee teacher is 'able to plan lessons' implies that he has a degree of understanding of what is involved. The need for understanding may not always be spelled out, but the assumption is that it can be unpacked from the performance statement.
>
> *Fleming (2009: 7)*

The emphasis on behaviours as indicators of understanding and as performance skills would, in the same vein, allow us to observe and to measure people's interculturality as a state of mind, as well as their ability to act interculturally. Intercultural competence is increasingly used as a concept to plan and evaluate learning and teaching as the more general change to using competences has taken place throughout formal education.

Thus far, we have focused on people acting as mediators among groups with different languages and cultures. A fine-grained analysis would show that different groups apparently speaking the same language also have different discourses, and that intercultural mediation is just as relevant here as when languages and cultures are visibly and obviously different. Families, for example, have their own family language – often with specific words or expressions – in which they refer to their shared knowledge and past. In this sense, a mediator between two families might have to explain the one to the other. The fact that they believe they speak the same language, where there is indeed much in common, would make the task of the mediator, in fact, more difficult than when languages are obviously different, because mediation would require sensitivity to fine-grained differences. Sometimes indeed, the capacity to speak two varieties of 'the same' language is referred to as being bilingual, and this adds a dimension to bilinguality that needs to be recognized, just as this kind of example adds a dimension to interculturality.

Where two groups have languages and cultures that are mutually incomprehensible,[2] the linguistic competences of the mediator are of a different kind. The mediator needs to be bilingual (and bicultural) in the ordinary sense. It is to emphasize this fact that the distinction is made between 'intercultural competence' and 'intercultural (communicative) competence', the latter referring to mediation between mutually incomprehensible languages. The latter combines the use in recent decades of the concept of 'communicative competence' in another language – with emphasis on the ability to use a language not only with correct application of knowledge of its grammar but also in socially appropriate ways (Savignon 2004; Chapter 24, this volume) – with 'intercultural competence'. It also recognizes the importance of the relationship between language and culture.

The nature of that relationship is, however, not simple. It has been much debated since the first part of the nineteenth century when Humboldt drew specific attention to it. Risager's (2006) comprehensive and authoritative analysis starting from Agar's notion of 'languaculture' has shown that a language spoken by a specific group of people – be they 'native speakers' or not – is not necessarily tied to a specific set of beliefs, values and behaviours, a specific culture. Furthermore, in foreign language use, the relationship between a language and the culture it embodies may be highly complex, as Risager shows in her example:

> The language in question is used with contributions from the languacultures of *other* languages. So there is a kind of language mix in the linguistic resources that, for example, makes use of the expression side of the one language (the target language) and of the content side of the other language (the first language). When one migrates to another country, one takes this particular, more or less individual, language mix with one. This means that the linguistic flows and languacultural flows do not move along precisely the same paths. If I, with Danish as my first language, travel round the world, I take my Danish idiolect with me, with the personal languaculture I have developed during my life. But I also take my special forms of English, French and German with me – the languages I have learnt as foreign languages. My foreign language resources are, without a doubt, influenced to a great extent by my Danish languaculture. So I contribute to the spreading of Danish languaculture, but to a lesser extent to the spreading of English, French and German languaculture.
>
> *Risager (2006: 134)*

However, this complexity is difficult to handle in pedagogical terms and, for teaching purposes, which requires a gradual development from initial simplification to increasing complexity, it is best to focus on one languaculture and to help learners to develop their linguistic and cultural competences with one focus. In this way, learners can acquire bilingual and bicultural competences in a systematic way, even though the constant interplay between languacultures (linguacultures) that Risager describes will be the inevitable experience of language in use. Learners also acquire a systematic way of developing intercultural competences by concentrating on the relationships between their own languaculture and one other. At the same time, they develop competences that are transferable to other languacultures they may learn subsequently.

Before we can develop further what the components of intercultural competence are, it is relevant to clarify the relationship of the person with intercultural competence to the native speaker. As said earlier, the ways in which the term 'bilingual' is used include the notion that individuals can pass for and identify themselves as a native speaker[3] in two or more languages. The aim that learners of another language should become, or attempt to become, native speakers has long dominated language teaching and been implanted in the minds of most language learners. Whatever the merits of this aim with respect to mastery of the grammar and phonetics of a language, having native speaker competence is not sufficient for the mediator with the third perspective on two or more languacultures. It is not even necessary. A mediator can be successful without native speaker language competence. It is for this reason that the phrase 'intercultural speaker' was coined (Byram 2008: 57–77) to indicate that intercultural competence is worthwhile in itself and should not be considered a poor imitation of native speaker competence. The intercultural speaker needs intercultural communicative competence, i.e. both intercultural competence and linguist/communicative competence, in any task of mediation where two distinct languacultures are present, and this is something different from and not comparable with the competence of the native speaker.

It is therefore surprising that many attempts to conceptualize and model the competences needed by those who wish to be and act interculturally do not take account of linguistic competence. In a major review of models of intercultural competence, Spitzberg and Changnon (2009: 10) decided to classify models as 'compositional, co-orientational, developmental, adaptational, and causal process'. It is only in the 'co-orientational' models 'devoted to conceptualising the interactional achievement of intercultural understanding' that linguistic competences are found. Other types of models are primarily concerned with psychological traits, with the success of adaptation to new circumstances, to change over time, and are often focused on describing the processes involved in longer or shorter sojourns in an environment that is experienced as culturally and perhaps linguistically different and challenging. Furthermore, in most models, including some they categorize as 'co-orientational', the relationships described are between two people or groups. The notion of a third party with a third perspective – the intercultural speaker – is not included.

## 4. Citizenship

Contrary to many of the models Spitzberg and Changnon analyse, the concept of the intercultural speaker was developed in the context of specifying competences for planning learning and teaching in a general education system, rather than for the specific preparation of people for living in a new environment. In the latter case, preparation may include acquiring the knowledge and other competences expected of residents in another country. Indeed, in the face of contemporary migration, many states require this, and include linguistic competence as a *sine qua non* of permission to stay and reside. There is often an assumption, implicit or explicit, that new residents should attempt to imitate the natives of the state in a way parallel to the expectations of language learners that they imitate native speakers. The futility of this aim – and the inbuilt failure awaiting language learners and new residents – is recognized even less in the expectations placed on new citizens than in those language teachers place on their learners, and is a major weakness of many concepts of citizenship used in processes of accepting or rejecting immigrants to a country; however, this is a point we cannot pursue in depth here.

On the other hand, just as it is useful to acknowledge that people can be bilingual and bicultural in ways that are different from being and acting as if they were two native speakers of two languacultures within the same person, it is also possible to conceive competence and identification with citizenship in two different states as being different from being two different citizens within the same person.[4] In an educational context, where citizenship is systematically learnt as both competence and identification, this would mean teaching citizenship of two or more states, parallel to the teaching of the national language and foreign languages. At the moment, this is unlikely to happen in most states where, historically and contemporarily, 'our' schooling is seen as necessarily focused on creating citizenship of 'our' state. This has been the case since the inception of state-supported schools in Europe and America in the nineteenth century, and is evident in the contemporary world, sometimes in virulent forms, wherever new states appear. As Heater (2004: 152) points out, the phrase 'totalitarian citizenship education' may appear to be an oxymoron but nonetheless exists in the world. Heater discusses Nazi Germany and the Soviet Union. Contemporary cases do not yet appear except in travel literature, such as the description of nation-building in Turkmenistan around the personality cult of the president and his literary works on which students take compulsory tests (Brummell 2005: 13).

Any attempt to develop citizenship competences for other states would be seen, even in less virulent cases, as subversive to the 'nation-state', which provides and depends on schooling for the development of future citizens. Teaching of another language, although comparable in principle, has never been seen as subversive, except in times of (hot or cold) war, when the language of the enemy is often removed from schools. Even when the teaching of another language involves taking seriously the notion of a languaculture and learning (about) different values, beliefs and behaviours, the threat to identification with the dominant values, beliefs and behaviours purveyed by schooling is not felt to be significant. In fact, it is often stated, with hope rather than evidence, that learning (about) other cultures will strengthen commitment to the culture of the state, as this statement from the Norwegian curriculum claims:

> By learning languages, pupils have the opportunity to become familiar with other cultures. Such insight provides the basis for respect and increased tolerance, and contributes to other ways of thinking and broadens pupils' understanding of their own cultural belonging. In this way pupils' own identity is strengthened.
>
> *www.utdanningsdirektoratet.no/dav/78FB8D6918.PDF (accessed 5 January 2005)*

The significance of 'learning *about*' rather than simply 'learning' in all this is that the former does not involve any sense of identification with the values, beliefs and behaviours of other languacultures. Furthermore, 'learning about' continues to be the dominant mode of engagement with other cultures in schools, whereas 'learning' other values, beliefs and behaviours would involve some degree of identification. Where this experience introduces learners to phenomena that conflict with existing values, beliefs and behaviours already acquired in their home and wider social environment, it could be the basis of reappraisal of 'the familiar' in the light of 'the strange'.[5]

Parallel to the misconceived image of 'the' native speaker of language, the concept of 'the' citizen of the state implies a unitary and uniform set of expectations of what each is, and can do. However, there is increasing recognition by the vast majority of states that, although they have one dominant social group on which expectations are based and which is the model for education and citizenship, they also have within their borders many other groups with their own vision of what citizenship entails. This recognition has been formalized in some countries where the rights of minorities to be different while continuing to be full citizens are acknowledged in law and international convention. In these circumstances, the relationships among groups are crucial and the ability of individuals and groups to live and interact with individuals and groups of other identifications has been described as 'intercultural citizenship':

> the idea of intercultural citizenship points to the building of political and social institutions by which culturally diverse communities within a multiethnic and multilingual nation can solve their differences democratically by consensus without tearing apart the common structures and values or having to abandon their particular cultural identities, such as language, culture and ethnicity.
>
> *Stavenhagen (2008: 176)*

The notion is developed, it is claimed, from the UNESCO definition of interculturality, i.e. 'the existence and equitable interaction of diverse cultures and the possibility of generating shared cultural expressions through dialogue and mutual respect' (quoted in Stavenhagen 2008: 175) – but the focus in the definition of intercultural citizenship limits the scope of the definition to interculturality within the limits of the state. Crucially, there is an assumption, as with some discussions of intercultural competence, that all those engaging in intercultural citizenship will speak the same language.

## 5. Intercultural (communicative) competence and intercultural citizenship

A contrasting concept of intercultural citizenship is not confined to dialogue and action with other groups within a state. It takes into account the permeability of state frontiers, whether it is formalized, as in the European Union (EU), or not. Within the EU, the right to reside and work in any member state for citizens of the states of the EU reduces the significance of frontiers, although the presence of many languages – and the experience citizens have of other langua-cultures as they move from country to country – is a constant reminder that there are many groups within Europe, just as there are many groups within every member state. The concept of intercultural citizenship within a state can thus be extended to the whole EU, but only if the significance of communicative competence is recognized.

In other cases, there is no formal recognition of the permeability of frontiers. Nonetheless, mobility across frontiers, both physical and virtual, is constant. Individuals may identify with their national (state) group, but also with international groups to which they belong. They may even identify with the whole of humanity and see themselves as 'global' or 'world' or 'cosmopolitan' citizens (Osler and Starkey 2005); the notion of cosmopolitanism has a long pedigree (Carter 2001; Heater 2004). These other concepts of supranational citizenship, unlike European citizenship, are not legal concepts but aspirations to identification with supranational communities.

The question then arises as to the concept of (supranational) citizenship itself and the role of schooling. For, just as in the early stages of schooling for citizenship in a state, the role of schooling in creating or developing citizenship beyond the state is crucial. Just as the people in nineteenth-century France, for example, did not know they were French until they went to school (and, for men, served in the army), similarly today schooling can – and perhaps should – create a sense of citizenship beyond the state.

How this might be done can be seen from current education for citizenship. As Himmelmann (2006) has shown, there is much coincidence in citizenship education in different countries, at least in those that are democratic. There is some focus on knowledge about the society and its elements and processes.[6] There is also some focus on attitudes and identification, which again may be more or less explicit.[7] Third, this emphasis on 'active' citizenship and activity implies certain competences in living and interacting together to achieve some aims in the development of society. This is encapsulated, for example, in the English National Curriculum where the aims of education for citizenship are described as:

1. Social and moral responsibility: Pupils learning – from the very beginning – self-confidence and socially and morally responsible behaviour both in and beyond the classroom, towards those in authority and towards each other.
2. Community involvement: Pupils learning about becoming helpfully involved in the life and concerns of their neighbourhood and communities, including learning through community involvement and service to the community.

3. Political literacy: Pupils learning about the institutions, problems and practices of our democracy and how to make themselves effective in the life of the nation, locally, regionally and nationally through skills and values as well as knowledge – a concept wider than political knowledge alone.

The outcomes of citizenship education are then summarized in the following terms:

> Pupils develop skills of enquiry, communication, participation and responsible action … through creating links between pupils' learning in the classroom and activities that take place across the school, in the community and the wider world.
>
> *www.dfes.gov.uk/citizenship/section.cfm?sectionId=3& hierachy=1.3*
> *(accessed 5 December 2006)*

What is particularly noticeable here is the limitation of activity to levels of society, to sense of community, which are within the state borders, with a minimal reference to 'the wider world'. And yet it is precisely in this wider world that people live today.

There are many similarities among the elements of citizenship and those of the intercultural speaker, as we have shown in detail elsewhere (Byram 2008). There are also differences. Models of citizenship tacitly assume that communication with fellow citizens is linguistically and culturally unproblematic. Models of intercultural competence and the concept of the intercultural speaker, as stated earlier, limit the activity of the individual to mediation. Intercultural citizenship goes beyond this, involving both activity with other people in the world and the competences required for dialogue with people of other languacultures.

Education for active citizenship beyond the constraints of the state would require competences for interaction with people of other languacultures. Intercultural citizenship would involve not only the competences of citizenship itself, as set out, for example, by Himmelmann (2003) and writers such as Audigier (1998), Duer *et al.* (2000) and Birzea (2000) at the Council of Europe, but also the competences of intercultural communication.

## 6. Theory and practice

Acting together with other people can, historically, take two forms, at least in the European tradition. Gellner (1998) refers to Tönnies' well-established distinction between an organic togetherness of the *Gemeinschaft* (community) and the tendency to rationalist individualism of the *Gesellschaft* (society), and argues that we need a middle way between the conservatism and the tendency to fascism of the *Gemeinschaft* and the individualism of the *Gesellschaft* which ignores the need for human comity. His suggestion that we need 'cultural pluralist nationalism and ( … ) political internationalism' (Gellner 1998: 187) is an attempt to combine a sense of belonging and identification with the promotion of political activity both nationally and internationally. An intercultural citizen would meet this intention as he/she is someone who can identify with a group of people who are of different languacultures but wish to act together.

Action can take two forms nationally: within the political system of the state or within civil society, 'the whole body social, namely the private sector, the market, and non-governmental organisations (NGOs)' (Wicht 2004: 202). The question then arises how action may take place internationally, as civil societies are usually constrained by the borders of the state, working in parallel with the state. However, transnational communities are evolving that take on the functions of civil society organisms, and simultaneously offer the possibility of identifying with social groups that are international. Such groups may be permanent, but need not be so. They may form around a specific issue in order to promote activity to resolve a problem. Teachers may, for example, encourage their learners to form an international group to discuss and take action on topics of mutual interest. Modern technologies allow individuals to form networks across international boundaries with great ease.

Networks remain alive only as long as communications pass along their connections, and this again brings us to the question of intercultural communicative competence. Language choices are crucial. Shall there be one or many? Are the network members bilingual and bicultural? Are they able to build on the intercomprehension of the languages they speak? Do they need a lingua franca where nobody claims to be a native speaker? Which lingua franca shall be used?

Whatever the choices made, our earlier argument suggests that intercultural competence will be important. Risager (2006; Chapter 6, this volume) argues that 'linguistic practice in a foreign language will typically show a blend of languaculture from both the (target) language and the learners' first language'. Where two or more people are using the target language as a lingua franca, this implies that there will be a common ground in the lingua franca to which both participants bring their own blend from their first language; they will then need their intercultural competence to tease out their mutual understanding of their original langua-cultures on the basis of their shared understanding of the lingua franca. This is to assume that all have learnt about a languaculture from which the lingua franca has been derived; for example, that all have learnt the languaculture of France if French is the lingua franca. The fact that French is the languaculture of other native speaker countries complicates matters in principle but, in practice, the dominance of France in *francophonie* probably means that it is the target languaculture for all learners of French.

The same cannot be said of English where several countries – the UK, the USA, Australia and so on – might be the reference point, the target languaculture. Empirical research in which lingua franca speakers of English from Thailand and Malaysia discussed topics of mutual interest shows that 'successful intercultural communication ( … ) cannot take place without a *similarity in connotative meaning* between interlocutors in relation to key words and phrases' (Taylor 2006: 257; our emphasis). Unfortunately, the acquisition of connotative meaning is haphazard and therefore unlikely to be shared, leading to a stronger risk of misunderstanding in any civil society network. Even though Meierkord (2002) argues that lingua franca speakers are likely to help each other and seek mutual understanding, her database is from face-to-face interactions, and these conclusions may not extend to electronic networks. Taylor's (2006) findings therefore have implications for teaching, e.g. that there should be a systematic approach not only to the teaching of denotative meanings but also of connotations.

The practical implications of intercultural citizenship may be handled by individuals participating in international civil society activities as they arise. On the other hand, the teaching and learning process in formal education has the potential to prepare learners for practical matters: to ensure that lingua franca users are aware of potential misunderstandings and that they develop strategies suitable to the media they are using to overcome problems that arise. Second, and crucially, teachers may encourage learners to become active as intercultural citizens. This means that educators of all kinds take the responsibility for stimulating activity in the community and society around them, whether at local, regional, national or international level. The principles of education for citizenship require this, as can be seen in the curriculum documents from many national education systems, although they usually encourage activity only within the frontiers of the state. The concept of international civil society is not found in national curricula. As pointed out earlier, in the context of education for citizenship, there is little or no attention to differences and potential difficulties of diverse languacultures. The practical solution might be for cooperation between teachers of citizenship and teachers of languacultures.

A proposal to facilitate such cooperation has been made in Byram (2008) with a 'framework for political and language education' where the complementarity of the orientations and objectives of citizenship and language education is identified as a basis for planning teaching and learning. This is summarized in four axioms of education for intercultural citizenship (especially in the final one).

Intercultural citizenship education involves:

- causing/facilitating intercultural citizenship experience, and analysis and reflection on it and on the possibility of further social and/or political activity, i.e. activity that involves working with others to achieve an agreed end;
- creating learning/change in the individual: cognitive, attitudinal, behavioural change; change in self-perception; change in relationships with others (i.e. people of different social groups); change that is based in the particular but is related to the universal.

*Byram (2008: 187)*

It is clear from this and in particular from the notion of 'causing/facilitating. ... reflection. ... on the possibility of further social and/or political activity' that teachers' responsibilities are complex and involve commitment beyond the traditions and conventions of many education systems hitherto. Some teachers may find this too demanding; others may wish to 'cause activity' in more direct ways than simply stimulating reflection on its possibility.

The training for teachers of intercultural citizenship has yet to be developed, as have the teaching materials to support them. The readiness of teachers to be involved in intercultural citizenship education was investigated in the Interact Project (Guilherme *et al.* 2007). The conclusions revealed that gaps in this area were 'widespread and noticeable' because the great majority of the teachers consulted 'had not received academic or pre-service education programmes focused on intercultural citizenship education' (p. 101). It is also disappointing that Ministry of Education officials in three countries (England, Spain and Portugal) but not in a fourth (Denmark) give higher priority to school achievement results, as determined in international comparisons, than to the development of intercultural competence as an educational purpose for all pupils. The value of international studies as a basis for drawing attention to citizenship education is evident from this. However, such studies do not yet pay attention to the concept of intercultural citizenship (e.g. Grossman *et al.* 2008; Schweisfurth *et al.* 2002; Zajda *et al.* 2009).

As for the development of materials for the teaching and assessment of intercultural citizenship competences, there is clearly a need to create materials that are founded on a thorough theoretical basis combining intercultural competence and a focus upon active citizenship. The *Autobiography of Intercultural Encounters* (www.coe.int/lang) is an attempt to do this. It is based on a model of intercultural citizenship that defines and describes competences required to be successful as an active citizen, as a social agent in an intercultural context. It is an instrument for self-analysis and evaluation by individuals who have had intercultural experiences that have been significant for them. It may be used by individuals autonomously, but can also be introduced and used as a pedagogical instrument by teachers and other educators. The characteristics and competences needed are listed in the Notes for Facilitators as follows:

Attitudes and feelings

- Acknowledging the identities of others: noticing how others have different identities and accepting their values and insights.
- Respecting otherness: showing curiosity about others and being willing to question what is usually taken for granted and viewed as 'normal'.

- Having empathy: being able to take someone else's perspective, to imagine their thoughts and feelings.
- Identifying positive and negative emotions and relating them to attitudes and knowledge.

Behaviour

- Being flexible: adapting one's behaviour to new situations and to what other people expect.
- Being sensitive to ways of communicating: recognising different ways of speaking and other forms of communication that exist in other languages or other ways of using the same language.

Knowledge and skills

- Having knowledge about other people: knowing facts about people whom one meets, and knowing how and why they are what they are.
- Discovering knowledge: using certain skills to find out about people one meets, by asking questions, seeking out information, and using these skills in real-time encounters.
- Interpreting and relating: understanding people or places or things by comparing them to familiar people, places, things in one's own environment, seeing similarities and differences.
- Being critical: noticing how other people think and act and distancing oneself from one's own ways of thinking and acting, and being able to explain one's judgements about both.
- Becoming aware of one's own assumptions, preconceptions, stereotypes and prejudices.

Action

- Taking action: as a consequence of all the rest, being willing and able to become involved with other people in making things different and better.

On the basis of this model, users of the *Autobiography* are led through a series of questions and stimuli to help them analyse their intercultural experience from a number of perspectives, to reflect on its meaning for them and to consider what action to take as a consequence. The main headings of Attitudes and feelings, Behaviour, Knowledge and skills are similar to other descriptions of intercultural competence, but the final heading, Action, is crucial. It refers to the competences of active citizenship, and in the *Autobiography*, it is realized as a series of questions that encourage users to take action as a consequence of their analysis and reflection. Action may be simply informing someone else about the encounter, but it may also be more complex and involve, for example, a decision to become involved in civil society organizations. It encourages activity in the world, but it leaves open the question of whether that activity should be together with others, in an international network, acting at a level that ignores the limitations of national frontiers.

## Related topics

Biculturalism; bilingualism; citizenship; cosmopolitanism; identity; intercultural speaker; interculturality, languaculture; third place

## Further reading

Byram, M. (2008) *From Foreign Language Education to Education for Intercultural Citizenship*, Clevedon: Multilingual Matters (a presentation of the relationship of competences in a foreign language and in citizenship).

Carter, A. (2001) *The Political Theory of Global Citizenship*, London: Routledge (a theoretical and philosophical analysis of concepts of citizenship).
Deardorff, D.K. (ed.) (2009) *The SAGE Handbook of Intercultural Competence*, Thousand Oaks, CA: Sage (essential introductory chapters on the concept of interculturality).
Heater, D. (2004) *A History of Education for Citizenship*, London: Routledge (an introduction to the concept of citizenship education and its evolution).

## Notes

1 Those who speak more than two languages are variously called multilingual or plurilingual, or the term 'bilingual' is used to cover all cases, on the grounds that the phenomenon is the same irrespective of the number of languages. Here, for the sake of clarity, we shall refer to individuals who speak and understand two languages at some level of competence.

2 The fact that some languages are intercomprehensible because they are related, and speakers of one can to some degree, and especially with training, understand speakers of another introduces a complicating factor to the discussion. For clarity's sake, we will not pursue this dimension in any detail here.

3 The concept of native speaker is itself complex, as Davies (2003) has said. It is used here, as Davies argues, as a necessary if somewhat mythical concept that is widely used in both professional and everyday discourse.

4 Many states, although not all, allow their citizens to have two citizenships, two passports, but this implies that they keep their two citizenships as separate entities in their lives.

5 The special case of education for European citizenship that is expected to develop identification with another entity than the state, in addition to and not in conflict with national identity, cannot be explored in detail here.

6 Although what is to be learnt may not be fully specified in curricula, the tests that new citizens have to pass are an indication of what is expected by authorities.

7 An example of explicit statements of attitude and identification can be found in Singaporean documents for citizenship education, which describe the aims of 'National Education' as:

- First, to develop an *awareness of facts, circumstances and opportunities* facing Singapore so that they [students] will be able to make decisions for their future with conviction and realism.
- Second, to develop a *sense of emotional belonging and commitment* to the community and nation so that they will stay and fight when the odds are against us.

*www.moe.gov.sg/ne/aboutne/approach.htm (accessed 4 December 2006)*
*(emphasis in original)*

## References

Audigier, F. (1998) *Basic Concepts and Core Competences of Education for Democratic Citizenship*, (DECS/CIT (98) 35), Strasbourg: Council of Europe.
Birzea, C. (2000) *Education for Democratic Citizenship: A Lifelong Learning Perspective*, (DG IV/ EDU/ CIT (2000) 21), Strasbourg: Council of Europe.
Brummell, P. (2005) *Turkmenistan*, London: Bradt.
Byram, M. (2008) *From Foreign Language Education to Education for Intercultural Citizenship*, Clevedon: Multilingual Matters.
Carter, A. (2001) *The Political Theory of Global Citizenship*, London: Routledge.
Council of Europe (2008) *White Paper on Intercultural Dialogue*, Strasbourg: Council of Europe.
Davies, A. (2003) *The Native Speaker: Myth and Reality*, Clevedon: Multilingual Matters.
Duer, K., Spajic-Vrkaš, V. and Martins, I.F. (2000) *Strategies for Learning Democratic Citizenship*, (DECS/ EDU/ CIT, 2000, 16), Strasbourg: Council of Europe.
Fleming, M. (2009) 'The challenge of "competence"', in A. Hu and M. Byram (eds) *Interkulturelle Kompetenz und fremdsprachliches Lernen. Modelle Empirie Evaluation*, Tübingen: Gunter Narr.
Gellner, E. (1998) *Nations and Nationalism*, Ithaca, NY: Cornell University Press.
Grossman, D.L., Lee, W.O. and Kennedy, K.J. (eds) (2008) *Citizenship Curriculum in Asia and the Pacific*, Hong Kong: Comparative Education Research Center, The University of Hong Kong.
Guilherme, M., Pureza, J.M., Osler, A., Starkey, H., Meyer, B. and Haas, C. Interact Project Final Report (2007) *Intercultural Active Citizenship Education*. Online. Available: www.ces.uc.pt/interact/documents/final_activity_report.pdf (accessed 4 June 2007).

Heater, D. (2004) *A History of Education for Citizenship*, London: Routledge.

Himmelmann, G. (2003) '*Zukunft, Fachidentität und Standards der politischen Bildung*', unpublished manuscript. Braunschweig: TU Braunschweig, Institut für Sozialwissenschaften.

——(2006) 'Concepts and issues in citizenship education: a comparative study of Germany, Britain and the USA', in G. Alred, M. Byram and M. Fleming (eds) *Education for Intercultural Citizenship: Concepts and Comparisons*, Clevedon: Multilingual Matters, pp. 69–85.

Meierkord, C. (2002) '"Language stripped bare" or "linguistic masala"? culture in lingua franca conversation', in K. Knapp and C. Meierkord (eds) *Lingua Franca Communication*, Frankfurt: Peter Lang, pp. 109–34.

Osler, A. and Starkey, H. (2005) *Changing Citizenship: Democracy and inclusion in Education*, Maidenhead: Open University Press.

Risager, K. (2006) *Language and Culture: Global Flows and Local Complexity*, Clevedon: Multilingual Matters.

Savignon, S. (2004) 'Communicative language teaching,' in M. Byram (ed.) *The Routledge Encyclopedia of Language Teaching and Learning*, London: Routledge, pp.124–29.

Schweisfurth, M., Davies, L. and Harber, C. (eds) (2002) *Learning Democracy and Citizenship: International Experiences*, Oxford: Symposium Books.

Spitzberg, B.H. and Changnon, G. (2009) 'Conceptualizing intercultural competence', in D.K. Deardorff (ed.) *The SAGE Handbook of Intercultural Competence*, Thousand Oaks, CA: Sage, pp. 2–52.

Stavenhagen, R. (2008) 'Building intercultural citizenship through education: a human rights approach', *European Journal of Education*, 43(2): 161–79.

Taylor, R. (2006) 'Investigating the role of connotation in communication and miscommunication within English as a lingua franca and consequent implications for teaching', unpublished PhD thesis, University of Durham, UK.

Wicht, B. (2004). 'Civil society or "everyone for themselves"? Culture as an agent for democracy in Europe'. Online. Available: www.coe.int/e/cultural-cooperation/education/E.D.C. (accessed 6 October 2004).

Zajda, J., Daun, H. and Saha, L.J. (2009) *Nation-building, Identity and Citizenship Education: Cross-cultural Perspectives*, Heidelberg: Springer.

# Section II
# Core themes and issues
## Verbal/nonverbal communication and culture

# 6

# Linguaculture and transnationality

## The cultural dimensions of language

*Karen Risager*

## 1. Introduction

The concept of linguaculture (or languaculture) is an offshoot of a cultural movement originating in the German-speaking areas of Europe at the end of the eighteenth century. This movement emphasized that language should be seen as intimately related to nation, people, and culture. During the nineteenth century, this idea gained a National–Romantic form stressing the intimate relations between the national language and the national culture. Since the 1990s, however, this national paradigm has been questioned because of the rise of interest in globalization and transnationality, and this has led to a rethinking of the relationship between language and culture.

The concept of linguaculture has been an important element in this recent development. It was invented around 1989 as a new term by linguistic anthropologists who saw it as a useful tool for a more precise analysis of the interface between language and culture. Since then, the term has been spreading in various fields of language studies such as language teaching and learning, and sociocultural linguistics.

This chapter presents some historical perspectives on the idea of an intimate relationship between language and culture, and then focuses on the current research strands that use the term linguaculture/languaculture.[1]

## 2. Historical perspectives

### The Herder/Humboldt tradition

Johann Gottfried von Herder was the first to formulate the idea of an intimate relationship between language and nation and—in a certain sense—culture. He was a central figure in connection with the emerging German national consciousness among the German-speaking liberal bourgeoisie and intellectuals in the period known in literary and cultural history as the *Sturm-und-Drang* period (1765–85). It is important to note that the concepts of culture and nation had a different content then than they have today. The concept of culture in Herder's age was partly an individual and partly a collective concept, and both were hierarchical: one generally distinguished between individuals/peoples who had culture and individuals/peoples who did not.

Herder was perhaps the first person to de-hierarchize the concept of culture. The word nation was almost synonymous with the word people (*Volk*), and it did not then have the political meaning it was to acquire with the French Revolution. The population of the entire world was seen as consisting of peoples/nations. The concept of nation at the time had, then, similarities with the present concept "ethnic group"/"ethnie".

Herder expressed a consistently humanist conception of history and humanity. For example, he wrote (Herder 1952 (1782): 141): "Although the human race appears in such different forms on the earth, it is nevertheless everywhere one and the same human genus". He believed that all peoples have culture, but to varying degrees. As did other writers of his time, Herder used the word nation as a synonym for people, and each people had a language that played a decisive role in its degree of culture and enlightenment. By language, he understood the mother tongue, the spoken and written "language of the people".

Herder probably did not use the word culture in the plural at any point, and he apparently did not explicitly ascribe a particular independent culture to any people. He did not talk about "Chinese culture", "Finnish culture", etc., but he did talk about European culture. So he did not use the concept of culture differentially to the extent one does today, although the differential meaning is latent in his views. One could say that Herder thought differentially, with the aid not of the concept of culture but of the concept of the nation. He was far in advance of his time by virtue of his humanist, anti-hierarchical conception of culture. This conception did not seriously re-emerge until the first decades of the twentieth century.

Wilhelm von Humboldt further developed Herder's idea of a correlation between language and people/nation (especially Humboldt 1907/1836). He was a politician/diplomat and academic, strongly influenced by the ideas of neo-humanism concerning the value of clarity and harmony in spiritual cultivation (*Bildung*), and he was particularly interested in language as a creative activity that was made possible because of the power of the human mind (*Geisteskraft*). He was, then, most interested in the psychological aspect of language, especially in the role of language for thought: "Language is the formative organ of thought" (Humboldt 1907/1836: 53) and for a worldview (*Weltansicht*): " ... so there lies in every language a particular worldview" (Humboldt 1907/1836: 60). Humboldt was one of the first to reflect on the role of language diversity in relation to our thoughts (an idea that was later to be known as "linguistic relativity"; see below).

Humboldt was also interested in what happens to one's worldview when one learns a foreign language. He thought that the new language marks a new standpoint, a different approach to an understanding of the world. Here, we have an approach to linguistic relativity that does not claim that language determines thought (which has sometimes been claimed by people working in the Sapir–Whorf tradition; see below), rather it involves a new perspective.

Humboldt was way ahead of his time in his interest in the form of language and the correlation between language and worldview. His posthumously published work on language did not have any major impact before it was revived by the neo-Humboldtians, particularly Leo Weisgerber in the 1940s and 1950s (Weisgerber 1953–54).

Neither Herder nor Humboldt were National Romantics. But there was an important "interlude" between Herder and Humboldt, namely German Romanticism proper, from c. 1795 to 1830. During this period, the idea of a unity between language and people was romanticized so that one spoke of a national soul and a mysterious, intimate connection between language, people and national soul. This romantic idea of a fusion between language and people/nation gained considerable general support in connection with the nationalist tendencies that became increasingly strong and widespread throughout eighteenth-century Europe, first as a progressive liberal movement, and later on in various right-wing nationalist and socialist versions (Risager 2006).

## The Sapir–Whorf tradition

Edward Sapir was a student of German-born Franz Boas, who in the first decades of the twentieth century introduced the German tradition of culture studies and studies of language as a part of culture to the USA and organized the study of anthropology there. Boas laid the foundation for empirical studies of American Indian cultures and culture areas, including languages, and he was the one who first formulated the idea of cultural relativism as opposed to racism and classical evolutionism (the idea that all societies in the world are moving toward the same evolutionary goal, but at different speeds).

Sapir was active in many parts of anthropology, including the study of language (Sapir 1921). He was deeply interested in the relationship between language and culture, but it should be noted that he was not an adherent of the national paradigm and its insistence on the inseparability of language and culture. Actually, he emphasized that languages can spread across cultural areas.

Sapir was also very interested in the more psychological question of the relationship between people's language and their worldview (cf. Humboldt's *Weltansicht*):

> Human beings do not live in the objective world alone, nor alone in the world of social activity as ordinarily understood, but are very much at the mercy of the particular language which has become the medium of expression for their society. It is quite an illusion to imagine that one adjusts to reality essentially without the use of language and that language is merely an incidental means of solving specific problems of communication or reflection. The fact of the matter is that the "real world" is to a large extent unconsciously built up on the language habits of the group. ... We see and hear and otherwise experience very largely as we do because the language habits of our community predispose certain choices of interpretation.
>
> *Sapir, quoted in Whorf (1956/1939: 134)*

This quotation functions as an introduction to one of Benjamin Lee Whorf's articles that appeared in 1939. Whorf was originally a chemical engineer, but became interested in linguistics in the mid-1920s and began studying Aztec and other American Indian languages. He enrolled in Sapir's classes at Yale, and in 1937–38, he was a Lecturer in Anthropology at the same institution. It was in his work on the Hopi language that he developed his ideas of the role of language in relation to thought and worldview, strongly inspired by Sapir's psychological approach, as can be seen in this well-known quotation from Whorf:

> We cut nature up, organize it into concepts, and ascribe significances as we do, largely because we are parties to an agreement to organize it in this way – an agreement that holds throughout our speech community and is codified in the patterns of our language.
>
> *Whorf (1956/1940: 213)*

The patterns of language that Whorf was especially interested in were grammatical categories such as tense, aspect, mood, and number, and he saw them as having a strong influence on language users' perception of the world, including perceptions of time, validity, and matter. For the idea that different languages influence thought differently, he introduced the term "linguistic relativity", with reference to Einstein's theories of relativity.

However, in his various articles, he was not very clear on the nature and strength of the influence of linguistic categories on thought: Both thought as process and as product? Both thought content and thought form? Both perception, memory, and production? How strong is the influence, are we dealing with a strict determination or a more open influence? (cf. "largely" in the quotation referred to above). Since his premature death in 1941, his idea of linguistic relativity (which is generally referred to as the Sapir–Whorf hypothesis or the Whorfian hypothesis) has been the object of intense discussions. Often a distinction is made between a strong and a weak version of linguistic relativity: the strong version hypothesizes that linguistic categories determine our thought, whereas the weak version hypothesizes that linguistic categories may have an influence on our habitual thought—a hypothesis that must, of course, be operationalized before it can be researched (for neo-Whorfian research, see below).

In his work on the relationship between language and culture, Whorf chose a psychological angle. The focus was on peoples' thoughts or worldview. This approach is also cultural to the extent that we think that the patterns of a language lead all members of a particular language community to think in the same way, i.e., they (tend to) have the same worldview and therefore share the same culture. But it is important to say that this use of the concept of culture foregrounds culture as something located in our minds (a psychological, cognitive concept of culture), not as something that is produced in interaction between people, such as rituals, sports events, family socialization, classroom teaching, media consumption, etc. (for a dynamic, practice-oriented concept of culture, see below).

## 3. Current contributions and research

### Paul Friedrich

The term linguaculture was introduced by the linguistic anthropologist Paul Friedrich in a 1989 article on the relationship between political economy, ideology, and language (Friedrich 1989). (He also used the term in a manuscript in 1988.) In the article, he writes that "the many sounds and meanings of what we conventionally call 'language' and 'culture' constitute a single universe of its own kind" (Friedrich 1989: 306), and he describes the concept of linguaculture with these words: "a domain of experience that fuses and intermingles the vocabulary, many semantic aspects of grammar, and the verbal aspects of culture" (Friedrich 1989: 306)

Thus, the concept of linguaculture does not encompass all of culture, but only "the verbal aspects of culture". Friedrich adds that this terminological innovation can "help to get rid of the decades-long balancing act between 'language *and* culture' ('how much of each?'), 'language *in* culture' ('culture *in* language?'), … " (Friedrich 1989: 307; italics in the original). Friedrich was the first to emphasize that there are dimensions of culture that are not related to language. At the same time, he also indirectly says that there are dimensions of language that are not cultural. He tries to carve out a concept that lies in the interface of language and culture.

### Michael Agar

The linguistic anthropologist Michael Agar borrowed the concept from Friedrich, but changed it to "languaculture". He justified his alteration of the term as follows: "I modified it to 'langua' to bring it in line with the more commonly used 'language'" (Agar 1994: 265). In his book *Language Shock: Understanding the Culture of Conversation* (1994), Agar presents, in a metaphoric style and with many anecdotal illustrations, the linguistic and anthropological basis for ideas about the interrelation between language and culture, and here he refers repeatedly to the Sapir–Whorf discussion. He deals with the misunderstandings and cultural awareness that can arise in connection with conversations, both when it is a question of "different languages" and when it is a question of "the same language". Whereas Friedrich refers to locally defined variation such as southern Vermont linguaculture, Agar expands the range of languacultural variation to all social groups.

Agar introduces the concept of languaculture in order to be able to sum up culture and language in one word:

> Language, in all its varieties, in all the ways it appears in everyday life, builds a world of meanings. When you run into different meanings, when you become aware of your own and work to build a bridge to the others, 'culture' is what you're up to. Language fills the spaces between us with sound; culture forges the human connection through them. Culture is in language, and language is loaded with culture.
>
> *Agar (1994: 28)*

The term languaculture, then, stresses two relations: "The *langua* in languaculture is about discourse, not just about words and sentences. And the *culture* in languaculture is about meanings that include, but go well beyond, what the dictionary and the grammar offer" (Agar 1994: 96; italics in the original). Thus, Agar focuses on meaning in discourse, particularly in conversation. But he is not as clear as Friedrich about the idea that there are dimensions of culture that are not related to language (or discourse).

Agar spent some time explaining what the Whorfian discussion is about. As with so many people within modern linguistic anthropology and socio- and psycholinguistics, he was in favor of the weak version of the Whorfian hypothesis, with such formulations as: "Language carries with it patterns of seeing, knowing, talking, and acting. Not patterns that imprison you, but patterns that mark the easier trails for thought and perception and action" (Agar 1994: 71). Agar proposed that what Whorf was really talking about was "languaculture".

Agar also introduced the concept of "rich points" to refer to the places in conversation where people misunderstand one another. It is there that there is the opportunity to glimpse "culture", to become conscious of cultural differences. He writes about "the Whorfian Alps" in linguistic communication in the sense that between people who have different languacultures (which ultimately everyone has) a number of cultural differences rise up—some small, some large—and that it is a question of bringing these out into the open and trying to go beyond them.

The concept of languaculture is developed in several of Agar's publications (e.g., Agar 2008). In this article, he argues that one should think of ethnography as second languaculture learning and translation. He suggests that the usual abbreviation L2 should be replaced by LC2 (second languaculture), and similarly that translation should be seen as a relation between LC1 (first languaculture) and LC2. He argues that ethnographic work is both a process whereby ethnographers learn a LC2, including experiences with significant rich points, and a product in which the ethnographers struggle with communicating their interpretation of LC2 in a translation to an LC1 public.

## Karen Risager

Whereas Agar focuses on ethnographic studies of languaculture in local settings, I introduce a transnational perspective in the book *Language and Culture: Global Flows and Local Complexity* (2006) (see also Risager 2007). My background is the study of culture teaching as a dimension of language teaching, and I combine sociolinguistics/the sociology of language with cultural and social anthropology in a rethinking of the relationship between language and culture. In this theory, the concept of languaculture is an ingredient. (I have used the term "languaculture", but in my recent writings I prefer "linguaculture" as a perhaps more straightforward term for linguists.)

Concerning the relationship between language and culture, two opposite positions are struggling within linguistics (in the broad sense, i.e., all studies of language). One position maintains that language and culture are inseparable, referring to the above-mentioned traditions associated with Herder, Humboldt, Sapir, and Whorf, and especially the National–Romantic form, which stresses the intimate relationship between national language and national culture. The other position maintains that language is culturally neutral in the sense that it is possible to study language as a structure or a functional system without reference to cultural and historical contexts of use. In my work, I define a third position, a position that maintains that: (1) language and culture can, in fact, be separated; and (2) language is never culturally neutral. It changes the perspective from the traditional national paradigm to a transnational view of both language and culture (and linguaculture). It argues that we need at least two different concepts in the interface between language and culture: linguaculture (associated with a particular language) and discourse (always expressed in a language, but potentially moving across languages). The following sections give an outline of this third position.

## A transnational view of culture

As I basically see human language as a part of human culture in general, I take my point of departure in a theory of culture, particularly a theory that departs from the national paradigm and takes a transnational and global perspective, namely that of the anthropologist Ulf Hannerz. In his book *Cultural Complexity: Studies in the Social Organization of Meaning* (1992), Hannerz describes his theory of the social organization of meaning, with particular reference to cultural flows and cultural complexity. He begins by giving the following summary of his understanding of culture:

The three dimensions of culture, to be understood in their interrelations, are thus:

1. *ideas and modes of thought* as entities and processes of the mind—the entire array of concepts, propositions, values, and the like, which people within some social unit carry together, as well as their various ways of handling their ideas in characteristic modes of mental operation;
2. *forms of externalization*, the different ways in which meaning is made accessible to the senses, made public; and
3. *social distribution*, the ways in which the collective cultural inventory of meanings and meaningful external forms, that is (1) and (2) together, is spread over a population and its social relationships.

*Hannerz (1992: 7; italics in the original)*

In Hannerz's opinion, then, culture has two loci, an external and an internal. The external locus is meaningful, externalized forms such as speech, gestures, song, dance, and decoration (cf. the dynamic, practice-oriented concept of culture mentioned above). The internal locus of culture is meaning in consciousness—not perceived as an idealized consciousness but as that of concrete human beings. The individual's share in culture he mainly describes with the aid of the hermeneutical concepts of perspective and horizon. Each human being is unique in his or her experience-based, socially influenced perspective on the outside world, and his or her horizon is reflected by personal life experiences and education. At the individual level, society is thus seen as a network of perspectives. The two loci of culture are each other's prerequisites, and the cultural process takes place in the interaction between them. Finally, meaning in consciousness and the externalized forms of this find themselves in a constant distribution process, and this means that "people must deal with other people's meanings" (Hannerz 1992: 14). Thus, Hannerz takes interaction at the micro level as his point of departure, describing cultural flow as a constant alternation between externalization and interpretation, with the flow passing from person to person in a constant process of distribution and transformation.

The cultural process takes place at both the societal micro and macro levels. It occurs partly in the concrete interaction between people in interpersonal situations, but also at higher levels, right up to the highest level: the global level, i.e., via the distribution of goods and mass communication. Hannerz, then, adopts a macro-anthropological perspective. He studies, among other things, how cultural distribution processes of various, possibly global, extent result in local mixes. Therefore, he contributes to current critiques of essentialist and static notions of culture.

## A transnational view of language

Hannerz only deals with language in passing, but his model is very useful for the development of a transnational view of language that foregrounds global linguistic flows and linguistic complexity, and also contributes to current critiques of essentialist notions of language.

Referring to Hannerz's two loci for culture, an external and an internal, I would also consider language as a two-sided phenomenon. The external locus is linguistic practice, oral or written (or some kind of a mixture), and the internal locus is linguistic resources in the individual subject, developed during his or her socialization and total life history. But in addition to this, I would include a third locus that has a more deliberately constructed or "artificial" nature, namely the idea of "the language" or "the language system" conceived as a coherent whole, or maybe an object, or even an organism or a person.

The two first-mentioned loci of language presuppose each other. Linguistic practice cannot be produced and received without linguistic resources carried by individual people, and the linguistic resources of the individual cannot be developed without the experience of linguistic practice. Whereas these two loci of language are both natural and necessary, the idea of the "language system" is not. We have to deconstruct the idea that there is a language "out there" that we can use and study as a natural object. The "language system" is a construct or, in other words, a family of historically and discursively constructed notions ("French", "Arabic", etc.). At the same time, it is important to note that this construct has consequences for linguistic practice and linguistic resources. The idea of the language system interacts with both linguistic practice and linguistic resources, being a kind of—more or less conscious—normative factor.

The use (linguistic practice) of a specific language may be seen as flows (and change) in social networks of people and groups of people. These networks may be located physically in individuals acting together, or they may be located in virtual space as communication networks made possible by information technologies such as the telephone, the internet, etc. These networks develop further through migration and language learning. The Danish language, for example, spreads in social networks all over the world where there are Danish-speaking people as settlers, tourists, sojourners, students, soldiers, sports people, etc. People carry their Danish language resources with them into new cultural contexts and perhaps put them to use in new ways under the new circumstances. People around the world are learning Danish as a foreign language, for instance, in Scandinavian Departments, and thus the Danish language is spread to new individuals and new social networks. It is also spread to new users via the learning of Danish as a second language (L2) in Denmark. Seen from this perspective, quite a large number of the world's languages are spreading in large global networks and can indeed be said to be world languages—not on the basis of their numbers of speakers, but on the basis of the extent of the networks using them.

These transnational linguistic flows of a large number of different languages create local multilingual situations of great complexity, characterized by language hierarchies and struggles among language users for power and recognition. Almost every country (state) in the world is multilingual in some sense. In a small country such as Denmark, for instance, over 120 languages are spoken as first languages. (For the sake of simplicity, I will not deal with the issues of language alternation and language mixing in this chapter, although this is clearly also relevant to the question concerning the relationship between language and culture.)

The transnational view of language makes it possible to describe how language and culture can be separated. Linguistic practice flows in social networks that may reach from one cultural context to another across the world. Or in other words—focusing on the internal locus: when people move around in the world, they carry their linguistic resources with them from one cultural context to another (cf. Sapir's position cited above).

## Linguaculture: three interrelated dimensions

The description of linguistic flows has implicitly focused on language codes. It is codes that are seen as flowing and intermingling in social networks—irrespective of the meanings to which they give rise. With the concept of linguaculture, the focus switches to the content or meaning side of language.

In relation to Agar's (1994) concept of languaculture, which focuses on the semantics and pragmatics of language (in discourse), I expand the concept to include two other dimensions as well: the poetics of language and the identity dimension of language. Together, they are meant to encompass the full range of culturality of a language.

The semantics and pragmatics of language is the dimension specifically explored by Agar and his antecedents in linguistic anthropology represented by Sapir and Whorf, as well by many linguists and language specialists interested in contrastive and intercultural semantics and pragmatics. This dimension is about the interplay of constancy and variability in the semantic and pragmatic potentials and practices of specific languages as opposed to other languages. As regards constancy; it could be more or less obligatory distinctions between (in English) "sister" and "brother", between "he" and "she", between "red" and "orange", between "hello" and "how are you", and the denotative (dictionary) meanings of culturally specific words such as "Christmas", "race", "lecturer", "done". As regards variability, it could be the social and personal variability that is found in concrete situations of use in different parts of the world. This is a vast and well-explored field of study.

The poetics of language is the dimension related to the kinds of meaning created in the exploitation of the interplay between form and content in the language in question—different kinds of rhymes, puns based on the relationship between speech and writing, etc.—areas that have interested literary theorists focusing on literary poetics, style and the like, for example Roman Jakobson. The poetic potentials and practices of particular languages can be very different, basically because of the arbitrary/conventional relationship between form and content (in Saussurean terms: "signifier" and "signified")—as illustrated by the challenges of translating poetry from one language to another.

The identity dimension is also called social meaning by some sociolinguists, for example, Dell Hymes. It is related to the social and personal variation of the language in question, not least its pronunciation. With a specific accent, for instance, you identify yourself and make it possible for others to identify you according to their background knowledge and attitudes. Like Le Page and Tabouret-Keller (1985), I see linguistic practice as a continuing series of "acts of identity" where people project their own understanding of the world onto the interlocutors by their choice of language variety (dialectal form, code alternation, etc.) and consciously or unconsciously invite them to react. The identity dimension has generally been explored by those scholars within sociolinguistics who are interested in the relationship between language and identity in multilingual society.

## Linguaculture in first, second, and foreign language use

When we consider linguaculture in the linguistic resources of the individual subject (the internal locus), it is important to distinguish between the functions of language as first, second, or foreign language. It should be noted that the idea of an intimate relationship between language and culture refers to the language only in its function as a first language (L1), even if this is rarely explicitly stated. The National–Romantic idea of an inner association between the language and the people (the nation) is in fact about people who have grown up from childhood with the L1 (the mother tongue) and the first language culture.

When the language in question functions as a second or foreign language, the relationship between language and culture is, in any case, of a different nature. A Dane who is learning German as a foreign language, for instance, especially in the first stages of learning, must draw on his/her cultural and social experiences related to the Danish language (cf. Humboldt's position cited above: " ... one always transfers into a foreign language, more or less, one's own worldview") (cf. also Lantolf 1999 from another, Vygotskyan, perspective; see below). There are some semantic/pragmatic distinctions that are obligatory in using German, such as an appropriate distribution of *du* and *Sie*. But besides such clearcut distinctions, it will be natural to build on the linguaculture developed in relation to the first language. Personal connotations to words and phrases will be transferred, and a kind of language mixture will result, where the foreign language is supplied with linguacultural matter from the first language (and possibly other languages learnt). From the learner's perspective, the alleged intimate association between German language and culture is normative, not descriptive. The learner's task is to establish an association between his/her new language and his/her life experiences and cultural knowledge, and this task has to be accomplished on the basis of a growing understanding of some of the life experiences and cultural knowledge common among first language speakers. But even when the learner reaches a high level of competence, his/her linguaculture will always be the result of an accumulation of experiences during his/her entire life history, some of which may have taken place outside the target language community.

Linguaculture is, as already said, both structurally constrained and socially and personally variable. It is a bridge between the structure of language and the socially constituted personal idiolect. When I speak English, I draw on the meaning structures and conventions of the English language, shared by others, and at the same time embody my personal connotations and life experiences in my speech. The most interesting potentials of the concept of linguaculture may lie in the study of the personal idiolect with a focus on individual (but not necessarily idiosyncratic) semantic connotations, and on language learning as a process that is integrated in the life history of the individual subject, as a speaker–hearer, a reader, and a writer (see Kramsch 2009; Risager 2006, 2007; the last of these deals with the linguaculture (languaculture) concept in the context of foreign and L2 teaching and learning, and analyzes the international history of culture pedagogy with special reference to the transition from a national to a transnational paradigm).

When we consider linguaculture in linguistic practice, oral or written (the external locus), there is usually a high degree of semantic and pragmatic variability in the process, even when all participants speak the language in question as a first language. When a text, oral or written, is produced, linguacultural intentions are laid down in the text, i.e., intentions concerning how this text is going to function semantically and pragmatically in that specific communicative activity. These intentions are restricted or expanded in the course of reception of the text. The addressees or the readers interpret the text according to their personal linguacultures and their knowledge of the world. In situations where the language in question is used as a foreign language or L2, there are many opportunities to add even more variability to the text or communication than is the case with L1 use, because of the wider range of linguacultural experiences.

When we distinguish between language used as first, second, or foreign language, it becomes clear that linguacultural flows do not follow exactly the same routes as linguistic flows. For example, when I as a Dane move around in the world, I tend to build on my Danish linguaculture, when I speak English, French, or German. I thereby contribute to the flow of Danish linguaculture across languages.

The linguaculture concept makes it possible to describe how languages are never culturally neutral. Any language (and language variety and language mixture) carries meaning potentials that are to some extent specific for this language. This also applies to English, of course, a language that carries a wealth of meaning from its diverse and conflictual histories in colonial expansion, in postcolonial settings, and in the more or less global spread of domains of use such as commercial and scientific communication.

## Discourse across and within language communities

Linguaculture in the senses presented above cannot stand alone when we want to consider all meaning carried by human language. The linguaculture concept in my perspective is bound to specific languages (mainly, but not only, in their use as first languages). But language also carries and forms discourses.

In this context, I propose to draw on the concept of discourse that has been developed by critical discourse analysts such as Fairclough (1992). This concept is content oriented: discourses are characterized by topics constructed in relation to perspectives, and more specifically ideological positions. They are mainly linguistically formed (although often incorporated in wider semiotic practices), but they are in principle not restricted to any specific language or language community. This means that discourses may transmit content from one language community or network to another. Discourses may spread from language community to language community by processes of translation and other kinds of transformation. Thus, discourses (sometimes called knowledge discourses) on nationalism, on agriculture, on Islam, on education, on democracy, on culture, on health, on intercultural communication, etc., etc., spread transnationally all over the world. But any discourse is at any time embodied in a specific language, and consequently formed by the linguacultural potential of that language. In the translation process, what one tries to keep constant is the discourse, while the linguaculture changes.

Some discourses may circulate only in a particular language community and never get out as, for example, certain discourses of opposition in dominated (language) groups, but the point is that these discourses are not bound to that particular language; they can, in principle, be translated into other languages if needed.

## The language–culture interface

Whereas Agar uses languaculture as an umbrella term for the unity of language and (parts of) culture, I divide the field into four different concepts in order to be able to describe different cultural flows that do not necessarily take the same routes in the world:

1. linguistic flows: codes such as English, Swahili, Tok Pisin, etc.;
2. linguacultural flows: meaning related mainly to first language use of particular languages;
3. discursive flows: meaning not necessarily related to particular languages;
4. other cultural flows: non-language meaning, including visual, architectural, musical, behavioral, etc., etc.

Thus, in studies of intercultural communication that include the language aspect, there will always be two meaning levels to consider: linguaculture and discourse. What dimensions of understanding may be attributed to different linguacultures (cf. Agar's rich points), and what dimensions may be attributed to different discourses, not necessarily related to the languages in question?

## 4. Related research

Among other researchers who use the term linguaculture, one can mention Mackerras (2008), who includes the concept of linguaculture in a discussion of how a sociocultural approach can help students become intercultural learners who can weave together everyday and scholarly concepts.

Sometimes an expression is used that serves as an alternative to linguaculture, namely "culture-in-language", for example in Crozet and Liddicoat (2000), who deal with the teaching of culture as an integrated part of language. The expression "culture-in-language" may be used in opposition to another expression: "language-in-culture", which focuses on the role of language in the wider culture. A third kind of expression is "language-and-culture" (also with an adjectival form: "language-and-cultural"). This term emphasizes the general inseparability of language and culture, irrespective of the specific part–whole relationship. This term has, for example, been used in Byram et al. (1994) on the learning of (foreign) language and culture as an integrated whole. In the French context, the expression langue-culture is often used, for instance by Galisson (1991), who focuses on cross-cultural lexical semantics with reference to French. In the German context, the most usual (near-)equivalent for linguaculture would be Kultur in der Sprache, or alternatively Sprachkultur, but Sprachkultur traditionally has another meaning, namely the cultivation of the language.

In continuation of the Sapir–Whorf tradition, we find the neo-Whorfians conducting experimental and theoretical investigations on the relationships between linguistic categories and cognition, among them Lucy (1992). Gumperz and Levinson (1996) provide a comprehensive overview of different approaches to linguistic relativity, including sociolinguistic studies of the production of meaning in context and critiques of idealizations such as "language", "culture", and "community".

Many other linguists and language specialists are working with linguaculture without using any of the expressions mentioned above, including the term linguaculture. Among these, the following can be mentioned: Wierzbicka (1997) on cross-cultural semantics; Blum-Kulka et al. (1989) on cross-cultural pragmatics; Dovring (1997) on the political consequences of semantic diversity in the English language; Ochs (1988) on language socialization in culture; Lantolf (1999) on second culture acquisition from a sociocultural perspective; Kramsch (1993) on the teaching of language and culture as discourse; and Müller-Jacquier (2000) on intercultural teaching. In Stubbs (1997), one can find a sociolinguistic interpretation of linguistic relativity, focusing on relations between language use in discourse and stereotypical thinking, as can be seen, for example, in racist and sexist discourse. Thus, quite a large number of different issues and approaches can be described as linguacultural studies.

## 5. Research methods

We are dealing here with a vast field characterized by a large number of research methods, and I will just mention three methods: an ethnographic approach to the study of linguacultural practices; a sociocultural approach to the study of linguacultural resources; and a semiotic/symbolic and biographic approach to the practices and resources of the multilingual subject.

Agar's work can be described as a highly language-sensitive and also practically oriented approach to intercultural communication. In his 1994 book, he provides an introduction to ethnographic studies of linguacultural and discursive practices (in my terms) in everyday conversation. The focus is on how as a layman one can build up one's cultural awareness by collecting rich points and investigating whether they form patterns, by investigating linguistic practice in certain situations in order to define frames (the typical example is what are also referred to as "scripts", e.g., concerning typical sequences of acts when visiting a restaurant): "Frames take language and culture and make them inseparable. The 'and' disappears, and we're left with *languaculture*" (Agar 1994: 132; italics in the original). His opinion, then, is that one ought to work inductively, empirically, and build up an increasingly comprehensive set of interrelationships between frames. This is an approach that underscores the search for coherence between language and culture in different settings.

The linguacultural resources of individuals have been investigated (without using terms such as linguaculture or culture-in-language) in a number of cognitive studies inspired by socio-cultural and sociohistorical theory (the Vygotskyan tradition). Lantolf (1999) gives an overview of such studies in the context of second language acquisition, where a number of researchers have conducted experimental studies in order to examine what they call "second culture acquisition", mainly by comparing word association or the use of metaphors in groups varying according to language use (use of the language in question as first or second/foreign language) and according to contexts of learning (the language learnt in school in their own country or by immersion in a target language country). These approaches, in their focus on "second language and culture acquisition", also tend to underscore the intimate relationship between language and culture but, at the same time, some of the studies show that learners of an L2 tend *not* to learn the second culture unless they are immersed in it, i.e., are living in a target language country (Lantolf 1999). This is an approach that primarily looks for similarities and differences between groups of language learners/users.

Another kind of approach is represented by Kramsch (2009), who deals with the subjective aspects of language learning. It focuses on the multilingual subject and his/her language learning biography and practices in a semiotic/symbolic perspective, including links with identity, memory, emotion, and imagination. The data are mainly spoken and written data from individual language learners, including online data from, for example, electronic chatrooms, and published testimonies and memoirs of former language learners.

## 6. Future directions

Studies of linguaculture can draw on quite a long, originally European tradition of interest in language in relation to culture (people, nation, history), and there are many researchers active in the field today, although only a few use the specific term linguaculture or related expressions. One of the central methodological concerns of the field, in my view, is the question of choosing between a search for coherence and a search for complexity. Agar's approach is a good example of the search for coherence in the study of the role of languaculture in situated intercultural communication, and that is clearly a fruitful approach. But I would suggest that one should try to raise awareness of complexity as well and, in doing so, I would take the concept of the language–culture nexus as a point of departure. This concept is defined in Risager (2006) as follows: "a local integration of linguistic, languacultural, discursive and other cultural flows in more or less differing social networks" (Risager 2006: 186). In the language–culture nexus, language and culture can blend in a great variety of ways, and this mix can be described as relatively convergent or relatively divergent.

A fairly convergent language–culture nexus could be the following: a conversation at Rønne Tourist Office (Rønne is the main town on the small Danish island of Bornholm). Those engaged in conversation were born in Rønne and speak modern Rønne dialect with Rønne linguaculture, and the discourse has to do with summer tourism in Rønne. A fairly divergent language–culture nexus could be the following: a telephone conversation between an office employee at the Berlin Zoo and an employee at the Aalborg Zoo (Aalborg is a city in Northern Jutland in Denmark). The person talking in Berlin speaks German with a tinge of Hungarian linguaculture because she is a Hungarian immigrant. The person talking in Aalborg speaks German with some Aalborg linguaculture. They discuss a project involving an exchange of lions. In this last example, the identities "point in different directions", so to speak. They exemplify (electronically mediated) local complexity as a result of transnational processes (the examples are taken from Risager 2006).

If one investigates only convergent situations, one can easily come to the conclusion that there is, generally speaking, a close connection or coherence between language and culture. But if one turns one's gaze to divergent situations, exhibiting greater cultural complexity, such a conclusion is less likely. So you cannot take the relationship between language and culture for granted. The specific blend or integration of language, linguaculture, discourse, and other culture in a given situation is always an empirical question. The methods of investigation of the language–culture nexus therefore have to be sensitive to this complexity.

This also applies to studies of the language–culture nexus in the subject (the internal locus), i.e., the unique integration of language(s), linguaculture(s), discourses, and other cultural meanings constructed as part of the life history of the subject. This calls for more qualitative research into subjects' complex personal language histories over time (e.g., Kramsch 2009).

Studies of linguaculture and discourse have already become incorporated into the larger field of intercultural communication and may have a promising role in contributing to an increased awareness of language complexity as a product of transnational practices and processes.

## Related topics

Culture, communication, context, and power; intercultural citizenship; intercultural competence; intercultural contact, hybridity, and third space; L2 education and citizenship; translation, interpreting, and intercultural communication; world Englishes

## Further reading

Kramsch, C. (1998) *Language and Culture*, Oxford: Oxford University Press (an introduction to the complex relationship between language and culture).

Risager, K. (2006) 'Culture in language: a transnational view', in H.L. Andersen, K. Lund and K. Risager (eds) *Culture in Language Learning*, Aarhus: Aarhus University Press, pp. 27–44 (a presentation of the two levels of meaning in language: linguaculture and discourse).

## Note

1 This chapter draws on parts of Risager (2006; forthcoming).

## References

Agar, M. (1994) *Language Shock: Understanding the Culture of Conversation*, New York: William Morrow.

——(2008) 'A linguistics for ethnography. Why not second languaculture learning and translation?', *Journal of Intercultural Communication*, 16. Online. Available: www.immi.se/jicc/index.php/jicc/article/view/66/38 (accessed 20 May 2010).

Blum-Kulka, S., House, J. and Kasper, G. (eds) (1989) *Cross-cultural Pragmatics*, Norwood, NJ: Ablex.

Byram, M., Morgan, C. and colleagues (1994) *Teaching-and-Learning Language-and-Culture*, Clevedon: Multilingual Matters.

Crozet, C. and Liddicoat, A.J. (2000) 'Teaching culture as an integrated part of language', in A.J. Liddicoat and C. Crozet (eds) *Teaching Languages, Teaching Cultures*, Applied Linguistics Association of Australia, Melbourne: Language Australia, pp. 1–18.

Dovring, K. (1997) *English as Lingua Franca: Double Talk in Global Persuasion*, Westport, CT: Praeger.

Fairclough, N. (1992) *Discourse and Social Change*, Cambridge: Polity Press.

Friedrich, P. (1989) 'Language, ideology, and political economy', *American Anthropologist*, 91: 295–312.

Galisson, R. (1991) *De la langue à la culture par les mots* [From language to culture via words], Paris: CLE International.

Gumperz, J.J. and Levinson, S.C. (eds) (1996) *Rethinking Linguistic Relativity*, Cambridge: Cambridge University Press.

Hannerz, U. (1992) *Cultural Complexity: Studies in the Social Organization of Meaning*, New York: Columbia University Press.

Herder, J.G. (1952; 1st edn 1782–91) 'Ideen zur Philosophie der Geschichte der Menschheit', in J.G. Herder, *Zur Philosophie der Geschichte. Eine Auswahl in Zwei Bänden*, Berlin: Aufbau-Verlag.

Humboldt, W. von (1836; 2nd edn 1907) 'Über die Verschiedenheit des menschlichen Sprachbaues und ihren Einfluss auf die geistige Entwicklung des Menschengeschlechts', in *Wilhelm von Humboldts Gesammelte Schriften*, Band VII, Berlin: B. Behr's Verlag, pp. 1–344.

Kramsch, C. (1993) *Context and Culture in Language Teaching*, Oxford: Oxford University Press.

——(2009) *The Multilingual Subject*, Oxford: Oxford University Press.

Lantolf, J.P. (1999) 'Second culture acquisition: cognitive considerations', in E. Hinkel (ed.) *Culture in Second Language Teaching and Learning*, Cambridge: Cambridge University Press, pp. 28–46.

Le Page, R. and Tabouret-Keller, A. (1985) *Acts of Identity: Creole-based Approaches to Language And Ethnicity*, Cambridge: Cambridge University Press.

Lucy, J. (1992) *Language Diversity and Thought: A Reformulation of the Linguistic Relativity Hypothesis*, Cambridge: Cambridge University Press.

Mackerras, S. (2008) 'Linguaculture in the language classroom: a sociocultural approach', *Babel*, November. Online. Available: http://findarticles.com/p/articles/mi_6934/is_2_42/ai_n28469145/ (accessed 21 May 2010)

Müller-Jacquier, B. (2000) 'Interkulturelle Didaktik' [Intercultural Didactics], in M. Byram (ed.) *Routledge Encyclopedia of Language Teaching and Learning*, London/New York: Routledge, pp. 303–7.

Ochs, E. (1988) *Culture and Language Development: Language Acquisition and Language Socialization in A Samoan Village*, Cambridge: Cambridge University Press.

Risager, K. (2006) *Language and Culture: Global Flows and Local Complexity*, Clevedon: Multilingual Matters.

——(2007) *Language and Culture Pedagogy: From a National to a Transnational Paradigm*, Clevedon: Multilingual Matters.

——(forthcoming) 'Linguaculture', in C. Chapelle (ed.) *Encyclopedia of Applied Linguistics*, Oxford: Wiley-Blackwell.

Sapir, E. (1921) *Language: An Introduction to The Study Of Speech*, New York: Harcourt, Brace, and Co.

Stubbs, M. (1997) 'Language and the mediation of experience: linguistic representation and cognitive orientation', in F. Coulmas (ed.) *The Handbook of Sociolinguistics*, Oxford: Blackwell, pp. 358–73.

Weisgerber, L. (1953–54) *Vom Weltbild der deutschen Sprache I–II*, Düsseldorf: Pädagogischer Verlag Schwann.

Whorf, B.L. (1939; 2nd edn 1956) 'The relation of habitual thought and behavior to language', in J.B. Carroll (ed.) *Language, Thought, and Reality: Selected Writings of Benjamin Lee Whorf*, Cambridge, MA: MIT Press, pp. 134–59.

——(1940; 2nd edn 1956) 'Science and linguistics', in J.B. Carroll (ed.) *Language, Thought, and Reality: Selected Writings of Benjamin Lee Whorf*, Cambridge, MA: MIT Press, pp. 207–19.

Wierzbicka, A. (1997) *Understanding Cultures Through their Key Words*, New York: Oxford University Press.

# 7

# Intercultural rhetoric and intercultural communication

*Dwight Atkinson*

## 1. Introduction

Intercultural rhetoric (IR) compares writing across languages for signs of cultural influence, ultimately for pedagogical purposes. Its original incarnation, 'contrastive rhetoric' (CR), began in 1966. Contrastive rhetoric entered an extended period of critique and development in the 1990s, resulting in its reformulation as intercultural rhetoric in 2004. This chapter reviews the historical development and current state of IC/CR, with emphasis on the vexed notion of culture.

## 2. Contrastive rhetoric

CR was first proposed by the applied linguist Robert B. Kaplan (1966). As an English as a second language (ESL) administrator at a large US university, Kaplan was concerned with problems ESL students had in organizing their academic texts. He hypothesized that these difficulties resulted from cultural differences in organizing and presenting ideas. Here, I describe Kaplan (1966) and its background in detail because, beyond providing CR's original conceptual basis, it has been a prime target of its critics.

Kaplan's article was basically a thought-piece, informed particularly by three concepts. The first was 'contrastive analysis' – the feature-by-feature comparison of two languages in order to predict difficulties speakers of one might have in learning the other. Structural similarities between linguistic features were assumed to predict ease of learning and differences difficulty. Kaplan extended contrastive analysis directly into the rhetorical domain, proposing a 'contrastive analysis of rhetoric' (Kaplan 1966: 15).

The second major concept influencing Kaplan was 'linguistic relativity', also known as the Sapir–Whorf hypothesis. Whorf (1956) proposed that a language's grammatical form determines its (native) speakers' thought, as reflected in the following quotation:

> Every language offers to its speakers a ready-made *interpretation* of the world. ... Take for example a simple sentence such as 'I see him'. ... This means English ... presents the impression made on our senses predominantly as human *activities*, brought about by our *will*. But the Eskimos in Greenland say not 'I see him' but 'he appears to me. ... '. Thus

the Indo-European speaker conceives as workings of his [self-willed] activities what the fatalistic Eskimo sees as events that happen to him.

*Spitzer (1953), quoted in Kaplan (1966: 3)*

In fact, Kaplan (1966) expressed ambivalence regarding the language–thought relationship. He later (e.g. 1992) described his position as a 'weak' version of Sapir–Whorf, i.e. that language influences but does not determine worldview.

The third main concept influencing Kaplan was 'culture'. The anthropological culture concept had achieved perhaps its greatest academic popularity in the 1960s. By then, its main popularizer, Franz Boas, had been dead for 20 years, leaving his students to turn it into an all-encompassing explanation of human difference (Stocking 1992). Kaplan adopted the concept, treating it as a causal variable: culture causes people to think in certain predictable ways.

Having reviewed the concepts underlying Kaplan's paper, let me summarize it. It begins by proposing that the key to ESL writing instruction is understanding cultural differences in rhetoric. Rhetoric – treated narrowly as arrangement of ideas in discourse – reflects the cultural logic whereby people intepret their worlds. In English, 'normal paragraph development' starts with a topic statement, divides it into parts and develops each part, so that the central idea/topic is 'relate[d] ... to all the other ideas in the whole essay ... to prove ... or ... argue something'.

Kaplan next presents and discusses nine illustrative examples, including five culled from 'some 700 foreign student compositions ... [he] carefully analyzed' (Kaplan 1966: 6). The first example, illustrating English paragraph development, is from Macaulay's *History of England*, and the second, exemplifying Semitic languages' complex parallelism, from the *King James Bible*. Two paragraphs by Arabic-speaking students illustrating parallelism and a short composition by a Korean student indicating an 'Oriental ... approach by indirection' (Kaplan 1966: 10) follow. Next, an excerpt from a professionally translated French essay, a short composition by a French-speaking student and two paragraphs by a Spanish-speaking student illustrate Romance languages' 'much greater freedom to digress ... than in English' (Kaplan 1966: 12). Finally, a translated Russian passage reveals 'a series of parallel constructions ... and subordinate structures, at least half of which appear to be irrelevant to the central idea of the paragraph' (Kaplan 1966: 12). Kaplan summarizes: 'These paragraphs may suffice to show that each language and culture has a paragraph order unique unto itself, and that part of the learning of a particular language is the mastering of its logical system' (Kaplan 1966: 14).

Kaplan next states that such rhetorical differences must be taught, but first they must be researched and better understood. He (confusingly) adds that all forms of paragraph development can occur in all languages, but preferred expository patterns deserve primary attention. Kaplan then presents diagrams of the paragraph patterns discussed, qualifying the diagrams as superficial and heuristic: a straight vertical vector for English; four parallel horizontal vectors connected by dashed lines for Semitic; a curved vector moving concentrically inward for 'Oriental'; a vector starting and ending vertically but zigzagging in the middle for Romance; and a Romance-like diagram but with the middle section dashed for Russian. Kaplan then concludes by stating that his approach usefully teaches both English form and logic, offering two techniques for doing so and describing his proposal as a response to student needs.

## Subsequent contrastive rhetoric studies

By Kaplan's account (e.g. 1972), his article initially received scant attention. However, this did not deter him from trying to build a conceptual base for CR and connect it with other research traditions. Prominent themes in Kaplan's many subsequent CR writings include: (1) CR's lineage in text and discourse analysis vs. sentence-based linguistics; (2) The understanding that writing, and especially 'writing with composing' (Kaplan 1987), requires explicit instruction, particularly for second language (L2) speakers; (3) Increasing emphasis on asking the following situation-specific questions to support cross-language textual comparison: 'Who has the authority to write? Who may be addressed? What may be discussed? What form may the writing take? What constitutes evidence? How can evidence be convincingly arranged?' (Kaplan 2005: 378–79); and (4) CR as a form of linguistic and rhetorical consciousness-raising rather than pedagogy, dealing not just with idea arrangement but also topic-marking, intersentential syntax, reader vs. writer responsibility (see below), textual conventions and audience awareness.

In later writings, Kaplan (e.g. 1992, 2005) qualified or clarified many of his original claims and assumptions, to the effect that:

- All languages have multiple discourse styles, but some are culturally preferred;
- The paragraph is not a useful unit for CR analysis, whereas the 'discourse bloc', in which 'every item is related to every other item by either coordination, subordination, or superordination' (1972: 27), is;
- Rhetoric involves more than just idea arrangement in texts;
- The representation of 'English rhetoric' as maximally direct was flawed – basically 'all' readers may view their culturally preferred rhetorical styles as natural and direct;
- The conflation of disparate linguistic groups, particularly Chinese, Korean and Japanese, made for 'rather artificial categorization' (Kaplan 1988: 299);
- The issue of genre was not considered, leading to illegitimate textual comparisons;
- The focus on textual products neglected composing processes;
- L2 writings were compared without considering their writers' first language (L1) literacy experience;
- No unified model of written discourse exists, thereby preventing objective cross-language comparisons.

In the late 1970s, due substantially to growing interest in ESL writing, CR began to attract adherents. One was John Hinds, a linguist specializing in Japanese. Hinds (1983a) discussed four 'major' rhetorical styles in Japanese expository prose. One was the subject of a follow-up study (1983b) – the four-part *ki-sho-ten-ketsu* style, 'which is consistently valued highly and is different from any pattern in English expository writing' (Hinds 1983a: 183). According to Takemata (1976, quoted in Hinds 1983b: 188), *ki* presents the beginning of 'one's argument', *sho* develops it, *ten* 'turn[s] the idea to a subtheme' with 'a connection, but not a directly connected association (to the major theme)' and *ketsu* 'brings all this together' and concludes. Hinds presented examples from a Japanese newspaper column, translated in a structure-preserving way for the paper's English language edition and so yielding parallel Japanese and English texts. Hinds also described a small survey study (minus key methodological information) appearing to show *ki-sho-ten-ketsu* texts being evaluated more positively by Japanese than by English readers for unity, focus and coherence.

Within the framework of linguistic typology, Hinds (1987) proposed a 'reader-vs.-writer responsibility' parameter on which the world's languages may vary. English, he suggested, tends to be 'writer-responsible', in that writers exert great effort in making their meaning clear to readers, whereas Japanese places the interpretive burden on readers. Analysing a text from the above-mentioned newspaper column, Hinds asserted that the Japanese particle *wa*, generally thought to mark noun phrases as old (i.e. already known) information, was used in the example's *ten* to signpost new information that readers should nonetheless treat as old, thereby signalling that the *wa*-marked noun phrase 'may seem unrelated to the major point, but the connection … will become clear in due time' (Hinds 1987: 150). On this basis, Hinds suggested that writer responsibility be taught in ESL writing classes.

In a final contribution before his untimely death, Hinds (1990) investigated 'semi-inductive' writing styles in Japanese, Korean, Chinese and Thai, which represented, in his view, a 'regional preference' (Hinds 1990: 89) for organizing text. By semi-inductive, Hinds meant texts that flowed naturally from beginning to end for native readers, but without initially and directly stating a main point, or necessarily having one at all. The central purpose of such texts was 'not necessarily to convince, … but to stimulate the reader into contemplating an issue [they] might not have … considered' (Hinds 1990: 100). Hinds presented texts from the four languages involved, indicating how all had distinctive discourse structures which nonetheless violated English norms of coherence and unity – the Japanese text was again from the above-mentioned newspaper column.

In the early 1980s, a US-based Finnish applied linguist named Ulla Connor was studying how cognitive schemas affected reading comprehension. On encountering the CR concept, which resonated with her experience as an ESL student (1999a), Connor began working with Kaplan, first organizing annual colloquia at the Teachers of English to Speakers of Other Languages (TESOL) conference and then producing the first-ever edited volume of CR studies (Connor and Kaplan 1987). Over time, Connor became CR's most active researcher and promoter, contributing many papers and four single-authored or co-edited books, presenting tirelessly on CR throughout the world, establishing a research institute devoted partly to CR issues and founding the Intercultural Rhetoric and Discourse Conference, which held its sixth meeting in 2010.

Connor has substantially developed CR as a field, building on Kaplan's pioneering efforts:

1. She forged links between CR and European text linguistics; whereas early CR depended on notional accounts of rhetorical styles, careful text-analytical studies now exist.
2. Connor strengthened CR's connections with the field of rhetoric and composition, such that a core of rhetoric/composition scholars now work in the field (e.g. Li 1996; Matsuda 1997; You 2010).
3. Connor brought recent innovations in linguistics and writing, such as corpus analysis, into the field.
4. She connected CR with English for specific purposes (ESP), the study and teaching of professional languages to L2 English users, and its main research methodology, genre analysis.
5. Connor promoted the development of CR research methods – as mentioned above, early studies were weak methodologically, but starting with Connor (1996), a concerted effort was made to develop tools for researching CR.
6. Connor moved CR beyond its primary focus on texts by encouraging broad consideration of context, including qualitative research approaches.
7. Connor has continued to lead the field away from its original focus on students' L2 texts, a trend begun by Hinds.
8. Connor's identity as an L2 speaker has encouraged broad international participation in the field. Charges of ethnocentricity permeate critiques of CR (see below), but they carry less weight when international scholars are leading the field.

More recent research in the CR framework reflects many of the developments promoted by Connor. Owing to space limitations, a single example must suffice. Li (1996) employed text-based interviews and a survey to study what 'good writing' meant to Chinese and American high school writing teachers. She asked two highly experienced teachers in each country to choose exceptional essays written by their students in their first languages, and then, after all four teachers had read the same essays (appropriately translated), she interviewed them. Li found both differences and similarities in the teachers' evaluative criteria, some falling along cultural lines:

> It is safe to conclude that ... Mr. Wang and Mr. Zhang think better of pieces that convey clear and positive moral messages and demonstrate a good mastery of conventional forms and the features of Chinese poetry. Jack and Jane, on the other hand, prefer writing that impresses them as 'unique', demonstrating the writer's intellectual rigor and originality. The irony is: while Jack and Jane genuinely encourage students to depart from rutted tracks, they enforce new standards ... just as rigorously.
>
> Li (1996: 95)

Li's (1996) survey, which asked a total of forty-five high school writing teachers from both countries to rank-order four essays, yielded diverse responses. Li nonetheless extracted three generalizations which, in her opinion, distinguished the two groups' evaluations: (1) Good writing tended to stress moral values and have 'social significance' for the Chinese teachers; (2) Good writing was concrete writing wherein 'show, don't tell' (Li 1996: 118) was the reigning ethic for the American teachers, whereas the Chinese teachers preferred fewer but more poetic details; (3) Form and expression should at least 'appear' emergent for the American teachers, whereas competent form/expression for the Chinese teachers resulted from training in *wen* – 'patterns and embellishment' (Li 1996: 125). Relatedly, the Americans preferred more colloquial, speech-like (but actually highly crafted) language.

In fact, mere summaries cannot do justice to the complexity of Li's findings. At the same time as the Chinese and American teachers were expressing different norms for good writing, they rated the essays quite similarly. Li's greatest strength is that she does not settle for simple answers – the inevitably reductive conclusions noted above were complemented by rich, in-depth discussion and interview data. More recent work on writing in China (e.g. Li 2002; You 2010) reveals further complexities.

## Critiques of contrastive rhetoric

CR has undergone extensive criticism in the past 25 years, and one of its current challenges is to respond to these critiques. If 'invention is always born of dissension' (Lyotard 1984: xxv) or, 'as with any promising model, in order to develop it further, we need to construct [and respond to – Author] significant critical perspectives on it' (Lemke 1997: 39), then the critiques reviewed below present opportunities to improve the field.

## Early critiques

Apart from Kaplan's own self-critiques, Hinds (1983b) offered the first serious criticisms: L2 essays are not the best source for CR comparisons; 'Oriental' is not a legitimate language group; and English should not constitute the norm for comparison. Mohan and Lo (1985) followed, asserting that: (1) rhetorical variation in L2 texts may result from incomplete control of the language, so straightforward attribution to cultural influence is unwarranted; and (2) CR descriptions of Chinese rhetoric highlight classical traditions, whereas current Chinese rhetoricians prescribe English-looking forms.

Mauranen (1993) echoed the above critiques, suggesting that CR ignored likely causes of textual variation. She instituted a three-way comparison among L1 English research articles, L1 Finnish research articles and L2 English research articles written by Finns: If the first group differed from the others, then 'cultural effects' existed; if the second group differed, 'linguistic effects' existed, that is the differing linguistic structure of Finnish and English caused the variation; and if the third group differed, a 'foreign language effect' existed à la Mohan and Lo. Although Mauranen's approach has itself been criticized, she deserves credit for spurring the development of CR research methods, including the insight that valid comparisons can only occur within genres.

Matsuda (1997) critiqued classic CR for its static assumptions: writers are culturally programmed to produce their L1 rhetorics, and writing contexts are predetermined by audience expectations. CR-informed pedagogy thus becomes a reprogramming task. Matsuda presented an alternative 'dynamic model of L2 writing', wherein writers are individual agents and writing is mediated by discourse community and genre as well as audience expectations. These influences all contribute to the rhetorical shaping of texts, leading to a dynamic composing process. Implications include an enhanced focus on writing contexts in research and context analysis and context-rich assignments in the classroom.

After praising CR as a 'liberating concept' (Leki 1997: 235) – for alerting teachers that their own standards for good writing may not be universal – Leki (1997) raised the following issues. Conceptually, the claim that writing (and L2 writing in particular) directly reveals cultural thought patterns is problematic, nor are particular cultures' rhetorical patterns finite or discrete. Methodologically, the focus on L2 student essays, a rare and contrived genre, limits CR's explanatory power and pedagogical usefulness. Regarding CR's findings, they have been 'overgeneralized, overinterpreted, and oversimplified' (ibid.: 239) in attributing writing differences to cultural influence and finding supposedly cultural characteristics in texts – even English has been oversimplified in CR descriptions. CR has also valorized textual products at the expense of composing processes. Finally, Leki criticized CR for ignoring its own ideological consequences, and for enforcing norms based on dominant varieties of English. These last points prefigure later criticisms of CR.

## Later critiques

Following a 'critical turn' in academics, recent critiques have focused on CR's implications for ideology, power and social inequality. Since 1997, CR's leading critic has been the applied linguist Ryuko Kubota.

Kubota (1997) questioned characterizations of Japanese writing as unique and exotic *vis-à-vis* other cultural rhetorics. She argued that Hinds was selective and idealizing in highlighting the 'unique' features of Japanese writing – especially *ki-sho-ten-ketsu* – because although presented as 'preexisting cultural codes', they were not 'unitary and homogenous' (Kubota 1997: 464). Hinds' description therefore had an ideological thrust – to demonstrate maximal difference and, implicitly, inferiority *vis-à-vis* the West. To support her argument, Kubota cited Japanese writing specialists who interpreted *ki-sho-ten-ketsu* variously and prescribed English-like discourse structures. She also provided historical background, suggesting that a tradition of direct English-to-Japanese translation has powerfully affected Japanese. Kubota concluded that Hinds and others had stereotyped Japanese writing, focusing wholly on differences and thereby 'dichotomizing *us* and *them* and constructing, instead of discovering, cultural differences' (Kubota 1997: 475).

Kubota (1998) examined whether Japanese university students writing in both Japanese and English transferred rhetorical structures cross-linguistically. Of twenty-two writers for an expository and twenty-four for an argumentative writing task, approximately half in each group employed different styles of rhetorical organization, including location of main ideas, in their Japanese vs. English essays. Kubota also found strong correlations between rhetorical organization scores for essays by the same writers across languages. She interpreted these findings as problematizing CR's assumption that readers automatically transfer L1 rhetorical structures to their L2; instead, what transferred seemed to be writing ability. Kubota also found that students generally reported having little experience writing in English, which she took to support Mohan and Lo's (1985) claim that L1–L2 writing differences are primarily developmental.

Kubota and Lehner (2004) critically reviewed CR research and proposed a new framework, 'critical contrastive rhetoric' (CCR), on the following principles:

- CCR deconstructs 'standard average European' norms of language and culture because traditional CR 'keeps standard English in its place of authority and positions second language student writers as needing correction' (Kubota and Lehner 2004: 17);
- CCR emphasizes linguistic and cultural diversity while interrogating essentialized constructions of language, culture, rhetoric and identity. Yet these phenomena are in fact 'dynamic sites of political struggle' (Kubota and Lehner 2004: 17), so their essentialized versions must be questioned regarding their underlying political motives;
- Binary colonialist representations of superior (Western) Self vs. inferior (non-Western) Other are reinforced by CR and have racist implications, so CCR 'requires teachers to reflect critically on how classroom dialogue that underscores cultural difference in rhetoric ... could perpetuate Othering, cultural stereotyping, and unequal relations of power' (Kubota and Lehner 2004: 18);
- CCR rejects an "English-only" approach to teaching and research' (Kubota and Lehner 2004: 19), encouraging full appreciation of the linguistic experience that students bring to learning situations;
- CCR critically examines how colonialist and assimilationist discourses and their accompanying linguistic ideologies influence language change and writers' identities. Traditional CR encouraged ESL learners to 'believe that English is more logical and advanced than their native language' (Kubota and Lehner 2004: 19) and, on account of these and other influences, some languages are acquiring English-like characteristics;
- CCR supports the postmodernist rejection of absolute (scientific) truth, viewing knowledge as situated, partial and dynamic. The proliferation of English throughout the world and its rapid conventionalization in postcolonial contexts suggest rhetorical hybridity rather than a single 'correct' English owned by 'native speakers';
- At the pedagogical level, CCR encourages critical questioning of dominant texts, rhetorics and their political backgrounds for the purpose of resistance, appropriation and empowerment. CCR is thus a form of critical pedagogy that examines '*what, why.* ... [and] *how* [something] is taught/learned, *who* decides, etc. It is not a neutral undertaking' (Kubota and Lehner 2004: 21);
- CCR promotes 'self-validation of a student's first language and culture' (Kubota and Lehner 2004: 21). Writing instruction is therefore additive, honouring bilingualism and multiple literacies while opposing CR's either/or dichotomies and rhetorical exotica;
- CCR emphasizes student agency, encouraging the exploration of supposed rhetorical differences based on students' literate experience. An anti-othering 'pedagogy of difference' emerges from students asking questions such as: '*How can I add English literacy to my existing literacies? Do I want to add English to these? What do I intend to achieve with such an addition?*' (Kubota and Lehner 2004: 22; italics in original).

Additional criticisms of CR have come from critical researchers. Pennycook (1998) compared Kaplan's (1966) diagram of 'Oriental' rhetoric with the musings of a nineteenth-century colonial schoolmaster in Hong Kong, who asserted that 'the average Chinese student was 'incapable of sustaining an argument, starting with false premisses [sic] and cheerfully pursuing a circuitous course to the point from which he started' (Pennycook 1998: 160). For Pennycook, Kaplan thus 'reproduces ... the view of the Other as deviant and ... as locked in ancient and unchanging modes of thought and action' (Kaplan 1966: 189), i.e. Orientalism (Said 1978).

Cahill (2003) questioned CR descriptions of Chinese and Japanese writing featuring a 'turn' – a conventional point at which their logic appears (at least to some Western scholars) radically discontinuous. *Ten* in the Japanese *ki-sho-ten-ketsu* style, described above, is a paradigm example. Cahill argued that Orientalist mischaracterization of turn elements was rampant in the CR literature, beginning with Hinds. Cahill found confirmatory evidence in Chinese and Japanese style guides and writing specialists who presented differing interpretations of the turn element – some similar to those Cahill was criticizing and others resembling, in Cahill's view, common rhetorical functions in English, such as expanding an argument:

> What the widely varying accounts of *zhuan/ten* ... reveal is that the original Chinese character of the third step, *zhuan*, can mean literally a turn or, figuratively speaking, a kind of change or shift. These scholars argue against arriving at exact definitions of *zhuan* and *ten* ... because *qi cheng zhuan he* and *ki sho ten ketsu* thereby retain their rich polysemy and metaphoricity. ... In the context of essay writing, the turn may be loosely defined as the occasion to develop an essay or paragraph further by alternative means. This redefinition demythologizes the turn from something mysteriously 'Eastern' into something closer to the Western rhetorical notion of amplification, broadly understood. The significant pedagogical implication is that the Chinese and the Japanese essay are more like the English essay than is commonly accepted.
>
> *Cahill (2003: 173)*

## 3. Intercultural rhetoric

Connor (2004, 2008) proposed that the field's name be changed from contrastive to intercultural rhetoric. Here, I summarize Connor's stated reasons for her proposal, others' assessments of it and related implications.

1. CR has undergone considerable development since Kaplan (1966), especially in the range of text types and contexts studied and research methods employed (Connor 2004). The call for a new name thus reflects CR/IR's field-internal development.
2. Critical scholars have radically rethought the culture concept. Connor and others (see next section) have started to bring these critiques into CR/IR, thereby providing an impetus to reconceptualize – and rename – the field.
3. If cultures are considerably more dynamic and negotiated than previously believed, then language is close behind. Connor (2008) advocated studying 'the interactive situations in which writers with a variety of linguistic and social/cultural backgrounds *negotiate* L2 writing in a great variety of situations for a variety of purposes' (Connor 2008: 312; italics added). In other words, 'contrastive' analysis is not the sole basis of CR/IR; it must also study the 'inters' – the 'in-between' spaces in which negotiation and accommodation occur among cultural/linguistic worlds. Connor (1999b) was a preliminary attempt to enact this vision, using accommodation theory as a conceptual lens. This study focused on spoken – not written – language, however.

4. Connor *et al.* (2008) viewed CR's critics as preoccupied with outmoded versions of it. A new name may therefore emphasize that the field has changed substantially over its nearly 50-year history. At the same time, Connor (2008: 313) welcomed 'the continuation of polemics' as a means of developing the field.

Connor's proposal has been assessed by other scholars in the field. Li (2008), a strong defender of CR, welcomed the change: 'A name denotes and connotes, describes and prescribes, connects and limits. It not only tells our colleagues who we are and what we do, but, more importantly, disposes what we tell ourselves we should do and will do' (Li 2008: 12). Welcoming critical questioning of CR/IR and its assumption of discrete cultures, Li nonetheless noted, regarding her research in China that, although much had changed there in recent years, much remained the same, and that 'fluidity is a valid concept only in relation to stability, just as permeability ... exists only when there are still borders' (Li 2005, quoted in Li 2008: 15).

In a transcribed academic conversation on CR, Matsuda and Atkinson (2008) discussed the prospect of an intercultural rhetoric. Matsuda argued that, although a new name might be useful, it needed to be accompanied by serious theoretical work – if CR's empirical efforts continued without developing its conceptual foundations, a name change would be counterproductive. At the same time, he called for broader (empirical) investigation of rhetorical practices across languages and cultures to provide a baseline for understanding how such practices come into 'contact or ... might influence each other' (ibid.: 284). Matsuda likewise suggested that the 'cultural' in 'intercultural' raises major issues: the need for a more complex understanding of culture in CR/IR and the rejection of culture as a straightforward explanatory construct.

Atkinson (2004), for his part, viewed the new name as suggesting 'that no rhetorical tradition is pure or purely indigenous. ... Therefore everything exists in an in-between space. ... [and] all social and cultural practices are deeply infused and penetrated by other cultural practices' (ibid.: 285). He argued that rhetorical differences could still be studied in CR/IR, but that studying 'only' differences was insufficient.

As these assessments suggest, IR is a work-in-progress. This may open it up to accusations that it is basically old wine in new bottles – that it continues some of the 'bad old ways' of CR. This makes it imperative to distinguish IR from its predecessor, without losing Kaplan's initial insight that, just as languages differ at the linguistic level, they 'may' differ at the level of textual organization, taking fully into account such complicating factors as context, genre, discourse community, individual preferences and experience, cross-linguistic influence, etc. Most importantly, the sheer complexity of confirming IR claims needs to be emphasized, as well as the extreme care that needs to be taken in doing so. As Matsuda and Atkinson also suggest, contrast, although a powerful way of looking, is only one way of looking – other approaches are also needed. In this sense, Xiaoye You's (2010) history of English writing in China – of how an alien rhetorical tradition was gradually but profoundly indigenized – may be a model for the future.

An additional goal for IR should be to respond to the field's critics. As valuable as their criticisms may be, they require dialectical engagement to test their usefulness and to aid progress in the field. To conclude this section, I therefore address work by two of CR's main critics.

Kubota (e.g. 1997) has built much of her critique of CR on the claim that Hinds 'overgeneralized' *ki-sho-ten-ketsu* to all Japanese expository prose, thus stereotyping Japanese rhetoric as unique and/or maximally different. Yet Hinds (1983a) introduced *four* 'major' Japanese expository prose forms, including *jo-ha-kyu*, which 'is similar to normal English rhetorical style' (Hinds 1983a: 80) – he had also described some of these forms in earlier writings (e.g. 1980).

Hinds' subsequent focus on *ki-sho-ten-ketsu* may be regrettably narrow, but it was hardly a claim for a single Japanese expository prose style. In addition, Hinds had moderated his view that *ki-sho-ten-ketsu* was maximally different from 'English rhetoric' well before Kubota appeared on the scene: 'The [*ki-sho-ten-ketsu*-organized] articles examined employ rhetorical conventions shared by English as well as … not used in English' (Hinds 1990: 93), and 'This is not to say that [*ki-sho-ten-ketsu*-like prose] cannot be found in languages other than Japanese, Korean, and Chinese. In fact, Mo (1982) has suggested that this pattern appears in many English paragraphs' (Hinds 1990: 100).

Pennycook's (1998) attempt to portray Kaplan as an Orientalist has similar problems. Pennycook claimed that Orientalist stereotyping of the 'illogical Other' and notions of cultural fixity pervaded both the writing of a nineteenth-century colonial headmaster and Kaplan (1966), as described above. Yet Kaplan nowhere claimed that Asian students were 'illogical'. He did consider the possibility, in asking whether a Korean student's supposed non-linear writing indicated a cultural lack of abstract thinking skills, but quickly dismissed it: 'This appears quite unlikely … in view of the fact that other native speakers of Korean have not demonstrated that shortcoming' (Kaplan 1966: 11). Pennycook claimed that Kaplan supported 'the view of the Other as locked in ancient and unchanging modes of thought and action' (Pennycook 2001: 189). Kaplan (1966) was, in Pennycook's (2001: 145) words, the 'locus classicus' of 'cultural fixity'. Kaplan, however, explicitly rejected such views: 'Rhetoric … varies … from time to time within a given culture. It is affected by canons of taste within a given culture at a given time' (Kaplan 1966: 2).

Pennycook and Kubota have thus essentialized CR by building straw-man arguments. This does not simply invalidate their critiques – Hinds did overstate the case for *ki-sho-ten-ketsu*, for instance, and he put his arguments in 'us-vs.-them' terms – but the rush to condemn on the flimsy 'evidence' described above does nothing to help us understand complex phenomena such as language and culture. If criticism is to be useful, it must be made fairly and responsibly.

## 4. Intercultural rhetoric and culture

Scholars (e.g. Hirvela 2009; Matsuda in Matsuda and Atkinson 2008) have argued that an adequate notion of culture is required for a viable IR. If culture is claimed to influence writing style, they suggest, then we need to know what culture is and how it does it.

Culture is, without question, a fraught and complex concept. This is true to the point that it is currently 'half-abandoned in anthropological theory' (Mazzarella 2004: 345) – by the very field that spent the twentieth century developing it. But the 'half-' is significant here; its sense was accurately captured by the culture critic James Clifford: 'Culture is a deeply compromised concept I cannot yet do without' (1988: 10). Having worked on culture theory intensively from 2000 to 2005, it is my sense that no adequate, unitary notion of culture will suddenly appear – that we must do what we can with what we have. I therefore briefly review culture theory below.

Franz Boas and his students originally developed the anthropological culture concept, based on German sources, to oppose race. Earlier anthropologists had ranked the 'races of man' by their supposed levels of cultural (including intellectual) development, with white Europeans on top and black Africans at or near the bottom. Boas attacked this pseudo-science, arguing that bloodlines had been so thoroughly mixed across human history that racial rankings were meaningless. Instead, people organized themselves 'culturally' – by the values, beliefs, arts, institutions, technologies and behaviours developed from dwelling together over long periods of time. Yet cultures were only stable-for-the-moment for Boas – they were mere collections of borrowings from neighbouring peoples, as described in Boas's favoured theory of cultural development, diffusionism. Boas's first doctoral student, Robert Lowie, defined culture (and civilization) as 'that planless hodgepodge, that thing of shreds and patches' (1920: 441), a definition strongly reflecting Boas's own views (Kuper 1999).

Boas's later students, however, took the concept in more deterministic directions (Stocking 1992). Ruth Benedict argued that cultures had their own distinctive 'personalities', whereas Margaret Mead wrote that 'a given temperamental approach to living could come so to dominate a culture that all ... born in it would become the willing or unwilling heirs to that view of the world' (1959/1989, quoted in Stocking 1992: 298). Such influential statements helped to cement the idea of deterministic cultural configurations and, in so doing, popularized culture as the master concept of what was increasingly called 'cultural anthropology'.

The 1970s saw the beginning of a backlash against the anthropological culture concept, based on both its own limitations and the growth of critical theory. Anthropologists had furthermore participated in neo-colonial adventures such as the Vietnam War and neo-colonial institutions such as the US Bureau of Indian Affairs. An additional contributing factor was Edward Said's (1978) theory of Orientalism, which viewed Western literary descriptions of 'the Orient' as ideological attempts to construct a dynamic, creative, individualistic and democratic West against the foil of a static, reproductive, groupist and despotic Orient.

In the 1980s and 1990s, cultural descriptions were criticized as the constructions of anthropologists embedded in ideologies of discrete, primitive, non-Western peoples. In the face of massive 'cultural flows' (Appadurai 1996), e.g. globalization, immigration and internationalized Western pop culture, the culture concept looked increasingly inadequate. Neo-Marxist, postmodernist, postcolonialist and feminist alternatives were proposed to fill the gap, some dispensing with the culture concept altogether. For academics still using culture in a received way (Atkinson 1999), these were dangerous times.

CR/IR has historically been one of those areas. As a direct result, it has been increasingly critiqued, spurring efforts in turn to update its culture concept. Atkinson (2004) proposed a range of culture concepts that might be useful in CR: (1) postmodernist views, which foreground the intense fragmentation of modern society; (2) neo-Marxist/cultural studies views, which treat cultures as sites of ideological struggle; (3) 'culture as process', which views cultures as ever-changing, ever-evolving phenomena; (4) 'culture in the head/culture in the world', which argues for a synthetic head–world space as culture's proper location (cf. Atkinson 1999, 2010); and (5) 'big cultures versus small cultures' (Holliday 1999), which conceptualizes cultures in all shapes and sizes, from single classrooms, to institutions, to professional–disciplinary cultures, to national cultures, and examines their interactions.

Yet Boas's original conceptualization also appears to contain many of the seeds of these later views, and so may help IR to think more deeply about culture. (1) Boasian culture is inherently unstable – or simply stable-for-the-moment. Chaos- and complexity-theoretic views of culture and society (e.g. Lyotard 1984), which explore the nature of communities in postmodern social orders, may have a role to play here. Thus, when Connor *et al.* (1995) began by assuming that Finnish grant writers applying for European Union grants followed English grant-writing conventions (they were, after all, writing in English), but ended up asking whether there were any conventions at all, one gets a sense of the complex instabilities inherent in current linguistic–cultural scenes. (2) Boasian culture is patched together out of 'other' cultures – Kubota's (1997) description of the possible historical effects of English (not to mention Chinese) on Japanese is one likely example. (3) Despite its unstable, patchwork character, Boas did view culture as powerfully influencing peoples' lives: It held them together and made them 'believe', at least, that they were one and the same people (cf. Anderson 1983). This suggests a combination of serious cultural influence – individuals are not just atoms floating freely in sociocultural space (e.g. Li 2008) – and ideological force – cultures are social constructions, and all constructs are 'interested' – i.e. political – as they are constructed by people themselves (e.g. Pennycook 2001) and likewise imposed by people on people. In speculating on these connections, I have doubtless stretched Boas's original culture concept beyond where it was meant to go, but what are concepts for if not stretching? At the same time, it is clear that only multiple efforts from multiple directions will suffice to develop a viable concept of culture for IR (and applied linguistics more generally – problems with the culture concept are by no means exclusive to IR).

## 5. Conclusion

Intercultural rhetoric has developed significantly since its founding almost 50 years ago. It began with notional analyses of L2 student essays, but now looks at writing in a variety of genres, by a variety of writers, in various situations, using various research tools (Connor 2008). If a field's success is marked by its ability to adapt to the times, then in generic, contextual and methodological terms, IR has been very successful. But growth is still needed at the theoretical/ conceptual level – this is where the biggest challenges now lie: What do IR scholars mean by culture? How does (this notion of) culture influence rhetorical–linguistic behaviour? What is language itself from a culturally and socially contextualized viewpoint, and how are global cultural flows changing this conceptualization? What, indeed, should be retained from Kaplan's classic insight, and what must be done to complexify, trouble and in some ways perhaps even overturn it? Without confronting these questions, IR will remain a promise (or a threat), but will not produce a better understanding of culture–writing connections or how to teach them, no matter how important those connections may be.

## Acknowledgements

I would like to thank Ulla Connor, Paul Kei Matsuda and Xiaoye You for thoughtful comments on an earlier version of this chapter.

## Related topics

Critical pedagogy; culture; identity; in-betweenness; language–thought relationship; language, power and identity; Othering; race; stereotyping; world Englishes

## Further reading

Connor, U., Nagelhout, E. and Rozycki, W. (eds) (2008) *Contrastive Rhetoric: Reaching to Intercultural Rhetoric*, Amsterdam: Benjamins (a collection of recent theoretical and empirical papers).
You, X. (2010) *Writing in the Devil's Tongue: A History of English Composition in China*, Carbondale, IL: Southern Illinois University Press (a historical account of an 'in-between' rhetoric, and a possible model for where IR can go in studying such phenomena).

## References

Anderson, B. (1983) *Imagined Communities: Reflections on the Origin And Spread of Nationalism*, London: Verso.
Appadurai, A. (1996) *Modernity at Large: Cultural Dimensions of Globalization*, Minneapolis, MN: University of Minnesota Press.

Atkinson, D. (1999) 'TESOL and culture', *TESOL Quarterly*, 33: 625–54.

——(2004) 'Contrasting rhetorics/contrasting cultures: why contrastive rhetoric needs a better conceptualization of culture', *Journal of English for Academic Purposes*, 3: 277–89.

——(2010) 'Extended, embodied cognition and second language acquisition', *Applied Linguistics*, 31(5): 599–622.

Cahill, D. (2003) 'The myth of the "turn" in contrastive rhetoric', *Written Communication*, 20: 170–94.

Clifford, J. (1988) *The Predicament of Culture: Twentieth-century Ethnography, Literature, and Art*, Cambridge, MA: Harvard University Press.

Connor, U. (1996) *Contrastive Rhetoric*, Cambridge: Cambridge University Press.

——(1999a) 'Learning how to write prose in a second language: a literacy autobiography', in G. Braine (ed.) *Non-native Educators in English Language Teaching*, Mahwah, NJ: Erlbaum, pp. 29–42.

——(1999b) 'How like you our fish: accommodation in international business communication', in M. Hewings and C. Nickerson (eds) *Business English: Research into Practice*, Harlow, UK: Longman, pp. 115–28.

——(2004) 'Intercultural rhetoric research: beyond texts', *Journal of English for Academic Purposes*, 3: 291–304.

——(2008) 'Mapping multidimensional aspects of research: reaching to intercultural rhetoric', in U. Connor, E. Nagelhout and W. Rozycki (eds) *Contrastive Rhetoric: Reaching toward Intercultural Rhetoric*, Amsterdam: Benjamins, pp. 219–315.

Connor, U. and Kaplan, R.B. (eds) (1987) *Writing across Languages: Analysis of L2 Text*, Reading, MA: Addison-Wesley.

Connor, U., Helle, T., Mauranen, A., Ringbom, H., Tirkkonen-Condit, S. and Marjo, Y-A. (1995) *Tehokkaita EU-Projectiehdotuksia. Ohjeita Kirjoittajille* [Successful European Union Grant Proposals: strategies for writers], Helsinki: TEKES.

Connor, U., Nagelhout, E. and Rozycki, W. (2008) 'Introduction', in U. Connor, E. Nagelhout and W. Rozycki (eds) *Contrastive Rhetoric: Reaching to Intercultural Rhetoric*, Amsterdam: Benjamins, pp. 1–8.

Hinds, J. (1980) 'Japanese expository prose', *Papers in Linguistics*, 13: 117–58.

——(1983a) 'Linguistics and written discourse in English and Japanese: a contrastive study (1978–82)', *Annual Review of Applied Linguistics*, 3: 78–84.

——(1983b) 'Contrastive rhetoric: Japanese and English', *Text*, 3: 183–95.

——(1987) 'Reader versus writer responsibility: a new typology', in U. Connor and R. B. Kaplan (eds) *Writing across Languages: Analysis of L2 Text*, Reading, MA: Addison-Wesley, pp. 141–52.

——(1990) 'Inductive, deductive, quasi-inductive: expository writing in Japanese, Korean, Chinese, and Thai', in U. Connor and A. Johns (eds) *Coherence in Writing: Research and Pedagogical Perspectives*, Alexandria, VA: TESOL, pp. 87–109.

Hirvela, A. (2009) 'Review of "Contrastive Rhetoric: Reaching to Intercultural Rhetoric"', *English for Specific Purposes*, 28: 286–88.

Holliday, A. (1999) 'Small cultures', *Applied Linguistics*, 20: 237–64.

Kaplan, R.B. (1966) 'Cultural thought patterns in intercultural education', *Language Learning*, 16: 1–20.

——(1972) *The Anatomy of Rhetoric: Prolegomena to a Functional Theory of Rhetoric*, Philadelphia: Center for Curriculum Development.

——(1987) 'Cultural thought patterns revisited', in U. Connor and R.B. Kaplan (eds) *Writing across Languages: Analysis of L2 Texts*, Reading, MA: Addison-Wesley, pp. 9–21.

——(1988) 'Contrastive rhetoric and second language learning: notes toward a theory of contrastive rhetoric', in A. Purves (ed.) *Writing across Languages and Cultures: Issues in Contrastive Rhetoric*, Newbury Park, CA: Sage, pp. 275–304.

——(1992) 'Contrastive rhetoric', in W. Bright (ed.) *International Encyclopedia of Applied Linguistics*, Oxford: Oxford University Press.

——(2005) 'Contrastive rhetoric', in E. Hinkel (ed.) *Handbook of Research in Second Language Teaching and Learning*, Mahwah, NJ: Erlbaum, pp. 375–91.

Kubota, R. (1997) 'A reevaluation of the uniqueness of Japanese written discourse', *Written Communication*, 14: 460–80.

——(1998) 'An investigation of L1–L2 transfer in writing among Japanese university students: implications for contrastive rhetoric', *Journal of Second Language Writing*, 7: 69–100.

Kubota, R. and Lehner, A. (2004) 'Toward critical contrastive rhetoric', *Journal of Second Language Writing*, 13: 7–27.

Kuper, A. (1999) *Culture: The Anthropologist's Account*, Cambridge, MA: Harvard University Press.

Leki, I. (1997) 'Cross-talk: ESL issues and contrastive rhetoric', in C. Severino, J. Guerra and J.E. Butler (eds) *Writing in Multi-cultural Settings*, New York: Modern Language Association of America, pp. 234–44.

Lemke, J. (1997) 'Cognition, context, and learning: a social semiotic perspective', in D. Kirshner and J.A. Whitson (eds) *Situated Cognition: Social, Semiotic, and Psychological Perspectives*, Mahwah, NJ: Erlbaum, pp. 37–55.

Li, X-M. (1996) *"Good Writing" in Cross-cultural Context*, Albany, NY: State University of New York Press.

——(2002) 'Track (dis)connecting: Chinese high school and university writing in a time of change', in D. Foster and D.R. Russell (eds) *Writing and Learning in Cross-national Perspective*, Urbana, IL: NCTE, pp. 49–87.

——(2005) 'Composing culture in a fragmented world: the issue of representation in cross-cultural research', in P.K. Matsuda and T. Silva (eds) *Second Language Writing Research: Perspectives on the Process of Knowledge Construction*, Mahwah, NJ: Erlbaum, pp. 121–31.

——(2008) 'From contrastive rhetoric to intercultural rhetoric: a search for collective identity', in U. Connor, E. Nagelhout and W. Rozycki (eds) *Contrastive Rhetoric: Reaching to Intercultural Rhetoric*, Amsterdam: Benjamins, pp. 11–24.

Lowie, R. (1920) *Primitive Society*, New York: Boni and Liveright.

Lyotard, J-F. (1984) *The Postmodern Condition*, Minneapolis, MN: University of Minnesota Press.

Matsuda, P.K. (1997) 'Contrastive rhetoric in context: a dynamic model of L2 writing', *Journal of Second Language Writing*, 6: 45–60.

Matsuda, P.K. and Atkinson, D. (2008) 'A conversation on contrastive rhetoric: Dwight Atkinson and Paul Kei Matsuda talk about issues, conceptualizations, and the future of contrastive rhetoric', in U. Connor, E. Nagelhout and W. Rozycki (eds) *Contrastive Rhetoric: Reaching to Intercultural Rhetoric*, Amsterdam: Benjamins, pp. 277–98.

Mauranen, A. (1993) *Cultural Differences in Academic Rhetoric*, Berlin: Peter Lang.

Mazzarella, W. (2004) 'Culture, globalization, mediation', *Annual Review of Anthropology*, 33: 345–67.

Mead, M. (1959/1989). 'Preface', in R. Benedict, *Patterns of Culture*, Boston, MA: Houghton-Mifflin, pp. xiii.

Mohan, B. and Lo, W. (1985) 'Academic writing and Chinese students: transfer and development', *TESOL Quarterly*, 19: 515–34.

Pennycook, A. (1998) *English and the Discourses of Colonialism*, London: Routledge.

——(2001) *Critical Applied Linguistics*, Mahwah, NJ: Erlbaum.

Said, E. (1978) *Orientalism*, New York: Vintage.

Stocking, G. (1992) *The Ethnographer's Magic and Other Essays in the History of Anthropology*, Madison, WI: University of Wisconsin Press.

Takemata, K. (1976) *Genko Shippitsu Nyumon* [An Introduction to Writing Manuscripts], Tokyo: Natsumesha.

Whorf, B.L. (1956) *Language, Thought, and Reality*, Cambridge, MA: Technology Press of MIT.

You, X. (2010) *Writing in the Devil's Tongue: A History of English Composition in China*, Carbondale, IL: Southern Illinois University Press.

# 8

# Nonverbal communication

## The messages of emotion, action, space, and silence

*David Matsumoto and Hyi-Sung Hwang*

## 1. Introduction

Although "language" often comes to mind first when considering communication, no discussion of communication is complete without the inclusion of nonverbal behaviors. These are all the behaviors that occur during communication that do *not* involve verbal language, and include facial expressions, nonverbal vocal cues, gestures, body postures, interpersonal distance, touching, and gaze. Some authors even consider the way you dress, the placement of your office within a building, the use of time, blinking, or the arrangement of your room as aspects of nonverbal communication (Henley 1977).

Collectively, nonverbal behaviors (NVBs) serve many functions. They signal emotions, attitudes, physiological states, and other mental states; they illustrate speech and regulate conversation; they convey verbal messages; and they manipulate the body. Given the wealth of information that they communicate, it is no wonder that studies that have compared the relative contributions of verbal vs. NVB in conveying messages report that the vast majority of the messages communicated are nonverbal (Friedman 1978). This is ironic, especially because most people consciously attend to the verbal language when interacting with others (Ekman *et al.* 1980; O'Sullivan *et al.* 1985). NVB is part of the "hidden dimension" of communication, a silent language (Hall 1966, 1973), and not paying attention to it means that one misses many messages that are being conveyed. Thus, although active listening is always good, active observation is also necessary.

Although there are some NVBs that have universal and probably biologically rooted bases, culture influences NVB in profound ways. Just as members of every culture learn to communicate with verbal language, they also learn to communicate nonverbally in culture-specific ways as well. When interacting with people of different cultures, one deals not only with different verbal languages, but with different NVBs. Understanding and even performing the mannerisms and associated NVBs of a language aids in becoming culturally as well as linguistically fluent (akin to the intercultural communicative competence of intercultural mediators described by Byram, Chapter 5, and Wilkinson, Chapter 18, this volume). These differences make intercultural interactions more complex and difficult than intracultural interactions, and lead to greater potential difficulties in relationships. We will return to this point at the end of the chapter. First, we review the main research findings from literature examining the influence of culture on the various NVBs and discuss how these influences contribute to the intercultural communication process. We begin our presentation with a discussion of culture and facial expressions.

## 2. Culture and facial expressions of emotion

### The universality of facial expressions

Questions concerning the universality of facial expression find their roots in Darwin's (1872) work, where he suggested that emotions and their expressions had evolved across species, were evolutionarily adaptive, biologically innate, and universal across humans and even non-human primates. According to Darwin, all humans, regardless of race or culture, possess the ability to express emotions in exactly the same ways, primarily through their faces. Darwin's position was not without its detractors, most notably anthropologists such as Margaret Mead, who argued that facial expressions of emotion were culture specific, learned differently in each culture like verbal language. Until the 1960s, only seven studies attempted to test the universality of facial expression. Unfortunately, these studies were inconclusive, so that unequivocal data speaking to the possible universality of emotional expression did not emerge at that time (Ekman et al. 1972).

It was not until the mid-1960s that psychologist Sylvan Tomkins, a pioneer in modern studies of human emotion, joined forces independently with Paul Ekman and Carroll Izard to conduct what is known today as the "universality studies". In the first set of studies, these researchers obtained judgments of faces thought to express emotions panculturally and demonstrated that all cultures agreed on the emotions portrayed in the expressions (Ekman 1972, 1973; Ekman and Friesen 1971; Ekman et al. 1969; Izard 1971). Collectively, these findings demonstrated the existence of six universal expressions—anger, disgust, fear, happiness, sadness, and surprise—as judges from around the world agreed on what emotion was portrayed in the faces.

The results from these early studies were open to criticism because the cultures studied were relatively industrialized, and participants may have learned to interpret the faces shown because of shared visual input through mass media, such as movies or magazines. To address this limitation, Ekman and colleagues (Ekman and Friesen 1971; Ekman et al. 1969) conducted two studies with two preliterate tribes—the Fore and the Dani—in the highlands of New Guinea. In the first study, Ekman showed that the tribespeople could recognize the faces of emotion posed by Westerners; in the second, films of the tribespeople expressing emotions were shown to Americans who had never seen New Guineans before, and the Americans recognized the emotions portrayed by the New Guineans. Thus, the ability to recognize facial expressions of emotion did not occur because of learning through mass media or other shared visual input.

One of the most important findings related to universality came from Friesen's (1972) cross-cultural study of expressions that occurred spontaneously in reaction to emotion-eliciting films. American and Japanese participants viewed neutral and highly stressful films while their facial behaviors were recorded. Coding of those behaviors that occurred when viewing the films identified the same expressions associated with the six emotions mentioned previously; they corresponded to the facial expressions portrayed in the stimuli used in the previous judgment studies. This study provided the first evidence that facial expressions of emotion were universally produced.

After the original universality studies, a seventh facial expression—contempt—was found to be universally recognized (Ekman and Heider 1988; Matsumoto 1992b). Over the past four decades, there have been well over 100 judgment studies that have demonstrated the pancultural recognition of these seven expressions (Elfenbein and Ambady 2002; Matsumoto 2001). And there have been over seventy-five studies that have demonstrated that these very same facial expressions are produced by individuals all over the world when emotions are elicited spontaneously (Matsumoto et al. 2008a). These findings are impressive, given that they have been produced by different researchers around the world, in different laboratories using different methodologies, but all converging on the same set of results. Thus today, there is strong evidence for the universal facial expressions of seven emotions (see Figure 8.1).

These expressions appear to be biologically innate. In one of our most recent studies, we examined the spontaneous facial expressions of congenitally blind judo athletes from the 2004 Athens Paralympics Games immediately after they had either won or lost a match for a medal, and compared their expressions with sighted athletes at the 2004 Athens Olympic Games in exactly the same contexts (Matsumoto and Willingham 2006, 2009). The blind athletes produced exactly the same expressions as the sighted athletes. Because they could not possibly have learned to produce them visually from birth, humans must be born with the innate capacity to produce them when they are spontaneously elicited.[1]

## Cultural differences in expressing emotion

Despite the existence of universal facial expressions of emotion, people around the world express emotions differently. The first evidence for cultural differences in expression occurred in Friesen's (1972) study. In the first condition described above, the Americans and Japanese viewed highly

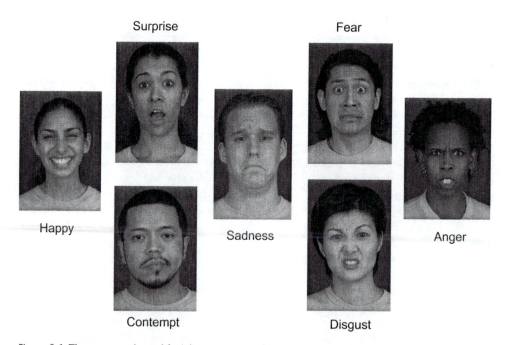

*Figure 8.1* The seven universal facial expressions of emotion
*Source*: Reproduced with permission from David Matsumoto.

stressful films alone, and produced the same expressions. In a subsequent condition, they viewed the films in the presence of an older, male experimenter. In this second condition, the Americans continued to express their negative emotions, but the Japanese were more likely to smile.

Ekman and Friesen (1969) coined the term "cultural display rules" to account for cultural differences in facial expressions of emotion. These are rules learned early in childhood that help individuals manage and modify their emotional expressions depending on social circumstances. This concept explained the cultural differences observed in Friesen's (1972) study. In the first condition of the experiment, there was no reason for display rules to modify expressions because the participants were alone and their display rules were inoperative; in the second condition, display rules dictated that the Japanese mask their negative emotions in the presence of the experimenter (Friesen 1972).

When the concept of display rules was proposed originally as a mechanism of expression management, Ekman and Friesen (1969) noted six ways in which expressions may be managed when emotion is aroused. Individuals can express emotions as they feel them with no modification. But individuals can also amplify (exaggerate) or demulsify (minimize) their expressions; for instance, feelings of sadness may be intensified (amplification) at funerals or minimized (deamplification) at weddings. People can mask or conceal their emotions by expressing something other than what they feel, as when nurses or physicians hide their emotions when speaking to patients with terminal illness, or when employees in service industries (e.g., flight attendants) interact with customers. Individuals may also learn to neutralize their expressions, expressing nothing, such as when playing poker (poker face), or to qualify their feelings by expressing emotions in combination, such as when feelings of sadness are mixed with a smile, with the smile commenting on the sadness, saying "I'll be OK". All these behavioral responses have been found to occur when spontaneous expressive behaviors have been studied (Cole 1986; Ekman and Rosenberg 1998).

As other studies documenting cultural differences in expression began to pepper the literature (e.g., Argyle et al. 1986; Edelmann et al. 1987; Gudykunst and Nishida 1984; Waxer 1985), a consensus in the field emerged that, when emotions are aroused, the displays are either universal or culture specific, depending on context. Recent research has shown that emotional displays can be both for the same person in the same context if displays are examined "in sequence across time". To demonstrate this possibility, we reanalyzed the data from the study of Olympic judo athletes (Matsumoto and Willingham 2006) by examining changes in the athletes' expressions after their initial reactions (Matsumoto et al. 2009a). We classified the subsequent expressions into one of several regulation strategies, and examined the relationship between these expressive styles and cultural variables, such as Hofstede's (2001) cultural dimensions, and country demographics such as population density and affluence. Although the athletes' initial reactions were universal, their subsequent expressions were culturally regulated and reliably associated with population density, affluence, and individualism. Athletes from urban, individualistic cultures expressed their emotions more; athletes from less urban, more collectivistic cultures masked their emotions more. Thus, emotional expressions can be both universal and culture specific in the same individuals in the same context, provided that expressions are examined across time. Expressive styles involving greater modification of the original initial reaction require more time for display than expressive styles involving relatively less modification, likely because the former recruit greater neurocognitive resources. Expressive modes that allow for the continued expression of the initial emotion or only slight modifications of its intensity (deamplification) require less such modification, and thus result in shorter elapsed times from initial response.

| Immediately at match competition | A few seconds later... | A few seconds after that... |

*Figure 8.2* An example from the 2004 Athens Olympic Games
*Source*: Reproduced with the kind permission of © Bob Willingham.

The fact that expressions change across time and are more culturally variable subsequent to an initial, immediate, universal emotional reaction explains why beliefs about the pervasiveness of cultural differences in expression exist. When intense emotions are aroused, attention is often drawn to the stimulus event and *not* the expressive behaviors of the individuals in that event (Figure 8.2a). Although attention is given to the eliciting event, immediate universal reactions occur but are missed. When attention returns to the individuals, they are already beginning to engage in culturally regulated behavior (Figure 8.2b). Such a process may perpetuate beliefs about the cultural variability of expressive behavior. Because we tend to believe our experiences, it is easier to believe the existence of cultural differences in expressive behavior, because that is what we often see.

## A worldwide mapping of cultural display rules

After the original inception of display rules, published cross-cultural research was dormant until Matsumoto's (1990) study examining display rules in Americans and Japanese and a similar study documenting differences in display rules among four ethnic groups within the US (Matsumoto 1993). Fifteen years ago, we created the Display Rule Assessment Inventory (DRAI), in which participants choose a behavioral response when they experience different emotions in different social situations (Matsumoto *et al.* 1998, 2005). Preliminary studies using this measure demonstrated cultural differences in display rules, and provided evidence for its internal and temporal reliability and for its content, convergent (with measures of emotion regulation), discriminant (correlations with personality controlling for emotion regulation), external, and concurrent predictive validity with personality.

Working with many collaborators, we (Matsumoto *et al.* 2008b) administered the DRAI in over thirty countries, examining universal and culture-specific aspects to display rules, and linking the cultural differences to culture-level individualism–collectivism. Despite the large potential range of scores, most countries' means on overall expression endorsement fell around the midpoint, and there was relatively small variation around this mean, suggesting a universal norm for expression regulation. Individuals from all cultures endorsed expressions toward in-groups more than toward out-groups, indicating another universal effect. Collectivistic cultures were associated with a display rule norm of less expressivity overall than individualistic cultures,

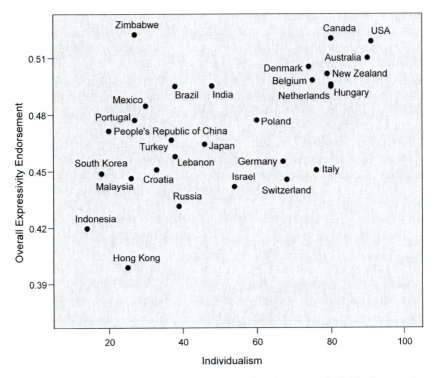

*Figure 8.3* Graphical representation of the relationship between individualism and overall expressivity endorsement

*Source*: Matsumoto et al. (2008b: 66). Reproduced with permission.

suggesting that overall expressive regulation for all emotions is central to the preservation of social order in these cultures (Figure 8.3). This finding is commensurate with the behavioral findings from previous studies (Friesen 1972; Matsumoto and Kupperbusch 2001; Matsumoto *et al.* 2009a). Individualism was also positively associated with higher expressivity norms in general, and for positive emotions in particular. And it was positively associated with endorsement of expressions of all emotions toward in-groups, but negatively correlated with all negative emotions and positively correlated with happiness and surprise toward out-groups. Cumulatively, these findings suggest a fairly nuanced view of the relationship between culture and expression endorsement that varies as a function of emotion, interactant, and overall expressivity endorsement levels.

A secondary analysis of the DRAI dataset allowed us to compute indices of variability according to context. We examined the relationships between these indices and Hofstede's (2001) and Schwartz's (2006) value dimensions. The findings indicated that context variability was positively correlated with power distance, embeddedness, hierarchy, and mastery, and negatively correlated with individualism, affective autonomy, egalitarianism, and intellectual autonomy (Matsumoto *et al.* 2009b). Based on these findings, we coined the term "context differentiation" as a potential, stable dimension of variability, at both cultural and individual levels.

## Cultural similarities and differences in judging emotion

There is overwhelming evidence that the seven universal facial expressions are panculturally recognized (Elfenbein and Ambady 2002; Matsumoto 2001). Cultures are similar in other aspects of emotion judgment as well. For example, there is pancultural similarity in judgments of relative intensity among faces; that is, when comparing expressions, people from different countries agree on which is more strongly expressed (Ekman *et al.* 1987; Matsumoto and Ekman 1989). There is also pancultural agreement on the association between perceived expression intensity and inferences about subjective experiences (Matsumoto *et al.* 1999). People from different cultures also agree on the secondary emotions portrayed in an expression (Biehl *et al.* 1997; Ekman *et al.* 1987; Matsumoto and Ekman 1989), suggesting pancultural agreement in the multiple meanings derived from universal faces. This agreement may exist because of overlap in the semantics of the emotion categories, antecedents and elicitors of emotion, or in the facial configurations themselves. There are cultural differences in emotion judgments as well, for instance, on the absolute levels of recognition across cultures (Matsumoto 1989, 1992a; Matsumoto *et al.* 2002), and attributions about the intensity of expressions (Biehl *et al.* 1997; Ekman *et al.* 1987; Matsumoto *et al.* 1999, 2002).

## An in-group advantage to facial emotion recognition?

One type of cultural difference in emotion judgment that has received attention recently concerns the possibility of an "in-group advantage" in emotion recognition (Elfenbein and Ambady 2002). This refers to the tendency for individuals to more accurately recognize emotional expressions produced by members of their own culture rather than those produced by another. Researchers arguing for the existence of this effect have suggested that it occurs because of "emotion dialects"—culturally derived, minor variants of emotional expressions (Elfenbein *et al.* 2007; Wickline *et al.* 2009). Presumably, people are more accurate when judging such expressions because those expressions are used differently in their culture. For instance, raising an eyebrow could be a sign of skepticism in one culture. If people of that culture judged the expressions of encoders raising an eyebrow, they are likely to respond that the expression was one of skepticism. People from another culture, however, may not because the expression may not be used in that culture, or it may have a different meaning in that culture. Unfortunately, none of the research reported to date claiming to support the in-group hypothesis has utilized spontaneous expressions that would support a dialect theory; instead, all the research cited to support the hypothesis has involved expressions that were posed by members of different cultures, and were not equivalent across cultural groups.

Recently, we tested the dialect theory of the in-group effect using spontaneous expressions produced by members of different cultures in a naturalistic field setting (Matsumoto *et al.* 2009c). The expressions came from Matsumoto and Willingham's (2006) study of athletes during the judo competition of the 2004 Athens Olympic Games. Across all emotions studied, the in-group advantage hypothesis was *not* supported, suggesting that the effect reported in previous studies may be localized to non-equivalent, posed expressions. That is, the cultural in-group advantage hypothesis may not be ecologically valid because they have occurred only with posed mimes. Mimed expressions may not be valid analogs of actually occurring expressions when emotions are aroused because they may include extraneous muscle movements, or not include muscle movements that would occur spontaneously. Innervated muscles may also be at different intensity levels or symmetries from spontaneous expressions. Any of these possible characteristics of posed expressions may be sufficient to produce the dialects proposed by Elfenbein and colleagues (2007), which, in turn, produced the in-group effect in the past. Future studies need to examine whether the cultural dialects Elfenbein and colleagues suggest occur actually do occur in real life, and if these truly produce in-group advantages in emotion recognition. The data to date suggest they do not.

## Judging faces in context

Despite the fact that facial expressions always occur in context in real life, most mono- or cross-cultural judgment studies, including those described above, present them fairly acontextually. Writers have long debated the relative contribution of face and context in contributing to emotion messages by studying congruent and incongruent face–context combinations (Bruner and Tagiuri 1954; Ekman and O'Sullivan 1988; Fernberger 1928). One type of study in this genre is that which examines the linkage between an emotion-eliciting context and a facial expression, which we have called "response linkage" (Matsumoto and Hwang 2010). Studies involving congruent response linkages have found an additive effect (Bruner and Tagiuri 1954; Knudsen and Muzekari 1983), which probably occurred because of the increased signal clarity in the overall emotion message when two different signal sources provide the same message. Interestingly, studies involving incongruent response linkages have demonstrated a face superiority effect, indicating that the signals in the face tend to override the signals provided by the context (Ekman and O'Sullivan 1988; Ekman et al. 1991; Nakamura et al. 1990).

But do these effects exist across cultures? We conducted two studies involving observers from three cultures (the US, Japan, and South Korea) who judged facial expressions of anger, sadness, and happiness presented together with a congruent or incongruent emotion-eliciting context (Matsumoto et al. in press). When faces were congruent with contexts, the agreement rates in judgments were near perfect, with no cultural differences. This suggests that our (and others') previous work documenting cultural differences in emotion recognition rates may have been the result of methodological artefacts, at least partially that is, of the fact that observers were asked to make judgments of emotion solely from faces. In reality, such judgments are made from multiple cues from both faces and contexts, and it makes sense that, when multiple cues are given, cultural differences are eliminated. When faces and contexts were incongruent, there were both face and context effects, and the relative contributions of each were moderated by culture. American judgments were more influenced by faces, whereas Japanese and South Korean judgments were more influenced by context. The results provided a more nuanced view of how both culture and emotion moderate judgments of faces in context—by showing how face and context effects occur simultaneously—and how cultural differences existed in the judgments.

## 3. Culture and gestures

Gestures are primarily hand movements that are used basically for two purposes—to illustrate speech and to convey verbal meaning. (There are also facial gestures that are used for the same purposes as well.) "Speech illustrators" are movements that are directly tied to speech, and illustrate or highlight what is being said. Illustrators can be classified into six categories (Efron 1941; Freedman and Hoffmann 1967):

1. Batons—movements that emphasize a word or phrase, sometimes temporally;
2. Ideographs—movements that draw a thought or sketch a path;
3. Deictic movements, such as pointing;
4. Spatial movements, which illustrate spatial relationships;
5. Kinetographs, which depict bodily action;
6. Pictographs, which draw a picture of their referent.

Batons and ideographs typically have no meaning without the accompanying words. The other illustrators may have some verbal content, even without the accompanying words. But all illustrative gestures are associated with verbal behavior on a moment-to-moment basis (Kita *et al.* 2007), and are directly tied to speech content, verbal meaning, and voice volume. They likely occur outside of or with minimal conscious awareness and intention.

Cultures differ in both the amount and type of these various illustrative gestures. Some cultures, such as Latin and Middle Eastern cultures, strongly encourage the use of large, illustrative gestures when speaking; they are highly expressive in their gesticulation. Others, such as East Asian cultures, discourage the use of such gestures, especially when in public; they are relatively less expressive in their gesticulation. Cultural differences exist not only in the overall frequency of usage, amplitude, and duration, but also in forms. When counting, for example, Germans use the thumb for one, whereas Canadians and Americans use the index finger (Pika *et al.* 2009).

The other purpose of gestures is to convey verbal meaning without words. These are known as "emblematic gestures" or "emblems". Every culture develops its own emblem vocabulary in gestures, which are tied to words or phrases; emblems, therefore, are culture specific (and some are gender specific within cultures). This is true not only of national cultures, but also of organizational cultures (e.g., the military, sports teams). Unlike illustrative gestures, emblematic gestures can stand on their own without speech and convey verbal meaning, such as the American A-OK sign, the peace sign (two fingers up, palm facing outward), or OK (thumb up, hand in fist). Emblems are an important part of any cultural language because they allow for communication across distances when voices cannot be readily heard, or when speech is not allowed or wise.

The study of culture and gestures has its roots in the work of Efron (Boas *et al.* 1936; Efron 1941), who examined the gestures of Sicilian and Lithuanian Jewish immigrants in New York City. Efron found that there were distinct gestures among traditional Jews and Italians, but that the gestures disappeared as people were more assimilated into the larger American culture. This work was followed initially by that of Ekman and his colleagues (Ekman 1976; Friesen *et al.* 1979), who documented cultural differences in emblematic gestures between Japanese, Americans, and New Guineans. Morris and his colleagues (Morris *et al.* 1980) have also documented many cultural differences in gestures.

| Apology in Nepal | "Too hot to touch" in China | "Oh my eye! (You liar!)" in Iran |

*Figure 8.4* Examples of culturally unique emblems
*Source*: Reproduced with permission from © David Matsumoto, author.

Because emblems are culture specific, their meanings across cultures are often different and sometimes offensive. The American A-OK sign, for example, is an obscene gesture in many cultures of Europe, having sexual implications. Placing both hands at the side of one's head and pointing upwards with the forefingers signals that one is angry in some cultures (such as Japan); in others, it refers to the devil; and in others, it means that one wants sex. The inverted peace sign—two fingers up in a fist pointed inward toward oneself—is an insult in England and Australia. (See Figure 8.4 for examples of other emblems.)

Although emblems are culture specific, our latest research suggests that a number of them are becoming universally recognized, such as come, go, hello, goodbye, yes, and no (Hwang *et al.* 2010). These results are likely being driven by the strong influence of mass media around the world, particularly television and the internet, where people can view the behaviors of others of different cultures and begin learning how to decode behaviors. We predict that it is only a matter of time before a universal set of emblematic gestures is also produced panculturally as well.

## 4. Culture and gaze

Gaze is a powerful NVB, most likely because of its evolutionary roots in animals. Research in both humans and nonhuman primates has shown that gaze is associated with dominance, power, or aggression (Fehr and Exline 1987), as well as affiliation and nurturance (Argyle and Cook 1976). The affiliative aspects of gazing begin in infancy (Fehr and Exline 1987), as infants attend to adults as their source of care and protection. The power of gaze is exemplified in "the staring game", in which two individuals stare at each other until one breaks off the stare or smiles; the individual that does so is the loser. Interestingly, such staring games are also done in animal societies, and establish dominance hierarchies.

Cultures create rules concerning gazing and visual attention because both aggression and affiliation are behavioral tendencies that are important for group stability and maintenance. Cultures differ in these rules. Arabs, for example, gaze much longer and more directly at their partners than do Americans (Hall 1963; Watson and Graves 1966). Watson (1970), who classified thirty countries as either a "contact" culture (those that facilitated physical touch or contact during interaction) or a "noncontact" culture, found that contact cultures engaged in more gazing and had more direct orientations when interacting with others, less interpersonal distance, and more touching. Within the US, ethnic groups differ in gaze and visual behavior (Exline *et al.* 1977; LaFrance and Mayo 1976).

Gaze is often used as a nonverbal sign of respect. But because different cultures produce different rules concerning gaze, respect is conveyed differently with gaze. In the US, individuals are taught to "look the other person in the eye" or to "look at me when you're talking". In the US, looking directly at the individual to whom one is talking is a sign of respect. In many other cultures, however, that behavior is a sign of disrespect, and looking away or even looking down is a sign of respect. Thus, it is easy to understand how Americans may judge people of other cultures as disrespectful or insincere, whereas individuals from other cultures may judge Americans to be aggressive or arrogant.

Stereotypes about gaze also belie judgments of deception and credibility. In the US, a commonly held belief is that, when people are not looking one straight in the eye, they are likely to be lying. Not only is that probably not true (there is little or no empirical support for this myth), but the cultural differences mentioned immediately above compound the situation even more, allowing Americans to believe that foreigners are lying when in fact they might simply be acting deferentially.

## 5. Culture and voice

The voice is another important channel of NVB, and conveys many different messages. Of course, words are communicated through speech and the voice, but the voice also contains many characteristics that go well beyond the speech in communicating messages. These characteristics are called "paralinguistic cues", and include the tone of voice, intonation, pitch, speech rate, use of silence, and volume.

Early work on paralinguistic cues provided evidence that some specific emotional states were conveyed through the voice across cultures (Beier and Zautra 1972; McCluskey and Albas 1981; Matsumoto and Kishimoto 1983; Scherer 1986), a view that has garnered even more support in recent work (Sauter and Eimer 2010; Sauter et al. 2010; Simon-Thomas et al. 2009). Anger, for instance, produces a harsh edge to the voice; the voice gets louder, and speech rates increase. Disgust produces "yucch" sounds, whereas fear produces higher pitch and sudden inhalations. Sadness produces softer voices and decreased speech rates.

The voice and verbal style are also used to illustrate and amplify speech, and culture moderates the use of these vocal characteristics in social interaction. Expressive cultures use louder voices with higher speech rates, whereas less expressive cultures use softer voices with lower speech rates. Additionally, the pronunciations of some languages require the production of different sounds and rhythms in the voice that may be associated with different emotions (e.g., the guttural quality of some Germanic languages, the up and down rhythms of Mandarin). Whereas in the cultures in which these vocal cues originate they sound normal, in other cultures, it is easy to have negative reactions to these because they sound different and are associated with aversive emotions.

## 6. Culture, interpersonal space, and touch

The use of space in interpersonal interactions is another important NVB, and is called "proxemics". Hall's (1966, 1973) classic work in this area specified four different levels of interpersonal space use depending on social relationship type: intimate, personal, social, and public. He suggested that interpersonal distance helps to regulate intimacy by controlling sensory exposures, because the possibility of sensory stimulation (smells, sights, touch) is enhanced at closer distances. For this reason, it makes good sense that cultures regulate the use of space, as such regulation is necessary for social coordination; violations of space bring about aversive reactions (Sussman and Rosenfeld 1978).

People of all cultures appear to use space according to the four major distinctions proposed by Hall (1966, 1973), but they differ in the spaces they attribute to them. Arab males, for example, tend to sit closer to each other than American males, with more direct, confrontational types of body orientations (Watson and Graves 1966). They also use greater eye contact and speak in louder voices. Arabs, at least in the past, learned to interact with others at distances close enough to feel the other person's breath (Hall 1963, 1966). Latin Americans tend to interact more closely than do students from European backgrounds (Forston and Larson 1968), and Indonesians tend to sit closer than Australians (Noesjirwan 1977, 1978). Italians interact more closely than either Germans or Americans (Shuter 1977), and Colombians interact at closer distances than do Costa Ricans (Shuter 1976). When interacting with someone from their same culture, Japanese sat the farthest away, Venezuelans the closest, with Americans in the middle (Sussman and Rosenfeld 1982); interestingly, in the same study, foreigners who spoke in English adopted the American conversational distance compared with when speaking with others from their home country in their native language. Cultural differences in the use of space even occurs when individuals set dolls to interact with each other (Little 1968).

A logical extension of interpersonal space is touch, as touch requires close physical contact. Touch is another powerful NVB, and is known as "haptics". Recent research has demonstrated that touch communicates distinct emotions, such as anger, fear, disgust, love, gratitude, and sympathy across cultures (Hertenstein *et al.* 2006, 2009). Just as cultures regulate space, they also regulate touch. As mentioned above, Watson (1970) classified thirty countries as either a "contact" culture (those that facilitated physical touch or contact during interaction) or a "noncontact" culture. Violations of the cultural rules regarding touch are likely to be interpreted in the same way as those of space, producing aversive consequences.

## 7. Culture, postures, and gait

Postures communicate attitudinal states and general affect, as opposed to the very specific emotions communicated by face and voice. These attitudinal and general affective states include liking vs. disliking, orientation (closed or open), attention (direct or indirect), and openness vs. closedness. These various dimensions can be summarized as communicating general positivity as well as status relationships (Mehrabian 1968a, 1968b, 1969).

There is surprising little systematic research on the production or interpretation of the meaning of postures across cultures. The studies that do exist suggest that people of different cultures interpret postures according to the same dimensions (i.e., positivity, status), but place different weights of importance on specific aspects of these dimensions (Kudoh and Matsumoto 1985; Matsumoto and Kudoh 1987).

Another aspect of NVB related to whole body movement is gait, which is the pattern of movement of the body when walking. To our knowledge, there are no direct studies that examine cultural similarities or differences in gait. But, there has been some interesting research on the speed with which individuals across cultures typically move through their cities (Kirk-caldy *et al.* 2001; Levine and Bartlett 1984; Levine *et al.* 1989; Levine and Norenzayan 1999). These studies have demonstrated that pace is associated with punctuality, coronary heart disease, and a variety of attitudinal and personality traits. These studies, and the relative lack of studies on culture, posture, and gait, suggest that this area is ripe for study.

## 8. Conclusion

The existing literature strongly suggests that culture influences NVB in important and profound ways. We believe that cultural differences in NVB can be summarized according to cultural norms associated with overall expressivity that is encouraged or discouraged in specific cultures (see Table 8.1). Expressive cultures are likely to facilitate the use of facial expressions and gestures more frequently, with greater intensity and duration; the use of louder voices, direct gaze, with relaxed and open postures, at closer distances. On the other hand, reserved cultures are more likely to facilitate the use of fewer facial expressions and gestures, softer voices, avoid direct gaze, with more rigid, closed postures at relatively greater distances.[2]

Clearly, cultural differences in NVB make intercultural interactions and communications more difficult than intracultural communication. Intercultural communication is likely to be marred by uncertainty and ambiguity, not only because of questions concerning the verbal messages, but also because of cultural differences in the NVBs associated with the verbal messages. These are likely to lead to aversive reactions that increase the potential for misunderstanding, miscommunication, and misattributions about intent or character, which disrupts social coordination and increases the potential for conflict. It is easier for people from expressive cultures to judge those from reserved cultures as being untrustworthy, inscrutable, sly, or shifty.

*Table 8.1* Cultural norms associated with expressivity

| Channel | Type of culture | |
|---|---|---|
| | Expressive | Reserved |
| Face | Many facial expressions, animated, regularly show emotions, use of face to amplify and illustrate speech | Fewer facial expressions, fewer emotions, more controlling expressions |
| Gesture | Many illustrating gestures, large motions, higher frequency of emblem usage | Fewer illustrating gestures, smaller motions, lower frequency of emblem usage |
| Voice | Louder voices, deeper range, higher speech rate | Softer voices, diminished range, lower speech rates |
| Gaze | Direct gaze at eyes of person to whom one is speaking | Less direct gaze at eyes of person to whom one is speaking |
| Interpersonal space and touch | Closer distances in interaction, more likely to touch | Farther distances in interaction, less likely to touch |
| Posture | More relaxed, open postures | More rigid, closed postures |

At the same time, it is easier for people from reserved cultures to judge those from expressive cultures as arrogant, loud, rude, immature, or vulgar. Many of these aversive reactions occur unconsciously and automatically, because they are rooted in cultural filters for interpreting the appropriateness of behavior that are developed from early on through the process of enculturation.

Many of these interpretations and attributions, however, may be incorrect because the cultural filters that one uses to interpret the NVBs of others may or may not be the cultural framework within which the person's behavior is rooted. When considering NVBs in the context of intercultural interactions, it is important to realize that cultural differences in NVBs exist, that engaging with such differences may produce negative emotional reactions, and that these differences and reactions are a normal and inevitable part of the communication process. By creating these kinds of expectations, we can begin to ensure that intercultural interactions are not an obstacle, but instead a platform, for staging the development and exchange of ideas and the sharing of goals in new and exciting ways not actualized by intracultural communication.

## Related topics

Culture; facework; intercultural communicative competence; linguaculture, politeness; speech acts

## Further reading

Darwin, C. (1872) *The Expression of Emotion in Man and Animals*, New York: Oxford University Press (explores the roots of most modern-day studies and understanding of emotion and nonverbal behavior).

Efron, D. (1941) *Gesture and Environment*, Oxford: King's Crown Press (one of the earliest surveys of emblematic gestures).

Ekman, P. and Friesen, W.V. (1969) 'The repertoire of nonverbal behavior: categories, origins, usage, and coding', *Semiotica*, 1: 49–98 (provides an extended discussion of nonverbal behaviors).

Henley, N. (1977) *Body Politics: Power, Sex, and Nonverbal Communication*, Englewood Cliffs, NJ: Prentice-Hall (a discussion of many aspects of nonverbal communication not covered in this chapter).

Morris, D., Collett, P., Marsh, P. and O'Shaughnessy, M. (1980) *Gestures: Their Origins and Distribution*, New York: Scarborough (a broad survey of gestures).

## Notes

1 Evidence for the biological bases of facial expressions of emotion also come from studies of nonhuman primates, which have demonstrated that the expressions that are universal to humans also occur in animals, and that animals have many different yet stable signals of emotion (Chevalier-Skolnikoff 1973; Geen 1992; Hauser 1993; Snowdon 2003). Likewise, the emotions portrayed in the universal facial expressions correspond to emotion taxonomies in different languages around the world (Romney *et al.* 1996, 1997; Shaver *et al.* 1992, 2001). There is also cross-cultural similarity in the physiological responses to emotion when these facial expressions are used as markers, in both the autonomic nervous system and brain activity (Davidson 2003; Ekman *et al.*1983; Levenson *et al.* 1990, 1992; Tsai and Levenson 1997). This similarity exists in people of such widely divergent cultures as the United States and the Minangkabau of West Sumatra, Indonesia. There is also universality in the antecedents that bring about emotion (Scherer 1997a, 1997b).

2 The distinction between expressive and reserved cultures is related to Hall's (1966, 1973) distinction between high-context and low-context cultures, as well as Watson's (1970) classification of contact and noncontact cultures. Our distinction is different, however, as we believe there is sufficient evidence to suggest that cultural differences extend beyond any single channel of NVB, and encompass the entire constellation of NVBs involved in interaction. At the same time, we do not believe that there is a unidimensional, positive relationship among all the various channels of NVB; some cultures may facilitate more or less expression differentially across channels. Differences in the relationships among channels across cultures may be an interesting avenue of research in the future.

## References

Argyle, M. and Cook, M. (1976) *Gaze and Mutual Gaze*, New York: Cambridge University Press.

Argyle, M., Henderson, M., Bond, M., Iizuka, Y. and Contarello, A. (1986) 'Cross-cultural variations in relationship rules', *International Journal of Psychology*, 21: 287–315.

Beier, E.G. and Zautra, A.J. (1972) 'Identification of vocal communication of emotions across cultures', *Journal of Consulting and Clinical Psychology*, 39(1): 166.

Biehl, M., Matsumoto, D., Ekman, P., Hearn, V., Heider, K., Kudoh, T. *et al.* (1997) 'Matsumoto and Ekman's Japanese and Caucasian facial expressions of emotion (JACFEE): reliability data and cross-national differences', *Journal of Nonverbal Behavior*, 21: 3–21.

Boas, F., Efron, D. and Foley, J.P. (1936) 'A comparative investigation of gestural behavior patterns in "racial" groups living under different as well as similar environmental conditions', *Psychological Bulletin*, 33: 760.

Bruner, J.S., and Tagiuri, R. (1954) 'The perception of people', in G. Lindzey (ed.) *Handbook of Social Psychology*, Vol. 2, Cambridge, MA: Addison-Wesley, pp. 634–54.

Chevalier-Skolnikoff, S. (1973) 'Facial expression of emotion in nonhuman primates', in P. Ekman (ed.) *Darwin and Facial Expression*, New York: Academic Press, pp. 11–89.

Cole, P.M. (1986) 'Children's spontaneous control of facial expression', *Child Development*, 57: 1309–21.

Darwin, C. (1872) *The Expression of Emotion in Man and Animals*, New York: Oxford University Press.

Davidson, R.J. (2003) 'Parsing the subcomponents of emotion and disorders of emotion: perspectives from affective neuroscience', in R.J. Davidson, K.R. Scherer and H.H. Goldsmith (eds) *Handbook of Affective Sciences*, New York: Oxford University Press, pp. 8–24.

Edelmann, R.J., Asendorpf, J., Contarello, A., Georgas, J., Villanueva, C. and Zammuner, V. (1987) 'Self-reported verbal and non-verbal strategies for coping with embarrassment in five European cultures', *Social Science Information*, 26: 869–83.

Efron, D. (1941) *Gesture and Environment*, Oxford: King's Crown Press.

Ekman, P. (1972) 'Universal and cultural differences in facial expression of emotion', in J.R. Cole (ed.) *Nebraska Symposium on Motivation*, 1971, Vol. 19, Lincoln, NE: Nebraska University Press, pp. 207–83.

——(ed.) (1973) *Darwin and Facial Expression: A Century of Research in Review*, New York: Academic Press.

——(1976) 'Movements with precise meanings', *Journal of Communication*, 26(3): 14–26.

Ekman, P. and Friesen, W.V. (1969) 'The repertoire of nonverbal behavior: categories, origins, usage, and coding', *Semiotica*, 1: 49–98.

——(1971) 'Constants across culture in the face and emotion', *Journal of Personality and Social Psychology*, 17: 124–29.

Ekman, P. and Heider, K.G. (1988) 'The universality of a contempt expression: a replication', *Motivation and Emotion*, 12(3): 303–8.

Ekman, P. and O'Sullivan, M. (1988) 'The role of context in interpreting facial expression: comment on Russell and Fehr (1987)', *Journal of Experimental Psychology: General*, 117(1): 86–88.

Ekman, P. and Rosenberg, E.L. (eds) (1998) *What the Face Reveals: Basic and applied Studies of Spontaneous Expression Using the Facial Action Coding System (FACS)*, New York: Oxford University Press.

Ekman, P., Sorenson, E.R. and Friesen, W.V. (1969) 'Pancultural elements in facial displays of emotion', *Science*, 164(3875): 86–88.

Ekman, P., Friesen, W.V. and Ellsworth, P. (1972) *Emotion in the Human Face: Guidelines for Research and an Integration of Findings*, New York: Pergamon Press.

Ekman, P., Friesen, W.V., O'Sullivan, M. and Scherer, K. (1980) 'Relative importance of face, body, and speech in judgments of personality and affect', *Journal of Personality and Social Psychology*, 38: 270–77.

Ekman, P., Levenson, R.W. and Friesen, W.V. (1983) 'Autonomic nervous system activity distinguishes among emotions', *Science*, 221(4616): 1208–10.

Ekman, P., Friesen, W.V., O'Sullivan, M., Chan, A., Diacoyanni-Tarlatzis, I., Heider, K. *et al.* (1987) 'Universals and cultural differences in the judgments of facial expressions of emotion', *Journal of Personality and Social Psychology*, 53(4): 712–17.

Ekman, P., O'Sullivan, M. and Matsumoto, D. (1991) 'Confusions about context in the judgment of facial expression: a reply to "the contempt expression and the relativity thesis"', *Motivation and Emotion*, 15(2): 169–76.

Elfenbein, H.A. and Ambady, N. (2002) 'On the universality and cultural specificity of emotion recognition: a meta-analysis', *Psychological Bulletin*, 128(2), 205–35.

Elfenbein, H.A., Beaupré, M.G., Levesque, M. and Hess, U. (2007) 'Toward a dialect theory: cultural differences in the expression and recognition of posed facial expressions', *Emotion*, 7(1): 131–46.

Exline, R.V., Jones, P. and Maciorowski, K. (1977) 'Race, affiliative-conflict theory and mutual visual attention during conversation', paper presented at the American Psychological Association Annual Convention, San Francisco, August 1977.

Fehr, B.J. and Exline, R.V. (1987) 'Social visual interactions: a conceptual and literature review', in A.W. Siegman and S. Feldstein (eds) *Nonverbal Behavior and Communication*, Vol. 2, Hillsdale, NJ: Lawrence Erlbaum, pp. 225–326.

Fernberger, S.W. (1928) 'False suggestions and the Piderit model', *American Journal of Psychology*, 40: 562–68.

Forston, R.F. and Larson, C.U. (1968) 'The dynamics of space: an experimental study in proxemic behavior among Latin Americans and North Americans', *Journal of Communication*, 18(2): 109–16.

Freedman, N. and Hoffmann, S.P. (1967) 'Kinetic behavior in altered clinical states: approach to objective analysis of motor behavior during clinical interviews', *Perceptual and Motor Skills*, 24: 527–39.

Friedman, H.S. (1978) 'The relative strength of verbal versus nonverbal cues', *Personality and Social Psychology Bulletin*, 4: 147–50.

Friesen, W.V. (1972) 'Cultural differences in facial expressions in a social situation: an experimental test of the concept of display rules', unpublished doctoral dissertation, University of California, San Francisco.

Friesen, W.V., Ekman, P. and Wallbott, H. (1979) 'Measuring hand movements', *Journal of Nonverbal Behavior*, 4(2): 97–112.

Geen, T. (1992) 'Facial expressions in socially isolated nonhuman primates: open and closed programs for expressive behavior', *Journal of Research in Personality*, 26: 273–80.

Gudykunst, W.B. and Nishida, T. (1984) 'Individual and cultural influences on uncertainty reduction', *Communication Monographs*, 51(1): 23–36.

Hall, E.T. (1963) 'A system for the notation of proxemic behaviors', *American Anthropologist*, 65: 1003–26.

——(1966) *The Hidden Dimension*, New York: Doubleday.

——(1973) *The Silent Language*, New York: Anchor.

Hauser, M. (1993) 'Right hemisphere dominance for the production of facial expression in monkeys', *Science*, 261, 475–77.

Henley, N. (1977) *Body Politics: Power, Sex, and Nonverbal Communication*, Englewood Cliffs, NJ: Prentice-Hall.

Hertenstein, M.J., Keltner, D., App, B., Bulleit, B.A. and Jaskolka, A.R. (2006) 'Touch communicates distinct emotions', *Emotion*, 6(3): 528–33.

Hertenstein, M.J., Holmes, R., McCullough, M. and Keltner, D. (2009) 'The communication of emotion via touch', *Emotion*, 9(4): 566–73.

Hofstede, G.H. (2001) *Culture's Consequences: Comparing Values, Behaviors, Institutions and Organizations Across Nations*, 2nd edn, Thousand Oaks, CA: Sage.

Hwang, H.S., Matsumoto, D., LeRoux, J.A., Yager, M. and Ruark, G.A. (2010) 'Cross-cultural similarities and differences in emblematic gestures', paper presented at the Biannual Conference of the International Association for Cross-Cultural Psychology, Melbourne, July 2010.

Izard, C.E. (1971) *The Face of Emotion*, East Norwalk, CT: Appleton-Century-Crofts.

Kirkcaldy, B., Furnham, A. and Levine, R. (2001) 'Attitudinal and personality correlates of a nation's pace of life', *Journal of Managerial Psychology*, 16(1): 20–34.

Kita, S., Ozyurek, A., Allen, S., Brown, A., Furman, R. and Ishizuka, T. (2007) 'Relations between syntactic encoding and co-speech gestures: implications for a model of speech and gesture production', *Language and Cognitive Processes*, 22(8):1212–36.

Knudsen, H.R., and Muzekari, L.H. (1983) 'The effects of verbal statements of context on facial expressions of emotion', *Journal of Nonverbal Behavior*, 7(4): 202–12.

Kudoh, T. and Matsumoto, D. (1985) 'Cross-cultural examination of the semantic dimensions of body postures', *Journal of Personality and Social Psychology*, 48(6): 1440–46.

LaFrance, M. and Mayo, C. (1976) 'Racial differences in gaze behavior during conversations: two systematic observational studies', *Journal of Personality and Social Psychology*, 33(5): 547–52.

Levenson, R.W., Ekman, P. and Friesen, W.V. (1990) 'Voluntary facial action generates emotion–specific autonomic nervous system activity', *Psychophysiology*, 27(4): 363–84.

Levenson, R.W., Ekman, P., Heider, K. and Friesen, W.V. (1992) 'Emotion and autonomic nervous system activity in the Minangkabau of West Sumatra', *Journal of Personality and Social Psychology*, 62(6): 972–88.

Levine, R.V. and Bartlett, K. (1984) 'Pace of life, punctuality, and coronary heart disease in six countries', *Journal of Cross-Cultural Psychology*, 15(2): 233–55.

Levine, R.V. and Norenzayan, A. (1999) 'The pace of life in 31 countries', *Journal of Cross-Cultural Psychology*, 30(2): 178–205.

Levine, R.V., Lynch, K., Miyake, K. and Lucia, M. (1989) 'The type A city: coronary heart disease and the pace of life', *Journal of Behavioral Medicine*, 12(6): 509–24.

Little, K.B. (1968) 'Cultural variations in social schemata', *Journal of Personality and Social Psychology*, 10(1): 1–7.

McCluskey, K.W. and Albas, D.C. (1981) 'Perception of the emotional content of speech by Canadian and Mexican children, adolescents and adults', *International Journal of Psychology*, 16: 119–32.

Matsumoto, D. (1989) 'Cultural influences on the perception of emotion', *Journal of Cross-Cultural Psychology*, 20(1): 92–105.

——(1990) 'Cultural similarities and differences in display rules', *Motivation and Emotion*, 14(3): 195–214.

——(1992a) 'American–Japanese cultural differences in the recognition of universal facial expressions', *Journal of Cross-Cultural Psychology*, 23(1): 72–84.

——(1992b) 'More evidence for the universality of a contempt expression', *Motivation and Emotion*, 16(4): 363–68.

——(1993) 'Ethnic differences in affect intensity, emotion judgments, display rule attitudes, and self-reported emotional expression in an American sample', *Motivation and Emotion*, 17(2), 107–23.

——(2001) 'Culture and Emotion', in D. Matsumoto (ed.) *The Handbook of Culture and Psychology*, New York: Oxford University Press, pp. 171–94.

Matsumoto, D. and Ekman, P. (1989) 'American–Japanese cultural differences in intensity ratings of facial expressions of emotion', *Motivation and Emotion*, 13(2): 143–57.

Matsumoto, D. and Hwang, H.-S. (2010) 'Judging faces in context', *Social and Personality Psychology Compass*, 3: 1–10.

Matsumoto, D. and Kishimoto, H. (1983) 'Developmental characteristics in judgments of emotion from nonverbal vocal cues', *International Journal of Intercultural Relations*, 7(4): 415–24.

Matsumoto, D. and Kudoh, T. (1987) 'Cultural similarities and differences in the semantic dimensions of body postures', *Journal of Nonverbal Behavior*, 11(3): 166–79.

Matsumoto, D. and Kupperbusch, C. (2001) 'Idiocentric and allocentric differences in emotional expression and experience', *Asian Journal of Social Psychology*, 4: 113–31.

Matsumoto, D. and Willingham, B. (2006) 'The thrill of victory and the agony of defeat: spontaneous expressions of medal winners at the 2004 Athens Olympic Games', *Journal of Personality and Social Psychology*, 91(3): 568–81.

——(2009) 'Spontaneous facial expressions of emotion of congenitally and non-congenitally blind individuals', *Journal of Personality and Social Psychology*, 96(1): 1–10.

Matsumoto, D., Takeuchi, S., Andayani, S., Kouznetsova, N. and Krupp, D. (1998) 'The contribution of individualism-collectivism to cross-national differences in display rule', *Asian Journal of Social Psychology*, 1: 147–65.

Matsumoto, D., Kasri, F. and Kooken, K. (1999) 'American–Japanese cultural differences in judgments of expression intensity and subjective experience', *Cognition and Emotion*, 13: 201–18.

Matsumoto, D., Consolacion, T., Yamada, H., Suzuki, R., Franklin, B., Paul, S. *et al.* (2002) 'American–Japanese cultural differences in judgments of emotional expressions of different intensities', *Cognition and Emotion*, 16(6): 721–47.

Matsumoto, D., Yoo, S.H., Hirayama, S. and Petrova, G. (2005) 'Validation of an individual-level measure of display rules: the display rule assessment inventory (DRAI)', *Emotion*, 5(1), 23–40.

Matsumoto, D., Keltner, D., Shiota, M.N., Frank, M.G. and O'Sullivan, M. (2008a) 'What's in a face? Facial expressions as signals of discrete emotions', in M. Lewis, J. M. Haviland and L. Feldman Barrett (eds) *Handbook of Emotions*, New York: Guilford Press, pp. 211–34.

Matsumoto, D., Yoo, S.H., Fontaine, J., Anguas-Wong, A.M., Arriola, M., Ataca, B. *et al.* (2008b) 'Mapping expressive differences around the world: the relationship between emotional display rules and individualism v. collectivism', *Journal of Cross-Cultural Psychology*, 39(1): 55–74.

Matsumoto, D., Willingham, B. and Olide, A. (2009a) 'Sequential dynamics of culturally-moderated facial expressions of emotion', *Psychological Science*, (2010): 1269–74.

Matsumoto, D., Yoo, S.H. and Fontaine, J. (2009b) 'Hypocrisy or maturity: culture and context differentiation', *European Journal of Personality*, 23: 251–64. 181–91.

Matsumoto, D., Olide, A. and Willingham, B. (2009c) 'Is there an ingroup advantage in recognizing spontaneously expressed emotions?', *Journal of Nonverbal Behavior*, 33:

Matsumoto, D., Hwang, H.-S. and Yamada, H. (in press) 'Cultural differences in the relative contributions of face and context to judgments of emotion', *Journal of Cross-Cultural Psychology*. Published online 15 December 2010 (doi: 10.1177/0022022110387426).

Mehrabian, A. (1968a) 'Inference of attitudes from the posture, orientation, and distance of a communicator', *Journal of Consulting and Clinical Psychology*, 32(3): 296–308.

——(1968b) 'Relationship of attitude to seated posture, orientation, and distance' *Journal of Personality and Social Psychology*, 10(1): 26–30.

——(1969) 'Significance of posture and position in the communication of attitude and status relationships', *Psychological Bulletin*, 71(5): 359–72.

Morris, D., Collett, P., Marsh, P. and O'Shaughnessy, M. (1980) *Gestures: Their Origins and Distribution*, New York: Scarborough.

Nakamura, M., Buck, R.W. and Kenny, D.A. (1990) 'Relative contributions of expressive behavior and contextual information to the judgment of the emotional state of another', *Journal of Personality and Social Psychology*, 59(5): 1032–39.

Noesjirwan, J. (1977) 'Contrasting cultural patterns on interpersonal closeness in doctors: waiting rooms in Sydney and Jakarta', *Journal of Cross-Cultural Psychology*, 8(3): 357–68.

——(1978) 'A rule-based analysis of cultural differences in social behavior: Indonesia and Australia', *International Journal of Psychology*, 13: 305–16.

O'Sullivan, M., Ekman, P., Friesen, W.V. and Scherer, K.R. (1985) 'What you say and how you say it: the contribution of speech content and voice quality to judgments of others', *Journal of Personality and Social Psychology*, 48(1): 54–62.

Pika, S., Nicoladis, E. and Marentette, P. (2009) 'How to order a beer: cultural differences in the use of conventional gestures for numbers', *Journal of Cross-Cultural Psychology*, 40(1): 70–80.

Romney, A.K., Boyd, J.P., Moore, C.C., Batchelder, W.H. and Brazill, T.J. (1996) 'Culture as shared cognitive representations', *Proceedings from the National Academy of Sciences*, 93: 4699–4705.

Romney, A.K., Moore, C.C. and Rusch, C.D. (1997) 'Cultural universals: measuring the semantic structure of emotion terms in English and Japanese', *Proceedings from the National Academy of Sciences*, 94: 5489–94.

Sauter, D.A. and Eimer, M. (2010) 'Rapid detection of emotion from human vocalizations', *Journal of Cognitive Neuroscience*, 22(3): 474–81.

Sauter, D.A., Eisner, F., Ekman, P. and Scott, S.K. (2010) 'Cross-cultural recognition of basic emotions through nonverbal emotional vocalizations', *Proceedings from the National Academy of Sciences*, 107(6): 2408–12.

Scherer, K.R. (1986) 'Vocal affect expression: review and a model for future research', *Psychological Bulletin*, 99: 143–65.

——(1997a) 'Profiles of emotion-antecedent appraisal: testing theoretical predictions across cultures', *Cognition and Emotion*, 11(2): 113–50.

——(1997b) 'The role of culture in emotion-antecedent appraisal', *Journal of Personality and Social Psychology*, 73(4): 902–22.

Schwartz, S.H. (2006) 'Value orientations: measurement, antecedents, and consequences across nations', in R. Jowell, C. Roberts, R. Fitzgerald and G. Eva (eds) *Measuring Attitudes Cross-nationally: Lessons from the European Social Survey*, Thousand Oaks, CA: Sage, pp. 161–93.

Shaver, P.R., Wu, S. and Schwartz, J.C. (1992) 'Cross-cultural similarities and differences in emotion and its representation', in M.S. Clark (ed.) *Emotion: Review of Personality and Social Psychology*, Vol. 13, Thousand Oaks, CA: Sage, pp. 175–212.

Shaver, P.R., Murdaya, U. and Fraley, R.C. (2001) 'The structure of the Indonesian emotion lexicon', *Asian Journal of Social Psychology*, 4(3): 201–24.

Shuter, R. (1976) 'Proxemics and tactility in Latin America', *Journal of Communication*, 26(3): 46–52.

——(1977) 'A field study of nonverbal communication in Germany, Italy, and the United States', *Communication Monographs*, 44(4): 298–305.

Simon-Thomas, E.R., Keltner, D., Sauter, D.A., Sinicropi-Yao, L. and Abramson, A. (2009) 'The voice conveys specific emotions: evidence from vocal burst displays', *Emotion*, 9(6): 838–46.

Snowdon, C.T. (2003) 'Expression of emotion in nonhuman animals', in R.J. Davidson, K. Scherer and H.H. Goldsmith (eds) *Handbook of Affective Sciences*, New York: Oxford University Press, pp. 457–80.

Sussman, N.M. and Rosenfeld, H.M. (1978) 'Touch, justification, and sex: influences on the aversiveness of spatial violations', *Journal of Social Psychology*, 106: 215–25.

——(1982) 'Influence of culture, language, and sex on conversational distance', *Journal of Personality and Social Psychology*, 42(1): 66–74.

Tsai, J.L. and Levenson, R.W. (1997) 'Cultural influences of emotional responding: Chinese American and European American dating couples during interpersonal conflict', *Journal of Cross-Cultural Psychology*, 28: 600–625.

Watson, O.M. (1970) *Proxemic Behavior: A Cross-cultural Study*, The Hague, Netherlands: Mouton.

Watson, O.M. and Graves, T.D. (1966) 'Quantitative research in proxemic behavior', *American Anthropologist*, 68: 971–85.

Waxer, P.H. (1985) 'Video ethology: television as a data base for cross-cultural studies in nonverbal displays', *Journal of Nonverbal Behavior*, 9: 111–20.

Wickline, V.B., Bailey, W. and Nowicki, S.J. (2009) 'Cultural in-group advantage: emotion recognition in African American and European American faces and voices', *Journal of Genetic Psychology*, 170(1): 5–29.

# 9

# Speech acts, facework and politeness

## Relationship-building across cultures

*Winnie Cheng*

## 1. Introduction

This chapter examines face, facework, politeness, and impoliteness from historical perspectives, beginning with Smith's (1894), Hu's (1944) and Goffman's (1955) notions of face and Goffman's (1955) facework. Drawing on empirical studies, relevant critical issues and topics in cross-cultural and intercultural communication are discussed to raise awareness of current contributions and suggest areas for future research. Although 'cross-cultural communication' and 'intercultural communication' both refer to communication across cultures, they are not exactly the same. Cross-cultural communication compares native discourse across cultures (for example, management meetings of Japanese and those of Americans), whereas intercultural communication involves an investigation of the discourse of people of different cultural and linguistic backgrounds interacting either in a lingua franca or in the native language of one of the participants (Bargiela-Chiappini and Harris 1997; Lustig and Koester 2009).

In the literature on speech acts, speech acts have been examined as 'linguistic carriers of politeness' (Meier 1996: 345), and politeness is considered to be inherent in some speech acts. Speech act theorists (Austin 1962; Searle 1965, 1969, 1975) are concerned with the functional value of utterances rather than the form of utterances. Austin (1962: 14–15) describes the 'felicity conditions' that must be met if performatives are to be successful in the real world. Hymes (1972) defines speech act as 'the level [which] mediates immediately between the usual level of grammar and the rest of a speech event or situation in that it implicates both linguistic form and social norms' (ibid.: 57). Searle (1969) emphasizes the importance of the social institution within which speech acts are produced, and proposes a typology of speech acts for classifying the functional value of utterances: representatives, directives, commissives, expressives and declarations. Searle's approach to speech acts was modified by Weigand (2000), who combined the active and reactive speech act into a dialogue principle, with active and reactive speech acts forming a unit called 'the minimal action game', incorporating 'the individual and cultural imprint of each human being' (Grein 2007: 111).

Very often, in speech act studies, particularly those involving cross-cultural and intercultural speech acts, linguistic realizations in English and conversational strategies are interpreted as a manifestation of universal sociolinguistic rules of politeness. An increasing number of studies have, however, discussed speech acts as culture specific and language specific, with a focus on the relationships between different cultural norms, values and assumptions, different languages and different speech acts.

In Brown and Levinson's (1987) view, 'certain kinds of acts intrinsically threaten face' (ibid.: 65). Face-threatening speech acts have received much attention in research as they are potentially the source of intercultural communication breakdowns or what Thomas (1983) refers to as 'pragmatic failure' or 'the inability to understand "what is meant by what is said"' (ibid.: 91). Brown and Levinson (1978, 1987) argue for the universality of politeness and, at the same time, 'acknowledge its cultural specification' (Liebersohn *et al.* 2004: 922). Facework strategies, which are considered to be largely motivated by politeness in face negotiation in everyday human interaction, have also been examined across cultures and discussed in terms of such factors as cultural variability in values, interaction scripts and language.

## 2. The notions of 'face', 'face-threatening acts', 'facework' and 'politeness'

Politeness consists of strategies used by speakers and writers to best achieve their communicative goals in an appropriate manner in a particular context. To understand pragmatic politeness, it is necessary to understand another term, 'face'. Gu (2008) discusses the Chinese origin of face in the *Book of Odes* about 2,500 years ago, reporting that the first Western author who wrote about Chinese face was A.H. Smith (1894) in *Chinese Characteristics*. Smith (1894) drew the attention of both Westerners and Chinese scholars to Chinese face. Fifty years later, in his paper 'The Chinese concepts of Face', Hu (1944) defines 'face' as *mien tzu* and *lien*: *mien tzu* refers to 'the kind of prestige that is emphasized in this country: a reputation achieved through getting on in life' (ibid.: 45), and *lien* as 'the respect of the group for a man with a good moral reputation: the man who will fulfil his obligations regardless of the hardship involved, who under all circumstances show himself as a decent human being' (ibid.: 45). Committing immoral acts is considered *tiu lien* ('lose face') (ibid.: 46). Not only does the person 'lose his own face' but 'public disgrace or ridicule of a serious nature is bound to have an effect on the reputation of the family' (ibid.: 50).

According to Gu (2008), Goffman's (1955: 5) article 'On face-work' is the first attempt 'to examine Western interpersonal behavior by using the Chinese concept'; Gu (2008) refers to this as the 'westernization of Chinese face'. Goffman (1955) defines face as 'the positive social value a person effectively claims for himself by the line others assume he has taken during a particular contact. Face is an image of self delineated in terms of approved social attributes'. For Goffman (1955), 'facework' refers to 'the actions taken by a person to make whatever he is doing consistent with face' and to counteract 'events whose effective symbolic implications threaten face' (ibid.: 12). He suggests that 'the person will have 2 points of view − a defensive orientation toward saving his own face and a protective orientation toward saving the others' face' (ibid.: 14). He then proposes two face-saving practices: 'avoidance process' and 'corrective process'. The avoidance process is used by a person to prevent threats to his or her face by avoiding potentially threatening contacts (ibid.: 15); the corrective process, which consists of the four moves of challenge, offering, acceptance and thanks, is adopted to ratify the threat and 'correct for its effects' (ibid.: 19).

Brown and Levinson's (1978, 1987) work on politeness phenomena remains 'the most seminal and influential starting point for studying cross-cultural and interlinguistic politeness' (Leech 2007: 167). Brown and Levinson view 'face' as 'the public self-image that every member wants to claim for himself' (ibid.: 61). They differentiate between 'negative face', defined as 'the want of every "competent adult member" that his actions be unimpeded by others' and 'positive face', defined as 'the want of every member that his wants be desirable to at least some others' (ibid.: 62). Their 'cognitive model of "face"' is based on 'Western ethnocentric assumptions such as the existence of a predominantly rational actor and the strategic, goal-oriented nature of "face-work" and social interaction. This explains their model's obsession with face threatening acts (FTAs)' (Bargiela-Chiappini 2003: 1454). Brown and Levinson (1978, 1987) regard all speech acts to be potentially face threatening, to either the speaker's or the hearer's face, or both. They identify facework as a crucial influence on the ways in which messages are constructed, and politeness phenomena explain how politeness is used to redress the performance of FTAs. Hence, politeness entails the use of redressive language that aims to compensate for face-threatening behaviour.

An illocutionary act has the potential to damage the hearer's positive face (by, for example, insulting H (hearer) or expressing disapproval of something that H holds dear) or H's negative face (an order, for example, will impinge upon H's freedom of action); or S's (speaker's) positive face (if S has to admit to having botched a job, for example) or S's negative face (if S is cornered into making an offer of help). In order to reduce the possibility of damage to H's face or to the S's own face, he or she may adopt certain strategies. The choice of strategy will be made on the basis of the S's assessment of the size of the FTA. The speaker can calculate the size of the FTA on the basis of the parameters of power (P), distance (D) and rating of imposition (R). These combined values determine the overall 'weightiness' of the FTA, which in turn influences the strategy used (Thomas 1995: 169).

Based on the assessment of weightiness, a speaker/writer can choose from five superstrategies of politeness (Brown and Levinson 1987: 69). They are: (1) do the FTA 'on record' baldly, without any redressive action of any kind; (2) do the FTA 'on record', but with redressive action in the form of positive politeness; (3) do the FTA 'on record', but with redressive action in the form of negative politeness; (4) do the FTA 'off record', in other words indirectly; and (5) the speaker/writer does not do the FTA because the risk of face loss may be considered too great, so impossible to redress. The above superstrategies are presented in rank order, beginning with the superstrategy used when the estimation of face loss is lowest. Table 9.1 summarizes the realizations of the second, third and fourth politeness superstrategies.

Leech (2007) reformulates his maxims of politeness (Leech 1983) – the maxims of tact, generosity, approbation, modesty, agreement and sympathy – into the 'grand strategy of politeness (or GSP)' that 'comprehends all the above maxims' (Leech 2007: 180). GSP is explained in this way: 'in order to be polite, S expresses or implies meanings which associate a high value with what pertains to O (O = other person(s), mainly the addressee) or associates a low value with what pertains to S (S = self, speaker)' (Leech 2007: 181).

In addition, Leech (2007) proposes scales of value that can be used to assess the appropriate degree of (pragmatic) politeness:

- Vertical distance between S and O (in terms of status, power, role, age, etc.) [cf. Brown and Levinson's P];
- Horizontal distance between S and O (intimate, familiar, acquaintance, stranger, etc.) [cf. Brown and Levinson's D];
- Weight or value: how large is the benefit, the cost, the favour, the obligation, etc. [cf. Brown and Levinson's R], i.e. the real socially defined value of what is being transacted;
- Strength of socially defined rights and obligations (e.g. a teacher's obligations to a student; a host's obligations to a guest; a service providers' obligations to their clients or customers);
- 'Self-territory' and 'other-territory' (in-group membership vs. out-group). There are degrees of membership of 'self-territory' and 'other-territory'.

Leech (2007: 194)

*Table 9.1* Realizations of positive, negative and off-record superstrategies

| Positive politeness strategies | Negative politeness strategies | Off-record strategies |
| --- | --- | --- |
| Notice/attend to hearer's wants | Be conventionally indirect | Invite conversational implicatures |
| Exaggerate interest/approval | Question/hedge | • Give hints |
| Intensify interest | Be pessimistic | • Give association clues |
| Use in-group identity markers | Minimize imposition | • Presuppose |
| Seek agreement | Give deference | • Understate |
| Avoid disagreement | Apologize | • Overstate |
| Presuppose/assert common | Impersonalize | • Use tautologies |
| ground | State the imposition as a general | • Use contradictions |
| Joke | rule | • Be ironic |
| Assert knowledge of hearer's | Nominalize | • Use metaphors |
| wants | Go on record as incurring debt | • Use rhetorical questions |
| Offer, promise | | Be vague or ambiguous: Violate |
| Be optimistic | | the manner maxim |
| Give (ask for) reasons | | • Be ambiguous |
| Assume/assert reciprocity | | • Be vague |
| Include speaker and hearer in the | | • Overgeneralize |
| activity | | • Displace H |
| Give gifts to hearer (goods, | | • Be incomplete, use ellipsis |
| sympathy, etc.) | | |

Source: Adapted from Brown and Levinson (1987).

Leech (2007) concludes that, even though 'the Eastern group-orientation and the Western individualistic-orientation are felt to be strong influences on polite behaviour' (ibid.: 201), there is 'no East–West divide in politeness' (ibid.: 202). Rather than different theories of politeness for the East and West, he maintains that we need to use the scales of politeness (ibid.: 194) to express quantitative and qualitative differences in values (ibid.: 201).

Brown and Levinson (1978, 1987) have been criticized, 'both from a theoretical and empirical point of view' (Jansen and Janssen 2010). Theoretically, their model is thought to be Western biased (e.g. Gu 1990; Mao 1994; Matsumoto 1988; Yu 2005), particularly in 'their construal of the concept of "face" … their overemphasis on face-threat and their assumptions of individualistic and egalitarian motivations, as opposed to the more group-centred hierarchy-based ethos of Eastern societies' (Leech 2007: 167). It is argued that members in collectivist cultures 'define themselves in relation to the social group they belong to' (Ogiermann 2009: 13). In particular, 'negative face' is viewed as 'a form of *deference* – the way an individual adheres to social and situational determined rules' (Bargiela-Chiappini 2003; Jansen and Janssen 2010). Empirically, Brown and Levinson's PDR model is criticized for its simplicity that 'made empirical testing easy' (Jansen and Janssen 2010); however, most of the studies only 'provide indirect evidence' about language production, i.e. 'etic', but do not involve language users directly evaluating the use of politeness in specific situations characterized by various P, D and R variables, i.e. 'emic' (Jansen and Janssen 2010).

## Chinese face and politeness

Ji (2000: 1060) suggests that 'for face to operate as a motivating factor for politeness at all, it must be related to each member of a community as a self-image'. Scollon and Wong Scollon (2001) compare the Western 'self' and the Asian 'self', suggesting that the Western self is highly individualistic, self-motivated, open to ongoing negotiation and emphasizing independence, whereas the Asian self is more collectivistic, connected to the family, the social circle and the workplace, and more conscious of the consequences of one's actions on the addressee. Different from the Western self, the Chinese equivalent of 'individualism' implies selfishness and often carries a negative connotation (Hu and Grove 1999), and the true Chinese self is defined by hierarchy (rank and position) and multiple prescribed relationships and social and ethical responsibility, rather than individuality (Gao and Ting-Toomey 1998).

Gu (2008) remarks that Brown and Levinson's (1978, 1987) 'positive face' is similar to Chinese *lian*, and 'negative face' is 'foreign to the Chinese mind' (Gu 2008). The Chinese 'face' is characterized by *lian* ('face') that 'embodies a moral dimension and often is internalized' and *mian zi* ('image'), which 'signifies a social image and often is externalized' (Gao and Ting-Toomey 1998: 53–56). The Chinese face is hence defined as '(a) a sense of one's social self-worth or others' assessments of our social "worthiness" or both and (b) a vulnerable resource in social interactions given that it can be threatened, attacked, maintained, and enhanced' (Gao and Ting-Toomey 1998: 56). Gu (2008) conceptualizes *lian* as 'a moral standard', 'ideal attributes', 'attributes earned from power, position, status, wealth, achievements, etc.' and the 'values one possesses which are held dear to a community/group'; *mianzi* refers to 'interpersonal or inter-organizational' dimensions, 'seen as the other's appreciation of the self's *lian*' and 'shareable (i.e. among insiders), borrowable, transferable (i.e. from the insider to the outsider via a third mediator')'.

Chinese 'facework' is considered to be the communicative strategies used to enact self-face and to uphold, support or challenge the other person's face (Ting-Toomey 1988). Gao and Ting-Toomey (1998: 60–68) discuss five face-directed communication strategies in order to achieve effective facework management in Chinese culture: being non-confrontational, compliance strategies, provisional responses, using intermediaries and *Yi lun* ('to gossip', 'to make remarks behind one's back' (ibid.: 63)). In conflict management situations, for example, non-confrontational means being obliging and compromising. Compliance strategies include avoiding arguing or disagreeing overtly with others in public, adopting an unassertive style of communication and complying even at the cost of truthful and honest communication (Gao and Ting-Toomey 1998: 63). Provisional responses refer to neither affirmative 'yes' nor negative answers 'no' (Gao and Ting-Toomey 1998). As for using intermediaries, the Chinese, as observed by Sun (1991), rely on others for solutions to avoid direct confrontations, which often cause face damage and disruption of interpersonal harmony among the conflicting parties. The last strategy *Yi lun* is practised to 'satisfy their curiosity about others' private lives and the need to speak their true feelings' (Gao and Ting-Toomey 1998: 67). Ye (2004) argues for the use of Chinese categories – 'acquaintance' vs. 'stranger' and 'insider' vs. 'outsider' – to describe and analyse interpersonal relationships.

When discussing Chinese politeness (*limào*), Gu (1990) draws attention to the two principles of *limào* – sincerity and balance – remarking that the essence of *limào* in modern China has assumed two new duties, namely the enhancement of social harmony and the diffusion of interpersonal tension or conflict. Gu (1990) believes that Chinese politeness centres on self-denigration and other elevation.

## 3. Cultural variability in speech act performance

Studies of speech acts across cultures have so far shown cultural variability in the manifestations of speech act performance. As noted by Morand (1995: 59), '[a]cross a range of face-threatening speech acts, and across a range of cultures, there exists significant variation in normative levels of politeness', using 'varying culture' as the same independent variable and politeness as the studies' dependent or 'value-free', variable (ibid.: 68).

The most famous study of cross-cultural speech acts must be the Cross-Cultural Speech Act Realization Project (CCSARP) (Blum-Kulka and Olshtain 1984; Blum-Kulka et al. 1989), which investigated 'cross-cultural and intralingual variation' (Blum-Kulka et al. 1989: 11) using a discourse completion test (DCT). The CCSARP incorporates all three approaches to the investigation of universality vs. culture specificity in speech act behaviour, namely:

> first, the theoretical, speech act theory oriented approach, which seeks to validate claims in regard to the universality of the basic structure of speech acts; second, the ethnographically oriented approach pursued by cultural anthropologists, who seek to highlight the differences in the conceptualization and actual use of speech acts across different societies; and third, the more linguistically oriented approach, which debates the question of universality within specific contrastive analyses of particular speech acts.
>
> *Blum-Kulka* et al. *(1989: 23)*

Another research team, Takahashi and Beebe, investigated many face-threatening speech acts between American and Japanese, including disagreement (Beebe and Takahashi 1989a, b), refusals (Beebe et al. 1990; Takahashi and Beebe 1987), announcing embarrassing information (Beebe and Takahashi 1989a), chastisement (Beebe and Takahashi 1989b) and correction (Takahashi and Beebe 1993).

## Apology

In Brown and Levinson's (1978, 1987) terms, making an apology is face-saving for the hearer and face-threatening for the speaker. In terms of Leech's (1983) tact maxim, 'apology is a convivial speech act (ibid.: 140) whose goal coincides with the social goal of maintaining harmony between S and H ... the realization of an apology provides benefit for the H and is to some degree at cost to the S' (Olshtain 1989: 157). Goffman (1971) defines apology as 'the offender's device to remedy a social breach and to establish social harmony; to apologize is to admit the offense, express remorse, and request forgiveness from the offended person' (Park and Guan 2006: 184–85). Guan et al. (2009) investigated the relationship between national cultures (US, China and Korea) and social distance on apology, and found that, although the three cultures do not differ in the intention to apologise to a friend, compared with Koreans, American and Chinese differ much more for 'feeling obliged to apologize to a stranger' (ibid.: 32).

Olshtain (1989) investigated seven apology situations of cross-culturally similar contexts in four languages – Hebrew, Australian English, Canadian French and German – and concluded that 'given the same social factors, the same contextual features, and the same level of offence, different languages will realize apologies in very similar ways' (ibid.: 171). Fahey (2005) conducted a corpus study of apologising in Irish and Chilean soap operas and found that cultural differences in the setting, social distance and power relations impacted on the apologising strategies the speakers used to restore a relationship. The perceived seriousness of the offence was also a factor. Comparing the expressions of South Korean and Australian English apologetic speech acts *mianhada* and *sorry*, Kim (2008: 257) found different attitudinal meanings and illocutionary acts associated with the expressions.

Park and Guan (2006) compared the effects of national culture and face concerns in the intention to apologise in the US and China. The researchers asked the participants to read vignettes that differed in 'relationship types (in-group vs. out-group members) and situation types (negative face vs. positive face threatening)' (ibid.: 183). They found that, in contrast to the US Americans, the Chinese participants had stronger intentions to apologise when the act threatened H's positive face, and concluded that '[c]ulture, relationship, and situations are interwoven with each other, influencing individuals' decision to apologize' (ibid.: 202).

Bataineh and Bataineh (2008) found culture-specific behaviours in American English speakers and Jordanian Arabic speakers' use of apologies, including the tendency of the latter to use '*proverbs* and *sayings* in order to ease their responsibility and pacify the victim'. These respondents employed non-apology strategies more frequently 'to deny responsibility to avoid having to apologize to or compensate the victim for an offense' (ibid.: 816); they also used both negative and positive assessment of responsibility when assigning blame to both themselves and others. In contrast, their American counterparts use only negative assessment of responsibility when blaming others (ibid.: 816). Apology strategies in Sudanese Arabic were also studied (Nureddeen 2009), and the results confirm both the universality of apology and the culture-specific choice of strategies to perform the speech act of apology.

Although the majority of research on speech acts uses a DCT to collect respondents' self-proclaimed language and strategy uses, Liebersohn *et al.* (2004) analysed the public apologetic speech of the former American President Clinton and the former Israeli Prime Minister Barak, and concluded that 'the pretensions of universality underlying the study of apology are incorrect' (ibid.: 941). Based on the results, Liebersohn *et al.* (2004) suggest a new perspective about what constitutes politeness. Their notion of the 'rhetorical persuasive act' (ibid.: 942) expands on Fraser's (1990) four perspectives: the 'social norm view', 'conversational maxim view', 'face saving view' and 'conversational contract view'.

## Complaint

The speech act of complaining is inherently face-threatening towards H as 'its conflictive nature might result in a breach of social goals of maintaining comity and harmony between S and H (Leech 1983)' (Olshtain and Weinbach 1993: 108). In Olshtain and Weinbach's (1993) study, the Hebrew speakers tended to choose central strategies when making a complaint: disapproval, complaint and warning. When complaining to lower status speakers, they most often used less severe strategies (disapproval and complaint) but, when complaining to equals or higher status speakers, they tended to use more severe strategies (complaint and warning). Olshtain and Weinbach (1993) compared the complaint strategies used by British, American and Israeli speakers, and observed interlanguage features in their speech act behaviour, particularly in complaining. Their most interesting discovery was that the Israeli learners of English 'sound less offensive and less face-threatening' (ibid.: 120), but when there is explicit social obligation by law or convention, the learners are 'less concerned with being polite and cautious' (ibid.: 121). Olshtain and Weinbach's (1993) results support the relevance of 'contextual parameters such as social factors and situational factors' in speech act behaviours.

Daly *et al.* (2004) investigated the uses and functions of the expletive *fuck* in the FTAs of direct complaints and refusals in team worker interaction in a New Zealand soap factory. Contrary to the politeness phenomena, they found that, among team workers, the expletive was used 'to create solidarity and provide face-attention' and 'to boost rather than attenuate the threat to face posed by these speech acts' (ibid.: 950). This finding lends further support to Eelen's (2001) argument that 'Politeness Theory can be criticized as overtly "normative" in some respects' (Daly *et al.* 2004: 950).

## Compliment response

Compliments can be 'very big FTAs in societies where envy is very strong and where witchcraft exists as a sanction' (Brown and Levinson 1987: 247). Previous studies on compliment and compliment response have shown that cross-cultural differences are manifested in the topics, structure, lexical choice, functions, response types, distribution and intent in the complimenting behaviour (see, for example, Chen 1993; Creese 1991; Herbert 1991; Holmes 1988; Knapp *et al.* 1984; Manes and Wolfson 1981; Pomerantz 1978; Wieland 1995; Wolfson 1989). In Western cultures, compliments are often associated with personal appearance, ability, performance and possessions (Creese 1991; Wolfson, 1989). Egyptian speakers tend to favour the topic of personality (Nelson *et al.* 2002), whereas Polish compliments are mainly about possession (Herbert, 1991).

Pomerantz (1978) was the first researcher to study compliment responses. Working with American data, Pomerantz (1978) noted that responding to a compliment poses a dilemma for the speaker. Most compliment responses in American English depart from the model or standard norm of acceptance; instead, there is a 'prevalence of rejections and disagreements' (Pomerantz 1978: 88). The non-accepting behaviour, which may constitute 'noticeable, reportable, puzzling, troublesome' phenomena, has been found to be predominant. Compliments are repeatedly rejected, downgraded or only accepted with qualification.

Chen (1993) compared the compliment response behaviour between American English and Chinese speakers. American English speakers were found to be less likely to reject compliments on appearance than on ability (or 'achievement' in Chen's word) and possessions, as they associate appearance with their self-image, and are reluctant to damage it by declining compliments on their appearance. Conversely, the Chinese tend to accept compliments on possessions, but reject compliments on appearance and achievement, as 'looks are more intimate and private to a person than achievement and possession' (Chen 1993: 69). The Chinese feel that being modest helps to enhance their face and self-image. When being constrained by the conditions of 'agree with the complimenter' and 'avoid self-praise', the Chinese subjects tend to adopt the 'self-praise avoidance' strategy, such as shifting credit to the complimenter (Chen 1993: 59).

The analysis of more than 1,000 compliment responses in a DCT administered to British and Spanish male and female undergraduates revealed similarities as well as cross-cultural and cross-gender differences in the use of strategies (Lorenzo-Dus 2001). For example, the Spanish males were inclined to 'upgrade compliments ironically' (ibid.: 107), which was not evident in the British data. Tang and Zhang (2009) reported on a contrastive study of compliment responses (CR), with a hypothesis that 'no universal pattern can be generalized regarding the use of CRs by Mandarin Chinese and Australian English speakers' (ibid.: 341). Their analysis of DCTs showed that, compared with their Australian counterparts, the Chinese participants consistently used fewer 'accept' and more 'evade' and 'reject' strategies, due to prevailing Chinese cultural values of modesty and collectivism.

## Correction

Using a DCT, Takahashi and Beebe (1993) examined the use of such politeness strategies as positive remarks, softeners and expressions of regret by status-unequal American and Japanese speakers to make each correction less face threatening. Their conclusion confirms the findings of their earlier studies on refusals (Beebe *et al.* 1990; Takahashi and Beebe 1987, 1993). That is, although both Americans and Japanese are conscious of status, the former downplay status differences, whereas the Japanese do not. Depending on the status of the interlocutor, when speaking English, the Japanese shift their style of correction in both disagreement and refusal situations more than Americans speaking English. As the behaviour of the Japanese is similar when speaking Japanese, this supports the notion that both semantic transfer and 'the patterns of style shifting' are taking place (ibid.: 154).

## Greeting

The speech act of greeting is positive politeness that meets the speaker's need for approval and belonging (Brown and Levinson 1978: 183). Feller (2007) investigated the speech act of greeting, based on Weigand's (2000) notion of the dialogic action game. Feller (2007) invited English, German and Peruvian native speakers to complete a DCT with sixteen descriptions of different greeting situations, and found culture-specific functions of greeting, namely promotion of togetherness for Peruvian Spanish, appreciation of one's privacy for Californian English and high regard for the individual *vis-à-vis* the group for German speakers (ibid.: 185–87). Despite these culture-specific functions, Feller (2007) argues that language and culture should be orientated more towards the single individual, in line with Rodriguez's (2002) notion of 'culturing beings', and argues against making general statements about '*the* culture' (Feller 2007: 187) and 'any kind of oversimplification which abstracts from the complexity of human life' (ibid.: 188).

## Promise

Egner (2006) examined the different cultural premises underlying the conditions of the use of the speech act of promising in Western and African cultures, observing that 'different pragmatic norms reflect different hierarchies of values characteristic of different cultures' (Wierzbicka 1985: 173; cited in Egner 2006: 449) and that 'interactional maxims and their hierarchical ordering are culture-specific' (ibid.: 449). Egner (2006) argues that the Western promise, which is associated with the notions of sincerity and commitment that underlie human interaction in Western culture, and the African promise, which is related to politeness and cooperativeness, are 'two different kinds of illocutionary acts' (ibid.: 462). Egner (2006: 448) quotes Brown and Levinson (1987) in support of the conclusion: 'even if they [the promises] are false ... they demonstrate S's good intentions in satisfying H's positive face wants' (ibid.: 125).

## Refusal

Nelson *et al.* (2002) adapted the DCT developed by Beebe *et al.* (1990) and used it to investigate similarities and differences between Egyptian Arabic and American English refusals in terms of 'frequency types of strategies, the direct/indirect dimension of communications style, gender, and status' (Nelson *et al.* (2002: 39). They found no difference in the frequency of use of direct and indirect strategies as well as specific indirect strategies, and the effect of interlocutor status, but discovered that Egyptian males use less indirection than Americans in refusals. These researchers, however, question the usefulness of the DCT for revealing 'the sociopragmatic complexities of fact-threatening acts such as refusals' (ibid.: 163).

Cho (2007) compared refusals by Koreans and Germans, incorporating four social settings (one's family, workplace, circle of friends and the public space) and four subtypes of refusals of an order, a request, a 'big petition' and a 'small petition' (ibid.: 195) into the DCT. The study's main finding is that the German participants were more concerned about pursuing their own communicative goals effectively, whereas the Koreans were more mindful of demonstrating 'respect of the interlocutor's social status and the establishment of a harmonious relationship with the other people around' (ibid.: 211).

Using Weigand's (2000) notion of 'minimal action game', Grein (2007) examined the dialogic usage of language as sequences of active speech acts (directives: requests, orders, invitations, proposals) and reactive speech acts (refusals) within German and Japanese languages. Grein (2007) analysed refusal data collected by a DTC and found both similarities and differences in the refusal behaviours of German and Japanese speakers. Japanese use very polite language towards children but avoid overt sympathy towards intimates; whereas Germans are indifferent to children but communicate sympathy towards intimates. The results are attributed to the different cultural imprinting, primarily dependent on face concepts, in that Japanese pass on their cultural values to children at the start of socialization and the harmony principle is perceived as the most effective interaction principle (Grein 2007: 99). In contrast, Germans teach children linguistic strategies for persuasion and techniques to avoid disharmony. Japanese also use diverging rules of language behaviour based on social distance, by being direct with family members and intimate friends (ibid.: 99).

## Request

The speech act of requesting, central to Brown and Levinson's (1978, 1987) politeness phenomena, is an FTA as the H can interpret a request as threatening her or his negative face by intruding upon her or his freedom of action, and S may fear that making a request exposes a need or risks the H's loss of face (Kim and Wilson 1994; Ogiermann 2009). Requests are 'the most frequently studied speech act in cross-cultural and interlanguage pragmatics' (Ogiermann 2009: 190). Blum-Kulka and House (1989) compared requests in Australian English, Canadian French, German, Hebrew and Argentinian Spanish, and concluded that 'cultural, contextual external and context internal factors' interact in intricate ways 'to determine choices of requestive behaviour' (ibid.: 151).

In Kim and Wilson's (1994) cross-cultural comparison of implicit theories of requesting, they compared the way 296 Koreans and 299 Americans conceptualized five interactive requestive constraints: clarity, perceived imposition, consideration for the other's feelings, risking disapproval for self and effectiveness (ibid.: 210). They discovered two main cross-cultural differences: first, the Americans perceived the direct statement strategy to be the most effective way of making a request, whereas the Koreans perceived it as the least effective; and second, the Americans perceived clarity of strategies as most effective, whereas the Koreans perceived it as counterproductive to effectiveness (ibid.: 210).

Kachru (1998) compared the use of request strategies by speakers of Indian and Singaporean English in 'identical' situations, using a modified DCT, to find out whether the request strategies used varied significantly according to the social parameters of 'relative' social distance and social status (ibid.: 82). The study found that the most favoured strategy for both groups was the same, i.e. query preparatory; the second one, direct request, was used by Indian speakers more frequently; and the third, the hint, was preferred by Singaporean speakers (ibid.: 84). Kachru (1998) also found intercultural differences. For instance, when Indian speakers interact with strangers of non-equal status, they tend to use impositives more often than query preparatory as the request strategy; however, when interacting with strangers of equal status, Indians tend to use hints more often than query preparatory. In similar contextual situations, the Singaporean group also behave differently (Kachru 1998).

In another study, comparing requests among Chinese speakers in Melbourne, Singapore and the People's Republic of China, Lee-Wong (2000) found a preference for on-record direct strategies that concur with the Chinese emphasis on clarity, explicitness and upfront sincerity in daily face-to-face requestives, except 'where the request has a high Wx in imposition or where H is S's superior, either in age and/or social position' (ibid.: 108). Lee-Wong's study, therefore, supports the importance and relevance of culture-specific and context-internal and context-external factors.

Byon (2006) analysed Korean request head act forms in the DCT responses of fifty Korean native speakers to ascertain 'the link between politeness and the indirectness of speech acts' (ibid.: 247). The study supports viewing the relation between linguistic indirectness and politeness from a language- and culture-specific perspective (ibid.: 247), as it found that Korean politeness is morphologically marked 'e.g. the honorific suffix, speech levels, hedges' (Byon 2006: 270), unlike the syntactically marked requests in English (Blum-Kulka *et al.* 1989), and the Korean politeness requests that are context dependent.

Ruzickova (2007) analysed a corpus of fifty-one requestive hints in 150 hours of 'spontaneous, non-directed speech' of 'Cuban men and women of all age groups, socio-economic status, educational levels, and regional and ethnic backgrounds' (ibid.: 1178) in order to observe what 'politic' speakers actually do to observe 'socioculturally determined conventions of linguistic action' (Kasper 1990: 198). Ruzickova's (2007) study confirmed the existence of culture-specific 'norms of facework and face behaviour' (ibid.: 1170), as evidenced in the exclusively positive politeness strategies employed by the Cuban Spanish speakers in the corpus. Previous studies in cross-cultural pragmatics showed language- and culture-specific preferences in the way requests are realized (Byon 2006; Ogiermann 2009).

## 4. Impoliteness

Politeness, in its pragmatic sense, is the way language functions to convey the most appropriate relationship, as perceived by the speaker/writer, in order that the speaker/writer enhances the likelihood of achieving the communicative goal, while maintaining the face of the participants. The notion of pragmatic politeness is linked to the default context of communication in which the speaker/writer tries to save, or enhance, her/his own face and/or the face of the hearer/reader. However, this is not always the context of communication. What about contexts in which the speaker/writer has to reprimand someone who repeatedly underperforms, or is angry or upset with the hearer/reader for some reason, or simply dislikes the hearer/reader?

In the special issue of the *Journal of Pragmatics* on 'Identity Perspectives on Face and (Im)Politeness' (Spencer-Oatey and Ruhi 2007), Graham (2007) reports on the speech act of disagreement with reference to (im)politeness and identity in a computer-mediated community (Graham 2007). In these contexts, the default objective is not to save or enhance the face of the hearer/reader, but to cause the hearer/reader to lose face. In such contexts, it is possible to analyse the impoliteness strategies used by the speaker/writer. Obviously, the use of impoliteness strategies is far less frequent than the use of politeness strategies, and there are far fewer studies of impoliteness (see, for example, Bousfield 2008; Culpeper 1996, 2005; Spencer-Oatey 2005). Just as studies of politeness have identified strategies in various categories, studies of impoliteness have done the same. Bousfield (2008) offers a framework for analysing impoliteness largely based on the work of Culpeper (1996, 2005). As with politeness, impoliteness consists of five 'superstrategies' together with specific positive and negative face-damaging strategies. Culpeper (2005) also adopts the formula advocated by Brown and Levinson (1987) to assess the extent of the face threat and, subsequently, to determine how best to damage the face of the hearer/reader. The calculation for how to achieve face loss is thus:

Power + distance + imposition = degree of face loss to be achieved by appropriate impoliteness strategy

Impoliteness superstrategies (in rank order, highest first) are:

1. Bald on record: used when much face is at stake and the speaker/writer does not have the power to (safely) speak directly and unambiguously;

2. Positive impoliteness + on record: the use of strategies to damage other's positive face;
3. Negative impoliteness + on record: the use of strategies to damage other's negative face;
4. Off-record impoliteness: the damage to face is done indirectly using implied meaning which can then be denied by the speaker/writer;
5. Withhold politeness: the speaker/writer keeps silent or fails to act where politeness is expected.

*Culpeper (2005)*

Table 9.2 summarizes Culpeper's (1996) realizations of positive and negative impoliteness superstrategies.

Limberg (2009) examined 'verbal threats and their immediate (elicited) responses' (ibid.: 1376) as manifestations of impoliteness, with impoliteness defined as 'an intentional form of face-aggravation caused by verbal and nonverbal means and interactively construed in a particular context' (ibid.: 1376). The study found that most threat responses are either compliance or non-compliance, occurring to various degrees; they support the success of the threat; they show evidence of the social power variable at work; and 'combinations of mitigating and aggravating moves occur in the same turn' (ibid.: 1392).

## 5. Conclusion

This chapter has reviewed a number of cross-cultural and intercultural research studies on speech act performance with a focus on the impact of differing cultural norms, values, assumptions and linguistic elements on facework and politeness. A review of the results demonstrates both the culture-specific and language-specific nature of speech acts and highlights key interactional and linguistic features. Although the majority of studies still employ written DCTs, a wider range of methodologies may be used. For example, oral DCTs, discourse role play talks, discourse self-assessment, videotaped role plays, ethnographic studies and the analysis of real-life interactions can also play a role in providing rich data in current and future cross-cultural and intercultural communication studies.

*Table 9.2* Realizations of positive and negative impoliteness superstrategies

| Positive impoliteness strategies | Negative impoliteness strategies |
|---|---|
| Ignore, snub, fail to attend to other's interests, wants, needs, goods, etc. | Frighten: instil a belief that action detrimental to other will occur |
| Exclude the other from activity | Condescend, scorn or ridicule: emphasize own power, use diminutives to other (or other's position), be contemptuous, belittle, do not take the other seriously |
| Disassociate from the other | |
| Deny common ground or association | |
| Be disinterested, unconcerned, unsympathetic | |
| Use inappropriate identity markers | Invade the other's space: literally (positioning closer than relationship permits) or metaphorically (ask for intimate information given the relationship) |
| Use obscure or secretive language | |
| Seek disagreement: select sensitive topic or just disagree outright | |
| Avoid agreeing with the other (even if S does) | Explicitly associate the other with negative aspect: personalize, use pronouns, 'I' and 'you' |
| Make the other feel uncomfortable | Put the other's indebtedness on record |
| Use taboo language: swear, be abusive, express strong views opposed to other | Hinder: physically (block passage), conversationally (deny turn, interrupt) |
| Call other names: use derogatory nominations | |

*Source*: Adapted from Culpeper (1996), cited in Bousfield (2008: 85–6). Reprinted with permission.

Research on speech acts, facework and politeness can be of great value in intercultural education and professional communication. In order for students and professionals to enhance their intercultural communicative competence, they need to have knowledge of face and facework, the diversity of speech acts and the relations between face, (im)politeness and the linguistic realizations of speech acts in the immediate (local) and wider (global) contexts of interaction. Further, they need to be culturally sensitive and approach intercultural communication with a positive attitude. Explicit instruction in intercultural pragmatics that draws on empirical studies can help students and professionals take steps towards interculturality.

## Related topics

Assessing and evaluating intercultural competence; gender, language, identity and intercultural communication; intercultural communication in context; intercultural conflict; interculturality and intercultural pragmatics

## Further reading

Cheng, W. (2003) *Intercultural Conversation*, Amsterdam: John Benjamins (this book describes a study of compliment response and disagreement, among other interactional analyses, in authentic intercultural conversations of Hong Kong Chinese speakers of English).

Fraser, B. and Turner, K. (2009) (eds) *Language in Life, and a Life in Language: Jacob Mey – A Frestshrift*, Bingley, UK: Emerald (many of the fifty-six articles discuss face, politeness and speech acts).

## References

Austin, J.L. (1962) *How to Do Things with Words*, Oxford: Clarendon Press.

Bargiela-Chiappini, F. (2003) 'Face and politeness: new (insights) for old (concepts)', *Journal of Pragmatics*, 35: 1453–69.

Bargiela-Chiappini, F. and Harris, S. (1997) *Managing Language: The Discourse of Corporate Meetings*, Amsterdam/Philadelphia: Benjamins.

Bataineh, R.F. and Bataineh, R.F. (2008) 'A cross-cultural comparison of apologies by native speakers of American English and Jordanian Arabic', *Journal of Pragmatics*, 40: 792–821.

Beebe, L.M. and Takahashi, T. (1989a) 'Do you have a bag? Social status and patterned variation in second language acquisition', in S.M. Gass, C. Madden, D. Preston and L. Selinker (eds) Variation in Second Language Acquisition: Discourse and Pragmatics, Clevedon: Multilingual Matters, pp. 103–28.

——(1989b) 'Sociolinguistic variation in face-threatening speech acts: chastisement and disagreement', in M. Eisenstein (ed.) *The Dynamic Interlanguage: Empirical Studies in Second Language Variation*, New York: Plenum Press, pp. 199–218.

Beebe, L.M., Takahashi, T. and Uliss-Weltz, R. (1990) 'Pragmatic transfer in ESL refusals', in R.C. Scarcella, E.S. Anderson and S.D. Krashen (eds) Developing Communicative Competence in a Second Language, New York: Newburry House, pp. 55–94.

Blum-Kulka, S. and House, J. (1989) 'Cross-cultural and situational variation in requesting behavior', in S. Blum-Kulka, J. House and G. Kasper (eds) *Cross-cultural Pragmatics: Requests and Apologies*, Vol. XXXI, Norwood, NJ: Ablex, pp. 123–54.

Blum-Kulka, S. and Olshtain, E. (1984) 'Requests and Apologies: a cross-cultural study of speech act realization patterns (CCSARP)', *Applied Linguistics*, 5(3): 196–213.

Blum-Kulka, S., House, J. and Kasper, G. (eds) (1989) *Cross-cultural Pragmatics: Requests and Apologies*, Vol. XXXI, Norwood, NJ: Ablex.

Bousfield, D. (2008) *Impoliteness in Interaction*, Amsterdam: John Benjamins.

Brown, P. and Levinson, S.C. (1978) 'Universals in language usage: politeness phenomena', in E.N. Goody (ed.) *Questions and Politeness: Strategies in Social Interaction*, Cambridge/New York: Cambridge University Press, pp. 56–311.

——(1987) *Politeness: Some Universals in Language Usage*, Cambridge: Cambridge University Press.

Byon, A.S. (2006) 'The role of linguistic indirectness and honorifics in achieving linguistic politeness in Korean', *Journal of Politeness Research*, 2: 247–76.

Chen, R. (1993) 'Responding to compliments: a contrastive study of politeness strategies between American English and Chinese speakers', *Journal of Pragmatics*, 20(1): 49–75.

Cho, Y. (2007) 'Refusals and politeness in directive action games: cultural differences between Korean and German', in M. Grein and E. Weigand (eds) *Dialogue and Culture*, Amsterdam/Philadelphia: John Benjamins, pp. 95–113.

Creese, A. (1991) 'Speech act variation in British and American English', *PENN Working Papers*, 7(2): 37–58.

Culpeper, J. (1996) 'Towards an anatomy of impoliteness', *Journal of Pragmatics*, 25: 349–67.

——(2005) 'Impoliteness and the weakest link', *Journal of Politeness Research*, 1(1): 35–72.

Daly, N., Holmes, J., Newton, J. and Stubbe, M. (2004) 'Expletives as solidarity signals in FTAs on the factory floor', *Journal of Pragmatics*, 36: 945–64.

Eelen, G. (2001) *A Critique of Politeness Theory*, Manchester: St Jerome Publishing.

Egner, I. (2006) 'Intercultural aspects of the speech act of promising: Western and African practices', *Intercultural Pragmatics*, 3–4: 443–64.

Fahey, M.P. (2005) 'Speech acts as intercultural danger zones: a cross-cultural comparison of the speech act of apologizing in Irish and Chilean soap operas', *Journal of Intercultural Communication*, 8. Online. Available: www.immi.se/intercultural/nr8/palma.htm (accessed 23 May 2010).

Feller, S. (2007) 'Cultural differences in the speech act of greeting', in M. Grein and E. Weigand (eds) *Dialogue and Culture*, Amsterdam/Philadelphia: John Benjamins, pp. 95–113.

Fraser, B. (1990) 'Perspectives in politeness', *Journal of Pragmatics*, 14: 219–36.

Gao, G. and Ting-Toomey, S. (1998) *Communicating Effectively with the Chinese*, Thousand Oaks, CA: Sage.

Goffman, E. (1955) 'On face-work: an analysis of ritual elements in social interaction', *Psychiatry: Journal for the Study of Interpersonal Processes*, 18: 213–31.

——(1971) *Relations in Public: Microstudies of the Public Order*, New York: Harper and Row.

Graham, S.L. (2007) 'Disagreeing to agree: conflict, (im)politeness and identity in a computer-mediated community', *Journal of Pragmatics, Special Issue: Identity Perspectives on Face and (Im)politeness*, 39(4): 742–59.

Grein, M. (2007) 'The speech act of refusal within the minimal action game', in M. Grein and E. Weigand (eds) *Dialogue and Culture*, Amsterdam/Philadelphia: John Benjamins, pp. 95–113.

Gu, Y.G. (1990) 'Politeness phenomena in modern Chinese', *Journal of Pragmatics*, 14: 237–57.

——(2008) 'Collective face, public image and politeness in Chinese organizational discourse: an indigenous approach', paper presented at Partnerships in Action: Research, Practice and Training, Inaugural Conference of the Asia-Pacific Rim LSP and Professional Communication Association, 8–10 December 2008.

Guan, X., Park, H.S. and Lee, H.E. (2009) 'Cross-cultural differences in apology', *Intercultural Journal of Intercultural Relations*, 33: 32–45.

Herbert, R.K. (1991) 'The sociology of compliment work: an ethnocontrastive study of Polish and English compliments', *Multilingua*, 10(4): 381–402.

Holmes, J. (1988) 'Paying compliments: a sex-preference politeness strategy', *Journal of Pragmatics*, 12: 445–65.

Hu, H.C. (1944) 'The Chinese concept of "face"', *American Anthropologist*, 46: 45–64.

Hu, W. and Grove, C. (1999) *Encountering the Chinese: A Guide for Americans*, Yarmouth, ME: Intercultural Press.

Hymes, D. (1972) 'Models of the interaction of language and social life', in J.J. Gumperz and D. Hymes (eds) *Directions in Sociolinguistics: The Ethnography of Communication*, New York: Holt, Rinehart and Winston, pp. 35–71.

Jansen, F. and Janssen, D. (2010) 'Effects of positive politeness strategies in business letters', *Journal of Pragmatics*. Online. Available: doi:10.1016/j.pragma.2010.02.013 (accessed 23 May 2010).

Ji, S.J. (2000) 'Face and polite verbal behaviors in Chinese culture', *Journal of Pragmatics*, 32(7): 1059–62.

Kachru, Y. (1998) 'Culture and speech acts: evidence from Indian and Singapore English', *Studies in the Linguistic Sciences*, 28(1): 79–98.

Kasper, G. (1990) 'Linguistic politeness: current research issues', *Journal of Pragmatics*, 14(2): 193–218.

Kim, H. (2008) 'The semantic and pragmatic analysis of south Korean and Australian English apologetic speech acts', *Journal of Pragmatics*, 40: 257–78.

Kim, M.-S. and Wilson, S. (1994) 'A cross-cultural comparison of implicit theories of requesting', *Communication Monographs*, 61(3): 210–35.

Knapp, M.L., Hooper, R. and Bell, R.A. (1984) 'Compliments: a descriptive taxonomy', *Journal of Communication*, 34(4): 12–31.

Lee-Wong, S.M. (2000) *Politeness and Face in Chinese Culture*, Frankfurt am Main, Germany: Peter Lang.

Leech, G. (1983) *Principles of Pragmatics*, London/New York: Longman.

——(2007) 'Politeness: is there an East–West divide?', *Journal of Politeness Research*, 3: 167–206.

Liebersohn, Y.Z., Neuman, Y. and Bekerman, Z. (2004) 'Oh baby, it's hard for me to say I'm sorry: public apologetic speech and cultural rhetorical resources', *Journal of Pragmatics*, 36: 921–44.

Limberg, H. (2009) 'Impoliteness and threat responses', *Journal of Pragmatics*, 41: 1376–94.

Lorenzo-Dus, N. (2001) 'Compliment responses among British and Spanish university students: a contrastive study', *Journal of Pragmatics*, 33: 107–27.

Lustig, M.W. and Koester, J. (2009) *Intercultural Competence: Interpersonal Communication across Cultures*, 6th edn, New York: Longman.

Manes, J. and Wolfson, N. (1981) 'The compliment formula', in F. Coulmas (ed.) *Conversational Routine: Explorations in Standardized Communication Situations and Prepatterned Speech*, The Hague/New York: Mouton, pp. 115–32.

Mao, L.M.R. (1994) 'Beyond politeness theory: "face" revisited and renewed', *Journal of Pragmatics*, 21(5): 451–86.

Matsumoto, Y. (1988) 'Reexamination of the universality of face: politeness phenomena in Japanese', *Journal of Pragmatics*, 12: 403–26.

Meier, A.J. (1996) 'Two Cultures Mirrored in Repair Work', *Multilingua*, 15: 149–69.

Morand, D.A. (1995) 'Politeness as a universal variable in cross-cultural managerial communication', *International Journal of Organizational Analysis*, 3(4): 52–74.

Nelson, G.L., Carson, J., Al-Batal, M. and El-Bakary, W. (2002) 'Cross-cultural pragmatics: strategy use in Egyptian Arabic and American English refusals', *Applied Linguistics*, 23(2): 163–89.

Nureddeen, F.A. (2009) 'Cross cultural pragmatics: apology strategies in Sudanese Arabic', *Journal of Pragmatics*, 40: 279–306.

Ogiermann, E. (2009) 'Politeness and in-directness across cultures: a comparison of English, German, Polish and Russian requests', *Journal of Politeness Research*, 5: 189–216.

Olshtain, E. (1989). 'Apologies across languages', in S. Blum-Kulka, J. House and G. Kasper (eds.) *Cross-cultural Pragmatics*, Norwood, NJ: Ablex, pp. 155–73.

Olshtain, E. and Weinbach, L. (1993) 'Interlanguage features of the speech act of complaining', in G. Kasper and S. Blum-Kulka (eds) *Interlanguage Pragmatics*, New York/Oxford: Oxford University Press, pp. 108–22.

Park, H.S. and Guan, X. (2006) 'The effects of national culture and face concerns on intention to apologize: a comparison of USA and China', *Journal of Intercultural Communication Research*, 35: 183–204.

Pomerantz, A. (1978) 'Compliment responses: notes on the co-operation of multiple constraints', in J. Schenkein (ed.) *Studies in the Organization of Conversational Interaction*, New York: Academic Press, pp. 79–112.

Rodriguez, A. (2002) 'Culture to culturing: re-imagining our understanding of intercultural relations', *Journal of Intercultural Communication*, 5. Online. Available: www.immi.se/intercultural/nr5/rodriguez.pdf (accessed 22 May 2010).

Ruzickova, E. (2007) 'Strong and mild requestive hints and positive-face redress in Cuban Spanish', *Journal of Pragmatics*, 39: 1170–1202.

Scollon, R. and Wong Scollon, S. (2001) *Intercultural Communication: A Discourse Approach*, 2nd edn, Oxford: Blackwell.

Searle, J. (1965) 'What is a speech act?', in P.P. Giglioli (ed.) *Language and Social Context*, Harmondsworth, UK: Penguin Books, pp.136–54.

——(1969) *Speech Acts: An Essay in the Philosophy of Language*, Cambridge: Cambridge University Press.

——(1975) 'Indirect speech acts,' in P. Cole and J.L. Morgan (eds) *Syntax and Semantics, Vol. 3: Speech Acts*, New York: Academic Press, pp. 59–82.

Smith, A.H. (1894) *Chinese Characteristics*, New York: F.H. Revell Co.

Spencer-Oatey, H. (2005) '(Im)politeness, face and perceptions of rapport: unpacking their bases and interrelationships', *Journal of Politeness Research*, 1(1)L 95–119.

Spencer-Oatey, H. and Ruhi, S. (2007) 'Identity, face and impoliteness', *Special issue of Journal of Pragmatics on 'Identity perspectives on face and (im)politeness'*, 39(4): 635–38.

Sun, L.K. (1991) 'Contemporary Chinese culture: structure and emotionality', *The Australian Journal of Chinese Affairs*, 24: 1–41.

Takahashi, T. and Beebe L.M. (1987) 'The development of pragmatic competence by Japanese learners of English', *JALT Journal*, 8: 131–55.

——(1993) 'Cross-linguistic influence in speech act of correction', in G. Kasper and S. Blum-Kulka (eds) *Interlanguage Pragmatics*, New York: Oxford University Press, pp. 138–57.

Tang, C.H. and Zhang, G.Q. (2009) 'A contrastive study of compliment responses among Australian English and Mandarin Chinese Speakers', *Journal of Pragmatics*, 41: 325–45.

Thomas, J. (1983) 'Cross-cultural pragmatic failure', *Applied Linguistics* 4(2): 91–112.

——(1995) *Meaning in Interaction: An Introduction to Pragmatics*, Harlow, UK: Longman.

Ting-Toomey, S. (1988) 'Intercultural conflict styles: a face-negotiation theory', in Y. Kim and W.B. Gudykunst (eds) *Theories in Intercultural Communication*, Thousand Oaks, CA: Sage, pp. 213–35.

Weigand, E. (2000) 'The dialogic action game', in M. Coulthard, J. Cotterill and F. Rock (eds) *Dialogue Analysis VII: Working with Dialogue*. Selected papers from the 7th IADA Conference, Birmingham 1999, Tübingen: Niemeyer, pp. 1–18.

Wieland, M. (1995) 'Complimenting behavior in French/American cross-cultural dinner conversations', *French Review*, 68(5): 796–812.

Wierzbicka, A. (1985) 'Different cultures, different languages, different speech acts', *Journal of Pragmatics*, 9: 145–78.

Wolfson, N. (1989) 'The social dynamics of native and nonnative variation in complimenting behaviour', in M. Eisenstein (ed.) *The Dynamic Interlanguage: Empirical Studies in Second Language Variation*, New York: Plenum Press, pp. 219–36.

Ye, Z.D. (2004) 'Chinese categorization of interpersonal relationships and the cultural logic of Chinese social interaction: an indigenous perspective', *Intercultural Pragmatics*, 1(2): 211–30.

Yu, M.C. (2005) 'Sociolinguistic competence in the complimenting act of native Chinese and American English speakers: a mirror of cultural value', *Language and Speech*, 48(1): 91–119.

# Language, identity and intercultural communication

# Gender, language, identity, and intercultural communication

*Xingsong Shi and Juliet Langman*

## 1. Introduction

This chapter intends to demonstrate the breadth and development of research regarding gender, language and identity in ways that may be relevant to intercultural communication research. It begins with a brief introduction of the major topics and theoretical approaches that have shaped language and gender studies since the 1970s, with a particular focus on the intercultural difference model of the 1980s. Next, research and theoretical shifts that problematize the early work in language and gender are discussed. Specifically, current research, which draws on insights from feminist poststructural theory and social constructivist theory, allows for a re-examination of the assumed and essentialized duality that sees "women" and "men" as different but undifferentiated groups. New work examines language through the lens of discourse and identity, and gender through the lens of performativity. A selection of recent work in intercultural and multilingual contexts illustrates these new perspectives. Finally, a brief discussion of implications and future directions is outlined.

## 2. Historical perspectives

Research on language and gender gained its voice as an independent field of inquiry in the 1970s, with an attempt to explore the relationship between language, gender, and power. Early work in gender studies was conducted primarily in monolingual contexts and sought to understand differences in language use between women and men—bringing women and their language as sources of language data to the forefront. Beginning with the notion that one should not take men's language as the standard from which to examine women's language, early work in the field of language and gender can be roughly divided into two types on the basis of the explanations provided for the perceived and recorded differences between women's and men's language. These two approaches can be characterized as the "dominance" and "difference" paradigms (Coates and Cameron 1998).

In the "dominance" framework, scholars usually concentrate on phonetics, phonology, syntax, and morphology as core features of language. Their studies suggest that, due to the social force of being appropriately "feminine", women tend to speak a "powerless language", which is described as uncertain, weak, and excessively polite, relying on hedges, tag questions, emphatic stress, and hypercorrect grammar. Consequently, women are often presented as inferior language users or a silenced group (e.g., Bradley 1988; Brown 1980; Lakoff 1975).

Early researchers in the "dominance" paradigm also examine conversational strategies in interaction between men and women. They outline how women and men do not have equal rights to the conversational floor. A variety of social contexts have revealed asymmetrical conversational patterns, in which men tend to use diverse competitive or non-cooperative strategies, for example no response, interruption, inadequate or delayed response, and silence, to control conversation (Leto DeFrancisco 1991; Swann 1989; West and Zimmerman 1983). Researchers believe that men use these strategies to exhibit and accomplish socially sanctioned patriarchic relations of dominance and submission. In other words, the institutionalized social status of men encourages them to adopt particular linguistic strategies to retain their power and to enhance women's relatively powerless social position. Similarly, this research paradigm examines the forms of talk women typically use and explains how these forms of talk represent and support their powerlessness.

For example, some early work on gender took on a variationist approach common to the developing field of sociolinguistics as articulated by William Labov. Such work focused on particular marked forms of language and compared the use of such forms across social groups, most often distinguished from one another in terms of gender, social class, and age. Findings from such work typically characterized women as using more standard and/or prestigious language forms in comparison with men from the same social contexts. The explanation for such differences, and in particular the more prestigious form, pointed to women's lack of "real" social power and the resultant sense of social insecurity (e.g., Trudgill 1983). In this research approach, gender is usually treated as a binary concept (male/female) and cross-correlated with other social factors (e.g., race, ethnicity, social class). In such a view, gender is seen as a fixed preexisting aspect of an individual's identity that therefore allows for predictions of behavior.

In response to the somewhat negative or secondary status that the dominance approach placed on women, the "difference" approach emerged as an alternative explanation for the observable differences between men's and women's talk. The difference paradigm explores gender-specific communicative norms by examining how gender is performed differentially in same-sex interactions (Maltz and Borker 1982; Tannen 1990). This approach proposes that males and females are socialized in different cultural groups, and therefore adopt different communicative styles and norms, and employ different communicative strategies. In essence, the difference paradigm characterizes talk between women and men in terms of intercultural communication and explains miscommunication in terms of different norms of language use and language interpretation that the two groups employ.

Major conclusions stemming from research in this paradigm outlines how women's speech is structured for the purpose of supporting "cooperative" social roles and relationships, whereas, in contrast, men's speech is seen as structured in ways that support a "competitive" orientation to social relations (Tannen 1990). Much of this work explains the differences in men's and women's speech in terms of how boys and girls are socialized from earliest childhood to be "competitive" and "cooperative" respectively (Coates 1998; Swann 1992).

Drawing on the field of linguistic anthropology (e.g., Hymes 1974), the difference paradigm examined language use in a cultural context and employed constructs such as the speech community and identity to explain differences in patterns of language use. Although researchers in the difference paradigm did not disagree with the notion that language reflects the power and dominance of men in society, they did challenge the notion that women's language, by definition, that is seen from the "norm" of men's language, is "deficient" or "anormal" in all contexts. Rather, in addition to the real power-related differences in status between men and women in society, these researchers also examined the ways in which language helped to shape women's and men's identities.

These two paradigms, which spanned the time period from the 1970s to the 1990s, have provided a rich array of research studies examining women's language use and later men's language use in both mixed-sex (cross-cultural or intercultural) interactions as well as in same-group intracultural interactions. A number of criticisms of this research have emerged over time; such criticisms have led to a complexification and deeper understanding of the relationship between language and gender, particularly through the added lenses of identity, discourse, performance, and power. Criticisms centered first, as outlined above, around the tendency of some work in the dominance paradigm to depict women's language in deficit terms, and as unchangeably weak. These critics had a clear political agenda of uncovering and addressing inequality between men and women. Additional criticisms, this time directed more at work within the difference model, questioned the validity of research carried out primarily among white middle-class English speakers to explain how language operates in connection with gender in a variety of different social groups and societies. The claim is that all research that examines "women" and "men" as members of groups will invariably lead to stereotyping of behavior and essentializing of the categories of "men" and "women" in ways that assume that there are no differences among women as a whole, and men as a whole, and, in contrast, vast differences between women and men.

## 3. Critical issues and topics

Within the field of language and gender, a number of critical issues and topics have helped to move the field forward from its beginnings in the 1970–90s. The key issues include a concern with the 'essentializing' orientation of much early work (Coates 1998, Ehrlich 2001; Pavlenko 2001a). In addition, concern about the generalizability of findings from early work came from the fact that the scope of research was restricted, to a great degree, to studies of white, American, or Western culture, middle-class women, in interaction either with one another or with white middle-class men. Drawing conclusions from such a limited sample of the diversity of human experience makes the likelihood of extending the findings to other groups questionable. In addition, criticisms of the early work also pointed to the focus on "women's" language, and calls were made to examine the nature of "men's" language and the link between men's language and masculinity as another focus of study.

Beginning in the 1990s, research taking a feminist poststructural perspective has resulted in a reconfiguration of key questions and issues in language and gender research. The feminist poststructuralist approach focuses on the role of gendered social practices in the (re)production of identities and social inequalities. The basic tenet of feminist poststructuralist theory, the notion of unequal symbolic power, has been used to explain (1) why the conventions of a dominant sociocultural group are most often seen as the norm, whereas subordinate groups are more likely to have to adapt to majority norms; (2) why it is usually the dominant group that determines what is legitimate, who is legitimate (Blackledge 2001); "who is in", "who is out", "how to be", or "how to act" (Sarangi and Roberts 2002: 197); (3) why there are usually damaging links between languacultural (Agar 1994) misunderstandings and deficits, as well as between cognitive incompetence and second language (L2) practices; and (4) why it is usually members of the dominated group who suffer the negative consequences of any languacultural differences and miscommunications. Thus, cultural capital (of which linguistic resources are a major part) can replace real capital to construct power relations among individuals, institutions, and communities, through which symbolic and material resources in a society are (re)produced, validated, and distributed.

In addition to power, key terms within the new paradigm focus on seeing gender as performance, which further links gender to identity and ideology. Drawing on the work of Butler (1990), gender is defined as a performance that is accomplished through "the repeated stylization of the body, a set of repeated acts within a highly rigid regulatory frame that congeals over time to produce the appearance or substance of a natural sort of being" (Butler 1990: 33).

Seeing gender as performance bounded by particular contexts helps to explain both the diversity of social practices that are seen as "gendered" as well as how the same practices, when performed by men on one occasion and by women on another occasion, are evaluated differently. With gender now viewed as "constructed" or "performed" rather than a "given" fixed component of an individual, the role of identity comes to the forefront of research. Norton, in her investigation of the L2 learning of five immigrant women in Canada, uses the term identity "to reference how a person understands his or her relationship to the world, how that relationship is constructed across time and space, and how the person understands possibilities for the future" (Norton 2000: 5).

Ideology, in turn, helps to explain the ways in which different social practices are differentially evaluated based on who says them, at which time. What previously were conceived of as "norms" of gendered behavior are now seen as ideology or belief systems about how gender operates in a society. As Philips (2005: 272) outlines:

> When we see gender ideology manifest in a bounded speech genre or form of talk, such as story and song, we should think of it not as some representative of a whole. Rather we should think of it as a piece of a larger puzzle, where we need to understand not only the piece, but the entire picture of the larger puzzle.

Further, Philips reminds researchers that, when considering individuals and the social contexts in which they live:

> the early work on gender ideologies was written as if there were only one gender ideology for each society. This was a problem, because the actual existence of multiple gender ideologies in all societies made it easy to counter claims of any one such position.
>
> *Philips (2005: 260)*

With the joining of research from a feminist poststructural approach and sociocultural approaches that examine language and learning as sociohistorically situated in context, a second shift in research urges researchers to examine language, often referred to as discourse in this new paradigm, as a socially constructed phenomenon that serves as a key tool in gender performance.

These new perspectives have resulted in a broadening of research questions and subjects. In what follows, we expand on the feminist poststructural perspective on language, gender, and identity with a particular focus on research that examines processes of gender performance and identity transformation in intercultural contexts such as those that arise in the context of L2 learning and multiple language use.

## 4. Current contributions and research

Recent work urges the perspective that gender is "performed" in locally situated and socially constructed contexts. Such work further introduces the concept of identity as socially constructed in discourse and urges researchers to think in terms of how individuals use language to construct identity rather than how members of a gendered group enact their gender by using the scripts and codes of that group. As such, the question of access to communities in which new language forms are used becomes of primary importance.

An important advance in current theorizing of language and gender examines access and success in language learning among immigrant minority women. As Pavlenko and Piller (2001: 25) point out, "immigrant and minority women's access to education in majority languages may be significantly constrained by language and gender ideologies and practices of both majority and minority communities". The pervading unequal gender relations (Pavlenko and Piller 2001), the restricted mobility and financial dependence due to daycare issues (Warriner 2004), and the threat of sexual harassment (Ehrlich 2001) may restrict females' access to L2 resources (Polanyi 1995) as well as educational and employment opportunities (Goldstein 2001; Menard-Warwick 2004). Even when immigrant and minority women do have access to the classroom, they may be doubly marginalized in the class, both as ethnic minority members and as females, and thus get significantly less classroom interaction time in the target language.

Norton Peirce (1995) first introduced a feminist poststructural approach in her analysis of the process of acquiring a new identity in a new language, through an in-depth series of case studies examining the process of learning how to be "oneself" in a new language. In her work, she further introduced the concept of investment as a way of understanding how individuals make choices, constrained by the social contexts in which they move, which serve either to provide them with access or to prevent them from access to speakers of a new language. Through observing women in different communities of practice, Norton found that "power relations play a crucial role in social interactions between language learners and target language speakers" (Norton 2000: 12), which in turn support or limit access to language practice. Influenced by Bourdieu (1991), feminist poststructuralists contend that linguistic resources possess symbolic power, because they "can be converted into economic and social capital" by providing "access to more prestigious forms of education, desired positions in the workforce or the social mobility ladders" (Pavlenko 2001a: 123). Thus, learners gaining access to an additional language are concomitantly engaged in the (re)creation of their social identities.

Unequal power relations based on gender as practices in diverse sociocultural contexts can serve to mediate L2 learners', often female learners', access to linguistic resources and interactional opportunities. In the process of L2 socialization in the new discursive communities, L2 learners/ users may easily find themselves positioned as incompetent students (Martin 2003), workers (Katz 2000), or adults/parents (Blackledge 2001), which may entail significant changes in ways some L2 users perceive themselves and are perceived by others (Pavlenko 2001b). Unable to feel confident that they are able to match the proficiency in the majority language of the dominant group, they may be reduced to silence in the majority language market (Blackledge 2001).

In the last 10 years, a range of work (Davis and Skilton-Sylvester 2004; Langman 2004; Norton and Pavlenko 2004; Pavlenko et al. 2001) has analyzed and theorized the relationship between L2 learning and gender, as well as between multilingualism and gender. Central to this work was a call to avoid essentializing gender as a fixed category, and to avoid oversimplifying the role of gender in L2 learning and teaching by making a priori assumptions about what difference gender "obviously" makes in the ways "men" and "women" adjust, adapt, or resist new languages and identities. This research further urged the field not to oversimplify the complex relationship between gender and other identity factors such as race, ethnicity, age, sexual orientation, and community status.

Pavlenko (2001a: 117), taking a poststructural approach, argues that "it is not the essential nature of femininity or masculinity that defines the patterns of bilingualism, language maintenance or language shift, but rather the nature of gender, social, and economic relations, and ideologies of language and gender that mediate these relations". Based on these under-standings, poststructuralist theorists recommend that the interaction between language and (gendered) identity be examined context-sensitively in the everyday "social practices" of particular local communities.

The "community of practice" (Lave and Wenger 1991) represents one such unit of analysis introduced into language and gender studies (Eckert and McConnell-Ginet 1999) on account of its ability to capture the multiplicity of gendered identities at work in specific contexts. Such an approach allows researchers to study the development of interactive practices within dynamic groups, and to understand how those acquiring additional languages are brought into or excluded from various activities that shape language learning.

Relevant to intercultural communication studies on the role of gender identity in the process of learning a L2 is work that sees the process of L2 learning as a process of taking on a new voice with associated gendered practices (Langman 2004; Pavlenko and Lantolf 2000; Pavlenko et al. 2001). Pavlenko and Piller (2001) examined the role of gender specifically in the context of bilingual and multilingual communities in which the process of L2 learning can be seen as taking place in a series of contexts in which one individual's agency and the power of societal norms are in a dynamic tension.

Vitanova (2004) examines differential ways in which partners in four heterosexual adult immigrant professional couples negotiated their identities in a new language. Drawing on the work of Bakhtin (1981[1930s]), she explores how individuals author themselves through avail-able language and other resources. Vitanova examines the intersection of gender in relation to two important types of participants: native speakers of English, on the one hand, and the immigrant's partner, on the other. Her analysis reveals that "gender is enacted on two planes of discourse: sensitivity to social positionings, with a particular focus on emotions, and linguistic expertise within the couples" (Vitanova 2004: 262). Although the women both presented themselves and were acknowledged as the linguistic experts in the couple, they tended to experience negative emotions of fear, shame, and nervousness in their interactions with native speakers, whereas the men "aligned themselves with the 'legitimate' members of their L2 community" (ibid.: 267) and expressed confidence in their interactions with native speakers. Vitanova concludes, however, that, although immigrant women routinely occupy doubly marginalized positions as women and as L2 learners, their discourses of emotion do not necessarily represent a sign of weakness. Rather, their discourse also encodes resistance and potential future action; by expressing their emotions, "they are engaging in a complex rhetorical relationship with a specific audience and at the same time are expressing a socioideological position" (Vitanova 2004: 274). Present in Vitanova's work is examination of both macro-level ideological con-siderations of gender, as well as micro- or local-level interactional considerations of gender in practice. In addition, Vitanova's work highlights the role of emotion and desire, a focus new to research in language and gender (see Keisling 2005; Kulick and Schieffelin 2004).

## 5. Renegotiating gender identity in intercultural contexts

For many adult L2 learners, L2 socialization begins with a robust sense of (gendered) social identity linked to particular culturally based ideologies of gender and gendered communicative practices. When they start a boundary-crossing journey, L2 learners are faced with performing gender in a new form and in a new context. How do they learn to do this? That is, how do they learn to "translate" their gender practices and/or change their identity practices in ways that align with their desires? In new cultural contexts, cross-cultural newcomers may find sharp differences or even clashes between their home and host communicative practices and gender ideologies. Hence, at times, learners adopt or adapt to new norms of behavior that code their previously established identities to represent themselves in gendered ways, whereas at other times they resist. L2 learners, who can be seen as novices in new communities of practice, are involved in a reciprocal process, one in which they actively co-construct their social identities. Although novices participate in new social and linguistic practices, in which they both learn and contribute, they do not simply co-construct agreement through assimilation (e.g., Menard-Warwick 2004; Norton 2000; Warriner 2004); they can sometimes resist and reframe their participation in L2 interactions (e.g., Goldstein 2001; McKay and Wong 1996; Siegal 1996; Skapoulli 2004). At other times, newcomers may find the new language and cultural context freeing in contrast to more strictly defined role expectations for women (Piller and Takahashi 2006).

In previous language and gender studies, scholars found diverse forms of L2 practices prompted by dynamic gendered identities in intercultural contexts. For example, in Norton Peirce's (1995), Menard-Warwick's (2004), and Warriner's (2004) studies on immigrant women, the research participants were all, to different degrees, motivated to invest in L2 learning to claim their "right to speak" (Norton Peirce 1995: 25). In Siegal's (1996) study, however, the white Western woman, Mary, who was learning Japanese in Japan, refused to use certain pragmatic features to "perform culturally appropriate rituals" (p. 365) in Japanese in order to resist the dominant gender ideologies encoded in Japanese female language. She wanted to keep her identity as a middle-aged professional "on almost equal standing with the professor" (p. 367), although her identity-maintenance efforts were at the cost of her being regarded as an inappropriate Japanese speaker with incomplete L2 transformation.

The resistance to complete assimilation or integration to the target culture was also found in Skapoulli's (2004) study in a more complicated interaction between gender and ethnicity. In Skapoulli's study, Nadia, an Egyptian adolescent girl in Cyprus, found her native Cypriot peers' gender practices conflicted with her more traditional gender ideologies. In her home culture community, she practiced "reserved and modest speech behavior" to meet expected behavioral norms, but among her peers at school, she adopted a more "extrovert and carefree speech style". Instead of seeking complete integration into the mainstream peer group, Nadia managed to take a "balanced" position between her two worlds. She used the youth register at school but took care to keep multiple and hybrid positionings in her discursive performance of gender. She made a clear differentiation between her activities at school and her practices in her own community. Consequently, even though Nadia had native-like L2 competence, she resisted complete assimilation to the gender practices in the mainstream youth culture. Her balanced bilingual bicultural competence gave her a wide repertoire of identities to choose from. This flexibility in gender practices that facilitates transitions between communities is what Bucholtz and Hall (2003) refer to as 'adequation'.

Similarly, Ek (2009) examines a Guatemalan American adolescent's construction of ethnic and gender identities across educational contexts and shows how this young woman negotiates the conflictive socializations to ethnicity and gender at home, church, and school by using her various languages to construct multiple identities. She shows, in a way similar to that of Nadia in the Cypriot context, that "[a]s Latino/a immigrant youth in the United States move in and across different contexts in their daily lives, they are continually engaging in actions and behaviors that are taken up as markers of their ethnicity and gender" (Ek 2009: 418). Because such youth are socialized in the home to gendered behaviors that are richly tied to their ethnic identity, "Latino/a students may find themselves in contexts like school that do not reflect nor validate their constructions of ethnicity or gender and create tensions for them" (Ek 2009: 418).

When examining older women immigrants from Central America to the United States enrolled in a community English language course, Menard-Warwick (2008) examines and compares narratives drawn from in-class conversations in adult ESL classrooms through positioning theory. She neatly juxtaposes examples of narratives that accept and reject traditional positioning of Latin American women as homemakers together with a careful analysis of how her participants vary their linguistic practices to mark themselves as either traditional or not, thus arguing how discrete elements of grammar can serve to be clear indicators of social power in the case of language learning.

In Shi's (2010) study of Chinese MBA exchange students in an American negotiation class, Cai, a female Chinese negotiator, felt extremely frustrated because she was criticized repeatedly by the professor for engaging in aggressive positional negotiations. In the class, aggressive and positional negotiators were cautioned against because a "win–win principle" was promoted as the ideal negotiation strategy. In this local community of practice, Cai could hardly ignore the criticisms, on the one hand, because she felt her face was threatened in the public sphere and, on the other hand, because the criticisms of her aggressive negotiation strategy made her highly self-conscious of the double bind experienced by Chinese women in business. In order to become a successful businesswoman, she was cultivated socioculturally and professionally to be tough and aggressive. To be a traditional Chinese woman, however, she was supposed to be tender, submissive, nurturing, and in no way tough or aggressive. Partly because her gendered identity as a soft and traditional Chinese woman was openly questioned by the professor's criticisms, Cai took deliberate measures to change her negotiation strategy, moving from aggressive positional debating to making quick and ready concessions in later class simulations. However, an unintended result of this strategy was the limiting of access to L2 practice that her earlier strategy had provided. In other words, Cai was faced with a mismatch between her practices and the competing ideologies associated with gender and business savvy in the American MBA program.

From the above, we can see that one's previously socialized home-cultural social identity and gender mentality could, to a considerable extent, mediate and reorient one's trajectory of intercultural language socialization (Shi 2010). Owing to different subjectivities and diverse sociocultural beliefs, individuals may face dynamic and unpredictable dilemmas with respect to their gender identities in intercultural language contexts. As such, their intercultural language socialization may not present a fixed or inevitable trajectory of development. Rather, L2 practices will likely show fluctuating, discursive, and sometimes contradictory characteristics.

## 6. Educational implications

As has been pointed out by many scholars, in the complex and multifaceted L2 socialization processes, the host culture's institutions play a crucial role in maintaining or challenging structures of power in society (Blackledge 2001; Bourdieu 1991; Heller 2001; Martin 2003). Schools are often the only arenas for L2 learners to practice their agencies, to (re)establish their identities, and to negotiate and prepare themselves as bicultural bilingual individuals in new societies. As educators, we need to consider how institutional interventions such as classroom instructions can facilitate or lead to resistance of L2 learners' development of new social identities, as well as how to mitigate the powerful social factors that impede their L2 socialization in certain communities. Based on this research, some recommendations are proposed in the following.

### Empowering L2 learners with cross-cultural communicative competence

To facilitate L2 learners' intercultural language socialization and social identity reestablishment, scholars have suggested that gatekeepers and stakeholders in the target culture institutions should help novices become not only linguistically or professionally proficient, but also socioculturally empowered in the process (Cummins 1994; Pavlenko and Piller 2001; Warriner 2004).

In order to empower L2 learners, educators need to take measures to reduce the negative effects of asymmetric power distributions existing in L2 sociocultural contexts. To achieve this purpose, one method is to inform L2 learners of target sociocultural norms, together with the difficulties, forms, and stages of cross-cultural transformations that learners often go through during their immersion into L2 contexts (Pavlenko and Lantolf 2000). Understanding such processes and associated gender practices can help students to uncover the often hidden social expectations for participation in new communities. As gendered identity and gendered learning are historically, culturally, and socially established, a general knowledge of the target culture, together with its historical and current expectations on gendered behavioral norms, may be invaluable to L2 learners. This can help them become conscious of the existing relations of power, prepare for frustrations they may face, and try to seek practices to transform or mitigate asymmetric power relations.

## Extending L2 learners' access to host languacultural resources

As has been argued in previous literature, L2 learners' complex renegotiation of their social identities in the new society "has profound implications for their attitudes to their own language and the learning of the majority group's language" (McNamara 1997: 561), which may mediate their investment in (McKay and Wong 1996; Norton 2000) and access to linguistic resources and interactional opportunities available in the target language and cultural contexts (Blackledge 2001; Menard-Warwick 2004; Pavlenko and Piller 2001; Warriner 2004). These factors can directly influence L2 learning and language contact outcomes, which, in turn, may have an impact on the learners' processes of engagement with and participation in new communities of practice. Deliberate intervention by educators and elaborate efforts on the part of learners themselves are both crucial in L2 socialization.

To promote learners' investment in and access to L2 resources, scholars have highlighted the benefits of guiding learners to conduct mindful self-reflexivity in mediational contexts. Learners are prompted to engage in self-reflection and critical thinking in diaries/journals (Norton 2000), autobiographies (Pavlenko 2001b), and narratives of life experience (Menard-Warwick 2004). With the L2 as the medium, and the negotiation between their home and host cultural identities as content, such self-reflection processes may stimulate investment in L2 usage. This process may help learners to reflect on unequal social power in L2 learning contexts and to recognize and respect the social, cultural, and political roots in their primary culture. This enhanced awareness may then facilitate their repositioning and renegotiation of social identities in the new society.

At a variety of levels, classroom teachers may offer intercultural communication courses that include both native and non-native students, which may provide a favorable platform for intercultural interaction and the examination of culturally bound practices. Representing different cultures, all students can benefit, by helping each other to examine the underlying roots of potential and actual miscommunications in a two-tiered way, by examining not just the "ways things are often said" but also the underlying ideologies that lead to "interpretations of meaning" based on a particular worldview. Collective intercultural reflexivity can construct a rich zone of collaboration to break unhealthy stereotypes and facilitate students' development in intercultural communicative competence, which would be beneficial to all participants.

175

## *Providing instructions according to specific conditions of L2 learners*

Ehrlich (2001) emphasizes that the way that gendered identities are constructed in particular communities may have very concrete consequences for the kinds of L2 proficiency developed by males and females. The target language interactions in which learners are reduced to silence or made to feel humiliated and degraded, as Polanyi (1995) describes, may crucially affect the foreign/L2 input that learners receive and the types of output they must learn to produce. For example, restricted movement within a target culture (e.g., due to daycare problems or fear of sexual assault) may enhance the development of female learners' literacy skills within an L2, but reduce their opportunities for oral proficiency improvement (Ehrlich 2001). Sensitive to the potential multiple, dynamic, and gendered nature of language access and investment, L2 educators can be better prepared to adopt flexible and multifaceted pedagogies that will create more meaningful and effective learning opportunities (Menard-Warwick 2009).

## 7. Future directions

In the early years (the 1960s and 1970s) of language and gender studies, research relied predominantly on an essentialist paradigm that characterized speakers according to biological sex, and used mainly quantitative research methods. In the 1970s and 1980s, gender was recognized as one of the categories of cultural construction, and more qualitative, ethnographic approaches predominated during that period. Since the 1990s, a more dynamic social constructionist and poststructuralist approach has emerged, which makes possible the combination of quantitative and qualitative research. This mixed method of combining qualitative and quantitative methods is highly recommended for future gender and language studies in intercultural communication contexts.

Intercultural communication studies has a tradition of using survey techniques, which have the advantage of collecting data from a large group of research participants for problem enumerating or variable testing. However, the usually one-point-in-time nature of quantitative research can hardly capture the highly dynamic, fluctuating, and developmental changes to be shown in cross-cultural individuals' identity (re)establishment processes. To overcome the problems of past designs, it is essential to integrate qualitative research methods to ascertain individual differences and cross-cultural influences. The "thick", triangulated, and substantial bodies of data collected from qualitative studies can help expound the intricate and complex nature of individuals' gender identity repositioning process in intercultural communication contexts. In addition to quantitative studies' strength of achieving generalizability, integrating the qualitative research approach can help to capture, uncover, document, and describe the richness of the experiences of individuals on their way to acquiring an L2, reconstructing (gendered) social identities, and becoming intercultural.

Thus, future language and gender studies may benefit from a more tightly integrated theoretical framework, which combines the strengths of feminist poststructuralist theories and intercultural communication theories. An integration of these two research approaches can not only compensate for the dearth of research in this interdisciplinary field, but also remedy existing deficiencies in either paradigm to provide more comprehensive and multifaceted insights into language, gender, identity, and intercultural communication issues.

In the paradigm of intercultural communication, as we know, there are two broad domains of interest: (1) the comparative examination of communicative similarities and differences across cultures; and (2) the communicative adaptations made by individuals when they move between cultures. The latter line of reasoning has made very informative generalizations on stages, patterns, and outcomes of intercultural adaptations, which align in kind with the types of transformational trajectories, based on a sociocultural theory, that are outlined by Pavlenko and Lantolf (2000).

Feminist poststructuralist theories envision language and cultural encounters as a process of negotiation situated within the prevailing power relations, either at the disposal of the cultural strangers themselves to make choices or on the part of the competition between host and home cultures to impede, to impel, or, at least, to complicate newcomers' cross-cultural adaptation process. By integrating the feminist poststructuralist approach into intercultural adaptation studies, the research may be attuned to both the constructive force of sociocultural contexts and individuals' capability of exercising their own agencies or subjectivities. Through this lens of examination, individuals are not regarded as static social products with a fixed identity and a predetermined developmental trajectory, but as individuals engaged in rich and varying identity practices as they develop new language practices in new sociocultural settings. Examining individual trajectories may help us better understand variations in discursive practices and differing degrees of adaptation in newcomers, which entail resistance or rejection of social practices and identities associated with a new culture.

On the flip side of the coin, introducing the well-developed conceptual tools of intercultural communication theories into feminist poststructuralist studies may provide interpretive insights into the potential competition between the coexisting home and host cultural systems, a competition that can have a significant impact on L2 learners' language behavior and their renegotiation of gender identities in the host society. One viewpoint developed in intercultural adaptation studies (Gudykunst and Kim 1997; Kim 2001) could be informative to feminist poststructuralist studies. That is, no matter how challenging or even frustrating a cross-cultural experience might be, it may offer an invaluable opportunity for individuals to expand their repertoire of knowledge, improve their L2 skills, enrich their personal experience/expertise, and develop their self-awareness and intercultural sensitivity. In other words, the stress caused by interactions with people from other cultures can be used as a vehicle to stimulate personal development (Kim 2001). This insight by Kim (2001) aligns with current work in language and gender that focuses on the importance of desire. Kulick and Schieffelin (2004) outline a focus on desire as a cognitive construct that explains the motivation for individuals' action to either socialize or not into the sets of practices that constitute normative behavior for particular individuals in particular communities. They further propose that researchers continue to examine not only "how speakers encode desire in language, but also how that desire is articulated with different kinds of authority and power" (Kulick and Schieffelin 2004: 362), arguing that "(o)nce we understand the structures through which this occurs, we are in a better position to also understand the ways in which those structures may be challenged, resisted, changed – or entrenched" (p. 362).

## 8. Conclusion

To sum up, feminist poststructuralists argue that gender cannot be understood as an individual attribute, a variable, or a role, but as a socioculturally constructed product or system of being. Gendered identities are not fixed and static, but are dynamic across social, situational, and interactional contexts. After reviewing the previous and current literature of language and gender studies, this chapter has outlined current research focusing on multiple identities and ideologies, and suggested ways in which such work may be further enriched through insights from intercultural communication studies. The integration of the two research paradigms holds promise to explore the complicated negotiation of language, gender, and identity both at macro cross-cultural and micro individual levels. With a more profound and comprehensive understanding of L2 learners' discursive negotiation of gendered identities and language practices in intercultural contexts and institutions, there will be a better chance of mitigating the sociocultural barriers that complicate the newcomers' development in the host communities. Cross-cultural newcomers may thereby achieve quicker and smoother integration into the new society.

## Related topics

Biculturalism; community of practice; cross-cultural adaptation and transformation; essentialism; identity; ideology; languaculture (linguaculture); language, power, and intercultural communication; poststructuralism; second language socialization; sociocultural theory; stereotyping

## Further reading

Cameron, D. and Kulick, D. (2003) *Language and Sexuality*, Cambridge: Cambridge University Press (presents current theorizing on language and sexuality as a key component in language and gender research).

Coates, J. (ed.) (1998) *Language and Gender: A Reader*, Malden, MA: Blackwell (a collection of classic and revised papers spanning the research from the 1970s through 1990s).

Eckert, P. and McConnell-Ginet, S. (2003) *Language and Gender*, Cambridge: Cambridge University Press (written by two leading scholars in this field, covering the main topics on language and gender studies).

Pavlenko, A. Blackledge, A., Piller I. and Teutsch-Dwyer, M. (eds) (2001) *Multilingualism: Second Language Learning, and Gender*, New York: Mouton de Gruyter (a collection of current debates on language and gender, mainly from feminist poststructuralist viewpoints and focused on multilingual contexts).

Talbot, M. (2010) *Language and Gender*, 2nd edn, Cambridge: Polity Press (a revised textbook covering the range of topics associated with language and gender research in the last three decades).

## References

Agar, M. (1994) *Language Shock: Understanding the Culture of Conversation*, New York: William Morrow.

Bakhtin, M.M. (1981[1930s]) *The Dialogic Imagination: Four Essays*. Ed. by Michael Holquist. Trans. by C. Emerson and M. Holquist. Austin, TX/London: University of Texas Press.

Blackledge, A. (2001) 'The wrong sort of capital? Bangladeshi women and their children's schooling in Birmingham, U.K.', *International Journal of Bilingualism*, 5: 345–69.

Bourdieu, P. (1991) *Language and Symbolic Power*, London: Polity Press.

Bradley, J. (1988) 'Men speak one way, women another', *Aboriginal Linguistics*, 1: 126–34.

Brown, P. (1980) 'How and why are women more polite: some evidence from a Mayan community', in S. McConnell-Ginet, R. Borker and N. Furman (eds) *Women and Language in Literature and Society*, New York: Praeger, pp. 111–36.

Bucholtz, M. and Hall, K. (2003) 'Language and identity', in A. Duranti (ed.) *A Companion to Linguistic Anthropology*, Malden, MA/Oxford, UK: Blackwell, pp. 369–94.

Butler, J. (1990) *Gender Trouble: Feminism and the Subversion of Identity*, New York: Routledge.

Coates, J. (1998) 'Gossip revisited: Language in all-female groups', in J. Coates (ed.) *Language and Gender: A Reader*, Oxford: Blackwell, pp. 226–53.

Coates, J. and Cameron, D. (eds) (1998) *Women in Their Speech Communities: New Perspectives on Language and Sex*, London: Longman.

Cummins, J. (1994) 'From coercive to collaborate relations of power in the teaching of literacy', in B.M. Ferdman, R. Weber and A.G. Ramirez (eds.) *Literacy across Languages and Cultures*, Albany, NY: State University of New York Press, pp. 295–330.

Davis, K. and Skilton-Sylvester, E. (eds) (2004) *TESOL Quarterly*, 38(3), Special Issue: Gender and Education.

Eckert, P. and McConnell-Ginet, S. (1999) 'New generalizations and explanations in language and gender research', *Language in Society*, 28: 185–201.

Ehrlich, S. (2001) 'Gendering the "learner": sexual harassment and second language acquisition', in A. Pavlenko, A. Blackledge, I. Piller and M. Teutsch-Dwyer (eds) *Multilingualism, Second Language Learning, and Gender*, New York: Mouton de Gruyter, pp. 103–30.

Ek, L.D. (2009) '"It's different lives": a Guatemalan American adolescent's construction of ethnic and gender identities across educational contexts', *Anthropology and Education Quarterly*, 40(4): 405–20.

Goldstein, T. (2001) 'Researching women's language practices in multilingual workplaces', in A. Pavlenko, A. Blackledge, I. Piller and M. Teutsch-Dwyer (eds.) *Multilingualism, Second Language Learning, and Gender*, New York: Mouton de Gruyter, pp. 77–101.

Gudykunst, W.B. and Kim, Y.Y. (1997) *Communicating with Strangers: An Approach to Intercultural Communication*, 3rd edn, New York: McGraw-Hill.

Heller, M. (2001) 'Gender and public space in a bilingual school', in A. Pavlenko, A. Blackledge, I. Piller and M. Teutsch-Dwyer (eds) *Multilingualism, Second Language Learning, and Gender*, New York/Berlin: Mouton de Gruyter, pp. 257–83.

Hymes, D.H. (1974) *Foundations in Sociolinguistics: An Ethnographic Approach*, Philadelphia, PA: University of Pennsylvania Press.

Katz, M. (2000) 'Workplace language teaching and the intercultural construction of ideologies of competence', *Canadian Modern Language Review*, 57: 144–72.

Keisling, S. (2005) 'Homosocial desire in men's talk: balancing and re-creating cultural discourses of masculinity', *Language in Society*, 34: 695–726.

Kim, Y.Y. (2001) *Becoming Intercultural: An Integrative Theory of Communication and Cross-cultural Adaptation*, London: Sage Publications.

Kulick, D. and Schieffelin, B.B. (2004) 'Language socialization', in A. Duranti (ed.) *The Handbook of Linguistic Anthropology*, Oxford: Blackwell, pp. 349–68.

Lakoff, R. (1975) *Language and Woman's Place*, New York: Harper and Row.

Langman, J. (ed.) (2004) '(Re)constructing gender in a new voice: An introduction', *Journal of Language, Identity and Education*, 3(4): 235–43.

Lave, J. and Wenger, E. (1991) *Situated Cognition: Legitimate Peripheral Participation*, New York: Cambridge University Press.

Leto DeFrancisco, V. (1991) 'The sounds of silence: how men silence women in marital relations', *Discourse and Society*, 2: 413–24.

McKay, S.L. and Wong, S.C. (1996) 'Multiple discourses, multiple identities: Investment and agency in second language learning among Chinese adolescent immigrant students', *Harvard Educational Review*, 3: 577–608.

McNamara, T. (1997) 'What do we mean by social identity? Competing frameworks, competing discourses', *TESOL Quarterly*, 31: 561–67.

Maltz, D.N. and Borker, R.A. (1982) 'A cultural approach to male–female miscommunication', in J. Gumperz (ed.) *Language and Identity*, Cambridge: Cambridge University Press, pp. 196–216.

Martin, D. (2003) 'Constructing discursive practices in school and community: bilingualism, gender and power', *International Journal of Bilingual Education and Bilingualism*, 6: 237–52.

Menard-Warwick, J. (2004) '"I always had the desire to progress a little": gendered narratives of immigrant language learners', *Journal of Language, Identity and Education*, 3: 295–312.

——(2008) '"Because she made the beds. Every day": social positioning, classroom discourse, and language learning', *Applied Linguistics*, 29(2): 267–89.

——(2009) *Gendered Identities and Immigrant Language Learning*, Bristol: Multilingual Matters.

Norton, B. (2000) *Identity and Language Learning: Gender, Ethnicity and Educational Change*, Harlow, UK: Longman/Pearson Education.

Norton, B. and Pavlenko, A. (eds) (2004) *Gender and English Language Learners*, Alexandria, VA: TESOL.

Norton Peirce, B. (1995) 'Social identity, investment, and language learning', *TESOL Quarterly*, 29(1): 9–31.

Pavlenko, A. (2001a) 'Bilingualism, gender and ideology', *The International Journal of Bilingualism*, 5(2): 117–51.

——(2001b) '"In the world of the tradition, I was unimagined": negotiation of identities in cross-cultural autobiographies', *The International Journal of Bilingualism*, 5(3): 317–44.

Pavlenko, A. and Lantolf, J.P. (2000) 'Second language learning as participation and the (re)construction of selves', in J.P. Lantolf (ed.) *Sociocultural Theory and Second Language Learning*, 2nd edn, Oxford: Oxford University Press, pp. 155–78.

Pavlenko, A. and Piller, I. (2001) 'New directions in the study of multilingualism, second language learning and gender', in A. Pavlenko, A. Blackledge, I. Piller, and M. Teutsch-Dwyer (eds) *Multilingualism, Second Language Learning, and Gender*, New York: Mouton de Gruyter, pp. 17–52.

Pavlenko, A., Blackledge, A., Piller, I. and Teutsch-Dwyer, M. (eds) (2001) *Multilingualism, Second Language Learning, and Gender*, New York: Mouton de Gruyter.

Philips, S.U. (2005) 'The power of gender ideologies in discourse', in J. Holmes and M. Meyerhoff (eds) *The Handbook of Language and Gender*, Malden, MA: Blackwell, pp. 252–76.

Piller, I. and Takahashi, K. (2006) 'A passion for English: desire and the language market', in A. Pavlenko (ed.) *Languages and Emotions of Multilingual Speakers*, Clevedon: Multilingual Matters, pp. 59–83.

Polanyi, L. (1995) 'Language learning and living abroad: stories from the field', in B. Freed (ed.) *Second Language Acquisition in a Study Abroad Context*, Amsterdam/Philadelphia: John Benjamins, pp. 271–91.

Sarangi, S. and Roberts, C. (2002) 'Discourse (mis)alignments in professional gatekeeping encounters', in C. Kramsch (ed.) *Language Acquisition and Language Socialization*, London: Continuum, pp. 197–227.

Shi, X. (2010) 'Intercultural language socialization of a Chinese MBA student in an American negotiation class', *Journal of Pragmatics*, 42: 2475–86.

Siegal, M. (1996) 'The role of learner subjectivity in second language sociolinguistic competency: Western women learning Japanese', *Applied Linguistics*, 17: 356–82.

Skapoulli, E. (2004) 'Gender codes at odds and the linguistic construction of a hybrid identity', *Journal of Language, Identity and Education*, 3: 245–61.

Swann, J. (1989) 'Talk control: an illustration from the classroom of problems in analysing male dominance of conversation', in J. Coates and D. Cameron (eds) *Women in Their Speech Communities*, London: Longman, pp. 122–40.

——(1992) *Girls, Boys and Language*, Oxford: Blackwell.

Tannen, D. (1990) *You Just Don't Understand: Women and Men in Conversation*, New York: Morrow.

Trudgill, P. (1983) *On Dialect: Social and Demographic Perspectives*, Oxford: Blackwell.

Vitanova, G. (2004) 'Gender enactments in immigrants' discursive practices: bringing Bakhtin to the dialogue', *Journal of Language, Identity and Education*, 3: 261–78.

Warriner, D. (2004) '"The days now is very hard for my family": the negotiation and construction of gendered work identities among newly arrived women refugees', *Journal of Language, Identity and Education*, 3: 279–95.

West, C. and Zimmerman, D. (1983) 'Small insults: a study of interruptions in cross-sex conversations between unacquainted persons', in B. Thorne, C. Kramarae and N. Henley (eds) *Language, Gender and Society*, Rowley, MA: Newbury House, pp. 102–17.

# 11

# Cultural identity, representation and othering

*Fred Dervin*

## 1. Introduction

It's easier to split an atom than a prejudice.

Einstein

Globalization is not a new experience. The anthropologist Jan Nederveen Pieterse (2004) maintains that anthropologists, economists, historians, political scientists and sociologists see it as a long-term historical process, which has witnessed, among others, the ancient population movements across and between continents and the diffusion of technologies (military technologies, numeracy, literacy, sciences … ). All these have led to intense intercultural encounters. Yet, under the pressures of contemporary globalization, meanings are multiplied and being put into question more than ever before. Consequently, individuals and groups experience bigger uncertainty as to who they are and where they belong (Hermans 2001).

For the fields related to intercultural communication, and the social and human sciences as a whole, this means that objects, theories and methods have to be reviewed in order to scrutinize this new *episteme*. Many concepts that have been central to the study of the Human, and the interdisciplinary domain that concerns us here, have been questioned over the past 30 years: culture, identity, community and society. The French anthropologist Maurice Godelier (2009: 7) goes as far as asking whether these concepts, whose meanings and usages are more and more complex, are still useful for the production of scientific knowledge. Let us try to see how this burning issue applies to intercultural communication.

## 2. Reconceptualizing culture and identity

This chapter looks at the concept of cultural identity and its relations to representation and Othering. The combination of the adjectives 'cultural' and 'identity' makes the concept a contended one, as the two words are polysemic, slippery and 'illusory' as analytical categories (Bayart 2005).

A review of the concept of cultural identity as a whole shows, first of all, that it is a 'floating signifier', which seems to encompass many different things. For Jonathan Friedman (1994: 29), for instance, cultural identity refers to 'the attribution of a set of qualities to a given population', who act as cultural beings. He adds that, in practice, i.e. as it is experienced by individuals, cultural identity is equivalent to ethnicity – another concept that is highly contested today (Brubaker 2006). Chen's definition (2006: 12) complexifies the concept: 'personal, sexual, national, social, and ethnic identities all combined into one'. In intercultural communication (be it research or teaching), cultural identity often refers to a localized national culture. Herzfeld (1997: 192) has demonstrated how, since their creation in the late eighteenth century in Europe and later on elsewhere, nation-states have made every effort to promote a sense of national cultural identity in order to limit communitarian divisions within their own space and to help people to identify with each other (cf. also Bauman 2004). This is often referred to as 'imagined communities' after Anderson's study on the creation of national imaginaries (1991).

In dealing with cultural identity, we are faced with the immensely challenging concept of culture. Many scholars have tried, unsatisfactorily, to define it. Some others have even asked for it to be 'banned' in research (Bayart 2005). Many issues are at stake with the concept, and I shall spend a bit of time here trying to specify some of them.

Let us first take a detour via anthropology. This field, which was created in the eighteenth century, used to aim at grasping the Human by proposing objective accounts of cultures through ethnographying exotic, strange and foreign places. This approach is now called 'culturalism' or 'essentialism', i.e. 'pretending that knowing the other takes place through knowing her culture as a static object' (Abdallah-Pretceille 2003: 13). According to Denzin and Lincoln (1994), anthropology has gone through at least five different historical movements that have shaped what it has become today. I will not summarize all these movements but concentrate briefly on the last two movements, as it will help us to see in what ways anthropology has changed. From about the 1980s, anthropology went through an important period, which is often called the 'crisis of representation' (Clifford and Marcus 1986). Through this, meanings were put into question by anthropologists themselves, especially in relation to their methodology, i.e. ethnography and the derived data: Who makes meanings? How do people represent these meanings? Who can interpret them and how? The basic question of 'what is culture?' was then put aside as it became more and more problematic as the core of human experience. This was also the time when postmodern thoughts (and all its declensions: queer theory, postfeminism, postcolonialism … ) became increasingly influential and started questioning and deconstructing how the human and social sciences had worked over the last two centuries. In fact, what these sciences are criticized for is their trying to imitate 'hard sciences' through scientific rigour, even though working on the Human implies not being able to attain truth and reason (Maffesoli 1996; cf. also Chapter 2, this volume).

It is quite interesting that many domains that work with interculturality seem to have remained 'stuck' in the first movements of anthropology (Dahlén 1997). Although, to be fair and avoid essentializing the field, as we shall see later on, many changes are occurring.

## From culture to culturality

Why is culture problematic then in both scholarly work and quotidian conversation? For Bhatia (2007: 49), the meaning of culture is related to power relationships; it is also composed of conflicting representations. For the Norwegian anthropologist Unni Wikan (2002: 75), culture is 'both over and underrated', and its definition depends on the researcher's vantage point (ibid: 84). Also, she asserts that culture is too often used as an agent in explaining intercultural encounters, whereas it has no autonomous or material existence (ibid.: 87). In fact, it is the acting subject only who does, thinks, behaves … (ibid.: 84). For Eriksen (2001: 141), culture is a 'cosy blanket', which can be misused and abused. Culture is also often depicted as though it were unchangeable and representative of all its 'members', whereas it is an object of power, which provides some people with the 'right to define what is to count and for what' and 'truth' (Wikan 2002: 86).

But culture cannot be but plural, changing, adaptable, constructed … (Clifford and Marcus 1986). A culture that does not change and exchange with other cultures is a dead culture. That applies to anthropological daily-life culture but also to 'high culture' (cinema, arts, etc.). Another aspect of culture that should be reviewed is the fact that cultures should be less defined as a certain amount of characteristics and cultural traits than relations and interactions between people and groups (Abdallah-Pretceille 2003: 15).

As a direct result of these criticisms and the dubious analytical utility of the concept of culture, many other concepts have been proposed to replace it. French intercultural educationalist Martine Abdallah-Pretceille (2003, 2006) has put forward the concept of 'culturality' to express these vital aspects of culture. Wikan suggests using 'knowledge/experience' (2002: 86), whereas Eriksen (2001: 141) simply explains that 'Instead of invoking culture, if one talks about local arts, one could simply say "local arts"; if one means language, ideology, patriarchy, children's rights, food habits, ritual practices or local political structures ( … )'.

Many postmodern phenomena are confusing for the individual: the retreat of nation-states; the speed at which things occur; the transformation of human relations ('new families', new sociality); confusing changes that often appear to be uncontrollable; identity crises … . These all trigger in our 'liquid individuals' (to borrow Z. Bauman's definition of contemporary individuals) a tendency 'to group around primary identities: religious, ethnic, territorial, national' (Castells 1996: 3) and thus a reduction in the complexity around them.

Now, if we come back to the concept of cultural identity, it is easy to see how such a concept can be problematic and difficult to define. At a recent conference on multicultural education in Europe, I was very surprised to notice that one session was about 'multicultural education to help develop cultural identity'. Based on what has been said until now, this goal does not make much sense: 'to develop a cultural identity' (if based on a solid/culturalist comprehension of the concept) will lead to the strengthening of identities – and thus possibly a closing up of the individual. Then how can one accept, respect and deal with different others, if one is strengthened in one's identity? This leads me to a proposal concerning cultural identity. This concept could refer to the acceptance that we all process along culturality and that we are thus plural. So cultural identity is what we construct whenever we are in contact with other human beings – regardless of the fact that they are from the same 'environment' or not. Some scholars have started to assert that this plurality means that we have different cultures. But this does not solve the problem. What are their boundaries? Can they be named?

I mentioned that anthropology, the study of the human par excellence, had moved away from culture as a central phenomenon to study. According to Eriksen (2001: 45), the field has recently shifted to the study of identities. Identity, which also constitutes the concept we are trying to understand here, cultural identity, is a complex and much disputed one.

## 'The daunting task of "squaring a circle"' (Bauman 2004: 10): identity work

Questions of identities – be they cultural, national, ethnic, religious … identities – have never mattered more than with current complex practices of intercultural communication. As such, the concept of identity is now omnipresent in research on interculturality. According to Levi-Strauss (1977: 331), any usage of the notion of identity must start with a criticism of the concept. Identity has been widely theorized and studied in many different fields, from the human and social sciences to the 'hard' sciences. For Bauman (2004: 17), 'identity is the "loudest talk in town", the burning issue on everybody's mind and tongue'. Cooper and Brubaker (2000: 1), in an article entitled 'Beyond identity', tell us that the social sciences and humanities have 'surrendered to the word "identity"'. They argue that it is an ambiguous concept that is either meaningless or too weak or strong (ibid.). Besides, the fact that it is both an analytical and a practical category makes it complex to work with (ibid.). The concepts of identification and categorization, self-understanding and social location, commonality, connectedness, groupness, among others, are often used interchangeably (Cooper and Brubaker 2000).

In practice, identity allows individuals to stratify their social experiences by linking with various others and groups or communities. Although the last two concepts have to be put into question (what are their 'boundaries'? Aren't they mere constructs? cf. Amit 2002), they allow people to 'compose and decompose their identities' (Bauman 2004: 38). In the age of 'crisis of belonging', where national identity is competing with other global, alternative identities, globalization leads towards some sort of pluralization of identities (Bauman 2004: 20).

It is important to note that some identities become strengthened in reaction to the feelings of emptiness or loneliness but also threat and uncertainty that globalization can trigger (ibid.). This has led to the revival of traditional cultural and religious practices or even the creation of new identities to maintain continuity (Jovchelovitch 2007: 76). In the field of intercultural education, this often translates through helping students to develop their cultural identity. However, by organizing activities within closed communities, emphasizing sameness and difference, geographical, physical, linguistic, religious boundaries are then produced (cf. Jovchelovitch 2007: 76). These boundaries are both physical and psychological (ibid.), and they often lead to representations on the actors involved (cf. below). All in all, this allows 'communities and individuals to develop knowledge about themselves and others, to recognize a history that is handed down by previous generations and give to self an identity, i.e. a coherent narrative that connects events, actions, people, feelings and ideas in a plot' (Jovchelovitch 2007: 79). Yet when identity is reduced in such ways, the consequences can be quite strong: 'conflicts and barbarities' (Sen 2006: XV) but also 'stereotyping, humiliating, dehumanizing, stigmatizing identities … ' (Bauman 2004: 38). When expressing an identity, there is always an issue of power at hand (Duncan 2003: 150).

What has become clear in terms of research and practice recently is that identity cannot be reduced to a single element; in other words, there is no such thing as a singular identity. This is shared by all postmodern thinkers such as Z. Bauman, M. Maffesoli, Ch. Taylor … . This discourse of the plural Self and Other also resonates in intercultural research, as we shall see later.

This understanding of identity related to the recognition that people cross various collective and individual positioning and voices on a daily basis, which can be opposed, seems contradictory (Hermans 2001). As such, the individual is torn apart between various networks, multiple interdependences … . For the anthropologist K.P. Ewing (1990), this is not just something that is happening in the Western world or in affluent countries. She writes:

> I argue that in all cultures people can be observed to project multiple, inconsistent self-representations that are context dependent and may shift rapidly. At any particular moment a person usually experiences his or her articulated self as a symbolic, timeless whole, but this self may quickly be displaced by another, quite different 'self', which is based on a different definition of the situation. The person will often be unaware of these shifts and inconsistencies and may experience wholeness and continuity despite their presence.
>
> *Ewing (1990: 251)*

Ewing explains that anthropologists have started looking at these inconsistencies (rather than consistencies) and contradictions in their work and, more specifically, at situational contexts involving 'experiencing actors' (1990: 262). This is a potential agenda for research on intercultural communication.

Inconsistencies are related to our next concept: representation. Complexity needs to be reduced on a permanent basis as the human mind needs to box and categorize experiences, ideas, others ... to 'survive'. Howarth (2002: 20) reminds us that 'identities are always constructed through and against representations'. She also argues that, when dealing with identity, if one does not incorporate representations, one does not work on a complex understanding of it. Social psychology has been working on these notions for a very long time now and can provide us with the tools to study them in intercultural communication (Jodelet 1991).

## 3. Representing the self and the other

The concept of representation has been extensively studied by social psychology and has had a great impact on other fields (cf. Scollon and Wong Scollon 2001 for intercultural communication). A worldwide phenomenon, the study of social representations started with Moscovici's seminal study of the perceptions of psychoanalysis (1961) and has reached nearly all fields of social experience (Howarth 2002: 3). Trying to define social representations is a difficult task as it is a very rich domain (ibid.: 4) and is very close to quite similar notions such as stereotypes and attitudes (Moore 2003: 9). The classic definition given by Moscovici himself (1961: xiii) is:

> Social representations are systems of values, ideas and practices which enable communication to take place among the members of a community by providing them with a code for social exchange and a code for naming and classifying unambiguously the various aspects of their world and their individual and group history.

For Jodelet (1991), another main theorist of social representations, meanings are condensed in social representations and help people to construe their experiences.

Social representations have many usages. They are a sociocognitive practice that allows us to create sociality, position ourselves, assert identities and defend ourselves when 'attacked' by others (Howarth 2002). As such, representations are 'particular presentations' of experiences, people, voices ... that are reinterpreted and re-presented and 'constitute our realities' (Howarth 2002: 8). Jovchelovitch (2007: 11) goes as far as telling us that 'the reality of the human world is in its entirety made of representation: in fact there is no sense of reality for our human world without the work of representation'. For Brubaker (2006: 79), representations and other phenomena such as perceptions, interpretations, etc., are 'perspectives on the world – not ontological but epistemological realities'.

So representations allow us to grasp sociality and the world, but they also help us to interact with other people (Gillespie 2006). Whatever representation is shared is also co-constructed with others; it re-presents 'what reality is intersubjectively agreed to be' (Howarth 2006: 8). The consequence of this is the instability, hybridity and multiplicity of representations, which compete with each other (Moscovici 1961).

Among the social representations that are co-constructed, some have a macro aspect whereas others are more micro. In other words, there are 'hegemonic representations' that are widely circulated and that dominate sociality, whereas 'oppositional representations' can be less circulated, more micro (Howarth 2006: 22). Yet these two types of social representations can combat and influence each other. This means basically that representations do have an ideological component and that an exercise of power is always present in representations (especially representation of the Other; cf. Duncan 2003).

All in all, representations emerge from the interrelations between 'self, other and the object-world' (Jovchelovitch, 2007: 11). They are not copies from originals but a symbolic, arbitrary means of putting meaning on people, ideas ... (ibid: 3). Also, representations do not always correspond to acts/actions or behaviours. This makes studying representation a complex and forcibly unfinished business; but also, it reorients research in intercultural communication and education from questioning 'what is people's cultural identity?' to 'how do they construct/re-present their cultural identity?'.

## The formation of stereotypes

Several types of social representations have been studied by both social psychologists and other fields (psychology, cognitive psychologists, but also linguistics, language educationalists ... ): prejudice, delegitimization, collectivizing and, more relevant to our field, stereotypes and Othering. Let us review these two concepts.

The study of stereotypes emerged in the 1950s. Stereotypes are 'a set of beliefs about the characteristics of a social category of people' (personality traits, attributions, intentions, behavioural descriptions ... (cf. Allport 1954; Bar-Tal 1996: 342). The images that emerge from stereotypes are often stable and decontextualized (Moore 2003: 16). Although often described as having 'negative connotations', human and social sciences have preferred to emphasize their constructive functions, as 'collective meta-attitudinal' discourses that lay boundaries between groups (Moore 2003: 14). In acts of interaction, people are guided in their behaviours and discourses through the cognitive order of the stereotypes that they have formed and learnt within their groups (Bar-Tal 1996, 1997: 493). Usually, two types of stereotypes are put forward: autostereotypes, which are linked to people's in-group; and heterostereotypes, which are related to an out-group ('the Other'). Stereotypes are often described as being static, limited and inert, but they often change as their content is not shared by everybody but is contextually and individually determined (Bar-Tal 1997). They can help to show the superiority of one's group and to differentiate. They also have an ideological aspect (Scollon and Wong Scollon 2001: 169).

As such, the study of stereotypes can constitute a sound basis for understanding intergroup behaviours (Bar-Tal 1997). Many theories have tried to explain stereotypic contents held by various groups: realistic conflict theory, scapegoat theory, belief congruence theory, social learning theory or authoritarian personality (ibid.). Bar-Tal (1989: 170), who has done extensive work on stereotypes based on the Israeli–Palestinian conflict, criticizes studies of stereotypes for failing to pinpoint how they guide behaviours towards groups – while concentrating on cognitive and affective components of relations. What he then finds important is to examine how stereotypes are formed and how they change by investigating the factors allowing this process (Bar-Tal 1997: 492). The researcher has proposed an integrative model that is very useful in this sense as it allows us to look at the factors that contribute to the creation of stereotypes: background variables (sociopolitical and economic conditions and historical relations), transmitting mechanisms (societal channels such as the political, the social, the cultural, the educational ... ) and mediating variables (ibid.: 494–95). All these aspects allow researchers using the model to identify individual and contextual differences in stereotypes. Bar-Tal adds that the model cannot predict particular contents (ibid.: 517).

For intercultural communication, both researchers and teachers should endeavour not to try to 'break' stereotypes or merely present a list of stereotypes, hoping that these will help to get rid of them – or paradoxically substitute them with the 'Truth'. This approach is flawed as stereotypes as such cannot be suppressed (cf. Einstein's quote at the very beginning of this chapter). What is interesting instead is to see how stereotypes are created and co-constructed and what they tell us about the people who resort to them (Abdallah-Pretceille 2006). In other words, working on stereotypes allows researchers and teachers to reflect on the notion of identity.

## Othering: making differences

Othering is another form of social representation, which is very much related to stereotypes. According to Kitzinger and Wilkinson (1996), theories on Othering have been developed in relation to women and representations of race and ethnicity (Clifford and Marcus 1986; Said 1978). Othering consists of 'objectification of another person or group' or 'creating the other', which puts aside and ignores the complexity and subjectivity of the individual (Abdallah-Pretceille 2003). In intercultural research, culturalism and essentialism, among other things, have tended towards Othering by imposing cultural elements as explanations for people's behaviours, encounters, opinions … (Dervin 2008, 2010; Holliday 2006; Virkama 2010). A good example of this is studies directed by Hofstede on the business world (cf. McSweeney's (2002) excellent criticism). Resorting to cultures or mere 'Culturespeak' (Hannerz 1999) will lead to Othering. This is shared by Abu-Lughod (1991: 143) when she writes in a famous critique of the notion of culture that it is 'the essential tool for making other'. Just like stereotyping, Othering allows individuals to construct sameness and difference and to affirm their own identity (ibid.: 87). Thus, Othering is not just about the other but also about the self. For A. Gillespie (2006), Othering leads people towards a widespread tendency to differentiate in-group from out-group and Self from Other in such a way as to reinforce and protect Self.

As a summary of the points made up to now, it is clear that, when working with the concepts of cultural identity and representations, we are walking on many slippery slopes. On the one hand, intercultural communication should strive to work against stereotypes, biases, racism, etc., but, on the other, we know that non-Othering, for example, is impossible (Abdallah-Pretceille 2006).

## 4. Critical issues and topics

In the social and human sciences, and increasingly in the field of intercultural communication, researchers are now moving away from transcendentalist/structuralist concepts of identity and dispelling the idea that identity is a given or an artefact. If we have a look at the fields that work with the concept of culture (or concepts that are related to it), there is a tendency to move beyond it: in anthropology, Gupta and Ferguson (1997: 2) call for ethnography without the *ethnos*; Philipps (2007) multiculturalism without 'culture', Brubaker (2006) ethnicity without groups. So what intercultural studies should increasingly concentrate on is interculturality without culture (Dervin 2010). This may sound paradoxical. It means that we should put aside solid visions of culture, or culture as a 'catch-all explanation for everything' (Philipps 2010: 65) to explain encounters, and examine how culture is used in discourse and actions to explain and justify one's own actions and thoughts (Dervin 2010). In other words, it is all about moving from façade diversity based on cultural unicity to the diversities that each and every one of us have in us to see the potential constructive and manipulatory power of culture. Anne Philipps, in a book entitled *Gender and Culture*, gives some examples of how culture is used for example in courts (or what is called 'cultural defence'; Philipps 2010: 86–87) to provide prosecutors with easy explanations and often successfully to reduce sentences (e.g. he killed his wife because that's what people would do in China).

So what is interesting for researchers working on interculturality is to look at how representations that are presented to interlocutors (be they teachers, researchers, friends, enemies ... ) are expressed and constructed. This is already a clear agenda for fields such as anthropology, linguistics, social psychology ... . Since the 1970s, intercultural education in language learning and teaching has been about identifying representations, stereotypes and signs of prejudice in order to crush them. What some researchers have noticed is that the 'crushing' usually leads to replacement with other representations or stereotypes, which are as unreliable, as constructed as the others. As such, if we take the Finnish context, some teachers would assert that Finns are not shy (as the auto- and heterorepresentation goes) but that they are more reserved than others. The problem remains: it is through such discourse that one way of conceptualizing, 'inventing' the Self and the Other, takes place (Virkama 2010). In her study on 'black pupils' in a London school, C. Howarth (2002: 6) shows how multiple representations of the same social object ('black pupil') are constructed and manipulated. She summarizes by writing that 'representations have to be seen as alive and dynamic – existing *only* in the relational encounter, in the in-between space we create in dialogue and negotiation with others'. And this is what researchers and teachers should endeavour to examine: this creation – but also why they are constructed and how they lead to possibilities for communication, negotiation, resistance, transformation ... (ibid.: 6). We should also bear in mind that not everything can be explained and that we are often dealing with hypotheses only (Maffesoli 1996).

The importance of intersubjectivity in the construction of identities and thus representations, stereotypes and Othering should be explored further. As asserted before, representations are unstable and co-constructed; this co-construction means that it is only through relations that meanings occur (Howarth 2006). This is an important point for researchers and teachers alike: as identities and representations require 'some other in and through a relationship with whom self-identity is actualized' (Laing 1961: 81–82) (which may be accepted, rejected, imposed, etc.), the influence of this other should be included in analyses, exercises, etc., as much as possible to open up the focus (Howarth 2002: 17).

The field of humanistic–experiential psychotherapy (Cooper 2009), among others, argues that experiencing does not reside in individuals but that it is always 'inter', i.e. an intersubjective phenomenon. Cooper (2009: 86) explains that:

> the fact that we experience others who experience us experiencing them, *ad infinitum*, means that our experiences are fundamentally embedded within a complex, multidirectional 'interexperiential' web, in which our 'own' experiences can never be entirely disentangled from the experiences of others.

Various fields in linguistics share this vital point: pragmatics or the study of how people do things with words (Levinson 1983); conversation analysis (Psathas 1995), which looks at how discourses and representations are jointly created and negotiated through topic development, turn-taking, etc.; critical discourse analysis (Barker and Galasinski 2001), which examines how power intervenes in the construction/questioning of meaning through intertextuality, control ... ; theories of enunciation (Dervin 2011; Marnette 2005), which looks at how intersubjectivity leads to the construction of objective–subjective discourses. These various approaches, which can complement each other, can help us to look at how people opt in and out of identities; the kinds of strategies that lead people to resist representations and protect themselves (Howarth 2002); the ways people manipulate (tone down/emphasize) identities, etc.

This leads us to one final aspect: the researcher's and educator's positions in the identity/representation game. As an 'other' (and any other 'other'), researchers and educators impact on other people, be they their research participants, the people who read them, their learners, etc., and, as people themselves, they circulate ideas, representations … . A good example of this is given by Kumaravadivelu (2008: 60) when he details how Asian students are reduced to (often negative) representations in L2 education and especially in ESL/TESOL research and teaching. He cites the following examples: they show blind obedience to authority; they lack critical thinking skills; and they do not actively participate in classroom interaction. Although this is often heard from teachers and learners alike, this needs to be questioned, as the author rightfully does: 'the language teaching profession has shown a remarkable readiness to forge a causal connection between the classroom behavior of Asian students and their cultural beliefs even though research findings are ambiguous and even contradictory' (Kumaravadivelu 2008: 54). This means that representations such as stereotyping and Othering are often put forward in the field by people who should work towards interculturality (i.e. culture and identity as changing objects) but who in fact seem to be working against it by 'boxing' their students or informants. I have proposed a critical analysis of research on intercultural communication to reveal Othering or the potential for it. This is what I have done in one of my studies by looking at how researchers working on student mobility have dealt with Chinese students theoretically, methodologically and analytically (Dervin 2011). This is also an important research agenda for the field.

## 5. Current contributions and research

Intercultural communication and education are not fixed fields, which makes it difficult to review the current literature. Some choices need to be made. In this section, I propose to review six studies, derived from various fields that have dealt with the issue of representations and questions of cultural identity. The fields represented here are linguistics (De Fina, Pepin), social psychology (Gillespie, Bhatia) and anthropology (Baumann, Dahlén). The studies are: Nicolas Pepin's (2007) publication in French about French nationals' experiences in Switzerland; Anna De Fina's (2003) examination of illegal Mexican immigrants in the USA; Alex Gillespie (2006) with his study on tourists in northern India; Sunil Bhatia (2007) and professional Indians in the USA; Gerd Baumann (1996) and his famous study of Southall in London; Tommy Dahlén (1997) and his book entitled *Among the Interculturalists* where he looks at the professional field of intercultural consultants in Sweden and the USA. Although all these studies are varied and diverse in terms of themes, contexts, theoretical backgrounds and approaches, they all have in common the fact that they are interested in examining how cultural identity is constructed and represented in intercultural contexts.

The first two studies presented here are derived from linguistics. Nicolas Pepin's book (2007) is about the identities of French people who live in Switzerland. Pepin brings together research on membership categorization analysis (influenced by the work of Harvey Sacks) and conversation analysis. The following specific research question is addressed: how do French migrants in Switzerland express, construct and support their memberships in interaction with a researcher and other participants? The subtitle of the book, *Eléments pour une grammaire de l'identité* ('Towards a grammar of identity'), is explained by the author as follows: 'the presence of recurring linguistic forms and devices used by speakers to activate, manage and show identities' (ibid.: 13, my translation). The corpus is based on twelve interviews led in dyads, in triads or in groups with French nationals who settled in the French-speaking part of Switzerland. The following elements compose his 'grammar of identity': various linguistic, paraverbal, nonverbal or spatial elements through which categorizations can take place; linguistic forms (nomination/identification) and categorization procedures (stabilization/dynamization; stereotyping … ) but also intersubjective devices, which can allow formulation and reformulation, categorization and re-/de-categorization of memberships (the enunciative multiplicity of 'I', reported speech, category affiliation, typicality, etc.). Pepin (2007) offers an analysis of what the participants consider as 'Swiss-French' and how they insert the words *septante*, *huitante* and *nonante* in their speech (70-80-90 in Swiss-French as opposed to *soixante-dix*, *quatre-vingt* and *quatre-vingt dix* in 'French' French). Pepin shows that their use of these words is not neutral as they serve emotional purposes and impact on the situated identities in the interviews. Another analysis is based on the role of accents in the construction of identities. It is clear, from Pepin's analysis, that accents in one language do allow categorizing people, be they participants in the act of interaction or 'absent third parties'. In addition, Pepin shows that accents have an imitative function as they are used in interaction to document and authenticate various accents; but also to caricaturize and dramatize them. All in all, this study is very useful to understand how language interacts with 'culture' in the creation of identity.

The second study is derived from Anna De Fina's (2003) work on fourteen Mexican undocumented immigrants' experiences of border crossing in the USA. The author examines through a discursive analysis (narratives) how group identity (e.g. ethnic identity, 'ethnic labelling') is represented, constructed and negotiated and how the relationships between identities and actions build up group self-representations. For the author, there are strong relationships between narrative and identity. The scholar explores various linguistic and rhetorical resources that can allow identifying the narrators' identification in their story-telling (pronoun switches, tempo, pitch, reported speech … ). She argues (ibid.: 352): 'by telling stories, narrators are able not only to represent social worlds and to evaluate them but also to establish themselves as a member of particular groups through interactional, linguistic, rhetorical and stylistic choices'. Through pronominal choice, De Fina evaluates how the immigrants present themselves in relation to others through an examination of the pronouns 'I' and 'we' in Spanish to express distance from or solidarity. She noticed that more than half the narratives are constructed with we, thus showing that the migration process could lead to strong relationships between migrants themselves. Also, she looks at the kinds of categories that the narrators use to talk about the Self and the Other. In the narratives, ethnic identity, through the use of different ethnic terms, is the only clear identity that is identified by the researcher. It is often used to generalize about the Self and the Other and to oppose them (e.g. 'there is no sense of community among Hispanics'; 'Americans think that Hispanics are ignorant'; ibid.: 152).

With the next two studies, we move on to the field of social psychology. The first study, written by Alex Gillespie (2006), evolves around the context of tourism, more precisely in Ladakh, which is located in the northernmost part of India, in the Himalayas. This site welcomes well over 12,000 tourists per year. Using informal group discussions led in Ladakh, the author maps the discourses of two groups: the tourists and the Ladakhis' 'experience of being toured'. The scholar looks at how encounters between the two groups have an impact on their self-reflection and the emergence of new identities. Based on George Herbert Mead's ideas, what the scholar does in terms of research method is that he resorts to a dialogical overtones approach (or 'population of discourse' such as quotes, semiotic elements such as books, films, narratives, the mentioning of a social act … ; ibid.: 159). The idea is to search for traces of social interactions in the discourses that are presented to the researcher. Based on these traces, he asks the following questions: 'What is the meaning of the trace? What is it doing in the speaker's discourse? Whose voice is it? What do tourists say among themselves about themselves and Ladakhis?' (ibid.: 160). All in all, Gillespie (2006) looks at uncertainty, points of debate and clash of differing perspectives in people's discourse (between people, groups or within themselves). The author shows that the image of the tourist as a naïve and unreflective individual is quite wrong as, even though one can easily get the impression that they search for authenticity, their discourse is evolving between various (often contradictory) positions and dimensions. For example, the tourists are well aware that the local Ladakhis are actually 'inventing' their cultural identity for them.

In a different context, the USA, the cultural psychologist Sunil Bhatia (2007) resorts to a similar approach but grounded in reflexive, critical and 'postmodern' ethnography to examine first-generation, professional middle-class Indians living in a northeastern suburb. The author is interested in how his informants understand the racial, ethnic and cultural labels created by the 'other'. Using a dialogical self approach, which challenges static identities, he argues that studying the polyphonic construction of Self can help researchers review canonical 'culturalist' and static approaches to acculturation and assimilation, often used in immigration studies (ibid.: 39). Based on interviews, the study is a good example of how 'the "culture concept", as made of contested codes, concerns the ways in which different modes of interpreting culture are tied to the historical, institutional and social contexts in which these interpretations are produced' (ibid.: 41). The study shows how solid identities are imposed on these professional Indians – even though they have well-paid jobs and a good status in American society. Yet many of Bhatia's informants try to tone down any form of racism that some say they have experienced. Also, interestingly, Bhatia shows in chapter 6 how his informants reject identification with 'blackness' and put forward their resemblance to 'whiteness' instead.

These contradictions and instabilities in identification are also very much present in the anthropologist Gerd Baumann's study on Southall (1996), a multiethnic suburb of London near Heathrow airport, UK. Baumann rented a house in the very centre of Southall for 6 years and involved himself in the life of the suburb. Talking to youngsters and adults of any 'origins' ('Asians', 'Whites', 'Afro-Caribbeans' … ), the anthropologist looks at the interplay of various discourses on culture and identity and shows how both 'groups' presented him with shifting identities during his fieldwork. He writes: 'the same person could speak and act as a member of the Muslim community in one context, in another take sides against other Muslims as a member of the Pakistani community, and in a third count himself part of the Punjabi community that excluded other Muslims but included Hindus, Sikhs, and even Christians' (ibid.: 5). Starting with a criticism of the concepts of culture and community, which are related to dominant discourses that 'equates ethnic categories with social groups under the name "community", and identifies each community with a reified culture' (ibid.: 188), Baumann demonstrates how the two concepts are renegotiated in the informants' discourse. On the one hand, discourse of community was presented as the basis of ethnicity or 'self-evident communities of culture', where people emphasized their belonging to a specific ethnic group. But on the other hand, he identified what he calls demotic discourse, which contradicts the dominant one by putting forward an image of community as creation, 'culture as process', where 'communities' or identities cut across the canonical ones.

The final study that I would like to mention is a bit different from the others, but it will allow me to wrap up this chapter on cultural identity and representations. As noted at the beginning of this chapter, there is often some confusion as to how culture and identity could be understood, and I mentioned earlier that anthropology, for example, has moved away from a reified and essentialized vision of these two concepts. The following study by Tommy Dahlén (1997) will help readers who still feel confused about this issue to understand what has happened to these notions. The study, entitled *Amongst the Interculturalists*, was written by Swedish anthropologist Tommy Dahlén. Having done an ethnography of intercultural consultants represented in the book by the Society for Intercultural Education, Training and Research (SIETAR), Dahlén shows how specialists in intercultural communication function and how they themselves create representations of the Self and the Other. The author explains, for example, how the SIETAR meetings are an important place for spreading models and ideas on intercultural communication (ibid.: 27), which are often derived from interculturalists such as Hofstede or Trompenaars. The latter have been much criticized for leading to a generic, essentialist and representational view of cultures. What the anthropologist notices is that the ideas and concepts that are borrowed by interculturalists from anthropology are derived from the 1930s to 1950s and that they can be labelled structural–functionalist, where culture is seen as a 'stable value system' (Dahlén 1997: 159); this is a notion that anthropology abandoned many decades ago to concentrate on 'internal diversity within various kinds of social units' (ibid.: 174). The author concludes that, as the interculturalist field (unlike anthropology) is practically oriented and situated in the marketplace, they need to be able to offer to their customers ways of predicting the behaviour of 'people from different cultures' (ibid.), and this might explain why they stick to these concepts.

For us, researchers and educators, these pressures are not present. The world is changing all the time; our conception of intercultural encounters is in the midst of a revolution. As we have demonstrated in this chapter, the concepts we have been used to working with (culture, identity, cultural identity) are very slippery, and the research tools offered by the fields that have worked on representations, stereotypes and Othering are very useful to take a critical stance towards them. The future of research on intercultural communication, if it follows the changes other fields that deal with Otherness (anthropology, psychology, sociology, philosophy … ) have witnessed, lays within further reflexivity, criticality and the idea of 'diverse diversities' (Dervin 2010).

## Related topics

Cross-cultural adaptation and transformation; culture, communication, context and power; language, identity and intercultural communication; learning the language of 'the Other'; identity, conflict and intercultural communication

## Further reading

Block, D. (2007) *Second Language Identities*, London: Continuum (the author reviews theories of identity in applied linguistics and presents several studies on the concept in intercultural contexts).

Breidenbach, J. and Nyíri, P. (2010) *Seeing Culture Everywhere, from Genocide to Consumer Habits*, Washington, DC: University of Washington Press (in this book, the authors describe a worldwide obsession with cultural difference).

Dahl, Ø, Jensen, I. and Nynäs, P. (eds) (2006) *Bridges of Understanding: Perspectives on Intercultural Communication*, Oslo: Unipub (this multidisciplinary volume gathers Scandinavian scholars who use a critical and reflexive approach to intercultural communication).

De Fina, A., Schiffrin, D. and Bamberg, M. (2006) *Discourse and Identity*, Cambridge: Cambridge University Press (This volume explores how social practices shape our identity through applying various research methods. Many chapters are related to intercultural communication).

Higgins, C. (2007) '"Interculturality" in talk-in-interaction', Pragmatics, 17 (special topics issue of *Pragmatics* dedicated to the construction of identity in intercultural contexts).

## References

Abdallah-Pretceille, M. (2003) *Former en Contexte Hétérogène. pour un Humanisme du Divers*, Paris: Anthropos.

——(2006) 'Interculturalism as a paradigm for thinking about diversity', *Intercultural Education*, 17(5): 475–83.

Abu-Lughod, L. (1991) 'Writing against culture', in R.G. Fox (ed.) *Recapturing Anthropology: Working in the Present*, Santa Fe, NM: School of American Research Press, pp. 137–62.

Allport, G.W. (1954) *The Nature of Prejudice*, Reading, MA: Addison-Wesley.

Amit, V. (2002) *Realizing Community*, London: Routledge.

Anderson, B. (1991) *Imagined Communities: Reflections on the Origin and Spread of Nationalism*, London: Verso.

Barker, C. and Galasinski, D. (2001) *Cultural Studies and Discourse Analysis*, London/New Delhi: Sage.

Bar-Tal, D. (1989) 'Delegitimization: the extreme case of stereo-typing and prejudice', in D. Bar-Tal, C. Graumann, A.W. Kruglanski and W. Stroebe (eds) *Stereotyping and Prejudice: Changing Conceptions*, New York: Springer-Verlag, pp. 169–88.

——(1996) 'Development of social categories and stereotypes in early childhood: the case of "the Arab" concept formation, stereotype and attitudes by Jewish children in Israel', *International Journal of Intercultural Relations*, 20: 341–70.

——(1997) 'Formation and change of ethnic and national stereotypes: an integrative model', *International Journal of Intercultural Relations*, 21: 491–523.

Bauman, Z. (2004) *Identity*, Cambridge: Polity Press.

Baumann, G. (1996) *Contesting Culture*, Cambridge: Cambridge University Press.

Bayart, J.-P. (2005) *The Illusion of Cultural Identity*, London: Hurst and Co. Publishers Ltd.

Bhatia, S. (2007) *American Karma*, New York/London: New York University Press.

Brubaker, R. (2006) *Ethnicity without Groups*, Cambridge, MA: Harvard

Castells, M. (1996) *The Power of Identity*, Malden, MA: Blackwell.

Chen, L.L. (2006) *Writing Chinese: Reshaping Chinese Cultural Identity*, Gordonsville, VA: Palgrave Macmillan.

Clifford, J. and Marcus, G.E. (1986) *Writing Culture: The Poetics and Politics of Ethnography*, Berkeley, CA: University of California Press.

Cooper, F. and Brubaker, R. (2000) 'Beyond identity', *Theory and Society*, 29: 1–47.

Cooper, M. (2009) 'Interpersonal perceptions and metaperceptions', *Journal of Humanistic Psychology*, 59: 85–99.

Dahlén, T. (1997) *Among the Interculturalists*, Stockholm: Stockholm Studies in Social Anthropology.

De Fina, A. (2003) *Identity in Narrative: A Study of Immigrant Discourse*, Amsterdam: John Benjamins.

Denzin, N.K. and Lincoln, Y.S. (1994) *Handbook of Qualitative Research*, Thousand Oaks, CA: Sage.

Dervin, F. (2008) *Métamorphoses Identitaires en Situation de Mobilité*, Turku: Humanoria.

——(2010) 'Assessing intercultural competence in language learning and teaching: a critical review of current efforts', in F. Dervin and E. Suomela-Salmi (eds) *New Approaches to Assessment in Higher Education*, Berne: Peter Lang, pp. 155–72.

——(2011) 'A plea for change in research intercultural discourses: A "liquid" approach to the study of Chinese students', *Journal of Multicultural Discourses*, 6(1): 37–52.

Duncan, N. (2003) '"Race" talk: discourses on "race" and racial difference', *International Journal of Intercultural Relations*, 27(2): 135–56.

Eriksen, T.H. (2001) 'Between universalism and relativism: "a critique of the UNESCO concept of culture"', in Cowan et al. (eds) *Culture and Rights. Anthropological Perspectives*, Cambridge: Cambridge University Press, pp. 127–47.

Ewing, K.P. (1990) 'The illusion of wholeness: culture, self, and the experience of inconsistency', *Ethos*, 18(3): 251–78.

Friedman, J. (1994) *Cultural Identity and Global Process*, London: Sage.

Gillespie, A. (2006) *Becoming Other*, Greenwich: Information Age Publishing.

Godelier, M. (2009) *Communauté, Société, Culture*, Paris: CNRS.

Gupta, A. and Ferguson, J. (eds) (1997) *Culture, Power, Place*, Durham, NC: Duke University Press.

Hannerz, U. (1999) 'Reflections on varieties of culturespeak', *European Journal of Cultural Studies*, 2(3): 393–407

Hermans, H.J.M. (2001) 'The dialogical self: toward a theory of personal and cultural positioning', *Culture and Psychology*, 7: 243–81.

Herzfeld, M. (1997) *Cultural Intimacy: Social Poetics in the Nation-State*, London: Routledge.

Holliday, A. (2006) 'Native-Speakerism', *ELT Journal*, 60(4): 385–87.

Howarth, A. (2006) 'Social representation is not a quiet thing: exploring the critical potential of social representations theory', *British Journal of Social Psychology*, 45(1): 65–86.

Howarth, C. (2002) 'Identity in whose eyes? the role of representations in identity construction', *Journal for the Theory of Social Behaviour*, 32(2): 145–62.

Jodelet, D. (1991) *Madness and Social Representations*, Hemel Hempstead, UK: Harvester Wheatsheaf.

Jovchelovitch, S. (2007) *Knowledge in Context*, London: Routledge.

Kitzinger, S. and Wilkinson, C. (1996) 'Theorizing representing the Other', in C. Wilkinson and S. Kitzinger (eds) *Representing the Other: A Feminism and Psychology Reader*, London: Sage, pp. 1–32.

Kumaravadivelu, B. (2008) *Cultural Globalization and Language Education*, New Haven, CT/London: Yale University Press.

Laing, R.D. (1961). *The Self and Others*. London: Penguin.

Levinson, S.C. (1983) *Pragmatics*, Cambridge: Cambridge University Press.

Levi-Strauss, C. (1977) *L'identité*, Paris: Grasset.

McSweeney, B. (2002) 'Hofstede's model of national cultural differences and their consequences', *Human Relations*, 55: 89–117.

Maffesoli, M. (1996) *Ordinary Knowledge: Introduction to Interpretative Sociology*, Cambridge: Polity Press.

Marnette, S. (2005) *Speech and Thought Presentation in French: Concepts and Strategies*, Philadelphia, PA: John Benjamins.

Moore, D. (2003) *Les Représentations des Langues et de leur Apprentissage*, Paris: Didier.

Moscovici, S. (1961) *La Psychanalyse, son Image, son Public*, Paris: Presses Universitaires de France.

Nederveen Pieterse, J. (2004) *Globalization and Culture: Global Mélange*, Chicago, IL: Rowman and Littlefield.

Pepin, N. (2007) *Identités Fragmentées. Eléments pour une Grammaire de l'Identité*, Berne: Peter Lang.

Philipps, A. (2007) *Multiculturalism without Culture*, Oxford: Oxford University Press.

——(2010) *Gender and Culture*, Cambridge: Polity Press.

Psathas, G. (1995) *Conversation Analysis: The Study of Talk in Interaction*, London: Sage.

Said, E. (1978) *Orientalism*, New York: Pantheon.

Sen, A. (2006) *Identity and Violence*, New Delhi: Penguin.

Scollon, R. and Wong Scollon, S. (2001) *Intercultural Communication*, Oxford: Blackwell.

Virkama, A. (2010) 'From othering to understanding', in V. Korhonen (ed.) *Cross-Cultural Lifelong Learning*, Tampere: Tampere University Press, pp. 39–60.

Wikan, U. (2002) *Generous Betrayal*, Chicago, IL: Chicago University Press.

# 12

# Other language learning, identity and intercultural communication in contexts of conflict

*Constadina Charalambous and Ben Rampton*

## 1. Introduction

This chapter examines the relation between language learning and intercultural communication by exploring the interface of language, identity and culture in conflict-ridden contexts. Focusing on languages associated with interethnic animosity, it aims to identify the challenges to established theories of language and culture teaching presented by contexts of conflict. Further, it discusses the role of language education in overcoming such hostility.

'Intercultural awareness' and 'intercultural competence' are major issues in recent modern foreign language (MFL) debates (Ager *et al.* 1993; Byram 1997; Kaikkonen 1997; Phipps and Gonzalez 2004), and language learning has been considered one of the key subjects for developing intercultural understanding. For example, the recently published Council of Europe Guide for the development of Language Education policies states:

> For individuals, [foreign languages] contribute to quality of life, the multiplication of personal contacts, *access to other cultural products*, and personal development and achievement. *For societies, knowing each other's languages may provide the basis for peaceful coexistence*, while multilingualism can be an enrichment of the environment and recognition of minority and foreign languages a precondition of democracy [ ... ] The acquisition of language thus involves acquisition of cultural competence and *the ability to live together with others*.
>
> *Beacco and Byram (2003: 46, 34; our italics)*

But what happens when the language to be taught and learnt is the language of a current or recent enemy, or is associated with a traditionally hostile ethnic group? What are the constraints that such situations impose on language teachers, and how are the politics and ideologies of 'Us' and 'Them' entangled with language lessons and language teaching practices?

To answer these questions, we first offer a detailed example, namely other language learning in Cyprus, which we then use to discuss established theories of language and culture in MFL teaching and learning. After that, we draw on evidence from language education programmes in conflict-ridden Israel and Macedonia, as well as bilingual programmes in Canada, exploring the role of language education in intercultural communication and peace education. Our guiding assumption is that close examination of the particularities of specific interethnic and ideological contexts throws valuable light on issues and complications that often escape the attention of more loosely focused language learning theories, and that these insights are important for policy makers, teacher educators and educational practitioners.

## 2. A critical case: Cyprus

### A history of conflict

In Cyprus, the Greek- and Turkish-Cypriot communities have a long history of conflict and, according to scholars studying Cypriot nationalist discourses, the two communities have actually constructed their identity in direct opposition to each other (Bryant 2004; Kizilyurek 1993; Mavratsas 1996).

Interethnic conflict on the island dates back to the beginning of the twentieth century, when the hitherto religious communities of Christians and Muslims came to imagine themselves as part of two broader groups – the rival Greeks and Turks (Bryant 2004). For both, language played an important role in the development of ethnolinguistic identities. It confirmed sameness with their respective 'motherlands' and difference from the other group in Cyprus, and it was perceived as a precondition for their survival (Karoulla-Vrikki 2004: 19; for discussion of the Turkish-Cypriot community, see Kizilyürek and Gautier-Kizilyürek 2004). According to Karoulla-Vrikki, language became 'a matter of ethnic hegemony' (ibid: 30), and this was obvious in the early twentieth-century press.

Before these nationalist discourses became established, the local variety of Greek, the language of the majority on the island, had served as the lingua franca–Greek-Cypriots were seldom communicatively competent in Turkish (Ozerk 2001). With rising nationalism and growing hostility in the mid-twentieth century, Turkish–Greek/Greek–Turkish bilingualism declined, and with the ascendance of nationalist perspectives, speaking the language of the 'Other' came to be seen as not only undesirable, but also a sign of betrayal (Kizilyürek and Gautier-Kizilyürek 2004; Ozerk 2001). As Ozerk observes, 'Turkish-Cypriots began to interpret physical nearness to Greek-Cypriots as a risk of *loss of life, loss of language, and loss of identity*' (2001: 258; original emphasis).

When Cyprus gained independence in 1960, both Greek and Turkish languages were recognized as official languages, and a degree of linguistic equality was ensured through the parallel use of both languages in all state bodies, organizations and documents. Education, however, remained monolingual and 'strictly communal' (Karyolemou 2003: 364). In both communities, schools were responsible for maintaining the links with the respective 'mother-lands', creating what Bryant (2004) calls 'true Greeks' or 'true Turks'. Even after the formation of the Republic of Cyprus, covering both communities, there was never any functional bilingualism. Furthermore, the intercommunal conflicts, which started as early as 1963, led to the separation of the two communities and their concentration in different areas. This undermined the unifying sovereignty of the Cyprus Republic as an independent state, and what bilingualism there was declined further with limited contact between the two communities (Ozerk 2001). Finally, the events of 1974 – what Greek-Cypriots call the 'Turkish invasion' (in line with UN resolutions [365(1974)]), and what Turkish-Cypriots call the 'the peace operation' (Papadakis 2005; see Killoran 1998, 2000 on the different local historical narratives) – resulted in the total division of the two communities with real, physical borders, and these remained impassable until 2003.

This historico-political sketch is important for a consideration of other language learning in Cyprus, because it gives an idea of both the symbolic value that language came to acquire in both communities and the powerful identity discourses that have since dominated education. Even after independence when the constitution considered both Greek and Turkish as official languages of the republic, Turkish had never been part of Greek-Cypriot curricula (Karoulla-Vrikki 2004; see also Karyolemou 2003). Indeed, the Greek-Cypriot educational system has continued to be responsible for preserving the Greekness of Greek-Cypriots, simultaneously pro-jecting a particularly hostile image of the 'Turks' (Charalambous 2009a, 2009b; Spyrou 2006) and, as we shall see, this severely restricts the reconciliatory potential of language learning.

## Introducing 'other language learning' with EU accession: the experience in Greek–Cypriot formal education

In April 2003, the Cyprus Republic signed the EU Accession Treaty. The whole island of Cyprus entered the EU, but the *acquis* (the body of the European law) was suspended in the areas not under the control of the Republic of Cyprus government (i.e. the northern part).[1] It was clearly stated, however, that the accession should benefit *all* Cypriot citizens, and that 'the suspension [of the acquis] has territorial effect, but does not concern the personal rights of Turkish-Cypriots as EU citizens ( … ) even though they may live in the areas not under government control.'[2] A week later, the Turkish-Cypriot authorities decided to lift some of the restrictions on movement across the Buffer Zone in Nicosia, which had been in place since 1974 (and in some areas since 1963) and, very soon after, the republic responded by announcing that it would offer a package of 'Measures of Support to the Turkish-Cypriots'.[3] Among these, the Turkish language was introduced in Greek-Cypriot secondary education as an optional MFL course, and free Greek and Turkish language classes were established for Turkish-Cypriot and Greek-Cypriot adults respectively. This was the first time in Greek-Cypriot history that the Turkish language was recognized and legitimized in formal education. According to senior Ministry of Education officials, this language teaching initiative was expected to contribute to the two communities' peaceful coexistence:

> We are a bicommunal state and it is definitely good … the knowledge of Turkish for our side, for us Greeks … *will definitely help the cohabitation in this island*, the *peaceful and harmo-nious cohabitation* (. … ) if the accession of Turkey to EU proceeds and the Cyprus Problem gets resolved, we will definitely have to be taught Turkish and they will have to be taught the Greek language in their schools … *It is the best way to come closer,* I believe.
>
> *Interview with Charalambous (9 January 2007; emphases added)*

This statement is consistent with the Council of Europe Guide mentioned in Section 1 and, at least at first sight, the reconciliatory intentions behind these lessons seem to conflict with the ethnocentric discourses traditionally dominant in Greek-Cypriot formal education.

To explore this potential tension, Charalambous conducted an ethnographic study that involved a total of 95 hours of observation in other language learning classes both in secondary educational settings and in adult afternoon classes, from September 2006 to January 2007 (see Charalambous 2009a). Things appeared to work well with the adult learners who, for the most part, attended the classes deliberately in order to signal their opposition to nationalist discourses. But when this policy was enacted in Greek-Cypriot secondary classrooms, the dominance of Hellenocentrism in formal education had a very significant impact, and the history of conflict was salient as a constant backdrop.

So, for example, during their Turkish language lessons, secondary students often made negative comments about the Turks or Turkish-Cypriots and resisted their teacher's attempt to introduce positive representations. Outside the lessons, the focal case teacher (Mr A) faced negative comments, often from fellow teachers and even from family friends, and indeed like-wise, all twenty-one students reported in interviews that they had been called traitors because they were learning the language of the enemy.

This created significant complications for the language pedagogy. On the one hand, the teacher could not endorse traditional discourses of interethnic hostility, as these would construct Turkish as the language of the enemy. But at the same time, explicit talk of reconciliation would generate negative reactions from the students and was likely to be seen as introducing political bias (see, for example, Charalambous 2009b; also Zembylas *et al.* 2011). The strategy the teacher developed was to 'disassociate the language from its speakers and its cultural con-text', as well as from the political situation on the island. In the first instance, he explicitly forbade any kind of 'political discussion' in the lessons, and then he also focused virtually all his teaching (29 out of the 32 hours observed) on grammar, vocabulary and reading exercises – in effect, on language as a decontextualized code. As far as possible, he avoided any reference to Turks or Turkish-Cypriots, referring to them explicitly only four times in the thirty-eight grammar-oriented lessons that Charalambous attended. Indeed, in two of the four instances when he named these groups, he did so in order to emphasize the irrelevance of Turks/Turkish-Cypriots to their language lessons, constructing 'a lack of communication' with them as the local norm, as in the following example:

Extract 1

MR A:   You can't learn a language without studying it unless you live with people who speak it. For example you learn English while living in England. We ... in our country (*pause*) well we *do* have Turkish-Cypriots but we do not have contact with them. (*pause*)
(*NO REPLY FROM STUDENTS*)
Ok now how can we say 'look at me'.

Even when the teacher classified two lessons as 'teaching culture', he still managed to avoid talking about these 'Others'. In the first case, he did a session on Islamic traditions and cele-brations, and here he restricted his talk to 'Muslims', in this way creating an ambivalent category, which sometimes implicitly included Turks or Turkish-Cypriots but, for the most part, explicitly excluded them:

Extract 2

MR A:   Children (.) all the Turks are Muslims (.) almost ...
But when we say Muslims we do not mean the Turks we mean *all* the *Muslims* who are almost all the Arabic- the ... Arabian countries.

The second 'culture' lesson involved a Turkish song that he brought into the class, but in fact, this was the adaptation of a Greek song, so that again, the 'Turkishness' of the lesson's content could be limited to the language.

It was clear that the historical and political connotations of Turkish created significant com-plications for the language teacher, and that he dealt with this by trying to keep these cultural associations outside the classroom. This active disconnection of language from its social context and its deliberate reconstruction as an autonomous abstract system are highly significant, not just because it appeared to run counter to the rapprochement aspirations driving this Greek-Cypriot curriculum innovation, but also because it was at odds with contemporary pedagogic theories which argue strongly for the language-and-culture link. In fact, the theoretical implications of this case study demand further examination, and we turn to this in the next section.

## 3. Locating the Cyprus case in contemporary language theory

The Cyprus case study is not hard to understand with theories of sociolinguistics and linguistic anthropology, but it is harder to reconcile with prevailing theories of language pedagogy, and so we will take each of these in turn.

### Sociolinguistics and linguistic anthropology

The links between language, culture, politics and ethnic identity are obviously complex, but there is a good deal of research in applied linguistics, sociolinguistics and linguistic anthropology that helps to make sense of the Cyprus case.

The social symbolic significance of language has been studied by numerous scholars, generating many detailed descriptions of how language can function as a salient feature in perceptions of ethnic identity (see e.g. Edwards 1985; Fishman 1991; May 2001), and research on language ideology has examined the role of language in nation building, providing insights into how language can be used to create 'difference' and 'sameness'. Blommaert and Verschueren (1998), for example, assess the role of language in European nationalist ideologies and identify the 'dogma of homogeneism' as a basic nationalist principle that treats any difference among the members of a 'nation' as a threat, assuming that linguistic and cultural homogeneity is necessary for a community to function as a nation. Gal and Irvine (1995) attend to the ideologies embedded in beliefs about linguistic difference and the creation of linguistic boundaries, pointing out their inexorable links to social, political and moral issues. And behind popular ideologies of linguistic sameness and difference, Jaffe (2009) identifies a 'foundational ideology' about language itself, seeing language as a homogeneous bounded code that can be mapped onto and equated with a particular social group (see also Gal and Irvine 1995). Relating these accounts back to the Cyprus example, it is clear that comparable ideological processes constructed 'language' as essentially linked to a group's 'culture' and 'identity'. Mr A tried hard to oppose, subvert and neutralize these assumptions in his lessons, but the ideology was so strong that Turkish was still sensed as the language of the enemy, with language learners and teachers seen as 'traitors'.

Similarly, there are many studies of language education policy that examine the ways in which politicians and governments use languages to construct an identity or sense of sameness or difference. Baker points out, for example, that 'bilingual education has become associated with political debates about national identity, dominance and control by elites, power relationships amongst politicians and civil servants, questions about social order, and the perceived potential subversiveness of language minorities' (2003: 101). And turning specifically to MFL policy, Pavlenko (2003) draws on the US, USSR and Eastern Europe to show how modern language curricula contribute to the shaping of national identity – 'a country's current allegiances and oppositions [can] impact the choice of languages to be offered for modern language study' (ibid.: 329). Again, this was certainly the case in Cyprus – as we have seen, the introduction of Turkish to the formal Greek-Cypriot MFL curriculum had political motives, forming part of a series of 'measures for building trust', as they were often called in the Greek-Cypriot media and press.

So there is a good deal of research on language policy and ideology that is able to accommodate the kinds of symbolic value associated with Turkish in the Greek-Cypriot case. But what about research focusing on MFL education?

## MFL research and theory

MFL classrooms have received hardly any attention from sociolinguists and linguistic anthropologists (cf. Rampton 2006: ch. 4), and instead, they have usually been investigated by drawing on the theories and approaches of language education and educational applied linguistics. Admittedly, a lot of this work has been influenced by sociolinguistics; there is sometimes a good deal of familiarity with perspectives on language policy and ideology such as the ones above (e.g. Kramsch 2009); and over at least the last 20 years, there has been a substantial shift in emphasis from linguistic structure to culture in MFL pedagogic theory. There is also a growing sense that language cannot be taught without regard to contexts of use, and 'culture [is] becom[ing] the very core of language teaching' (Kramsch 1993: 8), emerging as 'a particularly strong theme currently in language teaching debates' in both UK-based and American language teaching journals (Broady 2004: 68).

However, MFL scholarship has to operate in the difficult territory between research and teaching, between analysis and practical implementation, academic and professional discourse, and in this environment, it is quite common for an initially theoretical or descriptive concept to be reconstructed as a policy target, a curriculum ideal or an assessment metric. Within language education generally, this certainly happened to Hymes's originally ethnographic notion of 'communicative competence' (Dubin 1989; Leung 2005), and in recent years in MFL, the notion of 'intercultural communicative competence' (ICC) has become very influential, particularly through the work of Byram and colleagues (Byram 1997; Byram and Risager 1999; Byram et al. 2001).

Intercultural communicative competence is conceptualized as embracing the skills, knowledge and abilities needed for successful communication, either between native and non-native speakers or between non-native speakers using the target language as a common code. Byram (1995) criticizes MFL pedagogies that aim for a 'near-native' speaker model, and instead introduces the idea of the 'intercultural speaker', defined as:

> Someone who can operate their linguistic competence and their sociolinguistic awareness of the relationship between language and the context in which it is used, in order to manage interaction across cultural boundaries, to anticipate misunderstandings caused by differences in values, meanings and beliefs, and thirdly to cope with the affective as well as cognitive demands of engagement with otherness
>
> *Byram (1995: 25)*

According to Mughan (1999: 64), 'a key characteristic of intercultural competence is the fact that it prepares the learner for exposure to all cultures, not just the one whose language is being learned'. Similarly, Cortazzi and Jin (1999) envisage learners being made aware of the differences in behaviour, expectations, perceptions and values of another cultural group, also coming to understand the cultural structures that generate these differences. By developing ICC, learners are expected to be able to recognize the existence of different ways of viewing the world, to start to reflect upon their own culture and to realize that their own way of thinking is neither the only nor necessarily the best one. In sum,

Learning another language can contribute to people's understanding of and interest in people of other cultural origins whether in their own society, in geographically and politically related societies, or in distant and unfamiliar societies.

*Byram and Risager (1999: 4)*

Pedagogically, Byram and colleagues (Byram 1997; Byram and Risager 1999; Byram *et al.* 2001) propose a framework of four *savoirs*. *Savoir être* forms the base of ICC, and involves the development of positive attitudes towards 'otherness' and 'the ability to "decentre"' (Byram *et al.* 2001: 5). *Savoir apprendre* is the ability to learn and acquire new cultural knowledge, while *savoirs* on their own consist of general knowledge of 'the system of references which structures the cultural identity and spaces within which native-speakers live' (Byram and Risager 1999: 66). Finally, *savoir faire* refers to the capacity to integrate the three other *savoirs* in particular situations of bilingual contact (ibid.: 67). To support the implementation of this framework, there are a number of guides and edited volumes, and these often carry practical lesson illustrations that include, for example, visits abroad, teaching literature, the use of technology to communicate with people of the target community (see e.g. Byram *et al.* 1994: Ch. 4, 2001; Byram *et al.* 2002; Cortazzi and Jin 1999). Overall, such activities stress the importance of avoiding 'static' representations of culture. Instead, they offer 'contrasting views' of the target culture, using authentic texts and engaging students in critical discussions of the materials, textbooks and the situations they are presented with, and the use of insights from cultural studies and ethnography is also encouraged (Byram 1989; Roberts *et al.* 2001).

The impact of these ideas has been considerable. Many countries are adopting an intercultural perspective in language teaching and learning, seeking to broaden MFL education beyond its traditional focus on grammar and vocabulary. The Council of Europe's *Common Framework of Reference for Languages* is being applied in EU member countries (including Cyprus), and it now includes a series of sociocultural and intercultural objectives that embrace the four *savoirs* (Council of Europe 2001). And as already noted above, learning MFL is also expected to 'provide the basis for peaceful coexistence' and to contribute to democratic citizenship (Starkey 2002, 2005).

There are some obvious links here to the Cyprus case, at least at the policy level, where the introduction of Turkish language to Greek-Cypriot schools operated as a gesture of 'goodwill' and was accompanied by a rhetoric linking language to the promotion of 'mutual under-standing' and 'peaceful coexistence'. Indeed, we can also say that, in view of recent Cypriot history, there is a particularly intense need for the kinds of cultural disposition that these theories aspirationally associate with ICC, a need in Cyprus that is far greater than for, e.g., Britons learning French, or Italians learning German. Even so, it is hard to connect ICC's vision of intercultural learning and teaching with the classroom realities of teaching Turkish to Greek-Cypriot secondary students. Mr A may not have been a model of good practice, but he certainly was not unrepresentative, and subsequent observation of Greek-Cypriot teachers' classroom talk about Turkish-Cypriots confirms that his strategies were not unique (for an account of Greek-Cypriot teachers' difficulties in promoting 'peaceful coexistence' in their classrooms, see Zembylas *et al.* 2011). Outside the lessons described above in Section 2, the rest of the curriculum was heavily Hellenocentric, even anti-Turkish; anyone associating with the Turkish language risked accusations of being a 'traitor'; and in fact, the exchange of visits, frequently mentioned in language-and-culture teaching guides, has been officially denounced by the Greek-Cypriot teachers' trade union and prohibited by the Ministry of Education. In this context, the teacher's first-hand practical sensitivity to cultural relations dictated the evasion of 'culture' as a topic, and far from embedding one in the other, grammar and vocabulary had to be isolated from anything to do with Turkish (-Cypriot) ways, speakers or concerns.

So even though it is an environment in which the ideals of ICC look appealing in the abstract, ICC theory does not resonate with current Cypriot realities, and cases such as Cyprus do not actually appear to have held much significance in the development of ICC theory. In the Greek-Cypriot case, the very legitimacy of learning Turkish is in question, and rather than looking for growth in students' active 'understanding of and interest in' the Other, a compelling argument could be made for treating a shift from hostility to mere indifference as a significant achievement. In, say, Anglo-Spanish relations, a student's expression of 'goodwill' might be taken as a nice but lightweight token, but in any recent or current conflict setting, such symbolic gestures have to be treated much more seriously. Indeed, there are grounds for asking how far ICC theory has an analytical vocabulary capable of capturing the range and complexity of the manoeuvres involved in 'rapprochement' following conflict, and to enrich this understanding, we would propose sociolinguistic research on 'crossing' as a potentially useful resource (Rampton 1995; see also Rampton and Charalambous 2010).

'Crossing' refers to the use of a language that feels anomalously other, and it involves a sense of movement across sharply felt social or ethnic boundaries, often raising acute questions of legitimacy. Even though such practices seldom generate more than limited forms of language learning or proficiency, empirical descriptions of crossing document a variety of social and interactional strategies that permit and sustain these transgressive ventures into another language, and these include respectful avoidance, jocular abuse, the strategic manipulation of ignorance, the identification of privileging genres and relationships, and a number of interaction rituals. Most of this research focuses on informal, recreational and popular cultural activity, and there is absolutely no guarantee that these practices could be incorporated into new intercultural curricula at school (Rampton 1995: Ch. 13.5). Nevertheless, there are good grounds for claiming that language crossing can contribute to the development of new feelings of community. Going much further than any other tradition of language study in its description of the range and intricacy of sociolinguistic practice in the risky borderlands between ideologically counterposed ethnic groups, this is a tradition of research that would be worth consulting in efforts to develop officially/institutionally sponsored classroom crossing. Indeed, even if it is hard to see how the types of practice described in the literature could be transposed into educational curricula, engagement with this work can still help to reset our expectations about intercultural language learning in recent/current conflict situations, and thereby diminish the possibility of a highly committed teacher such as Mr A being misinterpreted as a culturally insensitive grammar-and-translation conservative.

So far, we have dwelt on the situation in Cyprus, and case study methodology can be invoked to justify this, careful consideration of a single instance being sometimes sufficient to point to the limitations in prevailing theories, generalizations or orthodoxies (Mitchell 1984). In fact, however, Cyprus is not the only context in which strong cultural and political ideologies interfere with language teaching and learning.

Multilingual settings in which language groups have unequal social status and compete over access to institutions such as government and education can often experience language conflict that is also closely related to political and ethnic conflict (Nelde 1997). Belgium is frequently cited as an example where status competition between French and Dutch has taken on political dimensions, impeding the workings of the federal state (Mettewie and Janssens 2007; Swing 2000; Treffers-Daller 2002). Brussels is officially a bilingual city, but societal bilingualism does not necessarily entail individual bilingualism, and the use of both official languages as media of instruction in schools is still prohibited by linguistic laws, despite several initiatives by non-profit organizations advocating bilingual education (Bollen and Baten 2010).[4] Outside Europe, similar conflict may be encountered in postcolonial settings between English and indigenous languages, and research in English teaching classrooms has revealed some similar patterns to those observed in Cyprus (cf. Canagarajah 1993).[5]

Returning to the specific concerns of this chapter, there are also several cases of intractable conflict in which language education has featured in efforts to achieve reconciliation. Both to give a broader sense of some of these possibilities and to place the Cyprus case in a wider context, it is worth taking a look at other reconciliatory initiatives in language education in other parts of the world.

## 4. Comparative cases: Israel, Macedonia and Canada

There have been a number of empirical studies in conflict-ridden contexts that have focused on other language teaching programmes designed to address societal conflict and reduce prejudice and discrimination (e.g. Bekerman 2005; Bekerman and Horenczyk 2004; Bekerman and Shhadi 2003; Genesee and Gándara 1999; Tankersley 2001). In Israel, bilingual Hebrew–Arabic schools for both Israeli and Palestinian students were established in 1997, with the aim of 'building a cooperative framework structured on the basis of equality and mutual respect' (Bekerman 2005: 6; see also Bekerman and Horenczyk 2004). Broadly in line with the responses in Cyprus, parents sometimes found that their friends and relatives reacted negatively to the decision to send their children to an integrated school, interpreting this as 'joining with the enemy' (Bekerman 2005: 11), and the different status of the two languages in Israeli society generated further complexities, in spite of extensive efforts to ensure equality between them. With Hebrew having much higher prestige than Arabic, Israeli and Palestinian parents had different expectations about the educational outcomes for their children, and the students' linguistic achievement in the two languages also appeared to be affected (Bekerman 2005; 2004). For Palestinian parents, the schools offered their children access to an education in Hebrew that could improve their future socioeconomic position, whereas for Israeli parents, Arabic was seen as 'a worthwhile addition but not necessarily an essential one', their main concern being to 'bring the two people together' (Bekerman and Horenczyk 2004: 394).

In Macedonia, Tankersley (2001) reports on an integrated kindergarten school, established by the 'Common Ground Foundation in Macedonia' as an intervention to improve relations between Macedonians and Albanians. As in Israel, the low status of minority Albanian had a negative impact on the Macedonian children's linguistic competence in that language, despite teachers' efforts to establish linguistic equality in class. Still, parallel use of the two languages in the classroom helped both groups of children to develop positive attitudes and interethnic friendships, and it created 'an atmosphere where interethnic conflicts could be brought up and discussed' (Tankersley 2001: 117).

In Canada, bilingual immersion programmes were initially established in a context of conflict directly linked to the issues of unequal access to power that French and English offered to their speakers (Genesee and Gándara 1999), and rather than being the sole purpose, language learning 'was intended to be an intermediate goal leading to improved relationships between English-speaking and French-speaking' Canadians (Genesee and Gándara 1999: 670). Reporting on studies conducted in the 1970s, Loveday (1982: 15–31) describes how the learning or use of the Other language was often regarded as either 'a gesture of solidarity' or the activity of 'a kind of ethnic "traitor"' (p. 27) but, according to Genesee and Gándara (1999), these programmes produced positive changes in intergroup attitudes. Indeed, even though they sometimes also resulted in increased intergroup contact, Genesee and Gándara (1999) suggest that learning the language of the Other could be sufficient on its own – 'direct contact, though desirable, is not necessary for changes in intergroup perceptions' (Genesee and Gándara 1999: 680).

Although any programme of this kind must first be analysed in its own specific social and historical context and any prediction is vulnerable to a wide range of both local and global contingencies, the descriptions here offer a longer and/or broader view than the Cyprus case affords, and they suggest that, despite the kinds of difficulty detected in Charalambous's study, other language learning in conflict situations can in fact make some contribution to intercultural understanding. But it is clear that in all four cases other language learning is itself highly charged with symbolism, standing for political alignments that run counter to the dominant evaluation of the languages being targeted, and that the complexity of sociopolitical dynamics defies the use of a reductive term such as 'integrative' to classify the powerful non-instrumental motivations that are involved. Maybe it is in later, post-initial stages of other language learning that more orthodox frameworks for the discussion of proficiency and intercultural communication become relevant but, in the early phases, the bilingualism promoted in these programmes seems as much emblematic as functional, and indeed this might even be sufficient in the transitional first steps towards rapprochement.

What about research methodology?

## 5. Research methods

Although there are descriptions of best practices in teaching addressed to education professionals (e.g. Byram *et al.* 2001), there is very little empirical research on MFLs and interculturality in Europe that looks closely at foreign language classroom practices and interaction. Certainly, there are a number of studies examining the links between politics and other language learning and teaching, and this includes studies of the impact of European integration on MFL teaching in different countries (Byram and Risager 1999), as well as analyses of how language policies and choices relate to different sociopolitical and historical backgrounds, language attitudes and intergroup relationships (Ager *et al.* 1993). But these generally only involve interviews with learners and teachers and quantitative measurement of, for example, learners' attitudes to the foreign language and culture. Indeed, interviews and attitude measurement also predominate in the studies of conflict-linked other language education described in the previous section (although there is also classroom observation in e.g. Bekerman 2005; and Tankersley 2001). Here, however, we would like to argue the case for more linguistic ethnography, partly because we consider it best suited to the subtlety of the processes involved in conflict situations, and partly because, as already noted, there is a serious shortage of descriptive sociolinguistic research on classroom MFL learning much more generally (Rampton 2006: 137–44, 171).

Surveys using questionnaires can certainly produce a broader image of the sociolinguistic landscape, pointing to large-scale attitudinal trends, and interviews can often provide a useful window on influential discourses currently in circulation. But none of these methods overcome the fact that claims may not coincide with actual acts (see, for example, Spyrou 2006), and nor do they penetrate beyond their informants' verbal reifications of ethnic and social categories. In rather sharp contrast to the empirical view of social processes provided by these methods, contemporary linguistic anthropology and interactional sociolinguistics generally regard everyday practices as dynamic and multifaceted, allowing people to negotiate different memberships and positionings of 'us' and 'them' simultaneously, and 'ethnicity' and 'identity' are viewed as socially and interactionally constructed situated practices. Theoretically contextualized in this way, 'classrooms emerge as sites where, day-in-day-out, participants struggle to reconcile themselves to each other, to their futures, to political edicts and to the movements of history' (Rampton 2006: 3), and these processes are likely to be especially complex in other language classrooms in conflict-ridden or post-conflict societies, where participants have to deal with powerful ideologies, contradictory expectations and the renegotiation of heavily watched boundaries.

The procedures and frameworks that linguistic anthropology and interactional sociolinguistics provide for the analysis of these situated practices are well described elsewhere (e.g. Duranti 1997, 2001, 2004; Gumperz 1982, 1999; Hymes 1980, 1996), but perhaps there are two points worth adding. First, in the recent development of 'linguistic ethnography' as an approach (evident in, for example, the UK Linguistic Ethnography Forum (www.uklef.net), in a rolling programme of training workshops (www.rdi-elc.org.uk) and in publications such as Rampton *et al.* 2007, there has been a concerted effort to synthesize a range of linguistic anthropological, socio- and applied linguistic subtraditions in order to facilitate an outward-facing dialogue across disciplines and beyond the academy, and this seems especially relevant to the kinds of situation detailed above, where the resolution of conflict requires analysis and debate from a wide spectrum of different contributors (and also where a critical mass of subdisciplinary specialists interested in detailed refinements in specific theories or techniques may be lacking). Second, in this commitment to close-up analysis of interactional practice, there is no retreat from the concern with policy. According to Ball, '[educational] policies are textual interventions into practice … The point is that we cannot predict or assume how they will be acted on, what their immediate effect will be, what room for manoeuvre actors will find for themselves' (Ball 1993: 12). In other words, educational policies are not simply 'implemented' – they are enacted, interpreted and re-created by different actors in educational practice, and it takes ethnography, not just the analysis of policy texts, to understand this (see Ball 1990, 1993; Bowe *et al.* 1992; Vidovich 2007).

Admittedly, linguistic ethnography is not necessarily relevant to every research question but, for the reasons sketched above, it should play a significant part in at least two lines of research that we see as a priority for the future.

## 6. Future directions

### Researching language learning, teaching and intercultural communication in contexts of conflict

Other than the studies reported in Section 4, there does not seem to have been much academic research examining language learning and teaching processes in contexts of conflict. As we saw with Mr A's politically attuned concentration on language structure to the exclusion of 'culture', there may be configurations in the links between language teaching practice and wider social forces that look quite different from those encountered in more politically relaxed environments, and there is still much to be learnt about, for example, the ways in which teachers and students do and do not manage to interactionally transform different discourses, how they negotiate representations of 'us' and 'them' and, equally, the kinds of structure that remain resistant to transformation. It is also likely that research of this kind would facilitate productive dialogue between sociolinguistics and both theory and practice in peace education and conflict resolution.

### Comparative and longitudinal studies in different conflict-ridden contexts

There is considerable need for further investigation of differences and similarities in other language learning and teaching, both across different contexts and within contexts over time. From the descriptions in Section 4, we can see some common trends (e.g. the 'traitor' theme), but both cross-sectional and longitudinal comparison of data and teaching practices could tell us much more, illuminating the possibilities and limits of language education as a means for promoting reconciliation and peaceful coexistence, and assisting in the development of teaching, materials and training guides.

## 7. Recommendations for practice

The practicalities of teaching a language associated with an interethnic conflict, as well as the design of appropriate materials, requires a lot more investigation, and this needs to be grounded not just in MFL pedagogic theory but in research that sheds light on the particularities of each context and on problems such as those illustrated above. Based on these examples, we would recommend the following.

### Understand teachers' emotional and practical difficulties

It is clear from the evidence that teachers face a range of potential problems, including student resistance during lessons and parents' expectations and hostile reactions in society at large. There is research to suggest that teachers can experience emotional difficulties employing reconciliation discourses and may reject interethnic/intercultural communication (Bar-Tal 2004; Murphy and Gallagher 2009) – recent research on teachers' perceptions of reconciliation in Cyprus, for example, revealed Greek-Cypriot teachers facing practical, ideological and emotional difficulties that seriously encumbered the implementation of reconciliatory ideas in class (Zembylas et al. 2011). It is crucial for both policy makers and teacher educators to understand these issues – failure to do so can endanger any peace education initiative, including 'other language' classes such as those described in this chapter.

### Peace and reconciliation pedagogies

As we have argued, teaching a language associated with interethnic animosity involves complications that are not usually taken into consideration in MFL guides and training. However, there is an extensive literature on peace and reconciliation pedagogies, and this can be used together with MFL theories of intercultural awareness to help teachers to deal with conflict. Although it is obviously not easy, several studies suggest that addressing rather than ignoring conflict can help children deal with it and develop a more critical perspective (Bekerman et al. 2009; Gallagher 2004; Tankersley 2001; Zembylas 2008) and, according to Zembylas (2008), there is evidence that engaging with 'trauma' in classrooms can be a 'transformative form of pedagogical engagement … [that] creates openings for different affective relations with others … by enabling new directions for a radical reinterpretation of trauma and its implications, individually and socially' (Zembylas 2008: 1, 5).

### Explore and build on students' experiences

Students choosing to attend other language classes have often either had experience of contact with the opposite community or have parents who are positively inclined towards the possibility of this (Bekerman 2005; Charalambous 2009a). Teachers can draw on students' experience and exploit it constructively by, for example, developing classroom dialogues around encounters that could actually happen, by asking students to use their contacts for classroom assignments (see e.g. Roberts et al. 2001) or by guiding students to draw on their experiences in critical reflection on different ideological representations of 'us' and 'them'.

## Related topics

Cultural identity, biases, and Othering; culture; intercultural citizenship; intercultural (communicative) competence; intercultural pedagogy/praxis; language, identity and intercultural communication; intercultural speaker

## Further reading

Bekerman, Z. (2005) 'Complex contexts and ideologies: bilingual education in conflict-ridden areas', *Journal of Language, Identity and Education*, 4(1): 1–20 (a comprehensive account of other language classes in Israel).

Byram, M. (1997) *Teaching and Assessing Intercultural Communicative Competence*, Clevedon: Multilingual Matters (a detailed description of the intercultural communicative competence (ICC) framework).

Rampton, B. and Charalambous, C. (2010) 'Crossing: a review of research', *Working Papers in Urban Language and Literacy*, 58 (a review of the literature on 'crossing' and a discussion of how this concept can be used for other language classes in Cyprus).

Salomon, G. and Nevo, B. (eds) (no date) *Peace Education*, London: Lawrence Elbrum Associates (a collection of peace-education studies in different conflict-ridden contexts).

## Notes

1 See http://europa.eu/eur-lex/pri/en/oj/dat/2003/l_236/l_23620030923en09310956.pdf#page=25.
2 See http://ec.europa.eu/enlargement/turkish_cypriot_community/index_en.htm.
3 Other measures of the same package included the issuing of official documents (ID, passports, etc.), access to public health care, movement of persons, goods and vehicles across the Buffer Zone, employment of Turkish-Cypriot personnel, etc.
4 Negative attitudes towards the French language by Dutch speakers have also been documented in the literature (see Dewaele 2005; Mettewie and Janssens 2007).
5 For a collection of papers dealing with situations in which indigenous languages have been oppressed by colonial languages, see SIT Occasional Papers Series, Vol. 4, http://www.sit.edu/SITOccasionalPapers/ops04.pdf.

## References

Ager, D.E., Muskens, G. and Wright, S. (eds) (1993) *Language Education for Intercultural Communication*, Clevedon: Multilingual Matters.

Baker, C. (2003) 'Education as a site of language contact', *Annual Review of Applied Linguistics*, 23: 95–112.

Ball, S.J. (1990) *Politics and Policy Making in Education: Explorations in Policy Sociology*, London: Routledge.

——(1993) 'What is policy? Texts, trajectories and toolboxes', *Discourse: Studies in the Cultural Politics of Education*, 13(2): 10–17.

Bar-Tal, D. (2004) 'Nature, rationale, and effectiveness of education for coexistence', *Journal of Social Issues*, 60(2): 253–71.

Beacco, J.C. and Byram, M. (2003) *Guide for the Development of Language Education Policies in Europe: From Linguistic Diversity to Plurilingual Education*, Strasbourg: Council of Europe.

Bekerman, Z. (2004) 'Potential and limitations of multicultural education in conflict-ridden areas: bilingual Palestinian–Jewish schools in Israel', *The Teachers College Record*, 106(3): 574–610.

——(2005) 'Complex contexts and ideologies: bilingual education in conflict-ridden areas', *Journal of Language, Identity and Education*, 4(1): 1–20.

Bekerman, Z. and Horenczyk, G. (2004) 'Arab–Jewish bilingual coeducation in Israel: a long-term approach to intergroup conflict resolution', *Journal of Social Issues*, 60(2): 389–404.

Bekerman, Z. and Shhadi, N. (2003) 'Palestinian–Jewish bilingual education in Israel: its influence on cultural identities and its impact on intergroup conflict', *Journal of Multilingual and Multicultural Development*, 24(6): 473–84.

Bekerman, Z., Zembylas, M. and McGlynn, C. (2009) 'Working toward the de-essentialization of identity categories in conflict and postconflict societies: Israel, Cyprus, and Northern Ireland', *Comparative Education Review*, 53(2): 213–34.

Blommaert, J. and Verschueren, J. (1998) 'The role of language in European nationalist ideologies', in B. Schieffelin, K.A. Woolard and P.V. Kroskrity (eds) *Language Ideologies: Practice and Theory*, Oxford: Oxford University Press, pp. 189–210.

Bollen, K. and Baten, K. (2010) 'Bilingual education in Flanders: policy and press debate (1999–2006)', *The Modern Language Journal*, 94: 1–22.

Bowe, R., Ball, S.J. and Gold, A. (1992) *Reforming Education and Changing Schools: Case Studies in Policy Sociology*, London: Routledge.

Broady, E. (2004) 'Sameness and difference: the challenge of culture in language teaching', *Language Learning Journal*, 29: 68–72.

Bryant, R. (2004) *Imagining the Modern: The Cultures of Nationalism in Cyprus*, London: I.B. Tauris.

Byram, M. (1989) *Cultural Studies in Foreign Language Education*, Clevedon: Multilingual Matters.

——(1995) 'Intercultural competence and mobility in multinational context: a European view', in M.L. Tickoo (ed.) *Language and Culture in Multilingual Societies: Viewpoints and Visions*, Singapore: SEAMEO Regional Language Centre, pp. 21–36.

——(1997) *Teaching and Assessing Intercultural Communicative Competence*, Clevedon: Multilingual Matters.

Byram, M. and Risager, K. (1999) *Language Teachers, Politics, and Cultures*, Clevedon: Multilingual Matters.

Byram, M. and Morgan, C. and colleagues (1994) *Teaching-and-Learning Language-and-Culture*, Clevedon: Multilingual Matters.

Byram, M., Nichols, A. and Stevens, D. (eds) (2001) *Developing Intercultural Competence in Practice*, Clevedon: Multilingual Matters.

Byram, M., Gribkova, B. and Starkey, H. (2002) *Developing the Intercultural Dimension in Language Teaching: A Practical Introduction for Teachers*, Strasbourg: Council of Europe.

Canagarajah, A.S. (1993) 'Critical ethnography of a Sri Lankan classroom: ambiguities in student opposition to reproduction through ESOL', *TESOL Quarterly*, 27(4): 601–26.

Charalambous, C. (2009a) 'Learning the language of "The Other": a linguistic ethnography of Turkish-language classes in a Greek-Cypriot school', unpublished PhD thesis, King's College, London.

——(2009b) '"Others" and "Brothers": Hellenocentric education and Turkish language lessons in Greek-Cypriot schools', *Cyprus Colloquium: Discourse and Education in the Process of Reconciliation*, London Metropolitan University, May 2009.

Cortazzi, M. and Jin, L. (1999) 'Cultural mirrors: materials and methods in the EFL classroom', in E. Hinkel (ed.) *Culture in Second Language Teaching and Learning*, New York: Cambridge University Press, pp. 196–220.

Council of Europe (2001) *Common European Framework of Reference for Languages: Learning, Teaching, Assessment*, Cambridge: Cambridge University Press.

Dewaele, J.M. (2005) 'Sociodemographic, psychological and politicocultural correlates in Flemish students' attitudes towards French and English', *Journal of Multilingual and Multicultural Development*, 26(2): 118–37.

Dubin, F. (1989) 'Situating literacy within traditions of communicative competence', *Applied Linguistics*, 10(2): 171–81

Duranti, A. (1997) *Linguistic Anthropology*, Cambridge: Cambridge University Press.

——(ed.) (2001) *Linguistic Anthropology: A Reader*, Oxford: Blackwell Publishers.

——(ed.) (2004) *A Companion to Linguistic Anthropology*, Oxford: Blackwell.

Edwards, J. (1985) *Language, Society and Identity*, Oxford: Blackwell.

Fishman, J.A. (1991) *Reversing Language Shift: Theoretical and Empirical Foundations of Assistance to Threatened Languages*, Clevedon: Multilingual Matters.

Gal, S., and Irvine, J. (1995) 'The boundaries of languages and disciplines: how ideologies construct difference', *Social Research*, 62(4): 967–1001.

Gallagher, T. (2004) *Education in Divided Societies*, London: Palgrave Macmillan.

Genesee, F. and Gándara, P. (1999) 'Bilingual education programs: a cross-national perspective', *Journal of Social Issues*, 55(4): 665–85.

Gumperz, J.J. (1982) *Discourse Strategies*, Cambridge: Cambridge University Press.

——(1999) 'On interactional sociolinguistic method', in S. Sarangi and C. Roberts (eds) *Talk, Work and Institutional Order: Discourse in Medical, Mediation and Management Settings*, The Hague: Mouton, pp. 453–71.

Hymes, D.H. (1980) *Language in Education: Ethnolinguistic Essays. Language and Ethnography Series*, Washington, DC: Center for Applied Linguistics.

——(1996) *Ethnography, Linguistics, Narrative Inequality: Toward an Understanding of Voice*, London: Taylor and Francis.

Jaffe, A. (2009) 'The production and reproduction of language ideologies in practice', in N. Coupland and A. Jaworski (eds) *The New Sociolinguistics Reader*, New York: Palgrave Macmillan, pp. 390–404.

Kaikkonen, P. (1997) 'Learning a culture and a foreign language at school – aspects of intercultural learning', *Language Learning Journal*, 15: 47–51.

Karoulla-Vrikki, D. (2004) 'Language and ethnicity in Cyprus under the British: a linkage of heightened salience', *International Journal of the Sociology of Language*, 168: 19–36.

Karyolemou, M. (2003) '"Keep your language and I will keep mine": politics, language, and the construction of identities in Cyprus', in D. Nelson and M. Dedaic-Nelson (eds) *At War with Words*, Berlin/New York: Mouton de Gruyter, pp. 359–84.

Killoran, M. (1998) 'Nationalism and embodied memory in Northern Cyprus', in V. Calotychos (ed.) *Cyprus and Its People: Nation, Identity and Experience in an Unimaginable Community, 1955–1997*, Boulder, CO: Westview Press, pp. 159–70.

——(2000) 'Time, space and national identities in Cyprus', in M. Yashin (ed.) *From Nationalism to Multiculturalism: Literatures of Cyprus, Greece and Turkey*, London: Middlesex University, pp. 129–46.

Kizilyürek, N. (1993) *Hi Kypros Peran tou Ethnous [Cyprus Beyond the Nation]*, Nicosia: G. Kasoulides and Son.

Kizilyürek, N. and Gautier-Kizilyürek, S. (2004) 'The politics of identity in the Turkish Cypriot community and the language question', *International Journal of the Sociology of Language*, 168: 37–54.

Kramsch, C. (1993) *Context and Culture in Language Teaching*, Oxford: Oxford University Press.

——(2009) *The Multilingual Subject*, Oxford: Oxford University Press.

Leung, C. (2005) 'Convivial communication: recontextualizing communicative competence', *International Journal of Applied Linguistics*, 15(2): 119–44.

Loveday, L. (1982) *The Sociolinguistics of Learning and Using a Non-native Language*, Oxford: Pergamon.

Mavratsas, C. (1996) 'Approaches to nationalism: basic theoretical considerations in the study of the Greek-Cypriot case and a historical overview', *Journal of Hellenic Diaspora*, 22(1): 77–102.

May, S. (2001) *Language and Minority Rights: Ethnicity, Nationalism and the Politics of Language*, Harlow: Longman.

Mettewie, L. and Janssens, R. (2007) 'Language use and language attitudes in Brussels', in D. Lasagabaster and Á. Huguet (eds) *Multilingualism in European Bilingual Contexts: Language Use and Attitudes*, Clevedon: Multilingual Matters, pp. 117–43.

Mitchell, J.C. (1984) 'Typicality and the case study', in R.F. Ellen (ed.) *Ethnographic Research: A Guide to General Conduct*, London: Academic Press, pp. 238–41.

Mughan, T. (1999) 'Intercultural competence for language students in higher education', *Language Learning Journal*, 20: 59–65.

Murphy, K. and Gallagher, T. (2009) 'Reconstruction after violence: how teachers and schools can deal with the legacy of the past', *Perspectives in Education*, 27(2): 159–68.

Nelde, P.H. (1997) 'Language conflict', in F. Coulmas (ed.) *The Handbook of Sociolinguistics*, Oxford: Blackwell, pp. 285–300.

Ozerk, K.Z. (2001) 'Reciprocal bilingualism as a challenge and opportunity: the case of Cyprus', *International Review of Education*, 47(3–4): 253–65.

Papadakis, Y. (2005) *Echoes from the Dead Zone: Across the Cyprus Divide*, London: I.B. Tauris.

Pavlenko, A. (2003) '"Language of the enemy": foreign language education and national identity', *International Journal of Bilingual Education and Bilingualism*, 6(5): 313–31.

Phipps, A. and Gonzalez, M. (2004) *Modern Languages: Learning and Teaching in an Intercultural Field*, London: Sage

Rampton, B. (1995) *Crossing: Language and Ethnicity among Adolescents*, London: New York: Longman.

——(2006) *Language in Late Modernity: Interaction in an Urban School*, Cambridge: Cambridge University Press.

Rampton, B. and Charalambous, C. (2010) 'Crossing: a review of research', *Working Papers in Language and Literacy*, 58.

Rampton, B., Maybin, J. and Tusting, K. (eds) (2007) 'Linguistic ethnography: links, problems and possibilities', Special issue of *Journal of Sociolinguistics*, 11(5).

Roberts, C., Byram, M., Barro, A., Jordan, S. and Street, B. (2001) *Language Learners as Ethnographers*, Clevedon: Multilingual Matters.

Spyrou, S. (2006) 'Constructing "the Turk" as an enemy: the complexity of stereotypes in children's everyday worlds', *South European Society and Politics*, 11(1), 95–110.

Starkey, H. (2002) *Democratic Citizenship, Languages, Diversity and Human Rights*, Strasbourg: Council of Europe.

——(2005) 'Language teaching for democratic citizenship', in A. Osler and H. Starkey (eds) *Citizenship and Language Learning: International Perspectives*, Stoke on Trent: Trentham, pp. 23–39.

Swing, E.S. (2000) 'Schools, separatism, and assimilation: the education of "others" in Europe', in E.S. Swing, J. Schriewer and F. Orivel (eds) *Problems and Prospects in European Education*, Westport, CT: Praeger Publishers, pp. 219–43.

Tankersley, D. (2001) 'Bombs or bilingual programmes?: dual-language immersion, transformative education and community building in Macedonia', *International Journal of Bilingual Education and Bilingualism*, 4(2): 107–24.

Treffers-Daller, J. (2002) 'Language use and language contact in Brussels', *Journal of Multilingual and Multicultural Development*, 23(1): 50–64.

Vidovich, L. (2007) 'Removing policy from its pedestal: some theoretical framings and practical possibilities', *Educational Review*, 59(3): 285–98.

Zembylas, M. (2008) *The Politics of Trauma in Education*, London: Palgrave Macmillan.

Zembylas, M., Charalambous, C., Charalambous, P. and Kendeou, P. (2011) 'Promoting peaceful coexistence in conflict-ridden Cyprus: teachers' difficulties and emotions towards a new policy initiative', *Teaching and Teacher Education*, 27(2): 332–41.

# 13

# Intercultural contact, hybridity, and third space

*Claire Kramsch and Michiko Uryu*

## 1. Introduction

Intercultural communication research in applied linguistics has traditionally been based on the assumption that cross-cultural encounters between individuals who have been socialized in one culture and who come into contact with individuals from another culture are more often than not a source of problematic talk, fraught with potential difficulties. The phrase "intercultural contact" (IC) itself evokes colonization or tourism. But, as modern societies have ceased to be the stable homogeneous communities they were imagined to be, IC occurs not only when abroad, but is a fact of life within industrialized societies between *autochtones* and immigrants, as it has always been among people from different ethnic groups in African countries, for example. Although some feel threatened by the contact with people whose culture is different from their own, IC has come to be seen as an opportunity to put into question one's own cultural assumptions and as a source of enrichment. Indeed, IC is seen by some as the very condition for the survival of culture.

The colonialist origins of the term still adhere to the way culture has been largely conceived in applied linguistics. IC has been associated with asymmetrical relations of linguistic proficiency and technological power. The positivistic, structurally oriented descriptions offered by anthropologists trying to make sense of the logic of IC between natives and non-natives has been echoed in the studies of native and non-native speakers in second language acquisition (SLA) research and research on study abroad. In the same manner as anthropologists studied how the Spaniards went about making the Indians into Christian subjects of the Spanish crown (Hanks 2010; Pratt 1992), applied linguists have been interested in exploring how immigrant non-native speakers can be helped to better understand and adopt the native speakers' ways of talking. Students in study abroad programs are encouraged to be ethnographers of foreign customs and ways of life. Professionals view IC as the encounter between speakers from various languacultures (Risager 2006: Ch. 8) or discourse systems (Scollon and Wong Scollon 1995/2001) and the way they manage the cross-cultural "traffic in meaning" (Pratt 2002).

However, in our current era of globalization, IC has become more complex than just speakers of different languages encountering one another. Nowadays, many of these intercultural encounters take place in English, which does not necessarily make cross-cultural understanding any easier. Applied linguistics research has become interested in the location of culture in "third spaces" (Bhabha 1994) that defy the neat national territorializations of yesteryear. Culture has become deterritorialized, crystallized in the forms of memories, identifications, and projections that people carry in their heads. It is passed on in the form of stories, images, and films, multi-modal creations, and multilingual speech productions that problematize the one language = one culture equation and that foster hybridity, *mestizaje*, and the shape-shifting avatars of the inter-net (Pennycook 2007). Rather than focusing on IC as a problem, sociolinguists and linguistic anthropologists, following the cultural theories of Bakhtin, Butler, Weedon, and others, are now interested in exploring the potential of IC for personal and discursive growth on various scales of time and space (Blommaert 2005; Lemke 2002) and various degrees of heteroglossia (Briggs and Bauman 1992). The study of IC today brings to the fore issues of power and ideology, historicity, and subjectivity, within a poststructuralist perspective.

## 2. Definitions

### Intercultural contact (IC)

IC refers to a state of affairs that occurs when people from different cultures come in touch with one another. It takes place in what Mary Louise Pratt calls "contact zones", i.e., "social spaces where disparate cultures meet, clash, and grapple with each other, often in highly asymmetrical relations of domination and subordination" (Pratt 1992: 12). IC necessarily brings about linguistic, cultural, and social change.

The phenomenon of "contact" has generally been observed to be either a voluntary or an involuntary physical contact between two or more people who belong to discrete linguistic or cultural communities in human history. In voluntary cases, one makes a contact with another (others), driven by one's interest in a cultural Other (e.g., travel) or the needs of social life and survival (e.g., trade). In contrast, in involuntary cases, intercultural contacts are often driven by rather negative elements such as power struggles between different ethnic or cultural groups (e.g., war) or a powerful group's political, economic, ideological, and cultural imposition and domination of the less powerful Other (e.g., colonization). Although IC is generally considered to be physical and thus face-to-face, this limited view has included other modalities such as textual and observable contacts (e.g., telecommunications, internet, etc.) resulting from modern technological development. In individuals who speak more than one language and belong to more than one culture, IC could refer to multilingual/multicultural identities and subjectivities within one and the same person.

Regardless of its voluntariness and modalities, IC brings about cross-cultural entanglements and often causes miscommunication because of interlocutors' socially and culturally different norms for interpreting others. In voluntary contacts, these issues can be managed by inter-locutors who attempt to negotiate meanings and understand the cultural other in a rather symmetrical manner. Involuntary contacts, however, tend to allow the more powerful group to impose its meanings and cultural norms upon less powerful others (e.g., Fanon 2004; Said 1978). As a consequence, it is usually the latter who are affected by drastic and unwelcomed changes in their language, culture, and society, e.g., through linguistic and cultural imperialism (see Canagarajah 1999; Phillipson 1993), although intercultural contacts may alter both parties' linguistic, cultural, and social spheres (Pratt 2002). Power differentials in IC can lead to practices of inclusion and exclusion studied by anthropologists and the creation of stereotypes on as small a scale as tourist brochures (Thurlow and Jaworski 2009) or on the scale of vast and durable ideologies such as orientalism (Said 1978) or occidentalism (Buruma and Margalit 2004).

## Hybridity and third space

The dualities, us/them, native speaker/non-native speaker, self/other, in/voluntariness, in/exclusion, orientalism/occidentalism, have been rendered more complex by economic globalization, large-scale migrations, and electronic modes of communication. As national, popular, and professional cultures have become deterritorialized, denationalized, and commodified for marketing purposes (Kramsch 2009a), and representations of other cultures on the internet have made the foreign both more familiar and more stereotypical, cultures seem to increasingly resemble one another, and to perform themselves for the tourist's or the consumer's gaze.

But such a view is deceptive; in fact, the boundaries between cultures have only been reshuffled. Intercultural contacts have become more complex and have led to more subtle kinds of cultural infiltration and mutual contamination around the world (Pennycook 2007). For example, Moroccans now living in France and returning to Morocco on vacation do not get charged native rates by local vendors, but tourist rates, even though they speak and act as natives (Wagner 2010). The spread of English and computer technology have exacerbated existing social class differences within societies and made contact between global and local cultures more pronounced and even less easily bridged than the national cultures of yesteryear. Global migrations have changed the nature of IC as well. The large-scale migrations from former colonies to their industrialized metropoles have enhanced cultural difference within former colonial powers. In multicultural societies such as the US, immigration has become an intractable issue, as traditionally the US economy could not survive without the cheap labor provided by its 12 million low-skill, low-wage, illegal workers, but national interests demand that illegal immigration be prosecuted.

In the postcolonial era, notions such as "hybridity" and "third space" have caught the imagination of cultural critics and educators alike. For cultural critics such as Homi Bhabha (see below), because culture is all about meaning-making and the struggle to make one's meanings heard and accepted, "all cultural statements and systems are constructed in a contradictory and ambivalent space of enunciation" (Bhabha 1994: 37). The meaning constructed by speaking subjects and given to events is a site of social and political difference and contestation in the margins of power structures. Difference and contestation, i.e., hybridity, is the essence of culture. In this sense, all cultures are "hybrid". Culture's hybridity creates the possibility of challenging, appropriating, and resignifying the meanings of a culture, in what Bhabha calls "the third space of enunciations" (p. 38). The Australian educator Alex Kostogriz has developed a "thirdspace pedagogy of literacy" (Kostogriz 2002) that makes the students aware of contradictions and ambivalences, a pedagogy he calls "thirding" which focuses on cultural difference (see below).

For American literacy educators such as Gutierrez et al. (1999), hybridity characterizes new learning environments adapted to the multiethnic, multivoiced populations of learners in school settings. Third spaces are, to use a Vygotskyan term, new "zones of proximal development" (Vygotsky 1978: 84). They are zones of collaboration and learning or reorganized activities to accommodate different learning styles and to transform conflict and disharmony into fruitful dialogue. For Gutierrez et al., hybridity and diversity serve as the building blocks of third spaces. The difference between the way literacy educators and cultural critics view hybridity and third space is the difference between a structuralist and a poststructuralist perspective on culture, as we shall see below.

## 3. Historical perspectives

In the 1970s and 1980s, applied linguistic research on IC drew primarily on the field of psycho- and sociolinguistics. In psycholinguistics, IC was one aspect of the study of language contact (e.g., Haugen 1972; Lado 1957; Weinrich 1990/2001) and interlanguage (Selinker 1972) in SLA. In sociolinguistics, it was concerned with such phenomena as pidginization and creolization code-switching, acculturation, bilingualism and multilingualism, and language maintenance and policy studies. These studies largely shared common interests and goals, that is, they aimed to reveal how the larger social context, which allows such contact to take place, affects the structure of linguistic systems and the variations in their use.

## On the micro level: interaction studies

Although the aforementioned studies focused on contact between linguistic systems, in the 1990s, applied linguists became more concerned with intercultural encounters between speakers, both at the micro and at the macro level of interactional exchanges. On the micro level, researchers in interactional sociolinguistics and pragmatics revealed what and how one's sociocultural know-ledge affects one's interactions and the process of interpretations in intercultural contacts. The indispensable connection between language and culture found its expression in interactional sociolinguistics and linguistic anthropology in the large body of research on context (Duranti and Goodwin 1992; Hanks 1996). As interlocutors in contact zones usually have dissimilar socio-cultural knowledge accompanied by differing expectations of mutual understanding, potential communication breakdowns are understood to stem from differences in social, historical, and ideological backgrounds. Gumperz and Roberts (1991), for instance, studied how socioculturally different expectations of participants impair the conversation between the British and Indians in job interviews. Scollon and Wong Scollon (1990) showed how culturally different ways of speaking can not only impair conversation between Anglo-American and Athabaskans, but also reinforce negative stereotypes about each other.

With respect to the vital impact of social and cultural factors upon one's communicative practices, linguistic anthropology has had an important influence on studies of IC in applied linguistics. According to Gumperz, texts are "indexically" made to fit into a particular socio-cultural context by addressers, in order to further help addressees properly understand the full meaning of a given text. Such social and cultural elements that serve meta-communicative functions are "contextualization cues", i.e., "any verbal and nonverbal signs that help speakers to hint at, or clarify, and listeners to make such inference" (Gumperz 1992: 229). As the interpretive process of the situated utterance is highly reliant on the context, the addressee is required to pick up those contextualization cues designating both linguistic and paralinguistic signals for the situated understanding of the sociocultural aspects of meaning. Hanks's studies of the encounter between Maya Indians and the Spanish conquistadores (Hanks 2010) highlights the historical, social, and religious dimensions of intercultural discourse in colonial Yucatan.

Similarly, the field of cross-cultural pragmatics research found social and cultural variables in universal rules governing contextual influence upon textual meaning. The work done in cross-cultural psychology and cross-cultural semantics has enriched conversational analysis with a cultural component it did not have originally (Moermann 1988). Revealing how cultural variables impact upon interlocutors' communicative practices in intercultural encounters, some studies discerned that there is a cultural relativity in terms of showing one's politeness to others in conversation (e.g., Matsumoto, 1988). Through comparative discourse analysis, Tannen (1984) found differences in the narratives of different cultural groups—not only national and ethnic cultures such as Greek vs. Americans but also different gender cultures. Lakoff (1990) showed how the conversational strategies for conveying distance, deference, or camaraderie differ from cul-ture to culture. These findings are significant, as sociocultural factors that impact upon inter-locutors' communicative practices may cause miscommunication or a sense of discomfort in IC.

Influenced by interactional sociolinguistics and pragmatics, SLA research has contributed to the research body of IC as well. Cross-cultural pragmatics was prominent in SLA in the 1980s, as part of the effort to define communicative competence. SLA researchers specifically focused on studying how language learners' cultural knowledge affects their pragmalinguistic behaviors in a target language and possibly causes communication breakdowns (e.g., Blum-Kulka *et al.* 1989; Chapter 4, this volume). The study of language learners' differences in expectations based on different cultural knowledge or "interlanguage pragmatics" referred to a non-native speaker's use and acquisition of speech act realization in a second language. These studies have emerged from the increasing opportunities for intercultural contact and communications. Because of the rapid globalization of economy and trade, the accompanying global migrations, and the recent innovations in global information/communication technologies, people now live in multiple and shifting spaces while communicating with linguistic and cultural others in the global lingua franca, English, but their pragmatics and conversational style often remain different from those of native English speakers.

## On the macro level: critical discourse studies

While the studies mentioned above focus on the communicative aspects of IC on the micro level, others are concerned with how discursive practices add up to larger discourse systems that shape our identities as social actors as they enter into contact with one another within the larger social context. Drawing heavily on Bourdieu and Foucault, James Gee conceptualized the notion of cultural actor as one who partakes in multiple Discourses with a capital D.

> A Discourse is composed of ways of talking, listening, reading, writing, acting, interacting, believing, valuing, and using tools and objects, in particular settings and at specific times, so as to display or to recognize a particular social identity. Law school teachers and students enact specific social identities or "social positions" in the Discourse of law school. The Discourse creates social positions (or perspectives) from which people are "invited" ("summoned") to speak, listen, act, read and write, think, feel, believe and value in certain characteristic, historically recognizable ways, in combination with their own individual style and creativity (Bourdieu 1979, 1984, 1991; Foucault 1980).
>
> *Gee* et al. *(1996: 10)*

This definition of Discourse has been equated with a poststructuralist definition of culture as a process of meaning creation and attribution mediated by symbolic systems (see below; Kramsch 1998). Responding to the need to consider an interlocutor's affiliation with multiple discourse systems, Scollon and Wong Scollon (1995/2001) offered a new analytical approach to understanding IC in an increasingly global economy. Targeting professional communicators across discourse systems in the global business world, Scollon and Wong Scollon first presented the major tenets of discourse analysis at the interactional level (i.e., speech acts, politeness phenomena, facework, inferences, frames, turn-taking) and then suggested connecting these analyses to a larger discourse level. This approach is quite useful for those who study IC as it allows for disentangling the complexity of multiple discourses that each interlocutor brings to the contact zone.

In the last two decades, research on IC in applied linguistics has taken on a critical edge as issues of power and ideology have entered the picture. One of the leading theorists who advocates combining social and cultural theories with the field of applied linguistics is Norman Fairclough (1989, 1992). Fairclough primarily pooled the Foucauldian notion of discourse and power and Bourdieu's theory of habitus and symbolic capital to theorize how power comes into play in discourses through social institutions and sociocultural practices. In his view, texts produced at the interactional level are part of a larger discourse system, which is highly ideologized to support the existing power structure and system in a particular society. Therefore, whenever one speaks, one inevitably reinforces the existing social structure by reproducing its supporting ideology. Note that, in Fairclough's view, a speaker is not the one depicted by Saussure, who encodes and decodes texts when communicating with others, but a social actor, whose body is subjugated to the existing social system while his/her perceptions of the world are essentially regulated, controlled, and normalized (i.e., technologized) through knowledges and discourses that support dominant ideologies.

Fairclough's re-conceptualization of language as social practice and interlocutors as social actors has significantly affected the study of IC. Within the field of critical applied linguistics, Phillipson (1993) called into question the uncontested notions surrounding IC, such as the global spread of English, the increasing opportunities for intercultural exchanges, and the contemporary trend of learning English as a prioritized subject at educational institutions. Phillipson first argued that the global spread of English is aimed at promoting the expansion of particular ideologies that belong to certain societies while allowing those who possess English as capital to exploit the linguistic Other and construct structural and cultural inequalities. Pennycook (1994) further argued that the general view of the global spread of English as neutral, natural, and beneficial is not only false, but also masks the prevailing colonialism practiced through the teaching of English. Although Fairclough's and Phillipson's work has been crucial for understanding the inherently political and ideological nature of IC, it seems insufficient to capture the "transcultural flows" (Pennycook 2007) and "layered simultaneities" (Blommaert 2005: 126) that we witnessed at the end of the first decade of the twenty-first century. Because IC today is experienced on the multiple timescales of the global and the local, the real and the virtual, the actual and the imagined, it has to be conceptualized within an ecological perspective that also takes into account the changed axes of time and space brought about by computer technology.

In sum, the interest of applied linguists in IC has followed the general shifts in focus of the field in the last 40 years. In the 1970s and 1980s, applied linguistics was mainly interested in the acquisition of foreign and second languages, and viewed culture as the communicative context in which SLA unfolded. IC was the extension of a contact between two linguistic systems and their social context of use. In the 1980s and 1990s, interest shifted to the interaction between native and non-native speakers who did not share the same social and cultural background. In the early 1990s, culture became a major topic in language studies. Applied linguistics not only broadened the range of fields it drew upon, to include sociolinguistics, linguistic anthropology, and critical cultural studies, but experienced a social and cultural turn that gave increasing prominence to discourse and conversation analysis in the study of both language acquisition and language socialization. At the end of the first decade of the twenty-first century, the study of IC in applied linguistics is ecological in its scope, critical in its approach, and is opening up its methods of analysis to include poststructuralist perspectives that the anthropologist Clifford Geertz had anticipated 30 years earlier (see below).

## 4. Critical issues and topics

In the last 10 years, critical trends in the applied linguistic study of IC have grown in importance and so have their theoretical underpinnings. The term "critical" refers to both the controversies that are going on in the field (Seidlhofer 2003) and the importance of the issues they raise. Critical applied linguistics (CAL) (Pennycook 2001) interrogates the complexities of power relations in IC in postcolonial and diasporic situations and in interethnic group conflicts. As the term "critical" suggests, CAL studies culture and IC through the symbolic systems that both constitute and represent it, one of which being language in discourse.

## Critique of structuralist approaches to IC

It is this foregrounding of culture as discourse that gives CAL its poststructuralist edge. One of the major issues that CAL has with traditional applied linguistics research is the latter's structuralist views of language, culture, and society in understanding IC. First, although applied linguistics has acknowledged the interrelationship of language, culture, and identity, it has not taken into account the power of language and other symbolic systems to "create" the very cultures it studies. Second, as Block (2009) and Kramsch (2009b) point out, by confusing identity and subjectivity, it has ignored the symbolic dimension of discourse, and the subjective and ostensive nature of verbal performance (Pennycook 2007, Ch. 4). Third, as Blommaert (2005) notes, these studies do not connect the micro level of interactional analyses and the sociohistorical context of contact zones on the macro level. Consequently, they do not fully capture the dialectic and dynamic relationship between changes at different levels, as they tend to examine how the form of power comes into play in the given context only in a linear way. Fourth, they have conceived of IC only as social and cultural, but not political and ideological practice (Pennycook 2001). In short, the findings of these studies are not holistic and comprehensive because they ultimately fail to capture the complex ecology of language, culture, and society.

In literacy education, the multiliteracies movement in literacy research has dealt with intercultural conflicts in schools, but because it is focused on helping schoolchildren from various ethnicities and abilities to become integrated into a multicultural society, it is more interested in "transforming conflict and difference into rich zones of collaboration and learning" (Gutierrez et al. 1999: 287). The construct of "third space" helps realize the transformative potential of complex and hybrid learning environments; conflict and miscommunication in the zone of proximal development can be made to result in new opportunities for learning. But what is not interrogated in the multiliteracies framework is the very notion of difference. By striving to neutralize "difference" and glorify "diversity", the ultimate goals of a neo-liberal capitalistic society are not put into question and the possibility of imagining other worlds is not conceived, indeed it is often viewed as inconceivable.

This criticism is related to the structuralist perspective taken by most IC research. By conceptualizing one's identity only as attributable to one's linguistic, cultural, ethnic, national, or social background, one runs the risk of essentializing such characteristics and making them into stable, non-negotiable features of the Self. As we have seen in American literacy education research, the solution proposed through the creation of hybrid third places does not necessarily do away with the dichotomy us vs. them, Self vs. Other, but strives to find a way of coexisting together around a common task. Indeed, as Gutierrez et al. (1999) claim, "From the perspective of activity theory, the third space can be also be considered an expanded activity … in which the object of activity is extended and the activity itself is re-organized, resulting in new opportunities for learning" (ibid.). But what if the activity itself is put into question, its purpose, its goals, its structure? With the increasingly frequent crises in the capitalistic market economy, the possibilities of one individual bettering his/her chances of success if only he/she plays by the rules and collaborates with others on a common task are not as clear as was once believed.

## Poststructuralist approaches to IC

In the age of globalization, CAL and cultural critics have become interested not in the resolution of conflict nor in the transformation of marginal individuals into mainstream society, but in the contact zone itself and its potential to transform both the discourse of marginalized individuals and the dominant discourse of mainstream society. Although appreciating the legacies of earlier studies, the study of IC needs to search for an alternative approach that goes beyond the constraint of traditional views of nation, culture, language, and identities in contemporary contact zones. As Pratt notes, "In talking about cross-cultural meaning making, it's essential to attend to fractures and entanglements, their makeup, asymmetries, ethics, histories, interdependencies, distributions of power and accountability" (Pratt 2002: 33).

Pratt calls for considering "cultural translation" as the *sine qua non* of IC. Such a translation has to be seen, she says, as a *desdoblamiento* or multiplying of the Self (Pratt 2002: 35). The stranger is, indeed, in ourselves. The problem is no longer a juxtaposition of various identities working in harmony with one another, but an entanglement of subjectivities, refracted in one another, historically interdependent, and morally accountable to one another. Her argument echoes that of Clifford Geertz who wrote in *Local Knowledge*:

> Translation [.] is not a simple recasting of others' ways of putting things in terms of our own ways of putting them (that is the kind in which things get lost), but displaying the logic of their ways of putting them in the locutions of ours; a conception which brings it rather closer to what a critic does to illumine a poem than what an astronomer does to account for a star.
>
> *Geertz (1983: 10)*

> The experience of understanding other cultures is "more like grasping a proverb, catching an allusion, seeing a joke − or, as I have suggested, reading a poem − than it is like achieving communion".
>
> *Geertz (1983: 70)*

Such a description of IC is much less optimistic about the possibility of working together than American literacy educators would suggest. There is no way we can fully understand one another, even though we have no other recourse than to try again and again to translate the untranslatable, and thereby gain sympathy for and acceptance of one another.

The postcolonial and poststructuralist cultural critic Homi Bhabha makes the important distinction between cultural diversity and cultural difference. Whereas the former is often hailed as the peaceful coexistence of people from various origins, creeds, and ethnicities under one national banner (e.g., in the US, *e pluribus unum*), the term "cultural difference" serves to underscore the importance of the "foreign" in understanding ourselves and others. In *The Location of Culture*, Bhabha draws attention to the in-between character of cultural mediation.

> A willingness to descend into that alien territory ... may open the way to conceptualizing an *inter*national culture, based not on the exoticism of multiculturalism or the *diversity* of cultures, but on the inscription and articulation of culture's *hybridity*. To that end we should remember that it is the "inter" − the cutting edge of translation and negotiation, the *in-between* space − that carries the burden of the meaning of culture.
>
> *Bhabha (2010: 55)*

In Bhabha's poststructuralist perspective, "hybridity" is conceived as a space of contested meanings always open to translation, negotiation, resignification, and the struggle for the power to acquire and impose knowledge. Bhabha called this space a "third space"—a metaphor for a discursive subject position that speakers create by referring to events in the outside world, and in so doing, giving these events meaning through language. Echoing Bakhtin's "heteroglossia" and Foucault's "order of discourse", Bhabha sees third spaces as both constituting and resignifying cultural meanings.

> Third Space, though unrepresentable in itself, ... constitutes the discursive conditions of enunciation that ensure that the meaning and symbols of culture have no primordial unity or fixity; that even the same signs can be appropriated, translated, rehistoricized and read anew.
>
> *Bhabha (2010: 55)*

Bhabha's Third Space has been adapted to critical foreign language education (Kramsch 1993, 2009c) and critical literacy education (Kostogriz 2002). Postcolonial theory, as represented for example by the work of Edward Said and Homi Bhabha, has focused on the multiplex nature of this Third Space. Within a discourse-based view of culture as a sociohistorical meaning-making system, IC is conceptualized as the process of translation itself—a process that is inscribed in the very condition of possibility of being a speaking subject. One feminist cultural critic, Chris Weedon, who has had a major influence on the thinking of critical applied linguists, captures the essence of IC as a site of struggle in which we are as much the active producers of discourse as we are the speakers of discourses beyond our control.

> Discourse is a structuring principle of society, in social institutions, modes of thought and individual subjectivity ... Meanings do not exist prior to their articulation in language and language is not an abstract system, but is always socially and historically located in discourses. Discourses represent political interests and in consequence are constantly vying for status and power. The site of this battle for power is the subjectivity of the individual and it is a battle in which the individual is an active but not sovereign protagonist. ... To speak is to assume a subject position within discourse and to be subjected to the power and regulation of the discourse.
>
> *Weedon (1997: 41)*

Hybridity is, in this view, a fundamental heteroglossia or multiplicity of voices, histories, worldviews that is inherent in any culture, because of the different ways in which members of a given speech community experience and interpret history. It is inextricably linked to an engagement with one's own and other people's memories, perceptions, and worldviews, rather than a collaborative partnership on a common task that has been defined and assigned by a third party.

## 5. Current contributions and future directions

Current research has expanded on this more ecological way of viewing IC—a view that stresses the relationality and non-linearity of cross-cultural entanglements and their links to historicity and subjectivity. A recent event can serve as an illustration (see Kramsch 2009d).

### IC as historicity and subjectivity: an example

On his visit to the US on April 17, 2008, Pope Benedict XVI, addressing the American bishops at the Basilica of the Shrine of the Immaculate Conception in Washington, DC, decried both the recent clerical abuses and the current secular materialism that he sees seeping into every area of

American life. Invoking the notions of secularism and materialism, he added: "It is easy to make the mistake of thinking we can obtain by our own efforts the fulfillment of our deepest needs. This is an illusion ... In a society which values personal freedom and autonomy, it is easy to lose sight of our dependence on others as well as the responsibilities that we bear towards them ... ".

If we consider the visit of Pope Benedict XVI, a German theologian steeped in the doctrinal culture of the Catholic Church, as an encounter with the predominantly Protestant culture of the US, we could say that we have here an IC that was bound to create some tensions. On both occasions, the Pope juxtaposed the culture of American capitalism and the alternative culture of the Gospel. Indeed, he was less juxtaposing than resignifying the very tenets of American democracy—freedom, faith, wealth, scientific and technological progress—and showing them wanting. "Individual enterprise", he said, is "an illusion", "personal freedom" is not "true freedom".

The same day, on *Newshour*, Jeffrey Brown interviewed two American Catholic priests and asked them how one was to interpret the words of the Pope. Considering the delicate nature of this intercultural encounter, the priest was in a tight spot. Should he show support for the beliefs of his Church or for the core values of his country? Here is how one of the priests solved the dilemma.

JEFFREY BROWN:  What do you think? When he's talking about the increasingly secular and materialistic culture, this is a ... you know him well. This is a very cultured man himself. He knows the culture of the United States. What is he saying?

PRIEST:  Well ... what I think he's saying is ... he recognizes how important freedom is to the American people. ... The Pope is for freedom, he loves our freedoms. But he talks about ... that ... with freedom comes responsibility, and that we have to use our freedom for the common good, not just for selfish self-interest, that we have to use our freedom to make the world a better place, to work for justice, to work for peace in our country and around the world.

By reframing the question of materialism and secularism into a question of freedom, the priest was able to reassert the American discourse excoriated by the Holy Father and reframe it in the discourse of morality and responsibility intoned by the Pope himself.

In a second, the priest had grasped the negative historic connotations of terms such as "secularism" and "materialism", their subjective resonances, offered a different frame for the events, and assuaged the millions of American viewers of *Newshour*. A third space of enunciation was reached by implicitly acknowledging the different timescales on which terms such as "materialism" and "freedom" were operating and resignifying the former to accommodate the latter in a new hybrid utterance: "Materialism in America *is* the freedom to make money. There is not necessarily a contradiction between making money and loving God, providing you work to make the world a better place".

Of course, even though Pope Benedict was speaking English, his thoughts were steeped in German theology. Translating "materialism" with "freedom" required a deep understanding on the part of the priest of the various subjective resonances of words such as "materialism" vs. *Materialismus*, the capacity to place them into their proper historic context, and an ability to reframe the question in such a way that it would be comprehensible and acceptable to an American audience. Such an approach is characteristic of critical discourse analysis but within the poststructuralist orientation that sociolinguists such as Jan Blommaert have proposed in recent years. Blommaert (2005) re-conceptualized the relation among interlocutor, text, and context by adding the historical dimension in the study of discourse. According to Blommaert, each society or system to which an interlocutor belongs has its own historical foundation consisting of multiple timescales, each of which further develops at different speeds and with various processes of transformation. IC contexts are therefore far more complicated than they appear at first glance because a particular ideological discourse that one can observe "here and now" is only a synchronized form of multiple, separate, and individual discourses, which are in fact simultaneously occurring in each historical layer of the same context. Given this fact, Blommaert argues, the real work of the discourse analyst is to identify from which historical perspective participants perform their social, cultural, and ideological identities in discourse in response to others.

## Ecological perspectives on IC

This kind of critical discourse analysis echoes many of the tenets of language ecology. The growing interest in language ecology comes from European linguists interested in linguistic variety and environmental diversity (Fill and Mühlhäusler 2001), and from American linguists concerned about the maintenance and revitalization of endangered languages. In SLA, language ecology is of interest to educational linguists anxious to bridge the psycho- and the socio- in language acquisition research (Kramsch 2002; van Lier 2003). An ecological approach has much in common with recent applications of complexity theory to understand multilingual phenomena (Larsen-Freeman and Cameron 2008). It stresses the relationality of Self and Other in IC, the non-linearity between illocutionary intentions and perlocutionary effects in intercultural exchanges, and the fractal nature of discourse events (e.g., terms such as "materialism" and "freedom" are metonymies for much larger historical discourses). It points to the open-endedness of any cultural meaning that can be resignified and reframed by participants in intercultural dialogue, especially when crossing over into other languages.

Recent studies have used a critical ecological approach to ethnographic data on intercultural encounters. Whiteside's (forthcoming) study of Yucatec Maya illegal immigrants in San Francisco's Mission district documents the way they maneuver the symbolic connotations of words in Maya, Spanish, and English in Chinese and Vietnamese grocery stores and underground soup kitchens. The multilingual encounters between immigrants with varying degrees of linguistic and social legitimacy and various lengths of stay provide a rich context in which to study IC among migrant populations in a global economy. Boner's (2011) study of micro enterprises in Tanzania that are funded and supported by American non-governmental organizations (NGOs) and international funding agencies reveals the invisible discourses that speak through the mouths of the protagonists and the limits of individual agency in controlling these discourses. The ability of English-speaking Tanzanian community leaders to resignify the neo-liberal discourse of the NGO representatives is a vivid illustration of the power struggle that goes on in situations of IC in global contexts. Uryu's (2009) study of international spouses of visiting scholars at an American university's Thanksgiving dinner, organized precisely to foster intercultural understanding, shows the crucial role played by history and memory in enabling participants to make sense of current events. Such a Thanksgiving dinner, originally conceived by Americans to bring former adversaries together—in this case, a German, a Russian, and a Japanese—to "get to know America and its customs", gets resignified in the post-Cold War era by participants who interrogate history in the light of globalization. What all these studies have in common is an ecological approach to their object of study and an attempt to eschew facile dichotomies.

Language ecology also offers a useful poststructuralist framework to examine intercultural contacts online. Having been mainly interested up to now in the linguistic aspects of online communication, applied linguistics has assumed that internet users share the same internet and social networking culture across languages. As online sites proliferate, it will be interesting to see

221

to what extent IC becomes as stratified as it is in real life. Although many hail the potential of virtual environments to increase intercultural contacts and bring about world peace, some are expressing concern that the ease of IC online fosters an illusion of understanding that conceals the growing commodification of meaning and cultural alienation.

## 6. Research methods and pedagogic practice

### Research methods

The implications of IC research in applied linguistics can be found in research methods and pedagogic practice. As far as research methods are concerned, applied linguistics has traditionally been more inclined to use structuralist approaches of the quantitative and the qualitative kind. Structuralist approaches to IC research have readily found applications in the studies of immigrant ESL learners, and Vygotsky-inspired contact zones of proximal development have been amply put to use in literacy research for native and non-native speakers alike. Even though there is definitely an interest right now for poststructuralist, hermeneutic research approaches (see below), the pressure to produce research that conforms to the criteria of reliability and validity of the hard sciences has discouraged many a young researcher from adopting truly ecological or post-structuralist methods of inquiry. Moreover, the expectation among policy makers and the educational establishment that applied linguistic research will yield direct results in the classroom has put pressure on researchers to produce quantifiable and measurable results that help language policy makers and educators to predict outcomes, make decisions, and plan ahead.

However, given the increased unpredictability of the job market and of language policies regarding intercultural contacts, applied linguists feel attracted to more complex descriptive approaches that do justice to the increasingly complex phenomena under study. These phenomena reveal non-linear, relational, and emergent subjectivities and historicities that need to be approached through more ecological and dynamic research designs that bring applied linguistics closer to the human sciences. The essentialization of cultures that was prevalent in applied linguistics 20 years ago has given way to a more nuanced understanding of the "foreign". The growing interest in multilingualism has made IC into a multidimensional affair that calls for a variety of modes of analysis and interpretation (e.g., see Zarate *et al.* 2010). For example, the growing interest in reflexive approaches in the social sciences encourages researchers to objectify their subject position rather than adopt the positivistic stance typical of the natural sciences. Furthermore, the study of IC in virtual spaces not only realigns the time and space axes of human interaction, but affects its degree of reality as well. Research on online exchanges has now to account for symbolic dimensions of intercultural encounters that, like the one between Pope Benedict and his American audiences, offer various possibilities of authentic, citational, actual, ostensible, animated, simulated discourse and its interpretations.

### Pedagogic practice

Pedagogic practice is also affected by IC research. In 2007, the Ad Hoc Committee for Foreign Languages of the American Modern Language Association, chaired by Mary Louise Pratt, issued a report that defined the goal of foreign language majors at American colleges and universities as follows:

> The language major should be structured to produce a specific outcome: educated speakers who have deep translingual and transcultural competence … The idea of translingual and

transcultural competence [ ... ] places value on the ability to operate between languages
[ ... ] This kind of foreign language education systematically teaches differences in meaning, mentality, and worldview as expressed in American English and in the target language.
[ ... ] In the course of acquiring functional language abilities, students are taught critical
language awareness, interpretation and translation, historical and political consciousness,
social sensibility, and aesthetic perception.

*MLA Ad Hoc Committee on Foreign Languages (2007: 237–38)*

The notion of transcultural competence that Pratt (1992) coined in the course of her study of
the IC between Incas and Spanish conquistadores in colonial times intends to go beyond
grammatical accuracy and communicative appropriateness to capture the difficult and sometimes
painful work of cultural translation from one worldview into the other—what Geertz referred
to by the phrase: "displaying the logic of their ways of [thinking] in the locutions of ours" (see
above). The injunction of the MLA Report for students to learn how to "operate between
languages" sets an inordinately greater challenge than just learning how to approximate the
native speaker. Operating between languages means knowing which language to use with
whom, to what effect, when to talk, when to remain silent, when to speak about what and in
the presence of whom, and the significance of code-switching. It requires becoming aware of
such discursive practices as: intertextuality, interdiscursivity, recontextualization (Briggs and
Bauman 1992). As in the *Newshour* interview about Pope Benedict's statements, operating
between languages requires an ability to reframe the ongoing discourse and find satisfactory and
symbolically powerful subject positions for oneself and others. It also entails an awareness of the
multiple timescales on which the discourse unfolds and an ability to capitalize on the layered
simultaneity of various historical discourses operating in the present. This kind of ability has
been called "symbolic competence" (Kramsch 2009d) to further characterize the third place of
the language user in a situation of IC.

## Related topics

Culture; discourse; essentialism; identity; ideology; interaction studies; language ecology;
othering; pragmatics; poststructuralism; power; stereotyping; structuralism

## Further reading

Grosjean, F. (2010) *Bilingualism: Life and Reality*, Cambridge: Harvard University Pres (a realistic treatment
of what it means to grow up bilingual).
Hoffman, E. (1989) *Lost in Translation: A Life in a New Language*, New York: Penguin (a classic autobiographical
account of an immigrant's encounter with a new language and culture).
Lugones, M. (1987) 'Playfulness, "world"-travelling, and loving perception', *Hypatia*, 2(2): 3–19 (a moving
testimony about living between cultures).

## References

Bhabha, H.K. (2010) 'Dissemination. Time, narrative and the margins of the modern nation', in *The
Location of Culture*, London: Routledge, pp. 199–244.
Block, D. (2009) 'Identity in applied linguistics: the need for conceptual exploration', in Li We and Vivian
Cook (eds) *Contemporary Applied Linguistics*, London: Continuum, pp. 215–32.
Blommaert, J. (2005) *Discourse*, Cambridge: Cambridge University Press.
Blum-Kulka, S, House, J. and Kasper G. (eds) (1989) *Cross-Cultural Pragmatics: Requests and Apologies*,
Vol. XXXI, Norwood, NJ: Ablex.

Boner, E. (2011) 'The making of the "entrepreneur" in Tanzania: experimenting with neo-liberal power through discourses of partnership, entrepreneurship, and participatory education', unpublished PhD thesis, University of California, Berkeley, CA.

Briggs, C. and Bauman, R. (1992) 'Genre, intertextuality, and social power', *Journal of Linguistic Anthropology*, 2(2): 131–72.

Buruma, I. and Margalit, A. (2004) *Occidentalism: The West in the Eyes of its Enemies*, London: Penguin.

Canagarajah, A.S. (1999) *Resisting Linguistic Imperialism in English Teaching*, Oxford: Oxford University Press.

Duranti, A. and Goodwin, C. (eds) (1992) *Rethinking Context*, Cambridge: Cambridge University Press.

Fairclough, N. (1989) *Language and Power*, London: Longman.

——(1992) *Discourse and Social Practice*, Cambridge: Polity Press.

Fanon, F. (2004) 'On national culture', in F. Fanon, *The Wretched of the Earth*; trans. R. Philcox, New York/Harmondsworth: Penguin, pp. 145–80.

Fill, A. and Mühlhäusler, P. (eds) (2001) *The Ecolinguistics Reader: Language, Culture and the Environment*, London: Continuum.

Gee, J.P., Lankshear, C. and Hull, G. (1996) *The New Work Order: Behind the Language of the New Capitalism*, Boulder, CO: Westview Press.

Geertz, C. (1983) *Local Knowledge*, New York: Basic Books.

Gumperz, J.J. (1992) 'Contextualization and understanding', in A. Duranti and C. Goodwin (eds) *Rethinking Context: Language as an Interactive Phenomenon*, Cambridge: Cambridge University Press, pp. 229–52.

Gumperz, J.J. and Roberts, C. (1991) 'Understanding in intercultural encounters', in J. Blommaert and J. Verschueren (eds) *The Pragmatics of Intercultural and International Communication*, Amsterdam: John Benjamins, pp. 51–90.

Gutierrez, K., Baquedano-Lopez, P. and Tejeda, C. (1999) 'Rethinking diversity: hybridity and hybrid language practices in the third space', *Mind, Culture and Activity*, 6(4): 286–303.

Hanks, W. (1996) *Language and Communicative Practices*, Boulder, CO: Westview Press.

——(2010) *Converting Words: Maya in the Age of the Cross*, Berkeley, CA: University of California Press.

Haugen, E. (1972) *The Ecology of Language*, Stanford, CA: Stanford University Press.

Kostogriz, A. (2002) 'Teaching literacy in multicultural classrooms: towards a pedagogy of "thirdspace"'. Online. Available: www.aare.edu.au/02pap/kos02346.htm (accessed 1 June 2010).

Kramsch, C. (1993) *Context and Culture in Language Teaching*, Oxford: Oxford University Press.

——(1998) *Language and Culture*, Oxford: Oxford University Press.

——(ed.) (2002) *Language Acquisition and Language Socialization: Ecological Perspectives*, London: Continuum.

——(2009a) 'Cultural perspectives on language learning and teaching', in W. Knapp and B. Seidlhofer (eds) *Handbook of Foreign Language Communication and Learning*, Berlin: Mouton de Gruyter, pp. 219–46.

——(2009b) *The Multilingual Subject*, Oxford: Oxford University Press.

——(2009c) 'Third culture and language education', in L. Wei and V. Cook (eds) *Contemporary Applied Linguistics*, Vol. 1, *Language Teaching and Learning*, London: Continuum, pp. 233–54.

——(2009d) 'Discourse, the symbolic dimension of intercultural competence', in A. Hu and M. Byram (eds) *Intercultural Competence and Foreign Language Learning*, Tübingen: Gunter Narr Verlag, pp. 107–22.

Lado, R. (1957) *Linguistics across Cultures*, Ann Arbor, MI: University of Michigan Press.

Lakoff, R. (1990) *Talking Power: The Politics of Language*, New York: Basic Books.

Larsen-Freeman, D. and Cameron, L. (2008) *Complex Systems and Applied Linguistics*, Oxford: Oxford University Press.

Lemke, J. (2002) 'Language development and identity: multiple timescales in the social ecology of learning', in C. Kramsch (ed.) *Language Acquisition and Language Socialization*, London: Continuum, pp. 68–87.

Matsumoto, Y. (1988). 'Reexamination of the universality of face: politeness phenomena in Japanese', *Journal of Pragmatics*, 12(4): 403–26.

MLA Ad Hoc Committee on Foreign Languages (2007) 'Foreign languages and higher education: new structures for a changed world', *Profession*, 2007, 234–45.

Moerman, M. (1988) *Talking Culture: Ethnography and Conversation Analysis*, Philadelphia, PA: University of Pennsylvania Press.

Pennycook, A. (1994) *The Cultural Politics of English as an International Language*, London: Longman.

——(2001) *Critical Applied Linguistics: A Critical Introduction*, Mahwah, NJ: Erlbaum.

——(2007) *Global Englishes and Transcultural Flows*, London: Routledge.

Phillipson, R. (1993) *Linguistic Imperialism*, Cambridge: Cambridge University Press.

Pratt, M.L. (1992) 'Introduction: criticism in the contact zone', in *Imperial Eyes: Travel Writing and Transculturation*, London: Routledge.

——(2002) 'The traffic in meaning: translation, contagion, infiltration', *Profession*, 2002, 12: 25–36.

Risager, K. (2006) *Language and Culture*, Clevedon: Multilingual Matters.

Said, E. (1978) *Orientalism*, New York: Vintage.

Scollon, R. and Wong Scollon, S. (1990) 'Epilogue to "Athabaskan–English interethnic communication"', in D. Carbaugh (ed.) *Cultural Communication and Intercultural Contact*, Hillside, NJ: Lawrence Erlbaum, pp. 287–90.

——(1995; 2nd edn 2001) *Intercultural Communication: A Discourse Approach*, Oxford: Blackwell.

Seidlhofer, B. (ed.) (2003) *Controversies in Applied Linguistics*, Oxford: Oxford University Press.

Selinker, L. (1972) 'Interlanguage', *International Review of Applied Linguistics*, 10: 209–41.

Tannen, D. (1984) *Conversational Style*, Mahwah, NJ: Ablex.

Thurlow, C. and Jaworski, A. (2009) *Tourism Discourse: Language and Global Mobility*, London: Palgrave Macmillan.

Uryu, M. (2009) 'Another Thanksgiving dinner: language, identity and history in the age of globalization', unpublished PhD dissertation, University of California, Berkeley, CA.

van Lier, L. (2003) *The Ecology and Semiotics of Language Learning: A Sociocultural Perspective*, Dordrecht: Kluwer Academic.

Vygotsky, L.S. (1978) *Mind in Society: The Development of Higher Psychological Processes*, M. Cole, V. John-Steiner, S. Scribner, E. Souberman (eds), Cambridge, MA: Harvard University Press.

Wagner, L. (2010) '"We are children of this country": linguistic practice, territorial identity, and economic power of diasporic visitors in Morocco', paper presented at the 16th annual conference on Language, Interaction and Culture, UCLA, May 8, 2010.

Weedon, C. (1997) *Feminist Practice and Poststructuralist Theory*, 2nd edn, Oxford: Blackwell.

Weinrich, H. (1990; 2nd edn 2001) 'Economy and ecology in language', in A. Fill and P. Mühlhäusler (eds) *The Ecolinguistics Reader*, London: Continuum, pp. 91–100.

Whiteside, A. (forthcoming) 'Complexity theory/language ecology and linguistic data analysis', in P. Benson and L. Cooker (eds) *The Applied Linguistic Individual: Sociocultural Approaches to Autonomy, Agency and Identity. Studies in Applied Linguistics*, London: Equinox.

Zarate, G., Lévy, D. and Kramsch, C. (eds) (2010) *Handbook of Multilingualism and Multiculturalism*, Paris: Editions des Archives Contemporaines.

Understanding intercultural transitions: from adjustment to acculturation

# 14

# Beyond cultural categories

## Communication, adaptation and transformation

*Young Yun Kim*

## 1. Introduction

'You cannot step into the same river twice, for fresh water is forever flowing towards you', observed Heraclitus of Ephesus, a Greek philosopher of the late sixth century BCE. This ancient insight into the human condition is relevant today more than ever before. Spurred by the globalization of human activities and the increasing interface of cultural traditions, we are in the midst of a historically unprecedented scope and pace of change. Some of the most profound and all-encompassing changes are being experienced by people who move across cultural boundaries. Countless immigrants and refugees leave their familiar milieu to build a new home in a foreign land, along with numerous temporary sojourners – from diplomats, military personnel, missionaries and business employees to construction workers, athletes, artists, musicians, writers, professors and students.

Although unique in individual circumstances and varied in scope, intensity, and duration, all strangers in a new and unfamiliar environment embark on the common project of establishing and maintaining a relatively stable and reciprocal relationship with the environment. Even relatively short-term sojourners must be at least minimally concerned with building a level of fitness that is necessary for their daily functioning. Given sufficient time, even those with the intention of confining themselves to only superficial relationships with the host environment are likely to be changed by the experience 'in spite of themselves' (Taft 1977: 150). This, in a nutshell, describes the phenomenon of cross-cultural adaptation at the individual level being addressed in this chapter.

## 2. Historical overview

Academic enquiry into the phenomenon of cross-cultural adaptation has been vast and varied across social science disciplines. This field of study became formalized in the 1930s when the Social Science Research Council adopted the term 'acculturation' to represent the new enquiry in cultural anthropology. The Council provided the parameters for this new field, which dealt with 'those phenomena which result when groups of individuals have different cultures and come into first-hand contact with subsequent changes in the original pattern of either or both groups'

(Redfield *et al.* 1936: 149). Accordingly, anthropologists such as Herskovits (1958) have approached the acculturation phenomenon largely at the level of cultural groups, focusing on the dynamics of change in traditional cultures and the presence of kin, friends and social organizations within immigrant communities. Sociologists, likewise, have focused on group-level issues pertaining to the structural 'assimilation' of immigrant groups within and across generations, employing indicators such as intermarriage and socioeconomic status (e.g. Anderson and Saenz 1994).

Paralleling the macro-level approaches to cross-cultural adaptation are a wide range of individual-level approaches employed by researchers mainly in psychology and communication. Major developments in the micro-level studies of long-term and short-term cross-cultural adaptation are briefly described below, along with a number of more notable theoretical accounts thereof.

## Long-term adaptation: strain, change, strategy

One of the central issues addressed in studies of long-term cross-cultural adaptation is the psychological and social strain immigrants and other settlers experience in response to their cultural uprooting and dislocation. Various terms have been employed to refer to such strain including 'marginality' (Park 1928; Stonequist 1937), 'cultural fatigue' (Taft 1977), 'acculturative stress' (Berry 1975) and 'adaptive stress' (Kim 1988, 2001, 2005). Others in psychiatry have focused on severe symptoms of mental illness such as emotional trauma and paranoia (e.g. Kinzie *et al.* 1980).

By far the most dominant issue in long-term adaptation studies is the cumulative nature of adaptive change that takes place over time within individuals and in their relationship to the host environment. Taft (1966) delineated seven stages of 'assimilation' of individual immigrants, moving progressively from the 'cultural learning' stage to the 'congruence' stage. A similar directionality of change towards assimilation was demonstrated by Nagata (1969) across successive generations of Japanese Americans. Many other studies have documented a similar long-term assimilative trend (e.g. Van Oudenhoven and Eisses 1998).

Based on cross-sectional comparisons according to the length of residence, numerous studies such as these have provided a substantial body of largely consistent empirical evidence for an incremental and progressive trend of adaptation. A common assumption underlying these studies has been that most, if not all, long-term settlers who live and work in a new environment need, and want, to be better adapted to the local language and cultural practices, so as to achieve some level of efficacy in their daily lives.

An alternative to the traditional perspective on long-term adaptive change has been employed in the bidimensional model of acculturation proposed by Berry (1980, 1990), among others. Rather than looking at the adaptive changes in individuals over time, Berry offers a psychological and pluralistic way of understanding immigrant experience. The theory is built on two central issues that immigrants confront: (1) cultural maintenance; and (2) contact and participation in the host society and its culture. With respect to cultural maintenance, the subject is asked to respond to the question: 'Are cultural identity and customs of value to be retained?' With respect to contact and participation in the host society, the subject is asked to respond to the question: 'Are positive relations with the larger society of value and to be sought?' By combining the response types (yes, no) to these two questions, four 'acculturation strategies' are identified: 'integration' (yes, yes), 'assimilation' (no, yes), 'separation' (yes, no) and 'marginality' (no, no). As a model to assess the state, or location, of an individual on the orthogonal domains of home and host culture identification, Berry's theory has been utilized widely in a variety of cultural contexts (e.g. Berry 2008).

## Short-term adaptation: culture shock, U-curve and W-curve

By and large, studies of short-term adaptation of sojourners have investigated the experience of 'culture shock' and the related 'U-curve' and 'W-curve' processes of psychological adjustment. Oberg (1960: 177) coined the term 'culture shock' to describe 'the anxiety that results from losing all our familiar signs and symbols of social intercourse'. Subsequently, a number of alternative conceptions of culture shock have been offered. Bennett (1977), for example, expanded the meaning of culture shock, and regarded it as part of the general 'transition shock', a natural consequence of individuals' inability to interact with the new environment effectively. Zaharna (1989: 501) added to the discussion the notion of 'self-shock', emphasizing 'the double-binding challenge of identity'.

Although culture shock is typically associated with negative psychological impacts, many investigators have highlighted that most sojourners eventually achieve satisfactory adjustment. The idea of a 'U-shaped curve' of psychological adjustment was first introduced by Lysgaard (1955). Based on his study of Norwegian Fulbright scholars in the United States, Lysgaard observed that psychological adjustment followed a U-curve, that is, the individuals who experienced the most difficulty during their sojourn in the US were those who had stayed for between 6 and 18 months, compared with those who had stayed for either less than 6 months or more than 18 months. Oberg (1960) subsequently identified the four stages of a U-curve leading to an eventual satisfactory adjustment: a 'honeymoon' phase, followed by a period of crisis, a period of adjustment, integration and enjoyment of the new environment. The U-curve hypothesis has been extended further to the 'W-curve' (Gullahorn and Gullahorn 1963) by adding the re-entry (or return-home) phase, during which the sojourner once again goes through a similar process.

Although the U- and W-curve hypotheses have proven to be heuristic to the extent that they remain popular and are intuitively appealing, these theories have demonstrated inconsistent results when applied to different research contexts. Comprehensive reviews of culture shock research (e.g. Anderson 1994; Ward *et al.* 1998, 2001) have concluded that support for the U- and W-curve hypotheses is limited and that evidence for the theories' claims tends to be inconclusive. Arguments have also been made that the cultural shock experience must be viewed in a broader context of learning and personal development. Adler (1972/1987: 29), for example, explained that culture shock should not be viewed as a 'disease for which adaptation is the cure, but is at the very heart of the cross-cultural learning experience, self-understanding, and change'. Consistent with this view, Ruben and Kealey (1979) reported that, among Canadian technical advisors and their spouses on 2-year assignments in Kenya, the magnitude of culture shock was positively related to the individuals' social and professional effectiveness within the new environment.

## Factors explaining the level of cross-cultural adaptation

Given that no two individuals adapt identically even under similar circumstances, a large number of theoretical models have been proposed to explain or predict differing levels or rates of individual adaptation. Factors identified in such models range widely from country of origin, pre-departure expectations and preparedness, personality characteristics (e.g. patience, empathy and flexibility) and psychological orientations (e.g. perception, attitude, motivation, uncertainty and anxiety), communication patterns/skills (e.g. language competence/preference, listening skills, interpersonal relationship development/preference, mass media behaviours and job-related technical skills) to demographic characteristics (e.g. age, age at the time of resettlement, socioeconomic status, length of residence and marital status). For example, Coelho (1958) focused on the complexity of sojourners' perception of members of the host society, whereas Epstein *et al.* (1996)

assessed 'linguistic acculturation' and Gudykunst (2005) focused on two psychological factors, uncertainty and anxiety. Mass communication researchers, meanwhile, have examined the patterns of mass media usage in relation to degrees of change in cultural values (e.g. Stilling 1997).

Over the years, efforts have been made to explain the level of cross-cultural adaptation based on a broader range of factors. Shuval (1963), for example, included a variety of factors from demographic factors (such as age and sex) and psychological factors (such as knowledge of the host language, motivation for acculturation and positive attitude towards the host society) to factors of social integration (including interpersonal relationships with the natives).

More recent efforts to explain cross-cultural adaptation broadly include the two-tiered conceptions proposed by Berry et al. (2006) and by Ward (1995, 2001). According to Berry et al. (2006: 13), 'psychological adaptation' refers to 'good mental health' reflected in 'few psychological problems of anxiety, depression, and psychosomatic symptoms' and 'a high sense of well being (i.e., self-esteem and life satisfaction)', whereas 'sociocultural adaptation' refers to 'the quality of relationships between individuals and their sociocultural contexts'. Building on a similar two-tiered conception, Ward (1995, 2001) has proposed a theoretical model that identifies psychological and sociocultural forms of acculturation as outcomes of societal-level and individual-level factors. Included within Ward's framework are macro-level factors related to the sociopolitical, socioeconomic and demographic characteristics of both the acculturating individual's society of origin and the society of settlement, as well as micro-level factors that reflect both characteristics of the acculturating individual and situational elements of the acculturative experience.

## 3. An integrative communication approach

As suggested in the above historical overview, cross-cultural adaptation as a field of social scientific enquiry has been, and continues to be, one of many varied perspectives and conceptions. The field as a whole reflects wide-ranging interests, perspectives and foci that are specific to the individual investigators. With respect to individual-level adaptation across cultures, a variety of concepts and models have been employed to investigate specific types and aspects of the phenomenon – from long-term, cumulative–progressive adaptive changes and accompanying stresses and bidimensional psychological strategies of acculturation to the experience of culture shock and associated patterns of short-term psychological adaptation.

As an effort to seek greater conceptual cohesion in the field, the present author (Kim 1988, 2001, 2005) has proposed an integrative communication theory of cross-cultural adaptation. Predicated on a set of open systems assumptions about human nature (Bertalanffy 1968; Ford and Lerner 1992; Jantsch 1980), this theory brings together many of the existing perspectives, concepts, theoretical accounts and research findings with respect to short-term and long-term adaptation into a comprehensive communication framework. As such, this theory is discussed here in some detail as a way of examining the phenomenon of cross-cultural adaptation in its full dynamism and complexity.

### Integration of key terms

From the open systems perspective, human beings are self-organizing living systems that are equipped with the capacity to maintain an overall integrity in the face of the continual instability created by multiple influences from the environment. Such systemic integrity is possible because of the human capacity to adapt, that is, to develop new forms of relating to a given milieu. Placed at the intersection of the person and the environment, adaptation is essentially a communication process that occurs as long as the individual remains in contact with a given environment.

Accordingly, 'cross-cultural adaptation' is defined as the phenomenon in which individuals who, upon relocating to an unfamiliar cultural environment, strive to establish and maintain a relatively stable, reciprocal and functional relationship with the environment. At the core of this definition is the goal of achieving an overall 'fit' between their internal conditions and the conditions of the environment. In this perspective, cross-cultural adaptation refers to the 'entirety' of the phenomenon that includes both the person and the environment, as well as both the process and the outcomes of communication activities. As such, the term cross-cultural adaptation serves not as an independent or dependent variable, but as a 'superordinate conceptual category' representing all facets of the phenomenon, a higher level abstraction in which other commonly used terms such as acculturation and assimilation can be subsumed and their interrelationships identified.

First, cross-cultural adaptation is a phenomenon that occurs subsequent to the process of childhood 'enculturation' of individuals into recognizable members of a given cultural community. As children, we learn to relate to our social environment and its culture; that is, the universe of information and operative linguistic and non-linguistic communication rituals that gives coherence, continuity and distinction to a communal way of life. The familiar culture is the 'home world', which is associated closely with the family or significant others.

Second, all individuals entering a new and unfamiliar culture undergo some degree of new cultural learning, that is, the acquisition of the native cultural patterns and practices, particularly in areas of direct relevance to the daily functioning of the individual – from attire and food habits to behavioural norms and cultural values. The re-socialization activities are the very essence of 'acculturation', consistent with the definition offered by Marden and Meyer (1968: 36), among many others: 'the change in individuals whose primary learning has been in one culture and who take over traits from another culture'.

Third, acculturation is not a process in which new cultural elements are simply added to prior internal conditions. As new learning occurs, 'deculturation' (or unlearning) of some of the old cultural habits has to occur, at least in the sense that new responses are adopted in situations that would previously have evoked old, habitual ones. The act of acquiring something new is inevitably the 'losing' of something old, in much the same way as 'being someone requires the forfeiture of being someone else' (Thayer 1975: 240).

Fourth, as the interplay of acculturation and deculturation continues, the individual undergoes an internal transformation in the direction of 'assimilation', a state of the highest degree of acculturation and deculturation theoretically possible. Whether by choice or by circumstance, individuals vary in the distance they travel in their own adaptation process. For most people, assimilation remains a lifetime goal rather than an obtainable outcome, one that often requires the efforts of multiple generations.

Generally speaking, measurable degrees of assimilation are unlikely among temporary visitors or sojourners engaged in relatively short-term cross-cultural adaptation experiences. In comparison, numerous empirical studies focusing on historical change in immigrants have amply demonstrated the acculturative, deculturative and assimilative trend both within and across generations. A study by the American Jewish Committee, for example, reported a significant increase in the members' merging into non-Jewish organizations and a substantial decrease in their Jewish identification (Zweigenhalf 1979–80). Likewise, Suro (1998) found both acculturative and deculturative trends among Hispanics in the United States: long-term Hispanics showed diminished Hispanic cultural patterns in their judgements and increased social interactions with non-Hispanics.

Based on these basic considerations, Kim's integrative communication theory addresses two central questions: (1) what is the essential nature of the adaptation process individual settlers undergo over time?; and (2) why are some settlers more successful than others in attaining a level of psychosocial fitness in the host environment? The first question is addressed in the form of a process model – a process of personal evolution towards increased functional fitness and psychological health and a gradual emergence of intercultural identity. The second question is addressed by a structural model in which key dimensions of factors that facilitate or impede the adaptation process are identified and their interrelationships specified.

## The process of cross-cultural adaptation

The process model identifies a cumulative–progressive trajectory of an individual's adaptive change over time, highlighting the juxtapositions of the experiences of 'adaptation' with those of 'stress'. Faced with uncertainty and anxiety, individuals are temporarily in a state of stress, a condition of internal disequilibrium or 'symmetry breaks' (Jantsch 1980: 79). The state of internal flux is often met by the tendency to use various defence mechanisms such as denial, hostility, cynicism, avoidance and withdrawal, all of which are particularly acute during the initial phase of sojourn or immigration.

At the same time, stress experiences are the very force that drives individuals towards adaptation. It is through the impetus of stress that they are compelled to engage in adaptive activities of new learning and making adjustments in the existing cultural habits, which enables them to handle the transactions of daily living with greater efficacy. The interplay of stress and adaptation thus serves as a dialectic between disintegration and reintegration, between regression and progression and between permanence and change. Each stress experience presents strangers with an opportunity to recreate themselves. Over time, most people manage to achieve an increasing capacity to detect similarities and differences between the new surroundings and the home culture and better able to manage their changed circumstances. What accompanies successful and cumulative management of the stress adaptation disequilibrium is a subtle and often imperceptible psychological 'growth', a form of internal change in the direction of increased perceptual and cognitive complexity with respect to the host culture.

Together, stress, adaptation and growth constitute the 'stress–adaptation–growth dynamic', a three-pronged conceptual representation of the psychological underpinning of the cross-cultural adaptation process (see Figure 14.1). The overall upward–forward process does not unfold in a smooth, arrow-like linear progression, but in a cyclic and fluctuating pattern of drawback-to-leap: each stressful experience is responded to with a temporary setback which, in turn, activates adaptive energy to reorganize and re-engage in the activities of cultural learning and internal change, bringing about a new self-reintegration. Integrated in this model of the stress–adaptation–growth dynamic is the traditional linear–progressive conceptions of long-term adaptation and the U-curve model of short-term adaptation. This model also presents additional information about the adaptation process, that is, large and sudden changes occur during the initial phase when the severity of difficulties and disruptions is likely to be high. Over time, the fluctuations of stress and adaptation are likely to subside, leading to an overall calming in the individual experiences of interacting with the host environment.

## The structure of cross-cultural adaptation

We now turn to the question of differential adaptation rates, or speeds, at which cross-cultural adaptation occurs in individual cases. As depicted in Figure 14.2, Kim's structural model identifies key dimensions and factors that interactively facilitate, or impede, a given individual's adaptive change over time. The interlocking bilateral functional relationships between and among these constructs are specified in twenty-one theorems (e.g. 'Theorem 1: the greater the host communication competence, the greater the participation in host social (interpersonal, mass)

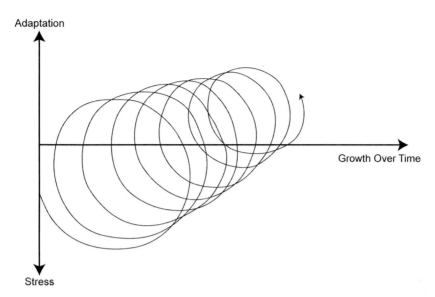

Figure 14.1 The process of cross-cultural adaptation
Source: Kim (2001: 59). Reproduced with permission.

communication'; 'Theorem 7: the greater the host receptivity and host conformity pressure, the greater the host communication competence'; Kim 2001: 91–92).

## Communication factors

At the heart of the structure of cross-cultural adaptation is the individual's personal and social communication activities, that is, host communication competence and his or her engagement with the host environment through participation in host interpersonal and mass communication activities.

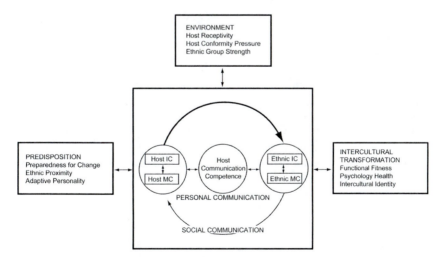

Figure 14.2 The structure of cross-cultural adaptation
Source: Kim (2001: 87). Reproduced with permission.
Notes: IC = Interpersonal Communication
      MC = Mass Communication

'Host communication competence' refers to the overall internal capacity of a stranger to decode and encode information in accordance with the host cultural communication practices. It is composed of three interrelated subcategories: cognitive, affective and operational. 'Cognitive competence' includes the knowledge of the host language and culture, history, social institutions and rules of interpersonal conduct. Knowledge of the host language, in particular, serves as the primary conduit for adaptation, enabling strangers to access the accumulated records of the host culture, including an understanding of how to communicate with native speakers in ways that are appropriate in local contexts.

'Affective competence' refers to the emotional and motivational capacity to deal with the various challenges of living in the host environment. A positive, willing and flexible self–other orientation helps to engender greater openness and lessen unwarranted negativism towards new cultural experiences. Also included in affective competence is the development of a capacity to appreciate and participate in the local people's emotional and aesthetic sensibilities, thereby making it possible for strangers to establish a meaningful psychological connection with the native inhabitants. The cognitive and affective capabilities work side by side with the 'operational competence', the capacity to express outwardly by choosing a 'right' combination of verbal and nonverbal acts in specific social transactions of the host environment.

Host communication competence is directly and reciprocally linked to participation in the social communication processes of the host society through interpersonal and mass communication channels. 'Host interpersonal communication' activities involving cultural native people offer opportunities for 'corrective exchanges' with respect to the use of the host communication system, including its verbal and nonverbal codes. Through active participation in host interpersonal communication activities, non-natives can begin the process of constructing a set of potentially satisfying and supportive relationships with natives. Host communication competence further facilitates, and is facilitated by, participation in 'host mass communication' activities. Through a wide range of mediated communication systems such as radio, television, newspaper, magazine, movie, art, literature, music and drama, non-natives interact with their host cultural milieu without direct interpersonal involvements. Such mass communication activities help broaden the scope of new cultural learning beyond one's immediate social context.

In many societies and communities today, non-natives' social communication activities involve their co-ethnics or co-nationals and home cultural experiences as well. Some form of 'ethnic interpersonal communication' activities through ethnic mutual aid or self-help organizations, including religious organizations, may be available to render assistance to those who need material, informational, emotional and other forms of social support. In addition, opportunities to participate in 'ethnic mass communication' activities through ethnic newspapers, radio stations and television programmes may be accessible via the internet or in pre-recorded audio- and videotapes and computer disks. Participation in ethnic interpersonal and mass communication activities can be helpful in the initial phase of the cross-cultural adaptation process when newly arrived strangers lack host communication competence and access to host interpersonal resources.

Beyond the initial phase, however, heavy and prolonged reliance on co-ethnics is likely to be either an insignificant influence on, or impede, the long-term adaptation process with respect to the host society at large.

## Environmental factors

The adaptive function of the individual's host communication competence and social (interpersonal, mass) communication activities cannot be fully explained in isolation from the conditions of the host environment. As different societies and communities present different environments for cross-cultural adaptation, a given stranger can be more successful in adapting to a certain environment than to another one. Of various environmental characteristics, three key factors are identified in Kim's theory as significant with respect to an individual's adaptation process: (1) host receptivity; (2) host conformity pressure; and (3) ethnic group strength. These three factors help define the relative degrees of 'push-and-pull' that a given host environment presents to the individual.

'Host receptivity' refers to the degree to which the receiving environment welcomes and accepts strangers into its interpersonal networks and offers them various forms of informational, technical, material and emotional support. A society or a community can be more hospitable towards certain groups of strangers while unwelcoming towards certain others. Along with receptivity, individuals face differing levels of conformity pressure from the host environment.

Individual sojourners and immigrants face 'host conformity pressure' to the extent to which the host environment challenges them, implicitly or explicitly, to act in accordance with the normative patterns of the host culture. Different host environments show different levels of acceptance and appreciation of strangers and their ethnic characteristics. In general, people in heterogeneous and cosmopolitan societies such as the United States tend to hold more pluralistic and tolerant attitudes towards ethnic differences, thereby exerting less pressure on strangers to change their habitual ways.

The third environmental factor, 'ethnic group strength', refers to the relative status or standing of a particular ethnic group in the context of the surrounding host society. Depending on relative group size or status, stronger ethnic groups are likely to provide their members with a more vibrant subculture and practical services to their members. In doing so, however, a strong ethnic community tends to encourage the maintenance of ethnic culture and communication, and even exert its own pressure to conform to the ethnic cultural norms, thereby discouraging individual community members' active social engagement with the host environment at large.

## Predisposition factors

New arrivals begin the cross-cultural adaptation process with a different set of backgrounds that help to set the parameters for the way they relate to the new environment and their own subsequent adaptive changes. The various predispositional differences are grouped into three categories: (1) preparedness; (2) ethnic proximity/distance; and (3) personality predisposition. Together, these characteristics help define the degree of a stranger's adaptive potential.

'Preparedness' includes the level of readiness to undertake the process of cross-cultural adaptation by developing host communication competence and participating in host social communication activities. Influencing the individual's readiness are differing levels of formal and informal learning of the host language and culture prior to moving to the host society. In addition, preparedness is often influenced by whether the move to the host society is voluntary or involuntary and for how long. Voluntary, long-term immigrants, for example, are likely to enter the host society with greater willingness to make the necessary efforts to adapt, compared with temporary visitors or those who relocate unwillingly for reasons other than their own volition.

The second factor, 'ethnic proximity/distance', addresses the extent to which the ethnicity of an individual immigrant or sojourner plays a role in the cross-cultural adaptation process by serving as a certain level of advantage or handicap. The individual's visual (such as height, skin colour and facial features) and audible (such as accents and other speech patterns) ethnic markers, as well as intrinsic ethnic characteristics (such as religious beliefs and cultural values), potentially influence the degree of host receptivity in terms of the native peoples' willingness or preparedness to welcome them into their interpersonal networks.

Along with preparedness and ethnicity, the non-native's 'adaptive personality', or a set of more or less enduring traits of sensibilities, facilitates his or her own adaptation process. Adaptive personality serves as the inner resource, based on which the individual pursues new cultural experiences with enthusiasm and success. Of particular interest are three interrelated personality resources that would help facilitate the strangers' adaptation by enabling them to endure stressful challenges and to maximize new learning: (1) openness, an internal posture that is receptive to new information; (2) strength, the quality of resilience, patience, hardiness and persistence; and (3) positivity, an affirmative and optimistic outlook that enables the individual to better endure stressful events with a belief in the possibilities of life in general.

## Three facets of intercultural transformation

Through the interactive workings of the above-described factors of personal and social communication, of the environment and of the individual's backgrounds, the process of cross-cultural adaptation unfolds. Emerging in the adaptation process are three interrelated facets of adaptive change and intercultural transformation of the individual: (1) increased functional fitness in carrying out daily transactions; (2) improved psychological health in dealing with the environment; and (3) emergence of an intercultural identity orientation. These three facets are interrelated developmental continua, in which individual strangers can be placed at different locations reflecting the different levels of adaptive change at a given point in time.

Most individuals who find themselves in an unfamiliar environment instinctively strive to 'know their way around'. Through repeated activities resulting in new learning and internal reorganizing, they achieve an increasing 'functional fitness' in the host environment. Well-adapted individuals would be those who have accomplished a desired level of effective functional relationship with the host environment – particularly with those individuals with whom they carry out their daily activities.

Along with functional fitness, everyone needs the ongoing validation of his or her social experience, thereby maintaining a satisfactory level of 'psychological health', a term that integrates related concepts such as culture shock and psychological adaptation. In the absence of adequate host communication competence, engagement in host social communication activities and functional fitness, individuals are subject to frustration, leading to the symptoms of maladaptation such as marginalization and alienation. Conversely, those individuals who have acquired high-level host communication competence, who actively participate in host social processes and who are proficient in their daily transactions in the host society are likely to enjoy a greater sense of fulfilment and efficacy.

Adaptive changes also include the emergence of an 'intercultural identity', a gradual and often unintended psychological evolution beyond the boundaries of childhood enculturation, an orientation towards self and others that is no longer rigidly defined by either the identity linked to the 'home' culture or the identity of the host culture. Intercultural identity transformation manifests itself in the progressive attainment of a self–other orientation that is increasingly 'individuated' and 'universalized'. As an individual's cultural identity evolves towards intercultural identity, that person's definition of self and others becomes simultaneously less restricted by rigid cultural and social categories and more broadened and enriched by an increased ability to, at once, particularize and humanize his or her perception of each communicative event.

## Empirical evidence

An extensive number of studies across the social sciences were examined and incorporated into the original formal construction (Kim 1988), and the subsequent elaboration (Kim 2001), of the above-described integrative communication theory of cross-cultural adaptation. Additionally, a substantial number of studies have tested directly both the process model and the structural model of this theory in a variety of research contexts. The latter group of studies includes those of Southeast Asian refugees (Kim 1989) and Haitian immigrants in the United States (Walker 1993), international university students in the United States (Tamam 1993) and in Japan (Maruyama 1998), American university exchange students overseas (Milstein 2005; Pitts 2009), Turkish employees of an American military organization in Germany (Braun 2001) and Korean expatriates in the United States and their counterparts in South Korea (Kim and Kim 2004), as well as native-born subcultural groups such as Native Americans (Kim *et al.* 1998) and Hispanic high-school students in the United States (McKay-Semmler 2010).

Perhaps one of the most succinct and eloquent testimonials to Kim's conception of the cross-cultural adaptation process and intercultural transformation was offered by Yoshikawa (1978). As someone who grew up in Japan and had lived in the United States for many years, Yoshikawa reflected on his own intercultural transformation as follows:

> I am now able to look at both cultures with objectivity as well as subjectivity; I am able to move in both cultures, back and forth without any apparent conflict. ... I think that something beyond the sum of each [cultural] identification took place, and that it became something akin to the concept of 'synergy' – when one adds 1 and 1, one gets three, or a little more. This something extra is not culture-specific but something unique of its own, probably the emergence of a new attribute or a new self-awareness, born out of an awareness of the relative nature of values and of the universal aspect of human nature. ... I really am not concerned whether others take me as a Japanese or an American; I can accept myself as I am. I feel I am much freer than ever. ...
>
> *Yoshikawa (1978: 220)*

## 4. Looking forward

Since the early twentieth century, academic enquiry in cross-cultural adaptation has been continuous and active across social science disciplines. Today, the field offers many different theoretical accounts and models to guide empirical studies with varying degrees of comprehensiveness, including some of the notable ones that have been examined in this chapter. On the whole, the theorizing activities have contributed to a significant advancement of the field towards a fuller understanding of how individuals, socialized in one culture, strive to forge a new life away from their familiar grounds, and how, in this process, they are changed by the cumulative communication experiences *vis-à-vis* the host environment.

Looking forward, we may foresee the continuing vitality of cross-cultural adaptation as a research domain. As long as people continue to interface across the boundaries of cultural and subcultural differences and engage each other in communication activities, issues of cross-cultural adaptation in general, and of identity transformation in particular, will be likely to have relevance and significance.

### Emerging research issues

One of the emerging research issues pertains to the advent of new communication technologies and their potential role in the cross-cultural adaptation process. A number of studies have begun to examine the potential influence of the rapid spread of various new forms of computer-based interpersonal and mass communication technologies on how sojourners and immigrants maintain relational ties back home and how they orient themselves to the host environment. For example, Cemalcilar *et al.* (2005) report that computer-mediated interpersonal communication activities (such as e-mail and the internet) have become the primary vehicle for maintaining relationships with folks back home, replacing many of the more traditional activities of making long-distance telephone calls and writing letters. Several other studies (e.g. Kim *et al.* 2009; Wang and Sun 2007) have suggested that mediated interpersonal communication may not change the positive theoretical relationship between active participation in host social processes and successful adaptive changes in the host society at large. Future studies in a variety of research contexts can produce a clearer and more in-depth understanding of the role that new communication technologies play in shaping the nature of an individual's direct engagement with local people and their psychological and functional relationship with the host environment.

Another promising research avenue yet to be explored is the phenomenon of 'stay home' cross-cultural adaptation. In many parts of the world, particularly in large metropolitan areas, people no longer have to leave home to experience the acculturative and deculturative pressures. Physical distance no longer dictates the extent of exposure to the images, sounds and events of once distant cultures.

Moreover, many urban centres present their own contexts of new cultural learning, as the native inhabitants are routinely coming into direct or indirect contacts with various groups of cultural strangers. Such everyday encounters are likely to challenge some of the cultural assumptions and practices of the local people, thereby compelling them to undertake the stress–adaptation–growth process of cross-cultural adaptation themselves, just as the non-natives do.

## Reaching beyond categories

Even as academic enquiry in cross-cultural adaptation continues to evolve, it is clear from the existing knowledge base, and specifically from Kim's integrative communication theory, that cross-cultural adaptation is a journey that ultimately rests on the conscious and unconscious decisions each individual makes. By resisting change, one can minimize the change. By accelerating adaptive efforts, one can maximize it.

Should we choose to adapt successfully, we need to recognize the critical importance of host communication competence and work to cultivate it. Host communication competence is, indeed, the *sine qua non* of successful adaptation, as both the quality and the quantity of our social engagement, functional fitness and psychological fitness in the host community hinges on it. The full benefit of acquiring host language competence, in particular, is the access it gives to the advantages that native speakers enjoy. In addition to the host language, we need to strive to understand the aesthetic and emotional sensibilities of local people, so that we may partake in their experiences meaningfully and intimately. We need to form and practice new habits of behaviour that will allow us to carry out our social activities closely aligned with those of the natives.

Each time we cross cultural boundaries, we are presented with multitudes of the challenge, as well as the opportunity, to learn and acquire new cultural categories. As we keep our sights on the goal of successful cross-cultural adaptation, we are able to reach beyond the conventional habit of defining ourselves and others according to cultural categories. We would want to embrace the real possibility of a gradual internal transformation along the way – a subtle internal change leading to a way of being in our rapidly changing world that is less monocultural and more intercultural, less categorical and more individuated and universalized, with an increasing blurring of lines between 'us' and 'them'.

Modern history presents countless cases of successfully adapted immigrants and sojourners. They demonstrate to us that personal transformation beyond cultural categories is not only a theoretical possibility but an empirical reality. They show us that cultivating an intercultural identity does not require us to be disloyal to our home culture, that cross-borrowing of identities is often an act of appreciation that leaves neither the lender nor the borrower deprived and that the experiences of going through adaptive challenges bring about a special privilege and freedom – to think, feel and act beyond the confines of any single culture. The Indian-born British author Salman Rushdie speaks to this freedom in *East, West* (1994: 211) in the voice of the book's narrator: 'I, too, have ropes around my neck, I have them to this day, pulling me this way and that, East and West, the nooses tightening, commanding, *choose, choose.* … Ropes, I do not choose between you. … I choose neither of you, and both. Do you hear? I refuse to choose'.

## Related topics

Accommodation; acculturation; hybridity; identity; intercultural competence; intercultural contact; mobility; technology; third space

## Further reading

Berry, J.W. (1990) 'Psychology of acculturation: understanding individuals moving between cultures', in R. Brislin (ed.) *Applied Cross-cultural Psychology*, Newbury Park, CA: Sage, pp. 232–53 (a presentation of Berry's theory of psychological acculturation).

Kim, Y.Y. (2001) *Becoming Intercultural: An Integrative Theory of Communication and Cross-cultural Adaptation*, Thousand Oaks, CA: Sage (an extensive literature review and a formal explication of Kim's theory of cross-cultural adaptation).

Ward, C. (1995) 'Acculturation', in D. Landis and R.S. Bhagat (eds) *Handbook of Intercultural Training*, 2nd edn, Thousand Oaks, CA: Sage, pp. 124–47 (a presentation of Ward's theory of psychological and sociocultural forms of adaptation as outcomes of acculturation).

## References

Adler, P.S. (1972/1987) 'Culture shock and the cross-cultural learning experience', in L. Luce and E. Smith (eds) *Toward Internationalism*, Cambridge, MA: Newbury, pp. 24–25.

Anderson, L. (1994) 'A new look at an old construct: cross-cultural adaptation', *International Journal of Intercultural Relations*, 18: 293–328.

Anderson, R. and Saenz, R. (1994) 'Structural determinants of Mexican American intermarriage, 1975–80', *Social Science Quarterly*, 75: 414–30.

Bennett, J.M. (1977) 'Transition shock: putting culture shock in perspective', in N. Jain (ed.) *International and Intercultural Communication Annual*, Vol. 4, Falls Church, VA: Speech Communication Association, pp. 45–52.

Berry, J.W. (1975) 'Ecology, cultural adaptation, and psychological differentiation: traditional patterning and acculturative stress', in R. Brislin, S. Bochner and W. Lonner (eds) *Cross-cultural Perspectives on Learning*, New York: Sage, pp. 207–28.

——(1980) 'Acculturation as varieties of adaptation', in A. Padilla (ed.) *Acculturation: Theory, Models and Some New Findings*, Boulder, CO: Westview Press, pp. 9–25.

——(1990) 'Psychology of acculturation: understanding individuals moving between cultures', in Brislin, R. (ed.) *Applied Cross-cultural Psychology*, Newbury Park, CA: Sage, pp. 232–53.

——(2008) 'Globalization and acculturation', *International Journal of Intercultural Relation*, 32(4): 328–36.

Berry, J.W., Phinney, J., Kwak, K. and Sam, D. (2006) 'Introduction: goals and research framework for studying immigrant youth', in J.W. Berry, J. Phinney, D.L. Sam and P. Vedder (eds) *Immigrant Youth in Cultural Transition: Acculturation, Identity, and Adaptation across National Contexts*, Mahwah, NJ: Lawrence Erlbaum, pp. 1–14.

Bertalanffy, L. (1968) *General Systems Theory: Foundations, Developments, Applications*, New York: Braziller.

Braun, V. (2001) 'Intercultural communication and psychological health of Turkish workers in an American–German workplace in Germany', unpublished doctoral dissertation, Norman, OK: University of Oklahoma.

Cemalcilar, Z., Falbo, T. and Stapleton, L. (2005) 'Cyber communication: a new opportunity for international students' adaptation?', *International Journal of Intercultural Relations*, 29(1): 91–110.

Coelho, G. (1958) *Changing Images of America: A Study of Indian Students' Perceptions*, New York: Free Press.

Epstein, J., Botvin, J., Dusenberry, L., Diaz, T. and Kerner, T. (1996) 'Validation of an acculturation measure for Hispanic adolescents', *Psychological Reports*, 79: 1075–79.

Ford, D. and Lerner, R. (1992) *Developmental Systems Theory: An Integrative Approach*, Newbury Park, CA: Sage.

Gudykunst, W.B. (2005) 'An anxiety/uncertainty management (AUM) theory of strangers' intercultural adjustment', in W.B. Gudykunst (ed.) *Theorizing about Intercultural Communication*, Thousand Oaks, CA: Sage, pp. 419–57.

Gullahorn, J.T. and Gullahorn, J.E. (1963) 'An extension of the U-curve hypothesis', *Journal of Social Issues*, 19: 33–47.

Herskovits, M. (1958) *Acculturation: The Study of Culture Contact*, Gloucester, MA: Peter Smith.

Jantsch, E. (1980) *The Self-organizing Universe: Scientific and Human Implications of the Emerging Paradigm of Evolution*, New York: Pergamon.

Kim, Y.Y. (1988) *Communication and Cross-Cultural Adaptation: An Integrative Theory*, Clevedon: Multilingual Matters.

——(1989) 'Personal, social, and economic adaptation: the case of 1975–79 arrivals in Illinois', in D. Haines (ed.) *Refugees as Immigrants: Survey Research on Cambodians, Laotians, and Vietnamese in America*, Totowa, NJ: Rowman and Littlefield, pp. 86–104.

——(2001) *Becoming Intercultural: An Integrative Theory of Communication and Cross-cultural Adaptation*, Thousand Oaks, CA: Sage.

——(2005) 'Adapting to a new culture: an integrative communication theory' in W. Gudykunst (ed.) *Theorizing about Intercultural Communication*, Thousand Oaks, CA: Sage, pp. 375–400.

Kim, Y.Y. and Kim, Y.S. (2004) 'The role of the host environment in cross-cultural adaptation: a comparative analysis of Korean expatriates in the United States and their American counterparts in South Korea', *Asian Communication Research*, 1(1): 5–25.

Kim, Y.Y., Lujan, P. and Dixon, L. (1998) '"I can walk both ways": identity integration of American Indians in Oklahoma', *Human Communication Research*, 25(2): 252–74.

Kim, Y.Y., Izumi, S. and McKay-Semmler, K. (2009) 'The role of direct and mediated interpersonal communication in cross-cultural adaptation: a study of educated and long-term non-native residents in the United States', paper presented at the annual conference of the National Communication Association, Chicago, November 2009.

Kinzie, J., Tran, K., Breckenridge, A. and Bloom, J. (1980) 'An Indochinese refugee psychiatric clinic: culturally accepted treatment approaches', *American Journal of Psychiatry*, 137: 1429–32.

Lysgaard, S. (1955) 'Adjustment in a foreign society: Norwegian Fulbright grantees visiting the United States', *International Social Science Bulletin*, 7: 45–51.

McKay-Semmler, K. (2010) 'Cross-cultural adaptation of Hispanic youth: a study of communication patterns, functional fitness, and psychological health', unpublished doctoral dissertation, Norman, OK: University of Oklahoma.

Marden, C., and Meyer, G. (1968) *Minorities in America*, 3rd edn, New York: Van Nostrand Reinhold.

Maruyama, M. (1998) 'Cross-cultural adaptation and host environment: a study of international students in Japan', unpublished doctoral dissertation, Norman, OK: University of Oklahoma.

Milstein, T. (2005) 'Transformation abroad: sojourning and the perceived enhancement of self-efficacy', *International Journal of Intercultural Relations*, 29: 217–38.

Nagata, G. (1969) 'A statistical approach to the study of acculturation of an ethnic group based on communication oriented variables: the case of Japanese Americans in Chicago', unpublished doctoral dissertation, Urbana-Champaign, IL: University of Illinois.

Oberg, K. (1960) 'Cultural shock: adjustment to new cultural environments', *Practical Anthropology*, 7: 170–79.

Park, R. (1928) 'Human migration and the marginal man', *American Journal of Sociology*, 33(6): 881–93.

Pitts, M. (2009) 'Identity and the role of expectations, stress, and talk in short-term student sojourner adjustment: an application of the integrative theory of communication and cross-cultural adaptation', *International Journal of Intercultural Relations*, 33(6): 450–62.

Redfield, R., Linton, R. and Herskovits, M. (1936) 'Outline for the study of Acculturation', *American Anthropologist*, 38: 149–52.

Ruben, B. and Kealey, D. (1979) 'Behavioral assessment of communication competency and the prediction of cross-cultural adaptation', *International Journal of Intercultural Relations*, 3(1): 15–27.

Rushdie, S. (1994) *East, West: Stories*, New York: Pantheon.

Shuval, J. (1963) *Immigrants on the Threshold*, New York: Atherton Press.

Stilling, E. (1997) 'The electronic melting pot hypothesis: the cultivation of acculturation among Hispanics through television viewing', *Howard Journal of Communication*, 8: 77–100.

Stonequist, E. (1937) *The Marginal Man*, New York: Scribner's.

Suro, R. (1998) *Strangers among Us: How Latino Immigration is Transforming America*, New York: Knopf.

Taft, R. (1966) *From Stranger to Citizen*, London: Tavistock.

——(1977) 'Coping with unfamiliar cultures', in N. Warren (ed.) *Studies in Cross-Cultural Psychology*, Vol. 1, London: Academic Press, pp.121–53.

Tamam, E. (1993) 'The influence of ambiguity tolerance, open-mindedness, and empathy on sojourners' psychological adaptation and perceived intercultural communication effectiveness', unpublished doctoral dissertation, Norman, OK: University of Oklahoma.

Thayer, L. (1975) 'Knowledge, order, and communication', in B. Ruben and J.Y. Kim (eds) *General Systems Theory and Human Communication*, Rochelle Park, NJ: Hayden, pp. 237–45.

Van Oudenhoven, J.P. and Eisses, A.-M. (1998) 'Integration and assimilation of Moroccan immigrants in Israel and the Netherlands', *International Journal of Intercultural Relations*, 22(3): 293–307.

Walker, D. (1993) 'The role of the mass media in the adaptation of Haitian immigrants in Miami', unpublished doctoral dissertation, Bloomington, IN: Indiana University.

Wang, Y, and Sun, S. (2007) 'Internet use among Chinese students and its implications for cross-cultural adaptation', paper presented at the annual conference of the International Communication Association, San Francisco, May 2007.

Ward, C. (1995) 'Acculturation', in D. Landis and R. Bhagat (eds) *Handbook of Intercultural Training*, 2nd edn, Thousand Oaks, CA: Sage: pp. 124–47.

——(2001) 'The A, B, Cs of acculturation', in D. Matsumoto (ed.) *The Handbook of Culture and Psychology*, New York: Oxford University Press, pp. 411–45.

Ward, C., Okura, Y., Kennedy, A. and Kojima, T. (1998) 'The U-curve on trial: a longitudinal study of psychological and sociocultural adjustment during cross-cultural transition', *International Journal of Intercultural Relations*, 22: 277–91.

Ward, C., Bochner, S. and Furnham, A. (2001) *The Psychology of Culture Shock*, 2nd edn, Philadelphia, PA: Routledge.

Yoshikawa, M. (1978) 'Some Japanese and American cultural characteristics', in M. Prosser, *The Cultural Dialogue: An Introduction to Intercultural Communication*, Boston, MA: Houghton Mifflin, pp. 220–39.

Zaharna, R. (1989) 'Self-shock: the double-binding challenge of identity', *International Journal of Intercultural Relations*, 13(4): 501–25.

Zweigenhalf, R. (1979–80) 'American Jews: in or out of the upper class?', *Insurgent Sociologist*, 9: 24–37.

# 15

# Acculturating intergroup vitalities, accommodation and contact

*Howard Giles, Douglas Bonilla and Rebecca B. Speer*

## 1. Introduction

A compelling issue challenging many societies is the movement of people across their national and cultural boundaries. This can happen for many reasons, from planned tourism (Ward 2008) and educational exchanges to the sudden displacement of frightened refugees avoiding oppression and genocide (see Berry 2006). The current case of Uzbeks fleeing Kyrgyzstan constitutes a tragic example; the recent free movement of individuals across national borders in the European Union to seek more gainful employment prospects is another. Such movements are linked to cogent political dynamics and emotional reactions. PEW (2002) showed that, although 49 percent of Americans and 77 percent of Canadians felt immigration was "good", only 25 percent of Italians and 24 percent of Poles felt the same. In sum, immigration is an important, global, and sometimes contentious, issue.

Sometimes, the process of adapting to another culture works well for both the receiving and the immigrating groups. In such instances, the host society, with an enhanced standard of living, benefits economically from much-needed professionals and/or cheap labor and émigrés; each party is also enriched by the cultural patterns (e.g., music and food) of the other (Cleveland et al. 2009). Despite potential positive outcomes, acculturative stress (see Kim 2001; this volume) is an almost inevitable component of the adjustment process, exacerbated when there is little family cohesion (Luek and Wilson 2010). Transactively, too, emergent acculturation gaps between generations can negatively impact family bonds and relational satisfaction (Ho 2010).

On other occasions, and where large-scale linguistic and cultural dissimilarities are evident (Triandis 1994), such intergroup contact can be plagued by miscommunications, misattributions, and misunderstandings (e.g., Li 1999), especially so if acculturators are labeled intruders, outsiders, or invaders and perceived as straining the original integrity of the system (Dandy and Pe-Pua 2010). In still others, and for highly complex sociopolitical reasons—as exemplified by the position of many Muslim immigrants in Western countries—alienation, distrust, and intergroup discrimination violence can prevail (see Luek and Wilson 2010). Despite varying circumstances, both foreigners and hosts in a given environment undergo acculturation, involving adaptation to one another's presence.

Although the concept of acculturation dates back to ancient Greek philosophy, it has only in the last couple of centuries been explored to better understand the interaction and potential clashing of cultural groups (Triandis 2007). In the 1930s, cultural anthropologists adopted the term "acculturation" to describe the process by which two autonomous cultural groups mutually influence one another through direct intergroup contact (Redfield *et al.* 1936). Since then, researchers in the fields of anthropology (e.g., Herskovits 1958), sociology (e.g., Glazer and Moynihan 1963), social psychology (e.g., Bourhis *et al.* 2009), and intercultural communication (e.g., Kim 2001) have continued investigating acculturation issues experienced at the individual rather than the group level. Multidisciplinary work in this area has seen exponential growth in recent decades (Berry and Sam 2006).

Although the term acculturation typically connotes immigrant groups' adaptation to host cultures distinct from their heritage cultures, this chapter demonstrates (via a new integrative model) how theoretical and applied acculturation research would benefit from a perspective that highlights the roles of group vitality, communication accommodation, and intergroup contact. Before introducing these perspectives, it is important to review past conceptualizations of acculturation phenomena.

## 2. Extant frameworks

Although many acculturation theories exist across the social sciences, such frameworks can be classified into two core approaches (Liebkind 2001). The original approach conceptualizes acculturation as a unidimensional process whereby immigrant individuals abandon their heritage culture upon assimilating into mainstream society. Gordon's (1964) unidimensional assimilation model, for example, posited that immigrants adapt to the dominant host society over time in a linear, unidirectional fashion, depicted as movement along a bipolar continuum between maintenance of the culture of origin to complete adoption of the dominant host culture. Rather than a desired strategy or outcome, biculturalism, denoting the preservation of some aspects of the heritage culture and the achieved adoption of some fundamental features of the host culture, represents the midpoint on Gordon's continuum. Unidimensional models thus conceptualize biculturalism as a passing phase in the assimilation process, assuming that successful assimilation requires losing identification with the heritage culture to successfully adapt to the dominant host culture.

Criticism of such conceptualizations (e.g., their failure to account for cultural plurality and mutual influence between immigrants and members of the dominant host society) engendered alternative, bidimensional acculturation approaches (Bourhis *et al.* 1997). Berry's (1980a) framework was the first to account for multiculturalism (Phinney *et al.* 2001), positing that immigrants' heritage and host cultural identities should be depicted as independent dimensions rather than bipolar opposites on a continuum.

Two primary questions/dimensions with which immigrants must contend upon settling into a host society drove his framework: "is it valuable to retain one's traditional culture, and is it valuable to have positive relations with the larger society?" (Berry 1980b: 258). From these two questions, a four-quadrant classification emerged (see Figure 15.1); the quadrants describe four possible acculturation outcomes: integration, assimilation, separation, and marginalization. Integration denotes the simultaneous acceptance of the new culture and adherence to the values and norms of the culture of origin.

Assimilation, like integration, involves accepting the new culture, but differs in its rejection of the original culture. Tajfel and Turner's (1986) theory of social identity speaks to this strategy in terms of social mobility. The theory argues that an initial tactic that subordinate group

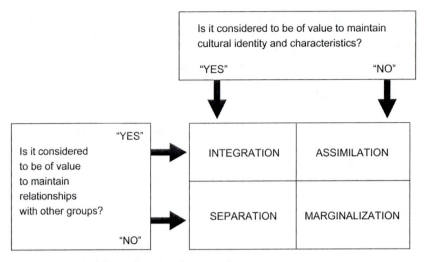

*Figure 15.1* Berry's (1980a) acculturation framework
*Source*: Reprinted with the permission of the author.

members use when seeking a more positive social identity is to abandon the dissatisfactory group for the dominant group to gain the social rewards associated with such an allegiance (see Mummendey *et al.* 1999). To achieve this elevated status, integrators have to acquire an array of skills, such as the out-group language and dialect, appropriate nonverbals, dress code, and espousing as well as investing in different ideologies and values. Such action requires a belief in boundary permeability for cultural passage (Reid *et al.* 2004). However, this undertaking is often unsuccessful given the complexities involved (see Taylor 1992), let alone enduring the emotional charge from certain members of one's ethnic in-group of cultural traitorhood (Hogg *et al.*1989).

In line with common in-group identity theory, assimilation usually involves de-categorizing one's ethnic identity and re-categorizing as a valued member of the superordinate national category (see Dovidio *et al.* 2005). However, although dominant groups enjoy encouraging specific individuals to assimilate, thereby underscoring their own values of meritocracy, if sufficient members of the subordinate groups do so successfully, this can diminish the superiority and privileges the dominant entity enjoys. Under such conditions of intergroup threat where intercultural boundaries between the in- and out-group are now deemed impermeable, the dominant group may likely restore its supremacy by recourse to various strategies of social competition and confrontation (Tajfel and Turner 1986).

Berry's (1980a) acculturative framework provides predictive power for intercultural interaction. Understanding the diverse outcomes possible in the acculturation process is crucial for capturing the phenomenon's complexity and the stress immigrants face when resolving the existence of conflicting cultural norms. Berry (1980b) claims that "differences between native groups indicate that the degree of cultural incongruity or disparity may be a factor in inducing stress, and analyses within groups suggest that stress may decline after a decision to further assimilate" (p. 264). Typically, the ability to adjust to the norms and values—and we would add, along with Kim (2001), the "communicative practices"—of the new culture yields the most satisfactory outcomes, including reducing adaptation stress and enhancing well-being (De Saissey 2009), for both younger (Sam and Berry 2009) and older immigrants (Jang and Chiriboga 2010). Further, this strategy, namely integration, is most immigrants' preference, as it is facilitated by acceptance and tolerance on the part of the dominant host society (Berry 1990).

The opposite of assimilation is the acculturative strategy of separation, whereby the original culture is upheld and the host culture is rejected. Both assimilation and separation orientations are, however, typically less preferred options than integration, as these often reflect mainstream pressure on immigrants to abandon their heritage cultural identity or to exist in isolated exclusion. Finally, marginalization is considered to be the least favorable of the four conditions with respect to acculturative stress and well-being, as it is often the result of the dominant host society's rejection of immigrants' heritage and, in the worst cases, rejection of immigrants as legitimate members of the host society. Perhaps for these very reasons, it appears that such a state is not commonly found (e.g., Schwartz and Zamboanga 2008). That said, work relating to the latter has focused on national cultural groupings; however, other kinds of intercultural contact, such as transitioning into police culture or moving into another cultural phase of the lifespan (e.g., elderliness), may also produce marginalization inclinations. Nonetheless, Bourhis et al. (1997) argued that, whichever acculturative path immigrants undergo, some minimal adaptation to the host culture occurs, even when strong ties to the heritage society are still embraced.

Although Berry's (1980a) model has made an invaluable contribution to understanding issues of identity and intercultural relations inherent to the acculturation process, it has faced scholarly criticism (e.g., Chirkov 2009; however, see Berry 2009). Ward (2008) argues, for example, that, despite widespread acknowledgment that acculturation occurs as a process, "it has most often been examined as a static outcome in itself", and it remains unclear "how people arrive at these orientations, and if they change overtime" (p. 107). Further, the model has been critiqued for failing to highlight the importance of contextual factors (e.g., Liebkind 2006) as well as "the fact that the host majority is also changed by the presence of culturally distinctive immigrants" (Bourhis et al. 1997: 376).

Consequently, Bourhis and colleagues (1997) proposed amendments to Berry's acculturation framework. The first was to ensure that both immigrants' attitudes and behavioral intentions were incorporated into the frame as Berry had intended. As such, Bourhis et al. reworded the question posed in the second dimension to read "Is it considered to be of value to adopt the culture of the host community?" (p. 378).

Bourhis et al.'s (1997) second refinement pertained to revising the marginalization orientation to reflect two distinct experiences of immigrants who reject both their heritage culture and the dominant host culture (see also Pickett and Brewer 2005). For some immigrants, the rejection of both cultures may result in "cultural alienation known as anomie", which may increase acculturative stress, negatively impact self-esteem, and thwart successful adaptation to the host society (p. 378). For other immigrants, however, the rejection of both cultures may be due to a preference for self-identifying as an individual rather than as a member of either cultural group. These individualists, in contrast to immigrants who experience anomie, may exhibit high levels of self-esteem and low levels of acculturative stress (Bourhis et al. 1997). Consequently, Bourhis et al.'s interactive acculturation model (IAM) features five strategies that can be assessed at individual or group levels: integration, assimilation, separation, anomie, and individualism.

Further, to demonstrate the mutual influence between members of immigrant groups and members of the dominant host society in the acculturation process, Bourhis et al. (1997) include 'host' acculturation orientations toward immigrant groups in their model. This component of the model is also driven by two primary questions (i.e., dimensions) to be assessed by members of the host community: "(1) Do you find it acceptable that immigrants maintain their cultural heritage? (2) Do you accept that immigrants adopt the culture of your host community?" (p. 380). Responses to these two questions produce five possible host community member acculturation orientations toward immigrant groups mirroring those proposed previously:

integration, assimilation, segregation, exclusion, and individualism. Host members who prefer integration support biculturalism for immigrants, whereas those who favor assimilation accept immigrants with the expectation that they will eventually fully adopt the host culture at the expense of their heritage culture. Segregationists prefer that immigrants maintain their heritage cultural identity rather than assimilating to mainstream society, and would rather avoid interacting with members of immigrant groups. Exclusionists are intolerant of the presence of immigrants in the host society, prefer that immigrants conceal or abandon their heritage culture, and, in extreme cases, advocate deportation. Finally, similar to immigrant individualists, host society members who favor individualism prefer to view themselves and immigrants with whom they come into contact as autonomous and independent of group membership classifications.

Notably, each of the host community acculturation orientations in Bourhis et al.'s (1997) IAM corresponds to specific state integration ideologies, or host community members' beliefs about how and whether immigrants should be integrated into the host society. Such ideologies generate distinct integration policies dictating the treatment and financial support of immigrant groups' cultural activities and identity expression. The integration orientation corresponds to a pluralistic ideology, whereby the state values and provides social and financial support to both immigrant cultural activities and those of the mainstream society. The assimilation orientation can be paired with policies reflective of either the civic or the assimilationist ideologies. The difference between the two ideologies is that the civic ideology suggests respect for the cultural activities of immigrant groups *and* the dominant host society, but only financially supports the activities of the latter. Policies reflecting the assimilationist ideology not only dictate that the cultural activities of immigrant groups will not receive public funding, but may also impose limitations on immigrants' public demonstrations of elements of their heritage cultural identity. The segregation orientation correlates with either the assimilationist or the ethnist ideology, with the latter associated with policies denying immigrants rightful citizenship (see Dandy and Pe-Pua 2010). Individualists, in contrast, likely endorse policies reflective of pluralistic or civic ideologies in which voluntary community involvements and national patriotism are more salient than nativist notions of birthright (see Esses et al. 2005).

The four ideological clusters depicted in Bourhis et al.'s (1997) model importantly illustrate that the acculturation orientations of immigrants and members of the host community "do not emerge in a social or political vacuum but rather are influenced by the integration policies adopted by the state which, in turn, may also reflect the acculturation orientations of the dominant group within the host society" (p. 373). Thus, the inclusion of host community members' acculturation orientations and the insertion of varying immigrant integration ideologies in the model further exemplify the interactive, dynamic nature of the acculturation process.

The final component of Bourhis et al.'s (1997) IAM, which has received support in Canadian, Israeli, and French contexts, is that of predicted relational outcomes resulting from contact between immigrants and members of the dominant host society of each acculturation orientation. Concordant combinations, or contact between immigrant and host community individuals who uphold similar acculturation orientations, yield consensual (i.e., positive) relational outcomes. Such consensual outcomes are characterized by positive intergroup attitudes and behaviors, a general lack of negative out-group stereotypes and discrimination, and low levels of acculturative stress. Conversely, discordant acculturation orientation combinations between immigrants and members of mainstream society may result in problematic or conflictual relational outcomes. Problematic relational outcomes transpire when immigrants and members of the host community who only partially share acculturation orientations engage in intercultural contact, which can potentially result in misunderstandings, tension and discomfort, increased acculturative stress, negative out-group stereotypes and discrimination. Conflictual relational

*Table 15.1* Toward a communication-relevant typology of acculturation

|  | *Assimilation* | *Integration* | *Separatism* |
|---|---|---|---|
| Host ideologies | Civic or assimilationist | Civic | Ethnicist |
| Acculturation orientations | Concordant | Concordant | Discordant |
| Immigrant vitality | Low | Medium/high | High |
| Host vitality | High | High | High |
| Immigrant communication | Fully accommodative | Accommodative | Non-accommodative |
| Host communication | Non-accommodative | Accommodative | Non-accommodative |
| Host prejudice | Potentially discriminatory | Social tolerance | Discriminatory |
| Intergroup contact spaces (inclusion of host community in self) | High | Medium | Low |
| Richness of self{-}host experiences | High | Medium | Low |

outcomes, the most negative of the three intergroup contact outcomes, emerge when immigrants and members of the dominant mainstream society who maintain completely disparate acculturation views interact. In addition to the aforementioned negative consequences associated with problematic relational outcomes, conflictual relational outcomes could include racist attacks and retaliatory behaviors on the part of individuals from both groups.

As acknowledged by Bourhis and colleagues (1997), the group vitalities of immigrant and mainstream social categories play a fundamental role in the relational outcomes of intercultural contact. Immigrants with low group vitality are more likely to experience acculturative stress and to be vulnerable to abuse and persecution than immigrants from groups with high vitality. Nonetheless, neither vitality nor intergroup contact is afforded representational significance in schematic representations of the IAM (see, for example, Bourhis *et al.* 2009). It is our contention that work in both these domains, together with that on communication accommodation, should assume more theoretical bite in this important applied intercultural domain (see Table 15.1), and it is to an overview of these domains that we turn next.

## 3. Complementary new perspectives

### Ethnolinguistic vitality

Since its inception (Giles *et al.* 1977), the concept of group vitality has received a great deal of attention globally in the multicultural (e.g., Bourhis and Landry 2008; Sayahi 2005) and, more recently, in the acculturation (Ehala 2010) literatures. Vitality refers to the amount of social advantages a group has or has not attained in terms of pride in its history, membership numbers, and the visibility of its culture and communicative codes within society. It is made up of three separate, but interrelated, dimensions of status, demographics, and institutional support. Revisiting social identity theory (Tajfel and Turner 1986), an in-group member may determine achievement of a positive group identity or lack thereof through intergroup comparisons of group characteristics along these vitality dimensions. The vitality of a group can be measured objectively, for example, by the percentage of in-group members living, as well as the number of media outlets, in the ethnic tongue.

Arguably, more cogent for predicting intergroup communication than objective vitality is its subjective counterpart (for a measure, see Abrams *et al.* 2009); that is, how people "perceive" their own and other groups' vitalities (Liebkind *et al.* 2007). It has been argued that we are aware of the vitalities of all the social groups to which we belong by mere (yet continual) perusals of media depictions and reports of relevant intergroup scenes. Further, ethnolinguistic identity theory (e.g., Giles and Johnson 1987) contends that the higher one's in-group vitality, the more members are willing to invest in their in-group emotionally, psychologically, and with respect to collective action to foster their own group's interests. In-groups and their cultures including their languages and literatures will survive and flourish (e.g., Catalan, Navaho, and Luxembourgish), continue to be creative and innovative, and expand and be socially influential, provided that they have "high" perceived in-group vitality. In general, high-vitality groups are usually those in the upper echelons of any intergroup status hierarchy (i.e., dominant groups), whereas low-vitality groups are those relegated toward the bottom end of this continuum (i.e., marginalized groups). It is important to note that, for dominant groups to maintain their social privileges and advantages, they might need to control public information (e.g., via the media) that perpetuates low subjective vitality among subordinate groups. Members of low-vitality groups, for their part, may be disposed to assimilate into other more prestigious collectivities to enhance personal worth and dignity.

One important dimension of group vitality has been labeled "status", which refers to the influence and power a group is believed to have economically, historically, socially, and linguistically. A group possessing high status would have control over its own collective fate and a high degree of esteem as well as pride in its history, which can be reflected in school texts, TV serials, monuments, murals, and so forth. However, sometimes, flawed historical events, such as military defeats, can be mobilizing even hundreds of years later (e.g., the Battle of Bannockburn for the Scots) as the in-group ponders its cultural survival in the face of colonializing influences and aggression.

Demographics (i.e., the population and location features of groups) are another key dimension of vitality. Demographic vitality can be manifest in a range of different means besides the membership numbers and their relative proportion *vis-à-vis* potent other immigrant communities and the host society. For example, in-group sanctions against those engaged in ethnically-mixed marriages can be interpreted as one way of maintaining in-group vitality. Attempted massacres, genocide, and ethnic cleansing perpetrated against certain groups can also be seen as a concrete means of delimiting the violated group's perceived strength.

Interestingly, having a territory of its own replete with ethnically distinctive scents and signage (e.g., Little Italy or Chinatown neighborhoods in large US urban cities) advances a group's vitality and aids in social cohesion and the maintenance of a distinctive communicative code and set of cultural values. Mainstream backlashes often result as a way of ameliorating the threat of increasing immigrant vitality. Oftentimes, immigrating groups and refugees (such as the Hmong in the US) are strategically dispersed across a nation's territory along with their cultural solidarity by the host government agencies so as not to have them concentrated in demographically, economically, and politically strong enclaves.

Institutional support, vitality's third dimension, refers to the extent to which a group and its culture are reflected in the main structures of society, such as in the media, politics, law, etc. The use of the in-group language in various ethnic media outlets is a potent form of high vitality (Abrams *et al.* 2003). Knowledge of and talk about (see Harwood *et al.* 1994) a group's presence in the educational curriculum, its continued use in religious settings, and even the growth of its own unique places of worship can make profound statements about its cultural capital. In addition, the group's festivals, music and song, sculptures and fine art, as well as many other cultural artefacts in the home are markers of in-group solidarity and valued distinctiveness. By these means, separation as an acculturative strategy would be bolstered by such activities and practices. By utilizing such resources (Kim 2001), acculturating groups can either afford themselves the opportunity to learn mainstream values and language (Somani 2010) or, in complete contrast and in search of separatist inclinations, avoid selecting media channels that offend their ethnic sensibilities (Abrams and Giles 2007).

It can be appreciated that groups are continually under pressure in a changing world to vie for an increasing share of overall vitality, as it is that, in part, which contributes to their survival in the local—and oftentimes global—intergroup scene. Clearly then, the perceived relative vitalities of an immigrant group should predictably affect its acculturative orientations as well as potentially shape those of the host community toward them (see below). Currie and Hogg (1994) found that the vitality of immigrants was predictive of their degree of larger scale social adaptations beyond that of proficiency in the host language, such as educational or occupational advancement and life satisfaction. Although research on group vitality has been devoted mostly to interethnic group settings, it is important to underscore that other forms of cultural groupings—including the genders, generations, organized street gangs, hearing impaired (and deaf culture), police, and so forth—all lend themselves to cogent analysis in these terms. Given power disparities and vitality disparities, intergroup accommodation (Gallois 2008) is, more often than not, unidirectional to the extent that subordinate groups communicatively align themselves more with dominant groups than vice versa. This is, of course, yet another facet of the acculturative process, and it is to issues of intergroup accommodation that we now turn.

## Communication accommodation

Communication accommodation theory (CAT) is a framework for describing and explaining why people adapt their communication practices. More specifically, it explores the reasons for, and consequences arising from, speakers converging toward and diverging away from each other (see Giles and Ogay 2006). CAT now has a 40-year history, and has been revised and elaborated many times, yet many of its propositions have received empirical support across an array of diverse languages and cultures, applied settings as well as electronic media (see Gallois et al. 2005).

Convergent moves are generally performed to reduce social distance and are received favorably by recipients, although the inevitable variability of people within any single cultural group requires an accommodative sensitivity (see Gallois and Callan 1997). As Horenczyk (2009) argues, many immigrant groups around the world do not simply have to acculturate to one host community but, in some situations (e.g., in Quebec), need to adapt to more than one ethnic dominant group and contend with other minorities vying for relative social advantages. Returning momentarily to the vitality of the mainstream media, this is the means whereby immigrants can ascertain and learn more precisely when to accommodate to whom and why.

"Accommodative resources" are an integral feature of what actually defines the construct of intercultural communicative competence itself. Such convergent acts as simple hellos and expressions of gratitude convey respect and effort which, in turn, renders appreciative responses, such as liking and altruism. For recipients, the effects of interactional satisfaction via intergroup accommodation can also generalize to broader and more positive feelings about the entire culture and group to which the converger belongs. All this notwithstanding, such affiliative approaches would have to be "viewed" as accommodative. Indeed, an important feature of the theory is that individuals accommodate (toward or away from others) to where they "believe" others reside communicatively.

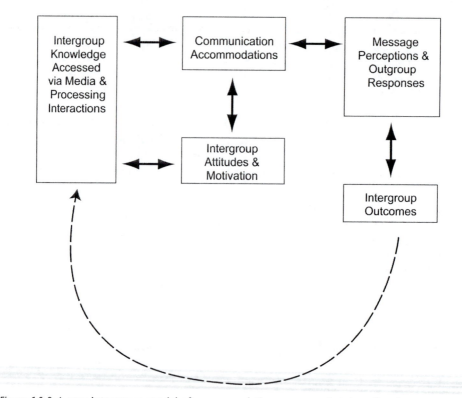

*Figure 15.2* A new intergroup model of accommodative processes in intercultural encounters
*Source*: Giles and Giles (in press). Reproduced with permission.

Conversely, the strategy of "divergence" leads to increases in social distance through an accentuation of language (and cultural) differences, as in switching to an ethnic dialect or language when speaking to a host national (Giles and Johnson 1981). Typically, such moves are negatively valued by recipients and often taken quite personally. However, given the importance of language to ethnic identity (Gaudet and Clément 2008; Giles 1977), it is not uncommon for people to diverge their communicative patterns when their ethnicity is contextually salient and, once again in social identity theory terms, when they are seeking a positive group identity. Clearly, accommodative acts are important means and symbols of acculturative orientations. Rarely, however, has CAT been drawn upon in the acculturative literature, and it is our contention (as delineated below) that it has some merit and potential in this regard.

The model depicted in Figure 15.2 is a summarized way of schematizing some of the intercultural communication processes just discussed (Giles and Giles, in press).

Starting with the top left box, intergroup knowledge can be gained by direct face-to-face interactions, vicarious observations of, and even imagined contact with out-group members (see Turner 2010). As seen above, intergroup contact can be achieved through conversations with and observations of the host culture through its media (Harwood 2010; Kim 2001), literature, and knowledge of its history and collective memory (Pennebaker *et al.* 1997).

Enriched by this intergroup knowledge, more positive attitudes toward the out-group and increased motivations to be communicatively involved with them can be engendered (as well as perhaps new insights evoked about the individual's in-group). This (Figure 15.2, middle lower box) then allows one to be better placed to make appropriate communicative accommodations with the out-group, be it in terms of dialect, key words, phrases, and/or accepted dress styles for particular contexts, etc. In the ideal world, these accommodations with the out-group will be recognized by them, and should reciprocal accommodations follow, positive outcomes (e.g., intercultural satisfaction) will ensue.

Sometimes, however, we are placed into cultural groupings erroneously by others based on inferences about the perceived character of our communicative styles. Many Sikh immigrants in the US, for example, have recently been categorized as Muslims and suffered discriminatory outcomes. Leading to "accommodative dilemmas", speakers have to communicatively manage others' potentially abusive miscategorizations of them, or just reluctantly accommodate, and this is a challenge if one wishes to amend an out-group's intergroup beliefs.

The nature of intergroup settings and the communication practices that typify them (see Giles et al. 2010) are critical to the acculturation process. The arrows in Figure 15.2 are bilateral to indicate feedback cycles, as in the case of intercultural satisfaction promoting future, and perhaps, more extensive accommodations as well as encouraging the pursuit of further intergroup knowledge. Thus, the acquisition of intergroup knowledge throughout the acculturation process can be furthered by a review of recent developments in intergroup contact research. Surprisingly, this is a rarely invoked, yet highly relevant, element in the complex acculturative equation; an overview of this area of research with special focus on a communication perspective within it follows next.

## Intergroup contact

Although researchers in the early 1930s began working on intergroup relations in terms of acquaintanceship and racial attitudes as determining factors of social tolerance (Zeligs and Hendrickson 1933), Williams (1947) carved out 102 testable propositions that formed the early foundation of what would become intergroup contact theory during this early period of research. Allport (1954) then expanded on the proposed inverse relationship of contact and prejudice when he proposed the intergroup contact hypothesis. He posited four facilitating conditions required for positive outcomes ensuing from contact: equal status within the situation; common goals; intergroup cooperation; and the institutional support of authorities, law, and/or customs. Since then, the hypothesis has had several major theoretical outgrowths, including the decategorization model (Brewer and Miller 1984), the common in-group identity model (Gaertner and Dovidio 2000), and the social identity model (Hewstone and Brown 1986).

More recently, Harwood (2010) drew attention to the "communicative" dynamics underlying various forms of intergroup contact, behavioral issues strangely neglected from the cognitively and affectively dominated contact literature. Referred to as contact space (see Figure 15.3), he focuses on the dimensionality of contact (involvement of the self against the richness of the experience) across the more prominently researched forms of intergroup contact, including face-to-face, extended, mass-mediated, mediated interpersonal, and imagined (see below).

The two-dimensional framework of contact space situates these five contact forms on continua of involvement of self and richness of the self–out-group experience. This first dimension deals with the level of personal involvement an individual commits to when engaging in one of the forms of contact. The self, however, can be extended to close relationships, thereby extending the level of personal involvement across those relationships (Aron et al. 1991). A close in-group friend would then be incorporated into an individual's sense of self and, subsequently, that individual's personal involvement in the interaction. On the other hand, the level of intimacy achieved with an in-group stranger would be much lower, causing the individual to feel

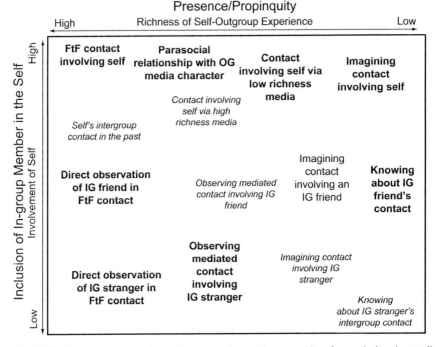

*Figure 15.3* The contact space: a two-dimensional model accounting for variation in studies of intergroup contact

*Source*: Harwood (2010: 155). Reproduced with permission from Sage Publications.

*Note*: IG, in-group; FtF, face-to-face. Contact is always used to refer to some form of contact between an in-group member (the self in some areas) and a member of an out-group. The axes are labeled with both objective labels (underlined) and subjective labels (gray outline font). In the body of the contact space, items in bold are areas already studied in the intergroup contact literature; items in italics are contexts of contact that have not previously been examined.

less personally involved in the interaction. The second dimension, richness of the self–out-group experience, refers to the number of cues and channels that are available to an individual in an interaction and, hence, that individual's ability to have access to and immediacy of feedback (Daft and Lengel 1984). Here (see Figure 15.3), moving across the richness continuum from high to low, one finds varying degrees of interactivity that the form affords with direct interaction being the highest, leftmost activity, then direct observation, then imagining, and then finally, knowing, the lowest, rightmost activity.

The five forms, however, can be embedded within each other, such that face-to-face contact, for example, can be found in extended contact. In other words, one can directly observe an in-group friend in face-to-face contact with an out-group member. Likewise, to observe an in-group friend engaging in an online chat with an out-group member would entail extended contact within mediated contact. Imagining the preceding examples of embedded contact would constitute imagined contact. Harwood (2010) states that contact space allows for the many combinations of these forms, highlighting many more empirical avenues to be taken in future contact research.

Face-to-face contact is understood to be the most direct form an individual can utilize when actually participating in an interaction. At its strongest along both continua, face-to-face contact involving the self would have the individual engaging in the interaction with an out-group member in a very rich, multisensory experience with immediacy. A face-to-face interaction with extended contact (i.e., mere observance of an in-group stranger) would be lower in self-involvement, but still high in richness. In accordance with the notion of others as an extension of the self, having an in-group friend experience an intergroup interaction would then be more involving of the self than if it had been with an in-group stranger.

Mass-mediated contact addresses the individual as a consumer of out-group media characters and the positive or negative portrayals of these characters (Schiappa *et al.* 2005). This is less involving of the self than the previous two forms, although still great in its potential for para-social relationships with the characters involved. The richness of the experience would also be lower because of the lower amount of sensory input and feedback.

Mediated interpersonal contact refers to an intergroup interaction that has reduced cues and less immediacy than face-to-face contact such as in computer-mediated communication (see Walther 2009). The level of richness is even lower than the preceding forms, although the exact amount of richness would depend on the technology used. A video chat, for example, is far richer than a text-based chat, but far less rich than face-to-face or extended contact. The level of personal involvement depends on who is the primary interactant in the intergroup interaction—the self, the in-group friend, or the in-group stranger. The notion of others as part of the self also applies here. In this case, observing mediated contact with an in-group stranger is low on the involvement continuum, and somewhat in the middle of the richness continuum.

Imagined contact occurs when an individual envisions a positive interaction with an out-group member (Turner 2010). Imagining is quite low in richness but can be high in personal involvement, depending on who is being imagined in the intergroup interaction. Below even imagining, at the lower rightmost corner of the contact space model (see Figure 15.3), sits knowing about an in-group stranger's intergroup contact, where both involvement and richness are at their lowest. Although too detailed for current purposes, Harwood (2010) discusses an array of moderators and mediators impinging on the contact space. This agenda-setting framework is a seminal springboard for more communication-oriented work on intergroup contact in order to further tease apart the acculturation process, both quantitatively as well as qualitatively (Halualani 2008).

## 4. Epilogue: a communication-oriented model of acculturation

In this chapter, we have overviewed past work on acculturation psychology, with an emphasis on Berry's and Bourhis's models. Thereafter, we discussed theory and research on group vitality, communication accommodation, and intergroup contact, providing schematic models that represent important aspects of these frameworks. In Table 15.1, we summarily draw upon all these frameworks and their attending research by means of a polythetic typology. Therein, we highlight some of the major bilateral forces propelling those encountering a new culture toward the more major ubiquitous acculturation inclinations of assimilation, integration, and separatism. Regarding these, we posit in Table 15.1 the host community's positions, both subordinate and dominant groups' accommodative strategies, and the kinds of contact spaces associated with them.

As with other acculturation frameworks (see again, Horenczyk 2009), other inclinations are possible. For instance, a so-called problematic type could be where the acculturation orientations of the parties are discordant to the extent that each side sees the inclinations of the others as mixed. In this sense, the heterogeneity of communication patterns and presumed values differs among the various subgroups of each party making prototypical inferences uncertain, anxious, stressful, and uncomfortable. Indeed, the typology could be embellished further with the addition of other language ingredients—in terms of the valence and complexity of ethnophaulisms directed toward immigrants (e.g. Mullen and Smyth 2004) and the kinds of ethnonyms or in-group labels fashioned by both parties for exclusion or inclusion (Mullen *et al.* 2007)—as well as other immigrant psychological outcomes (e.g., life satisfaction, well-being, depression, and occupational success).

Admittedly, there may be challenges in operationalizing and measuring some of the components. Indeed, the constructs apparent in Table 15.1 were formulated so as to be heuristically generic for this overview forum, and it would be premature at this stage in theorizing to concoct the relationships between them, causal or otherwise. The components of perceived vitality would likely vary by intergroup setting, the accommodative–nonaccommodative practices might differ too, and the contact spaces might be differentially available. Whatever, the typology is potentially testable, malleable in its potential for expansion and elaboration and, at the very least, affords communication a central place in theorizing about these very pervasive social phenomena across the entire range of settings deemed intercultural.

## Related topics

Biculturalism; cross-cultural adaptation; cross-cultural values; intercultural communicative competence; language and cultural identities; language learning; minority language maintenance; multiculturalism

## Further reading

Bourhis, R.Y. and Landry, R. (2008) 'Group vitality, cultural autonomy and the wellness of language minorities', in R.Y. Bourhis (ed.) *The Vitality of the English-speaking Communities of Quebec: From Community Decline to Revival*, Montréal: CEETUM, Université de Montréal, pp. 185–211 (a useful discussion about factors influencing the health of ethnolinguistic communities).
Dovidio, J.F., Gaertner, S.L. and Kawakami, K. (2003) 'Intergroup contact: the past present and future', *Group Process and Intergroup Relations*, 6: 5–21 (an extensive overview of intergroup contact research).
Gallois, C., Ogay, T. and Giles, H. (2005) 'Communication accommodation theory: a look back and a look ahead', in W.B. Gudykunst (ed.) *Theorizing about Intercultural Communication*, Thousand Oaks, CA: Sage, pp. 121–48 (a review of the history of the communication accommodation theory).
Giles, H., Bourhis, R.Y. and Taylor, D.M. (1977) 'Towards a theory of language in ethnic group relations', in H. Giles (ed.) *Language, Ethnicity and Intergroup Relations*, London: Academic Press, pp. 307–48 (a discussion of the role of group vitality factors influencing intercultural accommodation strategies).
Liebkind, K. (2006) 'Ethnic identity and acculturation', in D.L. Sam and J.W. Berry (eds) *The Cambridge Handbook of Acculturation Psychology*, New York: Cambridge University Press, pp. 78–96 (an excellent account of acculturation research and theory).

## References

Abrams, J.R. and Giles, H. (2007) 'Ethnic identity gratifications selection and avoidance by African Americans: a group vitality and social identity gratifications perspective', *Media Psychology*, 9: 115–35.
Abrams, J.R., Eveland, W.P., Jr and Giles, H. (2003) 'The effects of television on group vitality: can television empower nondominant groups?', in P. Kalbfleisch (ed.) *Communication Yearbook*, 27: 193–219.
Abrams, J.R., Barker, V. and Giles, H. (2009) 'An examination of the validity of the Subjective Vitality Questionnaire', *Journal of Multilingual and Multicultural Development*, 30: 59–72.
Allport, G.W. (1954) *The Nature of Prejudice*, Cambridge/Reading, MA: Addison Wesley.
Aron, A., Aron, E., Tudor, M. and Nelson, G. (1991) 'Close relationships as including other in the self', *Journal of Personality and Social Psychology*, 60: 241–53.
Berry, J.W. (1980a) 'Acculturation as varieties of adaptation', in A. Padilla (ed.) *Acculturation: Theory, Models, and Some New Findings*, Boulder, CO: Westview, pp. 9–25.
——(1980b) 'Social and cultural change', in H.C. Triandis and R. Brislin (eds) *Handbook of Cross-Cultural Psychology*, Boston, MA: Allyn and Bacon, pp. 211–80.

——(1990) 'Psychology of acculturation: understanding individuals moving between cultures', in R.W. Brislin (ed.) *Applied Cross-cultural Psychology*, Newbury Park, CA: Sage, pp. 232–53.

——(2006) 'Contexts of acculturation', in D.L. Sam and J.W. Berry (eds) *The Cambridge Handbook of Acculturation Psychology*, Cambridge: Cambridge University Press, pp. 27–42.

——(2009) 'A critique of critical acculturation', *International Journal of Intercultural Relations*, 33: 361–71.

Berry, J.W. and Sam, D.L. (2006) 'Acculturation and adaptation', in J.W. Berry, M.H. Segall, and C. Kagitçibasi (eds) *The Cambridge Handbook of Acculturation Psychology*, Cambridge: Cambridge University Press, pp. 181–97.

Bourhis, R.Y. and Landry, R. (2008) 'Group vitality, cultural autonomy and the wellness of language minorities', in R.Y. Bourhis (ed.) *The Vitality of the English-speaking Communities of Quebec: From Community Decline to Revival*, Montréal: CEETUM, Université de Montréal, pp. 185–211.

Bourhis, R.Y., Moise, L.C., Perreault, S. and Senecal, S. (1997) 'Towards an interactive acculturation model: a social psychological approach', *International Journal of Psychology*, 32: 369–86.

Bourhis, R.Y., Montreuil, A., Barrette, G. and Montaruli, E. (2009) 'Acculturation and immigrant–host community relations in multicultural settings', in S. Demoulin, J.C. Leyens, and J.F. Dovidio (eds) *Intergroup Misunderstandings: Impact of Divergent Social Realities*, New York: Psychology Press, pp. 39–61.

Brewer, M.B. and Miller, N. (1984) 'Beyond the contact hypothesis: theoretical perspectives on desegregation', in N. Miller and M.B. Brewer (eds) *Groups in Contact: The Psychology of Desegregation*, Orlando, FL: Academic Press, pp. 281–302.

Chirkov, V. (ed.) (2009) 'Critical acculturation psychology: what do we study and how do we study it, when we investigate acculturation?', *International Journal of Intercultural Relations*, 33(2): 94–105.

Cleveland, M., Laroche, M., Pons, F. and Kastoun, R. (2009) 'Acculturation and consumption: textures of cultural adaptation', *International Journal of Intercultural Relations*, 33: 196–212.

Currie, M. and Hogg, M.A. (1994) 'Subjective ethnolinguistic vitality and social adaptation among Vietnamese refugees in Australia', *International Journal of the Sociology of Language*, 108: 97–115.

Daft, R.L. and Lengel, R.H. (1984) 'Information richness: a new approach to managerial behavior and organizational design', in L.L. Cummings and B.M. Staw (eds) *Research in Organizational Behavior 6*, Homewood, IL: JAI Press, pp.191–233.

Dandy, J. and Pe-Pua, R. (2010) 'Attitudes to multiculturalism, immigration and cultural diversity: comparison of dominant and non-dominant groups in three Australian states', *International Journal of Intercultural Relations*, 34: 34–46.

De Saissy, C.K.M. (2009) 'Acculturation, self-efficacy and social support among Chinese immigrants in Northern Ireland', *International Journal of Intercultural Relations*, 33: 291–300.

Dovidio, J.F., Gaertner, S.L., Hodson, G., Houlette, M.A. and Johnson, K.M. (2005) 'Social inclusion and exclusion: recategorization and the perception of intergroup boundaries', in D. Abrams, M.A. Hogg and J.M. Marques (eds) *The Social Psychology of Inclusion and Exclusion*, New York: Psychology Press, pp. 245–64.

Ehala, M. (2010) 'Ethnolinguistic vitality and intergroup processes', *Multilingua – Journal of Cross-Cultural and Interlanguage Communication*, 29: 203–21.

Esses, V.M., Dovidio, J.F., Semenya, A.H. and Jackson, L.M. (2005) 'Attitudes toward immigrants and immigration: the role of national and international identity', in D. Abrams, M.A. Hogg and J.M. Marques (eds) *The Social Psychology of Inclusion and Exclusion*, New York: Psychology Press, pp. 317–38.

Gaertner, S.L. and Dovidio, J.F. (2000) *Reducing Intergroup Bias: The Common Ingroup Identity Model*, Philadelphia, PA: Psychology Press.

Gallois, C. (2008) 'Intergroup accommodative processes', in W. Donsbach (ed.) *International Encyclopedia of Communication* VI, Oxford: Blackwell, pp. 2368–72.

Gallois, C. and Callan, V.C. (1997) *Communication and Culture: A Guide for Practice*, Chichester: Wiley.

Gallois, C., Ogay, T. and Giles, H. (2005) 'Communication accommodation theory: a look back and a look ahead', in W. Gudykunst (ed.) *Theorizing about Intercultural Communication*, Thousand Oaks, CA: Sage, pp. 121–48.

Gaudet, S. and Clément, R. (2008) 'Forging an identity as a linguistic minority: intra and intergroup aspects of language, communication and identity in Western Canada', *International Journal of Intercultural Relations*, 33: 213–27.

Giles, H. (ed.) (1977) *Language, Ethnicity, and Intergroup Relations*, London: Academic Press.

Giles, H. and Giles, J. (in press) 'Ingroups and outgroups communicating', in A. Kuyulo (ed.) *Inter/cultural Communication: Representation and Construction of Culture in Everyday Interaction*, Thousand Oaks, CA: Sage.

Giles, H. and Johnson, P. (1981) 'The role of language in ethnic group relations', in J.C. Turner and H. Giles (eds) *Intergroup Behavior*, Oxford: Blackwell, pp. 199–243.

——(1987) 'Ethnolinguistic identity theory: a social psychological approach to language maintenance', *International Journal of the Sociology of Language*, 58: 66–99.

Giles, H. and Ogay, T. (2006) 'Communication accommodation theory', in B. Whaley and W. Samter (eds) *Explaining Communication: Contemporary Theories and Exemplars*, Mahwah, NJ: Erlbaum, pp. 293–310.

Giles, H., Bourhis, R.Y. and Taylor, D.M. (1977) 'Towards a theory of language in ethnic group relations', in H. Giles (ed.) *Language, Ethnicity and Intergroup Relations*, London: Academic Press, pp. 307–48.

Giles, H., Reid, S.A. and Harwood, J. (eds) (2010) *The Dynamics of Intergroup Communication*, New York: Peter Lang.

Glazer, N. and Moynihan, D. (1963) *Beyond the Melting Pot*, Cambridge, MA: MIT Press.

Gordon, M.M. (1964) *Assimilation in American life*, New York: Oxford University Press.

Halualani, R.T. (2008) 'How do multicultural university students define and make sense of intercultural contact? A qualitative study', *International Journal of Intercultural Relations*, 32: 1–16.

Harwood, J. (2010) 'The contact space: a novel framework for intergroup contact research', *Journal of Language and Social Psychology*, 29:147–77.

Harwood, J., Giles, H. and Bourhis, R.Y. (1994) 'The genesis of vitality theory: historical patterns and discoursal dimensions', *International Journal of the Sociology of Language*, 108: 168–206.

Herskovits, M. (1958) *Acculturation: The Study of Culture Contact*, Gloucester, MA: Peter Smith.

Hewstone, M. and Brown, R.J. (1986) 'Contact is not enough: an intergroup perspective on the "contact hypothesis"', in M. Hewstone and R. Brown (eds) *Contact and Coflict in Intergroup Encounters*, Oxford: Blackwell, pp. 1–44.

Ho, J. (2010) 'Acculturation gaps in Vietnamese immigrant families: impact on family relationships', *International Journal of Intercultural Relations*, 34: 22–33.

Hogg, M.A., d'Agata, P. and Abrams, D. (1989) 'Ethnolinguistic betrayal and speaker evaluations among Italian Australians', *Genetic, Social and General Psychology Monographs*, 115: 153–81.

Horenczyk, G. (2009) 'Multiple reference groups: towards the mapping of immigrants' complex social worlds', in I. Jasinskaja-Lahti and T.A. Mähönen (eds) *Identities, Intergroup Relations and Acculturation*, Helsinki: Gausdeamus Helsinki University Press, pp. 67–80.

Jang, Y. and Chiriboga, D.A. (2010) 'Living in a different world: acculturative stress among Korean American elders', *Journal of Gerontology: Psychological Sciences*, 65B:14–21.

Kim, Y.Y. (2001) *Becoming Intercultural: An Integrative Theory of Communication and Cross-cultural Adaptation*, Thousand Oaks, CA: Sage.

Li, H.Z. (1999) 'Communicating information in conversation: a cross-cultural comparison', *International Journal of Intercultural Relations*, 23: 387–410.

Liebkind, K. (2001) 'Acculturation', in R. Brown and S. Gaertner (eds) *Blackwell Handbook of Social Psychology: Intergroup Processes*, Oxford: Blackwell, pp. 386–406.

——(2006) 'Ethnic identity and acculturation', in D.L. Sam and J.W. Berry (eds) *The Cambridge Handbook of Acculturation Psychology*, New York: Cambridge University Press, pp. 78–96.

Liebkind, K., Jasinskaja-Lahti, I. and Teräsaho, M. (2007) 'Ingroup vitality and intergroup attitudes in a linguistic minority', *Scandinavian Journal of Psychology*, 48: 409–18.

Luek, K. and Wilson, M. (2010) 'Acculturative stress in Asian immigrants: the impact of social and linguistic factors', *International Journal of Intercultural Relations*, 34: 47–57.

Mullen, B. and Smyth, J.M. (2004) 'Immigrant suicide rates as a function of ethnophaulisms: hate speech predicts death', *Psychosomatic Medicine*, 66: 343–48.

Mullen, B., Calogero, R.M. and Leader, T.I. (2007) 'A social psychological study of ethnonyms: cognitive representations of the ingroup and intergroup hostility', *Journal of Personality and Social Psychology*, 92: 612–30.

Mummendey, A., Klink, A., Mielke, R., Wenzel, M. and Blanz, M. (1999) 'Socio-structural characteristics of intergroup relations and identity management strategies: results from a field study in East Germany', *European Journal of Social Psychology*, 29: 259–85.

Pennebaker, J.W., Pàez, D. and Rimé, B. (eds) (1997) *Collective Memory of Political Events: Social Psychological Perspectives*, Mahwah, NJ: Lawrence Erlbaum.

PEW (2002) *What the world thinks in 2002: The PEW Global Attitudes Report*, Washington, DC: The PEW Research Center Press for the People and the Press.

Phinney, J.S., Horenczyk, G., Liebkind, K. and Vedder, P. (2001) 'Ethnic identity, immigration, and well-being: an interactional perspective', *Journal of Social Issues*, 57: 493–510.

Pickett, C.L. and Brewer, M.B. (2005) 'The role of exclusion in maintaining ingroup inclusion', in D. Abrams, M.A. Hogg and J.M. Marques (eds) *The Social Psychology of Inclusion and Exclusion*, New York: Psychology Press, pp. 89–112.

Redfield, R., Linton, R. and Herskovits, M. (1936) *Acculturation: The Study of Cultural Contact*, Gloucester, MA: Peter Smith.

Reid, S., Giles, H. and Abrams, J. (2004) 'A social identity model of media usage and effects', *Zeitschrift für Medienpsychologie*,16: 17–25.

Sam, D.L. and Berry, J.W. (2009) 'Adaptation of young immigrants: the double jeopardy of acculturation', in I. Jasinskaja-Lahti and T.A. Mähönen (eds) *Identities, Intergroup Relations and Acculturation*, Helsinki: Gausdeamus Helsinki University Press, pp. 191–205.

Sayahi, L. (2005) 'Language and identity among speakers of Spanish in northern Morocco: between ethnolinguistic vitality and acculturation', *Journal of Sociolinguistics*, 9: 95–107.

Schiappa, E., Gregg, P.B. and Hewes, D.E. (2005) 'The parasocial contact hypothesis', *Communication Monographs*, 72: 92–115.

Schwartz, S.J. and Zamboanga, B. L. (2008) 'Testing Berry's model of acculturation: a confirmatory latent class approach', *Cultural Diversity and Ethnic Minority Psychology*, 14: 275–85.

Somani, I.S. (2010) 'Becoming American', *Journal of International and Intercultural Communication*, 3: 59–81.

Tajfel, H. and Turner, J.C. (1986) 'An integrative theory of intergroup conflict', in S. Worchel and W.G. Austin (eds) *Psychology of Intergroup Relations*, Chicago, IL: Nelson-Hall, pp. 2–24.

Taylor, D.M. (1992) 'The social psychology of racial and cultural diversity: issues of assimilation and multiculturalism', in A.G. Reynolds (ed.) *Bilingualism, Biculturalism, and Second Language Learning*, Hillsdale, NJ: Erlbaum, pp. 1–20.

Triandis, H.C. (1994) *Culture and Social Behavior*, New York: McGraw-Hill.

——(2007) 'Culture and psychology: a history of the study of their relationship', in S. Kitayama and D. Cohen (eds) *Handbook of Cultural Psychology*, New York: Guilford Press, pp. 59–76.

Turner, R.N. (2010) 'Imagining harmonious intergroup relations', *The Psychologist*, 23: 289–301.

Walther, J.B. (2009) 'Computer-mediated communication and virtual groups: applications to interethnic conflict', *Journal of Applied Communication Research*, 37: 225–38.

Ward, C. (2008) 'Thinking outside the Berry boxes: new perspectives on identity, acculturation and intercultural relations', *International Journal of Intercultural Relations*, 32: 105–14.

Williams, R.M., Jr. (1947) *The Reduction of Intergroup Tensions*, New York: Social Science Research Council.

Zeligs, R. and Hendrickson, G. (1933) 'Racial attitudes of 200 sixth grade children', *Sociology and Social Research*, 18: 26–36.

Intercultural communicative competence:
multiple conceptual approaches

# 16

# Language

## An essential component of intercultural communicative competence

*Alvino E. Fantini*

## 1. Language as mediator

A different language is a different vision of life.

*Federico Fellini*

No one doubts the importance of language in our lives. In fact, it would be hard to imagine life without the ability to communicate. Yet, because language has always been present—for as long as we can remember—we seldom consider the role and impact of the specific system of symbols that we use on a daily basis. This is true for our native language system, and it is just as true when dealing with people across different language–culture backgrounds.

To understand more fully the role and impact of our native language (L1), as well as that of a second language (L2) during intercultural contact, let us consider how language mediates absolutely everything we do: consider the notion that language makes the anthropoid "human". And consider language as a sort of "original sin" in the sense that language is not really about what it "is" but rather what it "stands for". The markings you are "reading" on this page (and the sounds they suggest), for example, represent something other than simply "markings" on the page or "sounds" in the air. They are the formulaic vehicles we use to transmit meaning from one person to another. Language is a convenient and efficient way to do just that.

Moreover, in addition to representing something other than itself, the words of a language actually represent abstractions from experience, formed into thoughts, shaped by our linguistic system, and conveyed through discrete graphic markings or sound bites, conjoined in a stream. Through these representational symbols, we perform an amazing range of functions: we can specify and designate individual units or concepts (e.g., tears, milk, steam, water, Coke, all manifestations of the category "liquids"), or we can generalize phenomena by employing a single word label to group together even dissimilar things (e.g., "animals" to lump together dogs, cats, porcupines, and cows). In other words, we can distinguish things from each other or group them together at will (and as our language permits). We can also label something as a "whole" entity (e.g., tree) or cite its separate "parts" (e.g., leaves, bark, trunk, roots). All these abilities form part of a linguistic system we learned from infancy and on into childhood, a continuing process throughout life, and one that we seldom give any thought to at all.

Yet, language arises from and shapes our experience, so much so that some say we are less than "human" without language. Consider *Victor the Wild Child*, found in Aveyron, France, in 1797, as well as accounts of other feral children reported throughout history (Lane 1976). These children were "feral" precisely because they were raised apart from human societies and possessed no language ability. It is clear that language arises from interactions with others in social situations and that communication is indispensable for membership of a culture. The use of symbolic behaviors, then, renders us intelligible and acceptable to those around us. The use of language, in fact, is our ticket to "membership" into a cultural enclave. These examples illustrate how language and culture are intertwined and how the habits and thoughts of its speakers are inseparable from both. No one creates language in isolation.

To pursue this notion further, consider that our entire view of the world is shaped in our minds, aided and influenced by the linguistic system to which we were exposed from birth. Indeed, all languages do just that. Nonetheless, we react with surprise when we learn that other systems function differently. The Inuit of Canada, for example, have created many names for designating varieties of snow. Why should they name and label the generic "snow" in so many ways? It turns out that all speakers in all cultures categorize and classify, segment and specify, whatever is of interest and importance to them. Asians, for example, name and label rice in more ways than English speakers, and *campesinos* in Bolivia do the same with potatoes, a food staple of the Andean region. Americans name and label automobiles with an even greater range of words for makes and models. And Italians, given their penchant for "pasta", employ this word as a superordinate label under which they group a variety of gastronomic experiences, all pasta, yet each instance precisely codified in accordance with shape, method of preparation, and whether stuffed, placed in soup, or baked. As illustrated in Figure 16.1, the result is a hierarchy of terms from general to specific producing nearly 200 possibilities (consequently, speaking Italian requires recognition and classification of phenomena in the Italian way).

But verbal hierarchies exist in all languages (cf. Anglin 1970). What differs is what we organize and classify and how we name and label. In the end, hierarchies are determined by speakers and vary significantly from language to language in accordance with their cultural context. There can be no doubt that language is an important aspect of every culture. Language is that proverbial two-edged sword—it arises from culture and, conversely, it influences and affects culture.

*Figure 16.1* A hierarchy of terms from general to specific

Consider some further mediating aspects: language has the dual effect of both liberating and constraining us. It liberates by permitting us to move figuratively beyond the "here and now" (represented by words such as: am, is, are) and allows us to retrieve past events conceptually (using words such as: was, were, used to) or project into the future (with words such as: going to, will, shall, tomorrow). That is, we can convey a sense of future intent through language (although affirming something linguistically is obviously no assurance that it "will" happen). Through language, we can also "know" (cognitively) even what we do not know (directly) at all or have never experienced (e.g., dinosaurs and Franz Josef of Austria). So, we are also beneficiaries of a collective heritage stored in language, gaining access to the thoughts of generations of speakers over hundreds of years and in diverse places, people we have never even met. All of this is possible vicariously (albeit not experientially) through linguistic symbols and through a process we seldom ponder.

And there is more: language influences our perceptions, but it can also contradict them. In the first case, for example, the child is "told" that an airplane is faster than an elephant and most accept that as fact. However, the child who has peered out the window of an airplane may dispute this fact based on his own experience (not having yet conformed to conventional wisdom). He explains what he "saw", demonstrating the speed of the airplane with slow movements of his hand. In contrast, he says, elephants run really, really fast, showing this with quick hand motions. He knows this, he says, because he watched them rampage through a village in a Tarzan movie on television. Through language, he is informed or contradicted and, eventually, his direct perceptions are converted into conventional ones.

Through language, we can even bring into creation what may not exist at all. The child describes in detail a "witch" he has seen in his mommy's closet. Real or fantasy? No matter, it can be spoken about and brought into existence through language. Language even allows us to transcend the boundaries of our very existence (mentally, of course) by questioning and speaking about alternatives to life's end: after learning about the concept of death, for example, the child expresses his concerns and his yearning: "Si yo me voy a morir, ¿por qué yo nací? ¿Por qué nací como nene? ¿Por qué no nací como Dios, o como el sol … como una bola de fuego"? [If I am going to die, why was I born? Why was I born a little child? Why wasn't I born instead like God, or like the sun … like a ball of fire?] (Fantini 1985: v).

In summary, every human language is capable of all these things (and more); however, each language does so "differently": all languages encode the human experience but in varying ways; they segment and classify into different structures and hierarchies, encode differing societal aspects, invent and create what may or may not be and, in the process, each child of each culture is socialized in the way of that culture through language. Conversely, because languages all provide a particular way of facilitating thoughts (within their own cultures), they also prevent one from grasping possibilities inherent and encoded in other systems. In the end, the specific language (our native tongue), which serves us so well throughout our entire life, becomes the biggest impediment to another view of that same world.

## 2. Language, culture, and worldview: the nexus

We have just explored some ways in which language mirrors culture. It also reflects and affects how we view the world. In short, language, culture, and the worldview they create are all parts of the same phenomenon—one that we take for granted, seldom think about, and fail to recognize; that is, until we come into contact with individuals from a different language–culture—individuals with a different worldview, one unlike our own. And in this moment of cross-cultural contact arise both great challenges and opportunities.

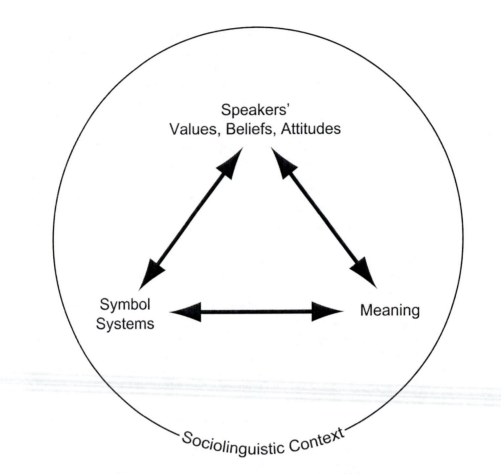

*Figure 16.2* The relationship between language, culture, and worldview

But as each society possesses its own particular view of the world—a *weltanschauung*, a *cosmovisión*—how might they differ (the "particulars") and what also might they share (the "universals")? Figure 16.2 illustrates, first of all, how language, culture, and worldview are related.

Three components are depicted: speakers (with their attendant values, beliefs, and attitudes), the speakers' symbol systems (or language), which include linguistic, paralinguistic, and extralinguistic (i.e., nonverbal) dimensions, and meaning (a semantic component). The linguistic component is made up of the sounds, words, script, grammar, etc.; the paralinguistic of tone, pitch, stress, speed, volume, and affect; and the extralinguistic includes patterns of physical contact (haptics), space (proxemics), gestures and movements (kinesics), eye contact (oculesics), smell (olfactics), and timing in discourse (chronemics, which varies from mono- to polychronic preferences, i.e., speaking one at a time or overlapping during discourse). Finally, meaning resides in our head, but we express and communicate it to others through the use of language symbols. Whereas the worldview of every society arises from combinations of these components, each worldview configures them differently. If one were to layer one worldview over the other, for example, their three components would not coincide. Whereas components are "universal", how they are configured is "particular" to each group.

In the end, each worldview is a cultural–linguistic construct—a way of perceiving, conceptualizing, expressing, and interacting within a sociolinguistic context (represented by the circle). Each context represents a social circumstance—a set of social factors of significance to its speakers, and embedded in their culture, that result in requiring varying styles of speech (e.g., baby talk, polite speech, informal speech, familiar talk, etc.), as appropriate for that context. What is more, sociolinguistic determinants and the resultant speech styles vary from language to language and culture to culture, and these variations are accessible only through knowledge of the language system.

Once again, we see how language reflects and reinforces the speakers' view of the world. In language, we find encoded whatever speakers consider important in their culture. If a society of speakers is concerned with hierarchy, their language reveals and builds in hierarchy (e.g., *tu/vous* in French or *tu/Lei* in Italian). If they are concerned with maintaining formal and informal distinctions, this too is reflected in the way they speak (e.g., *você/o Senhor* in Portuguese). If sexism, racism, or classism prevail, these also are reflected and reinforced in language (degrees of which are found in most languages through the ways they refer to gender, other people, and forms for talking up or down the social system). In other words, styles are linguistically expressed and culturally bound.

In summary, language is our most fundamental human paradigm. It reflects and affects all our thoughts, our behavioral patterns, our societal norms, and more. Edward T. Hall expressed this succinctly when he wrote: "Culture *is* communication" (Hall 1973: 97) and, conversely, I would add, "communication *is* culture". But as each language–culture (I prefer a compound word "linguaculture" to assure their interrelatedness and inseparability) configures worldview components differently, many cross-cultural challenges are revealed only through access to the host language. This notion raises important issues related to the topic of this chapter—the nexus between L2 development and intercultural competence.

## 3. Second language development

Second language "development" refers to both "acquiring" language in naturalistic settings and "learning" in classroom situations, two distinctly different processes often producing differing results. From the previous section, we see that acquiring an L2 naturally exposes one to more than what is normally taught in traditional classrooms. It provides exposure to linguistic, para-, extra-, and sociolinguistic aspects, as well as to how L2 symbol systems relate to other components forming its worldview. But whether the L2 is acquired or learned, it initiates a gradual process of entering a new paradigm (more easily done in natural settings than in the artificiality of a classroom). As one gains in proficiency, the more likely one will begin to transcend and transform one's native system for, as one learns to see things anew, it becomes increasingly difficult to maintain a monocular vision of the world. Either way, grappling with the host language is key to understanding others "on their own terms". To convey this point another way, we might ask: is one language (and one culture, one worldview) adequate for dealing across language and culture groups? And, given increasing heterogeneity in most societies plus globalizing trends around the world, can a single language be adequate? Finally, how interculturally competent can one be without (at least some) ability in the host tongue?

This said, we must recognize that the task of developing an L2, while formidable, is not impossible. Developing proficiency is not a quick or easy process, but takes considerable time and effort. Yet, the higher the proficiency level achieved, the greater the rewards. Educators, however, often fail to take into account the length of time required to attain varying ability levels. The terms "beginning, intermediate, and advanced" applied to language courses are usually relative to each other and misleading, so that "advanced" may not be very advanced at all in terms of actual performance.

*Table 16.1* Time commitments for learning various languages

| Time | Average level attained |
| --- | --- |
| *Group I: Dutch, French, Italian, Spanish, etc.* | |
| 8 weeks (240 hours) | 1/1+ |
| 16 weeks (480 hours) | 2 |
| 24 weeks (720 hours) | 2+ |
| *Group II: German, Greek, Farsi, Urdu, etc.* | |
| 16 weeks (480 hours) | 1/2+ |
| 24 weeks (720 hours) | 2 |
| *Group III: Bengali, Czech, Hebrew, Russian, etc.* | |
| 16 weeks (480 hours) | 1 |
| 24 weeks (720 hours) | 2 |
| *Group IV: Arabic, Chinese, Japanese, Korean, etc.* | |
| 16 weeks (480 hours) | 1 |
| 24 weeks (720 hours) | 1+ |

A projection chart helps to determine the amount of time required to attain varying levels of functioning in a new language. Excerpts from one chart, compiled originally by the US Foreign Service Institute, indicate the time needed for an average student to develop ability in various other languages (Liskin-Gasparro 1982). In Table 16.1, languages are listed in four groups (according to levels of difficulty for English-speaking students) and the number of weeks and hours required to achieve levels from 0 to 5 (5 represents a native speaker) are indicated.

Although this chart is based on English speakers learning other languages, one might hypothesize that speakers of other languages might take about the same time in reverse to learn English. Of course, this does not take into account cases of historically and linguistically related languages such as Spanish speakers learning Portuguese or German speakers learning Dutch. In any case, the projection chart gives some initial insights about the time commitments required to achieve increasingly higher levels of proficiency in classroom situations.

## 4. Beyond monolingualism

Today, the importance of developing a second, third, even a fourth language, moving beyond monolingualism to multilingualism, is well established. Whereas psychologists in the early 1900s viewed dual language development as producing potentially negative effects, research in the last half century (and changing world circumstances) underscore the desirability of bilingual/multilingual abilities and point to cognitive and other benefits.

When referring to bilingualism (and multilingualism), we are speaking of degrees of proficiency along a continuum, not absolutes. Many types of bilinguals have been identified by linguists (e.g., simultaneous, sequential, alternating, balanced, active, passive, coordinate, compound, and so forth); however, the hypothetical bilingual as equilingual does not in fact exist. In other words, no individual, no matter the level of proficiency, commands two or more languages in identical ways—to the same degree, on all topics, and in every context (Fantini 2007: 263–77).

In addition to degrees and types of bilinguals, there are also varying profiles of abilities. For example, encountering the following text (or possibly having someone approach you on the street uttering these sounds), what might be your reaction?

Desculpe, o senhor, pode-me ajudar? Eu estou perdido e não posso encontrar o meu hotel. Pode-me explicar como chegar lá? Estaria muito agradecido. Muito obrigado.

One reaction might be to skip over the text entirely (or ignore the person seeking your assistance in a strange tongue). Another might be to show interest, feel intrigued, and try to communicate in creative ways. Moving beyond monolingualism, in fact, begins with what I term "incipient" bilingualism. Simply put, this stresses an attitude of willingness to engage with others with no common tongue (not an uncommon situation) and attempting to communicate. In this view, bilingualism begins with attitude, a willingness to engage, even when no skill exists. Such a disposition begins the process and allows one to move forward toward eventually developing the needed skills. The Portuguese text above also underscores another aspect of language—that, although languages communicate, they also excommunicate; they include those who share the system but exclude those who do not. Many focus on language primarily as a tool or academic subject and fail to consider this dual nature of language use.

Aside from bilingual types, degrees, and profiles, varying combinations are also possible when we consider bilingualism +/− biculturalism: one might be bilingual without substantial biculturalism, bicultural without bilingualism, or bilingual and bicultural. The last combination links L2 to second cultural competence, similarly to how they are linked in our native paradigm: we are competent in our native language (L1) and competent in our native culture (C1). Complete entrance into a new language–culture requires much the same—L2 + C2, or LC2 (albeit only to varying degrees of proficiency in accordance with factors such as exposure, duration, motivation, opportunity, etc.). Clearly, we do not have another lifetime to achieve the same level as in our first system.

In summary, developing LC1 and LC2 assures the most complete type of intercultural communicative competence. Those able to participate in more than one linguaculture, in fact, obtain something more. Through this duality, they possess two vantage points. In addition to LC1 and LC2, the individual has a way of comparing and contrasting both LCs—something that no monolingual of either language–culture can ever hope to achieve.

## 5. Language education and intercultural communication

Given their common and overlapping areas, language education and intercultural communication (ICC) are inextricably linked. The two fields, however, developed quite separately. Whereas language education has existed for centuries, ICC is a relatively new discipline. In fact, ICC was formalized only a little over 50 years ago when US Peace Corps trainers met to compare notes about their evolving practices (cf. Wight *et al.* 1999: 11–15). Although the field has made considerable progress, intercultural educators and trainers generally leave language concerns to their colleagues in the language field. This separation is apparent in most ICC educational programs and training models, and reflected in the tools used for assessment.

Some interculturalists support this separate approach; others reproach fluent L2 speakers who lack intercultural depth as "fluent fools" (Bennett 1997: 16–21). Indeed, individuals exist who are fluent in other languages, perhaps dilettantes intrigued by linguistic systems, without knowledge of the cultures they represent. And there are also individuals who have entered other cultures to varying degrees without host language knowledge, but it is easier to imagine that entry and acceptance are facilitated and accelerated when one speaks the target language. The ideal proposed here is the person competent in both the language and the culture. Clearly, both L2 and intercultural competence are desirable whether the fields are separate or not.

Although language educators often refer to the cultural dimensions of language, they have been mostly concerned with big "C" culture (i.e., art, music, literature, history, etc.). Conversely, interculturalists, despite their focus on cross-cultural communication, seldom refer to the specific languages through which this communication takes place. Yet, given the role of language in communicating, it seems ironic to focus attention on intercultural interactions and ignore the language that directly mediates every transaction.

Despite increasing globalization, which has caused more people around the world than ever before to have direct and indirect contact with each other, this separatist approach to ICC remains common today. And despite the prevalence of English worldwide, certainly not all cross-cultural communication takes place in English. More commonly, it transpires in one, two, or several languages. We need to rethink how to prepare individuals for intercultural participation using multiple languages. This requires new goals that include the ability of individuals to make themselves understood linguistically as well as to gain acceptance behaviorally. Expanded goals will lead to rethinking about how best to prepare and assist individuals for an intercultural sojourn. Both ICC and language education may develop new models that address common areas, enhance positive redundancies, and reinforce each other. When culture-specific orientation is conducted, the target language would be included. When culture-general orientation is conducted, language learning strategies (and general communicative strategies) would be addressed. In both cases, language is acknowledged as a vital aspect of preparation.

The new paradigm, however, must be based on a more comprehensive and consistent notion of intercultural communicative competence than currently exists in the field. Interculturalists still employ varied terms to refer to the abilities appropriate for successful intercultural contact. In addition to varied terms, they also stress differing aspects of ICC and measure and monitor differing components. These inconsistencies are reflected in the variety of terms and differing portrayals of ICC described in the literature. The concept of ICC needs refinement and greater consensus among practitioners in addition to correcting the inattention to language. The section that follows explores these issues—first, examining ICC and its components, followed by thoughts about measuring and monitoring this complex phenomenon.

## 6. Cultural and intercultural competence

To understand intercultural competence, it might be useful to think first about cultural communicative competence (or cultural competence, for short). Cultural competence (CC) is something we all have—it is the ability that enables us to be members within our own society. Like language, this is something we do not think much about because we have been culturally competent for as long we can remember. And like language, cultural competence developed through a gradual process of enculturation beginning at birth. Both evolved together and so quickly that, by the age of five, we were already native speakers and members of our society. We communicated in comprehensible and intelligible ways. Our native tongue was an important aspect—not the only aspect—but certainly an indispensable aspect to becoming a member of our society. Without it, we could certainly not have access to everything that we do. In fact, we became intelligible, acceptable members of our societies because of our participation through a specific communication system. We mastered our native language–culture (linguacultural) system and, without realizing it, our native linguaculture system mastered us (a phenomenon sometimes termed "language unawareness").

Given this background, we turn now to our encounter with a second linguaculture, some time later in life. Whereas all children acquire the language (and culture) that surrounds them, not all adults do likewise when entering a new society. Various factors—social, psychological, biological, and others—account for this. But perhaps the very existence of our native language–culture becomes the biggest impediment to entering a second language–culture.

Yet, intercultural contact (in positive contexts) affords the possibility of entering a new language–culture. This experience can be both powerful and enriching because, through the development of a second linguaculture, we can not only know more, we can also know differently. It permits contact and interaction with representatives of another worldview. It opens up choices, each of which bears consequences and thereby allows us, if we choose, to transform our original understanding of the world, while entering another worldview. Two proverbs circulating among interculturalists capture this thought: "if you want to know about water, don't ask a goldfish" (in other words, a goldfish is unaware of its own medium) and "looking out is looking in" (which is to say that, upon entering a new paradigm, we are able to compare and contrast this with our initial worldview, something not possible without a second vantage point).

Although the notion of cultural communicative competence is easy to grasp, the notion of intercultural communicative competence is not always entirely clear, hence the many labels used with varying meanings. These terms include global competence, international competence, multicultural competence, and so forth. Some writers stress global knowledge, others emphasize sensitivity, and still others point to certain skills. The characterization of ICC synthesized below, however, reveals a phenomenon that is more complex than any one of these views.

Briefly defined, ICC is a complex of abilities needed to perform "effectively" and "appropriately" when interacting with others who are linguistically and culturally different from oneself (Fantini 2006: 12). Whereas "effective" relates to one's own view of one's LC2 performance (i.e., an "etic" or outsider view of the host culture), "appropriate" relates to how this performance is perceived by one's hosts (i.e., an "emic" or insider view). Although these perceptions may differ, it is instructive to compare, contrast, and account for them precisely because they arise from differing views of the same cultural situation.

ICC encompasses multiple components: (1) a variety of characteristics; (2) three areas or domains; (3) four dimensions; (4) host language proficiency; and (5) degrees of attainment that evolve through a longitudinal and developmental process. Following are comments about each.

## Characteristics

First of all, it is useful to distinguish acquired characteristics (related to one's cultural and situational context) from traits (i.e., innate personal qualities)—a sort of "nurture vs. nature" distinction. This distinction is important for training and educational programs because it poses the question: which abilities form part of an individual's intrinsic personality and which can be developed or modified through training and educational efforts? Commonly cited ICC characteristics include flexibility, humor, patience, openness, interest, curiosity, empathy, tolerance for ambiguity, and suspending judgments, among others.

## Three areas or domains

ICC also involves ability in three areas or domains (which, not surprisingly, are just as relevant to success in one's own native LC1 as well). These are: (1) the ability to establish and maintain relationships; (2) the ability to communicate with minimal loss or distortion; and (3) the ability to collaborate in order to accomplish something of mutual interest or need.

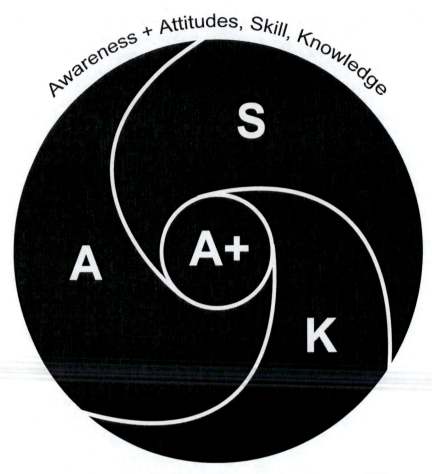

*Figure 16.3* The four dimensions of intercultural communicative competence (ICC)

## Four dimensions

The four dimensions of ICC are knowledge, (positive) attitudes/affect, skills, and awareness, shown in Figure 16.3.

Of these dimensions, awareness is central and especially critical to cross-cultural development. It is enhanced through reflection and introspection in which the individual's LC1 and the LC2 are contrasted and compared. Awareness differs from knowledge in that it is always about the "self" *vis-à-vis* everything else in the world (other things, other people, other thoughts, etc.), and ultimately helps to clarify what is deepest and most relevant to one's identity. Awareness is enhanced through developments in knowledge, positive attitudes, and skills, while it in turn also furthers their development.

## Host language proficiency

Ability to communicate in the host language enhances ICC development in quantitative and qualitative ways. This was clearly substantiated in an international research project testing assertions regarding intercultural competence (Fantini 2006: 44–49). One assertion read: "Learning the host language affects ICC development". After assessing levels of host language proficiency attained by sojourners, they gave testimonies when interviewed about how levels of proficiency affected their intercultural adjustments:

- my ability to communicate in the host language helped in many ways;
- it helped to know how to react in different situations and to overcome ambiguities;
- language was vital to overall intercultural success;
- it would have been impossible to perform my duties without it;
- if I were not capable of communicating, my work would have failed;
- it opened a new world of opportunities and experiences;
- things changed as I gained proficiency in the language;
- it was the main medium for everything, boosting my confidence and allowing integration;
- it enabled me to take part in conversations; I was not excluded;
- it allowed integration and helped me enjoy the experience;
- otherwise, I would have been closed to communication and culture;
- I am grateful that I was able to talk to hosts and co-workers;
- I was able to perform my job and would have been hindered without language;
- although I felt like a child, it would have been impossible to perform without language;
- without language, I would have missed so much;
- without language, it would have been frustrating, boring, and difficult;
- language was key to everything, to communicating, and to understanding the culture.

The sojourners also provided eloquent and insightful written narratives attesting to the significance of host language ability, and this from individuals who were initially monolingual and unsophisticated with foreign languages. Their thoughts derived not from linguistic study but from their own field experiences. They wrote of the importance of host language ability and also of the limitations imposed without it.

In summary, it is clear that increased host language proficiency enhances entry possibilities, whereas lack of proficiency constrains entry, adaptation, and understanding of the host culture. Grappling with another language also fosters the development of alternative communication strategies "on someone else's terms", a humbling and challenging process. Lack of an L2—even at a minimal level—constrains one to continue to think about the world and act within it entirely in one's native system, depriving the individual of one of the most valuable aspects of the intercultural experience.

## Degrees of attainment

ICC is a process that develops over time, occasionally with moments of stagnation and even regression. Much depends on the strength of one's individual motivation (instrumental vs. integrative) and attitudes regarding the host culture. Establishing benchmarks can help to monitor and measure one's progress in this journey, for example:

- Level I: educational traveler—e.g. a participant in a short-term exchange program (1–2 months);
- Level II: sojourner—a participant engaged in extended cultural immersion, e.g., an internship of longer duration (3–9 months);

| Global | Discrete |
|--------|----------|
| Direct | Indirect |

*Figure 16.4* Quadrant of multiple assessment strategies

- Level III: professional—an individual working in intercultural or multicultural contexts, e.g., staff employed in international institutions or organizations;
- Level IV: intercultural/multicultural specialist—a trainer or educator engaged in training, educating, consulting, or advising multinational students.

As the criteria on which intercultural competence is identified, monitored, and assessed are not always clear or consistent, assessment is an especially challenging task. Because it is complex, multiple assessment strategies are required to evaluate this multifaceted phenomenon. Figure 16.4 depicts a chart with varying modes and strategies that produce multiple indicators—global (using performance criteria), discrete (assessing specific items typical of quizzes, examinations, etc.), direct (when attention is focused on the evaluation process itself), and indirect (when attention is focused on an activity that can be used concurrently for assessment purposes).

Whereas many assessment tools exist to aid in assessing ICC, most assess specific components and most omit any reference to language proficiency (cf. Fantini 2009: 456–76). For this reason, a comprehensive tool was developed, known as the Assessment of Intercultural Competence (AIC), to ensure that all ICC components, including language proficiency, are addressed (Fantini 2006: 95–116).

The AIC serves a guide for use before, during, and after an intercultural sojourn, assisting in three ways: (1) establishing and critically examining intercultural objectives; (2) serving as a guide during the intercultural sojourn; and (3) providing a tool for assessment at various stages of the process as well as at the end. As such, the assessment approach is normative, formative, as well as summative. The tool can be used for both the sojourner and the hosts, looks at both etic and emic perspectives, and produces quantitative and qualitative data. Finally, the tool includes the assessment of language development as an important area of competence, an area omitted in most other forms.

## 7. Trends in language education and intercultural communication

Language education has made enormous strides over the past 50 years. Breaking tradition with a centuries-old grammar–translation approach, the audiolingual method shifted the focus from practices that emphasized memorization and grammar–translation to newer principles founded on behaviorism. Other ideas quickly ensued, leading to a succession of innovative methods—the Direct Method, Silent Way, CLL (Community Language Learning), Situational Reinforcement, Suggestopedia, and Total Physical Response (TPR), among others. These methods were based increasingly on theories of how language was learned. Although each new method experienced varying degrees of success, today, most educators have moved beyond a single "method" as attention has shifted from pedagogy (or teaching) to acquisition and learning (i.e., how individuals develop languages, differences in learning styles and strategies, and eventually to the crux of the matter—communicating).

Today, a "communicative approach" is widespread, stressing language proficiency and developing the learner's ability to perform specific tasks or functions in the second language–culture, e.g., greeting, asking/giving autobiographical information, asking/giving directions, requesting, commanding, negotiating, apologizing, etc. Although this represents an important step toward communicating in a second tongue, many language educators still focus mainly on "linguistic" aspects of communicating and neglect the concomitant interactive and behavioral dimensions required for communicating "appropriately". There are, however, some hopeful signs of change. A recent issue of the *Foreign Language Annals* (Spring 2010), for example, contains several articles for language educators that promote language awareness, social interaction, and pragmatic development, all steps in the right direction.

One explicit tool is the process framework, which posits cycles of seven stages for lesson plan development—from presentation of new material to practice, grammar exploration, transposition or use, sociolinguistic exploration, culture exploration, and, finally, intercultural exploration (comparing and contrasting target and native linguacultures) (Fantini 1997: 40–44). Use of this framework ensures that teachers address language, interactions, behaviors, and cultural aspects in each lesson plan cycle before beginning the next.

This said, the implementation of a communicative approach is spotty, and its use varies from institution to institution and country to country. Although many countries are making serious commitments to integrate foreign languages into their curriculum, the quality of language teaching varies dramatically. In recent years, China, Korea, and Chile have mandated the study of English as part of public education. Although Japan has followed this example, its instructional approach is mostly ineffective at present as teachers are inadequately prepared, speak mostly in Japanese, and focus almost entirely on grammar. This attempt contrasts with the European Union's recent policy designed to make all students minimally trilingual within a few years by beginning English as a second language in the early years and adding a third language a few years later.

In most cases, however, language is still taught without adequate cultural context, although increasing attempts are being made. Several educators are helping to redefine the role of the foreign language teacher. In Europe, an article by Sercu (2006), for example, speaks of "The Foreign Language and Intercultural Competence Teacher: The Acquisition of a New Professional Identity". This, plus works by Byram *et al.* (2002), Sercu *et al.* (2005) and Usó-Juan and Martínez-Flor (2006) all address this same issue. In the United States, the American Council on the Teaching of Foreign Languages (ACTFL) adopted new standards in 1996, which explicitly incorporate context. These standards include a model labeled the 3 Ps (products, practices, and perspectives), which also expands the teaching paradigm (based on a model developed by Fantini and Fantini 1997: 57–61). ACTFL also produced a series of thirty videos featuring exemplary teachers in language classrooms across the country who demonstrate communicative teaching activities situated in cultural contexts (cf. ACTFL FL Video Series, Pinker 2003). Both are signs of the language field moving in a direction that begins to overlap and reinforce the efforts of intercultural educators and closer to a more integrated model of intercultural competence.

Concurrently, unease about the spread of languages of wider communication as a form of imperialism (especially English, Spanish, and French) seems to have diminished in some quarters. This may be because minority language speakers increasingly choose to learn these languages. In many cases, L2 ability (especially in "world" languages) is viewed as a sign of prestige, opportunity, and modernity, affording advantages to bilingual and multilingual speakers (Graddol 2006). A recent article, moreover, points out that there are now more French speakers in the world outside of France than in France itself and that speaking French no longer relates only to French culture (Kimmelman 2010). Certainly, the same must be true of English. Esperanto (an auxiliary language developed over 100 years ago) presents a contrasting scenario as it was artificially created and pertains to no specific culture; yet, its spread continues around the world for quite different reasons. In general, Esperantists simply wish to get to know others from many cultures and find Esperanto a vehicle that makes this possible. Curiously, using a language that transcends all cultures makes most Esperantists into a new type of interculturalists themselves.

As with language education, the intercultural field has also spread around the world, and changes in how it is conceptualized and practiced are being witnessed. Assisting intercultural educators and trainers to develop the field is the professional organization, SIETAR (the Society for Intercultural Education, Training, and Research), akin to TESOL, ACTFL, and others. Through conferences and publications, SIETAR provides a venue and network through which interculturalists can share models, methods, and techniques for preparing people to live, study, and work interculturally.

Today, intercultural communication courses are well established in most universities in North America and Europe, and many institutions offer degrees in this field as well (Fantini and Smith 1997: 125–45). Courses and training programs are commonplace for students, business people, and professionals preparing for overseas sojourns. Often, these programs are offered concurrently with language courses. Cross-cultural orientation is provided not only for pre-departure, but also during and upon return from an overseas experience. Orientation efforts are both culture specific and culture general as the context requires; they are content and process oriented, and typically they employ interactive and participatory techniques and offer significant experiential and/or field-based activities.

## 8. Summary and conclusion

How can the frog know of the sea if it has never left its pond?

*Chuang Tzu, fourth century* BCE

Intercultural experiences contribute important educational dimensions to human development. Just as entry into one's initial language–culture paradigm is fundamental for every being to become human, access to a second linguaculture can also be quite powerful, opening up further possibilities and expanding upon that original view of the world. As one develops competences, it enhances these possibilities even further. Essential to these competences, however, is the development of proficiency in an L2. In Whorf's words, "a change in language can transform our appreciation of the Cosmos" (Carroll 1956: vii). Conversely, ignorance of the host tongue seriously constrains participation, impedes the ability to fully grasp alternative ways of being, and leaves us with monocular vision.

Developing ICC competences, however, is not a simple task. Despite modern language teaching approaches that stress communication, developing L2 proficiency requires time, effort, and consistency. In addition, it is not easy for most adults to question, introspect, and reconfigure the view that they hold of the world. For this reason, intercultural sojourns provide arguably one of the most provocative educational experiences imaginable, challenging the sojourner on every level. And although significant intercultural learning may occur without knowledge of the host language, it is qualitatively different. One is dependent on those willing and able to converse with the sojourner in his/her own tongue. Without host language ability, one cannot directly access their thoughts, their culture, their worldview. One can only learn about these things vicariously and intellectually, but not experientially. L2 completes the whole and provides total access, completely and directly.

Developing intercultural competences with language, then, facilitates full entrance into a new society. It allows participation and interaction in ways otherwise not possible. It extends relationships, evokes new sentiments, weakens stereotypes, and crumbles prejudices. It provokes new questions and stimulates reflection and introspection. And, in the end, it leads toward bilingualism+biculturalism. And if an L2 serves as a road map to another view of the world, then trilingualism is even better. A third language (and still others) breaks down a potentially polarized view of the world common to bilinguals (Mexicans are this and Americans are that) and promotes the understanding that cultural aspects may be shared by several groups instead of contrasting only two.

Moreover, intercultural experiences are multidimensional: many returnees from a sojourn abroad affirm its provocative and educational nature with comments like: "I learned a lot about my host culture but, surprisingly, I learned even more about myself". Such statements underscore the two-way nature of intercultural contact—in learning about others, we learn more about ourselves. And in learning about differences, we gain insights into our common humanity, despite the many linguacultures around the globe. For all these reasons, intercultural experiences are typically transformative, resulting in a profound paradigm shift.

Paradigm shifts of this magnitude would be difficult to imagine in a monolingual, monocultural individual, shifts so profound that they produce that "crack in the cosmic egg" that Pearce described over 40 years ago (Pearce 1971), shifts that give new meaning to the challenge from Don Juan when he admonished:

> Who the hell do you think you are to *say* the world is so and so ... just because you *think* it is so and so? Who gave you the authority? To believe that the world is only as you think it is, is stupid. The world is a strange place ... full of mystery and awe.
>
> *Castaneda (1972: 88)*

To summarize, language is fundamental to participation in society. This is true in our initial cultural experience; it is just as true in our second cultural experience. L2 development must be understood as essential to a full range of intercultural competences, which it is. When speaking about the abilities needed for effective and appropriate cross-cultural interactions, the languages of both parties must form part of the equation. Where both are not included, an imbalance results.

Monolinguals (especially those born to languages of wider communication) must recognize their language as both asset and liability. We cannot allow our languages of influence and power to prevent us from engaging in the dramatic experience that results when we attempt to communicate through other systems. The process must be direct, experiential (as well as "intellectual"), reflective, and introspective, and focus on learning to be and to do in alternative ways. As a result, we will profit maximally from the benefits of an intercultural educational experience—an experience that is unequaled, that changes our approach to the world, and that enriches us for the rest of our lives.

## Related topics

Learning the language of "the Other"; identity, conflict, and intercultural communication; the intercultural speaker and the acquisition of intercultural/global competence; an intercultural approach to second language education and citizenship; linguaculture

## Further reading

Fantini, A.E. (ed.) (1995) *Special Issue: Language, Culture and World View, International Journal of Intercultural Relations*, 19(2) (a collection of articles that explore the nexus between language, culture, and worldview).
Kramsch, C. (1994) *Language and Culture*, Oxford: Oxford University Press (a general work that investigates connections between language and culture).
Pinker, S. (1994) *The Language Instinct: How the Mind Creates Language*, New York, NY: William Morrow and Co. (a classic work that explores the role of language in the human experience).
——(2003) *Teaching Foreign Languages K-12: A Library of Classroom Practices*, ACTFL FL Video Series. Online. Available: www.learner.org/resources/series185.html (accessed 5 June 2010) (a video library for K-12 teachers).
Todeva, E. and Cenoz, J. (2009) *Multiple Realities of Multilingualism*, Berlin, Germany: Mouton de Gruyter (a compilation of narratives relaying the experiences of sixteen multilingual speakers and the impact on their lives).

## References

Anglin, J.M. (1970) *The Growth of Word Meaning*, Cambridge, MA: MIT Press.
Bennett, M.J. (1997) 'How not to be a fluent fool,' in A.E. Fantini (ed.) *New Ways in Teaching Culture*, Alexandria, VA: TESOL, pp. 16–21.
Byram, M., Gribkova, B, and Starkey, H. (2002) *Developing the Intercultural Dimension in Language Teaching*, Strasbourg: Council of Europe.
Carroll, J.B. (1956) *Language, Thought and Reality: Selected Writings of Benjamin Lee Whorf*, Cambridge, MA: Massachusetts Institute of Technology.
Castaneda, C. (1972) *Journey to Ixtlán: The lessons of Don Juan*, New York: Simon and Schuster.
Fantini, A.E. (1985) *Language Acquisition of a Bilingual Child: A Sociolinguistic Perspective*, Clevedon: Multilingual Matters.
——(ed.) (1997) *New Ways in Teaching Culture*, Alexandria, VA: TESOL.
——(2006) 'Exploring and Assessing Intercultural Competence', Brattleboro, VT. Online. Available: www.experiment.org/resources.html and www.sit.edu/graduate/7803.cfm (accessed 6 August 2010).
——(2007) 'Exploring bilingualism: its development, use and effects', in U.D. Scheu Lottgen and J. Saura Sánchez (eds) *Discourse and International Relations*, Berne: Peter Lang, pp. 263–77.
——(2009) 'Assessing intercultural competence,' in D.K. Deardorff (ed.) *The SAGE Handbook of Intercultural Competence*, Thousand Oaks, CA: Sage, pp. 456–76.
Fantini, A.E. and Fantini, B. (1997) 'Artifacts, sociofacts, mentifacts: a sociocultural framework', in A E. Fantini (ed.) *New Ways in Teaching Culture*, Alexandria, VA: TESOL, pp. 57–59.
Fantini, A.E. and Smith, E.M. (1997) 'A survey of intercultural communication courses', *The International Journal of Intercultural Relations*, 21(1): 125–45.
Graddol, D. (2006) *English Next 2006*, British Council. Online. Available: www.britishcouncil.org/learning-research-englishnext (accessed 5 August 2010).
Hall, E.T. (1973) *The Silent Language*, Garden City, NY: Doubleday and Co.
Kimmelman, M. (2010) 'Pardon my French', *The New York Times*, 21 April 2010.
Lane, H. (1976) *Victor, the Wild Boy of Aveyron*, Cambridge, MA: Harvard University Press.
Liskin-Gasparro, J.E. (1982) *ETS Oral Proficiency Testing Manual*, Princeton, NJ: Educational Testing Service.
Pearce, J.C. (1971) *The Crack in the Cosmic Egg*, New York: Washington Square Press.
Pinker, S. (2003) *The Language Instinct: How the Mind Creates Language*, New York, NY: William Morrow and Co.
Sercu, L. (2006) 'The foreign language and intercultural teacher: the acquisition of a new identity', *Intercultural Education*, 17(1): 55–72.
Sercu, L., Bandura E., Castro, P., Davcheva, L., Laskaridou, C., Lundgren, U., del Carmen, M., Méndez García, M. and Ryan, P. (2005) *Foreign Language Teachers and Intercultural Competence: An International Investigation*, Clevedon: Multilingual Matters.
Usó-Juan, E. and Martínez-Flor, A. (2006) *Approaches to Language Teaching and Learning: Towards Acquiring Communicative Competence through the Four Skills*, Berlin: Mouton de Gruyter.
Wight, A.R., Wasilewski, J., Arzac, A. and Jones, D. (1999) 'SIETAR's past, present, and future', in A.E. Fantini and J. Blohm (eds) *The SIETAR International Journal*, 1(1): 11–15.

# 17

# Understanding intercultural conflict competence

## Multiple theoretical insights

*Stella Ting-Toomey*

## 1. Introduction

Intercultural conflict frustrations often arise because of our lack of necessary and sufficient knowledge to deal with culture-based conflict communication issues competently. When a second language is involved, the situation may be exacerbated. Our cultural ignorance or ineptness oftentimes clutters our ability to communicate appropriately, effectively, and adaptively across cultural and linguistic lines. As the global economy becomes an everyday reality in most societies, individuals will inevitably encounter people who are culturally different in diverse workplaces and relationship-building situations. Learning to manage such differences mindfully, especially in intercultural conflicts, can bring about multiple perspectives and expanded visions in the conflict-encountering process.

This chapter is developed in six sections. The first provides an overview of the contents of the different sections. The second summarizes three theoretical approaches that hold potential promise for explaining and organizing the complex layers of intercultural conflict issues: social ecological theory, integrated threat theory, and face negotiation theory. The third section discusses critical issues related to the criteria and components of intercultural conflict competence. The fourth addresses the critical role of mindfulness and offers a set of reflective questions to stimulate a mindful transformation process by shifting our ingrained, culture-based conflict assumptions to alternative insights and viewpoints. The fifth section recommends specific identity threat management and facework management strategies to build intercultural conflict competence. The sixth section proffers directions for future theorizing and researching on the motif of intercultural conflict competence.

Intercultural conflict is defined in this chapter as the perceived or actual incompatibility of cultural values, situational norms, goals, face orientations, scarce resources, styles/processes, and/or outcomes in a face-to-face (or mediated) context (Ting-Toomey and Oetzel 2001). Both the appropriateness and the effectiveness features, together with the interaction adaptability feature, are part of the intercultural conflict competence criteria (Cupach *et al.* 2010). If inappropriate or ineffective conflict behaviors continue, the miscommunication can very easily spiral into a complex, polarized intercultural conflict situation.

More specifically, intercultural conflict competence refers to the mindful management of emotional frustrations and conflict interaction struggles due primarily to cultural, linguistic, or ethnic group membership differences. The larger the cultural distance, the more likely the escalatory conflict spirals will spin into an entangled, chaotic mode of biased attributions and defensive emotional reactions. The outcome goal of competent conflict practice is to transform ingrained culture-based conflict knowledge, habits, and skills from an ethnocentric viewpoint to an ethnorelative perspective.

Culture, from this backdrop context, is defined as a learned system of traditions, symbolic patterns, and accumulative meanings that fosters a particular sense of shared identity-hood, community-hood, and interaction rituals among the aggregate of its group members. Both cultural and individual conditioning factors in conjunction with multilayered situational factors shape intercultural conflict competence antecedent factors, process, and outcome.

## 2. Three intercultural conflict-related theories

After half a decade of researching and theorizing about intercultural conflict, many scholars have developed well-designed and well-tested theories to explain intergroup attitudes and general communication and particular conflict styles across languages and cultures (Gudykunst 2005a). For the purpose of this particular chapter and because of space limitations, I have selected three theories that hold theoretical and research promise for explaining intercultural conflict and intercultural conflict competence for the next generation.

The four criteria for my selection of theories include: (1) the theory has strong explanatory or framing potential in deepening our understanding of a complex, intercultural conflict case on multiple levels of analysis; (2) the theory covers some intriguing aspect of intercultural/inter-group conflict encounter and can be connected in a meaningful way with the intercultural conflict competence theme; (3) the theory has been systematically researched in a variety of cross-cultural or intercultural–intergroup conflict settings and displayed a reasonable sense of cross-cultural validity; and (4) the theory has heuristic function for bridging intercultural conflict theorizing process with conflict competence practice issues. I have selected the following three theories for a synoptic review and discussion in this section: social ecological theory; integrated threat theory; and conflict face negotiation theory.

### The social ecological theory

Intercultural conflict is a multilevel and multicontextual phenomenon. Although past inter-cultural studies tend to use either a macro-level lens or a micro-level view to analyze intercultural conflict, the social ecological perspective pays particular attention to multiple levels of analysis of a complex intercultural conflict case. A multilevel, contextual perspective in analyzing an intercultural conflict case provides the opportunity to understand (and possibly challenge) what are the deeply held assumptions of a particular cultural conflict worldview or practice (Kim 2001, 2005; Oetzel et al. 2006a). A multilevel theorizing process may illustrate that a particular inter-cultural conflict case contains both consistencies and inconsistencies at multiple levels of analysis. Additionally, a multilevel perspective helps to illustrate the multitude of factors that shape the cultural worldview level, institutional level, immediate community level, and individual level concerning conflict decoding process within and across distinct levels (Oetzel et al. 2006b).

More specifically, in utilizing a social ecological multilevel theoretical framework, there are four levels of research analytical units: macro-, exo-, meso-, and micro-level analysis. Brofenbenner (1979) viewed these four social ecological contexts as nested Russian dolls with reciprocal causal effects influencing each sphere. The "macro-level" analysis refers to the larger sociocultural and linguistic contexts, histories, worldviews, beliefs, values, and ideologies that shape the individual outlooks and the various embedded systems under this broad umbrella. The term "exo-level" (external environment emphasis) analysis refers to the larger, formal institutions (e.g., government agency system, courtroom system, health care system, or school system) that hold power resources and established personnel to enforce or modify policies, standards, and existing procedures (e.g., set language polices for education or legal systems). These exo contexts often have filtered (as opposed to direct) influence on individual conflict behaviors and reactions. On the other hand, the "meso-level" analysis refers to the broad-based, non-immediate units (e.g., media influence) to the immediate units' influence such as local church group, extended family unit, workplace setting, third-party witnesses, which have a direct impact on the individual's conflict attitudes and behaviors and the recurring conflict interactions. Finally, the "micro-level" analysis refers to both intrapersonal-level (i.e., personal and social identity-based issues, attributions, and conflict emotions) and interpersonal-level features (e.g., the ongoing team conflicts or the discourse and nonverbal face-to-face conflict encounters, which may take place in a second language) plus the actual settings in which the individuals live out their daily lives. It also emphasizes the importance of how individuals act as active agents to construct meanings and interpretations of a given conflict communication event. In addition to the macrosystem, exosystem, mesosystem, and microsystem of analysis, Brofenbrenner (1979) also later added a fifth context, the "chronosystem-level" of analysis—this level refers to the evolution phases, transitions, patterns, and consequences of developmental conflict changes over time.

The social ecological framework is an interdisciplinary approach that gained momentum in the mid-1960s and early 1970s to better address the influences of cultural and social contexts on human behavior and development (Brofenbrenner 1977; Stokols 1996). In recent years, for example, Ihinger-Tallman and Cooney (2005) used the social ecological framework to discuss the family system both as an institution and as a small group, and to describe how the study of family should be understood within the nested historical, linguistic, social class, and racial contexts.

## Core principles and analytical concepts

On a broad level, Stokols (1996) explains that the social ecological perspective consists of five core principles. First, communication outcomes are influenced by the cumulative effects of multiple physical, cultural, linguistic, social, and temporal factors. Second, communication outcomes are also affected by individual attributes and specific situations. Third, social ecology incorporates concepts from systems theory, such as interdependence and homeostasis, which helps to further understand the relationship between individuals and their broader contexts. Fourth, social ecology recognizes not only the interconnections among multiple settings, but also the interdependence of conditions within particular settings. Fifth, the social ecological perspective is interdisciplinary, involves multilevel domain analysis, and incorporates diverse methodologies. The key analytical concepts in the social ecological perspective are parallels and discontinuities, and cross-level effects.

## Parallels and discontinuities

In examining the reciprocal causation between the individual and the environment (e.g., intergroup conflict in a bilingual community setting), two specific types of relationships between and among levels of analysis can be probed: (1) parallels and discontinuities; and (2) cross-level effects (Klein et al. 1999). On the "parallels and discontinuities" relationship type, "parallel models" (also known as "isomorphic models") posit that the relationship between and among variables (e.g., concepts such as apology and forgiveness) at one level (e.g., interpersonal reaction level) will be the same or similar at another level (e.g., the larger institutional/governmental reaction level) in terms of magnitude and direction. In contrast, when different types of relationships or reactions are found among concepts at different (or in opposite direction) levels, these are described as "discontinuities".

## Cross-level effects

In the "cross-level" relationship type, studying intercultural conflict at any single level underestimates the fact that individuals, organizations, communities, and cultures are interconnected. Multilevel theorizing is influenced by the principles of interdependence and hierarchy from general systems theory. General systems theory emphasizes that different analytical levels are nested structures organized hierarchically. Given this assumption, three types of cross-level effects should be considered: (1) top-down effects; (2) bottom-up effects; and (3) interactive effects (Rousseau and House 1994).

"Top-down effects" refer to how the larger cultural/institutional forces shape the intercultural conflict stance or practice—from the macro, the exo, and the meso to the micro level. From this top-down effect viewpoint, individual conflict ideologies and practices are shaped by the various layered structures in which people are nested hierarchically (e.g., does the larger cultural worldview or institutional level emphasize the communication phenomenon of apology or forgiveness and does the effect spill downward to the lower levels?). "Bottom-up effects" focus on how lower levels (e.g., individuals and interpersonal relationships) affect higher levels (e.g., workplace/media, institutional policies, language use, and then cultural change). These types of effects are not as prevalent in the literature as top-down effects, but they are no less important. "Interactive effects" involve simultaneous and mutual effects at more than one level. In some cases, the effects at one level (e.g., culture) moderate the outcomes at another level (e.g., family policies, language choice). Top-down or bottom-up effects differ from interactive effects in that the former assume some sort of cumulative effect passing down (or up) from one level to the next in a systematic fashion, and interactive effects assume simultaneous process impacts at multiple contextual levels.

In any intercultural conflict situations, group membership identity threats and communicative face threats can occur at multiple levels of conflict struggles.

### The integrated threat theory

Throughout the years, Stephan et al. (1999) have collaborated closely together and influenced each other's ideas in their respective development of the integrated threat theory and the anxiety/uncertainty management theory. Integrated threat theory (Stephan 1999; Stephan and Stephan 2003) fuses various affective theories in the social identity and intergroup prejudice literature, and emphasizes one key causal factor in prejudice and intergroup conflict—namely, feelings of fear or threat. Feelings of fear or identity threat prompt intergroup animosities and conflicts. Feelings of fear or threat are closely aligned with Gudykunst's (2005b) notions of anxiety management issues and ineffective communication concepts.

The integrated threat theory can serve as a combined macro-level and exo-level conflict theory that explains intergroup or intercultural antagonism. Macro-level and exo-level theory factors refer to the "big picture" historical, socioeconomic, linguistic, and institutional factors that frame intergroup relations in a society. According to the integrated threat theory, "four antecedent conditions" prime the various perceived threat types: prior conflict history, ignorance or knowledge gap, contact, and status. According to Stephan (1999), "intergroup conflict history" is "the single most important seedbed of prejudice" (p. 32). Significantly, past intergroup conflict history serves as a backdrop to current intergroup contact relations. The more damaging and protracted the past conflict, the more perceived threats and prejudiced attitudes exist in the intergroup relations.

The second, the "intergroup knowledge gap" or "ignorance of the out-group" refers to the fact that, when intergroup members know very little of each other or assume they know more than they do (i.e., based on their overgeneralized, stereotypic lens), they are likely to perceive the other group as threatening in an intergroup hostility situation. A key element may be lack of language fluency, especially when a second language is involved. Interlocutors may have insufficient knowledge about the sociopragmatic dimensions of the target language in context. They may lack the ability to convey respect through the use of appropriate linguistic codes and tone of voice; they may have insufficient situational knowledge fluency (e.g., being unaware of when and to whom and in what situational context disrespect or identity threat codes should be directed or restrained). They may lack cultural fluency (e.g., a deep mastery of cultural dimensions such as individualism–collectivism values or small–large power distance values) in communicating with unfamiliar others during the antagonistic conflict situation. By not having adequate cultural knowledge and sociopragmatic competence in the target language, they may use inappropriate and ineffective discourse strategies in a polarized conflict context. Consequently, even minor intergroup irritations can escalate into major conflict misunderstandings and explosions.

Third, the "type (positive vs. negative) and frequency of intergroup contact" also shape feelings of security or insecurity, familiarity or unfamiliarity, and trust or mistrust between members of different language and identity groups. The more positive and personalized the contact, the more likely that members of both groups can see the "human face" beyond the broad-based identity group categories. The more negative and surface level the contact, the greater the perceived negative stereotypes and prejudice justifications. Fourth, "societal/group membership power status" refers to both institutional power dominance/resistance issues and individual power perception issues. At the institutional power level, dominant group members in a society can be perceived as controlling the key political, economic, linguistic, and media functioning of a society. On the individual power level, it can refer to how high-status group members view low-status group members in a society or in a particular institutional setting (and vice versa). Oftentimes, "high-status" or dominant group members may want to reinforce their own power positions (e.g., through the use of a "high-prestige" language) and not want to give up their power resources. They might also worry about hostility or competition from "low-status" (i.e., in the pecking order of the societal or institutional power scheme) minority group members who they fear will snatch away their precious resources in the community.

Minority group members might, indeed, resent the power resources (e.g., linguistic capital) or positions amassed by the dominant group members. They might have already experienced the historical legacy of inequality, injustice, prejudice, and unfair treatment weighted on them (e.g., due to national or institutional language policies). Thus, some minority group members are often emotionally frustrated because of the uneven playing field. The wider the cultural relation schism and the wider the perceived power schism, the more anxiety or fear is generated in the escalatory conflict cycles. These antecedent conditions can either escalate or de-escalate the perceived threat level in intergroup conflict.

## Identity threat types

The four basic identity threat types that lead to escalatory prejudice and conflict cycles are intergroup anxiety, negative or rigid stereotypes, tangible/realistic threats, and perceived value/symbolic threats. The theory also emphasizes "subjectively" perceived threats posed by the other "enemy" group (Stephan 1999). The first type of threat, "intergroup anxiety/anticipated consequences", often arises in unfamiliar intergroup encounter processes (Gudykunst 1995, 2005b). In intergroup encounters, people can be especially anxious about anticipated negative consequences such as negative psychological consequences (e.g., confusion, frustration, feeling incompetent in a second language), negative behavioral consequences (e.g., being exploited, harmed), and negative evaluations by out-group members (e.g., rejection or being identified with marginalized out-group members). Individuals have anticipated intergroup anxiety because they are concerned about potential face threats or their identities being stigmatized, embarrassed, rejected, or even excluded in intergroup contact situations. Non-native speakers, for example, may fear that their linguistic skills are inadequate to convey their ideas and emotions and they will be ridiculed by more proficient speakers. Emotional fear or anxiety is usually heightened and intensified when there exists intergroup historical grievances, low or little prior intergroup contact, or contact that is consistently antagonistic or reinforcing existing negative stereotypes.

The second type of threats, "rigid stereotypes or negative stereotypes", pose threats to the in-group (especially the dominant in-group) because in-group members typically learn negative images and traits of out-groups through the mass media and secondhand sources. These negative images can generate negative self-fulfilling prophecies and expectations and thus arouse negative intergroup encountering processes and outcomes. Rigid positive stereotypes can also be considered as a potential intergroup threat because of the fear that this particular group is taking over the technological field, the health care profession, or the educational system (e.g., by enforcing a medium-of-instruction policy). Overly positive and negative stereotypes can activate both dominant–minority and minority–minority intergroup conflicts in a multicultural society. This rigid or inflexible stereotypic mentality leads to a third type of identity threat.

"Tangible/realistic threats" refer to perceived content threats from the out-groups such as the battle for territory, wealth, scarce resources, and natural resources and also the perceived threats and competitions of economics, housing, education placements, and/or political clout. The fourth type of threats, "perceived values/symbolic threats", is founded in cultural/ethnic membership differences in morals, attitudes, beliefs, values, standards, and norms (e.g., differing linguistic norms of politeness). These are threats to the "standard way of living" and the "standard way of behaving" of the dominant in-group. Out-groups who hold worldviews and values that are different from the in-group threaten the core value systems of the in-group, which may then lead to fossilized in-group ethnocentrism and out-group avoidance or rejection. Values or symbolic threats can be experienced by linguistic/ethnic minorities, disadvantaged groups, and subordinate groups, as well as by majority groups. Research studies testing the four threat types demonstrated that three (i.e., intergroup anxiety, tangible threats, and values/symbolic threats) of the four threat types consistently predicted prejudice and attitudinal animosity from mainstream, dominant groups (e.g., European Americans) toward minority groups (e.g., African American, Asian American, and Mexican American groups; Stephan and Devine 2003) and also immigrant groups (e.g., Cuban American immigrants/second language speakers of the official language; Spencer-Rodgers and McGovern 2002) in a multicultural society.

In sum, intergroup anxiety and fear can color our biased expectations and intensify our perceived identity threat levels in dealing with culturally and linguistically dissimilar strangers or what we consider as our "enemies". At the macro level of analysis, if the backdrop of the intergroup relations evokes continuous, acrimonious hostilities, it is difficult for identity group members to come together with a clean slate. With historically tainted glasses and competition for scarce resources, members from dominant and minority language groups might view each other with certain mistrust, suspicions, disrespect, and face annihilation outlook (e.g., vicious verbal attacks and name-calling cycles).

## The conflict face negotiation theory

Intercultural conflict often involves different face-losing and face-saving behaviors. Face-losing and face-saving behaviors are situated discourse and nonverbal concepts (see Chapter 9, this volume). In order to practice competent facework in an intercultural conflict situation, the importance of practicing a sociopragmatic perspective in communication action is critical. This perspective takes into account the prescriptive or culture-based expectancies concerning the social setting, identity roles, statuses, language choice, and the speech event topic or goal of the situation from both conflict parties' and eye witnesses' viewpoints.

In the context of the conflict face negotiation theory, "face" refers to a claimed sense of desired social self-image in a relational or international setting (Ting-Toomey 1988, 2005a). The conflict face negotiation theory has been utilized on all four levels (macro, exo, meso, and micro) along the social ecological framework as presented earlier. Owing to space limitation, I will discuss the theory from an interactional macro-level (culture-level value dimensions' influence) and micro-level conflict facework perspective. In an antagonistic conflict situation, face loss occurs when we are being treated in such a way that our identity claims are being directly or indirectly challenged or ignored. Face loss can occur at the individual level, the identity group level, or both. Repeated face loss and face threat often lead to escalatory conflict spirals or an impasse in the conflict negotiation process (Ting-Toomey 2009a).

The facework collision process in a conflict encounter is often a direct result of sociopragmatic expectancy violation (e.g., perceived inappropriate language usage that clashes with self-ascribed status or role identity). Individuals from two contrastive cultural communities may have very different ideas about what discourse and nonverbal behavior are appropriate in a particular "activity type" such as a workplace feedback appraisal session or a motivational speech decoding process (Culpeper et al. 2003; Ting-Toomey 2009b). Members within an in-group language and cultural community have often developed a set of shared meanings and co-constitution process of what counts as proper or improper face-related conflict behaviors in a given emotionally laden, disagreement situation (Arundale 2006).

In fact, Spencer-Oatey (2005; van Meurs and Spencer-Oatey 2010) proposes that the study of facework can be understood via four relational interaction categories: a rapport enhancement orientation (a desire to strengthen or enhance harmonious relations between interlocutors); a rapport maintenance orientation (a desire to maintain or protect harmonious relations); a rapport neglect orientation (a lack of concern for the quality of interpersonal relations perhaps because of a focus on the self); and a rapport challenge orientation (a desire to challenge or impair harmonious relations between the interlocutors). Conflict facework collision is often part of a rapport-challenging or a rapport-neglecting speech event—whether it occurs intentionally or unintentionally. In particular, when a second language is involved in the facework clash process, the tone of voice, the nonverbal nuances, the situated linguistic codes, and the conflict assumptions that are being used and interpreted in the social disagreement episode can further derail the conflict management process.

To address some of the above concerns and in response to the heavy reliance on individualistic Western assumptions that underpin various conflict approaches, Ting-Toomey (1988) developed a cross-cultural conflict theory, namely, the conflict face negotiation theory. This theory emphasizes a collectivistic, Asian orientation perspective to understanding intercultural conflict and was intended to expand the theorizing process of existing, individualistic, Western-based conflict approaches (Ting-Toomey and Kurogi 1998).

## Core theoretical assumptions

Ting-Toomey's (2005a) conflict face negotiation theory assumes that: (1) people in all cultures try to maintain and negotiate face in all communication situations; (2) the concept of face is especially problematic in emotionally threatening or identity-vulnerable situations when the situated identities of the communicators are called into question; (3) the cultural value spectrums of individualism–collectivism (Ting-Toomey 2010; Triandis 1995, 2002) and small–large power distance (Hofstede 2001; House *et al.* 2004) shape facework concerns and styles; (4) individualism and collectivism value patterns shape members' preferences for self-oriented facework vs. other-oriented facework; (5) small and large power distance value patterns shape members' preferences for horizontal-based facework vs. vertical-based facework; (6) the value dimensions, in conjunction with individual, relational, and situational factors, influence the use of particular facework behaviors in particular cultural scenes; and (7) intercultural facework competence refers to the optimal integration of knowledge, mindfulness, and communication skills in managing vulnerable identity-based conflict situations appropriately, effectively, and adaptively. For a recent review of research findings in testing the conflict face negotiation theory, readers may consult Oetzel *et al.* (2008), Oetzel and Ting-Toomey (2003), and Ting-Toomey and Takai (2006).

## 3. Intercultural conflict competence: critical issues

Drawing on Spitzberg and Cupach's (1984) original conceptualization of interpersonal communication competence and also research in the broader intercultural communication competence domain, Wiseman (2003) conceptualizes general intercultural communication competence as involving the "knowledge, motivation, and skills to interact effectively and appropriately with members of different cultures" (p. 192). Deardorff (2006), in interviewing twenty-three scholars and trainers in the intercultural communication field, identifies the most preferred definition of intercultural competence as "the ability to communicate effectively and appropriately in intercultural situations based on one's intercultural knowledge, skills and attitudes" (p. 249). Canary and Lakey (2006) argue for the importance of the twin criteria of "appropriateness" and "effectiveness" in assessing conflict competence. They comment that communication can be judged as competent "only within the context of a relationship or situation because the context determines the standards of appropriateness that must be met" and that "communication can be appropriate without being effective and effective without being appropriate" (p. 187).

Thus, conflict facework competence can best be understood as a contextual package that includes the development of a deep knowledge structure of the cultural-framed social setting, the key conflict parties' sociocultural and personal identities, the conflict speech event, and the activation of culturally/linguistically appropriate and effective facework negotiation skills in respect to all the situational and multilayered features.

## Conflict competence criteria

The criteria of perceived interactional appropriateness, effectiveness, and adaptability can serve as the evaluative yardsticks of whether an intercultural communicator has been perceived as behaving competently or incompetently in a conflict situation (Cupach *et al.* 2010). "Appropriateness" refers to the degree to which the exchanged behaviors are regarded as proper and match the expectations generated by the insiders of the linguistic community. To behave appropriately in any given cultural situation, competent communicators need to have the relevant value knowledge patterns of the larger culture that frame the particular conflict situation. They also need to apply the specific situational knowledge schema of what constitutes proper or improper, and respectful or disrespectful communication patterns that promote an optimal constructive outcome. Thus, the criterion of "appropriateness" is conceptualized as a culture-sensitive application process in which individuals have mastered the deep knowledge structures and situated language codes of the culture-based values and behaviors.

The criterion of "effectiveness" refers to the degree to which communicators achieve mutually shared meaning and integrative goal-related outcomes through skillful interactional strategies in the various intercultural negotiation phases. To be perceived as effective inter-cultural communicators, individuals need to have a wide range of verbal and nonverbal repertoires to make mindful choices and cultivate creative options. Interactional effectiveness has been achieved when multiple meanings are attended to with accuracy and in an unbiased manner, and mutually desired interaction goals have been conjointly worked out in a strategic and inclusive manner.

More important, appropriateness and effectiveness criteria are positively interdependent. When one manages a problematic situation appropriately, the "good faith" proper and respectful behaviors can induce interaction effectiveness. Likewise, when one promotes an integrative-inclined mutual goal outcome, the integrative posture can maximize the perceived effectiveness criterion and further induce cooperative interaction responses from the other cultural party.

In addition, Ting-Toomey (2005a) argues that the criterion of perceived communication adaptability should be included as a third yardstick in assessing intercultural conflict competence. To behave both appropriately and effectively in managing a diverse range of intercultural con-flict situations, one needs to be mentally and behaviorally flexible and adaptive. "Communication adaptability" refers to our ability to change our interaction behaviors and goals to meet the specific needs of the situation. It implies cognitive, affective, and behavioral flexibility in dealing with the intercultural conflict situation. It signals our attunement of the other conflict party's perspectives, interests, goals, and conflict communication approach, plus our willingness to modify our own behaviors (e.g., second language use) and goals to adapt to the emergent conflict situation. Communication adaptability connotes dynamic code-switching ability in an intercultural conflict interaction scene. Dynamic cross-cultural code switching refers to the intentional learning and moving between culturally ingrained systems of behavior (Molinsky 2007).

## Conflict competence components

Individuals from contrasting cultural communities often bring with them different value patterns, verbal and nonverbal habits, and conflict interaction scripts that influence the punctuation points of competent vs. incompetent conflict behaviors. Sharpening the knowledge, mindfulness, and conflict communication skills of intercultural negotiators can enhance their pragmatic compe-tences. According to the conflict face negotiation theory (Ting-Toomey 2005a), culture-sensitive knowledge, mindfulness, and constructive communication skills constitute the key features of the intercultural conflict competence components.

Of all the components, knowledge is recognized as the most important component that underscores the other components of competence (Ting-Toomey 2004). With "culture-sensitive knowledge", communicators can learn to uncover the implicit "ethnocentric lenses" they use to evaluate the "bizarre" behaviors in an intercultural conflict scene. With culturally grounded knowledge, individuals can develop an accurate culture-sensitive perspective and learn to reframe their interpretation of a conflict situation from the other's cultural frame of reference.

"Mindfulness", from the intercultural conflict competence component framework, means the willingness to attend to one's internal cultural, linguistic, and personal communication assumptions, cognitions, and emotions and, at the same time, becoming exquisitely attuned to the other's communication assumptions, cognitions, language use, and emotions (LeBaron 2003; Ting-Toomey 1999). Mindful fluency requires us to tune into our own cultural, linguistic, and personal habitual assumptions in scanning a problematic interaction scene. It also refers to the willingness to learn from the unfamiliar other. To be mindful of intercultural differences, individuals have to learn to see the unfamiliar behavior from multiple cultural angles (Langer 1989, 1997). The discussion of the particular characteristics of mindfulness and mindful transformation process are presented in the next section.

"Constructive communication skills" refer to our operational abilities to manage a conflict situation appropriately and effectively via skillful language, verbal, and nonverbal behaviors, whether in a first or second language. Many communication skills are useful in enhancing intercultural mediation competences. Of the many possible operational competence skills, for example, skills such as deep listening, mindful reframing, de-centering, face-sensitive respectful dialogue skills, and collaborative conflict negotiation skills (Barge 2006; Coleman and Raider 2006; Ting-Toomey 2004) are competent communication practices, and are imperative when a second language is involved. In hooking the knowledge component with the conflict skills component, the theme of mindfulness plays a critical role in moving an intercultural conflict negotiator to enhanced ethnorelative consciousness.

## 4. The role of mindfulness in developing conflict competence

### Mindfulness: Eastern and Western orientations

According to Langer (1989, 1997), mindfulness can include the following characteristics: (1) learning to see behavior or information presented in the conflict situation as novel or fresh; (2) learning to view a conflict situation from several vantage points or perspectives; (3) learning to attend to the conflict context and the person in whom we are perceiving the behavior; and (4) learning to create new categories through which conflict behavior may be understood. Applying this Western mindfulness orientation to intercultural conflict, the perspective suggests a readiness to shift one's frame of reference from an ethnocentric lens to an ethnorelative lens, and the possibility of understanding a conflict episode from the other person's cultural frame of reference.

On the other side of the spectrum, mindfulness, from an Eastern Buddhist orientation, means "emptying our mindset" and learning to listen deeply without preconceived notions, judgments, and assumptions. Through an Eastern philosophical lens (Chogyam 1976; Kabat-Zinn 1994; Thich 1991, 1998), mindfulness means learning to observe an unfolding conflict episode with one-pointed wakefulness and watchfulness. It means being fully present—attending fully to our own arising emotions and the cultural disputants' conflict assumptions, worldviews, language usage, positions, interests, and arising emotions. It also means listening deeply with all our senses open and all our perceptual filters unclogged.

### Mindful transformation questions

We can also use some critical reflective questions to guide our conflict transformative "U" learning process (Fisher-Yoshida 2005; Mezirow 2000). For example, if a second language disputant in an intercultural mediation session was constantly using "silence" or indirect response to every question a mediator asked during the conflict storytelling phase, the mindful transformative questions that the mediator can process within herself or himself are: first, what are my cultural, linguistic, and personal assessments about the use of "silence" in this particular mediation scene? (a content reflection question). Second, why do I form such assessments and what are the sources of my assessments? (a process critical reflection question). Third, what are the underlying assumptions or values that drive my evaluative assessments? (a premise value question). Fourth, how do I know that they are relevant or valid in this second language conflict context? (a premise self-challenge question). Fifth, what reasons might I have for maintaining or changing my underlying conflict premises? (an identity transformation question). Sixth, how should I shift my cultural, linguistic, or personal premises into the direction that promotes deeper intercultural understanding? (a mindset transformation question). Seventh, how should I flex adaptively on both verbal and nonverbal conflict style levels in order to display facework-sensitive behaviors and to facilitate a productive common interest outcome? (a behavioral transformation question). The first three questions are based on Fisher-Yoshida's work (2005) concerning the importance of engaging in deeper double-loop thinking in analyzing the role of self-in-conflict context. The last four are an extension of Ting-Toomey's (2005b) mindful identity transformation work.

We engage in an ethnocentric viewpoint when we view our own cultural way of communicating as the most proper way, and we view the unfamiliar conflict communication practices of other linguistic and cultural groups as improper and incorrect. Ethnorelativism, on the other hand, means the capacity to view conflict communication behaviors from the other person's cultural premise and understand why people behave the way they behave from their cultural value orientations' perspective (Bennett and Bennett 2004). These seven questions can also be applied to our own intentional transformational process in dealing with diverse individuals (e.g., non-native speakers) in the intercultural mediation session.

## 5. Recommendations for competent conflict practice

### Managing identity threats

The focal ideas on intergroup conflict competence focus on the reduction of emotional or identity threat and promoting accurate knowledge between the two polarized identity groups. Stephan and Stephan (2003) recommended some possible remedies to lighten the perceived emotional anxiety and intergroup threat loads: (1) gaining accurate knowledge of major cultural value difference dimensions to enhance mutual understanding and decrease ignorance; (2) promoting information about overriding human values (such as family security, respect, and compassion) common to all cultures in order to decrease prejudice about out-group members; (3) pursuing accurate data concerning the exaggerated nature of people's beliefs concerning the scarcity of resources in a conflict situation; (4) creating or developing superordinate identities so that both cultural groups can realize the connected humanistic souls that exist between them; and (5) reminding people of the multiple social categories or overlapping circles to which they belong.

Additionally, setting up opportunities for two or more identity groups to engage in cooperative learning techniques (e.g., team-building activities and working on positive interdependent tasks) would help both groups to see the "human face" beyond the broad-based stereotypic group membership labels. Cooperative learning techniques include face-to-face active communication engagements between dominant group and minority groups in solving an interdependent problem, and that the outcome holds positive reward incentive.

More importantly, both groups should be able to experience some concrete interdependent contributions to the problem-solving task. Cooperative learning techniques also have built-in semi-structured time to promote friendships and a mutual personalized sharing process. Thus, the contact condition should allow individuals to get to know each other on a personalized, culture-sensitive sharing level as opposed to a superficial, stereotypic level. Lastly, the intergroup contact process should be strongly supported by key authority figures or change agents in the organization or the community and, hopefully, with adequate resource funding. In these cooperative settings, the "positive goal interdependence" between cultural/ethnic/linguistic groups has been identified as the key causal factor in accomplishing positive interpersonal relationship and achievement outcomes (Stephan and Stephan 2001).

## Managing facework vulnerability

According to assumption 7 of the conflict face negotiation theory, intercultural facework competence refers to the optimal integration of knowledge, mindfulness, and communication skills in managing vulnerable identity-based interaction scenes appropriately, effectively, and adaptively. Intercultural mediation competence can also borrow from the twin standards of communication appropriateness and effectiveness. An intercultural mediator has acted appropriately when both cultural disputants view that the mediator has communicated skillfully and displayed adaptive facilitation styles so that both disputants feel included in the mediation session. Concurrently, the mediator has also moved the conflict parties forward productively or effectively and helped them to reach a do-able, mutual interest outcome.

To behave appropriately in a mediation session, competent mediators need to internalize the relevant value knowledge patterns and the in situ operational language patterns of the larger cultures and the ethnic heritages of both conflict parties. They also need to apply culture-sensitive situational norms in understanding the holistic conflict story. To be perceived as effective mediators, the intercultural mediators need to have linguistic, verbal, and nonverbal elastic skills to confront, to conjure, and to know when to "manage" the mediation process and when to "let go" of the mediation process and let the disputants take over the process.

More important, appropriateness and effectiveness criteria reciprocally influence one another. When the mediator uses a culture-sensitive approach to mediate the mediation session, the "good faith" respectful behaviors can induce a cooperative and effective outcome. Likewise, when the mediator skillfully moves the disputants from one stage of the mediation process to another stage, her or his effective facilitation skills can elicit respect from both the disputants toward each other and toward the mediator herself or himself.

For example, in mediating conflicts with Asian cultural members, mediators may want to heed the following guidelines: (1) Asian disputants may emphasize a strong benevolent conflict approach in entering a mediation session; (2) they may expect that the mediator is there to serve as a benevolent, authoritative figure and to give them the solution to a conflict problem; (3) Asian disputants are oftentimes face sensitive in disclosing private information—they may not feel comfortable engaging in direct conflict storytelling and self-disclosure unless some emotional ties or trust have been established; (4) they may not see the distinction between substantive conflict issue and relational conflict issue—they may tend to see both datasets as an integrative whole; (5) they may not feel comfortable with the free-wheeling brainstorming techniques in the problem-solving phase especially under time pressure; and (6) they may need to claim "face victory" in front of their own in-groups.

On the other hand, competent intercultural mediators must also learn to validate the face claims or social self-images of the Western disputants via the following strategies: (1) culturally astute mediators need to spend more time in the "introduction" mediation stage to educate both Asian and Western disputants about the importance of displaying cultural sensitivity to all conflict parties in the mediation session; (2) they may want to address the possibility that individuals in the room may have different culture-based, language-based, and personal-based conflict style approaches and preferences; (3) they may also want to emphasize that their mediator role is neutral, impartial, and objective so that they can match the expectancies and concerns of disputants who subscribe to a strong "impartial" conflict approach; (4) they need to develop full mindfulness in serving as well-balanced traffic conductors in balancing talk times between potentially Western individualists and reticent Asian collectivists; (5) they may want to educate Western disputants about the difference between low-context and high-context communication tendencies (Hall 1983)—with Asian disputants' possible tendency to "context" their conflict story before getting to core substantive conflict issues; and (6) they may also need to role model adaptive communication styles so that both the Asian and the Western disputants can observe firsthand how to engage in appropriate and effective culture-sensitive dialogue. Finally, mediators may want to team up with other intercultural experts and conduct co-mediation sessions when there are strong linguistic and deep-rooted cultural animosities between the polarized cultural group factions.

## 6. Directions for future theorizing and research

This section presents some promising research directions drawing from the integrated threat theory and the conflict face negotiation theory. In addition, under each theory, research directions related to the prime criteria of "conflict appropriateness" and "conflict effectiveness" are addressed. The research directions proposed under each theoretical umbrella can also be equally applied to the macro, exo, meso, and micro levels of the social ecological framework.

### Researching integrated threat theory

In terms of further testing of the integrated threat theory in the context of intercultural conflict, there are three clusters of research directions. The first addresses the identity threat antecedent conditions. The second revolves around testing the relationship between different identity threat types and conflict escalation and de-escalation. The third appeals to the connection between identity threat management and conflict competence.

The first cluster research questions ask: what are the necessary and sufficient knowledge blocks that intergroup members need to master in order to reduce identity threat and increase identity security? What are the knowledge structures that are deeply needed to increase intergroup identity familiarity and reduce perceived identity threats? How can trust be restored and repaired when the intergroup relationship is severely broken? How can power be balanced at the institutional and individual levels so that social justice and fair treatment can be genuinely experienced by disenfranchised group members (e.g., non-native speakers)?

The second cluster research questions ask: which threat type triggers the most competitive intergroup discourse climate? How do negative or positive intergroup stereotypes affect the use of different verbal and nonverbal conflict strategies? What are some creative language strategies that can be deployed to counteract biased, stereotypic conflict messages? How do identity threat emotions such as fear, jealousy, resentment, bitterness, or hatred get translated into toxic language types and trigger further escalatory conflict spirals? How do all these threat types get played out in intergroup (e.g., dominant–minority group conflict) and intragroup (e.g., minority–minority group conflict) conflict situations?

In discussing the competences that are needed in managing identity threats appropriately and effectively, cooperative learning techniques and interdependent positive goals were mentioned.

Here are some fruitful directions for future research: what are some appropriate and effective discourse strategies that can be used to instill superordinate identities and interdependent fates among separate cultural/ethnic/linguistic group circles? What is the role of a competent translator or interpreter in the diplomatic multitrack negotiation process or in the interpersonal peace-building process in second language contexts? What architectural layout serves as optimal temporal, spatial, and seating arrangements in order for effective international diplomacy dialogues to take place? How can bilingual or multilingual mediators create a secure "third space" through the artful use of sociopragmatic language to promote mutual culture learning and mutual cultural respect in diverse identity groups?

## Researching conflict face negotiation theory

In light of existing findings and gaps in the face negotiation theory, the following three research areas hold promise and merit attention in future research: facework situations; facework emotions; and facework competence criteria. The study of face negotiation in conflict would definitely benefit from examinations of the relationship among "situations", face concerns, and facework language code usage. Questions such as the following need more systematic research investigations: under what specific situational conditions would conflict disputants be more interested in mutual face protection rather than self-face protection? Under what triggering mechanisms would conflict negotiators be more concerned with mutual face protection as opposed to mutual face annihilation? What are the language codes of honor, dignity, insult, and sabotage in different speech communities and in different social class strata? Under what situational conditions would face-threatening vs. face-honoring messages have a more powerful impact on the "enemy" recipients in the global stage? In connecting with different value dimension issues, what constitutes the most persuasive sequence of facework message delivery in moving both relationship-based and task-based conflict issues on track?

If we dig deeper, face concerns are directly linked to affective-based identity issues in conflict. We need more systematic studies in understanding the developmental flows of the facework defensive and supportive emotions. We need to pay more astute attention to the situational norms and rules that regulate conflict emotions' display and conflict emotions' reception in a diverse range of cultural/linguistic situations. We need to understand the repeated core metaphors, symbols, psychosomatic changes, conflict rhythms, plus verbal and nonverbal signals that surround the onset of affective facework embarrassment and affective peace-building resolution. Furthermore, the emotions of pride, shame, guilt, and redemption are all powerful emotional concepts lacking sufficient linguistic treatment in the intercultural conflict literature. These are complex, affective responses generated and experienced in reaction to others and related to the cognitive appraisals of the worthiness of self-face and other-face issues. More detailed studies of the role of nonverbal affective messages that accompany the rapport-challenging or rapport-neglecting conflict discourse may also help to expand the theoretical boundary of the conflict face negotiation theory.

Furthermore, both qualitative and quantitative research studies via a co-orientation approach will greatly facilitate the theory development phase of understanding "intercultural conflict competence". From analyzing real-life intercultural conflict case studies to conducting situated discourse analysis studies in second language conflict situations to using videotaped conflict interaction approaches, a methodological pluralistic perspective at this juncture can truly enhance our explanation of the intricate conflict face-saving, conflict face-compensation, conflict face-concession, and conflict face-honoring processes. An insider emic perspective in understanding the situated features and discourse meanings of terms such as identity respect or identity insult should also yield rich culture-specific face competence insights.

## 7. Conclusion

This chapter advocates the importance of understanding the multiple layers of intercultural conflict—from a macro identity threat perspective to the micro level of how individuals manage facework violation issues across languages and cultures. It also emphasizes the importance of understanding sociopragmatic discourse usage in promoting skillful intercultural conflict management. Both international insider and outsider research collaboration efforts are urgently needed to understand the rich fabric of the different designs and the golden threads that constitute the complex intercultural conflict competence system. From the narrative approach to the functional–quantitative approach, more theoretical efforts from both indigenous and cross-cultural comparative perspectives are needed for us to truly hear the multiplicity of voices, stories, and melodies of the storytellers from diverse situational conflict contexts, and from a diverse range of gendered, social class, and racial/ethnic/linguistic global communities.

## Related topics

Culture and contexts; facework and communication; identity and cultural communication; intercultural pragmatics; intercultural theory and practice; intergroup communication; intercultural training; sociopragmatics

## Further reading

Cupach, W., Canary, D. and Spitzberg, B. (eds) (2010) *Competence in Interpersonal Conflict*, 2nd edn, Long Grove, IL: Waveland Press (an up-to-date text on the central issues of conflict competence in interpersonal, family, organizational, intercultural, and mediation contexts).

Oetzel, J.G. and Ting-Toomey, S. (2003) 'Face concerns in interpersonal conflict: a cross-cultural empirical test of the face-negotiation theory', *Communication Research*, 30: 599–624 (a direct test of the conflict face negotiation theory with empirical evidence).

Stephan, W.G. and Stephan, C.W. (2001) *Improving Intergroup Relations*, Thousand Oaks, CA: Sage (a concise book on how to manage intergroup identity threats and improve intergroup relations).

Ting-Toomey, S. and Oetzel, J.G. (2001) *Managing Intercultural Conflict Effectively*, Thousand Oaks, CA: Sage (a classic book on managing intercultural conflict effectively in intercultural-intimate, team, and organizational conflicts).

## References

Arundale, R. (2006) 'Face as relational and interactional: a communication framework for research on face, facework, and politeness', *Journal of Politeness Research*, 2: 193–216.

Barge, J.K. (2006) 'Dialogue, conflict, and community', in J.G. Oetzel and S. Ting-Toomey (eds) *The SAGE Handbook of Conflict Communication: Integrating Theory, Research, and Practice*, Thousand Oaks, CA: Sage, pp. 517–48.

Bennett, J.M. and Bennett, M.J. (2004) 'Developing intercultural sensitivity: an integrative approach to global and domestic diversity', in D. Landis, J. Bennett and M. Bennett (eds) *Handbook of Intercultural Training*, 3rd edn, Thousand Oaks, CA: Sage, pp. 147–65.

Brofenbrenner, U. (1977) 'Toward an experimental ecology of human development', *American Psychologist*, 32: 513–31.

——(1979) *The Ecology of Human Development*, Cambridge, MA: Harvard University Press.

Canary, D. and Lakey, S.G. (2006) 'Managing conflict in a competent manner: a mindful look at events that matter', in J.G. Oetzel and S. Ting-Toomey (eds) *The SAGE Handbook of Conflict Communication*, Thousand Oaks, CA: Sage, pp. 185–210.

Chogyam, T. (1976) *The Foundations of Mindfulness*, Berkeley, CA: Shambhala.

Coleman, S. and Raider, E. (2006) 'International/intercultural conflict resolution training', in J.G. Oetzel and S. Ting-Toomey (eds) *The SAGE Handbook of Conflict Communication*, Thousand Oaks, CA: Sage, pp. 663–90.

Culpeper, J., Bousfield, D. and Wichman, A. (2003) 'Impoliteness revisited: with special reference to dynamic and prosodic aspects', *Journal of Pragmatics*, 35: 1545–79.

Cupach, W., Canary, D. and Spitzberg, B. (eds) (2010) *Competence in Interpersonal Conflict*, 2nd edn, Long Grove, IL: Waveland Press.

Deardorff, D.K. (2006) 'Identification and assessment of intercultural competence as a student outcome of internationalization', *Journal of Studies in International Education*, 10: 241–66.

Fisher-Yoshida, B. (2005) 'Reframing conflict: intercultural conflict as potential transformation', *Journal of Intercultural Communication*, 8: 1–16.

Gudykunst, W.B. (1995) 'Anxiety/uncertainty management (AUM) theory: current status', in R. Wiseman (ed.) *Intercultural Communication Theory*, Thousand Oaks, CA: Sage, pp. 8–58.

——(ed.) (2005a) *Theorizing about Intercultural Communication*, Thousand Oaks, CA: Sage.

——(2005b) 'An anxiety/uncertainty management (AUM) theory of effective communication: making the mesh of the net finer', in W.B. Gudykunst (ed.) *Theorizing about Intercultural Communication*, Thousand Oaks, CA: Sage, pp. 281–322.

Hall, E.T. (1983) *The Dance of Life*, New York: Doubleday.

Hofstede, G.H. (2001) *Culture's Consequences: Comparing Values, Behaviors, Institutions, and Organizations Across Cultures*, 2nd edn, Thousand Oaks, CA: Sage.

House, R.J., Hanges, P.J., Javidan, M., Dorfman, P.W. and Gupta, V. (eds) (2004) *Culture, Leadership, and Organizations: The GLOBE Study of 62 Societies*, Thousand Oaks, CA: Sage.

Ihinger-Tallman, M. and Cooney, T. (2005) *Families in Context: An Introduction*, Los Angeles, CA: Roxbury.

Kabat-Zinn, J. (1994) *Wherever You Go, There You Are: Mindfulness Meditation in Everyday Life*, New York: Hyperion.

Kim, Y.Y. (2001) *Becoming Intercultural: An Integrative Theory of Communication and Cross-Cultural Adaptation*, Thousand Oaks, CA: Sage.

——(2005) 'Adapting to a new culture: an integrative communication theory', in W.B. Gudykunst (ed.) *Theorizing about Intercultural Communication*, Thousand Oaks, CA: Sage, pp. 375–400.

Klein, K.J., Tosi, H. and Cannella, A.A. (1999) 'Multilevel theory building: benefits, barriers, and new developments', *Academy of Management Review*, 24: 243–48.

Langer, E. (1989) *Mindfulness*, Reading, MA: Addison-Wesley.

——(1997) *The Power of Mindful Learning*, Reading, MA: Addison-Wesley.

LeBaron, M. (2003) *Bridging Cultural Conflicts: A New Approach for a Changing World*, San Francisco, CA: Jossey Bass/John Wiley.

Mezirow, J. (2000) *Learning as Transformation: Critical Perspectives on a Theory in Progress*, San Francisco, CA: Jossey Bass.

Molinsky, A. (2007) 'Cross-cultural code-switching: the psychological challenges of adapting behavior in foreign cultural interactions', *Academy of Management Review*, 32(2): 622–40.

Oetzel, J.G. and Ting-Toomey, S. (2003) 'Face concerns in interpersonal conflict: a cross-cultural empirical test of the face-negotiation theory', *Communication Research*, 30: 599–624.

Oetzel, J.G., Ting-Toomey, S. and Rinderle, S. (2006a) 'Conflict communication in contexts: a social ecological perspective', in J.G. Oetzel and S. Ting-Toomey (eds) *The SAGE Handbook of Conflict Communication*, Thousand Oaks, CA: Sage, pp. 727–39.

Oetzel, J.G., Arcos, B., Mabizela, P., Weinman, A.M. and Zhang, Q. (2006b) 'Historical, political, and spiritual factors of conflict: understanding conflict perspectives and communication in the Muslim world, China, Colombia, and South Africa', in J.G. Oetzel and S. Ting-Toomey (eds) *The SAGE Handbook of Conflict Communication*, Thousand Oaks, CA: Sage, pp. 549–74.

Oetzel, J.G., Garcia, A. and Ting-Toomey, S. (2008) 'An analysis of the relationships among face concerns and facework behaviors in perceived conflict situations: a four-culture investigation', *International Journal of Conflict Management*, 19: 382–403.

Rousseau, D.M. and House, R.J. (1994) 'Meso organizational behavior: avoiding three fundamental biases', in C.L. Cooper and D.M. Rousseau (eds) *Trends in Organizational Behavior*, Vol. 1, New York: John Wiley and Sons, pp. 13–30.

Spencer-Oatey, H. (2005) '(Im)politeness, face and perceptions of rapport: unpacking their bases and interrelationships', *Journal of Politeness Research*, 1: 95–119.

Spencer-Rodgers, J. and McGovern, T. (2002) 'Attitudes toward culturally different: the role of inter-cultural communication barriers, affective responses, consensual stereotypes, and perceived threat', *International Journal of Intercultural Relations*, 26: 609–31.

Spitzberg, B.H. and Cupach, W. (1984) *Interpersonal Communication Competence*, Beverly Hills, CA: Sage.

Stephan, C.W. and Stephan, W.G. (2003) 'Cognition and affect in cross-cultural relation', in W.B. Gudykunst (ed.) *Cross-cultural and Intercultural Communication*, Thousand Oaks, CA: Sage, pp. 111–26.

Stephan, W.G. (1999) *Reducing Prejudice and Stereotyping in Schools*, New York: Teachers College Press/Columbia University.

Stephan, W.G. and Devine, P. (2003) 'The antecedents and implications of interracial anxiety', *Personality and Psychology Bulletin*, 29: 790–801.

Stephan, W.G. and Stephan, C.W. (2001) *Improving Intergroup Relations*, Thousand Oaks, CA: Sage.

Stephan, W.G., Stephan, C.W. and Gudykunst, W.B. (1999) 'Anxiety in intergroup relations: a compar-ison of anxiety/uncertainty management theory and integrated threat theory', *International Journal of Intercultural Relations*, 23: 613–28.

Stokols, D. (1996) 'Translating social ecological theory into guidelines for community health promotion', *American Journal of Health Promotion*, 10: 282–98.

Thich, N.H. (1991) *Peace is Every Step: The Path of Mindfulness in Everyday Life*, New York: Bantam Books.

——(1998) *Mindful Living*, Berkeley, CA: Parallax Press.

Ting-Toomey, S. (1988) 'Intercultural conflicts: a face-negotiation theory', in Y.Y. Kim and W.B. Gudykunst (eds) *Theories in Intercultural Communication*, Newbury Park, CA: Sage, pp. 213–35.

——(1999) *Communicating across Cultures*, New York: Guilford.

——(2004) 'Translating conflict face-negotiation theory into practice', in D. Landis, J. Bennett and M. Bennett (eds) *Handbook of Intercultural Training*, 3rd edn, Thousand Oaks, CA: Sage, pp. 217–48.

——(2005a) 'The matrix of face: an updated face-negotiation theory', in W.B. Gudykunst (ed.) *Theorizing about Intercultural Communication*, Thousand Oaks, CA: Sage, pp. 71–92.

——(2005b) 'Identity negotiation theory: crossing cultural boundaries', in W.B. Gudykunst (ed.) *Theorizing about Intercultural Communication*, Thousand Oaks, CA: Sage, pp. 211–34.

——(2009a) 'Intercultural conflict competence as a facet of intercultural competence development: multiple conceptual approaches', in D.K. Deardorff (ed.) *The SAGE Handbook of Intercultural Competence*, Thousand Oaks, CA: Sage, pp. 100–120.

——(2009b) 'Facework collision in intercultural communication', in F. Bargiela-Chiappini and M. Haugh (eds) *Face, Communication and Social Interaction*, London: Equinox Publications, pp. 227–49.

——(2010) 'Applying dimensional values in understanding intercultural communication', *Communication Monographs*, 77(2): 169–80.

Ting-Toomey, S. and Kurogi, A. (1998) 'Facework competence in intercultural conflict: an updated face-negotiation theory', *International Journal of Intercultural Relations*, 22: 187–225.

Ting-Toomey, S. and Oetzel, J.G. (2001) *Managing Intercultural Conflict Effectively*, Thousand Oaks, CA: Sage.

Ting-Toomey, S. and Takai, J. (2006) 'Explaining intercultural conflict: promising approaches and directions', in J.G. Oetzel and S. Ting-Toomey (eds) *The SAGE Handbook of Conflict Communication*, Thousand Oaks, CA: Sage, pp. 691–723.

Triandis, H.C. (1995) *Individualism and Collectivism*, Boulder, CO: Westview Press.

——(2002) 'Individualism and collectivism', in M. Gannon and K. Newman (eds) *Handbook of Cross-cultural Management*, New York: Lawrence Erlbaum, pp. 16–45.

van Meurs, N. and Spencer-Oatey, H. (2010) 'Multidisciplinary perspectives on intercultural conflict: the Bermuda Triangle of conflict, culture, and communication', in D. Masumoto (ed.) *APA Handbook of Intercultural Communication*, Washington DC: American Psychological Association, pp. 59–77.

Wiseman, R.L. (2003) 'Intercultural communication competence', in W.B. Gudykunst (ed.) *Cross-cultural and Intercultural Communication*, Thousand Oaks, CA: Sage, pp. 191–208.

# 18

# The intercultural speaker and the acquisition of intercultural/ global competence

*Jane Wilkinson*

## 1. Introduction

The 'intercultural speaker' has been a key protagonist in intercultural communication research and practice during the last 20 years. The term was coined by Michael Byram in the 1990s in the long process of redefining the goals of foreign language education away from the often elusive and, according to Davies (2004: 431–32), necessarily 'ambiguous' ideal of the 'native speaker'. The 'intercultural speaker' concept was soon adopted and adapted by many scholars and practitioners to describe the language learner who 'has an ability to interact with "others", to accept other perspectives and perceptions of the world, to mediate between different perspectives, to be conscious of their evaluations and differences' (Byram *et al.* 2001: 5). The intercultural speaker is, therefore, not only linguistically, but also interculturally, competent, i.e. he/she has a command of the grammar and vocabulary of the language he/she is learning and is also both sensitive towards other peoples and cultures and aware of his/her own cultural positioning. Significantly, the intercultural speaker is not bound to specific cultures or languages, but is competent in mediating across multiple borders. It is for this reason that intercultural competence is increasingly defined as global competence: the ability to be 'at home in the world'.

The aim of this chapter is threefold. First, the extant literature on the intercultural speaker is reviewed. It is, of course, beyond the scope of this chapter to review every scholarly contribution to the debate, so consideration is given to key contributors, with particular focus on the seminal work of Michael Byram. The focus then shifts to the acquisition of intercultural or global competence through foreign language education and the progression towards intercultural speaker status. Although recognizing the multiple opportunities for developing intercultural or global competence by alternative means, including work and leisure, this chapter focuses on formal secondary and, in particular, tertiary education. Both the employment of culture-based tasks in the language classroom and the role of residence abroad, during which language learners have the opportunity to become ethnographers of the languages and cultures they are studying, are discussed. Finally, the chapter reflects on the problems inherent in the concepts of the intercultural speaker and global competence. Although born of a desire to replace the idealism of the native speaker concept, the intercultural speaker has itself become a somewhat idealistic and overly theorized concept that does not apply to all language learners and to all contexts.

## 2. Conceptualizing the intercultural speaker

As already mentioned, one of Byram's primary concerns has been to encourage a shift in teachers and learners away from the almost obsessive desire to achieve so-called native speaker competence in the foreign language. Writing with Risager in 1999, he comments that language learners can only ever 'pretend' to be native speakers, but that they can more profitably and more realistically aspire to becoming intercultural speakers. The progression towards intercultural speaker status is not a progression towards perfection in the foreign language, unlike the progression towards the ideal of the native speaker. Furthermore:

> We have also recognised that the competence involved [in speaking with native speakers] is significantly different from that of the native-speaker because it involves the ability to see the relationships between the learner's and the native-speaker's languages and cultures, to perceive and cope with difference, rather than attempting to cast off one's existing social identities and pretending to be a native-speaker.
>
> Byram and Risager (1999: 2)

This more refined and developed definition of the intercultural speaker clearly draws on Byram's earlier discussions of intercultural communicative competence (ICC) in foreign language teaching:

> Foreign language teaching can be a major factor in what might be called – as an extension of the notions of primary and secondary socialisation – the process of tertiary socialisation, in which young people acquire an intercultural communicative competence: the ability to establish a community of meanings across cultural boundaries. [ ... ] this involves both cognitive and affective processes.
>
> Byram (1989: 5)

In this model of language learning, also proposed by Risager (2006: 7–8) and Roberts et al. (2001: 9–10), Byram acknowledges that exposure to national school curricula (secondary socialization) does little to foster intercultural competence. He therefore proposes the need for a third stage of 'socialization' to be introduced through foreign language education during which school pupils are (re-)educated to think and act interculturally, i.e. to be open to the possibilities of other peoples, languages and cultures and therefore able to communicate across boundaries, even without perfect or native speaker language skills. Moreover, as well as being open to and accepting of other cultures and languages, Byram (1997) later suggests that 'critical cultural awareness' plays a significant role in instances of intercultural communication. He defines 'critical cultural awareness' as 'an ability to evaluate, critically on the basis of explicit criteria, perspectives, practices and products in one's own and other cultures and countries' (Byram 1997: 53; see also Byram 2008: 162–66). He thus emphasizes the intercultural speaker's ability to engage critically and reflectively with his/her own and other cultures, to be able to interpret, analyse and evaluate familiar and unfamiliar cultural phenomena.

We see here the development of the idea that the intercultural or interculturally competent speaker not only 'communicates' but also 'mediates' across linguistic and cultural boundaries. In other words, the intercultural speaker possesses linguistic and cultural knowledge and awareness and also interpreting and negotiating skills. He/she therefore not only acts on behalf of him/herself and his/her interlocutor(s), but also on behalf of the larger sociocultural groupings to which they belong. Indeed, in 2008, Byram goes so far as to suggest that 'the phrase "intercultural speaker" can be paraphrased as an "intercultural mediator"', but maintains that 'the emphasis on speaker is useful because it reminds us of the importance of language, and the implication that mediation pre-supposes some linguistic competence' (Byram 2008: 68). It is not possible to mediate or negotiate cultural boundaries and differences without some knowledge of a shared or common language. The use of the term 'speaker' may, however, be somewhat misleading in its implicit emphasis on oral language skills. Like the literate native speaker who can speak, read and write fluently in his/her native language(s), the successful intercultural speaker is expected to be able to communicate and negotiate via both spoken and written media. The intercultural speaker is thus also the intercultural writer and the intercultural reader.

It should also be emphasized that the intercultural speaker or mediator is not limited to negotiating the boundaries between specific cultures, but rather between multiple cultures and contexts, or even on behalf of a 'common humanity' (cf. Byram and Fleming 1998: 8). Intercultural competence here is a general rather than a culturally specific skill. Unlike the learner who is taught specific linguistic and cultural knowledge in preparation for encounters with a specific new or foreign culture, the intercultural speaker or mediator is able to thrive in multiple situations: he/she is globally competent. This acknowledgement of global competence is particularly important in a world defined by the dissolution of national boundaries and the intensification of 'global flows' (Appadurai 1996; Bauman 2000; Risager 2006) or 'transnational connections' (Hannerz 1996). The globally competent intercultural speaker is at home and happily mobile in this increasingly borderless world.

Byram's extensive work on the intercultural speaker and intercultural competence has been formative in much concomitant and subsequent research and practice in languages and intercultural communication. Another key player in this field is Claire Kramsch, who similarly propounds the need to incorporate intercultural competence within language teaching. Like Byram, Kramsch (1998a: 27) clearly rejects the native speaker model, arguing that the 'characteristic of a "competent language user"' is 'the adaptability to select those forms of accuracy and those forms of appropriateness that are called for in a given social context of use'. This, she argues further, 'is precisely the competence of the "intercultural" speaker, operating at the border between several languages or language varieties, moving his/her way through the troubled waters of cross cultural misunderstandings' (Kramsch 1998a: 27). Kramsch's intercultural speaker is thus also an intercultural mediator or, in her own words, a 'broker between cultures of all kinds' (ibid.: 30), capable of communicating or mediating across language, and presumably also cultural, borders.

She usefully elaborates on Byram's work in two key areas: first, in her focus on multilingual, multicultural settings and, second, in her development of the idea of 'symbolic competence'. Looking at 'the increasingly grey zones of our multilingual, multicultural societies' (Kramsch 1998a: 27) and specifically of 'multilingual, multicultural foreign language classrooms' (Kramsch 1998a: 30) in which, she argues, 'the dichotomy between native versus non-native speakers has outlived its use' (Kramsch 1998a: 27), Kramsch reflects on the appropriateness of the intercultural speaker concept. Here, she draws on her experiences of multilingual and multicultural foreign language classrooms in the USA, but the argument is equally relevant to Europe, where the (selective) opening of borders and growth in foreign travel are giving rise to increasingly culturally and linguistically heterogeneous societies. It is increasingly the case that teachers of foreign languages are working with ethnically, culturally and linguistically diverse groups of students, who do not necessarily share the same 'mother tongue' or 'native language' and who, in some cases, bring two or more 'native languages' into the classroom with them. Teachers and pupils therefore require intercultural competence and the skills of the intercultural speaker already at the point of departure – the foreign language classroom – as they are already crossing multiple boundaries here, long before they cross the nation-state border into the country of the foreign language they are learning.

Indeed, Kramsch and Whiteside (2008) argue that they need more than intercultural competence. They maintain that 'global migration and deterritorialized living conditions in late modern societies [ … ] complicate[s] the teaching of communicative competence' because 'successful communication comes less from knowing which communication strategy to pull off at which point in the interaction than it does from choosing which speech style to speak with whom, about what, and for what effect' (Kramsch and Whiteside 2008: 646). This ability to move consciously and selectively between languages and dialects according to the context in which one is communicating, Kramsch and Whiteside (2008: 664) call 'symbolic competence'. Importantly, symbolic competence not only facilitates communication across linguistic and cultural borders, it enables speakers to choose the language or language variety that gives them advantage or power in interactions such as business transactions. Kramsch and Whiteside (2008) provide several examples of communicative situations in which Maya-speaking immigrants from Yucatan in Mexico now living in San Francisco negotiate the complex linguistic and cultural boundaries involved in visits to shops in the city, many of which are run by immigrants from other countries. However, the authors' conclusions could equally be applied to multilingual foreign language classrooms. Kramsch's intercultural speaker is thus not only interculturally but also symbolically competent.

Karen Risager (2006) shares Kramsch's interest in the multicultural or, to use her preferred term, 'transnational' milieu of the intercultural speaker. She too emphasizes that foreign language education often takes place in multicultural classrooms, in which students do not share the same first or even second language or the same cultural background. She illustrates this in her analysis of a German language lesson focusing on the *Tour de France* in a Danish class including a Dutch and an Iranian student, and argues that the 'composition of the participants' (as well as the theme) introduces 'European and global dimensions' (Risager 2006: 23) to an apparently 'bilateral' (Risager 2006: 28) learning context – German being taught in a Danish school. Although she does not use the term intercultural speaker to describe the interculturally competent language learner, she does suggest that 'language teaching socialises the learners involved to assume a number of roles or "figures" that are typical in the globalization perspective, such as "the tourist", "the vagabond" and "the cosmopolitan"' (Risager 2006: 25). I would therefore argue that Risager's globally competent 'cosmopolitan' shares many of the characteristics of Byram's and Kramsch's intercultural speaker.

In her work on ethnography and 'cultural translation' Shirley Jordan (2002), following Kramsch (1993: 231–59), usefully proposes Homi K. Bhabha's (1994) 'third space' as the space of the intercultural speaker. She builds on Byram's (2008) notion of the 'intercultural mediator' and Kramsch's (1998a, b) concept of the 'broker between cultures' in her discussion of cultural translation as 'a holistic process of provisional sense making', which 'implies trying to render accessible and comprehensible, first to the self and then to others, one's experience of aspects of ways of life – either one's own life made strange, or lives which are different from one's own' (Jordan 2002: 101). Jordan's 'cultural translator', like the intercultural speaker, thus needs to be both self-aware (aware of him/herself and of his/her language and culture) and sensitive to other cultures and languages, i.e. without preconceptions and prejudices.

According to Jordan (2002), successful cultural translation can lead to the creation of a productive new or 'third' space of communication and interaction, which she defines as:

> a highly reflexive and constructive breathing space – a space for reflection on intercultural issues in need of resolution, on political issues concerning dominance and inequality. It is

also the creative, dynamic space of action and interaction, the space for negotiating worlds through words. It is an ethical space, demanding self-knowledge, clear-sightedness, a readiness to listen and a preparedness to change.

*Jordan (2002: 101–2)*

The third space is, therefore, not merely in between two clearly defined cultures and languages – a miscomprehension arising from the use of the numerical descriptor 'third', for which Bhabha's (1994) concept has been frequently maligned – but is a dynamic, new space created through intercultural encounter and communication. Kramsch (1993: 235) similarly describes a 'third place' or 'third culture, made of a common memory beyond time and place among people with similar experiences' and argues the need to move on from the view that interlingual and intercultural communication takes place across a 'dichotomous boundary' or 'fence' between 'only two different cultures, that of our past and that of our present, or the culture we left behind and the one we have moved into' (Kramsch 1993: 34). The intercultural speaker or translator plays a key role in creating or facilitating this third space, place or culture and can therefore, I would argue, be understood as a 'liminal persona'. In his seminal work on liminality, anthropologist Victor Turner (1969: 95) maintains that 'liminal personae' 'elude or slip through the networks of classifications that normally locate states and positions in cultural space'. Building on this definition, border scholar Barbara Morehouse defines the liminal figure as being:

instrumental in negotiating otherwise intractable situations. In folk tales and cultures around the world, liminal figures such as shape changers, shamans, frogs, and coyotes populate this in-between space, this borderland of what may – or may not – be. They are important for they mediate differences, absorb contradictions into themselves, draw away the dangers of in-betweenness.

*Morehouse (2004: 31)*

We cannot fail to note striking similarities between Turner's and Morehouse's liminal figure or 'shape changer' and the intercultural speaker, mediator, broker or translator as introduced above. They all 'mediate differences' (Morehouse 2004: 30) or 'mediate between different perspectives' (Byram *et al.* 2001: 5), and they are able to 'draw away the dangers of in-betweenness' (Morehouse 2004: 30) or to move 'through the troubled waters of cross-cultural misunderstandings' (Kramsch 1998b: 27). For being 'in between' is an uncertain and, for many, dangerous state that requires careful negotiation and navigation to reach the other side or to create a sea of calm upon which new relationships can be forged. Successful negotiation of the liminal or in-between space can, I would argue with Jordan (2002) and Kramsch (2003), result in the creation of a new, shared, 'third space'.

## 3. Acquiring intercultural/global competence

We have seen above that the intercultural speaker is necessarily equipped with intercultural or global competence, but have not yet given sufficient thought to 'how' or 'to what degree' such competence can be acquired. The acquisition of intercultural or global competence will be the focus of the remainder of this chapter, but let us first consider the use of the terms 'intercultural' and 'global'. 'Intercultural' connotes exchange 'between' (*inter*) at least two cultures and therefore suggests that these cultures exist as definable and more or less bounded entities, often (but not always) locatable within politically determined nation-states. Discussions of intercultural communication and competence have tended to reinforce this view with the argument that '(t)he term "cross-cultural" or "intercultural" usually refers to the meeting of two cultures or two languages across the political boundaries of nation-states' (Kramsch 1998b: 81). Byram (1999: 54) similarly maintains that 'when a foreign language is involved [ ... ] the interaction is usually across a state or national boundary'. At the same time, however, both Kramsch and Byram are keen to emphasize that intercultural competence does not equate to learned knowledge about a specific culture, but rather to a general set of skills that enable the learner to interact even with 'new people from other contexts for which they have not been prepared directly' (Byram and Fleming 1998: 9). Risager (2006: 25) seems to share this view in her argument that language teaching 'plays a part in the cultural and linguistic globalization process' and 'lets students "out" into the world outside the country's borders'. Her language learners are not being prepared for specific cultural contexts and encounters, but for a world characterized by 'global flows and local complexity', as stated in the title of her book.

This conceptualization of intercultural competence is clearly a response to the opening of (nation-state) boundaries and advances in international travel and communication associated with globalization (see Risager 2006). Indeed, Byram and Risager (1999) refer explicitly to the changing shape of the world and its impact on our understanding of the aims of foreign language teaching and the role of intercultural competence when they suggest that:

> For foreign language teachers, the changes in the nature of the nation-state and its rela-tionships to other states is crucial, since the very notion of 'foreign' depends on the clear definition of frontiers and boundaries. When these frontiers and boundaries become less clear-cut, when opportunities for crossing them are made easier, the purposes of language teaching change.
>
> *Byram and Risager (1999: 1)*

Not only are there now more opportunities for learners to travel more easily and more often to the countries of the languages they are learning, they are more likely to encounter speakers of those languages 'at home' in their own countries, as already discussed (see Kramsch 1998a,b; Kramsch and Whiteside 2008; Risager 2006), or through the myriad channels of communication available via the worldwide web. As Jordan (2002: 101) points out: 'time–space compression, global mobility and communication technologies mean that sites of otherness are in the path of the everyday self which passes through them and that the field is everywhere.' Because 'sites of otherness are in the path of the everyday self' and intercultural competence may be called for anywhere and at any moment, it is perhaps more appropriately defined as global competence. Much of the current scholarship on global competence deals with the acquisition of the skills desirable for successful operation in a globalized business environment (see, for example, Sherman 1999; Vance 2005), but the term is also useful when defined more broadly as the ability to negotiate communication and interaction with people of multiple linguistic, cultural and social backgrounds or the ability to be 'at home in the world', like Risager's (2006: 25) 'cosmopolitan' (for more on global competence, see Baumgartz 1995; Cushner and Brennan 2007; Olson and Kroeger 2001).

## The acquisition of intercultural/global competence in the language classroom

There is broad agreement in the intercultural communication literature that the teaching of language has to be complemented by the teaching of culture, and that for this to be effective, culture needs to be broadly and anthropologically defined (see, for example, Byram 1991, 2008;

Roberts et al. 2001; Risager 2006; this volume). The tradition in much secondary education is to introduce 'the culture' of the 'foreign country' through the insertion of 'cultural texts', often in the learners' native or first language, into foreign language textbooks. These texts, which deal, for example, with food or festivals, are included in foreign language lessons when time allows, as addenda to the 'real' task of learning the language, but are rarely integrated into the curriculum. Byram (1991: 18) pinpoints precisely this problem in his early discussions of the vital role of culture in the foreign language classroom. He argues that it is impossible to separate language and culture as they are part of the same whole. Nevertheless, this separation often continues into the higher levels of secondary and into tertiary education when the teaching of culture becomes associated predominantly with the teaching of literature.

In my own language area, German, it is traditional that canonical texts by authors such as Goethe, Schiller, Brecht and Grass are studied by undergraduate students in literature/culture modules that run parallel to but are not incorporated into the core language modules. Despite the many benefits and joys of studying literature in a foreign language, in terms of both language and cultural knowledge, this persistent separation often leads students to question the reasons for studying literature. 'Why do I need to study literature when I just want to be better at German?' is a common complaint. There are, of course, many ways to better incorporate language and literature teaching so that students see and reap the benefits. Using a discourse analytical approach, for example, enables students both to analyse the language of the text in question and to discover the multiple layers of cultural meaning in the text (see Kramer 1990; Kramsch 1993, 1996). Roberts et al. (2001: 28–29) argue further that the growth of cultural studies has also changed the position of culture in foreign language curricula by broadening the range of texts deemed worthy of study and thereby opening up more of the culture associated with the language in question.

Taking the cultural studies approach further, it can be argued that the effective acquisition of intercultural/global competence through foreign language learning requires a redefinition of culture in anthropological rather than aesthetic terms. Culture is not just literature, but rather all aspects of how people live their lives. Risager (2006: 39) is particularly keen to underline the importance of a broad anthropological conceptualization of culture in foreign- or second-language learning contexts because anthropology's 'gaze is turned on "the unfamiliar", on unfamiliar cultures and societies, as is language and culture pedagogy'. Buttjes (1991: 9) therefore suggests that 'even in the early phases the motivation for learning another language can be raised through cultural awareness, and language acquisition can be facilitated through culturally "thick" and socially realistic textbook presentation'. Byram (1991: 27) goes a step further in suggesting that active 'cultural experience' can be facilitated in the foreign language classroom 'when pupils are taught through the foreign language'. He provides a number of examples, including cooking lessons in which pupils learn to cook dishes from the country of the language they are learning, or geography lessons in which the pupils learn aspects of the country's geography in the language of the country and also using teaching methods and concepts from that country. In their proposal that ethnography be introduced as a fundamental element of the language curriculum, Roberts et al. (2001: 29–30) similarly support an anthropological understanding of culture that 'shifts the emphasis away from written and audio-visual texts and towards the fashioning of texts out of participant observation'. 'In this way', they argue, 'it can connect texts and practices, the cognitive and the palpable, learning about and living/doing culture' (Roberts et al. 2001: 30). This ties in with Holliday's (2004: 64) notion of 'small culture', which 'refers to the composite of cohesive behaviour within any social grouping' or 'a discernable set of behaviours and understandings connected with group cohesion'. In sum, culture should be understood as the full gauntlet of social experience that students of foreign languages both learn about and participate in.

At the same time as broadening our understanding of culture, it is suggested that 'the cultural dimension [has] become the intercultural dimension' (Byram *et al.* 2001: 3). Although some culturally specific examples may be used, the aim of teaching culture is not to provide exhaustive, or even complete small parcels of, knowledge of the foreign culture, which, argues Byram (1991: 19), provides 'pupils with a consumer-tourist competence which offers them the opportunity to reach a critical threshold, enabling them to survive in the foreign and, by implication, hostile environment of the foreign country'. Roberts *et al.* (2001: 22–23) similarly argue that 'it [cultural learning] is not simply a question of acquiring facts about another country, although such facts are indeed useful. Nor is it about "reading off" from particular events generalized beliefs, values and attitudes in an unproblematic way'. Like Byram, they believe that 'this can only foster the misconception that there is some essential set of national characteristics which add up to French, Japanese or Spanish culture and which are waiting prone to be "discovered" by students on their arrival'. Instead, the aim should be to make students aware of and sensitive to instances of cultural difference that they will inevitably encounter through foreign travel and through virtual interactions with other cultures, i.e. to create intercultural speakers with global competence. In this way, Risager (2006: 25) argues, language teaching 'plays a part in the cultural and linguistic globalisation process'.

## Developing intercultural/global competence during periods of residence abroad

For many language students, the year or semester abroad is a turning point in the acquisition of both linguistic and intercultural competence. However, residence abroad does not inevitably and automatically churn out globally competent intercultural speakers. If students are to take full advantage of their time abroad, they need, argue Byram *et al.* (2001: 4), to be 'well prepared pedagogically' for the experience so that they do not simply return with reinforced prejudices and stereotypes, as Coleman (1997, 1998) suggests is often the case. To this end, ethnography is proposed as a teaching and learning method (see, for example, Holliday 1994, 2007; Roberts *et al.* 2001). Ethnography is the research methodology of 'professional' observers and interpreters of foreign cultures: anthropologists. It usually involves an extended period of fieldwork in the (foreign) culture, during which the anthropologist–ethnographer lives among the people he/she is studying, participates in aspects of their daily lives, possibly interviews certain members of the society and keeps a detailed record of everyone and everything observed. Importantly, however, the ethnographer maintains enough of a distance from the culture he/she is observing to enable critical reflection. In other words, he/she does not 'go native' to the extent of being completely absorbed into that culture. Byram (2008: 115) suggests that it is precisely this critical distance that language learners need to maintain during their time abroad if they are to become intercultural rather than native speakers. It is therefore argued that we as language teachers need to train our students as ethnographers in order to encourage the acquisition of intercultural/global competence during periods of residence abroad.

There exist some excellent examples of active research into the benefits of ethnography prior to and during the year/semester abroad, not least the work of Celia Roberts and Shirley Jordan, which is collated in the volume *Language Learners as Ethnographers* (2001). Here Roberts *et al.* provide a detailed description of the 'Ealing ethnography research project' conducted at Thames Valley University in the 1990s. The core of the research project consisted of an 'ethnography programme' divided into three integral parts: first, students were prepared for the year abroad in a second-year module called 'Introduction to ethnography'; second, students were required to conduct an ethnographic study during their year abroad; and third, students were asked to submit a written ethnography in the foreign language when they returned to university in their final year (see Barro *et al.* 1998: 81–82; Roberts *et al.* 2001: 13 and Ch. 6–10). The idea behind this programme was not only to equip students with the ethnographic tools to facilitate general observation of aspects of daily life in the foreign country, but to encourage a deeper engagement with a particular aspect of that culture through researching and writing up a specific ethnographic project. Examples of student projects included a study of transsexual prostitutes in Cadiz, Spain, and a sociolinguistic analysis of compliments in Las Palmas, Gran Canaria (Barro *et al.* 1998: 94–95). By conducting original cultural research with human participants, students on the Ealing ethnography programme were, according to Roberts *et al.* (2001: 12), able to acquire the cultural sensitivity and self-reflexivity that define intercultural competence: 'language teachers and students can use ethnography to develop their cultural learning in general, and their capacity to mediate between different cultural groups in particular'. In other words, as ethnographers, language learners could develop the mediating skills of the intercultural speaker.

In her later work on cultural translation, Shirley Jordan (2002: 107–8) further emphasizes that such ethnographic training and experiences provide students not only with the ability to understand and mediate between specific cultures, but with the global competence necessary to communicate and interact across multiple borders. This global competence is particularly important when we consider the rapidly increasing 'interconnectedness' (cf. Hannerz 1996) of the world in the early twenty-first century. This 'interconnectedness' enables more international travel and communication across long distances via multiple media, meaning that students can be in almost constant contact with people from all over the world. Moreover, opportunities for travel are also available to people in other parts of the world, meaning that 'home cultures are no longer comfortably bounded as the word "home" implies but are, in most cases, rapidly transforming multicultural and multilingual fields' (Jordan 2002: 208), so that students encounter 'difference' without having to leave their home towns (see also Kramsch 1998a, b; Kramsch and Whiteside 2008; Risager 2006). Jordan therefore also emphasizes the opportunities for and benefits of 'home' and 'auto' ethnography when helping students to acquire intercultural or global competence in preparation for a period of residence abroad. Of course, the global flows that have transformed students' 'home cultures' into 'multicultural and multilingual fields' (cf. Jordan 2002: 208) have also had their influence on the places students visit when they study or work abroad. This means that language students are asked to carry out local ethnographies in multilingual, multicultural and multireligious societies, for which they require global competence rather than specific cultural knowledge.

The results of the *Interculture Project* led by Robert Crawshaw at Lancaster University similarly demonstrate the ways in which ethnography can be used to support and enhance periods of residence abroad, and thus to help students acquire intercultural competence. In grossly simplified terms, this collaborative project, which ran between 1997 and 2000, collated a large corpus of materials used by UK universities to prepare students 'interculturally' for periods of residence abroad, devised and developed new materials suited to preparing students to go abroad, collected data from students using new materials and methods during their time abroad, and analysed these data in order to reflect upon how students develop – and can be supported in developing – intercultural competence. Crawshaw *et al.* (2000) found that students who were, for example, encouraged to observe and reflect on aspects of the culture(s) they encountered in ethnographic diaries – a concept similar to Jordan's (2002) autoethnographies – developed greater awareness and understanding of cultural similarities and differences and found themselves better able to communicate across the multiple boundaries encountered during periods of residence abroad.

## 4. Problematic concepts?

The extensive work on intercultural/global competence and the development of the intercultural speaker concept over the last two decades has irrefutably contributed much to the methods and aims of foreign language education. Nevertheless, the intercultural speaker is an imperfect concept, and it is necessary to reflect on these imperfections in order to complete the present discussion.

A repeated criticism of both the intercultural speaker and the intercultural competence concepts as they presently stand is that they are too general, to the point of being somewhat empty. In her work with Chinese students studying at university in New Zealand, Prue Holmes (2006: 19) suggests that 'current understandings of ICC are problematic because they do not sufficiently account for culture- and context-specific understandings of ICC'. She then argues the need for a 'culture-specific approach', which

> enables us to focus on the deep structure of culture (including world view, religion, community and social/political/economic structures), and the contemporary changes that influence rules for interpersonal communication. It also enables a closer examination of the individual and the idiosyncratic.
>
> *Holmes (2006: 19)*

I agree with Holmes that studying the acquisition of ICC (intercultural communicative competence) in specific contexts may well be a valid means by which to ground the theorizing in this area, and therefore support the use of specific case studies to demonstrate the theory at work. However, I wonder whether culturally specific understandings of intercultural competence might turn us back in the direction of facilitating understanding and communication between specific cultural groups through the teaching and sharing of specific cultural knowledge – the 'become interculturally competent in three days' model favoured by cross-cultural 'trainers' in business and commercial contexts that has long been rejected by Byram, Kramsch and others.

Although not arguing for culturally specific conceptualizations of intercultural competence and the intercultural speaker, Alison Phipps (2003: 9) does present a comparable critique when she defines Byram's space 'of the intercultural speaker, or sojourner, or ethnographer' as an 'empty space'. She acknowledges the possibilities opened up by this empty space 'for envisioning languages at work in new ways without determining what this may actually look like on the ground' (Phipps 2003: 19), i.e. for helping us to think about language learning and intercultural communication on an abstract level before applying that thinking to specific contexts and situations. However, Phipps argues further that envisaging the language learner in an empty space of intercultural speaking/communication:

> minimises the role that languages play as agentic markers of identity that may radically, even magically, change both who a speaker (or listener) is and, importantly, who that speaker is understood to be. It renders the cultural power of languages and the various modes of intercultural communicative agency invisible. It masks the marks and the marking.
>
> *Phipps (2003: 19)*

The criticism here is twofold. First, Phipps suggests that the concept of the intercultural speaker ignores the important role that languages play in defining our identity – in marking us as the same as or different from the people we are in dialogue with. In his later work – published after Phipps's essay – Byram (2008: 131) explicitly underlines the role that languages play as markers of identity: 'language is one of the most important means by which groups identify themselves and others, i.e. it is one of the most important "markers" of difference or "boundaries" between groups'. However, as Phipps argues further, he continues to hesitate to acknowledge the ways in which language learning and intercultural speaking can have a transformative effect on learners' identities (their sense of self and how they are perceived by others). Writing in 1991, Byram maintains that, in acquiring intercultural competence, language learners 'shall not change identity and abandon their own cultural viewpoint' (Byram 1991: 27). This is part of his critique of the native speaker goal, which asks learners to 'become' (like) native speakers and thus to change their identity (see, for example, Davies 2004). In 2008, Byram still maintains that 'to go native', i.e. to take on or at least imitate 'the native speaker in their identity', should not be the aim of the intercultural speaker (Byram 2008: 115). Phipps, on the other hand, believes that language learning and intercultural speaking are transformative and do give rise to changes in identity, and that the specific languages being learned and spoken are formative in shaping that identity. However, far from suggesting a return to the similarly problematic ideal of adopting the identity of the native speaker, Phipps proposes that we borrow Pierre Bourdieu's theory of 'habitus' as 'an enduring, learnt disposition for action, with implicit and explicit cultural commentaries' (Phipps 2003: 11), in order to understand the transformations experienced by language learners in intercultural situations. Reading the actions of language learners and their interlocutors as a form of habitus means that: 'The result is not some essential or idealized identity as a "sojourner", and "intercultural speaker" or even as a "Chinese, Arabic, French or Gaelic speaker". The result is a disposition for action, a *habitus* formed and forming' (Phipps 2003: 11). This understanding concomitantly grants learners agency in shaping their own identities and imbues languages (specific languages) with a certain transformative power.

In acknowledging the 'cultural power' of languages, Phipps also points to another determining factor in instances of intercultural communication: the often unequal power dynamic. Prue Holmes (2006: 19) similarly and more explicitly argues that much current research does not 'fully account for the power relations embedded in intercultural communication'. These power relations are often determined by perceptions of the language(s) being spoken and particularly by the apparent 'prestige' or 'value' of one language (and culture) over another, a fact acknowledged by Kramsch and Whiteside (2008) in their discussion of symbolic competence. To explain this further, I find it useful to turn again to research conducted into cross-border relations at nation-state borders and specifically along the former Iron Curtain dividing 'western' and 'eastern' or 'old' and 'new' Europe. Werner Holly *et al.* (2003) describe relations across this border as 'asymmetrical' on a number of levels (economic, social, political, cultural) and maintain that this asymmetry gives rise to attitudes of dominance in the communities on the western side of the border and an inferiority complex in their eastern neighbours. I find that the concept of asymmetry is also helpful when looking at the relationship between languages along this border. Because the western languages are often seen on both sides as more 'prestigious' or of 'higher value', in both economic and cultural terms, there is generally a greater motivation for inhabitants on the eastern side of the border to learn the language(s) of their western neighbours than vice versa. This in turn serves to exacerbate an already asymmetrical relationship and means that intercultural encounters across the border are inevitably influenced by a certain power dynamic predetermined by the language(s) being spoken and the cultures those languages represent (see Wilkinson 2009). In this context, which is mirrored at 'real' and 'virtual' borders across the world, the intercultural speaker, free from cultural and linguistic baggage and completely sensitive to cultural difference, does indeed seem to be an idealistic concept. However, if we turn again to Kramsch and Whiteside's (2008: 664) notion of symbolic competence – 'the ability not only to approximate or appropriate for oneself someone else's language, but to shape the very context in which the language is learned and used' – we can again grant agency to speakers in multilingual and multicultural settings. Kramsch and Whiteside (2008: 664) acknowledge the linguistic or symbolic capital (cf. Bourdieu 1991) embodied by certain languages or language varieties, but argue that successful intercultural speakers are not only aware of this capital, but are also able to negotiate and manipulate it to their own advantage by adopting a particular language or way of speaking for a particular context. A speaker with 'symbolic competence', a further layer of intercultural competence, is therefore not disadvantaged by linguistic asymmetries or unequal power relations, but knows how to gain advantage and power in a range of communicative situations.

## 5. Directions for future research

Much current and developing work on the intercultural speaker and intercultural/global competence focuses on the ethical issues inherent in instances of intercultural communication. The importance of considering the ethical dimension is clear when we take into account the previously mentioned power relations often at work when representatives of different languages and cultures come together. The intercultural speaker must be aware of his/her relation to his/her interlocutors and seek to avoid potential dominance or exploitation. Moreover, many scholars are concerned with intercultural communication as action research or as intervention (see, for example, Giroux 2006; Jack 2004; Tomic and Thurlow 2002). In other words, they see intercultural communication not only as a way of understanding and interpreting the world, but also as an ideology or way of changing the world, and the intercultural speaker as a form of moral or political activist. Such a viewpoint inevitably has an impact upon how we as teachers help our students to become interculturally competent, a central concern in the growing field of 'intercultural citizenship' or 'critical language and intercultural communication pedagogy' (see Chapters 5, 20 and 22, this volume; also Byram 2008), which explores the political dimensions and possibilities of intercultural communication.

Writing in the journal *Language and Intercultural Communication*, Malcolm MacDonald and John O'Regan (2007: 269) provide a very helpful summary of existing calls for action in intercultural communication and surmise that, in fact, 'we do intercultural work because we want to empower people, to raise their awareness about exploitation, manipulation, prejudice and abuse, and to *move* them to act upon this awareness – we want to provoke a *transformational* response'. However, they also warn us of the dangers of constructing and propagating an intercultural 'truth' as an, or possibly the only, alternative to other truths, ideologies or meta-narratives. They suggest that to propose the intercultural truth as the best or only truth is to enter the realms of totalitarianism that interculturalists are so keen to criticize in others. Instead, they argue, interculturalists and the intercultural speaker have a 'responsibility' to remain open to 'the Other' in all his/her guises (MacDonald and O'Regan 2007: 275). They thus conclude by asserting the need to rethink our notions of 'truth' and our attitudes towards 'others' if we are going to achieve an ethical and responsible discourse of intercultural communication, paving the way for future research in this area and giving scholars, teachers and learners substantial food for thought as they prepare for and reflect on encounters with the Other (see also Chapter 35, this volume).

I would also suggest further exploitation of the synergies between theories of intercultural communication and border theories as developed in geography, sociology and anthropology. We have already seen that the intercultural speaker is understood to be operating at and capable of communicating and mediating across multiple linguistic and cultural borders. I have therefore proposed the potential of understanding the intercultural speaker or mediator as a 'liminal' or 'border persona' (cf. Morehouse 2004). I believe that further exploration of the 'borderland' concept as developed by geographers such as Barbara Morehouse (2004) and Henk van Houtum, Olivier Kramsch and Werner Zierhofer (2005), who respectively describe geographical borderlands as in-between and potentially transformative spaces (Morehouse 2004: 31) or as spaces of 'openness, porosity, travelling and fecund hybridity' (van Houtum *et al.* 2005: 8), could prove fruitful in understanding and conceptualizing the space of the intercultural speaker.

## Related topics

Identity; intercultural citizenship; education abroad; intercultural (communicative) competence; intercultural contact; second language learning

## Further reading

Byram, M. (2008) *From Foreign Language Education to Education for Intercultural Citizenship: Essays and Reflections*, Clevedon: Multilingual Matters (in this monograph, Byram collates, reflects on and further develops his earlier work on the intercultural speaker and intercultural competence and stresses the importance of the political dimensions of foreign language education).

Kramsch, C. (1998) *Language and Culture*, Oxford: Oxford University Press (a detailed study of the changing role and importance of culture in foreign language education and the challenges of educating students to become intercultural speakers).

Roberts, C., Byram, M., Barro, A., Jordan, S. and Street, B. (2001) *Language Learners as Ethnographers*, Clevedon: Multilingual Matters (the most comprehensive study of the role of ethnography in the acquisition of intercultural competence during periods of residence abroad).

## References

Appadurai, A. (1996) *Modernity at Large: Cultural dimensions of globalization*, Minneapolis, MN: University of Minnesota Press.

Barro, A., Jordan, S. and Roberts, C. (1998) 'Cultural practice in everyday life: the language learner and ethnographer', in M. Byram and M. Fleming (eds) *Language Learning in Intercultural Perspective: Approaches through Drama and Ethnography*, Cambridge: Cambridge University Press, pp. 76–97.

Bauman, Z. (2000) *Liquid Modernity*, Cambridge: Polity Press.

Baumgartz, G. (1995) 'Language, culture and global competence: an essay on ambiguity', *European Journal of Education*, 30(4): 437–47.

Bhabha, H.K. (1994) *The Location of Culture*, London: Routledge.

Bourdieu, P. (1991) *Language and Symbolic Power*, Cambridge: Polity Press.

Buttjes, D. (1991) 'Mediating languages and cultures: the social and intercultural dimension restored', in D. Buttjes and M. Byram (eds) *Mediating Languages and Cultures: Towards an Intercultural Theory of Foreign Language Education*, Clevedon: Multilingual Matters, pp. 3–16.

Byram, M. (1989) 'Intercultural education and foreign language teaching', *World Studies Journal*, 7(2): 4–7.

——(1991) 'Teaching language and culture: towards an integrated model', in D. Buttjes and M. Byram (eds) *Mediating Languages and Cultures: Towards an Intercultural Theory of Foreign Language Education*, Clevedon: Multilingual Matters, pp.17–30.

——(1997) *Teaching and Assessing Intercultural Communicative Competence*, Clevedon: Multilingual Matters.

——(1999) 'Teaching Landeskunde and intercultural competence', in R. Tenberg (ed.) *Intercultural Perspectives: Images of Germany in Education and the Media*, Munich: Iudicium, pp. 54–70.

——(2008) *From Foreign Language Education to Education for Intercultural Citizenship: Essays and Reflections*, Clevedon: Multilingual Matters.

Byram, M. and Fleming, M. (1998) 'Introduction', in M. Byram and M. Fleming (eds) *Language Learning in Intercultural Perspective: Approaches through Drama and Ethnography*, Cambridge: Cambridge University Press, pp. 1–10.

Byram, M. and Risager, K. (1999) *Language Teachers, Politics and Cultures*, Clevedon: Multilingual Matters.

Byram, M., Nichols, A. and Stevens, D. (2001) 'Introduction', in M. Byram, A. Nichols and D. Stevens (eds) *Developing Intercultural Competence in Practice*, Clevedon: Multilingual Matters, pp. 1–8.

Coleman, J.A. (1997) 'Residence abroad within language study', *Language Teaching*, 30:1–20.

——(1998) 'Language learning and study abroad: the European perspective', *Frontiers: The Interdisciplinary Journal of Study Abroad*, 4: 1–21.

Crawshaw, R., Callen, B., Clapham, C., Hall, S., Jones, B., Lewis, T., Steel, D., Toll, S. and Tusting, K. (2000) *The Interculture Project*, Online. Available: www.lancs.ac.uk/users/interculture/index.htm (accessed 27 July 2010).

Cushner, K. and Brennan, S. (2007) *Intercultural Student Teaching: A Bridge to Global Competence*, Lanham, MD: Rowman and Littlefield Education.

Davies, A. (2004) 'The native speaker in applied linguistics', in A. Davies and C. Elder (eds) *The Handbook of Applied Linguistics*, Oxford: Blackwell, pp. 431–50.

Giroux, H.A. (2006) 'Is there a role for critical pedagogy in language/culture studies? An interview with Henry Giroux by Manuela Guilherme', *Language and Intercultural Communication*, 6(2): 163–75.

Hannerz, U. (1996) *Transnational Connections*, London: Routledge.

Holliday, A. (1994) *Appropriate Methodology and Social Context*, Cambridge: Cambridge University Press.

——(2004) 'Small cultures', in A. Holliday, A. Hyde and J. Kull (eds) *Intercultural Communication: An Advanced Resource Book*, London: Routledge, pp. 62–64.

——(2007) *Doing and Writing Qualitative Research*, 2nd edn, London: Sage.

Holly, W., Nekvapil, J., Scherm, I. and Tišerová, P. (2003) 'Unequal neighbours: coping with asymmetries', *Journal of Ethnic and Migration Studies*, 29(5): 819–34.

Holmes, P. (2006) 'Problematising intercultural communication competence in the pluricultural classroom: Chinese students in a New Zealand university', *Language and Intercultural Communication*, 6(1): 18–34.

Jack, G. (2004) 'Language(s), intercultural communication and the machinations of global capital: towards a dialectical critique', *Language and Intercultural Communication*, 4(3): 121–31.

Jordan, S. (2002) 'Ethnographic encounters: the processes of cultural translation', *Language and Intercultural Communication*, 2(2): 96–110.

Kramer, J. (1990) *Cultural and Intercultural Studies*, Frankfurt am Main: Peter Lang.

Kramsch, C. (1993) *Context and Culture in Language Teaching*, Oxford: Oxford University Press.

——(1996) 'The cultural component of language teaching', *Language, Culture and the Curriculum*, 8(2): 83–92.

——(1998a) 'The privilege of the intercultural speaker', in M. Byram and M. Fleming (eds) *Language Learning in Intercultural Perspective: Approaches through Drama and Ethnography*, Cambridge: Cambridge University Press, pp. 16–31.

——(1998b) *Language and Culture*, Oxford: Oxford University Press.

——(ed.) (2003) *Language Acquisition and Language Socialization: Ecological Perspectives*, London: Continuum.

Kramsch, C. and Whiteside, A. (2008) 'Language ecology in multilingual settings: towards a theory of symbolic competence', *Applied Linguistics*, 29(4): 645–71.

MacDonald, M.N. and O'Regan, J.P. (2007) 'Cultural relativism and the discourse of intercultural communication: aporias of praxis in the intercultural public sphere', *Language and Intercultural Communication*, 7(4): 267–78.

Morehouse, B. (2004) 'Theoretical approaches to border spaces and identities', in V. Pavlakovich-Kochi, B. Morehouse and D. Wastl-Walter (eds) *Challenged Borderlands: Transcending Political and Cultural Boundaries*, Aldershot: Ashgate, pp.19–39.

Olson, C.L. and Kroeger, K.R. (2001) 'Global competency and intercultural sensitivity', *Journal of Studies in International Education*, 5(2): 116–37.

Phipps, A. (2003) 'Languages, identities, agencies: intercultural lessons from Harry Potter', *Language and Intercultural Communication*, 3(1): 6–19.

Risager, K. (2006) *Language and Culture: Global Flows and Local Complexity*, Clevedon: Multilingual Matters.

Roberts, C., Byram, M., Barro, A., Jordan, S. and Street, B. (2001) *Language Learners as Ethnographers*, Clevedon: Multilingual Matters.

Sherman, H.D. (1999) 'Pursuing global competence in undergraduate business education: use of an international consulting experience', *Teaching in International Business*, 10(3/4): 29–41.

Tomic, A. and Thurlow, C. (2002) 'Editorial', *Language and Intercultural Communication*, 2(2): 81–85.

Turner, V. (1969) *The Ritual Process: Structure and Anti-structure*, Chicago, IL: Aldine.

van Houtum, H., Kramsch, O. and Zierhofer, W. (2005) 'Prologue: B/Ordering space', in H. van Houtum *et al.* (eds) *B/Ordering Space*, Aldershot: Ashgate, pp. 1–13.

Vance, C.M. (2005) 'The personal quest for building global competence: a taxonomy of self-initiation career path strategies for gaining business experiences abroad', *Journal of World Business*, 40(4): 374–85.

Wilkinson, J. (2009) 'Die härteste Sprachgrenze Europas? Negotiating the linguistic divide in theatres on the German–Polish border', in J. Carl and P. Stevenson (eds) *Language Discourse and Identity in Central Europe*: The German Language in a Multilingual Space, Basingstoke: Palgrave Macmillan, pp. 73–95.

# 19

# World Englishes, intercultural communication and requisite competences

*Farzad Sharifian*

## 1. Introduction

For better or worse, by choice or force, English has 'travelled' to many corners of the globe, making some people's lives easier, while making others' more complex. Worldwide, English serves many purposes, including acting as a medium for international and intranational communication. English has not 'spread' as a monolithic code, but has become a pluricentric language: many new varieties have developed, and are still being developed, as a result of contact-induced processes, such as pidginization, creolization and decreolization. Thus, today, we speak of 'Englishes', rather than 'English'. In recent years, due to the rapid expansion of globalization and the development of more and more varieties of English, many publications have appeared on World Englishes (e.g. Jenkins 2003; Kachru *et al.* 2006; Kachru and Nelson 2006; Kirkpatrick 2007, 2010).

The phrase 'world Englishes' has not been used consistently by the scholars who have studied various aspects of the varieties of the English language worldwide. Bolton (2005) finds three usages of the term 'world Englishes'. In one sense, it has been used to refer to all varieties of English across the globe. In the second sense, it is used to refer to 'new Englishes' that have developed in the Caribbean, Africa and Asia (e.g. Kenyan English, Cameroon English, Singaporean English and Malaysian English). In the third sense, it refers to World Englishes (WE), capitalized, a paradigm associated with the work of Braj B. Kachru and others who associate themselves with this framework. This paradigm is affiliated with the journal *World Englishes* (Wiley-Blackwell) and the International Association for World Englishes (IAWE). As Bolton (2005: 240–41) mentions, this paradigm has been characterized by an underlying philosophy that argues for the importance of inclusivity and pluricentricity in approaches to the linguistic study of English worldwide, and involves not merely the description of national and regional varieties, but many other related topics as well, including contact linguistics, creative writing, critical linguistics, discourse analysis, corpus linguistics, lexicography, pedagogy, pidgin and creole studies and the sociology of language.

Bolton (2005) provides a summary of the studies that have in one way or another addressed the issues surrounding the notion of World Englishes, or related terms such as 'New Englishes'. In general, he identifies a number of approaches to research and publication in the field of

*Table 19.1* Sociolinguistic approaches and their objectives (based on Bolton 2005)

| Approach | Objectives |
| --- | --- |
| The sociology of language | To do research on English in relation to issues such as language maintenance, shift and ethnolinguistic identities |
| 'Linguistic features' | To describe varieties of English through variationist methodologies |
| 'Socially realistic' or Kachruvian | To promote a pluralistic approach to world Englishes highlighting both the 'sociolinguistic realities' and the 'bilingual creativity' of outer circle and expanding circle societies |
| Pidgin and Creole studies | To describe and analyse 'mixed' languages and the dynamics of linguistic hybridizations |

World Englishes including English studies, sociolinguistics, applied linguistics, lexicography and critical linguistics. Bolton associates the 'English studies' approach with scholars such as Quirk and Crystal, and identifies the major aim of this approach as the description of varieties of English from eclectic, descriptive and historical perspectives. The work of more recent scholars in the field of English corpus linguistics, such as Greenbaum (1996) and Kortmann and Schneider (2004), is seen as an extension of this approach.

Under 'sociolinguistic approaches', Bolton (2005) includes studies associated with (1) 'sociology of language' (e.g. Fishman *et al.* 1977), (2) 'linguistic features' (and dialectological) approach (e.g. Trudgill and Hannah 1982), (3) pidgin and creole studies (e.g. Romaine 1988) and (4) 'socially realistic' studies of world Englishes (e.g. Kachru 1983, 1986 and his many other publications). In Table 19.1, Bolton (2005) presents the aims of the scholars under the general rubric of 'sociolinguistic approaches'.

Bolton (2005) associates 'applied linguistic' approaches with attempts made to explore the implications of world Englishes for language learning and teaching (e.g. Brumfit 1982; Kachru 1982; Strevens 1980). 'Lexicographical approaches' mainly focus on the compilation of dictionaries and glossaries, often for the expression of a national linguistic identity (e.g. Allsopp 1996; Butler 1981). Bolton (2005) also refers to the work of both linguists (e.g. Crystal 1988) and non-linguists (McCrum *et al.* 1986) who made attempts to 'popularize' studies of English.

Under 'critical linguistic' approaches, Bolton (2005) includes the work of scholars such as Phillipson (2000, 2003) and Pennycook (1994, 1998, 2001), who presented provocative arguments in relation to the politics of the spread of English. The last category that Bolton (2005) refers to is what he terms 'futurology', or the study of future trends in the spread of English and English pedagogy worldwide (e.g. Graddol 1997). It should be added here that Bolton (2005) acknowledges that there are significant overlaps between these approaches. For example, many sociolinguists, including most Kachruvian scholars, have also pursued the pedagogical implications of their findings.

In general, Bolton's (2005) review reveals the remarkable attention paid in the last 50 years to the study of English and its varieties mainly by scholars in the fields of linguistics, sociolinguistics, lexicography and applied linguistics. The growing spread of English throughout the world, particularly through technologies such as the internet, is expected to boost the amount of research on various aspects of World Englishes. In the following section, I focus on a more elaborate description of the Kachruvian paradigm of World Englishes (from now on WE), as it comprises the main body of research and scholarship about varieties of English worldwide.

## 2. Kachruvian paradigm

The main names that are usually associated with the WE paradigm are Braj Kachru, Yamuna Kachru, Larry Smith and some of their associates, although the main pioneer has always been acknowledged to be Braj Kachru. The paradigm as a whole has been concerned with the spread of English, the stratification of English, the contexts in which WEs are used, description of WEs, the politics and policies regarding the English language, the teaching and testing of English and fallacies about the users and uses of English (e.g. standard/non-standard debates) (Kachru 1992). A major development in this area was the conceptualization of the contexts affecting the use of English in terms of three circles (e.g. Kachru 1986, 1992). This model has three concentric circles: inner circle, outer circle and expanding circle countries (for an illustration of this model, see Jenkins 2009: 19; Kachru 1992: 356). In inner circle countries, such as the US, the UK, Australia and Canada, English is used as the primary language. Countries located in the outer circle, such as India and Singapore, are multilingual and use English as a second language (ESL), mostly as a result of their colonial history. In expanding circle countries, the largest circle, such as China, Japan, Korea and Egypt, English is learned as a foreign language (EFL).

Kachru classifies the norms associated with the three circles in the following way. He considers inner circle varieties as 'norm providing', outer circle varieties as 'norm developing' and expanding circle varieties as 'norm dependent'. According to this classification, the inner circle varieties provide norms to the expanding circle varieties, whereas the outer circle varieties develop their own local norms. In other words, in expanding circle varieties, norms are external or 'exocentric' (being drawn from American or British English), whereas in outer circle varieties, norms are internal or 'endocentric'.

The three circles metaphor has been very popular in studies of WEs, producing much debate and controversy. Recently, some scholars have questioned the current validity and usefulness of the three-circle model on several grounds. Jenkins (2009: 20–21) provides a summary of these concerns as follows:

- The model is geography–history based, rather than based on how the language is used and how speakers identify with the language.
- Some countries do not neatly lend themselves to the classification of inner circle and outer circle. For example, for some people in countries such as India and Singapore, English is the main language, used both at home and outside.
- Some countries, such as Argentina, Belgium and Denmark, are changing status from expanding circle to outer circle, as speakers shift from using English as a foreign language to a second language.
- Many speakers of English around the world grow up bilingually or multilingually and, in many cases, it is difficult to decide whether English is their L1, L2, L3, etc.
- The classification employed in the model does not provide any indication about speakers' proficiency level. So-called 'native speakers' of English are not necessarily more competent in all areas of the language.
- The model suggests uniformity of use and function for countries within a particular circle, whereas this is not the case. For example, the use of English in India, Singapore and Bangladesh is not exactly the same. In India, English is used mainly by an elite group, whereas in Singapore, it is used by more than half the population from all different levels of the society.
- Some scholars have suggested that the term 'inner circle' gives supremacy to the so-called 'native speakers' of English and places them at the centre, in terms of control of the language.

My own objection to the three-circle model (Sharifian 2009b) is that it uses political borders as the basis for classification, whereas in many countries, especially inner circle countries, there are English users from all different circles. For example, in Australia, Australian English was developed out of dialect mixing (e.g. Irish English, British English, Scottish English), but that is not the only variety used in Australia. Many Aboriginal people speak Aboriginal English[1] in Australia, and many migrants and refugees in Australia speak other varieties of English such as African Englishes, Indian English, China English, etc. Thus, it would be very simplistic to classify countries such as Australia in terms of a particular circle.

## 3. Recent approaches to the study of WEs

As mentioned above, traditional approaches to the study of WEs have mainly followed a sociolinguistic perspective. Recently, however, with the rise of cognitive linguistics, some scholars, including myself, have proposed a cognitive approach to the study of varieties of English (Sharifian 2006; Wolf and Polzenhagen 2009). These studies can generally be classified under the rubric of cognitive sociolinguistics (Kristiansen and Dirven 2008). As Kristiansen and Dirven (2008: 4) put it, cognitive sociolinguistics focuses 'on the way in which language usage in different regional and social groups is characterised by different conceptualisations, by different grammatical and lexical preferences, and by differences in the salience of particular connotations'. In this context, Wolf (2008: 355) explores the potential of cognitive sociolinguistics 'to become a new model within the wider context of WE, especially with respect to the higher-order research targets of cultural identity and cultural variation'. Wolf's work, either by himself or with Polzenhagen (e.g. Polzenhagen and Wolf 2007; Wolf 2008; Wolf and Polzenhagen 2009), has explored conceptualizations of the African cultural model of community in African varieties of English. He maintains that this 'cultural model involves a cosmology and relates to such notions as the continuation of the community, the members of the community, witchcraft, the acquisition of wealth, and corruption, which find expression in African English' (Wolf 2008: 368). For example, by examining a number of expressions in Cameroon English (e.g. 'they took bribers from their less fortunate brothers'), Wolf observes that the central conceptual metaphors in that variety of English are KINSHIP IS COMMUNITY and COMMUNITY IS KINSHIP (p. 370).

Another cognitive linguistics-based model for the study of WE is the theoretical framework of 'cultural conceptualizations' which I have developed over the last decade (Sharifian 2003, 2008, 2009a, 2011). In this model, language is viewed as deeply rooted in the ways in which different cultural groups conceptualize experiences of different kinds mainly through developing conceptual units such as 'cultural schemas', 'cultural categories' and 'cultural metaphors'.

Traditionally, in cognitive science, schemas have been viewed as conceptual units that we use to interpret, organize and predict information. For example, we have a schema for the word 'restaurant'. As soon as we hear the word, this schema is evoked and we interpret subsequent information accordingly. Thus, when someone says, 'we went to a restaurant last night and it was very expensive', we correctly identify 'expensive' with the price of the food that was served and not the price of the restaurant itself, as this corresponds to our schema.

'Categories' are conceptual structures that are used to put everything in the world in a particular mental 'folder'. Thus, 'food' is a category in our mind, in which instances such as pasta, rice, bread, etc. are associated. Conceptual metaphors help us understand one idea or domain in terms of another one (e.g. Lakoff 1987; Lakoff and Johnson 1980). For example, 'time' is metaphorically conceptualized in some cultures as a 'commodity', reflected in expressions such as 'I need to save some time' and 'I need to spend some time on it'.

Although, in traditional cognitive science, such conceptual structures are viewed as existing only in the individual human mind, in the model of cultural conceptualizations, I view them to be properties of broader, group-level cognition. The group-level cognition model that I have proposed, and called cultural cognition, is not just the sum of individual-level cognitions. It has a life that is more than the sum of its elements. Cultural cognition is heterogeneously represented across the minds in a cultural group. In other words, a particular cultural schema is not equally imprinted in the minds of all the people across a group, but is to some extent present differently in different people. In simple terms for the sake of the discussion in this chapter, what it means is that people from a particular cultural group 'more or less' share elements from a cultural schema. The group-level conceptual units arise out of the interactions between members of a cultural group across time and space, and are, so to speak, 'negotiated' and 'renegotiated' across generations of people.

In my work, I have employed the model of cultural conceptualizations to examine features of Aboriginal English, a variety of English that is spoken by Indigenous people in Australia (e.g. Arthur 1996; Eades 1991; Harkins 1994, 2000; Malcolm 2000), as well as an emerging variety among speakers of Persian, which I have called 'Persian English' (Sharifian 2010a, 2010b). In this chapter, I focus on my research on Aboriginal English for the sake of brevity.

Aboriginal English was developed out of a need by Aboriginal Australians to communicate with the white settlers upon contact. They also used it among themselves when they were displaced from their original places of settlement. Aboriginal English reflects the cultures and the worldview of Aboriginal Australians and is a strong marker of identity for many of them. Many features of Aboriginal English encode Aboriginal cultural conceptualizations (Sharifian 2006). Even everyday words such as 'family' and 'home' evoke cultural schemas and categories among Aboriginal English speakers that characterize largely Aboriginal cultural experiences (e.g. Sharifian 2005, 2006, 2007). The word 'family', for instance, is associated with categories in Aboriginal English that move far beyond the usual referent of the 'nuclear' family in Anglo-Australian culture. A person who comes into frequent contact with an Aboriginal person may be referred to using a kin term such as 'brother' or 'cousin' or 'cousin brother' (Malcolm and Sharifian 2007: 381). The word 'mum' may be used to refer to people who are referred to as 'aunt' in Anglo-Australian culture. Such usage of kinship terms does not stop at the level of categorization but usually evokes schemas associated with certain rights and obligations between those involved. The word 'home' in Aboriginal English usually evokes categories that are based on family relationships more than the building occupied by a nuclear family. For instance, an Aboriginal English speaker may refer to their grandparents' place as 'home'.

Many words in Aboriginal English, such as 'sing', 'smoke' and 'light', encode cultural conceptualizations associated with Aboriginal spirituality (see later in this chapter). In the Aboriginal worldview, the relationship between land, animals and human beings is understood to be very close, as during the Dreamtime (Aboriginal Australia Art and Culture Centre 2000), Ancestor Beings, who appeared as an amalgam of animal and human features, travelled the land. At that time, they created landforms and laid down customs, finally transforming into part of the land themselves, taking on the shape of stones, trees, etc. (e.g. Bain 1992; Elkin 1969; Stanner 1965, 1979). Thus, the land now embodies the 'spirits' of Ancestor Beings and, as such, is connected to people via kinship.

The following two sentences reflect the difference in which the relationship between land and human beings is understood, in terms of cultural–conceptual metaphors.

ABORIGINAL ENGLISH:  This land is me.
AUSTRALIAN ENGLISH:  This land is mine.

One conceptualization may appear patently ridiculous from the point of view of another. The Aboriginal English sentence draws on a schema according to which people and the land are identified in various ways, such as by totemic connection. Often, in response to 'this land is mine', Aboriginal people respond, 'but the land owns us'. When questioned about this difference, an Aboriginal person remarked that the land was there before he was born, so how could 'he' own it? From the perspective of Aboriginal cultural conceptualizations, people and the land have reciprocal responsibilities towards each other. The land provides food for people and people are supposed to 'look after' the land. The Australian English sentence, on the other hand, encodes the Anglo conceptualization of the relationship between the individual and the land, in which an individual's possession of a piece of land involves being able to transfer it to other individuals, usually for money. From a different perspective, the Australian sentence may also suggest political possession, that is, 'This land is mine because I am Australian' (Ian Malcolm, personal communication). This example clearly shows how different cultural conceptualizations are encoded in the two varieties of English.

## 4. World Englishes and intercultural communication

What is the relevance of studies of WEs to intercultural communication? According to Crystal (2003), estimates of the number of L1 and L2 speakers of English were 329,140,800 and 430,614,500, respectively, in 2003, and the numbers are surely higher today. English is now spoken in more than seventy countries in all three Kachruvian circles. Crystal (2003: 61) provides estimates of speakers of English in each circle: 320–80 million in the inner circle, 300–500 million in the outer circle and 500–1,000 million in the expanding circle countries. Based on these figures, the largest number of speakers is found in the latter. The situation nowadays is that speakers from each circle may use English to communicate locally where English is a medium of intranational communication, or they may use it to speak to speakers from other countries from the same circle or with speakers from other circles. Graddol (2006) refers to 'people on the move', including migrant workers, refugees, immigrants, tourists and international students, and notes that, between 1960 and 2000, the number of international migrants had doubled (to 175 million). As for tourism, there were around 763 million international travellers in 2004. He notes that 4 per cent of these were people from the so-called 'native' English-speaking countries to other 'native' English-speaking countries, whereas 74 per cent were from non-English-speaking countries to other non-English-speaking countries. He comments that '[t]his demonstrates the scale of need for face-to-face international communication and a growing role for global English' (Graddol 2006: 29).

English has become a major language of 'intercultural' communication *par excellence*, used as a language of international and intranational communication between speakers of WEs from all three circles. In Kachru's words, English is now a 'repertoire of cultural pluralism' (Kachru 1995, online document). This pluricentric language is now a vehicle for the cultural conceptualizations of many speech communities around the world as communication proceeds in many contexts and through many channels such as face-to-face, phone and internet. Furthermore, as different WEs influence each other with contact, blended systems of cultural conceptualizations are expected to emerge.

Clearly, the similarities and differences between cultural conceptualizations encoded in the multiple varieties of Englishes can either facilitate or impede intercultural communication. This has several implications. On the one hand, the pluricentricity of English and the use of multiple varieties by speakers of WEs in what Canagarajah (2006) calls a 'postmodern context of communication' has significant implications for the notion of 'proficiency' in English as a language of international and intercultural communication. As Canagarajah (2006: 233) puts it:

[i]n contexts where we have to constantly shuttle between different varieties and communities, proficiency becomes complex. To be really proficient in English today, one has to be multidialectal. This does not mean that one needs production skills in all the varieties of English. One needs the capacity to negotiate diverse varieties to facilitate communication.

In other words, he characterizes multidialectal competence as including 'passive competence to understand new varieties [of English]' (Canagarajah 2006: 233).

Varieties of English such as China English, Hong Kong English, Singaporean English, etc., are not just relevant within these countries as their speakers now live in and travel to all parts of the world. It is not enough today to understand British English or American English; one must be able to negotiate the other varieties of English with which one may come into contact. This observation has serious implications for the English language teaching (ELT) industry. Given the fact that about three-quarters of international travel takes place between non-native-speaking countries, where 'English' means varieties of English from outer and expanding circle countries, many learners do not need English for the purpose of communicating with inner circle speakers. This means that ELT curricula today need to expose learners to more than just the traditional varieties of English. In the following section, I shall focus on examples of how speakers of WEs can instantiate their cultural conceptualizations in English during intercultural communication.

## 5. Cultural conceptualizations in intercultural communication in English

To repeat, human languages serve to communicate and encode cultural conceptualizations of their speakers, and English is no exception. However, as English has become a highly pluricentric language as a result of the development of its many varieties, English is now associated with many systems of cultural conceptualizations and as such serves to satisfy speakers' local as well as international communicative needs. When speakers of WEs come into contact with each other, they are likely to draw on their cultural conceptualizations in varying degrees. In this section, I give examples from my research on Aboriginal English using Aboriginal English expressions for the Aboriginal worldview, a major part of which is known as 'the Dreamtime'. As was noted above, during the Dreamtime journeys, Ancestor Spirits emerged from the earth and made everything including the land, animals, plants and the people (Aboriginal Australia Art and Culture Centre 2000) and finally became part of nature. However, their spiritual powers are still present today and play a significant role in the life of Aboriginal people. Consider the following excerpt from a conversation between an Aboriginal English speaker and the author:

> C: that, that rain, the rain 'ere, the 'angry rain', das when some, you done somethin or someone's done somethin, that did bad an it's like it's not rainin and it comes and it's like bangin, loud, sort of lashin, makes the trees go shshsht, you know, hittin out that sort of rain an it can come out like that but then you find out after someone doin somethin, and you go thas what it was ...

Here, when the speaker talks about 'angry rain', she is referring to rain as an expression of the anger of Ancestor Beings, or 'old fallas'. According to the cultural conceptualization of 'rain as the anger of spirit beings', this anger is likely to have been caused by a wrongdoing, such as trespassing on a 'country', or by an omission according to Aboriginal law. Similar conceptualizations of Ancestor Beings are observed in African varieties of English. For example, Wolf (2008: 371) observes that, 'ancestors, which are conceptualized as spirits or ghosts, are understood as members of the community who still exert a considerable influence on the (physiologically) living'. This is reflected in sentences such as 'Cruelty to children is ... punishable by ancestral spirits' (Wolf 2008: 317).

In Aboriginal English, words such as 'sing' and 'smoke' are used in association with spiritual experiences that arise from the Aboriginal worldview, and as such they capture cultural conceptualizations that are often unfamiliar to non-Aboriginal speakers. The following comes from a conversation between an Aboriginal English speaker and the author:

> A: My sister said, 'when you go to that country, you not allowed to let 'em take your photo, they can *sing* you'.

After a series of verbal exchanges, it became clear that the word 'sing' in this context refers to an action similar to casting a spell over something associated with the target of the spell, such as a piece of their hair, and in this case a photograph. The following is an example of the use of the word 'smoke' from another Aboriginal English speaker:

> C: That's when I wen' up to up [name of a region], that was years ago, old fallas, there's couple of old girls an couple of old blokes was there but the old girl said, 'we gotta go an *smoke* that that one there' an I said, 'me?' and they said, 'yeah, you get *smoked'* an I said, 'no no, nex' time I come back', bu' the next time I went back I already knew then that was my Dad's family, they must already knew but I didn't an' they wanted to *smoke* me to protect me from the other umm mobs that ways, they knew who I was but I didn't know.

The use of the word 'smoke' in this instance refers to a ritual that involves rubbing special burnt leaf on the body of the person, carried out to welcome a visitor and mark them as an insider and protect them against the local groups of Aboriginal people. Arthur (1996) notes that smoking may also be used for 'cleansing' purposes by some Aboriginal people. In such cases, a person may be required to walk through the smoke of a fire. Arthur notes that '[t]hese practices are most often carried out after a death, to dissuade the spirit of the recently dead from disturbing the living' (1996: 57). Such examples clearly show how English is now used to express cultural conceptualizations that were not originally associated with the language. And it is clear these can lead to miscommunication or misapprehension. This observation brings up the question of when English is being used for intercultural 'communication' and when for 'miscommunication', and how we can offer strategies that diminish the latter.

## 6. WEs, intercultural competence and metacultural competence

The demographic changes that increasingly characterize the use of English around the globe require skills to facilitate the communication between people coming from different cultural backgrounds. In the previous section, I referred to 'multidialectal competence' as an essential element of proficiency in English within international contexts. Another relevant notion proposed in the literature is that of 'intercultural competence' or 'intercultural communicative competence' (ICC) (for the distinction between the two terms, see Chapter 5, this volume; see also Byram 1997, 2000; Byram *et al.* 2001). For Byram (2000: 10), ICC involves the following five elements:

1. Attitudes: curiosity and openness, readiness to suspend disbelief about other cultures and belief about one's own.
2. Knowledge: of social groups and their products and practices in one's own and in one's interlocutor's country, and of the general processes of societal and individual interaction.
3. Skills of interpreting and relating: ability to interpret a document or event from another culture, to explain it and relate it to documents from one's own.
4. Skills of discovery and interaction: ability to acquire new knowledge of a culture and cultural practices and the ability to operate knowledge, attitudes and skills under the constraints of real-time communication and interaction.
5. Critical cultural awareness/political education: an ability to evaluate critically and on the basis of explicit criteria perspectives practices and products in one's own and other cultures and countries.

Byram's conception of ICC has the strength of recognizing that success in intercultural communication requires a combination of attitudes, knowledge, skills and critical awareness. Often, developing the right attitude towards 'others' and 'other cultures' is the most essential requirement necessary to facilitate cross-cultural understanding and sympathy. And perhaps it is the most difficult to gain.

Despite its comprehensive approach to the components that are essential for the development of ICC, Byram's model requires fine-tuning of the content of each component as well as suggestions for how each could be developed. Here, I propose the notion of 'metacultural competence' (e.g. Sharifian 2009c) be included under the knowledge component of Byram's model. Metacultural competence involves knowledge of, and familiarity with, more than one system of cultural conceptualizations. These may be associated with either one language or more than one language, depending on whether the interlocutors are bilingual or multilingual. Key to the metacultural competence is the understanding that one language may be used to encode several systems of cultural conceptualizations. For example, as has been shown above, English can be used to draw on cultural conceptualizations of several, in fact many, speech communities.

As WEs enable contact between speakers who deploy different systems of cultural conceptualizations, metacultural competence is arising spontaneously in some speakers/learners. This, in turn, facilitates intercultural competence by making speakers conscious of the fact that the same words and expressions may be used to instantiate different cultural conceptualizations in different varieties of English. As an example, consider the following exchange between a speaker of China English and her supervisor, an Australian English speaker:

A (AUSTRALIAN ENGLISH SPEAKER):   Good luck with your presentation!
B (CHINA ENGLISH SPEAKER):   Thank you, I will try my best to protect your face.
A:   (bewildered for a few seconds), Oh you mean Chinese face! Thanks for that.

*(Personal data)*

In the above exchange, the speaker of China English uses the word 'face' in the sense that it is used in China English. In referring to China English, Qiong (2004: 28) observes that 'the word *face* is strongly stressed in Chinese culture; it means honour, dignity, pride, or even identity. So expressions like *give face*, *save face*, *no face*, *lose face* are very often used [in China English]'. The Australian English speaker is a bit surprised at first at the student's use of the word 'face' in association with himself, but then quickly realizes that here the English word 'face' has been used according to the Chinese cultural schema of 'face'. This cultural schema gives rise to a complex set of cultural meanings in different contexts, but the way it is used here implies that the supervisor's academic reputation is tied to his students' knowledge and thus, by trying to do her best for the presentation, the student is in fact making an attempt to protect her supervisor's academic face. This meaning is not necessarily readily evoked by the use of the word 'face' in such contexts in inner circle varieties of English. However, the supervisor shows awareness of the Chinese schema, which may have come about through interactions with Chinese speakers. This is how metacultural competence is realized and, once realized, can facilitate smoother inter-cultural communication. Metacultural competence can underlie intercultural 'negotiation' skills, which are essential for successful intercultural communication.

Obviously, it would be impractical to expect speakers to learn each system of cultural con-ceptualization associated with different WEs. However, exposure to and awareness of several systems of cultural conceptualizations should enable the speakers to develop the type of meta-cultural competence that I refer to above. If one understands that three different varieties of WEs are associated with partially different systems of cultural conceptualizations, it would not be difficult to predict that other varieties of WEs may have similar differences. This knowledge and awareness, together with proper attitudes, would lead to openness and willingness to negotiate diversity during intercultural communication. This is the basis for the development of ICC, as Byram and others have envisaged it.

## 7. Concluding remarks

In summary, successful communication in English in the context of the globalized world where there is intercultural communication between different varieties of WEs requires competences that go beyond learning the basic skills of a language and what was traditionally termed com-municative competence. Success in international/intercultural communication is now tied to competences such as multidialectal competence, intercultural competence and metacultural competence.

On the one hand, the rapid development of more and more WEs calls for systematic studies of the new varieties, in terms of features such as phonetic/phonological characteristics, syntactic structures and so on. On the other hand, at a deeper level, both the more established varieties and the new varieties need to be examined in terms of their associated cultural conceptualiza-tions. The results of such studies need to be used to produce resources (e.g. cross-WEs glossaries of key conceptualizations) to develop the competences that have been discussed in this chapter. The relevance of World Englishes to more practical areas such as intercultural communication and English language teaching cannot be overestimated. It is very timely and exciting to see the topic of World Englishes now finding its way into the books and journals published and conferences held in these areas.

## Related topics

English as an international language; English as a lingua franca; identity, intercultural (communicative) competence; multidialectalism

## Further reading

Jenkins, J. (2009) *World Englishes*, 2nd edn, London: Routledge (a textbook on world Englishes for postgraduate students).
Kachru, B.B., Kachru, Y. and Nelson, C.L. (eds) (2006) *The Handbook of World Englishes*, Oxford: Black-well Publishing Ltd (a collection of articles focusing on selected critical dimensions and case studies of the theoretical, ideological, applied and pedagogical issues related to English as it is spoken around the world).

Kirkpatrick, A. (2007) *World Englishes: Implications for International Communication and English Language Teaching*, Cambridge: Cambridge University Press [with an accompanying audio CD] (the book describes selected varieties of English, and discusses the issues of the choice of a model for language teaching).

——(2010) *Routledge Handbook of World Englishes*, London/New York: Routledge (a comprehensive introduction to the study of world Englishes drawing on the expertise of key authors in the field).

Wolf, H. and Polzenhagen, F. (2009) *World Englishes: A Cognitive Sociolinguistic Approach*, Berlin/New York: Mouton De Gruyter (an in-depth study of African English following a cultural conceptual approach).

## Notes

1 Technically speaking, varieties of English spoken by Aboriginal people should be referred to as Aboriginal Englishes but, as the contrast explored in this paper is between Australian English and English spoken by Aboriginal people, I collectively refer to them as Aboriginal English rather than Aboriginal Englishes. From the perspective of cultural conceptualizations, the varieties of Aboriginal English are very similar. A major difference between them is in the area of lexical items that they have absorbed from Aboriginal languages.

## References

Aboriginal Australia Art and Culture Centre (2000) The Dreamtime-2, Alice Springs: Aboriginal Australia Art and Culture Centre. Online. Available: www.aboriginalart.com.au/culture/dreamtime2.html (accessed 25 August 2010).

Allsopp, R. (1996) *The Dictionary of Caribbean English Usage*, Oxford: Oxford University Press.

Arthur, J. (1996) *Aboriginal English: A Cultural Study*, Melbourne: Oxford University Press.

Bain, M.S. (1992) *The Aboriginal–White Encounter: Towards Better Communication*, Darwin, Australia: Summer Institute of Linguistics.

Bolton, K. (2005) 'Where WE stand: approaches, issues, and debates in world Englishes', *World Englishes*, 24(1): 69–83.

Brumfit, C. (ed.) (1982) *English for International Communication*, Oxford: Pergamon Press.

Butler, S. (ed.) (1981) *The Macquarie Dictionary*, Sydney: Macquarie Dictionary Company Limited.

Byram, M. (1997) *Teaching and Assessing Intercultural Communicative Competence*, Clevedon: Multilingual Matters.

——(2000) 'Assessing intercultural competence in language teaching', *Sprogforum*, 18(6): 8–13.

Byram, M., Nichols, A. and Stevens, D. (eds) (2001) *Developing Intercultural Competence in Practice*, Clevedon: Multilingual Matters.

Canagarajah, A.S. (2006) 'Changing communicative needs, revised assessment objectives: testing English as an international language', *Language Assessment Quarterly*, 3(3): 229–42.

Crystal, D. (1988) *The English Language*, London: Penguin.

——(2003) *English as a Global Language*, 2nd edn, Cambridge: Cambridge University Press.

Eades, D. (1991) 'Aboriginal English: an introduction', *Vox*, 5: 55–61.

Elkin, A.P. (1969) 'Elements of Australian Aboriginal philosophy', *Oceania*, 40: 85–98.

Fishman, J.A., Cooper, R.L. and Conrad, A.W. (1977) *The Spread of English: The Sociology of English as an Additional Language*, Rowley, MA: Newbury House.

Harkins, J. (1994) *Bridging Two Worlds: Aboriginal English and Cross-cultural Understanding*, St Lucia, Qld: University of Queensland Press.

——(2000) 'Structure and meaning in Australian Aboriginal English', *Asian Englishes*, 3(2): 60–81.

Graddol, D. (1997) *The Future of English?* London: British Council.

——(2006) *English Next*, London: British Council

Greenbaum, S. (ed.) (1996) *Comparing English Worldwide*, Oxford: Clarendon Press.

Jenkins, J. (2003) *World Englishes*, London: Routledge.

——(2009) *World Englishes*, 2nd edn, London: Routledge.

Kachru, B.B. (ed.) (1982) *The Other Tongue: English across Cultures*, 1st edn, Oxford: Pergamon.

——(1983) *The Indianisation of English: The English Language in India*, New Delhi: Oxford University Press.

——(1986) *The Alchemy of English: The Spread, Functions, and Models of Non-native Englishes*, Oxford: Pergamon Press.

——(ed.) (1992) *The Other Tongue: English across Cultures*, 2nd edn, Urbana, IL: University of Illinois Press.

——(1995) 'The intercultural nature of modern English', 1995 Global Cultural Diversity Conference Proceedings, Sydney. Online. Available: www.immi.gov.au/media/publications/multicultural/confer/04/speech19a.htm (accessed 5 May 1996).

Kachru, Y. and Nelson, C.L. (2006) *World Englishes in Asian Contexts*, Hong Kong: Hong Kong University Press.

Kachru, B.B., Kachru, Y. and Nelson, C.L. (eds) (2006) *The Handbook of World Englishes*, Oxford: Blackwell Publishing Ltd.

Kirkpatrick, A. (2007) *World Englishes: Implications for International Communication and English Language Teaching*, Cambridge: Cambridge University Press.

——(2010) *Routledge Handbook of World Englishes*, London/New York: Routledge.

Kortmann, B. and Schneider, E.W. (2004) *A Handbook of Varieties of English: A Multimedia Reference Tool* (2 volumes), Berlin/New York: Mouton de Gruyter.

Kristiansen, G and Dirven, R. (eds) (2008) *Cognitive Sociolinguistics*, Berlin/New York: Mouton de Gruyter.

Lakoff, G. (1987) *Women, Fire and Dangerous Things*, Chicago, IL: University of Chicago Press.

Lakoff, G. and Johnson, M. (1980) *Metaphors We Live By*, Chicago, IL: University of Chicago Press.

McCrum, R., Cran, W. and MacNeil, R. (1986) *The Story of English*, London: Faber and Faber, BBC Publications.

Malcolm, I.G. (2000) 'Aboriginal English research: an overview', *Asian Englishes*, 3(2): 9–31.

Malcolm, I.G. and Sharifian, F. (2007) 'Multiwords in Aboriginal English', in P. Skandera (ed.) *Phraseology and Culture in English*, Berlin/New York: Mouton De Gruyter.

Pennycook, A. (1994) *The Cultural Politics of English as an International Language*, London: Longman.

——(1998) *English and the Discourses of Colonialism*, London/New York: Routledge.

——(2001) *Critical Applied Linguistics*, Hillsdale, NJ: Lawrence Erlbaum.

Phillipson, R. (ed.) (2000) *Rights to Language: Equity, Power, and Education*, Mahwah, NJ: Lawrence Erlbaum.

——(2003) *English-only Europe? Challenging Language Policy*, London: Routledge.

Polzenhagen, F. and Wolf, H. (2007) 'Culture-specific conceptualisations of corruption in African English: linguistic analyses and pragmatic applications', in F. Sharifian and G. Palmer (eds) *Applied Cultural Linguistics*, Amsterdam: John Benjamins, pp. 125–68.

Qiong, H.X. (2004) 'Why China English should stand alongside British, American, and the other "world Englishes"', *English Today*, 20(2): 26–33.

Romaine, S. (1988) *Pidgin and Creole Languages*, London: Longman.

Sharifian, F. (2003) 'On cultural conceptualisations', *Journal of Cognition and Culture*, 3(3): 187–207.

——(2005) 'Cultural conceptualisations in English words: a study of Aboriginal children in Perth', *Language and Education*, 19(1): 74–88.

——(2006) 'A cultural–conceptual approach and world Englishes: the case of Aboriginal English', *World Englishes*, 25(1): 11–22.

——(2007) 'Aboriginal language habitat and cultural continuity', in G. Leitner and I.G. Malcolm (eds) *The Habitat of Australia's Aboriginal Languages*, Berlin/New York: Mouton De Gruyter, pp. 181–96.

——(2008) 'Distributed, emergent cultural cognition, conceptualisation, and language', in R.M. Frank, R. Dirven, T. Ziemke, and E. Bernandez (eds) *Body, Language, and Mind*, Vol. 2, *Sociocultural Situatedness*, Berlin/New York: Mouton de Gruyter, pp. 109–36.

——(2009a) 'On collective cognition and language', in H. Pishwa (ed.) *Language and Social Cognition: Expression of Social Mind*, Berlin/New York: Mouton de Gruyter, pp. 163–82.

——(2009b) 'English as an international language: an overview', in F. Sharifian (ed.) *English as an International Language: Perspectives and Pedagogical Issues*, Bristol: Multilingual Matters, pp. 1–18.

——(2009c) 'Cultural conceptualisations in English as an international language', in F. Sharifian (ed.) *English as an International Language: Perspectives and Pedagogical Issues*, Bristol: Multilingual Matters, pp. 242–53.

——(2010a) 'Semantic and pragmatic conceptualisations in an emerging variety: Persian English', in A. Kirkpatrick (ed.) *Routledge Handbook of World Englishes*, New York/London: Routledge, pp. 442–58.

——(2010b) 'Glocalization of English in World Englishes: an emerging variety among Persian speakers of English', in T. Omoniyi and M. Saxena (eds) *Contending with Globalisation in World Englishes*, Clevedon: Multilingual Matters, pp. 137–55.

——(2011) *Cultural Conceptualisations and Language: Theoretical Framework and Applications*, Amsterdam/Philadelphia: John Benjamins.

Stanner, W.E.H. (1965) 'Religion, totemism and symbolism', in R.M. Berndt and C.H. Berndt (eds) *Aboriginal Man in Australia*, Sydney: Angus and Robertson, pp. 207–37.

——(1979) *White Man Got No Dreaming: Essays 1938–1973*, Canberra: Australian National University Press.

Strevens, P. (1980) *Teaching English as an International Language*, Oxford: Pergamon.

Trudgill, P. and Hannah, J. (1982) *International English: A Guide to Varieties of Standard English*, London: Arnold.

Wolf, H. (2008) 'A cognitive linguistic approach to the cultures of World Englishes: the emergence of a new model', in G. Kristiansen and R. Dirven, (eds) *Cognitive Sociolinguistics: Language Variation, Cultural Models, Social Systems*, Berlin/New York: Mouton de Gruyter, pp. 353–85.

Wolf, H. and Polzenhagen, F. (2009) *World Englishes: A Cognitive Sociolinguistic Approach*, Berlin/New York: Mouton de Gruyter.

# Section III
# Theory into practice

Towards intercultural (communicative)
competence and citizenship

# 20

# An intercultural approach to second language education and citizenship

*Peih-ying Lu and John Corbett*

## 1. Introduction

As intercultural language education has developed over the past few decades, it has become increasingly apparent that its practitioners share a set of concerns with the burgeoning area of citizenship education. This chapter surveys some of the links between citizenship education and intercultural language learning, and then proceeds to a discussion of the articulation of this common ground in influential documents issued as guidelines to language teachers in America, Australasia and Europe. The chapter concludes with a brief consideration of how broad curriculum guidelines relate to language classroom resources and practices.

## 2. Politics, language, identity and 'bounded' citizenship

The definition of citizenship employed by institutions and educators varies, in part because of the different historical processes that have moulded different communities, and partly because the goals of educators may affirm or resist institutional goals. In the literature on citizenship, a distinction is made between global or 'cosmopolitan' and local or 'bounded' forms of citizenship (cf. Miller 1999). Here, we take 'bounded' citizenship to exist within institutional, legally defined borders. The boundaries usually correspond to national borders; however, in cases such as the Special Administrative Regions of Hong Kong and Macao, or the four constituent nations of the United Kingdom, citizenship may relate to a locality either within or beyond the geographical 'nation'.

The nature of 'bounded' citizenship is necessarily complex. Ichilov (1998: 11) observes that citizenship 'consists of legal, cultural, social and political elements, and provides citizens with defined rights and obligations, a sense of identity, and social bonds'. Osler (2005: 4), in turn, states that 'citizenship is essentially about belonging, about feeling secure and being in a position to exercise one's rights and responsibilities'. Although reasonable working definitions, it is clear that notions such as 'belonging', 'security' and 'rights and responsibilities' are contingent. The migrant who aspires to citizenship of another country is faced with a range of contested subject positions with which he or she is expected to align. For example, a UK 'citizen' is also a British 'subject' and can be a member of the national communities of England, Northern Ireland, Scotland or Wales. Meanwhile, a citizen who was born and remains resident in Northern Ireland might feel affinities of belonging with fellow Irish citizens over the border in the south, or he or she might have ancestral roots in Scotland or England. The Irish language and Scots dialect both contribute to the language mix of the nine counties of Ulster, a region that maps awkwardly onto the six counties that make up Northern Ireland today. Issues of belonging, security, rights and responsibilities and language are thus difficult to navigate.

Alred *et al.*'s (2006) collection of case studies from around the world vividly demonstrates that the nature of citizenship within particular nations and regions depends on their historical development and contemporary political structures. For example, Guilherme *et al.* (2006) focus on the rise of citizenship education in Portugal after a period of dictatorship that ended in 1974. They demonstrate that Portuguese pupils' sense of belonging has to negotiate Portuguese nationality, degrees of affiliation to a transnational lusophone community, membership of an economic and political union that encourages plurilingualism and the fostering of a pan-European identity, while adopting an attitude of 'openness and tolerance' towards migrants and foreign languages and cultures. Not surprisingly, there are shifts, inconsistencies and lacunae in official documents that have attempted to direct citizenship education in post-totalitarian Portugal over the past 40 years.

In the same volume, Leung and Lee (2006) discuss the nuanced interplay between citizenship and language politics in Hong Kong, a city that 'belonged' to the UK, and whose last colonial governor afforded it only a brief glimpse of democracy before it was assimilated into China as a Special Administrative Region in 1997. They argue that an evolving sense of identity and belonging in the new Hong Kong is associated with the maintenance and enhancement of Cantonese as a civic language in the SAR. Although Mandarin might have been expected to be the preferred medium of many of the public and institutional functions in Hong Kong after the handover to China, this language shift has not occurred, and the continuing popularity of Cantonese in Hong Kong may be read as an assertion of the territory's continued distance from China. To complicate matters, English remains widely used as a lingua franca and a medium of higher education. In both Portugal and Hong Kong, the dynamics of a colonial history and the regional politics of the present day mould language practices and policies.

Complicated histories and the pressure of political realities also impact upon the construction of identity, which is crucial to the 'sense of belonging' that Ichilov and Osler refer to. Pavlenko and Blackledge (2004: 21) propose three types of identity relevant to individuals in multilingual contexts: 'imposed' identities, which are enforced by institutions and their representatives, irrespective of the desires of the individual; 'assumed' identities, which are accepted by the individuals and not negotiated; and 'negotiable' identities, which are contested by individuals and groups. The status of these identities is variable over time; for example, racial constructs such as 'black', 'white' or 'mixed race' might be imposed, affirmed or negotiated by different institutions and individuals at different times, and they become particularly salient when individuals migrate across territorial boundaries. And so citizenship might be imposed on an individual as an accident of birth, bestowed as a by-product of a social ritual such as marriage or actively sought through persuasion or submission to assessment. In these circumstances, 'individuals are agentive beings who are constantly in search of new social and linguistic resources which allow them to resist identities that position them in undesirable ways, produce new identities, and assign alternative meanings to the links between identities and linguistic varieties' (Pavlenko and Blackledge 2004: 27). Benwell and Stokoe (2006) examine the role of discourse in doing 'identity work' in different environments, including institutional settings and domestic and public spaces. Pertinent to citizenship's discourse of 'belonging' are their analyses of 'spatial identity' and how everyday interaction, such as disputes between neighbours, socially constructs and polices boundaries:

> In terms of identity, places and boundaries are constructed in order to channel human activity and produce spaces of inclusion or exclusion. Within these places, different categories of people are constructed as belonging or not belonging; as legitimate or illegitimate occupants of space.
>
> *Benwell and Stokoe (2006: 240)*

The case of Taiwan affords a particularly rich illustration of the interplay between identity, politics, language and citizenship (e.g. Law 2004). Colonized by the Japanese for over half a century until 1945, Taiwan was then governed by a Nationalist Party (the Ko Ming Tong, or KMT), which retreated to the island during the Chinese civil war. Although the KMT lost China to the Communist Party in 1949, it continued to govern Taiwan as a one-party state until democratic elections in 1996. Despite greater economic cooperation between Taiwan and China, political relations between them remain sensitive, with each side nursing an unresolved historical claim to the other's territory. Like the citizens of Northern Ireland, Portugal and Hong Kong mentioned above, Taiwanese pupils of Chinese descent have to negotiate a complex sense of 'belonging': to the Taiwanese state and to the wider Mandarin-speaking community that includes mainland China. The situation is further complicated by the presence on the island of aboriginal communities and their indigenous languages, sometimes referred to as Southern Ming. These languages influence the local variety of Taiwanese-accented Mandarin, which contains loans from Southern Ming. Educational attitudes to Taiwan's indigenous languages, particularly Southern Ming, have changed over the past few decades. Whereas Southern Ming and even Taiwanese-accented Mandarin were both discouraged in schools and virtually absent from Taiwanese media until the 1980s, the rise of a democratic Taiwan has raised the social status of Southern Ming and the Taiwanese accent. Speaking standard Mandarin is no longer deemed prestigious; instead, the use of Southern Ming or a Taiwanese-accented Mandarin can be a way of showing the degree of solidarity among Taiwanese citizens. It is a way of redeeming the local values that were threatened in the long period of colonization by Japan and, to a lesser extent, by the KMT governments in the postcolonial era. Today, even politicians of the second generation of mainlanders use Southern Ming to signal their solidarity with the people and to demonstrate their shared commitment to the island – effectively performing 'identity work' through their employment of a local language variety.

The complexities caused by lingering and changing attitudes to languages and their social roles were vividly demonstrated by the heated debate in Taiwan over the signing of a trade agreement with China, the ECFA (Economic Cooperation Framework Agreement) in 2010. The ECFA was supported by China and the governing KMT but was opposed by Taiwanese nationalists, who suspected that the agreement would contribute to Taiwanese economic dependence on China, and eventually lead to political assimilation. President Ma Ying-jiou, a second-generation mainlander, used Southern Ming on several occasions to support the ECFA, a language variety that he has had to learn. This move attracted press attention and resulted in two contrasting interpretations: one that his adoption of Southern Ming served to assert Taiwanese solidarity; and another that, in using Southern Ming to promote the ECFA, he was implying that its opponents are uneducated speakers of a local dialect. The controversy was intensified by a series of cartoon strips sponsored by the KMT to promote the benefits of the ECFA: they featured a young, educated multilingual woman explaining, in standard Mandarin, the meaning and benefits of ECFA to a middle-aged, male speaker of Southern Ming with no ambitions. After accusations of discrimination, the cartoon strips were discontinued. The Chinese media report on the press conference and a news report on the controversial strip cartoon can be found at the following websites: www.chinareviewnews.com/doc/1012/2/5/4/101225497.html?coluid=7andkindid = 0anddocid = 101225497 (accessed 24 June 2010) and http://www.youtube.com/watch?v=ibxJmb4YtT8 (accessed 6 May 2011).

Although the status of Southern Ming and Taiwanese-accented Mandarin have both risen as markers of local identity, and now contribute to contested notions of citizenship in Taiwan, English is also promoted because of its role as an international language and a means to improve the nation's global competitiveness and visibility. Recent educational initiatives include 'immersion' elementary schools in several cities, where pupils are educated through the medium of English. In its promotional literature, one such initiative, Fong Shan English Village, states its terms that incorporate values common to citizenship education:

> We expect our students to learn about unfamiliar cultures and respect the differences between various cultures. Providing immersion in an English environment makes students utilize English naturally and brings up students' interests and confidence so that they can use English to explore the world.

Further information on Fong Shan and other English villages can be found at www.loxa.edu.tw/schoolweb.html?webId=494; http://news.bbc.co.uk/2/hi/uk_news/education/6992823.stm and http://ev.dewey.com.tw/data/homepage/english/f.html (all accessed 24 June 2010).

As the case of Taiwan shows, citizenship involves various concentric, overlapping and contested identities that are realized through language choices. Within the island, regional and national identities are identified with Southern Ming and a Taiwanese accented-Mandarin. The use of standard Mandarin signals an affiliation with the larger Chinese-speaking community, an affiliation that may be disputed. In historical terms, pan-Chinese identity in Taiwan has moved from being imposed to being assumed or negotiable, depending on the political stance of the individual. Also negotiable is membership of a broader international community, of which English is a symbolic marker.

Citizenship education, then, involves a nuanced understanding of and active engagement with imagined communities that have complex and competing histories, diverse social structures and often ambitious linguistic demands. These demands operate at different legal and institutional levels. Aspiring UK citizens are currently required to take a citizenship test that assumes a particular level of proficiency in English (see www.lifeintheuktest.gov.uk/htmlsite/background_10.html; accessed 20 June 2010). Meanwhile, UK-born citizens are encouraged, but not required, to learn the languages and cultures of other member states of the European Union, as stated in Article 2 of the European Cultural Convention:

Each Contracting Party shall, insofar as may be possible,

> a. encourage the study by its own nationals of the languages, history and civilisation of the other Contracting Parties and grant facilities to those Parties to promote such studies in its territory, and
>
> b. endeavour to promote the study of its language or languages, history and civilisation in the territory of the other Contracting Parties and grant facilities to the nationals of those Parties to pursue such studies in its territory.

*http://conventions.coe.int/Treaty/en/Treaties/Word/018.doc*
*(accessed 20 June 2010)*

Issues raised by language tests and citizenship have been scrutinized, for example, in collections of articles edited by Extra *et al.* (2009), Hogan-Brun *et al.* (2009) and Shohamy and McNamara (2009). McNamara and Shohamy (2008) survey recent practices in a number of countries around the world, raising the issue of how best language teaching associations might respond to the potentially discriminatory policies being formulated by different nations. They contrast the 'largely symbolic' test currently operating in the United States with recent policy changes in Australia and the UK that have significantly raised the language bar. They conclude that language testing for citizenship has less to do with identifying and assessing the competences required to survive and prosper in the new community, and more to do with symbolic affiliation to the new state and the perceived political need to control the flow of immigration.

## 3. Education for global citizenship

Language testing in 'bounded' citizenship education focuses either on excluding particular immigrant groups or in enabling the symbolic articulation of membership of the community among those groups who are afforded access. However, most educational authorities, such as the administrators of the English Villages in Taiwan, look beyond national boundaries and advocate some form of language teaching for 'cosmopolitan' or 'global' citizenship, sometimes with reference to transnational institutions or human rights legislation. The interests of the global community, from which, by definition, no social group can be excluded, may come into conflict with the interests of 'bounded' institutions such as nation-states, which may use linguistic or other tariffs to exclude certain groups. Furthermore, among educators, advocacy of a global citizenship often coincides with a critical stance, particularly towards nationalist ideologies, and may place this type of citizenship education in opposition to 'bounded' citizenship. Guilherme (2002) puts it thus:

> The *critical* intercultural speaker must [ ... ] be aware that the development of ethnic identities, national or otherwise, involves a constant negotiation between remembering and forgetting, idiosyncrasies and common interests. Furthermore, s/he must be aware that the process of modernisation, on the other hand, has made societies more interdependent and populations more interactive.
>
> *Guilherme (2002: 126–27)*

The postmodern, critical citizen, in Guilherme's terms, is aware of the contingent nature of national and other identity formations, even while he or she may subscribe to them. The critical citizen continues to uphold ideals, such as 'equality of rights, freedom, social justice or general ethical principles that guide modern societies in the search for such ideals' (Guilherme 2002: 114). As there is no world government, some educators, such as Risager (2007), look to transnational institutions such as UNESCO and charities such as Amnesty International and Greenpeace to safeguard the ideals that Guilherme refers to. In arguing that language education has for too long been limited by national perspectives, Risager (2007) draws attention to topics and resources that offer a broader perspective on citizenship:

> Some people have supplemented more nationally oriented literature with various forms of transnational literature: postcolonial literature, travel literature, exile literature, etc., possibly in translation. Or the focus has been on forms and fusions of music from various parts of the world, e.g. Rastafari and reggae.
>
> *Risager (2007: 208) (see also Cates 2000 on global education)*

Although educators who favour global forms of citizenship focus on universal ideals, there remain differences in perspective on the content and aims of education for global citizenship. Guilherme (2002) summarizes the goals of critical cultural awareness as:

> [ … ] a reflective, exploratory, dialogical and active stance towards cultural knowledge and life that allows for dissonance, contradiction, and conflict as well as for consensus, concurrence and transformation. It is a cognitive and emotional endeavour, that aims at individual and collective emancipation, social justice and political commitment.
>
> *Guilherme (2002: 219)*

For Osler (2005), the goal of what she terms 'cosmopolitan citizenship' is to explore the relationship between bounded and global concerns. Her focus is on promoting democratic principles, from the classroom to the national and global institutions that regulate them:

> Preparing young people to participate as cosmopolitan citizens, capable of shaping the future of their own communities and of engaging in democratic processes at all levels, has become an urgent task. The nation state is no longer the only locus for democracy. The challenge is to develop democratic processes at all levels from the global to the local.
>
> *Osler (2005: 19)*

Among citizenship educators, a few cast doubt upon whether an explicit affirmation of democratic ideals is necessary to underpin citizenship education (Feng 2006; Heater 2004). Arguing that concepts of democracy are relative, and that they are interpreted differently in Eastern and Western cultures, Byram (2008:186–87) proposes what he terms 'intercultural citizenship', as distinct from 'intercultural democratic citizenship'. Although the latter may involve 'people of different social groups and cultures engag[ing] in social and political activity founded on democratic values and practices', the former, broader form of citizenship is focused on people of different backgrounds experiencing contact with others and striving to 'work towards an agreed end'. This mutual collaboration will necessitate reflection on the contingent nature of the self and the other, and the ability to analyse evolving relationships with people from different social groups. Byram (2008) sums up his position thus:

> Becoming an intercultural citizen involves psychological and behavioural change, including change in self-perception and understanding of one's relationships to others in other social groups. Where a particular emphasis is placed on learning to be a democratic citizen, the educational purpose is to enable individuals to recognise the particularity of all groups and their cultures, whilst seeing them in the context of universal human values and aspirations.
>
> *Byram (2008: 187)*

Concepts of global citizenship, then, turn out to be as nuanced and complex as those pertaining to situated, 'bounded' citizenships. Educators for democracy focus on the way learners are positioned in a complex web that links local, national and global institutions, and on how the classroom can become a space where learners practise agency in all three domains. Postmodern educational theorists find themselves affirming universal rights and responsibilities, such as freedom of speech, equal opportunities and social justice, even as they embark on discussions of how these rights and responsibilities might be differently understood in different cultures.

Acknowledgement of diversity rubs up awkwardly against avowals of our common humanity and our shared custodianship of the planet. Critical pedagogues urge learners to treat concepts of self and other with ironic detachment, while rousing them to challenge, with undiminished commitment, the oppressive forces of privilege and vested interests (see, for example, the articles collected in Norton and Toohey (2004) and Phipps and Guilherme (2004)). Byram's solution to the paradoxes of global citizenship education is focused on action in the here-and-now: he suggests that people from different cultural backgrounds agree on goals that are to the common good, and then establish protocols for working together that will, over time, change our understandings of the self and the other.

## 4. Intercultural communicative competence

Intercultural language education, like citizenship education, grew out of the political changes of the 1980s and 1990s, which contributed to ongoing pedagogical reflections on the means and purpose of language education, particularly with respect to the teaching of English, which was rapidly becoming a global lingua franca (cf. Byram 1997; Corbett 2003; Pennycook 1994). Harber (1997) discusses the educational impact of exhilarating social changes in Africa, Asia, Europe and South America towards the end of a turbulent decade. The enthusiasm for progressive reforms, kindled by events like the 'Velvet Revolutions' and the more recent 'Arab Spring', tends to be tempered by the consequent economic and social challenges, for instance, mass migration and the rise of religious and political extremism. Even so, energetic enquiry into education for democratic citizenship has continued, and it has increasingly informed models of intercultural language education (e.g. Alred et al. 2006; Byram 2008; Guilherme 2002; Osler and Starkey 2005).

The impulse towards intercultural language education arises from the recognition that there is more to language use than the transfer of information from one set of language speakers to another. Information transfer was the cornerstone of 'communicative' approaches to language education that held sway during the 1970s and 1980s. This move beyond information transfer elicited a variety of responses from different educational traditions. Cognitive approaches focused on the development of interlanguages according to universal instincts and the diversity of individual learning strategies (e.g. Cook 1993; Griffiths 2008). The nascent intercultural approach drew more on linguistic anthropology and, in particular, ethnographic descriptions of situated communicative events.

Ethnographic studies of intercultural *mis*communication investigate the ways that language signals assumptions about the identity and attitudes of the other. For example, Roberts et al. (1992) studied the communication practices of South Asian immigrant workers and their Anglo-British line managers; their discourse analyses of workplace settings led to training sessions with both groups that addressed issues such as their different interpretations of indirect questions in job interviews. Roberts et al. (2001) moved from teaching materials informed by workplace ethnography to training advanced learners to be ethnographers. By preparing language students in further and higher education to be active and reflective participant–observers in their year abroad, Roberts et al. (2001) put into practice one of the tenets of European citizenship, Article 2b of the European Cultural Convention, quoted above.

Intercultural language education addresses the now common situation in which individuals from different cultural backgrounds find themselves living and working together, discursively renegotiating their identities and critically reflecting on and reshaping their own ideological and value systems. Barnett (2000) coined the term 'supercomplexity' to express the condition in which this constant renegotiation and reshaping occurs. Intercultural language curricula generally attempt to address the issue of supercomplexity in one of two ways: by promoting a model of intercultural communicative competence that builds models of skills and competences; or by promoting an experiential mode of learning that aims to encourage 'intercultural being' (e.g. Phipps and Gonzalez 2004). Models of intercultural communicative competence have envisaged the goals of the curriculum as developing skills and knowledge, which Byram labels *savoirs*, or as linguistic and cultural 'resources' that learners develop and draw upon (see Byram 1997; Risager 2007). Byram's *savoirs* model is perhaps better known and can be summarized as follows (see Byram (1997, 2008: 69), Chapters 5 and 26, this volume):

- Attitudes: curiosity and openness, readiness to suspend disbelief about other cultures and belief about one's own (*savoir être*);
- Knowledge: of social groups and their products and practices in one's own and in one's interlocutor's country, and of the general processes of societal and individual interaction (*savoirs*);
- Skills of interpreting and relating: ability to interpret a document or event from another culture, to explain it and relate it to documents from one's own (*savoir comprendre*);
- Skills of discovery and interaction: ability to acquire new knowledge of a culture and cultural practices and the ability to operate knowledge, attitudes and skills under the constraints of real-time communication and interaction (*savoir apprendre/faire*);
- Critical cultural awareness/political education: an ability to evaluate critically and on the basis of explicit criteria perspectives, practices and products in one's own and other cultures and countries (*savoir s'engager*).

Risager (2007) suggests that Byram's model and discussion are too closely associated with a nation-based concept of culture; in other words, that Byram's intercultural communicative competence assumes that intercultural communication takes place between citizens of different countries. Her 'competences and resources' model builds on Byram's and extends it in the direction of cosmopolitan citizenship enjoyed by proficient users of a second language who have the following (adapted from Risager 2007: 227):

- Structural linguistic competence;
- Semantic and pragmatic competence and resources;
- Competence and resources in poetics;
- Competence and resources in linguistic identity;
- Competence in translation and interpretation;
- Competence in interpreting texts (discourses) and media products in a broad sense;
- Competence in using ethnographic methods;
- Competence in transnational cooperation;
- Knowledge of language and critical language awareness, also as a world citizen;
- Knowledge of culture and society and critical cultural awareness, also as a world citizen.

Risager's model extends some of Byram's formulations, for example into the domains of linguistic identity and poetics. Each relates to the language learner's stance towards the language, both as a creative agent and as someone who might wish to signal affinity with or distance from the linguistic norms of a given speech community. She also makes some of Byram's formulations more explicit, for example in proposing ethnography as a mode of cultural 'discovery and interaction', or translation as a mode of 'interpreting and relating'. Risager's final two types of 'knowledge' make explicit the goal of positioning the learner as a 'world citizen', whose linguistic proficiency is linked to his or her participation in topics raised in the discussion of cosmopolitan citizenship above, namely topics such as 'human rights, cultural diversity, the global environment, social inequality in the world, the peace issue, terrorism, etc.' (Risager 2007: 232).

## 5. Institutionalizing intercultural language education

It will be clear from the foregoing sections that 'bounded' citizenship education usually acknowledges that learners are simultaneously members of larger, transnational, cosmopolitan or global communities. Intercultural language education offers a means of extending 'bounded' citizenship education in the direction of 'global citizenship'. The competences and skills expected of the global citizen, such as openness to diversity, critical cultural awareness and the ability to deal with the conditions of supercomplexity, are those, given individual differences in emphasis and perspective, promoted by intercultural language educators such as Byram, Guilherme, Gonzalez, Phipps and Risager. Over the past two decades, similar ideas have increasingly influenced mainstream language education, supported by institutional documents such as the Council of Europe's *Common European Framework of Reference for Languages: Teaching, Learning and Assessment*, hereafter 'CEFR' (Council of Europe 2001); the USA's *National Standards in Foreign Language Education: Preparing for the 21st Century*, hereafter the *Standards*, published by four American language organizations (ACTFL 1996); and the *National Statement for Languages Education in Australian Schools*, hereafter the *National Statement* (Ministerial Council on Education, Employment, Training and Youth Affairs Australia 2005).

The Australian *National Statement* moves easily back and forth from bounded to global citizenship, noting that good national citizens must now also be 'inter-cultural':

> Education in a global community brings with it an increasing need to focus on developing inter-cultural understanding. This involves the integration of language, culture and learning. Inter-cultural language learning helps learners to know and understand the world around them, and to understand commonality and difference, global connections and patterns. Learners will view the world, not from a single perspective of their own first language and culture, but from the multiple perspectives gained through the study of second and subsequent languages and cultures. For learners who study their background or heritage language, it provides a strengthened sense of identity.
>
> *Ministerial Council on Education, Employment, Training and*
> *Youth Affairs Australia (2005: 3)*

The *National Statement* is effectively a strategy document rather than a detailed guide to the implementation of the aspirations it articulates. Its seventeen pages assert the purpose of language learning in a multicultural society and globalized world, before addressing issues such as teacher retention, programme development, quality assurance and advocacy of language learning, including the identification of 'national champions from various walks of life' (Ministerial Council on Education, Employment, Training and Youth Affairs Australia 2005: 17).

The more detailed American *Standards* document is also based on the rationale that 'the USA must educate its citizens to be equipped linguistically and culturally to communicate successfully both in a pluralistic American society and abroad' (ACTFL 1996: 7). Overall, the *Standards* emphasize both linguistic and cultural insights that come with foreign language study and consider such study 'a requisite for life as a citizen in the worldwide neighborhood' (ACTFL 1996: 12). The *Standards* document notes at the beginning that it is not a curriculum guide; instead, it provides a logically ordered sequence of language study and some recommendations for course framework development and reasonable expectations for the students in different parts of the country. Rather than discussing the language skills of listening, speaking, reading and writing discretely, the document formulates broadly conceived standards, based on 5 Cs: 'Communication, cultures, connections, comparisons and communities'. The *Standards* document assumes that competence in more than one language and culture enables people to develop awareness of self and other cultures and look beyond their customary borders, that is, effectively to become cosmopolitan citizens. Three key concepts are evident in the formulation of the *Standards* (ACTFL 1996: 43–48):

1. Perspectives: attitudes, values and ideas;
2. Practices: patterns of social interaction and patterns of behaviour accepted by a society; and
3. Products: books, foods, laws, music ... etc.

These aspects of culture are consistently woven into the *Standards* framework generally. Learners are also expected to explore the relationships among the products, practices and perspectives of the target culture. The *Standards* also emphasize that teaching cultural similarities as well as differences in the language classroom is important.

As with the *National Statement* and the *Standards*, the general aim of the CEFR is for learners to be able to deal with everyday life in another country and to help immigrants to do so in their country. However, unlike its Australian and American counterparts, the Council of Europe is a transnational body, concerned to harmonize distinct national identities within a larger imagined community. By acquiring some of the languages of other European member states, learners are expected be able to exchange information and ideas with speakers of other languages, as well as to achieve a wider and deeper understanding of the life and thought of fellow Europeans from different national traditions. Unlike the American and Australian documents, the CEFR includes English among the languages it promotes; the *Standards* and *National Statement* are concerned with languages other than English, including, in the case of Australia, aboriginal and heritage languages.

One of the concerns of the developers of the CEFR was explicitly 'preparation for democratic citizenship', again defined in terms familiar to intercultural language education:

> To promote methods of modern language teaching which will strengthen independence of thought, judgement and action, combined with social skills and responsibility.
>
> *Council of Europe (2001: 4)*

All three documents, then, implicitly or explicitly, seek to support the integration of language learning with those skills associated with intercultural citizenship.

Although the *Standards* document acknowledges that it is not a curriculum guide, it gives examples of different types of curricular experience. More ambitiously, the CEFR aims to provide a common basis for 'elaboration of language syllabuses, curriculum guidelines, examinations, textbooks, etc. across Europe' (Council of Europe 2001: 1). Compared with the *Standards*, the CEFR places a greater emphasis on the learning of language skills – what Risager (2007) refers to as 'languastructure'. Levels of language skill are assessed independently of intercultural skills and competences. Where sociocultural knowledge does appear in the CEFR, it is broken down into several concrete concepts that are characterized as distinctive features of a society, namely everyday living, living conditions, interpersonal relations, value, body language, social conventions and ritual behaviours (Council of Europe 2001: 101–3). For example, everyday living includes food and drink, meal times and public holidays, etc. Values, beliefs and attitudes cover issues such as social class, occupational groups and regional cultures. Levels of intercultural communicative competence draw upon Byram's *savoirs*. Emphasis is placed on knowledge, skills and know-how (*savoir-faire*) and 'existential' competences that include *savoir être* and *savoir apprendre* Risager (2007) notes that:

> It is [ … ] not surprising, perhaps, that *Framework* is characterised by a Eurocentrism that favours the majority languages in Europe and the European majority cultures – and that it ignores the entire rest of the world outside Europe, where, of course, the major European languages also happen to be widespread.
>
> *Risager (2007: 115)*

Although, as Risager observes, the CEFR makes no claims beyond the boundaries of Europe, its influence has been felt elsewhere in the world. For example, in Taiwan, in 2005, the Ministry of Education (MoE) posted the CEFR's levels of linguistic skills on its website (www. edu.gov.tw). At the time, the MoE strongly recommended in a press release that the CEFR's skills levels be used as a benchmark for English language assessment in Taiwan. This move was in response to public concern following the ROC Fair Trade Commission's criticism of the Language Training and Testing Center in Taiwan for providing inadequate descriptors of different levels of English proficiency in its own instrument of assessment, the General English Proficiency Test (GEPT). However, neither the overall objectives of the CEFR nor its sociocultural knowledge indicators were endorsed by the MoE. Sociocultural knowledge and intercultural communicative competence are absent from the excerpts it posted, and the CEFR was used primarily as a linguistic resource rather than as a resource to guide language and citizenship education. Furthermore, the MoE did not provide information about how teachers and materials developers based in Taiwan could make good use of the 260-page CEFR document, and there was no discussion of why a Eurocentric set of standards should be so privileged. Despite these absences, as a result of the MoE's intervention, the language level descriptors used in the CEFR document are, at the time of writing, still publicized on the websites of numerous Taiwanese educational institutions. For example, the website of the Language Training and Testing Center of the National Taiwan University includes the CEFR Language Levels as one of several descriptors of language proficiency. The British Council in Taiwan also makes available a Chinese translation of the CEFR language levels, itself taken from the MoE directive (websites accessed on 24 June 2010): www.lttc.ntu.edu.tw/english comparativenew.htm and www.britishcouncil.org/tw/taiwan-exams-common-reference-levels-global-scale.htm.

Despite the challenges of using them outside their original domains, the CEFR and similar documents can act as aspirational models for educators elsewhere who wish to integrate language with issues of culture and citizenship. The American *Standards* provide adaptable models of how culture and language can be addressed in the language classroom. As the *Standards* indicate, 'The true content of the foreign language course is not the grammar and the vocabulary, but the cultures expressed through that language' (ACTFL 1996: 43). This provides a chance for educational authorities and language professionals to look at the feasibility of changing the emphasis from memorization of words and grammar rules to the exploration, development and use of 'communicative strategies, learning strategies, and critical thinking skills as well as the appropriate elements of the language system and culture' (ACTFL 1996: 97). As Byram indicates, language teachers are not necessarily experts in the culture of the target language. Therefore, rather than attempting to teach facts, intercultural language teachers aim to teach the attitudes, competences and skills that are equally relevant to the learner becoming: (1) a global citizen, which involves understanding of and active engagement with different communities; and (2) what Met and Byram (1996: 68) call 'an independent cultural learner'. Such clear models of classroom practice provide accessible opportunities for developing these competences.

Despite the fact that, in comparison with the American *Standards*, its descriptors may seem convoluted and difficult to implement, the CEFR can also be used for scaling not only language proficiency but also the different kinds of intercultural knowledge demanded of global citizens. The detailed intercultural dimension of the CEFR can be considered alongside the discussion of culture learning found in the *Standards*. Where appropriate, Byram's five *savoirs*, particularly *savoir être*, *savoirs* and *savoir s'engager*, can be referenced together with the exemplars of activities found in the *Standards*. Thus, educators elsewhere who are interested in combining language and citizenship education can adapt the American and European models to suit their local needs. However, these institutional frameworks also need to be used critically, with an understanding of the political and philosophical aspirations of their creators.

## 6. Language and citizenship: pedagogical practices

Whatever the concept of citizenship that prevails, 'bounded' or 'global', most educators agree that the language classroom can be a privileged site for the exploration of identity and belonging, key aspects of citizenship. At best, language classrooms can function as 'safe houses' in Pratt's (1991) formulation:

> social and intellectual spaces where groups can constitute themselves as horizontal, homogeneous, sovereign communities with high degrees of trust, shared understandings, and temporary protection from legacies of oppression.
>
> *Pratt (1991: 40) (see also Andreotti 2005; Canagarajah 2004)*

In the 'safe house' of the ideal classroom, learners from different backgrounds and of different ages can develop their command of another language while exploring issues of identity and citizenship.

In practice, materials developed to promote citizenship education in the language classroom extend from 'bounded' notions of belonging to broader concerns of common humanity. For example, *Citizenship Materials for ESOL Learners in Scotland* (National Institute for Adult Continuing Education 2006) begins with a unit that looks specifically at UK citizenship in terms of knowledge about the parliamentary, legal and health systems, but also extends to issues of human rights and community involvement. Further units interrogate stereotypes and balance topics associated with symbolic affiliation to the British community (e.g. knowledge of flags, and kings and queens) with an acknowledgement that Britain is a diverse society, racially and culturally, and discussion of human rights legislation internationally. The assumption is that the user of these materials will wish to prepare for the 'Life in the UK' test that aspiring UK citizens must now take, but also that the learners' interests will be engaged by the intercultural exploration of topics such as body language, women's rights and the role of charities in public life.

The ethnographic exploration of everyday life, behaviour, attitudes, beliefs and responsibilities also underlies ELT textbooks developed for particular regions, such as *Changing Skies: The European Course for Advanced Level Learners* (Pulverness 2001) and the *Intercultural Resource Pack: Latin American Perspectives* (Morgado de Matos *et al.* 2006). Topics addressed in these materials include European emigration and exile, the 'idea of Europe', poverty in Rio and the representation of women in the Argentinian and American media.

ELT resource books such as *Global Issues* (Sampedro and Hillyard 2004) and *Intercultural Language Activities* (Corbett 2010) represent the fusion of communicative language teaching, with its focus on role plays, discussions and tasks, with content developed with cosmopolitan citizenship and cultural exploration in mind. Topics covered in *Global Issues* include child poverty, green issues and bullying, whereas *Intercultural Language Activities* draws upon the increasing availability of global communications to link classrooms virtually and engage in online ethnography. One task in Sampedro and Hillyard (2004: 19–20), called simply 'The global citizen', asks learners to visualize communities, local and global, as a set of concentric circles with 'family' at the core. As learners identify the communities represented by the ever-widening circles, they discuss the 'duties, rights and responsibilities' of members of those communities. For the largest circle – 'the global community' – learners are specifically invited to consider the principles they think should govern that community. The step not usually taken by such classroom resources is actually to engage the learners in community action; this move from language learning to social action remains for some the point at which intercultural language learning becomes citizenship education (e.g. Byram 2008; Guilherme 2002).

Classrooms that operate as 'safe houses' for citizenship and intercultural language education generally address issues of relevance to the learners' lives as members of the local and international communities – and do so in ways that model constructive modes of collaboration. Starkey (2005) proposes a set of characteristics of the class as 'safe house', again drawing on institutional frameworks such as those drawn up by the Council of Europe. A Council of Europe recommendation on 'Education for democratic citizenship' (Council of Europe 2002: 3; cited in Starkey 2005: 37) suggests that citizens learn how to:

- settle conflicts in a non-violent manner;
- argue in defence of one's viewpoint;
- recognize and accept differences;
- make choices, consider alternatives and subject them to ethical analysis;
- shoulder shared responsibilities;
- establish constructive, non-aggressive relations with others;
- develop a critical approach to information, thought patterns and philosophical, religious, social, political and cultural concepts [ … ].

Citizenship education, then, offers language teachers and learners content that is relevant to their lives as engaged members of different communities. One of the challenges facing the current generation of language educators is to ensure that classrooms do act as 'safe houses' and to design further resources and classroom tasks that specifically expose learners to the scenarios and resources that will equip them to develop the kinds of competences suggested in this chapter, and to express themselves in ways that allow them to assume their responsibilities and exercise their rights as active intercultural citizens.

## Related topics

Cosmopolitanism; global competency; identity; intercultural citizenship; intercultural communicative competence; second or foreign language education

## Further reading

Byram, M. (2008) *From Foreign Language Education to Education for Intercultural Citizenship*, Bristol: Multilingual Matters (a collection of essays that analyze the construct of intercultural communicative competence and discuss the relationship between foreign language education and education for citizenship).

Extra, G., Spotti, M. and Van Avermaet, P. (eds) (2009) *Language Testing, Migration and Citizenship: Cross-national Perspectives on Integration Regimes*, London: Continuum (essays offering a critical perspective on the role of applied linguists in developing tests on language and citizenship around the world).

Guilherme, M. (2002) *Critical Citizens for an Intercultural World: Foreign Language Education as Cultural Politics*, Clevedon: Multilingual Matters (theoretical foundations and practical proposals for the development of critical cultural awareness and intercultural communication competence).

Heater, D. (2004) *A History of Education for Citizenship*, London: Routledge (a broad historical overview of citizenship, considered from its classical origins through to contemporary ideas of world citizenship and multiculturalism).

Osler, A. and Starkey, H. (eds) (2005) *Citizenship and Language Learning*, Stoke on Trent: Trentham Books/British Council (a set of accessible essays discussing the nature of citizenship and the relevance of citizenship for language teachers and learners).

## References

Alred, G., Byram, M. and Fleming, M. (eds) (2006) *Education for Intercultural Citizenship: Concepts and Comparisons*, Clevedon: Multilingual Matters.

American Council on the Teaching of Foreign Languages (ACTFL) (1996) *Standards of Foreign Language Learning: Preparing for the 21st Century*, Lawrence, KS: Allen Press.

Andreotti, V. (2005) 'Reclaiming the right to question: language teachers in Brazil', in A. Osler and H. Starkey (eds) *Citizenship and Language Learning*, Stoke on Trent: Trentham Books/British Council, pp. 83–93.

Barnett, R. (2000) 'Supercomplexity and the curriculum', *Studies in Higher Education*, 25(3): 255–65.

Benwell, B. and Stokoe, E. (2006) *Discourse and Identity*, Edinburgh: Edinburgh University Press.

Byram, M. (1997) *Teaching and Assessing Intercultural Communicative Competence*, Clevedon: Multilingual Matters.

——(2008) *From Foreign Language Education to Education for Intercultural Citizenship*, Bristol: Multilingual Matters.

Canagarajah, A.S. (2004) 'Subversive identities, pedagogical safe houses', in B. Norton and K. Toohey (eds) *Critical Pedagogies and Language Learning*, Cambridge: Cambridge University Press, pp. 116–37.

Cates, K.A. (2000) 'Global education', in M. Byram (ed.) *Routledge Encyclopedia of Language Teaching and Learning*, London/New York: Routledge, pp. 241–43.

Cook, V. (1993) *Linguistics and Second Language Acquisition*, London: Macmillan.

Corbett, J. (2003) *An Intercultural Approach to English Language Teaching*, Clevedon: Multilingual Matters.

——(2010) *Intercultural Language Activities*, Cambridge: Cambridge University Press.

Council of Europe (2001) *Common European Framework of Reference for Languages: Learning, Teaching and Assessment*, Strasbourg: Council of Europe.

——(2002) *Recommendation (Rec 2002)12 of the Committee of Ministers to Member States on Education for Democratic Citizenship*, Strasbourg: Council of Europe.

Extra, G., Spotti, M. and Van Avermaet, P. (eds) (2009). *Language Testing, Migration and Citizenship: Cross-national Perspectives on Integration Regimes*, London: Continuum.

Feng, A. (2006) 'Contested notions of citizenship and citizenship education: the Chinese case', in G. Alred, M. Byram and M. Fleming (eds) *Education for Intercultural Citizenship: Concepts and Comparisons*, Clevedon: Multilingual Matters, pp. 86–105.

Griffiths, C. (2008) *Lessons from the Good Language Learner*, Cambridge: Cambridge University Press.

Guilherme, M. (2002) *Critical Citizens for an Intercultural World: Foreign Language Education as Cultural Politics*, Clevedon: Multilingual Matters.

Guilherme, M., Pureza, J.M., Paulos da Silva, R. and Santos, H. (2006) 'The intercultural dimension of citizenship education in Portugal', in G. Alred, M. Byram and M. Fleming (eds) *Education for Intercultural Citizenship: Concepts and Comparisons*, Clevedon: Multilingual Matters, pp. 213–31.

Harber, C. (1997) 'International developments and the rise of education for democracy', *Compare: A Journal of Comparative and International Education*, 27(2): 179–91.

Heater, D. (2004) *A History of Education for Citizenship*, London: Routledge.

Hogan-Brun, G., Mar-Molinero, C. and Stevenson, P. (eds) (2009) *Discourses on Language and Integration: Critical Perspectives on Language Testing Regimes in Europe*, Amsterdam: John Benjamins.

Ichilov, O. (1998) *Citizenship and Citizenship Education in a Changing World*, London: Woburn Press.

Law, W.W. (2004) 'Globalization and citizenship education in Hong Kong and Taiwan', *Comparative Education Review*, 48(3): 253–73.

Leung, S.W. and Lee, W.O. (2006) 'National identity at the crossroads: the struggle between culture, language and politics in Hong Kong', in G. Alred, M. Byram and M. Fleming (eds) *Education for Intercultural Citizenship: Concepts and Comparisons*, Clevedon: Multilingual Matters, pp. 23–46.

McNamara, T. and Shohamy, E. (2008) 'Language Tests and Human Rights', *International Journal of Applied Linguistics*, 18(1): 89–98.

Met, M. and Byram, M. (1996) 'Standards for foreign language learning and the teaching of culture', *Language Learning Journal*, 19(1): 61–68.

Miller, D. (1999) 'Bounded citizenship', in K. Hutchings and R. Dannreuther (eds) *Cosmopolitan Citizenship*, Basingstoke: Palgrave Macmillan, pp. 60–80.

Ministerial Council on Education, Employment, Training and Youth Affairs Australia (2005) *National Statement for Languages Education in Australian Schools*, Hindmarsh, SA: Department of Education and Children's Services.

Morgado de Matos, A., Assenti del Rio, A., Aparicio, N., Mobilia, S. and Martins, T.H.B. (2006) *The Intercultural Resource Pack: Latin American Perspectives*, Rio de Janeiro: British Council.

National Institute for Adult Continuing Education (2006) *Citizenship Materials for ESOL Learners in Scotland*, Leicester: NIACE.

Norton, B. and Toohey, K. (eds) (2004) *Critical Pedagogies and Language Learning*, Cambridge: Cambridge University Press.

Osler, A. (2005) 'Education for democratic citizenship', in A. Osler and H. Starkey (eds) *Citizenship and Language Learning*, Stoke on Trent: Trentham Books/British Council, pp. 3–22.

Osler, A. and Starkey, H. (eds) (2005) *Citizenship and Language Learning*, Stoke on Trent: Trentham Books/British Council.

Pavlenko, A. and Blackledge, A. (eds) (2004) *Negotiation of Identities in Multilingual Contexts*, Clevedon: Multilingual Matters.

Pennycook, A. (1994) *The Cultural Politics of English as an International Language*, Harlow: Longman.

Phipps, A. and Gonzalez, M. (2004) *Modern Languages: Learning and Teaching in an Intercultural Field*, London: Sage.

Phipps, A. and Guilherme, M. (eds) (2004) *Critical Pedagogy: Political Approaches to Language and Intercultural Communication*, Clevedon: Multilingual Matters.

Pratt, M.L. (1991) 'Arts of the contact zone', *Profession*, 91: 33–40.

Pulverness, A. (2001) *Changing Skies: The European Course for Advanced Level Learners*, Peaslake, Surrey: Delta Publishing.

Risager, K. (2007) *Language and Culture Pedagogy: From a National to a Transnational Paradigm*, Clevedon: Multilingual Matters.

Roberts, C., Davies, E. and Jupp, T.C. (1992) *Language and Discrimination: A Study of Communication in Multi-Ethnic Workplaces*, London: Longman.

Roberts, C., Barro, A., Byram, M., Jordan, S. and Street, B. (2001) *Language Learners as Ethnographers: Introducing Cultural Processes into Advanced Language Learning*, Clevedon: Multilingual Matters.

Sampedro, R. and Hillyard, S. (2004) *Global Issues*, Oxford: Oxford University Press.

Shohamy, E. and McNamara, T. (eds) (2009) 'Language testing for citizenship, immigration and asylum', Special issue of *Language Assessment Quarterly*, 6(1): 1–5.

Starkey, H. (2005) 'Language teaching for democratic citizenship', in A. Osler and H. Starkey (eds) *Citizenship and Language Learning*, Stoke on Trent: Trentham Books/British Council, pp. 23–40.

# 21

# Intercultural communicative competence through telecollaboration

*Robert O'Dowd*

## 1. Introduction/definitions

In the context of foreign language education, 'telecollaboration' refers to the application of online communication tools to bring together classes of language learners in geographically distant locations to develop their foreign language skills and intercultural competence through collaborative tasks and project work. The interaction has traditionally been text based and asynchronous (i.e. not in real time). However, recent advances in online connections and communication tools have meant that synchronous (i.e. in real time) oral communication as well as multimodal exchanges involving combinations of different media are becoming increasingly popular. Telecollaboration has come to be seen as one of the main pillars of the intercultural turn in foreign language education (Thorne 2006), as it allows educators to engage their learners in regular, (semi-)authentic communication with members of other cultures in distant locations and also gives learners the opportunity to reflect on and learn from the outcomes of this intercultural exchange within the supportive and informed context of their foreign language classroom. In the words of Kern *et al.* (2004), telecollaboration offers educators the opportunity to

> ... use the Internet not so much to teach the same thing in a different way, but rather to help students enter into a new realm of collaborative enquiry and construction of knowledge, viewing their expanding repertoire of identities and communication strategies as resources in the process.
>
> Kern et al. *(2004: 21)*

Over the past two decades, this activity has been referred to in many ways, including informal terms such as 'e-pals' or 'key-pals' or, in more academic contexts, as e-tandem (O'Rourke 2007), online intercultural exchange (O'Dowd 2007; Thorne 2010), internet-mediated intercultural foreign language education (Belz and Thorne 2006) and in France as EIEGL (*Échanges interculturels exolingues en groupe en ligne*) (Audras and Chanier 2008). Each of these terms tends to carry its own connotations and implications, depending on the educational context in which it is used. For example, the terminology 'e-pal' or 'key-pal' stems from the traditional activity of 'pen pals', which linked together young learners in different countries through letter exchanges. As a result, these terms are generally used in primary and secondary school contexts and on websites that aim to link pre-university classes of learners in different countries (see, for example, http://www.epals.com/).

The term 'e-tandem', on the other hand, comes from the tradition of 'tandem language learning', which has been widely practised in many European universities. Tandem learning is essentially a language learning activity that involves language exchange and collaboration between two partners who are native speakers of their partners' target language. Its online equivalent, e-tandem, thus involves two native speakers of different languages communicating together and providing feedback for each other through online communication tools with the aim of learning the other's language. E-tandem gained popularity throughout European universities in the early 1990s, and a centralized internet site with resources, bibliography and guidelines was financed by European project funding during this time (O'Rourke 2007). However, in the mid-1990s, the growth in interest in online interaction as a tool for foreign language education in the USA and Asia and the increased importance attributed to the social and intercultural aspects of foreign language learning led to the emergence of more complex exchange set-ups, which were referred to under the umbrella terms of 'telecollaboration' and 'internet-mediated intercultural foreign language education'. These terms described the different formats and structures of online intercultural exchange being carried out in classrooms around the globe, which had the dual aims of developing both linguistic competence and intercultural communicative competence. It is these practices that are the main focus of this chapter.

## 2. Historical perspectives

The origins of online intercultural exchanges in foreign language education can be traced to the learning networks pioneered by Célestin Freinet in 1920s France and later by Mario Lodi in 1960s Italy, decades before the internet was to become a tool for classroom learning (Cummins and Sayers 1995: 119–36). Freinet made use of the technologies and modes of communication available to him at the time to enable his classes in the north of France to make class newspapers with a printing press and to exchange these newspapers along with 'cultural packages' of flowers, fossils and photos of their local area with schools in other parts of France. Similarly, Lodi motivated his learners and helped to develop their critical literacy by encouraging them to create student newspapers in collaboration with distant partner classes. The link between the principles and activities of these educators and the online work being carried out today is discussed in detail by Cummins and Sayers (1995) and Müller-Hartmann (2007). However, the connection can be clearly seen by comparing Freinet's 'cultural packages' activity with popular contemporary online exchange tasks such as the 'E-Twinning Culture in a Box' activity. In both activities, students are asked to gather information about their own country and send it to their partner school. However, in the modern version, the partner class then becomes responsible for producing a PowerPoint presentation on their partner country's culture.

Upon the emergence of the internet as a potential tool for learning in the early 1990s, online intercultural exchange became one of the first activities to be explored by educators. Early reports of projects such as the Orillas Network (Cummins and Sayers 1995), the AT&T Learning Circles (Riel 1997) as well as in-depth research studies (Eck *et al.* 1995) demonstrated the potential of intercultural exchange for developing intercultural awareness. However, the cost of computer hardware and the lack of reliable internet access in schools and universities meant that reports of activities were scarce and often involved brief exchanges in which, for example, classes exchanged one jointly written message on a weekly basis. By the mid-1990s, the first reports of e-tandem exchanges were beginning to appear (Brammerts 1996), and Mark Warschauer, one of the pioneers of online foreign language education, had published *Virtual Connections* (1995), a vast collection of practitioners' reports on how online communication tools were being used to engage learners in intercultural communicative activities. At this stage, a number of webpages, including Intercultural E-mail Classroom Connections (IECC) and E-Tandem, also became available online in order to link up classrooms across the globe and to provide practitioners with activities and guidelines for their projects, while practitioners such as Ruth Vilmi in Finland and Reinhard Donath in Germany helped to make the activity better known by publishing practical reports of their students' work online.

Since this initial period, online intercultural exchange has gone on to become one of the main pillars of computer-assisted language learning (CALL) or network-based language teaching (NBLT), and the contribution of online contact and exchange to the development of inter-cultural awareness and intercultural communicative competence (ICC) has been one of the main areas of research in this area (Müller-Hartmann 2000; O'Dowd 2003; Ware 2005). Initi-ally however, the intercultural learning outcomes of such contact tended at times to be exaggerated or oversimplified. For example, it was common to read that intercultural learning could be 'easily achieved through [e-mail] tandem learning' (Brammerts 1996: 122), whereas Richter (1998) was justifiably critical of Lixl-Purcell (1995) for suggesting the following:

> As we cast our communicative nets wider, searching for contacts to foreign cultures across the globe, the spectrum of voices from otherwise obscure individuals helps us learn tolerance for difference as well as similarities.
>
> *Cited in Richter (1998: 3)*

Furthermore, many of the initial publications in the literature involved rather superficial e-mail exchanges, in which information was exchanged without reflection and students were rarely challenged to reflect on their own culture or their stereotypical views of the target cul-ture. In many reports, the mere fact that students referred in their mails to such topics as food, restaurants and holidays was considered to be 'cultural learning', and many writers seemed to assume that learners would develop intercultural competence simply by being exposed to information from the target culture (Gray and Stockwell 1998).

Soon, however, a more critical and in-depth body of research was producing findings that demonstrated the difference between intercultural contact and intercultural learning. Kern sug-gested that, in the context of on-line learning, '[ ... ] exposure and awareness of difference seem to reinforce, rather than bridge, feelings of difference' (Kern 2000: 256). Similarly, Meagher and Castaños (1996) found in their exchange between classes in the USA and Mexico that bringing the students to compare their different attitudes and values leads to a form of culture shock and a more negative attitude towards the target culture. Furthermore, Fischer (1998), in his work on German–American electronic exchanges, warned that very often students, instead of reflecting and learning from the messages of their distant partners, simply reject the foreign way of thinking, dismissing it as strange or 'typical' of that particular culture.

In an attempt to exploit more successfully the intercultural learning potential of such exchanges, the late 1990s saw the emergence of more complex and structured online projects and tasks. These tasks involved requiring students, for example, to work together with their international partners to produce websites or presentations based on comparisons of their cul-tures. Belz (2002), for example, reports on a USA–German exchange that involved developing a website which contained bilingual essays and a bilingual discussion of a cultural theme such as racism or family. Another popular intercultural task for telecollaborative exchanges has been the analysis of parallel texts. Belz defines parallel texts as ' ... linguistically different renditions of a particular story or topic in which culturally-conditioned varying representations of that story or topic are presented' (2005: n.p.). Popular examples of parallel texts that have been used in telecollaborative exchanges include the American film *Three Men and a Baby* and the French original *Trois hommes et un couffin*. In German, telecollaborative projects have engaged learners in the comparison of the German fairy tale *Aschenputtel* by the Brothers Grimm and the animated Disney film *Cinderella*.

Another intercultural task adapted to telecollaboration was the application of ethnographic interviewing in synchronous online sessions. O'Dowd (2005) trained a group of German EFL students in the basic techniques of ethnographic interviewing, and the students then carried out interview sessions with American informants in the USA via videoconference before writing up reflective essays on their findings. Hanna and de Nooy (2009) criticized the limited authenticity of simply engaging L2 learners with other classrooms and proposed as an alternative the activity of requiring learners to participate in the online asynchronous discussion forums that are provided by the websites of international newspapers such as *Le Monde* and *The Guardian*. The authors suggested that getting learners to take part in such forums would take them beyond the limitations of learner-to-learner communication and provide them with opportunities to join with native speakers in authentic interaction, which required an awareness of the cultural rules and register of this genre of communication.

A further telecollaborative practice that has become very popular in recent years is the 'Cultura' model (Furstenberg *et al.* 2001; O'Dowd 2005). This model for intercultural exchange uses the possibility of juxtaposing materials from two different cultures together on webpages in order to offer a comparative approach to investigating cultural difference (see Table 21.1). When using Cultura, language learners from two cultures (e.g. Spanish learners of English and American learners of Spanish) complete online questionnaires related to their cultural values and associations. These questionnaires can be based on word associations (e.g. What three words do you associate with the word 'Spain'?), sentence completions (e.g. A good citizen is someone who ... ) or reactions to situations (e.g. Your friend is 22 and is still living with his parents. What do you say to him?). Each group fills out the questionnaire in their native language. Following this, the results from both sets of students are then compiled and presented online. Under the guidance of their teachers in contact classes, students then analyse the juxtaposed lists in order to find differences and similarities between the two groups' responses. Following this analysis, students from both countries meet in online message boards to discuss their findings and to explore the cultural values and beliefs that may lie behind differences in the lists. In addition to the questionnaires, learners are also supplied with online resources such as opinion polls and press articles from the two cultures, which can support them in their investigation and understanding of their partner class's responses. The developers of this model (Furstenberg *et al.* 2001) report that this contrastive approach helps learners to become more aware of the complex relationship between culture and language and enables them to develop a method for understanding a foreign culture. It is also important to point out that, in this model, as in most telecollaborative projects, although the data for cultural analysis and learning are produced online, the role of contact classes and the teacher is considered vital in helping the learners to identify cultural similarities and differences and also in bringing about reflection on the outcomes of the students' investigations on the Cultura platform.

In an attempt to organize the wide variety of tasks being employed in telecollaborative exchange, O'Dowd and Ware (2009) categorized twelve telecollaborative task types that they had identified in the literature into three main categories – information exchange, comparison and collaboration (see Table 21.2). The first category, information exchange tasks, involved

*Table 21.1* Cultura: A comparative approach to investigating cultural difference

| Español | English |
|---|---|
| *A good citizen is one who...* ||
| Sin entrometerse en la vida de los demás está integrado más o menos en su comunidad. | follows the law and participates in civic responsiblities. |
| no tiene problemas con los demas ciudadanos normalmente y que no altera el orden publico | respects the space and comfort of others. Does their part to protect the environment. Votes. Helps others. |
| Respeta los derechos de los demás ciudadanos y cumple con su deber como ciudadano. | questions the role of her government nationally and internationally and actively works to improve both. |
| intenta comprender los diferentes puntos de vista del resto, siempre respetando a loas demás. | abides by the law, treats his or her neighbors like he or she wants to be treated and tries to help out anyone he or she can. |
| Participa en los deberes de la comunidad. | works for the good of others. |
| es tolerante, respetuoso y sabe convivir. | abides by the law and does whatever he or she can to help others in the community. A good citizen is one whose voice is heard. |
| acude al auxilio de otro ciudadano, ayuda a los turistas y respeta las instalaciones de su ciudad | is peaceful. |
| respeta las normas | pays their taxes, serves on jury duty, votes for politicians, and is active in their community. |
| respeta y cumple las leyes, sean o no de su agrado. | thinks of the bigger picture and his/her fellow citizens; he is not only interested in what is good for him. |
| no molesta a los demás | works to better society. |
| fundamentalmente repeta a los demás. | partakes in elections. |
| tiene respeto por los demas, vive y deja vivir | abides by the laws, unless the laws are arbitrary. |
| es educado, respeta a la mayoría y su entorno. | is fair and respectful of others, obeys the law, and tries to better his community. |
| | takes care of their community and supports others. |
| | takes an active role in the democratic process and stands up for what they believe in. A good citizen is not passive. |
| | is honest, pays taxes, and contributes to their country. |

learners providing their telecollaborative partners with information about their personal biographies, local schools or towns or aspects of their home cultures. These tasks often functioned as an introductory activity for two groups of learners who were not yet familiar with each other. Tasks in this category were usually 'monologic' in nature, as there was usually little negotiation of meaning (either cultural or linguistic) between the interlocutors. The second task type, comparison and analysis tasks, were seen to be more demanding as they required learners not only to exchange information, but also to go a step further and carry out comparisons or critical analyses of cultural products from both cultures (e.g. books, surveys, films, newspaper articles). These analyses or comparisons could have a cultural focus and/or a linguistic focus. These tasks generally required learners to provide their partners with explanations of the linguistic meaning or cultural significance of certain cultural products or practices and then to engage in dialogue in order to establish similarities or differences between the two cultures. The final task type, collaborative tasks, required learners not only to exchange and compare information, but also to work together to

*Table 21.2* Overview of telecollaborative task types

(1) Information exchange

| No | Task | Description | Examples | Intended outcomes | Potential pitfalls |
|---|---|---|---|---|---|
| 1 | Authoring 'cultural autobiographies' | Students present themselves and their home cultures to their (future) partners through 'cultural autobiographies' (Kern 1996), which can take the form of various visual and textual formats | Belz (2007) | Establishment of personal relationship with partners/ increased awareness of cultural differences | Students reify stereotypes in their presentations (students are not always that aware of their own L1 cultural situatedness)/ often restricted to single genre of narration/ primary reliance on personal narrative limits functionality across class contexts |
| 2 | Carrying out virtual interviews | Students take turns to interview each other on a certain cultural theme and produce a class presentation/written report based on the interview process | O'Dowd (2006); Wilden (2007) | Development of intercultural communicative competence (ICC) | Relies on the information provided by only one partner – requires a great deal of reciprocity and responsibility |
| 3 | Engaging in informal discussion | Students are provided with general questions (e.g. 'How do the new technologies influence your life?') or with a cultural product from C1 or C2 (e.g. a newspaper article or film) and are asked to discuss these with partners | Lee (2006); Vinagre (2005) | Learner independence/ development of fluency in TL | Can easily turn into an information exchange without significant processing or without challenging input |
| 4 | Exchanging story collections | Each class takes turns to collect legends, folk tales or accounts of local historical events from their partner class. A class magazine or website can then be published with the resulting collection | Warschauer (1995) | Increased factual/cultural knowledge about C2 | Can easily turn into an information exchange without significant processing or without challenging input |

Table 21.2 (continued)
(2) Comparison and analysis

| No | Task | Description | Examples | Intended outcomes | Potential pitfalls |
|----|------|-------------|----------|-------------------|-------------------|
| 1 | Comparing parallel texts | Both classes compare and analyse pieces of literature, film or fairy tales from both cultures that are based on a common theme (e.g. 'Three men and a baby' and the French original) | Belz (2002); Müller-Hartmann (2000) | Increased awareness of target culture and one's own culture | Superficial contrasts made unless the instructor guides the conversation |
| 2 | Comparing class questionnaires | Both classes complete questionnaires (e.g. related to word associations, reactions to situations) and then compare the answers of the two groups.[1] Findings by both groups are then discussed online | Furstenberg et al. (2001); O'Dowd (2005) | Development of awareness of different cultural meanings and connotations of words and concepts in C1 and C2 | Superficial contrasts made unless the instructor guides the conversation; requires a significant amount of participation using the L1, which not all teachers/students/institutions agree to do |
| 3 | Analysing cultural products | Cultural products from either C1 or C2 (e.g. films, pieces of literature, items in tourist shops) are analysed and discussed by both groups | Liaw (2006); Meskill and Ranglova (2000); O'Dowd (2003) | Greater awareness of target culture/one's own culture | Superficial contrasts made unless the instructor guides the conversation |
| 4 | Translating | Students translate text from their L1 to L2. Without seeing the original, C2 partners help to refine and correct the translation | Ware and Pérez Cañado (2007) | Improved language awareness/development of linguistic accuracy and fluency in TL | Tends to reduce the exchange to an information/linguistic exchange and is less rich in opportunities for cultural learning; relies on comparable metalinguistic awareness on both sides of the exchange |

Table 21.2 (continued)
(3) Collaboration and product creation

| No | Task | Description | Examples | Intended outcomes | Potential pitfalls |
|----|------|-------------|----------|-------------------|-------------------|

| # | Activity | Description | Sample studies | Outcome | Possible challenges |
|---|----------|-------------|----------------|---------|---------------------|
| 1 | Collaborating on product creation | Students in both classes work together to produce a document (e.g. essay) or multimedia product (e.g. website or Powerpoint presentation) | Belz (2007); Zaehner et al. (2000) | Development of ICC/ electronic literacy | Requires technology-savvy teacher or context because of the tendency towards multimedia; requires teamwork among students and therefore reciprocity (lack of participation on one side jeopardizes the whole project/grade) |
| 2 | Transforming text genres | Students in C1 help C2 partners to rewrite texts in a different genre in their TL | O'Rourke (2007); Ware and Pérez Cañado (2007) | Improved metalinguistic awareness/linguistic accuracy and fluency in TL | Tends to reduce the exchange to an information/linguistic exchange and is less rich in opportunities for cultural learning; relies on comparable metalinguistic awareness on both side of the exchange |
| 3 | Carrying out 'closed outcome' discussions | Students in C1 and C2 share and compare information in order to complete an information gap activity (e.g. a 'spot the difference' activity based on different versions of pictures) | Lee (2006); Pellettieri (2000) | Negotiation of meaning/ development of linguistic accuracy and fluency in TL | Requires elaborate set-up by the instructor in the absence of easily available online gap activities; research tends to show that students mainly negotiate at the lexical level when online |
| 4 | Making cultural translations/ adaptations | Students in C1 and C2 collaborate to make a culturally appropriate translation/ adaptation of a product from C1 to C2 (e.g. film scene/TV advertisement) | Ware and O'Dowd (2008) | Development of ICC | Requires off-task involvement (discussion, debriefing, etc.) by the teacher in order for most students to develop cultural awareness beyond stereotypes |

Source: O'Dowd and Ware (2009: 176–7). Reproduced with permission.

Notes:
[1] For the sake of clarity, in this table, it is assumed that the telecollaborative exchange involves only two groups – C1 and C2 – and that each of these is studying the 'languaculture' of the partner group. However, we are aware that many exchanges can involve three or more collaborating groups of learners, and that these exchanges may also involve the use of a language as a lingua franca.

produce a joint product or conclusion. This could involve the co-authoring of an essay or presentation or the co-production of a linguistic translation or cultural adaptation of a text from the L1/C1 (first language/first culture) to the L2/C2 (second language/second culture). These types of activities were seen to involve a great deal of coordination and planning, but the authors suggested that they also brought about substantial amounts of negotiation of meaning at both linguistic and cultural levels as learners attempted to reach agreement on their final products.

As will be seen in the following sections, telecollaborative exchange has been found to be a very complex and difficult activity to integrate and use in the foreign language classroom. However, it is important to clarify the beneficial outcomes that telecollaboration has been demonstrated to have for intercultural learning in foreign language education. First, telecollaborative exchanges have been found to contribute to culture learning by providing learners with a different type of knowledge from that which they usually find in textbooks and in other traditional cultural studies resources (O'Dowd 2006). As opposed to objective factual information, the accounts that students receive from their partners tend to be of a subjective and personalized nature. For this reason, exchanges can be particularly useful for making students aware of certain aspects of cultural knowledge (Byram 1997), such as how institutions are perceived in the target culture and what significant events and people are in the target culture's 'national memory'.

Second, it has been found that telecollaboration can also contribute to the development of critical cultural awareness as learners have opportunities in their online interaction to engage in intense periods of negotiation of meaning in which they can discuss cultural 'rich points' and elicit meanings of cultural behaviour from 'real' informants in the target culture. Learners are also led to become more aware of the relativity of their own cultural beliefs and values as they try to make them explicit for their partners. However, researchers emphasize that this is only the case when online exchange involves explicit comparison of the two cultures and the expression of direct opinions and reactions to the submissions of others (O'Dowd 2003). Such dialogue between partners contrasts with interaction that involves an unreflective exchange of information between partners.

Third, Belz and Kinginger (2002, 2003) have highlighted the potential of telecollaborative exchange for making learners aware of cultural differences in communicative practices, and their work has demonstrated how online exchange can contribute to the development of L2 pragmatic competence in foreign language learning. The authors found that this is the case because interaction with native peers can lead to the exposure of the learner to a broad range of foreign language discourse options and also because learners consider their partners to be 'people who matter' and therefore are more motivated to establish successful working relationships with them in the foreign language.

## 3. Critical issues

As mentioned earlier, the literature on online intercultural exchange is littered with findings which demonstrate that these practices often result in negative attitudes towards the partner group and their culture, misunderstandings and unachieved objectives. The main question that has occupied many researchers is why this is the case and whether these instances of intercultural communication breakdown should be seen as something problematic or as opportunities for learning.

Kramsch and Thorne (2002) found that the reasons for online communication breakdown between their French and American students was due to both groups trying to engage in interaction with each other using not merely different language styles, but culturally different discourse genres, of the existence of which both groups appeared to be unaware. Whereas the

French students approached the exchange as an academic exercise and used factual, impersonal, restrained genres of writing, the American group regarded the activity as a very human experience that involved bonding with their distant partners and taking a personal interest in finding solutions to the problems that arose. An exchange that involved two such different approaches interacting together was bound to end in disappointment and frustration for both sides. The authors conclude that:

> The challenge is to prepare teachers to transfer the genres of their local educational systems into global learning environments, and to prepare students to deal with global communicative practices that require far more than local communicative competence.
>
> *Kramsch and Thorne (2002: 96)*

Several other studies also looked at how the outcomes of intercultural exchanges could be influenced by both macro- as well as micro-level aspects of the environments in which they take place. Belz (2002), reporting on a semester-long e-mail exchange between third-level German and American foreign language students, found that the context and the setting of the two partner groups had a major influence on the success and results of the exchange. Issues such as different institutional and course demands and varying levels of access to technology led to misunderstandings with regard to deadlines for team work and therefore hindered the development of relationships on a personal level. Ironically, the author found that the American students reported that the principal intercultural learning experiences of the exchange had been increased awareness of the different institutional requirements and the different online behaviour of their German partners. Belz suggested sensitizing students to such institutional and cultural differences before engaging them in exchanges – although she also insisted that students should not be completely protected from them. According to the author, this awareness can be achieved by looking at theoretical textbooks on intercultural communication, as well as personal accounts on the internet that report on the experiences of foreigners in the target culture.

Looking at the influence of institutional demands on intercultural exchanges from another perspective, Müller-Hartmann writing alone (2000) and together with Belz (Belz and Müller-Hartmann 2003) suggested that institutional pressures and requirements will influence the developing relationship of teachers who organize intercultural e-mail exchange and that the teachers' ability to adapt to the extra challenges of such an exchange will influence the outcomes of the intercultural learning process for their students.

Other research has revealed how individual students' motivation and intercultural communicative competence can have an important influence on the outcome of online partnerships. With reference to motivation, Ware (2005) identified individual differences in motivation as being an important factor in the limited impact of an exchange. In her study, success in the asynchronous exchange required students to spend a substantial amount of time reading and replying to correspondence, and this often clashed with the amount of time students had put aside for such an academic activity. The importance of individual students' intercultural competence is illustrated in O'Dowd's study (2003) of five Spanish–English e-mail partnerships. He found that the essential difference between the successful and unsuccessful partnerships was whether students had the intercultural competence to develop an interculturally rich relationship with their partners through the creation of effective correspondence. This type of correspondence took into account the sociopragmatic rules of the partner's language, provided the partner with personal opinions, asked him/her questions to encourage feedback, tried to develop a personal relationship with the partner and was sensitive to his/her needs and questions. Fischer's work on high school e-mail exchanges (1998) also highlighted the importance of the students' level of intercultural competence. In this case, he underlined the need for students to bring tolerance and appropriate attitudes of curiosity and openness to their exchanges.

In order to prepare educators for the challenges that await them in their telecollaborative exchanges, O'Dowd and Ritter (2006) provided a structured inventory of possible reasons for the breakdown of telecollaborative exchanges (see Figure 21.1). The inventory organized the reasons for failed communication into four different levels, including the socioinstitutional, the classroom, the individual and interaction levels. The individual level referred to the learners' psychobiographical and educational background; the classroom level referred to how the exchange was organized and carried out in both classes; the socioinstitutional level dealt with the different levels of access to technology, institutional attitudes to online learning, etc.; and the interaction level looked at the actual quality and nature of the communication that takes places between the partner classes.

The question remains as to whether the repeated cases of communication breakdown and intercultural misunderstanding should be seen as a negative aspect of telecollaborative exchange or rather as a potential 'jump-off' point for exploring why members of different cultures interpret behaviour differently and how different cultural perspectives can be reconciled. Intercultural communication in face-to-face contexts and out of the classroom is also often characterized by misunderstandings and the need to deal with different behaviour and beliefs. It

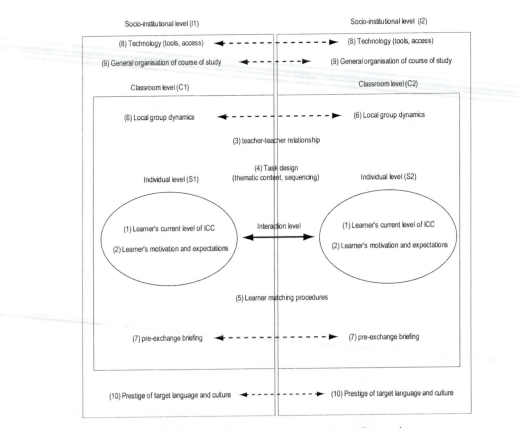

*Figure 21.1* Inventory of reasons for 'failed communication' in online exchanges
*Source:* O'Dowd and Ritter (2006: 629). Reproduced with permission.

is therefore fair to argue that these cases of 'failed communication' should be exploited as 'rich points' for learning in the classroom. Belz (2002: 76) goes so far as to argue that

> the clash of cultural fault lines in telecollaborative learning communities … should not be smoothed over or avoided based on the sometimes negative results of a study such as this one; indeed, they should be encouraged.

Apart from the question of dealing with intercultural communication breakdown in tele-collaborative exchanges, two other critical issues have emerged in recent years. First, there has been a growing criticism of the underlying belief in the research on online intercultural exchange that members of different cultures use different genres and cultural communication styles in their online intercultural interactions and that it is this 'clash of culturally specific genres' that often leads to dysfunctional exchanges. As was seen earlier, Kramsch and Thorne (2002: 99) described the breakdown in communication that occurred between classes of French and American students as 'two local genres engaged in global confrontation'. Similarly, Belz (2003), in her study of German–American online interaction, found that the online inter-action style of an American student, described as being uncommitted and self-depreciating, led his German partners to dismiss him as someone who was unwilling to engage in debate and confrontation. The American student's interpretation of the Germans' correspondence, which was characterized by directness and categorical assertions, led him to reject them as being rude and aggressive. However, Goodfellow and Lamy (2009: 6), point out that ' … the assumption that a coherent "genre" or "style" is characteristic of national cohorts is rarely interrogated'. In other words, the authors question whether it is possible to speak about something that can be called 'French communicative style' and whether it is oversimplistic to describe one mono-lithic cultural communicative style 'clashing' or causing misunderstandings with another. Although it is important not to overgeneralize and reduce online interaction to a simplistic picture of online behaviour being determined by nationality, the existence of culturally specific genres would appear to be at least one of the factors that contributes to how groups of learners interact online.

Finally, there is also the question of the level of authenticity in class-to-class telecollaborative exchange. Although many educators have been drawn to telecollaboration because of its potential to bring learners into contact with 'authentic' texts written by native speakers and to give them the experience of 'real' intercultural communication, the authors Hanna and de Nooy (2009) have pointed out that, in class-to-class telecollaboration,

> … [i]nteraction is restricted to communication with other learners, a situation that is safe and reassuring for beginners and younger learners, but somewhat limiting for more advanced and adult learners, who need practice in venturing beyond the classroom.
>
> *Hanna and de Nooy (2009: 88)*

The authors propose that it is more authentic and more advantageous to engage learners in interaction in authentic L2 discussion forums such as those related to L2 newspaper and maga-zine publications. For example, they report on studies of their own learners of French as a foreign language who participated in the discussion forums of French magazines such as *Nouvel Observateur*. Their criticism of class-to-class telecollaboration reflects a more general preoccupa-tion in foreign language pedagogy about the definitions of authenticity and authentic task (Lamy and Goodfellow 2010), and the question here is essentially whether structured class-to-class interaction is something that brings the classroom to genuinely intersect with the 'real' world or whether it simply engages learners in tasks that 'approximate' or 'replicate' real world activity. In the following section, it will be seen that new Web 2.0 models of online intercultural exchange may go some way to dealing with this perceived lack of authenticity in tele-collaboration, but it is likely that there will also continue to be an important role for class-to-class partnerships. Not only can the type of interaction and language generated in such school-to-school projects provide plenty of rich material for intercultural learning, but the possibility of structuring and organizing class-to-class exchanges will also provide a necessary reliability for educators that online interaction in public forums could not guarantee. Furthermore, the fact that learners in class-to-class exchanges have the opportunity to develop relationships of trust with their distant partners over time may in fact mean that the quality of the communication between the interlocutors may be more honest and more detailed than the anonymous style of interaction that is common to public message boards.

## 4. Current contributions

Recent years have seen a third 'generation' or model of telecollaborative exchanges emerging, which reflects in many ways a more flexible and adaptable interpretation of how online inter-cultural interaction and exchange can take place in contemporary foreign language learning contexts. Described by Guth and Helm (2010) as Telecollaboration 2.0, this model is based on the 'social web' that has emerged with the rise of Web 2.0 tools such as blogging, wikis and social networking sites, and is characterized by a less text-based and more multimodal form of com-munication (see Guth and Helm 2010; Lankshear and Knobel 2006). Certain variations of this model also involve a type of intercultural exchange that is more classroom independent than previous models. This emerging model of online exchange therefore allows for a much greater spectrum of possible partners, language set-ups and forms of interaction. For example, instead of linking up with other classes, learners may collaborate in specialized interest communities or environments that focus on specific hobbies or interests. Thorne et al. (2009), for example, describe the potential for intercultural contact and learning in online fan communities where learners can establish relationships with like-minded fans of music groups or authors and can even use Web 2.0 technologies to remix and create new artistic creations based on pre-existing books, films and music. Learners also have increasing opportunities to use their foreign language skills and hone their intercultural communicative competence through participating in online multicultural communities such as multiplayer online games and public discussion forums, such as those described by Hanna and de Nooy (2009). This emerging model requires learners to assume greater responsibility for how their intercultural learning progresses online as they are given greater freedom in their choice of potential intercultural learning partners and learning envir-onments – many of which may be completely independent of organized classroom activity. Thorne (2010: 144) describes this form of telecollaborative learning as 'intercultural communication in the wild' and speculates that this learning may be

> … situated in arenas of social activity that are less controllable than classroom or organized online intercultural exchanges might be, but which present interesting, and perhaps even compelling, opportunities for intercultural exchange, agentive action and meaning making.
>
> *Thorne (2010: 144)*

## 5. Recommendations for practice

The research findings reviewed to date undoubtedly illustrate the complexity of online inter-cultural exchange, and many educators are often discouraged by the many challenges that emerge during the organization and execution of a telecollaborative project. However, it is important to remind the reader of the richness of the learning that can take place in an online exchange and of the fact that this is probably the closest a learner can come to experiencing intercultural communication within the supportive environment of the classroom. Telecollaboration is an enlightening example of how the learning spheres of class work and fieldwork can be melded together into a rich intercultural learning experience. Nevertheless, it is important to keep in mind some guidelines for good practice for educators entering into telecollaborative exchange for the first time.

Educators, for example, will not only need to be familiar with practical areas such as where to find partner classes or what online tools could be used in an exchange, but they will need to work on areas of their own online intercultural competence as they try to liaise and coordinate their telecollaborative exchange with a teaching partner who they have probably never met in person. This involves, in the first place, being able to articulate to their partner teacher the learning objectives and pedagogical beliefs that they are bringing to the exchange. But educators should also bring with them an openness to alternative pedagogical beliefs and aims and a willingness to adapt as much as possible to other approaches to task design and project structure. Furthermore, educators need to have the ability to find common ground with their partner and to find compromises in task design that can suit them both.

Educators also need to be aware of the different options with regard to telecollaborative task design. Apart from being familiar with the different task types that exist (O'Dowd and Ware 2009), it is necessary to understand that, within the various constellations of task design and sequencing, there are options that will better suit certain institutional and learning contexts. For example, tasks that emphasize intercultural learning may be questioned by institutions or by students used to more grammar-driven approaches to language learning. Furthermore, there are also tasks that are more suited to teachers and learners that have more or less experience with technology.

Finally, teachers need to keep in mind that, in the context of telecollaboration, although the intercultural contact takes place in online contexts between learners, it is often in the classroom, in the related activities before and after the online interaction, that intercultural learning takes place. Studies have shown repeatedly that learners need the guidance and informed insight of their teachers to create their own online correspondence and to interpret and respond to the messages, blog posts and video recordings that they receive from their partners. It is in the classroom analysis of these authentic foreign texts that cultural 'rich points' emerge and the skills of intercultural interaction and ethnographic interviewing can be honed.

## 6. Future directions

Telecollaboration has been shown to hold great potential for the development of intercultural communicative competence and to be a powerful tool for putting the principles of intercultural learning into practice within the supportive context of the classroom. However, as a pedagogic activity, research has shown that it is not yet considered an integrated or 'normalized' part of study programmes and syllabi at university level (O'Dowd 2010). Stephen Bax defines the normalization of computer-assisted learning activity in the following way:

> when computers ... are used every day by language students and teachers as an integral part of every lesson, like a pen or a book ... without fear or inhibition, and equally without an exaggerated respect for what they can do. They will not be the centre of any lesson, but they will play a part in almost all ... They will go almost unnoticed.
>
> *Bax (2003: 23)*

353

If telecollaboration is to become a long-term, integral part of foreign language education, it needs to be seen as a fundamental part of classroom activity and language programmes rather than an extra or supplementary activity. It also needs to avoid unfounded expectations that the activity will have magical transformative effects on students' linguistic skills and intercultural awareness. Various impediments currently exist that are hindering this normalization of tele-collaboration. These include a lack of stability in project partners, the limited support and understanding of practitioners' institutions and the practical difficulties in integrating online exchanges in course syllabi and course evaluation schemes. Until these barriers are overcome, telecollaboration is destined to remain on the periphery of foreign language teaching and its potential is likely only to be exploited by teachers and students who are willing to take it on as an 'add-on' activity along with traditional skills-based language tasks and exercises.

## Related topics

Intercultural approaches to foreign language education; intercultural communicative competence; intercultural contact; intercultural pragmatics

## Further reading

Belz, J.A. and Thorne, S.L. (eds) (2006) *Internet-mediated Intercultural Foreign Language Education*, Boston, MA: Heinle and Heinle (an insightful collection of chapters that reports on research in online inter-cultural interaction and the potential for intercultural learning in this context).

Guth, S. and Helm, F. (2010) *Telecollaboration 2.0: Language, Literacies and Intercultural Learning in the 21st Century*, Berne: Peter Lang (a recent volume that presents a comprehensive overview of the 'third' phase of telecollaborative exchange. The research and case studies reported here demonstrate how online exchange is being used in Web 2.0 environments and in 'out of class' scenarios).

Kern, R., Ware, P. and Warschauer, M. (2004) 'Crossing frontiers: new directions in online pedagogy and research', *Annual Review of Applied Linguistics*, 24: 243–60 (a brief and concise overview of the main outcomes of research related to online intercultural exchange and online L2 interaction in general).

## References

Audras, I. and Chanier, T. (2008) 'Observation de la construction d'une compétence interculturelle dans des groupes exolingues en ligne', *Revue Apprentissage des Langues et Système d'Information et de Communication (ALSIC)*, 11: 175–204. Online. Available: http://alsic.revues.org/index865.html (accessed 1 November 2009).

Bax, S. (2003) 'CALL – past, present and future', *System*, 31(1): 13–28.

Belz, J.A. (2002) 'Social dimensions of telecollaborative foreign language study', *Language Learning and Technology*, 6(1): 60–81. Online. Available: http://llt.msu.edu/vol6num1/BELZ/default.html (accessed 11 May 2010).

——(2003) 'Linguistic perspectives on the development of intercultural competence in telecollaboration', *Language Learning and Technology*, 7(2): 68–99. Online. Available: http://llt.msu.edu/vol7num2/BELZ/default.html (accessed 11 May 2010).

——(2005) 'Telecollaborative language study: a personal overview of praxis and research', Selected Papers from the 2004 NFLRC Symposium. Online. Available: http://nflrc.hawaii.edu/networks/nw44/belz.htm (accessed 11 May 2010).

——(2007) 'The development of intercultural communicative competence in telecollaborative partnerships', in R. O'Dowd (ed.) *Online Intercultural Exchange*, Clevedon: Multilingual Matters, pp. 127–66.

Belz, J.A. and Kinginger, C. (2002) 'The cross-linguistic development of address form use in tele-collaborative language learning: two case studies', *Canadian Modern Language Review/Revue Canadienne des Langues Vivantes*, 59(2): 189–214.

——(2003) 'Discourse options and the development of pragmatic competence by classroom learners of German: the case of address forms', *Language Learning*, 53: 591–647.

Belz, J.A. and Müller-Hartmann, A. (2003) 'Teachers negotiating German–American telecollaboration: between a rock and an institutional hard place', *Modern Language Journal*, 87(1): 71–89.

Belz, J.A. and Thorne, S.L. (eds) (2006) *Internet-mediated Intercultural Foreign Language Education*, Boston, MA: Heinle and Heinle.

Brammerts, H. (1996) 'Language learning in tandem using the internet', in M. Warschauer (ed.) *Telecollaboration in Foreign Language Learning*, University of Hawai'i: Second Language Teaching and Curriculum Centre, pp. 121–30.

Byram, M. (1997) *Teaching and Assessing Intercultural Communicative Competence*, Clevedon: Multilingual Matters.

Cummins, J. and Sayers, D. (1995) *Brave New Schools. Challenging Cultural Literacy Through Global Learning Networks*, New York: St. Martin's Press.

Eck, A., Legenhausen, L. and Wolff, D. (1995) *Telekommunikation und Fremdsprachenunterricht: Informationen, Projekte, Ergebnisse*, Bochum: AKS-Verlag.

Fischer, G. (1998). *E-mail in Foreign Language Teaching: Towards the Creation of Virtual Classrooms*, Tübingen: Stauffenburg Medien.

Furstenberg, G., Levet, S., English, K. and Maillet, K. (2001) 'Giving a virtual voice to the silent language of culture: the Culture Project', *Language Learning and Technology*, 5(1): 55–102. Online. Available: http://llt.msu.edu/vol5num1/furstenberg/default.html (accessed 11 May 2010).

Goodfellow, R. and Lamy, M.-N. (2009) 'Introduction: a frame for the discussion of learning cultures', in R. Goodfellow and M.-N. Lamy (eds) *Learning Cultures in Online Education*, London: Continuum, pp. 1–14.

Gray, R. and Stockwell, G. (1998) 'Using computer-mediated communication for language and culture acquisition', On-CALL, 12(3). Online. Available: http://www.cltr.uq.edu.au/oncall/gray123.html (accessed 12 May 2010).

Guth, S. and Helm, F. (eds) (2010) *Telecollaboration 2.0: Language, Literacies and Intercultural Learning in the 21st Century*, Berne: Peter Lang.

Hanna, B. and de Nooy, J. (2009) *Learning Language and Culture via Public Internet Discussion Forums*, New York: Palgrave Macmillan.

Kern, R. (1996) 'Computer-mediated communication: Using e-mail exchanges to explore personal histories in two cultures', in W. Marschauer (ed.) *Telecollaboration in Foreign Language Learning*, Honolulu, HI: Second Language Teaching and Curriculum Center, pp. 105–9.

——(2000) *Literacy and Language Teaching*, Oxford: Oxford University Press.

Kern, R., Ware, P. and Warschauer, M. (2004) 'Crossing frontiers: new directions in online pedagogy and research', Annual Review of Applied Linguistics, 24: 243–60.

Kramsch, C. and Thorne, S.L. (2002) 'Foreign language learning as global communicative practice', in D. Block and D. Cameron (eds) *Globalization and Language Teaching*, London: Routledge, pp. 83–100.

Lamy, M.-N. and Goodfellow, R. (2010) 'Telecollaboration and learning 2.0', in S. Guth and F. Helm (eds) *Telecollaboration 2.0: Language and Intercultural Learning in the 21st Century*, Berne: Peter Lang, pp. 107–39.

Lankshear, C. and Knobel, M. (2006) *New Literacies: Everyday Practices and Classroom Learning*, 2nd edn, Maidenhead/New York: Open University Press.

Lee, L. (2006) 'A study of native and nonnative speakers feedback and responses in panish-American networked collaborative interaction', in J. Belz and S. Thorne (eds) *Internet-mediated Intercultural Foreign Language Education*, Boston, MA: Heinle and Heinle, pp. 147–76.

Liaw, M-L. (2006) 'E-learning and the development of intercultural competence', *Language Learning and Technology*, 10(3): 49–64.

Lixl-Purcell, A. (1995) *Foreign Language Acquisition and Technology*. Online. Available: www.uncg.edu/~lixlpurc/publications/whitmanpresentation.html (accessed 18 February 2001).

Meagher, M. and Castaños, F. (1996) 'Perceptions of American culture: the impact of an electronically-mediated cultural exchange program on Mexican high school students', in S. Herring (ed.) *Computer-mediated Communication: Linguistic, Social and Cross-cultural Perspectives*, Amsterdam: John Benjamins Publishing Company, pp. 187–201.

Meskill, C. and Ranglova, K. (2000) 'Sociocollaborative language learning in Bulgaria', in M. Warschauer and R. Kern (eds) *Network-based Language Teaching: Concepts and Practice*, Cambridge: Cambridge University Press, pp. 20–40.

Müller-Hartmann, A. (2000) 'The role of tasks in promoting intercultural learning in electronic learning networks', *Language Learning and Technology*, 4(2): 129–47. Online. Available: http://llt.msu.edu/vol4num2/muller/default.html (accessed 11 May 2010).

——(2007) 'Teacher role in telecollaboration: setting up and managing exchanges', in R. O'Dowd (ed.) *Online Intercultural Exchange*, Clevedon: Multilingual Matters, pp. 167–93.

O'Dowd, R. (2003) 'Understanding "the other side": intercultural learning in a Spanish-English email exchange', *Language Learning and Technology*, 7(2): 118–44. Online. Available: http://llt.msu.edu/vol7num2/odowd/default.html (accessed 10 May 2010).

——(2005) 'Combining networked communication tools for students' ethnographic research', in J. Belz and S.L. Thorne (eds) *Computer-mediated Intercultural Foreign Language Education*, Boston, MA: Heinle and Heinle, pp. 86–120.

——(2006) *Telecollaboration and the Development of Intercultural Communicative Competence*, Berlin: Langenscheidt.

——(ed.) (2007) *Online Intercultural Exchange: An Introduction for Foreign Language Teachers*, Clevedon: Multilingual Matters.

——(2010) 'Online foreign language interaction: moving from the periphery to the core of foreign language education?' *Language Teaching Journal* (available on Cambridge Journals Online (CJO) 05 May 2010; doi: 10.1017/S0261444810000194).

O'Dowd, R. and Ritter, M. (2006) 'Understanding and working with "failed communication" in telecollaborative exchanges', *CALICO Journal*, 23: 623–42.

O'Dowd, R. and Ware, P. (2009) 'Critical issues in telecollaborative task design', *Computer Assisted Language Learning*, 22(2): 173–88.

O'Rourke, B. (2007) 'Models of telecollaboration (1): eTandem', in R. O'Dowd (ed.) *Online Intercultural Exchange*, Clevedon: Multilingual Matters, pp. 41–61.

Pellettieri, J. (2000) 'Negotiation in cyberspace: The role of chatting in the development of grammatical competence', in M. Warschauer and R. Kern (eds) *Network-based Language Teaching: Concepts and Practice*, Cambridge: Cambridge University Press, pp. 59–86.

Richter, R. (1998) 'Interkulturelles Lernen via internet?', *Zeitschrift für interkulturellen Fremdsprachenunterricht*, 3 (2). Online. Available: http://zif.spz.tu-darmstadt.de/jg-03-2/beitrag/richter1.htm (accessed 12 May 2010).

Riel, M. (1997) 'Learning circles make global connections', in R. Donath and I. Volkmer (eds) *Das Transatlantische Klassenzimmer*, Hamburg: Koerber-Stiftung, pp. 329–57.

Thorne, S.L. (2006) 'Pedagogical and praxiological lessons from internet-mediated intercultural foreign language education research', in J. Belz and S.L. Thorne (eds) *Internet-mediated Intercultural Foreign Language Education*, Boston, MA: Heinle and Heinle, pp. 2–30.

——(2010) 'The intercultural turn and language learning in the crucible of new media', in S. Guth and F. Helm (eds) *Telecollaboration 2.0: Language and Intercultural Learning in the 21st Century*, Berne: Peter Lang, pp. 139–65.

Thorne, S.L., Black, R.W. and Sykes, J. (2009) 'Second language use, socialization, and learning in internet interest communities and online games', *Modern Language Journal*, 93: 802–41.

Vinagre, M. (2005) 'Fostering language learning via email: an English–Spanish exchange', *Computer Assisted Language Learning*, 18(5): 369–88.

Ware, P. (2005) 'Missed communication in online communication: tensions in fostering successful online interactions', Language Learning and Technology, 9(2):64–89. Online. Available: http://llt.msu.edu/vol9num2/default.html (accessed 10 May 2010).

Ware, P. and O'Dowd, R. (2008) 'Peer feedback on language form in telecollaboration', *Language Learning and Technology*, 12(1): 43–63.

Ware, P. and Pérez Cañado, M. (2007) 'Grammar and feedback: turning to language form in tele-collaboration', in R. O'Dowd (ed.) *Online Intercultural Exchange*, Clevedon: Multilingual Matters, pp. 107–27.

Warschauer, M. (ed.) (1995) *Virtual Connections*, Honolulu, HI: University of Hawai'i, Second Language Teaching and Curriculum Center.

Wilden, E. (2007) 'Voice chats in the intercultural classroom. The ABC's online project' in R. O'Dowd (ed.), *Online Intercultural Exchange*, Clevedon: Multilingual Matters, pp. 269–76.

Zaehner, C., Fauverge, A. and Wong, J. (2000) 'Task-based language learning via audiovisual networks: the LEVERAGE project', in M. Warschauer and R. Kern (eds) *Network-based Language Teaching: Concepts and Practice*, Cambridge: Cambridge University Press, pp. 186–203.

# 22

# Critical language and intercultural communication pedagogy

*Manuela Guilherme*

## 1. Introduction

Intercultural communication became established as an academic area of study and has become increasingly relevant in the English-speaking academy since the 1960s, mainly following Hall's publication entitled *Silent Language* (1959). Traditionally, the study of intercultural communication has adopted a particular perspective and implementation according to the discipline of the particular researcher or theorist. Increasingly, work on intercultural communication is involving scholars from all over the world, even if the field is still more or less related to and influenced by the English-speaking academy. Different social, epistemological and onto-logical visions are now emerging from different linguistic, cultural and territorial geographies and communities. This is providing multiple understandings of language, intercultural communica-tion and interaction. Therefore, differences between tradition-based epistemologies have become more influential than discipline-based theory and practice in intercultural communication, thus giving way to a more pressing need for a critical approach in its study. This diversity of visions has progressed beyond the North–South and East–West divides and cut across them through narratives of hybrid experiences and theorizations, not only in the form of accounts of social life but also in academic research. Furthermore, 'the once clear definitions of "us" and "them" are being blurred' as 'the tightly knit system of communication and transportation has brought differing cultures, nationalities, races, religions, and linguistic communities closer than before in a web of interdependence and a common fate' (Kim 2008: 359). This is happening especially in the academic world, causing a gradual, but evident, change in the criteria of scientific value in the social sciences. This follows from increased cross-cultural contact and is resulting in the valorization of a wider variety of models for carrying out intercultural dialogue and establishing intercultural relations that aim to be equitable, mutually respectful *and* reciprocally profitable.

Having this in mind, we may start from the principle that intercultural experience does not equate with intercultural competence and, furthermore, there is no single model of inter-cultural competence that fits every intercultural experience. There is, however, a need for the development of certain principles and strategies that may provide the person and the group, both from an individual and a collective point of view, with the knowledge and predispositions towards multiculturalism, interculturality and intercultural dialogue that will allow the intercultural experience to turn into an opportunity for personal, societal and professional reflection and enrichment. As noted by Deardorff (2009: xiii), 'there is no pinnacle at which someone becomes "interculturally competent"', as this involves an endless journey where each day brings more knowledge and more questions. In this spiral-shaped unfolding process, formal education ought to provide guidance. A critical pedagogy is expected to pave the way for that development to happen in a given direction, while promoting a plurality of itineraries.

## 2. The meanings of intercultural competence

The term 'competence' first emerged in vocational education, where the emphasis on skills and behaviours, rather than on content knowledge, was prioritized. However, it has since acquired a broader scope, in particular in international guidelines for schools and professional education, which are expected to include 'a combination of knowledge, skills, attitudes, values and behaviours' (Council of Europe 2005: 2). This trend is evident in educational projects, for example, the PISA (Programme for International Student Assessment; OECD, www.pisa.oecd. org) and the DeSeCo (Definition and Selection of Key Competences; OECD, www.oecd.org/ dataoecd/47/61/35070367.pdf); the latter singles out the 'ability to interact in heterogeneous groups' as one of its three key competences. The DeSeCo Project was primarily designed to define and select 'individually based key competences in a lifelong learning perspective' (Rychen and Salganik 2003: 2). While identifying such key competences, this project also included a 'criticism of an overemphasis on knowledge in general education and specialization in vocational education' (Salganik and Stephens 2003: 19). It underlined the need to respect and appreciate the 'values, beliefs, cultures, and histories of others', within a subcategory it identified as 'the ability to relate well to others', which focused on personal relationships. The need to acknowledge and value diversity was also mentioned in the project's country reports (Rychen 2003: 87). In sum, the idea of competence has become ever broader, expanding into the understanding that 'the evolution of competence frameworks has the potential to pose questions about the purpose of knowledge and how it contributes to the good of society and the individual' (Fleming 2007: 54).

Similarly, the idea of intercultural competence continues to develop in different directions, whether in more abstract or in more specific terms and, in the case of the latter, attempts to respond to different needs in different contexts and at different stages. Some general but brief definitions of intercultural competence have brought some consensus to the field. For example, this concept has been defined as 'the ability to interact effectively with people from cultures that we recognize as being different from our own' (Guilherme 2000: 297) or 'the appropriate and effective management of interaction between people who, to some degree or another, represent different or divergent affective, cognitive, and behavioural orientations to the world' (Spitzberg and Changnon 2009: 7). Spitzberg and Changnon then go on to describe various contemporary models that they aggregate in a taxonomy of 'compositional', 'co-orientational', 'developmental', 'adaptational' and 'causal path' models. Risager also broadens the concept as she states that

> intercultural competence is very much the competence of navigating in the world, both at the micro-level of social interaction in culturally complex settings, and at macro-levels through transnational networks like diasporas and media communications.
>
> *Risager (2009: 16)*

Other descriptions tend to focus on specific context demands or build competence lists 'that are just that, a lengthy listing of the many competences that are part of intercultural effectiveness' (Pusch 2009: 67). Nevertheless, some would argue such lists 'provide an excellent starting point for assessing the appropriate characteristics for the specific situation', even though, of course, 'no list fits all cultures, all contexts, all conditions' (Bennett 2009: 122).

As pointed out above, more recently, there have been some voices calling our attention to different world visions that generate other parameters for assessing intercultural communication competence. These may be based on 'different dimensions of self' that make it 'quite legitimate and "real" in many Asian societies to interact at the level of role and face' (Parmenter 2003: 128ff). Another claim made by authors who 'have looked to the communitarian theories and practices of indigenous social movements in Latin America' is that 'to be truly effective, intercultural communication should move beyond the limits of individualistic and interpersonal concerns' (Medina-López-Portillo and Sinnigen 2009: 260). There have been some attempts to overcome dichotomies and tensions, for example those between development programmes for education and training (Feng *et al.* 2009), those between quantitative and qualitative methodologies (Alasuutari *et al.* 2008) and those giving a combined perspective of different world visions (Deardorff 2009).

## 3. A critical pedagogy of intercultural competence

Language education and cultural studies have more recently made an important contribution to the development of a theory of intercultural communication and interaction and, consequently, given more elasticity to the definition of competence in the field. This discussion originally began to expand following Byram and Zarate's contribution to the Council of Europe's *Common European Framework* when they introduced a new concept, 'the intercultural speaker', which Byram developed further in his later work (Byram and Zarate 1997; Byram 1997). This Framework has provided great inspiration for language educators and researchers all over the world who started to focus on intercultural communication and interaction issues in their language education programmes. Around these issues, scholars and researchers have developed other subtopics, according to their own individual research interests, including identity, migration, globalization or textual hermeneutics. There has also been a tendency for educators and researchers to increasingly attempt to introduce a critical approach to language, culture and intercultural communication and to clarify what this means to them. Their theorization of critical pedagogy has, however, followed different philosophical and sociological sources and assumed various interpretations, postulates, dispositions and positions.

The term 'critical', with its various interpretations, has gained meaning from preceding theorizations, mainly in philosophy, sociology, literature and political science, each one of them acting as the primary source of inspiration for various definitions of the concept of a critical pedagogy. The notion of critical pedagogy/ies thus encompasses several definitions depending on the focus adopted. This focus may be educational, sociological, political, ethical, aesthetic and even methodological, e.g. dialogical, interactional, and therefore, each theory of a critical pedagogy will take a different perspective on the teaching/learning praxis it advocates. With regard to methodology, critical theories have provided more arguments to qualitative methodologies in education and stimulated more in-depth analysis and, as a result, methodology has grown into a research field itself rather than simply playing an instrumental role. Moreover, critical pedagogy views teaching as part of the learning process and, therefore, as a dialectical and dialogical reproduction as well as production of knowledge. Having this in mind, the implementation of a critical pedagogy always takes into consideration the 'situatedeness' of the individual in place and in time. Place is to be understood in its various concentric circles – from local to global and vice versa – and time in relation to its historical layers, and both place and time may offer possibilities of empowerment or represent processes of oppression. A critical pedagogy is consequently very much concerned with identity issues, with the learner's individual and collective heritage and with her/his social and political position as a subject of knowledge, as 'critical pedagogy identifies the subjects who form the discursive community of learners and knowers' (Hovey 2004: 248).

Language and culture are important elements to consider in critical pedagogy, mainly in relation to the processes of power and the shaping of identities within multilingual and multicultural cosmopolitan societies. In addition, although critical pedagogy has proved essential for the full accomplishment of intercultural education, the latter may also contribute to the implementation of a critical pedagogy, especially within the context of language education. Giroux is very clear on this:

> … you cannot decouple issues concerning language usage from issues of dialogue, communication, culture and power, matters of politics and pedagogy become crucial to how one understands pedagogy as a political issue and the politics of language as a deeply pedagogical consideration.
>
> *Giroux (2006: 174)*

A critical approach to experiences of cultural difference is vital both for the development of a critical pedagogy and for the effectiveness of language and intercultural education, leading to the development of 'critical cultural awareness', a notion put forward by Byram (1989, 1997, 2008). The idea of 'critical cultural awareness' first emerged from the reintroduction of cultural studies in language classes and was later developed within the conceptual framework of critical intercultural education and the acknowledgement of a complementary relationship between language/culture education, intercultural education, citizenship education and critical pedagogy (Guilherme 2002). Critical cultural awareness entails *savoir s'engager*, according to Byram's definition, and goes beyond an understanding and interpretation of difference and intercultural relations into commitment and action. Nevertheless, Byram reminds us that 'the definition of critical cultural awareness emphasizes the importance of individuals being aware of their own ideology – political and/or religious – and the need to be explicit in one's criteria of evaluating other people's action' (Byram 2008: 165). Furthermore, critical cultural awareness may propel individuals towards 'a philosophical, pedagogical, and political attitude towards culture' (Guilherme 2002: 219). Not only is it geared towards self-awareness or one-to-one communication, but also to collective micro and macro contexts and, therefore, is sensitive and attentive to ontological, epistemological, social and pedagogical issues and to changes in language and culture education. In sum, the development of critical cultural awareness through 'a critical pedagogy of (foreign) language/culture education and of intercultural communication/interaction (which) implies a critical use of language(s), a critical approach to one's own and other cultural backgrounds and a critical view of intercultural interaction' (Phipps and Guilherme 2004: 3). Therefore, critical pedagogy constitutes an impressive element and makes a valuable contribution to intercultural citizenship education.

## 4. A glimpse of the past

In the modern world, language has become one of the main symbols of national ethnicity and one of the main instruments of citizenship. The homogenization and standardization of national language has introduced a hierarchy into the practice of citizenship based on linguistic norms. This development results from the definition of political territorial borders, institutional stabilization and the structuring of educational systems and the media. The result is that those who are proficient in the official language, at the level of a mother tongue and in a standardized register, have more power than others.

All languages have been confronted in their historical and social development by issues of power while competing with each other and dealing with divergent forces within themselves, at both intra- and international levels. Over the last two centuries, sociologists, philosophers and linguists have increasingly emphasized the historical and social construction of language, which Vygotsky summarized in one simple statement: 'A word is a microcosm of human consciousness' (Vygotsky 1986: 256). Although there are some voices opposed to the nationally based citizenship model, such as multiculturalists who emphasize the linguistic and cultural rights of groups while requiring a 'differentiated citizenship' (Hall 2000; Young 1998) and radical democrats who possess a so-called postmodernist view and argue for an active integration of difference in the public sphere, the national perspective is, in one way or another, still prevalent in the notion of citizenship. However, globalization and mobility have been changing the order of things – the world has become more inter- and transnational and, above all, language and cultural diversity has become more and more visible and increasingly varied intranationally. National borders have become more porous and national authorities have had to become more flexible while using their powers both inside and outside their borders, as their decisions may contradict or be contradicted by transnational agreements.

Mobility is by no means a new feature of human behaviour. On the contrary, it has given birth and shape to civilizations throughout history. However, nowadays, we feel the need, probably more pressing than ever, to equip citizens with a set of competences, at both a personal and a professional level, that will enable them to fully explore the opportunities of a world that seems, although only to a privileged few (Bauman 1998), to have become wide open to them. Why do we bother? Don't we become naturally intercultural by being physically mobile? Why do we care? Can we be interculturally mobile without being physically mobile? Ethnic groups and isolated individuals have moved across regions, countries and continents for very different reasons: in search of material growth, religious survival, political freedom, adventure or intellectual enrichment. The higher and lower socioeconomic classes have been the most mobile, the former as a result of abundant resources and the latter to escape deprivation. This is the reason why there is a socially evident difference in terminology – migration and mobility – that does not simply address the apparent difference between groups of people moving only one or both ways. It emphasizes, we suggest, the underlying perceptions of status, which account for the positive connotations of terms such as 'expatriates' (or 'foreigners' in some languages) and the negative connotations of the term 'migrants'. Applying the term immigrant to a particular group is influenced not only by the host country's perceptions of the immigrant's country of origin, but also by the individual's socioeconomic status in the host country. This difference in terminology is based on the image (i.e. status) of developing countries, in particular, as well as that of the southern and eastern European countries that have joined the core group of the European Community; these labels affect the lives of individuals in society and, especially, in the workplace. Nevertheless, the common feature of both immigrants and expatriates, that is of all mobile people, is that they are both carriers and producers of culture. They carry their cultural baggage and they adapt, accommodate, resist and create culture, although not in a linear, chronological manner.

Throughout history, people have moved mostly in groups, with the exception of the occasional lone adventurers. With modernity, the development and the ubiquity of new means of transport, media and technologies have encouraged individuals to venture further and to move, either virtually or physically, alone or only with their nuclear families. However, most people do tend eventually to settle in or, at least, build relations with communities of individuals who are ethnically and culturally alike or equally foreign. On the other hand and despite this tendency to converge on such networks, some individuals move increasingly across different ethnic communities and cultures, both within and outside their local contexts, in both their private and public spaces. Thus, individuals move not only across cultures but also on the edge of the host and the immigrant community as they attempt to construct new communities in their everyday lives, at work and at home, as well as in-between.

Although research on intercultural relations is very recent, several scholars have attempted to identify and critically examine its nature, models and components. Arasaratnam and Doerfel (2005) also recognize Hall's (1959) *Silent Language* as the starting point for the scientific interest in intercultural communication. They also identify key components from multicultural perspectives developed during the last four decades, mainly by North American scholars and published in the English language, namely the ethnography of speaking approach, the cross-cultural attitudes approach, the behavioural skills approach and the cultural identity approach, developed by Geertz, Gudykunst, Wiseman, Ting-Toomey and Kim respectively. By analysing each of the selected models, the authors began to doubt the possibility of arriving at a culture-general conceptual model of intercultural communicative competence that may respond to every situation and therefore increase the probability of a general model of competence that is reciprocally perceivable as effective (ibid.: 141–43). In addition, Smith (1999) identified three research paradigms in intercultural relations prevalent from the 1970s onwards: (1) the logical empiricist approach, focusing on the individuated, psychological characteristics of subjects and influenced by behaviourist research; (2) the social interpretivist approach, inspired by cultural studies, centred on context and the subject's role in creating that context; (3) the rhetorical approach, which identifies historical motives (Smith 1999). This author proposed a paradigm bridge that he called 'the social network perspective', which is based 'on the assumption that behavior can be explained through relationship analysis' (ibid.: 633). This view led us to assume that intercultural communication and interaction is more complex and intricate than it has been perceived and, therefore, it requires both a critical theory and a critical pedagogy that account for its contingencies, constraints and possibilities.

The notion of a 'critical pedagogy', as it is understood nowadays, gained momentum in the United States in the late 1980s and early 1990s, mainly based on North and South American thinking. It was also inspired by European thinking, such as the Frankfurt School's critical theory and the French so-called postmodernism, as well as by American feminists; but the real source has mainly been South American postcolonial writing. The works of Freire – the Brazilian philosopher and educator (1921–97) who travelled widely, living and working in Europe and Africa – have provided the most solid and innovative ideas for the theorization of critical pedagogy. This is in large part due to the notion of *conscientização* that he disseminated throughout the academic field of education studies to draw attention to the political responsibility of education and educators and the perception of education as cultural politics. This concept represents more than critical awareness. It includes the purpose of informed and committed agency towards social justice and represents a fundamental contribution of critical pedagogy to language education and intercultural communication, by providing the link that changes their nature and makes them irreversibly intertwined in the forging of multiple identities and, consequently, multicultural citizenship agency in contemporary societies.

## 5. The impact of globalization on identity and citizenship

While decoding the relationship between language, communication and pedagogy, it is impossible to ignore the role that issues of identity and citizenship play within it, and how this relationship affects these issues in turn. These are indeed intertwined elements; but simply recognizing this fact is not sufficient and a critical understanding of the various ways in which this relationship may develop certainly provides more fertile ground for research and for the accomplishment of interculturality and criticality in language, communication and pedagogy. The concept of 'intercultural personhood', put forward by Kim (2008), responds to this line of thought and is described as 'the way of relating to oneself and others that is built on a dynamic, adaptive, and transformative identity conception – one that conjoins and integrates, rather than separates and divides' (ibid.: 360). This, according to Kim, leads to the emergence of an '*intercultural identity* – an open-ended, adaptive, and transformative self-other orientation' (ibid.: 364). From this point of view, Kim explains, 'cross-borrowing of identities is not an act of "surrendering" one's personal and cultural integrity, but an act of respect for cultural differences that leaves neither the lender nor the borrower deprived' (ibid.: 366). This leads us to assume that interculturality, if a critical approach is adopted, may generate and promote the suggested dynamic and transformative conceptions of identity and citizenship.

The Council of Europe describes intercultural dialogue 'as a process that comprises an open and respectful exchange of views between individuals and groups with different ethnic, cultural, religious and linguistic backgrounds and heritage, on the basis of mutual understanding and respect' (2010: 23). However, in the same document – the *White Paper on Intercultural Dialogue* – it adds that 'the universal values upheld by the Council of Europe are a condition for intercultural dialogue. No dialogue can take place in the absence of respect for the equal dignity of all human beings, ... ' (ibid.: 26). In fact, these statements may be mutually contradictory, as the former statement accounts for diversity whereas the latter implies universality, and a critical pedagogy would address this. Either the affirmed universal values are understood to be mutually endorsed within a common conceptual framework or they are uniformly translated. Here lies the cornerstone of critical intercultural dialogue.

According to Santos, 'the central task of emancipatory politics of our time, in this domain [a counter-hegemonic human rights discourse and practice], consists in transforming the conceptualization and practice of human rights from a globalized localism into a cosmopolitan project' (Santos 1999: 220). Among the five premises that he identifies as necessary for that transformation to take place, it is the second premise that focuses on the recognition that 'all cultures have conceptions of human dignity but not all of them conceive it as human rights' (ibid.: 221). The third and fourth premises state that 'all cultures are incomplete and problematic in their conceptions of human dignity' and 'all cultures have different versions of human dignity' (ibid.: 221). Having this in mind, a critical pedagogy tackles the idea of universal values by assuming that they encompass the discussion of a variety of perspectives in their essence, interpretation and implementation. The linguistic and cultural processes described above may be understood as coinciding with the four forms of globalization identified by the same author: (1) 'globalized localism' – 'the process by which a given local phenomenon is successfully globalized, be it ... the transformation of the English language into the *lingua franca*'; (2) 'localized globalism' – 'the specific impact of transnational practices and imperatives on local conditions that are thereby destructed and restructured in order to respond to transnational imperatives'; (3) 'cosmopolitanism' – 'the opportunity for subordinate nation-states, regions, classes or social groups and their allies to organize transnationally in defence of perceived common interests and use to their benefit the capabilities for transnational interaction created by the world system';

and finally (4) 'common heritage of humankind' – 'the emergence of issues which, by their nature, are as global as the globe itself' (Santos 1999: 217–18). Moreover, given that 'the new rich do not need the poor any more' (Bauman 1998: 72) in an economy that has lately grown more virtual than real, it is essential that communities and their citizenry are aware of the levels available to them in the new globalized society and the tricks that may be played upon them. In addition, 'while non-Western communities were busy working on one project (decolonisation), the carpet has been pulled from under their feet by another project (globalisation)' (Canagarajah 2005: 195–96) and, therefore, while new nation-states were emerging, they were also being pressed from the outside by economic forces that make them vacillate in their own freedom and autonomy.

## 6. Interculturality and criticality in language, communication and pedagogy

As a result, although some individuals were, everywhere, greedily using the circumstances of globality to become obscenely wealthier and others were struggling to survive starvation and violence, policy makers and academic knowledge producers were trying to figure out innovative directions for yet untravelled paths. New hegemonies and dominations have, as ever before, been established and critical pedagogies of language and communication aimed at the education of cosmopolitan citizens, integrating broader educational frameworks, such as human rights education and education for democratic citizenship, are increasingly necessary. The human rights education dimension focuses on the basic rights of every human being in the world, as stated in the documents of transnational organizations, which have been ratified by a number of nation-states, but are nevertheless open to different cultural interpretations, according to local contexts. A critical approach to language and communication is therefore expected to meet these goals and, furthermore, to add a multiple-perspective view, as well as a discussion about the power relations that underlie the surface differences within and beyond the limits of the nation-state (Guilherme 2002).

However, national and cosmopolitan citizenship are not mutually exclusive. Nor are learning foreign languages/cultures and developing one's home language(s)/(culture(s) or, via that process, having the opportunity to meet and deepen one's knowledge of other less powerful languages/cultures. Neither is citizenship a monolithic structure with clearly separate levels of identification. Besides, being an active cosmopolitan citizen does not start only beyond national borders, nor does the fact that one is bilingual or an expatriate make one a critical and active cosmopolitan citizen, for this depends on 'the level of conscious awareness involved' in acting interculturally (Byram 2003: 64). Here Byram makes a distinction between 'being intercultural' and 'acting intercultural', stating that 'acting interculturally involves a level of analytical awareness which does not necessarily follow from being intercultural', despite the fact that the condition (being intercultural) may be a strong factor for the development of the capacity to act according to that attitude (acting interculturally) (ibid.: 64–65). Nevertheless, 'being intercultural' may also be viewed as an ontological, existential perspective through which one sees the world and positions oneself within it that may be interpreted as utopian and consists of no less than 'the heart of languages' (Phipps and Gonzalez 2004). All these authors, therefore, envisage a critical cultural awareness and a disposition to act that is developed through education. The notion of agency is an important one when considering the idea of citizenship, and it corroborates the reinforcement of the notion of participative democracy that is so central in a critical pedagogy of intercultural communication (Guilherme 2002).

Furthermore, there has been an overall, increasing and more pervasive awareness that 'the recognition that a society had become multiethnic or multicultural was not simply about demographics or economics' and that it went beyond that into 'an understanding that a new set of challenges were being posed for which a new political agenda was necessary (or alternatively, had to be resisted: the view of certain conservatives ... )' (Modood 2007: 5). However, a change in the political rhetoric alone is insufficient. As the information- and knowledge-based society was constructing a new paradigm, leaving the goal of cultural hegemony behind and moving into an intercultural construct of society, this intercultural ideal also began to impact on organizational spaces and modify the prevailing paradigms of interaction. The information-based society, economic globalization, networking and mobility have changed both professional and personal relationships in society as well as in the workplace. Global exchanges have generated more than wider information and business interchange, they have also affected 'every aspect of communities, including beliefs, norms, values and behaviors, ... ' (Banks 2009: 308), in that they have made communities challenge each other's horizons.

Education for cosmopolitan citizenship, which here encompasses critical language and intercultural communication pedagogy, is ultimately geared to promoting participation that shapes the present in order to also shape the future. It opens up the citizens' horizon beyond territorial and ethnic boundaries, while striving to maintain their cultural roots, and ensures these dimensions reinforce one another. Thus, critical language and intercultural communication pedagogy carries the responsibility of simultaneously promoting a shared identity, the appreciation of diversity, the respect for difference, the pride in one's own identifications and the commitment to taking action in the interests of the weaker members of our communities. Language necessarily plays an important role in articulating and connecting multiple experiences and identifications both individually and collectively.

## 7. From intercultural competence to intercultural responsibility

Power relations rely on assumptions of status that depend on different variables present in each cultural framework, such as social class, age, gender, race, ethnicity, geographical region or physical features. In situations of multicultural interaction, these power relations may incorporate new cross-cultural and intercultural possibilities and generate new communicative dynamics. Moreover, the range of contacts and experiences that are now accessible has widened, and their intensity has also increased as a result of greater mobility and advances in communication technologies. For example, these developments have considerably facilitated cultural exchange. Within this context, intercultural competence, as it has been theorized, is considered to be lagging behind the potential and the demands of intercultural relations. Therefore, I have proposed a new term, 'intercultural responsibility', subsequently developed by the international ICOPROMO (Intercultural Competence for Professional Mobility) project team and specifically by the Portuguese team. This notion adds a social, relational, civic and ethical component to the conception of 'intercultural competence', in that it 'raises issues concerning the negotiation between the similar and the contrasting aspects of different ethical frameworks, in particular how this negotiation is verbalised and performed' (Guilherme et al. 2010: 83). Furthermore, it delves more deeply into a commitment to social justice and an active involvement in matters of individual dignity and collective interest. The development of the concept of intercultural responsibility may therefore respond to this need for restructuring one's bonds in a cosmopolitan society and its implications for the reorganization of language use, cultural premises and intercultural communication.

From our point of view, the development of intercultural competences requires an awareness of the meaning-making mechanisms – *conscientização*, a recurrent theme in Freire's works – and dialogical tools available when engaging in cross-cultural interaction and communication. Further, it is also necessary to develop an ability to manage and explore these mechanisms and tools in order to achieve effective intercultural communication and interaction competence. This is fundamental for living in new and emerging communities and being active citizens in those communities (Guilherme 2000). The conceptual framework of critical pedagogy strongly influences the definition of 'effective' intercultural communication and interaction, in that it develops the concept of dialogue in complexity, by moving beyond the idea of apparent consensus and superficial harmony. If language education enlightened by critical pedagogy gives way to the development of critical cultural awareness, then a critical pedagogy may also lead intercultural communication and interaction into intercultural responsibility. Once critical pedagogy looks suspiciously upon power dialectics, dialogue is no longer 'naïf', in Freire's words, and therefore, 'it cannot exclude conflict' as they 'interact dialectically' (Freire 1979/ 2007, my translation). Within this view, 'effective' critical intercultural dialogue does not aim at final consensus or expect enduring harmony throughout. Instead, it is built upon unstable and dynamic platforms of understanding/misunderstanding and temporary agreements/disagreements, based on reciprocal and respectful communication and collaboration, to be negotiated again and again with an eye on the power issues to be fought for and against. Moreover, within the scope of intercultural responsibility, intercultural contact is not limited to communication and interaction between two independent parties. It is applicable to interdependent participants and, therefore, necessitates cooperation, concurrence, sharing, collective synergy, congeniality and dependability among partners.

During this first decade of the twenty-first century, the notion of 'pedagogies' has in fact been supplanted by the requirements of 'standards' and, therefore, the focus on process has been replaced by a concern for results, seen as a product. However, even though critical pedagogies have tended to be overlooked, they have nonetheless been recognized as increasingly indispensable in order to ensure that education does not betray its nature and intention. Although the notion of critical pedagogy and the 'standard mania' dominant nowadays are, in principle, radically incompatible, a knowledgeable and critical combination of the two may set limits to simplified overstatements of each of them. In this case, standards should be used within a wider framework of a critical pedagogy, and not the other way round, as the latter provides a philosophical underpinning – both ontological and epistemological – and a political understanding of diversity in education, whereas the former offers a number of general guidelines aimed at homogenizing education, which can also be helpful, provided they are treated as complementary, rather than as a priority. They are also radically divergent in their goals, as a critical pedagogy aims to create an active citizen prepared to intervene in society, whereas a 'standards technocracy' produces a 'competent' individual ready to adapt to and serve society as it has been structured by dominant and established powers.

Although these are opposing visions of education theory in essence, they are nevertheless condemned, in practice, to cohabit in the same educational system and, therefore, in each individual 'educatee'. The education system, including lifelong learning programmes, must provide space for educators and educatees to develop both visions, according to moral, civic and professional patterns that are offered to them by their families and communities, the organizations where they work, their democratic societies, their critical educational institutions and free world. This is then the reasoning that suggests a move beyond the concept of 'intercultural competence' towards a notion of 'intercultural responsibility' (Guilherme et al. 2010). The ICOPROMO project, within which this concept was created, aimed to build a bridge between pedagogy and training, producing materials for professional development in intercultural communication and interaction. In the same line as the work of Phipps and Gonzalez (2004) and

Byram (2008) on the idea of an 'intercultural being', as mentioned above, Fleming, although mentioning 'key aspects of the holistic concept of intercultural competence such as empathy, openness, tolerance of ambiguity, readiness to decentre, willingness to engage with others and to try anything new ... ', recognizes that 'to say that someone possesses such traits is implicitly to say something about their propensity, ... ' and 'it is also to make a statement about how they will be rather than just how they will perform' (Fleming 2009: 9). In fact, the notion of 'intercultural responsibility' encompasses the idea of 'intercultural being' as well as some of the premises of 'an interculturally competent being'; however, it moves forward into the require-ments of critical intercultural dialogue and collaboration, which imply reciprocal commitment and cooperative agency.

The issue at stake here is how a critical pedagogy may suit professional development pro-grammes in intercultural communication. Critical pedagogy, as initiated by Paulo Freire in Brazil, was originally implemented with adult learners, so-called illiterate, rural workers. A few decades later, Raymond Williams was also developing a critical pedagogy of cultural studies with adult learners in England. Their theories, as well as the ways in which they have devel-oped, provide us with a scientific and practical background for a praxis that gives adequate responses and stimuli to contemporary challenges put to professional development programmes in critical language and intercultural communication. In the unsettling *Pedagogy of the Oppressed,* Freire explains that a critical pedagogy is an 'instrument for their [the oppressed] critical dis-covery that both they and their oppressors are manifestations of dehumanization', and therefore, it is the situation itself that demands to be changed as 'the very structure of their thought has been conditioned by the contradictions of the concrete existential situation by which they were shaped' (Freire 1970: 30–32); that is, 'cultural conquest leads to the cultural inauthenticity of those who are invaded' (ibid.: 150). Although speaking of oppressors and oppressed among those for whom these educational/training programmes are meant seems exaggerated, we do recognize signs of the same kind of 'symbolic violence' defined as 'the imposition of a cultural arbitrary by an arbitrary power', in this case, by the cultural arbitrary created and maintained by an organization or by a professional class, be it a school or other, that determines the evaluation criteria of competence (Bourdieu 1977: 5).

Moreover, given that, for example, 'TNCs [transnational corporations] are no longer the monolithic, vertically organized entities they were in most of the twentieth-century' and that, in fact, 'they have undergone fundamental changes in the last decades, facilitating the hor-izontalization of their corporate structures' (Palacios 2004: 390), this negotiation, if there is one, is increasingly implemented at the grassroots level. All the more so as 'the workplace as a venue of communication simply changes the location of the interaction, not the predispositions and stereotypes that human beings bring to the situation' (Asante and Davis 1989: 376) and, as mentioned above, the organizational structures have, to a great extent, kept these challenges hidden beneath other more pressing constraints related to corporate profit and political or individual interests. In the meantime, the social responsibility of both governmental and non-governmental organizations is perceived to be untouchable, in the case of the former because of their legal status and in the latter as a result of their soundly established goals. Therefore, in none of them is the intercultural responsibility of their workers opened for discussion, and their responsibility to be interculturally committed is not always a seriously taken commitment.

Intercultural responsibility is therefore understood, in this context, as a conscious and reci-procally respectful, both professional and personal, relationship among those who work or otherwise interact in a team/group where they have different ethnic backgrounds, whether national or subnational. This means that members-in-interaction demonstrate that they are aware of the particularities of collaborating with their co-workers, in either an inter- or an intranational context, recognizing that their identities have been socially and culturally constructed based on different ethnic elements and influences that have been, at different stages, more or less preponderant. Furthermore, intercultural responsibility implies that every member is responsible not only for identifying and recognizing the cultural idiosyncrasies of every other member-in-interaction, but also for developing full and reciprocally demanding professional relationships with them. The notion of intercultural responsibility adds a moral element to global ethics, although intercultural and cosmopolitan and, therefore, not dogmatic or absolute.

## 8. Conclusion and recommendations for practice

A critical language and intercultural communication pedagogy in professional education, for both teaching and other professions, is certainly expected to overcome avoidance, suspicion, prejudice and misunderstanding. First and foremost, it unsettles deep-rooted values and principles, unquestioned concepts and automated routines, all of which lead to unconscious criteria and uncontested judgements. It may, therefore, cause some discomfort and disturbance. Second, a critical language and intercultural communication pedagogy in professional education does not need intensive training; on the contrary, it requires time for reflection, experiential learning, dialogue, maturation, all of which can and should be done over time, with periods for individual search and musing and moments for group discussion. This process accounts for the difference between functional training and critical learning. Professional development programmes are too short (Hayman 2010), unless they involve postgraduate university qualifications; therefore, these programmes should be longer, although they need not demand full physical attendance by the trainees. Third, and as a result of the above, a critical language and intercultural communication pedagogy in professional education deals with complex ideas, although eventually they have to be expressed in a simple, organized and clear way, as students can be quick to reject ideas that seem abstract, inaccessible or even disturbing. It is always a challenge to attempt to deconstruct and uncover ideas, feelings and behaviours that are generally taken for granted or are often hidden from view and to invite students to address and explore them. Finally, examining the implicit as well as the explicit meanings of our cultural behaviours leads us beyond the visible, immediate, obvious and often deceptive aspects that may generate hasty and incorrect judgements. People can be discriminated against for motives other than material conditions, for example, because they do not, in different and subtle ways, adjust to dominant criteria and standards. Diversity and discrimination can emerge in elusive and intangible forms, linger beyond immediately obvious evidence and go unnoticed to most, except those who enjoy their attributes or suffer their consequences.

A critical pedagogy is relevant for education for language and intercultural communication as it allows us to go beyond a simple 'translation of linguistic and cultural differences' (Shi-xu 2001: 280), despite the limits that it involves and its shortcomings. If the aim is intercultural dialogue, a critical pedagogy takes into account the unequal relations of power in discourse. It also builds the bridge between the achievement of intercultural competence and intercultural responsibility, as these concepts are not incompatible and may complement one another. Although a critical pedagogy of language and intercultural communication recognizes multiculturalism, defined as 'the culturally diverse nature of human society', it also promotes interculturality, which 'refers to evolving relations between cultural groups' as, once again, one should not go without the other (UNESCO 2006: 17). The notion of 'intercultural competence' is based on the former vision of a diverse society and of intercultural contact, assuming the recognition of multiculturalism and of a multicultural framework, in that it 'may be defined as complex abilities that are required to perform *effectively* and *appropriately* when interacting with others who are linguistically and culturally different from oneself' (Fantini 2009: 458). This understanding of intercultural competence certainly encompasses the components of dialogue and interaction, but it does not necessarily ensure that a critical pedagogy is required or that a critical approach to intercultural dialogue or interaction is implemented. The idea of 'intercultural responsibility' attempts to respond to the need to consider cooperation in the fulfilment of a goal and a task, the need for solidarity with the weaker, for commitment to social justice, for active agency in the achievement of democratic societies in a global world through intercultural exchange and collaboration.

## Related topics

Cosmopolitanism; critical pedagogy; intercultural citizenship; intercultural competence; intercultural communication pedagogy; multiculturalism

## Further reading

Benhabib, S. (2008) *Another Cosmopolitanism*, Oxford: Oxford University Press (a theorization of the concept of cosmopolitanism).

Norris, P. and Inglehart, R. (2009) *Cosmopolitan Communications: Cultural Diversity in a Globalized World*, Cambridge: Cambridge University Press (a discussion about the complexities of globalization and intercultural communication).

Oetzel, J.G. and Ting-Toomey, S. (2006) *The SAGE Handbook of Conflict Communication: Integrating Theory, Research, and Practice*, Thousand Oaks, CA: Sage (a discussion of different kinds and contexts of intercultural conflict).

Phipps, A. (2007) *Learning the Arts of Linguistic Survival: Languaging, Tourism, Life*, Clevedon: Multilingual Matters (a philosophical and anthropological account of language use and intercultural experience).

Risager, K. (2007) *Language and Culture Pedagogy: From a National to a Transnational Paradigm*, Clevedon: Multilingual Matters (an account of recent developments of culture pedagogy in Europe and Northern America and of a transnational paradigm).

## References

Alasuutari, P, Bickman, L. and Brannen, J. (2008) *The SAGE Handbook of Social Research Methods*, Thousand Oaks, CA: Sage.

Arasaratnam, L.A. and Doerfel, M.L. (2005) 'Intercultural communication competence: identifying key components from multicultural perspectives', *International Journal of Intercultural Relations*, 29: 137–63.

Asante, M.K. and Davis, A. (1989) 'Encounters in the interracial workplace', in M.K. Asante and W.B. Gudykunst (eds) *Handbook of International and Intercultural Communication*, Newbury, CA: Sage, pp. 374–91.

Banks, J.A. (2009) 'Diversity, group identity, and citizenship education in a global age', in J.A. Banks (ed.) *The Routledge International Companion to Multicultural Education*, New York: Routledge, pp. 303–22.

Bauman, Z. (1998) *Globalization: The Human Consequences*, Cambridge: Polity Press.

Bennett, J.M. (2009) 'Cultivating intercultural competence: a process perspective', in D.K. Deardorff (ed.) *The SAGE Handbook of Intercultural Competence*, Thousand Oaks, CA: pp. 121–40.

Bourdieu, P. (1977) *Outline of a Theory of Practice*, Cambridge, MA: Cambridge University Press.

Byram, M. (1989) *Cultural Studies in Foreign Language Education*, Clevedon: Multilingual Matters.

——(1997) *Teaching and Assessing Intercultural Communicative Competence*, Clevedon: Multilingual Matters.

——(2003) 'On being bicultural and intercultural', in G. Alred, M. Byram and M. Fleming (eds) *Intercultural Experience and Education*, Clevedon: Multilingual Matters, pp. 50–66.

——(2008) *From Foreign Language Education to Education for Intercultural Citizenship*, Clevedon: Multilingual Matters.

Byram, M. and Zarate, G. (eds) (1997) *The Sociocultural and Intercultural Dimension of Language Learning and Teaching*, Strasbourg: Council of Europe.

Canagarajah, A.S. (2005) 'Accommodating tensions in language-in-education policies: an afterword', in A.M.Y. Lin and P. Martin (eds) *Decolonisation and Globalisation: Language-in-education Policy and Practice*, Clevedon: Multilingual Matters, pp. 194–201

Council of Europe (2005) *The Competency Workbook: Mobility and Competence Project (2001–4)*, Strasbourg: Council of Europe.

——(2010) *White Paper on Intercultural Dialogue*, Strasbourg: Council of Europe.

Deardorff, D.K. (2009) 'Preface', in D.K. Deardorff (ed.) *The SAGE Handbook of Intercultural Competence*, London: Sage, pp. xi–xiv.

Fantini, A.E. (2009) 'Assessing intercultural competence', in D.K. Deardorff (ed.) *The SAGE Handbook of Intercultural Competence*, London: Sage, pp. 456–76.

Feng, A., Byram, M.S., and Fleming, M. (eds) (2009) *Becoming Interculturally Competent through Education and Training*, Clevedon: Multilingual Matters.

Fleming, M. (2007) 'The use and misuse of competence statements with particular reference to the teaching of literature: towards a common European framework of reference for language(s) of school education', Proceedings of an international conference organized by the Council of Europe and the Jagiellonian University in Kraków, Poland, 27–29 April 2006.

——(2009) 'The challenge of competence', in A. Hu and M. Byram (eds) *Interkulturelle Kompetenz und Fremdsprachlices Lernen/Intercultural Competence and Foreign Language Learning*, Tübingen: Gunter Narr Verlag, pp. 3–14.

Freire, P. (1970) *Pedagogy of the Oppressed*, New York: The Continuum Publishers.

——(1979; 2nd edn 2007) *Educação e Mudança*, Sao Paulo: Paz e Terra.

Giroux, H.A. (2006) 'Is there a role for critical pedagogy in language/culture studies?: an interview with Henry A. Giroux by Manuela Guilherme', *Language and Intercultural Communication*. 6(2): 163–75.

Guilherme, M. (2000) 'Intercultural competence', in M. Byram (ed.) *Routledge Encyclopedia of Language Teaching and Learning*, London: Routledge, pp. 297–300.

——(2002) *Critical Citizens for an Intercultural World: Foreign Language Education as Cultural Politics*, Clevedon: Multilingual Matters.

Guilherme, M., Keating, C. and Hoppe, D. (2010) 'Intercultural responsibility: power and ethics in intercultural dialogue and interaction', in M. Guilherme, E. Glaser and M.C. Méndez-García (eds) *Intercultural Dynamics of Multicultural Working*, Clevedon: Multilingual Matters, pp. 77–94.

Hall, E.T. (1959) *The Silent Language*, New York: Doubleday.

Hall, S. (2000) 'Multicultural citizens, monocultural citizenship?', in N. Pearce and J. Hallgarten (eds) *Tomorrow's Citizens: Critical Debates in Citizenship and Education*, London: Institute for Public Policy Research, pp. 43–51.

Hayman, J. (2010) 'Talking about talking: comparing the approaches of intercultural trainers and language teachers', in G. Forey and J. Lockwood (eds) *Globalization, Communication and the Workplace*, London: Continuum International, pp. 148–58.

Hovey, R. (2004) 'Critical pedagogy and international studies: reconstructing knowledge through dialogue with the subaltern', *International Relations*, 18(2): 241–54.

Kim, Y.Y. (2008) 'Intercultural personhood: globalization and a way of being', *International Journal of Intercultural Relations*, 32: 359–68.

Medina-López-Portillo, A. and Sinnigen, J.H. (2009) 'Interculturality versus intercultural competence in Latin America', in D.K. Deardorff (ed.) *The SAGE Handbook of Intercultural Competence*, Thousand Oaks, CA: Sage, pp. 249–63.

Modood, T. (2007) *Multiculturalism: A Civic Idea*, Cambridge: Polity Press.

Palacios, J.J. (2004) 'Corporate citizenship and social responsibility in a globalized world', *Citizenship Studies*, 8: 383–402.

Parmenter, L. (2003) 'Describing and defining intercultural communicative competence – international perspectives', in M. Byram (ed.) *Intercultural Competence*, Strasbourg: Council of Europe, pp. 119–47.

Phipps, A. and Gonzalez, M. (2004) *Modern Languages: Learning and Teaching in an Intercultural Field*, London: Sage.

Phipps, A. and Guilherme, M. (2004) *Critical Pedagogy: Political Approaches to Language and Intercultural Communication*, Clevedon: Multilingual Matters.

Pusch, M.D. (2009) 'The interculturally competent global leader', in D.K. Deardorff (ed.) *The SAGE Handbook of Intercultural Competence*, Thousand Oaks, CA: Sage, pp. 6–84.

Risager, K. (2009) 'Intercultural competence in the cultural flow', in A. Hu and M. Byram (eds) *Interkulturelle Kompetenz und Fremdsprachliches Lernen/Intercultural Competence and Foreign Language Learning*, Tübingen: Gunter Narr Verlag, pp. 15–30.

Rychen, D.S. (2003) 'Key competencies', in D.S. Rychen and L.H. Salganik (eds) *Key Competencies for a Successful Life and Well-functioning Society*, Toronto: Hogrefe and Huber, pp. 63–107.

Rychen, D.S. and Salganik, L.H. (2003) 'Introduction', in D.S. Rychen and L.H. Salganik (eds) *Key Competencies for a Successful Life and Well-functioning Society*, Toronto: Hogrefe and Huber, pp. 1–12.

Salganik, L.H. and Stephens, M. (2003) 'Competence priorities in policy and practice', in D.S. Rychen and L.H. Salganik (eds) *Key Competencies for a Successful Life and Well-functioning Society*, Toronto: Hogrefe and Huber, pp. 13–40.

Santos, B.S. (1999) 'Towards a multicultural conception of human rights', in Lash, S. and Featherstone, M. (eds) *Spaces of Culture: City, Nation, World*, London: Sage, pp. 214–19.

Shi-xu (2001) 'Critical pedagogy and intercultural communication: creating discourses of diversity, equality, common goals and rational moral motivation', *Journal of Intercultural Studies*, 22(3): 279–93.

Smith, L.R. (1999) 'Intercultural network theory: a cross-paradigmatic approach to acculturation', *International Journal of Intercultural Relations*, 23(4): 629–58.

Spitzberg, B.H. and Changnon, G. (2009) 'Conceptualizing intercultural competence', in D.K. Deardorff (ed.) *The SAGE Handbook of Intercultural Competence*, Thousand Oaks, CA: Sage, pp. 2–52.

UNESCO (2006) *UNESCO Guidelines on Intercultural Education*, Paris: UNESCO. Online. Available: http://unesdoc.unesco.org/images/0014/001478/147878e.pdf accessed 2006 (accessed 5 May 2007).

Vygotsky, L.S. (1986) *Thought and Language [Myshlenie I rech]*, A. Kozulin (transl./ed.) Cambridge: MIT Press.

Young, I. (1998) 'Polity and group difference: a critique of the ideal of universal citizenship', in G. Shafir (ed.) *The Citizenship Debates*, Minneapolis, MN: University of Minnesota Press, pp. 263–90.

# 23

# Intercultural training in the global context

*Kathryn Sorrells*

## 1. Introduction

In the past 30 years, revolutionary changes in communication and transportation technologies have coalesced with neo-liberal economic and political policies to dramatically accelerate intercultural interaction around the world. The forces of globalization have catapulted people, practices and beliefs from different cultures into shared and contested physical and virtual spaces in workplaces, communities and schools in unprecedented ways. Our world, at the beginning of the new millennium, is a world in motion. More people are on the move today crossing cultural boundaries and national borders than ever before in the history of humankind. The International Organization for Migration reported in 2009 that 214 million people live outside their country of origin (International Organization for Migration 2009). Over 922 million people crossed international borders for business and leisure in 2008 despite rising oil prices, fluctuating exchange rates, global political uncertainty and threats of terrorism (World Tourism Organization 2008).

Driven by the global economy, collaboration in multicultural teams at home and abroad is increasingly the norm rather than the exception. Multinational managers are required to move more rapidly and frequently across multiple and varied cultural contexts than in the past. The growing diversity of student populations in educational institutions at all levels presents immense intercultural opportunities and challenges. Sojourns of international students are more multidirectional today as the value of 'international experience' gains currency globally and universities around the world compete for students in the educational marketplace. Additionally, the rapid de-territorialization and re-territorialization of migrants and refugees creates contested and hybrid cultural spaces as longstanding norms in countries of origin and destination are disrupted. With increased contact across cultural boundaries, greater complexity in cultural constellations and exacerbated potential for misunderstanding and conflict, the need for intercultural training, in the new millennium, is more critical than ever before.

This chapter begins with a historical overview of intercultural training. I then turn to the contemporary context of globalization to describe the complex, contradictory and inequitable conditions in which intercultural communication occurs today. Explicating the implications of the global context for intercultural training, I explore four critical trends in intercultural training and address the ways theoretical shifts manifest in terms of practice. The chapter concludes with a discussion of future directions for intercultural training in the global context.

## 2. Historical perspective

The following overview highlights the roots and critical developments of intercultural training over the last 70 years. The foundations of intercultural training can be traced back to the growth in international student exchange programmes and US government-sponsored international development programmes in the post WWII period. Edward T. Hall, often referred to as the originator of the field of intercultural communication, was hired by the US Foreign Service Institute in 1955 (Leeds-Hurwitz 1990). Recognizing that training focused primarily on verbal language and country-specific information was not sufficient preparation for work abroad, Edward T. Hall, along with others at the Foreign Service Institute, developed training programmes that were practical and situation based, with an emphasis on implicit culture. Hall's concentration on the tacit dimensions of culture, such as the use of time, space and context, later popularized in his work, the *Silent Language* (1959) and the *Hidden Dimension* (1966), continue as key concepts in intercultural communication training today. In addition, Hall's emphasis on applied and situational learning, his use of experiential teaching methods, the value he placed on the self as an instrument and focus of analysis as well as the important shift from studying cultures in isolation to studying communication interactions among cultures all established the groundwork for intercultural training (Pusch 2004; Sorrells 1998).

The Peace Corps initiated by President John F. Kennedy in the early 1960s enabled thousands of volunteers from the US to serve in countries around the world. Although Peace Corps training originally focused on country-specific information and was conducted on university campuses, training eventually moved to centres in host countries. Training techniques were developed and codified by Albert Wight and Mary Anne Hammons (1970) in the first intercultural training manual, *Guidelines for Peace Corps Cross-cultural Training: Philosophy and Methodology*. As Pusch (2004) notes, the emphasis on 'learning how to learn' that proved possible in host country training for the Peace Corps continues today in intercultural training. Several sources, *Culture Matters: The Peace Corps Cross-cultural Workbook* (Storti and Bennhold-Samaan 1998) and *Culture Matters: Trainer's Guide* (Storti and Bennhold-Samaan 1999), outline the strategies and technologies used by the Peace Corps to train volunteers about culture, and to value differences across cultures and cultural self-awareness. The Experiment for International Living, now called World Learning, began administering study abroad programmes starting in the 1930s and founded the School for International Training Graduate Institute in Brattleboro, Vermont, USA, in the 1960s as a training centre for Peace Corps volunteers (now called the SIT Graduate Institute). Their experiential-based graduate and continuing education programmes focus on building skills in language, intercultural communication and global citizenship. *Beyond Experience*, edited by Donald Batchelder and Elizabeth Warner (1977), and a second edition edited by Ted Gochenour (1995) consolidated the concepts, methods, experiential learning activities and assessment tools for intercultural training that have been developed over the years.

Another critical site for experimentation and the development of intercultural training occurred at the University of Pittsburgh starting in the mid-1960s and extending for about 10 years. David Hoopes and Stephen Rhinesmith, in conjunction with the Regional Council for International Education, developed what came to be known as Intercultural Communication Workshops (ICW), which brought international and US students together to learn from each other and to explore intercultural interactions. ICW, aimed at assisting participants in understanding culture and challenging communication barriers, were typically several days long and drew on a variety of training methods such as lectures, exercises, group experiences, discussions and film. David Hoopes (1970, 1972, 1973) edited *Readings in Intercultural Communication*, volumes that compile chapters on research, theory and training.

ICW at the University of Pittsburgh and a similar model developed at Cornell University by Clifford Clark enabled the development of an expanding network of trained intercultural facilitators. At Portland State University, Le Ray Barna developed an innovative academic model of ICW bringing international students in English as a Second Language courses together with students in communication classes to assist with language learning and to understand what helped and hindered intercultural communication. Barna's (1972) article 'Stumbling blocks in intercultural communication', based on her work with the ICW model, was first published in *Readings in Intercultural Communication* and continues as a standard today. In the late 1970s, Milton Bennett established a version of ICW at Portland State University and, along with Janet Bennett, developed a systematic train-the-trainer programme for graduate students. ICWs across the US were pivotal in developing and testing a wide range of approaches and strategies for intercultural training that were shared and refined through growing groups of trained facilitators such as the Intercultural Network and the Society for Intercultural Education, Training and Research (SIETAR). SIETAR, established in 1974 and later becoming SIETAR International, has held annual conferences in different locations for several decades and has played a central role in facilitating collaboration among intercultural practitioners and researchers around the world. SIETAR Japan was organized in 1985 and SIETAR Europa founded in 1991. In 1998, the first SIETAR Global Network international conference was held in Japan.

Although the field of intercultural communication emerged with a central focus on international contexts, it is important to note that developments in ethnic studies, multicultural education and interracial/interethnic relations in the US paralleled and influenced intercultural communication training. Out of the Civil Rights Movement, departments of ethnic studies emerged in US universities to challenge Eurocentric curricula, to construct knowledge from the position of silenced and disadvantaged groups and to empower non-dominant groups. Drawing on interdisciplinary fields of study such as ethnic and women's studies, multicultural education, an educational reform movement led by James Banks (1988; Banks and Banks 2003), aims to create equal educational opportunities for students from diverse racial, ethnic, class and cultural groups. Although a broad range of principles are essential to multicultural education, the emphasis on developing an awareness of stereotypes and biases, gaining skills to reduce prejudice and creating environments that foster interethnic and interracial relations increasingly intersects with goals of intercultural training particularly in educational contexts. The emergence of critical theoretical approaches in intercultural communication in the last decade (Nakayama and Halualani 2010) highlights the increasing importance of understanding cultural differences and intercultural communication within the context of inequitable relations of power and privilege.

With a few exceptions, intercultural training in multinational corporate contexts began to gain footing and momentum in the 1980s in Europe, the US and Japan. In 1980, Geert Hofstede created the Institute for Research on Intercultural Cooperation in the Netherlands. Based on his pioneering research at IBM, Hofstede's (1980, 1991) dimensions of culture – power distance, uncertainty avoidance, individualism–collectivism, masculinity–femininity and Confucian dynamism – and diagnostic tools have found broad appeal in multinational corporate settings around the world to identify cultural differences and develop intercultural communication skills. In the late 1980s, Fons Trompenaars, founder of the Centre for Intercultural Business Studies also in the Netherlands, developed an approach to intercultural training and consulting based on seven dimensions of culture, which address the way people relate to each other, solve problems and view time (Trompenaars 1993; Trompenaars and Hampden-Turner 1997). Although open to a range of critiques discussed later in the chapter, the work of these researchers and practitioners has had a tremendous impact on intercultural training in multinational business contexts.

Managing 'diversity' in the workplace, ubiquitous today in multicultural organizations and corporate boardrooms, was a new idea in the early 1990s. With roots in the Affirmative Action and Equal Opportunity Employment policies of the 1970s in the US, the notion of managing diversity attempted to move beyond numbers and quotas for the inclusion of non-dominant groups towards recognizing diversity as a resource (Thomas 1990). Trends in diversity training in the mid-1990s in the US (Abramms and Simons 1995, as cited in Lee Gardenswartz and Anita Rowe 1998) indicate that definitions of diversity were becoming more inclusive, 'victims versus oppressors' and affirmative action paradigms were used less frequently and there was a shift towards concepts and language that focused on ethnic and organizational culture. By the end of the 1990s, globalization, evidenced by radical demographic shifts in the workforce, required corporate diversity consultants and trainer/practitioners to adopt increasingly more fluid and flexible approaches, pay closer attention to differences in ethics across cultures and alter training methods, content and format to address changing demands (Gardenswartz and Rowe 1998).

Notable global trends at the end of the millennium, which continue today, include an increase in the number of women, immigrants and minorities in the workplace as well as an ageing workforce. Worldwide, the global economy and population projections also point to an increasingly heterogeneous workforce. Heterogeneity in the workforce, although often targeted, is not itself the problem; rather, the issue is a lack of knowledge and skills to manage diversity effectively and creatively to leverage strategic advantage (Gardenswartz and Rowe 1998).

## 3. Critical issues and topics

### The global context

The phrase 'global context' is used here to refer to the conditions of globalization that shape intercultural communication today. Although the term 'globalization' came into common usage in the 1990s to describe our rapidly changing world, the various factors and forces that constitute and shape globalization have been in play for a much longer time (Nederveen Pieterse 2009). Globalization is a complicated and contested concept with multiple and layered meanings that is understood and experienced in a broad array of ways by individuals and groups with different interests, positionalities and points of view. I define globalization as the complex web of economic, political and technological forces that have brought people, cultures and markets, as well as beliefs, practices and ideologies, into increasingly greater proximity to and con/disjunction with one another within inequitable relations of power (Sorrells 2010). The word 'globalization' is used here to address the contested processes that contribute to the vastly inequitable conditions of living in our contemporary world.

The frequent and multidirectional movement of capital, commodities, services, information, labour and ideologies in the global context is driven by shifts in international economic policies and global political governance that have taken place since WWII, and have accelerated dramatically since the 1980s (Stiglitz 2002). Economic liberalization, also known as 'free' trade, is the cornerstone of neo-liberal globalization. Neo-liberalism is based on government deregulation, a shift of responsibility from the public sector to individuals and the privatization of public space, issues, industries and resources (Harvey 2005). Characterized by growth in multinational corporate power, an intensification of international trade and international webs of production, distribution and consumption and the displacement of hundreds of thousands of people from their homes, jobs and countries, neo-liberal globalization has exponentially increased and dramatically affected intercultural interactions worldwide.

In the context of neo-liberal globalization, wealth concentration has intensified and economic inequity exacerbated both within and across nations, resulting in vastly disparate access to resources and deepening racial inequities (Toro-Morn and Alicea 2004). Today, between 15 and 22 per cent of the people on our planet wake up each morning assured of instantaneous communication with others around the globe (Shoenfeld 2009), whereas more than 50 per cent of the world's population lives below the internationally defined poverty line, starting their day without the basic necessities of food, clean water and shelter (United Nations 2004). In an era of instant messages and global communication, one out of five adults in the world does not have the skills to read and write (UNESCO 2010). Today, for every dollar an average white family owns in the US, the average family of colour has less than a dime, magnifying the racial wealth gap accrued from centuries of discriminatory and exclusionary laws and practices (Lui *et al.* 2006). In the global context, friends, migrants, tourists, business people and students from diverse cultures come into contact more rapidly than ever before in the history of human interaction; yet, some have the privilege of experiencing intercultural interactions in corporate boardrooms, in universities and through tourism, whereas other people, displaced from their home, are forced to eke out their basic survival as refugees of the global economy.

Clearly, the global context has dramatically altered the conditions that enable, shape and constrain intercultural communication. First, intercultural interactions and exchange have increased exponentially as a result of advanced communication, information and transportation technologies. Second, global intercultural interdependence has escalated as changes in economic and political policies, governance and institutions usher in a new era of shared interests, needs and resources. Third, as intercultural and transnational interdependence increases, intercultural misunderstanding, tension and conflict have also intensified. Fourth, economic disparity has magnified within and across nation-states based on flows of capital, labour and access to education and technology exacerbating existing inequalities. Finally, asymmetrical geopolitical and economic relationships of power forged through colonization, Western domination and US hegemony, although reconfigured today, continue to define and shape intercultural relations.

In the global context, the 'West' and the US are not by any means the only centres of economic, political and cultural production and power (Ong 1999; Shome and Hegde 2002); yet, the field of intercultural communication that provides the theoretical knowledge, conceptual framework and practical strategies for intercultural training is rooted in Western, white perspectives, colonial modes of thinking and imperial knowledge production (Asante 1987; Mendoza 2005; Miike 2003). The implications for intercultural training of the complex, contradictory and increasingly inequitable global context are explicated through a discussion of four critical trends.

## 4. Current contributions and research

First, I explore how the central concept of 'culture', as theorized in intercultural communication and operationalized in intercultural training, is undergoing a process of redefinition to more adequately address the complexities of culture in the global context. Second, I discuss the emerging emphasis in the intercultural communication field on broader historical contexts and geopolitical relationships of power, resulting in more systemic approaches to training in intercultural communication. Third, I address the increasing importance of technology and the focus on various forms of 'intelligences' in intercultural training today. Finally, I discuss the turn towards social justice and global engagement in intercultural training.

## Redefining culture

Historically anthropological perspectives, defining culture as shared values, norms, behaviours and ways of thinking, have provided the foundation for the field of intercultural communication and intercultural training. Much of intercultural training is based on concepts, models and dimensions of culture developed by anthropologists and cross-cultural psychologists (Bhawuk and Brislin 1992; Hofstede 1991; Triandis 1995; Trompenaars and Hampden-Turner 1997) that are typically operationalized in terms of national culture. Recently, the strong reliance on such models for intercultural training in the global context has been questioned for a number of reasons. Values orientation models based on dichotomous dimensions (high/low context, individualistic/collectivistic, high/low power distance, for example) are criticized as oversimplified, limiting and potentially counterproductive for addressing the complex dimensionality and multifaceted identities that characterize intercultural interactions in the global context.

Consider the following training situations:

- US students from various ethnic, racial and class backgrounds participate in a pre-departure orientation training programme preparing them for their sojourns in Europe and Latin America.
- A culturally diverse group of managers from a multinational corporation who move frequently and for short periods of time in and out of various multicultural team contexts in Europe and Asia gather in Amsterdam for intercultural leadership training.
- International business management students from various countries in Asia attend an intercultural communication training course in New Zealand.

In each case, useful generalizations may undoubtedly be made based on national culture of origin, location or destination; yet, the subcultural ethnic, racial, religious, class and/or organizational influences shaping the participants and the environments they will enter in the global context are likely to be as salient as national cultural characteristics. US students studying abroad today represent the multicultural diversity of the country. The environments where students are placed – in the scenario above, in families, communities and universities in Europe and Latin America – are characterizes by increasing hybridity and diversity as well. Given the complexities of intercultural interactions in the twenty-first century, the diversity of cultural tendencies within nations and the dramatic geopolitical shifts that have occurred in the last 20 years, frameworks of cultural variation based on national culture often lead to overgeneralizations and stereotypes that are counterproductive in intercultural training.

Historically, intercultural training has prepared managers to work in one new culture, often focusing on culture-specific knowledge. Yet, researchers and practitioners Earley and Peterson (2004) argue that knowledge of culture-specific values does not translate into effective interpersonal interactions when managers in the global workforce move rapidly across various and diverse multicultural contexts, such as the participants in the intercultural leadership training described above. Too easily, sophisticated stereotypes of national cultures are substituted for multidimensional cultural realities with the result of limiting rather than explaining the effects of culture on human interaction (Thomas 2008).

Asian students studying international management in New Zealand, as described above, may argue that the values orientation frameworks are not only inaccurate based on their knowledge of their own cultures but also that the frameworks can perpetuate neo-colonial perspectives that normalize global economic asymmetry and injustice, promote ethnocentrism and Western hegemony and devalue the humanity of countries who are less firmly articulated in global capitalism. Like European colonial cartographers who positioned the West as the geopolitical centre of the world and misrepresented the sizes and shapes of continents, the uncritical use in intercultural training of theories and models that de-historicize and de-politicize intercultural communication produces systematic distortions of the world (Munchi and McKie 2001).

Thus, a redefinition of our concept of culture in the global context is required. Culture necessarily implies shared meaning; yet, attention only to shared meaning privileges dominant readings or majority group experiences and obscures the dynamic, multifaceted and negotiated aspects of culture (Appadurai 1996). Critical/cultural studies perspectives define culture as a site of struggle where meanings are continually negotiated and contested within inequitable relations of power (Grossberg *et al.* 1992). This definition reveals how culture can function as a form of hegemony, or domination through consent, as articulated by Italian Marxist theorist Antonio Gramsci (1973). Hegemony operates when the goals, ideas and interests of the ruling group or class are so thoroughly normalized, institutionalized and accepted that people consent to their own domination, subordination and exploitation.

Cultural studies theorists argue that individuals and groups have the potential to challenge, resist and transform meanings in their subjective, everyday lives. Fiske (1992: 157) states, 'The social order constrains and oppresses people, but at the same time offers them resources to fight against those constraints', noting that individuals and groups are consumers and producers of cultural meanings and can act in counter-hegemonic ways. Culture, then, is the 'actual, grounded terrain' of everyday practices, representations, discourses and institutions where meanings are produced, consumed, negotiated and contested (Hall 1997).

Emerging approaches in intercultural training define culture as *both* 'shared meaning' *and* as 'contested meaning', which challenges static and dichotomous notions of culture, · disrupts essentialized concepts of cultural identities and addresses the complexities of culture in the global context (Sorrells and Nakagawa 2008; Sorrells 2010). Specifically, dichotomous cultural variation frameworks traditionally used in training are now more frequently accompanied by clear and directed discussions regarding the limitations and potential pitfalls of these models. Countering firm correlations between nationality and cultural orientation and acknowledging the de-territorialized and re-territorialized nature of culture in the global context (Appadurai 1996; Inda and Rosaldo 2002), intercultural trainers are moving towards approaches that highlight the complex, multidimensional and dynamic nature of culture and intercultural interactions in the global context (Earley and Peterson 2004; Englebert 2004). Although typologies of cultural variation can provide a first yet limited step towards the understanding of difference in intercultural business and other environments, attention to situational contexts and cultural histories is increasingly emphasized (Osland and Bird 2000).

## Taking contextual and systemic approaches

Following approaches in the field of intercultural communication, intercultural training has traditionally de-emphasized or ignored the roles that history and power play in intercultural interactions. Intercultural training, with its roots in the US, has generally stressed pragmatic approaches that facilitate effective interpersonal communication without much attention to how interpersonal communication is shaped and affected by intergroup or international interactions – either historical or current. Although attention to face-to-face interpersonal interaction in the present moment is important, this orientation often neglects and obscures critical historical dynamics as well as present-day events that have a tremendous influence on communication in business, relational, intergroup and international contexts. Extracting intercultural communication from historical, political and economic contexts also masks the inequitable relations of power between individuals, groups, organizations and countries that often play a major role in contouring intercultural relations. The introduction of the textbook, *Intercultural Communication in Contexts*, in the late 1990s by Judith Martin and Thomas Nakayama (1997) and emerging attention to critical perspectives on intercultural communication (Nakayama and Halualani 2010) provide the theoretical and conceptual foundations for teaching and training about intercultural communication within broader historical, economic and political contexts.

Returning to the brief scenarios introduced above illustrates the significance of broader contexts for intercultural communication training. Leaders in global corporations must be aware of the impact of situational contexts, historical alliances and enmities as well as existing configurations of geopolitical power in order to manage a diverse multinational workforce. Additionally, it is important to ask who has access to intercultural training. Is the knowledge and information imparted about effective intercultural communication the privilege of global elites? Szkudlarek (2009: 981) notes that the disproportionate access to intercultural training in the West compared with the training available in Asia, African and South America can, itself, serve as a 'manipulative tool, a new instrument for maintaining inequalities'.

Similarly, students studying abroad, like all sojourners, whether students, business people or refugees, are subject to attitudes and treatment based on the assumptions and perceptions held by members of host or receiving countries. Historical and current intergroup relations and geopolitical configurations can and do affect everyday intercultural interactions. This seems obvious; yet, although some emphasis has been placed on host culture environmental influences on sojourner or migrant adaptation (Kim 2001), intercultural training has often neglected to address the ways intercultural communication is inextricably interwoven and articulated in historical and current intergroup relations as well as macro-level geopolitical contexts.

It is also important to note the attitudes of host country members towards a particular national group: 'Americans', for example, are not homogenous, nor are the identities of the students travelling with US passports. The experiences of white American, black American, Latino/a, Arab American and Asian American students studying abroad in Europe or Latin America will vary, notably based on how each is perceived racially, how constructs of 'race' are understood locally as well as on intersecting gender, class, religious and sexual orientation identities. The experiences of students of diverse ethnic, racial and religious backgrounds who participate in a study abroad programme are also inevitably linked to historical and current events. Situating intercultural communication within historical, political and economic contexts highlights the links between historical and contemporary conditions and acknowledges the role power, privilege and positionality play in intercultural communication. Increasingly, training and curricula for study abroad programmes focus at least some attention on broader macro-level geopolitical, economic and historical contexts.

Taking an even broader view, the historical context of the past 500 years of colonization, which includes the anti-colonial and independence struggles, civil rights and alter-globalization movements, is also critical for understanding intercultural communication and implementing intercultural training programmes today. How can we address issues that arise in intercultural training, for example regarding South to North migration patterns today – from former colonies to centres of imperial power – without situating globalization within the broader context of colonization? What are the implications of training global managers in intercultural relations in the global context where 'free' trade policies enable the outsourcing of jobs by wealthier more powerful nations to poorer less powerful nations without acknowledging how these policies and practices recreate conditions for the exploitation of labour, the consolidation of economic wealth and political power parallel to the colonial period? How can we train for effective intercultural communication and grapple with the intercultural challenges facing our world today – racial and ethnic discrimination, intensified economic inequity and disputes over immigrant rights and immigration policies – without recognizing how these struggles are embedded in and structured by ideologies about race, class and nation forged and institutionalized through the last 500 years of colonization and Western hegemony?

As noted by Judith Martin and Teresa Harrell (2004), the emergence of critical approaches to intercultural communication and the dramatic impact of globalization on intercultural communication are influencing research on cultural adaptation and re-entry scholarship. Intercultural training for study abroad programmes, in pre-departure orientations and re-entry training, is gradually incorporating a degree of focus on broader macro-level historical, social and political contexts as pertinent to students' international experience. Depending upon the type of study abroad programme and the sponsoring university or organization, intercultural training designs are addressing relationships of geopolitical and economic power between sending and host countries. To varying degrees, study abroad programmes engage participants in discussions about the roles privilege based on nationality, class, race, ethnicity, gender and sexual orientation may have on their study abroad experience.

Increasingly, attention to the micro-level interpersonal level of interactions is coupled with broader views that take macro-level historical relationships as well as present-day events into account. An emerging approach for intercultural communication trainers in multinational corporate settings employs a systems approach to facilitate the analysis of issues and development of effective plans of action. Loosely based on general systems theory (Bertalanffy 1968) and systems thinking (Senge 1990), multinational and multicultural organizations are viewed as systems that are situated within larger economic, political and cultural systems. Introducing a systems approach or systems thinking in intercultural training highlights the complexity of the whole while viewing the interrelationship between and influence among increasingly larger systems from the organizational culture to the broader global business culture.

## Integrating teams, technologies and intelligences

Advances in communication, information and transportation technologies are defining characteristics of the global context that significantly alter the conditions of intercultural communication. The compression of space and time that accompany advanced technologies translates into workplaces and work teams that are not only increasingly culturally diverse but also geographically dispersed, which has resulted in the emergence of virtual global teams. As working effectively in multicultural and multinational teams gains priority in organizations, research and training directed towards intercultural teams has increased (Adler 2008; Guilherme *et al.* 2010).

Thomas (2008) notes that the cultural composition of work groups affects group effectiveness in three interrelated ways: (1) cultural norms about how work groups function and how they are structured; (2) cultural diversity or the number of different cultures in the group; and (3) relative cultural distance or the degree to which members of the group are culturally different from one another. Cultural diversity tends to increase the time required for multicultural groups to complete tasks and initially lowers performance rates compared with homogeneous groups;

yet, over time, greater cultural diversity can also increase creativity, broaden a group's perspectives and resources, resulting in higher quality decision making (Adler 2008; Earley and Mosakowski 2000). In brainstorming, culturally diverse groups generate more creative, high-quality ideas and are more effective than homogeneous teams in identifying problems and producing solutions.

Virtual teams that must communicate across time zones, national borders and cultural frames use a wide variety of technologies to bridge potentially vast differences and discontinuities. According to *Virtual Teams Survey Report 2010: The Challenges of Working in Virtual Teams*, 80 per cent of corporate managers work in virtual teams part of the time, and over 60 per cent consider themselves part of virtual teams. Yet, only 60 per cent of the respondents indicated that virtual teams were successful, citing time zones, language, communication styles and cultural differences as the biggest challenges (Solomon 2010). Survey respondents called for more face-to-face communication interaction and the use of collaborative technologies such as videoconferencing to bridge the challenges of cultural differences and distance in the global workplace.

Based on in-depth qualitative and quantitative research on virtual teams across national and organizational cultures, Gibson and Manuel (2003) emphasize trust as critical in virtual teams. Many factors that contribute to building and repairing trust, such as proximity, similarities in background and experience as well as interpersonal affective cues, are lacking in virtual interactions. Although cultural differences are identified as a significant impediment to building trust in virtual multicultural teams, intercultural training that provides knowledge and skills about communication style differences and focuses on creating supportive communicative climates, developing active listening skills, empathy and giving constructive feedback can improve the effectiveness of virtual teams.

In the global context, where managers, workplace teams, educators and leaders interact with multiple and varied cultural groups, a trend towards developing and enhancing intelligences for managing individual, team and organizational diversity is evident. Specifically, research and training on emotional intelligence and diversity (EID) (Gardenswartz et al. 2008) and cultural intelligence (CQ) (Earley and Ang 2003) are summarized here.

Extending the notion of emotional intelligence (Goleman 1995) to address today's diverse world, 'EID encompasses the ability to feel, understand, articulate, manage and apply the power of emotions to interactions across lines of cultural difference' (Gardenswartz et al. 2010: 76). Differences can and often do trigger powerful emotional reactions and behaviours in the highly diverse contexts in which individuals and groups engage and work today requiring emotional intelligence. The EID model is composed of four interdependent dynamics: (1) 'affirmative introspection' is an ongoing process combining self-awareness and insight with self-reflection on one's own values, preferences, biases and worldviews; (2) 'self-governance' is the act of managing one's reactions to difference in such a way that enables behavioural choices and responses that are constructive rather than destructive; (3) 'intercultural literacy' focuses on investigating and understanding the norms, beliefs, behaviours and values of others; (4) 'social architecting' involves consciously structuring our interactions and environments as intercultural communicators and interpreters to create mutually beneficial and productive relationships (Gardenswartz et al. 2010).

EID is useful in developing effectiveness and leveraging creativity for diverse teams who may experience differences as impediments or barriers.

EID provides an approach to creating and reinforcing healthy norms, which empowers teams to perform closer to their potential. Applying EID at the team level requires developing skills, competencies, and norms for creating teams that embrace differences in style, priorities, viewpoints, motivations, and talent.

*Gardenswartz* et al. *(2010: 80)*

At the organizational level, balancing shared organizational values with respect for individual uniqueness is at the centre of an emotionally intelligent workplace.

Earley and Ang (2003) first described cultural intelligence (CQ) in their book *Cultural Intelligence: Individual Interactions across Cultures* as the capacities of a person to adapt to new cultural settings through cognitive, motivational and physical means. CQ can be developed to improve cultural perceptions, gain knowledge and appreciation of differences and guide culturally appropriate behaviour, which increases success in business practices in the global context (Earley and Mosakowski 2004). The Cultural Intelligence Scale is used to measure an individual's cultural quotient or cultural intelligence, with a higher score indicating greater capacities for intercultural competence. The three fundamental elements of CQ are: metacognition and cognition (thinking, learning and strategizing); motivation (efficacy, confidence, value congruence and affect for the other culture); behaviour (social mimicry and behavioural repertoire) (Earley and Peterson 2004: 105).

Proponents of CQ argue that it is a particularly useful tool for assessing and training global managers who frequently and rapidly move through diverse cultural contexts. Intercultural training designed with attention to particular managers' unique strengths and weaknesses increases the effectiveness of training interventions. In addition to developing global managers, CQ competences are presented as critical for diverse work teams.

Our point here is success for multinational teams does not lie with cultural values training or broad orientations to diversity. Rather, it requires specific CQ competencies held by members to uncover commonality across its membership, effective and appropriate role allocations, and clearly defined rules for interaction based on the specific needs (i.e., some cultural and some individual) and interests of team members.

*Earley and Peterson (2004: 112)*

## Engaging global citizenship and social justice

As economic and political landscapes are restructured through globalization, educational institutions around the world are increasingly focusing on and allocating resources for global education and internationalization as well as the development of multicultural, global and cosmopolitan citizenship. To address the complex and shifting dynamics of inclusion and exclusion in global, national and local communities, these programmes, to varying degrees, are grounded in civic engagement, democratic participation, equality and social justice. Regional, national and institutional educational policies and curricula as well as teacher training, foreign language and study abroad programmes have been affected (Banks 2004; Guilherme 2002).

Although discussion and critique of these broad educational initiatives is beyond the scope of this chapter, it is important to note the emergence, in the context of globalization, of an 'activist turn' in the field of intercultural communication that links scholarly efforts with

action that attempts to make a positive difference in situations where people's lives are affected by oppression, domination, discrimination, racism, conflict, and other forms of cultural struggle due to differences in race, ethnicity, class, religion, sexual orientation, and other identity markers.

*Broome* et al. *(2005: 146)*

Drawing on existing research and practices, the field of intercultural communication is particularly well positioned to contribute to knowledge, attitudes, practices and strategies to engage multiple and diverse voices, build alliances and solidarity across various and shifting positionalities and contribute to a world where equity and justice are the norm not the exception (Allen *et al.* 2002; Broome *et al.* 2005; Collier *et al.* 2001).

In the global context, as intercultural scholars, teachers, trainers and practitioners draw more frequently on critical theoretical and pedagogical approaches, teaching and training goals are augmented to include informed action for social change. A central goal in critical approaches to intercultural communication includes challenging systems of domination, critiquing hierarchies of power and confronting discrimination to create a more equitable world (Nakayama and Halualani 2010).

As a critical practice, pedagogy's role lies not only in changing how people think about themselves and their relationship to others and the world, but in energizing students and others to engage in those struggles that further possibilities for living in a more just society.

*Giroux 2004: (63–64)*

Study abroad and re-entry training programmes illustrate the increasing importance of civic engagement and social change in intercultural training. Levin (2009: 9) argues that, although the US lags behind European and Asian study abroad programmes in leveraging international education for workforce preparedness and economic competitiveness, 'it stands in front in using the study abroad experience to instil in students a sense of civic responsibility and action'. More frequently today, study abroad programmes require students to work in community service organizations and research projects addressing critical social and environmental issues. Gradually, more and more students returning to the US from study abroad programmes are encouraged to engage their heightened social consciousness by networking with organizations and activists, educating people in their local communities about their experiences and linking their experiences in host countries with social and political issues at home. For example, after Peter Quaranto studied in 2005 in Uganda with SIT Study Abroad and witnessed the horrors of the war in northern Uganda, he and other SIT alumni formed UgandaCAN, the Uganda Conflict Action, to raise awareness of the conflict, advocate for the victims and bring peace through political pressure from the US (World Learning SIT 2008: 10–11).

Noting that study abroad programmes cultivating civic engagement and social justice are still the minority, Levin (2009: 9–11) offers several recommendations for higher education administrators and study abroad practitioners, which include: promoting study abroad as a means to prepare students to meet the challenges of globalization; integrating global citizenship-oriented study abroad programmes into the university curriculum such that students gain an understanding of global systems and knowledge of the culture, history, geography and politics of host countries; structuring study abroad programmes to achieve global learning goals and encourage international teamwork and promote civil participation; and broadening the inclusiveness so that study abroad programmes are available to all students not only those who are more economically advantaged.

Following earlier landmark research projects on cross-cultural effectiveness (Kealey 1989) and intercultural competence (Fantini 2006), *Beyond Immediate Impact: Study Abroad for Global*

*Engagement* (SAGE) examines the ways in which intercultural experiences, in the form of study abroad during college years, influence participants' long-term globally oriented behaviours, referred to as 'global engagement' in the study (Paige *et al.* 2009).

> Global engagement, as conceptualized by the SAGE project, is expressed by civic commitments in domestic and international arenas; knowledge production of print, artistic, online, and digital media; philanthropy in terms of volunteer time and monetary donations; social entrepreneurship, meaning involvement in organizations whose purpose and/or profits are to benefit the community, and the practice of voluntary simplicity in one's lifestyle.
>
> *Paige* et al. *(2009: 29)*

The study, surveying 6,000 study abroad participants, found that study abroad programmes are one of the most important and meaningful experiences undergraduate students can have. SAGE clearly documents the multiple ways in which returnees are engaged globally and provides empirical evidence for the positive impact of study abroad on global engagement. Through quantitative and qualitative data, the study demonstrates the profound influence that study abroad experiences have on developing global engagement (Paige *et al.* 2009).

## 5. Recommendations for practice

In the previous section, I explicated four trends in intercultural communication and training in the global context, including redefining the notion of 'culture,' emphasizing broader historical and geopolitical contexts, focusing on teams, technology and 'intelligences' and turning towards social justice and global engagement in intercultural training today. Some of the ways in which these trends are translated into practice and manifest in intercultural training design have already been mentioned. Yet, several broad recommendations are useful in developing effective intercultural training in the global context.

First, the methods used to address cognitive, behavioural and affective aspects of intercultural learning such as critical incidents, case studies, role play and simulations – to name a few of the most common – need to be adapted and modified to address the complex, contradictory and often contested nature of intercultural communication today. For example, methods for intercultural training commonly used to engage cognitive learning – critical incidents and case studies – need to reflect the complicated and multifaceted nature of cultural identities and intercultural interactions today; otherwise, intercultural trainers risk reinforcing stereotypes, creating hierarchies of difference and participating in the construction of the 'Other'.

Additionally, facilitation of intercultural training in the global context requires sufficient knowledge and skills to unpack multifaceted, layered and potentially contentious issues that emerge when questions of power and privilege as well as broader historical and current economic and geopolitical concerns are addressed. In other words, intercultural trainers need training and practice to learn how to effectively facilitate difficult dialogues, to address contrasting standpoints and positionalities and to foster participants' interest and commitment to social justice and global engagement. Reaffirming a foundational premise of the field, intercultural trainers must embrace and foster a 'learning how to learn' approach to adequately address the rapidly changing conditions, tremendous challenges and creative potential of intercultural communication in the global context.

Finally, to translate theory into practice, I recommend engaging in and training for intercultural praxis, a process of critical, reflective enquiry and engaged analysis that leads to informed action for social justice (Sorrells and Nakagawa 2008; Sorrells 2010). Intercultural praxis operates as engaged communicative action informed by an understanding of the positionalities and standpoints of the communicators and is exercised within and is responsive to particular, concrete temporal and spatial contexts that produce historical and sociopolitical as well as local and global conditions.

Through six interrelated points of entry – enquiry, framing, positioning, dialogue, reflection and action – intercultural praxis utilizes our multifaceted identity positions and shifting access to privilege and power to develop allies, build solidarity, imagine alternatives and intervene in struggles for global engagement, social responsibility and justice. From these points of entry, intercultural praxis may be manifest in a range of forms such as simple or complex communication competences, oppositional tactics and creative, improvisational and transformational interventions. All moments in our day – when we make choices about what we consume, when we are confronted with sexist, racist, homophobic, classist and other discriminatory language, structures and inequitable conditions and when we develop relationships and build alliances with friends, co-workers, bosses and strangers – provide opportunities to engage in intercultural praxis.

Intercultural praxis offers trainers, educators and learners a conceptual framework along with the skills and strategies to address the complexities of intercultural communication in the global context. Intercultural praxis focuses attention on issues of power, privilege and positionality and utilizes a systemic approach that requires practitioners to think, reflect and act critically and multidimensionally. Engaging in intercultural praxis calls for multifocal vision that emphasizes the links between the local and global as well the connections between historical and contemporary conditions. Lastly, intercultural praxis offers a blueprint for envisaging intercultural training as a site for global engagement and social justice.

## 6. Future directions

The trends outlined in the earlier section indicate some future directions for intercultural training as practitioners – trainers and educators – grapple with the challenges and opportunities of the global context. Clearly, the multiple uses and, perhaps, misuses of technologies in our late-capitalist global world will continue to amaze, confound and demand innovation from intercultural trainers and practitioners. Addressing the challenges of virtual communication, virtual team-building and management as well as ways to maximize the potential for training opportunities through technology will, based on current trajectories, increasingly require attention. Additionally, as organizations in business, education, non-profit and governmental contexts recognize the importance of intercultural communication in the global context and wrestle with challenging budget constraints, intercultural training will likely find itself more integrated into other types of training such as resource management, public and community relations and organizational development. Although this trend towards 'mainstreaming' intercultural training indicates an acknowledgement and acceptance of intercultural issues as central in a variety of arenas, it could also result in diluted and canned versions of intercultural training as well as facilitators whose main knowledge area is not intercultural communication.

Additionally, the use of various instruments to quantify intercultural competence and intelligence will probably continue and gain even greater importance in the future. This future direction can contribute in significant ways to our understanding of intercultural effectiveness and, in turn, inform intercultural training programmes. One danger that can be foreseen is that instruments that claim to measure innate tendencies for intercultural competence will be used in predictive and restrictive ways rather than as means to point to areas that need development.

Specifically, tools that claim to offer employers the ability to predict employees' innate capacities to function effectively in intercultural settings can easily be used to exclude employees from international assignments rather than as tools to identify areas for enhancement and training. In contexts where economic interests are the main criteria for decision making, assessment tools will probably serve as exclusionary gate-keeping mechanism rather than as a means to identify areas for growth.

Propelled by powerful forces into a fast-paced, technologically driven and yet devastatingly inequitable twenty-first century, the future direction of intercultural training exemplifies to a large extent the competing interests that frame our global context. The goals, role and direction of intercultural training occupy a precarious space between serving the interests of bottom-line marketability in business and education and serving the interests of social and economic justice. Although the challenges we face are never clearly delineated or dichotomous, an important question remains for the future: who benefits from the work of scholars and practitioners of intercultural training?

## Related topics

Citizenship; cultural history; culture; education abroad; essentialism; experiential learning; identity; intercultural praxis; power; race; stereotyping

## Further reading

Landis, D., Bennett, J.M. and Bennett, M.J. (2004) (eds) *The Handbook of Intercultural Training*, 3rd edn, Thousand Oaks, CA: Sage (the most comprehensive treatment of scholarship and practice related to intercultural training).

Nakayama, T.K. and Halualani, R.T. (eds) (2010) *The Handbook of Critical Intercultural Communication*, New York: Wiley-Blackwell (groundbreaking compilation of essays on critical/cultural studies approaches to intercultural communication).

Nederveen Pieterse, J. (2009) *Globalization and Culture: Global Mélange*, 2nd edn, Lanham, MD: Rowman and Littlefield (excellent review of competing theories and discourses on globalization and culture, where the author argues that cultural hybridization most accurately describes the complex processes of the global context).

## References

Adler, N. (2008) *International Dimensions of Organizational Behaviour*, 5th edn, Mason, OH: Thompson.

Allen, B.J., Broome, B.J., Jones, T.S., Chen, V. and Collier, M.J. (2002) 'Intercultural alliances: a cyberdialogue among scholar-practitioners', in M.J. Collier (ed.) *Intercultural Alliances: International and Intercultural Communication Annual*, Vol. 25, Thousand Oaks, CA: Sage, pp. 279–319.

Appadurai, A. (1996) *Modernity at Large: Cultural Dimensions of Globalization*, Minneapolis, MN: University of Minnesota.

Asante, M.K. (1987) *The Afrocentric Idea*, Philadelphia, PA: Temple University.

Banks, J.A. (1988) *Multiethnic Education: Theory and Practice*, 2nd edn, Boston, MA: Allyn and Bacon.

——(2004) *Diversity and Citizenship Education: Global Perspectives*, San Francisco, CA: Jossey Bass.

Banks, J.A. and Banks, C.A.M. (2003) *Handbook of Research on Multicultural Education*, 2nd edn, New York: Macmillan Publishing.

Barna, L. (1972) 'Stumbling blocks to intercultural communication', in D.S. Hoops (ed.) *Readings in Intercultural Communication*, Vol. 2, Pittsburgh, PA: Regional Council for International Education, pp. 27–34.

Batchelder, D. and Warner, E. (eds) (1977) *Beyond Experience: The Experiential Approach to Cross-Cultural Education*, Brattleboro, VT: Experiment Press.

Bertalanffy, L. (1968) *General Systems Theory*, New York: George Braziller.

Bhawuk, D.P. and Brislin, R.W. (1992) 'The measurement of intercultural sensitivity using the concept of individualism and collectivism', *International Journal of Intercultural Relations*, 16: 413–46.

Broome, B., Carey, C., De La Garza, S.A., Martin, J. and Morris, R. (2005) '"In the thick of things": a dialogue about the activist turn in intercultural communication', in W.J. Starosta and G.M. Chen (eds) *Taking Stock In Intercultural Communication: Where to now?*, International and Intercultural Communication Annual, Vol. 28, Thousand Oaks, CA: Sage, pp. 145–75.

Collier, M.J., Hegde, R.S., Lee, W.S., Nakayama, T.K., and Yep, G.A. (2001) 'Dialogue on the edges: ferment in communication and culture', in. M.J. Collier (ed.) *Trans-forming Communication about Culture: Critical New Directions*, International and Intercultural Communication Annual, Vol. 24, Thousand Oaks, CA: Sage, pp. 219–80.

Earley, P.C. and Ang, S. (2003) *Cultural Intelligence: An Analysis of Individual Interactions Across Cultures*, Palo Alto, CA: Stanford University Press.

Earley, P.C. and Mosakowski, E. (2000) 'Creating hybrid team cultures: an empirical test of international team functioning', *Academy of Management Journal*, 43: 26–49.

——(2004) 'Cultural intelligence', *Harvard Business Review*, October 2004: 139–46.

Earley, P.C. and Peterson, R.S. (2004) 'The elusive cultural chameleon: cultural intelligence as a new approach to intercultural training for the global manager', *Academy of Management Learning and Education*, 3(1): 110–15.

Englebert, S. (2004) '"Intercultural training" in exchange situations for experts and managers: a critical reflection', *Intercultural Education*, 15(2): 195–208.

Fantini, A.E. (2006) *Exploring and Assessing Intercultural Competence: Final Report of a Research Project*, Brattleboro, VT: Federation EIL.

Fiske, J. (1992) *Introduction to Communication Studies: Studies in Culture and Communication*, London: Methuen and Co.

Gardenswartz, L. and Rowe, A. (1998) *Managing Diversity: A Complete Desk Reference and Planning Guide*, New York: McGraw-Hill.

Gardenswartz, L., Cherbosque, J. and Rowe, A. (2008) *Emotional Intelligence for Managing Results in a Diverse World*, Mountain View, CA: Davies-Black.

——(2010) 'Emotional intelligence and diversity: a model for differences in the workplace', *Journal of Psychological Issues in Organizational Culture*, 1(1): 74–83.

Gibson, C.B. and Manuel, J.A. (2003) 'Building trust: effective multicultural communication processes in virtual teams', in C.B. Gibson and S.G. Cohen (eds) *Virtual Teams that Work: Creating Conditions for Virtual Team Effectiveness*, San Francisco, CA: Jossey-Bass, pp. 21–36.

Giroux, H.A. (2004) 'Cultural studies, public pedagogy, and the responsibility of intellectuals', *Communication and Critical/Cultural Studies*, 1(1): 47–59.

Gochenour, T. (ed.) (1995) *Beyond Experience: An Experiential Approach to Cross-cultural Education*, 2nd edn, Yarmouth, ME: Intercultural Press.

Goleman, D. (1995) *Emotional Intelligence: Why it Can Matter More Than IQ*, New York: Bantam.

Gramsci, A. (1973) *Selections from the Prison Notebooks*, New York: Harper and Row.

Grossberg, L., Nelson, C. and Treichler, P. (1992) *Cultural Studies*, New York: Routledge.

Guilherme, M. (2002) *Critical Citizens for an Intercultural World: Foreign Language Education as Cultural Politics*, Clevedon: Multilingual Matters.

Guilherme, M., Glaser, E. and Méndez-García, M.C. (eds) (2010) *The Intercultural Dynamics of Multicultural Working*, Bristol: Multilingual Matters.

Hall, E.T. (1959) *Hidden Silent Language*, New York: Doubleday.

——(1966) *Hidden Dimension*, New York: Doubleday.

Hall, S. (1997) 'Introduction,' In S. Hall (ed.) *Representation: Cultural Representations and Signifying Practices*, Thousand Oaks, CA: Sage, pp. 1–12.

Harvey, D. (2005). *A Brief History of Neoliberalism*, New York: Oxford University.

Hofstede, G.H. (1980) *Culture's Consequences: International Differences in Work-related Values*, Thousand Oaks, CA: Sage.

——(1991) *Cultures and Organizations: Software of the Mind*, London: McGraw-Hill.

Hoopes, D.S. (eds) (1970) *Readings in Intercultural Communication*, Vol. 1, Pittsburgh, PA: Regional Council for International Education.

——(1972) *Readings in Intercultural Communication*, Vol. 2, Pittsburgh, PA: Regional Council for International Education.

——(eds) (1973) *Readings in Intercultural Communication*, Vol. 3, Pittsburgh, PA: Regional Council for International Education.

Inda, J.I. and Rosaldo, R. (eds) (2002) *The Anthropology of Globalization: A Reader*. Cambridge: Blackwell.

International Organization for Migration (IOM) (2009) 'About migration'. Online. Available: www.iom.int/jahia/page3.html (accessed 29 January 2010).

Kealey, D.J. (1989) 'A study of cross cultural effectiveness: theoretical issues, practical application', *International Journal of Intercultural Relations*, 13(3): 387–428.

Kim, Y.Y. (2001) *Becoming Intercultural: An Integrative Theory of Communication and Cross-Cultural Adaptation*, Thousand Oaks, CA: Sage.

Leeds-Hurwitz, W. (1990) 'Notes on the history of intercultural communication: the Foreign Service Institute and the mandate for intercultural training', *Quarterly Journal of Speech*, 76: 262–81.

Levin, R. (2009) 'Transforming the study abroad experience into a collective priority', *Peer Review/AACandU*, Fall: 9–11.

Lui, M., Robles, B., Leondar-Wright, B., Brewer, R., and Adamson, R. (2006) *The Color of Wealth: The Story Behind the U.S. Racial Wealth Divide*, New York: New Press.

Martin, J.N. and Harrell, T. (2004) 'Intercultural re-entry of students and professions' in D. Landis, J.M. Bennett and M.J. Bennett (eds) *Handbook of Intercultural Training*, 3rd edn, Thousand Oaks, CA: Sage, pp. 309–36.

Martin, J.N. and Nakayama, T.K. (1997) *Intercultural Communication in Contexts*, Mountain View, CA: Mayfield.

Mendoza, S.L. (2005) 'Bridging paradigms: how not to throw out the baby of collective representation with the functionalist bathwater in critical intercultural communication', in W.J. Starosta and G. Chen (eds) *Taking Stock in Intercultural Communication: Where to Now?* Washington, DC: NCA, pp. 237–56.

Miike, Y. (2003) 'Toward an alternative metatheory of human communication: an Asiacentric vision', *Intercultural Communication Studies*, XII, (4): 39–64.

Munchi, D. and McKie, D. (2001) 'Toward a new cartography of intercultural communication: mapping bias, business and diversity', *Business Communication Quarterly*, 64(3): 9–22.

Nakayama, T.K. and Halualani, R.T. (eds) (2010) *The Handbook of Critical Intercultural Communication*, New York: Wiley-Blackwell, pp. 171–89.

Nederveen Pieterse, J. (2009) *Globalization and Culture: Global Mélange*, 2nd edn, Lanham, MD: Rowman and Littlefield.

Ong, A. (1999) *Flexible Citizenship: The Cultural Logics of Transnationality*, Durham, NC: Duke University.

Osland, J.S. and Bird, A. (2000) 'Beyond sophisticated stereotypes: cultural sense-making in context', *Academy of Management Executive*, 14: 65–79.

Paige, R.M., Fry, G.W., Stallman, E.M., Josić, J. and Jon, J. (2009) 'Study abroad for global engagement: the long-term impact of mobility experiences', *Intercultural Education*, 20: 29–44.

Pusch, M.D. (2004) 'Intercultural training in historical perspective', in D. Landis, J.M. Bennett and M.J. Bennett (eds) *The Handbook of Intercultural Training*, 3rd edn, Thousand Oaks, CA: Sage, pp. 13–36.

Senge, P. (1990) *The Fifth Discipline: The Art and Practice of the Learning Organization*, New York: Doubleday.

Shoenfeld, E. (2009) 'Internet Population Passes One Billion'. Online. Available: http://techcrunch.com/2009/01/23/comscore-internet-population-passes-one-billion-top-15-countries/ (accessed 22 September 2010).

Shome, R. and Hegde, R.S. (2002) 'Culture, communication and the challenge of globalization', *Critical Studies in Media Communication*, 19(2): 172–89.

Solomon, C. (2010) 'The challenges of working in virtual teams, Virtual teams survey report – 2010'. Online. Available: http://rw-3.com/VTSReportv7.pdf (accessed 5 December 2010).

Sorrells, K. (1998) 'Gifts of wisdom: an interview with Dr. Edward T. Hall,' *The Edge: The E-Journal of Intercultural Relations*, 1(3).

——(2010) 'Re-imagining intercultural communication in the context of globalization', in T.K. Nakayama and R.T. Halualani (eds) *The Handbook of Critical Intercultural Communication*, New York: Wiley-Blackwell, pp. 171–89.

Sorrells, K. and Nakagawa, G. (2008) 'Intercultural communication praxis and the struggle for social responsibility and social justice', in O. Swartz (ed.) *Transformative Communication Studies: Culture, Hierarchy and the Human Condition*, Leicester: Troubador, pp. 17–44.

Stiglitz, J. (2002) *Globalization and Its Discontents*, New York: W.W. Norton.

Storti, C. and Bennhold-Samaan, L. (1998) *Culture Matters: The Peace Corps Cross-cultural Workbook*, Washington, DC: Peace Corps.

——(1999) *Culture Matters: Trainer's Guide*, Washington, DC: Peace Corps.

Szkudlarek, B. (2009) 'Through Western eyes: insights into the intercultural training field,' *Organizational Studies*, 30: 975–86.

Thomas, D. (2008). *Cross-Cultural Management: Essential Concepts*, Thousand Oaks, CA: Sage.

Thomas, R.R. (1990) 'From affirmative action to affirming diversity', *Harvard Business Review*, 68: 107–17.

Toro-Morn, M.I. and Alicea, M. (2004) (eds) *Migration and Immigration: A Global View*, Westwood, CT: Greenwood.

Triandis, H.C. (1995) *Individualism and Collectivism*, Boulder, CO: Westview Press.

Trompenaars, F. (1993) *Riding the Waves of Culture: Understanding Diversity in Global Business*, 1st edn, Burr Ridge, IL: Irwin Professional.

Trompenaars, F. and Hampden-Turner, C. (1997) *Riding the Waves of Culture: Understanding Diversity in Global Business*, 2nd edn, New York: McGraw-Hill.

United Nations (2004) *World Economic and Social Survey 2003: Trends in the World Economy*, New York: United Nations.

UNESCO (2010) 'Literacy'. Online. Available: www.unesco.org/en/literacy/ (accessed 12 August 2010).

Wight, A.R. and Hammons, M.A. (1970) *Guidelines for Peace Corps Cross-cultural Training: Philosophy and Methodology*, Washington, DC: Peace Corps.

World Learning SIT (2008) *After Study Abroad: A Toolkit for Returning Students*. Online. Available at: www.worldlearning.org/OurWorld_documents/SITStudyAbroadReentryToolkit.pdf (accessed 18 September 2010).

World Tourism Organization (2008) *Statistics*. Online. Available: www.world-tourism.org/index.php (accessed 12 June 2010).

# 24

# Multiple strategies for assessing intercultural communicative competence

*Alvino E. Fantini*

## Overview

Assessment has sometimes been likened to "the tail that wags the dog". In other words, what we assess ultimately reflects what we consider to be most important. Assessment, therefore, solidifies the main purposes of a training or educational program—what we anticipate to be the outcomes, what participants are expected to know or to be able to do. Unfortunately, there is often a mismatch between assessment process and content, the assessment tools and strategies employed, and the objectives set forth. Stated another way, the assessment process and content, and tools and strategies employed, do not adequately nor appropriately measure what they should. Clearly, the purposes of training and education and the outcomes assessed must be inextricably linked; unfortunately, this is not always so in practice. This is especially the case when attempting to assess a complex phenomenon such as intercultural communicative competence (ICC).

A survey of intercultural communication courses in fifty American universities (Fantini 1997) and nearly 100 ICC assessment tools (Fantini 2006: Appendices F and G) reveals just this—that in many cases, course objectives and assessment processes are inadequately connected. And where external test instruments are also employed, many of these have a bias embedded that may or may not align with the course objectives. This bias arises from the particular view of intercultural competence held by the developers of the external tool, sometimes an incomplete or partial view, and often one that may or may not support the objectives set forth by trainers and educators. For these reasons, assessing intercultural competence is both an interesting and a challenging task, and many trainers and educators continue to search for better ways to monitor and measure the development of ICC in their participants.

Hence, although assessment may be "the tail", an examination of evaluative processes and content must start with "how" intercultural competence is conceptualized and the search for a definition of ICC that is holistic and complete: what is ICC? And what are the components that together contribute to such competence? Although these may appear to be basic questions, they are important ones, as a search of the literature and analysis of available assessment tools revealed a surprising array of responses to these questions, ones that are fundamental to our field, to our practices, and therefore to the assessment process itself.

## 2. The challenge

As stated above, lack of clarity about the nature of ICC makes its assessment especially challenging. This challenge is exacerbated by the myriad assessment instruments that have been developed in recent years, leaving many practitioners confused about what to assess, how to assess, and which tools to use. Some educators have even reported the experience of utilizing external assessment tools only to find that participants appeared to do less well at the end than at the beginning of an intercultural experience. Obviously, this is counterintuitive. Indeed, ICC is complex and, consequently, it is important to have a clear picture of what is involved, how to develop intercultural abilities in individuals preparing for a sojourn among people of other language–culture backgrounds, what these abilities are, and how to track their development and the eventual outcomes in sojourners during and following their experience.

Over the years, a number of important publications have attempted to answer these questions (e.g., Byram 1997; Deardorff 2004; Humphrey 2007; Martin 1989; Wiseman and Koester 1993, among others). A more extensive review of the literature, however, revealed a range of inconsistencies as well as commonalities that can help practitioners with these issues. Although Bennett (2008: 97) correctly reported some degree of convergence among researchers and practitioners, most often viewing intercultural competences " … as a set of cognitive, affective, and behavioural skills and characteristics … ", some inconsistencies cannot be easily dismissed. For example, the literature revealed an array of descriptive terms in use in addition to the term ICC. The terms included cross-cultural adaptation, cross-cultural awareness, cross-cultural communication, cultural competence, cultural or intercultural sensitivity, effective intergroup communication, ethnorelativity, intercultural cooperation, global competitive intelligence, intercultural interaction, intercultural effectiveness, metaphoric competence, transcultural communication, global mindedness, global mindset, and culture learning, among others. And this is only a partial list!

These terms and their underlying concepts find their way into the work of researchers and educators—in program literature, course objectives, lesson plans, and, of course, in approaches to assessment. A lack of general consensus (we have chosen to use the term ICC in this publication) leads to a diversity of approaches from start to finish. To make matters worse, one also finds that, having chosen a specific term, it is not uncommon to find that some practitioners address certain ICC components while ignoring others, use the terms inconsistently, and then proceed to focus on still other areas in their course or program.

Clearly, a higher degree of consensus is needed regarding what we believe to be the abilities and attributes that constitute intercultural competence and what makes up its component parts. Consensus around these areas will help us better state our training and educational objectives, our expectations, as well as aid in designing and implementing courses and programs to develop ICC in participants. Finally, it is fundamental to determining what and how to monitor and measure what is at the heart of our concern—the development of intercultural competence.

To help focus our approach to assessment, then, we revert to a definition of ICC cited earlier in this volume (see Chapter 16): intercultural competence is a complex of abilities needed to perform "effectively" and "appropriately" when dealing with others of a different language–culture background. This definition contains several aspects, each of which is important to assessing the results of our efforts: competence and perform/performance, complex of abilities, effectively and appropriately, and dealing with others. The following is a brief elaboration of each in terms of how they relate to assessment.

We normally interpret the "others" in this definition to refer to those of other languages and cultures (although it is also possible to consider individuals with the same language yet a

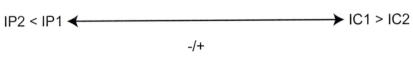

-/+

language-culture variables

*Figure 24.1* Continuum of social variables

different cultural background given the diversity found in many societies today). In fact, we find that whatever applies to inter*cultural* relations is also applicable to inter*personal* relations, i.e., dealing with others even within our own language–culture context. In the first case, where individuals are from "different" language–culture backgrounds, the number of sociocultural variables between interlocutors increases dramatically, whereas in the second situation, interlocutors may share many more common aspects, beginning with the same (or a similar) language. Even so, in every interaction, mediating variables always exist between interlocutors even despite similar backgrounds. These variables include factors such as age, gender, educational level, economic status, ethnic and religious differences, and so forth. Both of these possibilities are captured in Figure 24.1, which shows increasing or decreasing language–culture variables as one moves toward the right or left along the continuum.

To explain further, IP1 represents *inter*personal contact, whereas IC1 represents *inter*cultural contact. As one enters another culture more deeply (moving farther to the right), one possibly discovers IC2, representing the *intra*cultural aspect or the diversity that exists within most societies (aha! not all Greeks are alike!). At this point, generalizations and stereotypes often give way to more individualized distinctions. On the extreme left of the continuum, IP2 represents *intra*personal exploration, that is, the awareness of self, which increases as a result of the introspection and reflection that commonly ensues when dealing with people different from oneself. As one learns about others, one learns more about oneself.

Another important aspect of the definition above is the terms "effectively" and "appropriately". "Effectively" is an assessment made that is based on how one (and one's language–culture peers) judges one's competence in another culture, i.e., the "etic" or outsider's view. "Appropriately", on the other hand, is an assessment based on how one's competence is judged by one's hosts from their own cultural perspective, i.e., the "emic" or insider's view. Both perspectives are essential for a balanced, accurate, and complete assessment of abilities; unfortunately, the latter is seldom part of the assessment process. And although etic and emic perspectives often do not match, both are instructive in illuminating how each viewpoint is rooted in a differing perspective, a different worldview. Assessment that omits the emic perspective, however, whether in educational settings, training contexts, or field situations, results in a rather ethnocentric approach to the assessment of intercultural communication abilities in a foreign context. A more complete assessment, then, requires also obtaining information from one's hosts when evaluating cross-cultural abilities as their view is quite significant.

And finally, the terms "competence" and "performance" require some elaboration. In the Chomskyan sense, for example, "competence" refers to an abstraction and therefore it cannot be directly viewed. In this case, competences are inferred by observing "performance", and performance, of course, is evidenced by how one behaves, what one says, and what one does. Whether using this particular distinction or not, a degree of interpretation is involved when analyzing the data obtained and making sense of the evidence observed. These notions all have important implications for our discussion of assessment later on.

What type of performance, therefore, should be of concern? Should we infer competence from observable behaviors and interactions? The performance of individuals, in fact, includes a range of components consistently identified in the literature that are relevant to successful intercultural interactions, ones that facilitate intercultural entry and acceptance. These components are characteristics or attributes such as flexibility, humor, patience, openness, interest, curiosity, empathy, tolerance for ambiguity, and suspending judgments, among others; three areas or domains such as (1) the ability to establish and maintain relationships, (2) the ability to communicate with minimal loss or distortion, and (3) the ability to collaborate in order to accomplish something of mutual interest or need; four dimensions such as knowledge, (positive) attitudes/affect, skills, and awareness; and target language proficiency, an important component that is often ignored. All these components are directly affected, of course, by learner motivation, degree of contact, and duration of exposure in which interlocutors are able to develop these abilities (the longitudinal dimension) (Fantini 2006). Assessment, then, is dependent on devising ways to evaluate all these components. It becomes immediately apparent that assessment of each is not an easy task and, that assessment of multiple components will require multiple strategies conducted at various moments over time.

## 3. Coherence and quality

Once the basic ICC components are firmly established, we have solid ground on which to conceptualize, design, and implement training or educational programs, as well as to establish exactly what it is that we need to monitor and measure. Monitoring and measuring, of course, has to do with the entire assessment process. And, instead of "a tail that wags the dog", we now expand our view of assessment to think of it as a plan that must be an integral part of the entire educational design—from start to finish. In other words, assessment has to do with tracking the participants' movement toward the educational goals and their attainment of the stated objectives. Whereas the goals point to a long-term and future direction, the objectives are what we actually expect participants to achieve within the context of the program. As a future direction or orientation (extending beyond the course or program itself), goals are not measured, unlike objectives, which are. Objectives establish the outcomes expected of participants and, when attained, move the individuals closer in the direction of the goals. This is what assessment tries to determine.

The Gemstone model (Fantini 2000–2001), which is shown in Figure 24.2, depicts how the parts of a training or educational program are related, from needs assessment to evaluative assessment. Rather than list the parts sequentially, this model configures them around a circle, with intersecting lines that connect each item to every other one. Hence, although assessment is clearly linked to goals and objectives, it is also related to all other aspects of the curriculum plan.

Assessment is not something to be considered only at the middle or end of a process. It must be considered along with all the other parts, from the beginning. As one conducts a needs assessment and clarifies the educational precepts on which the program is based (e.g., inductive/deductive, teacher-centered/student-centered, traditional/experiential, etc.), which in turn guide the educational process, one is better able to establish clear goals and objectives. Clear goals and objectives facilitate curriculum and syllabus design, implementation (the content and process of each lesson plan), selection of the required resources, and the content and process of assessment (note that, although long-term assessment is included, it is normally what departments or institutions might do some time after the conclusion of the program to ascertain the long-term effects of the program cycle upon participants).

In the end, educational quality is a result of the degree to which all the curriculum parts cohere—the degree to which they are linked and support and reinforce each other. And quality

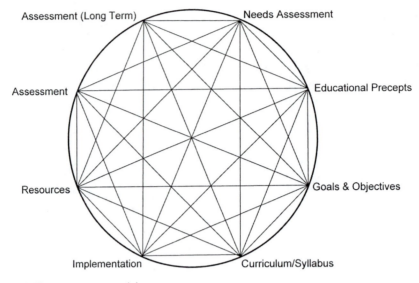

*Figure 24.2* The gemstone model
*Source*: Fantini (2000–2001: 100–5).

is further enhanced—like a precious gem placed into an appropriate ring mount—when the parts are appropriate for the context(s) for which they are designed.

## 4. Basic assessment principles

### Aspects of assessment

From among the multiple parts illustrated in the model above, we now turn our attention specifically to assessment. We begin by reviewing important aspects of the assessment process. Notice, first of all, that we speak of assessment as a "process", recognizing that we are not dealing solely with traditional sorts of assessment (i.e., tests or quizzes given at specific times, often at mid- and end-points of a course or program). Instead, our "process" approach bears a number of distinctive characteristics:

- as a process, it is ongoing and continuous (longitudinal);
- it is designed to monitor and measure the attainment of objectives over time;
- it utilizes both quantitative and qualitative measures;
- it measures competence by observing, interpreting, and documenting performance;
- it includes language proficiency as an essential component of ICC;
- it is multidimensional (i.e., self-evaluations, peer evaluations, teacher evaluations, and host evaluations);
- some of the tools and strategies are devised by the educator; externally designed instruments are used to support and supplement results, as appropriate;
- and assessment includes both etic and emic viewpoints in field situations.

In planning the assessment process, it is useful to keep in mind the following stages:

1. determine the purposes and uses for the assessment process;
2. identify the training or educational objectives (the what and the criteria to be used);

3. outline the assessment process (the when and how);
4. identify the items and tasks to be employed;
5. administer the assessment process at various stages;
6. score, rate, and document the results (ascertaining the relative weight of the different evaluative attempts);
7. analyze the items and tasks used for assessment;
8. distribute and report the results to all interested parties, as appropriate;
9. finally, use the findings to modify the training or educational design as needed.

Because the assessment process is used to evaluate a complex phenomenon, its implementation is necessarily multimodal, employing multiple strategies that are direct or indirect and/or discrete or global. For example, a "direct" strategy often takes the form of a quiz or test given at a designated time. Participants are told in advance and may have time to prepare for the test. "Indirect" assessment, on the other hand, is when assessment procedures are conducted during ongoing activities (e.g., a simulation, role play, discussion, etc.), during which students may or may not be aware of the assessment effort. Clear criteria must be established in advance to guide the assessor's observations and to reduce subjectivity. "Discrete" assessment refers to attempts to evaluate particular aspects and focuses on very specific items (e.g., a specific attribute, ability with a specific skill, knowledge of certain facts, etc.), whereas "global" assessment is concerned with holistic aspects of the participant's performance (the learner's motivation, attitude, engagement; how appropriate is the interaction, participation, etc.).

Strategies are often consciously and purposefully combined; however, in other cases, the choice of specific evaluative modes sometimes naturally combines strategies—for example, a quiz is both direct and discrete at the same time, and performative evaluation during a simulation may be both global and indirect. What is important, in either case, is that various strategies and tools are employed throughout the process to ensure a more accurate, more complete, and more reliable assessment result.

To summarize, assessing intercultural competence requires the combined use of a variety of modes and strategies. Examples of these include:

- strategies that involve objective scoring (e.g., matching items, true/false questions, multiple-choice questions, cloze or gap-filling items, etc.);
- oral and written activities (e.g., presentations, paraphrasing, essays, journals);
- active and passive activities (e.g., experiential activities, reports, problem-solving tasks, etc.);
- individual and interactive activities in pairs or small groups (e.g., discussions, debates, tasks, reflective activities, etc.);
- dialogs, interviews, presentations, etc.;
- demonstrations, poster sessions, simulations, role plays ;
- structured and unstructured field tasks and other experiential activities;
- questionnaires that require self-evaluation, peer evaluation, group evaluation, teacher evaluation, and/or host evaluation (triangulation).

Recent developments in the general field of assessment and in the specific areas of assessing intercultural competence provide further evaluative possibilities, facilitating the use of combinations of assessment types, modes, and strategies. These developments, in addition to more recent practices that include the learner in the evaluative process through self-evaluation, reflection, and feedback, help to generate better and more varied indicators of participant progress. Portfolio assessments, for example, constitute a now widely accepted approach that both improves the information obtained and enhances the learning process itself. When assembling a portfolio, a participant reviews materials and experiences, analyzes and synthesizes learning, selects salient aspects that best represent achievements, and reflects on the significance of the aspects chosen. Constructing a portfolio, then, is not only an assessment activity but enhances learning at the same time. When used together, portfolio and proficiency approaches provide an even more reliable assessment of intercultural competence. Finally, the increasing availability of a wide range of external assessment instruments enriches the possibility of combining teacher-devised assessment with other tools. These are discussed below.

## Assessing language proficiency

Target language proficiency, as important and relevant a component of competence as it is for an intercultural experience, is often left out of courses and programs designed to develop intercultural competence. This may occur because language is not always viewed as an ICC component and/or because language instruction may be treated as a separate area that is left to the purview of language educators. Yet, language is fundamental and integral to the notion of ICC discussed here (see also Chapter 16, this volume). Because of this expanded perspective, assessing the development of language proficiency is also treated here.

Despite numerous foreign language teaching methods that have emerged over the past 50 years, a communicative approach seems most effective where the main concern is the development of proficiency. A communicative approach emphasizes authentic communication and, consequently, it is interactive and participatory. It strives to develop proficiency in the four skill areas—comprehension, speaking, reading, and writing. And, in addition to abilities in linguistic aspects of language (i.e., grammar, vocabulary, etc.), it also addresses paralinguistic aspects (i.e., volume, pitch, tone, expressive dimensions, etc.), extralinguistic aspects (i.e., touching or haptics, kinesics or gesture and body movements, oculesics or eye contact patterns, proxemics or how space is used, olfactics or acceptable smells, and chronemics or the timing between the interactions of interlocutors) (see Chapter 8, this volume). Taken together, these several dimensions ensure effective and appropriate language use when interacting and communicating with one's hosts in their tongue (i.e., the sociolinguistic aspect). Viewed in this way, language educators and intercultural educators have much in common, and they must join together, overlap in their work, and provide useful and constructive redundancies that reinforce all the components that together constitute intercultural competence, albeit with differing emphases.

Developing foreign language abilities—especially with these expanded dimensions—is not a quick and easy task, and the amount of time required to achieve ascending levels of proficiency (whether in classroom or field situations) is usually underestimated. A more realistic idea of time can be obtained by consulting a language projection chart. One such chart (and assessment scale) was compiled by the US Foreign Service Institute (FSI) many years ago and later adapted for public education by the American Council on the Teaching of Foreign Languages (ACTFL) (a comparison of both systems may be viewed online at: www.sil.org/lingualinks/languagelearning/mangngyrlngglrnngprgrm/correspondenceofproficiencysca.htm).

Given a communicative approach, and the added possibility of field exposure, traditional assessment is clearly not adequate for evaluating language proficiency. Instead, proficiency assessment approaches are increasingly in use in places such as the United States (the ACTFL Proficiency Guidelines), the European Union (the Common European Framework of Reference for Languages or CEFR) (Council of Europe), and Australia (Australian Second Language Proficiency Ratings or ASLPR, later renamed the International Second Language Proficiency Ratings or ISLPR). These systems all stress communicative ability and employ several criteria for judging language development (e.g., comprehension, fluency, pronunciation, grammar control, and vocabulary in the ACTFL scale), and utilize scales that range from no proficiency to levels akin to that of a fluent or native speaker of the target language.

As will be seen in the examples provided below, most language assessment tools utilize a variety of modalities: dialoguing with the participant in the target language, questionnaires, portfolios, and so forth. In these tools, discrete details such as an incorrect verb form are subsumed within the total communication act and are important mostly for their effect on transmitting the message. In other words, importance is given to the global result of how well the learner communicates in the foreign tongue rather than on discrete linguistic items. The following are descriptions of five such instruments:

(1) ACTFL Proficiency Scale and Guidelines

*Purpose*: Measures foreign language proficiency
*Description*: This instrument establishes language proficiency levels that are based on five levels originally identified by the US Foreign Service Institute. The scale lists levels of communication functions, range of vocabulary, degree of accuracy, and conversational flexibility in four skill areas (comprehension, speaking, reading, and writing). Descriptions of each level help establish learning goals, plan learning activities, and evaluate proficiency.

Source: *American Council on the Teaching of Foreign Languages*
*(ACTFL), 1982, revised 1985. Information available online at:*
*www.sil.org/lingualinks/languagelearning/otherresources/*
*actflproficiencyguidelines/contents.htm*

(2) Assessment of Language Development (ALD)

*Purpose*: Measures foreign language development
*Description*: A questionnaire, in a YOGA format (Your Objectives, Guidelines, and Assessment), designed for self-assessment and also assessment by peers and teachers. This tool charts developing levels of language proficiency over time, providing normative, formative, and summative indicators.

Source: *SIT Graduate Institute. For copies and permission*
*to use, contact: alvino.fantini@sit.edu*

(3) European Language Portfolio (ELP)

*Purpose*: Assesses foreign language proficiency
*Description*: This tool, developed by the Council of Europe's Modern Languages Division, was piloted between 1998 and 2000 in fifteen countries, and launched throughout Europe in 2001. The instrument consists of a portfolio with three components—a language passport, a language biography, and a dossier—to help partners describe proficiency levels required by existing standards, tests, and examinations as well as to facilitate comparisons among differing systems of qualifications.

Source: *The Council of Europe's Modern Languages Division. Information available online at:*
*www.coe.int/t/dg4/portfolio/default.asp?l=e& m = /main_pages/welcome.html*

(4) International Second Language Proficiency Ratings (ISLPR) (formerly the Australian Second Language Proficiency Ratings (ASLPR); renamed in 1997)

*Purpose*: Assesses second language proficiency

*Description*: This instrument rates second language proficiency on a scale from zero to native-like, providing performative descriptors expressed in terms of practical tasks. Developed initially for English second language teaching, it was later adapted for English dialects in Australia and for use with various other languages.

Source: *Instrument developed by E. Wylie and D.E. Ingram in 1978 and revised in 1995. Information available online: www.apec.edu.tw/ research/eng_3_1.php*

(5) MAXSA (Maximizing Study Abroad) instruments

*Purpose*: Assesses foreign language strategies, culture learning strategies, and speech acts
*Description*: This tool consists of three instruments designed to assess strategies that learners use for language acquisition, intercultural development, and language gain. The first two, known as the Language Strategy Use Inventory and the Culture-Learning Strategies Inventory, were created for pre- and post-study abroad. The third is the Speech Act Measure available in English, Spanish, and French. All three instruments can be used as independent measures or within a broader study or program.

Source: *Website for the final report containing all three instruments (pp. 325–55) is www.carla.umn.edu/maxsa/documents/ MAXSAResearchReport.pdf*

## Assessing other components of intercultural competence

In addition to assessing target language proficiency, clearly, all the other components of intercultural competence cited above also need to be assessed. To reiterate, these include characteristics (or attributes), three areas (relationships, communication, and collaboration), and four domains (knowledge, attitudes/affect, skills, and awareness). All develop over time (hence the longitudinal dimension and the need to monitor and measure periodically). Because many of these are inferred through observations of performance, and because most components extend beyond cognitive areas (the usual focus of traditional education), multiple modes and multiple strategies in varying combinations are used throughout the assessment process. Although it is impossible to provide examples here of how each component might be assessed, examples can easily be accessed online. Here are some illustrations: (1) J. Mader (2009) *Testing the Untestable – Can Intercultural Competence Be Tested?* This presentation provides examples of good tests, criteria, and tasks to evaluate the three areas cited above in addition to several additional areas; (2) R. Camerer (2008) *Teaching and Testing Intercultural Competence*. This presentation also discusses various aspects of ICC and strategies for assessment; (3) K.M. Bailey (1998) *Learning about Language Assessment*. This publication discusses dilemmas, decisions, and directions for assessing language proficiency and provides abundant examples.

To further assist the multiple modes and strategies of assessment discussed above, it often helps to incorporate well-selected external assessment tools. The important thing to remember is that the assessment of intercultural competence needs to be multidimensional as well as multiperspective, ongoing, and integrated. By "integrated", what is meant is that the external tool must be carefully chosen to align and support the overall assessment effort. If the tool is not aligned, it may distract and confuse more than it may help.

To aid in this effort, then, let us consider a variety of examples of external instruments. Numerous instruments are available from several sources—some in journal publications, many are accessible online, and still others are available commercially. Commercially published instruments often require specialized training and/or are administered only by specialized agencies or organizations for a fee.

When selecting an instrument, investigate exactly what each instrument purports to measure and ensure that its purpose, approach, and content are compatible with the course or program objectives. The following questions may help guide you when selecting an external instrument (adapted in part from Deardorff 2004: 203):

- Is the external instrument compatible with your own goals and objectives?
- Does it contribute to the overall assessment plan?
- Does it share compatible theoretical foundations?
- Can it be used with any ethnic or national group, i.e., is it free of cultural bias?
- What is the instrument's validity and reliability (validity tells whether the test measures what it says it does, and reliability tells how well the instrument produces consistent results each time it is used)?
- Is it appropriate for the age and developmental level of those being assessed?
- What is required to administer the tool?
- How will the results be used (i.e., to inform the teaching/learning process, or for students, researchers, teachers, administrators, supervisors)?

The following are examples of twelve selected external instruments, followed by statements regarding their purpose, a description, and source. Upon comparison, the varied ICC conceptualizations (and the components measured) that are represented in each instrument become obvious. Some tools are predictive, whereas others are formative, normative, and/or summative. With the exception of the first instrument cited below, the remaining tools all assess intercultural competence without attention to language proficiency. Finally, although confirmed at the time of this writing, it goes without saying that URLs may change over time. (For a more extensive list of over ninety instruments, see Fantini 2006: 87–94.)

(1) Assessment of Intercultural Competence (AIC)

*Purpose*: To measure intercultural competence, including language proficiency
*Description:* This questionnaire, designed in a YOGA format (Your Objectives, Guidelines, and Assessment), is used for self-assessment and assessment by peers, teachers, and host mentors. The tool monitors the development of the intercultural competence of sojourners (and hosts) over time, providing normative, formative, and summative indicators. Long and short versions exist, and the tool is also available in English, British English, Swiss German, and Spanish. For the research on which the tool is based, go online to: www.experiment.org/resources.html (click on Final Report, then Appendix G); for a shorter version, go to: www.worldlearning.org/7803.htm (click on Occasional Papers Series Issue No. 1, scroll down to pp. 25–42).
Source*: For access and permission to use, contact: alvino.fantini@sit.edu*

(2) Behavioral Assessment Scale for Intercultural Communication (BASIC)

*Purpose*: Provides indicators of cross-cultural behavior
*Description:* This instrument explores cross-cultural equivalents of the Behavioral Assessment Scale for Intercultural Communication. Its eight scales are based on a study that identified significant skill profiles, validated with 263 university students.
Source: *Olebe and Koester (1989)*

(3) Beliefs, Events, and Values Inventory (BEVI)

*Purpose*: Measures personal disposition toward transformational experiences
*Description:* This tool is designed to predict various developmental, affective, and attributional processes and outcomes that explain the processes by which beliefs, values, and worldviews are acquired and maintained, why their alteration is typically resisted, and how and under what circumstances their modification occurs. It is proposed for assessing international learning and determines whether, how, and to what degree people are likely to be open to international experiences.

*Source: Craig N. Shealy, James Madison University (shealycn@jmu.edu).*
*Information available online at: www.acenet.edu/programs/international/fipse/*
*PDF/BEVI_Abstract.pdf*

(4) Cross-Cultural Adaptability Inventory (CCAI)

*Purpose*: Measures potential for cross-cultural adaptability
*Description:* A culture-general instrument designed to assess individual potential for cross-cultural adaptability based on the assumption that individuals adapting to other cultures share common feelings, perceptions, and experiences that occur regardless of their own cultural background or target culture characteristics. The tool contains fifty items that result in an individual profile with scores along four dimensions.

*Source: Kelley and Meyers (2010). Information available online*
*at: www.vangent-hcm.com/Solutions/ PerformanceManagement/*
*OrganizationalSurveys/CCAI/*

(5) Cross-Cultural Assessor (CCA)

*Purpose*: Assesses one's understanding of self and others
*Description:* Designed to improve one's understanding of self and others as well as to promote positive attitudes to cultural difference. The tool also provides a personal navigator system that allows individuals to conduct self-assessment to aid successful communication across cultures through a program of exercises and questionnaires that measures, builds, and manages cross-cultural skills and characteristics.

*Source: Richard Lewis Communications. Information available online at: www.crossculture.com*

(6) Cultural Orientations Indicator® (COI)

*Purpose*: Assesses cultural preferences
*Description:* A cross-cultural assessment tool to help individuals to assess personal cultural preferences and compare them with generalized profiles of other cultures. Cultural profiles are based on ten dimensions especially relevant to doing business in multicultural situations.

*Source: Information available online at: www.tmcorp.com*

(7) Development Communication Index

*Purpose:* Assesses communication quality and accuracy of perception
*Description:* A field instrument, developed during the Kealey study, designed to assess the quality of communication and the accuracy of perception between Canadian advisors and their national counterparts in development projects abroad. The

index presents thirty scenarios related to issues such as project progress and adaptation skills.

Source: *Information available online at: www.tamas.com/samples/ source-docs/ROI-Briefings.pdf*

(8) Global Mindedness Scale (GMS)

*Purposes:* Measures the effects of study abroad on student global mindedness
*Description:* Pre- and post-surveys designed to determine how study abroad influences the development of global mindedness among university students. The tool measures five dimensions: cultural pluralism, responsibility, efficacy, globalcentrism, and interconnectedness.

Source: *Hett (1993)*

(9) Intercultural Competence Questionnaire

*Purpose:* Assesses global literacy
*Description:* A brief questionnaire containing a self-test of intercultural competence described as global literacy.

Source: *Available online at: www.7d-culture.nl/ Content/cont053b.htm*

(10) Intercultural Development Inventory (IDI):

*Purpose:* Measures intercultural competence
*Description:* An instrument containing fifty items designed to measure individual and group intercultural competence along a developmental continuum focusing on the respondents' orientation toward cultural differences and their readiness for intercultural training. The tool is statistically reliable and is translated into twelve languages for use with people from various cultural backgrounds. Users must take a qualifying seminar to administer this instrument.

Source: *Mitchell R. Hammer, Hammer Consulting LLC. Information available online at: www.idiinventory.com/*

(11) Peterson Cultural Awareness Test (PCAT) and Peterson Cultural Style Indicator (PCSI)

*Purpose:* Assesses cross-cultural awareness and effectiveness
*Description:* Two tools designed to measure cross-cultural effectiveness and awareness of cultural differences. Both tools provide pre- and post-indicators of intercultural learning before and after training and help to promote global business success.

Source: *Brooks Peterson, Across Cultures, Inc. Accessible online at: www.acrosscultures.com*

(12) Schwartz Value Survey (SVS)

*Purpose:* Assesses compatible cross-cultural values orientation
*Description:* Based on use with more than 60,000 individuals in sixty-four nations, this tool explores the compatibility of a candidate's cultural orientation and the anticipated dominant cultural orientations of the region or country to which assigned. The tool also

provides information about differences in value orientations within a multicultural team and the effects on a team's work.

Source: *Information available online at: www.imo-international.de/englItisch/html/svs_info_en.htm*

## 5. Assessment and research challenges

Tracking the development of intercultural competence is important not only during training or educational courses or programs preparing individuals for an overseas sojourn, but also during the ensuing experience itself. Developing ICC is a longitudinal process that transpires over time, occasionally with moments of stagnation or even regression, but hopefully with forward movement over the long haul. In addition, it is also instructive to measure the impact of intercultural contact after a sojourn has ended as intercultural contact often provides some of the most important educational experiences of a person's life. For this reason, impact studies, which measure the outcomes of these experiences on an individual's life long after a sojourn is over, are extremely important. One, 5, 10, and even 20 years later, it is not uncommon to hear individuals say: "that experience was the most important educational experience I have ever had. It changed my entire life".

Indeed, impact studies are beginning to appear following the lead set by a Canadian project a number of years ago (see Kealey 1990). This is fortuitous as such studies are quite instructive and the results are useful in many ways. One recent study conducted by an international educational exchange organization measured the outcomes of volunteers participating in cross-cultural service projects, during, at the end, and up to 10 years after their program ended (Fantini 2006). Various assertions were tested in this systematic study, which collected rich quantitative and qualitative data through questionnaire surveys and follow-up interviews. Analysis of these data provided evidence that strongly supported the following assertions:

- intercultural competence involves a complex of abilities;
- learning the host language affects intercultural development in positive ways;
- intercultural experiences are life-altering;
- participant choices made during their sojourn produce certain intercultural consequences;
- all parties in intercultural contact, both sojourners and hosts, are affected;
- people are changed in positive ways as a result of this experience;
- returnees lean toward specific life choices, life partners, lifestyles, values and jobs as a result of their experience; and
- returnees often engage in activities upon return that further impact on others at home in positive ways.

Although almost everyone engaged in intercultural activities believes most of these assertions intuitively and perhaps experientially, the statistics and comments obtained through systematic research provide substantial evidence that garners further support for all assertions. For example, specific attributes were cited as extremely important to the success of an intercultural experience, attributes that conformed with many of those commonly cited in the literature, while also contributing several. Participants gained dramatic insights about the importance of being able to communicate in the host tongue, both to reduce barriers as well as to enable participation. As one alumna wrote, "Language was the key to everything, to communicating and understanding the local culture, and to my overall success". Another affirmed that: "Language was vital and very important to my success" (Fantini 2006: 46–47). These statements and many others support the view of language as an important component of intercultural competence.

Alumni also made abundant comments about how their lives were changed, and the directions their lives had taken after returning home. But what is really interesting is that their host mentors were also significantly affected through contact with foreigners, reinforcing the notion that both sojourners and hosts may be affected during the process of intercultural contact. And finally, as participants returned home and many engaged in social service types of activities, it became clear that they had significant impact in turn upon others (the multiplier effect). (Note: a report of this study is available electronically at: www.experiment.org/resources.html or www.sit.edu/graduate/7803.cfm.)

In the end, the evaluative results obtained from orientation programs, during sojourns abroad, as well as research studies of impact and outcomes might be compiled in an effort to create a projection chart of norms or expectations similar to the language projection chart mentioned above. Of course, it would seem easier to establish norms based on hours and weeks of input in classroom situations than for developments that ensue in natural settings and field situations given the host of variables that might arise in each individual case.

It would also be interesting to ascertain which competence aspects emerge that are common across cultural groups (universals), as well as those that might be specific or characteristic only of certain groups (particulars). In other words, in the research project cited above involving British and Swiss volunteers in Ecuador, are the results comparable? Which competences are most salient for both groups? And what differences emerge across groups? Is the impact of the British upon their Ecuadorian hosts similar to that of the Swiss? Did the multilingual Swiss have an easier adjustment than the mostly monolingual British? There are early indications that similarities exist, but differences also emerge. This promises to be an interesting area for future researchers as more investigators expand their work to include more and varied combinations of sojourners in cross-cultural contact.

Finally, several other research challenges persist that are worth adding or repeating (adapted in part from Van de Vijver and Leung 1997: 413–15). These are:

- the need for more widely shared definitions of crucial concepts;
- greater clarification regarding the conceptualization of ICC;
- recognition that ICC tests may not be as reliable predictors of success in intercultural encounters as IQ tests are of school performance;
- ensuring that the assessment plan is aligned with the objectives and vice versa;
- developing an assessment plan that is ongoing and uses a multimethod, multiperspective approach to track the multiple components of ICC, including language;
- selecting external test tools that demonstrate good psychometric properties (i.e., adequate internal consistency, generally considered to be above a threshold of 0.70 or 0.80);
- choosing instruments that are adequate from a cross-cultural perspective (in areas such as construct bias, method bias, and item bias);
- compiling and analyzing the results obtained for use in modifying the current plan or future program designs.

All these areas are reminders of the challenges facing the assessment of intercultural competence and of research studies designed to measure the impact on participants as a result of their experiences. Challenges, yes, but not insurmountable.

## 6. Summary and conclusion

In summary, assessment is important to our work, despite the challenges it may present. The basic challenge reiterated several times throughout this chapter is the need to define and refine the concept of intercultural competence as this notion is fundamental to curriculum design and implementation. And assessment forms an integral part of that process. In the end, assessment helps to ascertain how well we accomplish the objectives set forth and tracks their attainment by the learners involved. By monitoring and measuring their development as the program unfolds, assessment provides us with snapshots at various moments along the way. In this way, it provides feedback to the trainers and educators as well as to those being trained and allows us to modify efforts and to make adjustments as needed throughout our work.

Given the complex nature of intercultural competence, traditional assessment approaches are clearly insufficient. Multiple assessment modes and strategies are required. Quality assessment—assessment that is based on a thoughtful, varied, and explicit approach—generates an array of indicators that balance our subjective impressions. Happily, increasing assessment options are now available to help in our efforts. Aside from assessment activities devised by educators, external instruments, properly aligned with our objectives, can provide important additional information. An assessment process involving multiple strategies can yield rich and reliable information that enhances both educational practices and the results for students and sojourners.

In the end, intercultural experiences are extremely important because they provide valuable educational opportunities for human development. The benefits of intercultural education that includes opportunities to experience directly, holistically, and affectively, alternative ways of being in the world are well documented. For all these reasons, intercultural experiences are typically transformative; they change the rest of our life. Assessment helps to substantiate that all of this is so.

## Related topics

Language and intercultural communicative competence; education abroad; intercultural education pedagogy; outcomes-based assessment

## Further reading

Bolen, M. (2007) *A Guide to Outcomes Assessment in Education Abroad*, Carlisle, PA: Forum on Education Abroad (this work attempts to provide better data about learning outcomes in education abroad in addition to specific assessment tools that can help improve programs and advocate for the value of education abroad efforts).

Driscoll, A. (2008) 'Aligning pedagogy, curriculum, and assessment: support for student success', paper presented at North Carolina State University, Raleigh, NC, April 2008 (this paper explores the importance of aligning curriculum design, pedagogical approaches, and assessment strategies in order to guarantee student success in keeping with the increasing trend toward outcomes-based education (OBE)).

Fantini, A.E. (2000–2001) 'Designing quality intercultural programs: a model and a process', *Interspectives: A Journal on Transcultural Education*, 18: 100–105 (this publication presents a model for a curriculum process that will ensure quality in the design and implementation of intercultural educational programs in order to maximize the benefits of such experiences to participants and sojourners).

Serban, A.M. and Friedlander, J. (eds) (2004) *Developing and Implementing Assessment of Student Learning Outcomes*, San Francisco, CA: Jossey-Bass (this work responds to the increasing need for educational institutions to produce evidence of student learning and achievement and provides various models for developing and implementing ways to substantiate student learning outcomes. Although its focus is on community colleges, the material presented is relevant to all levels).

## References

ACTFL (1985) *ACTFL Proficiency Guidelines*, Hastings-on-Hudson, NY: ACTFL Materials Center. Online. Available: www.actfl.org/i4a/pages/index.cfm?pageid=4236 (accessed 12 October 2010).

Bailey, K.M. (1998) *Learning about Language Assessment*, New York, NY: Heinle and Heinle Publishers.

Bennett, J.M. (2008) 'Transformative training: designing programs for culture learning', in M.A. Moodian (ed.) *Contemporary Leadership and Intercultural Competence: Understanding and Utilizing Cultural Diversity to Build Successful Organizations*, Thousand Oaks, CA: Sage, pp. 95–110.

Byram, M. (1997) *Teaching and Assessing Intercultural Competence*, Clevedon: Multilingual Matters.

Camerer, R. (2008) *Teaching and Testing Intercultural Competence*, Bonn, Germany: BESIG Conference, 22 November 2008.

Council of Europe (2001) *Common European Framework of Reference for Languages (CEFR)*. Online. Available: www.coe.int/t/dg4/linguistic/cadre_en.asp (accessed 15 October 2010).

Deardorff, D.K. (2004) 'The identification and assessment of intercultural competence as a student outcome of internationalization at universities of higher education in the United States', unpublished dissertation, Raleigh, NC: North Carolina State University.

——(2009) *The SAGE Handbook of Intercultural Competence*, Los Angeles: CA: Sage.

Fantini, A.E. (1997) 'A survey of intercultural communication courses', *The International Journal of Intercultural Research*, 21(1): 125–48.

——(2000–2001) 'Designing quality intercultural programs: a model and a process', *Interspectives: A Journal on Transcultural Education*, 18: 100–105.

——(2006) *Exploring and Assessing Intercultural Competence*, Brattleboro, VT: Federation EIL. Online. Available: www.experiment.org/resources.html (accessed 1 November 2010).

Hett, E.J. (1993) *The Developing of an Instrument to Measure Global Mindedness*, San Diego, CA: The University of San Diego.

Humphrey, D. (2007) *Intercultural Communication Competence: The State of Knowledge*, London: The National Centre for Languages.

Kealey, D.J. (1990) *Cross-Cultural Effectiveness: A Study of Canadian Technical Advisors Overseas*, Hull, Canada: Canadian International Development Agency.

Kelley, C. and Meyers, J. (2010) *Cross-Cultural Adaptability Inventory (CCAI)*, Chicago, IL: Vangent.

Mader, J. (2009) *Testing the Untestable – Can Intercultural Competence be Tested?* Frankfurt, Germany: Frankfurt School of Finance and Management.

Martin, J.N. (ed.) (1989) 'Special issue on intercultural communication competence', *International Journal of Intercultural Relations*, 13(3).

Olebe, M. and Koester, J. (1989) 'Exploring the cross-cultural equivalence of the behavioral assessment scale for intercultural communication', *International Journal of Intercultural Relations*, 13(3): 333–47.

Van de Vijver, F.J.R. and Leung, K. (1997) 'Methodological issues in researching intercultural competence', in D. Deardorff (ed.) *The SAGE Handbook of Intercultural Competence*, Thousand Oaks, CA: Sage, pp. 404–18.

Wiseman, R.L. and Koester, J. (eds) (1993) *Intercultural Communication Competence*, Newbury Park, CA: Sage.

Wylie, E. and Ingram, D.E. (1995) *Australian Second Language Proficiency Ratings (ASLPR)*, Nathan, Queensland: Centre for Applied Linguistics and Languages (CALL), Griffith University.

# Section IV
# Language and intercultural communication in context

# 25

# Second language teacher education

*Michael Kelly*

## 1. Introduction

Education has always been called on to fulfil a contradictory role. On the one hand, it must pass on the core knowledge, skills and values that have been accumulated by preceding generations. On the other hand, it must provide the next generation of citizens with the knowledge, skills and values they will require to confront the challenges of the future. The role of the teacher is to manage these contradictions, straddling the generations and enabling their society to make a more effective transition from the past to the future. Over the past 20 years, the pace of social change has quickened, sharpening the contradictions that teachers must manage. Teachers are increasingly confronted with new demands, for which their own education has not prepared them. They therefore have a growing requirement to be better equipped, both in their initial teacher education and in their continuing professional development (CPD).

Other chapters in this *Handbook* show how the strategies and insights of intercultural communication have been called upon to address a range of social changes, including greater internationalization of economic activity, acceleration of migration, pressures on individual and social identities and increased linguistic and cultural diversity. The challenge to teacher education is to find ways of equipping teachers with strategies and insights that they can incorporate in their personal and professional practice, and can share with their pupils and students. This chapter examines how the challenge is being and can be addressed in the education of second or foreign language teachers. It focuses principally on the experience in Europe and deals mainly with initial teacher education. It also suggests that greater attention needs to be given to CPD.

## 2. Historical perspectives

Language teacher education in Europe is a complex and varied field. Each country has its own system, responding to the national needs, history and traditions, and often playing a significant social and political role in the life of the country. However, there are also common patterns, which are tending to converge in response to common international pressures and the development of increased cooperation at European level and more widely (Ager *et al.* 1993; Kelly *et al.* 2003).

Language teachers in secondary schools are usually trained by universities or teacher education institutions. Within universities, training is normally the combined responsibility of two academic units, one focusing on education and the other focusing on languages, although the degree of active cooperation between them is extremely variable. There are two main models of teacher education, one which situates the courses in the first cycle of higher education (undergraduate or equivalent), and the other which concentrates them in the second cycle (postgraduate or equivalent). In several countries, both alternatives exist. Undergraduate teacher training generally lasts for 4 or 5 years, whereas postgraduate teacher training takes between 1 and 2 years and follows on from 3- or 4-year undergraduate first degree studies, in which language studies are usually the main component. In postgraduate programmes, the link between education studies and subject studies is often quite limited. This can lead to a question about where intercultural communication should be taught. If it is located within the more academic context of a first degree, students may have more time to study and achieve a fuller understanding. If, on the other hand, it is taught within a vocational postgraduate degree, students may only be able to acquire limited knowledge and skills.

A growing minority of countries include aspects of intercultural or sociocultural pedagogy in the training of teachers. This can entail either specific courses or a general emphasis on themes such as intercultural relationships in Europe, education of minorities, promotion of minority or community languages and equal opportunities. A small but growing number of countries are establishing dual qualification programmes where trainees study in two countries. In those cases, intercultural cooperation tends to be a specific feature of the course aims, and includes preparation for teaching citizenship, moral education and similar subjects.

All students undertake courses in the history, literature and culture of the target community either as a specific component of their teacher training or else as part of their first foreign language degree. In about half the countries in Europe, comparative linguistics, sociolinguistics and psycholinguistics are incorporated in training, and may include elements of intercultural communication.

Language teaching is increasingly being undertaken in primary schools in all European countries, and debate is continuing over whether it should be carried out by specialist language teachers, or by generalist teachers, who are expected to teach over the full primary curriculum, or by semi-specialists, who are particularly trained in one or two subjects, but also expected to teach over a wider range. All primary school language teachers are required to acquire a wide body of knowledge in the course of their studies in higher education. The precise profile varies from country to country and from language to language, but the general areas of expected expertise are widely shared.

Primary-level language teacher training courses tend to focus mainly on language structure and practical language skills, building up prospective teachers' own communicative abilities and providing an advanced level of linguistic awareness (linguistics, stylistics, grammar, pronunciation, phonetics) as well as the specific didactic skills necessary for teaching the language at primary level. As a majority of primary teachers tend to be generalists and trained to teach all subjects, they have a more explicit role in fostering the values of tolerance and understanding, at the appropriate level for primary children, and a growing minority of countries are beginning to emphasize elements of intercultural or sociocultural pedagogy, particularly in primary training (Hawkins 2004; Zhu et al. 2007).

Outside the formal requirements of state education, there is a growing industry of training for language teachers in adult education for a wide range of purposes, including leisure and cultural pursuits, career development, business activity and social integration. Historically, this has been largely unregulated but, in recent years, a number of public agencies, industry bodies and professional associations have begun to introduce regulations and guidelines. This is an area where intercultural communication has emerged as a key issue, especially in the teaching of a native language as a foreign or second language, such as English as a Lingua Franca (ELF), Français Langue Étrangère (FLE), Italiano come Lingua Straniera (ITALS) and many equivalent approaches in other languages (Corbett 2003; Diadori 2010).

CPD (or in-service training) for language teachers is generally less systematic and more fragmented than initial training. By the same token, it is also more flexible and responsive to changing requirements. Whereas initial teacher training addresses only the new incoming cohort of language teachers, CPD can potentially involve the entire community of existing language teachers. It is consequently a key vector for change. In particular, it can refresh the existing expertise of teachers, and introduce them to new ideas and approaches, and it can act as a means of implementing new policies decided on by governments and other agencies. There is little evidence that intercultural communication is being introduced in an explicit way, although it may appear as a thread in refresher courses for language teachers.

On the other hand, it is common for intercultural issues to be broached in 'whole-school' training or in courses for school leaders. In this context, intercultural communication may be viewed as a helpful tool in responding to issues such as classroom diversity, literacy, involvement of parents and relations with other social groups. It figures widely in the extensive literature on multicultural approaches to education, or the role of education in a multicultural society, which is generally not focused specifically on language education (Brisk 2007; Lynch 1992). The issues are discussed in several chapters in this volume and are not developed here.

## 3. Critical issues

Although the field of intercultural communication was established internationally in the 1970s, it was not initially connected with language education. Conversely, the relationship between language teaching and culture was a long established and much debated topic in the literary and philological traditions. Views ranged between the position that cultural materials were essentially an aid to language learning and the contrary position that the purpose of language learning was to gain access to culture. In practice, many programmes in upper secondary and higher education resolved this by segregating the teaching of language and culture. A similar segregation takes place in research, where the predominant interest of language educators and applied linguists is to identify the ways in which 'second culture' teaching can support second language acquisition (Hinkel 1999).

During the 1980s, this dichotomy was challenged by a number of teacher educators, including Michael Byram, Geneviève Zarate and Joyce Valdes, who argued the need for a much more integrated approach to language and culture (Byram 1989; Valdes 1986; Zarate 1986). Their approach was integrated into the theoretical work undertaken by Byram, Zarate and others on behalf of the Council of Europe. It formed an important strand in the highly influential *Common European Framework of Reference for Languages* (Council for Cultural Cooperation 2001; Council of Europe 1996).

The *Common European Framework* was the first major European policy document to give significant emphasis to the intercultural nature of language learning. It emphasized that communication calls upon the whole human being and therefore requires teachers to develop, in themselves and in their students, intercultural awareness, intercultural skills and know-how, and the attitudes, values and other personal factors that contribute to an intercultural *savoir être* (Council of Europe 1996: 103–6). It was aimed at teachers and policy makers, but also offered to teacher educators a common vocabulary for articulating the intercultural dimensions of language learning.

Similar themes have been explored by the European Commission, through a series of projects. The Thematic Network projects, undertaken by the European Language Council, identified intercultural communication as a major issue in the wider area of languages (Kelly *et al.* 2001). The Languages and Cultures in Europe project made recommendations on strengthening intercultural competences in compulsory education (Languages and Cultures in Europe (LACE) 2007).

More widely, the connection between languages and intercultural communication was developed during the 1990s by organizations concerned with international education and training. These included the Society for Intercultural Education, Training and Research (SIETAR) and the European Association for International Education (EAIE). They played a significant role in promoting the education and training of intercultural trainers and education professionals. The growing interest of the research community in this area was reflected in the journal, *Language and Intercultural Communication*, and the linked association, the International Association for Languages and Intercultural Communication (IALIC), which were founded in 2001 to promote an understanding of the relationship between language and intercultural communication.

This work on the principles and policies of intercultural communication has gradually been integrated into language teacher education programmes across Europe (Garabato *et al.* 2003). However, the process has encountered challenges of two different kinds. The first concerns professional issues related to the context of language teacher education. The second concerns conceptual issues of the relationship between cultural and intercultural content in language teaching.

## 4. Professional issues

It is a potential issue that initial teacher education, and most professional development, takes place in a monolingual and monocultural context, which may be in tension with intercultural aspirations. One of the key aims of initial training is to familiarize student teachers with the specific education system in which they aim to be employed. Aside from their subject courses, most of the programme takes place in the home language of the institution and is designed to produce an acculturation into the home education system. This is vital for the students as they take the first steps in a career which most will expect to last through their whole working life. In this sense, teacher education may discourage an intercultural perspective.

This tendency is offset by two factors. First, teachers now need to be able to deal with a highly diverse range of students, who increasingly come from a wide variety of linguistic and cultural backgrounds. As a result, generic teacher education usually includes preparation for a multicultural school environment. Second, there is a growing emphasis in language teacher education on the need for partnerships and exchanges with schools in other countries. Student teachers are encouraged to develop the skills and contacts they will need to build up successful relationships. In a small, but growing number of cases, initial teacher education courses have been established that involve study in more than one country. These provide a basis for further work after qualification.

It is also a potential issue that, as language teachers develop their professional identity, they may tend to identify strongly with a single language. This affects teachers who are native speakers of the language they teach, as well as affecting teachers who have learned it as a second language. Native speaker teachers are equipped with a high level of linguistic and cultural competence, and often have a sense of embodying the language they teach. Non-native speakers, in contrast, have invested a great deal of time in learning a particular language and studying the related culture in order to attain a high level of competence. They too invest a good deal of their personal identity in that language. They have typically lived for a period in a country of their second language, where they have acquired social networks, and in some cases a partner in their personal life. Once they enter the teaching profession, they are presented with many opportunities to associate with teachers of the same language, whether as part of a teaching team or as a member of a national or international association. All these developments are likely to be beneficial to them in their development as language teachers, but they can also have the effect of compartmentalizing the language taught, restricting the teachers' engagement with other cultures and limiting interaction between teachers of different languages.

The effects of single-language identity are attenuated by other factors, which may encourage more multilingual attitudes. In many cases, students of different languages may be taught together during their teacher education. They may be invited to share their perception of language teaching questions from the perspective of experiences in different languages, fostering a spirit of intercultural working. A significant number of student teachers have acquired two or more second languages during their studies, and may intend to become teachers of both languages. In the UK, for example, many schools prefer to recruit teachers who can offer more than one language as it increases the flexibility with which the teacher can be deployed. And there are many examples of cooperation between teachers of different languages, in schools or in associations of language teachers. Undoubtedly, this cooperation is welcomed by policy makers at national and European levels, who are keen to encourage multilingualism.

## 5. Conceptual issues

An important issue that remains under discussion is how far the cultural dimension of language learning contributes to intercultural learning. There is a traditional view that the study of a foreign culture is an inherently intercultural activity, as it requires the student to confront a 'target culture'. The implications for language teacher education are then to ensure that the student teacher develops his or her knowledge of the relevant culture, together with the understanding and skills needed to relate to it. However, this view is open to challenge on the grounds that the study of national cultures and societies tends to encourage monocultural rather than intercultural education (Risager 2007). Students readily compartmentalize the culture studied and do not necessarily make connections with other areas of their experience.

These monolingual approaches to language teaching are often reinforced by target language methodologies, which are very widely used. There are clear benefits to methods that immerse the student in the target language and culture. However, this can be accompanied by an ethos of policing, which excludes the use of other languages in the classroom and discourages reference to other cultures. This issue is keenly felt in the teaching of English, where it is no longer evident that the language 'belongs' to a particular national culture, or indeed to any culture.

The predominant response to this difficulty is that teachers must explicitly invite language learners to compare and contrast the target culture with their own culture(s). This is reflected in the *Framework*, which argues:

> The learner does not simply acquire two distinct, unrelated ways of acting and communicating. The language learner becomes plurilingual and develops interculturality. The linguistic and cultural competences in respect of each language are modified by knowledge of the other and contribute to intercultural awareness, skills and know-how.

They enable the individual to develop an enriched, more complex personality and an enhanced capacity for further language learning and greater openness to new cultural experiences.

*Council of Europe (1996: 23)*

The authors insist that intercultural awareness includes an awareness of regional and social diversity within their own world and the one they are studying. Learners also bring an awareness of a wider range of cultures, which provides a richer contextualization. As Paolo Balboni has argued, this means that an apparently simple high-level concept such as intercultural communicative competence represents a deep and complex array of codes, values and events (Balboni 2006). Increasingly, this standpoint is becoming embedded in the aims of language programmes and of language teacher education programmes. It is reflected, for example, in the UK *Benchmark Statement*, which sets out the official expectations for degree programmes in languages.

A key form of knowledge and understanding developed among students of languages is the ability to compare the view of the world from their own languages and cultures with the view of the world from the languages and cultures they have studied. The analytical skills they have developed can be used equally well in the study of their own culture and, in particular, in comparing, contrasting and mediating between the two (or more) societies with which they are familiar (Quality Assurance Agency 2007: 6).

The approach taken in the *Common European Framework* was subsequently incorporated into the *European Language Portfolio*, which has been developed in more than 100 versions to cater for a variety of different kinds of learners in different countries. The *Portfolio* is a pedagogical tool, which incorporates a 'language passport', a language biography and a dossier of work. Both have been taken up very widely by language teachers, and it is clear that they are incorporated into many teacher education programmes. The success of these tools has mainly been led by their codification of language competence into six different levels. The valuable analysis they present of intercultural aspects to language learning has, in contrast, attracted the attention of researchers rather than practitioners or decision makers. However, it is a significant benefit of the *Portfolio* that teachers and learners are invited to consider the full range of languages they have encountered, rather than simply focusing on one specific second language.

## 6. Current contributions and research

The importance of intercultural communication in language teaching has been highlighted in the *European Profile for Language Teacher Education* (Kelly and Grenfell 2004), which deals with the initial and in-service education of foreign language teachers in primary, secondary and adult learning contexts. It offers a frame of reference for language education policy makers and language teacher educators in Europe. It serves as a checklist for existing teacher education programmes and a toolbox for those still being developed. It is harmonized with the *Common European Framework*, particularly in its use of terminology.

The *Profile* has played an important role in the European Commission's efforts to improve language teaching, recognizing that language teachers play a major part in working towards the European Union's objective that all EU citizens should have linguistic competence in their own mother tongue and two other languages. In the period since the *Profile* was first published, the importance of languages and intercultural communication has been recognized in a plethora of documents at the European level. They were given a sharp focus in the EU Commission's communication *A New Framework Strategy for Multilingualism* (European Commission 2005) and in the follow-up communication *Multilingualism: An Asset for Europe and a Shared Commitment*

(European Commission 2008). The EU declared the year 2008 to be the 'Year of Intercultural Dialogue' and sponsored programmes of activity across all member states.

The *Profile* describes forty important elements in foreign language teacher education in Europe. They concern the structure and organization of language teacher education, as well as the knowledge, skills and values that trainee language teachers should be able to acquire. Many of the elements have a bearing on the development of intercultural communication, which is threaded through as an integral part of language teacher education. The *Profile* does not propose a separate 'content' module on intercultural communication, although it does not dismiss the suggestion. It suggests that many aspects of teacher education courses can provide opportunities for thinking about intercultural issues and developing intercultural competence as an integral part of other activities.

An example of this approach is the suggestion made in the *Profile* that trainee teachers should be offered the opportunity to experience an intercultural and multicultural environment. There are two components to this suggestion. First, trainee teachers should have the experience of living, studying, working or teaching in a context characterized by distinctive or different social, cultural, ethnic, national, religious or linguistic groups. Second, trainee teachers should be taught that intercultural and multicultural approaches to teaching and learning involve teachers promoting dynamic interactions between teacher and learner and between learners.

The *Profile* recognizes that there are problems in defining the key terms, and suggests that, in this context, 'multicultural' should be understood as a descriptive term, referring to a range of different cultural perspectives and attitudes existing in parallel. In contrast, 'intercultural' refers to a dynamic state of exchange and interaction between these cultural perspectives. It notes that these processes take place both in the trainee teacher's own country and abroad. Even within one national context, learners have a wide range of cultural perspectives and attitudes, shaped by social, ethnic and political factors, as well as gender, age and sexual orientation. These affect how learners respond to teaching and learning. It suggests that one way to experience an intercultural environment is by teaching one's native language to non-native speakers (for example, children from immigrant communities), and argues that trainee teacher placements in multicultural classrooms help develop an intercultural mindset.

The *Profile* provides a number of suggestions for how this can be implemented, following the example of a number of teacher education programmes in different countries. They have found certain points to be helpful. For example:

- The training institution gives trainees the chance to teach different groups of students, for example, in urban areas as well as rural areas.
- Some training is offered in teaching one's native language to non-native speakers.
- Native trainees are encouraged to mix with non-native trainees. This can be done by partnering them up for group work together.
- Trainees are offered the experience of studying or working in another country and so are more culturally aware and are better equipped to face diversity in a non-judgemental manner. This can be reinforced by the content of the teacher education.
- Trainees are encouraged to build up and maintain networks with colleagues from other countries, and may spend a period abroad during their training.
- Trainees are led to understand the concepts of interculturalism and multiculturalism and can discuss the issues surrounding these two notions cogently and with clarity.
- Trainees work well in groups with colleagues from a variety of backgrounds. How they treat their colleagues is reflected in how they teach.

Kelly and Grenfell (2004: 31)

The *Profile* recognizes that trainees are sometimes educated in areas where there is little opportunity for intercultural or multicultural experience. Imaginative ways can be found to provide equivalent experiences, for example through online resources. It also warns that issues around interculturalism and multiculturalism can be difficult to address in certain learning contexts. How trainees are encouraged to deal with these issues will need to be context sensitive.

In the 6 years since it was first published, the *Profile* has been used in many different contexts to assist the development of language teacher education. It has been promoted by the Commission, for example in the 2008 communication (European Commission 2008). And it was a key source for development of the *European Portfolio for Student Teachers of Languages* (EPOSTL), a tool for reflection and self-assessment designed for use by students in the pre-service education of modern language teachers (Newby *et al.* 2007). The EPOSTL tool was developed for the European Centre for Modern Languages (ECML) of the Council of Europe, as part of their programme: 'Languages for social cohesion – Language education in a multilingual and multicultural Europe'. Along with a main focus on language teaching methodology, its concern is with culture and the plurality of cultures in a multicultural world, although it does make reference to the need for intercultural awareness (Newby *et al.* 2007: 12).

The *Profile* has been the starting point for a number of other European initiatives, funded by the European Commission's Lifelong Learning Programme. For example, the EUROPROF project produced a *European Foreign Language Teacher Professional Profile and Portfolio*, which aimed to enable student teacher mobility and to develop skills and intercultural competence (Paggiaro 2009). The LANQUA (Language Network for Quality Assurance) project (2007–10) has developed a tool kit for quality assurance in language programmes, in which intercultural communication and language teacher education play a significant role (www.lanqua.eu). The SemLang project (2009–10), led by the Centre International d'Études Pédagogiques at Sèvres, France, held a summer school and a series of dissemination conferences in different countries, in which issues of intercultural communication in language education were a frequent reference (www.semlang.eu). The project produced a series of recommendations for further action, which include a strengthening of the intercultural dimensions of language teacher education (Ziegler *et al.* 2009).

> In a parallel development in the UK, intercultural communication played a prominent role in the development of a new school qualification, entitled the Diploma in Languages and International Communication, which 'will blend theory and practice to show how languages can be applied at work and at leisure – bringing language learning to life. The innovative programme also aims to teach young people intercultural skills and translation and interpreting skills. It intends to help them learn about the way language works so that they can become independent language learners.'
>
> *(www.linksintolanguages.ac.uk/news/786, accessed 10 May 2011)*

## 7. Main research methods

The development of intercultural communication in European language teacher education has gained momentum from pragmatic rather than theoretical considerations. It has been a problem-solving exercise in which teacher educators have taken an eclectic approach, drawing on insights from a number of disciplines across the human and social sciences. The notion of the 'reflective practitioner' is widely adopted as a watchword in teacher education (Schön 1983), and forms the basis for action research, which has become perhaps the most widespread method for developing approaches to intercultural communication, together with the closely related approach of action learning (Byram 1997; James 2001). Action research involves identifying a particular issue or problem encountered while teaching, gathering information about it, developing a plan of action, evaluating its results and sharing them with colleagues. It has gained ground among practising teachers in several countries, and there is every reason to encourage trainee teachers to adopt it as part of their own self-development. As an effective tool of self-development, action research is usually carried out informally and on a small scale. Its results are typically shared at a local level and are rarely given wider dissemination.

Alongside the development of a greater intercultural focus to language teacher education, reflections on intercultural communication across Europe have explored the concept of a 'third space'. The notion is implicit in Byram's 'intercultural communicative competence' and its prolongations in the *Common European Framework*. But it was developed in North America, inspired by work in postcolonial theory and applied linguistics, by such writers as Homi Bhabha and Claire Kramsch (Bhabha 1988; Kramsch 1993). Imported into Europe, it offered the benefit of providing a solution to the confrontation of competing national cultures, without denying their legitimacy. However, the notion of third space remains largely a theoretical construct, which has as yet found little purchase in the practice of language teachers (Ikas and Wagner 2009; Kelly 2009).

## 8. Recommendations for practice

There is widespread agreement on the need for intercultural communication to play a larger role in language teaching, and therefore in language teacher education. The challenge is to embed it in practice. It has already been suggested that trainee teachers would benefit from the experience of an intercultural and multicultural environment, which would encourage them to reflect on the intercultural nature of language teaching. This approach could usefully be extended to several other areas of teacher education.

Greater opportunities need to be offered for trainee teachers to participate in links with partners abroad, including visits and exchanges. These can offer many benefits, and it is important that appropriate intercultural education should form part of the advance preparation. As well as visits to partner institutions, there are intercultural benefits to be gained from other forms of contact: written exchanges; 'e-twinning' of institutions; an interactive forum between institutions; e-mail; videoconferencing, skype; chat; social networking and other online methods. One of the challenges for teacher educators is to keep abreast of the technological avenues that are constantly opening up. Trainees may be better versed in such communications than their trainers. Trainees may also come to realize that their own pupils will most likely be similarly better able to deploy new technology. No doubt this is evidence of a new range of intercultural challenges.

A period of work or study in a country or countries where the trainee's foreign language is spoken as native is an essential part of teacher education, and opportunities are widely available. Trainees benefit in many ways from exposure to the target culture but, in order to derive intercultural benefits, it is important that they should be equipped to reflect actively on their experience. This should be assisted by explicit preparation in methods of reflection, such as learner diaries, and ethnographical approaches to participant observation in the host culture.

Trainees can draw many lessons from observing or participating in teaching in more than one country. Many aspects of school culture differ radically from one country to another and from one part of the education system to another. This may not be easily deduced from more general cultural differences and will enable trainees to reflect on the need to develop intercultural skills appropriate to a wider range of situations.

Intercultural communication would be strengthened by closer links between trainees who are being educated to teach different languages. Where they are taught in the target language, cooperation between trainees in different languages may be more difficult. Trainees in different languages are often based in different departments and locations, making cooperation between them logistically difficult. It would be beneficial for them to cooperate during lectures, seminars, workshops and other learning activities, as well as during their school-based teaching practice. Where they follow certain teacher education modules in common, they can be encouraged to explore and compare their methodological approaches. They can also do this during school-based practice, if they are placed in the same school, through peer observation or peer review, for example. This would promote intercultural exchange and the sharing of good teaching and learning practices. It would give them the opportunity to discuss their experiences with trainees in different languages, make comparisons and identify the differences in approaches employed.

Trainee teachers are often given formal classes on issues surrounding social and cultural values and citizenship, which they generally share with students of other disciplines. These are excellent opportunities to develop intercultural awareness. It would also be valuable for language teacher trainees to be offered a more systematic understanding of the diversity of languages, cultures and societies. A logical place to start would be an exploration of the linguistic profile of countries in which the languages they teach are spoken as native. This would help them to understand the importance of maintaining linguistic diversity in Europe. It would also give them a basis for discovering key concepts in intercultural communication and in languages, including notions such as multilingualism, plurilingualism and communicative competence. It might also motivate them to contribute to exploring these issues.

Although some materials are beginning to be available, there is still a shortage of learning materials and other resources to support intercultural classroom practices. Similarly, more information would be useful to facilitate comparative reflection on education systems, and practical experience of intercultural environments.

## 9. Future directions

There is some debate around the issue of whether there is a need to include explicit learning modules on intercultural communication in initial teacher training and CPD. The main argument for doing this is to equip teachers with the concepts and strategies that will support their reflective practice. The main argument against it is that intercultural communication could be presented as an alternative to language learning, and one that will appear more cost effective to policy makers. Both arguments carry weight in different ways. My view is that an intercultural module can be effective if it is well integrated in the language teacher education programme and connected in practical ways to the trainees' experience of language teaching and learning.

A good example is the ethnographic approach to language learning elaborated 10 years ago by a team of researchers and educators (Roberts et al. 2001). This has been used in several undergraduate programmes at British universities. It argues that learners who have an opportunity to stay in the target language country can be trained to do an ethnographic project while abroad. It borrows from anthropologists the idea of 'cultural fieldwork' and 'writing culture', and encourages language learners to develop their linguistic and cultural competence through the ethnographic study of a group in their locality.

This kind of course offers very useful tools to students who are planning to spend a period working or studying in the country where their language is spoken. However, it is not suitable for short intensive study. It would be very useful to have an appropriate short course designed for a crowded language teacher education curriculum. There would also be scope for a course within a professional development programme.

The incorporation of intercultural approaches into language teacher education is closely linked to the evolution of the languages curriculum in schools, universities and private language centres. Any curriculum is governed by a multiplicity of factors, not least the different cultural, social and economic purposes that language learning is required to serve. It is important that teachers and researchers should recognize the wide range of contexts in which language learning may take place, even though they may see their own teaching career as taking a very specific route. Intercultural communication is similarly a very different proposition when it is needed for travel abroad from when it serves social inclusion at home. The current surge in early language learning is introducing even more differences of approach, particularly where the learning of language is integrated into a broad curriculum taught by a single generalist class teacher. Different needs again arise from the development of bilingual learning approaches, such as Content and Language Integrated Learning (CLIL).

As a result, there is a growing need for flexible and well-tailored approaches to intercultural communication that will match the variety of language learning situations. Language teacher educators may well be able to address only the most general principles of intercultural communication, rather than the rich variety of provision, but there is an increasing requirement that they should give their trainees the basic tools needed to adapt intercultural approaches to whatever teaching they subsequently undertake. This is a difficult challenge, but one to which teacher educators must rise.

## 10. Conclusion

There is growing social demand for intercultural communicative competence, whether or not it is linked to linguistic competence. The challenge to language educators is to respond to this demand by enriching language learning and by integrating into it an informed awareness of intercultural issues. In their turn, they can enrich intercultural communication through the imaginative use of cultural materials, from the canonical literary heritage through to the demotic culture of everyday life. There is a clear need for CPD in these issues for language teachers and for language teacher educators. Educators are well placed to respond to this challenge, but they will certainly need to adapt their professional profile to meet the new needs.

## Related topics

Education abroad; Europe; intercultural communicative competence; language; multilingualism; teacher education; third space; transnationalism

## Further reading

Abdallah-Pretceille, M. and Porcher, L. (2001) *Éducation et communication interculturelle*, Paris: Presses universitaires de France (an excellent overview of intercultural issues in education from a French perspective, including language education among other things).

Alred, G., Byram, M. and Fleming, M. (eds) (2002) *Intercultural Experience and Education*, Clevedon: Multilingual Matters (a classic collection of essays by some of the leading scholars in this area, extending the concept of 'interculturality' beyond its usual frames of reference).

Corbett, J. (2003) *An Intercultural Approach to English Language Teaching*, Clevedon: Multilingual Matters (applies a range of theoretical approaches to ways of exploring cultural differences through language teaching).

Lázár, I. (ed.) (2003) *Incorporating Intercultural Communicative Competence in Language Teacher Education*, Strasbourg: Council of Europe (a review of the field, with some very useful examples of assessment tools).

Phipps, A. and Gonzalez, M. (2004) *Modern Languages: Learning and Teaching in an Intercultural Field*, London: Sage (an inspiring reconceptualization of the field).

# References

Ager, D.E., Muskens, G. and Wright, S. (eds) (1993) *Language Education for Intercultural Communication*, Clevedon: Multicultural Matters.

Balboni, P.E. (2006) *Intercultural Communicative Competence: A Model*, Perugia: Guerra.

Bhabha, H.K. (1988) 'The commitment to theory', *New Formations*, 5: 5–23.

Brisk, M.E. (ed.) (2007) *Language, Culture, and Community in Teacher Education*, New York: Routledge.

Byram, M. (1989) *Cultural Studies in Foreign Language Education*, Clevedon: Multilingual Matters.

——(1997) *Teaching and Assessing Intercultural Communicative Competence*, Clevedon: Multilingual Matters.

Corbett, J. (2003) *An Intercultural Approach to English Language Teaching*, Clevedon: Multilingual Matters.

Council for Cultural Cooperation (2001) *Common European Framework of Reference for Languages: Learning, Teaching, Assessment*, Cambridge: Cambridge University Press.

Council of Europe (1996) *Modern Languages: Learning, Teaching, Assessment. A Common European Framework of Reference*. Draft 2 of a Framework Proposal, Strasbourg: Council for Cultural Co-operation.

Diadori, P. (ed.) (2010) *Formazione Qualità Certificazione per la Didattica delle Lingue Moderne in Europa*, Milan: Le Monnier.

European Commission (2005) *A New Framework Strategy for Multilingualism: Communication from the Commission to the Council, the European Parliament, the European Economic and Social Committee and the Committee of the Regions*. Online. Available: http://europa.eu/languages/en/document/74 (accessed 24 April 2008).

——(2008) *Multilingualism: An Asset for Europe and a Shared Commitment*. European Commission. Online. Available: http://ec.europa.eu/education/languages/pdf/com/2008_0566_en.pdf (accessed 30 January 2009).

Garabato, C.A., Auger, N., Gardies, P. and Kotul, E. (eds) (2003) *Les Représentations Interculturelles en Didactique des Langues-Cultures: Enquêtes et Analyses*, Paris: L'Harmattan.

Hawkins, M.R. (ed.) (2004) *Language Learning and Teacher Education: A Socio-cultural Approach*, Clevedon: Multilingual Matters.

Hinkel, E. (ed.) (1999) *Culture in Second Language Teaching and Learning*, Cambridge: Cambridge University Press.

Ikas, K. and Wagner, G. (eds) (2009) *Communicating in the Third Space*, Oxford: Routledge.

James, P. (2001) *Teachers in Action: Tasks for In-Service Language Teacher Education and Development*, Cambridge: Cambridge University Press.

Kelly, M. (2009) 'A third space for Europe: intercultural communication in European language policy', *European Journal of Language Policy/Revue européenne de politique linguistique*, 1(1): 1–20.

Kelly, M. and Grenfell, M. (2004) *European Profile for Language Teacher Education: A Frame of Reference*. Online. Available: http://ec.europa.eu/education/policies/lang/doc/profile_en.pdf (accessed 2 January 2008).

Kelly, M., Elliott, I. and Fant, L. (eds) (2001) *Third Level, Third Space: Intercultural Communication and Language in European Higher Education*, Berne: Peter Lang.

Kelly, M., Grenfell, M. and Jones, D. (2003) *The European Language Teacher*, Berne: Peter Lang.

Kramsch, C. (1993) *Context and Culture in Language Teaching*, Oxford: Oxford University Press.

Languages and Cultures in Europe (LACE) (2007) *The Intercultural Competences Developed in Compulsory Foreign Language Education in the European Union*. Online. Available: www.lace2007.eu/ (accessed 31 January 2009).

Lynch, J. (ed.) (1992) *Cultural Diversity and the Schools*, London: Falmer.

Newby, D., Allan, R, Fenner, A.-B., Jones, B., Komorowska, H. and Soghikyan, K. (2007) *European Portfolio for Student Teachers of Languages. A Reflection Tool for Language Teacher Education*, Graz: Council of Europe.

Paggiaro, L. (ed.) (2009) *The Europrof Handbook*, SSIS Toscana, Italy. Online. Available: http://ucsyd.dk/fileadmin/user_upload/international/EUROPROF_HANDBOOK_Final_Version.pdf (accessed 5 June 2010).

Quality Assurance Agency (2007) *Languages and Related Studies Benchmarking Statement*. Online. Available: www.qaa.ac.uk/academicinfrastructure/benchmark/statements/languages07.pdf (accessed 30 May 2010).

Risager, K. (2007) *Language and Culture Pedagogy: From a National to a Transnational Paradigm*, Clevedon: Multilingual Matters.

Roberts, C., Byram, M., Barro, A., Jordan, S. and Street, B. (2001) *Language Learners as Ethnographers*, Clevedon: Multilingual Matters.

Schön, D.A. (1983) *The Reflective Practitioner: How Professionals Think in Action*, New York: Basic Books.

Valdes, J.M. (ed.) (1986) *Culture Bound: Bridging the Cultural Gap in Language Teaching*, Cambridge: Cambridge University Press.

Zarate, G. (1986). *Enseigner une culture etrangère*, Paris: Hachette.

Zhu, W., Seedhouse, P. Wei, L. and Cook, V. (eds.) (2007) *Language Learning and Teaching as Social Interaction*, London: Palgrave Macmillan.

Ziegler, G., Eskildsen,L., Coonan, C.M., Ludbrook, G., Bottin, C. and De Matteis, P. (2009) *Recommendations for Optimising Language Teacher Training In Europe*. Online. Available: www.semlang.eu (accessed 31 May 2010).

# 26

# The English as a foreign or international language classroom

*Phyllis Ryan*

## 1. Introduction

The English as a foreign language (EFL) classroom is typically associated with a physical location where the students, under the guidance of a teacher, follow a program that is designed to help them learn the target language, even though it is not widely spoken in the community. During the learning process, they may be exposed to other languages and cultures if their peers are from diverse backgrounds. In many cases, however, they will be sitting alongside classmates who share the same ethnicity and first language. The students may be in the class for a variety of reasons. Some may be obliged to take an EFL class as a program requirement. Others may have opted to enroll for personal reasons (e.g., to secure a better job, to prepare for study abroad, to facilitate travel to English-speaking countries, to gain exposure to another language and culture, for pleasure or literary pursuits). Whatever the driving force behind their presence in the classroom, the students will not only be exposed to linguistic features of the target language, but, willy-nilly, cultural elements as well.

The aim of this chapter is to consider the relationship between language and culture, and the cultivation of intercultural communicative competence within such a language learning context. For this purpose, we might imagine an English language classroom in an institution of higher education in Dubai, a language institute in Tokyo, or a secondary school in Mexico City. We may visualize a teacher, students, blackboards (or whiteboards), books, materials, and the requisite uncomfortable chairs. We might even see a computer or two, with a language laboratory nearby. As the target language is English, discussion must take into account the status and global spread of the language, including the development of world Englishes.

Within this classroom setting,[1] the learners are exposed to the dynamic created by interaction between the teacher, students, and language–culture learning materials. In the learning process, the students are apt to encounter new ideas and ways of being that may challenge their sense of self. Although this enhanced awareness of self and other may spur the development of inter-cultural competence, it may also be disquieting and raise uncomfortable questions about the positioning and status of their first language (L1) and local culture(s). The relationship between language and culture and intercultural development is very complex and has significant implications for the FL (foreign language) classroom, especially when the learning of a powerful, global language is involved.

This chapter begins with a discussion of the evolving status of English and its growing influence on the world stage. Attention is drawn to implications for the teaching of English as a foreign language (EFL) and English as an international language (EIL) in non-English-speaking communities. Drawing heavily on the work of Risager (2007), we look at the debate between the teaching of English as a national language and the more recent transnational paradigm and its implications for FL teaching. Discussion then centers on teacher thinking about culture and intercultural communicative competence in relation to the foreign language classroom and how it may affect the teaching of EFL/EIL. We then focus on the process of becoming an intercultural person, with particular attention paid to the classroom context. Relevant models of intercultural communicative competence are examined along with pedagogical implications for EFL/EIL classroom situations. Finally, suggestions are offered for research that could lead to further improvements in the teaching and learning of English in situations where the language is not widely used in the community.

## 2. The spread of English as an international language

English now has a very important, if not unique, position in that it has become an international language and tool of communication throughout most of the world. In recent decades, it has emerged as the de facto lingua franca for international education, scientific communication, business negotiations, diplomacy, and academic conferences in many nations on all continents. A problem sometimes mentioned with respect to English is the perceived "unfair advantage" native speakers have on the international stage. There is a long history of attempts to come up with a replacement for any national languages as a lingua franca. For instance, Latin was once used as an international means of communication which, as it was the language of a population who had disappeared, made everyone who used it a non-native speaker. This concept has also led to the invention of artificial languages such as Esperanto which have the same advantage. Unfortunately, these attempts have met with extremely limited success, so the world seems for the moment to have only English as its principal international language. Owing to this global spread of English, a growing number of applied linguists (e.g., Alptekin 2002; Alvarez 2007; Byram 1997; Corbett 2003; Holliday, 2005; Sharifian 2009, to name a few) are drawing attention to the shifting realities associated with the learning of the language in international settings. Traditionally, the EFL classroom has focused on the teaching of English with native speakers as the model (e.g., British English, American English) and, hence, there has been an emphasis on Western national Anglophone culture (Saraceni 2009). But is this an appropriate classroom model for students who are learning the language for international communication?

The term "English as an international language" (EIL) is used to emphasize the international, global character of the language and to recognize the reality that "the majority use of English is now outside the English-speaking West" (Holliday 2005: 8). In non-English-speaking countries, a great many non-native speakers need to communicate with other non-native speakers in English, and many only occasionally interact with native speakers. Nowadays, the number of speakers of English as an additional language is actually far greater than the number of native speakers worldwide. Questions are therefore being raised about the ownership of the language and, in many parts of the world, English is no longer viewed as being attached to a specific culture or nation. A growing number of scholars argue that the native speaker paradigm presents a problem in foreign language education if the emphasis is on a standard linguistic norm and a standard uniform sociocultural world. Intercultural theorists and educators who recognize language and culture learning as a complex cognitive, social, and emotional process have expressed strong opposition to what they consider an outdated native speaker paradigm in FL teaching (Alvarez 2007; Byram 1997; Holliday 2005; McKay 2002; Sharifian 2009).

Other applied linguists maintain that the traditional FL classroom, with a focus on a specific native speaker model of the language, is still appropriate for students who intend to live, study, or do business in a particular English-speaking country. They argue that there should be room for a range of classroom options for English language learners in non-English-speaking countries.

Risager (2007) proposes a transnational paradigm for language teaching, which rejects the notion that a connection with native speakers and national cultures is necessary and inevitable. Instead, this paradigm places language teaching and learning firmly within a global social context. Risager's vision of language and culture pedagogy, and world citizenship are the focus of the next section.

## 3. The emergence of national and transnational paradigms

The teaching of culture in language courses has generated a prolonged debate about the relationship between culture and language, especially in the case of English, a global language. As has been mentioned in the previous section, this struggle is particularly obvious in EFL settings, because of the powerful, international status of English and what this implies. It might be said that, in relation to languages other than English, the study of the life of the people who speak the language (the host speech community) guides the activities and events that are incorporated into the FL lessons. For example, in North America, learners of Italian, German, or Russian may study facets of culture linked to a particular nation (e.g., Italy, Germany, or Russia respectively). The learning and teaching of English as an additional language in non-English-speaking countries is much more complicated, however, because of the global status of the language and the emergence and growing acceptance of a variety of world Englishes (e.g., Indian English, Kenyan English, Singaporean English) (Crystal 2003; Jenkins 2009; Kachru et al. 2006; Kirkpatrick 2010; Sharifian 2009; see also Chapter 19, this volume).

Risager (2007) calls for language teachers to assess for themselves the relationship between culture and language in their teaching pedagogy. In her book, *Language and Culture Pedagogy: From a National to a Transnational Paradigm*, she provides the critical basis from which to make professional judgments related to aims for teaching. She argues for a vision of language teaching that sets long-term goals that will put in place the knowledge, strategies, and reflection necessary to help learners develop as world citizens. Her conception of intercultural competence includes critical multilingual and multicultural awareness with a global perspective.

Knowledge of national and transnational concepts, according to Risager (2007), is vital to understanding the evolution of language and culture pedagogy. In her landmark book, she discusses the history of how the transnational paradigm evolved from the national paradigm, delving into the complexity of the concepts upon which they are based. She traces key elements and events throughout the 1960s, 1970s, and 1980s leading up to the impact of internationalization and the intercultural approach to language teaching that emerged in the 1990s (Byram and Fleming 1998; Byram et al. 2002). Noting that, in recent decades, the national paradigm has been called into question, Risager is a strong proponent of a transnational approach. (Readers may consult her 2007 book for an in-depth discussion of the complexity of what might be called "phases of culture pedagogy" in relation to the history of different parts of the world, such as Europe, North America and Australia; see Chapter 6, this volume.)

The teacher in a foreign language classroom has traditionally been expected to teach the linguistic form of the target language, so that the student will be able to produce this form when needed, either orally or in writing. The communicative competence approach to teaching that emerged in the 1980s emphasized identifying and employing learning strategies that could facilitate genuine communication in the target language (Canale and Swain 1980; Hymes 1971; Savignon 1997). From the 1990s onwards, the introduction of the concept of intercultural competence has led to a focus on raising learners' awareness of how their own cultural background and cultural assumptions may impact on their attitudes towards and communication with people from other cultures (Alred *et al.* 2003; Byram 1997; Corbett 2003). This reflection or self-analysis is considered integral for the development of the learners' intercultural communication skills and knowledge of the world. Further, Risager (2007) distinguishes intercultural competence from cultural competence. For her, the latter involves the knowledge, skills, and attitudes of a specific cultural area associated with a particular target language country, whereas intercultural competence involves the knowledge, skills, and attitudes at the interface between several cultural areas, including the students' own culture and a target culture.

In her review of the relationship between language and the development of intercultural communicative competence, Risager (2007) drew attention to the impact of paradigms on FL teaching. The national paradigm refers to foreign language teaching that is primarily aimed at presenting a standard norm of native language use based on a particular national language and culture. In this orientation, the instructor is optimally a native speaker of the standard language, teaching only the target language in a standard form. This view of language implies that the world has monolingual language areas, each with its associated culture. There has been much debate and criticism about the national paradigm, especially in the case of English, as in traditional EFL classrooms the language is often narrowly linked to a single nation where it is spoken as a first language (e.g., England, the US). A focus on the "majority culture" in the target country, however, largely ignores cultural and linguistic diversity within the nation (Risager 2007; Saraceni 2009).

A transnational perspective, on the other hand, proposes the teaching of English or other foreign languages within a global social context (Risager 2007). The teacher does not need to be a native speaker, but should have a high level of competence in the target language. Within this orientation, the language teaching material should be contextualized transnationally (locally/globally) and only nationally if this is absolutely necessary. This mode of language teaching can take place anywhere in the world. Risager (2007) envisions transnational language and culture pedagogy as interdisciplinary, drawing on the complex relations between language, culture, and society and the individual. In addition to the relationship between language and culture, this orientation deals with national and transnational social structures and processes, including national and international political relations.

As well as turning away from the national paradigm, there is now more emphasis on cultural learning processes and the development of intercultural competence in classroom situations. In language teaching, there is more attention being directed toward helping language learners develop as intercultural speakers who can mediate between various languages and cultural contexts (see Chapters 5, 18, 20, 22, and 29, this volume).

## 4. Teacher thinking about culture and the EFL classroom

Some of the initial studies of intercultural competence have explored teachers' concepts of culture and language, perceptions of classroom teaching, and the goals driving language learning. It is useful to consider research on teacher thinking as it relates to teacher perceptions of culture and language. As their thinking impacts on their classroom teaching, it is important to be mindful of how teachers perceive the following elements: concepts of culture; the role of culture and intercultural communication in the EFL classroom; EFL teacher–student interaction; the roles and responsibilities of EFL teachers and learners; and foreign language learning. A good overview of the research on teacher thinking in the fields of general education, communication, and foreign language teaching can be found in Ryan (2004: 610–11), the *Routledge Encyclopedia of Language Teaching and Learning*, which provides a historical review of foreign language classroom studies. Numerous studies of teachers' beliefs have suggested that such beliefs strongly affect their behavior (Abelson 1979; Clark and Peterson 1986; Tabachnick and Zeichner 1984, to name a few). Furthermore, teachers' beliefs have been found to be highly resistant to change (e.g., Bandura 1986; Pajares 1992).

Since the 1990s, exploratory, descriptive, and interpretative ethnographic studies have drawn attention to the complexity of the sociocultural context of EFL classrooms and intercultural language learning. Qualitative methods have enabled researchers to focus on the meaning teachers give to culture, the relationship between language and culture, and intercultural competence. The findings help to explain what teachers believe is taking place with respect to this aspect of their classroom teaching. The search for an understanding of how teachers understand the word "culture" is often traced back to anthropological patterns described by Kroeber and Kluckhohn (1952) and Keesing (1981), who categorized elements of culture in terms of their linkage to cognitive, structural, and adaptive systems (descriptive, historical, and normative).

In the last two decades, studies of foreign language teachers have investigated perceptions of culture as a preliminary to exploring interculturality in classroom contexts. Ryan's (1994) ethnographic study at a major university in Mexico, for example, focused on teacher beliefs about culture and the teaching of culture in EFL classrooms The findings revealed that teachers' beliefs were linked to their pedagogical choices and student perceptions of cultural aspects in their language classes. This qualitative study drew attention to the relationship between university English teachers' beliefs about the nature of culture and their classroom instruction. A dichotome appeared between the teachers' perceptions of culture and how they handled it in their teaching. For some, their definitions of culture were broad, embracing many aspects of daily life; others limited their perception of culture to knowledge of world literature and the arts. Some used metaphorical language to capture their ideas in the form of photographic snapshots on which to hang definitions of culture, while conveying the highly personal nature of the concept (Ryan 1997).

Later studies of teacher perceptions, beliefs, attitudes, and knowledge have explored such aspects as: how teachers perceive the concept "intercultural"; to what extent interculturality is part of their teaching goals; and how they deal with intercultural communication in the classroom. Sercu et al. (2005) compiled data from researchers in seven countries (Belgium, Bulgaria, Poland, Mexico, Greece, Spain, and Sweden) to build up a comprehensive picture of how teachers' thinking and their perceptions, beliefs, attitudes, and knowledge relate to their current professional self-concepts, and how these self-concepts profile the intercultural FL teacher. Although this project did not specifically address the question of EIL, many, but not all, of the respondents were teachers of English in international settings where the language had various levels of use in the local community.

The second aim of this large-scale project was to determine to what extent current FL teaching is directed toward attaining intercultural competence. Third, the researchers wanted to know the degree of teacher willingness to interculturalize foreign language education. Sercu et al.'s (2005) project culminated in the production of country-specific case studies and a cross-country comparison of FL teachers and their perceptions (for example, see Ryan and Sercu 2003 for the complete analysis of a particular country, Mexico).

In general, the findings suggested that many teachers still perceived teaching and learning culture and intercultural competence in terms of the transmission of teacher knowledge, rather than in terms of assisting learners to develop as intercultural speakers. This is significant because research on teacher beliefs has shown a reasonably direct relationship between teacher perceptions of teaching and learning and the ways in which teachers shape their teaching. Interestingly, however, this study brought to light a mismatch between teachers' willingness to teach intercultural communication and the way in which they shaped their teaching practice. Sercu et al. (2005) speculated that FL teachers may not be clear in their own minds about what intercultural communication means and what their role(s) should be. Many FL teachers appear to define intercultural communication primarily as familiarity with some aspects of a foreign culture (Sercu et al. 2005: 166). Further, they are unsure how to cultivate intercultural competence in FL learners. Sercu et al. (2005) concluded that it is imperative that FL teachers move well beyond the traditional view that it is sufficient to broaden the minds of learners by simply transmitting culture-specific information to them.

In EIL contexts, McKay (2002) and McKay and Bokhorst-Heng (2008) argue for the concept of thinking globally, but acting locally. In particular, McKay and Bokhorst-Heng (2008) argue that "EIL should be relevant to the domains in which English is used in the particular learning contexts" and that "EIL should be taught in a way that respects the local culture of learning" (pp. 196–97). Teachers' views about this aspect of language and culture teaching can have a significant impact on what happens in English language classrooms in international settings.

## 5. The EFL classroom and the process of becoming an intercultural person

We now turn to the process of becoming an EFL speaker with intercultural communicative competence. In doing so, we must consider what approach and experiences can lead the student to reach intercultural awareness and competence. How can EFL teachers prompt students to think about their own culture and other cultures that they will come into contact with when using English? In the intersection of multiple native and target cultures, Kramsch (1993) maintains that learners of foreign languages need to "create a culture of the third kind in which they can express their own meanings without being hostage to the meanings of either their own or the target speech communities" (pp. 13–14). This "third place" may evolve as the learner makes sense of dialogues with "others" in intercultural encounters. This interaction may be facilitated by the EFL teacher in or outside of class (e.g., online pen pals, world literature in English, face-to-face meetings with English-speaking international students on campus). (For a discussion of telecollaboration and the development of intercultural communicative competence, see Chapter 21, this volume.)

Students often experience a heightened awareness of self through the challenges they face in their contact with different cultures inside the classroom or elsewhere. Initially, they may feel very strongly that their core culture is somehow the only "correct" or "natural" one; their ethnocentric stance can then lead to reluctance to integrate new cultural ideas into their worldview. In Ryan (2006), for example, three Mexican EFL speakers had very specific notions about their own identities; this impacted on their openness to other ways of being and their intercultural communicative competence. Adler (1975) intensely studied learning about oneself in what he termed "evolving psychocultural patterns of identity" that are affected by human diversity experiences. For him, at the core of the intercultural person's cultural identity is an image of self and culture intertwined with the individual's total concept of reality. The intercultural person stands out as an adaptive person undergoing personal transitions in a state of flux, with continual dissolution and reformation of identity and growth. This person, according to Adler (1975), has a multicultural identity and a psychological state of not owning or being owned by a single culture.

Intercultural communicative competence is linked to communicative competence in a foreign language, i.e., a person's ability to act in a foreign language in a linguistically, sociolinguistically, and pragmatically appropriate way. Hence, intercultural communicative competence enlarges communicative competence to include intercultural competence. In the early 1990s, one of the major contributions to our conception of intercultural competence was the model that Byram and Zarate (1997) presented as input for the *Common European Framework of Reference for Languages* (Council of Europe 2001). These FL specialists attempted to refine what was then called "sociocultural competence" (Canale and Swain 1980) by introducing what they termed four *savoirs* (Byram and Zarate 1997). This model incorporated: *savoirs* (declarative knowledge), *savoir faire* (skills and know-how), *savoir être* (existential competence), and *savoir apprendre*, which was further extended by Byram (1997) to include *savoir s'engager* (critical cultural awareness/political education), as illustrated in Figure 26.1. The five *savoirs* fall into categories of knowledge, skills, behavior, and attitudes/traits. (For further details about the origins of the intercultural speaker and the evolution of a cultural dimension in language teaching, see Byram 2009; Byram and Fleming 1998; Feng *et al.* 2009; Risager 2006, 2007; Sercu *et al.* 2005; see also Chapters 5 and 18, this volume.)

Byram's (1997) visual illustration of intercultural competence is a prescriptive, ideal model aimed at providing direction for the development of intercultural learning objectives for FL teaching and learning. In this model, the concept of "critical cultural awareness" is crucial. Byram defines this element as "an ability to evaluate critically and on the basis of explicit criteria perspective, practices and products in one's own and other cultures and countries" (Byram 1997: 53). Hence, an important objective of learning is to develop "the ability to decentre from one's own culture and its practices and products in order to gain insight into another" (Byram 2006: 117).

When discussing his model, Byram (1997) establishes a difference between "bicultural" and "intercultural" speakers. For him, the former tend to experience tension between their own values and identity in one culture *vis-à-vis* the other culture. The intercultural speaker, however, is more of a mediator, able to negotiate between both cultures, while possessing an individual identity that is flexible. In other words, this person can experience two cultures and possess motivation (attitudes), knowledge, and skills that enable him or her to interact in both cultures without experiencing identity conflict (Deardorff 2009: 18).

The purpose of Byram's (1997) model is to encourage language teachers to build into their teaching specific objectives that address the critical cultural awareness component. Byram (1997) recommends that teachers focus on the values or behaviors identified in his model and use them as specific standards or criteria for evaluation. He advocates that teachers train learners to adopt a reflective stance on intercultural interaction so that they draw their attention back on themselves in order to develop critical awareness of both self and other. He argues that learners should cultivate their own evaluative processes and consider ways to enhance their intercultural behavior. In early publications, Byram maintained that teachers should not try to change learner values when promoting intercultural communicative competence (Byram 1997; Byram *et al.* 2002).

Guilherme (2002: 166–207) holds a different position with respect to the role of FL education in changing learners' values. In her research, she proposed that teachers should bring

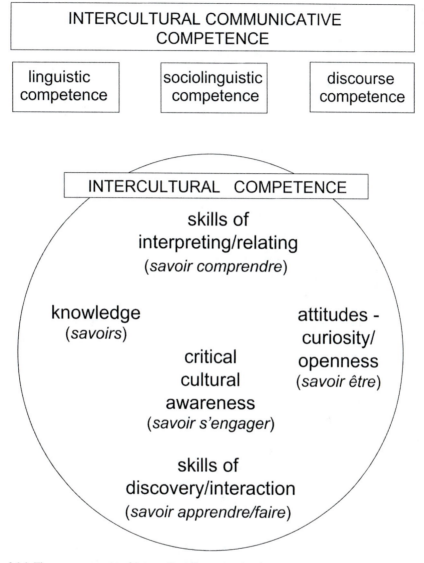

INTERCULTURAL COMMUNICATIVE
COMPETENCE

| linguistic competence | sociolinguistic competence | discourse competence |

INTERCULTURAL COMPETENCE

skills of
interpreting/relating
(*savoir comprendre*)

knowledge
(*savoirs*)

attitudes -
curiosity/
openness
(*savoir être*)

critical
cultural
awareness
(*savoir s'engager*)

skills of
discovery/interaction
(*savoir apprendre/faire*)

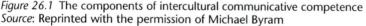

*Figure 26.1* The components of intercultural communicative competence
*Source*: Reprinted with the permission of Michael Byram

student values in line with democratic principles and human rights, promoting social justice and responsible global citizenship. In her view, it might be necessary to change learner values. Byram appears to be somewhat more open to such change later (Byram 2008; Byram and Guilherme 2002: 70–76) as discussion of intercultural competence, identity, and FL teaching began to merge with education for citizenship and democracy (Byram 2008; Osler and Starkey 1996).

Owing to its nature as a schematization, Houghton (2010: 324) argues that Byram's (1997) model "doesn't specify in every detail the intercultural speaker, the prescription of how learners should develop is limited". In her view, his model does not provide FL teachers with a clear understanding of ways in which to organize their teaching to foster intercultural communicative competence in their students. Houghton (2010) extended Byram's (1997) model in her empirical study of the development of critical cultural awareness in English language learners at a Japanese university. Her research project explored the issue of value judgment in critical cultural awareness and the ability of language learners to bring to different kinds of cultural experience a "rational and explicit standpoint from which to evaluate" the encounter. She explored the type of learning objectives that can and should be set when teachers deal with the complexity of values, prejudice, and evaluative processes. Her research design entailed three different teaching approaches. In the first, teachers trained students to adopt a non-judgmental stance toward difference, while engaging in intellectual empathy by taking the perspective of others. In the second, teachers trained learners to focus their attention back on themselves to develop critical awareness of their own evaluative processes and biases in order to control themselves. The teachers did not try to change the learners' values. In the third, the teachers followed the second approach but also aimed to bring student values in line with democratic principles and human rights, promoting social justice. Hence, the teachers aimed to change learner values, if necessary. Based on her findings, the model Houghton (2010) proposed centered on the complexity of issues of evaluation or judgment in foreign language education in relation to learning objectives (Barnett 1997; see Tables 4–6 in Houghton 2009b: 25–28). Her model revolves around the analysis of value systems and analytical consciousness-raising that can empower students to consciously reprioritize their own conflicting values.

Houghton (2010) compared her model with Byram's (1997) model of intercultural communicative competence and Barnett's levels of critical reflection (1997: 95–99) with the aim of identifying conceptual links between them. She proposed that *savoir se transformer*, knowing how to become, knowing how to develop oneself selectively through interaction with others, be added to Byram's (1997, 2008) models and be recognized in the *Common European Framework of Reference for Languages* (Council of Europe 2001: 101–6).

## 6. Conclusion

The intention of this chapter has been to draw attention to some of the primary issues of concern related to the teaching of EFL/EIL and the nurturing of intercultural communicative competence in these language classrooms. In particular, one cannot ignore the unique positioning and status of English and its impact on local languages and identities. The global spread of the language is bringing about the decentering of the native speaker and the emergence of EIL classrooms where varieties of English are recognized and used. This is a significant departure from traditional EFL classrooms that center on a native speaker model of English in a particular English-speaking nation. As noted by Risager (2007), in FL teaching, we are seeing a paradigm shift from a national to a transnational orientation, and this will continue to impact on the teaching and learning of English in non-English-speaking countries in years to come.

As more attention is being paid to the language and intercultural learning in non-Western settings, we are gaining more insight into elements that can affect the development of intercultural communicative competence in EFL/EIL settings. It is now apparent that more attention must be paid to the cultural element in FL teacher education programs as well as in in-service workshops or courses for practicing teachers. It is imperative that language teachers understand the core dimensions of intercultural communicative competence and are familiar with the models discussed in this chapter, as well as their pedagogical implications. We must be mindful of teacher perceptions about the relationship between language and culture and their key role in promoting and assessing the development of intercultural communicative competence in their students.

## 7. Future research

The discussion in this chapter suggests several lines of inquiry that should be pursued in empirical studies. For example, further research is needed that explores the construct of intercultural communicative competence within the context of EIL. We need more understanding of the concept of self in relation to "others" and EFL/EIL classroom environments. We could also benefit from investigations of inner conflicts in language learners as well as the analysis of reflective accounts of language and cultural learning experience that focus on changing values, identities, and perceptions. It is also important to study the fostering of critical cultural awareness in EFL/EIL classes as a basis for intercultural citizenship. Further development of pedagogical models that systematize intercultural learning and competences is also needed. Thick ethnographic description, as suggested by Holliday (2005), may be used to explore the development of intercultural awareness and self-understanding in FL learners.

It would also be worthwhile for researchers to study teacher/student thinking about facets of intercultural communicative competence in diverse language learning contexts (Han 2009; Ryan 1994; Ryan and Sercu 2003). Researchers could also explore student values and the development of critical cultural awareness in EFL/EIL classes (Houghton 2009a,b), and reading literary texts as a route to intercultural learning in FL education (Matos 2007). The findings should help us to better understand how language and culture interact with different language speakers in various settings, and lead to more awareness of how and to what extent interculturality occurs.

Research on teacher thinking and understandings of interculturality would benefit from more studies in FL classroom situations (e.g., ethnographic investigations, surveys, mixed method studies). The findings could offer additional insight into factors that affect the teaching and learning of FL and culture. Studies of this nature could help us to discover the most effective and appropriate ways to promote intercultural communicative competence in diverse settings where non-native speakers are learning English. This line of inquiry could lead to enhancements in the intercultural development of both EFL/EIL teachers and learners.

## Related topics

Culture and context; English as an international language; foreign language education; intercultural communicative competence; the intercultural speaker; linguaculture; SLA; L2 pedagogy; transnationalism; world Englishes

## Further reading

Byram, M. (2009) 'Intercultural competence in foreign languages, the intercultural speaker and the pedagogy of foreign language education' in D.K. Deardorff (ed.) *The SAGE Handbook of Intercultural Competence*, Thousand Oaks, CA: Sage pp. 321–32. (this chapter discusses the notion of the intercultural speaker, its origins and applications within foreign language education. It encourages language teachers to include objectives, materials, and methods that develop the specific elements of intercultural competence).

Byram, M., Gribkova, B. and Starkey, H. (2002) *Developing the Intercultural Dimension in Language Teaching: A Practical Introduction for Teachers*, Strasbourg: Council of Europe (this book provides foreign language teachers with useful, practical advice for embedding an intercultural dimension into their teaching).

Holliday, A. (2005) *The Struggle to Teach English as an International Language*, Oxford: Oxford University Press (this book discusses social and political issues related to the teaching of English in international contexts).

Risager, K. (2007) *Language and Culture Pedagogy: From a National to a Transnational Paradigm*, Clevedon: Multilingual Matters (this book offers an overview of the history of culture teaching and a new transnational perspective on language and culture pedagogy).

Sercu, L., Bandura, E., Castro, P., Davcheva, L., Laskaridou, C., Lundgren, U., Méndez García, M. and Ryan, P. (2005) *Foreign Language Teachers and Intercultural Competence: An International Investigation*, Clevedon: Multilingual Matters (this book reports on an investigation of teacher beliefs about the cultural dimension of foreign language teaching and learning).

## Note

1 Participants may also meet new cultures and languages among their peers in the classroom but, for the sake of clarity, we will not consider these complications.

## References

Abelson, R. (1979) 'Differences between belief systems and knowledge systems', *Cognitive Science*, 3: 355–66.

Adler, P.S. (1975) 'The transitional experience: an alternative view of culture shock', *Journal of Humanistic Psychology*, 15(4): 13–24.

Alptekin, C. (2002) 'Towards intercultural communicative competence in ELT', *ELT Journal*, 56(1): 57–64.

Alred, G., Byram, M. and Fleming, M. (eds) (2003) *Intercultural Experience and Education*, Clevedon: Multilingual Matters.

——(2006) *Education for Intercultural Citizenship, Concepts and Comparisons*, Clevedon: Multilingual Matters.

Alvarez, I. (2007) 'Foreign language education at the crossroads: whose model of competence?', *Language, Culture and Curriculum*, 20(2): 126–39.

Bandura, A. (1986) *Social Foundations of Thought and Action: A Social Cognitive Theory*, Englewood Cliffs, NJ: Prentice-Hall, Inc.

Barnett, M. (1997) *Higher Education: A Critical Business*, Buckingham: Open University Press.

Byram, M. (1997) *Teaching and Assessing Intercultural Communicative Competence*, Clevedon: Multilingual Matters.

——(2006) 'Developing a concept of intercultural citizenship', in D. Alred, M. Byram and M. Fleming (eds) *Education for Intercultural Citizenship: Concepts and Comparisons*, Clevedon: Multilingual Matters, pp. 109–29.

——(2008) *Foreign Language Education to Education for Intercultural Citizenship: Essays and Reflections*, Clevedon: Multilingual Matters.

——(2009) 'Intercultural competence in foreign languages, the intercultural speaker and the pedagogy of foreign language education' in D.K. Deardorff (ed.) *The SAGE Handbook of Intercultural Competence*, Thousand Oaks, CA: Sage, pp. 321–32.

Byram, M. and Fleming, M. (eds) (1998) *Language Learning in Intercultural Perspective*, Cambridge: Cambridge University Press.

Byram, M. and Guilherme, M. (2002) 'Human rights culture and language teaching', in A. Osler, (ed.) *Citizenship and Democracy in Schools: Diversity, Identity, Equality*, Stoke on Trent: Trentham Books, pp. 63–79.

Byram, M. and Zarate, G. (1997) 'Definitions, objectives and assessment of sociocultural competence', in *Sociocultural Competence in Language Learning and Teaching*, Strasbourg: Council of Europe, pp. 7–43.

Byram, M., Gribkova, B. and Starkey, H. (2002) *Developing the Intercultural Dimension in Language Teaching: A Practical Introduction for Teachers*, Strasbourg: Council of Europe.

Canale, M. and Swain, M. (1980) 'Theoretical bases of communicative approaches to second language teaching and testing', *Applied Linguistics*, 1: 1–47.

Clark, C.M. and Peterson, P.L. (1986) 'Teacher thought processes', in M.C. Wittrock, (ed.) *Handbook of Research on Teaching*, 3rd edn, New York: Macmillan, pp. 255–93.

Corbett, J. (2003) *An Intercultural Approach to English Language Teaching*, Clevedon: Multilingual Matters.

Council of Europe (2001) *Common European Framework of Reference for Languages*, Strasbourg: Council of Europe.

Crystal, D. (2003) *English as a Global Language*, 2nd edn, Cambridge: Cambridge University Press.

Deardorff, D.K. (ed.) (2009) *The SAGE Handbook of Intercultural Competence*, Thousand Oaks, CA: Sage.

Feng, A., Byram, M. and Fleming, M. (eds) (2009) *Becoming Interculturally Competent through Education and Training*, Bristol: Multilingual Matters.

Guilherme, M. (2002) *Critical Citizens for an Intercultural World: Foreign Language Education as Cultural Politics*, Clevedon: Multilingual Matters.

Han, H. (2009) 'An investigation of teachers' perceptions of culture teaching in secondary schools in Xinjiang, China', doctoral dissertation, University of Durham, UK.

Holliday, A. (2005) *The Struggle to Teach English as an International Language*, Oxford: Oxford University Press.

Houghton, S. (2009a) 'Intercultural mediation in the mono-lingual, mono-cultural foreign language classroom: a case study in Japan', *Cultus 2: Training and Competence*, 117–32.

——(2009b) 'The role of intercultural communicative competence in the development of world Englishes and lingua francas', *The South East Asian Journal of English Language Studies*, 15: 69–95.

——(2010) '*Savoir se transformer*: knowing how to become', in Y. Tsai and S. Houghton (eds) *Becoming Intercultural: Inside and Outside the Classroom*, Cambridge: Cambridge Scholars Publishing, pp. 194–228.

Hymes, D.H. (1971) *On Communicative Competence*, Philadelphia, PA: University of Pennsylvania Press.

Jenkins, J. (2009) *World Englishes*, 2nd edn, London: Routledge.

Kachru, B.B., Kachru, Y. and Nelson, C.L. (eds) (2006) *The Handbook of World Englishes*, Oxford: Blackwell.

Keesing, R.M. (1981) 'Theories of culture', in R. Chasson (ed.) *Language, Culture and Cognition*, New York: Macmillan.

Kirkpatrick, A. (2010) *Routledge Handbook of World Englishes*, London/New York: Routledge.

Kramsch, C. (1993) *Context and Culture in Language Teaching*, Oxford: Oxford University Press.

Kroeber, A.L. and Kluckhohn, D. (1952) *Culture: A Critical Review of Concepts and Definitions*, Cambridge, MA: Harvard University Press.

McKay, S.L. (2002) *Teaching English as an International Language*, Oxford: Oxford University Press.

McKay, S.L. and Bokhorst-Heng, W.D. (2008) *International English and its Sociolinguistic Contexts: Towards a Socially Sensitive EIL Pedagogy*, New York: Routledge.

Matos, A.A. (2007) 'Literary texts: a passage to intercultural learning in foreign language education', doctoral dissertation, Universidade Nova de Lisboa, Lisbon, Portugal.

Osler, A. and Starkey, H. (1996) *Teacher Education and Human Rights*, London: David Fulton.

Pajares, F. (1992) 'Teachers' beliefs and educational research: cleaning up a messy construct', *Review of Educational Research*, 62(3): 307–32.

Risager, K. (2006) *Language and Culture: Global Flows and Local Complexity*, Clevedon: Multilingual Matters.

——(2007) *Language and Culture Pedagogy: From a National to a Transnational Paradigm*, Clevedon: Multilingual Matters.

Ryan, P. (1994) 'Foreign language teachers' perceptions of culture and the classroom: a case study', doctoral dissertation, Department of Educational Studies, University of Utah, Salt Lake City, Utah (ERIC document: ED 385 135 1–25).

——(1997) 'Sociological goals for foreign language teaching and teachers' metaphorical images of culture', *Foreign Language Annals*, 29(4): 571–86.

——(2004) 'Teacher thinking', in M. Byram (ed.) *Routledge Encyclopedia of Language Teaching and Learning*, 2nd edn, London: Routledge, pp. 610–16.

——(2006) 'Interculturality, identity and citizenship education in Mexico', in *Education for Intercultural Citizenship: Concepts and Comparisons*, Clevedon: Multilingual Matters, pp. 11–22.

Ryan, P. and Sercu, L. (2003) 'Foreign language teachers and their roles as mediators of language-and-culture: a study in Mexico', *Estudios de Lingüística Aplicada*, 21(37): 99–118.

Saraceni, M. (2009) 'Relocating English: towards a new paradigm for English in the world', *Language and Intercultural Communication*, 9(3): 175–86.

Savignon, S.J. (1997) *Communicative Competence: Theory and Classroom Practice*, 2nd edn, New York: McGraw-Hill.

Sercu, L., Bandura, E., Castro, P., Davcheva, L., Laskaridou, C., Lundgren, U., Méndez García, M. and Ryan, P. (2005) *Foreign Language Teachers and Intercultural Competence: An International Investigation*, Clevedon: Multilingual Matters.

Sharifian, F. (ed.) (2009) *English as an International Language: Perspectives and Pedagogical Issues*, Bristol: Multilingual Matters.

Tabachnick, B. and Zeichner, F. (1984) 'Teacher beliefs and classroom behavior: some teachers responses to inconsistency', in M. Ben-Peretz, R. Bromme and R. Halkes (eds) *Advances of Research on Teacher Thinking*, Lisse: Swets and Zeitlinger, pp. 84–96.

# 27

# The multicultural classroom

*Jennifer Mahon and Kenneth Cushner*

## 1. Introduction

The American Association of Colleges of Teacher Education (AACTE 2010) has created a blueprint for what education should look like in the twenty-first century. They argue that educators must be able to prepare their students for a dynamic, changing, and global world. The authors explain:

> Whether a high school graduate plans to enter the workforce directly, or attend a vocational school, community college, or university, it is a requirement to be able to think critically, solve problems, communicate, collaborate, find good information quickly, and use technology effectively. These are today's survival skills – not only for career success, but for personal and civic quality of life as well.
>
> *AACTE (2010: 10)*

In order to prepare students for such a future, much is demanded of teachers. They must be effective and competent communicators, possess a critical understanding of the content they teach and the context in which it is taught, and command a wide variety of pedagogical and assessment techniques. And perhaps most of all, they must adapt such knowledge and skills to a wide range of culturally and linguistically diverse learners who inhabit an increasingly complex world. For, as we like to emphasize in our own work with pre-service and in-service teachers, all classrooms are multicultural, and teachers must be interculturally skilled mediators who enable learning to occur for everyone.

This chapter focuses on intercultural communication competence for the multicultural classroom. Based on our perspective from our years working in the United States, we have designed this chapter with the general education classroom in mind—a context in which one person must manage the academic and psychosocial needs of a large group of diverse students for the majority of the school day. Although this volume emphasizes linguistic and communicative contexts, we recognize that today's general education teacher wears many hats. She must reach not only English language learners (ELLs) but simultaneously individualize instruction across a broad variety of learner requirements such as academic readiness, cognitive abilities, learning disabilities, maturity levels, religious differences, behavioral and physical challenges. With such a guarantee of diversity in the classroom, it would seem that intercultural competence would be a generally agreed upon skill that should be demonstrated by all teachers. Unfortunately, although educators have attempted to address this area for decades, as a result of political and ideological debates, concepts related to intercultural understanding and communicative competence remain on the margins, rather than central to the preparation and development of teachers. These are some of the challenges we discuss en route to offering suggestions for the types of knowledge and skills teachers must possess to be successful in today's classroom.

## 2. Historical perspectives

A plethora of terminology exists that makes reference to culture in education including multicultural education (Banks and Banks 2004), global or international education (Hanvey 1975; Merryfield 1996), intercultural competence of educators (Cushner and Mahon 2010), peace education (Stomfay-Stitz 1993), and culturally relevant or responsive education (Gay 2000; Ladson-Billings 1994). For our purposes, we define intercultural competence as the critical knowledge and skills that enable teachers to be successful in culturally different contexts and to manage interactions between students and teachers in multicultural settings that represent such sociocultural factors as race, ethnicity, ability, sexuality, socioeconomics, and language. We will now turn our attention to the historical development of language and education in the US.

Although details of terminology are beyond the chapter's scope, suffice it to say that the interest in attending to culture in the teaching–learning process has been emphasized in the US at times when immigrants and minorities were most noticeable—that is, during waves of immigration at the turn of the century and during the Civil Rights Movement of the 1960s. Originally, such efforts were designed to help assimilate immigrants to an American (white, Protestant, middle-class) way of life and, to a lesser extent, to build peace and understanding between cultures. These concerns were not led by immigrants or minorities, as it was not until the 1960s that people of color began to have a say in the content and direction of schooling.

Ricento and Wright (2008) explain that, when public schooling began in the US in the late 1800s, the attitude toward linguistic diversity was negative. English as the language of instruction became mandated in thirty-four states by the early 1900s. Some of this began to change in the 1930s. The oppressive system of the Bureau of Indian Affairs boarding schools, which denounced Native American languages, began to "relax" and, as the Civil Rights era took root, bilingual education started to gain some support. The Bilingual Education Act of 1968 "authorized the use of non-English languages in the education of low-income language minority students" (Ricento and Wright 2008: 287). In 1974, the US Supreme Court in Lau v Nichols utilized the Civil Rights Act to find that the San Francisco School District failed to provide an adequate education to Chinese students because it did not address their linguistic needs. The Office of Civil Rights produced the Lau Remedies, which instructed school districts on the identification and instruction of ELLs. However, opposition arose to a remedy known as bilingual maintenance, which enabled students to keep their first language while acquiring English. Schools were soon required to transition students to English-only classrooms within 3 years.

In 2002, the federal government would repeal the Bilingual Education Act and replace it with the policy known as No Child Left Behind (NCLB). This policy mandated accountability, high stakes testing, and teacher quality for all students including ELLs, but "all references to 'bilingual education' were stripped from the law". The law implemented strict guidelines regarding the instruction, mainstreaming, and testing of ELLs. NCLB authorized states to provide testing accommodations to ELLs, and students may be tested in their native language for 5 years (Ricento and Wright 2008).

According to Waxman and Tellez (2006), preparing teachers to work with ELLs was "largely ignored" until the 1980s. Where bilingual education did exist, teachers were to speak as much of the language, generally Spanish, as possible, whereas in English education, teachers were told to teach in English as students would eventually "catch on". This changed for two reasons. As the demographics of ELLs increased, more teaching jobs opened to work with these students. Second, research (Garcia 1990) pointing to the dismal quality of teaching for ELLs across the country led educators and legislators to focus attention on teacher training. However, research (Alexander *et al.* 1999; Lewis *et al.* 1999) indicated that, despite the increased efforts, educators still reported feeling unprepared to work with culturally and linguistically diverse students. At the same time, national data on student achievement were continually showing the discrepancy in performance between ELLs and their English-speaking counterparts. According to Genesee *et al.* (2005), NCLB drew attention to this problem. "Although schools may exempt ELLs from achievement testing in English for up to three years, they must assess English language proficiency annually (with no exemption period)" (Genesee *et al.* 2005: 364).

## 3. Critical issues

With the passage of NCLB and its emphasis on teacher quality, logic dictates that greater attention would be put on the highly qualified teacher of ELLs as for other areas such as math or science. Gándara and Maxwell-Jolly (2006) hold that little has been done to define what "highly qualified" looks like for the English language teacher. Federal policy, they contend, has focused on efforts that can most quickly move students into mainstreamed classes.

Some of this urgency may be because language and language education are hot-button issues in the US as they relate to issues such as immigration, health care, and global economic competitiveness. The central issue involves the debate over whether a majority language should be a condition of citizenship (which, of course, then creates a definition of the good citizen) and if this requirement should be "at the *expense* of, or in *addition* to the maintenance of other languages" (May 2008: 15; emphasis in original). This has obvious implications for the role of second and foreign language instruction. Teachers have been considered the "guardians" of appropriate language—both implicitly and explicitly—through language policy, often placing them in a precarious position (Wiley 2008). On the one hand, the federal government provides latitude and funding for language initiatives, but educators must also follow state rules that may dictate the type of instruction used. For example, in California, Arizona, and Massachusetts, teachers have been subject to English-only language policies that prescribe appropriate methods for teaching ELLs.

There is copious research in second language acquisition that has "provided clear evidence" of such things as late-exit bilingual programs, immersion programs for native English speakers, issues of transferability of knowledge between languages, and the importance of utilizing student language and culture. Nonetheless, this research has been "distorted and politicized by opponents" (Ricento and Wright 2008: 295).

Wiley argues that teachers are not immune from such distortions. "Many educators tend to be influenced more by the political climate and common discourse related to citizenship and language diversity than they are informed by theory and research" (Wiley 2008: 231). Problems arise from "institutional practices and teachers' folk theories" regarding language use in the classroom and teaching. Discriminatory practices include unfair assessment and grading, prohibiting language minority students from enrollment in certain courses, and lack of identification of students needing language assistance.

In their report of the American Educational Research Association (AERA) Panel on Research and Teacher Education, editors Cochran-Smith and Zeichner (2005) examine the issues surrounding US teacher readiness to work with second language learners. The authors note that a major concern is the amount of training received by teachers. Citing a 2002 study by Gruber et al., they explain that, of the 41 percent of teachers who worked with limited English-proficient (LEP) students, only 12.5 percent had at least 8 hours of training. Seastrom et al. (2002) found that 36 percent of non-English-speaking students were taught by untrained teachers lacking "any earned credentials that researchers have identified as indicators of teacher qualifications" (p. 4). Additionally, 73 percent of teachers working with ELL students lacked both a major and certificate—"the two earned credentials that researchers have identified as elements of teacher qualifications that are associated with high student performance" (ibid. 2002: 4). State licensure requirements in this area are uneven (Morrier et al. 2007). Eleven states (Arizona, California, Florida, Colorado, Massachusetts, Minnesota, New Jersey, New York, North Dakota, Rhode Island, and Vermont) required competence for licensure when an individual was pursuing certification or endorsement in bilingual education or English as a Second Language (ESL). The remaining thirty-nine states had no specific requirements.

Beyond licensure, US schools of education look to the standards created by three national organizations. These include the Interstate New Teachers Assessment and Support Consortium (INTASC), the Association for Teacher Educators (ATE), and the National Council for Accreditation of Teacher Education (NCATE). Of these, the last organization, as the chief accrediting body, is the one most commonly consulted.

Each of these organizations includes some language regarding teachers' abilities to address diversity. Yet researchers have argued that none of these standards is extensive enough to ensure that teachers will be competent to meet the needs of students from culturally diverse backgrounds (Peterman 2005; Zeichner 2003). Beginning in the fall of 2007, NCATE modified its standards. Linguistic diversity was added for the first time, and "diversity" is now defined according to the US Census categories. Perhaps most significant is the addition of the following statement: "Candidates are helped to understand the potential impact of discrimination based on race, class, gender, disability, sexual orientation, and language on students and their learning" (NCATE 2008: 2). Thus, although teacher preparation has existed in the US for more than 100 years, it was not until 2008 that institutions were held accountable for instructing future educators on the impact of discrimination on the teaching and learning process.

Concerning the needs of language learners specifically, the major teacher education accrediting bodies such as NCATE, the International Reading Association (IRA), Teachers of English to Speakers of Other Languages (TESOL), and the National Council on the Teaching of English (NCTE) have adopted standards addressing the instruction of language minority students. However, Wiley (2008) argues that standards often lead to "overly prescribed curricula". Instead, educators should attend to the rationale behind the standards and the interests of those involved in their construction. Too often, such policies are grounded in notions of deficiency:

> To what extent do educational standards adequately take into consideration and reflect the language needs of all students? Advocates of educational standards contend that standards provide an explicit foundation for measuring student progress against national expectations as well as for cross-national educational comparisons. Student demographics, resources, and

materials, however, vary greatly between countries and within them. Language minority students can be disadvantaged by educational standards, particularly when their home and community languages are ignored or held in low regard by teachers. Therefore, in order for educational standards to be equitable, teachers must have an understanding of the specific linguistic and cultural resources all students bring with them to school.

*Wiley (2008: 235)*

In summary, the history and examination of critical issues surrounding the education and teaching of ELLs in the US has indicated substantial problems. Although such knowledge and skills are often stated in the rhetoric about what teachers should be able to know and do to best impact the learning and preparation of their students for an interdependent, global existence, the reality is that such skills are not tested and their teaching is inconsistent at best.

## 4. Current contributions and research

In our previous work (Cushner and Mahon 2010), we discussed the important aspects of intercultural competence as related to teaching and teacher education. Based on our own research as well as reviews of the literature, we identified the following elements necessary to being an interculturally competent educator:

- Perception, perspective, and relationship-building;
- Cognition, complexity, and conflict;
- Cultural knowledge, attitude, and efficacy;
- International worldview.

In the following section, we expand on these areas as they relate to the teaching of English language learners. Although we discuss all of the elements, due to space limitations, we will focus on perception, perspective, and relationship-building as being most salient to the teaching of ELLs.

### Perception, perspective, and relationship-building

A crucial skill for the culturally competent teacher is to understand the realities of her students. She must recognize how she may perceive events and knowledge differently than her students, and how different perspectives affect the teaching and learning environment. In order to broaden intercultural competence, teachers must engage in learning more about student experience in and out of the classroom. In this way, teachers can work to build safe and trusting relationships across cultures that are vital to successful learning and teaching. Communication is a central element in this equation. Concerning language learners, this involves recognizing the importance of culturally influenced factors such as communication contexts and styles.

### Perception and perspective

Many studies point to the power of teacher perception. Differences in perceptions of appropriate communicative behaviors, especially in regard to personal disclosure, discourse, and display (Gay 2006), have been shown to have clear effects on classroom interactions (McCarthy and Benally 2003; Powell and Caseau 2004). As in any context, a predominant pattern of communication and interaction can be found in classrooms. In classrooms around the world, typical interaction has been characterized as a game in which participants follow set rules with four fairly common moves: structuring and establishing a context for appropriate and expected behavior (e.g., "today we will discuss … "); soliciting aims to elicit a verbal response from students (e.g., "Did you bring your supplies for today's class?"); responses to student answers; and reacting moves, or statements used to modify or evaluate students' responses (Powell and Caseau 2004). When classroom communication unfolds in this manner, the teacher does most of the talking—in some cases, up to 70 percent or more—in relatively limited teacher-directed communicative behavior (Bellack *et al.* 1966; Cazden 1988; Haslett 1987).

Teacher questioning is one of the more frequent modes of interaction, designed to encourage students to participate and engage in the learning process. Frequent questioning by teachers correlates positively with student achievement (Brophy and Good 2000), with the maximum effect on learning related to the clarity of the questions and how the interaction is managed. Student achievement is enhanced when teachers ask clearly phrased questions, probe student responses, and provide feedback on the accuracy of their responses (Kindsvatter *et al.* 1996).

Yet communicative differences can confound this process. Hall (1976) suggested that, because people face so many daily stimuli, they develop filtering mechanisms to help simplify and make sense of things. Culture determines some of these filters, for example, how context can be used to facilitate communication. High-context communicators convey most of the information in the physical setting or internalized in the person, with much meaning implied. Thus, explicit, straightforward messages are not necessary to fully understand the intent. Low-context messages, on the other hand, demand that the message contains much explicit information. Most classroom communication exists in low-context exchanges, with teachers expected to be direct and linear in their instructions and expectations, and students to respond in kind. However, the further they diverge from these conventions, the more at risk they become.

Communication apprehension—a construct found to constrain learning in the classroom—is much discussed in the communication literature, but not much in the field of education. It is defined as "an individual's level of fear or anxiety associated with either real or anticipated communication with another person or persons" (McCroskey 1997: 82). People may have low communication apprehension in one context, among most teachers, for instance, who enter the profession fully aware of the high dependency on communication, but increased apprehension, perhaps, when communicating across cultures. The same occurs for children, who may be comfortable and facile in their home environment, thus experiencing low communication apprehension, yet exhibiting high anxiety and apprehension in a language-intensive classroom environment, especially for children from second language backgrounds.

In the instructional setting, students with high communication apprehension tend to have more difficulty in school than students with low communication apprehension (Powell and Caseau 2004). Such students may be less likely to seek the assistance of teachers, have difficulty articulating their instructional needs, have fewer friends, and are more likely to drop out of school (McCroskey and McCroskey 2002). Chesbro *et al.* (1992) studied communication apprehension in 2,793 at-risk US middle-school students in fourteen large, predominantly minority urban districts. They found that at-risk students were substantially more apprehensive about speaking in groups and in dyads—the most predominant means of classroom interaction. In the classroom, those high in communication apprehension may experience such intense internal discomfort and negative arousal that they attempt to avoid such situations by physically or psychologically withdrawing from the situation. For instance, instead of giving a required speech in a class, the student may feign illness and stay home, say that she or he does not understand the assignment, did not do it, or in rare circumstances, overparticipate in communication by attempting to talk through their anxiety. Those in second language or other interculturally stressed contexts will most certainly encounter communication apprehension to a higher degree than the general population of students.

Although some attribute communication apprehension to biological causes, Daly and Friedrich (1981) suggest that it may emerge as a consequence of the manner in which social skills (e.g., language use, sensitivity to nonverbal communication, and interaction management skills) are acquired or modeled. Here, perhaps ELLs, immigrant and refugee students in new cultural contexts, may not have acquired the requisite social skills and confidence to allow them to fully integrate and gain confidence in the classroom setting, thus resulting in anxiety, apprehension, or avoidance.

Among bilingual learners, those speaking a primary language at home while having to learn a new language for success in their schooling often encounter two levels of linguistic adjustment that were introduced by Cummins (1979) to draw attention to the different time periods typically required by immigrant children to acquire conversational fluency in their second language compared with grade-appropriate academic proficiency in that language. On one level, children may acquire Basic Interpersonal Communication Skills (BICS) relatively quickly and appear quite fluent within 2 or 3 years, at least on the surface. That is, second language learners in school may quickly be able to communicate effectively with other children during play, free time, and in informal interactions in the classroom. Yet, these same children struggle and may fail standardized tests of educational achievement as a secondary, deeper level of linguistic competence is at play. Students may require between 5 and 7 years to attain Cognitive Academic Language Proficiency (CALP)—the level of linguistic competence in a language typically required for school success.

Another area that needs further attention is in regard to communication skills and conflict resolution—topics that are thinly covered in the literature in regard to ELLs. Given the aforementioned issues of communication apprehension in learners and the saliency of communicative competence to a successful teaching and learning environment, it would seem logical that the communicative skills of teachers would be an important aspect of study in teacher education. Unfortunately, the research on communication skill training for teachers is generally outdated (see e.g., Applegate 1980; McCaleb 1987; Rubin and Feezel 1985, 1986; Willmington 1993). A lack of direct examination of communication competence is confusing given that research has shown the positive relationship between effective classroom communication and learning outcomes (Allen and Shaw 1990; Johnson and Roellke 1999; Wanzer and McCroskey 1998). Wubbels and colleagues (den Brok et al. 2002; Wubbels and Levy 1991; Wubbels et al. 1997) have published strong empirical research demonstrating the impact of teacher interpersonal behavior. Teachers with cooperative and dominant (assertive) interpersonal styles were perceived by students as more competent in the classroom. Empirical evidence shows that these same interpersonal styles positively affect student outcomes such as motivation and achievement (den Brok et al. 2002).

Teachers rarely see themselves as students do, often perceiving the learning environment more favorably than students, and seeing themselves as better leaders, more friendly, understanding, and cooperative than their students (Wubbels and Levy 1993). In one study looking at student perceptions of teacher communication style, students from Latin America who speak Spanish at home perceive teachers to be more dominant than do other cultural groups (e.g., Asians or domestic Anglo students). The more heterogeneity among the students, the more they perceived teachers to be submissive. The cultural makeup of a class, then, may affect teacher behavior—at least as perceived by students (Levy et al. 1997). Student interaction with culturally different teachers can also be a cause of concern. A study looking at communication between Thai secondary students and British teachers in an international school in Thailand found that, although students were aware that some differences existed between themselves and their teachers, they could rarely identify specific aspects of culture or communication differences in any consistent manner (Monthienvichienchai *et al.* 2002). The researchers attribute this to the fact that students were not likely to have much broad exposure to British culture, and were more likely to be interacting with individual teachers in a particular classroom setting. This is in contrast to the teachers who, interacting with Thai culture as a whole and with many Thai children in school, had far greater awareness of cultural differences. They knew, for instance, that they were more individualistic than their students, and talked about how their teaching strategies had to change in response to teaching their more collective students. Teachers were also aware that students sometimes found themselves walking in two worlds, so to speak. At home, they interacted in a more collectivist, high uncertainty avoidance, and high power distant context than they were encountering in their school. Although using a small sample size, they found a positive correlation between teachers' cultural awareness and communication competence.

Citing research by Chesterfield (1983), Genesee *et al.* (2005) contend that teacher interaction is especially important for less proficient ELLs. That is, students benefit more when talking with a teacher than with a peer. Second, the studies reviewed by the authors also suggest that such conversational interactions, whether between teacher/student or peers, needs to be well structured. It is not the conversation alone that offers benefits, but conversation that matches the needs and abilities of the ELL learner. Special attention needs to be given to "design of tasks, training of non-ELLs and language proficiency of the ELLs" (ibid. 2005: 368). Additionally, the authors noted that English use at school, rather than at home, has a stronger impact on English reading achievement. The literature shows that teachers must be aware of the importance of "carefully planned" strategies that combine direct instruction and interaction.

## Relationship-building

Just as student language abilities vary and may be influenced by communication apprehension, so do those of parents. Communication inside the school is as important as that outside of it. Research into parental involvement and home–school cooperation has received more attention in recent years. The Met Life Study of the American Teacher (Metropolitan Life 2005) found that 98 percent of teachers felt involvement with families was essential to good teaching. For new teachers, 31 percent admitted that parent communication and involvement was their greatest challenge.

Ramirez (2003) interviewed forty-three Latino parents regarding their interactions with their children's schools. Overwhelmingly, the parents reported wanting to be listened to. They also reported feeling frustrated, stereotyped, and that the teachers did not care about their children. In addition, they perceived that teachers tended to correlate showing up at school with being a "good parent", and that teachers lacked knowledge about cultural differences between Latino cultures such as Mexico and El Salvador. The author reported issues such as teachers pulling on ears when students misbehaved (in an all Spanish-speaking classroom), calling a student retarded because she did not speak in class, putting students in timeout when their parents brought them late to school, and advocating that parents needed to "turn off the TV and take care of their kids". When asked what the parents did in response, many reported feeling afraid to address issues in school because they feared retaliation.

## *Cognition, complexity, and conflict*

Educators need a more sophisticated and dynamic way of understanding and thinking about cultural interaction and communication. Coulby argues that educators need more complex understandings of culture in order to competently handle the difficult and tenuous aspects of intercultural interaction. He believes that intercultural education should be "an education able to negotiate between cultures rather than to show that there is more than one culture" (2006: 247). Further, he believes that "in order to make an academic contribution that goes beyond the parochial", educators must engage in debates around the central issues inherent in intercultural education including "identity and identity politics, government and governance, transitional economies and societies; nationalism and nation construction; and globalization" (p. 254).

Franson and Holliday (2009) argue that it is not enough for teachers to understand language acquisition, they must have a critical view of the ways in which language denotes power, the history of colonial oppression associated with English, and the relationship of racial and ethnic identity to language. They argue that teachers must not only understand the pressure put on linguistic minorities to play by the rules of English language acquisition, this knowledge must permeate their pedagogy. They advocate, for example, using case studies to make teacher candidates aware of the realities of language learning experienced by immigrants. "Student-teachers need to be made aware that learners bring multiple identities to the classroom, and to language learning and use, and to consider how they can use this knowledge to develop responsive curricula and pedagogy" (ibid.: 43).

## Cultural knowledge, attitude, and efficacy

Research into the attitudes and knowledge of pre-service teachers regarding English language learners appears to be mixed. Teacher candidates who were already proponents of bilingualism increased their support, whereas those who supported English-only approaches searched for evidence to buttress their beliefs (Katz 2000). In a school-wide study, Sharkey and Layzer (2000) found that teachers' attitudes, beliefs, and practices affected ELLs' placement in mainstream classes, teacher expectations and classroom interactions. The school was not providing an equitable learning environment, but practices were rationalized "in a discourse of well-meaning concern" for fear of overloading students who would be at risk for failure in too challenging conditions (Sharkey and Layzer 2000: 364). Citing Hatch (1992), the authors described this as a "benevolent conspiracy", wherein teachers attempt to create a comfortable environment, but not necessarily one that is capable of "facilitating academic content knowledge" (as cited in Sharkey and Layzer 2000: 361). For example, almost all of the ELL students were in lower tracks and would be given credit for completed work, regardless of correctness. Teachers emphasized that, in order to be successful, students needed to ask questions, try hard, and communicate, but less was said about mastering content. Researchers observed that ELL students "rarely spoke or were spoken to". Teachers attributed this to the fact that students were shy or timid and thus they did not want to push them. "Such attitudes place the burden of interaction on the students while leaving the classroom context unchallenged" (Sharkey and Layzer 2000: 362).

Teachers must not only have knowledge of cultural differences, and a positive attitude about those differences, they must also feel confident in their efficacy or ability to affect the learning environment. Pre-service teachers have shown positive attitudes toward cultural differences, but lack confidence in their knowledge of these differences. They were positive about different teaching techniques used to reach a diversity of learners, such as cooperative learning, but lacked confidence in how to address individual needs (Whitfield et al. 2007). With regard to ELLs, Tasan (2001) examined whether student language background had an effect on elementary teacher efficacy, finding that teachers reported lowest efficacy for non-standard English speakers, followed by non-English speakers, and finally native speakers. Others (e.g., Quach et al. 2007) examined 252 teachers in the southeastern United States, finding that teachers who reported fluency in another language had higher efficacy for working with ELLs as opposed to those with language study, regardless of the number of years.

## International worldview

Coulby argues that teachers "need an awareness that education is an international activity and neither its pupils nor its subject matter can be constrained by familiar boundaries" (Coulby 2006: 254). In our view, the importance of an international worldview is a critical component of intercultural competence for educators. Linguistic differences in students originate from many parts of the globe. Owing to the numbers of Hispanics in the US, many teachers may be guilty of assuming that a working knowledge of Spanish will enable them to reach the linguistic needs of their students. However, not only is there a great deal of variation in Spanish, there are a great many learners who speak Asian, Caribbean, Middle Eastern, and African first languages. Teachers must be familiar with working with these learners and understanding the significance of teaching learners from these countries, with their varied languages and cultures.

## 5. Recommendations for practice: building relationships and community in the multicultural classroom

Genesee *et al.* (2005) discuss factors that promote the academic success of ELLs. These include a positive school climate, challenging, consistent, and thematic content, cooperative learning, higher level thinking, standards-driven assessment, theoretically based practice, teachers' knowledge of language acquisition, as well as the goals and structure of the programs in which they were teaching and "high-quality exchanges between teachers and students" (ibid. 2005: 377). In the end, it is important to understand that no one approach is best for teaching ELLs as they have a diversity of backgrounds, achievement levels, and needs. A full examination of these areas is beyond the scope of this chapter; therefore, given our emphasis on intercultural competence for the multicultural classroom, we have chosen to focus here on the establishment of learning communities.

Effective multicultural learning communities are characterized by four qualities: (1) students and teachers have a mutual sense of belonging or personal connection to others in the group; (2) individual members respect one another, make a difference to the group, and the group matters to the members; (3) members are reinforced by their membership and feel that their needs are met; and (4) there is an emotional connection as members share a common history and similar experiences (Cushner *et al.* 2009; McMillan and Chavis 1986; Powell and Caseau 2004). A sense of belonging on the part of students results in them feeling both emotionally and physically secure in the classroom, both of which are fundamental to effective learning.

Learning is intimately linked to the social and emotional development of young people. Elias *et al.* (1997) defined social and emotional competence as:

> … the ability to understand, manage, and express the social and emotional aspects of one's life in ways that enable the successful management of life tasks such as learning, forming relationships, solving everyday problems, and adapting to the complex demands of growth and development.
>
> Elias et al. *(1997: 2)*

How students feel about school and their classes is in large part determined by the quality of the relationships they have with their teachers. Children must feel that they are cared for in the school environment in order to succeed both in their academics as well as in their sense of self-esteem in the classroom (Noddings 1995). Supportive, caring, and friendly teachers foster supportive relationships with their students. Spending time developing relationships with students, allowing them to talk about their problems, as well as guiding them toward sensitivity are significant teaching activities. Central to establishing meaningful interpersonal relationships between teacher and student is a common understanding through shared meaning-making. Thus, developing the capacity to communicate effectively across cultures becomes an essential skill in culturally diverse classrooms and communities. We might liken this to the fourth "R"—reading, 'riting, 'rithmetic, and relationships.

Two aspects of communication—breadth and depth—seem to influence the direction an interpersonal relationship will take (Altman and Taylor 1973). When teachers get to know about different arenas of a student's life—their family, academic strengths and weaknesses, as well as their out of school interests—they are developing breadth. As they begin to learn more details of a child's life circumstances, such as how they feel about a pending divorce, they are developing depth of understanding. Probing for reasons why a student may not have turned in a homework assignment, for instance, helps a teacher to better understand the context in which a child lives, and potentially offer assistance.

Another important skill to building a learning community is teacher immediacy—or the tendency for people to move toward people they like and away from those they dislike (Mehrabian 1971). Immediacy, communicated primarily through implicit nonverbal behavior (smiling, touch, eye contact) as well as through verbal behaviors (using humor, addressing students by name, and using personal examples), has a positive influence on student affect or their feelings about a teacher and a given course (Andersen 1979). Immediacy operates in two directions. That is, students indicate they are accurately receiving information through their nonverbal behaviors, with the result that teachers are more motivated to teach those who engage in immediate behaviors. As immediacy involves implicit codes, it is essential that teachers are able to interpret messages in the same way that they are intended by the sender. Although operating in both directions, Powell and Caseau (2004) report that there is no documented evidence that test scores or other cognitive measures are impacted by immediacy in any clear ways.

Finally, teachers need to learn the art of self-disclosure. Revealing something about oneself that the other would not know unless they were told has been argued as necessary for effective teacher–student relationships (Cooper and Simmonds 1999). Culture, however, plays a significant role in self-disclosure (Powell and Caseau 2004). In the US context, teachers from individualistic, low-context cultures tend to be more comfortable with self-disclosure, whereas those from more collective, high-context cultures (e.g., Native Americans, Asians, and Latinos) are less likely or feel it inappropriate to engage in this behavior as readily. Teachers need to gain more rapport with students and deeper cultural knowledge so they will recognize when it may be inappropriate, for example, to ask a student to share personal information in a class discussion.

## 6. Future directions

Although great strides have been made in the education of English language learners in the US in the past few decades, much more needs to be done. The persistent achievement gap at the K–12 level, the fewer number of ELLs enrolled in higher education, and the greater numbers of ELLs in poverty are just a few issues that attest to this fact. Teachers play an especially key role. More needs to be done to ensure that highly qualified teachers are working with ELLs. This is especially important for the regular classroom teacher who may not have professional education or certification in TESOL or ESL. More university preparation is needed in this area. Additionally, we need a better definition of the highly qualified ELL teacher, better professional development, and more consistent licensure requirements across the US. More specific research is also needed that is specifically related to the ELL context such as in teacher efficacy, parental involvement, and classroom management and conflict.

## 7. Conclusion

We have long argued that intercultural competences are a vital necessity to ensure that students receive an excellent and equitable education. The inclusion of linguistic differences in the classroom is one area where such competences are especially crucial. Teachers must call upon a variety of skills to enable students to use the strengths of their native languages to maintain their cultural identity and feel welcome and honored in the classroom. At the same time, they need to use those skills to assist students in the difficult process of second language acquisition in an academic context so they can reach their highest potential.

## Related topics

Diversity; identity; intercultural communicative competence; linguistic competence; multicultural education; teacher education; worldview

## Further reading

Cushner, K., McClelland, A. and Safford, P. (2009) *Human Diversity in Education: An Integrated Approach*, 6th edn, New York: McGraw-Hill (a research-based, comprehensive text designed to provide future teachers with an introduction to multicultural education and diversity in society).

Diaz-Rico, L.T. (2008) *Strategies for Teaching English Learners*, 2nd edn, Boston, MA: Allyn and Bacon (an introduction to teaching English to speakers of other languages, this text discusses the influence of culture on schooling and the sociopolitical context of education).

Santa Ana, O. (ed.) (2004) *Tongue-tied: The Lives of Multilingual Children in Public Education*, New York: Rowman and Littlefield (this anthology incorporates excerpts from well-known writers such as Maxine Hong Kingston and Amy Tan, along with articles by linguists and educators on aspects of multicultural education).

Wurzel, J. and Fischman, N. (1993) *A Different Place: The Intercultural Classroom*, The Intercultural Resource Corporation. Online. Available: https://irc-inte.ipower.com/InterculturalClassroom.html (accessed 5 November 2010) (a two-part video presentation that is designed to raise awareness of the challenges and advantages of student diversity in higher education).

## References

Alexander, D., Heavside, S. and Farris, E. (1999) *Status of Education Reform in Public Elementary and Secondary Schools: Teachers' Perspectives*, Washington, DC: US Department of Education, National Center for Educational Statistics.

Allen, J.L. and Shaw, D.H. (1990) 'Teacher's communication behaviors and supervisor's evaluation of instruction in elementary and secondary classrooms', *Communication Education*, 39: 308–22.

Altman, I. and Taylor, D. (1973) *Social Penetration*, New York: Holt.

American Association of Colleges of Teacher Education (AACTE) (2010) *Educator Preparation: A Vision for the 21st Century—Draft Paper*. Online. Available: http://aacte.org/email_blast/president_e-letter/files/02-16-2010/Educator%20Preparation%20and%2021st%20Century%20Skills%20DRAFT%20021510.pdf (accessed 27 February 2010).

Andersen, J.F. (1979) 'Teacher immediacy as a predictor of teaching effectiveness', in D. Nimmo (ed.) *Communication Yearbook*, Vol. 3, New Brunswick, NJ: Transaction Books, pp. 543–59.

Applegate, J.L. (1980) 'Adaptive communication in educational contexts: a study of teachers' communicative strategies', *Communication Education*, 29(2): 158–70.

Banks, J.A. and Banks, C.A.M. (2004) *Multicultural Education: Issues and Perspectives*, San Francisco, CA: Jossey-Bass.

Bellack, A., Kliebard, H., Hyman, R. and Smith, F. (1966) *The Language of the Classroom*, New York: Columbia Teachers College Press.

Brophy, J. and Good, T.L. (2000) 'Teacher behavior and student achievement', in M. Wittrock (ed.) *Handbook of Research on Teaching*, 3rd edn, New York: Macmillan, pp. 330–75.

Cazden, C. (1988) *Classroom Discourse: The Language of Teaching and Learning*, Portsmouth, NH: Heinemann.

Chesbro, J.L., McCroskey, J.C., Atwater, D., Bahrenfuss, R., Cawelti, G., Gaidino, J. and Hidges, H. (1992) 'Communication apprehension and self-perceived communication competence of at-risk students', *Communication Education*, 47: 82–91.

Cochran-Smith, M. and Zeichner, K.M. (eds) (2005) *Studying Teacher Education: The Report of the AERA Panel on Research and Teacher Education*, Mahwah, NJ: Lawrence Erlbaum.

Cooper, P.J. and Simmonds, C. (1999) *Communication for the Classroom Teacher*, 6th edn, Boston, MA: Allyn and Bacon.

Coulby, D. (2006) 'Intercultural education: theory and practice', *Intercultural Education*, 17(3): 245–57.

Cummins, J. (1979) 'Cognitive/academic language proficiency, linguistic interdependence, the optimum age question and some other matters', *Working Papers on Bilingualism*, 19: 121–29.

Cushner, K. and Mahon, J. (2010) 'Developing the intercultural competence of educators and their students: creating the blueprints', in K. Deardorff (ed), *The SAGE Handbook of Intercultural Competence*, Thousand Oaks, CA: Sage, pp. 304–20.

Cushner, K., McClelland, A. and Safford, P. (2009) *Human Diversity in Education: An Integrative Approach*, 6th edn, Boston, MA: McGraw-Hill.

Daly, J.A. and Friedrich, G. (1981) 'The development of communication apprehension: a retrospective analysis of contributory correlates', *Communication Quarterly*, 29: 243–55.

den Brok, P., Brekelmans, M., Levy, J. and Wubbels, T. (2002) 'Diagnosing and improving the quality of teachers' interpersonal behaviour', *The International Journal of Educational Management*, 16(4): 176–84.

Elias, M.J., Zins, J.E., Weissberg, R.P., Frey, K.S., Greenberg, M.T., Haynes, N.M., Kessler, R., Schwab-Stone, M.E., and Shriver, T.P. (1997) *Promoting Social and Emotional Learning: Guidelines for Educators*, Alexandria, VA: Association for Supervision and Curriculum Development.

Franson, C. and Holliday, A. (2009) 'Social and cultural perspectives,' in A. Burns and J.C. Richards (eds) *Cambridge Guide to Second Language Teacher Education*, New York: Cambridge University Press, pp. 40–46.

Gándara, P. and Maxwell-Jolly, J. (2006) 'Critical issues in developing the teacher corps for English language learners', in K. Waxman and H.C. Tellez (eds) *Preparing Quality Teachers for English Language Learners: Research, Policy and Practice*, Mahwah, NJ: Lawrence Earlbaum and Associates, pp. 99–120.

Garcia, E. (1990) 'Educating teachers for language minority students', in W.R. Houston (ed.) *Handbook of Research on Teacher Education*, New York: Macmillan, pp. 712–29.

Gay, G. (2000) *Culturally Responsive Teaching: Theory, Research, and Practice*, New York: Teachers College Press.

——(2006) 'Connections between classroom management and culturally responsive teaching', in C.M. Evertson and C.S. Weinstein (eds) *The Handbook of Classroom Management: Research, Practice, and Contemporary Issues*, Mahwah, NJ: Lawrence Erlbaum and Associates, pp. 343–70.

Genesee, F., Lindholm-Leary, K., Saunders, W. and Christian, D. (2005) 'English language learners in U.S. schools: an overview of research findings', *Journal of Education for Students Placed at Risk*, 10(4): 363–85.

Gruber, K., Wiley, S.D., Broughman, S.P., Strizek, G.A. and Burian-Fitzgerald, M. (2002) *Schools and Staffing Survey, 1999–2000: Overview of the Data for Public, Private, Public Charter, and Bureau of Indian Affairs Elementary and Secondary Schools* (NCES 2002–2313), Washington, DC: US Government Printing Office.

Hall, E.T. (1976) *Beyond Culture*, New York: Doubleday.

Hanvey, R.G. (1975) *An Attainable Global Perspective*, New York: New York Center for War/Peace Studies.

Haslett, B. (1987) *Communication: Strategic Action in Context*, Hillsdale, NJ: Lawrence Erlbaum Associates.

Hatch, E.M. (1992) *Discourse and Language Education*, New York: Cambridge University Press.

Johnson, S.D. and Roellke, C.F. (1999) 'Secondary teachers' and undergraduate education faculty members' perceptions of teaching effectiveness criteria: a national survey', *Communication Education*, 48: 127–38.

Katz, S.R. (2000) 'Promoting bilingualism in the era of Unz: making sense of the gap between research, policy, and practice in teacher education', *Multicultural Education*, 8(1): 2–7.

Kindsvatter, R., Wilen, W. and Ishler, M. (1996) *Dynamics of Effective Teaching*, White Plains, NY: Longman.

Ladson-Billings, G. (1994) *Dreamkeepers: Successful Teachers of African-American Children*, San Francisco, CA: Jossey-Bass.

Levy, J., Wubbels, T., Brekelmans, M. and Morganfield, B. (1997) 'Language and cultural factors in students' perceptions of teacher communication style', *International Journal of Intercultural Relations*, 21(1): 29–56.

Lewis, L., Parsad, B., Carey, N., Bartfai, N., Farris, E. and Smerdon, B. (1999) *Teacher Quality: A Report on the Preparation and Qualifications of Public School Teachers*, Washington, DC: US Department of Education, Office of Educational Research and Improvement, National Center for Educational Statistics.

McCaleb, J.L. (ed.) (1987) *How do Teachers Communicate?*, Washington, DC: ERIC Clearinghouse on Teacher Education, ED 282 872.

McCarthy, J. and Benally, J. (2003) 'Classroom management in a Navajo middle school', *Theory into Practice*, 42(4): 296–304.

McCroskey, J.C. (1997) 'Willingness to communicate, communication apprehension, and self-perceived communication competence: conceptualizations and perspectives', in J.A. Daly *et al.* (eds) *Avoiding Communication: Shyness, Reticence, and Communication Apprehension*, Cresskill, NJ: Hampton Press, pp. 75–108.

McCroskey, J.C. and McCroskey, L.L. (2002) 'Willingness to communicate and communication apprehension in the classroom', in J.L. Chesbro and J.C. McCroskey (eds) *Communication for Teachers*, Boston, MA: Allyn and Bacon, pp. 19–34.

McMillan, D.W. and Chavis, D.M. (1986) 'Sense of community: a definition and theory', *Journal of Community Psychology*, 14: 6–23.

May, S. (2008) 'Language education, pluralism, and citizenship', in S. May and N.H. Hornberger (eds) *Language Policy and Political Issues in Education*, Vol. 1: 15–29. *Encyclopedia of Language and Education*, 2nd edn, New York: Springer.

Mehrabian, A. (1971) *Silent messages*, Belmont, CA: Wadsworth.

Merryfield, M. (1996) *Making Connections between Multicultural and Global Education: Educators and Teacher Education Programs*, Washington, DC: American Association of Colleges of Teacher Education.

Metropolitan Life (2005) *The Metlife Survey of the American Teacher: Transitions and the Role of Supportive Relationships; The Role of Teachers, Principals and Students*, New York: Harris Interactive, Inc. Online. Available: www.metlife.com/WPSAssets/34996838801118758796V1FATS_2004.pdf (accessed 16 September 2006).

Monthienvichienchai, C., Bhibulbhanuwat, S., Kasemsuk, C. and Speece, M. (2002) 'Cultural awareness, communication apprehension, and communication competence: a case study of Saint John's International School', *The International Journal of Educational Management*, 16(6): 288–96.

Morrier, M., Irving, M.A., Dandy, E., Dmitriyev, G. and Ukeje, I.C. (2007) 'Teaching and learning within and across cultures: educators' requirements across the United States', *Multicultural Education*, 14 (3): 32–40.

National Council for the Accreditation of Teacher Education (2008) *NCATE Unit Standards Revisions*, Washington, DC: National Council for Accreditation of Teacher Education. Online. Available: www. ncate.org/documents/standards/SummaryMajorChangesUnitStd.pdf (accessed 2 February 2008).

Noddings, N. (1995) 'Teaching themes of care', *Phi Delta Kappan*, 76: 675–79.

Peterman, F.P. (ed.) (2005) *Designing Performance Assessment Systems for Urban Teacher Preparation*, Mahwah, NJ: Lawrence Earlbaum Associates.

Powell, R.G. and Caseau, D. (2004) *Classroom Communication and Diversity: Enhancing Instructional Practice*, Mahwah, NJ: Lawrence Erlbaum.

Quach, L.H., Heining-Boynton, A.L. and Wang, C. (2007) 'Language study matters for classroom teachers in diverse schools', *Multicultural Learning and Teaching*, 2(1): 10–19. Online. Available: www.bepress. com/cgi/viewcontent.cgi?article=1013& context = mlt (accessed 10 May 2011).

Ramirez, A.Y.F. (2003) 'Dismay and disappointment: parental involvement of Latino immigrant parents', *The Urban Review*, 35(2): 93–110.

Ricento, T. and Wright, W. (2008) 'Language policy and education in the United States', in S. May and N.H. Hornberger (eds) *Language Policy and Political Issues in Education*, Vol. 1. *Encyclopedia of Language and Education*, 2nd edn, New York: Springer, pp. 285–300.

Rubin, R.B. and Feezel, J.D. (1985) 'Teacher communication competence: essential skills and assessment procedures', *Central States Speech Journal*, 36: 4–13.

——(1986) 'Elements of teacher communication competence', *Communication Education*, 3: 254–68.

Seastrom, M.M., Gruber, K J., Henke, R., McGrath, D.J. and Cohen, B.A. (2002) *Qualifications of the Public School Teacher Workforce: Prevalence of Out-Of-Field Teaching, 1987–88 to 1999–2000. Statistical Analysis Report*, ERIC document reproduction no. ED468700. Online. Available: http://eric.ed.gov/ERICDocs/data/ericdocs2sql/content_storage_01/0000019b/80/1a/67/3d.pdf (accessed 29 May 2010).

Sharkey, J. and Layzer, C. (2000) 'Whose definition of success: identifying factors that affect English language learners' access to academic success and resources', *TESOL Quarterly*, 34(2): 352–68.

Stomfay-Stitz, A.M. (1993) *Peace Education in America, 1928–1990: Sourcebook for Education and Research*, Metuchen, NJ: Scarecrow Press.

Tasan, A.P. (2001) 'Teacher efficacy and diversity: implications for teacher training', paper presented at the annual meeting of the American Educational Research Association, Seattle, WA, April 2001 (ERIC document reproduction service no. ED453201).

Wanzer, M.B. and McCroskey, J.C. (1998) 'Teacher socio-community style as a correlate of student affect toward teacher and course material', *Communication Education*, 47: 43–52.

Waxman, K. and Tellez, H.C. (eds) (2006) *Preparing Quality Teachers for English Language Learners: Research, Policy and Practice*, Mahwah, NJ: Lawrence Earlbaum and Associates.

Whitfield, P., Klug, B.J. and Whitney, P. (2007) 'Situative cognition: barrier to teaching across cultures', *Intercultural Education*, 18(3): 259–64.

Wiley, T.G. (2008) 'Language policy and teacher education', in S. May and N.H. Hornberger (eds) *Language Policy and Political Issues in Education*, Vol. 1. *Encyclopedia of Language and Education*, 2nd edn, New York: Springer, pp. 229–41.

Willmington, S. (1993) 'Oral communication skills necessary for successful teaching', *Educational Research Quarterly*, 16(2): 5–10.

Wubbels, T. and Levy, J. (1993) *Do You Know What You Look Like? Interpersonal Relationships in Education*, London: Falmer Press.

——(1991) 'A comparison of interpersonal behavior of Dutch and American teachers', *International Journal of Intercultural Relations*, 15: 1–18.

Wubbels, T., Levy, J. and Brekelmans, M. (1997) 'Paying attention to relationships', *Educational Leadership*, 55(2): 82–86.

Zeichner, K. (2003) 'The adequacies and inadequacies of three current strategies to recruit, prepare, and retain the best teachers for all students', *Teachers College Record*, 105(3): 490–519.

# 28

# Education abroad

*Jane Jackson*

## 1. Introduction/terminology

In the last 30 years, we have witnessed an increase in the number of young people who are gaining some form of education outside their country of citizenship. By 2025, more than seven million tertiary-level students are expected to be educated transnationally, and a record number of secondary-level students are also going abroad for part of their education (American Council of Education 2006; Atlas of Student Mobility n.d.; Organization for Economic Cooperation and Development 2009). Education abroad options have also become more diverse (e.g. study abroad, internships, work placements, field research, service learning,[1] volunteering, directed travel linked to learning goals) and motivated by a wider range of goals (e.g. second language (L2) learning, exposure to other cultures, professional enhancement, disciplinary learning).

When education abroad involves formal L2 learning and immersion in the native speech community, it is widely believed to offer students the best opportunity to enhance their intercultural sensitivity and proficiency in the host language. Increasingly, however, education abroad researchers are discovering that the relationship between language proficiency, intercultural communicative competence (Deardorff 2006; Chapters 5 and 16, this volume), and intercultural contact is far from straightforward. The complexity and variability of the sojourn experience, in part due to individual differences in sojourners, can lead to strikingly different outcomes. Further, with more diversity in programmes, questions are being raised about the best ways to enhance the language and (inter)cultural development of L2 sojourners and extend their learning once they return home.

The field of education abroad is further complicated by the use of different terminology in different parts of the world. Several terms may represent the same concept and, in some cases, a single term may have multiple meanings. To reduce semantic ambiguity and facilitate comparisons of programmes and research findings, the Forum on Education Abroad[2] (2011) has published a glossary for education abroad professionals within and outside the US who work with American students abroad. Coleman (1997, 2007, 2009), Europa, the European Commission of Education, Training and Youth (European Commission 2010)[3] and Murphy-Lejeune (2008) offer insight into the education abroad (e.g. academic mobility) nomenclature that is prevalent in European contexts.

In this chapter, I begin by briefly discussing historical trends in education abroad, with an emphasis on programmes designed with L2 and (inter)cultural learning in mind. I then identify critical issues and topics that have emerged in the literature. I cite key studies and current contributions, highlighting variations in the theoretical underpinnings and methodologies that have guided research on the intercultural learning of L2 sojourners. I then discuss the practical implications of the findings for the enhancement of education abroad programming and, more specifically, the language and (inter)cultural development and 'whole person' learning of L2 students. I conclude the chapter by suggesting areas for further investigation.

## 2. Historical perspectives

Education abroad is not new. For centuries, students have left their home country to gain exposure to other languages and cultures and acquire the knowledge and credentials that were not available in their home institution.[4] A review of historical records reveals that ancient centres of learning (e.g. Athens, Cairo, Rome) were attracting students from other countries as early as 500 BCE. By the eighteenth century, the 'European Grand Tour' had become popular in Europe, whereby elite students (e.g. affluent children of aristocrats in England) travelled to Western European countries in search of cultural and social sophistication (Hoffa 2007; Medina 2008). Post World War II, the 'Junior Year Abroad' emerged as an option for American students (e.g. majors in the Arts and Humanities) to enhance their knowledge of another language and culture in the host speech community (Hoffa 2007). Since the 1960s, what was once an experience largely reserved for the privileged has become more accessible, varied and increasingly focused on disciplinary learning.

In the last few decades, with accelerating globalization, more institutions of higher education across the globe are embedding an international dimension into their teaching and research, and providing more opportunities for education abroad. Kälvermark and van der Wende (1997: 19) define this process of internationalization as 'any systematic sustained effort aimed at making higher education more responsive to the requirements and challenges related to the globalization of societies, economy and labor markets'. More specifically, it entails the integration of 'an international, intercultural or global dimension into the purpose, functions or delivery of post-secondary education' (Knight 2004: 11). In some quarters, secondary schools are also developing programmes to facilitate international exchange for both staff and students.

In Europe, internationalization policies are shaping the scope and direction of 'academic mobility'. The European Region Action Scheme for the Mobility of University Students (ERASMUS) was initiated in 1987 to cultivate 'European citizenship' and an international outlook (Byram and Dervin 2008). This scheme enables higher education students, teachers and institutions in thirty-one European countries to study for part of their degree in a European country that is foreign to them. By 2012, it is expected that three million European students will have taken part in this programme (European Commission 2010). ERASMUS has also inspired the establishment of the Bologna process, which is facilitating movement from one country to another within the European Higher Education Area by making academic degree standards and quality assurance standards more comparable and compatible throughout Europe.

In other parts of the world, there has been an increase in the number and diversity of education abroad programme options, including those in 'non-traditional' settings (e.g. Argentina, China, India, Israel). Further, the reasons why students venture abroad have become more varied. Some must study abroad to fulfil a requirement of their home institution. At the tertiary level in the UK and elsewhere, for example, modern language students may be obliged to spend part of their degree programme in a country where the target language is widely spoken (Coleman 1997, 2009). While in the host environment, student sojourners may take language or subject matter courses at a tertiary institution, serve as a teaching assistant, join a work placement scheme in the private sector, do volunteer work or undertake a combination of these options. On site, they may also carry out focused, small-scale research projects (e.g. ethnographic studies) or participate in other experiential activities to bring them into closer contact with the host speech community (Jackson 2006; Knight and Schmidt-Rinehart 2010; Ogden 2006; Roberts et al. 2001).

Another interesting phenomenon is that students at the secondary and tertiary levels are increasingly choosing to enhance their L2 proficiency by taking part in either a short-term[5] or micro-term sojourn[6] (Allen 2010; Institute of International Education 2010). Some venture abroad on their own, whereas others travel in a group with classmates. While in the host environment, they may take courses in the host language at a commercial language centre or other educational institution. Some participants study alongside L2 speakers from other countries, whereas others remain in intact groups, taking specially designed courses (e.g. literature, cultural studies, business English) with peers from their home institution. Some coursework may be credit bearing, allowing the transfer of credits back to the home institution.

Increasingly, short-term or micro-term programmes are faculty led, whereby a teacher or professor from the home institution accompanies the group abroad. A secondary school teacher of English in Japan, for example, may travel to Australia with her students for a 10-day intensive language and cultural enhancement programme. The micro-sojourn may include a homestay,[7] language and cultural lessons with host teachers, cultural site visits and informal activities with Australian peers. Thousands of miles away, a secondary school teacher of French as a second language in England may go to France with his students for a week-long cultural exchange programme. While in the host culture, the student visitors may reside in a dormitory, youth hostel or homestay. As well as classes in French language and civilization, the micro-sojourners may take part in activities and cultural excursions with French students of the same age. Later in the year, the English students may reciprocate by hosting their French counterparts.

At the tertiary level, a professor of Spanish in the US may accompany a group of her students to Mexico and teach Spanish language, literature or cultural studies courses alongside local professors. She may also supervise out-of-class activities (e.g. service learning, work placements, ethnographic fieldwork, survey/interview research) to encourage active participation in the host culture, and promote language and (inter)cultural development, global citizenship and disciplinary learning.

Exchange agreements with foreign counterparts are also making it possible for more students at the secondary and tertiary levels to join an exchange programme[8] and stay abroad for a longer period of time (e.g. a 14-week semester, an academic year). Participants with an advanced level of proficiency in an L2 (e.g. the host language) may take L2-medium courses alongside host nationals and other international students and then transfer credits to their home institution. With this arrangement, the participants can simultaneously enhance their L2 proficiency and academic knowledge in other areas of study (e.g. architecture, engineering). While abroad, they may also hone their professional skills (e.g. business, health care) in an L2 through coursework, service learning or a work placement. With intercultural contact, both in and outside the classroom, participants have the opportunity to bolster their intercultural communicative competence and take steps towards intercultural citizenship and a more global, cosmopolitan identity (see Chapters 5 and 18, this volume).

Owing to the emergence of English as the global language of internationalization, advanced English as an international language (EIL) students no longer need to travel to 'inner circle' countries[9] (e.g. Australia, England, the US) to pursue further studies in English. Many non-English-speaking countries now offer English-medium courses and exposure to local (and global) perspectives in a range of disciplines. Hong Kong Chinese business majors, for example, can travel to Sweden or the Netherlands to take English-medium courses in their area of specialization (e.g. marketing, management). Through interaction with international students and host nationals, they may hone their intercultural communication skills in English. Some participants may also choose to take language enhancement courses in Swedish or Dutch and gain more exposure to the local culture on campus and in the wider community. Within these exchange programmes, as in the short-term, faculty-led options, the quality and degree of contact with the host language and culture vary considerably.

Another element that can have a significant impact on the language and (inter)cultural learning of sojourners is the housing arrangement, which can take many forms (e.g. independent accommodation, living with a host family, residence in a boarding house, youth hostel or dormitory on campus, sharing an apartment off-campus with host nationals, other international students or L1 speakers from the home country). Some options may be more effective in facilitating relationship-building with people from other cultural/linguistic backgrounds.

The use of electronic tools of communication can also affect the degree of immersion in the host culture. Advances in technology (e.g. the use of e-mail, skype (an internet phone service), Facebook and other electronic means) are now enabling sojourners in many parts of the world to keep in regular contact with home, if they choose. This can make the 'immersion' experience far different from previous generations.

Besides variations in aims, duration, content and housing, there are other elements within programmes that can impact on sojourner development. The quality and amount of pre-sojourn preparation, sojourn support and re-entry debriefings differ greatly, ranging from no support to credit-bearing coursework at all stages that is designed to facilitate, deepen and extend sojourn learning. It is, therefore, important to be mindful of contextual elements when digesting publications that centre on intercultural communication/learning and the L2 sojourn.

## 3. Critical issues and topics in education abroad learning

A review of the literature on L2 education abroad reveals a number of issues and concerns that have captured the attention of researchers and practitioners. In particular, there is much more awareness today of the multiple variables that can impact on the language and (inter)cultural learning, identity expansion and 'whole person' development of participants: specific programme features (e.g. duration, mode of housing, guided cultural/experiential project work, degree of cultural immersion, quality and extent of pre-sojourn orientation/ongoing support/debriefings), elements in the host environment (e.g. host receptivity, quality and amount of exposure to the host language and culture, ease of access to technology and contact with the home country) and the characteristics of individual sojourners (e.g. personality, L2 competence, degree of openness to new experience, attitude towards cultural difference, motivation and investment in L2 enhancement, level of intercultural sensitivity/competence, previous intercultural/international experience, adaptive stress management).

Differing developmental trajectories and sojourn outcomes caution us not to make assumptions about education abroad learning. Researchers are discovering that simply being present in the host speech community does not guarantee the enhancement of a sojourner's L2 competence or interculturality. Further, an advanced level of proficiency does not necessarily mean that individuals possess a high level of sociopragmatic awareness and intercultural sensitivity or will easily make friends with people from other cultures (Jackson 2008, 2010, 2011a). The relationship between L2 proficiency and intercultural communicative competence is far from straightforward.

There is mounting recognition of the complex connection between sojourner learning and such variables as power, access, positioning and context (Byram and Dervin 2008; Byram and Feng 2006; Coleman 2009; Jackson 2008, 2010; Kinginger 2009). To fully understand the 'whole person' development of L2 sojourners, one must be sensitive to their status and positioning in the host environment. In a homestay situation, for example, on a daily basis, newcomers or 'novices' may be pressed to convey their thoughts and emotions in a foreign language, in what may be, for them, a rather intimidating and confusing setting. In contrast, their hosts are at home in their own surroundings and are typically positioned as 'experts' in both the host language and the culture. Host families who are mindful of this imbalance may make more of an effort to understand the adjustment process (e.g. psychological stress resulting from increased use of an L2, homesickness and other symptoms of culture shock) and frequently encourage their 'guests' to join in family or community activities. Other hosts, however, may fail to comprehend the needs and insecurities of the newcomers. Lack of empathy, patience and understanding may have a detrimental impact on the host–sojourner relationship and student learning (see Chapters 14 and 15 for more discussion on adjustment).

Agency plays a key role in how sojourns unfold. Students are individuals ('social agents') with their own aims, needs and concerns. Their mindset (e.g. degree of openness to other cultures) and the actions they take in the host environment can have a profound impact on sojourn outcomes. Some sojourners aspire to enhance their L2 social skills and actively cultivate friendships with host nationals. With resilience and a positive frame of mind, they take full advantage of linguistic and cultural affordances in the local speech community (e.g. frequently initiate conversations in the host language, make an effort to include host nationals in their social networks). In contrast, sojourners with a fear of cultural difference and a more rigid mindset may limit themselves to formal, academic contexts and shy away from social intercultural interaction, thereby curtailing exposure to the host language and culture. These individuals may even return home with heightened xenophobia. The learning situation of student sojourners is variable and complex.

Education abroad professionals have also become more aware of the potential impact of intercultural interaction on the sojourner's sense of self. A review of the literature reveals that sojourners who are open to the process of personal expansion and find their hosts welcoming may develop a broader, more cosmopolitan sense of self and revel in the acquisition of a global identity (Bennett 2008; Jackson 2008, 2010; Kinginger 2009). For some, this comes at the expense of the home language and culture. Feelings of cultural marginality (J.M. Bennett 1993) may ensue when sojourners reject their L1, local selfhood and traditional values. Others acquire an appreciation of *both* local and global identities and diverse ways of being. Recognizing and enjoying the benefits of a bilingual or multilingual self, they may hone their intercultural communicative competence, grow in self-confidence and take steps towards cosmopolitan, intercultural citizenship (see Chapters 5, 18 and 22, this volume).

If the preferred self-identity of newcomers is contested in the host culture, psychological distress may create barriers between them and their hosts. In her identity negotiation theory, Ting-Toomey (2005) posits that newcomers who find that their identities are continuously misunderstood may remain disconnected from the host culture (and language) and become less willing to engage. In the host environment, surrounded by more proficient speakers of the host language, some newcomers may also lose confidence in their L2 ability. They may continuously regard themselves as 'outsiders' and find it difficult to develop a sense of belonging in the host culture, especially if they are racially different from the majority for the first time in their life. Under threat, they may cling more tightly to their L1, 'local self' and friends from their home country who share the same ethnicity. As more L2 students from different parts of the world venture abroad, issues of agency, positioning, environmental affordances/constraints and identity will merit attention for decades to come.

## 4. Current contributions and research

Drawing on a variety of theoretical and methodological approaches, researchers from multiple disciplines have investigated the language and intercultural development of L2 students in education abroad programmes. Much of the early work of applied linguists measured linguistic gains in formal classroom situations, sometimes comparing language study at home and abroad. In Freed's (1995) volume on SLA research in a study abroad context, the majority of studies examined individual and group differences in terms of fluency, lexical and grammatical development and the use of communication strategies. Although the results were mixed, most supported the notion that study abroad can help learners become more fluent, confident speakers of the host language.

In the last two decades, large-scale, product-oriented studies of the sojourn experience have been criticized when they have ignored the sociocultural, political, linguistic and historical context of the learning situation. In view of that, Collentine and Freed (2004) advised education abroad researchers to pay close attention to contextual elements and the out-of-class, informal learning of sojourners. Accordingly, a number of applied linguists have been focusing on 'whole person development', including the processes involved in language and (inter)cultural learning using an array of introspective techniques (e.g. diaries, first-person narratives/blogs, in-depth interviews) and such approaches as case studies, ethnographies and mixed-method studies (Byram and Dervin 2008; Byram and Feng 2006; Coleman 2007; Jackson 2008, 2010, 2011b; Kinginger 2008). Their examination of the storied experiences of L2 sojourners within particular sociocultural contexts is helping us to better understand variations in developmental trajectories, which can ultimately lead to more effective interventions (e.g. curricular changes in study abroad programmes).

In the first in-depth qualitative investigation of student migration within Europe, Murphy-Lejeune (2002) investigated the experiences of 'year abroad' students in three different programmes: ERASMUS, bilateral language assistantships and a French business school programme. Interview data revealed that the experience of mobility can transform students' concepts of 'space' and 'home' as they adjust to an unfamiliar linguistic and cultural environment, 'mediate over sameness and difference', 'try out potential identities' and interact with host nationals in unfamiliar social scenes. Multiple variables impacted on their sojourn learning (e.g. motives, agency, duration of stay, type and degree of social, intercultural contact, L2 competence, attitudes, home links, personality) (see Byram and Dervin 2008; Byram and Feng 2006 for further analyses of the ERASMUS experience).

Drawing on sociocultural theory, Kinginger (2008) developed case histories of six American undergraduate learners of French who participated in a semester-long sojourn in France. Data consisted of journals, semi-structured interviews, a language use log and a standardized reading and listening comprehension test in French. Variations were discovered in the ways in which male and female participants perceived the sojourn experience, the degree of investment in language and cultural learning, the amount of computer-mediated communication with the home country, the frequency and quality of intercultural contact and gains in host language proficiency. Kinginger (2008: 106) concluded that, although study abroad is significantly shaped by 'the ways students choose to live their lives and by the values they bring to the experience', they may benefit from 'guidance in understanding the organic link between language and culture' and 'projects or assignments requiring engagement in social interaction within their host communities'.

Using a mixed-method approach, Medina (2008) examined the intercultural sensitivity development of twenty-eight American university students who took part in one of two study abroad language programmes: eighteen attended a 7-week programme in Taxco, Mexico, and ten took part in a 16-week sojourn in Mexico City. Pre- and post-sojourn surveys (the Intercultural Development Inventory (IDI),[10] the Intercultural Contact Questionnaire) were supplemented by interviews and journal writing. Data collected from the two programmes were then analysed by drawing on the contact hypothesis or intergroup contact theory[11] (Allport 1954/1979; Pettigrew 1998), Kauffmann et al.'s (1992) model of the transformation process,[12] and M.J. Bennett's (1993) developmental model of intercultural sensitivity (DMIS), which is linked to the IDI. Within this framework, intercultural sensitivity is thought to involve personal and cognitive growth and the gradual emergence of 'a mindset capable of understanding from within and from without both one's own culture and other cultures' (Bennett et al. 2003: 252). Medina (2008) discovered that longer term sojourners acquired a more sophisticated understanding of nuances in the host culture (e.g. discourse, politics) than those with less time abroad.

Following an ethnographic approach, Jackson (2008, 2010[13]) investigated the language and (inter)cultural development and self-identities of Hong Kong Chinese university students who participated in a faculty-led, short-term sojourn in England. Data consisted of semi-structured interviews, surveys (e.g. modified Language Contact Profile, Freed et al. 2004; weekly sojourn surveys), a pre-sojourn intercultural reflections journal, sojourn diary, a language use log and field notes. For the latter cohort, the IDI measured their intercultural sensitivity on entry, after the pre-sojourn preparation and post-sojourn. Following a mixed-method approach, Jackson (2011b[14]) later investigated the L2 and intercultural development of students from the same institution who took part in either a semester- or a year-long exchange programme.

In Jackson's studies (2008, 2010, 2011b), the trajectories of the participants were found to differ because of a complex mix of internal and environmental factors (e.g. host receptivity, investment in language and culture enhancement, degree of acculturation, personality attributes, social networks, quality of socioemotional support). Advanced knowledge of the grammar and vocabulary of the host language did not ensure intercultural communicative competence or satisfactory social intercultural interaction. Initially, many of the student sojourners possessed a very inflated perception of their intercultural sensitivity, according to the IDI; their recognition and response to cultural difference varied, accordingly. In general, the findings supported the primary assumption that underpins the DMIS: 'as one's experience of cultural difference becomes more sophisticated, one's competence in intercultural relations potentially increases' (Hammer and Bennett 2001: 12).

Dufon and Churchill's (2006) volume presents studies that traced the pragmatic development of student sojourners in a variety of cultural settings using a range of methodologies (e.g. ethnography, case studies, discourse/narrative analysis) and data sources (e.g. diaries, transcripts of intercultural conversations, informal and oral proficiency interviews, discourse completion tasks, classroom observations). Several of the chapters focus on the socialization processes that were collaboratively constructed at the dinner table in host family settings. The findings offer additional insight into the individual and programme variables that facilitate (or restrict) opportunities for sojourners to engage in successful intercultural interaction (e.g. informal conversations). This research highlights the role that language and cultural learning strategies can play in shaping the sojourn experience.

## 5. Main research methods

Researchers have employed an array of methods to investigate the language and cultural development of L2 students who participate in education abroad. The choice of method and research design is influenced by many factors: the aims of the study, the research questions, the type of programme being investigated (e.g. short term, faculty led; year-long exchange, service learning), the researcher's background and expertise, the availability of time and resources and the extent of the researcher's access to the participants and host environment.

Studies investigating student perceptions of international experience (e.g. L2 and intercultural learning) typically rely on surveys and interviews. Research of this nature may be large scale involving hundreds of participants in several education abroad programmes in different parts of the world or be limited to those in a single programme in one setting. Internationally recognized instruments such as the IDI and the Language Contact Profile may also be employed to provide measures of intercultural sensitivity or document L2 use, and facilitate comparisons with other studies (see Chapter 24 for a review of instruments used to assess L2/intercultural competence).

Intercultural, sociopragmatics research in education abroad contexts is also becoming more common as applied linguists recognize the importance of host–sojourner interaction in social settings and the challenge of intercultural relationship-building on stays abroad. More researchers are conducting discourse analyses or employing an ethnography of communication approach to examine host–sojourner speech behaviour (e.g. informal conversations, service encounters); this research is helping us gain a better understanding of what facilitates or hinders intercultural communication in education abroad contexts. More attention is being directed to the impact of intercultural contact and social networks on the participants' sociopragmatic awareness, intercultural communicative competence and evolving sense of self. Analyses of the quality and degree of social contact and linguistic interaction are providing much-needed direction for pre-sojourn programming and on-site support.

More recently, as noted in Section 4, a growing number of researchers are conducting small-scale, focused studies (e.g. case studies, ethnographies) of single education abroad programmes or individual L2 sojourners. Some of these studies are guided by a theoretical framework (e.g. the DMIS, intergroup contact hypothesis, the identity negotiation theory); others employ grounded theory, whereby models are generated from the analysis of data (e.g. coded and categorized sojourner narratives and interviews). Richly contextualized qualitative studies are facilitating a deeper understanding of variations in L2 and intercultural learning as we become better informed about what actually happens in the host environment. Qualitative research can raise questions that can be investigated later in larger scale, quantitative studies (e.g. experimental design studies that compare sojourn and home country learning) and vice versa. Mixed-method studies, which combine the collection and analyses of qualitative and quantitative data, are also becoming more frequent. For example, transcripts of semi-structured interviews with L2 sojourners and field notes from participant observation are being triangulated with survey data (e.g. the IDI) and study abroad blog entries to help track sojourner development over time and space.

In line with the recommendations of Coleman (1997, 2009) and other study abroad specialists, a small number of researchers are also adopting a longitudinal, retrospective approach to gain a better understanding of the long-term impact of sojourns on the linguistic, affective and cognitive development of student sojourners. Alred and Byram (2002) and Paige *et al.* (2009), for example, have investigated the prolonged effect of a sojourn experience on education abroad alumni in relation to such aspects as L2 use, career choice, global engagement and social networks (e.g. degree of intercultural contact).

## 6. Recommendations for practice

With more awareness of factors that enhance (or curtail) the linguistic and (inter)cultural development and global citizenship of sojourners, education abroad professionals and L2 students can make more informed decisions about the type of programme that will best suit their needs and expectations. Research on education abroad should provide direction for the design and refinement of specific programme features (e.g. pre-departure curricula, experiential learning activities) to optimize the L2 learning, intercultural sensitivity development and global engagement of student sojourners.

As international experience alone does not guarantee interculturality, intercultural communicative competence must be nurtured before, during and after a sojourn. When students are well prepared for the sojourn experience, they may set more realistic goals for their stay, cope better with the natural ups and downs of adjustment, employ more effective language and culture learning strategies, be more willing to interact with host nationals and, ultimately, reap the benefits of more satisfactory intercultural interaction. These 'intercultural speakers' (see Byram 2009; Chapters 5 and 18, this volume) may more successfully mediate between cultures and significantly enhance their intercultural communicative competence as they take steps towards a more open, global identity and intercultural citizenship.

Well-designed and sequenced pre-sojourn, sojourn and re-entry programming, based on empirical research, can foster more awareness of the complex connection between language, culture, identity and intercultural adjustment (see Chapter 14, this volume). Unfortunately, many institutions still provide no pre-sojourn education or offer only a very brief orientation that focuses on logistics (e.g. safety measures, health precautions, financial matters, basic survival vocabulary in the host language, academic credit transfer procedures).

In contrast, a small number of institutions have created intensive, credit-bearing pre-departure courses to better equip students for education/life abroad. Coursework addresses such issues as language/culture shock and coping mechanisms, language and culture learning strategies, cultural difference, strategies to enhance intercultural communication, sociopragmatic norms in the host language and unfamiliar teaching styles, among others (Jackson 2008, 2010). Students may be prompted to reflect on their cultural background, language use, communication style and preferred self-identities as well as their intercultural experiences and attitudes towards people from other cultures. Guided reflection and introspective writing can lead to more critical awareness of intercultural behaviour or what Byram (1997) refers to as 'critical *s'engager*'. This heightened awareness of self and other is a crucial element in the path to intercultural communicative competence and intercultural citizenship (see Chapters 5, 18 and 22, this volume)

In the pre-departure phase, it is vital that educators provide students with a framework to help them make sense of intercultural encounters and cultural difference (e.g. values, beliefs, communication styles and other behaviours). By developing the skills of observation, description, interpretation and analysis (Bennett *et al.* 1977), participants can be encouraged to resist the temptation to quickly label unfamiliar behaviours as 'weird' or 'rude'. As intercultural awareness and sensitivity are vital components of intercultural communicative competence, education abroad practitioners are well advised to incorporate language/culture learning strategies and sociopragmatic elements into pre-sojourn programming (e.g. Cohen *et al.* 2005;

Shively 2010). Explicit instruction in these areas can help sojourners develop the knowledge, skills and confidence needed to deal with culture shock, develop intercultural relationships and make the most of their stay in the host culture. Some materials may be culture general, focusing on the intercultural knowledge and skills that can enhance adjustment and communication in an unfamiliar setting (e.g. Mikk *et al.* 2009). If a group will go to the same speech community, L2 educators may incorporate a context-specific dimension into the pre-sojourn curriculum (e.g. instruction on sociopragmatic norms in the host culture with an awareness of individual variations).

Ideally, guided critical reflection should continue once the participants are in the host environment. In faculty-led programmes, for example, it may be feasible for regular on-site debriefing sessions to provide a safe haven for students to freely discuss their observations, concerns and sojourn experiences. The facilitator may field questions about the host environment and encourage the participants to view critical incidents from multiple perspectives. These group sharing sessions can foster personal growth and empower students to take a more active role in the host environment. Sojourners may also be prompted to describe, interpret and evaluate their sojourn experiences in diary entries, open-ended surveys and e-journals or blogs (web logs) (Elola and Oskoz 2008; Jackson 2010; Stewart 2010). The act of reflection can heighten awareness of their environs, their positioning and the potential impact of their own mindset and behaviour on intercultural relations. By becoming more attuned to their development (e.g. academic, intercultural, linguistic, interpersonal) and the affordances and constraints in their environment, the sojourners should be better equipped to adjust their learning goals to take full advantage of their stay in the host culture.

In some programmes, it may be possible to build in experiential activities that require sustained intercultural contact. With adequate pre-sojourn preparation, even short-term sojourners can carry out tasks (e.g. family interaction journal) or small-scale projects (e.g. ethnographic studies) that require them to closely observe a culturally scene and initiate informal conversations with host nationals (Jackson 2006; Knight and Schmidt-Rinehart 2010). As they negotiate relationships with people who have been socialized in a different cultural environment, the sojourners can apply their intercultural communication skills and evolving knowledge of local sociopragmatic norms. Provided there is sufficient scaffolding and ongoing support, projects of this nature can help newcomers develop a sense of belonging in the host environment, thereby facilitating both language and intercultural learning and adjustment.

Near the end of their stay, student sojourners should be encouraged to take stock of their learning and prepare for what they may experience when they return home (e.g. reverse culture shock, readjustment issues). In some programmes, debriefing sessions in the host culture may prompt participants to divulge their re-entry expectations and concerns. They may also write diary or blog entries or respond to open-ended survey questions that induce them to look back over their experiences in the host culture and assess their sojourn learning. For students in exchange programmes in different parts of the world, the home institution may prompt them to complete online reflective surveys at strategic intervals (shortly after their arrival, mid-sojourn, near the end of their stay).

Whatever the programme, once the students are back on the home campus, debriefings are vital to stimulate deeper reflection on sojourn learning and the re-entry experience. This process can facilitate the setting of realistic goals for further self-enhancement (e.g. L2/culture learning). All too often, however, returnees receive no support and quickly 'shoebox' their international experience as they become immersed in home culture happenings. Valuable opportunities for L2/intercultural/international learning are then lost. In contrast, a few institutions have developed re-entry workshops or courses for returning students, which may be credit bearing (e.g. Jackson 2011b). Designed to help returnees make sense of their international experience, these modules may ease the participants' integration into their home culture and campus, deepen and extend their learning and prompt reflection on ways to gain additional international/L2 experience. With or without these initiatives, institutions can encourage returnees to serve as a resource for other students who are planning to venture abroad.

## 7. Future directions

Education abroad has the potential to enhance the language, intercultural development and 'whole person' learning of L2 sojourners; however, much more research in a variety of contexts is necessary to fully understand the conditions that foster intercultural communicative competence and intercultural citizenship. In particular, we would benefit from further studies that systematically integrate qualitative and quantitative measures to explore the L2/intercultural learning and identity reconstruction of sojourners in a range of education abroad situations (e.g. service learning, study abroad, teaching assistantships). Studies are needed that include both male and female participants of varying proficiency levels and ethnic/linguistic backgrounds in diverse programmes, housing situations and locations. As the majority of research on education abroad has focused on the experiences of American or European sojourners, more attention should be devoted to the learning of L2 participants from other parts of the world. The results would help us develop a more comprehensive picture of the multifarious factors that can play a role in differing sojourn outcomes. These studies have the potential to bring to light variables that have been overlooked.

The field of education abroad could benefit from more knowledge about the impact of individual attributes and characteristics on sojourn learning. Researchers could consider: gender differences; level of L2 proficiency, degree of motivation and investment in L2/intercultural learning; personality traits; previous education abroad; intercultural sensitivity; sociopragmatic awareness; and aims and expectations for the stay abroad, among others. Close attention should also be paid to programme characteristics (e.g. duration, type, housing situation, content, experiential learning elements, facilitation of host–sojourner interaction) and environmental factors (e.g. host receptivity, cultural distance between the participants' home culture and the host culture).

Much remains to be discovered about the influence of specific programme elements on the intercultural (re)adjustment, host language acquisition, intercultural communicative competence and self-identities of L2 sojourners. The findings could provide further insight into how best to prepare participants, support their sojourn learning and extend their growth once they are back on home soil. As there are many types of education abroad options available today, comparative studies are essential to document differences in learning processes and sojourn outcomes. As we learn more about the variables involved, we will have a better grasp of the benefits and limitations inherent in each programme. This can help administrators and students choose which option best meets their needs and expectations.

More longitudinal studies are needed that track participants from the selection process until at least a year after their return home from an education abroad experience, whether an internship, a short-term sojourn or an international exchange programme. In particular, researchers could examine the long-term impact of stays abroad on the linguistic, (inter)cultural, cognitive development, global mindset and personal development (e.g. identity expansion) of L2 sojourners. More retrospective studies of education abroad alumni are a must to better understand the prolonged impact of the experience on such aspects as L2 usage, intercultural friendships, identity, social networks, sociopragmatic awareness, intercultural sensitivity, intercultural communicative competence and career choice.

Most studies on education abroad centre on sojourners and the perceptions of accompanying faculty (if present), largely ignoring the experience and perspectives of the hosts (e.g. host families, host 'buddies'[15]) even though these individuals often play a pivotal role in determining sojourn outcomes. Few researchers have studied host perceptions of their roles and responsibilities or examined how their behaviour can impact on the adjustment and L2/intercultural learning of sojourners. Scant attention has also been paid to the ways in which interaction with L2 sojourners impacts on the intercultural competence or identities of hosts.

More investigations of intercultural discourse in the host culture could help us to better understand: the types of interactions L2 sojourners routinely engage in; learner speech act behaviour in these situations; the nature of intercultural misunderstandings; and the negotiation strategies, if any, that participants employ to repair and build host–sojourner relationships. Although intrusive, audio- or videorecordings of intercultural interaction in naturalistic settings (e.g. host–sojourner conversations in homestays) and stimulated recall sessions with the interlocutors could enrich our knowledge of factors that influence intercultural relations. Data of this nature could supplement insights obtained through participant observation, diaries, interviews, blogs and surveys. The triangulated findings could then provide direction for the pre-sojourn preparation and ongoing support of future participants. The data would facilitate the development of 'real world material' (e.g. cases, critical incidents) for use in the preparation of both hosts and student sojourners.

More interdisciplinary research, involving the collaboration of applied linguists, cross-cultural psychologists, speech communication specialists and scholars from other disciplines, could deepen our understanding of the multifaceted education abroad experience of L2 sojourners. This triangulation of perspectives could facilitate theory-building, enrich research projects and foster improvements in education abroad programming. Ultimately, this collaboration could propel more L2 sojourners towards intercultural communicative competence and intercultural, global citizenship.

## Related topics

Cross-cultural adaptation and transformation; identity; intercultural adjustment; intercultural assessment; intercultural communicative competence; intercultural pedagogy/praxis/training; intercultural sensitivity; the intercultural speaker

## Further reading

Bolen, M.C. (ed.) (2007) *A Guide to Outcomes Assessment in Education Abroad*, Boston, MA: Forum on Education Abroad (a practical guide to measuring outcomes in education abroad; it includes a glossary of key terms and a review of instruments).

Kinginger, C. (2009) *Language Learning and Study Abroad: A Critical Reading of Research*, New York: Palgrave Macmillan (an overview and critical assessment of research on language learning and student mobility, including explorations of identity development and informal interactions in the host culture).

Lewin, R. (ed.) (2009) *The Handbook of Practice and Research in Study Abroad: Higher Education and the Quest for Global Citizenship*, New York: Routledge (a comprehensive survey of the field, with critical assessments of research, theory and practice).

Savicki, V. (ed) (2008) *Developing Intercultural Competence and Transformation: Theory, Research, and Application in International Education*, Sterling, VA: Stylus (a collection of eighteen chapters that explores the personal growth and intercultural transformation potential of international education).

Van de Berg, M. and Paige, R.M. (2009) 'Applying theory and research: the evolution of intercultural competence in U.S. study abroad', in D.K. Deardorff (ed.) *Handbook of Intercultural Competence*,

Thousand Oaks, CA: Sage, pp. 419–37 (a review of six study abroad intercultural training projects designed to enhance the intercultural competence of American sojourners).

## Notes

1 Service learning refers to 'a volunteer work placement combined with academic coursework, within the context of a study abroad program. The learning experience is given structure through the principles of experiential education' (Forum on Education Abroad 2009: 23).
2 Founded in 2001, the Forum on Education Abroad is an organization that aims to enhance the quality of education abroad programmes. To accomplish this mission, it has established standards of good practice, offers suggestions to improve study abroad curricula and actively promotes data collection and outcomes assessment in education abroad programmes. For further information, see: www.forumea.org/.
3 The European Commission Education, Training and Youth provides a glossary of key terms in international education that are used in European contexts. See http://ec.europa.eu/education/programmes/llp/guide/glossary_en.html.
4 For a detailed history of US study abroad, see Hoffa (2007) and Kinginger (2009); for an account of historical developments in academic mobility in Europe, see Coleman (2009), Murphy-Lejeune (2002, 2008) and Welch (2008).
5 According to the Forum on Education Abroad (2009), a short-term sojourn lasts 8 weeks or less and may include a summer session or the long break between semesters.
6 Micro-sojourns last 3 weeks or less (Forum on Education Abroad 2009).
7 In a homestay, a local family typically provides a visiting student with a private or shared bedroom, meals and laundry. This arrangement is intended to provide exposure to family life in the host culture and more opportunity to use the host language in an informal setting.
8 A student exchange programme involves two-way movement of participants between institutions or countries. At the post-secondary level, they are usually on a one-to-one basis (e.g. one American student spends time at an overseas institution while a student from that university is enrolled at the US university) (Forum on Education Abroad 2009).
9 In his concentric circles model, Kachru (1985) distinguishes between the 'the types of spread, the patterns of acquisition and the functional domains in which English is used across cultures and languages' (p. 12). In the inner circle, English is the primary language of the country (e.g. in Australia, Canada, the US, the UK).
10 The Intercultural Development Inventory (IDI) is a valid, reliable, cross-cultural tool for assessing intercultural competence at the individual, group and organizational level. It is frequently used in study abroad research (Hammer *et al.* 2003). For further details about the IDI, see www.idiinventory.com/.
11 Allport (1954) held that positive effects of intergroup contact occur only in situations marked by four key conditions: equal group status within the situation; common goals; intergroup cooperation; and the support of authorities, law or custom.
12 Focusing on the maturation process, Kauffmann *et al.*'s (1992) model of the transformation process helps explain the personal change process in students who study abroad (e.g. growth in the areas of cognitive, culture-related and psychological development) (Medina 2008).
13 Jackson's (2008, 2010) research was funded by direct grants from the Chinese University of Hong Kong (2010288, 2010312) and an earmarked grant from the Research Grants Council of the Hong Kong SAR (project no. 2110093).
14 This research on the international exchange experience has been generously supported by the Research Grants Council of the Hong Kong SAR (project no. 2110167; RGC ref. no. CUHK444709).
15 Host buddies are students from the host country who are a similar age to the L2 sojourners. These individuals may be paired with visiting students.

## References

Allen, H.W. (2010) 'Language-learning motivation during short-term study abroad: an activity theory perspective', *Foreign Language Annals*, 43(1): 27–49.
Allport, G.W. (1954; 2nd edn 1979) *The Nature of Prejudice*, Cambridge: Perseus Books.
Alred, G. and Byram, M. (2002) 'Becoming an intercultural mediator: a longitudinal study of residence abroad', *Journal of Multilingual and Multicultural Development*, 23(5): 339–52.

American Council of Education (ACE) (2006) *Students on the Move: The Future of International Students in the United States*. Online. Available: www.acenet.edu/AM/Template.cfm?Section=Search&section=issue_briefs&template=/CM/ContentDisplay.cfm&ContentFileID=7276 (accessed 10 May 2011).

*Atlas of Student Mobility* (n.d.) Online. Available: http://atlas.iienetwork.org/ (accessed September 20 2010).

Bennett, J.M. (1993) 'Cultural marginality: identity issues in intercultural training', in R.M. Paige (ed.) *Education for the Intercultural Experience*, Yarmouth, ME: Intercultural Press, pp. 109–36.

——(2008) 'On becoming a global soul: a path to engagement during study abroad', in V. Savicki (ed.) *Developing Intercultural Competence and Transformation: Theory, Research and Application in International Education*, Sterling, VA: Stylus, pp. 13–31.

Bennett, J.M., Bennett, M.J. and Allen, W. (2003) 'Developing intercultural competence in the language classroom', in D. Lange and M. Paige (eds) *Culture as the Core: Perspectives on Culture in Second Language Learning*, Greenwich, CT: Information Age Publishing, pp. 237–70.

Bennett, J.M., Bennett, M.J. and Stillings, K. (1977) *Description, Interpretation, and Evaluation: Facilitator's Guidelines*. Online. Available: www.intercultural.org/resources.html (accessed 26 April 2010).

Bennett, M.J. (1993) 'Towards ethnorelativism: a developmental model of intercultural sensitivity', in R.M. Paige (ed.) *Education for the Intercultural Experience*, Yarmouth, ME: Intercultural Press, pp. 21–71.

Byram, M. (1997) *Teaching and Assessing Intercultural Communicative Competence*, Clevedon: Multilingual Matters.

——(2009) 'Intercultural competence in foreign languages: the intercultural speaker and the pedagogy of foreign language education', in D.K. Deardorff (ed.) *The Handbook of Intercultural Competence*, Thousand Oaks, CA: Sage, pp. 321–32.

Byram, M. and Dervin, F. (eds) (2008) *Students, Staff, and Academic Mobility*, Newcastle: Cambridge Scholars Publishing.

Byram, M. and Feng, A. (eds) (2006) *Living and Studying Abroad: Research and Practice*, Clevedon: Multilingual Matters.

Cohen, A.D., Paige, R.M., Shively, R.L., Emert, H.A. and Hoff, J.G. (2005) *Maximizing Study Abroad Through Language and Culture Strategies: Research on Students, Study Abroad Program Professionals and Language Instructors*, Minneapolis, MN, USA: Center for Advanced Research on Language Acquisition, University of Minnesota. Online. Available: www.carla.umn.edu/maxsa/documents/MAXSAResearch Report.pdf (accessed 5 August 2010).

Coleman, J.A. (1997) 'State of the art article: residence abroad within language study', *Language Teaching*, 30(1): 1–20.

——(2007) 'A new framework for study abroad research', in C. Way, G. Soriano, D. Limon and C. Amador (eds) *Enhancing the Erasmus Experience: Papers on Student Mobility*, Granada: Atrio, pp. 37–46.

——(2009) 'Study abroad and SLA: defining goals and variables', in A. Berndt and K. Kleppin (eds) *Sprachlehrforschung: Theorie und Empire, Festschrift für Rüdiger Grotjahn*, Bochum: AKS-Verlag, pp. 181–96.

Collentine, J.A. and Freed, B. (2004) 'Learning context and its effects on second language acquisition', *Studies in Second Language Acquisition*, 26: 153–71.

Deardorff, D.K. (2006) 'Identification and assessment of intercultural competence as a student outcome of internationalization', *Journal of Studies in International Education*, 10(3): 241–66.

Dufon, M.A. and Churchill, E. (eds) (2006) *Language Learners in Study Abroad Contexts*, Clevedon: Multilingual Matters.

Elola, I. and Oskoz, A. (2008) 'Blogging: fostering intercultural competence development in foreign language and study abroad contexts', *Foreign Language Annals*, 41(3): 454–77.

European Commission (2010) *European Commission – Education and Training*. Online. Available: http://ec.europa.eu/education/lifelong-learning-programme/doc80_en.htm (accessed 5 May 2010).

Forum on Education Abroad (2011) *Education Abroad Glossary*, Carlisle, PA: Forum on Education Abroad.

Freed, B.F. (1995) *Second Language Acquisition in a Study Abroad Context*, Amsterdam: John Benjamins.

Freed, B.F., Dewey, D.P., Segalowitz, N. and Halter, R. (2004) 'The Language Contact Profile', *Studies in Second Language Acquisition*, 26(2): 349–56.

Hammer, M.R. and Bennett, M.J. (2001) *Intercultural Development Inventory Manual*, Portland, OR: The Intercultural Communication Institute.

Hammer, M.R., Bennett, M.J., and Wiseman, R. (2003) 'Measuring intercultural sensitivity: the intercultural development inventory', *International Journal of Intercultural Relations*, 27(4): 421–43.

Hoffa, W.W. (2007) *A History of US Study Abroad: Beginnings to 1965*, Carlisle, PA: Frontiers: The Interdisciplinary Journal of Study Abroad and The Forum on Education Abroad.

Institute of International Education (2010) *Open Doors: Report on International Educational Exchange*. Online. Available: www.iie.org/en/Research-and-Publications/Open-Doors (accessed 25 December 2010).

Jackson, J. (2006) 'Ethnographic preparation for short-term study and residence in the target culture', *International Journal of Intercultural Relations*, 30(1): 77–98.

——(2008) *Language, Identity, and Study Abroad: Sociocultural Perspectives*, London: Equinox.

——(2010) *Intercultural Journeys: From Study to Residence Abroad*, Basingstoke: Palgrave Macmillan.

——(2011a) 'Assessing the impact of a semester abroad using the IDI and semi-structured interviews', (Distinguished paper award). Proceedings of the 2nd Intercultural Development Inventory conference, Minneapolis, MN, USA.

——(2011b) 'Maximizing the impact of international experience through "practice-to-theory-to-practice" pedagogy', paper presented at the 6th Asia-Pacific Association for International Education conference, Taipei, Taiwan, March 2011.

Kachru, B.B. (1985) 'Standards, codification, and sociolinguistic realm: the English language in the outer circle', in R. Quirk and H.G. Widdowson (eds) *English in the World*, Cambridge: Cambridge University Press, pp. 11–30.

Kälvermark, T. and van der Wende, M.C. (1997) *National Policies for Internationalization of Higher Education in Europe*, Stockholm: National Agency for Higher Education.

Kauffmann, N.L., Martin, J.N. and Weaver, H.D. (1992) *Students Abroad: Strangers at Home*, Yarmouth, ME: Intercultural Press.

Kinginger, C. (2008) 'Language learning in study abroad: case studies of Americans in France', *Modern Language Journal*, 92(1): 1–131.

——(2009) *Language Learning and Study Abroad: A Critical Reading of Research*, New York: Palgrave Macmillan.

Knight, J. (2004) 'Internationalization remodeled: definition, approaches, and rationales', *Journal of Studies in International Education*, 8(1): 5–31.

Knight, S.M. and Schmidt-Rinehart, B.C. (2010) 'Exploring conditions to enhance student/host family interaction abroad', *Foreign Language Annals*, 43(1): 64–79.

Medina, A. (2008) *Intercultural Sensitivity Development in Study Abroad: Is Duration a Decisive Element in Cultural Learning Outcomes?*, Saarbrücken: Verlag.

Mikk, B.K., Cohen, A.D. and Paige, R.M. with Chi, J.C., Lassegard, J.P., Meagher, M. and Weaver, S. (2009) *Maximizing Study Abroad: An Instructional Guide to Strategies for Language and Culture Learning and Use*, Minneapolis, MN: Center for Advanced Research on Language Acquisition, University of Minnesota.

Murphy-Lejeune, E. (2002) *Student Mobility and Narrative in Europe: The New Strangers*, London: Routledge.

——(2008) 'The student experience of mobility, a contrasting score', in M. Byram and F. Dervin (eds) *Students, Staff and Academic Mobility in Higher Education*, Newcastle: Cambridge Scholars Publishing, pp. 12–30.

Ogden, A.C. (2006) 'Ethnographic inquiry: reframing the learning core of education abroad', *Frontiers: The Interdisciplinary Journal of Study Abroad*, VIII: 87–112.

Organization for Economic Cooperation and Development (OECD) (2009) *Education at a Glance 2009: OECD Indicators*. Online, Available: www.oecd.org/document/24/0,3343,en_2649_39263238_1_1_1_1,00.html (accessed 10 May 2010).

Paige, R.M., Fry, G.W., Stallman, E.M., Josić, J. and Jon, J. (2009) 'Study abroad for global engagement: the long-term impact of mobility experiences', Intercultural Education, 20(4): S29-S44.

Pettigrew, T. (1998) 'Intergroup contact theory', *Annual Review of Psychology*, 49, 65–85.

Roberts, C., Byram, M., Barro, A., Jordan, S. and Street, B. (2001) *Language Learners as Ethnographers*, Clevedon: Multilingual Matters.

Shively, R. (2010) 'From the virtual world to the real world: a model of pragmatics instruction for study abroad', *Foreign Language Annals*, 43(1): 105–37.

Stewart, J.A. (2010) 'Using e-Journals to assess students' language awareness and social identity during study abroad', *Foreign Language Annals*, 43(1): 138–59.

Ting-Toomey, S. (2005) 'Identity negotiation theory: crossing cultural boundaries', in W. Gudykunst (ed.) *Theorizing about Intercultural Communication*, Thousand Oaks, CA: Sage, pp. 211–34.

Welch, A. (2008) 'Myths and modes of mobility: the changing face of academic mobility in the global era', in M. Byram and F. Dervin (eds) *Students, Staff and Academic Mobility in Higher Education*, Newcastle: Cambridge Scholars Publishing, pp. 292–311.

# 29

# Business and management education

*Prue Holmes*

## 1. Introduction

The contemporary workplace includes new identifications and communication practices across cultural and national boundaries. Students of business/management, and others in the workplace, need intercultural communication skills and knowledge to handle this increasingly complex, ambiguous, and pluricultural context (Mintzberg 2004). They must also be able to account for individual distinctiveness in the local environment and foster the human engagement that enables development. How, then, is intercultural communication—as a theoretical concept, a practical tool, and an educational discipline within management education—to be conceptualized and delivered?

In this chapter, I attempt to answer this question. I begin by exploring conceptualizations of intercultural communication that have influenced its teaching and research in the management/business context. Next, I describe some critical responses to this situation and more recent approaches that seek to develop experiential learning and critical/reflective intercultural action. Then, I outline my own approach and research activities to promote student intercultural learning. I finish with implications and possible future directions.

## 2. Historical perspectives

The concept of intercultural communication, and the idea that people need to have some kind of intercultural competence, is a relatively new phenomenon in management education. It began in the 1950s when foreign nationals, who had been given language training as preparation for their overseas missions, discovered that language was but one aspect of the toolkit they required for their overseas work (Martin and Nakayama 2007). They also needed an understanding of the culture of the people with whom they were going to reside and work.

In this section, I describe the foundational orientations of intercultural competence—value orientation frameworks for understanding cultural difference—that have underpinned much intercultural communication research to date, in both business and management, and more generally. I then outline a model that sought to expand this approach in the face of globalization, with particular reference to global project management. I conclude the section by exploring other influential social science approaches.

## Foundational orientations: understanding cultural differences

As intercultural contact increased, through job mobility and migration, researchers became more interested in understanding how people understood difference. Thus, frameworks for under-standing culture evolved, often culture specific, rule based, and goal achievement oriented, on ways of communicating and behaving with people in another society/culture. Culture was understood as learned patterns of behavior, developed through interaction in a shared social environment and with various groups of individuals (Martin and Nakayama 2007). This line of thinking seeks to understand cultural differences in terms of shared value orientations. Martin and Nakayama (2007) described values as "the most deeply felt beliefs shared by a cultural group ... [and] a shared perception of what ought to be, and not what is". Four key models—Kluckhohn and Strodtbeck's (1961) five value orientations, Hall's (1976) high/low context communication, Hampden-Turner and Trompenaars' (1998) seven value dimensions, and Hofstede's (1984) value orientations framework—are discussed next.

## Kluckhohn and Strodtbeck's five value orientations

Drawing on the cultural patterns of ethnic groups in the United States, Kluckhohn and Strodtbeck (1961) identified five value orientations prevailing within all cultures. They concern: (1) the nature of human nature; (2) the relationship between humans and nature; (3) the rela-tionships between humans; (4) preferred forms of activity (e.g., "doing" or action oriented as opposed to "being" which is person oriented); and (5) time orientation (e.g., future, present, or past oriented ways of thinking and acting). This framework provided an understanding of the broad differences in values among various cultural groups.

## Hall's high/low context communication

A further value orientation framework is that of Hall (1976). He describes cultures as having either high- or low-context communication. Hall speaks of the difference between "conscious" and "unconscious" culture, that is, all that is explicit, highly visible, and "sensible" (i.e., able to be sensed) and that which is invisible and nonverbal and is unconsciously acquired. In the latter, he includes all aspects of nonverbal communication, for example, facial expressions, gestures, eye contact, "chronemics" (differences in time orientation), "proxemics" (use of personal space), and silence (Hall 1998). Conscious cultures fall into the low-context communication framework, where the majority of meaning is in the verbal code. In contrast, unconscious cultures have high-context communication, where the information tends to be located in the physical context or internalized within an individual and little information is in the coded, explicit part of the message.

## Hampden-Turner and Trompenaars' seven value dimensions

A second value orientation framework is the seminal work of Hampden-Turner and Trompe-naars (1998). They established seven dimensions that embody the deep values entrenched in different cultures, and from which generalizations can be derived as to how people in a culture are most likely to respond to everyday dilemmas and human interactions.

The seven dimensions were found using questions that were designed to portray different dilemmas of everyday life. The respective culture's most likely response to each dilemma can be seen to illustrate the deep values entrenched in different cultures, and are used to generalize each national culture's most likely response to everyday dilemmas and human interactions. The different dimensions are useful in understanding different interactions between people from different national cultures, and can give guidance to, for example, expatriates with managerial tasks in different cultures:

1. Universalism vs. particularism (What is most important—rules or relationships?)
2. Individualism vs. collectivism (Do we function in a group or as individuals?)
3. Neutral vs. emotional (Do we display our emotions, or do we hide them?)
4. Specific vs. diffuse (Do we handle our relationships in specific and predetermined ways, or do we see our relationships as changing and related to contextual settings?)
5. Achievement vs. ascription (Do we have to prove ourselves to receive status, or is status given to us?)
6. Sequential vs. synchronic (Do we do things one at a time or several things at once?)
7. Internal vs. external control (Do we believe that we can control our environment, or do we believe that the environment controls us?)

Value dimension frameworks could therefore be used by business managers to foresee how individuals from a particular culture are likely to behave and communicate. The implication for the workplace was that failure to recognize and understand differences in value orientations may lead to intercultural conflict. For example, by drawing on value orientation frameworks, Buzzanell (1994) concluded that individualistic relationships and "doing" behaviors, as demonstrated by white American professionals, tended to be rewarded rather than the more collaborative and yet equally productive work of their Chinese colleagues who share a collectivist approach where the goal is to complete the task for group/organizational reward or benefit rather than individual merit. Further, differences in power and attitudes toward traditional ways of doing things and the privileging of outsider values over local ones may often result in conflict, for example, in joint ventures between China and the West, and in international and nongovernmental aid programs to developing countries (e.g., United Nations programs in Nepal and African countries).

These outcomes suggest that concepts such as equality and fairness have varied interpretations in different cultural contexts. For example, in many Western nations, such as the United States, Australia, and New Zealand, the notion of equality suggests that, fundamentally, individuals are created equal, yet disparities in talent, intelligence, or access to material goods exist, and notions of fairness require that people be treated accordingly. Yet in cultures where history and tradition provide guidance for behavior, as evidenced in Asian cultures such as China, or in traditional African societies, respect and deference must be shown to those with greater knowledge and power, and relationships and interactions reflect such differences.

## Hofstede's value orientations framework

Perhaps the most widely cited value orientation framework is that of Hofstede (1984). His four dimensions or value orientations of cultural difference—power distance, femininity/masculinity, uncertainly avoidance, and individualism–collectivism (a binary first posited by Kluckhohn and Strodtbeck 1961)—have provided a theoretical model for much management/business research to date. Power distance refers to the extent to which less powerful members of institutions and organizations within a country expect and accept the unequal distribution of power. New Zealand, Denmark, and Israel value low power distance, minimizing adherence to hierarchies of power. In contrast, in countries such as India, China, and Mexico, hierarchies and decision-making processes and relationships among managers and their subordinates are transparent and formalized.

Femininity/masculinity refers to the extent to which gender roles are valued, and attitudes toward ascribed masculine values (e.g., achievement, ambition). Japan, Austria, and Mexico scored high here, valuing gender-specific roles, whereas northern European countries (Sweden, Denmark, Norway) demonstrated a tendency to value the feminine orientation (preferring gender equality and quality of life for all). The third binary—uncertainty avoidance—refers to a preference for unambiguous and uncertain situations and maintaining the status quo. Countries with weak uncertainty avoidance (the United Kingdom, Sweden, Hong Kong, and the United States) are more risk taking, accepting of dissent, and less rule structured. Countries with strong uncertainty avoidance (Japan, Portugal, Greece) favor rules and regulations and seek consensus about goals. The fourth dimension—individualism/collectivism—refers to individual vs. group orientation. Individualist countries (e.g., New Zealand, Australia, the United States) emphasize personal over group goals, weak group and organizational loyalty. Collectivist countries (e.g., Arab countries, Brazil, India) emphasize community, collaboration, shared interest, harmony, tradition, and maintaining face (Martin and Nakayama 2007).

Later, as a result of extensive criticism of the Western bias of this framework, Hofstede (2001) added a fifth dimension—long- and short-term orientation or "Confucian dynamism"—which emphasizes Confucian values such as persistence, thrift, personal stability, and respect for tradition. So, in the work context, employees who reflected long-term orientation (as in China, Japan, Korea) have a strong work ethic and show respect for status differences, whereas those with a short-term orientation (e.g., the United States, the United Kingdom, Canada) focus on short-term results, seek quick gratification of their needs, and show less concern for status.

Of all the cultural differences frameworks, Hofstede's model has been particularly influential in intercultural (management) training, as the model enables participants to identify the key values and assumptions of their own and the target culture, to identify the differences between the two and the most common issues these differences cause, and offer strategies to deal with these issues (Storti 2009). Yet, despite its application to research in many fields of management, notably in cross-cultural marketing research to assess potential customer values, and in intercultural management training, the model has been strongly criticized for its Western bias and methodological limitations. These criticisms, and those pertaining to value orientation models generally, are discussed later in the chapter.

## Responses to globalization: leading global projects

Transmigration and global trends in business and organizational practices have changed the world in which people now live and work. As organizations engage in manufacturing, marketing, and research and development, global alliances and their manifestation—global projects—are forged. In these contexts, project leaders must manage the project strategically, demonstrate effective cross-cultural management, and show project leadership skills (Moran et al. 2009). Moran et al. (2009) noted that project leaders invariably encountered the following challenges: (1) communication and understanding difficulties resulting from language differences; (2) different norms, values, and behaviors that can lead to conflict; (3) geographical dislocation (working in different countries), giving less time to become acquainted, which in turn leads to lack of trust and communication gaps; and (4) organizational policy and strategy differences across project team members who represent different companies. Acknowledging that much cultural behavior is hidden, they argue that successful project managers must "learn to 'read' between the lines and change their communication style to suit the listener, through being adaptive in their communicative styles" (Moran *et al.* 2009: 300). To this end, Moran *et al.* described Mintzberg's (1983) leadership strategy as a way for project leaders to develop effective coordination in multicultural teams:

> [P]roject members should mutually adjust to each other, at times applying direct supervision, and creating a standardized work process and output while reinforcing interdependence among tasks and objects.
>
> *Mintzberg (1983) cited in Moran et al. (2009: 297)*

The strategy highlights the adaptive processes required in recognizing and responding to cultural differences. However, this suggested leadership style reinforces notions of managerial control and Western dominance, neglecting the transformational potential of context-specific intercultural interaction.

## Other approaches to learning about culture and cultural difference

Martin and Nakayama (2007) categorize approaches to learning about culture and cultural difference into the social science, positivist, and functionalist approaches. By studying cultures objectively, from an outsider's position, researchers seek to make generalizations about communication and behavior. In a social science approach, researchers analyze difference according to a set of variables, such as value orientations (as described above), which are typically applied in sociological research and in cross-cultural psychology. Further examples include Gudykunst's (2005) anxiety uncertainty management theory, which explains how anxiety and uncertainty can influence the communication of strangers in their interactions with those in the host community. And Ting-Toomey's (2005) face negotiation theory uses variables of collectivism and individualism to measure the extent to which people in such cultures (e.g., China and the United States respectively) use face negotiation strategies to manage or avoid conflict.

Similarly, cross-cultural psychologists have focused on cultural difference by measuring these and other variables fundamental to the study of intercultural communication, including those of nationality, ethnicity, personality, and gender (Brislin 1999). The role of perception is important in developing learned patterns of thought and meaning that make up our culture. Allport's (1979) famous work on prejudice describes how the cognitive activities of categorization and generalization that occur normally in the human brain are an important way of making sense of the world around us. Although such categorizations are useful as sense-making strategies for human behavior, if unchecked, they can lead to more extreme understandings of cultural difference, such as ethnocentrism, stereotyping, and prejudice—the roots of racism. As a result, the social science approach to researching and understanding cultural difference has been heavily criticized, and it is to these critiques that I now turn.

## 3. Critical issues and topics

### Critiques of the "cultural difference" frameworks

Cultural difference frameworks (as described above) within the social science approach have prevailed in intercultural communication management/business training and education contexts because they provide new entrants with tools to make sense of culturally new phenomena, and with rules about how to communicate with clients and colleagues from other places and backgrounds. The implication is that, in knowing/learning about these cultures with these (predictable) patterns and observed ways of interaction and communication, people will then have the ability to enter into the culture and know how to communicate with its people (Chuang 2003; Martin and Nakayama 2007).

However, they have also been criticized. For example, McSweeny (2002) presented three main flaws in Hofstede's (1984) research design: (1) the population surveyed were employees of Hermes and IBM, a United States multinational whose employees represented their organizational goals; (2) the validity of the items used in constructing some of the indices was questionable, thus raising concerns about assessing any one group's (and especially Asians') attitudes and lived experiences; (3) the data were collected using a paper and pencil survey, a method that is laden with positivist constructs and approaches to representing understanding. Others added to the critique, namely, the Eurocentric bias of the research, with the researchers as "experts" and the exotic natives as others and not as co-owners and co-producers of knowledge (Chuang 2003). Further, the boundaries of these dichotomies of difference fail to account for globalization and economic progression (Guirdham 2005); instead, making sense of the other has been done through an imperial and colonial gaze. Finally, they tend to view culture as static and monolithic, with inherent patterns to be learned.

Studying cultural differences in this way, as real and tangible entities, alongside analyses of exotic examples of cultural behaviors, can result in "essentializing" people in cultures. That is, they presume "universal essence, homogeneity and unity in a particular culture … [and] reduce cultural behaviour down to a simple causal factor" (Holliday et al. 2004: 2). As students draw on these constructs to analyze the (exoticized) other, they ignore the intersubjective and negotiated processes that embody intercultural communication encounters. A further outcome of these approaches is otherization—"imaging someone as alien and different to 'us' in such a way that 'they' are excluded from 'our' 'normal,' 'superior' and 'civilised' group" (Holliday et al. 2004: 3).

Instead, Holliday et al. (2004) argue that students need skilled communication strategies and principles in a globalizing world. Still other scholars have called for context-specific analyses of intercultural communication and new tools for local contexts (Ting-Toomey 2010). These theoretical and methodological approaches shift the focus away from "differences between national cultures and the development of universalised competences within international groups, towards multiple identities and particular competences within local groups" (Lund and O'Reagan 2010: 56). Thus, the next section focuses on knowledge/skills building and training, approaches used by educators and trainers/coaches in the workplace.

## Intercultural education and training

Managers have come to recognize the need for all employees to receive management diversity training in their organizations (Landis et al. 2004). No longer are knowledge and skills in intercultural communication for others—that is, those on overseas assignments, or migrants entering the workplace—but for all gender, ethnic, and racial groups who come together for purposes of work. In these plurilingual/pluricultural contexts, new ways of connecting, working and learning are required (Edwards and Usher 2008). Rigid frameworks that essentialize people according to their culture and ethnicity have given way to more flexible approaches that require people to be responsive to changing contexts. This transcultural context requires research theories and methods that enable people to encounter interculturality in real world situations. In this new context, educators and trainers draw on a range of tools to simulate real world situations that highlight problematic intercultural communication and/or conflict, for example, vignettes, case studies, critical incidents, and other problem-solving activities. Other methods include reading about another culture, spending time with people from another culture (Mughan 2009), and more recently, learning about other cultures through various online or web-based training tools (Storti 2009) and online intercultural exchanges (O'Dowd 2007).

A further approach is to start with "self" by asking learners (whether workplace employees or students) to examine tacit values and norms that frame their own behaviors in their encounters with cultural others. This strategy would enable the exploration of stereotypes, ethnocentrism, prejudice, and the resultant essentializing and otherizing that evolve from these categories of difference (Jack 2009). Further, learners are encouraged to practice self-monitoring in intercultural interactions. Self-report studies and protocols that enable learners to self-assess their competence abound (for example, see the self-report protocols described in Spitzberg and Changnon 2009). However, self reports are limited in that they tend to develop learners' intercultural competence in generic terms, rather than culture-, context-, or individually specific terms. This limitation may result in part from self-report methodology, which relies on multichoice answers or Likert scales as their bases for self-assessment (see, for example, such models of intercultural competence in the review by Spitzberg and Changnon 2009), and not critical reflective self-evaluation (of both self and other) based on some intercultural encounter (which is the approach adopted by the "Autobiography of Intercultural Encounters" (Council of Europe 2010) and Holmes and O'Neill 2010).

However, education and training should not lose sight of its primary function. This is not to exonerate organizations from guilt or legal redress, purely because they have fulfilled managerial functions in training staff to manage diversity or risk assessment. Phipps (2010: 62) describes this as the "deficit" model of training which seeks to address "danger" in the workplace, thus forcing employees into "dominant and uncontestable models of good citizenship". Instead, she argues, the purpose of education and training should be to prepare people for "the mess and struggle of dialogue, human trust, subtlety of context-based understanding, a disposition that is enabled, through careful sensory perception, to be attuned to a new habitat, a new place, a different context" (Phipps 2010: 65). Intercultural understanding and knowledge is not acquired through the straitjacket training models found in contemporary organizations, but as Phipps argues, through processes of finding common ground, dialogue, discernment, and intercultural understanding.

## 4. Current contributions and research

Having discussed a range of social science approaches and considered their strengths and limitations, I now turn to interpretive and experiential approaches, and then critical intercultural action and reflexivity as responses to understanding intercultural interactions across languages and cultures.

### Interpretive/experiential approaches

More recent research has seen a focus on experiential learning. To this end, Bennett (1998) argues for the need to improve intercultural communication and sensitivity through education and training by exploring core concepts played out in intercultural exchanges. Therefore, trainees need to develop skillful facilitation where they have the opportunity to "acquire increased self-awareness and other-awareness" and to "confront emotional and communication challenges and practice context-pertinent communication skills" (Ting-Toomey 2010: 21).

Experiential learning has also been linked to real life, firsthand experience. For example, Mughan (2009), in his research on small- to medium-sized enterprises (SMEs), noted that investment in intercultural skills analysis and development has mostly focused on the foreign language needs of first-time exporters, largely ignoring the intercultural dimension. However, he found that much of the learning required to manage business across multiple markets and cultures lay in some foreign language skills, although not necessarily using them, but also in the higher education level of the owner–manager. Other ways include valuing prior professional experience in other cultural environments and frequent interactions in situ with members of other cultures both at home and abroad.

In the context of MBA education, Tomalin (2009) noted that experiential learning is embodied in the learning cycle—activity, debrief, conclusion, implementation. This model draws on Kolb and Fry's (1975) seminal work—the four-step learning cycle in experiential learning—which involves: (1) concrete experience; (2) observation and experience; (3) forming abstract concepts; and (4) testing in new situations. Although Kolb and Fry's model has been criticized for its Western assumptions of selfhood and does not sufficiently account for other cognitive and communicative styles (Tennant 1997), the model is commonly applied in intercultural education and training.

To conclude, these forms of experiential learning resonate with conceptually based intercultural learning, suggesting the importance of links between theory and practice in intercultural training and education (Mughan 2009). However, Jack (2009) notes the importance of teaching approaches that encourage critical transformation in learners. A scholarly response to this situation has seen, on the one hand, the emergence of critical theories of management education and business, and on the other, a greater emphasis on intercultural competence—the skills, behaviors, and knowledge required to understand and manage interaction with people who have other ways of thinking, doing, communicating, and being. In this context, developing sensitivity, mutual respect, and critical understanding in intercultural encounters is important in facilitating successful intercultural relationships and communication. As Byram notes in Chapter 5 (this volume), critical understanding includes knowledge of the conditions under which political activity can take place, which he describes as citizenship education. This line of thinking suggests that intercultural competence lies in skills of "critical" intercultural learning, which includes developing critical thought, critical self-reflection, and critical action (Alred et al. 2003; Guilherme et al. 2010; Jack 2009). Thus, students must be encouraged to "critically analyze the value assumptions of different knowledge systems, forms, and categories" (Banks 1991: 126), necessary steps in developing potential managers who demonstrate moral and political responsibility. This aspect of criticality is explored in the next section.

## Developing critical intercultural action and reflexivity

To prepare learners to become accountable to and for others through their ideas, communication, and actions, management educators must "provide the conditions for students to learn in diverse ways how to take responsibility for moving society in the direction of a more realisable democracy" (Giroux 2004: 20). This means requiring learners to draw on their (lived) experiences and values while attending to interpersonal relations, communication, conflicts, feelings, and politics (Grey 2004). Within this section, I discuss three approaches to developing critical intercultural action and reflexivity: an examination of hegemony and cultural imperialism, intercultural teamwork, and identity (re)construction and (re)negotiation.

## Hegemony and cultural imperialism

Jack (2009) argues that, although many of the courses in intercultural communication teach learners critical thought and critical self-reflection, they do not necessarily promote critical action.

Further, he states: "an obsession with the marketplace obscures and often distorts a broader discussion of values and relations to the Other". He interprets this limited vision as perpetuating the status quo, whereby "institutions shape and edit the managerial self to fit the institutional interest of the organisation" (ibid.: 101–2). In other words, the management academy, including both its teaching and its practice, is embedded in and constrained by Eurocentric thought and geographical location, and as such, legitimizes those in and with power to decide whose and what ideas count. Instead, drawing on Said's (1978) "orientalism", Jack invites learners to examine and question the hegemony and cultural imperialism of the dominating colonial structures responsible for this Eurocentric managerialism. He encourages them to develop, in Foucault's (1984: 102) terms, "practices of liberation", that is, other ways of relating to oneself (and others).

## Intercultural teamwork

This type of critical reflexivity can also be achieved through teaching about intercultural teamwork, for example, by encouraging learners to appreciate the complexity of teamwork processes, the inherent ethnocentric values of team members, the range of emotional responses engendered by teamwork, and issues of resistance (Cockburn-Wootten et al. 2008). For example, in teaching teamwork, my colleagues and I invite our students to question existing power structures, knowledge, and conditions in the wider society (Giroux 1997), and to engage in student/teacher dialogue and co-constructed learning. Communication in this learning context is thus characterized by negotiation, conflict, persuasion, and critique.

Guilherme et al.'s (2010: 2) recent study of intercultural teamwork reveals a new theoretical focus—intercultural mobility—where divisions between guest and host are diminishing and where we begin to "look for the Other in ourselves". In their investigation of the intercultural dynamics of heterogeneous groups in the cosmopolitan context of the European workplace, they found that people demonstrated intercultural mobility through processes of self and social discovery, and "languaging". That is, they engage in a critical cycle—"a reflective, exploratory, dialogical and active stance towards cultural knowledge and life" (Guilherme 2010: 4). The outcome, she argues, is intercultural personhood, where an individual becomes more inter-connected and networked, and is able to perceive, and I would add (ideally) manage, risk. She concludes that an individual's ability to recognize and manage intercultural dynamics is where his/her intercultural competence lies, but that such competence is a process of continuous transformation.

The emergent model from this extensive study extends understanding of intercultural com-petence in the professional context to include several aspects of intercultural communication: awareness, cross-cultural communication, cultural knowledge acquisition, sense-making, per-spective taking, relationship-building, and social responsibility. Therefore, as we have noted in our own work, focusing on intercultural teamwork has the value of educating learners to become managers who demonstrate moral, social, political, and cultural responsibility as well as flexibility (Holmes et al. 2005).

## Identity (re)construction and (re)negotiation

As people move from place to place, they take with them, or leave behind, aspects of their reconstructed and renegotiated identities that have evolved through their intercultural com-munication experiences. Instead of identity being framed more simply as in-/out-group differ-ences (Tajfel 1978), it is now possible to speak of multiple identities that account for religion, history, political and economic conditions, locality, region, and nationality, and in organizational diversity management, of gender, age, and (dis)ability (Martin and Nakayama 2007). Further, changes in how we communicate and through what media have resulted in what Martin and Nakayama (2007) describe as contested and fragmented identities. These identities are played out on the internet and in ever-changing spaces as people can be who they like across time and geographical location. Thus, knowledge about identity—both as a stable unifying force and as contested and negotiable—is an important aspect of developing intercultural communicative knowledge and skills.

To conclude, a critical approach to intercultural communication would seek understandings of intercultural communication that embrace questions of power, representation, and knowledge of the other, and just as importantly, questions about self in relation to other and whose interests are being served. These questions are important in the current global economic context as Western financial institutions seek to exploit the resources of poorer, developing nations. Such an approach also acknowledges the ambiguous and complex nature of intercultural communication.

## 5. Main research methods and implications for practice

In this section, I explore the central question: "How can teachers of intercultural communication encourage business/management students to be successful intercultural communicators?". To educate management students to become critical, culturally aware, and socially connected citizens, I use three key approaches—experiential learning, ethnographic inquiry, and praxis—which I describe next.

### My approach: developing intercultural competence in management education

### Experiential learning

To develop students' intercultural knowledge and skills, they require tasks that enable them to prepare for intercultural engagement and communicative interaction with others, and then to reflect on those experiences. These processes echo those described in Kolb and Fry's (1975) four-step experiential learning cycle (described earlier). Ramsden (1992: 40) notes that students need intellectual challenge and the opportunity to develop a sense of independence, but also active engagement with one another, which leads to the possibility of learning from one another. Students also need to engage in deep learning, which encourages them to relate prior, extant knowledge to new knowledge and everyday intercultural experience both within and outside the classroom (Biggs 1999). Finally, an experiential learning approach requires students to think for themselves as active agents in the learning process.

### Ethnographic inquiry

Noels, Yashima, and Zhang (Chapter 3, this volume) highlight the benefits of longitudinal, multilevel research designs that can account for changes over time, and describe intercultural communication processes in situ. Drawing on a tradition of students as researchers (Jackson 2006; Jordan 2001; Roberts et al. 2001), I also provide assignments where students become researchers/observers of intercultural communicative phenomena in both business and everyday communicative contexts. They engage in intercultural communication research with people from other cultures, and then write a research report of the experience. By applying theory they have studied in the course to their own intercultural communication experiences, they reflect not only on the competences of the other, but more importantly, on their own intercultural competence (Holmes and O'Neill 2010). As this research approach also engages international students, who are newcomers in most instances, it aligns with Holliday's goal, outlined in Chapter 2 (this volume), of the potential of newcomers in contributing toward, changing, and enriching the cultural practices that hosts encounter. Thus, this kind of student-led research is transformative in many ways.

## Praxis

Embedded in Kolb and Fry's (1975) experiential learning cycle is the notion of praxis. In the context of intercultural communication, praxis refers to the need for self-conscious and ethical actions where individuals question their past behavior as well as future possibilities. Praxis encourages students to reframe past behavior, which they have performed and examined in their intercultural encounters within the context of their research tasks. Then, by linking these experiences to theory they have been exposed to in their course work, they are able to open up new possibilities for engaging with cultural others (Holmes *et al.* 2005). Thus, my goal here is to teach students, through intercultural engagement, a process of reflection and analysis for future action.

Drawing on these three approaches, I require students to carry out research where they explore some aspect of interculturality. These research tasks involve intercultural experience, where students can begin by identifying who they are (to acknowledge their own socially constructed beliefs, values, and behaviors), and where they can critically analyze and reflect on that experience in order to take action (Alred *et al.* 2003). I now briefly outline three student-led research assignments that capture the above three approaches, and also seek to develop students' awareness of what successful intercultural communication might be.

The first research project emerged out of a need to improve understanding of the complexity of global professional communication. To investigate the complex cultural interpretations that producers and audiences apply to professional texts, a colleague in Israel and I developed a 2-year interactive project. Drawing on Pan *et al.*'s (2002) "communication display portfolio" methodology, the business students in our respective intercultural communication classes produced promotional "texts"—5-minute video clips of a "sales presentation" of an academic program (in this case, their respective business degrees)—which they exchanged with their counterparts overseas to receive feedback. Students in each country were asked to respond, following the same set of questions, to the video clip made by their counterparts in the other country. The responses of each group were then exchanged between countries for reflective discussion and feedback. Students' experiences suggested that, although written and spoken communication are important, cultural differences in the use of iconic messages, and in the promotion of dissimilar values about education, created confusion in the target audience (the students in the other country viewing the promotional video). The project enabled students to understand how people in another culture experience and interpret communication in their own culture. (This project is explained further in Zaidman and Holmes 2009, and the methodology we used is discussed in Holmes and Zaidman 2007.)

The second research project investigated how immigrants to New Zealand used information communication technologies (ICTs) (in this study, e-mail and the internet) to bridge the challenges they faced in adapting to and communicating with people in this new homeland. Each student researcher in the class undertook an e-mail and follow-up face-to-face interview with an immigrant to investigate how ICTs shaped the immigrants' communication practices, and consequently, how those practices impacted the settlement process (in terms of both work and social experiences). Aside from their active involvement as researchers discovering new knowledge, these students, in carrying out this research, learned valuable research skills and interviewing techniques. They also had to manage intercultural interactions within the interviews, including managing relationships and developing rapport and trust as they arranged and conducted the interviews. Student researchers encouraged participants to talk about their personal experiences of and attitudes toward e-mail and the internet, and also to provide examples and stories. These tasks were at times challenging in terms of developing their intercultural competence skills as they negotiated language differences, confronted their own stereotypes of the other, and learned appropriate ways of asking and responding to questions during the interview. The tasks were also challenging practically as students had to negotiate times and places for interviews, communicate via telephone, and gain the commitment of participants throughout the research process. (The process and outcomes of this study are described further in Holmes and Janson 2008.)

The third research project focused on developing students' self-understanding of their intercultural competence through intercultural encounters with a cultural other. Knowing about intercultural competence is important because it offers "the potential for taking action, for mediating and reflecting the values, beliefs and behaviours of one language group to another – and the opportunity for reflexivity, i.e., to critically analyse one's own values, beliefs and behaviours" (Byram 2008: 228). Therefore, finding ways for students to develop and evaluate their own intercultural competence is important in enabling them to become successful intercultural communicators in the workplace, and in society generally.

Students were assigned a research task requiring them to engage in extended intercultural interaction with someone from another culture over several encounters. Drawing on their intercultural communication and experience in the context of those encounters, they then wrote an autoethnography of their experience in which they reflected on and evaluated their intercultural competence. The findings from their autoethnographies suggested that defining, acquiring, and evaluating intercultural competence is complex, messy, and iterative. The findings indicated that communication is influenced and/or constrained by religious, cultural, ethnic, and value differences, and may involve (re)construction and (re)negotiation of an individual's intercultural communication and identity. The outcomes of the project indicated the importance of reflection on intercultural experience in understanding and assessing one's own competence. Further, the intercultural encounter proved to be a useful place for this experience. (See Holmes and O'Neill 2010 for further details of the project.)

Through the experiences students gain from these research projects, and in their reflections on them, students are in a better position to take action, to work with others to achieve an agreed end, and in the process, become better intercultural citizens. Their relationships with cultural others may enable them to (re)construct and (re)negotiate a more strongly developed sense of self; this may also enable them to retain important aspects of cultural, religious, historical, gendered, local/regional, etc. identity—an important transformative stage in developing students who can communicate responsibly with cultural others, engage in intercultural dialogue,[1] and act as intercultural speakers. Ultimately, their actions will work toward improving the human condition. Although these goals may be idealistic and not wholly achievable, they are, nonetheless, worth striving for.

A further objective of this approach, and one articulated by Sorrells (Chapter 23) is, ideally, to promote global engagement. Paige et al. (2009) describe global engagement as economic, sociocultural, political, and other forms of behavior intended to serve the common good locally, nationally, and globally. Whether or not, or to what degree, intercultural experiences promote global engagement has yet to be answered. However, formal and informal feedback from my students in these classes suggests that they benefit from the types of intercultural situations and problems they encounter through these student-centered teaching, learning, and research approaches.

## 6. Conclusion and future directions

An examination of the research on intercultural communication in business/management contexts recognizes a need to develop people who can span cultural and linguistic boundaries. On a basic level, they need the knowledge and skills of intercultural communication and competence. Current approaches have emphasized intercultural competence, focusing in particular on appropriateness and effectiveness (see, for example, recent evaluations in Deardorff 2009). However, given the cultural complexity of the workplace, people also need to be intercultural mediators who can negotiate cultural boundaries and differences, and collaborate and cooperate in their endeavors (for a discussion of this concept, see Chapter 18, this volume). Which knowledge and skills this mediation entails is, as yet, little understood. As MacDonald and O'Reagan (Chapter 35, this volume) point out, managing such communication requires competences that are localized and contextualized, and that focus on the self as much as on the other in the intercultural encounter. Research that provides this local, contextual, and embodied focus, and that captures experience and practice, is needed in order to better understand the meaning of the intercultural mediator/negotiator in the business context.

Future directions for research are required in several areas. One such area is the mediation/ negotiation skills and knowledge required to manage conflict, whether in interpersonal professional settings, intercultural teams, organizational hierarchies, or international negotiations. Guilherme (2010), in her re-evaluation of intercultural competence in the workplace, points out that models of intercultural competence exclude the idea of "rupture" (ibid.: 10). Further research that explores this concept and its relationship to conflict, and that moves it beyond competence as appropriateness and effectiveness in goal achievement, is necessary. For example, Guilherme (2010) summarizes other perspectives of intercultural competence: plasticity (Kim 2008); critical cultural awareness (Byram, 1997; Guilherme 2002); and perception of risk (Phipps 2007). These conceptualizations may be starting points for future research on intercultural conflict.

Another area for potential research concerns the importance of relationships and relationship-building. For example, Deardorff (2009) notes the dearth of research, particularly in Western models and contexts, that investigates the relational aspect of intercultural competence—where relationship-building and dialogue take place between the interactants in the intercultural encounter.

Further, understandings of the impact of multiple identities and identity construction and negotiation—across gender, religion, nationality, history, language, etc.—have yet to be fully explored. And the value of these perspectives in situations where conflict occurs also requires deeper understanding.

Within the European context, the recently articulated concept of "intercultural dialogue" reflects the emergence of the culturally diverse, yet communicatively connected society we now inhabit. Intercultural dialogue has been defined as "a process that comprises an open and respectful exchange or interaction between individuals, groups and organizations with different cultural backgrounds or world-views" (European Institute for Comparative Cultural Research, ERICarts 2008). Broadly, the definition highlights five key aspects: (1) communication should be open and respectful of ethnic, cultural, religious, and linguistic diversity; (2) intercultural dialogue requires a capacity to listen; (3) intercultural dialogue aims to develop integration across diversity through processes of cooperation and participation; (4) these processes allow for personal (and, by implication, societal) growth and transformation; (5) the dialogic process is underpinned by mutual tolerance and respect. These aspects resonate with the concept of the "intercultural speaker" (Byram 2009: 55), someone who has intercultural competence (which Byram conceptualizes as the five *savoirs*) and skills of mediation and conflict resolution, and can therefore demonstrate international political activity.

Linked to the notion of intercultural dialogue is intercultural ethics, basically understood as the rightness and wrongness of interactions among people from different value and morality systems. Although we may be motivated to act according to what we believe is right or serves our own needs, such actions may not be very helpful in intercultural interaction. While general guidelines, or meta-ethics, of the type offered in intercultural texts (see, for example, Martin and Nakayama 2007) may provide guidelines, to what extent do these universally inspired rules resonate with specific local, communal, and cultural practices? Or should there be tolerance toward ethical relativism, permitting people in a culture to make their own decisions about right and wrong actions? These questions are more difficult to answer and need deeper investigation. Further, developing guidelines that transcend cultural difference and that embrace the concept of intercultural dialogue requires empirical investigation and theoretical development.

Further challenges call for non-Eurocentric approaches to understanding intercultural communication and competence and the need for a paradigm shift that considers Eastern conceptualizations of communication (Miike 2007). To this end, Chen and An (2009) suggest a culture-specific (Chinese) model of intercultural leadership, marked by (Buddhist, Confucian, Tao) religious influences that decree a "holistic, interconnected, and transitional worldview"; the need for harmony as an ethical principle of leadership; and an "intuitive, sensitive, and indirect way of communication" (ibid.: 203). For example, the behavioral and communication styles that underpin successful business negotiation in the Chinese context would include: "emotional control, avoidance of aggressive behaviours, avoidance of the expression of 'no,' face saving, and the emphasis of particularistic relationships" (ibid.: 203). These communication styles are in direct contrast to Western conceptions, which Chen and An (2009) claim underline "atomistic, confrontational, reductionist, and logical views" (ibid.: 203). Chen and An conclude that there is a need to move beyond these dichotomized categories toward an integrated model of global leadership competence that embraces the universal values of humans, namely, "courage, kindness, hard work, honest integrity, love, and tolerance" (ibid.: 203). Thus, this Chinese approach reflects the need for paradigmatic conceptualizations and assumptions that both build on and expand Western ways of thinking, doing, and being.

The implications of these terms and concepts for business/management intercultural communication and research have yet to be realized. How do people make sense of the dialogue and interaction in intercultural encounters? How do these experiences impact on their own knowledge of their intercultural competence, and more broadly, on the outcomes and consequences of intercultural communication in the workplace more generally? As we prepare for and seek to understand the increasingly complex and pluricultural nature of the workplace, these questions will require answers.

## Related topics

Culture, communication, context, and power; ethnocentrism; experiential learning; identity; intercultural citizenship; intercultural (communicative) competence; intercultural conflict; intercultural mediator; intercultural training; professional and workplace settings; values

## Further reading

Deardorff, D.K. (2009) (ed.) *The Sage Handbook of Intercultural Competence*, Thousand Oaks, CA: Sage (an extensive survey of the literature, in particular a theoretical and methodological examination of the intercultural competence required in a range of contexts, including management and business, and the nature of this competence).

Feng, A., Byram, M. and Fleming, M. (eds) (2009) *Becoming Interculturally Competent through Education and Training*, Clevedon: Multilingual Matters (a selection of chapters highlighting theoretical and practical issues in intercultural communication for management education, training and business).

Guilherme, M., Glaser, E. and Méndez-García, M.C. (2010) *The Intercultural Dynamics of Multicultural Working*, Clevedon: Multilingual Matters (a new perspective on intercultural communication in the workplace, drawing together extensive research on intercultural interaction in European work contexts; also includes a new theoretical approach to mobility in transcultural Europe and exercises for developing intercultural competence).

Holliday, A., Hyde, M. and Kullman, J. (2010) *Intercultural Communication: An Advanced Resource Book*, 2nd edn, Routledge: London (a source book that offers a critical examination of intercultural contexts and theories, with many useful scenarios for practical use in the classroom).

Landis, D., Bennett, J.M., and Bennett, M.J. (2004) (eds) *Handbook of Intercultural Training*, 4th edn, Thousand Oaks, CA: Sage (a general book on methods of and approaches to intercultural communication and education).

## Note

1 The term "intercultural dialogue" was the focus of the National Communication Association's Summer Conference on Intercultural Dialogue, 22–26 July 2009, at Maltepe University, Istanbul, Turkey, and resulted in a special issue of the *Journal of International and Intercultural Communication* 4 (2), 2011.

## References

Allport, G.W. (1979) *The Nature of Prejudice*, Reading, MA: Addison-Wesley.

Alred, G., Byram, M. and Fleming, M. (2003) *Intercultural Experience and Education*, Clevedon: Multilingual Matters.

Banks, J.A. (1991) 'A curriculum for empowerment, action, and change', in C.E. Sleeter (ed.) *Empowerment through Multicultural Education*, Albany, NY: State University of New York, pp. 125–41.

Bennett, M.J. (1998) *Basic Concepts of Intercultural Communication*, Yarmouth, ME: Intercultural Press.

Biggs, J. (1999) *Teaching for Quality Learning at University*, Buckingham: SRHE and Open University Press.

Brislin, R. (1999) *Understanding Culture's Influence on Behavior*, 2nd edn, Belmont, CA: Wadsworth.

Buzzanell, P.M. (1994) 'Gaining a voice: feminist organizational communication theorizing', *Management Communication Quarterly*, 7: 339–83.

Byram, M. (1997) *Teaching and Assessing Intercultural Communicative Competence*, Clevedon: Multilingual Matters.

——(2008) *From Foreign Language Education to Education for Intercultural Citizenship*, Clevedon: Multilingual Matters.

——(2009) 'Intercultural competence in foreign language education', in D.K. Deardorff (ed.) *The Sage Handbook of Intercultural Competence*, Thousand Oaks, CA: Sage, pp. 321–32.

Chen, G.-M. and An, R. (2009) 'A Chinese model of intercultural leadership competence', in D.K. Deardorff (ed.) *The Sage Handbook of Intercultural Competence*, Thousand Oaks, CA: Sage, pp. 196–208.

Chuang, R. (2003) 'A postmodern critique of cross-cultural and intercultural communication research: contesting essentialism, positivist dualism, and eurocentricity', in W. Starosta and G.-M. Chen (eds) *Ferment in the Intercultural Field: Axiology/Value/Praxis*, Thousand Oaks, CA: Sage, pp. 24–55.

Cockburn-Wootten, C., Holmes, P. and Simpson, M. (2008) (eds) 'Teaching teamwork in business communication/management programs', Special Issue, *Business Communication Quarterly*, 71: 1–4.

Council of Europe (2010) 'Autobiography of intercultural encounters', Online. Available: www.coe.int/t/dg4/autobiography/default_EN.asp (accessed 10 November 2010).

Deardorff, D.K. (2009) 'Synthesizing conceptualizations of intercultural competence: a summary and emerging themes', in D.K. Deardorff (ed.) *The Sage Handbook of Intercultural Competence*, Thousand Oaks, CA: Sage, pp. 264–70.

Edwards, R. and Usher, R. (2008) 'Globalisation and pedagogy: space, place and identity', *British Journal of Educational Studies*, 56(4): 490–92.

European Institute for Comparative Cultural Research (ERICarts) (2008) 'What is intercultural dialogue?' Online. Available: www.interculturaldialogue.eu/web/intercultural-dialogue.php (accessed 13 October 2008).

Foucault, M. (1984) *The History of Sexuality: Volume 3 – The Care of the Self*, London: Penguin Books.

Giroux, H.A. (1997) *Pedagogy and the Politics of Hope: Theory, Culture, and Schooling*, Boulder, CO: Westview Press.

——(2004) 'Betraying the intellectual tradition: public intellectuals and the crisis of youth', in A. Phipps and M. Guilherme (eds) *Critical Pedagogy: Political Approaches to Language and Intercultural Communication*, Clevedon: Multilingual Matters, pp. 7–21.

Grey, C. (2004) 'Reinventing business schools: the contribution of critical management education', *Academy of Management Learning and Education*, 3: 178–86.

Gudykunst, W.B. (2005). 'An anxiety/uncertainty management (AUM) theory of effective communication: making the mesh of the net finer', in W.B. Gudykunst (ed.) *Theorizing about Intercultural Communication*, Thousand Oaks, CA: Sage, pp. 281–323.

Guilherme, M. (2002) *Critical Citizens for an Intercultural World: Foreign Language Education as Cultural Politics*, Clevedon: Multilingual Matters.

——(2010) 'Introduction', in M. Guilherme, E. Glaser and M.C. Méndez-García (eds) *The Intercultural Dynamics of Multicultural Working*, Clevedon: Multilingual Matters, pp. 1–20.

Guilherme, M., Glaser, E. and Méndez-García, M.C. (eds) (2010) *The Intercultural Dynamics of Multicultural Working*, Clevedon: Multilingual Matters.

Guirdham, M. (2005) *Communicating across Cultures at Work*, Basingstoke: Palgrave Macmillan.

Hall, E.T. (1976) *Beyond Culture*, New York: Random House.

——(1998) 'The power of hidden differences', in M.J. Bennett (ed.) *Basic Concepts of Intercultural Communication: Selected Readings*, Yarmouth, ME: Intercultural Press, pp. 53–68.

Hampden-Turner, C. and Trompenaars, F. (1998) *Riding the Waves of Culture: Understanding Diversity in Global Business*, New York: McGraw-Hill.

Hofstede, G.H. (1984) *Culture's Consequences*, Beverly Hills, CA: Sage.

——(2001) *Culture's Consequence: Comparing Values, Behaviors, Institutions and Organizations across Nations*, 2nd edn, Thousand Oaks, CA: Sage.

Holliday, A., Hyde, M. and Kullman, J. (2004) *Intercultural Communication: An Advanced Resource Book*, London: Routledge.

Holmes, P. and Janson, A. (2008) 'Migrants' communication practices with ICTs: tools for facilitating migration and adaptation?' *International Journal of Technology, Knowledge and Society*, 4: 51–62.

Holmes, P. and O'Neill, G. (2010) '(Auto)ethnography and (self)reflection: tools for assessing intercultural competence', in J. Tsau and S. Houghton (eds) *Becoming Intercultural: Inside and Outside the Classroom*, Cambridge: Cambridge Scholars, pp. 167–93.

Holmes, P. and Zaidman, N. (2007) 'The role of culture in persuasive presentations: an Israeli and New Zealand student video exchange', in M.B. Hinner (ed.) *The Influence of Culture in the World of Business*, Frankfurt am Main, Germany: Peter Lang, pp. 391–412.

Holmes, P., Cockburn-Wootten, C., Motion, J., Zorn, T. and Roper, J. (2005) 'Critical reflective practice in teaching management communication', *Business Communication Quarterly*, 68: 247–56.

Jack, G. (2009) 'A critical perspective on teaching intercultural competence in a management department', in A. Feng, M. Byram and M. Fleming (eds) *Becoming Interculturally Competent through Education and Training*, Clevedon: Multilingual Matters, pp. 95–114.

Jackson, J. (2006) 'Ethnographic preparation for short-term study and residence in the target culture,' *International Journal of Intercultural Relations*, 30: 77–98.

Jordan, S. (2001) 'Writing the other, writing the self: transforming consciousness through ethnographic writing', *Language and Intercultural Communication*, 1: 40–56.

Kim, Y.Y. (2008) 'Intercultural personhood: globalization and a way of being', *International Journal of Intercultural Relations*, 32: 359–68.

Kluckhohn, C. and Strodtbeck, F. (1961) *Variations in Value Orientations*, Evanston, IL: Row, Peterson.

Kolb, D.A. and Fry, R. (1975) 'Toward an applied theory of experiential learning', in C. Cooper (ed.) *Theories of Group Process*, London: John Wiley.

Landis, D., Bennett, J.M. and Bennett, M.J. (2004) (eds) *Handbook of Intercultural Training*, 4th edn, Thousand Oaks, CA: Sage.

Lund, A. and O'Reagan, J. (2010) 'National occupational standards in intercultural working: models of theory and assessment', in M. Guilherme, E. Glaser and M.C. Méndez-García (eds) *The Intercultural Dynamics of Multicultural Working*, Clevedon: Multilingual Matters, pp. 41–58.

McSweeny, B. (2002) 'Hofstede's model of national cultural differences and their consequences: a triumph of faith – a failure of analysis', *Human Relations*, 55: 89–118.

Martin, J.N. and Nakayama, T.K. (2007) *Intercultural Communication in Contexts*, 4th edn, New York: McGraw-Hill.

Miike, Y. (2007) 'An Asiacentric reflection on Eurocentric bias in communication theory', *Communication Monographs*, 74: 272–78.

Mintzberg, H. (1983) *Structures in Fives: Designing Effective Organizations*, Englewood Cliffs, NJ: Prentice Hall.

——(2004) *Managers not MBAs: A Hard Look at the Soft Practice of Managing and Management Development*, San Francisco: Berrett Koehler.

Moran, R., Youngdahl, W. and Moran, S. (2009) 'Intercultural competence in business – leading global projects: bridging the cultural and functional divide', in D.K. Deardorff (ed.) *The Sage Handbook of Intercultural Competence*, Thousand Oaks, CA: Sage, pp. 278–303.

Mughan, T. (2009) 'Exporting the multiple market experience and the SME intercultural paradigm', in A. Feng, M. Byram and M. Fleming (eds) *Becoming Interculturally Competent through Education and Training*, Clevedon: Multilingual Matters, pp. 32–51.

O'Dowd, R. (2007) *Online Intercultural Exchange: An Introduction for Foreign Language Teachers*, Clevedon: Multilingual Matters.

Paige, R.M., Fry, G.W., Stallman, E.M., Josić, J. and Jon, J. (2009) 'Study abroad for global engagement: the long-term impact of mobility experiences', *Intercultural Education*, 20: 29–44.

Pan, Y., Wong Scollon, S. and Scollon, R. (2002) *Professional Communication in International Settings*, Oxford: Blackwell Publishers.

Phipps, A. (2007) 'The sound of higher education: sensuous epistemologies and the mess of knowing', *London Review of Education*, 5(1): 1–13.

——(2010) 'Training and intercultural education: the danger in "good citizenship"', in M. Guilherme, E. Glaser and M.C. Méndez-García, *The Intercultural Dynamics of Multicultural Working*, Clevedon: Multilingual Matters, pp. 59–73.

Ramsden, P. (1992) *Learning to Teach in Higher Education*, London: Routledge.

Roberts, C., Byram, M., Barro, A., Jordan, S. and Street, B. (2001) *Language Learners as Ethnographers*, Clevedon: Multilingual Matters.

Said, E. (1978) *Orientalism: Western Conceptions of the Orient*, London: Penguin.

Spitzberg, B.H. and Changnon, G. (2009) 'Conceptualizing intercultural competence', in D.K. Deardorff (ed.) *The Sage Handbook of Intercultural Competence*, Thousand Oaks, CA: Sage, pp. 2–52.

Storti, C. (2009) 'Intercultural competence in human resources', in D.K. Deardorff (ed.) *The Sage Handbook of Intercultural Competence*, Thousand Oaks, CA: Sage, pp. 272–86.

Tajfel, H. (ed.) (1978) *Differentiation between Social Groups*, London: Academic Press.

Tennant, M. (1997) *Psychology and Adult Learning*, 2nd edn, London: Routledge.

Ting-Toomey, S. (2005). 'The matrix of face: an up-dated face-negotiation theory', in W.B. Gudykunst (ed.) *Theorizing about Intercultural Communication*, Thousand Oaks, CA: Sage, pp. 71–92.

——(2010) 'Intercultural conflict interaction competence: from theory to practice', in M. Guilherme, E. Glaser and M.C. Méndez-García (eds), *The Intercultural Dynamics of Multicultural Working*, Clevedon: Multilingual Matters, pp. 21–40.

Tomalin, B. (2009). 'Applying the principles: instruments for intercultural business training', in A. Feng, M. Byram and M. Fleming (eds), *Becoming Interculturally Competent through Education and Training*, Clevedon: Multilingual Matters, pp. 32–51.

Zaidman, N. and Holmes, P. (2009) 'Business communication as cultural text: exchange and feedback of promotional video clips', *International Journal of Intercultural Relations*, 33: 535–49.

# 30

# Professional and workplace settings

*Martin Warren*

## 1. Introduction

Intercultural communication in today's world has increased as a result of the communication needs stemming from the globalization of professional services and businesses. This process has led to an increasing number of studies aimed at a better understanding of these intercultural communication needs, and studies to help those involved to achieve an appropriate level of intercultural communicative competence (see, for example, Ball *et al.* 2010; Beamer and Varner 2008; Cheng *et al.* 2008; Ferraro 2010; Gesteland 2005; Martin and Nakayama 2010). Here, a distinction is made between 'intercultural' communication, which takes place when cultures are in contact, and 'cross-cultural' communication, which is when cultures are compared but are not in contact. All texts are subject to cultural variables in their construction, and also in their interpretation and, with the wide use of English as the language of choice in international professional and business communication, which is typically the case in most intercultural encounters in which English is not the first language of either party (Graddol 1999: 61–63), in theory the potential for miscommunication increases. The rationale for this is the premise that the more divergent the cultural values, norms and behaviours of the participants in an intercultural communication context, the greater the potential for miscommunication and misunderstanding. As Hall (n.d.) explains, such situations have implications for the otherwise successful benefits of intercultural collaboration among professions and businesses because breakdowns in communication can affect the bottom line. In other words, successful intercultural communication in professional and workplace settings is not solely about enhancing our understanding and appreciation of cultural diversity and, through a critical awareness of our own cultural background and that of our colleagues and business partners, creating a more facilitative environment for successful communicating, it is also seen as an essential tool to overcome potential operational difficulties and so, ultimately, as a means to improve profitability.

## 2. Historical perspectives

Two of the most widely cited researchers in this field are Hall (see, for example, 1976) and Hofstede (see, for example, 1991, 2001 and Hofstede and Hofstede 2005), who both focus on intercultural communication in professional and workplace settings. They are both associated with a view of intercultural communication as being between different nationalities, and have developed taxonomies that enable researchers to measure and plot the attributes of national cultures along various dimensions. For Hall, there is one main cultural dimension, which has low-context cultures at one end and high-context cultures at the other end of the dimension. Each of these forms of culture has a number of characteristics ascribed to it, and these characteristics are paired with their opposites at the other end of the dimension. For example, low-context cultures are more direct in their communication style, more monochronic in their attitude towards time (e.g. more concerned with punctuality, deadlines, agendas and completing each task before beginning the next), whereas high-context cultures rely more heavily on shared understanding and are therefore less direct when communicating, more collectivist, more relationship oriented rather than outcome oriented and so on. Hofstede proposes five dimensions: power distance, uncertainty avoidance, individualist vs. collectivist, feminine vs. masculine, and long-term vs. short-term orientation. Both these researchers are interested in intercultural communication in the workplace, and their findings are based on surveys conducted in such settings. Famously, Hofstede, in his role as a psychologist based at IBM, collected survey data from over 100,000 IBM employees working in seventy-one countries, whereas much of Hall's work compares workplaces in the USA with those in Europe and Japan. Hofstede's dimensions have been added to in light of research conducted in Confucian-based cultures (e.g. China, Singapore, Korea and Japan) with another researcher, Bond (see for example, Bond 1986). The result is the notion of low vs. high Confucian work dynamism. This is a dimension that refers to the selective promotion, or not, of a particular set of values found in Confucian teachings, such as thrift, perseverance, a sense of shame and hierarchical relationships. This dimension is said to explain the rapid economic development of a number of Confucian-based Asian countries as a result of these cultural values being pervasive in their workplaces and so enabling their economic success.

The approach typified by Hall and Hofstede emphasizes the shared values, norms, thought patterns and behaviours (including nonverbal behaviour) in intercultural communication and is criticized for paying insufficient attention to 'the role of language use, including multilingual language use, language learning and language proficiency' (Piller 2009: 321). Examples of the role of linguistic competence have received more attention recently in the work of, for example, Fujio (2004) and Vaara et al. (2005), who both look at the role of silence in workplaces in the USA and Finland where the senior management is in the hands of Japanese and Swedes respectively. The lack of consultation with their local colleagues, and the lack of senior positions allotted to local staff, is initially put down to the non-participation (silence) on one side of the workplace relationship, which is claimed to be characteristic of the national cultures of Japan and Finland. However, these two studies both come to the same conclusion, which is that it is the lack of linguistic competence in English on the part of the Japanese and the Finns that is the root cause of the non-participation (manifested in silent behaviour) and not the expression of a national cultural value. In other words, English language training in both these workplaces, for both workers and management, would go a long way to improving intercultural communication. These studies constitute a salutary reminder that intercultural communication problems can be attributed to a mismatch of cultural values when, in fact, the causes lie elsewhere.

The lack of attention to actual language use in the work of Hall and Hofstede is partly addressed in the work of ethnographers and discourse analysts (see, for example, Bhatia 2006; Cheng 2003; Pan et al. 2002; Poncini 2004; Sarangi and Roberts 1999; Scollon and Wong Scollon 2001; Warren 2011), who go beyond questionnaire data to include the observation of participants, interview data and, importantly, actual instances of naturally occurring intercultural communication discourses. These additional sources of data enable researchers to provide what are termed 'thick descriptions' (Geertz, 1973) of communication in action. Importantly, as Piller (2009: 320) points out, this approach is ideal for describing intercultural communication 'in a specific context such as a company', but is impractical when it comes to 'the description of a national culture'. This movement by some researchers away from general descriptions of the characteristics of national cultures to local sites of interaction is embodied in the work of Holliday (1999).

These days, studies tend to have a more textured approach to the notion of culture and are using the term 'culture' to include Holliday's (1999) notion of 'small culture' as opposed to 'large culture'. Holliday makes the case for adopting the term 'small culture' to describe 'small social groupings or activities wherever there is cohesive behaviour' (1999: 237). These small cultures stand in contrast to what Holliday terms 'large cultures', which he argues can lead to 'culturist ethnic, national or international stereotyping' (ibid.: 237). Hofstede's taxonomy of dimensions on to which large cultures are plotted, and the work of Hall (see, for example, 1976), which also attempts to capture the key components of 'national culture', both represent work that has attempted to describe 'large culture' across a range of behaviours. Holliday argues that 'ethnic, national or international difference provides only one lamination' (1999: 260) with respect to culture in what he describes as our increasingly 'multi-cultural at every level' (ibid.: 260) societies. Another criticism of an approach that is only concerned with large culture is made by Holliday (1999: 244), who argues that it runs contrary to our increasingly globalized world in which people lead cosmopolitan and multicultural existences and in which geographical boundaries are becoming less and less relevant.

Studies of small culture, which includes institutions such as 'work, leisure, interest and discourse' (ibid.: 260), are seen as appropriate in studies of groups of professional and workplace settings in which an institutionalized discourse of a particular speech community has patterns of language use that may be distinct from their interlocutors. Such discourses can therefore be viewed as the site of intercultural communication. Holliday (1999: 252) makes the case that the notion of English for specific purposes in applied linguistics, which is based on the existence of different speech communities, each with particular patterns of language behaviour, is an implicit acknowledgement of the existence of small cultures. This notion of culture is supported by others, such as Sarangi and Roberts (1999), who describe how institutional, professional and social discourses interact to form multilayered 'hybrid discourses' such as the discourses examined in this study where the highly routinized and institutionalized discourse of the operators meets the less routinized, but also institutionalized, discourse of the customers. As Holliday (1999) points out, the existence of small cultures, and a better understanding of their implications for language use, needs to be given more attention, and they have important implications in the field of English for specific purposes.

## 3. Critical issues and topics

The work of those involved in capturing and describing the characteristics of national cultures is criticized by some for 'overgeneralisation and essentialism' (Piller 2009: 319). Overgeneralization is potentially problematic because there is always the risk, when trying to describe national cultural characteristics based on an inevitably relatively small-scale survey, of overlooking the diversity that exists within any nation based on social class, religion, age, gender, profession and so on. Its essentialist nature is a product of seeing culture as a stable feature of an individual when in fact cultural identities are dynamic. This essentialism contrasts with the ethnographic and data-driven approach that sees culture as something that is performed through the process of communication rather than a static condition observable outside the communication process itself. The small culture approach is also non-essentialist in that it does not intend to map out national, ethnic or regional cultures, focusing instead on any cohesive social grouping that may or not have a relationship with the cultural values derived from large culture. This emphasis on small culture pushes the researcher examining instances of intercultural communication to look beyond large culture-based values and take into account professional and organizational cultural values to explain the communication processes and products.

A good example of such an approach is provided by Cheng's (2009) study of profession-specific competences across the main professional groups in Hong Kong. The study begins by analysing the key texts of the various professions and determining from them the values espoused by their members. Only by understanding the particular cultural values of a profession, Cheng (2009: 32–33) argues, can we begin to understand their communication practices and then intervene, if necessary, to improve their communicative competences. In a related study (Cheng and Mok 2008), the preference for inductive vs. deductive rhetorical strategies in written communication is investigated across a range of professionals from different countries. The findings raise the issue of whether such choices are in fact the product of national cultural values or are more likely to be the result of profession-specific conventions and preferences.

Sarangi (2002) encourages and practises a discourse-centred approach, as do Scollon and Wong Scollon (2001: xii), who describe what they term 'interdiscourse communication' as including 'the entire range of communications across boundaries of groups or discourse systems'. Pan et al. (2002: 2) adopt just such a situated discourse approach as the basis for training professionals to become more competent intercultural communicators by studying both their own use of professional communication resources and 'how to interpret the behavior and communication of other colleagues in these settings'. This is done through the compilation of 'communication display portfolios', which consist of instances of discourse types (e.g. reports, telephone calls, meetings) collected in different partner organizations and are representative of the main forms of communication between the different professionals based in their different organizations in different countries. The professionals are then encouraged to critically analyse these discourses to determine similarities and differences, which are then discussed among the various groups of professionals. This process is aimed at better preparing professionals to be critically aware of similarities and differences in how they realize the various discourse types, and thereby achieve more effective intercultural communication between all the participants.

In a study of intercultural communication in call centres (Warren 2007), it is argued that the patterns of language use identified manifest the institutionalized roles of the participants and hence the situated small culture within which communication takes place. For example, the use of self- and other-address forms is different, with the call centre operators using more other-address forms ('you', 'your', 'sir', 'ma'am' and 'you're') than the customers ('you' and 'you're') reflecting their role and status in the discourse. Warren (2007: 83–84) concludes that these differences in language use are a product of the roles of the two groups of speakers, which are determined by the power differential in the context of these small cultures interacting. The operators might have 'expert power' (Thomas 1995: 127) in that they have expertise in terms of knowledge and/or information that the customers usually do not have, but this is more than countered by the customers having 'legitimate power' (ibid.: 127) over the operators because of their designated roles in this small culture in which they are basically being served by the operators who have been trained to put into practice their customer care skills. Another difference is the use of the word 'just' by the two sets of speakers (Warren 2007: 87–88). The call centre operators mainly use 'just' to hedge a request made to the customers (e.g. 'just a moment', 'just give … ', 'just send … ', 'just try … ', 'let me just … '). Generally speaking, the operators use 'just' to mitigate requests or to mitigate the need to explain a procedural point of some kind. This use is described by pragmaticists as minimizing the imposition for the benefit of the hearer, and contributes to maintaining the face of the participants. The customers, on the other hand, mainly use 'just' to emphasize the immediacy of what is being said (e.g. 'I just … ', 'just + a moment ago', 'just + don't', 'just + can't'). There are no instances of customers saying 'let me just' to the operators. Instead, they use the word 'just' more often to intensify what is being said rather than to hedge it. This difference is explained by the institutional roles of the participants with the customers in a position where they do not feel the need to hedge when making a request to the operators. The operators, however, are clearly in a different role (i.e. one of relative subservience) in this small culture encounter and frequently hedge what they say. Warren (2007) argues that the identification of these patterns is of potential benefit to the call centre industry in general and to language trainers in particular. This example of workplace intercultural communication is a good example of what Sarangi and Roberts (1999) term multilayered 'hybrid discourses', in which the more highly routinized and institutionalized discourse of the operators meets the less routinized, but also institutionalized, discourse of the customers. In this sense, call centres constitute a workplace in which basically two small cultures, one internal and one external, communicate with one another.

In their study, Brew and Cairns (2004) seem to confirm, in part, the small culture notion of Holliday, but also the large culture and high power distance vs. low power distance dimension of Hofstede. They examine intercultural communication between Singaporeans and Australians working in Western-owned organizations in Singapore, and between Thais and Australians working in Western-owned organizations in Bangkok. Their original hypothesis was that the national cultural value of collectivism for the Singaporeans and Thais would result in them communicating more indirectly in all workplace contexts than their individualist Australian colleagues. Interestingly, this was only found to be true when the Thais and Singaporeans communicated with a superior, especially if the superior was an Australian. Power relationships rather than collectivism seem to be the main determinant of communication style. In contrast, the Australians communicated directly with each other and indirectly with local colleagues, irrespective of their position in the workplace hierarchy. The latter communication style is largely thanks to the orientation training provided to the Australians prior to taking up their jobs. This training emphasized the indirect communication style of their local colleagues based on an assumed collectivist culture in the workplace. Brew and Cairns (2004: 349) conclude that awareness training for all employees (not just incoming expatriates) should revisit some of the preconceived ideas of cultural norms and place more emphasis on actual situated instances of intercultural communication and the importance placed on power relationships in most workplace communication over and above other cultural values.

Other researchers have introduced cultural values specific to particular workplace sites in order to better describe intercultural communication behaviour and the implication of their findings. For example, Shi and Wright (2003) look at the impact of 'national feelings' in international negotiations in Chinese contexts between Chinese and Western (defined as Australian, European, and North American) negotiators. They argue (ibid.: 312) that previous studies have ignored an underlying aspect that may affect the negotiation process and business relationships, namely national feelings. They define these feelings as 'the felt need to promote the best interests of the Mother Country above either personal, or organizational concerns or needs' (ibid.: 312). Their hypothesis is that Western negotiators are solely concerned with the best outcome for their organization, whereas the Chinese have two competing needs: to promote their organization's interests and to promote and protect the nation's interests. They find that Westerners who are aware of this underlying construct are more likely to be successful because negotiations will be less contracted and miscommunication reduced (ibid.: 312). For example, Chinese negotiators, apart from their own mixture of organizational and national goals, are likely to involve local or even national government officials in the negotiation process either directly or indirectly, and their Western counterparts need to be aware of this. Also, both sides need to make explicit the advantages and disadvantages to the Chinese nation of their proposals and counterproposals (ibid.: 323) in order to address and satisfy these national feelings.

Most people who think of intercultural communication in the workplace tend to think of transnational communication, especially when there is so much discussion about the political, economic and social implications of globalization. As Loh and Dahles (2006: 130) observe, many professions and organizations have seen the process of globalization as an opportunity to grow beyond national borders, which then affects both internal and external communication. The challenges for successful intercultural communication already exist between management and their staff, across the gender divide, and between different professions and organizations, and now, as the workplace becomes more internationalized, between local and foreign staff. They caution that studies grounded in the notion of culture have to account for 'the complex interplay of culture with other factors, the most prominent being politics (competition for power and privilege) and economics (attaining organizational effectiveness and ensuring profitability of the business)' (ibid.: 131). They argue that culture can be used as 'a source of power where ethnic identity has been manipulated to achieve management ends'.

For example, a study of Japanese and Dutch co-workers in the Netherlands suggests that it is power that is central, and ethnicity is exploited as the source of that power (Byun and Ybema 2006). The Dutch staff had expatriate Japanese management, and this resulted in asymmetrical power relations with decision-making powers in the hands of the Japanese (Byun and Ybema 2006: 86). This was then compounded by national cultural differences in which the Japanese were cautious, implicit and courteous in the communication, passing decision making up the chain of command within the Japanese management team, whereas for the Dutch, explicitness, clarity, directness and constructive criticism are prioritized. Also, the Japanese emphasize knowing one's position in a group to be accepted and found the improper behaviour of the Dutch towards their superordinates problematic (Byun and Ybema 2006: 87). The Japanese then used these cultural differences as reasons for excluding Dutch staff from promotions to important posts in the organization along with resistance to working overtime, individualism, work–life balance vs. subordinating individual goals to group goals and loyalty to the organization.

## 4. Current contributions and research

Although there are those who are generally critical of the work of those who see culture in terms of national characteristics, it needs to be acknowledged that this approach is still widely adopted by researchers. Even among those who are critical, there are many who continue to find it useful in both their analyses and/or discussions of their findings, which are often based on thick, situated, data-driven descriptions, to refer to the cultural dimensions devised by Hall and Hofstede. For example, two studies of website content (Singh and Baack 2004; Wurtz 2005) set out to determine the cultural messages communicated by various forms of web content by organizations that are potentially communicating to customers, partners, shareholders, employees and competitors worldwide. Such studies demonstrate that, although the findings using these large culture analytical frameworks need to be updated as cultural values shift along the various dimensions, the dimensions themselves have proved to have a long methodological shelf life.

Wurtz (2005) makes use of Hall's taxonomy and identifies aspects of McDonald's websites in five different countries that identify the organizational culture as high or low context. For example, the use of animation, especially in connection with images of moving people, reflects a high context, less direct communication style compared with a text-dependent low context website. Likewise, the choice of images can promote values characteristic of individualistic or collectivist societies, with the high context websites using more family images and groups of McDonald's employees, and low context websites preferring images of solitary individuals. The use of hyperlinks, which promote an exploratory approach to navigation on the website, are more process oriented and are indicative of a high context culture. Conversely, clear and seemingly redundant cues placed on the website to aid with navigation are more goal oriented, and hence characteristic of a more low-context culture.

A comparison of company websites in the USA and Mexico by Singh and Baack (2004) uses four of Hofstede's dimensions (power distance, uncertainty avoidance, individualism/collectivism and masculine/feminine). It is of interest to briefly note some of the examples of what Singh and Baack looked for on the websites to determine where to position the different organizations on each of the dimensions. Collectivism is expressed through highlighting aspects of community relations policies, the provision of clubs or chat rooms, members' clubs and product-based clubs, newsletters and an emphasis on team building and collective work responsibility through the use of photographs of teams of employees, vision statements and so on. A strong need to avoid uncertainty is conveyed by having pages devoted to frequently asked questions, customer support, product return polices, detailed site navigation information and explicitly displayed links, and a tendency to draw attention to the history and traditions of the organization. High power distance is signalled through highlighting the organization's hierarchy with information about the ranks of company people, organizational charts, photographs of important people in the company, the use of full official titles and detailing the ranking of the organization relative to its competitors. The masculine end of the fourth dimension is made known by adopting a hard sell approach by means of discounts and promotions, explicit comparisons with competitors' products, the use of superlatives in organization and product descriptions and clear, traditional gender roles.

Mead (1998) uses two of Hofstede's dimensions to describe different kinds of bureaucracy to refer to the processes by which modern organizations operate. He shows how organizations vary across cultures and identifies four types of bureaucracy based on variations in power distance and the extent of the need to avoid uncertainty. For example, a full bureaucracy is an organization that sets up bureaucratic rules and procedures in order to make the behaviour of its members more predictable and so reduce uncertainties. Typically, a workplace culture that has the most need for these rules is a culture with wide power distances and a strong need to avoid uncertainty. In this kind of organization, functions are tightly distinguished, members attach most importance to maintaining line authority and communication is downward (i.e. 'executive led'). Criticism of the senior management is not formally facilitated; it is only possible using informal means. The opposite of a full bureaucracy is a market bureaucracy. Market bureaucracies are found in cultures where the desire for predictable behaviour and the need to reduce uncertainties are very weak. Such cultures have small power distances and weak needs for uncertainty avoidance. Employees in this kind of workplace rely heavily on personal relationships rather than their relative positions in the hierarchy. They have relatively greater control over how they perform their job duties, and power is less centralized and may come from a number of sources.

Other studies have looked at speech acts, such as directives in specific genres (e.g., hotel front desk service encounters) (Yuen 2009), to illustrate how the use of pragmatic politeness is dependent on the institutionalized cultural values of the hotel vs. the priorities of the guests. Again, as confirmed in a separate study (Cheng 2004) of hotel service encounters, it is confirmed that the nature of such intercultural communication events cannot be fully understood unless one understands the nature of the workplace, the institutionalized values of the hotel staff and the communicative agendas of the participants.

## 5. Main research methods

To describe the complex characteristics of intercultural communication in professional and workplace settings, rigorous empirical research is needed that accounts for both the contexts of interaction and the interactions themselves. One of the more elaborate research methodologies is proposed by Bhatia (2004) in his critical genre analysis of the intercultural language use of members of the legal profession around the world. He devises an elaborate multidimensional and multiperspective framework that encompasses four major perspectives: textual, ethnographic, sociocognitive and sociocritical.

We have seen how the development of taxonomies, surveys, observations, interviews and discourse-based data collection play a role in intercultural communication studies. Also, the use of a corpus has been shown to be useful in examining the notion of small cultures by informing the analysis of language use. Such corpora can provide real-life examples of best (and less than best) workplace practice, reveal patterns of language use to highlight in language training and be a source of real-world dialogues that can be edited and used in training programmes.

In a study of intercultural communication from a management perspective, Mead (1998) identifies three main aspects of how a message is communicated – language, medium and style – all of which may be influenced by cultural preferences and need to be thoroughly researched. A large-scale study by Evans (2010) examines exactly these three aspects of language use across a range of professions and workplace contexts by means of a survey, interviews and the collection of sample discourses to examine the use of English in Hong Kong. Evans is thus in a position to validate his claims based on a wide range of data collection instruments based primarily on a large-scale survey of over 2,000 professionals in Hong Kong. The study highlights how language use (both medium and discourse types) can vary across professions and workplaces and thus affects intercultural communication in a variety of ways.

In the literature, reference is made to the etic (outsider's view) vs. the emic (insider's view) approach to studying intercultural communication and, clearly, the approach adopted has implications for the findings of any study. Both approaches have their advantages and disadvantages and, ideally, the two can be combined. To achieve this, profession- and workplace-specific descriptions of intercultural communication need to involve the stakeholders in the process of research. A good example of a researcher who attempts to involve all the stakeholders in his studies of professional communication is Sarangi (2002). He points out the importance for researchers to study not only 'how language mediates professional activities' but also 'what constitutes professional knowledge and practice beyond performance' (Sarangi 2002: 99). In other words, Sarangi (2002: 99) emphasizes the importance of an understanding of 'professional practice and knowledge representations from their insiders' perspective'. The implication is that, as researchers, we need to understand the cultural values and discourse practices of the professions and workplaces we investigate in order to be able to critically analyse communication in action. He raises three issues for researchers to consider when collecting and analysing professional discourse, namely accessing, problematizing and interpreting professional discourse (Sarangi 2002: 100–103). 'Accessibility' refers to the ongoing problem for researchers of gaining access to business and professional data. Even when permission is granted by the subject and organization for the research team to collect data, it has to be made clear that the subject and the organization retain the right to censor or delete any data collected. With regard to the future use of the data, the subjects and organizations are asked to give their permission in principle to the research team for the data to be used for other academic research purposes. 'Salience/problem identification' is the mutual identification of salient issues and problems, and 'coding/interpretability/articulation' is the process by which the researcher, through collaborating with practitioners, gains insider knowledge in order to better interpret the data (Sarangi 2002).

A project that has embraced the approach outlined by Sarangi has collected all the discourses encountered by six professionals in the course of shadowing them for 1 week in their workplaces (Warren 2009). All the discourse events they engage in were collected together with detailed field notes and profiles of the professionals and their respective organizations to supplement the discourse data. The six professionals, although operating in mainly English medium environments in Hong Kong, communicated through a combination of spoken languages (i.e. Cantonese, English and Mandarin/Putonghua) and either English or written Chinese across a range of contexts. Theories drawn from literacy, discourse analysis, conversation analysis, critical discourse analysis, pragmatics and intercultural communication were adopted in the description and analysis of the discourse processes and products. In order to be able to fully analyse the data collected, the researcher had to have a thorough understanding of each professional's cultural identity and their workplace cultures. In addition, interpretation of the communicative events was only possible through collaborative research with the active participation of the six subjects.

## 6. Recommendations for practice

What does one do with the results of intercultural communication research and how can it be used to improve the intercultural communicative competence of those engaged in it? Training perspectives are coming under scrutiny. Do those involved in intercultural communication need cultural awareness training, language training or a mixture of the two?

First, we need to clarify what is meant by competence in this context. Communicative competence was first proposed by Hymes (1972) and later refined by van Ek (1986) in his model of communicative ability which is made up of six competences. The first of these is linguistic competence, which is the ability to produce and interpret meaningful utterances in accordance with the rules of the language and that carry conventional meaning. Sociolinguistic competence is the awareness of ways in which the choice of language forms is determined by factors such as setting, interpersonal relationships and communicative intention. This requires an understanding of the relationship between purely linguistic signals and their contextual meaning. Discourse competence is the ability to use appropriate strategies in the construction and interpretation of texts, and strategic competence is the ability to handle communication when it is problematic to convey or interpret a message; this involves communication strategies such as rephrasing and asking for clarification. Sociocultural competence is an awareness of the sociocultural context in which all languages are situated. The last of the six is social competence, which encompasses both the willingness and the skill set to interact with others. This involves the motivation, attitude, self-confidence, empathy and the ability to handle social situations.

van Ek's (1986) model is useful in that it identifies a number of aspects of communicative and interactional ability. However, it is criticized (see, for example, Byram 1997; Kramsch 1993) as using native speakers as the implicit yardstick for almost all the six competences. This implies that anything less than native speaker competence is insufficient to communicate effectively. It also implies that a non-native speaker has to be 'linguistically schizophrenic' (Byram, 1997: 11–12), abandoning one set of competences in one language to assume another set of competences accepted by the native speakers of the new language. Based on his identification of the above factors, Byram (1997: 48) revised three of van Ek's competences to better describe intercultural communicative competence. For Byram, linguistic competence is the ability to apply a knowledge of the rules of a standard version of the language to produce and interpret spoken and written language. Sociolinguistic competence is the ability to give to the language produced by the interlocutor, whether native speaker or not, meanings that are taken for granted by the interlocutor or are negotiated and made explicit by the interlocutor. Lastly, discourse competence is the ability to use, discover and negotiate strategies for the production and interpretation of monologue or dialogue texts that follow the conventions of the culture of an interlocutor or are negotiated as intercultural texts for particular purposes.

If you plan to raise awareness of the importance of large and/or small cultures for intercultural communicators, how do you determine what to highlight? The use of intercultural communication audits are considered useful in this regard (Mead 1998) for a number of reasons. They provide a descriptive instrument for modelling the internal and external communication patterns in the workplace, and enable the user to identify significant differences in typical communications patterns between cultures in specific contexts of interaction. In this sense, the intercultural communication audit is a diagnostic instrument because it can be used to predict the effects of these cultural differences and assist in planning appropriate communication systems and awareness, plus language training. However, as Mead (1998) advises, in order to be maximally effective, audits need to be conducted independently, comprehensively, systematically and regularly, underlining the dynamism of professional and workplace cultures.

The importance of communication in health services is widely acknowledged given its often high stakes outcomes, and so it not surprising that this has been the site for a number of intercultural communication studies (for more details, see Chapter 32, this volume). One such study conducted by Kagawa-Singer and Kassim-Lakha (2003) notes that all ethnic minorities in the USA 'lag behind European Americans (whites) on almost every health indicator', and they argue that part of the problem is that many clinicians lack an understanding of how 'culture influences the clinical encounter' and the skills to overcome the possible differences (Kagawa-Singer and Kassim-Lakha 2003: 577). They (ibid.: 581) note that the physician and patient have four communication alternatives:

1. the physician communicates only within the biomedical paradigm;
2. the patient and physician communicate exclusively within their own native cultures;
3. the physician could communicate within the patient's cultural paradigm;
4. the physician and patient negotiate the cause of the medical condition based on their own cultural concepts and the mutually desired goal of how best to treat it.

They argue that that the fourth alternative is the preferred one where there is an attempt to bridge potential cultural differences. This approach requires that the physician be trained to gather background information in order to determine the level and nature of cultural influence and, based on this information, arrive at a 'risk reduction assessment' (ibid.: 583). To do this, the physician needs to invest the time to find out the community resources available to the patient and the patient's family, the cultural identity of the patient and the degree of integration within the ethnic community, the skills available to the patient and the patient's family, and have an understanding of the ethnic group's health beliefs, values and behaviours, and communication norms and conventions (ibid.: 583). Kagawa-Singer and Kassim-Lakha (2003) give the example of how, in Western medicine, diseases are viewed mechanistically and the idea that they may have spiritual or metaphysical causes is not given credence. This is contrary to the beliefs of many cultural groups and can be an obstacle to the efficient treatment of medical conditions (ibid.: 584). What is needed is 'culturally competent practice' backed up by medical institutions providing the infrastructure to respond to and support cultural diversity (ibid.: 584). In a similar study, the kind of training advocated by Kagawa-Singer and Kassim-Lakha is implemented successfully by Betancourt and Cervantes (2009), who have made cross-cultural communicative competence an integral part of the curriculum at the Harvard Medical School.

The misinterpretation of impression management has also been examined by Bilbow (1997) in intercultural business meetings at a Hong Kong airline company. Impression management is behaviour aimed at projecting what is perceived as appropriate in a particular context. He finds that there are frequent misinterpretations of the impression conveyed by divergent communication styles between the meeting members. For example, the more direct style of communication of expatriate meeting members when employing directive speech acts (requests, suggestions, orders and questions) with the more indirect style of the local Hong Kong Chinese meeting members leads to miscommunication as a result of inaccurate inferencing. The Hong Kong Chinese interpret the direct style of their expatriate colleagues as 'aggressive' and 'rude' (ibid.: 462). For their part, the expatriate colleagues interpret the more indirect style of the Hong Kong Chinese as 'cautious, evasive and non-confrontational' (ibid.: 462). To overcome these misunderstandings based on differing cultural notions of what is appropriate behaviour, a workplace-specific training programme is advocated. He recommends a programme of cross-cultural impression training, using video-recordings of the trainees interacting in their professional roles in the workplace, with the proviso that such training be a long-term strategy to really bring about significant changes in behaviour and perceptions (ibid.: 485). This training programme is similar to that advocated by Pan et al. (2002) described earlier.

## 7. Future directions

The study of intercultural communication is becoming increasingly global itself with an increasing number of studies coming from colleagues working outside North America and Europe. This is particularly true of Asian researchers who have begun to look beyond the traditional study of intercultural communication between Asians and Westerners (typically North Americans) to examine intercultural communication between Asia-based professionals and Asia-based organizations (see, for example, a collection of papers in Bargiela-Chiappini and Gotti 2005). Intercultural communication studies are also becoming multimodal in orientation to more fully account for the richness of the intercultural communication process and product. A pioneer of the study of multimodal workplace discourse corpora is Gu (2006), who describes the extensive work required in the preparation of an accessible multimodal corpus of discourses. He includes orthographic transcription, prosody, speech acts, eye gaze, body language, gestures, elaborate descriptions of participant roles and relative positioning. Although the preparation of such data is an enormous and complex task, the rewards make the effort worthwhile. No doubt multimodal analyses will become the norm in future studies of professional and workplace intercultural communication.

Interdisciplinary approaches are likely to be more common in the future, and this is a welcome development and is best conceived of as 'partnership research' (Bargiela-Chiappini 2009: 29), in which each discipline brings its perspective to the analysis of communicative events and so enriches the findings and conclusions to be drawn. In order to embark on such an approach, Bargiela-Chiappini (2009: 29–30) puts forward a three-point agenda to address the challenges thrown up. The various disciplines need to explore and identify a set of shared analytical frameworks to examine discourse and its situated culture. Researchers also have to critically revisit some of the assumptions made in predominantly Western studies of intercultural communication to encompass those of others. Third, there is a need to evaluate 'ethical issues arising from collaboration with individuals and business organizations of different nationalities' (Bargiela-Chiappini 2009: 30). Certainly, an interdisciplinary approach, which also embraces situated, thick, data-driven descriptions of workplace intercultural communication, and intercultural communication between professionals, promises more comprehensive and applied studies in the future.

## Acknowledgement

The research work conducted by the author and described in this chapter was substantially supported by a grant from the Research Grants Council of the Hong Kong Special Administrative Region (project nos PolyU 5480/06H, B-Q02J).

## Related topics

Business and management; culture, communication, context and power; health care settings; intercultural communicative competence; intercultural training; legal contexts; pragmatics; speech acts; tourism; values

## Further reading

Bargiela-Chiappini, F. (ed.) (2009) *The Handbook of Business Discourse*, Edinburgh: Edinburgh University Press (a comprehensive look at business discourse, which often encompasses intercultural communication).

Bargiela-Chiappini, F. and Gotti, M. (eds) (2005) *Asian Business Discourses(s)*, Frankfurt: Peter Lang (intercultural business communication studied from an Asian perspective).

Cheng, W. and Kong, C.C.K. (eds) (2009) *Professional Communication: Collaboration between Academics and Practitioners*, Hong Kong: Hong Kong University Press (an interesting collection of papers that cover all of the stakeholders).

## References

Ball, D.A., Geringer, M.J., Minor, M.S. and McNett, J.M. (2010) *International Business: The Challenge of Global Competition*, New York: McGraw-Hill.

Bargiela-Chiappini, F. (2009) 'Business communication across cultures: a theoretical perspective', in W. Cheng, and C.C.K. Kong, (eds) *Professional Communication: Collaboration between Academics and Practitioners*, Hong Kong: Hong Kong University Press, pp.19–30.

Bargiela-Chiappini, F. and Gotti, M. (eds) (2005) *Asian Business Discourses(s)*, Frankfurt: Peter Lang.

Beamer, L. and Varner, I. (2008) *Intercultural Communication in the Global Workplace*, New York: McGraw-Hill/Irwin.

Betancourt, J. and Cervantes, M. (2009) 'Cross-cultural medical education in the United States: key principles and experiences', *Kaohsiung Journal of Medical Science*, 259: 471–78.

Bhatia, V.K. (2004) *Worlds of Written Discourse: A Genre-based View*, London: Continuum.

——(2006) 'Legal genres', in B. Keith (ed.) *The Encyclopedia of Language and Linguistics*, London: Elsevier, pp. 1–7.

Bilbow, G.T. (1997) 'Cross-cultural impression management in the multicultural workplace: the special case of Hong Kong', *Journal of Pragmatics*, 28: 461–87.

Bond, M.H. (1986) *The Psychology of the Chinese People*, New York: Oxford University Press.

Brew, F.P. and Cairns, D.R. (2004) 'Do culture or situational constraints determine choice of direct or indirect styles in intercultural workplace conflicts', *International Journal of Intercultural Relations*, 28: 331–52.

Byram, M. (1997) *Teaching and Assessing Intercultural Communicative Competence*, Clevedon: Multilingual Matters.

Byun, H. and Ybema, S. (2006) 'Cooperation and rivalry in a Japanese organization in the Netherlands', in H. Dahles and W.L. Loh (eds) *Multicultural Organizations in Asia*, London: Routledge, pp. 85–102.

Cheng, W. (2003) *Intercultural Conversation*, Amsterdam: John Benjamins.

——(2004) '// → did you // → from the mini*BAR* //: what is the practical relevance of a corpus-driven language study to practitioners in Hong Kong's hotel industry?', in U. Connor and T. Upton (eds) *Discourse in the Professions: Perspectives from Corpus Linguistics*, Amsterdam: John Benjamins, pp. 141–66.

——(2009) 'Bridging the divide between business communication research and business communication practice', in F. Bargiela-Chiappini (ed.) *The Handbook of Business Discourse*, Edinburgh: Edinburgh University Press, pp. 481–95.

Cheng, W. and Mok, E. (2008) 'Discourse processes and products: land surveyors in Hong Kong', *English for Specific Purposes*, 27(1): 57–73.

Cheng, W., Greaves, C. and Warren, M. (2008) *A Corpus-Driven Study of Discourse Intonation*, Amsterdam/Philadelphia: John Benjamins.

Evans, S. (2010) 'Language in transitional Hong Kong: perspectives from the public and private sectors', *Journal of Multilingual and Multicultural Development*, 31(4): 347–63.

Ferraro, G. (2010) *The Cultural Dimension of International Business*, Boston, MA: Pearson.

Fujio, M. (2004) 'Silence during intercultural communication: a case study', *Corporate Communications*, 9(4): 331–39.

Geertz, C. (1973) *The Interpretation of Cultures: Selected Essays*, New York: Basic Books.

Gesteland, R. (2005) *Cross-Cultural Business Behavior: Negotiating, Selling, Sourcing and Managing across Cultures*, Hendon: Copenhagen Business School Press.

Graddol, D. (1999) 'The decline of the native speaker', in D. Graddol and U.H. Hall (eds) *English in a Changing World*, AILA Review, 13: 57–68.

Gu, Y. (2006) 'Multimodal text analysis: a corpus linguistic approach to situated discourse', *Text and Talk*, 26(2): 127–67.

Hall, E.T. (1976) *Beyond Culture*, New York: Doubleday.

——(n.d.) *Hidden Dimensions: International Business Practices*. Information available online: www.irc-international.com/content/hidden-dimensions-international-business-practices (accessed 10 May 2011).

Hofstede, G.H. (1991) *Cultures and Organisations: Software of the Mind*, Maidenhead: McGraw-Hill.

——(2001) *Culture's Consequences: Comparing Values, Behaviors, Institutions, and Organizations across Nations*, Thousand Oaks, CA: Sage.

Hofstede, G. and Hofstede, G.J. (2005) *Cultures and Organisations: Software of the Mind: Intercultural Cooperation and its Importance for Survival*, 2nd edn, New York: McGraw-Hill.

Holliday, A. (1999) 'Small cultures', *Applied Linguistics*, 20(2): 237–64.

Hymes, D. (1972) 'On communicative competence', in J.B. Pride and J. Holmes (eds) *Sociolinguistics*, Harmondsworth: Penguin, pp. 269–93.

Kagawa-Singer, M. and Kassim-Lakha, S. (2003) 'A strategy to reduce cross-cultural miscommunication and increase the likelihood of improving health outcomes', *Academic Medicine*, 78(6): 577–87.

Kramsch, C. (1993). *Context and Culture in Language Teaching*, Oxford: Oxford University Press.

Loh, W.L. and Dahles, H. (2006) 'Organizational boundaries reconsidered', in H. Dahles and W.L. Loh (eds) *Multicultural Organizations in Asia*, London: Routledge, pp. 130–36.

Martin, J.N. and Nakayama, T.K. (2010) *Intercultural Communication in Contexts*, New York: McGraw-Hill.

Mead, R. (1998) *International Management: Cross-cultural Dimensions*, 2nd edn, Oxford: Blackwell.

Pan, Y.S., Wong Scollon, S. and Scollon, R. (2002) *Professional Communication in International Settings*, Malden: Blackwell.

Piller, I. (2009) 'Intercultural communication', in F. Bargiela-Chiappini (ed.) *The Handbook of Business Discourse*, Edinburgh: Edinburgh University Press, pp. 317–30.

Poncini, G. (2004) *Discoursive Strategies in Multicultural Business Meetings*, Berne: Peter Lang.

Sarangi, S. (2002) 'Discourse practitioners as a community of interprofessional practice: some insights from health communication research', in C. Candlin (ed.) *Research and Practice in Professional Discourse*, Hong Kong: City University of Hong Kong Press, pp. 95–133.

Sarangi, S. and Roberts, C. (1999) 'The dynamics of interactional and institutional orders in work-related settings', in S. Sarangi and C. Roberts (eds) *Talk, Work and Institutional Order: Discourse in Medical, Mediation and Management Settings*, Berlin: Mouton de Gruyter, pp. 1–57.

Scollon, R. and Wong Scollon, S. (2001) *Intercultural Communication: A Discourse Approach*, Oxford: Blackwell.

Shi, X. and Wright, P.C. (2003) 'The potential impacts of national feelings on international business negotiations: a study in the China context', *International Business Review*, 12: 311–28.

Singh, N. and Baack, D. (2004) 'Web site adaptation: a cross-cultural comparison of U.S. and Mexican web sites', *Journal of Computer-Mediated Communication* 9(4). Online. Available: http://jcmc.indiana.edu/vol9/issue4/singh_baack.html (accessed 5 August 2010).

Thomas, J. (1995) *Meaning in Interaction*, London: Longman.

Vaara, E., Tienari, J., Piekkari, R. and Säntti, R. (2005) 'Language and the circuits of power in a merging multinational corporation', *Journal of Management Studies*, 42(3): 595–623.

van Ek, J. (1986) *Objectives for Foreign Language Learning*, Vol. 1, *Scope*, Strasbourg: Council of Europe.

Warren, M. (2007) 'An initial corpus-driven analysis of the language of call-centre operators and customers', *ESP across Cultures*, 4: 80–100.

——(2009) 'The phraseology of intertextuality in English for professional communication', *Language Value*, 1(1): 34–56.

——(2011) 'Realisations of intertextuality, interdiscursivity and hybridisation in the discourses of professionals', in G. Garzone and M. Gotti (eds) *Discourse, Communication and the Enterprise: Genres and Trends*, Linguistic Insights Series, Vol. 134, Frankfurt am Main: Peter Lang, pp. 91–110.

Wurtz, E.A. (2005) 'A cross-cultural analysis of websites from high-context cultures and low-context cultures', *Journal of Computer-Mediated Communication*, 11: 1.

Yuen, W.L. (2009) 'An investigation of the politeness phenomena in hotel service encounters', unpublished PhD dissertation, Hong Kong: The Hong Kong Polytechnic University.

# 31

# Translation, interpreting and intercultural communication

*Juliane House*

## 1. Introduction

The aim of this chapter is to characterize and connect the fields of intercultural communication and translation and interpreting. Following a discussion of the phenomena of translation, interpreting and intercultural communication, I will describe two relevant opposing research strands. Given the importance of the notion of culture in both strands, I will then examine the relationship between language and culture, and present a functional–pragmatic theory of translation/interpreting as re-contextualization in intercultural communication. A cornerstone of this theory is the postulation of two fundamental translation types and the construct of a 'cultural filter'. Empirical evidence for this theory is provided in the form of contrastive pragmatic and discourse analyses conducted with a particular language pair. Finally, the increasing dominance of one particular language used as a lingua franca in intercultural communication and its impact on global communicative processes will be discussed briefly.

## 2. Translation and interpreting as intercultural communication

Translation and interpreting are linguistic–cultural practices known since earliest times. They can be defined as interlingual and intercultural processes or products of mediation facilitating intercultural communication between individuals or groups who do not share, or do not choose to share, the same language(s). Translation and interpreting can also be regarded as the replacement of something else, something that pre-existed them, ideas and expressions represented at second hand. In this sense, they have often been seen as 'second best', not the real thing, leading invariably to distortions and losses of what was originally 'meant'. They are essentially secondary communicative events. Normally, communicative events happen only once. With translation and interpreting, communicative events are reduplicated for persons or groups otherwise prevented from participating in or appreciating the original communicative event. So translation and interpreting can be seen as fulfilling an important service in that they mediate between different languages overcoming linguistic and cultural barriers.

Translation is the written form of mediation, interpreting the oral one. The term interpreting is preferred in the scientific community in that this term is distinct from 'interpretation' referring to understanding and explicating the meaning of a text. In the field of interpreting, one can distinguish between today's professional forms of simultaneous interpreting where the act of interpreting is carried out while the speaker is still talking (e.g. at international conferences or other meetings) and consecutive interpreting (where the interpreting occurs after the speaker has finished) at all sorts of get-togethers, and non-professional forms of interpreting in former times between colonizers and others who ventured into or invaded foreign lands and needed an interpreter to conduct their affairs with 'the natives', as well as today's ad hoc, dialogue or community interpreting conducted by bilingual individuals as a service to people or institutions in various professional or institutional contexts such as hospitals or government agencies. In translation, the written form of mediating practice, distinctions are often made according to the category of texts to be translated, e.g. broadly between pragmatic texts and literary texts, with the former being subdifferentiated into scientific, business, legal, advertising, etc.

Translation and interpreting are both similar and different activities: similar in that, obviously, both involve a language switch; different, in that in translation (usually) a fixed, relatively permanently available and, in principle, unlimitedly repeatable text in one language is changed into a text in another language, which can be corrected as often as the translator sees fit. In interpreting, on the other hand, a text is transformed into a new text in another language, but it is, as a rule, orally available only once (cf. Poechhacker and Shlesinger 2002). As the new text emerges chunk by chunk and does not 'stay' permanently with the interpreter (or the addressees), it is only controllable and correctable by the interpreter to a limited extent. Although some steps or phases in the interpreting process can be regarded as 'automatic' and need little reflective thought and strategic endeavour, others may be more complex and take more time. This requires a lot of cognitive effort and coordination, as the interpreter has to listen, understand and 're-code' bit by bit at the same time. All this is different in translating, where the translator can usually read and translate the source text at his or her own pace. And, very important, the source text is available for translation in its entirety, whereas, in simultaneous and consecutive interpreting, it is produced and presented bit by bit. This is an enormous challenge for the interpreter who must create an ongoing text out of these incremental bits – a text that must eventually form a coherent whole.

In written translation, as a rule, neither the author of a source text nor the addressees of the target text are present, so no overt interaction, and with it, the possibility of direct feedback, can take place. In interpreting, on the other hand, both author and addressees are usually co-present, so interaction and feedback is possible.

Over and above conference interpreting in national and international contexts, another kind of interpreting known as 'community interpreting', or 'dialogue interpreting', sometimes also referred to as 'public service interpreting', has recently gained importance (cf. e.g. Bührig and Meyer 2004; Bührig and Rehbein 2000; Wadensjoe 1998). Given increasing worldwide politically or economically motivated migration flows and the resulting multilingual populations, community interpreting fulfils important mediating functions as it facilitates communication between representatives of institutions and lay persons who speak different languages but need to interact for various reasons. Community interpreting is almost always carried out consecutively – face to face, over the phone or involving new media – with typical contexts being immigration departments, police stations, social welfare and other governmental as well as and non-governmental agencies, hospitals, prisons, schools. This type of interpreting is carried out either by professional experts in specialist domains (legal, medical, etc.) who have some knowledge of the languages involved or, more frequently, by untrained, lay 'natural interpreters' such as bilingual relatives, friends or volunteers who happened to be present when the need for interpreting arose. Mention must be made of the particularly deplorable practice of using children as interpreters – more often than not to avoid spending money on professional interpreters. Community interpreters interpret for both sides, switching between both languages. Understandably, community interpreters are more often than not neither objective nor neutral *vis-à-vis* the content of what they are interpreting for relatives or friends. Instead, they often sympathize with, or take the side of, whoever they are assisting in whatever institutional context they find themselves.

The relationship between translation and interpreting studies, on the one hand, and intercultural communication, on the other hand, has generally not been much researched. True, there have been several worthwhile previous attempts at providing such a link (e.g. by Katan 2004), and there is the important work by Bassnett (2002) on the intercultural dimension in the field of literary translation. However, these attempts have largely failed to place this linkage on a firm linguistic basis; this has been the major thrust of the volume edited by Bührig *et al.* (2009).

For the purpose of this chapter, which is mainly on translation and interpreting, intercultural communication can be simply characterized as communication between members of different cultures who presumably follow differing sociocultural rules for behaviour, including speaking, and who can include groups at the national level such as linguistic minorities as well as groups that have potentially differing rules for speaking determined by social class, age, gender. In the past, many studies of intercultural communication have been concerned with cases of failed intercultural communication, cases in which interactants fail to understand one another and thus cannot communicate successfully. The reasons for this were often ascribed to 'intercultural differences' such as values, beliefs, behaviours of culture members (cf. e.g. Gumperz 1982; House *et al.* 2003; Spencer-Oatey 2000). More recently, however, many researchers have shifted their focus to how interactants manage intercultural understanding (cf. Bührig and ten Thije 2006; Sarangi 1994). It is also intercultural understanding that is the basis for the single most important concept in translation and interpreting studies: functional equivalence. Functional equivalence is a condition for achieving a comparable function of a text in another context. So intercultural understanding is the success with which the linguistic–cultural transposition has been undertaken.

The link between functional equivalence (which is the conceptual basis of translation/interpreting) and intercultural understanding (which is the conceptual basis of intercultural communication) is highlighted when we consider the concept of the 'dilated speech situation' (Ehlich 1984). According to Ehlich, the main function of a 'text' is its role as an 'agent of transmission' providing a bridge between speaker and hearer who are not at the same place at the same time. It is a text's role as a sort of 'messenger' that makes it possible for the hearer to receive the speaker's linguistic action despite the divergence of the production and reception situations. Through such a 'transmission' carried out by a text, the original speech situation becomes 'dilated'. Because a speaker knows that her message will be 'passed on', she adapts her formulation accordingly, i.e. a speaker makes a 'text' out of her linguistic action. Texts are therefore not limited to the written medium, but can also exist in an oral form. The notion of the 'dilated speech situation' is highly relevant for oral and written intercultural communication, translation and interpreting. Both translation and interpreting can be characterized by a specific rupture of the original speech situation that is the result of a linguistic barrier between author and reader or between speaker (member of culture 1) and hearer (member of culture 2), which can only be bridged by acts of translation and interpreting. Bührig and Rehbein (2000) hypothesize an 'internally dilated speech situation' for the case of interpreting, where the primary communication participants are co-present but unable to communicate without mediating action on the part of the interpreter. It is the interpreter who will have to bridge the linguistically conditioned rupture. The translator/interpreter passes on the linguistic action in L1 (situation 1) to the L2 addressees (situation 2). This procedure is not without consequence for the transmitted linguistic action. Although already monolingual texts show signs of being prepared for transmission, this is, of course, particularly true of translated texts: they undergo a double transmission process. The linguistic action in an L2 in interpreting is likewise subject to this specific text construction. For instance, it is well known that, in interpreting processes, phatic or small talk often shows traces of a transition from discursive L1 action to a more textual L2 action.

Besides the importance of the general feature of the dilation of the speech situation in translation and interpreting, another characteristic of these two mediating modes is that both are essentially reflective activities, much more so than 'normal' monolingual communicative actions. Reflection is here aimed at the achievement of functional equivalence. On account of this inherent reflective nature, both translation and interpreting have a potential for intercultural communication and intercultural understanding.

## 3. Sociocultural vs. linguistic–textual views of translation and interpreting

In recent decades, a major shift in translation and interpreting studies has occurred away from text and linguistically oriented approaches to socially and culturally oriented ones. The recent work by scholars such as Robinson (1997) or Venuti (1995) are examples of a primarily sociopolitical and cultural orientation, a concern with translating and interpreting as a cultural procedure, touching upon such issues as race, class, gender, minority status, ideology and giving them a central place in analyses of translation and interpreting phenomena. The so-called 'cultural turn in translation studies' is epitomized in statements such as 'One does not translate languages but cultures'. How did this shift come about? Translation studies, I would suggest, is here simply following a general trend in the humanities and social sciences, whose contents and methodologies (at least in the so-called First World) have over the past decades been substantially influenced by postmodernist, postcolonial, feminist and other sociopolitically and philosophically motivated schools. Translation is no exception in this regard, and translation studies' history of mimicking fashionable trends is here, it seems to me, simply being replayed.

Another way of taking account of 'culture' in translation follows the model set by some linguistic schools, e.g. the Prague school of linguistics or British contextualism, schools that conceived of language as primarily a social phenomenon, which is naturally and inextricably intertwined with culture. In these and other sociolinguistically and contextually oriented approaches, language is viewed as embedded in culture such that the meaning of any linguistic item can only be properly understood with reference to the cultural context enveloping it. As 'meaning' is of particular importance in translation, it follows that translation cannot be fully understood outside a cultural frame of reference. The adherents of such an integrative view of language and culture (see e.g. Hatim and Mason 1997; House 1997; Koller 2004), although considering translation to be a particular type of culturally determined practice, also hold that it is, at its core, a predominantly linguistic procedure. They thus differ significantly from a radical cultural studies view in which translation is taken to be predominantly, or even exclusively, culture related.

## 4. Universality vs. culture specificity in translation and interpreting

### Culture, language and translation

The concept of 'culture' has been the concern of many different disciplines such as philosophy, sociology, anthropology, literature and cultural studies, and the definitions offered in these fields vary according to the particular frame of reference invoked. Two basic views of culture have emerged: the humanistic concept of culture and the anthropological concept of culture. The humanistic concept of culture captures the 'cultural heritage' as a model of refinement, an exclusive collection of a community's masterpieces in literature, fine arts, music, etc. The anthropological concept of culture refers to the overall way of life of a community or society, i.e. all those traditional, explicit and implicit designs for living that act as potential guides for the behaviour of members of the culture. Culture in the anthropological sense of a group's dominant and learned sets of habits, as the totality of its non-biological inheritance involves presuppositions, preferences and values – all of which are, of course, neither easily accessible nor verifiable.

Four analytical levels on which culture has been characterized can be differentiated (House 2004): the first is the general human level, along which human beings differ from animals. Human beings, unlike animals, are capable of reflection, and they are able to creatively shape and change their environment. The second level is the societal, national level, with culture being the unifying, binding force that enables human beings to position themselves *vis-à-vis* systems of government, domains of activities, religious beliefs and values in which human thinking expresses itself. The third level corresponds to the second level but captures various societal and national subgroups according to geographical region, social class, age, sex, professional activity and topic. The fourth level is the personal, the individual one relating to the individual's guidelines of thinking and acting. This is the level of cultural consciousness, which enables a human being to be aware of what characterizes his or her own culture and makes it distinct from others.

Along with the rise of postmodernist thinking in the humanities, the whole notion of culture has come under attack (see e.g. Holliday 1999). The critique formulated in postmodernist circles can be summarized as follows: the very idea of 'culture' is an unacceptable abstraction, there are no 'pure cultures' and there are no such things as 'social groups', because these groups are constantly destabilized by external influences, individual idiosyncrasies and actions. Cultures themselves are, in this view, mere ideologies, idealized systems simply serving to reduce real differences that always exist between human beings in particular socially and geographically delimited areas. Is the very concept of a 'culture' therefore useless, in particular for an eminently practice-oriented field such as translation? Surely not. In the empirical social sciences, attempts to 'problematize' and 'relativize' the concept of 'culture' have as yet not prevented solid ethnographic descriptions. Moreover, if such criticism were taken to its logical conclusion by social scientists, they would no longer exist.

One recent approach which seems to be particularly well suited to resolve the hotly debated issue of generalization vs. diversification and individualization of cultures is the one by Sperber (1996), who views culture in terms of different types of representations (which may be representations of ideas, behaviours, attitudes, etc.). Within any group, there exists a multitude of individual mental representations, most of which are fleeting and individual. A subset of these representations, however, can be overtly expressed in language and artefacts. They then become public representations, which are communicated to others in the social group. This communication gives rise to similar mental representations in others, which, in turn, may be communicated as public representations to others, which may again be communicated to different persons involving mental representations and so on. If a subset of public representations is communicated frequently enough within a particular social group, these representations may become firmly entrenched and turn into cultural representations. The point at which a mental representation becomes sufficiently widespread to be called 'cultural' is, however, still a matter of degree and interpretation, as there is no clear division between mental, public and cultural representations.

Members of a particular culture are constantly being influenced by their society's (and/or some of the society's cultural subgroup's) public and cultural representations (with regard to values, norms, traditions, etc.). This influence is exerted most prominently through language used by members of the society in communication with other members of the same and different sociocultural groups. Language as the most important means of communicating, of transmitting information and providing human bonding therefore has an overridingly important position inside any culture. Language is the prime means of an individual's acquiring knowledge of the world, of transmitting mental representations and making them public and intersubjectively accessible. Language is thus the prime instrument of a 'collective knowledge reservoir' to be passed on from generation to generation. But language also acts as a means of categorizing cultural experience, thought and behaviour for its speakers. Language and culture are therefore most intimately (and obviously) interrelated at the level of semantics, where the vocabulary of a language reflects the culture shared by its speakers.

As opposed to this view that language 'reflects' the culture of a social group, the ideas that came to be known as 'linguistic relativity' imply the very opposite: language in its lexicon and structure has an influence on its speakers' thinking, their 'worldview' and behaviour. The idea that an individual's mother tongue is an important source of cognitive and behavioural conditioning goes back to German idealistic philosophy and was most prominently formulated by von Humboldt, who propagated the view that every language as an a priori framework of cognition determines its speakers' *Weltansicht* (Humboldt also looked upon language as a self-contained creative symbolic organization, as *energeia* – an idea taken over in the twentieth century most prominently by Chomsky). The spiritual structure that language possesses is assumed to correspond to the thought processes of its users, language being situated at the interface between objective reality and man's conceptualization of it. The relativity postulate put forward in the first half of the twentieth century by Sapir and his disciple Whorf advanced basically similar ideas. Whorf, in particular, inferred mental and behavioural differences from differences between languages on the levels of lexis and, in particular, syntax.

The consequence of the Humboldtian and Whorfian postulate for translation and translatability seems to be the denial of its theoretical possibility – 'theoretical' because the practice of translation has, of course, been an undeniably present and, indeed, thriving business from time immemorial. This apparent contradiction can, however, be resolved by pointing out that linguistic relativity, although clearly affecting, in specified areas, some of our cognitive behaviour, can always be counteracted through language itself and its users' creativity, dynamism and flexibility. Further, it is necessary also to link linguistic diversity with external differences in historical, social and cultural background rather than one-sidedly insisting on the overriding importance of a link between cognitive and linguistic differences. If languages are seen to be structured in divergent ways because they embody different conventions, experiences and values, then the importance of what may be called linguistic–cultural relativity emerges. Such a notion of relativity is relevant for translation (cf. House 2000). Cultural knowledge, including knowledge of various subcultures, has long been recognized as indispensable for translation, as it is knowledge of the application linguistic units have in particular situational and sociocultural contexts that makes translation possible in the first place. 'Application' here refers to the relation holding between an expression and the cultural situation in which it is used – it is pragmatic meaning. In establishing equivalences between L1 and L2 linguistic units in translation, the notion of 'application' is crucial: if sense and reference differ for two linguistic units in translation, it is their application in particular knowable and describable cultural contexts that ensures translatability. Linguistic units, as argued above, can in any case never be fully understood in isolation from the particular cultural phenomena for which they are symbols.

Although differences in the 'worldview' of speakers of different languages resulting in different concepts in their minds may not be accessible to the translator, the intersubjectively determinable application of linguistic units in a particular cultural situation can. And even if cultural distances between languages are great, cultural gaps can, in theory, always be bridged via ethnographic knowledge. Conceptions of language within the broader context of culture, whereby meaning is seen as contextually determined and constructed, are not recent developments, but have a venerable tradition in Russian formalism, the Prague School and Firthian linguistics, as well as American sociology of language, speech act theory and discourse analysis. In particular, Firth and Halliday, both strongly influenced by the ethnographer Malinowski, regard language as 'language events' with meanings of utterances being defined in terms of their use and function in the context of a sociocultural situation.

Such a broad sociocultural view of language and translation is also adopted in the functional model of translation and translation criticism developed in House (1977, 1997, 2009), which is based on Hallidayan systemic–functional theory, and in which translation is conceived as a cross-linguistic cultural practice involving re-contextualization. Two fundamentally different types of re-contextualization are distinguished which lead to two distinct types of translation.

## Distinguishing two fundamental types of translation and interpreting

As mentioned in Section 2 above, 'functional equivalence' is the key notion in translation, interpreting and intercultural communication. Functional equivalence can be established by referring the original and translation to the context of situation enveloping the original and translation, and by examining the interplay of different contextual dimensions reflected in the text as well as shaping it. The dimensions are used to 'open up' the text in such a way that its textual profile, which characterizes its function, can be revealed. In order to determine the function of a text, consisting of an interpersonal and an ideational functional component which must be kept equivalent in translation, the text is analysed at the levels of language, register and genre. The relationship between these levels can be seen in terms of semiotic planes that relate to one another in a Hjelmslevian 'content-expression' way, with genre being the content-plane of register, and register being the expression plane of genre. Register, in turn, is the content-plane of language, and language is the expression plane of register. Register is divided in Hallidayan fashion into field, tenor and mode.

'Field' refers to the subject matter and the nature of the social action handled in the text. In the dimension of 'tenor', the author's temporal, geographical and social provenance is diagnosed, as is the author's stance (his/her 'personal viewpoint') *vis-à-vis* the content the author is portraying and the communicative task he or she is engaged in. Tenor also captures the social role relationship between author and addressee(s), and between fictive characters in the text as well as the 'social attitude' adopted, i.e. formal, consultative and informal style levels manifest in the text. As to 'mode', here Biber's (1988) distinctions between involved vs. informational text production, explicit vs. situation-dependent reference and abstract vs. non-abstract presentation of information are taken into account. Establishing linguistic–textual correlates of register, i.e. field, mode and tenor, and of the 'genre' they realize – with genre being understood as reflecting the communicative purpose shared by a collectivity of texts – yields a certain textual profile characterizing its textual function, which is to be kept equivalent in translation. Genre and register thus cover different aspects of the adaptation of language to the demands of its social use: registers are conglomerates of linguistic features in response to situational parameters; genres are types of linguistic objects. As linguistic objects, the texts that constitute a genre can be considered from a static or a dynamic perspective.

Equivalence of function, however, differs markedly in two empirically derived (House 1977, 1997) types of translation, 'overt' translation and 'covert' translation, and distinguishing these two translational types is thus indispensable in any discussion of functional equivalence. The distinction of these two fundamental translation types harks back to Schleiermacher's classic distinction between *einbürgernde* vs. *verfremdende Übersetzung*, a critical difference, however, being that the covert–overt distinction is tied to a well-argued theory of translation.

An 'overt' translation is, as the name suggests, quite overtly a translation, not a second original; hence, its target culture addressees are quite 'overtly' not being directly addressed. In an overt translation, the original is tied in a specific way to the culture enveloping it; it has independent status in the source culture, and is both culture specific and pointing beyond the source culture because the original text – independent of its source language origin – is also of potential general human interest. In a word, it also evidences 'universality'; source texts that call for an overt translation have an established worth or value in the source culture – and potentially in other cultures. In their universality, they are often 'timeless': as works of art and aesthetic creations, for instance, they transcend any distinct historical meaning. Although of timeless value, texts calling for overt translation are also and at the same time culture specific because they often reflect a particular *état de langue*, or a geographical or social variety, and because they have independent status in the language community through belonging to the community's cultural products. Many such texts are literary texts and can be characterized by their fictional nature, i.e. they are situationally abstract in that they do not immediately refer to a unique historical situation. Fictional texts describe a kind of 'fictive reality', which is, in every reception by an individual reader, newly related to the specific historical reality in the concrete situation in which the reader finds herself.

An overt translation is embedded in a new speech event in the target culture: it operates in a new frame, a new discourse world. An overt translation is thus a case of 'language mention' resembling a quotation or citation. In terms of the translation theory presented above, an original and its overt translation are equivalent at the levels of language and register as well as genre. At the level of the individual textual function, however, 'true' functional equivalence is not possible. At best, an equivalence of a 'removed' nature can be achieved: its function is to enable access to the function that the original has (had) in its discourse world or frame. As this access must be realized in the target 'linguaculture' via the translation, a switch in the discourse world becomes necessary, i.e. the translation operates in its own discourse world, and can thus reach only the aforesaid 'second level equivalence', featuring a sort of 'topicalization' of the original's textual function. Paradoxically, this type of functional equivalence is achieved through an equivalence at all three analytical levels, i.e. language/text, register, genre, which together facilitate the co-activation of the source text's frame and discourse world. It is through this co-activation of both discourse worlds and frames that members of the target cultural and linguistic community are put in a position to 'eavesdrop', as it were, i.e. they are enabled to appreciate the function the original text has – albeit at a linguistic and cultural distance. In overt translation, the translator must therefore quite 'overtly' produce a translation that allows culturally different people to gain an impression of the cultural impact that the original text has on source culture members, permitting them to observe and be worked upon by the original text. In the case of overt translation, we can speak with some justification of genuine cultural transfer. Transfer is here understood in Uriel Weinreich's (1953) sense, i.e. a result of a contact situation that results in deviations from the norm of the target language/culture through the influence of another language and culture. This means that, in overt translation, cultural transfer is often noticeable as a (deliberately) jarring deviation of the translation from target cultural norms.

The situation is very different in the case of 'covert' translation. A covert translation is a translation that enjoys the status of an original text in the receiving culture. The translation is covert because it is not marked pragmatically as a translation, but may, conceivably, have been created in its own right. A covert translation is thus a translation whose original is, in terms of status, not particularly tied to the target culture. An original and its covert translation are – one might say – 'universal' in the sense that they differ 'only' accidentally in their respective languages. The original is not culture specific, but rather of potentially equal concern for members of different cultures. Although certain texts are designed for 'ready consumption', ephemeral and transitory texts, such as e.g. instructions, commercial circulars, advertisements and other 'pragmatic texts' such as journalistic and scientific texts, are not culture bound; it is the covert type of translation that such texts (normally) require which presents more subtle cultural translation problems than overt translation. In order to meet the needs of the new addressees in their cultural setting, the covert translator must take different cultural presuppositions in the two cultures into account. This is, for instance, crucially important for media people who every day translate all manner of news from the world's major news bureaus and networks from English or other languages of wide dissemination into many different local languages.

In covert translation, the translator recreates an equivalent speech event and reproduces the function the original has in its linguistic–cultural framework, i.e. 'real' functional equivalence is the goal. A covert translation operates quite 'overtly' in the different frame and discourse world set up by the target culture without wishing to co-activate the discourse world in which the original had unfolded. Covert translation is thus psycholinguistically less complex than overt translation and more deceptive. It often results in a very real cultural distance from the original text, because the original is transmuted. As true functional equivalence is aimed at, changes at the levels of language/text and register may be freely undertaken, with the result being a different text. And this is why covert translations are often received as though they were original texts.

In order to achieve this 'originality', the translator employs a 'cultural filter'. With the use of this filter, the translator can take account of culture specificity accommodating differences in sociocultural norms and differences in conventions of text production and communicative preferences. This 'cultural filter' is thus the means by which the translator 'compensates for' culture specificity. It is often so expertly integrated into the fabric of the text that the seams do not show. As the notion of a cultural filter is crucial not only for covert translation, but also for problems of culture transfer and compensation, it will be dealt with more extensively in the next section.

## The cultural filter in translation

In the course of the analysis of a corpus of original and translated texts (German–English, English–German), which were classified as belonging to the broad functional categories interpersonal and ideational in the Hallidayan sense, House (1977) found that the translator had evidently placed a cultural filter between the source and target texts, viewing, as it were, the source text through the glasses of a target culture member. If the translator is to both meet the needs of the new addressees in their specific cultural setting and achieve an effect equivalent to the one the source text has had, she will have to take relevant cultural presuppositions in the two cultures into account. And these presuppositions are linked most frequently to the interpersonal functional component for which values along the dimensions of tenor and mode are particularly important. Therefore, whenever a text has a well-marked interpersonal functional component, the employment of the cultural filter is both particularly important and complicated, as one is dealing here with adjustments in social role relationships, social attitudes, the author's personal stance, involvement, etc. – phenomena that are notoriously difficult to capture. It is important to point out that, in any cultural filtering, empirically verified differences of presuppositions should be taken into account.

A glance at the rich anecdotal literature on translation describing numerous 'exotic' cultural oddities may lead one to believe that there are, indeed, many crucial cultural differences complicating the translation process. However, on closer examination, most of the impressive examples of cultural differences are drawn from comparisons of a European language and languages from Southeast Asia or American Indian languages, where the sociocultural differences are obviously remarkable. As concerns translations between European languages, however, it seems sensible to point out that cultural differences should not be exaggerated, because – as is well known by practising translators – expressions referring to culture-specific political, institutional, socioeconomic, historical and geographical phenomena, which can only be understood in the particular 'cultural situation' in which they are embedded, and which consequently lack a corresponding expression in the target culture, can nevertheless be translated by means of certain compensatory mechanisms. Indeed, there are a number of standard translational procedures for overcoming such cultural translation problems such as, e.g., using loan words or loan translations, adaptations, explications, commentaries, definitions and paraphrases. All these procedures have venerable traditions in ethnographic research and, of course, in the rich tradition of bible translations.

Elevating concrete, mundane differences between cultures such as e.g. differences in safety regulations or shopping routines to the rank of impenetrable cultural and translation barriers is both unnecessary and bordering on the ludicrous. One should not forget that, as de Waard and Nida (1986) rightly point out:

> all peoples share more cultural similarities than is usually thought to be the case. What binds people together is much greater than what separates them. In adjustments to the physical environment, in the organization of society, in dealing with crucial stages of life (birth, puberty, marriage, and death), in the development of elaborate ritual and symbolism, and in the drive for aesthetic expression [ … ] people are amazingly alike. Because of all this, translating can be undertaken with the expectation of communicative effectiveness.
>
> *de Waard and Nida (1986: 43ff)*

Despite this universality of the human condition, there are of course subtle if crucial differences in cultural preferences that need to be known to the translator in covert translation and cultural filtering. Such knowledge should be based on empirical research into language-pair specific cultural differences, which can give more substance to cultural filtering than intuition and tacit native speaker knowledge. In the following, an example of such research involving English and German discourse will be outlined.

## Substantiating the notion of a cultural filter

Over the past decades, a series of German–English intercultural discourse analyses were conducted inside larger projects, in which the discourse of German and English native speakers was compared (cf. summary in House 2006). Subjects were German and English students and experts in professional contexts. The data were collected in open, self-directed dyadic role plays, often followed by retrospective interviews, discourse completion tests combined with a variety of metapragmatic assessment tests, and naturalistic interactions between German and English native

*Table 31.1* Five dimensions of German-English differnces in communicative styles

| | | |
|---|:---:|---|
| Directness | | Indirectness |
| Orientation towards self | ⟷ | Orientation towards other |
| Orientation towards content | ⟷ | Orientation towards persons |
| Explicitness | ⟷ | Implicitness |
| Ad hoc formulation | ⟷ | Use of verbal routines |

speakers, comparative analyses of texts and their translations, field notes, interviews, diary studies and the examination of relevant background documents.

The following pragmatic and discursive phenomena were investigated in the various studies: speech acts, discourse strategies, realization of certain discourse phases, gambits and modality markers. The analyses provide converging evidence and point to hypotheses about German–English cultural preferences: German subjects tend to interact in ways that are more direct, more explicit, more self-referenced and more content oriented; they were also found to be less prone to resort to using verbal routines than Anglophone speakers.

This pattern of cross-cultural differences that has emerged from many German–English contrastive–pragmatic discourse analyses can be displayed along the five dimensions displayed in Table 31.1.

Along these dimensions, German speakers were found to prefer positions on the left hand side. It must be emphasized that we are dealing here with clines rather than dichotomies, reflecting tendencies rather than categorical distinctions.

In German discourse, then, a 'transactional' style focusing on the content of a message is often preferred, whereas in Anglophone discourse, speakers often prefer an 'interactional', addressee-focused style. In terms of the two Hallidayan functions of language, German discourse often leans towards the ideational function, with Anglophone discourse tending towards the interpersonal function. In terms of the well-known conversational maxims of Grice (1975), German speakers might be said to interpret the maxims of 'quantity' (make your contribution as informative as required) and manner (be brief) differently from Anglophone speakers.

By hypothesizing dimensions of cross-cultural difference in discourse orientations that give substance to the notion of a cultural filter, it is implicitly suggested that language use is linked to culture and mentality, and that linguistic differences in the realization of certain discourse phenomena may be taken to reflect deeper differences in communicative preference patterns at a conceptual–cognitive and emotive level.

The hypothesized dimensions of German–English cultural differences are supported by similar results from other research (see e.g. Clyne 1987). The following section gives a few examples of translations exhibiting German–English cultural filtering along the above dimensions.

## Examples of cultural filtering in translations

The first set of examples stems from a corpus of German signs put up in different domains of public life.

(1) Sign at Frankfurt Airport on display at a building site (original German):

Damit die Zukunft schneller kommt!

vs.

We apologize for any inconvenience work on our building site is causing you!

The difference in perspective, i.e. a focus on content in German, an interpersonal focus in the English translation, is noticeable here.

(2) Sign in a hotel bathroom (original German):

> Lieber Gast! Weniger Wäsche und weniger Waschmittel schützen unsere Umwelt. Bitte entscheiden Sie selbst, ob Ihre Handtücher gewaschen werden sollen. Nochmals benutzen: Handtücher bitte hängen lassen. Neue Handtücher: Handtücher auf den Boden legen.
>
> vs.
>
> Dear guests, will you please decide for yourself, whether your towels shall be washed. Use again: please leave your towels on the towel rack. Clean towels: please put your towels on the floor.

In the German original, but not in the translation, an explicit justification for the request is offered in the first sentence. The German original is also more direct than the translation, which inserts the marker 'please' in each of the three requests.

The following example stems from an instruction for using ovenware. A preference for greater explicitness in the German original is clearly noticeable here:

(3) Instruction leaflet, ovenware (original German):

> Kerafour ist in unabhängigen Prüfungsinstituten auf Ofenfestigkeit und Mikrowellenbeständigkeit getestet worden. Damit Sie lange Freude an ihm haben, geben wir Ihnen einige kurze Gebrauchshinweise: 1. Stellen Sie nie ein leeres, kaltes Gefäß in den erhitzten Ofen (als leer gilt auch ein nur innen mit Fett bestrichenes Gefäß) …
>
> vs.
>
> Kerafour oven-to-table pieces have been tested by independent research institutes and are considered ovenproof and microwave resistant. Here are a few simple rules for using Kerafour: 1. Never put a cold and empty piece into the heated oven …

In the second sentence, the German original gives an explicit reason for the instruction: 'Damit Sie lange Freude an ihm haben' ('such that you enjoy it for a long time'), which is, significantly, left out in the English translation. And under 1., the German original – unlike the translation – defines precisely the conditions under which the Kerafour pieces are to be considered 'empty'. One is reminded of Whorf's famous example of a fire breaking out because of an erroneous conception of a gas-filled vessel being 'empty' – but, whatever the reasons for the explicitness in the German text (perhaps s/he was considering potentially costly consequences of a customer's misinterpretation of 'empty'), the fact remains that the entire explicitizing bracket is left out in the translation.

The last example is a circular written by the president of a multinational firm to its shareholders, informing them about future developments that will not be to their advantage. The interpersonal functional component of the English original is transformed substantially in the translation such that the carefully orchestrated, distantly polite and non-committally indirect tenor in the English text is turned into a more undiplomatically direct tone in the German translation. Thus, the letter's recipients are often not personally addressed, e.g. 'as you know' is rendered as *bekanntlich*. See also the following extract:

(4) Letter to shareholder

> In order to avoid the possibility of accidental misdirection of your certificate … your assistance is required. We have enclosed a 'Dividend Instruction Form' for your completion; this should be returned in the pre-addressed form.
> vs.
> Um zu vermeiden, daß Ihre Zertifikate versehentlich fehlgeleitet werden. … bitten wir Sie, das beigefügte Dividendenzustellungsformular auszufüllen und in dem ebenfalls beigefügten adressierten Umschlag zurückzuschicken.

In the translation in (4), the letter writer appears more forceful and direct when expressing the action to be carried out by the addressees more abstractly and indirectly (nominally) in the English text. The utterance in the original has the illocutionary force of a subtle suggestion. The translation turns it into a request. And, although the original insinuates that it is not the company's president who wants something done but rather some abstract external necessity, the translation is far less subtle about who must do what. Thus, the German translation of 'Your bank (or broker) should indicate … ' reads: 'Sie müssen die Bank (oder einen Makler) bitten … '.

The analyses of German and English texts presented in House (1977, 1997, 2009) contain many more examples of cultural filtering, all of which attest to translators' attempts to accommodate in a patterned way the target addressees' differing presuppositions about cultural conventions.

## 5. Recommendations for practice

In looking at translation and interpreting as acts of intercultural communication, it is essential to consult language-pair specific contrastive pragmatic research before employing what I have called here a 'cultural filter'. Cultural filtering is appropriate in only one type of translation: covert translation, whereas the original text is to be kept as intact as possible in overt translation. These distinctions can serve as useful guidelines in the practical business of moving from one linguaculture to another.

## 6. Future directions

In the course of today's steadily increasing process of globalization in science, business, politics, culture, the media and technology, there is also a steeply rising demand for texts that are simultaneously meant for recipients in many different linguistic and cultural environments. Thus, ever more texts are needed that are either translated covertly or produced immediately as 'parallel texts' in different languages. In the past, translators and interpreters routinely used a cultural filter in such cases. However, owing to the worldwide dominance of English as a lingua franca – propelled by globalization processes and information technologies – a tendency towards 'cultural universalism', which is really a drift towards Anglophone norms – has been set in motion. It is thus reasonable to predict that the unstoppable spread of English in the decades to come will increase the conflict between cultural universalism and culture specificity in text production, on the one hand, and local, particular textualization conventions, on the other hand. Whereas cultural filtering in covert translation used to be a standard procedure, it will become rare in future, replaced by 'culturally universal' or 'culturally neutral' translation texts – texts that are, in reality, carriers of Anglophone cultural norms. A well-known example is Enid Blyton's children's books, which owe much of their popularity to their bland cultural 'universalism' – good for marketing them worldwide, but bad for presenting children with linguistic–cultural differences.

Although English influence on the lexicon of other languages has long been acknowledged, it has hardly ever been studied at the levels of pragmatics and discourse. The effect of the trend towards cultural universalism and neutralism in many languages and cultures (described above) is, however, an important research area. One first step into this new research direction is taken by the project 'Covert Translation' funded by the German Research Foundation, which examines the influence of English on German, French and Spanish texts (cf. e.g. Baumgarten *et al.* 2004; Becher *et al.* 2009). One of the aims of such research is also to close the gap between the two cultures – the linguistic and the cultural – as we are dealing here with linguistic–cultural phenomena that need to be explored in an interdisciplinary manner.

Rules of discourse, conventions of textualization and communicative preferences often remain hidden and act stealthily at deeper levels of consciousness. This does not mean, however, that they are less powerful and persuasive.

## Related topics

Cross-cultural communication; culture; English as a lingua franca; linguaculture; linguistic relativity; pragmatics

## Further reading

Baker, M. (2011) *In Other Words*, 2nd edn, London: Routledge (a practical course book on translation).
House, J. (2009) *Translation*, Oxford: Oxford University Press (a short readable overview).
Steiner, E. and Yallop, C. (eds) (2001) *Exploring Translation and Multilingual Text Production*, Berlin: de Gruyter (an overview of systemic functional thinking about translation).

## References

Bassnett, S. (2002) *Translation Studies*, Oxford: Routledge.
Baumgarten, N., House, J. and Probst, J. (2004) 'English as lingua franca in covert translation processes', *The Translator*, 10(1): 83–108.
Becher, V., House, J. and Kranich, J. (2009) 'Convergence and divergence of communicative norms through language contact in translation', in K. Braunmueller and J. House (eds) *Convergence and Divergence in Language Contact Situations*, Amsterdam: Benjamins, pp. 125–52.
Biber, D. (1988) *Variation across Speech and Writing*, Cambridge: Cambridge University Press.
Bührig, K. and Meyer, B. (2004) 'Ad-hoc interpreting and achievement of communicative purposes in doctor–patient communication', in J. House and J. Rehbein (eds) *Multilingual Communication*, Amsterdam: Benjamins, 43–62.
Bührig, K. and Rehbein, J. (2000) 'Reproduzierendes Handeln', *Arbeiten zur Mehrsprachigkeit*, No. 6.
Bührig, K. and ten Thije, J. (2006) *Beyond Misunderstanding: Linguistic Analyses of Intercultural Communication*, Amsterdam: Benjamins.
Bührig, K., House, J. and ten Thije, J. (eds) (2009) *Translational Action and Intercultural Communication*, Manchester: St Jerome.
Clyne, M. (1987) 'Cultural differences in the organization of academic texts: English and German', *Journal of Pragmatics*, 11: 211–47.
de Waard, J. and Nida, E. (1986) *From One Language to Another: Functional Equivalence in Bible Translating*, Nashville, TN: Nelson.
Ehlich, K. (1984) 'Zum Textbegriff', in A. Rothkegel and B. Sandig (eds) *Text-Textsorten-Semantik*, Hamburg: Buske, pp. 9–25.
Grice, H.P. (1975) 'Logic and conversation', in P. Cole and J. Morgan (eds) *Syntax and Semantics*, Vol. 3. *Speech Acts*, New York: Academic Press, pp. 41–58.
Gumperz, J.J. (1982) *Discourse Strategies*, Cambridge: Cambridge University Press.
Hatim, B. and Mason, I. (1997) *The Translator as Communicator*, London: Routledge.
Holliday, A. (1999) 'Small cultures', *Applied Linguistics*, 20: 237–64.

House, J. (1977; 2nd edn 1981) *A Model for Translation Quality Assessment*, Tübingen: Narr.

——(1997) *Translation Quality Assessment: A Model Revisited*, Tübingen: Narr.

——(2000) 'Linguistic Relativity and Translation', in M. Puetz and M. Verspoor (eds) *Explorations in Linguistic Relativity*, Amsterdam: Benjamins, 69–88.

——(2004) 'Linguistic aspects of the translation of children's books', in H. Kittel, A.P. Frank and N. Greiner (eds) Übersetzung-Translation-Traduction, *An International Encyclopedia of Translation Studies*. Berlin/New York: de Gruyter, 683–97.

——(2006) 'Communicative Styles in English and German', *European Journal of English Studies*, 10: 249–67.

——(2009) *Translation*, Oxford: Oxford University Press.

House, J., Kasper, G. and Ross, S. (eds) (2003) *Misunderstanding in Social Life*, London: Longman.

Katan, D. (2004) *Translating Cultures*, Manchester: St Jerome.

Koller, W. (2004) *Einführung in die Übersetzungswissenschaft*, 7th edn, Heidelberg: Quelle and Meyer.

Poechhacker, F. and Shlesinger, M. (eds) (2002) *The Interpreting Studies Reader*, London: Routledge.

Robinson, D. (1997) *Translation and Empire: Postcolonial Theories Explained*, Manchester: St Jerome.

Sarangi, S. (1994) 'Intercultural or not? Beyond celebration of cultural differences in miscommunication analysis', *Pragmatics*, 4: 409–27.

Spencer-Oatey, H. (ed.) (2000) *Culturally Speaking. Managing Rapport through Talk across Cultures*, London: Continuum.

Sperber, D. (1996) *Culture: A Naturalistic Approach*, Oxford: Blackwell.

Venuti, L. (1995) *The Translator's Invisibility*, London: Routledge.

Wadensjoe, C. (1998) *Interpreting as Interaction*, Linkoeping: Linkoeping University Press.

Weinreich, U. (1953) *Languages in Contact*, New York: Linguistic Circle of New York.

# 32

# Culture and health care

## Intergroup communication and its consequences

*Bernadette Watson, Cindy Gallois, David G. Hewett and Liz Jones*

## 1. Introduction

Health is a critical part of life, and the quality, safety and appropriateness of health care is of vital importance for both patients and providers. This context raises every type of intercultural matter, from national culture and ethnicity through to intergroup issues around professional, social and personal identity. Indeed, this setting points clearly to the similarity in communication across cultural divides and other intergroup contexts, and we argue that the same theoretical and methodological lens can clarify both.

In this chapter, we review the literature on health communication, with a particular emphasis on intercultural issues as they apply to the hospital setting. For many years, research in health communication was criticized for being atheoretical but, in more recent times, theories of identity and accommodation have gained more prominence (see also other chapters in this book, particularly Chapters 14 and 15). We believe that an intercultural lens is appropriate for understanding issues that, although not in the traditional domain of intercultural communication, can nevertheless best be considered as intercultural. These issues frequently involve miscommunication and problematic talk (Coupland *et al.* 1991), and intergroup models such as that of Coupland and colleagues are helpful in understanding them. In this chapter, we canvass issues of ethnic relations and communication issues arising from cultural and ethnic differences in hospital settings. Our main focus, however, is on the hospital environment as essentially one of different cultures coming together. These differences lead to intergroup conflict and miscommunication.

Hospitals are intercultural, or multicultural, entities in the traditional sense, as they include ethnically and culturally diverse staff. In particular, in Western countries, many members of staff are foreign or foreign trained, and patients (and their families) in these multicultural countries come from many places of origin. In this chapter, we will look, albeit briefly, at this aspect of intercultural communication. We propose, however, that this is only one layer in a multilayered and complex intercultural environment. Many challenges in the health context result from the diverse range of health professionals working together, who come from different professional and interspeciality backgrounds. Each health profession (nurses, doctors, physiotherapists, psychologists – the list is extensive) has its own language, rules and norms that coexist but are rarely shared between professions. In this sense, each profession has its own culture. In addition, and equally important, most individuals who enter hospital as patients are confronted with unfamiliar territory; that is, with a different culture. These cultural differences create and reflect an equally important set of issues as those of ethnic differences. In fact, when ethnic differences are combined with interprofessional and interspeciality cultural differences, the problems become more complex. We argue that, by using an intercultural lens for all aspects of the hospital context, it is possible to provide a parsimonious and insightful approach to these problems. Indeed, Teal and Street (2009) describe the physician–patient encounter as intercultural and propose a skills-based model of culturally competent communication (CCC) to deal with it.

The delivery of health care occurs in a complex sociotechnical environment with patients and professionals from different disciplinary, ethnic and social backgrounds. Navigating a safe and effective path through this complexity is challenging for patients seeking care and for health professionals seeking to provide care. We know that good communication is vital to effective health care and assists in accurate diagnosis and treatment. For example, a patient's lack of understanding of the treatment regimen has been linked to poor compliance (Ley 1988; Stewart 1995). In turn, poor compliance can impede patient health outcomes. Current research conducted by health communication scholars has also increasingly focused on patient safety and improving patient outcomes, demonstrating the key role of poor or problematic communication (e.g. Bleakley 2006b; Coiera and Tombs 1998; Edwards *et al.* 2009; Fewster-Thuente and Velsor-Friedrich 2008; Lingard *et al.* 2004a; Solet *et al.* 2005).

Improving communication, then, is a key factor in outcomes for patients. Trummer *et al.* (2006) conducted an experiment on the impact of improved communication. Patients due to undergo heart surgery were assigned to either a control or an intervention group. In the latter group, the medical and nursing staff were provided with training in patient empowerment strategies. The results indicated that improved communication from the medical staff led to significantly better health outcomes and shorter hospital stays for those patients in the intervention group.

We highlight the two main approaches to communication in health care: skills based (or intercultural communication competence: ICC, which includes Teal and Street's 2009 model of CCC) and system based (or macro-level critiques of the health sector). In our view, another key, but frequently missed, aspect is intergroup communication (IGC) (Giles and Watson 2008), the language and nonverbal behaviour characterizing interactions between health professionals and patients, on the one hand, and among health professionals, on the other. This includes intercultural and intergroup issues in doctor–patient communication (among them ethnicity, age, gender and the nature of illness), multidisciplinary team communication and interprofessional and interspeciality communication among health professionals.

In this chapter, we emphasize the intergroup nature of relationships in the health context. We discuss the ways in which cultural diversity contributes to interactions in hospital settings and presents barriers to effective communication. Furthermore, even when ethnic issues are not evident in health care communication, other cultural barriers in the medical social system may impede effective communication and lead to intergroup conflict.

First, we look at current issues in the health communication literature. We describe intergroup communication in this context and make a link with ethnicity and cultural diversity (which is most often studied in intercultural health communication). We argue that, by using an intercultural lens to examine all aspects of health communication, we can understand the barriers to effective communication in culturally diverse and other health-related encounters.

Before examining the intergroup dynamics in health communication, we briefly present research on the ICC approach in health communication.

## 2. Intercultural communication competence (ICC): a skills-based approach

Much of the focus in health communication has been on skills training and communication competence (see Cegala 2006; Cegala and Broz 2003; Wright *et al.* 2008). This focus mirrors work in traditional intercultural communication research (see Emry and Wiseman 1987). Historically, when communication improvement has been addressed in the delivery of health care, education has focused on training health professionals in interpersonal skills such as active listening, paraphrasing and assertiveness. It is clear that communication competence is a critical component of effective communication.

ICC training has much to recommend it, and it has been very popular with health professionals who want to get through difficult communication situations with colleagues or patients from other cultures, or where there is conflict. This approach focuses on interpersonal communication between individuals, and starts from the assumption that lack of skill on the part of one or more participants in an interaction leads to miscommunication and misunderstanding. Sometimes, the misunderstanding is caused by cultural differences. For example, there are very different attitudes to being treated by a doctor of the opposite sex among Anglo and Arab patients – in some cases, members of the latter group may refuse to see an opposite-sex doctor, which can be bewildering to majority members of Anglo-Celtic countries. In the same vein, pain is expressed through different behaviour by northern European (under-expressers) and southern European (over-expressers) patients; as doctors rely on patients to describe the type and extent of their pain precisely. Such culturally based differences can lead to miscommunication, inappropriate treatment and some degree of mutual stigma. Cases such as these can be addressed in a straightforward way through knowledge and skills training.

The ICC approach emphasizes the knowledge (usually culture-general knowledge, or knowledge about the impact of culture on communication and the dimensions on which cultures differ) and specific communication skills needed in difficult situations. As such, this approach is concrete and problem based, and assumes that more knowledgeable and more skilled communication will be more effective; that is, speakers will understand each other better and will solve problems better. ICC training works very well where this is the case in both intercultural and within-culture contexts, for example, in training doctors to give bad news (often a difficult and unfamiliar situation for them) or in history taking (e.g. Kaldjian *et al.* 2006; Radomski and Russell 2010).

What the ICC approach does not take account of is the importance of each speaker's attitudes towards the other speaker, and in general the intergroup context. Related to this, the ICC approach does not address the ways in which speakers' goals in an interaction influence their approach to the interaction. As we discuss below, these goals may not be directed at attaining mutually effective interactions. We argue that the application of competence training to intercultural communication problems without taking account of the interactants' motivations and cognitions makes the false assumption that interactants are always motivated to engage in effective communication. Just as two interactants from cultural groups in conflict (e.g. a militant Israeli and a Palestinian) may not desire a mutually effective interaction, so too this can be the situation in a hospital setting. Indeed, as in this case, people may be motivated to achieve bad outcomes (Gallois 2003). For example, in the case of non-compliant patients, interactants may be motivated to use hostile or unempathic communication in order to achieve their own goals. Such behaviour is not considered in the skills training approach.

## 3. Health encounters as intergroup communication

An ICC approach assists in some aspects of communication, such as managing some conflicts and misunderstandings through increased skills. Like other researchers, however, we believe that, by itself, the ICC approach is insufficient (e.g. see Cargile and Giles 1996; Gallois 2003; Gardner et al. 2001). It is essential in any intercultural or other intergroup encounter to consider the sociohistorical context of speakers, including their culture and belief systems (e.g. education, socioeconomic status, attitudes and norms about health). Often, it is these factors that motivate a speaker's communication behaviour, and achieving appropriate communication skills is not salient. An important component of the intergroup approach is the level of power one speaker has over others (Gallois 2003). In the health context, health professionals' power and how it is used in interactions with patients are critical to the intergroup dimension.

Intercultural communication problems may arise from issues of ethnicity, such as difficulty in understanding a patient's or health practitioner's accent, as well as lack of respect between majority group health providers and immigrant colleagues or patients. Alexis and Vydelingum (2005) found that immigrant nurses felt unwelcome, perceived a lack of opportunities and did not feel respected or appreciated. In a later paper, Alexis et al. (2006) found that minority group nurses experienced abusive behaviour from some white nurses in a white majority setting. Sheikh (2001) reported that minority groups experience intimidation at medical school and harassment by colleagues at work. This area of prejudice requires more investigation from an intergroup perspective. It is apparent that focusing on skills training does not address underlying issues of prejudice and discrimination such as these.

In research on intercultural contact between patients and health providers in the US, Reynolds (2004) elicited issues that differentiate ethnic minority groups from a majority (often white) group in their reactions to health care settings. These issues ranged from the actual health care system infrastructure (e.g. language and cultural barriers, such as the lack of inter-preting services) to poor health care plans for ethnic minorities and inferior physical locations of the clinics that cater for them. Reynolds (2004) also observed that health providers showed prejudice towards ethnic minorities, as well as a tendency to stereotype ethnic out-groups. In addition, she found that health providers reported high levels of uncertainty about their ability to communicate with ethnic out-groups. One consequence was lower quality care for these groups, compared with the majority, including poor medical history taking, inaccurate diagnosis and ineffective subsequent treatment. These poor outcomes were exacerbated by misunderstandings by patients that led to non-compliance with treatment instructions.

Other research has also revealed inequalities that ethnic minority groups face. For example, Diette and Rand (2007) noted that Puerto Ricans, non-Hispanic blacks and American Indians experience higher levels of asthma than whites in US settings. They argued that a key reason for this high incidence was poor health provider communication with the patient and subsequent inferior treatment. Medrano et al. (2005) reported on the complexities in a major multi-disciplinary and multimethodological study examining outpatient care in San Antonio, Texas. These issues included inadequate representation and voice for minority ethnic groups, lack of ethnic diversity among staff and lack of commitment to health care that takes account of cultural and linguistic issues. Schouten and Meeuwesen (2006) reviewed research between 1974 and 2004 on culture and ethnicity in interactions between health providers and patients. They found that, compared with majority groups, ethnic minorities were less likely to be referred for medical treatment, and also that there were lower levels of compliance with treatment instructions by patients. They concluded that there was inadequate attention paid to communication and its consequences, and that this area was inadequately theorized.

Finally, there is research concerning same- and different-race interactions between health professionals and patients (e.g. Cooper *et al.* 2003; Schnittker and Liang 2006). Schnittker and Liang (2006) compared discordant and concordant medical consultations from a large US national data set of white, black and Latino participants. They examined participants' beliefs about the frequency of racism, and found that perceptions were complex and multifactorial. For example, some minority group members felt that European American doctors were better trained and more trustworthy than members of their ethnic in-group. On the other hand, Doescher *et al.* (2000) found that, compared with the majority group, minority group members had more negative perceptions of (ethnic out-group) health professionals, as well as lower levels of trust and satisfaction.

Ethnic differences between interactants, of course, are only one part of understanding health communication as an intergroup encounter. In the next sections, we change the focus from geographical and ethnic issues and examine interactions between health professionals and patients and then interprofessional interactions among health professionals.

## 4. Interactions between health professionals and patients

To understand the communication process in any interaction requires a theoretical framework that explains each interactant's behaviour. Focusing on communication competence assists in some aspects of communication, such as managing conflicts and misunderstandings but, as noted above, it is insufficient by itself. We argue that interactions between health professionals and patients are essentially intergroup encounters (Street 2001; Watson and Gallois 2007). Individuals who become hospital inpatients are often ill prepared for managing the new environment in which they find themselves. They are faced with unfamiliar rules and regulations and are often unsure of how they should behave, attesting to Teal and Street's (2009) argument that 'at the most basic level, patient–physician encounters can be intercultural ... ' (p. 534). It is this very complexity and the coming together of patients and health professionals from different cultures that has led researchers to view communication between health providers and their patients as best understood as an intergroup rather than only an interpersonal phenomenon. This observation does not ignore the interpersonal dimensions of the interaction (which we return to at the end of this section), but rather looks to what is the most salient aspect of health professional and patient communication. For many interactants, the role of patient or practitioner is highly salient and drives the interaction process. Thus, health professionals and patients tend to keep their respective roles at the forefront. If interactants focus only on role, the consultation will be high in intergroup salience and low in interpersonal salience, and the communication will mainly concern the patient's condition and treatment regimen. Watson and Gallois (1998) found that, although patients perceive such encounters as acceptable, they are not rated as positively as interactions that are more interpersonal (e.g. if a doctor shares some personal information, such as supporting the same sports team as the patient).

Other group memberships also influence interactions between patients and health professionals. For example, age differences can mean that a patient talking to an older or younger doctor may feel uncomfortable or ill at ease (see Nussbaum and Fisher 2009). Similarly, different levels of education or socioeconomic status between practitioners and patients may also result in communication difficulties.

Other researchers have developed communication models that seek to explain intergroup communication and provide mechanisms to reduce inappropriate levels of intergroup salience. Ryan and colleagues' communication predicament of ageing (CPA) model (Hummert *et al.* 2004; Ryan *et al.* 1986) and the closely related communication predicament of disability (CPD) model (Ryan *et al.* 2005) provide a clear picture of intergroup communication and demonstrate how communication behaviours are influenced by communication and other goals. These models are concerned with the patterns of communication between elderly (CPA) or disabled (CPD) speakers and their speech partners. As this is an intergroup context, at least one of the speech partners, usually a carer, is not elderly (or disabled). The predicament model posits that carers accommodate to their stereotype of an elderly (or disabled) person, rather than to the interactant as an individual. The resulting, often patronising or hostile, behaviour means that the carer tries to distance him or herself from the less able person linguistically. This includes patronising speech, simplification of sentences, speaking to a third party or other communication moves that disempower or disadvantage the elderly or disabled person. People experiencing this non-accommodative communication must then choose to react through assertiveness, passivity or aggression; hence, the communication predicament. In all cases, the communicative options are narrowed, and the model posits a vicious circle leading to negative health consequences for the elderly or disabled person. Based on their CPD model, Ryan *et al.*'s (2005) solution to this dilemma is for the carer (or other able-bodied person) to begin the interaction by treating the other person as an individual, leading to a virtuous circle that empowers the person and leads to more and better communicative choices. The communication predicament model as it relates to both the elderly and the disabled readily transfers across to communication between health professionals and patients in hospitals, and reminds us that an intergroup context exists for patients in hospital. Both models propose that encounters that disempower patients reduce trust and rapport with health professionals.

Street (2001, 2003) developed the linguistic model of patient participation in care (LMOPPC) to address individual differences among patients in their approach to health encounters. His patient-centred model proposes that patients vary across two main dimensions, which in turn influence the level of patient participation. One dimension, predisposing factors, includes four components. The first of these is the patient's beliefs about active engagement with the doctors; the second is the importance patients place on their health needs (i.e. how important to them are the health issues they have come to discuss); the third involves personality variables; and the final component takes account of the relationship patients have with their doctors (rapport). Street's second dimension, enabling factors, includes a patient's knowledge about his or her illness and treatment, and the patient's ability to articulate information and concerns to the doctor. This latter component is related to good social skills. These two factors are linked in the model to a third factor, which focuses on the doctor's ability to engage and build a partnership with the patient. Street argues that the enabling and predisposing factors along with partnership building ultimately determine how much the patient participates in the consultation, and are predictive of the patient's perception of quality of care and health outcomes. Street's model implicitly recognizes the intergroup nature of interactions between doctors and patients through his emphasis on variables such as patient's beliefs in the legitimacy of contributing to the consultation process. Street notes that patients of low socioeconomic status may be more reticent about engaging with the doctor, given the latter's high social status and power. The LMOPPC model goes some way to unpacking some of the complexities inherent in medical consultations.

The study of the intergroup dynamics of interactions between health providers and their patients benefits from an exploration of intergroup and interpersonal salience. For different types of interactions, it is important to determine the extent to which role drives the communication process, and how much the individual characteristics of interactants influence it.

In line with Street's (2001) LMOPPC, Epstein (2006) also examined the complexity of encounters between patients and doctors. He noted that there are key issues for health communication researchers to consider. Four of these are relevant here. First, Epstein found that the first impression a patient has of a medical encounter is critical. Even an uncaring receptionist can adversely influence a patient's upcoming consultation. Second, the levels of attentiveness, care and interest shown by the doctor have a major effect on the patient's experience. A patient who has to argue for better care for a leg injury because she or he is a dancer experiences at least two outcomes. One is that the patient has actively made a difference to the treatment plan with his or her needs being met; this outcome is good. However, he or she may experience a loss of trust in the doctor who did not check this patient's needs; the outcome of loss of trust is not so good. Third, Epstein stated that context is everything. Who the patient is, the severity of the illness and the kinds of support that are in place for the patient change the doctor–patient dynamic. Finally, the perspective of each person involved in the consultation is different. This includes the perspective of doctors, patients, family members and health communication researchers.

Harris *et al.* (1985) found that particular behaviour by patients resulted in negative responses towards them. Some of these behaviours are not obviously negative. For example, Harris *et al.* (1985) found that patients who were talkative or could not clearly articulate their health problems were perceived negatively. This finding is in line with the communication predicament model outlined above and also points to ways in which doctors may categorize patients into groups that can disadvantage the patients. The tendency to categorize patients based on little information is at the very heart of the intergroup aspect of health communication.

In addition, individuals differ in their attitudes to seeking medical assistance. For example, some people believe they should refer to a medical doctor at the slightest indication of ill health; these people are likely to see the consultation process differently from those who would rather not 'bother the doctor'. The reason for their different viewpoints may be familial history or fear of illness; whatever the reason, it can usually be linked to a person's or family's, or group's, experiences. Moore *et al.* (2009) investigated differences between patients on a number of variables, one of which was self-efficacy. They found that, compared with patients who rated themselves as low in self-efficacy, patients who rated themselves as high on this variable differed in their reported levels of satisfaction with their doctor. Their findings suggest that more investigations into differences between patients should be conducted.

Although good communication is a vital part of good patient care, the study by Moore *et al.* (2009) described above shows how individual differences also matter. To examine interactions from an intergroup perspective is to recognize that two individuals similar in, say, age, gender and professional status may view a medical consultation in different ways. If patients feel trusting and friendly towards a doctor, they adopt different communication behaviour to achieve their goals from that of patients who are hostile and mistrustful.

An exploration of the interplay of group and individual salience and its influence on effective outcomes for health professionals and patients is an important research area. An intercultural lens is also useful for examining the ways in which health professionals interact with each other. In the next section, we discuss these interprofessional differences in culture and their consequences for communication and for health care.

## 5. Intergroup interactions among health professionals

Interactions among different types of health professionals, be they among doctors, nurses and others or among doctors (or nurses) with different speciality training, are especially likely to produce intergroup conflict. Hospital-based patient care requires the contribution of many types of care providers, who all bring their own perspective as they interact with one another. Clinical work has often been described as a process of interprofessional negotiation, in which professional culture, role and power conflicts have an important impact on teamwork (Degeling *et al.* 1999, 2003; Hall 2005; Horsburgh *et al.* 2006; Strauss *et al.* 1963), and collaboration between team members occurs through the exchange of clinical commodities (e.g. Lingard *et al.* 2004b).

Most research on interprofessional health communication in hospitals has concentrated on team interactions in confined, high-stakes, high-pressure clinical environments such as operating theatres, intensive care units or emergency departments. For example, ethnographic work by Lingard, Bleakley and their colleagues has provided a rich analysis of interprofessional interaction and communication failure in multiprofessional hospital contexts, where staff from various professional and speciality backgrounds are required to collaborate and coordinate patient care (Hawryluck *et al.* 2002; Lingard *et al.* 2004a,c, 2002a,b). Similarly, Eisenberg and colleagues (2005) examined the impact of communication on adverse events in emergency departments, and found that the admission of patients involved a political process that highlighted significant differences between two social or communicative worlds. They found that admission was an arena characterized by conflict between health professionals.

Lingard and colleagues (2002b) described a range of communication behaviours in the operating theatre that facilitated the maintenance of relationships and the minimization of tension. Using a rhetorical framework, they argued that incompatible discursive constructions and role simplification prevent people from identifying as interprofessional staff members, and instead promote socialization within a single profession. They formulated a descriptive rhetorical classification of communication failure, and subsequently implemented a preoperative team communication checklist and theory-based instrument to evaluate team communication in the operating room (Lingard *et al.* 2004a). In the intensive care unit, Lingard and colleagues found that team collaboration between what they called empowered actors occurred through understanding the rules of the game; interspeciality negotiation facilitated the exchange of role-based resources and generated team conflict (Lingard *et al.* 2004b).

Bleakley and colleagues (Bleakley 2006a,b; Bleakley *et al.* 2004) also explored the dynamics of operating theatre teams in the United Kingdom. In an analysis of near-miss patient incident reports, Bleakley (2006b), like Lingard, found that interactants used rhetorical strategies to construct an incident and the identities of participants, often through stereotyped or oversimplified descriptions of out-group members. Bleakley (2006a) analysed the ethical and value positions generated in this micropolitical setting. He argued that a distributed virtue ethic emerges in high-performing operating theatre teams through open dialogue ('collaborative intentionality'), in contrast to the authoritarian climate arising from professional socialization in medicine, which emphasizes heroic individualism and autonomous surgeon-led hierarchies. Bleakley drew on notions of hospitality and friendship (Aristotle, Levinas) to conceptualize good interprofessional communication, in which practitioners suspend self-centredness for patient-centredness.

Lingard, Bleakley and their colleagues have examined the social use of language from a rhetorical perspective, and have conceptualized team communication in various hospital settings as socially motivated. Their research shows that, in multiprofessional settings, role-based professional (or 'tribal') cultures and affiliations are salient and determine team membership (Hawryluck *et al.*

2002; Lingard *et al.* 2002a,b). These cultures lead to significant intergroup tension, particularly when interactants perceive differences in relative status and power. Health professionals in an intergroup context use strategic miscommunication to maximize differences between team members. In this way, as posited by social identity theory (e.g. Haslam 2004; Tajfel and Turner 1979), they can make intergroup comparisons that advantage their in-groups (positive intergroup comparisons), and can also optimize their power and status in intergroup conflicts.

There has been less research on interactions between health professionals involving care that is distributed in time and place. Increasingly, hospital patients have complex health problems and require shared treatment input from multiple specialities and professions. In research exploring the impact of interspeciality communication on patient care, Hewett *et al.* (2009a,b) studied interactions during the care of patients in complex contexts. Through interviews, examination of medical records and surveys, they found that speciality identity was salient in all forms of communication. For example, doctors consistently identified themselves and related to their colleagues as members of speciality groups. Speciality identity and intergroup conflict were particularly evident when there were ambiguous or contested responsibilities for patient care; examples included the admission process (see also Eisenberg *et al.* 2005) and the process of obtaining informed consent from patients for medical interventions. These findings are consistent with Lingard's; intergroup behaviour involving patient care was a commodity over which identities were negotiated and conflict enacted (Lingard *et al.* 2002a, 2004b).

Hewett *et al.* (2009a,b) also showed the impact of intergroup conflict and miscommunication on patient care (cf. Strauss *et al.* 1963). For example, they found that interspeciality communication was a better predictor of whether patients received treatment according to best practice guidelines than was severity of illness or other clinical indicators. In addition, medical records included cases of patients receiving delayed or no treatment because of disputes over the availability of beds or admission procedures.

## 6. Conclusion

It is clear that there is much to investigate in this area of communication. The issues of status, professional role and conflict are evident in many areas of patient care. Clearly, these behaviours do not serve the best interests of either patients or carers. Thus, we must examine why they occur and the purpose they serve in these intergroup interactions. We conclude by revisiting some of these issues, drawing on the above and our own recent research.

We argue that patient–doctor interactions are both intergroup and interpersonal encounters, but most often the intergroup dimension is more salient. Consultations are rated by patients as most effective and satisfying when the health professional shows expertise (intergroup salience) and recognition of the needs of the individual (interpersonal salience). Watson and Gallois found that the most important communication strategies for a health professional to engage in, which led to high patient satisfaction ratings, were appropriate emotional expression (appropriate reassurance and demonstration of concern) and discourse management, a strategy that allows the patient to actively engage in the conversation (Watson and Gallois 1998, 2002, 2004, 2007). These findings confirm that communication theory that takes account of the dynamics of the communication process is essential in this field of research. Specifically, communication accommodation theory (CAT) (see Chapter 15, this volume) and other related theories can be used by researchers to unpack the interpersonal and intergroup aspects of the dialogue and accurately describe patient and health professional interactions. Savundranayagam and colleagues (2007) highlight how status differentials can disempower the elderly. These researchers provide communication strategies that can empower the elderly and improve their interactions with carers. These findings transfer across to other groups such as the disabled.

With respect to interspeciality communication, we highlight the following issues. Hewett et al. (2009b) noted the first one: that speciality identity, like professional identity, was highly salient for hospital doctors. For example, doctors refer to medical colleagues in other specialities by the speciality name rather than the doctor's name. For example, doctors talked about what 'gastros' (gastroenterologists) do or what DEM (Department of Emergency) doctors think. This practice highlights the existing intergroup relationship. Hewett et al. also found that specific arenas were especially likely to lead to intergroup conflict and communication, with adverse consequences for the quality of care patients received. One of these contested arenas, as others have also found, concerned admission policies. In the hospital they studied, the policy was that the hospital department that admitted the patient was responsible for the patient, and had 'ownership' of his or her care. Problems arose when, as was often the case, a patient required multispeciality care, and no one was willing to take responsibility for the patient's course of treatment. The result was delay in care and reduced quality of care.

A second contested arena was related to informed consent (Hewett et al. 2009a). In this hospital, there were debates about whether the specialist performing a procedure or the admitting department should obtain consent for the procedure from the patient. This conflict, combined with another about who was responsible for providing a hospital bed for the patient (e.g. the Emergency department refused to take a patient back following a procedure), provide us with a picture of intergroup conflict. In considerable part, they result from resource constraints (time, number of available beds, etc.), but they are exacerbated by non-accommodative interspeciality interactions.

At present, Watson and Jones (in preparation) are addressing health professionals' perceptions of clinical handovers, yet another contested arena. They have found that there is a multiplicity of divergent perceptions and concerns about the handover of patients, and they have seen ample evidence of non-accommodative communication. These examples all make clear that hospitals are complex sociotechnical systems, whose professional teams and technical services form component subsystems characterized by distinct cultures and belief systems (Van Cott 1994). Under conditions of resource constraint or ambiguity, the strong professional identity leads to intergroup conflict and lower quality of care.

Future research in this area can most usefully focus on the organizational factors that support the current hospital system of care, along with the consequences for communication. We need to understand much better the impact of hospital and professional culture and hierarchy, the influence of identity on communication in these circumstances and the ways in which the health system affects them and consequent quality of care. One avenue of research for health communication researchers is the contexts in which interprofessional salience is heightened or attenuated. As Coupland et al. (1991) theorized, the most problematic communication comes when system factors produce an intergroup or intercultural arena – the cause of such communication problems is virtually impossible for people inside the system to see, and so is an especially important area for research.

As Gallois (2003) noted, intercultural communication competence is a key aspect of good communication in health as in other contexts such as the workplace and police–civilian encounters. Good intergroup and intercultural communication training will help, and in some cases will be sufficient, to deal with difficulties arising from cultural or group factors. Nevertheless, trainers and researchers in health communication must also raise awareness about the intergroup nature of all or almost all health communication encounters. As Gallois noted, ethnorelativism alone does not improve communication. Understanding the history of the relations between speakers and the power structure that is embedded in the health care system, particularly in the hospital setting, is paramount to effecting good communication.

## Related topics

Accommodation ethnicity; gender; identity; intercultural communicative competence; intergroup communication; intergroup conflict; language and intercultural communication; social identity theory

## Further reading

Gallois, C., Ogay, T. and Giles, H. (2005) 'Communication accommodation theory: a look back and a look ahead', in W. Gudykunst (ed.) *Theorizing about Intercultural Communication*, Thousand Oaks, CA: Sage, pp. 121–48 (provides a theoretical framework for understanding intergroup and intercultural communication).

Giles, H., Reid, S.A. and Harwood, J. (2010) 'Introducing the dynamics of intergroup communication', in H. Giles, S. Reid and J. Harwood (eds) *The Dynamics of Intergroup Communication*, New York: Peter Lang Publishing, Inc., pp. 1–17 (discusses the relevance of intergroup communication across a wide range of contexts).

## References

Alexis, O. and Vydelingum, V. (2005) 'The experiences of overseas black and minority ethnic registered nurses in an English hospital', *Journal of Research in Nursing*, 10(4): 459–72.

Alexis, O., Vydelingum, V. and Robbins, I. (2006) '"Overseas nurses" experiences of equal opportunities in the NHS in England', *Journal of Health Organization and Management*, 20(2): 130–39.

Bleakley, A. (2006a) 'A common body of care: the ethics and politics of teamwork in the operating theater are inseparable', *Journal of Medicine and Philosophy: A Forum for Bioethics and Philosophy of Medicine*, 31(3): 305–22.

——(2006b) 'You are who I say you are: the rhetorical construction of identity in the operating theatre', *Journal of Workplace Learning*, 17(7/8): 414–25.

Bleakley, A., Hobbs, A., Boyden, J. and Walsh, L. (2004) 'Safety in operating theatres: improving teamwork through team resource management', *Journal of Workplace Learning*, 16(1/2): 83–91.

Cargile, A.C. and Giles, H. (1996) 'Intercultural communication training review, critique, and a new theoretical framework.', in B. Burleson (ed.) *Communication Yearbook*, 19: 385–423.

Cegala, D.J. (2006) 'Emerging trends and future directions in patient communication skills training', *Health Communication*, 20(2): 123–29.

Cegala, D.J. and Broz, S.L. (2003) 'Provider and patient communication skills training', in T.L. Thompson, A. Dorsey, R. Parrott and K. Miller (eds) *Handbook of Health Communication*, London: Routledge, pp. 95–120.

Coiera, E. and Tombs, V. (1998) 'Communication behaviours in a hospital setting: an observational study', *British Medical Journal*, 316(7132): 673–76.

Cooper, L.A., Roter, D.L., Johnson, R.L., Ford, D.E., Steinwachs, D.M. and Powe, N.R. (2003) 'Patient-centered communication, ratings of care, and concordance of patient and physician race', *Annals of Internal Medicine*, 139(11): 907–15.

Coupland, N., Wiemann, J.M. and Giles, H. (1991) 'Talk as "problem" and communication as "miscommunication": an integrative analysis', in N. Coupland, H. Giles and J.M. Wiemann (eds) *'Miscommunication' and Problematic Talk*, Newbury Park, CA: Sage, pp. 1–17.

Degeling, P., Sage, D., Kennedy, J., Perkins, R. and Zhang, K. (1999) 'A comparison of the impact of hospital reform on medical subcultures in some Australian and New Zealand hospitals', *Australian Health Review*, 22(4): 172–88.

Degeling, P., Maxwell, S., Kennedy, J. and Coyle, B. (2003) 'Medicine, management, and modernisation: a "danse macabre"?', *British Medical Journal*, 32 (7390): 649–52.

Diette, G.B. and Rand, C. (2007) 'The contributing role of health-care communication to health disparities for minority patients with asthma', *Chest*, 132(5 suppl.): 802S–9S.

Doescher, M.P., Saver, B.G., Franks, P. and Fiscella, K. (2000), 'Racial and ethnic disparities in perceptions of physician style and trust', *Archives of Family Medicine*, 9: 1156–63.

Edwards, A., Fitzpatrick, L., Augustinea, S., Trzebucki, A., Chenga, S.L., Presseaua, C., Mersmannb, C., Heckmanc, B. and Kachnowskia, S. (2009) 'Synchronous communication facilitates interruptive work-flow for attending physicians and nurses in clinical settings', *International Journal of Medical Informatics*, 78: 629–37.

Eisenberg, E.M., Murphy, A.G., Sutcliffe, K., Wears, R., Schenkel, S., Perry, S. and Vanderhoef, M. (2005) 'Communication in emergency medicine: implications for patient safety', *Communication Monographs*, 72(4): 390–413.

Emry, R. and Wiseman, R.L. (1987) 'An intercultural understanding of ablebodied and disabled persons' communication', *International Journal of Intercultural Relations*, 11(1): 7–27.

Epstein, R.M. (2006) 'Making communication research matter: what do patients notice, what do patients want and what do patients need', *Patient Education and Counseling*, 60: 272–78.

Fewster-Thuente, L. and Velsor-Friedrich, B. (2008) 'Interdisciplinary collaboration for healthcare professionals', *Nursing Administration Quarterly*, 32(1): 40–48.

Gallois, C. (2003) 'Reconciliation through communication in intercultural enounters: potential or peril?', *Journal of Communication*, 53: 5–15.

Gardner, M.J., Paulsen, N., Gallois, C., Callan., V.J. and Monaghan, P. (2001) 'Communication in organizations: an intergroup perspective.', in W.P. Robinson and H. Giles (eds), *The New Handbook of Language and Social Psychology*, London:Wiley, pp. 561–84.

Giles, H. and Watson, B. (2008) *Intercultural and Intergroup Communication*, Blackwell, Oxford.

Hall, P. (2005) 'Interprofessional teamwork: professional cultures as barriers', *Journal of Interprofessional Care*, 19: 188–96.

Harris, I.B., Rich, E.C. and Crowson, T.W. (1985) 'Attitudes of internal medicine residents and staff physicians toward various patient characteristics', *Academic Medicine*, 60(3): 192–95.

Haslam, S.A. (2004) *Psychology in Organizations*, 2nd edn, Thousand Oaks, CA: Sage.

Hawryluck, L.A, Espin, S.L., Garwood, K.C., Evans, C.A. and Lingard, L.A. (2002) 'Pulling together and pushing apart: tides of tension in the ICU team', *Academic Medicine*, 77(10): S73-S6.

Hewett, D.G., Watson, B.M., Gallois, C., Ward, M. and Leggett, B.A. (2009a, 'Communication in medical records: intergroup language and patient care', *Journal of Language and Social Psychology*, 28(2): 119–38.

——(2009b) 'Intergroup communication between hospital doctors: implications for quality of patient care', *Social Science and Medicine*, 69: 1732–40.

Horsburgh, M., Perkins, R., Coyle, B. and Degeling, P. (2006) 'The professional subcultures of students entering medicine, nursing and pharmacy programmes', *Journal of Interprofessional Care*, 20(4): 425–31.

Hummert, M.L., Garstka, T.A., Ryan, E.B. and Bonnesen, J.L. (2004) 'The role of age stereotypes in interpersonal communication', in J.F. Nussbaum and J. Coupland (eds) *Handbook of Communication and Aging Research*, 2nd edn, Mahwah, NJ: Erlbaum, pp. 91–115.

Kaldjian, L.C., Jones, E.W., Rosenthal, G.E., Tripp-Reimer, T. and Hillis, S.L. (2006) 'An empirically derived taxonomy of factors affecting physicians' willingness to disclose medical errors', *Journal of General Internal Medicine*, 21(9): 942–48.

Ley, P. (1988) *Communicating with Patients: Improving Communication, Satisfaction and Compliance*, London: Croom Helm.

Lingard, L., Reznick, R., DeVito, I. and Esprin, S. (2002a) 'Forming professional identities on the health care team: discursive constructions of the "other" in the operating room', *Medical Education*, 36: 728–34.

Lingard, L., Reznick, R., Espin, S., Regehr, G. and DeVito, I. (2002b) 'Team communications in the operating room: talk patterns, sites of tension, and implications for novices', *Academic Medicine*, 77(3): 232–37.

Lingard, L., Garwood, S. and Poenaru, D. (2004a) 'Tensions influencing operating room team function: does institutional context make a difference?', *Medical Education*, 38: 691–99.

Lingard, L., Espin, S., Evans, C. and Hawryluck, L. (2004b) 'The rules of the game: interprofessional collaboration on the intensive care unit team', *Critical Care*, 8(6): 403–8.

Lingard, L., Espin, S., Whyte, S., Regehr, G., Baker, G.R., Reznick, R., Bohnen, J., Orser, B., Doran, D. and Grober, E. (2004c) 'Communication failures in the operating room: an observational classification of recurrent types and effects', *Quality and Safety in Healthcare*, 13: 330–34.

Medrano, M.A., Setzer, J., Enders, S., Costello, R.M. and Benavente, V. (2005) 'Self-assessment of cultural and linguistic competence in an ambulatory health system', *Journal of Healthcare Management*, 50(6): 371–85.

Moore, S.D., Wright, K.B. and Bernard, D.R. (2009) 'Influences on health delivery system satisfaction: a partial test of the ecological model', *Health Communication*, 24(4): 285 – 94.

Nussbaum, J.F. and Fisher, C.L. (2009) 'A communication model for the competent delivery of geriatric medicine', *Journal of Language and Social Psychology*, 28(2): 190–208.

Radomski, N. and Russell, J. (2010) 'Integrated case learning: teaching clinical reasoning', *Advances in Health Sciences Education*, 15(2): 251–64.

Reynolds, D. (2004) 'Improving care and interactions with racially and ethnically diverse populations in healthcare organizations', *Journal of Healthcare Management*, 49(4): 237–49.

Ryan, E.B., Giles, H., Bartolucci, G. and Henwood, K. (1986) 'Psycholinguistic and social psychological components of communication by and with the elderly', *Language and Communication*, 6: 1–24.

Ryan, E.B., Bajorek, S., Beaman, A. and Anas, A.P. (2005) '"I just want you to know that "them" is me: intergroup perspectives on communication and disability', in J. Harwood and H. Giles (eds) *Intergroup Communication: Multiple Perspectives*, New York: Peter Lang, pp. 117–40.

Savundranayagam, M.Y., Ryan, E.B. and Hummert, M.L. (2007) 'Communication, health and aging: promoting empowerment', in A. Weatherall, B. Watson and C. Gallois (eds) *Language, Discourse and Social Psychology*, Basingstoke: Palgrave Macmillan, pp. 79–107.

Schnittker, J. and Liang, K. (2006) 'The promise and limits of racial/ethnic concordance in physician–patient interaction', *Journal of Health Politics Policy and Law*, 31(4): 811–38.

Schouten, B.C. and Meeuwesen, L. (2006) 'Cultural differences in medical communication: a review of the literature', *Patient Education and Counseling*, 64(1): 21–34.

Sheikh, A. (2001) 'What's to be done about racism in medicine?', *Journal of the Royal Society of Medicine*, 94(10): 499–500.

Solet, D.J., Norvell, J.M., Rutan, G.H. and Frankel, R.M. (2005) 'Lost in translation: challenges and opportunities in physician-to-physician communication during patient handoffs', *Academic Medicine*, 80 (12): 1094–99.

Stewart, M. (1995) 'Effective physician–patient communicaiton and health outcomes: a review', *Canadian Medical Association Journal*, 152: 1423–33.

Strauss, A., Schatzman, L., Bucher, R., Ehrlich, D. and Sabshin, M. (1963) 'The hospital and its negotiated order', in E. Freidson (ed.) *The Hospital in Modern Society*, London: Collier-Macmillan, pp. 147–69.

Street, R.L. (2001) 'Active patients as powerful communicators', in W.P. Robinson and H. Giles (eds) *The New Handbook of Language and Social Psychology*, Chichester: Wiley, pp. 541–61.

——(2003) 'Interpersonal communication skills in health care contexts', in J.O. Greene and B.R. Burleson (eds) *Handbook of Communication and Social Interaction Skills*, Englewood Cliffs, NJ: Lawrence Erlbaum Associates, pp. 909–33.

Tajfel, H. and Turner, J.C. (1979) 'An integrative theory of intergroup conflict', in W.G. Austin and S. Worchel (eds) *The Social Psychology of Intergroup Relations*, Belmont, CA: Wadsworth, pp. 33–53.

Teal, C.R. and Street, R.L. (2009) 'Critical elements of culturally competent communication in the medical encounter: a review and model', *Social Science and Medicine*, 68(3): 533–43.

Trummer, U.F., Mueller, U.O., Nowak, P., Stidl, T. and Pelikan, J.M. (2006) 'Does physician–patient communication that aims at empowering patients improve clinical outcome?: a case study', *Patient Education and Counseling*, 61(2): 299–306.

Van Cott, H. (1994) 'Human errors: their causes and reduction', in M.S. Bogner (ed.) *Human Error in Medicine*, Hillside, NJ: Lawrence Erlbaum Associates, pp. 53–65.

Watson, B.M. and Gallois, C. (1998) 'Nurturing communication by health professionals toward patients: a communication accommodation theory approach', *Health Communication*, 10: 343–55.

——(2002) 'Patients' interactions with health providers: a linguistic category model approach', *Journal of Language and Social Psychology*, 21: 32–52.

——(2004) 'Emotional expression as a sociolinguistic strategy: its importance in medical interactions', in S.H. Ng, C.N. Candlin and C.Y. Chiu (eds) *Language Matters: Communication, Culture and Identity*, Hong Kong: City University of Hong Kong Press, pp. 63–84.

——(2007) 'Language, discourse, and communication about health and illness: Intergroup relations, role, and emotional support', in A. Weatherall, B.M. Watson and C. Gallois (eds) *The Social Psychology of Language and Discourse*, London: Palgrave Macmillan, pp. 108–30.

Watson, B.M. and Jones, L. (in preparation) *Perceptions of Clinical Handover*.

Wright, K.B., Sparks, L. and O'Hair, H.D. (2008) *Health Communication in the 21st Century*, Malden, MA: Blackwell.

# 33
# Legal contexts

*Christoph A. Hafner*

## 1. Introduction/definitions

Interactions in legal contexts, such as the legislature, police interview, or courtroom, typically involve participants from diverse cultural backgrounds. Each of these participants comes to the encounter imbued with their own assumptions about norms of communication, developed through their historical upbringing and grounded in their individual personal, professional, and other sociocultural affiliations. Participants in legal interactions must accommodate this cultural diversity in order to communicate effectively: a failure to do so can result in serious consequences for the individuals concerned. Research in legal discourse and intercultural communication in legal contexts has focused on three main arenas of intercultural contact: (1) interactions between legal professionals and lay people; (2) interactions between dominant culture and minority culture group members; (3) interactions in multilingual and multicultural legal contexts. The aim of this chapter is to provide an overview and critical review of this research.

In spite of the potential for intercultural contact, communication in legal contexts is characterized by its rigid adherence to the norms and conventions of legal discourse. However, many people are unfamiliar with these norms and conventions, and as a result, legal encounters can be a bewildering experience. This lack of familiarity with legal cultural norms can be attributed to a number of factors, which often combine with one another, depending on individual cultural background. In the first place, legal cultural norms conform to the norms of the legal professional domain, with its own specialist language, rituals, and practices, all informed by a particular legal worldview. Non-specialists who lack an appreciation of these legal ways may find communication in legal contexts to be challenging. Second, legal cultural norms conform to the norms of the dominant culture in society. Members of minority groups who are unfamiliar with this dominant culture may therefore experience additional challenges to communication in these contexts. Finally, legal cultural norms can vary from place to place, and from legal system to legal system. As a result, even individuals who are experienced in one legal culture may experience challenges when confronted with a foreign legal culture. With the globalization of trade and the dismantling of national borders that has come with it, it is becoming increasingly important for members of the legal profession to learn to operate in multilingual and multicultural legal contexts.

In this chapter, I adopt a broad approach to the notion of culture, to include the range of cultural factors described above. Culture is defined in its anthropological sense, as "any of the customs, worldview, language, kinship system, social organization, and other taken-for-granted day-to-day practices of a people which set that group apart as a distinctive group" (Scollon and Wong Scollon 2001: 139). It is important to note at the outset that the categories adopted, for example professional and lay culture or dominant and minority culture, are not intended to be applied in a simplistic or essentialist way to members of the groups concerned. Indeed, such cultural groups are made up of diverse individuals who typically have a variety of cultural affiliations. It would not be unusual to find members of minority groups who occupy a prominent position in the dominant cultural group by virtue of their status in society, and therefore operate competently in both cultures. Similarly, many lay people (e.g., business people) frequently deal with legal documents and legal processes, and through this contact develop a detailed understanding of legal discourse practices. Although this diversity is acknowledged in the literature, there is nevertheless a tendency to focus on clearcut cultural differences, and as a result, the literature in this area must be read with a critical eye.

In this chapter, I begin with a review of studies of legal discourse and intercultural communication in the three principal cultural contexts of interaction mentioned above: professional and lay culture; dominant and minority culture; multilingual and multicultural contexts. Then the practical implications of these studies are considered and suggestions for future research in this area are made.

## 2. Professional and lay culture

One kind of intercultural communication in legal contexts occurs when legal specialists interact with non-specialists in the legal process. In such interactions, non-specialists may encounter challenges to successful communication because the cultural norms and conventions of legal discourse are so different from those of ordinary spoken and written discourse. Such challenges to intercultural communication arise at two interrelated levels. First, at the level of formal features, legal discourse is characterized by heavy reliance on technical terms, archaic language, and complex syntax. Early studies of language and the law attempt to describe and explain these formal features. Second, at the level of beliefs and values, legal discourse is organized according to the norms and conventions of the legal community, i.e., following the rule-based logic of legal reasoning. More recent studies examine these underlying beliefs, values, and norms, and the way in which they reinforce divisions of social class.

### Formal features of legal discourse

The formal features of legal discourse, including its specialized rhetorical structure, grammar, and vocabulary, are notoriously difficult for non-specialists to penetrate. These formal features can be illustrated with reference to two prototypical contexts: (1) The written discourse of legal rules and relationships; (2) the spoken discourse of the courtroom.

Studies of the written discourse of legal rules and relationships aim to describe the specialist language of the law used in genres such as legislation and agreements, and explain how this technical language can be difficult for non-specialists to understand. Influential work in this area includes that by Bhatia (1987, 1993, 1994), Crystal and Davy (1969), Mellinkoff (1963), and Tiersma (1999). The studies suggest that one of the reasons why legal documents cause difficulties for lay people is that they are not primarily authored with non-specialists in mind. That is, legislation and agreements are written in order to achieve particular legal ends, such as the establishment of a legal rule or relationship. As a consequence, such texts are primarily intended to be read not by the lay people whom they govern, but by legal professionals fluent in the language of the law. In writing to this audience, legal draftspeople must construct legally effective texts that are expressed in a clear, precise, and unambiguous way, incapable of being misconstrued. At the same time, however, these texts must successfully anticipate and include the full range of possible real world scenarios to which the legal rule might apply (Bhatia 1993).

The formal features of legal discourse can be explained in relation to the aims of clarity, precision, unambiguity, and all-inclusiveness mentioned above. Although it is sometimes claimed that legal language is more precise than ordinary language, this claim has been severely criticized (Danet 1980, 1985; Mellinkoff 1963; Tiersma 1999). Scholars point out that all language, including the language of the law, is inherently indeterminate. Nonetheless, Bhatia (1987, 1993, 1994) describes numerous lexical and syntactic features that legal specialists employ in normative texts (e.g., legislation and contracts) in order to serve the competing aims of precision and all-inclusiveness. These include lengthy sentences, nominalization, complex prepositional phrases (e.g., "in accordance with"), binomial and multinomial expressions (e.g., "wholly and exclusively"), and complex conditional structures with frequent qualifications that introduce syntactic discontinuities. A range of other formal features characteristic of legal texts, such as the use of legal technical terms, archaic language, Latin phrases, and formulaic, ritualistic language, is described in other studies (Danet 1980, 1985; Mellinkoff 1963; Tiersma 1999). Such ceremonial language can be crucial to the legal meaning of the document. As Tiersma notes, "formal and ritualistic language in wills and similar documents can signal to the parties that this is a legal act with significant consequences" (1999: 102).

Like written legal discourse, spoken legal discourse can also provide a source of intercultural communication difficulty between lawyers and lay people. Eades (2010) provides a comprehensive overview of the research in this area. The problems can be illustrated with reference to two contexts: witness examination and judges' summaries and instructions for the jury. Studies of witness examinations investigate the way in which lawyers control courtroom interaction, using a range of linguistic devices (e.g., more or less coercive question types) in order to present and refute the evidence of witnesses (Atkinson and Drew 1979; Danet et al. 1980; Drew 1985; Gibbons 2003, 2008; Matoesian 2005; Woodbury 1984). Other research examines the linguistic speech style of witnesses themselves, identifying both "powerful" and "powerless" speech, and suggesting that the style of speech adopted influences impressions of a witness as truthful or trustworthy (Conley et al. 1978; O'Barr 1982; O'Barr and Atkins 1980). Finally, studies of jury instructions, where the judge instructs the jury on how to perform their role as fact-finders in the trial, highlight linguistic features, such as nominalization and technical vocabulary, that impede comprehension (Charrow and Charrow 1979; Heffer 2002, 2005, 2008).

## Beliefs, values, and norms in legal discourse

Even if a lay person is able to decode the formal features of legal discourse, successful communication is not guaranteed. Legal discourse is constructed from the perspective of a particular legal worldview, which makes assumptions about the legal process that are unlikely to be shared by lay people. This legal worldview is aptly characterized in Conley and O'Barr's (1990) study of the discourse of lay litigants in informal courts (e.g., small claims tribunals) in the USA. Their ethnographic study identified two principal orientations for lay litigants, namely "relational" and "rule oriented". According to Conley and O'Barr (1990), relational litigants tend to "analyze and describe legal problems in terms of social relations" (p. 61). Thus, in constructing their accounts, they "strive to introduce to the trial the details of their social lives" (ibid.: 58). In contrast, rule-oriented litigants understand their legal problems in terms of abstract rules, principles, and legal categories, which transcend details of the social context. Their accounts are presented as "a deductive search for blame" (ibid.: 59). It is this second orientation, that of the rule-oriented litigant, which most closely matches the beliefs, values, and norms of legal professionals.

The role of this legal worldview in interactions between legal professionals and lay people is further explored in a number of major studies: by Mertz (1996, 2007) in law school classrooms; by Maley et al. (1995), Felstiner and Sarat (1992), and Sarat and Felstiner (1986, 1988) in lawyer–client interviews; and by Merry (1990) in courtroom trials and mediation sessions. In general terms, the picture that emerges is of two (or sometimes more) distinct discourses in contact: the real world discourse of concrete experience, social relationships, and personal narratives; and the legal discourse of abstract rules, categories, and legal analysis. This is not to say that there is one style for lawyers and another style for lay people, however. In reality, different individuals, both lawyers and lay people, draw upon these discourses to frame their accounts in strategic ways. For example, Maley et al. (1995: 48) show how lawyers employ "empathy and the common touch" in order to make their points in a more accessible and persuasive way with their clients.

The rule-based ideology that underlies legal discourse can affect communication between legal professionals and lay people in subtle ways that are very difficult for either group to detect. This is because legal discourse is constructed according to particular assumptions about the legal problem-solving process (for a detailed description of this process and associated legal methods and legal conventions, see Holland and Webb 2010; Vandevelde 1996). As already suggested, legal accounts focus exclusively on those "facts" that are relevant to legal issues and rules, and omit much of the social background that would normally form part of a lay narrative. The kind of contextual information that lay people would normally rely on in order to form moral judgments is simply irrelevant when the dispute is viewed from a legal perspective. Mertz (2007: 132) refers to this process of selection and prioritization as "cultural dominance" and "cultural invisibility", arguing that "important aspects of social context and identity have become invisible ... [while] other aspects of dominant culture and assumptions become highly visible".

The fact that legal discourse is constructed according to different beliefs, values, and norms raises issues of power. First, there is the question of whether lay people can effectively communicate their legal problems to legal professionals. Lay people are often unable to provide the kinds of rule-oriented accounts required to engage effectively with the legal process (Conley and O'Barr 1990). As a result, they may be disadvantaged when courts are unable to understand their cases in legally meaningful terms. Thus, one role of the lawyer is to act as an interpreter who translates the lived experience of the client into the appropriate legal categories, in effect helping the client to tell an appropriate legal story (Maley et al. 1995; Mertz 2007). Second, the observation that some lay people approach the legal process from a more rule-oriented perspective than others suggests that the discourse of the law may act to re-enforce existing divisions of social class. Conley and O'Barr (1990) suggest that rule orientation is a skill that members of the dominant classes acquire, but members of the subservient classes fail to develop. In this sense, the rule-oriented nature of the discourse of the law acts as an agent of social inequality.

## 3. Dominant culture and minority groups

If communication between legal professionals and lay people is challenging, these challenges are compounded when members of minority groups, who may be unfamiliar with the discourse practices of the dominant culture as well as have limited proficiency in the majority language, are involved. Forensic linguistic studies investigate the issue of language and disadvantage before the law, focusing on two main kinds of participants: aboriginal groups/indigenous minorities; and limited proficiency individuals, often immigrants. The literature examines the way in which such culturally and linguistically diverse participants in the legal process interact with dominant culture legal professionals. In addition to the problems already identified above, these participants face additional cultural and linguistic barriers to effective communication.

## Limited proficiency individuals and interpreters

Studies of interactions with limited proficiency individuals examine issues related to complex legal language, first language (L1) interference, and the practice of interpreting. With respect to complex legal language, one area of focus that has received considerable attention is the context of police interviews, although the difficulties described are of course not restricted to limited proficiency individuals alone (see Heydon 2005; Kurzon 1996; Rock 2007; Shuy 1997). In common law jurisdictions such as Australia, Britain, and the United States, police are under a duty to provide suspects to a crime with a "warning" or "caution" (known in the US as a "Miranda warning"), informing the suspect of their right to silence and their right to a lawyer. Only when police have ascertained that the suspect has understood these rights and decided to waive them can the police proceed with the interview. However, the form of this police warning can be difficult for low proficiency individuals to understand, because of its use of police jargon, low-frequency lexis, complex syntax, passive voice, and nominalization (Brière 1978; Gibbons 1990, 2003; Roy 1990). Even if it can be demonstrated that the suspect was able to comprehend the text of the warning, suspects may be subjected to subtle, or not so subtle, linguistic coercion (Berk-Seligson 2002, 2009). For example, Pavlenko (2008) describes a case in which a police officer uses three types of deception in order to persuade a limited proficiency individual to sign an interview form waiving her Miranda rights. Pavlenko maintains that limited proficiency individuals appear to be particularly vulnerable to such tactics, as they lack the necessary cultural knowledge to understand the full significance of the police warnings.

In cases where no interpreter is provided, L1 interference is potentially responsible for far-reaching intercultural communication problems, both in police interviews and in the courtroom. The work of Cooke (1995, 2002) provides useful insights here. For example, the way in which negatively framed yes–no questions (e.g., "you didn't see him, did you?") are answered varies across languages. Cooke (2002: 24) notes that, in the Australian Aboriginal language, Yolngu, people "frequently say *yes* to confirm the veracity of a negatively framed proposition in a situation where the English speaker would say *no*". Cooke suggests that, in the context of witness examination, transferring this pragmatic strategy could lead to significant mis-communication, with serious consequences. In the same study, Cooke found that confusion between "don't have to" and "must not", a characteristic L1 transfer error for speakers of the Kriol language, resulted in communication difficulties in witness examination.

Interpreters are often employed in order to provide assistance to limited proficiency indivi-duals, both in police interviews and in courtroom contexts. The role of an interpreter is to "remove the language barrier and to the best of their skill and ability place the non-English speaker in a position as similar as possible to that of a speaker of English" (Hale 2004: 10). However, studies of interpreting situations show that certain linguistic issues cannot be resolved by the use of an interpreter. At the lexical level, some vocabulary can be difficult to interpret because it lacks a direct translation in the target language. The same applies to gram-matical categories. With respect to English and Korean, Lee (2009a, 2009b, 2010) shows how cross-linguistic differences in grammatical structure can lead to inaccuracies in interpretation, which may be exploited by lawyers as evidence of a lack of credibility on the part of the witness (see especially Lee 2009b: 393–94). Finally, at the pragmatic level, interpreters often fail to translate discourse markers such as "well", which serve to impart important information about attitude (Berk-Seligson 1999; Hale 1999, 2004; Rigney 1999). Thus, these studies highlight problems that arise in communication with culturally and linguistically diverse participants in the legal process as a result of different linguistic norms.

Aside from linguistic matters, communication with limited proficiency individuals can be complicated because they adhere to different underlying cultural values. As a result, interpreters are sometimes called upon to act as a kind of cultural broker (Hale 2007) in order to resolve challenges in intercultural communication. In this somewhat controversial role, interpreters may be asked to provide cultural information in order to explain the responses of limited proficiency individuals. In her research on community interpreting, Hale (2007: 133) acknowledges the possible influence of cross-cultural differences, but cautions that such differences "can be varied and complex, and ... interpreters need to be confident that the cause of the misunderstanding is a cross-cultural issue before deciding to offer an explanation".

## Aboriginal groups/indigenous minorities

Other studies of intercultural communication in legal contexts have focused their attention on participants from indigenous minority groups, for example aboriginal groups in Canada, the United States, or Australia, among others. The most extensive work in this area has been carried out in the Australian context, and describes disadvantages that indigenous Australians may experience as a result of cultural differences. Gibbons (2003) provides a useful overview of this work. Three kinds of cultural differences are described: (1) different norms of interaction (both verbal and nonverbal); (2) different assumptions about knowledge and questioning; (3) different assumptions about the legal process.

As was suggested earlier, the norms of interaction in police interviews and in the courtroom are considerably different from those of everyday conversation. In particular, courtroom inter-action is highly regulated, with precise rules about who can speak, what they can say, and how they can say it (Conley and O'Barr 1990). These norms, which are derived both from legal rules of evidence and from legal convention and ritual, conform to those of the dominant legal professional culture. Consequently, members of indigenous minority groups following their own culturally expected norms of interaction may behave inappropriately in the eyes of dominant culture legal professionals. As an example, consider the way in which conversational silence is valued differently by different cultural groups. Eades (2007) points out that it can be the case that indigenous Australians begin their answers to questions with silence. This cultural practice is not tolerated in courtroom interaction, where witnesses are expected to provide answers directly and without hesitation. Such a silence can contribute to the impression that a witness lacks confidence, coherence, and credibility, even if that witness has important information to impart. Similarly, indigenous Australians may sometimes avoid direct eye contact, which they perceive as threatening or rude (Eades 1994; Walsh 1994). However, in many legal contexts, a failure to make eye contact could be interpreted as a sign of dishonesty or guilt by dominant culture judges, lawyers, and jurors.

In addition to these cultural differences in nonverbal interaction styles, culture also plays a role in the norms of verbal interaction, in terms of what is said and how. For indigenous Australians, perhaps the most serious of all the cultural differences noted in the literature is the phenomenon that Liberman (1981) terms "gratuitous concurrence". According to Eades

(1994: 245), "a very common strategy for Aborigines being asked a number of questions by non-Aborigines is to agree, regardless of either their understanding of the question, or their belief about the truth or falsity of the proposition being questioned". Obviously, such a strategy can have disastrous consequences in legal contexts. Furthermore, Gibbons (2003) draws attention to the fact that indigenous Australians construct narratives according to different cultural assumptions about generic structure and rhetorical effectiveness (Christie and Harris 1985). Gibbons suggests that this cultural difference could lead to difficulties in police interviews or in the courtroom, both of which assume a Western-style narrative.

Different assumptions about knowledge and questioning can also lead to challenges in intercultural communication. For indigenous Australians, direct questioning of the kind that occurs in courtrooms can in some cases be considered an inappropriate way to solicit information, with more indirect methods being preferred (Eades 1994; note that Morrow 1993 reports similar values with respect to Central Alaskan Yup'iks). As noted earlier, such an observation can be an overgeneralization based on an essentialist supposition, and should not therefore be considered true for all people in this population. Where such differences in underlying assumptions are indeed evident, the individuals concerned may respond to direct courtroom questioning by saying "I don't know" or with a shrug, as a way of signaling the perceived inappropriateness of the questions. Furthermore, in contrast to Western societies where knowledge is freely available, knowledge in indigenous Australian societies is acquired only after lengthy initiation, and is therefore carefully guarded (Eades 1994; Walsh 1994). There are clear, culturally defined rules about who may gain access to particular information, and under what circumstances. The right to divulge such information is similarly limited. Again, these values are in direct conflict with the expectations of the dominant legal culture that information can be freely shared in response to direct questions from a lawyer in court.

Finally, differences can arise in terms of assumptions about the legal process itself. For example, Walsh (1999, 2008) documents the difficulties encountered in Australian land claims and native title hearings, which result from fundamentally different assumptions about such concepts as land ownership.

## 4. Multilingual and multicultural legal contexts

The discussion so far has focused on instances of intercultural communication that take place within the confines of the local legal system. However, the spread of globalization has led to the establishment of multilingual and multicultural legal contexts, in which different legal systems and cultures increasingly come into contact. Two examples in particular have attracted the attention of scholars. One is the establishment of the European Union (EU), a supranational political and economic entity that combines the different legal systems and cultures of its various member states. A second example is the practice of international commercial arbitration, an alternative dispute resolution process used primarily by multinational corporations for disputes that span national borders. In both these contexts, individuals from different legal cultures are directly or indirectly brought into contact: directly, if they are involved in political negotiations as legislators in the EU, or if they are acting in international commercial arbitration proceedings, as party, counsel, or arbitrator; indirectly, if they are involved in the translation of legal documents, especially legislation or regulations, related to EU government or to the administration of international commercial arbitration in different national contexts.

In order to understand the potential for intercultural communication difficulties in these contexts, it is necessary to appreciate the principal differences that may be observed across different legal cultures. At the risk of oversimplifying, two main legal traditions can be identified:

the common law tradition, derived from English law and practiced in the Commonwealth; and the civil law tradition, derived from Roman law and practiced elsewhere. Among other factors, these two traditions differ in their approach to sources of law (code or case law); trial procedures (inquisitorial or adversarial); and the mode of legal reasoning (deductive or inductive) (for a review of issues in the context of international commercial arbitration, see Frommel and Rider 1999). Because these legal cultures are based on very different assumptions, challenges to intercultural communication can arise when practitioners from different systems come into contact. For example, in international commercial arbitration, arbitrators from a civil law background may experience difficulties in understanding the assumptions made in arguments by common lawyers, and vice versa (Bernini 1998).

Research into communication in these multilingual and multicultural contexts is relatively recent (see Bhatia *et al.* 2003a, 2008a,b). Most of this research examines the linguistic features of normative texts, as implemented in a range of national contexts, and describes what I have referred to above as "indirect contact" between individuals from different legal cultures. With respect to "direct contact", two main contexts have been explored. First, Powell and Hashim (2011) examine interactions in international commercial arbitration proceedings based in Malaysia, and describe the practice of code-switching in that context. Second, Hafner (2011) provides a contrastive analysis of professional legal reasoning in extracts of common law and civil law International Chamber of Commerce arbitration awards. Hafner illustrates the way in which award writers use a range of discursive strategies in different cultural contexts, and highlights the importance of intercultural communicative competence as a professional skill for arbitrators.

Legal cultures also come into contact in a more indirect way where legal rules are drafted to apply internationally across a number of legal systems and cultures. This occurs with EU legislation and with supranational arbitration rules such as the UNCITRAL model law. In both instances, the normative texts created are implemented in a range of national contexts, each with its own distinct legal language and culture. Studies of such texts (e.g., Bhatia *et al.* 2003b) identify systematic discursive variation, which can be explained by differences in drafting conventions, linguistic constraints, and sociocultural constraints (Catenaccio 2008; Gotti 2008a). For example, in the common law tradition, great value is placed on precision in legal drafting. Consequently, the rules constructed tend to be more detailed and specific than the rules drafted in a civil law context (Catenaccio 2008; Garzone 2003).

Issues of intercultural communication arise when the kinds of rules described above are translated into the local legal language. In her study of translated arbitration rules, Garzone (2003) finds that common translation practices, such as simplification and explicitation, can lead to changes in the legal meanings of source texts. In fact, normative texts present great challenges to translators, because much of the time the required legal concepts and categories are simply missing from the legal lexicon of the target legal culture. In order to meet this challenge, a number of scholars advocate the adoption of a functional approach to translation (Chromá 2004, 2008; Gémar 2001; Šarčević 1997). According to this approach, the translator attempts to translate the text in terms that are not only formally equivalent, but also legally equivalent. In order to achieve such a functional translation, it is necessary for the translator to have a good understanding of the norms and conventions of the target legal culture.

## 5. Recommendations for practice

The review so far has shown that different participants in the legal process make different cultural assumptions when attempting to resolve legal problems. These differences can create barriers to effective participation in the legal process, and therefore raise important questions of access to the law by members of different cultural groups. The main question is whether anything can be done to minimize these barriers and improve access. In this section, I will review and evaluate suggestions for practical reform designed to achieve these ends.

Although most people would agree that it would be desirable to reform legal processes and make them more accessible, there are nevertheless powerful forces counteracting such reform. Viewed from the perspective of the legal professional, many (although by no means all) of the features of legal discourse that make it difficult to access also serve important legal functions. For example, the syntactic complexity of written legal discourse can be attributed to the need for legal instruments that are clear, precise, all-inclusive, and above all, achieve the desired legal effect. As noted by Tiersma (1999), legal language is resistant to change because, in legally significant contexts, the safest and most convenient thing for legal writers to do is to recycle existing forms and precedents, which have withstood the test of time and can therefore be relied on with confidence. Innovation is considered risky and to be avoided. Similarly, the extreme asymmetry of courtroom interaction can be attributed to legal rules of evidence whose aim is to ensure the reliability and trustworthiness of witness testimony. Any suggestions for reform of legal processes must take into account the communicative purpose of legal discourse practices, as well as legal professionals' extremely conservative approach to these practices.

In spite of this conservative approach, there have been some attempts originating within the legal profession to make legal language more accessible to non-specialists. The plain legal language movement is one such attempt (for a detailed account, see Asprey 2003). The movement has its beginnings in the early to mid-1970s in the insurance and banking sectors in the US and, over the past 40 years, it has gradually spread worldwide. The movement aims to encourage legal writing in "clear, straightforward language, with the needs of the reader foremost in mind" (Asprey 2003: 12). Among other things, this involves a movement away from the traditional, archaic language of legal documents to more modern language.

As suggested above, some legal professionals fear that using such innovative and untested language could lead to greater litigation, as the legal effect of plain language documents would be unclear. However, this does not appear to be the case at all. Asprey (2003: 33–44) describes a range of companies that have rewritten their agreements and forms in plain language, and argues that the new plain language forms have led to less, not more, litigation. Of course, the need for plain legal language is not restricted to written agreements, and is also felt in the highly formalized and ritualized language of police warnings and jury instructions. Gibbons' (2001) work on simplifying the language of police interviews is an example of the kind of effort that is needed in this domain. Thus, the plain legal language movement represents a practical response to the difficulties that lay readers face with the complexity of legal discourse.

As we have seen, the challenges of legal discourse are particularly acute for culturally and linguistically diverse participants in the legal process. As well as being unfamiliar with the legal system of the dominant culture, such participants often have limited proficiency in the dominant language and may therefore require the assistance of an interpreter. However, as Gibbons (2003) points out, there is considerable resistance to the use of interpreters in the court system. Furthermore, whether an interpreter is required is left to the discretion of individual judges and police officers, who typically make their judgment on the basis of a few quick questions to the individual concerned (Eades 2010). This practice can be problematic as the person involved may have good basic interactional competence, but lack the necessary linguistic and conceptual competence to participate in legal exchanges (on this distinction, see Eades 2003; Pavlenko 2008). There is therefore a need to create, pilot, and evaluate valid and reliable tests of language proficiency, which are capable of deciding this issue.

The observations made in discourse studies of the legal context further suggest a need for some form of intercultural training for participants in the legal process, especially with respect to the courtroom situation. Such training could be targeted at lay people from a variety of cultural backgrounds, and would aim to help prospective witnesses to understand the principles of courtroom interaction. In addition, legal professionals should be aware of cultural factors that may affect the way in which some witnesses respond to questions (e.g., indigenous Australians as described by Walsh (1994) and Eades (1994), among others). Eades' (1992) practitioners' guide on communicating with indigenous Australian clients is one example of an attempt to raise such cultural awareness.

With better cultural awareness, legal professionals would be able to examine witnesses from diverse cultural backgrounds in a more effective way. Furthermore, legal professionals would be better able to recognize cultural behavior that disadvantages a witness, such as the practice of "gratuitous concurrence" described earlier in association with some indigenous Australians. One possibility is that judges who recognize such cultural behavior take steps to warn a jury of their implications in their summing up. One could even argue that, in contexts with large numbers of culturally diverse participants, legal procedures should themselves be modified to accommodate culturally different interaction styles and values. One example of such cultural accommodation can be seen in the New Zealand legal system, which integrates elements of restorative justice following cultural practices that can sometimes be associated with indigenous Maori values (e.g., in the family court system; see Tauri 1998).

Finally, with increasing globalization and consequent contact between legal systems, there is a growing need for legal practitioners to develop the ability to operate in multilingual and multicultural contexts. In addition, it has been suggested that, where different legal systems come into contact, these systems should accommodate one another through a gradual process of "harmonization". For example, procedures developed in international commercial arbitration combine elements of the civil law system (e.g., an inquisitorial style) with elements of the common law system (e.g., cross-examination) (Lazareff 1999). However, the existing linguistic and discourse-based research suggests that complete harmonization will be difficult to achieve, because the cultural influences of different legal traditions are deeply ingrained in the discourse and operate at a level below consciousness (Gotti 2008a,b; Hafner 2011).

## 6. Future directions

This chapter has provided an overview and critical review of research into the role of culture in communication in legal contexts. We have seen how, in interactions in the legal context, a number of cultural factors may be present and combine to pose challenges to effective communication. In future, as an increasingly global and culturally diverse population comes into contact with the local legal system, culture is likely to grow in importance as a factor in communication in legal contexts. In response to this increasing diversity, the kind of research that has been described in this chapter will inevitably expand in scope.

The existing research into intercultural communication in legal contexts has yielded important insights into the kind of communication challenges that can occur, particularly from the perspective of participants in the legal process who are not members of the legal establishment. In future, such research could usefully develop in two main ways. First, there is a need for more studies that place greater emphasis on cultural awareness in legal settings. This includes a focus on whether participants in the legal process, especially legal professionals, are aware of particular cultural differences and their effects, and if so, how they seek to accommodate, exploit, or address these differences. Second, there is a need for research that investigates the possibility of raising cultural awareness through some form of intercultural training, documenting possible measures that can be taken, and evaluating their effect on communication in the legal context. Expanding the research agenda in this way should make it possible to explore in greater depth the kind of action that policy makers or concerned individuals can take in order to accommodate cultural differences in legal contexts.

## Related topics

Beliefs; intercultural communicative competence; intercultural rhetoric; intercultural training; professional and workplace contexts; translation, and interpreting; values; worldview

## Further reading

Atkinson, J.M. and Drew, P. (1979) *Order in Court: The Organization of Verbal Interaction in Judicial Settings*, Atlantic Highlands, NJ: Humanities Press (an early study of courtroom interaction).
Bhatia, V.K. (1993) *Analyzing Genre: Language Use in Professional Settings*, London: Longman (provides a methodological framework for the analysis of written legal text, from the point of view of specialists and non-specialists).
Conley, J.M. and O'Barr, W.M. (1990) *Rules versus Relationships: The Ethnography of Legal Discourse*, Chicago, IL: University of Chicago Press (influential ethnographic study of interaction in informal courts in the US, analysing the assumptions and expectations of lay litigants).
Eades, D. (2010) *Sociolinguistics and the Legal Process*, Bristol: Multilingual Matters (thorough overview of issues related to sociolinguistic studies of the legal context).
Gibbons, J. (2003) *Forensic Linguistics: An introduction to Language in the Justice System*, Malden, MA: Blackwell (thorough overview of issues related to language and the law, including language and disadvantage before the law).

## References

Asprey, M.M. (2003) *Plain Language for Lawyers*, 3rd edn, Sydney: Federation Press.
Atkinson, J.M. and Drew, P. (1979) *Order in Court: The Organization of Verbal Interaction in Judicial Settings*, Atlantic Highlands, NJ: Humanities Press.
Berk-Seligson, S. (1999) 'The impact of court interpreting on the coerciveness of leading questions', *Forensic Linguistics*, 6(1): 30–56.
——(2002) *The Bilingual Courtroom: Court Interpreters in the Judicial Process*, Chicago, IL: University of Chicago Press.
——(2009) *Coerced Confessions: The Discourse of Bilingual Police Interrogations*, Berlin: Mouton de Gruyter.
Bernini, G. (1998) 'Is there a growing international arbitration culture?', *ICCA Congress Series*, 8: 41–46.
Bhatia, V.K. (1987) 'Textual-mapping in British legislative writing', *World Englishes*, 6(1): 1–10.
——(1993) *Analyzing Genre: Language Use in Professional Settings*, London: Longman.
——(1994) 'Cognitive structuring in legislative provisions', in J. Gibbons (ed.) *Language and the Law*, London: Longman, pp. 136–55.
Bhatia, V.K., Candlin, C.N., Engberg, J. and Trosborg, A. (eds) (2003a) *Multilingual and Multicultural Contexts of Legislation: An International Perspective*, Bern: Peter Lang.
Bhatia, V.K., Candlin, C.N. and Gotti, M. (eds) (2003b) *Legal Discourse in Multilingual and Multicultural Contexts: Arbitration Texts in Europe*, Bern: Peter Lang.
Bhatia, V.K., Candlin, C.N. and Engberg, J. (eds) (2008a) *Legal Discourse across Cultures and Systems*, Hong Kong: Hong Kong University Press.
Bhatia, V.K., Candlin, C.N. and Evangelisti Allori, P. (eds) (2008b) *Language, Culture and the Law: The Formulation of Legal Concepts across Systems and Cultures*, Bern: Peter Lang.
Brière, E.J. (1978) 'Limited English speakers and the Miranda rights', *TESOL Quarterly*, 12(3): 235–45.
Catenaccio, P. (2008) 'Implementing council directive 1993/13/EEU on unfair terms in consumer contracts in Great Britain: a case for intra-linguistic translation?', in V.K. Bhatia, C.N. Candlin and P. Evangelisti Allori (eds) *Language, Culture and the Law: The Formulation of Legal Concepts across Systems and Cultures*, Bern: Peter Lang, pp. 259–80.

Charrow, R.P. and Charrow, V.R. (1979) 'Making legal language understandable: a psycholinguistic study of jury instructions', *Columbia Law Review*, 79(7): 1306–74.

Christie, M. and Harris, S. (1985) 'Communication breakdown in the Aboriginal classroom', in J. Pride (ed.) *Cross-cultural Encounters: Communication and Miscommunication*, Melbourne: River Seine, pp. 81–109.

Chromá, M. (2004) 'Cross-cultural traps in legal translation', in C.N. Candlin and M. Gotti (eds) *Intercultural Aspects of Specialized Communication*, Bern: Peter Lang, pp. 197–222.

——(2008) 'Semantic and legal interpretation: two approaches to legal translation', in V.K. Bhatia, C.N. Candlin, and P. Evangelisti Allori (eds) *Language, Culture and the Law: The Formulation of Legal Concepts across Systems and Cultures*, Bern: Peter Lang, pp. 303–15.

Conley, J.M. and O'Barr, W.M. (1990) *Rules versus Relationships: The Ethnography of Legal Discourse*, Chicago, IL: University of Chicago Press.

Conley, J.M., O'Barr, W.M. and Lind, E.A. (1978) 'The power of language: presentational style in the courtroom', *Duke Law Journal*, 6: 1375–99.

Cooke, M. (1995) 'Aboriginal evidence in the cross-cultural courtroom', in D. Eades (ed.) *Language in Evidence: Issues Confronting Aboriginal and Multicultural Australia*, Sydney: University of New South Wales Press, pp. 55–96.

——(2002) *Indigenous Interpreting Issues for Courts*, Carlton, Victoria: Australian Institute of Judicial Administration.

Crystal, D. and Davy, D. (1969) 'The language of legal documents', in D. Crystal and D. Davy (eds) *Investigating English Style*, Harlow: Longman, pp. 193–217.

Danet, B. (1980) 'Language in the legal process', *Law and Society Review*, 14(3): 445–564.

——(1985) 'Legal discourse', in T.A. van Dijk (ed.) *Handbook of Discourse Analysis*: Vol. 1, *Disciplines of Discourse*, London: Academic Press, pp. 273–91.

Danet, B., Hoffman, K.B., Kermish, N.C., Rahn, H.J. and Stayman, D.G. (1980) 'An ethnography of questioning in the courtroom', in R.W. Shuy and A. Shnukal (eds) *Language Use and the Uses of Language*, Washington, DC: Georgetown University Press, pp. 222–34.

Drew, P. (1985) 'Analyzing the use of language in courtroom interaction', in T.A. van Dijk (ed.) *Handbook of Discourse Analysis*, Vol. 3, *Discourse and Dialogue*, London: Academic Press, pp. 133–47.

Eades, D. (1992) *Aboriginal English and the Law: Communicating with Aboriginal English-speaking Clients: A Handbook for Legal Practitioners*, Brisbane: Queensland Law Society.

——(1994) 'A case of communicative clash: Aboriginal English and the legal system', in J. Gibbons (ed.) *Language and the Law*, London: Longman, pp. 234–64.

——(2003) 'Participation of second language and second dialect speakers in the legal system', *Annual Review of Applied Linguistics*, 23(1): 113–33.

——(2007) 'Aboriginal English in the criminal justice system', in G. Leitner and I. Malcolm (eds) *The Habitat of Australia's Aboriginal Languages: Past, Present and Future*, Berlin: Mouton de Gruyter, pp. 299–326.

——(2010) *Sociolinguistics and the Legal Process*, Bristol: Multilingual Matters.

Felstiner, W.L.F. and Sarat, A. (1992) 'Enactments of power: Negotiating reality and responsibility in lawyer-client interactions', *Cornell Law Review*, 77: 1447–98.

Frommel, S.N. and Rider, B.A.K. (eds) (1999) *Conflicting Legal Cultures in Commercial Arbitration: Old Issues and New Trends*, The Hague: Kluwer Law International.

Garzone, G. (2003) 'Arbitration rules across legal cultures: an intercultural approach', in V.K. Bhatia, C.N. Candlin, and M. Gotti (eds) *Legal Discourse in Multilingual and Multicultural Contexts: Arbitration Texts in Europe*, Bern: Peter Lang, pp. 177–220.

Gémar, J. (2001) 'Seven pillars for the legal translator: knowledge, know-how and art', in S. Šarčević (ed.) *Legal Translation: Preparation for Accession to the European Union*, Rijeka: University of Rijeka, pp. 111–38.

Gibbons, J. (1990) 'Applied linguistics in court', *Applied Linguistics*, 11(3): 229–37.

——(2001) 'Revising the language of New South Wales police procedures: applied linguistics in action', *Applied Linguistics*, 22: 439–69.

——(2003) *Forensic Linguistics: An Introduction to Language in the Justice System*, Malden, MA: Blackwell.

——(2008) 'Questioning in common law criminal courts', in J. Gibbons and M.T. Turell (eds) *Dimensions of Forensic Linguistics*, Amsterdam: John Benjamins, pp. 115–30.

Gotti, M. (2008a) 'Cultural constraints on arbitration discourse', in V.K. Bhatia, C.N. Candlin, and J. Engberg (eds) *Legal Discourse across Cultures and Systems*, Hong Kong: Hong Kong University Press, pp. 221–52.

——(2008b) 'The formulation of legal concepts in arbitration: normative texts in a multilingual, multi-cultural context', in V.K. Bhatia, C.N. Candlin, and P. Evangelisti Allori (eds) *Language, Culture and the Law: The Formulation of Legal Concepts across Systems and Cultures*, Bern: Peter Lang, pp. 23–45.

Hafner, C.A. (2011) 'Professional reasoning, legal cultures, and arbitral awards', *World Englishes*, 30(1): 117–28.

Hale, S. (1999) 'Interpreters' treatment of discourse markers in courtroom questions', *Forensic Linguistics*, 6(1): 57–82.

——(2004) *The Discourse of Court Interpreting: Discourse Practices of the Law, the Witness, and the Interpreter*, Amsterdam: John Benjamins.

——(2007) *Community Interpreting*, Basingstoke: Palgrave Macmillan.

Heffer, C. (2002) '"If you were standing in Marks and Spencers": narrativization and comprehension in the English summing-up', in J. Cotterill (ed.) *Language in the Legal Process*, Basingstoke: Palgrave, pp. 228–45.

——(2005) *The Language of Jury Trial: A Corpus-aided Analysis of Legal–Lay Discourse*, Basingstoke: Palgrave Macmillan.

——(2008) 'The language and communication of jury instruction', in J. Gibbons and M.T. Turell (eds) *Dimensions of Forensic Linguistics*, Amsterdam: John Benjamins, pp. 47–65.

Heydon, G. (2005) *The Language of Police Interviewing: A Critical Analysis*, Basingstoke: Palgrave Macmillan.

Holland, J.A. and Webb, J.S. (2010) *Learning Legal Rules: A Students' Guide to Legal Method and Reasoning*, 7th edn, Oxford: Oxford University Press.

Kurzon, D. (1996) 'To speak or not to speak: the comprehensibility of the revised police caution (PACE)', *International Journal for the Semiotics of Law*, 9(1): 3–16.

Lazareff, S. (1999) 'International arbitration: towards a common procedural approach', in S.N. Frommel and B.A.K. Rider (eds) *Conflicting Legal Cultures in Commercial Arbitration: Old Issues and New Trends*, The Hague: Kluwer Law International, pp. 31–38.

Lee, J. (2009a) 'Interpreting inexplicit language during courtroom examination', *Applied Linguistics*, 30(1): 93–114.

——(2009b) 'When linguistic and cultural differences are not disclosed in court interpreting', *Multilingua*, 28(4): 379–401.

——(2010) 'Interpreting reported speech in witnesses' evidence', *Interpreting*, 12(1): 60–82.

Liberman, K. (1981) 'Understanding Aborigines in Australian courts of law', *Human Organization*, 40: 247–55.

Maley, Y., Candlin, C.N., Crichton, J. and Koster, P. (1995) 'Orientations in lawyer–client interviews', *Forensic Linguistics*, 2(1): 42–55.

Matoesian, G. (2005) 'Nailing down an answer: participations of power in trial talk', *Discourse Studies*, 7(6): 733–59.

Mellinkoff, D. (1963) *The Language of the Law*, Boston, MA: Little, Brown.

Merry, S.E. (1990) *Getting Justice and Getting Even: Legal Consciousness among Working-class Americans*, Chicago, IL: University of Chicago Press.

Mertz, E. (1996) 'Recontextualization as socialization: text and pragmatics in the law school classroom', in M. Silverstein and G. Urban (ed.) *Natural Histories of Discourse*, Chicago, IL: University of Chicago Press, pp. 229–49.

——(2007) *The Language of Law School: Learning to Think like a Lawyer*, New York: Oxford University Press.

Morrow, P. (1993) 'A sociolinguistic mismatch: Central Alaskan Yup'iks and the legal system', *Alaska Justice Forum*, 10(2): 4–8.

O'Barr, W.M. (1982) *Linguistic Evidence: Language, Power, and Strategy in the Courtroom*, New York: Academic Press.

O'Barr, W.M. and Atkins, B.K. (1980) '"Women's language" or "powerless language"?', in S. McConnell-Ginet, R. Borker and N. Furman (eds) *Women and Language in Literature and Society*, New York: Praeger, pp. 93–109.

Pavlenko, A. (2008) '"I'm very not about the law part": nonnative speakers of English and the Miranda warnings', *TESOL Quarterly*, 42: 1–30.

Powell, R. and Hashim, A. (2011) 'Language disadvantage: Malaysian litigation and arbitration', *World Englishes*, 30, 1, 92–105.

Rigney, A.C. (1999) 'Questioning in interpreted testimony', *Forensic Linguistics*, 6(1): 83–108.

Rock, F. (2007) *Communicating Rights: The Language of Arrest and Detention*, Basingstoke: Palgrave Macmillan.

Roy, J.D. (1990) 'The difficulties of limited-English-proficient individuals in the legal setting', in R.W. Rieber and W.A. Stewart (eds) *The Language Scientist as Expert in the Legal Setting*, New York: New York Academy of Sciences, pp. 73–83.

Sarat, A. and Felstiner, W.L.F. (1986) 'Law and strategy in the divorce lawyer's office', *Law and Society Review*, 20(1): 93–134.

——(1988) 'Law and social relations: vocabularies of motive in lawyer/client interaction', *Law and Society Review*, 22(4): 737–69.

Šarčević, S. (1997) *New Approach to Legal Translation*, The Hague: Kluwer Law International.

Scollon, R. and Wong Scollon, S. (2001) *Intercultural Communication*, 2nd edn, Oxford: Blackwell.

Shuy, R.W. (1997) 'Ten unanswered language questions about Miranda', *Forensic Linguistics*, 4(2): 175–96.

Tauri, J. (1998) 'Family group conferencing: a case-study of the indigenisation of New Zealand's justice system', *Current Issues in Criminal Justice*, 10(2): 168–82.

Tiersma, P. (1999) *Legal Language*, Chicago, IL: The University of Chicago Press.

Vandevelde, K.J. (1996) *Thinking like a Lawyer*, Boulder, CO: Westview Press.

Walsh, M. (1994) 'Interactional styles in the courtroom: an example from northern Australia', in J. Gibbons (ed.) *Language and the Law*, London: Longman, pp. 217–33.

——(1999) 'Interpreting the transcript: problems in recording Aboriginal land claim proceedings in northern Australia', *Forensic Linguistics*, 6(1): 161–95.

——(2008) '"Which way?" difficult options for vulnerable witnesses in Australian Aboriginal land claim and native title cases', *Journal of English Linguistics*, 36(3): 239–65.

Woodbury, H. (1984) 'The strategic use of questions in court', *Semiotica*, 48(3–4): 197–228.

# 34

# Tourism

*Gavin Jack and Alison Phipps*

## 1. Introduction

This chapter provides an overview and critical discussion of the principal approaches to the study of language(s) and intercultural communication within the specific context of tourism. During the second half of the twentieth century, the number of people travelling has grown significantly, generating large revenues for the many and varied institutions of the tourist establishment and increasing opportunities for intercultural and multilingual encounters between tourists/guests and locals/hosts. Despite this fact, little scholarly attention has been devoted to the study of communication and language use in intercultural interactions between tourists and locals, although there is comparatively more research on the communicative strategies of the various intermediaries (e.g. tour guides, travel agents) that have an important influence on these interactions. This lack of research on naturally occurring intercultural communication in tourist settings is lamentable, not simply because of the potential economic contribution to be gained from effectively orchestrated interactions, but also because these interactions take place in contexts of power and status differentials that reproduce symbolic (and economic) inequalities between interlocutors in tourism settings.

There are, of course, many kinds of tourists with different motivations and modes for travelling, and thus different degrees of interest in interacting with locals. These variations in type and perspective on tourism influence the nature and extent of tourist engagement in intercultural communication. For some tourists, the opportunity to practice a foreign language while on holiday and to learn about new cultures and ways of life might be key to travel and the particular choice of destination. But how many of us actually take time to learn a second language – or at least much beyond a few key phrases or cultural curiosities from our guidebooks – before travelling? For others, perceived cultural and linguistic differences between themselves and their hosts might be viewed as potentially discomforting, even alienating or threatening, and can form the basis of prejudice. These emotional, or affective, elements of attitudes towards the culturally different can influence tourists' choice of holiday destination (e.g. avoiding certain countries or regions seen to be 'too different') or type of accommodation (e.g. choosing a large hotel complex with hosts who speak their language and offer a taste of the local culture that does not necessarily involve venturing far outside the confines of the resort).

Divergent attitudes might also be discerned in the perspective of the locals. For some, tourism can be threatening and viewed as corrosive of local cultural traditions and languages. For others, contact provides an opportunity not only for earning money by meeting tourist demands, but also for the preservation of their minority languages/ethnolinguistic communities and for intercultural and language learning. Indeed, in this latter regard, it is most typically locals who are expected to learn tourist languages and thus to engage in linguistic accommodation. There are, then, many competing perspectives on tourism as a sociocultural event (Murphy 1985), perspectives that have been studied to differing extents and with different theoretical and methodological resources. In this chapter, we begin by describing, illustrating and evaluating in three sections the principal approaches to the study of tourism and intercultural communication, which we label: the tourism impacts approach; the language of tourism approach; the intercultural encounters approach. The final section points to some future theoretical and methodological directions for scholars in this area of intercultural research.

## 2. Tourism impacts approach

Tourism scholars have dedicated considerable effort to identifying the economic impacts of tourist activity, but less to the cultural consequences. Brunt and Courtney define the cultural impacts of tourism as

> those which lead to a longer-term, gradual change in a society's values, beliefs, and cultural practices. To an extent, this is caused by the demand of tourists for instant culture and authentic souvenirs, and at the extreme may result in the situation whereby the host society becomes culturally dependent on the tourism generating country ( ... ). In other situations, however, local communities can be quite ambivalent towards its development.
>
> *Brunt and Courtney (1999: 496)*

The tourism impacts approach involves research that explores the sociocultural effects of tourism in terms of the attitudes (including ambivalence), beliefs and values held by both tourists and hosts.

The 'contact hypothesis' – a theory initially developed in the social psychology literature by Allport (1954) – is frequently used by researchers to study attitudinal impacts. According to Allport, intercultural or intergroup contact 'changes the attitudes and behaviours of groups and individuals towards one another and, in turn, will influence any further contact' (Dörnyei and Csizér 2005: 328). Contact theorists are primarily interested in identifying the positive and negative attitudinal and behavioural changes associated with tourism. Allport (1954) suggested that a number of so-called 'intergroup conditions' are needed to make it more likely that individuals and groups will develop positive attitudes to intergroup and intercultural communication. These conditions included equal status between groups, shared pursuit of common goals, a perception of common interests and institutional support for the contact.

However, as noted by Dörnyei and Csizér (2005), the typical nature of the tourist experience mitigates against the existence of many of these conditions for favourable attitudes to contact. The typically brief length of time that tourists stay in a local area means there is only a low possibility for real cooperation and for any friendship potential between tourist and hosts. Such a situation, these authors suggest, might also be compounded by the fact that tourists often have a higher economic status than locals. These conditions increase the likelihood that a one-sided and exploitative relationship between tourists and locals will develop, characterized by 'an orientation toward immediate gratification on the part of both hosts and tourists, with salient commercial, contrived, and even exploitative overtones' (Dörnyei and Csizér 2005: 330). The so-called 'demonstration effect' – where locals, over time, come to adopt certain values and behaviours exhibited by the tourists who visit an area – for example can be the basis for the development of positive or negative cultural impacts. In methodological terms, studies within the tourism impacts approach typically make use of questionnaire surveys, and a positivist, quantitative research paradigm, to record and analyse locals' attitudes and perceptions.

A number of studies have specifically examined the linguistic dimension of tourism's cultural impact, with notable regard to minority/threatened languages and attitudes to tourist/second language acquisition. We have chosen three to illustrate the tourism impacts approach. The first is Brougham and Butler's (1981) study of the attitudes and beliefs of residents of Sleat – the Gaelic-speaking southern part of the Isle of Skye, Scotland – regarding the impact of tourism on their Gaelic language and cultural life. Their study demonstrated variation among respondents' attitudes towards tourism's impact on local language and culture, attributable to a number of different variables. These variables included the extent to which respondents had contact with tourists (called 'degree of exposure') and certain demographic characteristics (notably length of residence, age and language).

With regard to the former, the study found that, although the majority of respondents held the view that tourism did not affect the status of Gaelic, variation in responses to this questionnaire item were associated with respondents' self-assessed 'degree of contact with second home users' (Brougham and Butler 1981: 580). Second home users will tend to stay for longer periods than other types of tourist in a particular place, with the effect that 'a certain decline in the amount of Gaelic spoken' (ibid.) was perceived to ensue. Respondents who had zero contact with second home users and resided in so-called zones of higher tourist pressure expressed the view that tourism had no impact on the local language. In contrast, most respondents in 'areas of lower tourist pressure but with frequent contact with tourists' (ibid.) perceived tourism to have an impact, with residents above 44 years of age in particular expressing this view strongly.

Dörnyei and Csizér's (2005) survey of 8,593 13- and 14-year-old Hungarian school pupils also explored attitudes to the contact effects of tourism. They investigated whether increased intercultural contact – promoted by the development of tourism in post-revolutionary Hungary – had enhanced language attitudes and language learning motivation. Their findings indicated that, for the most part, intercultural contact encouraged positive intergroup and language attitudes, and a motivation for language learning. School pupils who reported greater levels of self-confidence towards communicating in a foreign language exhibited the most positive attitudes to intercultural contact. As with Brougham and Butler's (1981) study, there was some variation within the attitudinal results connected to the case of German tourists in the most frequented tourist localities in Hungary. In these areas, local school pupils had the least positive attitudes and motivation to learn a language. The authors explained this finding in terms of the concept of intergroup and interpersonal 'salience', according to which 'superficial contact experiences that are personally unimportant (i.e., that have no value in themselves and are not instrumental in reaching a valued goal) will not bring about a significant improvement of intergroup relations' (Dörnyei and Csizér 2005: 353). In this dataset, the respondents who had the highest contact – more frequent, less personally important – were in Budapest and, here, attitudes and second language learning motivations were comparatively lower vis-à-vis respondents from rural Hungary where tourist contact is less frequent but more salient.

A third study by Prentice and Hudson (1993) also deployed a survey tool to investigate the language dimensions of tourism impact among Welsh- and non-Welsh-speaking residents of Porthmadog, Gwynedd, Wales. They framed their research in terms of broader debates that conceive of tourism either as a mechanism for linguistic and cultural conservation or as a threat to an ethnolinguistic community (Welsh speakers in Wales), especially from the adjacent English-speaking/Anglo culture in Wales. In this context, they wished to find out whether Welsh speakers, compared with non-Welsh speakers, were more likely to be negatively disposed to the linguistic dimensions of tourism impact, notably the threat of 'anglicization'. The results indicated that, although most respondents agreed that tourism did not affect Welsh lifestyle, a substantial minority (notably falling in the age groups 31–40 and 41–50 years) did; however, the language issue was a secondary one in their determinations. In this regard, linguistic competence in Welsh did not have a differential impact on respondents' views regarding the impact of second home ownership on community life. Based on these results, Prentice and Hudson (1993: 298) warned against 'ascribing too much influence to linguistic competence in Welsh to the causes of residents' perceptions of tourism impacts in Wales' and any resultant tendency to 'characterize impact perceptions in terms of Welsh and English traditions'.

The impact of divergent (national) 'cultural value systems' on tourist behaviour – and the perceived need for tourism providers to be sensitive to these differences – is also a key concern of researchers. Remaining with a psychological framework, scholars here have typically deployed Hofstede's cognitive model of national culture as a mental programme comprising a set of values that shape behaviour to investigate cultural differences between tourists. Three studies by Reisinger and Turner (1997, 1999, 2002) are illustrative of a Hofstedian approach to tourism and intercultural communication in the specific context of Asian tourists in Australia. They note that Asian markets became increasingly important to Australian tourism during the 1990s with the effect that non-English-speaking tourists outnumbered English-speaking ones for the first time. It also raised a multicultural challenge for tourism providers, as they reportedly struggled to deliver culturally sensitive tourist experiences, notably to Japanese tourists (Reisinger and Turner 1999). In order to help Australian tourism providers enhance the quality of the interpersonal elements of service delivery, Reisinger and Turner (1999) identified the following cultural issues and practical recommendations to enhance the 'psychological comfort' of Japanese tourists in Australia:

- As members of a high-uncertainty avoidance culture, Japanese tourists require adequate and reliable information and other risk reduction strategies.
- Prompt service is vital as punctuality is taken as a sign of good manners and a measure of professionalism.
- As members of a high-power distance culture that values authority and hierarchy, displays of respect for the particular social position and age of tourists are vital. Tourist providers might, for instance, use these variables to determine the order to serve individual tourists, to allocate hotel rooms or appropriate seating on tour buses, to provide special care and display respect for older tourists or wear uniforms with badges to indicate their own social/employment status.
- As a high-context culture in which indirect communication styles, silence and nonverbal cues are especially important, tourist providers should display humility (rather than directness and overconfidence) and an apologetic attitude. Confidence is regarded with suspicion and might be interpreted as rude, according to Reisinger and Turner (1999).
- Learn some basic phrases and principles of Asian languages.

Within this framework, cultural differences are viewed as aspects of host–tourist interactions that can, first, be isolated and identified using Hofstede's national culture framework and, second, be 'managed' by providing employees with pertinent knowledge and skills. Reisinger and Turner (1999) state that:

all tourism employees should be exposed to a broad multicultural training for cultural sensitivity to the international tourist's needs. Such training should include familiarization by tourism providers with the tourist's native language, the cultural aspects of the meanings of interpersonal and non-verbal communication cues such as symbols, signs, gestures, facial expressions, and messages contained in body language.

*Reisinger and Turner (1999: 146)*

This quote describes core components of 'communicative competence' (verbal and nonverbal language skills, familiarity with cultural meanings) as a vital skill for tourism workers to develop and enact. These elements typically form the basis for training courses not only for students of tourism, but also for practising professionals in the industry. As demonstrated by Leclerc and Martin (2004) with specific regard to tour guides, however, there are cross-national variations in the perceived importance of various communicative competences. Tour guides provide a number of important functions for tourists ranging from information provision and story-telling to go-between or a cultural/linguistic 'broker' facilitating interaction between locals and tourists. These roles demand various kinds of intercultural communication competence including, according to Leclerc and Martin (2004), four non-verbal factors (approachability, poise, attentiveness, touch) and three verbal ones (language adaptability, interpersonal inclusion, assertiveness). These authors collected 441 surveys from a sample of French, German and American tourists in the Southwest USA to assess the relative importance of these factors in their evaluations of tour guides in general. They found that all the communication skills were rated more important by the American compared with the European tourists. Leclerc and Martin (2004) explain this finding by pointing to the greater importance generally placed on interpersonal communication skills in the USA.

There are a number of limitations to these survey-based approaches to tourism and intercultural communication. These limitations are primarily methodological and associated with the use of a survey instrument that provides self-reported data at one point in time of locals'/tourists' attitudes, beliefs and perceptions of tourism. What actually happens in everyday communicative practice is left unexplored, thus posing the question of whether what respondents purport their attitudes and behaviours to be is truly reflective of what would actually occur in practice. Surveys thus provide decontextualized data that do not capture the dynamics and complexities of local contexts for interaction, notably the social impact of others on our own behaviours. Attitudes may also change over time, and respondents may 'impression manage' their responses to survey items in order to present what they might perceive to be the best or the right answer rather than the one that more accurately reflects their views. Turning to the culture management issues, Hofstede's (1980) framework has now been extensively criticized for: its use of the nation-state as a putative container of a national culture; the reduction and homogenization of intra-national diversity into portrayals of national culture; its essentialist characterizations of culture; methodological flaws with the sampling frame, 'the initial questionnaire design and statistical processing' (McSweeney 2002).

In offering a limited portrayal of intercultural communication in practice, or in context, the tourism impacts approach only takes us so far in understanding the relationship between culture, language and power. The next approach draws upon different conceptual and methodological premises and directly addresses some (although perhaps not all) of these shortcomings.

## 3. The language of tourism approach

Although the first approach focused on individual tourist attitudes and perceptions, the language of tourism approach encourages analysis of the content and effects of the textual and visual representations of tourist destinations and local populations found in the promotional materials produced and touristic practices deployed by the so-called 'actors' of the 'tourist establishment'. These materials and practices of the tourist establishment form the basis of a tourism discourse, i.e. 'a set of expressions, words and behaviour as well as particular touristic structures and activities that describe a place and its inhabitants' (Papen 2005: 79). Central to this approach is the notion that tourism discourse is a form of social control, as its aim is to manipulate individual and collective tourist behaviour in ways that help tourism providers to turn a profit.

In this respect, tourism marketers are in the business of producing 'induced images' of destinations through a variety of promotional media in a way that 'directs expectations, influences perceptions, and thereby provides a preconceived landscape for the tourist to "discover"' (Weightman 1987: 230). Tourism discourse is, then, hardly 'neutral work'; instead, the production of compelling images of 'the other' provokes political, ethical and historical questions at the heart of intercultural communication. In short, this second approach to exploring tourism and intercultural communication is one that asks questions about language, representation and power, and does so with recourse to sociolinguistic, discourse analytical and, to a lesser extent, postcolonial theory and method.

To unpack some of these questions, we turn first to a sociolinguistic tradition and the book that provides the title of this section, Graham Dann's (1996) *The Language of Tourism: A Sociolinguistic Perspective*. Dann starts his book (p. 2) with reference to notions such as 'the language of dance', 'the language of architecture' or 'the language of music', notions that call attention to the manner in which these domains of everyday life:

> have ways of communicating to us. They are structured. They follow certain grammatical rules and have specialized vocabularies. They are in many senses language-like in their properties. Analogically too, these languages convey messages, they have a heuristic or semantic content, they operate through a conventional system of symbols and codes. Many also include the equivalent of dialects and registers.
>
> *Dann (1996: 2)*

Dann's analogous use of language is (at least in this opening section of his book) part of a wider structuralist semiotic tradition. This tradition – whose perhaps most famous contributor is Roland Barthes – uses structuralist linguistic vocabulary (usually taken from de Saussure) to excavate and identify the underlying 'grammar' or *langue* (to use de Saussure's phrase) of a particular cultural system (such as clothing, fashion, photography, celebrity culture, etc.). Dann makes the case that tourism can also be compared with a language, suggesting 'that tourism, in the act of promotion, as well as in the accounts of its practitioners and clients, has a discourse of its own' (ibid.), the properties of which can be identified using sociolinguistic concepts and practices.

Dann identifies the various properties of this language of tourism with reference to tourism promotional material (including brochures, destination signage and the language used in organized tours) as well as practitioner/client accounts. Some of the properties he identifies are common to all languages, but others mark tourism as distinctive. The reason for this distinctiveness, and thus the reason why he impels us to think beyond tourism as 'just' being language-like, is that tourism is a language of social control. These distinctive properties are to be found in particular verbal and visual techniques of tourism production, and notably in the existence of multiple linguistic registers addressed to different types of tourist. These registers include: Ol'Talk (nostalgia tourism); Spasprech (health tourism); Gastrolingo (food and drink); and Greenspeak (ecotourism).

As noted in the introduction to this chapter, there are many different kinds of tourist and motivations for travel. The sociological and anthropological literature on tourism is characterized by a number of distinctive perspectives on the nature and motivation for tourism, perspectives that Dann uses to organize some of his analysis. Indeed, he argues that each of the four major perspectives from these disciplines has sociolinguistic correlates. These perspectives can be summarized as follows:

- The 'authenticity' perspective. Here, the search for 'authentic' social relations with the other is the primary driver of tourism. The language characteristic of this perspective involves enhancing the impression that the tourist will experience such authentic relations. As MacCannell (1976) famously argues, the tourist establishment is actually producing a 'staged' form of authenticity, one specifically manufactured for tourists, and based on the reduction, manipulation and commodification of other cultures. Drawing upon Marxist terminology, Dann (1996: 8) critiques such staged authenticity, arguing that it 'imbue[s] tourist with a false consciousness', with the result that 'far from becoming new persons as promised by advertising, tourists instead become victims of fantasy, prisoners of their own impulses, and mere imitators of those who supposedly represent the better life'.
- The 'strangehood' perspective. Here, the search for something strange, different and for new experiences is the primary driver of tourism. The language characteristic of this perspective is one of differentiation, and typically involves the use of binary oppositions (of contrasting nouns and verbs), similes, metaphors and other lexical means to produce representations of other places and people as 'strange' or 'different'. Interestingly, Dann notes that, although some tourism operators will play out the radical strangeness of a destination, others provide tourists with a more 'domesticated' view by promising a 'home away from home' and thus a familiar locale in the middle of a strange culture.
- The 'play' perspective. Associated with postmodern theory, tourism from this perspective is a spectacle or a game in which 'knowing' tourists are aware of, yet still enjoy, the consumption of artificially created cultural and linguistic experiences. Dann presents examples of research conducted in Barbados, where its slavery plantation heritage has been turned into a spectacle for tourists to enjoy called 'The Plantation Spectacular'. Dann critiques the manner in which such spectacles involve the distortion, sometimes even erasure, of historical and contemporary manifestations of colonial racism.
- The 'conflict' perspective takes an ideological lens and views tourism as a site of power struggle between different social groups especially with regard to questions of the economic benefits derived from tourist activity as well as ethical questions regarding which groups are responsible for representing and thus speaking on behalf of others. He illustrates these power struggles with reference to representations of Aboriginal and Native American cultures in tourism genres, and the manner in which the tourist establishment imposes the order and representations (e.g. through ethnocentric stereotyping, vocabularies and symbols) of mainstream society on minority groups. Dann labels tourism from this perspective as a language of appropriation that reproduces symbolic inequalities between cultural and ethnic groups.

We can extend the insights Dann offers into the language of tourism (especially as a language of social control) through these four perspectives, first with reference to Cardiff University's Centre for Language and Communication Research's project on Language and Global Communication. Over a series of publications, the multiple researchers on this project explored, among other things, the uses and representations of local languages and the social roles and negotiation of status in host–tourist interactions, in British TV holiday programmes. Using critical discourse analysis (CDA) and critical language awareness (CLA) as theoretical frames, their analyses illustrate the presence of all four perspectives on tourism within these TV programmes.

Jaworski *et al.* (2003a) discuss the discursive and performative deployment of the few languages other than English used in interactions between the TV presenters (proxies for tourists) and locals/hosts. The dataset comprised 106 episodes of two TV programmes and the detailed analysis of 246 examples of interaction. Although English is positioned in these programmes as a global language, they note how other languages are reduced to a few key phrases easily found in guidebooks and tourist brochures. Local languages are used for four key functions to authenticate the tourist experience of the presenter: expert talk (guided tours or explanations of local life); service encounters (such as buying food); phatic communion (to exchange greetings); naming and translating.

Jaworski *et al.* (2003a) critique the portrayal of local languages, and their speakers, in the programmes, arguing that they disempower the role of locals in interactions, and give the impression that communicating in the host language is effortless and requires little more than a few guidebook phrases. They develop a conflict perspective analysis in another piece published in the same year (Jaworski *et al.* 2003b), in which they conceptualize televised encounters as a site of power struggle where 'presenter-tourists ( ... ) construct for themselves parochial identities by adhering to stereotyped interpretations of local people and seeking "safe" interpretations of the host culture' (ibid.: 135).

The conflict perspective from Dann's framework can also be extended with reference to recent postcolonial analyses of tourism discourse, especially of so-called Third World tourism (usually tourism to formerly colonized societies in Africa, East Asia or Latin America). Postcolonial analyses, inspired by Edward Said's (1978) text *Orientalism*, set out to identify and critique the processes of othering that lead to the production of ethically problematic representations of other cultures. Underpinned by a constructionist notion of discourse (in which language serves to both enable and constrain, and therefore to regulate, understandings of concepts (in Said's text, the concept of 'the Orient')), othering refers to the ways in which linguistic representations serve to manufacture differences and inequalities between the self and the other. As Said illustrates in his text, these differences are constructed through the deployment of binary oppositions in which one side of the opposition (used to signify the self) is valued more positively, and thus comes to dominate, the other. In relation to tourism, Aitchison notes how:

> Tourist destinations as sites for tourists, and the people within them as sights for tourists, are frequently rendered Other by a tourist industry that has developed an unsigned colonialist and gendered hegemony in the form of a set of descriptors for constructing and representing 'Tropical Paradise'. These descriptors signify a colonial legacy where places are viewed as mystical or treasured landscapes preserved by time to be explored, and often exploited, in their natural state.
>
> *Aitchison (2001: 137)*

Aitchison is pointing to the continued presence of colonial imagery and ideology in contemporary tourism discourse, according to which the 'modern' tourists of the First World can be contrasted with a pre- or non-modern, timeless and unchanging Third World. The textual manufacturing of this contrast between the First and the Third Worlds is particularly well illustrated in Echtner and Prasad's (2003) analysis of the myths used in a corpus of tourism

*Table 34.1* Tourism myths

| Myths | Unchanged | Unrestrained | Uncivilized |
|-------|-----------|--------------|-------------|
| The place | Lands of legend | Lands of luxuriance | Lands at the limit |
| The time | Past | Present | Primordial |
| The natural | Significant silence | Soft | Savage |
| The built | Relics | Resorts | Significant silence |
| The host | Peasant (simple/stoic) | Pleasant (serving/smiling) | Primitive (savage/ surprising) |
| The tourist | Explorer into the past | Explorer into paradise | Expedition into the primitive |

*Source*: Echtner and Prasad (2003: 678). Reproduced with permission.

brochures to construct understandings of Third World destinations for First World tourists. They identified three principal 'Un'-myths in tourism marketing: the myth of the unchanged; the myth of the unrestrained; the myth of the uncivilized (see Table 34.1, which expands on the nature of these myths with regard to a number of different categories). These myths are an outcome of a set of binary oppositions where the other is signified as deficient or lacking, compared with the Western tourist (the self in this discourse). These myths therefore reproduce a colonial discourse in which the First World is constructed as superior (more civilized, more modern, etc.) than the Third World.

The language of tourism approach places an emphasis, then, on the identification and/or deconstruction of the discourses used by the tourist establishment. As with the tourism impacts approach, this second research perspective on tourism and intercultural communication has a number of limitations. First, the primary focus on textual analysis and critique means that scholars are perhaps overly concerned with exploring the content and forms of tourism discourse, rather than the structural and ideological interests and actors involved in the production and subsequent consumption/use/appropriation of these texts.

It is perhaps no surprise that these kinds of colonial image are present in contemporary tourism discourse given the fact that, as Echtner notes:

> Third World destinations are primarily promoted by multinational tour operators, travel agencies and other tourism corporations with origins in the First World. ( ... ) This situation creates a marketing system whereby the majority of the images used to represent Third World tourism destinations are selected by First World promoters in order to cater to the needs of consumers in developed countries.
>
> *Echtner (2002: 413–14)*

Taking a political economy approach to understanding the productive apparatus and ideological interests of the parties that provide tourism services offers an important way of contextualizing the language of tourism approach. Papen's (2005) ethnographic study of community-based tourism enterprises (CBTEs) in Namibia offers us an exemplar of how to combine a postcolonial discourse analytical lens with a global political economic one. Her study demonstrated the economic as well as the symbolic reproduction of a set of colonial structures and practices in the Namibian tourist context that create racially based inequalities between the country's white and black communities. Crucially, she shows that the marginalization of black tourism operators in Namibia is not just a consequence of local race relations but of the global nature of the tourist system. Most travellers to Namibia book their trip overseas through

multinational tour operators who already have links to predominantly white local tour operators, lodges and hotels, and certainly very few located in the black township areas of Windhoek.
Black CBTEs have little control over these material arrangements (and thus little capacity to get
into these tourist networks) and the destination images that position black Namibian life as
'culture' and fix it in time through the use of 'heritage' discourse.

The second limitation with the language of tourism approach is that it offers little insight into
how the constituent texts of a particular tourism discourse are mobilized and appropriated in
actual language use and intercultural communication. Evans-Pritchard's (1989) ethnographic
study of Native American (from the Pueblo and Navajo tribes) silversmiths in New Mexico,
and their perceptions and interactions with tourists visiting their shops, is another exemplary
work that can redress this limitation. She presents ethnographic data that not only demonstrate
the tribal members' awareness of the stereotypes that (American) tourists hold of them, but also
how they subverted and used these to profit from tourists' expectations. This intercultural
awareness was a prominent feature of Evans-Pritchard's informants' situationally specific interactions with tourists. Evans-Pritchard concludes that, in this instance, stereotypes can 'function
to defend' (1989: 89) the privacy of the tribal members, a view of stereotypes different from the
usually negative overtones they generate. These latter ethnographic data of intercultural
encounters provide an appropriate segue into the final approach covered in this chapter.

## 4. The intercultural encounters approach

The third approach is different from the individual and attitudinal focus of the first, and the
institutional and textual/discursive focus of the second. The intercultural encounters approach
takes 'interaction', and ideally 'naturally occurring' interaction, between locals and tourists as its
primary unit of analysis. Sociolinguistic and ethnographic research (characterized by the use of
participant observation methods in a cultural setting) constitute typical theoretical and methodological resources in this approach. Compared with the previous two perspectives, there is
significantly less research in/on tourism that falls within this approach, probably because of the
methodological challenges (notably gaining access and permission to record everyday interaction)
associated with it. We begin, however, with a well-known conceptual essay.

In the tourism studies literature, Cohen and Cooper's (1986) work on language and tourism – and in particular their notion of tourist talk (TT) – provides a detailed framework for
conceiving the contextual exigencies, linguistic differentiation and varieties of language spoken
in intercultural communicative encounters between tourists and locals. Their framework draws,
first, upon traditional sociolinguistic concepts beginning with foreigner talk (FT), which they
define as 'a *simplified register* which the members of a speech community consider appropriate for
use with outsiders who have imperfect mastery of the community's language' (Cohen and
Cooper 1986: 536, italics added). They call FT a 'register' as it comprises a language variety
linked to a specific use, and simplified as 'members of the community view it as a more basic
version of the normal adult vernacular' (ibid.) in terms of lexical variability and syntactic
complexity.

The authors supplement their sociolinguistic framework by drawing from the sociological
literature to suggest that, although it is often the case that users of FT typically have higher
status than those who receive it, the tourist context often involves a reversal of this situation that
impacts on the question of who speaks in which language to whom. That is to say, in the
tourist context, it is typically the foreigner rather than the local who is of higher status (usually
FT involves the opposite in the sociolinguistics literature, as in the case of migrant workers for
example) with the result that linguistic acculturation of the tourist to the local is unusual.

Cohen and Cooper (1986) label this type of speech tourist talk (TT) to differentiate it from FT, although it can still be considered a simplified register depending on context.

Also inspired by sociology, the authors critique sociolinguistic scholarship for its lack of consideration of the impact of the high degree of temporariness of tourists on patterns of linguistic accommodation and intercultural communication between locals and foreigners. They speculate that the linguistic reversal enacted in TT will be compounded by the fact that tourists typically have neither the time nor the opportunity to learn a language during their stay and that locals do not usually expect it. Indeed, the economic benefits to be derived from communicating with foreign tourists tend to provide sufficient motivation for many tourism providers to engage in foreign language learning. Having said this, the diversity of tourists, contexts and locals' language proficiency means that the specifics of language accommodation and thus intercultural communication will vary considerably.

In order to capture and describe some of the hypothesized linguistic diversity of touristic contexts, they draw upon some of Cohen's earlier work – a typology of tourist types – to organize their discussion. Cohen's typology describes two principal forms of tourism according to the extent to which 'a tourist exposes [sic] himself to the strangeness of the host society or, contrariwise, encloses himself within the familiarity of the "environmental bubble" of his home society provided by the tourist establishment' (ibid.: 539–40). The two principal forms of tourism and conjectured linguistic practices can be summarized as follows:

- 'Institutionalized' tourism (where tourists stay in the 'bubble'). Here, local tourist personnel will be expected to speak the tourist's language, or a lingua franca, with a high degree of competence. To this end, language learning is typically formally studied by personnel and will involve the acquisition of polite speech and specialized vocabulary. Host–tourist encounters will be formal (with formal role definitions) and instrumental (rather than personal) in orientation. For those tourists who leave the tourist bubble and enter the fringes of the tourist establishment (labelled individual mass tourists by the authors), such as local bars or shops, some competence will be required of hosts, but competence would be expected to be generally lower than in the central establishment. Sometimes, a pseudo-personalized style of speech will be developed by members of some tourist-related service occupations, and there may well be an element of playfulness, and metalinguistic awareness, between the host and the tourist as they interact with one another.
- 'Non-institutionalized' tourism (where tourists expose themselves to the local culture to a greater degree) involves individuals and groups that make limited or no use of the tourist establishment's services. Cohen and Cooper (1986) suggest that, in these contexts, there will be a great variety of local competence in tourist language, and tourists may well be required to engage in linguistic accommodation of their own. Locals will probably use a highly simplified register of TT and, together, these characteristics of language in non-institutionalized tourism may well create numerous communication problems for tourists. Cohen and Cooper encourage researchers to study the kinds of communication that emerge in situations of total linguistic strangeness for tourists, especially the development by tourists of a private patois or a spontaneous pidgin for purposes of intercultural communication.

The utility of Cohen and Cooper's framework lies, in part, in the fact that it is ripe for empirical application, testing and refinement. It provides researchers with a clear way of mapping out some potential sociolinguistic and sociological relationships between tourists, hosts and the intercultural communication that might ensue between them. However, there are inevitably limitations with such a conceptual framework that is rather sparing in its use of detailed empirical evidence. Huisman and Moore (1998), for instance, argue that many of Cohen and Cooper's suggestions depend on the specific national languages being talked about. Based on interviews and questionnaires with German tourists visiting New Zealand, they found that these particular tourists expressed little desire for their New Zealand hosts to accommodate their German language. In fact, they stated that it would reduce the enjoyment of the trip and the challenge of communicating in a foreign language, which they relished. For the tourists in this sample, they expected to adopt the host language and, in so doing, they expressed a desire to escape the dominant language of tourism and its various attempts at linguistic accommodation. One wonders whether these same tourists (who probably learned English in school) would have been so willing to communicate in a foreign language if they went to a country where they knew significantly less of the host language than is the case here.

Snow's (2004) study of the impact of international tourism in the village of Old Bank, on the island of Bastimentos, Panama, provides detailed empirical insights into the kinds of issues outlined by Cohen and Cooper (1986) within the specific historical national language context of Spanish and Panamanian Creole Englishes (PCEs). Until recently, and for geographical and historical reasons, Western Caribbean Creole English speakers in Panama have had to learn Spanish to participate fully in society, thereby creating a necessary bilingualism in communities such as Old Bank. Echoing the minority language issues in the Welsh case outlined earlier, local concerns have pertained to the question of whether, over time, varieties of English Creole would diminish as Spanish took firmer hold in the everyday life of Old Bank.

However, Snow argues, the development of international tourism in this part of Panama has fundamentally changed the conditions of contact between PCE speakers and those of other languages. Of the PCE spoken in Old Bank, he remarks that it is:

> proving to be an economically viable alternative to Spanish in interactions with tourists. Indeed, the variety of Panamanian Creole English spoken in Old Bank appears to be strengthening and may become even more vital as the region's economy shifts from bananas to tourism.
>
> *Snow (2004: 116)*

Snow draws upon data from his ethnographic study (60 hours of interviews; observations of interactions in homes and public spaces) to provide some fascinating insights into the language dimensions of international communication in a tourist context, notably the great utility of English in communicating with international tourists.

The transcripts of selected interactions between locals and tourists that Snow analyses illustrate how tourists and locals negotiate in situ the choice of language in which to communicate across cultures. The data demonstrate speakers' metalinguistic awareness as they initially negotiate language choice. Snow uses the concept of 'language ideologies' to interpret these insights, a concept that can be defined as 'any sets of beliefs about language articulated by the users as a rationalization or justification of perceived language structure and use' (Silverstein 1979: 193, in Snow 2004: 121). Snow takes the view that tourist encounters are sites in which language ideologies are produced and used to negotiate and articulate language choice. In his dataset, he shows how the deployment of language ideologies came to have the following outcomes for intercultural communication: English rather than Spanish becomes the preferred language for tourist communication; distinctions, and tensions, between different types of English language/Creole speakers are erased as a clear boundary is constructed in interaction between English and Spanish speakers; aware that many English-speaking international tourists will not understand their Creole, PCE speakers frequently accommodate by altering their speech.

## 5. Future directions

As noted in the introduction, tourism as a context for intercultural communication scholarship has been rather neglected. This is not to say that there is no research on the particularities of language(s) and intercultural communication in the distinctive context of tourism. Rather, it is surprising and disappointing, given the manner in which the rise in tourism has multiplied opportunities for transcultural linguistic encounters in recent decades, that not more has been done. This state of affairs represents a wonderful opportunity for new scholars to make a contribution and to take this multidisciplinary area of scholarship in exciting future directions.

First, future scholars might consider broadening and deepening the insights of extant research encapsulated by the three principal approaches. This task might involve adopting one of the theoretical and methodological approaches outlined above, be it that of social psychology and the survey questionnaire, critical discourse analysis/sociolinguistic analysis of the texts and visual materials of tourism discourse, or the careful linguistic analysis of transcripts of naturally occurring talk captured as part of an ethnographic study. Alternatively, scholars might consider combining and either integrating, or holding in productive tension, two or more of these theoretical and methodological approaches. Clarity will be required on the theoretical assumptions that researchers are making about tourism and intercultural communication, as well as some reflexivity about the impact of their presence and their own intercultural positions on that which they observe.

Second, we would highly recommend that more ethnographic research be conducted into tourism and intercultural communication, which can provide the lived and rich contextual insights that are currently missing from much of the tourism impacts and language of tourism approaches. In our own work (Jack and Phipps 2005), we adopted an ethnographic approach to the study of tourism and intercultural communication. The insights we provided regarding how, and with what effects, intercultural communication between tourists is/can be fostered drew attention to the vital role of material objects as well as story-telling in tourist contexts (e.g. youth hostel kitchens, hotel receptions, standing around at monuments and overhearing conversations in cafes) as a facilitator of intercultural communication. We would never have considered the importance of these objects and stories had we not had firsthand experience of participating in and observing their importance to tourism and intercultural communication.

## Related topics

Critical pedagogy; English as a global language; ethnography; ideology; intercultural communicative competence; intergroup contact; intercultural training; othering, postcolonialism

## Further reading

Dahles, H. (2002) 'The politics of tour guiding: image management in Indonesia,' *Annals of Tourism Research*, 29(3): 783–800 (an excellent, ethnographic insight into the political dimensions of tour guiding and its potential impact on intercultural communication).

Spencer-Rodgers, J. and McGovern, T. (2002) 'Attitudes toward the culturally different: the role of intercultural communication barriers, affective responses, consensual stereotypes, and perceived threat', *International Journal of Intercultural Relations*, 26: 609–31 (this is a good example of a social psychological, quantitative approach to intercultural communication research and especially its affective elements).

## References

Aitchison, C. (2001) 'Theorizing Other discourses of tourism, gender and culture: can the subaltern speak (in tourism)?', *Tourist Studies*, 1(2): 133–47.

Allport, G.W. (1954) *The Nature of Prejudice*, Cambridge, MA: Addison-Wesley.

Brougham, J. and Butler, R. (1981) 'A segmentation analysis of resident attitudes to the social impact of tourism', *Annals of Tourism Research*, 8(4): 569–90.

Brunt, P. and Courtney, P. (1999) 'Host perceptions of sociocultural impacts', *Annals of Tourism Research*, 26(3): 493–515.

Cohen, E. and Cooper, R. (1986) 'Language and tourism', *Annals of Tourism Research*, 13: 533–63.

Dann, G.M.S. (1996) *The Language of Tourism: A Sociolinguistic Perspective*, Wallingford, UK: CAB International.

Dörnyei, Z. and Csizér, K. (2005) 'The effects of intercultural contact and tourism on language attitudes and language learning motivation', *Journal of Language and Social Psychology*, 24: 327–57.

Echtner, C.M. (2002) 'The content of Third World tourism marketing: a 4A approach', *International Journal of Tourism Research*, 4: 413–34.

Echtner, C.M. and Prasad, P. (2003) 'The context of Third World tourism marketing', *Annals of Tourism Research*, 30(3): 660–82.

Evans-Pritchard, D. (1989) 'How "they" see "us": Native American images of tourists', *Annals of Tourism Research*, 16: 89–105.

Hofstede, G.H. (1980) *Culture's Consequences: International Differences in Work-related Values*, Beverly Hills, CA: Sage.

Huisman, S. and Moore, K. (1998) 'Natural language and that of tourism,' *Annals of Tourism Research*, 26 (2): 445–49.

Jack, G. and Phipps, A. (2005) *Tourism and Intercultural Exchange: Why Tourism Matters*, Clevedon: Channel View Publications.

Jaworski, A., Thurlow, C., Lawson, S. and Ylänne-McEwen, V. (2003a) 'The uses and representations of local languages in tourist destinations: a view from British TV holiday programmes', *Language Awareness*, 12(1): 5–29.

Jaworski, A., Ylänne-McEwen, V., Thurlow, C. and Lawson, S. (2003b) 'Social roles and negotiation of status in host–tourist interaction: a view from British television holiday programmes', *Journal of Sociolinguistics*, 7(2): 135–63.

Leclerc, D. and Martin, J. (2004) 'Tour guide communication competence – French, German and American tourist perspectives', *International Journal of Intercultural Relations*, 28: 181–200.

MacCannell, D. (1976) *The Tourist: A New Theory of the Leisure Class*, New York: Schocken Books.

McSweeney, B. (2002) 'Hofstede's model of national cultural differences and their consequences: A triumph of faith – A failure of analysis', *Human Relations*, 55(1): 89–118.

Murphy, P.E. (1985) *Tourism: A Community Approach*, London: Routledge.

Papen, U. (2005) 'Exclusive, ethno and eco: representations of culture and nature in tourism discourses in Namibia', in A. Jaworski and A. Pritchard (eds) *Discourse, Communication and Power*, Clevedon: Channel View Publications, pp. 79–97.

Prentice, R. and Hudson, J. (1993) 'Assessing the linguistic dimension in the perception of tourism impacts by residents of a tourist destination: a case study of Porthmadog, Gwynedd', *Tourism Management*, 14(4): 298–306.

Reisinger, Y. and Turner, L. (1997) 'Cross-cultural differences in tourism: Indonesian tourists in Australia', *Tourism Management*, 18(3): 139–47.

——(1999) 'A cultural analysis of Japanese tourists: challenges for tourism marketers', *European Journal of Marketing*, 33(11/12): 1203–27.

——(2002) 'Cultural differences between Asian tourist markets and Australian hosts', *Journal of Travel Research*, 40: 295–315.

Said, E. (1978) *Orientalism: Western Conceptions of the Orient*, London: Penguin.

Silverstein, M. (1979) 'Language structure and linguistic ideology', in P. Clyne, W. Hanks and C. Hofbauer (eds) *The Elements: A Parasession on Units and Levels*, Chicago, IL: Chicago Linguistics Society, pp. 93–247.

Snow, P. (2004) 'Tourism and small-language persistence in a Panamanian Creole village', *International Journal of the Sociology of Language*, 166: 113–28.

Weightman, B.A. (1987) 'Third World tour landscapes', *Annals of Tourism Research* 14: 227–39.

# Section V
# New debates and future directions

# 35

# A global agenda for intercultural communication research and practice

*Malcolm N. MacDonald and John P. O'Regan*

## 1. Introduction

This chapter identifies key issues and topics in intercultural communication set out in the preceding chapters and places them in the wider context of globalization and transnational mobility. It goes on to outline contributions that have been made in recent intercultural communication research, to highlight trends in research methods and to propose areas where further work can be carried out. These are tied in with some suggestions for pedagogic practice and continuing professional development, and we conclude with some thoughts about the possible future of intercultural communication.

Paradoxically, two concepts that remain problematic in intercultural communication are the idea of culture itself, and the ways in which this relates to the identities of human actors. As we have seen in this volume, the nation-state is still often regarded as the default signifier of cultural identification, although its centrality to the conceptualization of culture and to intercultural communication is contested (Holliday 2011). First, there are 'cultures' with which individuals identify that both exceed and traverse the boundaries of the nation-state. These include pan-national geographical and political groupings such as 'Asia', 'Africa' and 'Latin America', professional and academic associations such as those listed at the end of this chapter as well as the transnational networks described below. Second, it has been forcefully argued (e.g. McSweeney 2002) that members of any cultural grouping or network – be it national or transnational – do not actually subscribe in a monolithic fashion to sets of behaviours, values and attitudes that are *a priori* homogeneous and consistent over time, as suggested by the early survey research (Chapter 1).

Numerous qualitative studies in the field are now describing how more contingent facets of human agency and a person's sense of self are realized through communication in particular social contexts. On the one hand, social identity is arguably constituted through a series of performative acts that are responsive to the context of communication (Pennycook 2004). Here, 'culture' is performed by social actors in real time and, in a recent radical analysis of internet chatroom talk, only becomes noteworthy when made relevant in the talk of its Chinese and Korean interlocutors (Brandt and Jenks 2011). On the other hand, subjectivity is manifested in a phenomenological sense of self that unfolds through time and is becoming increasingly fluid and unstable as members of modern social elites engage in ever more fragmented forms of activity (Bauman 2000). Narrative accounts of the ambivalent experience of Japanese students returning from overseas study (*kikokushijo*) provide evidence of the conflicts and contradictions that can arise from a protracted engagement with another culture (Ford 2009). The relationship between identity and culture has been discussed extensively within this volume (e.g. Chapters 2, 11 and 13) and remains a recurrent theme in what follows.

## 2. Historical perspectives and emergent themes

The issues in the study of intercultural communication described in earlier chapters are coterminous with the phenomenon of globalization. For Turner (2010),

> globalization involves the compression of time and space, the increased interconnectivity of human groups, the increased values of the exchange of commodities, people and ideas, and finally the emergence of various forms of global consciousness which ... we may call cosmopolitanism.
>
> *Turner (2010: 5)*

A central feature of globalization is the movement of populations between nation-states, referred to as 'transnational mobility' (e.g. Faist 2004). Three features of transnational mobility simultaneously impact upon the conditions of intercultural communication and are constituted by it: the numbers of people migrating and the directions in which they move in a particular historical period; the social conditions under which migrants reside within the modern nation-state; and the sociopsychological relationship of migrants to their home country and their country of destination.

According to the International Organization for Migration (2010), 'there are now about 192 million people living outside their place of birth, which is about three per cent of the world's population'. Hoerder (2002) also estimated that there are also around 25 million refugees who live 'in transition'. Many migrants move to gain more lucrative work in Europe and North America, while large numbers travel from Asia to the Gulf States. Further movements of populations also take place internally across distinct regional zones within nation-states, for example in the recent movement of labour from rural to urban areas of China. However, in the twenty-first century, we are seeing an unexpected change in the dynamic of population flows. We are also witnessing not a continuing exponential increase but rather increasing attempts to regulate and inhibit the flow of populations, particularly in the case of movements to the North from the South. We anticipate that this change in the dynamic of transnational migration will impact upon the patterns of intercultural communication that take place both 'within borders' – between members of migrant and majority groups within destination countries – and 'across borders' – between migrant groups, their families and other social networks that they wish to maintain with their countries of origin.

Within borders, communication between minority and majority ethnic groups is inextricably linked to the accessibility of citizens and non-citizens to equal rights under law, and the positioning of members of minority ethnic groups within the nation-states in which they find themselves. The relationship between migration and the granting of citizenship to long-term migrant workers is complex and varies from country to country and region to region. For example, Australia and Canada pursue a policy of selective immigration through which it is possible for migrants in favourable circumstances to obtain citizenship after a prolonged period of residence. However, for guest workers coming from outside the EU to those European countries that pursue more open immigration policies, citizenship is less readily available; and, in many cases, such as for those seeking temporary work in the Gulf States, it is simply un-achievable (Hoerder 2002: 575–76). Recently, however, there has been an intensification of the barriers to be surmounted by migrant workers seeking citizenship. The most recent Migrant Integration Policy Index (2006–7) shows that eleven out of the then twenty-five countries in the European Union now set citizenship tests.

For immigrants who do achieve citizenship within a destination country, relations between majority and minority groups, as well as between different minority groups, remain problematic (Modood 2007). For some time, multiculturalism has been the policy of choice not only for states that have incorporated diverse ethnic, religious and linguistic groups from their inception (e.g. India, Indonesia, Malaysia, the Philippines and Singapore) but also for those that are pre-pared to grant citizenship to new arrivals (e.g. Australia, Canada, France, New Zealand and the UK). However, the realization of the policy of multiculturalism in different countries varies, and different forms have been contested over the years (Kivisto 2002). Ideally, multiculturalism recognizes diversity between different groups within a society or nation-state and upholds the rights of members of different ethnic groups to practise distinctive cultural practices such as religion, language, dress, music and cuisine. However, given asymmetries of power between majority and minority ethnic groups, the complex differentiation of cultural practices between minority groups and the challenges of incorporating an array of languages and religions, festivals and public holidays into any national public life, it is virtually impossible to recognize the cultural practices of different groups equally. Somewhere, certain groups are going to lose out – and these are unlikely to include the most dominant one. Thus, critics argue that multiculturalism still leans overmuch towards the assimilation of minorities towards one dominant set of cultural practices, rather than a process of multilateral integration where the cultural practices of every ethnic group are accorded equal place (Modood 2007).

The outcome of increasing doubts about multiculturalism from both functional and ethical viewpoints has lead to a radical shift in policy taking place within the European Union. Now it is intercultural communication that is placed at the heart of the social cohesion of multiethnic European states. The Council of Europe's (2008) White Paper on Intercultural Dialogue asserts that '… old approaches to the management of cultural diversity were no longer adequate to societies in which the degree of that diversity … was unprecedented and ever-growing'. Instead, the paper proposes that the pursuit of 'intercultural dialogue' both as policy and as social practice would uphold the values of diversity, human rights, freedom of expression and equality of opportunity more successfully than multiculturalism (ibid.: 25–27). For the Council of Europe, intercultural dialogue is understood as: ' … an open and respectful exchange of views between individuals, groups with different ethnic, cultural, religious and linguistic back-grounds and heritage on the basis of mutual understanding and respect' (ibid.: 10). This dialogue requires three areas of competence: participation in democratic citizenship; learning languages – particularly those that predominate in the state; and knowledge of the history of different ethnic groups. However, as Byram emphasizes, intercultural citizenship is not just limited to mediation within the single nation-state. It ' … goes beyond this, involving both activity with other people in the world, and the competences required for dialogue with people of other languacultures' (Chapter 5, this volume).

So far, we have been describing transnational mobility very much in terms of the 'container model' of nation-state, where individuals are conceived of as moving from one geographically and politically bounded space to another. However, more recent empirical research into the social and economic conditions of migration indicates that the migrant experience is less amenable to crude binaries of regional or national affiliation (Faist 2004), and it has been rede-scribed in ways that reflect the economic, social and communication conditions of globalization (Faist 2000; Hannerz 1996; Portes 1996; Pries 1999).

This has led to the reconceptualization of the idea of space, both as an analytical category and as the experience of individual actors. On this analysis, space is neither identical with state ter-ritories, nor indeed with particular physical or geographical locations. Instead, space stands for the 'cultural, economic and political practices' of territorially located actors, and constitutes the 'links' between different places (Faist 2004: 4). Where these practices are interactions that take place between individual actors who have bonds to two or more nation-states, they become part of 'transnational space'. These practices represent an expansion of social space across terri-torial boundaries, which has led to 'a transformation in the spatial organisation of social and symbolic relations' (Faist 2004: 3). The social aspect of space consists of 'ties', which are ongoing transactions between three or more people. Transactions are the symbolic aspect of social space including 'meanings, memories, expectations for the future and collective representations'.

Transnational spaces are classified by Faist into four ideal types: 'areas of diffusion', organiza-tions and communities, issue networks and small groups (2004: 3–10). Many of the intercultural communication contexts set out in Section IV of this volume entail a diffusion of social ties and symbolic relations between participants in which information, goods, services and capital are exchanged. These include forms of pedagogic activity and exchange, both formal and informal (Chapters 23, 25, 26, 27, 28 and 29); contexts that require mediation across languages such as translation and interpreting (Chapter 31); health care settings (Chapter 32); legal contexts (Chapter 33); and tourist excursions (Chapter 34). According to Faist, although the social ties of areas of diffusion remain relatively stable across national boundaries, they entail low levels of formalization and a relatively low intensity of relations between participants.

In contrast, transnational organizations, such as multinational corporations, and transnational communities, such as religious movements, operate over prolonged periods of time at high levels of formalization. Transnational communities chiefly comprise religious movements, par-ticularly the more populous worldwide religions of Buddhism, Christianity, Hinduism, Islam and Judaism. Religious diasporas also form distinctive transnational communities. These are distinguished by the 'closeness' of their symbolic ties (Faist 2004: 9), as these transnational communities achieve a certain emotional intensity and distinctive semiotic power from the symbolic content of their religious ceremonies, texts and practices.

Transnational issue networks involve the exchange of information and services between persons and organizations in order to attain some shared purpose (Faist 2004). Unlike transna-tional organizations and communities, they operate at relatively low levels of formalization. Issue networks include non-governmental organizations (NGOs), human rights organizations and networks focusing on particular scientific or technological issues.

Finally, 'small groups' that are dispersed across national boundaries include principally households or families. Although these kinship systems are scattered, they exhibit high degrees of formalization. Household or family members can become dispersed abroad to work within a multinational company, or travel to another country or region to seek employment as contract workers. Key to the communication between these networks is the remittance of income back to family members in their countries of origin.

## 3. Critical issues and topics

Here, we revisit the core issues featured in Section II of this book: language and identity, communication and culture, intercultural transitions and communicative competence.

For Kramsch and Uryu (Chapter 13), 'identity' is a term that refers to the sets of social relations that a human being creates and maintains within a social group or culture, whereas 'subjectivity' refers to a human being's sense of self. A parallel dualism is reflected in the way in which forms of relations are conceived of as being constituted between intercultural actors. From one perspective, intercultural communication is conceived as a form of dialogue that is able to render permeable the boundaries between individual actors derived from the hypostatized diversity of their cultures. However, we maintain that there are limits to dialogue. In our view, a fundamental condition of intercultural communication also arises from 'difference', whereby each individual social actor remains existentially separate. Difference is created and maintained not only through the types of linguistic and non-linguistic semiotic systems described in this book, but also through less contingent biological and social features such as corporeality, ethnicity and access to economic and cultural capital.

In the same vein, this volume has also considered the relationship between language and identity in order to consider the ways in which the 'diverse diversities' (Chapter 11) of participants are constituted through linguistic interactions and discursive practices executed in micro-contexts. For example, Shi and Langman (Chapter 10) analyse how the constitution of gendered identities is performed in the flow of communication in a hybrid context, where students negotiate the interstices between the performance of Chinese and American identities required of them in a US university management training seminar. The seminar thus becomes a site where relations of power are played out, not only as the participants interact in an adversarial role play but also as the communicative practices of the educational subject *qua* negotiator are constituted as a form of cultural capital. In contrast, Charalambous and Rampton (Chapter 12) address the ideological role that language choice plays in the creation and maintenance of the unified nation-state. Although the use of English and the assumption of 'Americanized' identities by Shi's subjects (Chapter 10) was socially and politically uncontroversial within the context of a US management training seminar, the introduction of the Turkish language to Greek-Cypriots by Charalambous's and Rampton's teacher was perceived as highly contentious by members of the social groups that interfaced with the class. On this account, the assumption that an encounter with another language and culture will necessarily lead to a harmonious dialogue seems rather less secure.

Preceding chapters have also considered written, spoken and nonverbal forms of communication and the extent to which these function at a universal level, a national–cultural level or at the level of the individual subject. However, a major question remains concerning the different levels at which these operate and the relationships between them. In Chapter 6, Risager posits four interrelated dimensions for the global flow of communication: that of the language system ('linguistic flows'); that of the relationship between meaning and L1 ('linguacultural flows'); and that of meaning not necessarily related to particular languages ('discursive flows'), as well as other cultural flows such as non-linguistic and behavioural meanings. The relationship between universal and context-specific behavioural meanings is also taken up by Matsumoto and Hwang in Chapter 8. Although earlier research has suggested that seven universal facial expressions of emotion can be identified, the authors present evidence of a battery of other behavioural displays of meaning – facial expression, gesture, gaze, voice, space, touch, posture and gait – which do suggest patterns specific to members of different cultural groupings. In a similar vein in Chapter 9, Cheng also challenges early conceptualizations of universal characteristics of 'facework' (e.g. Brown and Levinson 1978, 1987) and proposes that the negotiation of face might also reflect patterns specific to diverse national or ethnic groups. Here, it is suggested that the maintenance of politeness in verbal interactions displays patterns that are isomorphic with the cultural systems of different nation-states.

Evidence in this volume therefore supports the idea that, although some phenomena operate very much at a global level, some are contextualized much more narrowly within local contexts, relating to a national or regional culture or to 'smaller' cultures such as the language classroom or project team. Thus, it is possible to retain the proposition that there is some homogeneity of communicative behaviours that are shared by members of the same broadly defined cultural groupings but at the same time to acknowledge, first, that some features of human communication are more amenable than others to homogenized patterning within cultural groups and, second, that individual members of cultural groups might not share the personal sense of identification ascribed to them by their visible patterns of linguistic and non-linguistic behaviour.

A third critical issue in the study of intercultural communication is the conceptualization of intercultural competence. Chapter 18 has traced the emergence of the term 'intercultural speaker' and how the goal of intercultural competence came to challenge the idealized conceptualization of the native speaker as the goal of language education (Byram *et al.* 2001; Kramsch 1998). However, in our view, no modelling of intercultural competence is context free. This volume has described four types of social situations in which different modalities of intercultural competence are deployed: the teaching and learning of a foreign language as the goal of an educational programme (Chapters 5, 18, and 26); the use and acquisition of a second language as membership of an immigrant group (Chapter 15); the variation of a single language within a multidialectical speech situation (Chapter 19); and the use and acquisition of a foreign or second language in the workplace (Chapter 30). The challenge remains whether any one model of competence can be developed that can be applied reliably to every intercultural context, or whether multiple models of competence should be developed in particular contexts with high levels of specificity.

One of the most commonly held universal principles of intercultural communication is reflected by Wilkinson in Chapter 18 as 'sensitivity towards other people and cultures coupled with self-reflexivity', and it is this that leads to mediation as a form of intercultural praxis. Likewise, for Fantini, writing in Chapter 16, 'awareness' emerges as central to cross-cultural development. Whereas, for Fantini, different conceptualizations of culture are associated with different linguistic systems, for Sharifian in Chapter 19, these are also associated with different dialects within one language. Sharifian therefore suggests adding 'metacultural competence' under the knowledge category in Byram's classic model (1997; Byram *et al.* 2001) to reflect 'the understanding that one language may be used to encode several systems of cultural conceptualizations'. In Chapter 5, Byram himself expands these original precepts to combine competence in citizenship with communicative competence as a necessary goal so that subjects can participate in a broader political sphere than the singular nation state.

Byram and colleagues' framework for intercultural citizenship communication is very much envisaged from the 'inside looking out' – for members of an identifiable cultural entity, often a nation-state, aspiring to engage with a broader global context in terms of attitudes, beliefs and values as well as linguistic performance. For Giles *et al.*, intercultural communication is conceived from the 'outside looking in'. In Chapter 15, they describe intercultural competence from a social psychological perspective as communication accommodation theory in order to explain the reasons for convergence or divergence on the part of intercultural speakers in second language contexts, particularly while communicating with dominant social groups. Yet, like Wilkinson, a key component in Giles *et al.*'s description of communication accommodation remains sensitivity. For them, it is required for speakers to achieve the necessary variability in communication practices that is necessary for particular social situations.

However, in our view, three things need to be considered in order to understand the aetiology of different modalities of intercultural competence. First, any particular set of parameters for intercultural competence is coterminous with the specific social context in which communicative praxis takes place. At a micro-level, this includes 'small cultural' contexts such as the language classroom (Chapters 26 and 27), sites of study abroad programmes (Chapter 28) and tourism (Chapter 34). At a macro-level, they also include contemporary social, economic and political conditions. Second, a variety of disciplines have informed the descriptions of intercultural competence in this volume: social psychology (Chapter 15), social cognition and sociolinguistics (Chapter 19), education (Chapter 5), anthropology and ethnography (Chapter 18). The different constituents of intercultural communicative competence inevitably reflect the epistemological concerns of any one discipline. The third condition for a framework for intercultural competence is its evidence base, i.e. the extent to which it is based on data and the ways in which that data are used. Thus, the principles for intercultural communicative competence can be established deductively, in anticipation of the performance of intercultural interactions, and thereby act as criteria for its relative success; alternatively, they can be derived inductively, emerging from the analysis of sets of empirically collected data.

Other accounts of research and practice in intercultural competence have gone beyond the educational contexts described above. For example, the present authors were recently engaged in the research and design of the UK National Occupational Standards for Intercultural Working, and proposed the introduction of more inductive approaches in order to ground standards criteria in 'empirical data gleaned from workplace contexts' (MacDonald *et al.* 2009: 389). Coming from a very different perspective, Spencer-Oatey has also analysed transcripts of naturally occurring speech in intercultural business settings in order to establish empirically grounded descriptions of the pragmatic features of successful intercultural interaction (Spencer-Oatey and Franklin 2009). Further intercultural communication research using inductive data is required to understand the ways in which intercultural competence is constructed in real-time language. This would then sit alongside the existing curricular principles and the extensive introspective, attitudinal and psychological data derived from the disciplines of education and social psychology.

## 4. Current contributions and future directions

The sociological conceptualizations of transnational space described above have implications for research in intercultural communication, both present and future. To date, this research has engaged extensively with Faist's 'areas of diffusion' such as pedagogic contexts (e.g. Chapters 26 and 27) and tourism (Chapter 34), as well as transnational organizations such as multinational corporations (reflected in part in Chapters 29 and 30). However, intercultural communication within other types of transnational space remains underresearched, in particular within transnational communities, transnational issue networks and 'small groups'. Although Witteborn (2007a, b, 2008) has carried out research into the discursive practices of diasporic Arab communities resident in the USA, many features of intercultural communication within and between religious faiths are yet to be described. Witteborn (2010) has recently described how the notion of global citizenship is constituted as a discursive practice through the webpages of a major international NGO. However, little or no research has described intercultural communication either in the range of 'issue networks' described above, or in Faist's 'small groups' of transnational kinship systems and families.

Thus, there is scope for intercultural communication researchers to engage with the experiences of less privileged groups of sojourners such as migrant workers and those seeking asylum and refuge. For neither of these populations is travel a luxury, and accounts of their intercultural experience might be more challenging than those mainly recorded so far – of elite groups travelling for education, commerce or tourism. There is already an emerging engagement with these issues that often uses a case study approach. For example, Miles's (2010) study describes ways in which the identity of a multilingual male French citizen of Senegalese descent adopts the role of a mediator between immigrant workers and the native English speakers within a multinational corporation situated in the USA. And Alison Phipps's (2010) keynote conference speech to the International Association of Languages and Intercultural Communication gave a powerful account of a young Eritrean women struggling to gain political asylum in the UK.

Another context with which the academy has not traditionally engaged is the role of intercultural communication within warfare and security. The events of 9/11 and their aftermath have intensified the global visibility of the intercultural dimension to the conflict between different forms of fundamentalism – and particularly in relation to the wars currently being conducted by US and UK forces in Iraq and Afghanistan. There appears to be increasing awareness within the US and UK military of the potential for intercultural communication as a way of mediating conflict situations. However, the literature on this appears to be largely confined to periodicals that circulate within the military itself (e.g. Simpson 2007). There appear to be further possibilities here for both intercultural communication researchers and instructors.

Although the study of intercultural communication has persistently attempted to broaden the focus of language learning and teaching away from the dominance of hegemonic global languages, the range of languages addressed within intercultural communication research still remains limited. This volume has reflected a preoccupation with the teaching and use of predominantly European languages, inevitably English, but also the mainstream 'modern and foreign languages' such as French, German and Spanish. In particular, intercultural communication in other global languages such as Chinese and Arabic has yet to be extensively described, as well as Japanese, the language spoken by the third most powerful economy in the world. Thus, not only is there still a need to develop intercultural communication research in several of the historically and economically most important global languages, but also with regard to minority and aboriginal languages. This applies less perhaps to minority languages and aboriginal studies in multicultural societies in the North, such as Punjabi in the UK (e.g. Rampton 1999), Afro-American dialects in the USA (e.g. Alim and Perry 2011), Carbaugh's description of intercultural communication among the Blackfeet Native Americans (2005) as well as Aboriginal English in Australia (Chapter 19, this volume), but it certainly applies to languages that are spoken in smaller and less economically developed countries and regions of the globe, for example in parts of Latin America and the islands of the Pacific.

In its research paradigms, intercultural communication often seems riven with dichotomies that reflect the epistemological and ontological assumptions of its diverse disciplinary origins (Holliday 2010). Again, this applies in particular to the articulation of 'culture' within different theoretical frameworks. Thus, 'culture' can be an explanatory concept that precedes the phenomena analysed by empirical research (*a priori*/deductive), or 'culture' can be performed by agents as an effect of communication (*a fortiori*/inductive). Approaches informed by social psychology largely subscribe to *a priori* conceptualizations of culture, often conceived as forms of social representation, whereas critical and poststructuralist approaches generally subscribe to the notion of culture as 'performativity' (e.g. Pennycook 2004). In fact, for Dervin (Chapter 11), the concept of culture has become so problematic that he advocates the study of 'interculturality without culture'.

However, this volume reflects the longstanding trend in intercultural communication research towards the eschewal of more positivistic, social scientific approaches using quantitative research methods (e.g. experimental design, surveys, interaction and content analysis) towards more interpretive qualitative approaches that deploy methods such as ethnography, in-depth interviews and case studies. This approach is informed by an ontology and epistemology that is predominantly social constructionist (e.g. Chapter 10, this volume). Here, the world is inextricably bound up with the self and is, correspondingly, not amenable to objective verification. In this perspective, views of the world are socially constituted through semiotic systems or 'scapes': linguistic, ethnic, technological, financial, journalistic, ideological, etc. (Appadurai 1990; Fairclough 2010; Kress 2010; Shohamy and Gorter 2009). Given this and the close alliance of intercultural research with language learning, it is not surprising that many of the approaches described in this handbook have focused on the 'linguascape' of language and discourse. For example, Risager's language–sociological approach embraces semiotic approaches to culture and cultural complexity at a discursive level of analysis (Chapter 6), while Warren reports on the language of international exchanges in an international call centre (Chapter 30).

A noticeable move in current intercultural communication research methods is the increasing and – in our view – welcome use of what we call 'radical narrativity'. This is manifest in studies of extreme intensity and thick description, which can comprise accounts of just one subject such as the descriptions by Miles (2010) and Phipps (2010) mentioned above. These are often driven by a democratic, ethical imperative to empower the subject of the research and to disclose the phenomenological basis behind poststructuralist claims about the fluidity and hybridity of identities within postindustrial societies (Bauman 2000). Here, the researcher permits the subject to speak for him/herself, and astringently sets out his/her own position *vis-à-vis* the research subject. These studies are often informed by theories such as hermeneutics or phenomenology, and deploy methods such as narrative enquiry, life stories and life histories (Holstein and Gubrium 1999). By embracing the complexity and hybridity of intercultural subjects, these approaches have resisted the urge to quantify found in mixed methods approaches in favour of the radical subjectivism characteristic of much late modern culture.

In this conjuncture, we note an absence on the theoretical side, which is the need for a powerful theoretical and methodological paradigm from which to interrogate intercultural communication itself, from essentialist through to radical subjectivist accounts. Much has been written on the former; little, if anything, on the other hand, has been written about the latter. What is needed is a theory that can encompass both. The critique of the Hofstedean tradition is already well attended to in this volume and elsewhere, so we will not rehearse it here; however, on radical intercultural subjectivism, it is one thing to move to a position of poststructuralist performativity in the construction of (inter)cultural identities, but the move itself also calls for reciprocal engagement with counterrelativist and postpositivist theoretical paradigms. For this task, a reciprocal theory that 'speaks back' at essentialist, neo-essentialist and radical–constructivist positions simultaneously is potentially presented by critical realism and postpositivist immanent counter-critique (Bhaskar 1998, 2008). By rejecting both positivist essentialism and radical subjectivism, critical realism may offer a methodology that has the potential to interrogate the claims that are being made at both ends of the intercultural spectrum, from fixed nation-state views of cultural identity to the radical relativist narratives of intercultural 'becoming'.

Finally, it seems to us that the relocation of the institutional sites for intercultural communication research and pedagogic renewal still remains overdue. As set out in Chapter 1, the most visible traditions of intercultural communication research remain, first, the heirs (dissenting and otherwise) to the assimilationist language programmes in the USA set up in the 1950s; and second, the later promotion of multilingualism in education and commerce within the EU through research projects and educational exchange programmes. Further initiatives are necessary to set up truly global, multidisciplinary centres for intercultural communication, particularly those that are accessible to 'periphery' scholars and practitioners. Arguably, an early player in this regard was the World Communication Association located at the University of Manoa, Hawaii, USA. More recently, regular intercultural communication conferences have been held in China, for example by the China Association for Intercultural Communication (CAFIC), and regional research centres are also opening up fresh intercultural perspectives. One example of these is the Institut Kajian Oksidental (IKON) at the Universiti Kebangsaan (UKM) in Malaysia, which runs an entire project devoted to Eastern perspectives of the West (Hussin 2006). If the study of intercultural communication is to become truly intercultural and interdisciplinary, we anticipate – as economic influence relocates Eastwards – an even more radical decentring of its current Euro-American discourse.

## 5. Recommendations for practice

In our view, the move towards more interpretive and critical approaches to intercultural communication research (as described in Chapter 1) reflects a move from predicating the study of intercultural communication on the model of a natural science, which is value free, towards predicating it on the model of a social science, which is value laden (Winch 1990). We believe that there has been a corresponding shift towards engaging with the political and ethical dimensions of intercultural pedagogy and intercultural competence. As has been noted elsewhere, the values embedded in citizenship have become a central focus for intercultural education – not only for migrants seeking economic or political sanctuary, but also for learners who are engaging with a foreign language as a means of enhancing their democratic participation in a political milieu larger than the single nation-state. Thus, Lu and Corbett (Chapter 20) have opposed 'bounded' approaches to citizenship that create barriers to national citizenship, such as language tests, to foreign language teaching for 'global' citizenship which seeks to transcend national borders. However, they concede that there is a complexity to the conceptualization of global citizenship, as educationalists attempt to meld together the engagement of the intercultural citizen in democratic agency at a local, national and global level while simultaneously acknowledging the ways in which 'universal rights and responsibilities, such as freedom of speech, equal opportunities, and social justice' are understood and realized in different cultures. The trouble with universalism, however, is that there remain asymmetries of power that exist between political and national blocs, between institutions and agents within the nation-state and between groups of actors and individuals. In this, it seems to us that Guilherme's call for critical awareness as part of intercultural citizenship is particularly timely. But for us, this critical awareness would not only entail intercultural actors becoming aware of the role of their own ideology and standards of judgement in viewing the actions of other people (after Bryam in Guilherme, Chapter 22), but also enable them to become aware of the ways in which they are positioned through asymmetries of power created and maintained though the transmission of intercultural relations as 'discursive practice' (Foucault 1977).

This volume has referenced a range of textbooks for intercultural communication (e.g. Lu and Corbett, Chapter 20), some of which are produced not for global consumption, but for particular regions. Although these are doubtless well meaning, in our view, there is no substitute for language teachers and intercultural trainers developing a curriculum and set of materials specifically designed for a particular cultural context – be it a region, a town or just one's own class. We signal this in the light of the recent turn to local 'postmethod' approaches to language education in global English language teaching (Kumaravadivelu 2003; Pennycook 2010). It is necessary for the intercultural communication educator to reconfigure 'regionalized' as well as 'globalized' intercultural materials for the local context if s/he is going to engage honestly and comprehensively with the political and ethical issues, as suggested above. Specially designed intercultural materials in both formal and non-formal classrooms can address the particular identities of intercultural learners, just as they reflect the teacher's or instructor's own identity. In these circumstances, the classroom more readily becomes the sort of 'safe house' envisaged by Lu and Corbett (Chapter 20) (after Pratt 1991: 40).

The techniques available for these activities have already been described extensively. These include cultural studies and area studies for an etic view of culture (Byram 1989) and ethnography for an emic view (Roberts et al. 2001). Study abroad programmes (e.g. Chapter 28) can provide learners with an immersion experience of another language and culture, although well-designed, well-implemented orientation and debriefing programmes are important to ensure that learners achieve a positive and beneficial outcome. Forms of telecollaboration (Chapter 21) can enable learners in foreign language learning contexts to engage with members of other cultures either in personal intercultural dialogue or through collaborative projects. Within professional contexts, the type of experiential learning cycle described by Holmes (Chapter 29, after Kolb and Fry 1975) can be used for participants to reflect upon their experience and enhance their intercultural awareness. However, although intercultural educators who design their own locally developed materials are able to engage more meaningfully with particular groups of learners, the materials also have to be firmly focused on transcending conceptualizations of culture bounded by the nation-state (Holliday et al. 2010).

The development of skills and knowledge in curriculum and materials design, the ability to marshal the necessary resources for in-house materials development as well as the commitment and inspiration to implement them effectively often requires specialized training, either at certificate, diploma and postgraduate level or in in-service workshops for continuing professional development (CPD). If there appears to be a general dearth of CPD for intercultural pedagogy (Chapters 25 and 27), it appears to us that the provision of resources and training for intercultural communication curriculum design and materials development remains even more scarce.

## 6. New paradigms, new engagements

A paradigm shift appears to be taking place in intercultural communication, and it is a shift from the global to the local, from overarching templates to engagements with local knowledge and practice. To adapt a phrase from Pennycook (2010), we might call this interculturalism as a local practice. The move to localism in intercultural communication is exemplified by many of the contributions to this volume and is a welcome reminder that intercultural communication is an intimate, 'intersubjective' activity, in that it generally requires people and language for it to be enacted, either face to face – on the street, in classrooms, shopping malls, airports or holiday destinations – or at a distance in chat rooms, virtual worlds, through e-mail or online conferencing. It also occurs in much less amenable surroundings such as immigration detention centres, border crossings and war zones, and symbolically through acts of aggression and terror. Wherever the locale and whatever the symbols, issues of identity and 'interculture' (i.e. the economy of intercultural communication) are always at stake in these meetings. In personal exchanges, they are always potentially open to negotiation, although not necessarily freely or on the basis of equality. This is not simply because intercultural communication can occur in coercive circumstances, but because acts of communication are always bound up with power in some form, and with the historical and discursive forces in which the participants are embedded, whether they are hosts and study abroad students or border agency officials and asylum seekers, so that the locales are themselves complexly constituted from the linguistic and semiotic activities of the participants in them.

This is not a particularly new notion in discourse analysis or in language studies – it is a perspective that has run through systemic–functional, critical discourse and multimodal approaches to language for some time – but it is still relatively new to intercultural communication. We would suggest, then, that in addition to studying all the ways in which people can become, in Byram's words, 'intercultural speakers', there is still a need to examine the locales, spaces and contexts of intercultural communication – in terms of how these spaces came into being historically and how they function and reproduce themselves as centres of intercultural communication. This does not imply stepping away from language necessarily, but it does presage a more emphatic move towards 'discourse', or better still, 'semiosis' (i.e. human meaning-making in all its forms) in understandings of intercultural communication and, crucially, of the locales that are constituted (as well as construed) by it. An international call centre, as Warren (Chapter 30) demonstrates, is fairly meaningless without the practices, linguistic and otherwise, of the operators and callers for whom and by which it comes into being. We therefore wish to make an appeal for research into semiosis in intercultural communication, and into the constitution of the 'locales' (i.e. the spatial contexts – virtual, physical and conceptual) in which it occurs, and the relations between the two, in order to shed light upon the production and reproduction of the structures and practices of which they are a part.

Inasmuch as locales are constituted by semiotic and other causal means, the increased emphasis on localism should not obscure the necessary relation between the local and the global in intercultural communication, because all locales – particularly intercultural communication locales – are in one way or another globally situated and, for the participants in them, are inevitably and ineluctably referenced to wider personal imaginaries about the nature of the world they live in and where they are in it. Locales are thus also linked to intercultural communication participants' geocognitive conceptions of personal location, such as 'institution' (where the discourse is occurring), 'country' (Gabon, Haiti, Australia, etc.), 'state' (autocracy/democracy) and 'region' (East/West; North/South). In other words, intercultural communication locales may be 'local', but they cannot help but be bound up with the human desire for personal triangulation, both conceptually and physically, as a means of staving off feelings of intercultural insecurity and alienation (Jameson 1988; Lynch 1960). The interrogation and mapping of the relationship between the local and the global therefore remains an important aspect of the agenda for intercultural communication research and pedagogy, and following from this, of intercultural practice and action.

Clearly drawing on Williams's (1977) configuration of culture as dominant, residual and emergent, Holliday's *Intercultural Communication and Ideology* (2011) is a useful study of the local/global dialectic in intercultural communication. In contrast to Williams's tripartite conceptualization of culture, Holliday presents a view of 'competing worlds': an 'established' actual world of centre discourses and normalized cultural descriptions; a 'dominant' 'imagined' world of essentialized selves and demonized others that impinges directly upon the established world; a 'marginal' world of counterdiscourses that are spoken from the periphery (i.e. where the prejudices of the dominant world are deconstructed); and an 'emergent' world of alternative reflexive possibilities in which the self-certainties of the established and dominant 'centre' worlds have been refuted and eschewed. Here, the purpose is to 'open up the possibility of seeing something else' (ibid.: 190) – i.e. that which is unseen and presently out of view. The emergent world therefore encapsulates a form of hope that some day things interculturally might be other than they are now. It has always been in the nature of intercultural communication research and teaching that we have looked for the unseen and, as this volume has shown, we have done so from a range of identities, cultures and disciplinary perspectives, and by employing a wide variety of techniques. As Marx once said, '*Hic Rhodus, hic salta!*' (1961 [1887]: 166) – or, in a manner of speaking, 'Here's the problem, now get on with it!' It was good advice.

## Further reading

Below, we set out a fairly comprehensive list of peer-refereed academic journals to read for your research project. Where available, we have listed the publisher and the academic association to which they are affiliated.

*Communication, Culture, and Critique* (International Communication Association).
*Cross-Cultural Management: An Intercultural Journal.*
*Cross-Cultural Research*, Sage.
*Cross-Cultural Psychology Bulletin.*
*Culture and Psychology*, Sage.
*Intercultural Communication Review.*
*Intercultural Education*, Routledge.
*Intercultural Pragmatics*, De Gruyter.
*International and Intercultural Communication Annual.*
*International Journal of Cross-Cultural Management*, Sage.
*International Journal of Intercultural Relations*, Elsevier (International Academy for Intercultural Research).
*Journal of Cross-Cultural Competence and Management.*
*Journal of Cross-Cultural Psychology*, Sage.
*Journal of Intercultural Communication Research* (World Communication Association).
*Journal of Intercultural Studies*, Routledge.
*Journal of International and Intercultural Communication.*
*Journal of International and Intercultural Communication* (National Communication Association).
*Journal of Language, Identity and Education*, Routledge.
*Journal of Multicultural Discourses*, Routledge.
*Journal of Multilingual and Multicultural Development*, Routledge.
*Journal of Studies in International Education*, Sage.
*Language and Intercultural Communication*, Routledge (International Association of Language and Intercultural Communication).
*Review of Education, Pedagogy and Cultural Studies*, Routledge.
*The SIETAR International Journal* (Society for Intercultural Education, Training and Research).

## References

Alim, H.S. and Perry, I. (2011) 'Lost in translation: language, race and the DEA's legitimization of ebonics', *Anthropology News*, 52(1): 20.
Appadurai, A. (1990) 'Disjuncture and difference in the global cultural economy', in M. Featherstone (ed.) *Global Culture: Nationalism, Globalization and Modernity*, London: Sage, pp. 295–310.
Bauman, Z. (2000) *Liquid Modernity*, Cambridge: Polity Press.
Bhaskar, R. (1998) *The Possibility of Naturalism*, London: Routledge.
——(2008) *Dialectic: The Pulse of Freedom*, London: Routledge.

Brandt, A. and Jenks, C.J. (2011) "Is it okay to eat a dog in Korea … like China?' Assumptions of national foodeating practices in intercultural interaction', *Language and Intercultural Communication*, 11(1): 41–58.

Brown, P. and Levinson, C.S. (1978) 'Universals in language usage: politeness phenomena', in E.N. Goody (ed.) *Questions and Politeness: Strategies in Social Interaction*, Cambridge: Cambridge University Press, pp. 56–311.

——(1987) *Politeness: Some Universals in Language Usage*, Cambridge: Cambridge University Press.

Byram, M. (1989) *Cultural Studies in Foreign Language Education*, Clevedon: Multilingual Matters.

——(1997) *Teaching and Assessing Intercultural Communicative Competence*, Clevedon: Multilingual Matters.

Byram, M., Nichols, A. and Stevens, D. (eds) (2001) *Developing Intercultural Competence in Practice*, Clevedon: Multilingual Matters.

Carbaugh, D. (2005) *Cultures in Conversation*, New York: Routledge.

Council of Europe (2008) *White Paper on Intercultural Dialogue*, Strasbourg: Council of Europe.

Fairclough, N. (2010) 'Semiosis, ideology and mediation: a dialectical view', in Fairclough, N. (ed.) *Critical Discourse Analysis: The Critical Study of Language*, London: Longman, pp. 69–83.

Faist, T. (ed.) (2000) *The Volume and Dynamics of International Migration and Transnational Social Spaces*, Oxford: Oxford University Press.

——(2004) 'The border-crossing expansion of social space: concepts, questions and topics', in T. Faist and E. Özveren (eds) *Transnational Social Spaces: Agents, Networks and Institutions*, Aldershot: Ashgate, pp. 1–36.

Ford, K. (2009) 'Critical incidents in the experiences of Japanese returnees', *Language and Intercultural Communication*, 9(2): 63–75.

Foucault, M. (1977) *Discipline and Punish*, London: Tavistock.

Hannerz, U. (1996) *Transnational Connections: Culture, People, Places*, London: Routledge.

Hoerder, D. (2002) *Cultures in Contact: World Migrations in the Second Millennium*, Durham, NC: Duke University Press.

Holliday, A. (2010) 'Complexity in cultural identity', *Language and Intercultural Communication*, 10(2): 165–77.

——(2011) *Intercultural Communication and Ideology*, London: Sage.

Holliday, A., Hyde, M. and Kullman, J. (2010) *Intercultural Communication: an Advanced Resource Book for Students*, 2nd edn, London: Routledge.

Holstein, J.A. and Gubrium, J.F. (1999) *The Self We Live By: Narrative Identity in a Postmodern World*, Oxford: Oxford University Press.

Hussin, N. (2006) *The Easternization of the West: Europe meets Asia*, Bangi, Malaysia: IKON Publications.

International Organization for Migration (2010) About Migration. Online. Available: www.iom.int/jahia/Jahia/about-migration/lang/en (accessed 16 January 2011).

Jameson, F. (1988) 'Cognitive Mapping', in C. Nelson and L. Grossberg (eds) *Marxism and the Interpretation of Culture*, London: Macmillan Education, pp. 347–58.

Kivisto, P. (2002) *Multiculturalism in a Global Society*, Oxford: Blackwell.

Kolb, D.A. and Fry, R. (1975) 'Toward an applied theory of experiential learning', in C. Cooper (ed.) *Theories of Group Process*, London: John Wiley.

Kramsch, C. (1998) 'The privilege of the intercultural speaker', in M. Byram and M. Fleming (eds) *Language Learning in Intercultural Perspective: Approaches through Drama and Ethnography*, Cambridge: Cambridge University Press, pp. 16–31.

Kress, G. (2010) *Multimodality: A Social Semiotic Approach to Contemporary Communication*, London: Routledge.

Kumaravadivelu, B. (2003) 'A postmethod perspective on English language teaching', *World Englishes*, 22 (4): 539–50.

Lynch, K. (1960) *The Image of the City*, Cambridge MA: MIT Press.

MacDonald, M.N., O'Regan, J.P. and Witana, J. (2009) 'The development of national occupational standards for intercultural working in the UK', *Journal of Vocational Education and Training*, 61(4): 375–98.

McSweeney, B. (2002) 'Hofstede's model of national cultural differences and their consequences: a triumph of faith – a failure of analysis', *Human Relations*, 55(1): 89–121.

Marx, K. (1961 [1887]) *Capital*, Vol. 1, Moscow: Foreign Language Publishing House.

Miles, C. (2010) 'Discursive power and the new labor force: the metamorphosis of a speech community', *Language and Intercultural Communication*, 10(2): 150–64.

Modood, T. (2007) *Multiculturalism*, Cambridge: Polity.

Pennycook, A. (2004) 'Performativity and language studies', *Critical Inquiry in Language Studies*, 1: 1–19.

——(2010) *Language as a Local Practice*, London: Routledge.

Phipps, A. (2010) 'Fostering language: the bonds and borders of linguistic hospitality', unpublished keynote paper presented at the 10th Conference of the International Association of Language and Intercultural Communication, Leeds, UK, December 2010.

Portes, A. (1996) 'Transnational communities: their emergence and significance in the contemporary world system', in R.P. Korzeniewicz and W.C. Smith (eds), *Latin America in the World Economy*, Westport, CT: Praeger, pp. 151–68.

Pratt, M.L. (1991) 'Arts of the contact zone', *Profession*, 91: 33–40.

Pries, L. (ed.) (1999) *Migration and Transnational Social Spaces*, Aldershot: Ashgate.

Rampton, B. (1999) 'Dichotomies, difference, and ritual in second language learning and teaching', *Applied Linguistics*, 20(3): 316–40.

Roberts, C., Byram, M., Barro, A., Jordan, S. and Street, B. (2001) *Language Learners as Ethnographers*, Clevedon: Multilingual Matters/Routledge.

Shohamy, E. and Gorter, D. (eds) (2009) *Linguistic Landscape: Expanding the Scenery*, London: Routledge.

Simpson, D. (ed.) (2007) *Cultural Awareness and the Military*, Maxwell ADB, USA: Muir S. Fairchild Research Information Center.

Spencer-Oatey, H. and Franklin, P. (2009) *Intercultural Interaction: A Multidisciplinary Approach to Intercultural Communication*, Basingstoke/New York: Palgrave Macmillan.

Turner, B. (2010) *Routledge Handbook of Globalization*, London: Routledge.

Williams, R. (1977) *Marxism and Literature*, Oxford: Oxford University Press.

Winch, P. (1990) *The Idea of a Social Science and its Relation to Philosophy*, 2nd edn, London: Routledge.

Witteborn, S. (2007a) 'The situated expression of Arab collective identities in the United States', *Journal of Communication*, 57: 556–75.

——(2007b) 'The expression of Palestinian identity in narratives about personal experiences: implications for the study of narrative, identity, and social interaction', *Research on Language and Social Interaction*, 40: 145–70.

——(2008) 'Identity mobilization practices of refugees: the case of Iraqis in the United States and the war in Iraq', *Journal of International and Intercultural Communication*, 1: 202–20.

——(2010) 'The role of transnational NGOs in promoting global citizenship and globalizing communication practices', *Language and Intercultural Communication*, 10(4): 1–15.

# Index

# Exploring Intercultural Communication

# Language in Action

Edited by Zhu Hua

*Series: Routledge Introductions to
Applied Linguistics*

*Routledge Introductions to Applied Linguistics* is a series of introductory level textbooks covering the core topics in Applied Linguistics, primarily designed for those beginning postgraduate studies, or taking an introductory MA course as well as advanced undergraduates. Titles in the series are also ideal for language professionals returning to academic study.

The books take an innovative 'practice to theory' approach, with a 'back-to-front' structure. This leads the reader from real-world problems and issues, through a discussion of intervention and how to engage with these concerns, before finally relating these practical issues to theoretical foundations. Additional features include tasks with commentaries, a glossary of key terms, and an annotated further reading section.

*Exploring Intercultural Communication* investigates the role of language in intercultural communication, paying particular attention to the interplay between cultural diversity and language practice.

This book brings together current or emerging strands and themes in the field by examining how intercultural communication permeates our everyday life, what we can do to achieve effective and appropriate intercultural communication, and why we study language, culture and identity together. The focus is on interactions between people from various cultural and linguistic backgrounds, and regards intercultural communication as a process of negotiating meaning, cultural identities, and – above all – differences between ourselves and others.

2013 | 280 Pages | HB: 978-0-415-58550-7| PB: 978-0-415-58551-4
Learn more at: www.routledge.com/9780415585507

**Available from all good bookshops**

# Introducing Language and Intercultural Communication

By Jane Jackson

Written in an accessible and user-friendly style, this introductory book will be essential reading for undergraduates in English language, applied linguistics, TESOL and communication studies who are new to the area of intercultural communication. It provides a basic skill-building framework to enhance their understanding of the complexities of language and intercultural communication in diverse domestic and international settings.

This book:

- introduces foundational concepts of intercultural communication,

- raises awareness of the implications of English as a lingua franca and international language with many variations.

- draws upon current research and theories of particular relevance to applied linguistics

- incorporates real-life examples from around the world

- engages the reader through a variety of interactive exercises and discussion questions

- is accompanied by a companion website with material for lecturers and students

The text seeks to avoid the essentialisation of people and behaviours and allows readers to understand power relations, positioning, and the impact of social and political forces on language choice and the intercultural communication process. The book also raises awareness of the cognitive, affective, and behavioural dimensions of intercultural communicative competence and will serve as an essential resource for students studying this area.

2014 | 392 Pages | HB: 978-0-415-60198-6| PB: 978-0-415-60199-3
Learn more at: www.routledge.com/9780415601986

**Available from all good bookshops**

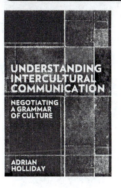